THE HEDAYA

COMMENTARY ON THE ISLAMIC LAWS

Translated by

CHARLES HAMILTON

Kitab Bhavan

New Delhi-110002

KITAB BHAVAN
Publishers, Distributors, Exporters & Importers
1784, Kalan Mahal, Darya Ganj,
New Delhi - 1100 02 (India)
Phones : (91-11) 23277392/93,23274686, 32906494
Fax : (91-11) 23263383
Website: www.nusratalinasri.com
Email : nasri@vsnl.com
: nusrat@bol.net.in

First Edition : 1870
3rd Reprint : 2014

ISBN : 81-7151-195-3
Book Code No. : H00001

Printed & Published in India by :
Nusrat Ali Nasri for KITAB BHAVAN
1784, Kalan Mahal, Darya Ganj,
New Delhi - 1100 02 [India]

ADVERTISEMENT TO THE SECOND EDITION

In further pursuance of the design to which I alluded in my Preface to the Third Edition of Menu's Institutes, I now present to the profession the Second Edition of the Hedaya. As this work has been made a text-book by the Council of Legal Education, for the examination of the students of the Inns of Court, who are qualifying themselves for call to the English Bar, with a view of practising in India ; as the First Edition, by Mr. Hamilton, has been some time out of print ; its bulk (four quarto volumes) is not calculated to assist reference to its pages ; and its price had increased in proportion to the difficulty of obtaining it, I felt it a duty to publish a new Edition, in order to bring it somewhat more within the reach of the students, not only with reference to its size, but its cost. I have accordingly, therefore, prepared this Edition for those enterprising Publishers, Messrs. W. H. Allen & Co. A large portion of the work having become obsolete, in consequence of the abolition of slavery, and from other causes, I have expunged the books containing those portions from the present Edition, they being more interesting to the antiquarian (who can consult the First Edition) than useful to the student or practitioner, and their insertion would not only have increased the bulk of the volume, but its expense also. I have, however retained in the "Introductory Discourse" the translators's epitome of those books from which the object and scope of the obsolete law may be learned. Where portions of the expunged subjects have been incidentally mixed up with others, I ave been constrained to retain such portions lest the context might, by their omissions, be involved in obscurity. The second edition is now comprised in one volume, printed in double columns, and in smaller type than the original, with a view of comprising it within that compass, but, as the type is clear, it is conceived that no disadvantage will result from this. Wherever any subject is omitted, I have inserted a note, expressing my reasons for expunging it. A large portion of the original translation had been printed in Italic letters. For the sake of uniformity and clearness, this plan has not been adopted in the present Edition. I have added a very copious Index, which will facilitate reference to the context ; and I should have embodied in foot-notes, reference to the cases that have been decided upon the various subjects of which the work treats, but that I have already done so in that portion of my work on "the Mahommedan Law of Inheritance and Contract," in which the same subjects are discussed, and where those cases will be found collected.

Although the present Edition has been published with a view of assisting the student to prosecute his studies, yet the hope is entertained that the Judge, as well as the Practitioner, will find it useful, particularly in those provinces where the Mahommedan law demands a great portion of the attention of the judiciai, as well as that of the practitioner. It is hoped, also, that it may be found useful in promoting the study of the law in the several Universities in India, it being advisable to assimilate the curriculum in both countries as much as possible.

2, *Plowden Buildings, Temple,*
April, 1870.

Standish Grove Grady.

DEDIATION OF THE ENGLISH TRANSLATION

TO WARREN HASTING, ESQ.

Late Governor-General of Bengal.

Sir,—After the labour of several years. I am at last enabled to present you with a translation of the Hedaya.

To you, Sir, I feel it incumbent on me to inscribe a word originally projected by yourself, and for some time carried on under your immediate patronage,—However humble the translator's abilities, and however imperfect the execution of these volumes may be, yet the design itself does honour to the wisdom and benevolence by which it was suggested ; and if I might be allowed to express a hope upon the subject, it is, that its future beneficial effects, in facilitating, the administration of Justice throughout our Asiatic territories and uniting us still more closely with Our Mussulman subjects, may reflect some additional lustre on your Administration,—I have the honour to be, with the utmost respect, and the most lively gratitude and esteem

Sir,

Your most obedient,

And most humbl Servant

CHARLES HAMILTON.

Contents

INTRODUCTORY ADDRESS

BY THE

COMPOSERS OF THE PERSIAN VERSION

PRAISE and glory unbounded is due to that adorable Being, in the investigation of whose ways; through several mazes the most learned theologians are exhausted, and the most contemplative philosophers in the wilderness of research, find the foot of comprehension shackled with the fetters of amazement !—Duly to return thanks for his favours (which to offer is a duty indispensably incumbent on every existent being) is impossible; and to touch the skirt of his intelligence (which exceeds the power of the finger of diligence) by force of reason and study, impracticable !—Salutations innumerable are also to be presented at the tribunal of HIM who is seated on the elect throne, to follow whose infallible institutes is a certain means of attaining the Divine favour, and whose world-illuminating Lamp of Law derives its sacred light from the morning beams of the Day of Judgment.—All honour and blessing upon him, and upon his holy family, and his worthy COMPANIONS !—Upon the tablets of the hearts of those who adorn the exordium of the book of knowledge and wisdom, and upon the minds of those who expound the collected mysteries of the creation, it is impressed,—that, from the day that the delightful region of BENGAL was cheered by the rays of Government of the Nawab Governor-General, MR WARREN HASTINGS, the whole of his wise and prudent attention was occupied and directed to this point,—that the case and protection of the country, and the administration of public affairs, should be placed on such a footing, that the community being sheltered from the scorching heat of the sun of violence and tyranny, might find the gates closed against injustice and oppression; and that the range of sedition in those who deviate from the road of truth might be limited and shortened :—and since this hope must be fulfilled through the influence of the holy LAW of the PROPHET, and the injunctions and inhibitions of the chosen sect,—this denizen of kingdom of humility and solitude, named GHOLAM YEHEE, was therefore instructed and empowered, together with Molla TAJ-ADDEEN, Meer MOHAMMED HOSSEIN, and Molla SHAREEAT OOLLA, to translate from the Arabic language into the Persian idiom certain treaties upon the LAW, but particularly that excellent work the HEDAYA (which, from its great subtlety, and the closeness of its style, is a species of miracle),—to which, accordingly, with their assistance, applying his attention, the Arabic text was, as much as it would admit, reduced into a Persian version; which they have entitled the HEDAYA FARSEE (Persian Guide).—hoping that mankind may thereby find their wants supplied, and that profit and advantage may thence accrue.

FROM those who travel in this fruitful garden let it not be concealed, that where, in the course of their investigation, the word Sheikhine (that two Elders) is mentioned, it signifies the two renowned Doctors, Imam ABOO HANEEFA. and the most illustrious of disciples, Imam ABOO YOOSAF :—where the word Tirrafine (the two extremes) is written, it imports the sublime name of ABOO HANEEFA (on whom be the peace of GOD) and Imam MOHAMMED, who stands next in rank to the two it Elders; and by the term Sahibine ithe two disciplesi are intended the two scholars of HANEEFA, upon both of whom be the blessing of GOD !

A HOPE is indulged, from the benevolence of those who shall persue the following pages, that if in passing over the valleys and the hills of this long journey, it should happen that the foot of meditation has anywhere slipped from its place, they will not treat it with severity, nor expose it to the finger of scorn or reprehension.—The guidance is with God.

PRELIMINARY DISCOURSE

By THE TRANSLATOR.

VOL. I.

Book I. Of Zakat

Zakat means the alms imposed by the Law, in opposition to Sadka (charity), which signifies the voluntary contributions of individuals, and which is treated of at large under the head of gifts,—As Alms, in our application of that word, is always used to denote something purely gratuitions, the translator, in treating of those imposen by the Mussulman law, has retained the original term, to which the English language does not afford any expression strictly analogous. Some writers have confounded Zakat and Sadka under one common meaning. The Arabian commentatcrs, however, make an essential difference between them; for the former is merely an indispeasable compliance with a legal obligation, claiming no merit in futurity; whereas the latter is as much an impulse of the mind as an act of the hand, and is of course entitled to its reward.—The impost of Zakat originated with Mohammed himself, who at first employed the revenue arising from it according to his discretion, is the support of his needly adherents; but the objects of it were afterwards ascertained by various passages in the Koran; and it is somewhat remarkable that the Prophet particularly excluded the members of his own family from any participation in it, and this in terms which sufficiently denote the arrogant superiority assumed by the tribe of Hashim.* To compensate, who ever, for this execution, he admitted them to fifth share in that proportion of the spoil which was alloted to the public treasury. For some generations after Mohammed this impost was regularly collected, and faithfully applied to its appointed purposes.—In most Mussulman territories it continues to be levied at the present day; but the original object of its disbursement have been long since disregarded, and what was intended as a relief to the poor is now, even in the best regulated governments, carried to the exchequer of the prince, who endeaveurs to satisfy his conscience by a sort of commutation, in the erection of mosques, or the support of a few indigent and idle Fakcers about his palace. That which commenced in the indigence or rapacity of the sovereign, has now acquired a sort of prescriptive authority; and the revenue derived from Zakat is universally considered as the right of the state. It has indeed, for several centuries past, ceased to be collected upon stationary property, the only tax which at present

---

*See his declaration upon this subject (Vol. I.), where the grossness of the metrhpors sued by him is worthy of remark.

bears the name of Zakat being that imposed on goods imported in the way of trade from one country or district into another, and levied in the name of a toll.—Many of its rules will be found to apply peculiarly to ARABIA and SYRIA, the countries in which these laws originated, and where flocks and herds have ever formed a chief part of the wealth of the inhabitants. Although the laws of Zakat have in a great measure been superseded, or become obsolete with respect to their original design, yet they are worthy of attention, as incidentally involving many of the laws of proparty in points not immediately connected with this subject.—Under this head is comprehended the Sadka Fittir or alms given to the poor on the festival of breaking Lent ; because the payment of those is considered as a divine ordinance, and the amonnt (contrary to other descriptions of Sadka) is particularjy prescribed by the Law.

Zakat is the only one of the five books upon the Abadat, or spiritual law, retained by the English translator. It is, therefore, immediately followed by the Maamilat, or temporal law,—commencing with MARRIAGE, and ending (properly) with BEQUIST, the last temporal act of MAN ;—though a short supplementary book upon Hermaphrodities is added.

BLOK II OF MARRIAGE.

THE preliminaries to this most important of all contract, as set forth in Chap. I, are stated in terms remarkably simple. No provision is made for the execution of any written engagement ; no particular form of ceremony is prescribed ; but the efficiency of the whole is made to depend merely upon the oral declarations of the parties, before sufficient witnesses. In fact, written engagements were not in common use until some time after the establishment of Islamism.—A section of this chapter is occupied throughout with the matrimonial prohibitions and restriction, with respect to which the Mohammedan and Levitical law have a close affinity. The principal of these restrictions are, that a man shall not marry his relation within the prohibited degrees ; that he shall not have more than four wives at a time ; and that he shall not marry, together, to women related to each other within the prohibited degrees.—To the political and speculative inquirer the most curious features in this book are, the passage which particularly concern WOMEN, as contained in Chap. II and III from which it appears, that the female sex are, among the Mussulmans, invested with many personel rights and independent privileges, such as certainly in some measure, compensate for the various hard conditions to which law or custom has subjected the daughters of Islam.—These, as they are fully discussed in the body of the work, it is needless to recapitulate. The most striking of them which occurs under this articles is, the liberty allowed to a woman to dispose of herself in marriage independent of her guardians, and the right of option which still remains to one contracted during infancy, after she shall have attained to maturity, which the law fixes at a very early age. A woman is also entitled to possess her dower, or marriage settlement,

---

See Vol. III.

as her own exclusive property, which she may dispose of by gift, will or other deed, altogether independent of her husband, or any claims which may lie against his estate.—Chapter VI exhibits a still more extraordinary regards, in the Mussulman legislator, for the feelings of the sex, upon a point of a very delicate nature, and in which he doubtless consulted the peace of the Haram as much as the dictates of abstract equity.—Concerning. this, however, we shali leave the text to speak for itself.

Book III. Of Fosterage.

In a state of society where fastidious refinement has not destroyed the genuine feeling of the heart, the lie of fosterage is, next to that of blood, of the strongest and most lasting nature.—Even in the more remote parts of our own country the Nurse is still considered rather in the light of an humble relative than a menial dependent. By the people of Asia this idea is carried still farther ; and the nursing is supposed to partake of the very nature of her from whose blood he receives his earliest nourishment. An affinity is therefore created by this circumstance, which operates to tender marriage illegol in the same manner as actual consanguinity. Hense the prohibitions occasioned by fosterage are analogous to those set forth in the second section of the preceding book,—to which this is a kind of supplement.

Book IV. Of Divorce.

The great variety of matter which this book embraces, and the many deviations which it admits from its main subject, the translator shall not undertake either to account for or to defend.—From the contents of the first six chapters the reader will perceive that the Mohommadan law of divorce bears a strong affinity throughout to that of Moses. In this, as in marriage, no written instrument is required, the repudiation being effected merely by the verbal declaration of the party.—Custom, indeed, and the municipal regulations of most Mussulman countries, following the example of the Jews, have made a writing of divorce, if not an essential, at least a circumstance which it would be highly indecorous to omit. What most forcibly strikes us on the perusal of this subject is the extreme facility with which a husband may rid himself of his female partner,—a facility which, when we consider the too frequent levity and fickleness of Man, seems at first sight calculated to expose the weaker sex to the most degrading insult which malice could dictate, of caprice put in practice.—The Arabian legislator has, however, established so many bars, and pride itself opposes such obstacle as, if they do not completely remedy, at least tend greatly to counteract this apparent defect.—Before a divorce becomes irreversible it must have been pronounced three times, allowing (according to the orthodox form) an interval of a month to pass between each sentence,—or such a period must have elapsed as affords ample room for reflection and repentance, in cases of anger or disgust ; and a reversal is, at any time before the expiration of that term, established by either word or deed, denoting a reconciliation. The husband, moreover, unless he can prove gross misbehaviour, must give up the dower.—But the most powerful obstacle to unjust or capacious repudiation is that part of the law which provides, that if a wife be once completely divorced, the husband cannot take her again, until she be previously married to, bedded with, and divcored by, another man.—To this salutary regulation chiefly is owing the dislike which obtains against divorce in all Mussulman countries, and the d shonour attached to it,—insomuch that the instances of it are very rare notwithstanding the liberty which is permitted by the LAW. The place and title of chap. XV. would naturally lead us to conclude, that it treats in particular of the alimony payable to a divorced wife during the term of probation. This, however, is by no means the case; for it is made to comprehend those rights of every person which some under the denomination of MAINTENANCE,—not of the wife alone. but also of parent, children, poor or disabled relatives and slaves.—With respect to domestic arrangements, this is perhaps, the most useful section of the whole work. It evinces, in many places, a considerable spirit of humanity, and very properly introduces.

BOOK V. OF MANUMISSION.

TENDERNESS towards SLAVES is certainly a prevalent principle in the Mussulman law, notwithstanding some passage which occur in this treatise concerning them them are directly repugnant to common feeling and to the natural rights of Man.—In the XXIVth chapter of the KORAN this tenderness is strongly enforced with respect to certain points in the domestic treatment of them* and it may also be traced in various parts of this commentary.—It is, indeed, in practice pretty much confined to the slaves professing the Mussulman faith, as it is natural to suppose that the followers of the Prophet do not entertain the same regard towards their bond-servants of other religious. Still, however, we shall be guilty of great injustice, if we form our ideas of Mussulman slavery from the treatment experienced by Christian captives among the barbarians of Tunis and Algiers. The precepts concerning manumission are injunctive with respect to believers only; but those which recommend kindness and good usage apply to all alike. The law in many instance affords them protection against injustice, and declares them to be "claimants of right." It in some particulars, moreover, provides an alleviation to this otherwise most hopeless and degraded state of MAN. unknown to the more polished inhabitants of Europe;—as may be perceived in perusing the laws with respect to Am-Walids, Mokatibs, Modabbirs, and Mazoons.—To the free-born denizen of BRITAIN, the very name of SLAVE carries with it something odious and disgustful : but the Mohammedan bondman, generally speaking, experiences in a very slight degree, if at all, the miseries which necessarily attend that state in some of the dependencies of EUROPE; where the riches of the community grow out of the incessant labour of wretches, whose shortened date of life is balanced against their earnings by rules of Algebra and calculations of Arithmetic! if the slaves of Mussulman appear, by their conduct. to be deserving of

*The passage referred to treats of matchings slaves who are single :—"CONTRACT in marriage) THOSE OF THEM WHO ARE SINGLE, SUCH AS ARE WORTHY, OF YOUR MALE AND FEMALE (slaves); IF THEY BE POOR, GOD WILL ENRICH THEM OF HIS BOUNTY——UNTO SUCH AS DESIRE A WRITTEN COVENANT for Kitabat), GRANT IT IF YE SEE GOOD IN THEM; AND GIVE THEM OF THE RICHES OF GOD, WHICH HE HATH GIVEN YOU," &c.

encouragement, they are frequently trea'ed rather as humble friends and confidents than as servile dependants ; and though inhibited from rising in the state, often, in the capacity of Mazoons, amass a degree of wealth which enables them to purchase their freedom.—The subject of manumission is discussed at large in the first five chapters of this book,—Chap. VI. treat of a practice which was common in ARABIA before the time of MOHAMMED, and was confirmed by his precepts. It affords a strong incentive to emancipation by cnabling a master to perform an act af piety which, being posthumous in its effect, cannot injure his circumstances.—Chap. VII. exhibits a branch of that most important article, "the establishment of parentage." It shows, that the children born to man by his female slaves are as legitimate as those begotten in marriage ; and also, that the Mussulman law, like the Raman does not acknowledge any affinity between a bastard and his father but throws him wholly upon the mother.

NOTE.—On turning to Book V. it will be seen that the subject treated of has been omitted, on the ground that slavery having been abolished by Act V. of 1843, there is no use in preserving the law upon the subject, which will be interesting to the antiquarian only and he can find the learning upon the subject in the earlier editions.

BOOK VI. OF VOWS.

OATHS are one of the bonds of society and in many instances the chief security for public integrity and private property. Perjury, therefore, has in all communities been justly reprobated as a most flagrant crime. It is remarkable, however, that the Musslman law has instituted no specific punishment for this species of offences except in the case of slander, the legislator seeming to think the apprehension of punishment a future state of itself sufficient to restrain men from the commission of it. This is evidently the case with respect to the expurgatory oaths required of accused or suspected persons. In matters of property, indeed, the magistrate is at liberty to punish it bv a slight discretionary correction ; but in those most enormous instances of it which implicate the life of MAN, the only ill consequence it induces, on discovery, is a fine adequate to the blood thus unjustly shed :—a very trifling atonement certainly ! in this defect. however (if it be such), of their law, the Mussulman do not stand alone.

NOTE.—The law of perjury is now regulated by the Penal Code.

VOL. II

BOOK VII. OF PUNISHMENTS

THIS book treats only of the punishment incurred by crimes of a spiritual nature, those instituted for offences against person or property being discussed under their respective heads. The punishment for adultery is certainly severe. Yet we will not, perhaps, be forward to condemn this severity, if we compare it for a moment with what is recorded in the twentieth chapter of Leviticus upon the same point—in fact, from the nature of the evidence required, it was next to impossible that the offence should ever be fully proved, even among the tents of the ARABS ; so that the institution of the prescribed punishment was in a great measure nugalory, exeept in eases of confession by the parties. That those confessions were sometimes made in the early days of Islamlsm, is a fact ; and made, as they were, at the certain expense of life, they offord a wonderful instance of devotod zeal among the first followers of MOHAMMAD. Still, however, even in those instances, every means that precaution could suggest is enjoined to aroid the necessity of inflicting the sentence.—The three first chapters of the book relate entirely to whoredom. and the penalties incurred by each species of illegal connexion.—Chap. III involves some curious matter concerning the retrospective limitations of testimony, which in practice extend to all cases of criminal accusation. Much here occurs, likewise, concerning the general laws of evidence, that may not be deemed unworthy of notice. Chap. IV. containing the penalties of drunkeness, exhibits a degree of lenient indulgence with respect to that vice which we should scarcely expect to meet in a Mussulman law-book, as it hence appears that a man may offend in this way. even to a considerable degree. without any danger of legal cognizance. Slander, as treated of in Chap. V. comprehends all expressions which may either affect the reputation of a man or womnn previously possessed of a fair character, or the legitimacv of their issue; and the punishment has added to it, an effect equally just and politic. namely, incapacitating the slanderer from appearing as an evidence on any future occasion.—Discretionary correction, which forms the subject of Chap. VI. extends to all petty descriptions of personal insult, even to abusive language. In fact, two-thirds of the punishment incurred under the Mussulman jurisdiction at the present day, whether in Turkay, Persia, or India, are inflicted under the name of Tazeer.—We must not pass this book without noticing the extraordinary indulgence show to slaves, in subjecting them, for all spiritual offence, to only half the punishment of freemen. The reasons alleged for this lenity manifest an uncommon degree of consideration and feeling for the state of bondage.

BOOK VIII OF LARCENY.

THE Translator has adopted the term Larceny, as the title of this book, because that work expreses every species of THEFT, from the most petty to the most atrocious. The uniform punishment annexed to Larceny is the amputation of a limb, unless where the act has been accompanied by murder, in which case the offender forfeits his life by the law of RETALIATION.—Many arguments might be adduced against the law of multilation in cases of Larceny, founded as well on the inhumanity as the inefficiency and inconvenience of that mode of correction. It is, however, the only method expressly authorized by the text of the KORAN ;—and if we consider the force of religious prejudice, and the effect of long habit, it may, perhaps appear very unadvisable to introduce any hasty alteration in the penal juricdiction in this particular,—especially as we have nothing better so offer by way of substitute (for surely our penal laws are still more sanguinary !), and also, as the Geutno laws, with respect to theft are strictly analogous to the Mussulman, in awarding mutilation under certain circumstances.—Chap. VII. of thls book is particularly worthy of attention, as it respects the most daring and outrageous branch which can be made against the peace and security of society. To enter fully into the spirit of the text, in this and many other parts under the head of larceny, it is requisite that we keep in mind the peculiar manners of the people in those parts of the world where the MUSSULMAN law operates. It is obserable that, at end of this book, a remarkable instance is incidentally introduced of the forbearance of the law in a case of homicide upon provocation.

NOTE.—Book VIII. has been omitted, as the question of larceny, as now applicable to India is regulated by the Penal Code, Act XLV. of 1860.

BOOK IX. THE INSTITUTES

THIS book contains a chief part of what may be properly termed the political ordinances of MOHAMMED, and is useful both in a historical and a legal view,—in the former, as it serves to explain the principles upon which the Arabinns proceeded in their first conquests (and in which they have been imitated by all successive, generations of Mussulmans), and in the latter, as many of the rules here laid down, with respect to subjugated countries, continue to prevail in all of that description at the present day. The nature and end of those regulations is so fully explained in the text, that they do not require any illustration or comment in this place.*

BOOK X. OF FOUNDLINGS

ONE of the earliest and most laudable attempts of MOHAMMED, in the prosecution of his pretended mission, was, to correct certain barbarous practices than prevalent among his countrymen, particularly with respect to infant children, whom it was common for the parents to expose or put to death, where they apprehended any inconvenience from the maintenance of them. The present book is to be considered merely as a comment upon his precepts in this particular.

BOOK XI. OF TROVES.

BOOK XII. ABSCONDING OF SLAVES.

NOTE.—This has been omitted for the same reason as Book V.

BOOK XIII. OF MISSING PERSONS.

THE rules laid down in these books will be found, in general strictly consonant to natural justice, and such as prevail (or ought to prevail) in all well-regulated communities.

BOOK XIV OF PARTNERSHIP.

THIS Book contains a number of subtle distinctions with respect to property, in many of which acute discrimination seems to be studied

*This book has been omitted, as it has hardly any practical effect ; and, if requisite, the former edition can be consulted.

more than practical utility. Several of them the reader may indeed be tempted to consider rather as the scholastic reveries of an abstracted divine, than as flowing from an active intercourse with the world, or dictated by the liberal spirit of commerce. Still, however, it will perhaps be found that in the mass of speculation much matter is interwoven of more substantial kind. The MUSSALMAN laws of property (to ascertain which is one great end of the present work) are in scme instances defined with considerable precisions ; and the various subdivision it exhibits to us of representative wealth, as opposed to real, gives us an interesting idea of the refinement which, so many centuries ago subsisted in Mohammedan countries with respect to those particulars.

BOOK XV. OF WAKF OF APPROPRIATIONS,

IN all Mohammedan countries (and in none more than in HINDOSTAN) it has been a common practice to dedicate lands, houses ; one other fixed as well as movable property to the use of the poor, or the support of religion. The founding of a mospue, the construction of a reservoir, and even the digging a well, for the public use, come all under the same head : and many noble monuments of these kinds are still to be seen in different parts of INDIA the useful effects of benevolence of superstition, in the more flourishing periods of the Mogul empire. That empire has, indeed, long since been hastening to decay ; and the monuments of Mussulman piety or magnificence have suffered, with it, a sympathetic dilapidation. Numberless grants of LAND, however, to pious or charitable uses, have been executed at different times, of which many are still in full force, under the general title of Aima ;—and these must give some interest to the subject of the present book, in which the various modes of alienation are discussed with considerable accuracy.

BOOK XVI. OF SALE.

BOOK XVII OF SIRF SALE.

To enter fully into the subjects of these books, would occupy more time and space than is consistent with the brevity of prefatory remark. The observations we have made concerning Book XIV. will equally apply to these throughout. The book of SALE is swelled by a vast accession of incidental matter. Of these, the most striking is USURY, the subject of Chap. VIII. The Mohammedans, in this particular, closely copy the Jewish law, by which the children of ISAREL were also strictly forbidden to exercise usury among each other.—To this chapter the book of SIRF SALE may in some measure be considered a supplement, since it seems chiefly calculated to guard and provide against the practice of USURY in the exchange of the precious metals.

BOOK XVIII, OF BAIL.

UNDER this head are comprehended all sorts of security, whether for persons or property. This book contains a good deal of practical matter (particularly in the laws concerning guarantees), and is therefore worthy of an attentive perusal.

BOOK XIX. TRANSFER OF DEBTS.

Is in some measure supplementary to the former, as the transaction of which it treats is performed by way of giving security to a creditor.

BOOK XX. DUTIES OF THE KAZEE.

THE subject of this book is of the utmost importance in all countries, as upon the conduct of the magistrates the welfare and happiness of every society must chiefly depend ; and indeed the Mohammedant esteem it of so must importance, that several large works have been written by their principal law commentators, under this title.—In Chap. I. and II. the proper conduct of a judge, and the behaviour required in him, are briefly defined.—In these, however, as well as in the subceeding chapter, the text wanders strangely from its professed subject, and goes into a variety of matter which would appear to fall more property under other heads.

BOOK XXI. OF EVIDENCE.

BOOK XXII. OF RETRACTATION OF EVIDENCE.

THESE are two as useful books as any in the whole work,—and develop some of the most important principles in judicial proceedings.—The last section of Book XXI. shows, that the punishment incurred by perjury are (as has been already noticed) of a very slight nature, and calculated to operate more upon men's feelings than their fears. The reasons for this lenity are of the same description with those urged by our lawyers. perhaps, indeed, the infamy and perpetual disqualifications to which the witness is subjected by it may operate as effectually as those penalties which the LAW prescribes ;—but it is certain that false testimony is regarded with less abhorrence by Mohammedans in general than among Christians.

VOL. III.

BOOK XXIII, OF AGENCY

BOOK XXIV. OF CLAIMS

IN the former of these books nothing very remarkable occurs, the laws with respect to agents being in general analogous to those which obtain in our own courts.—BOOK XXIV. chiefly relates to the conduct of suits at law and the rules to be observed in administering oaths, &c. It also comprehends much extraneous matter with respect to the various subjects of suits. Chap. V. treats of a point already mentioned. namely, the establishment of parentage. In all societies where polygamy and concubinage are allowed, this subject must necessarily afford frequent ground for litigation.

BOOK XXV. OF ACKNOWLEDGMENTS.

IT is only necessary to remark of this book, that Acknowledgment, in the Mussulman LAW, has the same effect, in the establishment or transfer of property, as a formal deed.

BOOK XXVI. OF COMPOSITIONS.

BOOK XXVII. OF MOZARIBAT.

THESE books contain a quantity of technical matter. Mozaribat seems to have been a device adopted in order to avoid the imputation of usury, by which the monied man was enabled to obtain a profit from his capital without the odium of receiving any interest upon it,— This species of contract is in common used in Hindostan.

BOOK XXVIII, OF DEPOSITS.

BOOK XXIX. OF LOANS.

BOOK XXX. OF GIFTS.

THESE books chiefly consist of plain rules, applied to ordinary cases.— It is to be remarked, however, that the Messlman law, with respect to gifts, differs considerably from the Roman, in leaving to the doner an unrestricted right of resumption.

BOOK XXXI. OF HIRE.

IT is a book of considerable practical utility, as it comprehends every deseription of valuable usufruçt, from the hire of land to that of a workman or an animal.

BOOK XXXII. OF MOKATIBS.

BOOK XXXIII. OF WILLA.

IT is probable that many of the laws in these books have now fallen into disuse, or are confined to Arabia, Persia, and Turkey. The privileges and immunities of WILFA, however, still obtain in all Mussulman countries, and are of considerable consequence, as involving many rights liable to become subjects of litigation. The privilege allowed to a slave, of covenanting for and purchasing his freedom, place the Mussulman laws of bondagc in a striking, but not a disagreeable light.

NOTE.—This book has also been omitted for the same reason as Book V·

BOOK XXXIV. OF COMPULSION.

IT is in general agreed, by most juridical writers, that a defect of the will arising from compulsion, is an excuse for any crime committed, and an annulment of any deed executed under it. In the Mussulman code this rule, however, does not invariably hold, as from what occurs under this head it appears, that compelled contracts or other acts are nevertheless valid in their effect ; and that offences committed under the influence of fear have still a degree of criminality attached to them.

Book XXXV. Of Inhibition.

The subject of this book comprehends every species of incapacity, whether natural or accidental. The secord chapter exhibits one of the most striking features in the institutes of Mohammedanism.—How far legal restrictions upon adult prodigals are calculated for the advantage of the community at large, is not our business to inquire. It is, however certain, that the imposition of wholesome limitations upon thoughtless extravagance, and every other species of folly, if more generally introduced, would operate powerfully to preserve the property and peace of families, and (perhaps) the virtue of individuals.—The iuhibition upon debtors, as contained in Chap. III. is well worthy of attention.

Book XXXVI. Of Licensed Slaves.

That regulation of the Mussalman law by which a master is empowered to endow his slave with alnost all the privileges and responsibilities of a freeman, preserving, at the same time, his property in him inviolate, affords a strong proof of its tenderness with respect to bondage. It in fact places the slave who obtains this advantage rather in the light of an attached dependant than of a mere servile instrument, deprived of privilege, and destitute of volition.

Bnok XXXVII. Of Usurapations.

Book XXXVIII. Of Shaffa.

The points of discussion which occupy these books are of some importance in every view. The regulations in the former are, for the most part, sanctified by natural justice, and those in the latter, by many considerations of conveniency and expedience. Several particulars which occur in treating of Usurpation must indeed be referred to certain customs prevalent in Arabia. The right of pre-emption enjoyed in virtue of community or contiguity of property, is perhaps peculiar to the interests and partialities of individuals, this privilege may neverthciess be considered as liable to some objection, on the score of affording room for endless litigation. Under certain restrictlons, it is both a just and a humane institntion.

VOL. IV

Book XXXIX. Of Partition.

This book relates chiefly to the divisiyn of inheritable property. By the Mussulman law, as by the Roman, partners in an estate may be constrained to make partition of their joint inheritance ; for which purpose proper officers are appointed by public authority.—The same rule also extends to other descriptions of partnerships property. The principal tendency of the disquisitions under this head is, to show what are proper objects of partition, and in what instances the magistrate is at liberty to compel the parties to accede to the separation of their joint possessions.—The laws of usufructury partition, as contained in Chap. V., possess much curious originality.

Book XL. Compacts Of Cultivation.

Book XLI. Compacts Of Gardening.

These books are of use chiefly on account of the regulations with respect to landed property which incidentally occur in them. They exhibit the farming of lands in a very imperfect state, aud at a time when money had as yet come little into current use. They, however, explain a number of principles upon this subject equally applicable to all ages.

Book XLII. Of Zabbah.

In the Mohammedan as in the Jewish Law, the eating of blood is strictly forbidden, and hence the various rules and precautions are set for under this head. It appears, from some passages, that the Arabian Prophet was desirous of inculcatlng not only a scrupulous regard to the purity of food, but also a humane and tender attention to the feelings of the animals destroyed for the purpose of supplying it.—This last is indeed a sentiment discoverable in many parts of his precepts.

Book XLIII. Of Sacrifice.

Sacrifice, whether as a memorial or an expiation, is one of the most mankind. The particular ceremony which is the subject of this book, was instituted in commemoration of Abraham's obedience to the Divine command by the intended sacrifice of his son. This son the Arabian commentators make to be their great progenitor Ishmael, and not Isaac, whom they assert to have been promised subsequent to that event. This conclusion they draw from the manner in which the whole circumstance is worded in the thirty-seventh chapter of the Koran, though the passage is certainly very equivocal. The anniversary of this rite falling on the tenth of Zee-al-Hidjee (the month of pilgrimage), it is performed by pilgrimage in the valley of Minna, and constitutes one of the prescribed ceremonies of pilgrimage.—It is, however, equally enjoined on all others possessed of the ability ; and may be performed by any man at his own habitation. The rules respecting it are few and simple ; and are, in fact, of little consequence in a civil light, farther than as they tend to affect property.

Book XLIV. Of Abominations.

A subject which involves a vast variety of frivolous matters, and must be considered chiefly in the light of a treatise upon propriety and decorum. In it is particularly exhibited the scrupulous attention paid to female modesty, and the avoidance of every act which may tend to violate it, even in though.—It is remarkable, however, that this does not amount to that absolute seclusion of woman supposed by some writers. In fact, this seclusion is a result of jealousy or pride, and not of any legal Injunction, as appears in this and several other parts of the Hedaya,

Neither is it a custom universally prevalent in Mohommedan countries.

Book XLV. Cultivation Of Waste Lands.

In most Mussulman governments, particular ecouragement has been held forth to the reclaiming of barren or deserted grounds, by the powerful incentive of granting to the cultivator a property in the soil,—A considerable portion of this book is occupied with discussions upon the right to water, that element being justly regarded as a most valuable commodity in' countries where, from the heat of the climate, the ground is liable, for the greatest part of the year, to excessive drought; and where of course, the success of tillage must chiefly depend upon an artificial supply of it.

Book XLVI. Prohibited Liquors.

In prohibiting the use of wine (under which term are included all descriptions or inebriating liquors), the prophet meant merely to restrain his followers from unbecoming behaviour. and other evil effects of intoxication. At first the precept was issued in the Koran simply against drunkenness which amounted only to a prohibition of excess in the use of strong liquors; but this not proving sufficient for the purposes of complete determent, the negative injunction was produced, by which inebriating fluids were altogether prescribed, and declared unlawful. The tendency of this book is chiefly, to exhibit the opinions of their divines concerning what kind of liquors those are which fall under the demonination of prohibted; in which we may trace the rigid scrupulosity of the more early Mussulmans upon this point, At present, however, they are not, in general, very strict observers of the Law in this particular, their modern doctors allowing that fluids various may be drunk, either medicinally or for pleasure, provided it be done with moderation, and so as to avoid scandal.

Book XLVII. Of Hunting.

This book is, properly, a supplement to Zabbah; any any reflections upou it may therefore be referred to the observations under that head.

Book XLVIII. OF Pawns

Book XLIX. Offnce Against The Persion.

In determining the measure of punishmant for offences committed upon the persons of men, the lex talionis seems at first sight to have been dictated by natural reason, and to be consistent with a justice, as affording the best means of a strict and equal retribution. Accordingly, we find it among the earliest institutes of every society approaching to a state of perfect civilization. Before the time of Mohammed, the administration of public justice being little known in Arabia, personal injuries were a fruitful source of private revenge and civil war, and preserved, among the descendants of Ishmael, a sanguinary ferocity of spirit, which was considered as a virtue rather than a blemish in their character. The Prophet soon perceived it necessary to the completion of his project, to introduce a reform in this particular ; and therefore, with a view at once to indulge his countrymen's propensity to revenge, and to preserve the peace of the community, shortly after his flight to Medina (as it is said), revealed that passage of the KORAN allowing of retaliation, in which he has nearly copied the law of MOSES. As equality is the professed ground of this institution, the Mussulman doctors, in their comments upon it seems, to have followed the literal acceptation of the text in all cases where the observance of this equality is possible, In practice however, retaliation is seldom or never inflicted upon a limb or member ; but a mulct is imposed in proportion to the injury, and according to the cricumstances by which it is excited or attended,—In fact, however equitable this mode of requital may appear in some instances of personal injury, yet, when applied to all without limitation' it certainly involves much gross absurdity and injustice, a charge from which it does not stand acquitted by all the distinctions which the commentators have established concerning it in this book. Hence it is that the Mussulman courts, following the example of the Jews, understand the words of the KORAN, in all cases short of life, in the same manner as those do the Pentateuch : that is, not as awarding an actual retaliation ; according to the strict literal meaning, but an atonement in exact proportion to the injury.—Thus much with respect to wilful offences. That law by which a man is made responsible in his property for offences unintentional or merely accidental, is certainly, in some instances, rather rigorous. It was, however, well calculated, in an irregular society, and a defective state of civilization, to guard men from acting carelessly, and has a strong tendency to support and inculcate the sacredness of the person of MAN.*—

BOOK. L. OF FINES.

ALTHOUGH the manner in which this subject is treated involves a considerable portion of frivolous absurdity, yet we also find, in the course of its discussions, many wise and salutary regulations, both for preserving the security of the person, and the peace and good order of society. We may perceive, from the persual of it, that a man is made responsible not only for his overt acts, but likewise, for any injury which may be more remotely occasioned by his carelessness, obstinacy, or wilful neglect. The degree of the fine was originally fixed at a certain amount, that for the life a man being determined at one hundred camel, and all others at a proportionable rate according to the injury. In later times however, the changes in manners, and in the value of property, introduced other modes of ascertaining amercement, and fines came to be levied not only in proportion to the injury sustained, but also according to the cricumstances of the case.—Chap. VI. exhibits the only species of inquest admitted by the Mussulman law in cases of uncertain homicide, consisting solely of expurgatory oaths, However well calcuated this may have been for the meridian of Arabia or Irak, and for the state

*This subject has been omitted, as it is now dealt with by the Indian Criminal Law.

of society in those countries at the time these laws were first systematized into a code, it is certainly but a poor device for the detection of guilt or the ascertainment of fact in a well-regulated community.—It is remarkable that a law strictly correspondent to what is mentioned in this chapter formerly prevailed among the Saxons and other northern nations of EUROPE, where the responsibility for unascertainable bloodshed lay with the master of the family, or with the people of the tithing in which the body was found.*

Book LI. THE LEVYING OF FINES.

THE subject of this book is purely of a local nature, relating entirely to the levying of fines upon the Arabian tribes for offences unintentionally committed by any individual of them.—These regulation serve to give us a pretty clear idea of the state of society in the native land of Islamism. However useless, and perhaps impracticable, in a more advanced state of refinement, these, as well as many regulation in the two preceding book, were well calculated to reduce a fierce people under the restraints of law and civil government.

NOTE.—See note to Book XLIX.

Book LII. OF WILLS.

WITH respect to the forms of wills, the same observations occur as have been already made in treating of MARRIAGE.—In fact, as writing was formerly very little in use among the Arabs, all deeds are, in the commentaries upon their laws regarded and mentioned as merely oral. Hence WILLS, as discussed in this book, are solely of the nuncupative description. The most remarkable features in this book are, the restrictions imposed upon testators with respect to the disposal of their property.

Book LIII. OF HERMAPHRODITES.

THIS book, and the succeeding chapter, which, because of its being detached from any particular subject, is termed CHAPTER THE LAST, are a kind of supplement to the rest of the work Hermaphrodites are probably a class of beings which exist in imagination rather than in reality. We shall therefore leave this book to speak for itself, —The fast chapter is worthy of particular notice, as (if we except bills of sale and judicial letters) it is the only part of the work in which anything mentioned concerning forms of WRITING.

———

IN concluding this short review, the translator esteems it his duty to add, that it is a very imperfect summary indeed of the work which is now presented to the public. The subjects of it would admit of a much more ample discussion.—But to enter into a comparative and analytical survey of topics so numerous and important would of itself require a lagre volume; and the patience of the reader is perhaps exhausted. The more particular investigation of them we shall therefore leave to his own reflections or inquiries; and hasten to conclude an essay, for the length of which no other apology can be

*See the note above.

offered, than an anxious wish to forward the chief end of this publication, by throwing some light upon a subject dry in itself, and not without its difficulties, and accommodating it to the preceptions of those whom duty or curiosity may lead to make it an object of their study.

Or the importance of a work in which the translator has borne so large a share, it may not become him to say much ; but as the objects of it are of a public nature and as it has been brought forward in some measure at the public expense, he feels himself called upon to hazard a few words in vindication of its probable utility.

With respect to the immediate and proposed by those who originally projected this translation, all that is necessary to be stated may be resolved into one summary argument. While the Mohammedan LAW is allowed to be the sole standard of criminal, and in a great measure of civil jurisprudence throughout our dominions* in INDIA (and it would perhaps be neither prudent nor possible hastily to introduce any other system), it appears indispensably necessary that those who are to project the rights of the people, and who are responsible for the proper administration of public justice, should possese the means of consulting the principles on which the decisions of the Mussulman courts are founded. This reflection acquires still greater weight, when we consider how very large a portion of subjects under the British government in INDIA are Mohammedans, upon whose attachment to their rules much of the prosperity of our Asiatic empire must necessarily depend.

The advantages to be derived from a development of the institutes of MOHAMMED are, however, not confined to the administration of justice in our Asiatic territories. The commerce of GREAT BRITAIN extends to almost every region where his religion is professed ; and as this work is a commentary upon the juridical code of the OTTOMAN as we as of the OTTOMAN as well as of the MOGUL empire, and is applicable to the customs and judicial regulations of Cairo, Aleppo, or Constantinople, as well as of Delhi or Moorshedabad,—it can scarcely fall to open a source of desirable knowledge to the merchant and the traveller. In a political view, likewise, it is humbly presumed that this work will not be found altogether uninteresting. At the present eventful period, when we have seen new empires springing in to birth, and the old indignantly throwing off the long rivetted chains of despotism, the grandest remaining fabric of Islamism seems hastening to its fall.—In expecting this mighty ruin, we are naturally led to inquire upon what principles the fabric was founded, and to what causes we are to attribute its decay.—Some parts of the following treatise are particularly calculated to assist us in such an investigation. We may there observe that however sagaciously it might be formed for the sudden extension of dominion, during an age when mankind were involved in the darkest gloom of superstition and ignorance, the Mussulman system, civil and religious, is but wretchedly adapted to the purposes of public security or private virtue. We may observe, with some degree of laudable exultation,

*See the Penal Code, and Cods of Criminal Procedure

its obvious inferiority, in every useful view, to that excellent system which we profess, and which is so admirably calculated to promote the temporal good of mankind, as well as their eternal happiness !

But it is time to close this address. The translator cannot however, conclude without paying that tribute which justice and gratitude demand— Concerning the public zeal, the penetrating and comprehensive mind of the Gentleman to whom the work is dedicated, in is unnecessary to enlarge in this place. From him the present translation derives its existence ; and the merit of his design received its best confirmation in the continuance of support it experienced from his immediate superiors, as well as from his successors in office.—To the liberal attention and honourable confidence of Sif John Macpherson and the Colleagues in the Bengal government it is owing, that the traslator was at all enabled to look forward to the completion of his labour. Yet this attention and confidence, flattering as they were, would not have sufficed to bear him through an arduous and expensive undertaking, had it not been aided by the generous and munificent support of the Court of Directors, whose regard to every effort which may tend to promote the interests of our Oriental dominions has been repeatedly experienced both by himself and others. Conscious of his own deficiences, he has only to hope it may appear, that what they have liberally granted has been faithfully and diligently employed. He entertains too humble an opinion of his abilities not to be sensible that, with all his assiduity aided by the many happy suggestions of the worthy and excellent friend who had for some time been his Colleague in the performance, it will still be found for short of perfection·—The chief business of a translator, when engaged in an undertaking of this kind, is scrupulous accuracy, and they only merit he can claim laborious application. The former these the present translator has endeavoured to preserve, and the latter he presumes to affirm has not been wanting. Nevertheless, there is undoubtedly much room for correction and amendment. The very nature of the work rendered the translation of it a business attended with no common degree of difficulty. Treating of an ostruse science, the technical terms of which but nakedly explained, and frequently not to be met with in any of his guides, all the light the translator could obtain to a knowledge of his subject necessarily sprung out of the text : and consequently, as he advanced, he saw continual occasion for retrospective alterations, which amounted to little less than a repetition of his labour. He found himself therefore frequently at a loss ; and repeatedly experienced the truth of an observation made by our immortal Lexicographer,—that "a writer may often in vain trace his memory, at the moment of need, for that whieh yesterday he knew with intuitive readiness. and which will come uncalled into his thoughts to morrow."

In confirmetion of his wish to renden this publication, as much as in his power, worthy of the patronage under which it has been conducted. the translator hopes he may be indulged in these egotism of the remarks.—that he has dedicated his three last years unremittedly to revisal or re-translation.—He now dismiss it with an anxious wish that that patronage may not appear to have been bestowed, or his own efforts applied, in vain ?

THE HEDAYA;

A

COMMENTARY ON THE MUSSULMAN LAWS.

BOOK I.

OF ZAKAT.

Definition of the term.—ZAKAT, in its primitive sense, means purification whence it is also used to express a contribution of a portion of property assigned to the use of the poor, as a sanctification of the remainder to the proprietor. It is by some commentators termed the indispensable alms.

CHAPTER I.

Obligation of Zakat and the conditions upon which it is incumbent.—ZAKAT is an ordinance of God, incumbent upon every person who is free, sane, adult and a Mussulman, provided he be possessed, in full propriety, of such estate or effects as are termed in the language of the law a Nisab, and that he has been in possession of the same for the space of one complete year, which is denominated Hawlan-Hawl. The reason of this obligation is found in the word of God, who has ordained it in the KORAN, saying, "BESTOW ZAKAT." The same injunction occurs in the traditions ; and it is moreover universally admitted. The reason for freedom being a requisite condition is, that this is essential to the complete possession of property. The reason why sanity of intellect and maturity of age are requisite conditions shall be hereafter demonstrated. The reason why the Mussulman faith is made a condition is, that the rendering of Zakat is an act of piety, and such cannot proceed from an infidel. The reason for the possession of a Nisab being a condition is that the Prophet has determined the obligation of Zakat upon that amount. The reasons for Hawlan-Hawl being made a requisite condition are twofold ; FIRST, because some space of time is necessary to increase* of property, and the law determines this at one year, because the Prophet has declared; "ZAKAT is not due upon property until the same shall have been possessed one year by the proprietor : "—SECONDLY, the proprietc of a Nisab is able, within such a period, to obtain an increase from it, since in a year there are four seasons, in each of which it most commonly happens that such property bears a different price ; wherefore the rule is determined accordingly. It is to be observed, that some maintain Zakat to be due immediately upon the completion of Hawlan Hawl, and others that it is so through, life.†

Zakat is not due from infants nor from maniacs.—ZAKAT is not incumbent upon infants or maniacs—Shafei declares Zakat to be an obligation connected with property and therefore that it is incumbent upon those, as well as upon other proprietors, in the same manner as subsistence to a wife, and Tythe and Tribute ; but to this our doctors reply that Zakat is an act of piety, and, as such, is fulfilled only by being paid with the option of those who are subject to it ; and infants and maniacs are not held in law to be possessed of option, this being necessarily connected with reason, which they are not endowed with ; but this does not apply to Tribute, as that is a provision arising from

---

*By increase is here understood that obtained by breeding, where the Nisab consists of cattle, or by profit, where it consists of merchandise.

†That is to say, annually, upon the same property, so long as it remains with the proprietor.

the soil, for the expenses of the state; nor to Tythe, as that is also in some shape of the same nature.

With certain exceptions. IF a lunatic have lucid intervals within the year, it is the same as if they happened within the month of Ramzan; that is to say, if he recovers his reason within the year, he is subject to Zakat, in the same manner as if he were to recover it within the month of Ramzan, in which case he would have to make up for the days of Lent he had omitted in consequence of his insanity.—Aboo Yoosaf has observed, that regard is to be paid to the length or continuance of the lucid intervals; that is to say, if they continue the greater part of the year, the lunatic is subject to Zakat; but if he be insane for the greater part, it is not incumbent upon him. It is to be observed, that original and supervenient insanity are here considered as the same; by original is understood that which appears in a person in infancy, and continues upon him as he grows up to puberty; and by supervenient, that which occurs after a person has attained the years of maturity. It is related as an opinion of Aboo Yoosaf that if a person attain maturity in a state of insanity, and then becomes sane, the year* is considered to commence from the instant of his recovery, the same as a boy attaining puberty, with whom it is regarded as commencing on the day of his majority.

Nor from Mokatibs.—Zakat is not incumbent upon a Makatib, he not being completely and independently possessed of property, since he is still a slave; whence it is that he is not at liberty to emancipate any of his own slaves.

Nor from insolvent debtors.—ZAKAT is not incumbent upon a man against whom there are debts equal to, or exceeding, the amount of his whole property. Imam Shafei alleges that it is incumbent, because the cause of the obligation, to wit, possession of an increasing NISAB, is established. To this our doctors reply that such a Nisab is not possessed by him clear of incumbrance, and is therefore held to be non-existent, the same as water, which, when provided for the sole purpose of drink,† is held to be non-existent with respect to performance of the Tammeem, and cloth provided for the purpose of apparel, which is held non-existent with respect to the obligation of Zakat. But if his property exceeds his debts, Zakat is due upon the excess, provided the same amount to what is sufficient to constitute a Nisab, and that it be free from incumbrance. By the debts here mentioned are understood those due to individuals; such, therefore, as are due in consequence of vows or on account of expiations, do not forbid the obligation to pay Zakat: pay Zakat in the continuance of the Nisab, as that would be thereby rendered defective: and, in like manner, a debt of Zakat forbids Zakat after the dissolution of the Nisab. The case of the continuance of a Nasib is, where the proprietor keeps it for two years without rendering any Zakat upon it, in which case no Zakat is due from him on account of the second year; because a Zakat, in the proportion of one in forty, is already due on account of the preceding year, whence the full amount necessary to constitute a Nisab does not remain in the second year: and the case of dissolution of the Nisab is, where the proprietor keeps the same for the full space of one year without paying Zakat, and then disposes of the Nisab, and afterwards becomes possessed of another Nisab, and this also continue in his possession for the complete space of one year; in which case, no Zakat is due upon this second Nisab because a proportion of one in forty is already occupied by the Zakat due on the former Nisab which has been disposed of. Ziffer controverts the rule in both these cases: and it is also said that Aboo Yoosaf controverts it with respect to the second case. The reason why a debt of Zakat thus forbids any further obligation to pay Zakat is, that the claimant of a debt of Zakat is, in fact an individual,* as the claimant thereof, in pastures, is the Imam, and, in articles of merchandise, the deputy of the Imam;† and the proprietor of the property, in all other articles, is the Imam's substitute.‡

Nor upon the necessaries of life.—ZAKAT is not due upon dwelling-houses or articles of clothing or household furniture, or cattle kept for immediate use, or slaves employed as actual servants, or armour, or weapons designed for present use; all these falling under the description of necessaries; neither are such considered as increasing property; and the same of books of science, with respect to scholars, and likewise of tools, with respect to handicrafts; these being to them as necessaries.

Nor upon uncertain property.—IF a man have a claim upon another for a debt, and the other dispute the same and some years thus pass away, and the claimant be destitute of proof, and the debtor afterwards make a de-

*For the establishment of Hawlan-Hawl in his possession.

†As in the caravans, where water is provided and carried upon camels for drink, but not for the purpose of purification, which in that or similar situations is permitted to be performed with sand.

*In opposition to God; for, if Zakat were claimed purely as a right of God, the payment of it would be absolutely and unconditionally incumbent.

†Because the Imam is always supposed to collect the Zakat upon pastures in person, and that upon merchandise by his deputies, *i.e.* by collectors placed at particular stations for that purpose.

‡As the payment of Zakat, upon all other articles, is committed to the proprietor himself.

claration or acknowledgment publicly, insomuch that there are witnesses of the same there is no obligation upon the claimant to render any Zakat* for so many years as have thus passed. This uncertain sort of property is termed, in the language of the law, Zimar: and trove property, and fugitive slaves, and usurped property, respecting which there is no proof, and property sunk in the sea, or buried in the desert and its place forgotten, and property tyrannically seized by the Sultan, are all of the description of Zimar: and all these articles are equally exempted from Sadka-fittir.† Ziffer and Shafei maintain, that all these articles are subject both to Zakat, and also to Sadka-fittir, as the cause of the obligation to pay Zakat (to wit possession of a Nisab) is established in each of them, although it was not in the immediate seisin of the proprietor whilst it fell under the description of Zimar, which does not forbid the obligation of Zakat; like the property of a traveller, which if it remain in his house, is nevertheless subject to Zakat, although it be not at the time in his hands. The arguments of our doctors herein are twofold: First, Alee declared that no Zakat is due upon Zimar property: Secondly, the cause of the obligation to pay Zakat is the possession of property in a state of increase, which cannot be the case but where the proprietor has an immediate power of management over it; but this does not apply to a traveller who has property at home, as he may manage it by agents.

Property buried in the home of the proprietor is not Zimar, because it is easily recovered; but with respect to property buried in any other ground than that on which the house actually stands (such as the garden, for instance) there is a difference among our modern doctors.

It is due upon unquestionable property.—Property which is acknowledged by a debtor to be owing to his creditor is subject to Zakat, whether such debtor be rich or poor, because the recovery of it is possible: or if the debtor dispute the demand, yet here also the property in question is subject to Zakat, provided there be proof sufficient to substantiate the creditor's claim, or that the Kazee himself be satisfied of the justice of it; because here also recovery is possible. And if the acknowledging debtor be poor,—that is to say, if the Kazee declare him insolvent;—yet here also the property in question is subject to Zakat, according to Haneefa,—he holding that a Kazee's declaration of the insolvency of a debtor is not approved: but Imam Mohammed maintains that the property in this case is not subject to Zakat,—he holding a Kazee's declaration of a debtor's insolvency to be approved.—Aboo Yoosaf agrees with Mohammed respecting the validity of a Kazee's decree of insolvency; but he, at the same time coincides with Haneefa, that the property of which the debt consists is not, in this case, subject to Zakat.

Intention of traffic in property subjects it to Zakat.—If a person purchase a female slave for the purpose of traffic, and afterwards retain her for his own use, declaring his intention, no Zakat is due upon her, because the intention is here connected with the act namely, the relinquishment of traffic in her; and an intention thus declared, when connected with an act, is to be credited:—and if he should afterwards declare a design of trafficking in her; yet no Zakat will be due upon her in virtue of such declaration, until he actually dispose of her by sale, because here the intention is not connected with the act, and consequently she is not held to be a subject of traffic from his declaration, unless he actually sell her, when Zakat is due upon her price.

If a person purchase a thing with an intention of traffic, it is to be considered as an article of traffic, on account of the connection of an intention of traffic with the act, to wit, purchase: contrary to a case where a person obtains possession of property by inheritance, and intends to traffic in the same, such not being considered an article of traffic merely from the intention, since that, in this case, bears no relation to the act*.

If a man become possessed of property by gift, or bequest, or marriage or Khoola, or composition for blood, and intend trafficking in the same, it becomes (and is, in virtue of his intention, considered as) an article of merchandise,—according to Aboo Yoosaf—, he holding the intention here to be connected with the act. It is related as an opinion of Imam Mohammed, that this property does not become as merchandise, because the intention is not here connected with the act of traffic, which is understood only by purchase and sale; some, however, have related this difference of opinion the reverse of what is here mentioned.

Intention of Zakat, in the payment, necessary to its validity.—The payment of Zakat is not lawful, except under an intention existing at the period of such payment, or at the period of setting apart the proportion of Zakat from the Nisab property, because the rendering of Zakat is an act of piety, to which the intention is essential; and a radical principle of the intention is that it be connected with the payment: but yet, inasmuch as the giving of Zakat to the poor is necessarily an act of frequent repetition and occurrence, it suffices that the intention exist at the period of setting apart the proportion of Zakat (as aforesaid), for the sake of convenience.

---

*Upon the property which is the subject of the claim.

†For an explanation of Sadka-fittir, see Chap. VIII.

*That is, to the means by which such property was acquired.

Excepting under certain circumstances;—If a man bestow his whole property in charity, without intention of Zakat, the obligation of Zakat, with respect to him, drops, upon a principle of benevolence, because such obligation extends to a certain part of his property only; and where the whole is thus bestowed, that part is necessarily included; whence it is that there is no necessity for his specifying the same by intention.

If a man give to the poor a portion of his Nisab property, without intention of Zakat, his obligation to Zakat drops with respect to such portion (according to Mohammed), because the part of his property due (on account of Zakat) affects the whole of his Nisab equally,—wherefore, when a part of the Nisab is thus bestowed the proportiondue upon such part goes along with it. Aboo Yoosaf maintains that the obligation to the Zakat of that portion does not drop, because no part thereof is particularly specified as Zakat, the remainder of the Nisab being the subject from which the obligation is to be discharged: contrary to where the whole Nisab has been bestowed, since there the proportion due on account of Zakat goes, a certiori, as being involved in the whole.

CHAPTER II.

OF ZAKAT FROM SAWAYEEM; THAT IS, HERDS AND FLOCKS.

Definition of Sawayeem,—Sawayeem is the plural of Sayeema; and Sayeema is, by the learned, understood to imply camels, oxen, goats and other animals which subsist for the greater part of the year upon pasture: wherefore, if they live but half the year in pastures, and are fed for the other half upon forage, they do not fall under the description of Sawayeem.*—And this chapter is divided into several heads.

Sect. 1.—Of the Zakat of Camels, &c.

One goat due upon five camels, &c—No Zakat is due on fewer than five camels; and upon five camels the Zakat is one goat, provided they subsist upon pasture throughout the year; because Zakat is due only upon such camels as live on pasture, and not upon those which are fed in the house with forage.

One goat is due upon any number of camels from five to nine; and two goats is the Zakat on any number from ten to fourteen; and three on any number from fourteen to nineteen and four upon any number from twenty to twenty-four; and upon any number of camels from twenty-five to thirty-five the Zakat is a Binnit-Makhass, that is a yearling camel's colt; and upon any number from thirty-six to forty-five, a Binnit-liboon, or camel's colt of two years; and upon any number from forty-six to sixty, a Hikka, or four-year old female camel; and upon any number from sixty-one to seventy-five, a Fazeeyat, or five-year old female camel; and for any number from seventy-six to ninety, the Zakat is two camel's colts of two years; and on any number from ninety-one to one hundred and twenty, two Hikkas. These proportions of Zakat upon camels are what were written by the Prophet in his letters and instructions to his public officers and Aumeels. And when the number of camels exceeds one hundred and twenty, the Zakat is calculated by the aforesaid rule; that is to say, where the whole number is one hundred and twenty-five (for instance), the Zakat is one goat for the odd five, and two Hikkas for the one hundred and twenty; and if the excess number be ten, two goats; and if it be fifteen, three goats; and if it be twenty, four goats; and if it be twenty-five, a yearling camel's colt; and if the whole number of camels be one hundred and fifty, the Zakat is three Hikkas; and if the number exceed one hundred and fifty by five, it is then one goat and three Hikkas, that is to say, three Hikka upon the hundred and fifty, and a goat upon the odd five; and upon one hundred and sixty camels, the Zakat is three Hikkas and two goats; and upon one hundred and seventy, three Hikkas and four goats; and upon one hundred and seventy-five, three Hikkas and one yearling colt; and upon any number from one hundred and eighty-six to one hundred and ninety-five the Zakat is three Hikkas and a two-year old colt; and upon any number from one hundred and ninety-six to two hundred, the Zakat is four Hikkas; and in this manner is the Zakat to be calculated upon every fifty camels exceeding one hundred and fifty.—This arrangement is according to our doctors. Shafei alleges that when the number exceeds the hundred and twenty by one only, the Zakat is three two-year old colts; and if it amount to one hundred and thirty, it is one Hikka and two two-year old colts; after which the Zakat is calculated at a two-year old colt upon every forty camels, and a Hikka upon every fifty: the Prophet, upon a particular occasion, having written to one of his Aumeels to this effect, without making any mention of a goat upon the odd five, and so forth. But our doctors, in support of their opinion, as above, cite the letters of the Prophet to Omar, where he says, "upon every five camels the Zakat is one goat."

Female camels only lawful in the payment of Zakat.—And it is to be observed that, in the payment of the Zakat of camels, females alone are lawful, because males are held to be lawful only in regard to their

*This term is in our dictionaries translated pastures, but the above is the precise definition of it.

value,* such being recorded both in the sacred writings and in the traditions.

Camels of all descriptions included.—Camels of every description, whether Bactrian, Arabian, or others, are all included in these rules of Zakat, as the term camel [Shutr] is common to all.

Sect. II.—Of the Zakat of Horned Cattle.

One yearling due upon thirty kine, &c.—No Zakat is due upon fewer than thirty kine; and upon thirty kine, which feed on pasture for the greater part of the year, there is due at the end of the year a Zakat of one Tubbee, that is, a follower, or yearling calf, male or female; and upon forty there is due one Misna, or calf of two years, male or female, on the authority of the Prophet; and where the number exceeds forty, the Zakat (according to Haneefa) is to be calculated agreeably to this rule, so far as sixty; that is to say, if there be one animal more than the forty, there is an additional Zakat of the fortieth part of a Misna; and if two, of the twentieth part of a Misna; and so on to the number sixty.—What is here advanced accords with the Mabsoot; and the ground upon which it proceeds is that, in the sacred writings, the Zakat is particularly specified for any number between thirty and forty, and also for those of sixty and above, but none for the numbers between forty and sixty, Hasan states the doctrine of Haneefa to be in this case, that, on the numbers from forty to forty-nine, no excess Zakat whatever is due; and that upon fifty kine the Zakat is one Misna, and the fourth of a Misna, or the third of a Tubbee; because upon every Akid, or drove of even number, in a Nisab of cattle, such as thirty, forty, or fifty head Zakat is due, but not upon any intermediate number.—The two disciples say that no Zakat whatever is due upon any odd number between forty and fifty; and there is also one tradition of the opinion of Haneefa to this effect; and the reason they allege is, that the Prophet said to Maaz. "Take not anything from an Owkas of kine," and he explained an Owkas to mean any number between forty and fifty. And upon sixty kine, the Zakat is two yearling calves, male or female: and upon seventy, one Misna and one Tubbee and upon eighty, two Misnas: and upon ninety, three Tubbees: and upon one hundred, two Tubbees and one Misna: and thus on every ten head, a Misna and a Tubbee alternately, the Prophet having ordained that the Zakat upon thirty kine should be a Tubbee; and that upon forty a Misna:—thus, upon one hundred and ten kine, the Zakat is two Misnas and one Tubbee; and upon one hundred and twenty, four Tubbees.

The usual method, however, of calculating the Zakat upon large herds of cattle, is by dividing them into thirties or forties, imposing upon every thirty one Tubbee; or upon every forty one Misna.

Buffaloes are included with other horned cattle.—It is to be observed that buffaloes are included with kine in the laws of Zakat, these being also considered as a species of black cattle; but yet, in our country,* the buffalo is not regarded as of the black cattle species; whence it is that if a person were to make a vow, saying, "I will not eat of the flesh of black cattle," and were afterwards to eat buffalo beef, he would not be forsworn

Sect. III.—Of the Zakat of Goats.

One goat due upon forty goats, &c.—No Zakat is due upon fewer than forty goats; and upon forty goats, which feed for the greater part of the year upon pastures, there is due, at the expiration of the year, a Zakat of one goat; and this Zakat suffices for any number from forty to one hundred and twenty: and if the number exceed one hundred and twenty, a Zakat of two goats is due from one hundred and twenty-one to two hundred: and if it exceed two hundred, a Zakat of three goats is due from two hundred and one to three hundred and ninety-nine: and if it amount to four hundred, the Zakat is four goats: and beyond four hundred the Zakat is one goat for every hundred: the Prophet having thus ordained, and all the doctors uniting in this opinion. It is also to be observed, that the same rules of Zakat are applicable to sheep as to goats, the term Ghannem, in the tradition equally implying both species.

Kids or lambs are not acceptable payment unless they be above a year old.—In the Zakat of goats or sheep, Sinnees are acceptable payment, but not Juzzas. This is the Zahir-Rawayet. Sinnees are kids which have entered on the second year; and Juzzas are such as have not yet completed their first year.—The two disciples have said that the Zakat may be paid with the Juzzas of sheep; and there is one opinion of Haneefa recorded to this effect; and the reasons are twofold; First the Prophet has said, "The Zakat upon them consists of Juzzas and Sinnees; Secondly, sacrifice is fulfilled by the immolation of a juzza, and therefore Zakat may be also discharged by it. The ground upon which the Zahir-Rawayet proceeds is also twofold; First, a saying of Alee, "In Zakat nothing is acceptable short of a Sinnee;"—Secondly, in the Zakat of goats it is incumbent to give those of a middling size, and the juzzas of sheep are not of that standard, being small; whence it is that the Juzzas of goats also are not acceptable in Zakat. With respect to the first reason urged by the two disciples, it may be replied, that by the term Juzza, as mentioned in the tradition, is to be understood the Juzzas of camels, that is, yearling colts:

*That is to say, the price of a male is held to be lawful in Zakat, but not the animal

*Meaning Persia or Hindostan.

and what they say of sacrifice is no rule, as that of a Juzza is approved (not by analogy, but) from the express words of the sacred text.

But males and females are equally acceptable.—IN paying the Zakat of goats or sheep, males and females are equally acceptable; the term Shat, in the traditions applying indiscriminately to both genders.

Sect. IV.—Of the Zakat of Horses.

One Deenar per head due upon horses, or five Deenars per cent on the total value.—WHEN horses and mares are kept indiscriminately together, feeding for the greater part of the year on pasture, it is at the option of the proprietor either to give a Zakat of one Deenar per head for the whole, or to appreciate the whole, and give five Deenars per cent upon the total value: and this last is the mode adopted by Ziffer. The two disciples maintain that no Zakat whatever is due upon horses, the Prophet having ordained that Mussulmans should not be subject to ZAKAT for their horses or slaves. Haneefa in support of his doctrine, as above, states an ordinance issued by the Prophet, in which he directed that the Zakat upon ordinary horses should be one Deenar, or ten Dirms, per head. And with respect to the ordinance above quoted by the two disciples, that applies solely to war-horses, and not to ordinary cattle.

Zakat not due upon droves consisting entirely either of males or of females.—No Zakat whatever is due upon a Nisab of horses consisting entirely of males, because in that there can be no increase by breeding; and, in like manner, there is no Zakat upon a Nisab consisting entirely of mares, for the same reason.—This is one tradition from Haneefa. There is another tradition from him, however, which says that a Zakat is due upon mares although there be no horses among them, as horses can be occasionally borrowed by the proprietor for the purpose of producing, whence increase may be had: but this is impossible with respect to droves consisting entirely of horses.

No Zakat due upon asses or mules, unless as articles of commerce.—THERE is no Zakat due upon asses or mules, the Prophet having said, "With respect to Zakat upon asses and mules, I have received no revelation." But yet, if these animals be as articles of merchandise, a Zakat is due upon them, because, in the present times, Zakat is imposed upon the property involved in them the same as upon any other articles of traffic.

Sect. V.—Of the Zakat of Kids, and Calves, and Camels' Colts.

No Zakat due upon the young of herds or flocks until a year old.—No Zakat whatever is due (according to Haneefa) upon the young of goats, kine, or camels, which are under one year; that is to say, if a man were to purchase twenty-five camels' colts (for instance) or forty kids, or thirty calves, and one complete year should pass from the period of possession, still no Zakat is due; nor does any become due until the expiration of the term of a year after they shall have been grown up.

One camel's colt due on 25, &c.—ABOO YOOSAF holds that Zakat is not due upon fewer than forty kids, or thirty calves or twenty-five camels' colts: and upon twenty-five camels' colts the Zakat is one colt: and there is no further Zakat due till the number amounts to seventy-six, when the Zakat is two colts; because upon seventy-six Misnas a Zakat is due of two Binnit-liboons; and there is no further Zakat till the number amounts to one hundred and forty-five when it is three colts; because upon one hundred and forty-five Misnas the Zakat is two Hikkas and one Binnit-makhass. There are other traditions of the opinion of Aboo Yoosaf herein; but the above, as being a posterior record, supersedes them.

Case of the payment of Zakat by substitution.—IF a person owe, as Zakat, a *Misna*, and it should happen that he is not possessed of one, having no cattle in his flocks but what are either under or over that description, the officer who collects the Zakat is at liberty either, in the former case to take an animal of the under rate, and the difference in money,—or, in the latter, to take one of a superior sort, paying the difference of value between that and a Misna to the proprietor. It is to be observed that, in the latter case, no constraint is to be put upon the collector, who is at liberty to insist upon either the actual thing due (to wit, a Misna), or the value of one in money, because the acceptance of an animal of the superior sort, on the terms above stated, wears the aspect of traffic; his acceptance of it, therefore, cannot be compelled, insomuch that if the proprietor were to give him no obstruction in taking it, yet he is not considered as being seized of it; but the collector may be compelled to accept of an animal of an inferior sort, and the difference in money, insomuch that if the proprietor merely give no obstruction to the officer, in thus taking the animal and the difference, he (the officer) is considered as being seized of the same; because here the transaction does not bear the aspect of purchase and sale, as the proprietor pays the inferior animal in part of the Misna, and consequently the difference along with it.

Substitution of the value lawful.—IF a proprietor, in Zakat, should, in lieu of the actual thing due, pay the value in money, it is approved, according to our doctors; and the same holds good in expiation, or in the payment of Sadka-fittir, or Tythe, or the fulfilment of a vow. Shafei maintains that this is unlawful, because it is not lawful to exchange, for a substitute, anything specified in the sacred writings; as in sacrifice (for instance) where a substitution of value for the victim is illegal. The argument of our doctors is, that God has himself ordained Zakat, and has directed the same to be distributed in alms to the poor, which plainly indicates that the intent of the institution is merely that the poor should derive a subsistence from it, so as that their wants may be thereby relieved; and to effect this the value will answer equally well with the specific animal, wherefore the substitution of the value in payment of Zakat is legal, the same as in payment of Jazzeeyat, or capitation-tax: but this reasoning does not apply to sacrifice as that is an act of piety, to the fulfilment of which the shedding of the blood of the victim is essential, wherefore no conclusion can be drawn from this instance, as there is no analogy between the two cases.

Labouring cattle exempt from Zakat.—CAMELS and oxen kept for the purpose of labour, such as carrying burthens, drawing the plough and so forth, are not subject to Zakat; neither is any Zakat due upon them where they are fed one half of the year or more upon forage. Malik controverts this doctrine; but the arguments of our doctors herein are threefold; FIRST, the Prophet has expressly ordained that these two species of cattle should be exempted from Zakat under such circumstances; SECONDLY, the cause of the obligation of Zakat consists in the possession of increasing property and the increase of cattle can be conceived only under two circumstances, that is, their being either kept in pastures,* or for the purpose of traffick, neither of which is the case with the cattle now under consideration; THIRDLY, in case where the cattle are fed upon forage, the keeping of them is attended with great expense, a circumstance which more than counterbalances any advantage to be derived from their breeding in such a situation, and therefore virtually prevents increase, although it may not actually do so.

Must be paid in animals of a medium Value.—THE officer, in collecting Zakat, is not at liberty either to insist upon the best or to accept of the worst sort of the property collected upon, but must take what is of a medium standard, because the Prophet has so ordained it; and also, because, in confining the Zakat to property of a medium value, regard is had at once to the interest of both the parties concerned, to wit, the poor and the proprietor.

Law respecting property acquired in the interim between the payments.—WHOEVER is possessed of a Nisab property, and obtains an addition of the same sort of species within the year, must add it to the Nisab, and pay Zakat upon the whole. Shafei objects to this, maintaining that the supervenient acquisition should not be added to the first Nisab, because the property of which that consists is original and independent with respect to propriety, and is therefore so with respect to Zakat likewise: contrary to acquisition by breed or profit obtained within the year, that being a dependant only of the original property, and, as such, not to be confounded with it. To this our doctors reply, that the reason for supervenient acquisition, by brood or profit, being added to the Nisab is homogeneity in the subject of it; since, where the original and supervenient property are of the same species, it is not easy to discriminate precisely between them, and consequently difficult to ascertain the Hawlan-Hawl with respect to any species of profitable acquisition arising from original property; and as the Hawlan-Hawl is regarded only for the sake of convenience, it therefore appears that homogeneity in the subject is a sufficient reason for the supervenient acquisition being added to the orginal property; and this reason exists in the present case.

Rules respecting the Afoo.—THE two Sheikhs hold Zakat to be due upon the Nisab only, and not upon the Afoo;* but Mohammed and Ziffer maintain it to be due upon both the Nisab and the Afoo, that is, upon the whole: the result of which difference in opinion is that, if the Afoo were to perish, and the Nisab to remain, then, according to the two Sheikhs, the whole Zakat that had been before obligatory still remains due; but, according to Mohammed and Ziffer, an adequate proportion of Zakat drops: and, in support of this latter opinion, Mohammed and Ziffer argue that Zakat is due as an acknowledgment for the blessings of Providence, and the Afoo is, a blessing the same as the Nisab; that is to say, they are both equally blessings, wherefore Zakat is equally due upon both. The argument upon which the Sheikhs support their opinion is twofold: FIRST, the Prophet has expressly said, "The ZAKAT upon five camels is one goat, and ZAKAT is due upon any further number till it amount to ten;" and in like manner the Prophet has ordained the Zakat upon every Nisab, and forbidden it upon the Afoo; SECONDLY, the Afoo is a dependant of the Nisab, whence, if a part of the whole Nisab and Afoo were to perish, the loss would be first calculated upon the Afoo, as being the dependant part; as in a contract of Mozaribat, where any accidental loss is first calculated upon the profit, and not upon the capital: and on this ground it is that Haneefa accounts the loss upon the Afoo to the extent thereof, and beyond that upon the Nisab property of the first (or highest) denomination, and beyond that upon the Nisab of the next lower denomination, and so on to the last (or lowest) denomination of Nisab; because the Nisab of the highest denomination is the principal, to which all the

* Meaning, that where the cattle are suffered to go at large, as in pastures, the males have free access to the females, which produces breed.

* Afoo literally means exempt. In the Zakat of cattle it is used to express any intermediate or odd number between one Nisab and another, as between twenty-five and thirty-six camels, for instance.

inferior Nisabs are dependants; and according to Aboo Yoosaf, the loss is calculated first upon the Afoo, and beyond that upon all the degrees or descriptions of Nisab collectively.

Case of Zakat being levied by the Rebels, or Schismaticks.—*If the rebels or schismaticks overcome any particular tribe of Mussulmans, and take from them the Zakat of their cattle, when these rebels are driven away, the rightful Imam must not impose another Zakat upon that tribe, because it appears from the above circumstances that the Imam has not protected them, and the right of imposing Zakat appertains to the Imam, in virtue of the protection he affords; the learned however have decreed, upon this case, that the tribe in question should repeat their Zakat, and pay it a second time, but not their Tribute, because the latter is declared, in the sacred writings, to be applicable to the use of the warriors who fight their enemies; and hence rebels may be considered as an object of its application, they also answering this description; whereas the only object of the application of Zakat is the poor, and rebels do not bestow what they may levy upon the tribe, under that denomination, to the use of the poor; wherefore it is necessary that the tribe should again pay Zakat, so as that it may be applied to its proper object; but not their Tribute. Some of our doctors say, that if the aforesaid tribe, at the period of paying Zakat to the rebels, intend in so doing to give them alms, in this case Zakat drops with respect to that tribe, and there is no necessity for their afterwards repeating it; and the giving of Zakat to any tyrant or plunderer whatever is capable of this construction, because persons of this description, whatever wealth they may be apparently possessed of are yet actually poor, on account of the retribution, which lies against them hereafter: but the former doctrine (that the tribe should repeat their Zakat) is preferable to this, because here the Zakat is rendered and applied, a certiori

How far the Toglib tribe are subject to Zakat.—The Zakat of cattle is not incumbent upon an infant of the tribe of Toglib;† and whatever is incumbent upon the men of that race is so upon the women also, because peace was made with them upon those terms, "that they should pay, of all public imposts, double what as paid by Mussulmans;" now the Mussulman women are subject to Zakat, and it follows that the women of the Toglib race are so in a double proportion; but on Zakat whatever is required of infant Mussulmans, wherefore the infants of the aforesaid tribe are not subject to it.

An accidental destruction of the property induces an exemption from Zakat.—If the property be destroyed, without being consumed by the proprietor after Zakat has become due (that is to say, after the completion of Hawlan-Hawl), the Zakat upon it drops. Shafei has said that if the property be destroyed after the proprietor has been enabled to pay the Zakat upon it, either by the claimant making his demand of Zakat, or by the proprietor finding a claimant, although such claimant should not have demanded it, in this case the proprietor is responsible for the Zakat, because it was due from him, and he did not pay it, although it was in his power to have done so; moreover, if he should not pay the Zakat upon the requisition of the claimant, this circumstance stands as a destruction of it on his part. The argument of our doctors is, that the Zakat due is a portion or part of the Nisab; and, as its destruction is involved in that of the Nisab, it drops of course, the same as where a slave commits a Janayat [offence against the person], in which case it is incumbent upon the proprietor to make over that slave to the Walee-Janayat, or person entitled to the composition; but, if the slave should die or be lost in the interim, the proprietor is no longer responsible for the transfer of him, and that consequently drops; and, with respect to the second argument of Shafei, it may be replied, that no person can be considered as the claimant of Zakat except a pauper whom the proprietor may have specified as the object of its application, and the case does not suppose the requisition to be made by such an one. But if the collector demand the Zakat, and the proprietor neglect payment, and the Nisab afterwards perish, there are various opinions among the Haneefite doctors, some alleging that the proprietor of the destroyed Nisab, in that case, still remains responsible for the Zakat due upon it whilst others maintain that, in this instance also, he is not responsible, because the Nisab does not here appear to have been destroyed by him.

A partial destruction includes a proportionable exemption—If, after Hawlan-Hawl, a portion of a Nisab (such as a third for instance) should be destroyed, the claim of Zakat is proportionably destroyed, in the same manner as where the whole Nisab is destroyed; in which case the whole Zakat drops.

Zakat may be paid in advance.—If the proprietor of a Nisab should pay the Zakat upon it, before Hawlan-Hawl, it is lawful, because

* This and the next following case are merely local in their application, and allude to the state of Arabia, shortly after the establishment of Islamism. The schismaticks were those who refused to submit to the law of the Prophet; whilst others (like the tribe of Toglib, mentioned in the next case) submitted and paid tribute.

†One of the Arabian tribes, who refused to embrace the faith, but agreed to pay tribute to the Prophet. The tribe itself is supposed to be long since extinct; but the laws to which the people of it were subject are applicable, in general, to all infidel tributarics

he has here paid it during the existence of the creative principle of obligation to Zakat, which is understood in his possession of a Nisab; this payment, therefore, is approved, the same as a discharge of a debt, under the existence of its cause; as where a Mohrim, for instance, pays expiation for wounding game whilst the animal is yet alive. This doctrine is controverted by Malik.

If the proprietor of a single Nisab should, before Hawlan-Hawl, make payment of Zakat upon the same for a certain number of years in advance, or should pay a Zakat upon a certain number of additional Nisabs, it is approved, because the first Nisab is the original with respect to the cause of the obligation of Zakat, and anything beyond that is as a dependant.

CHAPTER III.

OF ZAKAT FROM PERSONAL EFFECTS.

Sect. I.—*Of the Zakat of Silver.*

No Zakat due on less than 200 dirms.—No Zakat is due on less than two hundred Dirms,* because the Prophet has ordained that there shall be no Zakat upon fewer than five Awkiyat,† and an Awkiyat is valued at forty Dirms.

And upon 200 at the rate of two and an half per cent.—The Zakat Nisab of silver is two hundred Dirms; and if a man becomes possessed of two hundred Dirms, and the Hawlan-Hawl be completed, the Zakat due upon it is five Dirms, because the Prophet wrote to Maaz, saying, "Upon two hundred Dirms take a Zakat of five Dirms; and upon twenty Miskals of gold, half a Miskal."

And at the same rate upon every forty above two hundred.—No Zakat is due upon any excess above the two hundred Dirms, till such excess amount to forty, upon which the Zakat is one Dirm: and upon every succeeding forty the same Zakat is due, but not on fewer than forty. This is according to Haneefa. The two disciples have said that a proportionate Zakat is due on whatever excess may occur over and above two hundred Dirms; and Shafei coincides in this opinion, because in the traditions of Alee it is related that the Prophet has so ordained it; and also, because Zakat is rendered as a return of gratitude for the blessings of Providence; and the reason why it is expressed as a condition, in the beginning of this book, that the property, in order to cause an obligation of Zakat, amount to a Nisab, is that the proprietor may thence appear to be in easy circumstances; but where, from his being possessed of a Nisab, this appears to be already the case, it is not requisite that any excess amount to a Nisab; and hence Zakat is due upon such excess proportionably, whatever its amount may be.

Objection.—This would lead to a conclusion that, in the Zakat of cattle, the same is due upon any excess under a Nisab; whereas the rule is otherwise, no Zakat whatever being due upon such excess, since that is considered as Afoo, or exempt.

Reply.—Such is the conclusion from analogy; but the excess in cattle is made Afoo, because, if a proportionate Zakat were to be levied upon it, this would necessarily induce a copartnership in the subject, by the proprietor admitting the claimant of Zakat to a share in it:—for instance, the Zakat upon twenty-five camels is one yearling colt; now, if Zakat were due upon excess camels, and the drove consist of twenty-six there would be a Zakat upon this one excess camel of the twenty-fifth part of a yearling colt, which is not payable in any way than by admitting the claimant to a partnership in such colt; and this partnership, being compulsive, is illegal; but plate or cash not being liable to the same objection, a Zakat is due, proportionably, upon any excess whatever over two hundred Dirms.

Rules respecting the calculation of a Nisab of silver.—It is to be observed, that the Nisab of silver of two hundred Dirms is calculated by the Wazn-sebbayat, or septimal weight (which is in the proportion of ten Dirms to seven Miskals), as this was the weight used in the tribunal of Omar, and that of the Dirm is thence established.

Those Dirms in which silver predominates are to be accounted as silver; and the laws respecting silver apply to them, although they should contain some alloy; and the same rule holds with all articles whatever falling under the denomination of plate, such as cups, goblets, and so forth; but Dirms, in which the alloy predominates, are not to be accounted as silver, but only as trading property, estimable by its real value, to which alone regard is to be had; and accordingly, if the value of them amount to a Nisab, they are subject to Zakat, provided there be an intention of trafficking in them; as is the condition with respect to all other chattels. In all plate, therefore, in which the alloy prevails, respect is to be had to the intention of trafficking in it, excepting where the silver contained in it amounts to a Nisab, in which case the intention of trade is not a condition, nor is any regard paid to the estimated value, because in actual silver no respect is had to either of these. The above case is thus stated; because money always contains a small portion of alloy, as pure silver is unfit for coinage, since, without being hardened by an addition of some baser

---

* A silver coin, value about two pence sterling.

† An ounce of silver; or a silver coin of that weight, value between six and seven shillings.

metal, it cannot retain the mint impression; but the alloy is generally in the smaller proportion; regard therefore is had to excess; that is to say, if the proportion of silver be the greater it is accounted as silver, but not if the alloy be in greater proportion (that is, in a proportion above a moiety of the whole weight).

Sect. II. Of the Zakat of Gold.

No Zakat due upon less than 20 Miskals; and upon 20 at the rate of two and an half per cent—There is no Zakat on fewer than twenty Miskals of gold, this sum being the smallest that constitutes a Nisab in that metal; and the Zakat upon twenty Miskals of gold is one half Miskal, when the Hawlan-Hawl therein becomes established, on the authority of the tradition before quoted.—By the Miskal* here mentioned, is to be understood that which weighs in the proportion of seven Miskals to ten Dirms; and the Miskal consists of twenty Kerat,† and the Kerat of five grains.

And at the same rate upon every four above twenty.—When the quantity of gold exceeds twenty Miskals, on every four Miskals of such excess a Zakat of two Kerats is due, because the Zakat due is a fortieth of the whole, and two Kerats are the fortieth of four Miskals and upon any excess short of four Miskals no Zakat is due, according to Haneefa. The two disciples hold that on every excess there is a proportionable Zakat, the same as mentioned in the preceding section; and the foundation of their difference in opinion is also the same here as was there recited, to wit, Haneefa holds that broken numbers are free of impost, whereas the two disciples maintain the coutrary opinion. The ground upon which Haneefa proceeds, in the rule here cited, is this: the legal value of a Deenar is ten Dirms, and a Deenar and Miskal are of the same weight; the value of four Miskals in gold is therefore forty Dirms; and consequently no Zakat is due upon fewer than four Miskals, since these stand the same as forty Dirms: and it has been already shown that nothing short of forty Dirms is subject to Zakat, on account of the tradition of Amroo Bin Khurrm, as before recited.

General rule.—Zakat is due upon gold and silver bullion, which is termed Tebbur: and in like manner upon ornaments or utensils of gold or silver, whether the use thereof be allowable (such as rings, and so forth) or otherwise.‡—Shafei maintains there is no Zakat upon the gold or silver ornaments of women, nor upon rings worn by men, the use of which is allowable, and which are therefore the same in this respect as clothing or articles of apparel.—The argument of our doctors is, that the cause of the obligation to Zakat still continues in the present case:—moreover, articles of gold and silver do, in their own nature, afford an argument of increase in the subject, since these metals are brought into use principally for the purpose of facilitating exchanges by traffick, which affords an argument of increase; and it is the virtual and not the actual increase in any subject that creates the obligation to Zakat upon it; contrary to the case of articles of apparel, which afford no argument or probability of increase.

Sect. III. Of the Zakat of personal Chattel Property.*

Zakat due upon all merchandise.—Zakat is due upon articles of merchandise, of whatever description, where the value amounts to a Nisab either of gold or silver, because the Prophet ordained that articles of merchandise should be appraised, and that a Zakat be paid on the same, in the proportion of five Dirms upon every two hundred,† as the proprietor has prepared and keeps them with a view to increase, so that they resemble gold and silver, which the law holds to be kept for the same purpose; and, as Zakat is due upon the latter, it is in like manner due upon the former: but the intention of trade in these articles is made a condition, in order that it may be ascertained that they are kept with a view to increase.

Mode of ascertaining the Nisab of merchandise.—Mohammed says that, in estimating the value of articles of merchandise with a view to the imposition of Zakat upon them, they should be resolved into such Nisabs as may be most advantageous to the poor; thus if, in valuing an article by Dirms, it would amount to a Nisab of silver, and in valuing the same by Deenars, it would not amount to a Nisab of gold, it must be estimated by Dirms; and, vice versa, if its value should appear to amount to a Nisab of gold, it is to be estimated by Deenars.—The com-

* A dram and a half: also a coin of that weight.

† A Carat; the twenty-fourth part of an ounce.

‡ This alludes to prohibitions against the use of the precious metals in certain articles of personal ornament and household furniture, which have been at various times issued by the Prophet and his followers as checks upon luxury. (See Abominations.)

* In the original, personal chattels are expressed by the terms Rakht and Mata, of which it is not easy to give any literal translation; they express, in general, all articles which appertain to personal estate or effects [Mal]: articles of gold and silver, it is true, do also fall under this general description of Rakht and Mata; but they are introduced under a different head, as the laws of Zakat, with respect to them, are of a peculiar nature, and such as do not affect or apply to other articles of personal property.

† To wit, at the rate of two and an half per cent.

piler of the Hedaya observes that there is one opinion recorded from Haneefa to the same effect. Mohammed again, in the Mabsoot, has said that the proprietor of the article has it in his option to estimate it at whatever species of Nisab he pleases, because gold and silver are standards, and in estimating the value of effects are both equally proper.—It is recorded as an opinion of Aboo Yoosaf, than an article should be estimated by that with which it was purchased: thus, if it has been purchased with Dirms, it is to be appraised in Dirms; and if with Deenars it is to be appraised in Deenars: and if it should have been purchased with any other than either of these, it is to be estimated in money of the most general currency.—It is on the other hand recorded, as an opinion of Mohammed, that whatever the purchase may have been made with, the estimate is to be in current money, as above, in the same manner as that of property forcibly seized, which is thus estimated in all cases.

Property not exempted by an intervening defect in it.—IF a Nisab be complete in the beginning of the year, and also at the end, Zakat does not drop on account of its having been defective at any time within that period; because it is difficult to ascertain its completeness through the intermediate space; moreover, in the commencement of the year its completeness is requisite, in order to the establishment of the cause of obligation, and so also the close of the year, in order to Zakat becoming due; but it is not so within the interval.

Other chattel property may be united with money or bullion to form a Nisab.—THE value of personal effects, or other articles, may be united with gold or silver; that is to say, if (for instance) the proprietor should have effects estimated at the value of one hundred Dirms, and also one hundred Dirms in money, the value of the effects, as above, must be added to the one hundred Dirms, so as that the whole may make one Nisab; and Zakat is due thereon, because the obligation to Zakat, in such property, is occasioned by the circumstance of its being kept with a view to traffick, although the shape in which it is so kept be different with respect to each of the two descriptions of it, traffick in chattels being established by the act of the individual, but that in money by the construction of the law.

And also silver with gold.—GOLD and silver may in the same manner be united; both being in effect of one nature, as standards of estimation, and the possession of each equally causing the obligation to Zakat.

GOLD and silver may be united, according to Haneefa, in respect to their value;* but, according to the two disciples, in respect to their parts: and the consequence of this difference of opinion is, that if a man were possessed (for instance) of one hundred Dirms in silver, and five Miskals of gold (the value of which would amount to one hundred Dirms), this person would be subject to Zakat according to Haneefa, but not so according to the disciples; for these latter say that, in ascertaining the Zakat of gold and silver, regard is to be had to the quantity only, and not to the value; whence it is that Zakat is not due upon a vessel of silver, where the weight is short of two hundred Dirms, although the value should be to that amount, or beyond it: Aboo Haneefa, on the other hand, contends that gold and silver are united with each other on account of their homogeneity, which is established between them in respect to their value, but not in respect to their substance.

CHAPTER IV.

OF THE LAWS RESPECTING THOSE WHO COME BEFORE THE COLLECTOR.

Declarations respecting property, when made upon oath, to be credited.—IF a person come with his property* before the collector and say, "It is so many months since this property has come into my possession, and a year has not yet elapsed;" or, "I am indebted so and so" and make oath of the same, the collector is to credit him, and must not exact anything, because this person stands as a defendant denying his obligation to Zakat: and the declaration of a defendant, when supported by his oath, must be credited. So also, if a person were to declare that he had already paid the Zakat upon such property to a former collector, his declaration must be credited, because the collector, in taking Zakat, acts merely as a Trustee, and the Zakat comes to and remains with him as a deposit; and the declaration of the above person amounts only to his having deposited the trust in its proper place, and this is to be credited, provided there should have been another collector there within the year; but if, on the contrary, there should have been no other collector on that station within the current year, the affirmation and oath are not to be credited, since, in this case, the falsehood is manifest. And, in like manner, if the proprietor were to declare that he had already paid the Zakat upon such property in his own city, by having there bestowed the same upon the poor, his declaration must be credited, because a proprietor, whilst in his own city, is entrusted with the payment and distribution of the Zakat upon his property, and he continues to be so until he comes forth and brings his property before the collector, when the authority for levying

* That is to say, may be both resolved into one Nisab, not by the respective weight of each, but by a general valuation of both.

*Meaning merchandise, but not cattle; and the word bears the same sense throughout this chapter.

Zakat rests with the latter, as the property and the proprietor do both then come within his jurisdiction.*—In short, in all these four instances, the declaration of the proprietor is to be credited. And in the same manner the declaration of a proprietor, respecting Zakat upon cattle, is to be credited in the three first instances, but it is not so in the fourth, although he should confirm his attestation by an oath. Shafei maintains that it is to be credited here also, as the proprietor appears, by the tenor of his declaration, to have rendered the right duly to the claimant.—In opposition to this, our doctors argue that the right of exacting the Zakat upon cattle appertains solely to the Sultan, and the proprietor is not at liberty to preclude the Sultan's right; contrary to the case of property of other nature, such as is termed, in the language of the law, Batena [internal, or domestic], the rendering of the Zakat upon which is committed to the proprietor.—It is to be observed that some have said, respecting cattle, that the Zakat which was paid by the proprietor himself in the first instance is the true obligatory Zakat, and that whatever may be afterwards exacted of him under that denomination, is consequently an oppression; whilst others maintain that this latter is to be considered as the obligatory Zakat, and the former to be held as an act Nifl, or gratuitous; and this last doctrine is approved.—Now a question here arises, as the assertion of the proprietor is to be credited, whether he ought to produce his writing of discharge [voucher] or not?—Mohammed, in the Jama Sagheer, has not required this as a necessary condition; but in the Mabsoot he has made it a condition; and this latter opinion (according to a tradition of Hoosn) is that of Aboo Haneefa. The principle of this doctrine is, that as the proprietor pleads a discharge, and as he possesses a voucher of such discharge, he ought consequently to produce it; whilst the principle of the doctrine maintained in the Zahir-Rawayet is that as one writing resembles another writing, they are not admitted as proofs.

Declarations of Zimmees to be credited.—In whatever instance the declaration of a Mussulman, with respect to Zakat, is to be credited, that of a Zimmee† must be so likewise, because a Zimmee is subject to double the impost of a Mussulman: and hence all the conditions which are to be regarded, with respect to the property of the latter, must be equally so with respect to that of the former.

But not those of Aliens.—If an alien appear before the collector of the Sultan with articles of merchandise, it behoves that officer to exact from him what is usually exacted of aliens, without paying any regard to his declarations in those points in which the declarations of a Mussulman or Zimmee are to be credited, although he should swear to the same, excepting where he declares, concerning his female slaves, that those slaves are his Am-Walids;* for, in all other species of property, his affirmation is not worthy of attention, because the impost which is thus levied upon him is not in fact Zakat,† but rather a contribution exacted as a return for the protection he receives, and which is requisite for the safeguard of whatever he may possess; it is therefore proper to take from him the impost usually levied upon aliens, except where he declares, as above, with respect to his female slaves, that they are his Am-Walids, which declaration must be attended to and credited; because, if an alien were to declare, concerning any other persons who accompany him, that "they are his children," his declaration is approved; and so, in like manner, with respect to his female slaves, as the rights of the Am Walid are derived from the establishment of the child's descent, and consequently the female slaves do not appear to be transferable property; and nothing but transferable property is an object of taxation.

Proportion levied upon merchandise.—From a Mussulman is taken the fourth of the tithe of his property; and from a Zimmee the half of the tithe; and from an alien the tithe; Omar having instructed his collectors to this effect.

Zakat to be levied on the property of aliens, to the value of fifty Dirms, or upwards.—If an alien should come before the collector with property to the amount only of fifty Dirms, nothing whatsoever is to be exacted of him, except where aliens exact contribution upon an equally small property of Mussulmans; in which case a similar impost must be laid upon this amount, the property of an alien, because what is taken from aliens is merely in the way of reciprocity; contrary to the case of Mussulmans or Zimmees, as what is levied upon them is in fact Zakat, either single or twofold, whence it is indispensable that the property with them amount to a Nisab.—This is the doctrine of the Jama Sagheer. In the Mabsoot, under the title Zakat, it is written that if the property of an alien should be small (that is, short of a Nisab), nothing whatever is to be exacted of him, let the custom of aliens, in this respect, be what it may, because a proportion of property not amounting to Nisab is invariably to be considered as Afoo, or exempt; and also, because a trifle of this sort is not sup-

* This comment upon the law (as in many other instances) has reference to some local customs or circumstances which cannot now be ascertained.

† An infidel subject of the Mussulman government.

* Slaves who have borne children to him.

† Because, as being an act of piety, an infidel is held to be incapable of paying Zakat; wherefore it cannot be considered in that sense, although it be exacted under that denomination

posed to stand in need of the State's protection, as travellers must necessarily carry with them small sums for the purpose of expenses, and robbers do not pay any attention to such trifles, not considering them objects of their pursuit.

Proportion to be levied upon the property of aliens.—If an alien come before the collector with two hundred Dirms, and it be uncertain what tax foreigners levy upon a similar property of Mussulmans, in this case tithe is to be taken; and if it be known that foreign states exact only a twentieth or a fortieth, a similar proportion is to be taken; but if it be known that they take the whole, yet the Mussulman collector must not act accordingly, because this is an act of rapine. And if it be known that they take nothing of the Mussulmans, it is then proper that nothing be taken from them, in order that the Mussulman merchants, travelling into foreign countries, may remain free of impost; and also, because where foreign states observe kindness towards Mussulmans, and exact nothing of them, it is requisite that nothing be exacted of them in return, as it behoves the Mussulmans to preserve a character of benevolence towards all men.

Must not be exacted repeatedly.—If an alien come before the collector, and the latter exact the tithe of him, and he should again pass near the station of the collector, yet nothing more is to be exacted till the completion of the Hawlan-Hawl, because, if the tithe were to be repeatedly levied within the year, the property would be annihilated, and the impost is laid for the purpose of protecting the property; moreover, the protection which is first granted continues until the beginning of a new year, when the Aman, or protection, commences de novo, because it is not permitted to an alien to remain in a Mussulman territory beyond the space of a year. But the tax may be again demanded of him at the expiration of the second year, as this does not tend to annihilate his property.—What is here advanced proceeds upon a supposition that the alien has not returned into his own country within the period of the year, after this payment of the tithe, as aforesaid; but if he should return thither, it is to be again exacted of him upon his re-entering the Mussulman territory, even though he were to go there on the very day of payment, and to come again into the Mussulman territory on the same day, because every time he thus returns into the Mussulman territory, he returns under the virtue of a new protection; moreover, the repetition of exaction upon his return cannot be considered as tending to annihilate his property, since on every return he is supposed to acquire a profit.

Zakat-tithe to be levied on wine.—If a Zimmee, or infidel subject, pass the station of a collector with wine and pork, the collector is to levy a tithe upon the former article, but not upon the latter. By levying a tithe upon the wine, is to be understood (not on the actual article, but) upon the estimated value of the article. The distinction here made between wine and pork, is taken from the Zahir-Rawayet.—Shafei says, that nothing whatever should be levied on either pork or wine, neither being legally subjects of estimation. Ziffer, on the other hand, argues that it should be levied equally upon both, as both do actually constitute property among Zimmees. Aboo Yoosaf also says that the tax should be levied upon both, provided that they be found together upon the Zimmee; but possibly he is here to be understood as making the pork an appendage to the wine, whence it is that he adds "If the Zimmee were to come before the collector with either wine or pork, singly, the tenth would be levied on the former but not upon the latter."—The reasons upon which the Zahir-Rawayet proceeds, in this case, are twofold; First, the estimated value of a thing which falls under the description of Zooatal-Keem stands as the identical thing itself, and pork is of this class; whereas the value of an article belonging to the class of Zooatal-Imfel does not stand in place of the identical articles, and wine is of this description; Secondly, the right of exacting the tenth is vested in the collector in consequence of the protection afforded by the state; and a Mussulman has a right to take measures for the preservation of his wine, for the purpose of making vinegar of the same, whence it is also lawful for him to protect the wine of a Zimmee; whereas he is not permitted to take any of his pork, insomuch that if a Zimmee, being possessed of pork, were to be converted to the faith, it would be incumbent on him to destroy it or throw it away; and a Mussulman not being allowed to take care of his own pork, it follows that he is not competent to the protection of the pork of others; and hence the state not being considered as affording protection to the pork of a Zimmee, no tax can be levied upon it.

If a boy or a woman of the Toghleb tribe pass the station of a collector, with property, nothing is to be taken from the former, but he must exact from the latter the usual proportion of persons of that tribe, according to what is said concerning the Zakat of cattle.

If a person come to the collector with one hundred Dirms, declaring that he has another hundred at home, and that the Hawlan-Hawl has elapsed, yet the collector is not at liberty to take Zakat either upon those hundred or upon the other; because the one does not come under his protection, and the other is short of a Nisab.

No Zakat to be levied on Bazat or Mozaribat property.—If a person come to the collector with two hundred Dirms, which are with him as a Bazat, the collector must not impose any Zakat upon it,—because this person is not empowered by the actual proprietor to pay Zakat; and so also, if that property were in his hands in the way of Mozaribat.—This is the doctrine of the two disciples; and Haneefa has also subscribed to it; and the reason upon which it is founded is that the Mozarib is neither the actual proprietor nor the representative of the proprietor, with respect to the payment of Zakat: wherefore Zakat is not to be required, except where the Mozarib, by the nature of the contract, derives such a proportion of profit from the capital stock entrusted to him as amounts to a Nisab; in which case a proportionable Zakat must be levied, as he is the actual proprietor of such proportion.

Mazoon slaves subject to it.—If a Mazoon slave, not indebted to any person, come before the collector with two hundred Dirms, the Zakat must be levied.—Aboo Yoosaf says, that it is not known whether Haneefa ever retracted this opinion, and delivered another (that the collector should not levy Zakat upon a Mazoon) or not; but from his subscribing to the opinion of the two disciples in the preceding case (to wit, that no Zakat is to be levied upon a Mozarib), it may be presumed that he has also agreed that none is to be levied upon a Mazoon, as he is not the proprietor, but his master, the former having only a power of transaction, with respect to the property in question, so that he stands in the same predicament with a Mozarib.—Some have said, that between a Mazoon and a Mozarib there is this difference, that the former transacts with the property on his own account, and hence is subject to its obligations; for, as he cannot have recourse to his master, but may be sold, in order to the fulfilment of such of its obligations as he is legally liable to, it follows that he does stand in need of protection for it upon his own account: contrary to a Mozarib, for he manages the Mozaribat stock in the manner of an agent, and hence whatever may attach to him in the obligations thereof he takes again from the proprietor, wherefore the owner of the property is the person who requires protection for it: and there thus appearing an essential difference between a Mazoon and a Mozarib, no inference can be drawn of Haneefa's opinion respecting the former from what he has conceded concerning the latter.

Unless accompanied by their owner.—It is to be observed that if the master of the Mazoon accompany him, the collector must take the Zakat (not from the Mazoon, but) from the master, he being the actual proprietor; the Zakat, therefore, is to be taken from him, except where it appears that the slave is indebted to such an amount as comprehends the property in question; in which case no Zakat whatever can be required of the master, since (according to Haneefa) the master, in this circumstance has, in fact, no actual property in the Mazoon's hands:—and (according to the two disciples) the right of another is connected with the property, namely, the debt—and consequently no Zakat is due upon it, they holding that debt upon a property forbids the exaction of Zakat.

If a merchant, being in a country where the Schismaticks prevail, go to a collector of the Schismaticks, and there pay the Zakat upon his property, and afterwards come before a collecttor of the Orthodox, the latter may again exact Zakat of him, because in going before a collector of the Schismaticks, and there paying Zakat, he was in fault.

———

CHAPTER V

OF MINES AND BURIED TREASURES.

Distinctions.—There are three legal terms which particularly belong to these subjects, and which are employed for the use of distinction; Madin, Kanz, and Rikaz: by Madin is understood the place in which the ore or metal is naturally produced; by Kanz, treasure, or other property, buried in the ground;* and Rikaz applies equally to either, to Madin literally, and to Kanz metaphorically.

Mines subject to a Zakat of one-fifth.—If there be discovered, in Kherajee or Ashooree lands (that is, lands subject to tithe or tribute), a mine of gold, silver, iron, lead or copper, it is subject to a Zakat of one-fifth, according to our doctors; and this Zakat is termed Khams.†—Shafei has asserted that nothing whatever is due upon a mine, because it is free to the first finder indifferently, and is therefore the same as game; but yet if, the metal be produced from the mine, it is subject to Zakat independent of Hawlan-Hawl, that having been constituted as a condition of Zakat merely to afford time for increase, whereas here the identical subject itself (the metal) is increase of property; wherefore the lapse of Hawlan-Hawl is not in this instance required. The arguments of our doctors, on this subiect, are twofold;—First, the ordinance of the Prophet, who directed that upon Rikaz there should be imposed a fifth; and the term Rikaz applies to mines, as was already demonstrated:—Secondly, the mine, as being discovered in tithe or tribute lands, must at one period have been property of the infidels, and afterwards have fallen into poseession of the Mussulmans by conquest, wherefore the whole falls under the description of Ghaneemat, or plunder; and one-fifth is due upon plunder:—contrary to the case of game, the property in which cannot be traced to any antecedent proprietor.

Objection.—If the mine be thus resolved into plunder, it should follow that, as such the products of it is the common property of all the warriors.

Reply.—The property of the warriors is

*This is a common practice in all parts of Asia. Treasures are hidden in the ground on the commencement of a war, or other troubles; and it frequently happens that, the depositors perishing, the treasure remains concealed, perhaps, for many years, till it be discovered by accident, and at a time when no legal claimant can be found.

†Literally, a fifth. It is elsewhere translated double tithe.

established in the mine constructively, in virtue of the establishment of their property in the surface of the territory : but the discoverer of the mine is the actual acquirer of it ; wherefore the property of the warriors is established in one-fifth, their right being only constructive; and that of the discover is established in the remaining four-fifths, as his right is actual ; whence it is that those four-fifths are reserved to him.

Case of a mine within a house. If a person discover a mine within the precincts of his own habitation, nothing is due upon it, according to Haneefa. The two disciples hold that a fifth is due upon that also, in conformity to the traditionary ordinance already quoted, because that applies equally to the present case. Haneefa argues upon this, that a mine is a constituent part of the land in which it lies, as being supposed to have been originally created with it, and nothing being due upon the ground generally, it follows that nothing is due upon any particular portion of it (such as the mine, for instance), because a part does not differ from the whole: contrary to the case of a Kanz, which is no constituent part of the soil, as not having been originally created with it, but deposited there by some person.

Or in lands which are private property.—If the said mine be discovered, not actually in the house of the finder, but in lands, subject either to the tribute or tithe, which are his own especial and exclusive property, in this case there are two opinions recorded of Haneefa's doctrine ; one, that no Zakat what ever is due, any more than if the mine had been discovered within the house of the finder ; another, that a fifth is due upon it : the former of these opinions is mentioned in the Mabsoot, and the latter in the Jama Sagheer : and the principle upon which the latter opinion proceeds is, that between a house and lands there is a manifest distinction, because the ground on which a house stands is not supposed to be any way productive of the fruits of the earth (whence it is that no tax of any kind is levied upon it, insomuch that, if a date-tree were by accident to grow within a dwelling, and to produce fruit, yet nothing is due upon the fruit), whereas lands, on the contrary, as being productive, are not thus exempted from tithe and tribute, and consequently a fifth is due upon all mines which are found in them.

And of buried treasures.—If a person find a Kanz, or deposit, of buried treasure, a fifth is due upon it, according to the opinions of all the doctors, in conformity to the traditionary ordinance already quoted, the expression there used [Rikaz] applying to Kanz. It is to be observed, however, that if the treasure in question be coin, bearing the impression of Mussulman money (such as the words of the Creed*), the Kanz stands as a Lookta, or trove-property, the laws concerning which are explained elsewhere :—yet, if it bear the impression of infidel coinage (such as the image of a saint or idol), a fifth is due upon it in all cases,—that is to say, whether a person may have found the same in his own grounds, or in those of another, or in common lands which are not the property of any person ; and the fifth is thus due upon the authority of the traditionary ordinance to which we have just referred.—It is here proper to remark, that if the treasure be found in common land, four-fifths of it appertain to the finder, as having recovered it, because the other warriors had no information concerning it, and of course no share in the discovery ; and consequently he has an exclusive right to it :—and the same rule obtains if it be found in appropriated land, whether such be his own property, or belonging to another (according to Aboo Yoosaf), because the claim is established in virtue of salvage, or recovery, and the treasure has been recovered by the finder.—Mohammed and Haneefa maintain, on the contrary, that the treasure is the property of him upon whom the Imam had bestowed the lands, originally, at the period of subjugation, who is termed the Mokhuttut-le-hoo, or first grantee, upon the principle that whoever has the first exclusive property in a soil is the true proprietor of whatsoever may be contained in it, although he should not have obtained visible possession thereof, —the same as where a person catches a fish with a pearl in its maw, in which case he becomes the proprietor of the pearl, although he has not actually laid his hands upon it, nor knows of its being in the fish's belly.* And it is further to be observed, that if the first grantee should have sold his lands, yet he does not forfeit his right to any Kanz, or buried treasure, which may be afterwards discovered there, as that does not form a part of the soil like mines, which as being a constituent portion of it, upon a transfer by sale become the property of the purchaser. And if the first grantee be unknown, in this case, according to the opinion of the learned, the four-fifths go to him who was the first known proprietor from the period of the establishment of the Mussulman faith, that is to say, him beyond whom no antecedent proprietor can be discovered.—And if the treasure should consist of coin, the impression of which is so far effaced as to render it doubtful whether it be infidel or Mussulman

*Meaning the Kulma, or Mussulman Confession of faith, "There is no God, but one God, and Mohammed is the Prophet of God."

*This is a case of some curiosity, and affords an instance (among a multitude of others) of points of law adduced in elucidation of passages to which they do not appear to have an immediate reference.—From the above it appears, that if a man were to catch a fish with a jewel in its belly, and were to sell the fish (not knowing what it contained), he would have a right to recover the jewel of the purchaser.

money, in this case according to the Zahir-Rawayet) it is to be considered as of the former class: some however, have observed that, in modern times, it is held as Mussulman coinage.

Of mines or buried treasure found in a foreign country.—If a Mussulman go under protection into a foreign country, and there find a Rikaz within the house of an infidel, whether it be a Madin or a Kanz, let him deliver the same up to the proprietor, in order that treachery and breach of faith may not be induced; because whatsoever is in that country belongs of right to the people of it: but if he were to find the Rikaz in the open country or desert, it belongs to him, no person having any exclusive right in it so as to make his appropriation of it an act of treachery and here the fifth would not be due; as treasure, thus found, does not bear the construction of plunder, the person who finds it standing as a thief, and not as a warrior.

Precious stones not subject to impost.—No fifth is due upon turquoises, such as are found in mountainous places; because a turquoise is a stone; and the Prophet has said, "Upon stones there shall be no Khams."

Quicksilver subject to impost of a fifth, but not pearls or amber.—Upon quicksilver there is due a fifth, according to Haneefa, in his last opinion recorded upon this subject: contrary to the opinion of Aboo Yoosaf.—Upon pearls and amber there is no fifth due, according to Haneefa and Mohammed.-Aboo Yoosaf maintains that upon those, as well as upon all gems procured from the sea, there is a fifth; because Omar used to levy a fifth upon amber.—Haneefa and Mohammed argue, that the depths of the sea do not come under the description of parts subjugated by conquest; and hence anything procured thence cannot be defined plunder although it should consist of gold or silver; and the case of Omar levying a fifth upon amber existed only where that article was cast up by the sea upon the shores; and here also they coincide that the fifth may be levied.

If a person find, in common ground, a deposit of chattel property, such as vessels or cloths, the same is the property of the finder; and there is a fifth due upon it, because this comes under the description of plunder, the same as gold or silver.

CHAPTER VI.

OF ZAKAT UPON THE FRUITS OF THE EARTH.

A tithe due upon the product of lands watered by natural means.—Upon everything produced from the ground there is due a tenth, or tithe, which is termed Ashar; whether the soil be watered by the annual overflow of great rivers (such as the Oxus and Shyhoon), or by periodical rains: excepting the articles of wood, bamboos, and grass which are not subject to tithe—This is according to Haneefa. The two disciples say that tithe is not due except upon such things as are permanently productive,* which are subject thereto, provided the product amount to five Wusks, or sixty Saas; and they further hold that herbs are not subject to tithe. From this it appears that the difference of opinion between Haneefa and the two disciples exists with respect to two points in particular;—First, the specification of the quantity as a condition; Secondly, that of permanency in the subject. The arguement of the two disciples, with respect to the former of these, is twofold;—First, the Prophet has ordained that there should be no Zakat on less than five Wusks: Secondly, tithe being as alms, to render it obligatory it is requisite that some Nisab be ascertained and established, so as to confine the contribution to the rich.—The argument of Haneefa is that the Prophet ordained that an Ashar should be held due upon everything produced from the ground, which ordinance is general in its application, and without any specification of quantity; and, with respect to the ordinance quoted by the two disciples, it is to be taken as applying solely to articles of commerce; that is to say that "there is a Zakat upon those articles, as Merchandise, where the quantity amounts to five Wusks-;" because, in the time of the Prophet, fruits were sold by the Wusk, and the value of a Wusk was estimated at forty Dirms, so that the value of five Wusks was two hundred Dirms, the amount of a Nisab in estimated property:—and, with respect to their second argument, the obligation to tithe upon the fruits of the earth is connected with what it yields only, without respect to the proprietor (whence it is that a tithe is due upon the product of Wokf-lands), how, therefore, should any regard be had to the description of the proprietor as being rich? And hence also it is that Hawlan-Hawl is not requisite in the present case, that, having been established for the purpose of ascertaining increase; and the fruit of the earth does itself come under this description.—The argument of the two disciples, with respect to the second point is, that the Prophet has ordained that, "upon vegetables (that is, herbs) no alms are due;" and by alms is here to be understood, tithes; as Zakat is not forbidden here, since it is due provided the property amount to a Nisab.—In reply to these observations, the arguments of Haneefa are twofold;—First, the tradition before quoted;—and, with respect to the ordinance adduced by the two disciples, it is to be observed, that by the term Sadka [alms] there mentioned, is to be understood such alms as are taken by the collector, but not that contribution which falls under the denomination of Ashar; and in this Haneefa also agrees, that the collector is not to take

*Such as fruit-trees.

tithe from those articles ;—Secondly, articles of product are often cultivated which are not of a permanent nature, such as melons and cucumbers ; and these are the increase of the earth : and the cause of obligation to the payment of Zakat upon land is increase ; whence it is that the land is subject to tribute, and therefore tithe is also due : but, with respect to the articles of wood, bamboos, and grass, the ground is not tilled or prepared for the cultivation of them ; nay it is usual to clear them away ; yet, if a person were to till the ground with a view to the culture of such articles, his land would be subject to tithe.

And an half tithe upon the product of lands watered by artificial means.—Land watered by means of buckets, or machinery, or watering camels, are subject to half tithe,*—according to Haneefa and the two disciples :—the latter, however, coincide in this, under the restriction, conditional, that the product be of a permanent nature, and that the quantity of product amount to five Wusks ; whereas Haneefa does not specify any such condition.—The reason why such lands are made subject to half tithe only is, that the expense of tillage greatly exceeds that of lands watered by rains, or by the periodical overflow of great rivers.

Rule respecting lands which partake of both descriptions.—With respect to lands watered a part of the year by rivers and a part by labour, in regulating their proportion of impost, regard is to be had to the greater portion of the year ; that is to say, if the land be such as is watered by rivers for the greater part of the year, the impost is a tithe ; but, if it be watered for the greater part of the year by labour, it is only half tithe, or a twentieth.

Aboo Yoosaf has said that, upon every article the amount of which is not estimated by Wusks (such as saffron and cotton), tithe is due, provided its value be equal to that of five Wusks of an article of the lowest value so estimable (such as millet in the present times) ; because articles, the quantity of which the law does not hold to be estimable by Wusks, can have their Nisab ascertained only by estimation of the value ; as is the case with articles of merchandise.—Mohammed, on the other hand, alleges that tithe is due upon those articles, provided their quantity amount to the number five of the highest standard of ascertainment of quantity with respect to each ; for instance, cotton is weighed by Mans and Hamls, each Haml containing three Mans ; a Nisab of cotton therefore consists of five Hamls ; saffron, on the other hand, is weighed by Dirms, Astars, Rutls, and Mans ; and the latter being the greatest of these, a Nisab of saffron, consequently, consists of five Mans weight.—The reason upon which Mohammed proceeds herein is, that the Wusk is constituted the standard of estimation of Nisab in grain & c. only on account of its being the largest standard by which their quantities can be ascertained ; and the same principle operates with respect to all other articles.

A tithe due upon honey :—Tithe is due upon honey where it is collected in tithe-lands. Shafei maintains that nothing is due upon honey, because that is an animal production, the same as silk, which being tithe-free, honey is so likewise.—The arguments of our doctors are twofold : First, the Prophet ordained that honey should be subject to tithe ; Secondly, bees collect their honey from blossoms and fruits, which articles being subject to tithe, it follows that honey, which is extracted from those, must be so likewise : contrary to the case of silk worms, because those feed upon leaves of trees, which are not subject to tithe. Haneefa holds tithe to be due upon honey, whether the quantity be great or small ; he not regarding Nisab as essential in this article.—Aboo Yoosaf has reported it as an opinion of Haneefa, that the Nisab of honey is to be ascertained by estimate, according to his general tenet upon the subject of Zakat ; and he further says, that nothing is due upon honey, unless the quantity amount to ten Kirbs (a Kirb being fifty Mans), because this was the rule by which the trible of Syara paid tithe on their honey to the Prophet, Again, it is related as an opinion of Aboo Yoosaf, that a Nisab of honey consists of five Mans. According to Mohammed the Nisab in honey is five Sirks (a Sirk containing thirty-six Rutls), because the Sirk is the largest standard of quantity in honey, as the Wusk is in grain. And the same of sugar-cane ; that is to say, according to Mohammed, tithe is due upon sugar-cane where the quantity of sugar produced from it amounts to five Sirks.

And upon wild honey and fruits :—Honey and fruits, collected in the wilderness, are subjects of tithe. This is the doctrine of the Zahir-Rawayet.—It is related as an opinion of Aboo Yoosaf, that nothing whatever is due upon such articles, because the occasion of obligation to Zakat is the land being of a productive nature, which is not the case in this instance.—The principle upon which the Zahir-Rawayet proceeds herein is, that all that is required to constitute land being productive, is the circumstance of its affording produce of any sort ; and produce does appear in the articles above mentioned.

And upon all the product of tithe lands, indiscriminately :—Tithe is due upon all the produce of tithe-lands indiscriminately ; nor is any deduction to be made on account of the expense of men or cattle employed in tilling those lands, because the Prophet has ordained that dues should be different in proportion to the difference of expense, and also that lands watered by rain shall be subject to tithe and those watered by labour to half-tithe ; wherefore the deduction of expense is needless.

*To wit, a twentieth of the whole product.

And double tithe upon those lands when held by Toglibees.—Upon tithe lands, possessed by persons of the Toglib tribe, a twofold Ashar, or fifth, must be levied ; and in this all the doctors agree.—It is recorded, however, as an opinion of Mohammed, that upon tithe-lands which may have been purchased by a Toglibee of a Mussulsman, a single tithe only should be levied ; he holding that the imposition upon lands does not suffer any alteration in consequence of a transition of the property.

Cases of transition of property in land subject to double tithe.—If a Zimmee, or infidel subject, purchase land of a Toglibee, from which double tithe had used to be collected, the Zimmee must also pay double tithe upon it. In this all our doctors coincide, because it is lawful to require twice as much of a Zimmee as of a Mussulman,—whence it is that, if such an one were to come before the collector with merchandise, twice as much would be exacted of him as of a Mussulman. And the same rule obtains (that is to say, the same proportion of tithe continues to be imposed upon those lands) where a Mussulman purchases them of a Toglibee ; or where a Toglibee, being the proprietor, becomes a Mussulman. Haneefa holds this opinion in all cases, whether the land had originally belonged to a Toglibee, or the Toglibee had purchased them of a Mussulman,—for in either case the rule of double impost continues, with respect to them, where they are purchased by a Mussulman,—because he holds double impost upon those lands to have been already irreversibly established,* and, consequently that this incumbrance on the lands devolves to the Mussulman purchaser along with the property, in the same manner as obtains in the case of a sale of tribute-lands. Aboo Yoosaf maintains that, in the case here recited, a single tithe only is to be collected from the Mussulman proprietor ; nor will the lands, whilst in his possession, be subject to any further impost, since the only principle upon which double tithe had been exacted of the Toglibee was the infidelity of the proprietor; and this, upon the devolving of the property to a Mussulman, is done away, Aboo Yoosaf, in the Kadooree, has further said that (according to the Rawayet-Saheeh) the opinion of Mohammed is the same as that here recited. Our author, however, remarks that it is most certain that Mohammed coincides entirely with Haneefa in his general principle, that the impost upon the land continues as before ; but he [Mohammed] carries this still farther ; for, as where a Mussulman purchases lands, subject to double impost, of a Toglibee, the same continues upon him, so if a Toglibee were to purchase lands of a Mussulman, subject only to single impost, he will not have to pay any more than the said single impost, since a change in the property makes no alteration with respect to those rules to which the lands are subject.

Land devolving from a Mussulman to a Zimmee becomes subject to tribute.—If a Mussulman sell his lands to a Christian, who is a Zimmee and not a Toglibee, and the Christian aforesaid have seizin of those lands, Haneefa holds that tribute is to be collected from the same, the payment of tribute being a consequence of infidelity. According to AbooYoosaf, the double tithe collected therefrom is to be expended upon the objects of the expenditure of tribute, which is a mode of adjustment easier than that of thus exchanging tithe for tribute. Mohammed holds that the lands remain subject to tithe as before ; and he morever maintains that the tithe, collected from these lands, is to be applied to the purposes of Zakat.—It is to be observed that, if a Mussulman were to take those lands of a Christian in right of Shaffa,* or if the property in them were to revert to the seller, being a Mussulman, on account of the sale having been invalid, in either case the lands remain subject to tithe, as before ; in the first instance, because the Mussulman, as Shafee,† must effect his purpose (of obtaining the lands in right of Shaffa) by means of a contract of sale with the proprietor, wherefore the transaction here, in fact, amounts to his purchasing the lands ; and, in the second isntance, because, by the property in the land reverting to the Mussulman proprietor, on account of an invalidity in the sale, the case remains the same as if no transfer by sale had ever been made ; moreover the Mussulman's right is in no respect affected by such invalidity, since it is proper that that transaction be altogether disregarded ; whence the case remains the same as if no sale had ever taken place ; and for all these reasons the land will continue subject to tithe as before.

Case of a Mussalman.—If a Mussulman convert the ground of his habitation into a garden, the same having been his original property (that is to say, he being the first grantee), he owes tithe upon it where he waters it with tithe-water, or tribute where he waters it with tribute-water, because this land is not, in its original description, either tithe-land or tribute-land, and in such ground the mode of watering is the standard of the expense of cultivation.

Case of a Majoos.—A Majoos‡ does not owe either tithe or tribute for his habitation, because Omar exempted dwellings from all impost. But, if the Majoos were to convert the ground of his habitation into a garden,

*By original compacts between the Mussulmans and Toglibees. This is expressed at large under the head of Seyir.

*Neighbourhood, or conjunction of property, which gives a right of pre-emption.

†The person in whom the right of pre-emption lies.

‡Meaning a worshipper of fire ;—a Magujaian.

he owes tribute upon the same, although he should water it with tithe-water, as he cannot lie under any obligation to pay tithe, because that bears the sense of an oblation and act of piety, of which an infidel is held to be incapable; he is appointed, therefore, to pay tribute, which is conformable to his situation, as being a sort of infliction. Our author remarks that analogy (from the opinion of the two disciple), would suggest that the Majoos owes tithe where the land is cultivated with tithe-water; single tithe, according to Mohammed; and double, according to Aboo Yoosaf:—the reasons for this have been related before.

Definition of tithe-water and of tribute-water.—RAIN-WATER, and the water of wells and fountains, and of lakes which are not under the particular authority of any individual, is what is termed tithe-water; and the water of the artificial canals and aqueducts, constructed by the kings of Ajim (such as the river of Yezdejird), is tribute-water.

THE river of Kharzim, called the Jyhoon [Oxus is tithe-water, according to Mohammed; and so likewise is the Shyhoon, and also the Dijlet [Tigris] and the Firat [Euphrates], because those rivers are not under the authority of any person whatever, nor is any one entitled to an exclusive privilege with respect to them, wherefore they are the same as the open sea. Aboo Yoosaf considers the waters of all those rivers as tribute-water, because bridges of boats are occasionally thrown over them, which is an act of seizin, evincing that those who do so are the guardians of the stream; and hence the water of those rivers must necessarily be deemed tribute-water.

Impost upon land the property of Toglib women or infants.—THE lands of infants or women of the Toglib tribe are subject to the same laws as those of the men of that tribe: that is to say, upon their tithe-lands is imposed double tithe, and upon their tribute-land single tribute; because peace was made with them on the terms of double contribution to purposes of charity, but not to the service of the state: moreover, the lands of Mussulman infants or women are subject to a single tithe, and therefore the same is to be levied twofold upon the lands of Toglib women and children.

UPON fountains of pitch or bitumen, or wells of sulphur, nothing is due where they are found in tithe-lands, because those productions do not come under the description of growing out of the earth [vegetables], but are rather the same as the water of fountains, which sprung out of its bosom, and are not subject to any impost. The proprietor of such places, however, is subject to tribute where they exist in tribute-lands; but this is to be understood only provided the contiguous soil be capable of cultivation, because the imposition of tribute depends upon the proprietor of the land being able to cultivate the same.

CHAPTER VII.

OF THE DISBURSEMENT OF ZAKAT, AND OF THE PERSONS TO WHOSE USE IT IS TO BE APPLIED.

Persons to whose use Zakat is to be applied.—THE objects of the disbursement of Zakat are of eight different descriptions: FIRST, Fakeers;—SECONDLY, Miskeens;*—THIRDLY, the collector of Zakat, (provided he be not a Hashimee†);—FOURTHLY, Mokatibs, (upon whom Zakat is bestowed, in order to enable them, by fulfilling their contract of Kitabat, to procure their freedom);—FIFTHLY, debtors not possessed of property amounting to a Nisab;—SIXTHLY, Fee Sabeel Oola [in the service of God‡];—SEVENTHLY, Ibnus Sabeel, or travellers;—and EIGHTHLY, Mowlkfutal-kaloob.§ And those eight descriptions are the original objects of the expenditure of Zakat, being particularly specified as such in the KORAN; and there are, therefore, no other proper or legal objects of its application. With respect to the last, however (Mowlefutal-kaloob], the law has ceased to operate, since the time of the Prophet, because he used to bestow Zakat upon them as a bribe or gratuity to prevent them from molesting the Mussulmans, and also to secure their occasional assistance; but when God gave strength to the faith, and to its followers, and rendered the Mussulmans independent of such assistance, the occasion of bestowing this gratuity upon them no longer remained; and all the doctors unite in this opinion.

Definition of the terms Fakeer and Miskeen.—By the term Fakeers is to be understood persons possessed of property, the whole of which, however, amounts to somewhat less than a Nisab. By Miskeens is understood persons who have no property whatever. The comment upon the terms Fakeer and Miskeen is recorded from Aboo Haneefa. Some, however, hold the reverse description to be true.

Allowance to the collector.—THE Imam is to allow the officer employed in the collection of Zakat as much out of it as is in proportion to his labour: as much, therefore, is to be allowed as may suffice for himself and his assistants; and his allowance is not fixed to an eighth. Shafei argues that Zakat, being appropriated to eight different objects, be-

*Fakeer and Miskeen both apply to persons in want; the distinction between these two terms is fully explained in the definition of them a little lower down.

†A descendant from the tribe of the Prophet.

‡The meaning of this phrase is more particularly described in another part of this chapter.

§The translator is not able to find any precise meaning for this term in the lexicons. By Kuloob is understood an Asil Arbee, or original Arabian of the desert, and it is probable that some tribe of these is alluded to in this place.

comes thus divided into eight equal lots, of which one is the right of the collector, who is consequently entitled to an eighth of the whole. Our doctors argue that, as Zakat is paid to the collector, not as alms, but in the manner of a reward for service performed, it follows that the proportion paid him must be whatever may suffice for that purpose; and hence it is that the collector is entitled to pay himself out of the collections of Zakat although he should be rich.*

Definition of other terms.—By the phrase Feear-Rikab, mentioned in the KORAN (where it treats of the objects of expenditure of Zakat), is to be understood Mokatibs: this definition is taken from Seyid Ben Jeeroo. And by the term Gharumeen, in the same passage, are meant debtors: Shafei says that it means persons who have involved themselves in composing the differences of others. By the phrase Fee Sabeel Oola, in the same passage, is to be understood (according to Aboo Yoosaf) a person who, by proverty of estate, is incapacitated and cut off from taking a part in the wars of the faith; that is, in the Jihad Farz. Mohammed, on the contrary, argues that the phrase here mentioned applies to a person who, by poverty, is incapacitated from performing pilgrimage: the latter description, however, is necessarily implied and understood in the former; whence the phrase in question may be said to apply to both. It is to be observed that (according to our doctors) no portion of Zakat is to be paid to such warriors as are in a state of affluence, none being objects of its application but those who are poor.

BY the term Ibnus Sabeel [travellers] is to be understood persons, in a strange place, having left their property at home, and who are consequently destitute of means of support.

THE seven descriptions of persons here specified are the proper objects of the application of Zakat; and a proprietor (who chooses to disburse his Zakat himself, and not to pay it to the collector) is at liberty either to distribute it, in equal shares, among seven persons of those different descriptions, or to pay the whole to one of them.—This is the opinion of our doctors.—Shafei has said that a proprietor is not at liberty himself to disburse the Zakat upon his own property in any other way than bestowing a part upon three individuals of each several description. The arguments on both sides here turn on some peculiarities in the Arabic language. Our doctors take their opinion from Amroo Bin Abbas.

Zakat not to be bestowed upon Zimmees.—IT is not lawful to bestow Zakat upon a Zimmee, or infidel subject, because the Prophet directed Maaz, saying, "Take ZAKAT from the rich Mussulmans, and bestow it upon the poor Mussulmans."—But although infidel subjects are not entitled to share in Zakat, yet other alms may be bestowed upon them in the manner of Sadka, or almsgift.—Shafei says that they are prohibited from partaking of these also, as well as of Zakat: but our doctors ground their opinion on this point upon a precept of the Prophet, who has ordained that alms should be bestowed upon persons of every religion indiscriminately; and our doctors also allege, that if it were not on account of the directions to Maaz, before quoted, they should deem the bestowing of Zakat upon Zimmees to be legal.

Cases which do not constitute a payment of Zakat.—IF a person employ the Zakat upon his property in the erection of a mosque, or the burial of the dead, yet his Zakat is not considered as being thereby discharged, because, in the payment of Zakat, it is established as a principle that it shall be made over to the person or persons entitled to it; and such delivery does not appear in this case.

IF Zakat be employed in discharging the debts of a defunct, this is not considered as a payment of Zakat, because delivery does not appear in this instance.

IF a person employ the Zakat upon his property in the purchase of a slave, for the purpose of granting him his freedom, this is not a discharge of Zakat. Imam Malik maintains that this act amounts to a due discharge of Zakat: because he alleges that the phrase Feear-Rikab, which occurs in the KORAN, applies to a slave thus bought and liberated; but our doctors argue that the emancipation of a slave amounts simply to a dereliction of property, and does not in any respect bear the construction of delivery or transfer of possession.

Persons who are not the proper objects of its application.—IT is not lawful to bestow any part of Zakat upon the rich, the Prophet having declared that "alms are not lawful to the wealthy."—Shafei extends the use of Zakat to warriors, although they should be rich; but the precept here quoted is in proof against him.

IT is not lawful for an owner of property to pay the Zakat upon it to his father, grandfather, or great-grandfather; nor to his son, grandson, or great-grandson; because the use of property between him and those persons is conjunct,—that is to say, each of those relatives is entitled to the use of the other's property; and hence transfer of property, in its full sense, does not exist in these cases.

IT is not lawful for a proprietor to pay the Zakat upon his property to his wife, because the use of property is common between the husband and wife, according to general custom; nor is it lawful for a wife to pay the Zakat upon her property to her husband (according to Haneefa), for the same reason. The two disciples have said that it is lawful to give Zakat to the husband, because the

*An objection and reply are here omitted, as they turn solely upon points of verbal criticism, and consequently do not admit of an intelligible translation.

wife of Abd-'Oola-bin-Masood asked the Prophet whether she should give Sadka to her husband?—to which he replied,—"You have two duties, one, that of Sadka, the other, that of relationship."—But to this our doctors reply from Haneefa, that by the term Sadka, mentioned in this tradition, is to be understood the Sadka Nifl, or voluntary alms.*

It is not lawful for a proprietor to bestow the Zakat of his property upon his own Mokatib, or Am Walid, or Modabbir, because in none of these cases is there a transfer of property, since that which falls to a slave becomes the property of his master;—and a master has, in like manner, a superior right in the property of his Mokatib, whence the master's transfer of property to him cannot be established.

It is not lawful for a proprietor to bestow the Zakat of his property upon his slave, whom he may have partially emancipated, (according to Haneefa) because such a slave is held by him to stand as a Mokatib; but the two disciples maintain that the bestowing of Zakat upon such a slave is legal, because they hold this slave to be a debtor to his master.†

It is not lawful to bestow Zakat upon the slave of a rich man, because, if it be made over to the slave, it becomes the property of his master, and the master being rich, the delivery of Zakat to him is illegal. And, in like manner, it is illegal to bestow Zakat upon the child of a rich person, being an infant, since the child is supposed to be rich in the property of the father; contrary to the case of the child of a rich person, being an adult, who is poor, he not being accounted rich in the property of his father, although his subsistence be a debt upon his parents:' and also contrary to the case of the wife of a rich person, because she, if she be poor, is not accounted rich in the property of the husband, or in proportion to, or on account of, the subsistence she enjoys from him.

It is not lawful to bestow any part of Zakat upon persons of the tribe of Hashim; the Prophet having said, "O, descendants of Hashim! of a truth God hath rendered unlawful to you the Ghoosala [water dirted by ablution of men, and also their Chirk [fifth,] and in lieu thereof he hath ordained to you a fifth of the fifth of all plunder:" and by the term Ghoosala is here to be understood the Zakat upon property, which is not lawful to Hashimees: contrary to Sadka Nifl: and by the term Chirk is to be understood the same. By the tribe of Hashim are here to be understood the families of Alee, and Abbas, and Jafir, and Akleel, and Haris-Ibnal-Mootlib; all these deriving their descent from Hashim the son of Minaf. But by the same Hashim, in the words of the Prophet before quoted, is to be particularly understood Hashim the great-grandfather of the Prophet, who also gives a name to a tribe.*

Zakat is discharged by the erroneous application of it to an improper person.—If a person were to bestow Zakat upon another, erroneousuly supposing him to be a proper object of its application, and should afterwards discover him to be rich, or a Hashimee, or an infidel,—or, if he should give Zakat to a person in the dark, and afterwards discover that person to be his father, or his son,—in these cases Zakat is considered to be fully discharged, and no longer to remain due.—This is according to Haneefa and Mohammed.—Aboo Yoosaf has said that, in the cases here recited, Zakat is still held to remain due, because it was in the power of that person to inquire into, and discover the particulars concerning him upon whom he bestowed Zakat previous to making it over to him; and such being the case, where he is guilty of an evident neglect, his act is null, and consequently the Zakat is still a debt upon him; the same as where there are several vessels of water, some clean and others unclean,—or several garments, some pure and others defiled,—in which case, if a person, after due deliberation, select one of the pots of water, and perform his ablution with it, or put on one of the garments, and say his prayers, and he should afterwards appear to have committed an error, a repetition of the prayer or ablution is held to be incumbent upon him.—Haneefa and Mohammed support their opinion, in this case, upon a decision recorded of the Prophet in a similar instance; and they moreover argue, that a knowledge of the situation and circumstances of men is only to be formed from conjecture and cannot be easily obtained to a degree of decisive certainty, wherefore the matter is to be taken according to the donor's conception of it; the same as in a case of prayer, where if a man, intending to turn his face towards the Kaba, were to look in another direction, and pray and his mistake afterwards appear, a repetition of the prayer is not incumbent upon him. It is recorded as an opinion of Haneefa, that Zakat is to be held discharged if thus bestowed by mistake, upon a rich person, but not if bestowed upon a Hashimee, a parent, or a child; but the Zahir-Rawayet accords with what was before advanced.—What is here mentioned proceeds upon a supposition that the Zakat has been bestowed after due deliberation, in consequence of the donor conceiving that the receiver is a proper object of its applica-

*In opposition to Zakat, which comes under the description of Sadka Farz, or obligatory alms; and consequently what is quoted above by the two disciples does not in any respect apply to the present case.

†That is for the remainder of his bondage. For a full explanation of this, see Ittak.

*What follows of this passage relates merely to the Arabian tribes, and is therefore quite useless.

tion; but he should not have deliberated, or if, after deliberation, a doubt still remain, the Zakat is not discharged, unless it afterwards appear that the receiver was a proper object of its application.

Unless that person be the slave or Makatib of the donor.—If a person bestow Zakat upon another, and afterwards discover that this other is his own slave or Mokatib, this is not held to be a discharge of his Zakat, because, in this case, there is no transfer of property (according to what has been already remarked), and the discharge of Zakat rests upon a complete transfer of it, as was formerly explained.

It is not thought proper to bestow Zakat upon a person possessed of a complete Nisab in any property whatever, such an one being considered as coming under the description of Ghannee [rich], because this is the law term for any one possessed of a Nisab; but the condition on which any person is accounted a Ghannee is, that the Nisab which constitutes his property be exclusive of all demands or incumbrances (such as debts, and so forth); and on this precise quantity of absolute property no Zakat is legally due from the proprietor, the increase thereof (understood in the lapse of Hawlan-Hawl) being a condition of the obligation to Zakat.

Other persons upon whom Zakat may be lawfully bestowed.—It is lawful to bestow Zakat upon a person possessed of less than a Nisab, although he be sound in body and capable of labour, because such an one comes under the description of a Fakeer, who is one of the specified objects of its application, and also, because actual necessity in the situation or circumstances of the object is difficult to be ascertained, and therefore the rule is restricted to that description which affords argument of such necessity; and a deficiency in worldly property, to the amount of a Nisab, affords such argument of necessity with respect to the proprietor.

If a person were to bestow to the amount of two hundred Dirms, or upwards of the Zakat of his property, upon one individual, such a procedure is abominable, but yet is legal.—Ziffer has said that this is illegal; because in the act of bestowing that quantity of Zakat, the person who receives it becomes a Ghannee,* which would induce the idea of Zakat being bestowed upon a Ghanee; but to this our doctors reply, that the opulence of the person in question is an effect of the gift of Zakat to him, and therefore he does not come within the description of a Ghannee until after it has been bestowed,—yet, where discharge of Zakat tends to bring any one within the description of Ghannee, it is abominable, the same as prayer when performed near any filth.

*Literally, a rich person, in opposition to Fakeer, a poor person.

Aboo Haneefa has said, "I regard it as most laudable to bestow upon a Fakeer, Zakat to such an amount as may preclude him from the necessity of begging for that day."

Zakat of one city not transferable to another except in certain cases—The transfer of Zakat from one city to another is abominable, it being rather indispensable that the Zakat of every city be bestowed upon the claimants of that city; and also, because in this a regard is had to the rights or Jowar [neighbourhood]:—and hence, it is abominable in men to transfer the Zakat upon their property from their own city to another, except either for the use of their relations, or for the purpose of assisting those who may be in greater necessity than the inhabitants of their own city; because in the one case exists the peculiar duty of consanguinity, and in the other the application of relief where it is most required.—But although the transfer of Zakat from one city to another, excepting for the purposes here mentioned, be accounted abominable, yet it amounts to a valid discharge of Zakat because the term Fakeer, mentioned in the sacred writings as one of the proper objects of the application of Zakat, is not local but general.

CHAPTER VIII.

OF SADKA-FITTIR

Definition of the term.—By Sadka-fittir is understood the alms bestowed upon the poor on the Yd-al Fittir, or festival of breaking Lent.

Obligation of Sadka-fittir,—Sadka-fittir is incumbent upon all free Mussulmans possessed of property to the amount of a Nisab clear of incumbrance. The obligation to Sadka-fittir is founded on a precept of the Prophet, who, in a discourse upon the festival of breaking Lent, said, "Let every person, whether infant or adult bestow [upon the poor] half a Saa of wheat, or one Saa of millet or of barley." This saying is recorded by Salba-Adwee, but being of the class of Hidees Ahad,* it establishes only a moral but not a religious obligation.

Conditions of the obligation.—Freedom is made a condition, in order that the assignment [of the Saduka] may be complete: and Islam, or profession of the faith, is also made a condition, in order that this donation may bear the construction of an obligation and act of piety, of which infidels are held incapable: and the possession of a Nisab is

*The singular traditions:—that is, those which are not included among the approved traditions, and therefore are not supposed to be possessed of the same authority.

also made a condition, the Prophet having declared "Alms are not expected to be bestowed but from the ability of the RICH." Shafei has said that the Sadka-fittir is incumbent upon every person who possesses property to the amount or value of one day's subsistence for himself and family; but the above precept of the Prophet is in proof against him.—It is to be observed that wealth is determined at the rate of a Nisab, because that is the standard by which the law measures it; but this, with the reserve of its being exclusive of all incumbrances, as whatever may be so occupied is accounted non-existent; but increase in it is not a condition.—There are three things connected with the possession of a Nisab, such as here described; FIRST, prohibition against the acceptance of alms; SECONDLY, obligation to perform sacrifice; and THIRDLY, obligation to bestow Sadka-fittir.

Persons upon whom, or in whose behalf, it is incumbent.—THE Sadka-fittir is incumbent upon every individual respectively. Ebn Amir having recorded that the Prophet has constituted Sadka-fittir an absolute injunction [Farz] upon all mankind and both sexes, indiscriminately.

IT is incumbent upon a man to discharge the Sadka-fittir in behalf of his children, being infants, because he is their guardian, and their proivision is a debt upon him; wherefore the accomplishment of their duties of Sadka must also rest upon him, this being considered as a part of their provision. And, in the same manner, a man must discharge the Sadka-fittir in behalf of his male and female slaves, he being their guardian, and their subsistence depending upon him. What is here advanced proceeds entirely upon a supposition that the slaves are not held by the proprietor merely in the way of traffick; and also that his children are not possessed of any independent property; for, if the children be possessed of property, their Sadka-fittir is to be discharged out of that, according to the two Sheicks. Mohammed contradicts their opinion in this instance. The argument of the two Sheicks is that the lawgiver has considered Sadka-fittir the same as Nifka,* and therefore it is to be held as such.

Persons upon whom, or in whose behalf, it is not incumbent.—THE Sadka-fittir is not incumbent upon a man in behalf of his wife because his power of guardianship and provision, with respect to her, is incomplete, since a husband is not guardian over his wife any farther than respects the rights of marriage, nor does the provision for her rest upon him any further than with respect to food, clothing, and lodging, which are termed Rawatib [necessaries], any thing beyond which he is not accountable for.—And, in the same manner, it is not incumbent upon a man to disburse the Sadka-fittir for his children, being adults, although these form a part of his family, because he is not invested with any authority of guardianship over them.—But yet if a man was to disburse the Sadka-fittir on behalf of his wife, or adult children, without their desire, it is lawful, on a principle of benevolence, their consent being by custom understood.

IT is not incumbent upon men to pay the Sadka-fittir for their Mokatibs; neither is it incumbent on a Mokatib to pay it on his own account, such an one coming under the description of a Fakeer.

Exception.—IT is incumbent on men to pay Sadka-fittir on behalf of their Modabbirs and Am-Walids, as being invested with complete authority over them.

Not incumbent on behalf of slaves kept as articles of traffic.—IT is not incumbent upon men to pay Sadka-fittir on behalf of their male and female slaves designed for sale as merchandise. Shafei alleges that the Sadka-fittir is obligatory upon such slaves, and that the proprietor is to pay it for them; and that the Zakat upon them is due from the proprietor. In short, Shafei holds that Sadka-fittir is due from the slave, and Zakat from their proprietor, on two distinct and separate accounts; and consequently, that this does not induce the idea of a repetition of Sadka upon one and the same property; but with our doctors the obligation to Sadka-fitter, on behalf of slaves, is held to rest upon their owner, the same as Zakat; and consequently, if the payment of the former were incumbent, it would admit the idea of two Sadkas upon one property within the year, which is illegal.

Nor on behalf of a partnership slave.—No Sadka-fittir is incumbent upon any of the proprietors on account of a partnership slave, because none of them, individually, is invested with complete authority over him, nor obliged to furnish his entire provision. And, in the same manner, no Sadka-fitter is incumbent upon any of the proprietors, on account of two or more partnership slaves, according to Haneefa.—The two disciples have said that, in this case, Sadka-fittir is incumbent upon the proprietor; but in such a degree only, with respect to their shares, as may amount to a complete slave or slaves, and not to any fractional part or portion of them: for instance, if there were five slaves held in partnership by two men, each partner would have to pay Sadka-fittir for two slaves, and not for two and a half.—Some, however, have said that the two disciples agree with Haneefa in their doctrine upon this point, because the share of each partner, individually, cannot be collected into any particular slave or slaves, until a partition take place of the partnership stock, and consequently none of them appertains to either partner in particular.

Incumbent on behalf of infidel slaves.—IT is incumbent upon Mussulmans to pay the Sadka-fittir for their infidel slaves, on the

*The subsistence due to a wife, parent, child, and other relations.

authority of the tradition of Salba-Adwee, already quoted, because there the term slaves is used generally, and is not restrictively applied to Mussulman slaves : more over in the traditions of Abbas, it appears that the Prophet said "Render SADKA-FITTIR on behalf of every freeman, and also of every slave, be that slave a CHRISTIAN, a JEW, or a PAGAN :" and further, it is incumbent, because the occasion of the obligation is here established, and the proprietor [of the slave] is capable of taking upon him the responsibility for such obligations. Shafei maintains that, in this instance, no Sadka-fittir is due, because the obligation to Sadka-fittir rests upon a slave himself, and not upon his owner ; and the former (in the case here supposed) is incapable of such obligation, as being an infidel.

But not on behalf of a slave the property of an infidel.—IF the slave be a Mussulman, and his master an infidel, in this case no Sadka-fittir whatever is due for such slave, according to all the doctors ; according to our doctors, evidently, because they hold the obligation of Sadka-fittir, with respect to the slave, to rest upon the master, and here the master is an infidel ; and, according to Shafei, because he holds the obligation to rest upon the slave himself, to be discharged by his master ; and the master, in the present case, is incapable of discharging it, as being an infidel.

Case of a slave sold with a reserve of option.—IF a slave be sold with a reserve of option to one of the parties, the seller or the purchaser, determinable on the ensuing festival of Fittir, in this case the Sadka fittir, on behalf of that slave, is incumbent upon the party to whom he may ultimately belong. —Ziffer alleges that the discharge of the Sadka-fittir rests with the party in whose behalf reserve of option was made a condition, because the authority over that slave is in fact vested in him. Shafei maintains that it rests with him who has possession in the interim, whom he holds to be the purchaser, on this ground, that the furnishing Sadka-fittir is one of the rules of possession, the same as furnishing subsistence.—Our doctors argue that the possession of the slave in the present case, is a matter which remains in suspense, since, if he to whom the option was reserved choose to dissolve the sale, the property in the slave reverts to the seller ; but, on the other hand, if he confirm the sale and render it valid, the slave becomes the property of the purchaser from the period of the original engagement ; and the possession thus remaining in suspense, that which depends upon such possession must remain suspended also : contrary to the case of Nifka, which is requisite from day to day, to supply the wants of nature, and is consequently incapable of such suspension. And if this slave be an article of traffick, the same difference of opinion holds with respect to the Zakat upon him.

———

Section.—Of the measure of Sadka-fittir and of the Time of its Obligation and its Discharge.

Proportion of Sudka-fittir and the articles in which it may be discharged —THE measure of Sadka-fittir in wheat, or flour or bran, or in dried fruits, is an half Saa ; and in dates or barley it is one Saa. The two disciples say that dried fruits are the same as barley in this respect ; and there is also one tradition of the opinion of Haneefa to the same effect.—The former is the doctrine recorded in the Jama Sagheer. Shafei says that the measure of a Sadka-fittir, in all the articles here specified, is one Sea ; because Aboo Seyid Kadooree remarks that this was the customary Sadka-fittir in all articles in the time of the Prophet.—Our doctors support what was before advanced on the authority of the tradition of Salba Adwee, already repeatedly quoted ; and the doctrine of the whole of the companions (such as the Kholfa Rashidine* and others), is consonant to that of our doctors : the tradition, also, of Aboo Seyid, cited by Shafei, implies no more than that, in the time of the Prophet, people were accustomed in giving something over what was obligatory.—The two disciples allege (in support of their opinion, that dried fruits are the same as barley) that Khurma [dried dates] is one species of dried fruits ; and they being considered the same as barley, it follows that all dried fruits, as being of one general description,. should be subject to the same rule. The argument of Haneefa is, that dried fruits and barley are of a corresponding nature, because as the poor eat the flour of wheat with its bran, so do they dried fruit with its core or stone : contrary to dates, which are the same as barley, in as much as the stones of the one and the bran of the other are thrown away. —Barley-meal is the same as barley ; but it is best that, in discharging the Sadka-fittir in the flour or bran of either barley or wheat, attention be paid to the value ; that is to say if, for instance, the value of half a Saa of flour be equal to that of the same quantity of wheat, it will suffice to give half a Saa of flour, but otherwise not ; and the same with respect to barley-meal.—This is not noticed in the Jama Sagheer, because the value of meal or flour does not commonly fall short of that of the grain, but rather generally exceeds it.

IN discharging the Sadka-fittir with bread regard is to be had to the value only ; this is approved doctrine.

The half Saa now mentioned is to be ascertained by weight, according to Haneefa ; but the two disciples hold that it is to be ascertained by measure.

In discharging the Sadka-fittir, flour is preferable to wheat, and money is preferable to flour according to what is recorded from Aboo Yousaf ; because money satisfies the

*The immediate successors of the Prophet.

wants most amply, and flour most readily: contrary to wheat, which, after it is bestowed, requires to be made flour before it is fit for use.—It is recorded, as an opinion of Aboo Bikr Ayamush, that wheat is preferable either to flour or money, because this is universally admitted to be a proper article in which to discharge the Sadka fittir, whereas concerning money and flour there are various opinions.

THE Saa, according to Aboo Haneefa and Mohammed, consists of eight Ratls* of the Ratls of Irak.—Aboo Yoosaf has said that it is only five Ratls and one third; and this is also the doctrine of Shafei: the Prophet having said "Our SAA is smaller than that of others."—The arguement of the Tirrafine†, in this case, is, that it is recorded by the Prophet, that he performed the Woozo by the Mid (which is two Ratls), and the Ghosl by the Saa (which is eight Ralts); and the Saa of Omar was the same: moreover, this Saa is small compared with that of Hashimee, which was the Saa in common use, wherefore it is lawful to regard that mentioned in the tradition above quoted as the standard in Sadka-fittir.

*Time of the commencement of the obligation.*THE obligation to the performance of the Sadka fittir commences with the dawn of the morning of the festival of Fittir; that is to say, the arrival of that specified period is a condition of its obligation. Shafei alleges that the obligation commences with the sunset of the last day of Ramzan:—and the result of this difference of opinion is, that if (for instance) an infidel were to be converted, and to become a Mussulman,—or, if a child were to be born,—on the eve of the festival of Fittir, the Sadka-fittir would be due on account of the convert of the child, according to our doctors; but, according to Shafei, it would not be due: and, on the other hand, if a man's child, or male or female slave, were to die on the last night of Ramzan Sadka-fittir is incumbent upon him on their account, according to Shafei; but it would not be so, according to our doctors.—The argument of Shafei, in this case, is that the Sadka-fittir is essentially connected with, and bears relation to Fittir [the act of breaking of fast], as the connection of the terms evinces; and the sunset of the last day of Ramzan is the time of Fittir, because the fast may be then broken.—To this our doctors reply, by admitting that the Sadka-fittir is certainly connected with the act of fittir, but the Fittir has reference to the day, and not to the night, whence it is that this period is expressed by the words Yawm-al-fittir [day of breaking fast], and not by the words Lail-al-fittir [night of breaking fast]; and hence it follows that the obligation to the performance of Sadka-fittir if connected with the morning of the festival of Fittir, and not with the eve thereof.

IT is most laudable that men discharge their Sadka-fittir on the day of the festival of Fittir, before they proceed to the mosque to perform the prayers of that festival, because the Prophet did thus; and also, because the precept regarding Sadka-fittir was issued with a view that this donation might relieve the wants of the poor, and thereby enable them to enjoy the festival, and to unite in the duties of it with a cheerful mind; and the design is best answered by the donation being made before prayer.

IF tha Sadka-fittir be discharged previous to the day of the festival of Fittir, it is lawful; because the discharge of an obligation, at any time after the establishment of the cause of the obligation, is legal, in the same manner as that of Zakat previous to the lapse of Hawlan-Hawl.

IF a person were not to discharge the Sadka-fittir within the day of the festival of Fittir, yet the obligation still continues, and it is proper that it be made good afterwards, because the obligation of it is imposed with a view to the relief of the poor, which object still remains; contrary to sacrifice, the obligation to which, if it be neglected on the Yawm-al Nihr [the day of sacrifice, being the tenth of the month Zee-al Hidjee], drops altogether;—this being merely an act of piety, in which the wants or rights of others are no way concerned.

---

*A Ratl is about fourteen ounces.

†Literally, the two extremes, as being the oldest and youngest of the three orthodox doctors; namely, Hanneefa and Mohammed.

BOOK II.

OF NIKKAH, OR MARRIAGE.

Definition of the term.—NIKKAH, in its primitive sense, means carnal conjunction. Some have said that it signifies conjunction generally. In the language of the law it implies a particular contract used for the purpose rf legalizing generation.

CHAPTER I.

Forms under which marriage may be contracted.—MARRIAGE is contracted,—that is to say, is effected and legally confirmed,—by means of declaration and consent, both expressed in the preterite, because although the use of preterite be to relate that which is past, yet it has been adopted, in the law, in a creative sense, to answer the necessity of the case.*—Declaration, in the law, signifies the speech which first proceeds from one of two contracting parties, and consent the speech which proceeds from the other in reply to the declaration.

Marriage may also be contracted by the parties expressing themselves, one in the imperative, and the other in the preterite; as if a man were to say to another "Contract your daughter in marriage to me,"—and he were to reply. "I have contracted" [my daughter to you]—because his words "Contract your daughter to me" are expressive of a commission of agency, empowering to contract in marriage; and one person may be authorized to act on both sides in marriage (as shall be hereafter explained); wherefore the reply of the father, "I have contracted," stands in the place both of declaration and consent,—as if he had said "I have contracted, and I have consented."

Marriage may also be contracted by the use of the word Nikkah, or marriage,—as if a woman were to say to a man "I have married myself to you for such a sum of money,"† and the man were to reply "I have consented:" and, in like manner, by the word Tazweej, or contracting in marriage as if a woman were to say to a man "I have contracted myself in marriage unto you," and so forth:—and so also, by the word Hibba, or gift,‡ as if she were to say "I have bestowed myself upon you:" and likewise, by the word Tamleek, or consignment,—as if she were to say "I have consigned myself over to you:" and so also, by the word Sadka, or alms-gift, as if she were to say "I have given myself as an alms unto you."—Shafei is of opinion that marriage cannot be contracted except by the words Nikkah and Tazweej, because the term Tamleek (for instance) does not bear the construction of matrimony either in a literal or metaphorical sense;—evidently not in a literal sense, this term never being used to express marriage; nor in a metaphorical sense, because a metaphor is to be understood in a particular sense only from the propriety of its application, which is not the case here, the terms Nikkah or Tazweej implying conjunction (as was before observed), and between the possessor and the possession no conjunction whatever exists. The argument of our doctors, in this case, is that consignment operates as the principle of a right to a carnal conjunction in the subject of it, in virtue of a right in the person (as in the case of female slaves); and the right to carnal conjunction is also established by matrimony; wherefore, as marriage and consignment thus appear to be both principles operating to the same end, the latter may be metaphorically taken for the former.

Marriage may be contracted by the use of the term Beeya, or sale; as if a woman were to say to a man "I have sold myself into your hands," and this is approved, because sale operates as the principle of a right in the person; and a right in the person is the principle of a right to carnal conjunction, whence the proprety of the metaphorical application of sale to metrimony.

According to the Rawayet-Saheeh, marriage cannot be contracted by the use of the term Ijara, or hire—(as if a woman were to say "I have hired myself to you for so much;")—nor by Ibahit, or permission; nor by Ihlah, or rendering lawful; nor by Areet or loan; none of these operating as the principle of a right to a carnal conjunction.—Neither can marriage be contracted by the use of the term Waseeyate or bequest; because bequest does not convey any right of possession until after the testator's death:—and as a contract of marriage in express terms, referring the execution of it to a period subsequent to the decease of either of the parties would be null, so also, in the present case, a fortiori.

Must be contracted in the presence of witnesses.—Marriage, where both the parties are Mussulmans, cannot be contracted but in the presence of two male witnesses, or of one man and two women, who are sane, adult, and Mussulmans, whether they be of established integrity of character or otherwise, or may ever have suffered punishment as slanderers.—The compiler of this work observes that evidence is an essential condition of marriage, the Prophet having declared "no marriage is good without evidence;" and this precept is a proof against Malik, who maintains that in marriage notoriety only is a condition, and not positive evidence.

Qualification of a witness.—It is necessary that the witnesses be free, the evidence of slaves being in no case valid, because such are not competent to act in any respect sui juris: and it is also requisite that they be of sound mind and mature age, because minors or idiots are in capable of acting for themselves; and it is likewise necessary that they be Mussulumans; the evidence of infidels not being legal with respect to Mussulmans.

Persons may witness a marriage, whose testimony would not be received in other cases.—The sex of the witnesses is not an essential condition of their competency, insomuch that marriage may be lawfully contracted in the presence of one man and two women:—neither is the integrity of the witnesses an essential condition, insomuch that (according to our doctors) a marriage is valid if contracted in the presence of two Fasiks or unjust persons.*—Shafei maintains that

*Because the present and future being expressed, in the Arabic language, under one from, a contract expressed in the present would be equivocal.

† Meaning her dower.

‡ This, and the two following terms, are such as are used where the woman does not stipulate any dower.

*The word Fasik which throughout this work is used in contradistinction to Adil, has

the integrity of the witnesses is an essential condition, because evidence is entitled to reverence and respect, the Prophet having said "pay reverence to witnesses;" and Fasiks are not proper objects of such reverence, but rather the reverse.—To this our doctors reply that Fasiks are competent to act for themselves, and of course competency in evidence must also appertain to them, since they are not incapaitated from acting with respect to others; a Fasik, moreover, is capable of holding the office of a Sultan or an Imam, whence it follows that he is also capable of becoming a Kazee, or a witness.—A person who has suffered punishment for slander, as being still possessed of general competency, is also capable of bearing witness, so far as merely respects declaration and consent in matrimony, but no farther, there being a positive prohibition to the reception of such a person's evidence, which, however, admits of exception in the present case, like that of blind persons, or of the children of the parties, whose evidence, although not admissible in any other case, is yet allowed in marriage.

Infidels may witness the marriage of an infidel woman—If a Mussulman marry a female infidel subject in the presence of two male infidel subjects it is lawful, according to Aboo Yoosaf and Haneefa. Mohammad and Ziffer maintain that it is not lawful because their testimony, with respect to declaration and consent in marriage, amounts to evidence and the evidence of infidels regarding Mussulmans is illegal; whence it is the same in fact as if they had not heard the declaration and consent of the parties. The argument of the two elders, in reply to this objection, is, that evidence is required in matrimony, not with any view to the ascertainment of a point of property (such as dower), but merely in order to establish the husband's right of cohabitation, which is in this case the object.

The negotiator of the contract may also, in certain cases, be a witness to it.—If a man desire another to contract his daughter (being an infant) in marriage to a third person, and the other should accordingly contract his daughter, upon the spot, to the third person, in the presence of the person so desiring, and the act be witnessed by only one person besides these two, the marriage is lawful; because, in this case, the father, as being upon the spot, is considered as the actual contractor of the marriage [on behalf of his daughter]; wherefore the second person stands merely as the negotiator of the contract, and of course, not appearing as a party in it, is a competent witness with the therefore been rendered, in the translation, unjust, which is indeed the most common acceptation of the world; it must, however, be understood to relate to a person who neglects decorum in his behaviour and dress, and such other inferior points, rather than to one who is actually known to be dishonest.

other. But, if the father of the infant aforesaid should go away, and be not actually present at the execution of the contract, the marriage would be null; because the father, as not being present, cannot be considered as the contractor, that appellation properly applying to the other—who appears to act, in his absence, as his matrimonial agent on his daughter's behalf; consequently here would be only one competent witness present, and one evidence is not sufficient; whence the mariage would be illegal.—And the rule is the same where a father matches his daughter (being an adult), at her desire, in the presence of one other witness; that is to say, if the daughter be herself present at the execution of the contract it is legal, otherwise not.

Section—Of the prohibited degrees; that is to say, of Woman whom it is lawful to marry, and of those with whom Marriage is unlawful.

It is unlawful to marry a mother, or a grandmother.—A man may not marry his mother, nor his paternal or maternal grandmother; because the word of God in the Koran says, "Your Ams (that is, your mothers) and your daughters are forbidden to you;" and the primitive sense of the term Am [mother] being origin or root, the grandmothers are comprehended in this prohibition. The illegality of such a connexion is, moreover, supported upon the united opinion of all our doctors.

A daughter or a grand-daughter.—A man may not marry his daughter, on the authority of the text above quoted, nor his grand-daughter, nor any of his direct desendants.

A sister, a niece, or an aunt.—Neither may a man marry his sister, nor his sister's daughter, nor his brother's daughter, nor his paternal aunt, nor his maternal aunt; the prohibition of such in marriage being included in the text already quoted.

All the degrees of aunts are also included in this prohibition; to wit, maternal and paternal aunts, as well as the aunts of the father, and the aunts of the mother, both paternal and maternal:—so also the daughters of all the brothers; that is to say, of the full brother, and of the paternal* brother and of the maternal brother; and, in like manner, the daughters of all sisters, to wit, of the full sisters, and of the paternal sisters, and of the maternal sisters; because the terms Amma, Khala, Okh, and Okht, which occur in the passage of the koran already cited, apply to all those degrees of kinded.

Or a mother-in-law—It is not lawful for a man to marry his wife's mother, whether, he may have consummated his marriage with her daughter or not, the Almighty

* By the terms maternal or paternal applied to brothers and sisters, is to be understood half-brothers or half-sisters by the father's or mother's side.

having prohibited such a connexion in general terms, without any regard to that circumstance.

Or a step-daughter.—Neither is it lawful for a man to marry the daughter of his wife; but this only, provided he have already consummated his marriage with the latter, because the sacred text restricts the illegality of this union to that circumstance, wherefore marriage with the daughter of the wife is illegal, where carnal connexion has taken place with the latter, whether the daughter be an inmate of the husband's Haram, or not. It is here to be observed, that the text in the sacred writings which says "Your women who reside in your Harams, being the daughters of your wives with whom you have held cohabitation, are unlawful to you," has merely reference to custom, and does not imply that the residence of the daughter in the man's Haram along with her mother is unlawful; for it is usual, when a man marries a woman who has a daughter by a former husband, that the latter accompanies her mother to his house, and is thence considered as one of his Haram.*

Or a step-mother, or step-grandmother.—It is unlawful for a man to marry the wife of his father, or of his grandfather, God having so commanded, saying "Marry not the wives of your progenitors."

Or a daughter-in-law, or grand-daughter-in-law.—Neither is it lawful for a man to marry the wife of his son. or of his grandson, the Almighty having said "Wed not the wives of your sons, or your daughters who proceed from your loins:"

Or a nurse or a foster-sister.—It is not lawful for a man to marry his foster-mother, or his foster-sister, the Almighty having commanded, saying "Marry not your mothers who have suckled you, or your sisters by fosterage;" and the Prophet has also declared, "Every thing is prohibited by reason of fosterage which is so by reason of kindred."

Or two sisters.—It is not lawful to marry and cohabit with two women being sisters, neither is it lawful for a man to cohabit with two sisters in virtue of a right of possession [as being his slaves], because the Almighty has declared that such cohabitation with sisters is unlawful.

Case of two sisters.—If a man marry the sister of his female slave with whom he has not cohabited, such marriage is approved, the contract being, in this case, entered into by parties competent in every respect.—And this marriage being legal and valid, the man must not afterwards hold any carnal connexion with his female slave, even though he should never consummate his marriage carnally with her sister, because a wife stands in law, as Fœmina Fututa:—neither should the husband indulge in the connubial enjoyment with this wife until he shall previously have rendered her sister [the slave] unlawful to him, and relinquished his right of cohabitation with her, by some means or other, such as emancipating her, or marrying her to another man, in order to avoid the construction of cohabitation with sisters; but having so done, he may afterwards cohabit with his wife; because the no breach of the law would ensue, since a female slave is not held in the law, merely as such, to be a Fœmina Fututa.

Another case of two sisters.—If a man should happen to marry two sisters by two contracts,* and it be not known with respect to which marriage first took place, a separation from both the sisters must ensue; because it is evident that his marriage with one of the two is illegal, but it is impossible to ascertain with which, by reason of ignorance of priority; nor is it conceivable that a judgment should be pronounced legalizing the marriage of either, unspecified, since the marriage of both remaining unascertained. a rule to make the same valid would be illegal, as not leading to any good or advantage; for the adv ntage proposed in matrimony is procreation. which is unattainable without carnol connexion of the parties; and this connexion with a woman unspecified is inadmissible: moreover, allowing the marriage to be valid, it would be injurious to both, as laying them under the matrimonial restraints without the advantage of the connubial enjoyment, which neither could legally possess; for all which reasons their separation is indispensable. And in this case each sister is entitled to receive an half dower, because, if either could have been proved to be first married, she would have had a claim to her full dower, but the priority of marriage of either remaining unascertained, the dower is thus divided between them.—Some have said that this is only where each of the sisters respectively maintains the priority of her marriage without either being able to adduce any proofs; but that where they both declare their ignorance of such priority, nothing whatever is to be paid to either, until such time as both agree to receive an half dower, as above, because that is due to them in virtue of a priority unascertained, wherefore it is necessary either that each should respectively maintain her priority, or that both should agree, as above, before any decree for payment of an half dower to each should be passed.—But if each sister maintain her priority, and both produce equal

* This observation is introduced merely with a view to explain an ambiguity in the text referred to.

*This doubtless supposes a case where a man is contracted in marriage through the agency of others empowered by him for that purpose (as shall be shown in an ensuing chapter), and who may engage in the contract without his immediate knowledge.

evidence in support of it, an half dower is the right of each, according to all the doctors.

A man may not marry an aunt and niece.—It is unlawful for a man to marry two women, of whom one is the aunt or niece of the other, the Prophet having declared a precept, as recorded in the Zahir-Rawayet, to this effect.

Or two women related within the prohibited degrees.—IT is not lawful for a man to marry two women within such degree of affinity as would render a marriage between them illegal, if one of them were a man,—and for the same reason, because this would occasion a confusion of kindred.

A man may marry a woman and her step-daughter.—But a man may marry two women; one of them being a widow; and the other the daughter of that widow's former husband by another wife, because here exists no affinity, either by blood or fosterage.—Ziffer objects to this, and maintains that the marriage would be illegal; because, if the daughter were supposed a man, a marriage between her and the widow would be illegal, and these two consequently stand in the same predicament, with respect to each other, as those in the preceding case.—To this our doctors reply that the illegality there stated is supposed to exsist only in cases where this supposition, if applied to either of the women, would render their marriage illegal; but that does not hold in the persent instance, for if the widow were supposed to be a man, she could lawfully marry the daughter.—And it is moreover related, in the Nakl Saheeh, that Abdoola the son of Jafir married a wife and a daughter of Alee.

Cases which induce illeglity.—IF a man commit whoredom* with a woman, her mother and daughter are prohibited to him.—Shafei maintains that they are not prohibited; because whoredom does not induce Hoormat-Mooshahirat, or prohibition from affinity, as this law of prohibition is a peculiar distinction bestowed upon the servants of GOD through the divine favour, and whoredom being a crime, cannot possibly induce that which is a favour of GOD.—To this our doctors reply, that the carnal act operates as a principle or cause of a mutual participation of blood between the parties concerned in it, in vitrue of the child which is, or may be, the fruit thereof, that partaking of the father and the mother respectively, in toto, for it is usually said "This child is the offspring of such a man and of such a woman;" and this participation being thus established between the child and each of the parents respectively, it is virtually so between the parents themselves, because although a portion of the child be a part of the mother, yet it is attributed, in toto, to the father, whence a part of the mother is attributed to him; and vice versa; and a mutual participation of blood being thus established between the man and the woman, it follows that the mother or the danghter of the latter stands as the actual mother or daughter of the man, because the former would be the grandmother of the child produced by such act of whoredom; she is therefore the root of the root of such offspring, and the offpring is the branch of a branch from her; and it is inconceivable that the child should be a branch of a branch from her, unless the fornicator were considered as a branch from her, and the grandmother the root of the fornicator: and the same reasoning applies with respect to the daughter.

IF a woman touch a man in lust [*i.e.* manu penem fricans, stuprum excitat], the mother and daughter of that woman are thereby prohibited to him.—Shafei says that they are not prohibited. And the same difference of opinion obtains in cases where a man touches a woman in lust; or sees the pudendum of a woman; or where a woman sees the yard of a man in lust: in all which instances our doctors hold that the mother or daughter of such woman are rendered unlawful to the man; but Shafei maintains a contrary sentiment, arguing that seeing or touching do not amount to the absolute act, insomuch that the usual ceremonies required by the law after the carnal act* are not here necessary.—To this our doctors reply, that such acts as those, being a cause of copulation, stand as that constructively.—It is to be observed, that by touching in lust, with respect to a man, is meant producting a priapism with the hand, or increasing the turgidity of the virile member, by the same means where the priapism already exists.—This is an approved definition of that phrase, as to the term lust, with respect to young men in full vigour and equal to the performance of coition; but with respect to old men, and Inneens (or persons naturally impotent), the exciting of lust amounts only to causing the heart to beat more quickly than usual; or increasing that palpitation where it already exists.—By the exciting of lust in women or eunuchs is understood simply causing a desire of coition, or increasing that desire where it already exists.—These definitioins are recited at large in the Fatavee Alumgueeree. By seeing the pudendum of a woman is understood; seeing the entrance of the vagina, which is not supposed practicable unless she be in a reclining posture.

IF a man indulge in lewdness with a woman until he produce an emission, some have said that this occasions Hoormat-Moosahirat, or prohibition from affinity, [with respect to the kindred of that woman;] but it is certain that this does not occasion prohibition, because the man, by producing an ex-vulval emission, manifests that coition was not his intention; wherefore it does not

*Arab. Zinna, meaning either fornication or adultery—(Vide Sales's Koran)

*Such as ablution, and so forth.

stand as such. And, in like manner, if a man enter a woman in ano, some have said that this occasions prohibition from affinity as such an act amounts to touching in lust; but it is certain that this does not occasion prohibition, because the carnal conjunction of the sexes does not stand as procreation on any other principle than as it may be the occasion of offspring, which it cannot possibly be from the performance of the act as above described.

A man cannot marry the sister of his repudiated wife during her Edit.—If a man repudiate his wife, either by a complete or a reversible divorce, it is not lawful for him to marry her sister until the expiration of her Edit,*—Shafei maintains that is lawful, because by either of those forms of divorce the former marriage was completely dissolved, insomuch, that if a man were to have carnal knowledge of his repudiated wife during her Edit, knowing the illegality of the same; he would be liable to the punishment for whoredom.—To this our doctors reply, that whatever the nature of the divorce may have been, whether reversible or complete, the marriage with the first sister does still, in fact, continue during her Edit, in virtue of the continuance of several of its effects, such as maintenance, and custody, any inability to marry another man; neither does it appear, in the book of divorce, that and punishment for whoredom is specified in the case of the husband having carnal connexion with his repudiated wife within the term of her Edit; although, according to the book of punishments, he would incur it, because by the act of divorce, the husband's right of cohabitation is dissolved and consequently any subsequent cohabitation with her would bear the construction of whoredom; but yet his other rights are not dissolved (as was above observed), wherefore, if he were to marry the second sister before the expiration of the former's Edit, it would amount to a marriage with two sisters at one time, which is forbidden.

Marriage with slaves.—A MASTER may not marry his female salve, nor a mistress her bondsman, because marriage was instituted with a view that the fruit might belong equally to the father and the mother, and mastership and servitude are contradictory to each other, wherefore it is not admissible that offspring should thus be divided between the master and the slave.

And with Kitabees.—MARRIAGE with a Kitabee woman is legal, according to the word of GOD, "WOMEN ARE LAWFUL TO YOU, SUCH AS ARE Mahsanas OF THE SCRIPTURAL SECTS:", (the term Mahsana does not, in this passage, imply a Muslamite, but merely a woman of chaste reputation.*)—Free Kitabee women, and those who are slaves, are equal in point of matrimonial legality, as shall be demonstrated hereafter.

And with Majoosees.—IT is unlawful to marry a Majoosee woman, GOD having said "YE MAY HOLD CORRESPONDECE WITH Kitabees, BUT YE MUST NOT MARRY THEIR DAUGHTERS, NOR PARTAKE OF THEIR SACRIFICES."

And with Pagans.—IT is unlawful to marry a Pagan woman, according to the words of the KORAN, "MARRY NOT A WOMAN OF the Polytheists UNTIL SHE EMBRACE THE FAITH."

And with Sabeans.—A MUSSULMAN may marry a woman of the Sabeans, she believing the scriptures, and professing faith in the prophets; but if she worship the stars, and believe not in any of the divine scriptural revelations, it is unlawful to marry her —such being inolators.—The diversity of opinion which is recorded between Haneefa and the two disciples, originates in their different ideas with respect to the Sabeans; each arguing according to his own premises, for Haneefa accounts the Sabeans to be Kitabees; whereas the two disciples consider them as worshippers of the stars.

Marriage during pilgrimage.—IT is lawful either for a man or a woman to marry during the Ihram† of pilgrimage.—Shafei alleges that it is unlawful, And the same difference of opinion obtains in the case of a Mohrim‡ contracting in marriage a woman to whom he is guardian.—Shafei supports his opinion upon a precept of the Prophet, "MOHRIMS marry not, nor cause to marry." —In opposition to this, however our doctors produce the instance of the Prophet himself, who married Meyemoona whilst he was a Mohrim; and with respect to the traditionary precept cited by Shafei, as above, it is to be regarded as solely applying to the act of carnal conjunction, that is to say, the word Nikkah§ in that sentence is to be construed into Wuttee,||—as if he had said, "Let not MOHRIMS hold carnal connexion, nor MOHRIMAS admit men to such connexion"—This indeed is rather a weak comment, since the word Nikkah has never been construed into the admitting of man to the commission of the carnal act: but the better principle upon which to answer it is that from the grammatical construction of the sentence, the

*The time of probation which a divorced woman is to wait before she can engage in a second marriage, in order to determine whether or not she be pregnant by the former. See Book IV. Chap II.

*This comment upon the text is meant as an exception to the general definition of the term Mahsana, as explained in the laws concerning slander, Book VII. Chap. V.

†The period of the pilgrims remaining at Mecca.

‡A pilgrim, whilst he remains at Mecca.

§Meaning conjunction in its primitive sense, and marriage in its occasional sense.

||Literally conjunction, but generally applied to the carnal act.

words of the Prophet may be rendered into merely a negative remark rather than a positive prehibition,

Mossolmans may marry female slaves.—It is lawful for a Mussulman, who is free, to marry a female slave, whether she be a Muslima, or Kitabeea, although he be in circumstance to marry a free woman—that is to say, able to pay a dower, and afford an adequate maintenance to such a woman.—Shafei says that a man cannot lawfully marry a Kitabee slave, he holding that it is not lawful for a freeman to marry any slave except of necessity, because by such an act he incurs the consequence of subjecting a portion of his body to bondage; that is to say, his seed (which is a portion of his body) by entering the womb of a slave, is born in bondage; necessity, therefore, he holds can alone legalize such a marriage, and consequently, that ability to pay the dower and maintenance of a free woman prohibits a freeman from marrying a slave; but from this rule he excepts Muslima slaves.—With our daughters, on the other hand, marriage with female slaves of every description is legal, because the text of the Koran, on which the legality of marriage is founded, extends to all descriptions of women, to slaves as well as to those who are free:—and with respect to what Shafei objects, that "by such an act a man incurs the consequence of subjecting a portion of his body to bondage," it may be replied that by marrying a slave, a man is only withheld from producing free children; but it is not thence to be concluded that he, de facto, subjects a portion of his body to slavery, free nor otherwise; and as a man is at liberty to abstain from producing the child itself (either by not marrying, or by marrying a woman who is barren), it follows that he is certainly at liberty to abstain from producing it in a state of freedom.

A man already wedded to a free woman cannot marry a slave.—It is unlawful for a man already married to a free woman to marry a slave, the Prophet having issued a precept to this effect, "Do not marry a slave upon [along with] a free woman."—Shafei says that the marriage of a slave upon a free woman is lawful to a man who is a slave; and Malik likewise maintains that it is lawful, provided it be with the free woman's consent.—The above precept, however, is an answer to both, as it is general and unconditional:—moreover, the legality of marriage is a blessing to males and females equally, but the enjoyment of it is by bondage restricted to one half, insomuch that slaves can have only two wives, whereas freeman may legaly have four (as will be explained hereafter), and slavery operating thus restrictively upon males does so equally upon females;—upon the former it operates by a restriction in point of member, as above; but since, with respect to females, this is impossible, it has its effect by a restriction in point of circumstances; for instance, by restricting the legality of the marriage of female slaves to certain particular circumstances, as in the present case, where it is admitted only under the circumstance of the man not having any free wives.

But a man wedded to a slave may marry a free woman.—A man may lawfully marry a free woman upon a slave, the Prophet having so declared:—moreover, a woman who is free is lawful under all circumstances, the principle of restriction before mentioned not operating with respect to such a woman.

If a man marry a slave during the Edit of complete divorce of another wife who is free, it is null, according to Haneefa.—The two disciples allege that it is valid, as under the circumstances now recited it does not amount to marrying a slave upon a free woman; whence it is that if a man were to make a vow that he would not marry another woman upon his present wife, and he were afterwards to divorce his wife, and to marry another woman during her Edit, he would not forsworn. The argument of Haneefa, in this case, is that the marriage with the free wife does still in some shape remain, on account of the continuance of several of its effects; wherefore that with a slave during the term of the free woman's Edit is not admissible, on a principle of caution: contrary to the case of a vow, as recited above, because there the intention of the vower goes only to express that he would not introduce another wife to the prejudce of her right of Kissm; but her right of Kissm* is snnihilated by divorce.

Four wives allowed to freemen.—It is lawful for a foreman to marry four wives, whether free or slaves: but it is not lawful for him to marry more than four, because God has commanded in the Koran, saying "Ye may marry whatsoever women are agreeable to you, two, three, or four," and the numbers being thus expressly mentioned, any beyond what is there specified would be unlawful.—Shafei alleges a man cannot lawfully marry more than one woman of the description of slaves, from his tenet as above recited, that "the maraiage of freemen with slaves is allowable only from necessity:" the text already quoted, is, whoever, in proof against him, since the term Nissa [woman] applies equally to free women and to slaves.

And two to slaves.—It is unlawful for a man who is a slave to marry more than two women: Malik maintains that it is lawful for a slave to marry as many women as a freeman, he holding it as a principle, that a slave, with respect to marriage, is in every particular the same as a free person, insomuch that (according to him) a slave is authorised to marry whithout his proprietors' consent.—The argument of our doctors, in

*Impartiality in cohabitation with his wives. See Chap. VI.

this case, is that slavery operates to the privation of one half of the natural privileges and enjoyments and the legality of four wives in marriage being of this description, it follows that the privilege of a slave extends to the possession of two wives only, in order that the dignity cf freedom may be duly supported.

A man having the full number of wives allowed, cannot marry during the Edit of one of them.—IF a man, having four wives, repudiate one of them, it is unlawful for him to marry any other woman during the term of that wife's Edit, whether the divorce, under which she stands repudiated, be reversible or complete. Shafei's doctrine differs from this. His reasoning, and the reply to it, are the same as in the case of a man marrying a sister of his wife during the term of the latter's Edit.

A man may marry a woman pregnant by whordeom.—A MAN may lawfully marry a woman pregnant by whoredom, but he must not cohabit with her until after her delivery.—This is the doctrine of Haneefa and Mohammed.—Aboo Yoosaf says that a marriage made under such a circumstance is invalid: if, however, the descent of the Fœtus be known and established, the marriage is null, according to all the doctors.—The argument upon which Aboo Yoosaf supports his opinion as above, is, that the illegality of the marriage, in cases where the parentage of the Fœtus is established, originates purely in a principle of tenderness towards the Fœtus, and a Fœtus is an object of this tenderness, although it be begot in adultery since it is innocent of any offence; whence procuring the abortion of it is illegal; marriage, therefore, with a woman pregnant by adultery is invalid, equally with one where the parentage of the Fœtus is aesertained, and for the same reason. Our doctors, upon this point, argue that the woman is lawful in matrimony, on the authority of the sacred writings, the KORAN saying, "ALL WOMEN ARE LAWFUL TO YOU, EXCEPTING THOSE WITHIN THE PROHIBITED DEGREES:" and the prohibition of cohabitation until after delivery, is merely on account of the impropriety of sowing seed in a soil already impregnated by another, a prohibition which occurs in the traditions. With respect to what Aboo Yoosaf alleges, that "the illegality of the marriage in case where the parentage of the Fœtus is established originates purely in a principle of tenderness towards the Fœtus,"—it is altogether unfounded, because the nullity of the marriage in that case originates in a regard for the right, or the Fœtus, but of the father.

But not a captive taken in that state.—IT is unlawful to marry a woman taken in war, being pregnant at the time of her capture, because the parentage of her Fœtus is ascertained.*

*As necessarily proceeding from some one of the enemy.

A man cannot contract his Am-Walid (being pregnant) to another.—IF a man contract his Am-Walid, who is pregnant by him, to another man, it is null, because the Am-Walid is accounted as the Firash of her master, or partner of his bed, insomuch that the parentage of her child is established by the law in him, independent of any forma claim or acknowledgment thereof on his part, wherefore, if the marriage were valid, it would induce the existence of a right to cohabitation in two individuals with one and the same woman, a right which is null, as it would occasion a doubtful parentage.

OBJECTION.—The Am-Walid being declared the Firash of her master, it would appear that his marriage of her to another would not be legal, although she were not pregnant.

REPLY.—The Firash right of a master in his Am-Walid is of but weak consideration; whence it is, that if he were to deny her child's descent from him, it would become bastardized on the instant, without any asseveration. His Firash right in her, therefore, not being of any account, independent of pregnancy, is not prohibitory to her marriage, unless as connected with that circumstance.

But he may so contract his enjoyed female slave.—IF a man have carnal connexion with his female slave, and afterwards contract her in marriage to another man, it is lawful; because an absolute slave is not accounted as a Firash, or partner of her master's bed sinec, if she were to produce a child, the parentage would not be established in him unless he were to claim it.—But yet it is advisable that the master, previous to contracting her to another person, suffer one term of her courses to elapse, so as to guard against the possibility of his seed mixing with that of the other.—It is to be remarked, in this place, that the marriage of the slave, under the circumstance now mentioned, being valid, it is lawful for her husband to have carnal connexion with her immediately, and before her purification from her first succeeding courses, according to Haneefa and Aboo Yoosaf.—Mohammed alleges, however, that it will be laudable in the husband to abstain from carnal connexion with her until one complete term of her courses shall have elapsed, because it is possible that there may remain in her womb seed of her master.—wherefore it is requisite that it be purified of that seed, the same as in a case of the purchase of female slave.—The argument of the two Elders, in this case, is that the institute of the law, legalizing her marriage, is in itself a proof that her womb is unoccupied, as the law does not admit any marriage to be legal but under that supposition; wherefore purification, in the present instance, is not made a rule, either laudadle or injunctive: contrary to a case of purchase, that of a female slave being held lawful although she be pregnant.

IF a man marry a woman, knowing her to

have been guilty of whoredom, he may lawfully have carnal connexion with her immediately, before her purification from her courses, according to the two Elders: but Mohammed deems it laudable that he have no such connexion with her until after her purification.—The reasoning of each upon this point is to the same effect as in the preceding cas·.

An usufructuary marriage is void.—A NIKKAH MATAT, or usufructuary marriage, where a man says to a woman "I will take the use of you for such a time for so much," is void, all the companions having agreed in the illegality of it.—It is related in the Nakl Saheeh, that Ibn Abbas retracted from his first opinion and embraced that of the other companions:—for Ibn Abbas was first of opinion that the usufruct here mentioned is allowable; but Alee informed him that the Prophet had declared it unlawful, upon which he retracted from his opinion of usufruct being allowable:—and Ibn Abbas having thus retracted, all the companions appear to have agreed concerning its illegality.

And so also a temporary marriage.—A NIKKAH MOWOKKET, or temporary marriage, —where a man marries a woman, under an engagement of ten days (for instance) in the presence of two witnesses,—is null. Ziffer asserts that such marriage is valid and binding, the condition expressed of a specified period for its continuance being of no effect; because a marriage is not to be held null on account of a null or illegal condition therein expessed.—The argument of our doctors is that a temporary marriage is of the same nature with a usufructuary marriage; and in all contracts regard is had to the sense rather than to the latter, wherefore a temporary marriage, is null as well as a usufructuary marriage, whether the period specified be short or long; because the principle on which a contract of marriage falls under the description of Matat, or usufructuary is its containing a specification of time; and the same is found in a Nikkah Mowokket, or temporary marriage.

Case of a double marriage by one contract.—IF a man marry two women by one contract, one of whom is lawful to him, and the other prohibited, his marriage with the one who is lawful holds good, but that with the other is void because in that only a cause of nullity is found: contrary to where a man puts together a freeman and a slave, and sells them by one agreement, as such sale is null with respect to both, because sale is rendered null by an invalid condition, and the consent to the contract of sale is required with respect to the free person, in order to the legality of it with respect to the slave; this is therefore an invalid condition, as shall be demonstrated in treating of slaves;—It is to be observed that the whole of the stipulated dower, in the case now recited, goes to her with respect to whom the marriage is lawful, according to Haneefa.—With the two disciples, on the contrary, the dower is divided into the proper dower to each*, and therefore she with respect to whom the marriage is legal receives the amount of her proper dower, and the remainder drops in favour of the husband; and the same is recorded in the Mabsoot.

Case of marriage by a judicial decree.—IF a woman sue a man on a plea of marriage, declaring that such an one had married her, and produce evidence in proof of her affirmation, and the Kazee accordingly declare her to be the wife of such a man, and it should so happan that the man had never been actually married to that woman, yet he may, after this, lawfully reside with her;—and this is a sign of the authority of a judicial decree (or order of the Kazee) in regard to appearance; and if the woman desire carnal connexion, the man may lawfully hold such connexion with her;—and this is a sign of the authority of a judicial decree, in reality.—The authority of the judicial decree extending both to appearance and reality is a tenet of Haneefa; and is also found in a prior opinion of Aboo Yoosaf.—In a more recent opinion of Aboo Yoosaf, and with Mohammad and Shafei, it is not lawful for the man to have carnal connextion with this woman, because the Kazee has erred in his proof, as the witnesses bore false testimony, and an error in the proof destroys the authority of the decree in regard to reality; wherefore it is, in some measure, the same as if the witnesses were slaves or infidels, in which case the decree would have no authority either in appearance or reality; and so it would appear in the present instance likewise; but here the decree has authority in regard to appearance, on account that the witnesses gave a true testimony in appearance; yet it has no authority in reality, as their testimony is false in point of fact; whereas where the witnesses are slaves or infidels, the decree is destitute of authority in appearance also, as the proof remains unestablished even in appearance, since the discovery of their being slaves or infidels is practicable.—The arguement of Haneefa is that the witnesses are, held, with the Kazee, to bear true testimony and this is proof, as it is impossible to ascertain whether their testimony be actually true: contrary to the state of bondage, or the infidelity of witnesses, as those are circumstances easily known and ascertained, wherefore their evidence is not proof in any way.—Now the decree being founded on the proof, and the authority of the decree, in respect to reality, being here possible, by previously taking the marriage for granted, as a matter of necessity, it follows that the decree has authority in respect to reality, in order that the contradiction between the two may be obviated in every shape,—for if she

*That is to say, a dower suitable or proportioned to the rank and circumstance of each respectively.

were not lawful to him in reality, it would occasion a contradiction between the two, instead of obviating a contradiction; contrary to a case of property claimed generally (that is to say, without any mention of the cause of propriety), such as if a man were to claim a female slave generally, and bring false evidence, and the Kazee decree the slave to the plaintiff, and it afterwards appear that the witness bore false testimony, —for in this case the decr e has authority in appearnce, but not in reality, because the cause of propriety in the slave are several, such as sale, purchase, gift, and inheritance, and regard cannot legally be had to any one of these as being prior to the other, since no one of them has precedence of the others, and to regard the whole of them as prior, is impossible; wherefore the decree cannot possess any authority [in reality]. Observe that the previously taking the marriage for granted, as a matter of necessity, is on account that a decree signifies the promulgation of a thing which is established, and not the establishment of a thing which is not established—for, if it were not previously taken for granted, it would follow that a decree signfies the establishment of a thing which is unestablished, wherefore the marriage is necessarily first taken for granted; and this is possible in the case of a claim of marriage, but not in a case of general propriety, for the causes of propriety there are multifarious, and no one of these has priority over the other;—in such a case, therefore, the regarding of any one cause of propriety as prior to the others is impossible.

CHAPTER II.

OF GUARDIANSHIP AND EQUALITY.

An adult female may engage in the contract without her guardian's consent.—A WOMAN who is an adult, and of sound mind, may be married by virtue of her own consent, although the contract may not have been made or acceded to by her guardians; and this, whether she be a virgin or a Siyeeba.—This is the opinion of Haneefa and Aboo Yoosaf, as appears in the Zahir-Rawayet.—It is recorded, from Aboo Yoosaf, that her marriage cannot be contracted except through her guardian. Mohammed holds that the marriage may be contracted, but yet its validity is suspended upon the guardian's consent: on the other hand, Malik and Shafei assert that a woman can by no means contract herself in marriage to a man in any circumstance, whether with or without the consent of her guardians:—neither is she competent to contract her daughter or her slave, nor to act as a matrimonial agent for any one, so as to enter into a contract of marriage on behalf of her constituent; because the end proposed in marriage, is the acquisition of those benefits which it produces such as procreation, and so forth; and if the performance of this contract were in any respect committed to women, its end might be defeated, they being of weak reason, and open to flattery and deceit.—Mohammad argues that this apprehension is done away by the permission of the guardian being made a requisite condition.—The reasoning upon which the Zahir-Rawayet proceeds in this case is that, in marrying the woman has performed an act affecting herself only, and to this she is fully competent, as being sane and adult, and capable of distinguishing good from evil, whence it is that she is by law capacitated to act for herself in all matters of property and likewise to choose a husband; neither does a woman require her gurdian to match her for any other reason than is she may, by that means, avoid the imputation which might be thrown upon her modesty if she were to perform this herself; for all which reasons a woman contracting herself in marriage is valid, independent of her guardian, although it should be unequal match; but yet, in the latter case, the guardian is at liberty to dissolve the marriage.

Unless the match be unequal.—IT is recorded as an opinion of Haneefa and Aboo Yoosaf, that the marriage is illegal if there be an inequality between the parties.—It is also recorded that Mohammed afterwards adopted the sentiments of the two elders upon this point, and agreed with them, that the marriage here treated of is lawful, and that its validity is suspended upon the approbation of the guardian.

An adult virgin cannot be married against her will.—IT is not lawful for a guardian to force into marriage an adult virgin against her consent.—This is contrary to the doctrine of Shafei, who accounts an adult virgin the same as an infant, with respect to marriage, since the former cannot be acquainted with the nature of marriage any more than the latter, as being equally uninformed with respect to the matrimonial state, whence it is that the father of such an one is empowered to make seizin of her dower without her consent.—The argument of our doctors is that the woman, in this case, is free, and a Mokkatiba (that is, subject to all the obligatory observances of the law, such as fasting, prayer, and so forth), wherefore no person is endowed with any absolute authority of guardianship over her; contrary to the case of infants, over whom others are necessarily endowed with this authority, the understanding of such being defective, whereas that of an adult is held complete, in consequence of her having attained to years of discretion; for, if it were otherwise, she would not be subject to the obervances of the law: from all which it follows that this woman is the same as an adult son; and that all her acts with respect to matrimony are good and valid, the same as his with respect to property; neither is her father empowered to make seizin of her dower without her consent expressed of virtually understood, as he is not at liberty to do so where she has forbidden him.

Tokens of consent from a virgin.—Whenever a guardian, being the person empowered to engage in the contract, requires the consent of an adult virgin to a marriage, if she smile or remain silent, this is a compliance; because the Prophet has said, "A virgin must be consulted in every thing which regards herself; if she be silent it singifies assent;" and also because her assent is rather to be supposed as she is ashamed to testify her desire; and laughter is a still more certain token of assent than silence; contrary to weeping, as this manifests abhorrence, since tears are most commonly the effect of grief, and not of joy, which is rarely the occasion of them, and therefore not to be regarded. —Some have said that if her laughter be in the manner of jest or derision it is not a compliance; nor is her weeping a disappoval, if it be not accompanied with noise or lamentation.

But if a marriage be proposed to an adult virgin by any other than her guardians, or by a Walee Bayeed (or guardian of a more distant degree than her father, brother, or uncles), her silence or laughter are not sufficent, until she shall from her lips pronounce an explicit compliance, because here her silence might be construed to arise from shyness towards such a person as being a stranger, and not from her consent to the match; and if it were even to be considered as a token of approbation, yet, under such a circumstance, it must be regarded as doubtful; but this is not the case if the person who proposes the marriage be acting merely as a messenger from her parent, or other immediate guardian; because to such an one the same signs of assent or dissent suffice as were specified in the preceding case.—It is here to be observed that, in requiring the woman's consent as aforsaid, it is requisite that the husband proposed to her be particularly named and described, so as to enable her to form some idea of him, whereby to ascertain her liking or dislike; but it is unnecessary to name or specify the dower; and this is approved, because marriage may be effected independent of any dower, as that is not essential to it.

If a man contract an adult virgin in marriage to another without her knowledge, upon her receiving intelligence of it the same tokens suffice, to singify her compliance or approval, as were specified in the former case; that is to say, if she laugh or remain silent she consents, or if she weep she disapproves, provided the person contracting on her behalf be her guardian, and as such empowered so to contract; but if the contract be entered into by any other than her guardian, her consent is not understood until she shall have expressed the same in terms; and in this, as in the preceding case, the naming and describing of the husband to her is a requisite condition, but not the specification of the dower.—It is to be here observed that, if the person who conveys the intelligence to her be a Fazoolee (that is, one who is neither an agent nor guardian), number or integrity are conditions essential to the effect; that is to say, the information must be conveyed to her by two persons, or at least by one person of known good repute, according to Haneefa: but if the informer be acting merely as a messenger from the guardian, than neither number nor integrity are conditions; according to all the doctors. There are many cases similar to this with respect to the point at persent in question, such as the recall of an ambassador, and the revocation of the privileges of a Mazoon.

Token of consent from a Siyeeba.—If a guardian propose a marriage to a Siyeeba (or woman with whom a man has had carnal connexion), it is necessary that her compliance be particularly expressed by words, such as, "I consent to it," because the prophet has said, "Siyeebas are to be consulted," and also because a Siyeeba, having had connexion with man, haa not the same pretence to silence or shyness as a virgin, and consequently the silent signs before intimated are not sufficient indications of her assent to the proposed alliance.

Cases under which a woman is still considered as a virgin, in respect to the tokens of consent.—If the signs of virginity in a girl should happen to be effaced, either by leaping or any other exertion, or by a wound, or by frequent respetition of the menses, yet she is still to be considered as a virgin that; is to say, her silence is a sufficient sign of her acquiescence in a marriage proposed, because she is still in reality a virgin, the law accounting every woman such who has not had carnal connexion with the other sex, —and consequently subject to the same shyness and reserve, from her not being accustomed to male society.—And if the signs of virginity be effaced even by formication, yet she here also stands as a virgin, according to Haneefa. Aboo Yoosaf, Mohammed, and Shafei are of opinion that the silence of such an one is not a sufficient token of consent to a marriage proposed because she is actually a Siyeeba, since she has actually had connexion with man.—Haneefa in this case argues that people in general still suppose her to be a virgin, and hence consider her speaking as a breach of decorum, and consequently she will refrain from speech; her silence, therefore, must be held sufficiant, lest her delicacy be violated; contrary to a case where a woman has lost her virginity either in an erroneous or an invalid marriage, as such an one would not be held a virgin with respect to the point in question, the law having manifested her carnal connexion, by instituting, in her case, observance which are a consequence of it (such as Edit and Dower), and by establishing the parentage of her child, whereas it recommends as laudable, the concealment of fornication : this, however, is only where the case is not of a very notorious nature ; for if a woman be known to abandon herself to fornication publicly, her silence would not be deemed sufficient.

Case of allegtion and denial.—If a man should say to a woman, "You have heard of your being contracted to me by our friends, and remained silent" ; and she reply, "No, I refused you," or, "I dissented," her declaration is to be credited.—Ziffer says that the declaration of the husband is to be credited, on account that silence is the original state of man, wherefore the person who adheres to that is the defendant ; and the repulsion of the marriage is supervenient, wherefore the person who adheres to that is the plaintiff ; the case is therefore the same as where a person enters into a contract of sale under a condition of option, and pleads a rejection after the time of option has elapsed and the other denies the rejection,—for in that case the declaration of the denier is to be credited, as he adheres to what is original, to wit, silence. Our doctors, on the other hand, say that the husband, in the present case, on account of his plea of silence, pleads the obligation of the contract of marriage and consequently of his being the proprietor of the women's person;* and, that the wife by pleading the rejection, sets aside the claim of her husband, and must therefore be considered as the defendant, in the same manner as when a depositee pleads the restoration of a deposit, and the proprietor of the deposit declares that he had not returned it to him ; because, in such a case, the declaration of the trustee would be credited, since he is in reality the defendant, although in appearance he be the plaintiff, for he frees himself from responsibility, and the original state of man is freedom, and an exemption from responsibility:—it is otherwise with respect to the case of a condition of option in sale, because the obligation of a sale is manifested after the lapse of the time option, and therefore the person who pleads the rejection is plaintiff both in reality and in appearance. But here, if the husband should produce evidence in support of his silence, the marriage becomes established: if, however, he have no evidence, then an oath must not be imposed upon the wife, according to Haneefa.—This is one out of six cases in which an oath is incumbent upon the defendant according to Haneefa, in opposition to the opinion of the two disciples : as will be fully treated of under the head of sales.

Infants may be contracted by their guardians.—The marriage of a boy or girl under-age, by the authority of their paternal kindred, is lawful, whether the girl be a virgin or not, the Prophet having declared, "Marriage is committed to the paternal kindred." Malik alleges that this is a power the exercise of which does not appertain to any of the kindred except the father.—Shafei maintains that it belongs only to her father or grandfather : and he adds that this privilege does not appertain to any guardian whatever with respect to an infant Siyeeba, although he be her father or her grantfather.—Malik argues that power over freemen is estalished from necessity ; but in the present instance no such necessity exists, as infants are not subject to any canal appetite : yet it is vested in a father, on the authority of sacred writings contrary to what analogy would suggest :—but he also says that a grandfather, not being the same as a father, is not to be included with him. Our doctors, on the other hand, allege that the guardianship vested in a father is in no respect contrary, but is rather agreeable to analogy ; because marriage is a point which involves in it many considerations, both civil and religious ; and it is not perfect unless the parties be equal in degree according to the customary acceptation ; and this equality is not always to be found; wherefore authority is vested in the father to contract his children during their minority, lest an opportuniry of marrying them equally might be lost.—Shafei argues, that entrusting the power of contracting marriage to any others than the father or grandfather would be oppressive upon the child, since it is to be supposed that no others are equally interested in its welfare or happiness ; on which principle it is that kindred of a more distant degree are not empowered to act with respect to the property of infants, a matter of infinitely less importance than their persons, and consequently the acts of such, with respect to the latter, are unlawful a fortori—Our doctors argue, that affinity is a cause of affection in other relations the same as in the parents, and in whatever degree that may be defective, a provision is made against any evil consequence, by vesting in the child an option of acquiescence in the match after puberty, which acquiescence is necessary to constitute its validity ; contrary to the case of acts with respect to propety, because these are capable of repetition, since they are done with a view to the acquisition of gain, which cannot be obtained but by such repetition ; and such being the case, if any loss should happen in the property, it is irretrievable ; wherefore authority to act in respect to property is useless, unless it be absolute : and absolute authority cannot be established where there is any defect. The argument of Shafei, in support of his second proposition (to wit "that this privilege does not appertain to any guardian whatever with respect to an infant Siyeeba, although he be her father or grandfather"), is, that her becoming a Siyeeba is to be considered as endowing her with sufficient understanding and capacity to act and judge for herself, on account of her being thus accustomed to male society, wherefore the law operates upon this consideration

*Arab : Booza, i.e Genitale Mulieris. The phrase here adopted is to be thus understood in marriage and divorce, throughout.

without any regard to the absolute fact of her being endowed with such a portion of understanding or not, as that is a matter which does not readily admit of ascertainment. To this our doctor reply, that the infant requires a guardian whose tenderness and affection must be necessarily admitted; neither can her acquaintance with the other sex be considered as endowing her with any additional portion of understanding in regard to mankind, without concupiscence, which, in a child, does not exist.—It may also be farther observed that the precept of the Prophet already quoted is general and indiscriminate, and therefore includes all relations equally; which makes it a sufficient answer to Malik and Shafei.

RELATIONS stand in the same order in point of authority to contract minors in marriage as they do in point of inheritance; but this authority, in the more distant relatives, is superseded by the existence of those of a nearer degree.

Case in which the marriage of infants continues binding after puberty.—IF the marriage of infants be contracted by the father or grandfathers, no option after puberty remains to them; because the determination of parents in this matter cannot be supected to originate in sinister motives as their affection for their offspring is undoubted; wherefore the marriage is binding upon the parties, the same as if they had themselves entered into it after maturity.

Case which admits an option of acquiescence after puberty.—BUT if the contract should have been executed by the authority of others than their parents, each is respectively at liberty, after they become of age, to choose whether the marriage shall be confirmed or annulled.—This is according to Haneefa and Mohammad. Aboo Yoosaf maintains that, in this case also, no option remains to them, since he considers all guardians to be the same as parents. To this Haneefa and Mohammed reply, that the more distant the guardians stand in their affinity to the parties, the less warm are their affections supposed to be; whence it is to be apprehended that, in contracting the marriage, self interest, or some other sinister motive, might operate in their minds to the disadvantage of the infant under their guardianship, an evil which is provided against by leaving an option to the infant after maturity.—It is to be observed, however, that this case, applying generally to all except the father and grandfather, includes the mother of the infant, and also the Kazee because the former, as being a woman, is deficient in judgment; and the latter, as a stranger, in affection; and consequently a right of option must be reserved to the infant after maturity.—It is also to be remarked that, in dissolving the marriage, decree of the Kazee is a necessary condition in all cases of option exerted after maturity; contrary to the rule in the exertion of a similar right of option after manumission; that is to say, if a master marry his female slave to any person, and afterwards emancipate her, she will have a right of option upon her emancipation; if she please the marriage continues, but if she disapprove it is dissolved; and the decree of the Kazee is not essential to such dissolution: but it is otherwise in the case of option after maturity; because that option is reserved with a view to guard against injury to the other rights of the parties, which might occur in a variety of instances, and which if admitted (as, if the marriage were absolute, they must be), would be calculated to introduce many evils into the married state, since the guardian might, for instance, in executing the contract, agree to an inadequate dower, or to an unequal match; and as the dissolution of the marright thus tends to affect other rights, a decree of the Kazee is essential therein; but, in the case of the female slave, the right of option after emanciption is intended as a security against an evident injury to herself as the husband's power over her is extended, and his authority, as well as her obligations, in many respects enlarged, by her emancipation from slavery; whence it is that this right of option is restricted to female slaves only, and does not extend to males, to whom the above principle would not apply; and such being the case, the dissolution of her marriage is to be regarded merely as the removal of a hardship from herself, in which the decree of the Kazee is no way necessary, since all persons are entitled to relieve themselves from evil.

Token of acquiescence after puberty.—IF the female, thus contracted during infancy, be of age when the marriage is first mentioned to her, and she upon that occasion remain silent, her silence (according to Haneefa and Mohammed), is to be construed into consent; but if she continue ignorant of the contract, her right of option is still reserved to her, until such time as she is informed of it, and remain silent as above.—Mohammed, in this case, makes it a condition that the girl be duly informed of the marriage, because she cannot exert her right of option without a knowledge of the circumstance, as the guardian may effect the marriage altogether unknown to her, and it may consequently happen that she never hears of it, and of course she would remain excused (as to her silence) on the ground of ignorance; but he does not make a knowledge of her right of option a condition, because that is an institute of the law, and ignorance is no plea with respect to an institute of the law, with which it is supposed that every person ought to be acquainted; the case is otherwise with a female slave, who being employed in the service of her master has no opportunity to obtain any knowledge of the law, wherefore ignorance of this point is a good plea in favour of the continuance of her right of option.

Circumstances which annual the right of option.—THE right of option in a virgin, after maturity, is done away by her silence; but the right of option of a man is not done away by the same circumstance, nor until he express his approbation by word or by deed, such as presenting her dower, cohabiting with her, and so forth: and in like manner the right of option of the female after maturity (in a case where the husband has enjoyed her before she attained to that state), is not annulled until she express her consent or disapprobation in terms (as if she were to say "I approve," or "I disapprove)", or until her consent be virtually shown by her conduct, in admitting the husband to carnal connexion, and so forth.

Degree of the continuance of a right of option after maturity.—THE option of maturity of a virgin is not protracted to the end of the assembly;* but that of a Siyeeba, or a youth, is not annulled even by the rising from the assembly, because the option of maturity is established by dissent, on account of the apprehension of the ends of marriage being defeated; and whatever is established by dissent is annulled by assent, on account of its advantage being obtained; now the silence of a virgin is assent. but not that of a Siyeeba or a youth: wherefore the option of the former is annulled, but not that of the two latter:—moreover, a Siyeeba's option of maturity† has not been established by the act of her husband, as is evident; and a circumstance which is not established by the act of the husband is not restricted to that assembly, since that only which is delegated‡ is so restricted, as shall be hereafter demonstrated; § contrary to the option of manumission, as that is not annulled by silence, but is protracted to the end of the assembly, and annulled by the rising from the assembly, because the option of manumission is established by the act of the master, namely, emancipation: and hence regard is had to the Majlis in this case, as well as in that of a woman endowed by her husband with an option of divorce.

Separation in consequence of option is not divorce.—A SEPARATION between a husband and wife in consequence of option after maturity is not divorce, from whatever side it proceed, because it may with propriety proceed from the wife, whereas divorce cannot. And so also, separation in consequence of option after manumission is not divorce, for the same reason.

Rule inheritance in the marriage of infants.—IF a girl who has been contracted in marriage by her guardian, as already stated, should die before she attain maturity, her husband inherits of her: and, in like manner, if a youth so contracted should die before he attains maturity, his wife inherits of him;—and so also, if either should happen to die after maturity, without a separation having taken place;—because the marriage contract was regular and valid as origine, and would remain so, until dissolved to the dissent of one or both of the parties in the event of their arriving at maturity; but this being precluded by the demise of one of them, the marriage continues good for ever; and consequently all the mutual privileges established in the parties by the marriage are irreversibly confirmed by the decease of either of them:—contrary to the case of a marriage contracted by an unauthorized person, where, if either of the parties were to die before assent being duly expressed, the other would not inherit; because, in this case, the existence of the marriage is suspended upon the consent of the parties, and is consequently rendered null by the demise of either previous to the declaration of their will in it; whereas, in the other case, the decease of either party, previous to maturity or separation, as aforesaid, does not annul, but rather confirms their marriage.

Persons incapable of acting as guardians in marriage.—AUTHORITY to contract others in marriage is not vested in a slave, an infant, or a lunatic, because such persons, being considered in law as incapable of acting for themselves, are incompetent to exercise any authority over others, a fortiori; moreover, this authority is established in guardians and others out of tenderness to persons who, from their situation, require attention and care (such as infants and lunatics; but this would not be manifested by committing the execution of marriage, on their behalf, to persons of the above descriptions.

AN infidel cannot be vested with this authority with respect to a Mussulman, male or female because the word of GOD says "HE DOTH NOT ADMIT INFIDELS TO ANY CLAIM UPON BELIEVERS;" and, if this authority were vested in in infidels, it would be admitting them to such a claim. and hence also it is, that the evidence of infidels regarding Mussulmans is not admitted; and, upon the same principle, that Mussulmans and infidels cannot inherit of each other.

AN infidel is vested with this authority with respect to his children who are infidels, the word of GOD saying, "INFIDELS MAY EXERCISE AUTHORITY OVER INFIDELS;" whence it is that the evidence of infidels regarding infidels is admitted, and that inheritance obtains among them.

Maternal relations may act in defect of the paternal.—IN defect of paternal relations, authority to contract marriage appertains to the maternal (if they be of the same family or tribe), such as the mother, or maternal uncle or aunt, and all others within the prohibited degrees, according to Haneefa,

*Arab, Majlis, meaning the place or company in which she may happen to be at the time of her attaining maturity. It is treated of at large elsewhere. Vide Index.

†By option of maturity, and option of manumission, is meant, option of acquiescence after maturity, or after manumission.

‡Namely, a power of divorce.

§See Book of Divorce, Chap. III.

upon a principle of benevolence.—Mohammed alleges that this authority is not vested in any except the paternal kindred; and there is also an opinion of Haneefa on record to this effect.—Of Aboo Yoosaf two opinions have been mentioned; according to that most generally received, he coincides with Mohammed; and their arguments on this subject are twofold: First, the Prophet has declared "Marriage is committed to the paternal kindred" (as was before quoted); Secondly, the only reason for instituting this authority is that families may be preserved from improper or unequal connexion; and this guard over the honour of a family is committed to the paternal relatives, whose peculiar province it is to take care that their stock be not exposed to any mean or debasing admixture, so as to subject them to shame.—The argument of Haneefa is, that authority to contract marriage is instituted out of a regard to the interest of the child, which is fully manifested by committing it to persons whose relation to the infant is so near as to render them interested in its welfare.

Or the Mawla of an infant female slave.—If the Mawla* of an infant female slave, having emancipated her, should contract her in marriage, it is lawful, although she have relations within the prohibited degrees upon the spot, provided there be not among them any relations of the paternal description, because the Mawla stands as a paternal relation with respect to her.

Or the Magistrate in defect of a natural guardian.—Where persons are destitute of any natural guardian, the authority of contracting them in marriage is vested in the Imam or the Kazee; because the Prophet has, in his precepts, declared, "Persons being destitute of guardians have a guardian in the Sultan."

Or the nearest guardian present in the absence of others.—If the parents, or other first natural guardians of an infant, should be removed to such a distance as is termed Gheebat-Moonkatat, it is in that case lawful for the guardian next in degree to contract the infant in marriage.—Ziffer and Shafei allege that it is not lawful, because this authority is vested in the first guardian as a right, in order that the family may be preserved from the shame occasioned by the infant forming a degrading connextion; and this being a positive right, cannot be annulled by the absence of the party, as the law does not admit absence to be destructive of a right; and hence it is that if the absent guardian were to contract the infant in marriage on the spot where he may at that period happen to be, it is lawful; moreover, a relation of a more distant degree is not vested with authority in the existence of a nearer relative, since the more distant is precluded by the nearer.—The argument of our doctors is that authority to contract minors in marriage is instituted out of regard to their interest, as was already noticed; whence it is that this authority is not admitted over any, excepting such as are incapable of paying the necessary attention to their own interest; and the regard is not manifested in committing the business of marriage to the nearer guardian, who is absent, as from the exertion of his prudence or good sense no advantage can, in that situation, be easily derived; the authority, therefore, in this case, devolves to the guardian next in degree who is present:—moreover, as, in case the first guardian were to die, or to income, besane the authority, would devolve to the next in degree, so does it likewise in the present case. And with respect to what Ziffer and Shafei have advanced, that "If the absent guardian were to contract the infant in marriage on the spot where he may at that period happen to be, it is lawful,"—the assertion is not admitted: but even granting this, it is still to be observed, that although the more distant guardian be further removed from the infant in point of consanguinity, yet, being upon the spot, he is enabled to transact for the latter, with the advantage of immediate and local knowledge; and vice versa of the other guardians. Thus they stand upon an equal footing with respect to authority; and whoever of them may enter into a contract of marriage on behalf of the infant, the same, holds good, and is not liable to be set aside.—By the absence termed Gheebat-Moonkatat is to be understood the guardian being removed to a city out of the track of the caravans, or which is not visited by the caravan more than once in every year: some, however, have defined it to signify any distance amounting to three days' journey.

The guardianship over a lunatic woman rests with her son.—If a lunate woman have two guardians, one her son and the other her father, the authority of disposing of her in marriage rests with the former and not with the latter, according to Haneefa and Aboo Yoosaf. Mohammed says that the father is her guardian in this respect, as feeling a more lively interest in her than the son.—The argument of the two Elders is that a son is prior to all others of the parental kindred; and the right of guardianship goes by this right of priority, in preference to affection thus any paternal kinsman (such as the son of the father's brother, for instance), is in this respect prior to the maternal grandfather, although the natural affection of the latter be admitted to be the strongest.

Section.—Of Kafat, or Equality.

Definition of Kafat.—Kafat, in its literal sense, means equality.—In the language of the law it signifies the equality of a man with a woman, in the several particulars which shall be immediately specified

*Meaning the emancipator. For a full definition of this term, see the Emancipation of Slaves.

Equality necessary in marriage.—In marriage regard is had to equality, because the Prophet has commanded, saying, "Take ye care that none contract women in marriage but their proper guardians, and that they be not so contracted by with their equals; and also, because the desirable ends of marriage, such as cohabitation, society, and friendship, cannot be completely enjoyed except by persons who are each other's equals (according to the customary estimation of equality), as a woman of high rank and family would abhor society and cohabitation with a mean man; it is requisite, therefore, that regard be had to equality with respect to the husband; that is to say, that the husband be the equal of his wife; but it is not necessary that the wife be the equal of the husband, since men are not degraded by cohabitation with women who are their inferiors.—It is proper to observe, in this place, that one reason for attending to equality in marriage is, that regard is had to that circumstances in confirming a marriage and establishing its validity; for if a woman should match herself to a man who is her inferior, her guardians have a right to separate them, so as to remove the dishonour they might otherwise sustain by it.

In point of tribe or family.—EQUALITY is regarded with respect to lineage, this being a source of distinction among mankind; thus it is said, "a Kooraish is the equal of a Kooraish throughout all their tribes;" that is to say, there is no pre-eminence among them, between Hashmees and Niflees, Teyemees or Adwees; and in like manner they say, "an Arab is the equal of an Arab."—This sentiment originates in a precept of the Prophet to this effect; and hence it is evident that there is no pre-eminence considered among the Kooraish tribes: and with respect to what Imam Mohammed has advanced, that "pre-eminence is not regarded among the KOORAISH tribes or families, excepting where the same is notorious, such as the house of the KHALIFS," his intention in this exception was merely to show that regard should be had to pre-eminence in that particular house, out of respect to the Khilafet, and in order to suppress rebellion or disaffection; and not to say that an original equality does not exist throughout. The Kooraishees are the descendants of Nazir, son of Kanaan, as is universally known.—Ibn-Hijr has said that the Kooraishees are descended of Kihr the son of Malik. The term Kooraish is a diminutive of Kursh, which means a body of people, or congregation; and this appellation was originally applied to them, because they were accustomed to trade through different cities and countries, and after being thus scattered, used to reassemble at Mecca. The Arabs are those who derive their descent from a stock anterior to Nazir, or (according to Ibn Hijr) anterior to Kihr.

THE Binno Bahala tribe are not the equals of Arabs of any other description whatsoever, they being notorious throughout Arabia for every species of vice; and none of those before mentioned esteem them as upon an equality with themselves.

In point of religion.—MAWALEES, this is to say, Ajims, who are neither Kooraishees nor Arabs, are the equals of each other throughout, regard not being had among them to lineage, but to Islam.—Thus an Ajim whose family have been Mussulmans for two or more generations is the equal of one descended of Mussulman ancestors;—but one who has himself embraced the faith, or he and his father only, is not the equal of an Ajim whose father and grandfather were Mussulmans; because a family is not established under any particular denomination (such as Mussulman, for instance), by a retrospect short of the grandfather.—This is the doctrine of Haneefa and Muhammed. Aboo Yoosaf says that an Ajim whose father is a Mussulman is the equal of a woman whose father and grandfather are Mussulmans.

AN Ajim who is the first of his family professing the faith is not the equal of a woman whose father is a Mussulman.

In point of freedom.—EQUALITY in point of freedom is the same as in point of Islam, in all the circumstances above recited, because bondage is an effect of infidelity, and the properties of meanness and turpitude are therein found.

In point of character.—REGARD is to be had to equality in piety and virtue, according to Haneefa and Aboo Yoosaf; and this is approved because virtue is one of the first principles of superiority and a woman derives a degree of scandal and shame from the profligacy of her husband, beyond what she sustains even from that of her kindred.—Mohammad alleges that positive equality in point of virtue is not to be regarded, as that is connected with religion, to which rules regarding mere worldly matters do not apply, excepting where the party, by any base or degarding misconduct such as a man exposing himself naked and intoxicated in the public street, and so forth), may have incurred derision and contempt.

In point of fortune—EQUALITY is to be regarded with respect to property, by which is understood a man being possessed of a sufficiency to discharge the dower and provide maintenance; because if he is unable to do both, or either of these, he is not the equal of any woman; as the dower is a consideration for the carnal use of the woman, the payment of which is necessary of course; and upon the provision of a support to the wife depends the permanency of the matrimonial connextion; and this is therefore indispensable a fortiori—This, according to some, is found in the ability to support a wife for one month only; but others say for a year. By a man possessing sufficient to enable him to discharge the dower, is understood his ability to pay down that proportion of it which it is customary to give immediately upon the marriage, and which is termed

Moajil, or prompt; the remainder, termed the Mowjil, or deferred, it is not usual to pay until a future season; and hence it is that the ability to pay that part of the dower is not made a condition.—Aboo Yoosaf teaches that regard is to be had only to the man's ability to support his wife, and not to the discharge of the dower, because the latter is of a nature to admit of delay in the payment, but not the former; and a man is supposed to be sufficiently enabled to pay the dower where his father is in good circumstances. According to the doctrine of Haneefa and Mohammed, however, the fortune of the man is to be considered in general (without regard to any particular ability), insomuch that a man who may even be qualified both to pay the dower and to provide subsistence, yet may not be held the equal of a woman possessed of a large property; since men consider wealth as conferring superiority, and poverty as inducing contempt. Aboo Yoosaf, on the other hand, maintains that wealth is not to be regarded in this respect, since it is not a thing of a stable or permanent nature, as property may be acquired in the morning and lost before night

And in point of profession.—Equality is to be regarded in trade or profession, according to Aboo Yoosaf and Mohammed.—There are two opinions recorded of Haneefa upon this point; and there is also an opinion related of Aboo Yoosaf; that the profession is not to be regarded, unless where it is of such a degrading nature as to oppose an insurmountable objection; such, for instance, as barbers, weavers, tanners, or other workers in leather, and scavengers, who are not the equals of merchants, perfumers, druggists, or bankers.—The principle upon which regard is to be had to trade or professon is, that men assume to themselves a certain consequence from the respectability of their callings, whereas a degree of contempt is annexted to them on account of the meanness thereof.—But a reason, on the other hand, why trade or profession should not be regaded is, that these are not absolute upon a man, since he is at liberty to leave a mean profession for one of a more honourable nature.

Case of a woman contracting herself on an inadequate dower.—If a woman contract herself in marriage, consenting to receive a dower of much smaller value than her proper dower,* the guardians have a right to oppose it, until her husband shall agree either to give her a complete proper dower, or to separate from him.—This is according to Haneefa.—The two disciples maintain that the guardians are possessed of any such authority; and their argument is, that whatever the dower may be above ten Dirms is the right of the woman, and no person is to be opposed in relinquishing that which is her own as where a woman, for instance, chooses to relinquish a part of the dower, after the amount of it has been specifically stipulated.—To this Haneefa replies, that the guardians assume a certain degree of respect and consideration from the magnitude of shame to and its smallness is an occasion of shame to them; wherefore regard is had to that, as well as to equality: contrary to the case of a woman relinquishing her claim to any part of her dower after it has been specifically stipultated, because no disgrace falls upon the guardians from such dereliction.

Case of a father contracting his infant child on a disproportionate dower.—If a father should contract in marriage his infant daughter, agreeing to a very inadequate dower; or, if he should contract his infant son, engaging for an extravagant dower, yet this is legal and valid with respect to them.—This, however, is not lawful to any excepting a father or grandfather, according to all the doctors—The two disciples have said that diminution or excess in the dower is illegal only where it is very apparent; that is to say, a contract of marriage, involving any very disproportionate excess or deficiency of dower, is not held by them to be legal; because the authority of a father or grandfather to contract infants in marriage is founded upon the supposition of their regard for the interest of those infants, and therefore where this regard does not appear, the contract is null; and in agreeing for a deficient dower on behalf of a female infant; or for an excessive one on behalf of a male, no regard to their interest whatever is manifested.—Similar to this is a case of purchase or sale; that is to say, if a guardian were, on behalf of an infant, to sell a thing for less than its value, or to buy a thing for more than it is worth, at an excessive disproportion, such sale or purchase would be invalid; and so also in marriage:—and hence it is that no person is empowered, with respect to deficient or excessive dowers, excepting a father or grandfather — To this Haneefa replies, that the law here rests solely upon whatever affords an argument of tenderness for the infant. and that is found in nearness of affinity; and in marriage there are many considerations of more weight and moment than the dower, whereas, in transactions which concern property, that only is a consideration; and where that which is the end appears to be defeated, their authority is done away.—But with respect to other than the father and grandfather, no regard is had to affinity as an argument of tenderness in the persent case, since that exists in them in smaller degree.

A father may contract his infant child to a slave.—If a man contract his infant daughter to a slave, or his infant son to a female slave, it is lawful.—The compiler of the Hedaya observes that this is according to Haneefa, who argues that the father's neglect of equality in this instance must be supposed to arise from some other considerations of greater weight, wherefore the said contract of marriage is lawful; but if it should appear that the parent has adpoted such a

* The nature of the proper dower is fully explained in the next chapter.

match without any view to a particular advantage, the contract is in that case null: and the two Elders coincide with Haneefa in this opinion.—According to the two disciples the contract is illegal, because it involves a twofold disadvantage with respect to the infant;—a want of equality in the first instance; and secondly, a want of residence, as a slave cannot be or remain anywhere but with the owner's consent.

Section.—Of a Power of Agency to contract Marriage.

Agents in marriage, and their powers.—Agents in matrimony are persons employed and authorized by the parties concerned to enter into contracts of marriage on their behalf; and the power so delegated is termed Wikalit-ba-Nikkah.

It is lawful for a nephew to contract the daughter of his uncle in marriage with himself.— Ziffer alleges that this is unlawful.

If a woman give authority to a man to contract her in marriage with himself, and he accordingly execute the contract in the presence of two witnesses it is lawful. Ziffer and Shafei affirm that this is illegal, because no person is competent to transfer and make himself the proprietor of that which is transferred; as in a case of sale, for instance, where, if the proprietor constitute a person his agent of sale with respect to any particular property, and the agent sell the same to himself, both the agency and the sale are void, no man being competent to act as the transferrer of property, and to become himself the master of that property.— Shafei, however, alleges that a guardian may lawfully contract his word to himself on the plea of necessity, since, if he were not allowed this privilege, she might never be married; but a mere agent has no such plea because in this case her guardian will contract her.*—Our doctors, on the other hand, argue that an agent in matrimony is merely a negotiator, and the obligations of the contract do not, in any respect, affect the contractor of a marriage; neither would any objections which may arise apply to the simple negotiation, but to the rights and obligations which it involves: contrary to the case of sale, as cited by Ziffer and Shafei, because there the agent appears to be acting not merely as a negotiator, but also as a principal, in the contract of sale, and is consequently affected by its obligations. It may be remarked in this place, that as the contractor of a marriage is merely a negotiator, so where a person becomes empowered to contract on both sides, his single declaration "I have contracted," comprehends both the declaration and the acceptance, and consequently there is in this instance no occasion for two separate sentences.†

Cases of a contract executed by on unanthorized person.— If a man should contract in marriage the slave of another without the owner's consent, and validity of the deed is suspended upon the will of the Owner; if he approve, it is lawful; if he disapprove, it is null.

In the same manner, if a man contract a woman in marriage without her knowledge in the presence of two witnesses, or if a woman contract a man in marriage without his consent, the validity is suspended upon the same cirumstance.—This is an opinion of our doctors; because they hold that in a case of a contract entered into by a Fazoolee or unauthorized person, and to which there exists any person who has a right assent, the same stands as a complete contract, the validity of which is suspended upon that person's approbation.— Shafei maintains that all acts whatever of a Fazoolee are null; because the use of a contract is for the purpose of establishing its effect, like that of sale, for instance, which is used for the purpose of establishing a right of property, and that of marriage for the purpose of establishing a right of enjoyment; and Fazoolee is incapable of establishing the effect, on account of his want of authority; wherefore the act of the Fazoolee is nugatory.—The argument of our doctors is, that the foundation of the contract, namely, declaration and acceptance, has proceeded from a competent person (that is, from one who is sane and adult), and has reference to its proper subject; neither can any injury be sustained if the contract be executed, inasmuch as there exists; in respect to it, a person who has a right of assent, and who, if he think proper, will signify such assent, and give the contract force, or, if otherwise, will reject it: and in reply to what is urged by Shafei, we observe that the effect of a contract is sometimes deferred to a period subsequent to the time or date of the contract; as in a contract of sale under a condition of option, where possession is deferred until such time as the condition of option drops.

If an unauthorized person say to two persons, "Be ye witness that I have married such a woman who is absent;" and afterwards the woman should hear of it, and consent, yet the marriage is void: but if, on the unauthorized person speaking as above, a third person were to say, "I have married that woman to that man," and the woman on hearing it should consent, the marriage is lawful. And, in like manner, if a woman should say "Be ye witness that I have contracted myself to such a man who is absent," and the man should afterwards hear of it and consent, the marriage would, notwithstanding, be void; but if, on the woman thus speaking, a bystander were to say, "Be ye witness that I give consent on behalf of such a person;" and the man, on hearing of it, should give his consent, the marriage is valid. This is the doctrine of Haneefa. Aboo Yoosaf alleges that if a woman were to say, "I

* This proceeds upon a supposition that the guardian is not within the prohibited degrees, and that no other proper person offers.

† See the beginning of this Book.

have contracted myself to such a man" (he being absent), and the man, on afterwards receiving intelligence of this, were to declare his assent, the marriage is valid. In short, according to Haneefa and Mohammed, one person is not competent to act as a Fazoolee in a contract of marriage, either on behalf of both parties, or as a Fazoolee on one side, and a principal on the other; whereas Aboo Yoosaf holds a contrary opinion. But, if two unauthorized persons enter into a contract of marriage on behalf of both parties,—that is to say, one on the part of the man, and the other on that of the woman,—or, if the persons enter into such a contract, one as a Fazoolee, and the other as a principal,—it is lawful, with our doctors (Haneefa, Mohammed, and Aboo Yoosaf). The argument of Aboo Yoosaf, in the case before stated, is that one person may in marriage stand as two, and the declaration of that person may be considered as two declarations* (whence it is that if one person be authorized by both parties, the marriage is effected by his single declaration); and, in the case of an unauthorized person, the only difference is, that the validity of the contract remains suspended upon the ultimate consent of the parties, as in a case of Khoola, where if a man were to declare that "he had repudiated his wife by the form of Khoola for such a consideration" (the wife being absent), and she were afterwards to receive intelligence of this, and to assent, the Khoola is lawful; and so also, in a case of divorce or of manumission, where if a man were to declare that he had divorced his wife for one thousand Dirms (she being absent), and intelligence of this reach her, and she consent,—or, a man declare that "he has emancipated such an one, his slave, for a recompense of one thousand Dirms" (the slave being absent), and the latter, hearing of this assent, the proceeding is lawful.—To this Haneefa and Mohammad reply that, in the case before recited, the declaration of the unauthorized person, "I have contracted such a woman to such a man," or, "I have married such a woman," amounts to a contract on one part only, which is not valid, wherefore the legality of it is not suspended upon the consent of the parties, as its completion rests on the reply, which is not approved unless it proceed from a person present in the assembly or company where the contract is made, and during the continuance of that company; and, like a sale, it is incapable of being protracted to any person, on the contrary, acts on the authority of both parties, the contract is valid, because here his declaration applies equally to both; and where the contract is entered into by two unauthorized persons (acting for, or, as it were, representing the respective parties), it is complete, as it here possesses all the essential properties of contract; and so also in cases of Khoola or of divorce, or manumission for a compensation (as cited by Aboo Yoosaf), because in such instances the declaration stands as a conditional vow on the part of the husband or the master, so as to be binding upon him, and from which he cannot with propriety retract; and hence the engagement is completed solely by him.

Cases of the matrimonial agent exceeding or acting contrary to his commission.—If a man commission another, as his agent, to procure him a wife, and the agent should contract him to two women, by one declaration,* his marriage is not valid with either, for, being unlawful with both, on account of its contradicting the tenor of the commission with which he was charged, and unestablished with either, on account of unspecified priority, a separation from both must necessarily ensue.

If a person commission another, as his agent, to contract him in marriage to a woman, and the agent should contract him to a female slave the property of some third person, it is valid (according to Haneefa), because here the agent appears to have acted in strict conformity with the tenor of his commission, as the term woman is general, applying equally to the whole sex, to slaves as well as to others; nor can there be any doubt, since the case supposes the slave to be the property not of the agent, but of some third person;—neither is there any impropriety in it as the case supposes the authorizer not to be previously married to a free woman.—The two disciples allege that a marriage thus made by an agent is illegal. unless it be contracted with a woman who is the equal of the constituent; because, by the term woman, generally expressed, is to be understood such as it is customary to wed, and men commonly marry their equals; the term woman, therefore, thus indefinitely expressed, means such a woman as it is usual for such a man to marry.—To this Aboo Haneefa replies, that in custom there is an indefinite latitude, it being common for men, even of considerably rank, to marry female slaves, as well as free women who are their equals; and such being the case, the agent is not restricted to any particular description of women, as the term woman must be taken generally; and even admitting that custom does thus prevail in marriage, it may be replied that custom is of two different descriptions, one applying to words (as Daba, for instance, a term applying to beasts in general, but which custom hath restricted to a horse); and the other to actions (such, for instance, as men clothing themselves in new garments on the festival of Yd); now, in the present case, custom applies to facts, and not to terms, and therefore does not admit the construction of being restrictive.—It will hereafter be shown, in

*That is to say, "as the proposal and the acceptance," or, in other words, "as the declaration and the consent."

*That is to say, by one contract.

treating of Agency, that the two doctors regard equality, in the present case, upon another principle, to wit, that a man not being necessitated to marry any woman, of course his desire of being married by an agent relates only to a woman who is his equal.

CHAPER III.

OF THE MIHR OR DOWER.

Marriage without a dower is valid.—A MARRIAGE is valid, although no mention be made of the dower by the contracting parties, because the term Nikkah, in its literal sense, signifies a contract of union, which is fully accomplished by the junction of a man and woman ; moreover, the payment of dower is enjoined by the law, merely as a token of respect for its object (the man), wherefore the mention of it is not absolutely essential to the validity of a marriage :—and, for the same reason, a marriage is also valid, although the man were to engage in the contract on the special condition that there should be no dower : but this is contrary to the doctrine of Malik.

Ten Dirms the lowest legal dower.—THE smallest dower is ten Dirms*—Shafei says that whatever sum may be lawful as the price of a commodity in purchase and sale, is lawful as a dower, because the dower is the right of the woman, and consequently it must depend upon herself to determine the amount of it. The arguments of our doctors in this case are twofold ; FIRST, a precept of the Prophet, which expressly declares "There is no dower under ten Dirms," SECONDLY, the law enjoins a dower with a view to manifest respect for the wife, wherefore it must be fixed, in its smallest degree, at such a sum as may be respectable ; and this is ten Dirms, that being the lowest amount of a theft inducing the punishment of amputation of a limb, which shows that such sum is the least that can be regarded in an important or respectable light.

Case of a dower of ten Dirms.—IF a man assign, as a dower, a sum under ten Dirms, yet his wife shall receive the whole ten Dirms, according to our doctors.—Ziffer alleges that she shall receive a Mihr-Misl,, or proper dower ; because where the sum specified is so small as not to bear the construction of a dower, it is the same as if none whatever had been named.—The argument of our doctors is, that the impropriety of naming a stipulating so small a sum is on account of the injunction of the law, which cannot be fulfilled with less than ten Dirms, and the woman will certainly be satisfied with ten Dirms, as she had agreed to accept of less than ten : neither is it proper to take an example, in this case, from that in which no dower whatever has been named, because it may sometimes happen that a woman may grant the right of possession without any return, and out of pure love ; but no woman will agree to a trifling return. And here, if the husband were to divorce the wife before consummation, her due on account of the dower is five Dirms, according to our three doctors. Ziffer holds that she is in this case entitled only to a Matat, or present, the same as would be due where no dower had been named.—The meaning of the term Matat shall be hereafter fully explained.

The wife entitled to her whole dower upon the consummation of the marriage or the death of the husband.—IF a person specify a dower of ten or more Dirms, and should afterwards consummate his marriage, or be removed by death, his wife, in either case, has a claim to the whole of the dower specified, because, by consummation the delivery of the return for the dower, namely, the Booza, or woman's person,* is established, and therein is confirmed the right to the consideration, namely, the dower ; and, on the other hand, by the decease of the husband the marriage is rendered complete, and every thing becomes established and confirmed by its completion, and consequently is so with respect to all its effects.

And to one-half, upon divorce before consummation.—IF the husband, in the case now stated, were to divorce his wife before consummation, or Khalwas Saheeh,† she in this case, receives half her specified dower ; GOD having command, saying, "IF YE DIVORCE THEM BEFORE YE HAVE TOUCHED THEM, AND HAVE ALREADY SETTLED A DOWER ON WHAT YE SHALL PAY THEM ONE-HALF OF WHAT YE HAVE SETTLED."

OBJECTION.—It would here appear that the whole dower should of right drop, because the object of the contract reverts to the woman untouched, the same as in sale, where the whole price drops, if the buyer and seller break off the contract.

REPLY.—There are two analogical conclusions applicable to this subject ; FIRST, what is recited in the above objection : SECONDLY it would appear that the whole dower is due, because the husband did not make use of his possession, but suffered it to pass from him untouched of his own choice ; as in sale, where the whole price of a purchase is due, if the purchaser suffer the goods to perish in the hands of the seller ; and these two conclusions directly contradicting each other, they are both abandoned, and we adhere to the sacred text as above.—This case supposes

*The value of the Dirm is very uncertain. Ten Dirms, according to one account, make about six shillings and eightpence sterling.

*Literally, Genitale arvum Mulieris.

†Retirement, solus cum sola, where there is no legal or natural impedimens to the commission of the carnal act. It is elsewhere translated, complete retirement.

the divorce to take place before Khalwat, or retirement, because that with a wife is held by our doctors to amount to carnal knowledge, as shall be hereafter explained.

Where no dower is stipulated in the contract, the wife receives her proper dower.—If a man marry a woman without specifying any dower, or on the express stipulation that she shall not have a dower, and he either have carnal connexion with her, or die, she is in that case entitled to her Mihr-Misl, or proper dower.—Shafei alleges that where the husband dies, nothing whatever remains due: but many of his disciples and followers admit that the woman's proper dower is due in case of carnal connexion. The argument of Shafei is that the dower is purely a right of the woman; whence it is in her power to relinquish it a priori, for the same reason as she is at liberty to remit it afterwards.—To this our doctors reply that in the dower are involved rights of three different descriptions; the First, the right of the law, which is that it shall not consist of less than ten Dirms (as has been already said); the Second, the right of the guardians, which is that it shall not be short of the woman's proper dower; and the Third, the right of the woman, which is that it shall become her property. Now the right of the law and the right of the guardians are to be regarded in the execution of the contract, but not its continuance; consequently, in the continuance, the dower is the right of the woman solely; and hence it is that she is empowered to give it up or relinquish it in the continuance of the contract, but not a priori.

Or a present, in case of divorce before consummation.—If a man marry a woman without any specification of a dower, or on condition of there being no dower, and divorce her before carnal connexion, the woman in this case receives a Matat, or present; God having commanded, saying, "Give her a present, the rich according to his wealth, and the poor according to his poverty,:" thus a present is incumbent upon the husband on the authority of the sacred writings:—but this is contrary to the doctrine of Malik.—The Matat, or present, here mentioned, is to consist of three pieces of dress, composed of such materials as are suitable to the woman to whom it is given; and these are, the Dirra, or shift; the Khoomar, or veil; and the Mulhaffet, or outer garment. The quantity is determined at three pieces of dress, on the authority of Aysha and Ibn Abbas.—From the restriction of the present to such materials as are suitable to the woman, it would appear that, in the adjustment, regard should be had to the woman's state and condition (and such is the doctrine of Koorokhee), because it is a sort of substitute for the woman's proper dower:—but the more approved doctrine on this point is, that regard be had solely to the state and condition of the husband, because of the words of the sacred text before quoted,—"The rich according to his wealth, and the poor according to his poverty."—It is to be remarked, that the present must not exceed in value one-half of the woman's proper dower, or nor be worth less than five Dirms: the same is recorded in the Mabsoot.

Case of dower specified after marriage.—If a man marry a woman without naming any dower, and the parties should afterwards agree to a dower, and specify its amount, such dower goes to the woman, if the husband either consummate the marriage or die; but if he divorce her before consummation, she receives only a present. With Aboo Yoosaf she, in this case, receives one-half of the dower specified (and such also is the opinion of Shafei), because here the dower has been made obligatory and specifically determined, and consequently one-half is due according to the words of the text, "Ye shall pay them one-half of what ye have settled." The argument of our doctors is that, in the present case, the specification of the dower indentifies a thing which was due on account of the contract, to wit, the woman's proper dower, and as this is incapable of subdivision, consequently that which is its substitute cannot be halved.—With respect to the text above quoted, it is to be regarded as applying solely to what has been agreed to and specified at the period of the contract: this being agreeable to what is customary.

Case of an addition made to the dower after marriage.—If a man make any addition to the dower in behalf of his wife subsequent to the contract, such addition is binding upon him.—This is contrary to the doctrine of Ziffer, as shall be demonstrated in treating of an increase of price in a contract of sale.—But although such after-addition to the dower be thus approved, yet it drops in consequence of divorce before consummation.—According to an opinion of Aboo Yoosaf, the woman is entitled to the half of the additional together with that of the original dower.—The cause of this difference of opinion is that, with Haneefa and Mohammed, nothing is halved but what has been rendered obligatory, and specifically determined; whereas Aboo Yoosaf holds whatever is engaged for after the contract to be the same as that which is made obligatory in the contract, and therefore considers it as subject to the same rule.

A wife may remit the whole dower.—If a woman exonerate her husband from any part, or even from the whole, of the dower, it is approved; because after the execution of the contract, it is her sole right (as was already explained), and the case supposes her dereliction of it to take place at a subsequent period.

Case of Khalwat-Saheeh or retirement.—If a man retire with his wife, and there be no legal or natural obstruction to the commission of the carnal act, and he afterwards divorce her, the whole dower in this case goes to her.—Shafei maintains that she is here to receive no more than her half dower, because the husband cannot obtain possession of the object of the contract but by actual coition; and the right to the dower is not corroborated and confirmed without enjoyment.—The argument of our doctors is, that the woman has completed her part of the contract, by delivering up her person, and by removing all obstructions, which is the extent of her ability; her right to the recompense is therefore confirmed and corroborated; in the same manner as in a case of sale, where, if the seller have offered delivery of the goods sold, and there be nothing to obstruct seisin on the part of the purchaser, and the latter neglect to make seisin, he is considered as having made seisin, and the purchase is afterwards as a trust in the hands of the seller, and the whole of the price is obligatory upon the purchaser.

Circumstances in which retirement does not imply consummation.—If a man retire with his wife whilst one of them is sick, or fasting in the month of Ramzan, or in the Ihram of a pilgrimage, whether obligatory* or voluntary, or of a visitation at the shrine of the Prophet (termed an Amrit), or whilst the woman is in her courses—this is not regarded as a Khalwat-Saheeh, or complete retirement, insomuch, that if the man were to divorce his wife after such a retirement, the woman is entitled to her half dower only; because all the above circumstances are bars to the carnal act;—sickness, from the weakness and imbecility with which it is attended, or from its rendering the commission of the carnal act injurious to one or the other of the parties; —and fasting in Ramzan because it would induce upon the party a necessity of expiation and atonement;—and pilgrimage, or visitation, because it would induce a necessity of atonement by sacrifice;—and the woman's courses, because they oppose an obstruction both natural and legal.

Exception.—But if one of the parties be observing a Nifl [voluntary] fast only, the woman is entitled to her whole dower, because the breach of such a fast is a matter of indifference: a fast of atonement, or in consequence of a vow, is the same as a voluntary fast in this respect, and for the same reason.

Case of retirment of an eunuch.—If a Majboob eunuch retire with his wife, and afterwards divorce her, she is entitled to her whole dower, according to Haneefa.—The two disciples maintain that the half dower only goes to her, on account that a Majboob is still more incapacitated than a sick person: contrary to the case of an Ineen (or one naturally impotent), because the point of law rests upon the existence of the instrument of generation, which is there found, but not in the former case.—Haneefa on the other hand, argues, that all which is due on the part of the woman is the delivery of her person (by admitting the husband to feel and touch her), and this being, to the extent of her ability, completely performed, it follows that the consideration is completely due to her.

It is incumbent upon the woman to observe an Edit (or appointed term of probation), after the divorce, in all the cases here recited, for the sake of caution, on a principle of propriety, from the apprehension or possibility of her womb being occupied by seed. The Edit is, moreover, a right of the law and of the foetus; and credit is not to be given to the parties that they have not committed the carnal act, because this (in precluding the necessity of Edit) would amount to an extinction of rights (as above specified) distinct and separate from these of the parties: but it is otherwise with the dower, because that is a matter of property, the right in which cannot be decided upon principles of caution (like the Edit), nor under any circumstance admitting of doubt; the dower, therefore, is not due, where retirement is not of the description of Khalwat-Saheeh. Kadooree, in his commentary upon his own work, has observed that, if the obstruction to the carnal act be merely of a legal nature (such as fasting), the observance of Edit is incumbent, because here the natural ability to the performance of the act is supposed: but if the obstruction be of a positive nature (such as sickness or infancy), the Edit is not requisite, because the ability to perform the act does not here exist.

Case in which the present to the wife is laudable, or incumbent.—It is laudable to bestow a Matat, or present, upon every woman divorced by her husband, excepting two descriptions of woman, namely, one whose dower, has been stipulated, and whose husband divorce her before consummation.—and one whose dower has not been stipulated and who is also divorced before consummation; for in their behalf a present is not merely laudable, but incumbent. Shafei says, that a present is incumbent in behalf of every divorced woman, excepting one whose dower has been stipulated, and who is divorced before consummation; because the present is made incumbent in the way of a gratuity, or compensatory gift, from the husband, on account of his having thrown the woman into a forlorn state by his separation from her; but, in the excepted instance, the half dower is a substitute for the present, as divorce is here a dissolution of the contract, and the present need not be bestowed repeatedly. The argument of our doctors is, that the present is a substitute for the proper dower in the case of a resigned woman (that is, a woman who resigns herself to her husband without a dower), on account that, as the proper dower drops, the present becomes incumbent; because, in a contract of

*All Mussulmans are required, once in their lives, to make a pilgrimage to Mecca, which is termed Hidj-Farz, or ordailed pilgrimage.

marriage, a return is essential: the present, therefore, is a substitute for the proper dower and such being the case, it must not be required in addition either of the whole dower, which is the original thing, or to any part of it: whence the present is not incumbent where any part of the dower in due. As to what Shafei advances, that "the pesent is made incumbent in the way of a gratuity, or compensatory gift, from the husband, on account of his having thrown the woman into a forlorn state by his separation from her,"—we reply, that this act of his does not amount to an offence, as the husband is privileged by the law to do so, wherefore no recompense is due from him on that account; and hence it is that the present is regarded merely as respectful and laudable.

Case of a reciprocal bargain between two contractors.—If a person contract his daughter, or his sister in marriage to another, on the condition of the other bestowing a sister or daughter in marriage upon him, so as that such contract shall stand as a return for the other, respectively, both the contracts are lawful. Shafei maintains that both the contracts are null, as they make one half of the woman's person, reciprocally, a dower, and the other half the subject of marriage; because, where the person marries his daughter to the other, and also constitutes her the dower for the other's daughter, it follows that the daughter's person* is divided between the other person and his daughter.—one half to that person, as husband, in virtue of the marriage, and the other half to his daughter as her dower; and as the matrimonial possession, or propriety, is incapable of being participate (since it is ordained as a complete enjoyment, and not as a participated one), it follows that the bargain is nugatory." To this our doctors reply, that the contract or has named, as a dower, a thing incapable of being so (since a woman's person, in the sense it here bears, is incapable of being the property of a woman); —but yet the contract holds good, and a Mihr Misl, or proper dower, remains due [to each of the women], the same as where wine or a hog are assigned as a dower—With respect to what Shafei urges, that "the matrimonial propriety is incapable of being participated,"—it is admitted; but this participation is not induced in the present case, as the person of either of the daughters is not made the right of the other daughter in virtue of the contract.

Case of marriage on a condition of service from the husband.—If a free man marry a woman, on the condition, in return of serving her for a stated time (a year, for instance), or of teaching her the Koran, yet her proper dower is incumbent upon him notwithstanding, according to Haneefa and Aboo Yoosaf, Mohammad has said that she is, in this case, to receive a sum amounting to the estimated value of his service for one year. But if a slave, by his owner's consent, marry a woman on the same terms, it is lawful and the woman is entitled to the stipulated service only. Shafei is of opinion that the woman is entitled merely to the service whatever may be lawfully received as a fixed stipulated in either of these cases; because return, is capable of constituting a dower, since a mutual exchange may be thereby effected, and consequently the case is the same as if the man had married the woman on condition of a stated service to be performed by another person, or on a stipulation of himself watching her flocks for a stated period. The arguments of our doctors, on this point, are twofold:—First, the possession of a woman's person is not to be sought (that is to say, to desire, it is not lawful), except in lieu of property; and teaching the Koran is not property; neither does usufruct constitute property (according to the sentiments of our doctors), because that is not substantial or permanent, whereas property is a thing of a permanent nature, and what constitutes actual wealth; service therefore, not being property, to seek the possession, of a woman's person, in return for the services of a freeman, in unlawful:—contrary to a case where a slave obtains a woman in marriage on the condition of his serving her, since here possession is sought for that which is actual property, the service of a slave being considered as such because this comprehends a surrender or delivery of the slave's person, and the person of a slave is actual property, and of course the usufruct thereof; wherefore it is analogous to the bestowing of the slave himself as a dower: but with a husband who is free this cannot be the case: Secondly, it is not lawful that a woman should be in a situation to exact the service of her husband who is a freeman, as this would amount to a reversal of their appointed stations, for one of the requisites of marriage is, that the woman be as a servant, and the man as the person served; but if the service of the husband to the wife were to constiute her dower, it would follow that the husband is as the servant and the wife as the served: and this being a violation of the requisites of marriage, is therefore illegal; but it is otherwise with the service stipulated to be performed by another free person, with that person's consent, as this offers no violence to the requisites of the contract; and so also in the case of service of a slave, because the service performed by a slave to his wife is, in fact, performed to his master, by whose consent it is that he undertakes it; and the same with the case of tending flocks, because this is a service of a permanent nature, and admitted to be performed for wives, and therefore does not violate the requisites of marriage; for the service of the husband to his wife, as a dower, is prohibited only as it may be degrading to the former: but the tending of flocks is not a degrading office. Mohammed, according to his tenets, holds as)

*Arab. Booza, i.e., Genitale Mulleris.

was already observed) that the woman is, in this case, entitled to receive a sum amounting, to this estimated value of the service, because he maintains that what was stipulated (to wit, the service) is properly, but of such a nature as it is not in the husband's power to make delivery of, since by such an act he would violate the requisites of marriage; the case, therefore, is the same as if a man were to marry a woman, assigning, as a dower, a slave, the property of another, in which case he would have to pay the woman the value of such slave. Haneefa and Aboo Yoosaf, on the other hand, hold that the woman is entitled to a proper dower; because they maintained that the service here stipulated is not property, as a woman cannot legally exact service of her husband, being a freeman, in any situation whatever lest a reversal of stations should be induced, as was just observed; the naming, therefore, of service as a dower, is the same as naming wine, or a hog; for, not being capable of legal delivery, it is not a subject of appreciation; and such being the case, resourse is had to the original rule in defect of any dower, and this dictates a proper dower.

Cases of a wife remitting or returning the dower to her husband, either wholly or in part.—IF a man marry a woman on a dower of one thousand Dirms, and the woman make seisin of the said thousand, and then present the same to him, and he take possession of such gift, and afterwards divorce her before consummation, the husband, in this case, has a claim upon his wife for five hunderd Dirms, because he is not considered, in law, as having received, in the form of the gift, that identical thing which becomes obligatory upon his wife in consequence of divorce before consummation, since money is incapable of identification either in the fulfilment or the annulment of contracts. So also, if the dower consist not of money, but of articles of weight or measurement of capacity, as iron or copper.—But if the wife were to make a gift to her husband of the thousand Dirms, without having herself been in possession of the same,* and he were afterwards to divorce her before consummation, in this case neither party has any claim whatever upon the other. This proceeds upon a favourable construction; for analogy would suggest that the husband should receive from his wife the amount of half the dower, because the whole dower remains untouched with the husband in consequence of the gift, which amount to a discharge, but the wife does not appear to be discharged from what becomes obligatory upon her in consequence of divorce before consummation.—The reason for a more favourable construction of the law upon this point is that the identical thing which becomes obligatory upon the wife in favour of the husband, in consequence of divorce before consummation, has come to him, in his being discharged from half the dower (through the wife's gift), and the end being thus obatined, any difference in the manner in which it is obtained will not be regarded.—that is to say, the end was, that the husband should recover half the dower after divorce before consummation, and that end has been obtained, not indeed through divorce, but through antecedent gift, which answers the same purpose.

IF a man marry a woman on a dower of one thousand Dirms and the woman make seisin of five hunderd Dirms, and afterwards make a gift to her husband of the whole thousand, —as well of the portion in her possession, as of that which she has not received,—or of the latter only,—and the husband afterwards divorce her before consummation, neither party in this case, has any claim upon the other, according to Haneefa.—The two disciples maintain that the husband has, in this case, a claim upon the wife for one half of that proportion of which she had possession; because they conceive of a part from the whole; —that is to say, if the wife were to make a gift of the whole dower to her husband, without having herself made previous seisin of any part thereof, the husband has no claim to resume anytning out of it;—and, on the contrary, if she were first to make seisin of the dower, and then to make a gift of the same to her husband, he would have a claim of resumption upon her for one half; and consequently, when she has made seisin of any particular part or portion of it, has a claim of resumption upon her for the half of that part of which she had made seision; and again, on the other hand, because a gift of any part of the dower to the husband amounts to an abatement with respect to that part, and is therefore altogether excluded from the contract;* and consequently, when the gift is of that half which had remained unseised, it is the same as if the contract had regarded the half only (as where a seller, for instance, makes a gift of half the price of the commodity sold, in which case it is the same as if the price agreed upon were no more than the remaining half); and such being the case, it follows that the proportion of abatement (in consequence of gift) becomes altogether excluded from the dower, and that the half of which seisin had been made stands as the complete dower:—and as, where seizin had been made by the wife of her whole dower, and she had presented the same to her husband, he would still (upon divorce before consummation) have a claim of resumption upon her for one half (as has been shown in

*That is to say, relinquishes her right to to it.

*The phrase in the original is remarkable, "LEHAZA YEWLUKKO B'ASSIL AL AKID,"—"and therefore is connected with the origin of the contract;"—that is to say,—with a period antecedent to the contract, and consequently not included in it. The term here adopted appears to be the clearest by which the translator could express the sense.

a former case), so here, in like manner, he has a claim of resumption for a moiety of the seised proportion, that standing as the complete dower. The argument of Aboo Haneefa in this case is, that the end of the husband hath been already obtained, in a moiety of the dower remaining untouched with him without any return; wherefore, upon divorcing his wife before consummation, he would have no occasion to make any resumption: and with respect to what the two disciples advance, that "an abatement becomes altogether excluded from the contract," it may be replied, if this were to be admitted, it would follow that, in a case where a man marries a woman on a dower of twenty Dirms (for instance), and the woman makes a gift to him of fifteen Dirms out of the twenty, ten Dirms would remain obligatory upon the husband; because, the abatement being excluded from the contract, it would be the same as if he had married her upon a dower of five Dirms; and if he had married her upon such a dower, he would be bound for ten Dirms, on the principle of law, that if a man marry a woman on a dower of fewer than ten Dirms, ten Dirms are obligatory upon him; this idea would consequently lead to an unjust and unfounded conclusion, and is therefore inadmissible.

If a man marry a woman on a dower of one thousand Dirms, and she make a gift to him of a part less than the half—two hundred, for instance,—and take possession of the remainder, and the husband afterwards divorce her before consummation, he has, in this case (according to Aboo Haneefa), a claim of resumption upon her for such a sum as together with what she had proviously bestowed upon him, makes a moiety of the whole, namely (in the supposition before mentioned) three hundred Dirms:—according to the two disciples, on the contrary, his claim of resumption is for the half of what the woman had made seisin of, namely, four hundred Dirms.

The same when the dower consists of effects —If a man marry a woman on a dower consisting of certain specified effects, and she make a gift of the same to him, either before or after seisin, and he afterwards divorce her before consummation, he, in this case, has no claim of resumption whatever upon the woman—This proceeds upon a favourable construction.—Analogy would suggest that he should have a claim to the amount of the value of half the effects, because here it becomes obligatory upon the woman to make restitution of half the dower, as was already explained, and she is incapacited from making restitution by delivery of half the actual effects, in consequence of her gift; wherefore it would appear that she should make it by paying the estimated value of one half —But the reason for a more favourable construction of the law in this case is, that the husband who is entitled to recover from the woman one half of what she had taken possession of, in consequence of his having divorced her before consutmmation, has already actually obtained this (through her gift); whence it is that the woman would not be at liberty to give her husband any other thing in lieu of those effects, because the consideration consists of a thing capable of identical specification, and of course the said effects, which have been in possession of the woman, and by her made over in gift to her busband, constitute a dower of a certain specific description; thus the husband appears to have received that actual thing which had been rendered obligatory upon the wife by divorce before consummation:—contrary to the case of a dower consisting of a debt; for here, if the wife were to make seisin of such debt, and then to make a gift of the same to her husband, and he afterwaads to divorce her, as above, he would, in this case have a claim of resumption upon her for the value of one half of the dower, because a debt of this nature is, like money, incapable of identical specification:—and contrary, also, to a case where a woman, having taken possession of effects, as a dower (as was stated in the preceding case), sell such effects to her husband, because, in this case, they have come back to him for a consideration and his claim is to the recovery of the half of her dower without any consideration.—And if the dower consist of an animal, or of effects, which are a debt upon the husband,* the rule is the same as in the case of one consisting of specified effects; because the thing seised by the woman is of such a nature as, if she had herself borrowed it, must be restored by her in substance; and articles of this description are all capable of identical specification.

Cases of stipulation in behalf of the wife. —If a man marry a woman on a dower of one thousand Dirms,† on a condition that he is not to carry her out of her native city,—or that he is not to marry, during his matrimonial connexion with her, any other woman, in this case, if he observe the condition, the woman is entitled to the above specified dower only, as that consists of a sum sufficient to constitute a legal dower, and she has agreed to accept it; but if he should infringe the condition, by either carrying her out of her native city, or marrying another wife, she is in this case entitled to her proper dower, because he had acceded to a condition on behalf of the woman which was advantageous to her, and that not being fulfilled, the woman is nor supposed to be satisfied with the thousand Dirms, and must therefore be paid her complete proper dower; the same as in a case where a woman had agreed to accept of one thousand Dirms, as a dower, on condition of being treated with

*That is to say, an animal, or effects, which had been borrowed or procured upon credit by the husband.

†This case proceeds on the supposition of one thousand Dirms being of less value than the woman's proper dower.

reverence, and not subjected to any laborious work; or of being presented with a rich dress, and so forth.

If a man marry a woman, stipulating the dower at one thousand Dirms, provided he should not carry her out of her native city, but stay and reside there with her,—or at two thousand, if he should carry her thence,—in this case, if he continue to reside with her in the said city, she is entitled to the thousand Dirms only; but if he carry her thence she becomes entitled to her proper dower, where that does not exceed two thousand, nor fall short of one thousand.—This is according to Haneefa. The two disciples say that both conditions are equally valid, insomuch that, as if he were to continue to reside with her in the city aforesaid, she would receive the one thousand Dirms only, so if he carry her thence, she becomes entitled to two thousand.—Ziffer, on the other hand, maintains that both the conditions are null and that the woman shall, in either event, receive her proper dower, where that does not exceed two thousand Dirms, nor fall short of one thousand.—This case is founded upon what occurs in the book of Hire, where a man says to a tailor, "If you make me up this robe within the day, I shall pay you one Dirm; or if you finish it by to-morrow, you shall have half a Dirms;"—as will be hereafter explained.

Cases of a dower consisting of property unidentified.—If a man marry a woman, agreeing to give her, as a dower, either of two slaves unspecified,—as if he were to say—"Make one of these two the dower"—and the slaves be of different value,—in this case, where the woman's proper dower is under the rate of the slave of less value, she receives that on; or if it exceed the rate of the more valuable slave, she receives that one; and if it exceed the former, and fall short of the latter, she then receives her proper dower. This is according to Aboo Yoosaf.—The two disciples allege that the least valuable slave goes to her, in all these circumstances. But if the husband divorce her without consummation, she in that case becomes entitled to half the price of the least valuable slave only, according to all the doctors.—The argument of the two disciples, in this case, is that the proper dower is not to be held obligatory, unless where the stipulated dower is of such a nature as renders an obligation with respect to that impossible; but it is possible with respect to the least valuable slave, because that one is undoubted,* and is therefore obligatory; the same as in a case of Khoola, or of manumission, for a compensation "of one thousand, or of two thousand," or "of this slave, or of that slave;"* in which case, whatever is the least value named is held to be the compensation either for Khoola or for manumission, as there can be no doubt concerning it; and so in this case also.—The argument of Haneefa, in reply to the two disciples, is that the proper dower is the radical obligation in a contract of marriage, like the price of a purchase, in a contract of sale, as that is the most equitable, being a medium adjustment neither over nor under, and consequently it is not to be deviated from, except in cases where the specification of the dower is perfect and complete; but here the specification is not complete, since neither slave has been particularly mentioned by the husband, in settling the dower, but both indefinitely: contrary to a case of Khoola or of manumission for a compensation, since in neither of these is there any radical compensatory obligation understood, independent of some particular previous agreement; for if a slave were to say to his master, "emancipate me," and the master were to reply "thou art free" or if a wife were to say to her husband, "grant me Khoola," and the husband were to reply, "I have granted Khoola," no obligation whatever would remain upon the slave or the wife; whereas, on the contrary, if a woman were to say to a man, "marry me," and he were to reply, "I have married you, "her proper dower would be incumbent upon him: but where the rate of the more valuable slave falls short of the proper dower, the wife has virtually acceded to the abatement; and, in like manner, where the rate of the least valuable slave exceeds the proper dower, the husband has virtually agreed to the excess; and she then receives one or other of the slaves, as the case may be.—It is here to be observed that if divorce take place before emancipation, the wife is to receive from her husband a present in addition to half the price of the least valuable slave: this is a rule established by custom, and must be complied with, as an obligation on the part of the husband, although the value of the present should even exceed the half price of such slave.

Or undescribed.—If a man marry a woman, assigning her, as a dower, an animal undescribed, it is approved, and the woman shall receive an animal of a middling standard; but the husband has it at his option instead of this, to pay her the value of such an animal in money.—The compiler of the Hedaya observes that this is to be understood only where a man names the species of

*That is to say, although, with respect to the slave of greater value, a doubt might be entertained, yet with respect to the other there can be none, since that is the lowest terms offered by the party himself.

*This relates merely to the point of law in case of vague and indefinite expression; for instance, in Khoola, where the wife may say to her husband, "I will give you one or two thousand Dirms, or either of my slaves, Zeyd or Amir, for my divorce,"—in which case the law always determines the proposed compensation at the lowest value mentioned.

the animal in general, without any specific description (as if he were to say, "I will give you as a dower a horse." or "an ass," without describing whether it is to be an Arabee or a Toorkee) ; but where he does not mention the species of the animal (as if he were to say, "I will give, as a dower, a quadruped"), it is not lawful, and he in that case becomes liable to make good to the woman her proper dower.—Shafei maintains that a proper dower is obligatory in either of the above cases, he holding that nothing is fit to be assigned as dower, in a contract of marriage, but what would be capable of appreciation in a contract of sale ; and an animal underscribed, is incapable of appreciation, as being unknown, and consequently cannot constitute a dower.—The argument of our doctors is, that a contract of marriage includes an exchange of property for that which is not property (for the use of the woman's person, which is the return, cannot be termed such) :—now the law admits that animals may be a debt upon the person, in the course of an exchange, where there is no property in return, as in the case of Deeyat, where an hundred camels are rendered obligatory in law, their description being undefined: the dower is therefore to be considered, in this respect, as a property, concerning which the man has taken an obligation upon himself a priori, in the manner of an acknowledgment : now ignorance, with respect to the actual property, does not invalidate an acknowledgment by which a person takes upon himself a priori, an obligation concerning it ; as for example, if a person were to acknowledge that he owed a slave, or any thing else undescribed, his acknowledgment would be good, and the specification would rest with him.

Objection.—If the nomination of a dower be to stand the same as an acknowledgment, it follows that the nomination of an animal on account of dower is approved, although the species remain unknown,—the same as in an acknowledgment respecting property unknown,—which is not the case.

Reply.—A knowledge of the species of the animal is made a condition, in conformity with the rule, that a specified dower shall consist of property, the medium of which may be known, for the sake of both the parties ; now this cannot be ascertained, except where the species is unknown, which comprehends a best, a worst, and a medium of the kind, for if this be unknown, the distinction cannot be made, since no medium can be ascertained amidst an infinite variety of species.—But (as was already observed) the husband has it at his option, in discharging the dower, either to give the woman a medium animal of the species mentioned, or to pay her the value in money, because the medium cannot be ascertained precisely except by appreciation, and consequently the value of the animal is the standard of payment ; and, on the other hand, the actual animal is the standard according to nomination.

If a man marry a woman, assigning her a dower of cloth, undescribed, she, in this case, receives her proper dower. This is where the term cloth alone is mentioned by the man without any addition ; and the reason is, that the species of cloth is here unknown and unascertainable, since of that there are a variety of species.—But if he were to name the species of cloth, as if he were to say, "I will give, as a dower, a piece of Hirrooey,"* this manner of description is approved ; and the husband has it in his option either to give a piece of Hirrooey of a middling quantity, or to pay the value in cash, for the reasons already stated. In like manner he has it at his option either to give the cloth or to pay the value, where he has been still more particular, in his description, mentioning the length, breadth, and quality of it, in a way such as would suffice in a Sillim sale.—This is according to the Zahir Rawayet ; and the ground upon which it proceeds is that cloth is not of the class of things denominated Zooatal-Imsal, or things compensable by an equal quantity of the same species. In like manner he shall have the same option where the dower is assigned of goods, the quantity of which, is ascertainable by weight or measure, provided he should not have particularly described the quality, but only the species : but if he should particularly describe the quality, he then has no option, and must pay the actual thing mentioned, because, under such description, it becomes a debt upon him, of the specific weighable or measurable articles described.

Case of a dower consisting of unlawful articles.—If a Mussulman marry a woman, agreeing to give her, as a dower, wine or a hog, the woman has her proper dower, because a condition of assenting to receive such articles is invalid ; but as a contract of marriage is not rendered null by a nugatory condition being comprehended in it, it holds good, in this case, though the condition be null : contrary to a case of sale, which is rendred null by an invalid condition.—The assignment of the dower in either of the articles aforesaid is disapproved, because what is named is not property with Mussulmans ; and on this principle it is that a proper dower becomes due.

Cases of false assignment.—If a man marry a woman, assigning her, as a dower, a cask of vinegar, and the cask should afterwards appear to contain wine, she, in this case, has her proper dower, according to Haneefa.—The two disciples allege that, in this case, she is to receive vinegar of a medium quality, and the same in quantity as the wine.—And if the man were to name, as a dower, a certain specified slave (as if

*A particular species of cloth manufactured in Herat, a city of Khorasan.

he were to say, "I assign this slave as a dower"), and it should afterwards appear that the person so mentioned as a slave was at that time free, to this case a proper dower is due, according to Haneefa and Mohammed. Aboo Yoosaf says that here husband owes the estimated value of the free person aforesaid, supposing he were a slave; for he argues that the man has filled the woman with the expectation of a certain property, the delivery of which he afterwards finds impossible; the value therefore is obligatory upon him, or an article similar to that agreed for, if it be of the species of Zooatal Imsal, as in a case where a man marries a woman on a dower consisting of a specified slave, and the slave dies before delivery—Aboo Haneefa, on the other hand, says, that where nomination and pointed reference* are united, regard must be had to the latter, because indication is more clear and express under that form, and hence the case is the same as if the man had engaged to give, as a dower, wine or a hog.† Mohammed (coinciding with Haneefa with respect to the slave, and dissenting from him with respect to the vinegar, as aforesaid) says that it is a rule, that if the thing named be of the same species with the thing specified by pointed reference, the contract is connected with the latter; but if the thing named be of a species distinct and different from the thing pointedly specified, it [the contract] is connected with the thing named; because indication is more effectual from naming a thing, than it is from pointing that thing out, inasmuch as it is thereby known what that thing is, whereas by pointing it out the substance only is known:—on which principle it is that if a man purchase a ring stone, on the condition of its being a ruby, and it should prove to be only a garnet, the bargain is void, on account of the difference of species; but if a person were to purchase a stone on condition of its being a ruby, and it should prove to be an emerald, yet the bargain holds good, because these are held by lapidaries to be of the same species:—now, in the present instance, the slave and the free person are of one and the same species: the contract, therefore, is connected with the thing identically specified or pointed out, and on this principle her proper dower is due to the woman; but wine and vinegar being of distinct species, and totally different from each other (inasmuch as the latter is lawful in use, and the former prohibited) the contract is there connected with the thing nominally specified, and consequently the woman is entitled to vinegar equal in quantity to the wine.

If a man marry a woman, agreeing to give her, as a dower, two slaves specified, as if he were to say, "I assign, as a dower, those two slaves;" and it should happen that one of the persons so specified as slaves is free, in this case, according to Haneefa, the woman is not entitled to more than the single slave remaining, provided the value be equal to ten Dirms, because the slave is particularly assigned, and where the assigned dower is admitted to be incumbent, this prohibits the obligation to proper dower:—as where a man, for instance: marries a woman, assigning her, as a dower, a piece of cloth of the value of five Dirms, in which case the woman gets the piece of cloth aforesaid together with five Dirms in money, in such a manner as that the whole shall amount to ten Dirms, being the lowest legal dower, beyond which nothing is incumbent. Aboo Yoosaf alleges that, in this case, the woman gets the slave, together with the amount of the estimated value of the other person, supposing he were a slave, because here the man has filled her with expectation of two slaves, the delivery of one of which afterwards appears to be impossible; wherefore the value of the latter is obligatory upon him. Mohammed has said (and there is also one opinion recorded of Haneefa to the same effect) that the woman gets the salve, together with a property sufficient to complete her proper dower, if that should exceed the value of the salve; because, if both the persons named as slaves by the husband, in specifying the dower, were actually free, the whole proper dower (according to Mohammed) would be due; and consequently, where one only is a slave that slave is due, together with such property as (along with the slave) amounts to a proper dower.

A woman is not entitled to any dower under an invalid marriage dissolved before consummation.—If the Kazee separate a man from his wife, before cohabitation, on account of their marriage being invalid, the woman is not entitled to any part of her dower, because, where the marriage is invalid, no obligation with respect to dower is involved in the contract, as that, in such a case, is also null; nor is the dower held to be due on any other ground than the fruition of the connubial enjoyment, which is not found in the present instance.—In the same manner no dower is due after Khalwat Saheeh, or complete retirement, because, on account of the invalidity of the marriage, the law does not consider retirement as indicating the commission of the carnal act, and consequently it does not stand as such. It is, however, to be observed that in an invalid marriage a

*Tasmeeat and Isharet: the former term means simply naming a thing, or (as expressed above) nomination; by the latter is understood pointing a thing out, such as "This slave," &c.

†This is to say, the condition is altogether void, and a proper dower is of course due; for if the man were to say, "I will give as a dower this slave," and the person so spoken of should appear to be free, it is evident (regard being had to the relative "this," denoting pointed reference) that the condition or agreement is ipso facto null, as regarding a thing which does not exist.

separate dower is not due on account of every repetition of the carnal act, because here the right of possession is doubtful, and the case is therefore the same as where a man has repeated carnal connexion with the slave of his son,—or where a man has repeated carnal connexion with his wife, and it should afterwards appear that he had suspended the divorce of that woman upon the circumstance of his marrying her,—in either of which cases one dower only is due, because of a doubt respecting the right of possession; contrary to a case where a man has repeated carnal connexion with the slave of his father, his mother, or his wife and pleads his conception of the same being lawful; for in this case a dower is incumbent upon him for every repetition of the act, because here no doubt exists, as he appears, on every repetition, to have had carnal connexion with a slave who is the absolute property of another:—and, contrary also, to a case where a man has repeated carnal connexion with a female slave held in partnership between himself and another, for in this case an half fine is incumbent upon him for every repetition (according to the determination in the Burhanal Aima of Abdul-azeez-Bin Amroo), because he has every time committed the carnal act in the share of his partner.

But in case of consummation, she is entitled to her proper dower, not exceeding what is specified in the contract.—IF a man engage with a woman in an invalid marriage, and have carnal connexion with her, she is in this case entitled to her proper dower: but she is not entitled to more than the specified dower,*according to our doctors.—This is contrary to the opinion of Ziffer, who conceives an analogy between this and an invalid sale, that is to say, in an invalid sale, if the stipulated price of the thing sold be short of its actual value the latter is due to whatever amount; and so also in the present case.—The argument of our doctors, in this case, is that the thing which the husband has received (namely, the possession of the woman's person) is not property, and therefore is not appreciable in any other way than by the assignment of a dower; now if a dower assigned should exceed the proper dower, the excess is not incumbent, because of the invalidity of the assignment, for that is a part of the contract, which being invalid, the assignment is so likewise, and, on the other hand, if the dower assigned be short of the proper dower, the difference is not incumbent because, with respect to that, assignment has not been made; contrary to an invalid sale, because there the thing sold is appreciable, and consequently the amount of the return will be adjusted by its value.

And she must observe an Edit after separation.—THE observance of an Edit, after separation, is in-cumbent upon a woman with whom a man has had carnal connexion in an invalid marriage. And here the Edit is to commence as from the date of separation, and not from that of the last carnal connexion.

A child born in an illegal marriage is of established descent.—THE descent of a child born of a woman enjoyed in an illegal marriage is established [in the reputed father], because in this, regard is had to the child's preservation, since if the descent were not to be established, the child might perish for want of care.— Mohmmed holds (and decrees are passed agreeable to this doctrine) that, in the establishment of genealogy under an invalid marriage, the time* is calculated from the first carnal connexion, not from the date of the marriage, because one which is invalid does not give a claim to the carnal act, so as to stand as such, whereas the reverse is the case in a valid marriage, as that establishes such claim: and hence, in the establishment of genealogy, the time is calculated from the date of the marriage.

Rate of the Mihr Misl, or proper dower—THE Mihr Misl (or proper dower) of any woman is to be regulated, in its amount or value, by that of the dower of her paternal relations, such as her paternal sister or aunts, or the daughter of her paternal uncles, and so forth, according to a precept of Ibn Mussaood, "To the woman belongs such a dower as is usually assigned to her female paternal relatives :"—moreover, men are accounted of the class of their peternal tribe, and the value of a thing cannot be estimated but by attending to the value set upon its class.

A WOMAN'S proper dower is not to be estimated by the dower of her mother or her maternal aunt, where they are not descended of her father's family, on account of the precept of Ibn Mussaood already recorded; yet if her mother should be descended of her father's family (being for instance, the daughter or his paternal uncle), in this case a judgment may be formed from her dower, as being descended from the family of the father.

IN regulating the proper dower of a woman, attention must be paid to her quality with the woman from whose dowers the rule is to be taken, in point of age, beauty, fortune, understanding, and virtue, because it varies according to any difference in all these circumstances; and, in like manner, it differs according to place of residence, or time (that is to say, times of trouble and confusion, as opposed to time to tranquality); and the learned in the law have observed that equality is also to be regarded

*That is to say, if her proper dower should exceed in value the dower specified in the contract, yet the woman is entitled to the specified dower only, and not to her proper dower.

*The probable term of pregnancy, by which the child's descent is to be judged of and ascertained, (For a further elucidation of this point see Book of Divorce, Chap. XIII.)

in point of virginity, because the dower is different according as the woman may be a virgin or otherwise.

A woman's guardian may become surety for her dower.— IF the Walee [guardian] of a woman become surety for her dower, it is approved, because he is competent to such responsibility (that is, to take such obligation upon himself), and he is surety in a thing which is a legal subject of bail (namely, the dower), since that is a debt, in which bail is approved: and the woman is afterwards at liberty to require her dower either of her husband or of her guardian, as in all other cases of bail: and if the guardian pay the dower, he shall take the same from the woman's husband, where he has become surety at his desire, as is the invariable rule in bail. The bail is like manner approved, if the wife be an infant: contrary to where a father sells the property of his infant child, and becomes bail for the amount, which is not lawful, because a guardian is, with respect to marriage, a negotiator merely; but in sale, he is the executor of the contract (whence it is that its obligations rest upon him, and its rights appertain to him); and the father's discharge is also approved, if he clear the purchaser of the whole price of the infant's property; and he is moreover at liberty to take possession of the price after the infant shall have attained maturity; wherefore, if his bail were to be approved, it would admit the principle of a man becoming surety in his own behalf, which is absurd.

OBJECTION.—A father is at liberty to take possession of the dower of his infant daughter, in the same manner as of the price of his infant child's property; wherefore if the ball of the father with respect to the dower be approved, it follows that he is bail in his own behalf.

REPLY.—The authority vested in a father to take possession of the dower is because of his parental relation, and not on account of his being a party in the contract (for which reason it is that he is not at liberty to take possession of the dower after the maturity of his child), so that he does not in this case, appear to be bail in his own behalf.

A woman may resist consummation until she be paid the prompt proportion of the dower.—A WOMAN may refuse to admit her husband to a carnal connexion until she receive her dower of him, so as that her right may be maintained to the return, in the same manner as that of her husband to the object for which the return is given, as in sale.

A WOMAN is also at liberty to resist her husband carrying her upon a journey until she shall have received her dower of him, for the same reason

ON the other hand the husband has no power to restrain his wife from going on a journey, or from going abroad, or visiting her friends, until such time as he shall have discharged the whole of the Mihr Moajil, or prompt dower, because a husband's right to confine his wife at home is solely for the sake of securing to himself the enjoyment of her person, and his right to such enjoyment does not exist until after the payment of the return for it.

Unless the whole dower be deferable.—WHAT is here advanced proceeds upon a supposition of the whole dower, or a certain portion of it, being Moajil, or prompt; but if the whole be Mowjil, or deferred,* the woman is not at liberty to refuse the embraces of her husband, as she has dropped her right by agreeing to make her dower Mowjil, - the same as in a case of sale, where if the price of the article sold be made deferable, the seller is not at liberty to detain the article sold on account of the price.—Aboo Yoosaf controverts the doctrine which is her advanced, and maintains that, in this case also, the wife is at liberty to refuse to admit her husband to carnal connexion, as long as he omits to make payment of the dower.

And she may also resist a repetition of the connexion, after consummation, in the like circumstances.—IT is further to be observed, that even if the husband should have committed the carnal act, or should have been in complete retiremens with the wife, yet the rule is the same; that is to say, she is still at liberty to refuse to admit him to carnal connexion, or to resist his carrying her upon a journey, until such time as she shall have received the whole of her prompt dower from him.— This is the doctrine of Haneefa. —The two disciples, on the contrary, allege that the woman, in this case, has no such liberty of refusal or resistance. It is to be remarked, however, that this difference of opinion subsists only where the original carnal act, or complete retirement, has taken place with the woman's consent; but if she have been enjoyed by force, or if she be an infant or an idiot, her right of refusal or resistance, as above, does not cease, according to the united opinion of all our doctors.

But she is, notwithstanding, entitled to her subsistence.—IT is proper to observe, that where the woman refuses to admit the husband to a repetition of the carnal act, as above stated, yet she has, nevertheless (according to Haneefa), a claim to her subsistence, as her refusal does not, in this case, proceed from any stubbornness or disobedience, since it is not exerted in resistance to a right, but rather in maintenance of one. —The two disciples hold that she is not entitled to any subsistence; and their argument on this occasion is, that the sole object of the contract has been duly delivered to the husband, either by the single carnal act, or by the single complete retirement, as aforesaid; on which account it is that her right to her whole dower is confirmed and

*That is to say, if the stipulation fixes the payment of the dower at some future period, as a year, or so forth.

established, and consequently no right of further detention of her person remains with her: as in a case of sale, where the seller having delivered the article sold to the purchaser, before receiving the price, has no further right over it.—Haneefa, on the other hand, reasons that the woman in resisting refuses and withholds a thing which she has opposed to a return, and over which she has, of course a right of detention, until such return shall have been duly made to her: and with respect to what the two disciples allege, that "her right to her whole dower is confirmed and established by the single carnal act, and so forth," it may be replied, that the whole becomes confirmed to her by a single commission of the carnal act, or a single instance of complete retirement, necessarily, because every thing beyond that is then unknown, and consequently cannot obstruct the operation of what is known; but the right of resistance still remains because the dower is opposed to the whole, the same as to the single instance, of enjoyment.

The husband obtains full authority over his wife upon payment of her dower.—When the husband has duly paid to his wife the whole of her dower, he is at liberty to carry her wherever he pleases, because the word of God says, "Ye shall cause them to reside in your own habitations." Some have alleged that the husband is not at liberty to carry his wife to another city different from her own, although he should have paid her the whole dower, because journeying and travelling may be injurious to her; but he is at liberty to carry her to the villages in the vicinity of her city, as this does not amount to travelling.

Cases of dispute between the parties concerning the amount of dower.—If a man marry a woman and they afterwards dispute concerning the rate of her dower, the declaration of the wife is to be credited to the amount of her proper dower, and that of the husband, with respect to any excess. This proceeds upon a supposition of his having had carnal connexion with her: but if he should have divorced her before consummation, his declartion alone is to be credited with respect to the half dower. This is the doctrine of Haneefa and Mohammed. Aboo Yoosaf alleges that the declaration of the husband is to be credited, whether before divorce or after, unless where it goes to establish something trifling, that is to say, something so small as is known to be short of what such a woman has a right to expect in marriage according to general usage; and this is approved. The argument of Aboo Yoosaf is that, in the case in question, the woman is plaintiff suing for an excess, and the husband defendant; and the declaration of a defendant, when made upon oath, is to be credited; wherefore that of the husband, in the present instance, must be so, unless he testify to something so small as that apparent circumstances argue against him: and the ground upon which this proceeds, is that the appreciation of the woman's person is a matter of necessity; and, therefore, so long as it is possible that anything can be decreed from the stipulated dower, the proper dower is not regarded.—The argument of Haneefa and Mohammed in this case is that, in all claims, credit must be given to the declaration of that person in whose favour apparent circumstances bear testimony, and apparent circumstances do bear testimony with one who attests the proper dower, as that is the standard object in marriage:—similar to a case where dispute arises between a dyer and the owner of a piece of cloth, concerning the charge for dying, in which case the declaration of that person will be credited in whose behalf the value of the dye or colour bears testimony.* Concerning what is here advanced, that "if the husband should divorce his wife before consummation, his declaration alone is to be credited with respect to the half dower;" it is to be observed that this (which is recorded by Mohammed in the Jama Sagheer and Mabsoot) apparently contradicts what he has advanced in the Jama Kabeer, to wit, that "the woman must, in this case, be decreed a proportionable Matat, or present"—(which is conformable to the inference of Haneefa and Mohammed, who hold that, as a present is due, on account of a contract of marriage, after divorce, the same as a proper dower, before divorce, the one must be decreed her in the former case, as well as the other in the latter);—but this apparent contradiction between the above authorities may be reconciled by adverting to the different manner in which the case is put in them respectively; thus, in the Mabsoot, the case supposes one thousand Dirms and two thousand,—that is to say, the husband declares that the dower is only one thousand Dirms, and the wife claims two thousand; now the value of a customary present does not equal the half of those sums, of course, to decree a present here would be no advantage to the plaintiff:—in the Jama Kabeer, on the other hand, the case supposes ten Dirms, and one hundred Dirms—that is to say, the husband averts the dower to be only ten Dirms and the wife claims one hundred; and her proper † present may be estimated, suppose at twenty Dirms; here therefore a proper present may with propriety be decreed to her: and what occurs upon this subject in the Jama Sagheer being destitute of any mention of the amount of the dower, that rests upon what is said in the Mabsoot.

---

*Because, as different colours bear a different price, the value of the colour used is certainly the only standard by which the amount of the charge for dying can be judged of.

†Arab, Misl: that is, proportionable to her rank and circumstances, in the same manner as the proper dower.

—As a more full exposition of the doctrine of Haneefa and Mohammed, in a case where a dispute arises between the husband and wife concerning the amount of the dower on the continuance of the marriage, let us suppose that the husband declares one thousand Dirms, for instance, and the wife claims two thousand, in which case, if the proper dower of the woman do not exceed one thousand, the declaration of the husband is to be credited; but if it be two thousand, or upward, that of the wife: and whoever of the two produces evidence in support of his or her declaration, the same is to be credited, under either of the above circumstances: and if they both produce evidence under the first of the above circumstances (that is, the woman's proper dower not exceeding one thousand Dirms), the evidence on the part of the wife is to be credited, because by such evidence her right to the excess is established;—but if, under the second (that is the woman's proper dower being two thousand or upwards), the evidence on the part of the husband is to be credited, because that goes to prove that the wife has made an abatement in her dower: but if the proper dower be one thousand five hundred Dirms, both parties must be required to make oath, after which one thousand five hundred are to be decreed to the woman. This is according to the Takhreej of Razi. Koorokhee says that the oath must be tendered to both parties in all the three circumstances, after which the proper dower must be decreed.—All this applies to a case where the husband and wife dispute with respect to the amount of the dower itself, and not with respect to its specification: but if their dispute respect the latter one of the parties asserting that a dower had been named, and the other denying, in this case the proper dower must be decreed, according to all the doctors, that being the original dower, independent of any specification.

Or between one of the parties, and the heirs of the other.—If, after the death of the husband or wife, a dispute should arise between the survivor and the heirs of the deceased, concerning the amount of the dower, the rule in this case is the same as when the dispute arises between the parties during life, because a claim to the woman's proper dower does not cease in consequence of the demise of either.

Or between the heirs of both parties.—And if both husband and wife were to die, and a dispute to arise between their heirs with respect to the amount of the dower, in this case the declaration of the husband's heirs shall be credited, although they should declare a sum less than the usual and customary dower of such a woman as the wife deceased.—This is according to Haneefa. Mohammad holds that the rule is the same here as where the dispute arises between the parties during life.—And if the heirs dispute with respect to the specification of the dower, one party insisting that a dower had been named, and the other denying, the declaration of the latter is to be credited, according to Haneefa, In short, with Haneefa, the woman's proper dower is not at all regarded after the decease of both parties, as shall be hereafter demonstrated. The two disciples on the other hand, maintain that the proper dower should in that case be decreed.

The heirs of a deceased wife may take the amount of the specified dower out of the deceased husband's property.—In case of the death of both husband and wife, it belongs to the heirs of the latter to take the dower out of the estate of the husband, where it has been specifically named: but if it should not have been specified, they cannot claim anything whatever, according to Haneefa. The two disciples maintain that woman's heirs are entitled to her dower in either case, —that is to say, to the specified dower, in the former case, or to the woman's proper dower, in the latter;—in the former, because the specified dower was a debt upon the husband, confirmed by the circumstance of his decease, and consequently must be paid out of his estate, unless it should be known that the wife had died first, in which case the husband's portion of inheritance would drop from the dower [that is, must be deducted from it] on account that he also is an heir; —and, in the latter, because the woman's proper dower had become a debt upon the husband, the same as a specified dower, and therefore does not drop in consequence of his death, any more than where only one of the parties dies.—Haneefa argues that, in this case, a supposition of the death of both husband and wife affords a conclusion that their peers and contemporaries are already cut off by death, and no longer remain, because it is most probable that they would not both die until after a length of time; and after the lapse of such a period, their peers and contemporaries no longer remaining, from whom can the Kawzee judge of or decide what the value of the woman's proper dower ought to be?—Haneefa, however, holds also that where the husband and wife both happen to die before the lapse of any length of time, so as that their peers and contemporaries are still remaining, her heirs are entitled to her proper dower.

Case of a dispute concerning articles sent by a husband to his wife.—If a husband were to send anything to his wife, and she were to denominate it a present, while he asserts that he has given it in part payment of her dower, in this case the declaration of the husband must be credited, because he is the giver, and consequently must be supposed to know his own intentions best;—moreover, it is evidently the business of the husband to liquidate the obligation which lies against him before he proceeds to perform gratuitous acts; his declaration, therefore, must be credited, except where the thing sent consists of victuals ready dressed for eating (such as roasted, or boiled, or stewed, and so forth), in which case the assertion of the woman must be credited, because it is usual and customary for husbands to send such articles as presents to their wives, not counting it in the dower; but in respect to wheat or barley, the declaration of the husband should be credited for the reason above mentioned.—Some have observed that articles, the supply of which is generally held incumbent upon the husband, such as shifts, and robes, and veils, are not to be counted in the dower, apparen circumstances arguing against this

Section.

O the dower of infidel subjects and of aliens, where none has been stipulated, or where it consists of carrion.—If a Christian man marry a Christian woman without stipulating any dower, or marking it consist of carrion,* such as may be deemed lawful by those of their profession, and have carnal connection with her, or divorce her before consummation, or die and leave her, the woman is not entitled to any dower whatever, although both parties should have embraced the faith within the interim —And the law is the same where the parties are aliens married on like terms in a foreign country. The opinion of the two disciples concerning aliens as the same as that of Aboo Haneefa; but with respect to Christians, being Zimmees (that is, subjects of the Mussulman government), they hold that the woman is entitled to her proper dower, where the husband either consummates the marriage by committing the carnal act, or dies; and that she is entitled to a present when he divorces her before consummation.—Ziffer alleges that the alien woman is entitled to her proper dower in either case (that is, in the event either of the husband's death, or of divorce), because the law does not hold it allowable to seek or desire marriage but in return for property, and this rule equally affects Infidels and Mussulmans, as marriage forms a part of the temporal law, the obligations of which extend to all alike. To this the two disciples reply, that aliens do not take upon themselves any obligation to the observance of the laws of Islam, neither are they capable of so doing, on the account of a difference of country : contrary to the case of Zimmees, who are subject to the Mussulman law in all temporal concerns, or acts to which the temporal law has reference (such as whoredom, usury, and so forth), since they are fully capable of taking upon themselves an obligation to the observance of those laws, as being native subjects of the Mussulman country. Haneefa reasons upon this, that Zimmees do not subject themselves to any of the laws of Islam, either with respect to things which are merely of a religious nature (such as fasting and prayer) or with respect to such temporal acts as, though contrary to the Mussulman law, they may hold to be legal (such as the sale of wine, or of swine's flesh), because we are commanded to leave them at liberty, in all things which may be deemed by them to be proper; according to the percepts of their own faith; wherefore, with respect to all such acts, Zimmees are the same as aliens; but from these is to be excepted whoredom, that being held universally, and by all sects, to be a criminal act; and as to usury, no such thing can have legal existence, it being excepted from all the obligations to which the person can be subject, because of a saying of the Prophet, "Observe that between us, and whosoever takes usury, no engagements exist."—The compiler of the Hedaya remarks that what Mohammed has advanced in the Jama Sagheer, "If a Christian man marry a Christian woman without any dower"—and so forth,—may be understood in two ways,—one, the absolute exception of a dower (that is especially stipulating that there shall be none); and the other, merely the omitting to mention it in the contract. Some have said, concerning this case, that where the dower is either made to consist of unlawful articles, or is not mentioned in the contract, there are two traditions; according to one, the woman is entitled to her proper dower (as maintained by the two disciples), and according to the other, nothing whatever is due; and it is from this variance on the traditions that the difference of opinion arises between Haneefa and Muhammed.

Of the dower of infidel subjects, where it consists of wine or pork—If a Zimmee marry a Zimmeea, making the dower to consist of wine or pork, and one or both should afterwards embrace to the faith, yet the woman is nevertheless entitled to the unlawful article settled upon her, although the conversion take place previous to seisin, provided the unlawful article had been identically specified; but if this be not the case, the woman, in the instance of wine, is to receive the estimated value of such wine, or in that of pork, her proper dower —This is according to Haneefa. Aboo Yoosaf alleges that the woman is entitled to her proper dower in either instance. Mohammed, on the contrary, maintains that she is in either instance entitled to the estimated value of the unlawful article specified, whatever it be.—The reasoning upon which the opinion of the two disciples proceeds in this case is that by seisin, or possession, the right in the thing possessed becomes fully established and confirmed; seisin, therefore, is similar to a contract of marriage, since, like that, it produces a right which had not before existed.; and consequently the seisin of wine or pork by a Musslima, as a dower, if illegal, the same as a contract itself including a specification of such unlawful articles, as a dower; and this, whether those articles may have been indentically specified, or only

*Meaning the flesh or carcass of any animal which dies a natural death.—The original word signifies the flesh of any fowl or quadruped not being Game) which has not been lawfully slain.

generally mentioned.—Aboo Yoosaf further remarks that as, where the time of seisin is connected with the time of the execution of the contract, if both parties were then to embrace the faith, her proper dower would become due to the woman, so in the present instance likewise:—with Mohammad on the other hand, the mention of the unlawful article, as a dower, is approved; as being held, by the sect of the parties, to be property; but yet the delivery is forbidden, on account of the parties having embraced the faith; wherefore the value becomes obligatory upon the husband, the same as where a man makes dower of a slave who dies before the delivery.—The argument of Haneefa on this subject is that a dower identically specified becomes the property of the woman on the instant of the contract of marriage being executed, for which reason it is that a woman is empowered to make what use of her dower she may think expedient, by giving it away, or transferring her property in it, either for or without a return; and the only difference that possession makes is, that the husband is thereby exonerated from responsibility with respect to it, this being simply a transition of it from the possession of the husband to that of the wife, which does not become prohibited here by the Islam of the parties, any more than in the case of a claim of restitution of wine which had been forcibly seized:—that is to say, if a person were to make a forcible seizure of wine from a Zimmee, and this Zimmee should afterwards become a Mussulman, he is nevertheless still at liberty to claim restitution of the wine thus forcibly seized; and so likewise in the present case (contrary to a case where a Zimmee purchases wine or a hog, and afterwards becomes a Mussulman before he has taken possession of his purchase: for in this case it is unlawful for him to take possession, and the bargain becomes void, because, in sale, a right of transaction with respect to the property sold does not take place until after seisin is made of it by the purchaser, which becomes forbidden by his subsequent Islam):—but where the unlawful article is not identically specified, nothing but actual possession can establish a property in it, and this becoming prohibited by the subsequent Islam of the party, and being thereby precluded, the price or value of the pork would not be due to the woman, because the receipt of that is the same as of the property itself,—hog's flesh being of the class of things denominated Zooatal-Keem, whereas wine is not of this nature, being of the class of Zooatal-Imsal, for which reason, if the husband were to offer the value before Islam, the wife would be compelled to accept of that of the pork, but not of that of the wine.—It is to be remarked that if the husband, in the present instance, were to divorce his wife before consummation, the same difference of opinion exists among our doctors; those who (as above) determine for a proper dower, decreeing her a present; and those who make the value of the article obligatory upon the husband, decreeing her an half of such value.

CHAPTER IV.

OF THE MARRIAGE OF SLAVES.

Slaves cannot marry without the consent of their proprietor.—THE marriage of a male or a female slave is not lawful without the master's consent. Malik has said that the marriage of a male slave is valid independent of the consent of his master, because he is competent to pronounce divorce, and is therefore equal to the contracting of marriage. The arguments of our doctors on this subject are twofold:—FIRST, a precept of the Prophet says, "Whatever slave marries without his owner's consent is an adulterer;"—SECONDLY, marriage, with respect either to male or female slaves, is a blemish,* on which account they are not at liberty to enter into such a contract without the approbation of their owners.

Nor Mokatibs.—NEITHER is it lawful for a Mokatib to enter into a contract of marriage without his owner's consent; because a slave of this description, although he be, by virtue of his contract of Kitabat, rendered free with respect to acquistion, of necessity, he remains with respect to matrimony, subject to the laws of bondage. And, for the same reason, it is not lawful for a Mokatib to contract his own male slave in marriage without the consent of his owner.

Although such may contract their own female slaves in marriage nor Mokatibas, although they have the same privilege.—BUT he may lawfully contract his female slave, as hence arises an acquisition, in her dower.—In like manner, it is not lawful for a Mokatiba to marry without her owner's consent; but she may lawfully cantract her female slave in marriage, as hence arises an acquisition to her as above. Neither is it lawful for a Modabbir or Am-Walid to marry without their owner's consent, becasue his authority with respect to them still exists.

A slave may be sold for the discharge of his wife's dower.—IF a slave marry with his master's consent, the dower (to the woman whom he marries) is a debt upon his person, for the payment of which he may be sold, because the debt has become obligatory upon the slave on account of the existence of its cause (namely, marriage, proceeding from a competent person), and the obligation of the debt exends to the master also, he having consented thereto, and accordingly devolves upon him, in order that the creditor may be protected from injury, as in the case of debts contracted by a slave in mercantile dealing.

And a Modabbir or Mokatib are to discharge it by labour.—A MODABBIR or Mokatib (in case of marriage) must discharge the

*As tending to depreciate their value.

dower by labour, as not being liable to be sold, because the property in them is not capable of being transferred from one to another; this debt of the dower, therefore; is to be discharged by their acquisitions, so that the wife may not be subject to loss; but their persons are not liable to be attached for payment.

How far a master's desiring his slave to divorce his wife, is an argument of his assent to the slave's marriage.—IF a slave marry without his owner's consent, and the latter afterwards should say to him, "divorce" [your wife] or "put her away," his [the [owner's] assent to the marriage is not implied, because such a mode of address bears the construction of obstructing or resisting execution of the contract, as the terms divorce and separation apply to that, as well as to the dissolution of the contract of marriage already executed it is therefore to be thus construed, either because this is suitable to the state of disobedient and refractory slave, or because the prevention of a marriage is an act of less magnitude than the assenting to it. But if the owner were to say to his slave, "repudiate her by a divorce reversible," this implies his assent to the marriage, because a reversible divorce is not supposed but in a case of marriage [already executed], wherefore assent to the marriage, is hereby signified.

Obligation of the dower in a case of invalid marriage, contracted by a slave at the desire of his owner.—IF a person desire his slave to marry such a female slave, and he accordingly wed her by an invalid marriage,* and have carnal connexion with her, Haneefa holds that the slave shall be sold for the discharge of her dower. The two disciples, on the contrary, maintain that the dower shall be exacted of him (the slave) upon his becoming free.—The foundation of this difference of opinion is that, with Haneefa, assent applies equally to a legal and to an invalid marriage, and consequently the debt [of the dower] is upon the owner; but with the two disciples, assent applies to a valid and regular marriage only, wherefore the debt is not upon the owner (whence it is that it may be required of the slave on his becoming free at any subsequent period), for they argue that the intent of marriage is to guard against incontinence, and that end is obtained by regular, but not by invalid marriages, wherefore if a person were to make a vow that he will not marry, his vow applies solely to regular marriage: contrary to a case of sale; that is to say, if a person were to empower another in sale, such power extends both to regular and to invalid sale, a variety of privileges being therein involved, such as the right of emancipation, and so forth. Aboo Haneefa, on the other hand, argues that the word "marry" [in the owner's desire expressed to his slave] is general, and is therefore to be considered as having a general application, the same as sale; and there are a variety of points involved in an irregular, marriage, as well as in sale, such as genealogy [of children born in such, marriage], and the obligations to the payment of dower, and to the observance of Edit; and with respect to the instance of a vow, as produced by the two disciples, it is not admitted as applicable by Haneefa.

Case of an indebted Mazoon, contracted in marriage by his owner.—IF a man contract his Mazoon, or privileged slave, who is a debtor, to any woman in marriage, it is lawful; and the wife [in virtue of her right to her dower] becomes a joint creditor with the others; that is to say, the slave is to be sold for the discharge of all debts, and the price arising from the sale is to be divided between his wife and the other creditors, in proportion to their respective claims. The compiler of the Hedaya observes that this rule holds only where the marriage has been effected upon a Mihr Misl, or less; but if the dower exceed the Misl proportion, the other creditors are, in that case on an equality with the wife, so far as the amount of her Mihr Misl, or proper dower, and the payment of the excess must be postponed till after the discharge of the debt to the creditors; the ground of which is, that the owner's authority over his slave, with respect to matrimony, is founded on his having the property of his person (as shall be hereafter explained), and that right of property still remaining, the marriage of the slave is completely legal and valid.

OBJECTION.—In consequence of the marriage the right of the creditors is rendered null both by design, and in effect; wherefore it would be requisite that, in discharging the debts of the Mazoon, those due to the first creditors ought to be first paid; whereas it is otherwise in this case, for they are all put on an equality.

REPLY.—The right of the creditors is not designedly rendered null by the marriage: but the marriage being held valid, the debt of dower is due in consequence of the existence of its cause; and there is nothing to invalidate its existence; the dower, therefore, is the same as a debt of damage;—that is to say, where a Mazoon slave, being already in debt, destroys or wastes the property of a stranger, the latter comes in as a joint creditor; and the slave is as a sick debtor; that is to say, if a sick person, being in debt, marry a woman, she comes in as a joint creditor with the others, to the amount of her proper dower, and so in this case likewise.

A master may withhold permission from his female slave to dwell in the house of her husband.—IF a master contract his female slave in marriage to another man; he is not under any obligation to send her to the house of her husband, she still remaining attached in service to her master; and the husband shall be desired to visit his wife at oppor-

*That is, under such circumstances of affinity, &c., as invalidates the marriage.

tune seasons, at her masters house, because his right to her service still remains in virtue of his property in her; and if he were under any obligation to send her to the house of her husband, his right would be rendered null.

And if he so permit, her husband must support her, but not otherwise.—And if the master should give permission to his female slave to dwell in the house of her busband, her subsistence and lodging are incumbent upon the husband; but if he should not permit this, nothing whatever is incumbent, because subsistence is the recompense for the matrimonial restraint; and if she live in the house of her husband, she is under this restraint, but not otherwise. And if the master thus permit her to dwell with her husband, still he is at liberty, notwithstanding, to call for and require her legal service at any subsequent period, because his right of usufruct still continues, in virtue of his property in her; and this right is not relinquished by such permission any more than by her marriage.

The compiler of the Hedaya remarks that Imam Mohammed has said, "A master contracting his male or female slave in marriage is lawful," without making any mention of the consent of the slave to such marriage, which shows that this consent is not a condition; and such is the opinion of our doctors, who hold that a master is empowered to contract his slaves in marriage by compulsion; that is to say, that the marriage of such, where it is contracted by the master, holds good independent of their consent. According to Shafei, a master is also empowered to contract his male slave in marriage by compulsion; and there is also an opinion of Haneefa recorded to this effect: this doctrine proceeds upon the principle that marriage is a natural privilege of man, and a slave is a possession of his owner by the laws of property, but not by the laws of nature; wherefore the master is not endowed with any absolute authority with respect to his marriage, contrary to the case of a female slave, whose owner, as being entitled to the carnal use of her person, is at liberty to transfer the same to any other. The argument of our doctors on this subject is that a master, in causing his slave to marry, acts with a view to the preservation of his property, because, by marrying, the slave is withheld from the commission of whoredom which is a cause of destruction or damage;* the master, therefore, is fully empowered with respect to the marriage of his male slaves, the same as of his females; but he is not thus empowered with respect to his Mokatib, or Mokatiba, because these are, as to privileges the same as free persons, and their consent is therefore a condition; for if it were otherwise, their privileges and powers of action would be totally annulled.

An owner slaying his female slave before consummation has no claim to her dower.—If a man marry his female slave to another person, and afterwards put her to death, before her husband has had carnal connexion with her, no part of the dower whatever is, in this case, due from the husband, according to Haneefa. The two disciples hold that, in this case, the dower is due from the husband, in the same manner as it would be if the female slave had died a natural death; and the foundation of their opinion is that a person who is slain dies by his own fate, death implying merely the termination of life, and life being terminated by the act of killing. The case, therefore, is here the same as if the female slave had been slain by a stranger; that is to say; if the female slave had been slain by a stranger, her dower would remain due from the husband, and so also in the present case. The argument of Haneefa is, that the owner of the slave, who, as being her Mawla, claims the consideration, has by his act prevented the delivery of the return (to wit, the person of woman) and consequently his right to the consideration is extinguished, in the same manner as when a free woman apostatizes; that is to say, if a free woman apostatize from the faith before she has admitted her husband to the carnal embrace, no dower whatever is due to her, she [by her act of apostasy] having prevented the delivery of the return; and so likewise in the present instance. With respect to what is advanced by the two disciples, that "a person who is slain dies by his own fate," it may be answered, that although this be admitted, yet it holds with respect to a future state only, and not with respect to this world, murder, according to worldly institutes, being in the eye of the law considered as an act of destruction, inducing retaliation, fine, and so forth; and it is therefore to be regarded as an act of destruction with respect to the dower, that also being a temporal institution.

The dower of a free woman is due, although she kill herself before consummation.—If a free woman kill herself before she has admitted her husband to carnal connexion, her dower is nevertheless due from him, contrary to the opinion of Ziffer, who conceives an analogy between this case and that of a woman apostatizing before carnal connexion, or of a master slaying his female slave; for he argues that no dower whatever is here due from the husband, as the wife to whom the consideration belongs, has by her act of suicide, prevented the delivery of the return. The arguments of our doctors are that, in worldly institutes, no regard is paid to the offence committed by a man upon his own person, wherefore suicide is to be held as dying a natural death, contrary to the case of a man killing his female slave, that being an act to which worldly institutes have regard, and, as such, subjecting the perpetrator of the murder to the performance of acts of expiation.

*On account of the punishment which attends it.

IF a man marry the female slave of another and be desirous of committing the act of Azil with her (*i.e.* emissio seminis in ano, vel inter Mamillas), this shall depend upon her master's permission, according to Haneefa ; and such also is the Zahir Rawayet. According to the two disciples, the permission to this act rests with the slave, because [as being the man's wife] carnal connexion is her right ; but by Azil that carnal connexion which is her right is frustrated. Her consent, therefore, is a requisite condition to the legality of the act, the same as that of a free woman, contrary in the case of a female slave, who is the property af the person having such connexion with her,* because carnal connexion is not her right (whence it is that she is not entitled to claim the carnal act of her master or owner), and consequently her consent is not a condition. The principle upon which the Zahir Rawayet proceeds in this case is, that the act of Azil defeats the intention of marriage, which is the production of children, and this is a right of the master ;† whence it is that his consent is a condition, and not that of the slave. And herein appears a distinction between the state of a free woman and that of a slave [in marriage].

A female slave, upon obtaining her freedom, has a right to annul the marriage contract.—IF a female slave marry with her owner's consent,‡ and afterwards become free, she is then at liberty either to break off the marriage or to continue it, whether her husband be a slave of a freeman, because, upon Barreera (who was a Mokatiba of Aysha) becoming free, the Prophet said to her, "You are now mistress of your own person, and therefore at your own disposal," which tradition evinces that she is at liberty as above, whether her husband be a slave or a freeman, since the cause of her right of opinion, as there mentioned (that is ,her being mistress of her own person), exists equally in either case. Shafei maintains that she has no such right of option where her husband is a freeman. The tradition above quoted, however, is in proof against him ; moreover, the power of the husband with respect to his wife is greater after her emancipation, that it was before, because before she was free he had power to pronounce only a double sentence of divorce, whereas afterwards he is authorized to pronounce three divorces, on which account she is justly empowered to set aside the contract of marriage; so as that her husband may not obtain any additional authority with respect to her in consequence of her emancipation. And the rule is the same where a Mukatiba marries with her owner's consent, and afterwards becomes free. Ziffer says that a Mokatiba has no right of option, because the contract of marriage proceded by, and was excuted with, her especial consent, and she receives the dower,* and such being the case, she can have no subsequent right of option, contrary to the case of an absolute slave, whose consent in marriage is not regarded.—The argument of our doctors is that the reason for her right of option (to wit, the accession, to the husband, of an additional authority with respect to her) appears in the case of a Mokatiba, the same as in that of an absolute slave, for before freedom the term of her Edit was only two menstruations, and she was subject to no more than a duplicate sentence of divorce ; whereas, in her state of freedom, her Edit includes three menstruations, and she is subject to three divorces.

But not otherwise.—IF a female slave marry without her owner's consent, and be afterwards made free, her marriage then becomes legal and valid, because, being of sound mind and mature age, she is competent to the declaration and acceptance ; moreover, the illegality of the marriage was on account only of the owner's right, which being done away, it remains lawful ; and the woman has not any option, as in the former case, because the marriage is not in this case valid until after emancipation, which consequently occasions no accession of power to the husband ; and hence the case is the same as if she were to bestow herself in marriage after emancipation.

Case of a man marrying a female slave without her owner's consent.—IF a man marry a female slave, without her owner's concurrence, on a dower of a thousand Dirms, her proper dower being one hundred Dirms only, and he have carnal connexion with her, and her owner afterwards emancipate her, the specified dower goes to him [the owner], because the husband has here obtained possession of an article which was the property of the owner, who is therefore entitled to the return ; but if the marriage be not consummated until after emancipation, the specified dower goes to the woman, because in this case the husband appears to have obtained possession of an article which was her property, and she of course is entitled to the return, since tne marriage, in consequence of her emancipation, takes effect from the period of the contract ; and hence the specification of the dower is valid, and that which was specified is incumbent ; and accordingly, no other dower is due on account of carnal connexion previous to the efficiency of the marriage, ...here that has been suspended [upon the event of the owner's approbation, or the slave's freedom], because the marriage, deriving its legaltiy

*As where a master has connexion with his female slave in virtue of propriety.

†Because he has a propriety in the children born of his slave.

‡That is, at his instigation.

*In opposition to the case of an absolute slave, whose dower is received by her Mawala, or proprietor, and by him appropriated.

from the original contract, its efficiency is considered as existing from the instant the marriage takes place; nothing, therefore, but one dower can be due.

Case of a father cohabiting with the slave of his son.—IF a father enjoy the female slave of his son, and she produce a child, and he [the father] claim it, the slave becomes his Am-Walid, and he is answerable to his son for her value; but he is not so for her dower, because a father being at liberty to possess himself of the property of his son, whenever that may be requisite to his own preservation, it follows that he may possess himself of her son's slave, where he requires her for the preservation of his progeny, since he thereby provides for his own continuance, he being virtually continued in his offspring; but the preservation of his progeny being a matter of less immediate importance than that of his life, he must pay a price in exchange for the slave, whereas he might take his son's victuals without paying any price.—And here the father's property in the slave is established antecedently do his claim of the child, possession being a condition essential to such claim, which does not hold good unless he be either fully possessed of her in all respects, or at least have a right of possession in her; and neither of these exist in him (insomuch that he might legally marry her);—it is therefore requiste that his property in her be considered as existing a priori; and this being admitted, the father appears to have had carnal connexion with his own slave, and consequently is not subject to the payment of an Akir.—Ziffer and Shafei maintains that the slave's dower is a debt upon the father; because they hold that his property in her is a consequence of his Isteelad, or claim of the child,—that is, that his right of possession is thereby established the same as in a partnership slave; now the effect of a thing, is not found until after that thing has taken place; and such being the case, as the carnal connexion appears to have been had, in the first instance, with the property of another, a dower is due.

Case of a son contracting his female slave in marriage to his father.—IF a man marry his female slave to his father, and she produce a child, she does not become Am-Walid to the father, neither is her price a debt against him, because he is answerable for her dower; and the child born of her is free, such a marriage being approved by our doctors.—This is contrary to the doctrine of Shafei, according to whom a marriage of this kind is illegal. The argument of our doctors is, that the slave is not at all the property of the father, because, the son being her proprietor in every respect, it is impossible that the father should be so in any view; the son, moreover, is endowed with privileges [in regard to her] which do not appertain to his father, such as selling or bestowing her in marriage or emancipating her, which evinces that the father is not in any respect her proprietor, although, in a case where he has carnal connexion with her, punishment drops, on account of erroneous possession; and his marriage with her being admitted as legal, the conservation of his deed is effected by means of marriage, [not by means of Isteelad], so that his property in her is no way established [by the circumstance of her bearing a child to him], and consequently she does not become his Am-Walid.—And here the father is not answerable for the value either of her or of her child, as he does not become proprietor of either; but he owes her dower, he having taken that upon him by his marriage; and the child is free, because his owner would otherwise be his brother; and he is virtually emancipated of course.

The marriage of a free woman with a slave is annulled by her procuring his emancipation.—IF a free woman, being the wife of a slave, should say to the proprietor of such slave, "Emancipate him on my behalf for a thousand Dirms," and he accordingly emancipates him, the marriage is annulled.—Ziffer maintains that it is not annulled.—Our doctors argue, on this occasion, that the slave obtains his freedom from the woman, whence it is that the right of Willa rests with her, and also, that if she were under obligation to perform an expiatory act, and intend her husband's release to stand as such, her expiation is thereby fulfilled.—With Ziffer the emancipation is held to proceed from the owner, because the woman has required him to emancipate the slave "on her behalf," which is absurd, since manumission connot take effect upon a slave who is not the property of the emancipator; consequently, her requisition being improper, emancipation is to be regarded as proceeding solely from the owner.—Our doctors, on the other hand, say, that there is one mode in which the requisition of the woman may be rendered proper, viz. by considering her property in the slave to have existence previous to emancipation, as an essential (for her right of possession is a condition of the validity of emancipation on her behalf), and such being the case, her requisition "emancipate him, &c" bears the construction of her desiring the owner first to transfer to her his property in the slave for such a consideration, and then to emancipate him "from her," and the reply of the owner, "I have emancipated him," is as if he were to say that he had transferred him, and then set him free "from her;" and upon the woman's property in him being established, it necessarily follows that the marriage is annulled, the marriage of a free woman with her slave being illegal, since possession by right of property is irreconcilable with possession by matrimony.—But if the woman were to say to the owner of her husband, "emancipate him from me," without mentioning any consideration, in this case the marriage is not annulled, and the Willa rests with the master. This is according to Haneefa and Mohammad.—Aboo Yoosaf says that this and the preceding case are the same, and that the marriage is here likewise annulled, because in this instance also the transfer must be supposed to have previously taken place (though without any return), in order that the act may be lawful.

Objection.—Transfer of property, without a return, amounts to gift, and that is not valid without seisin; now here seisin does not appear; consequently how can the transfer be valid?

Reply —Seisin is not in this case regarded, any more than in Zihar; thus, if the expiation of Zihar were in-cumbent upon any person and he were to desire another to give the victuals,* as from him, and the other do accordingly, the gift is understood independent of seisin; and so here likewise.—The argument of Haneefa and Mohammed is that seisin being declared, in the ordinances of the Prophet, to be a condition of gift, cannot be dispenesed with; neither can it be established merely by supposing or assuming it, as an essential, because seisin is a sensible act,—contrary to sale, which is a legal transacation; and in the case of expiation, as cited by Aboo Yoosaf, the poor stand as the deputies of the expiator, in the seisin of the victuals, but the slave(in the case here treated of) cannot stand as the wife's deputy, because nothing is received by him, so as to constitute him her deputy in seisin.

CHAPTER V.

OF THE MARRIAGE OF INFIDELS.

The marriage of an Infidel couple is not dissolved by their jointly embracing the faith.—If an Infidel man and woman marry without witnesses, or whilst the woman is in her Edit from a former Infidel husband, and this be no objection by the rule of their own sect, and they afterwards embrace the faith together, their marriage remains valid.—This is according to Haneefa.—Ziffer maintains the marriage to be invalid in either case—(that is to say, whether it be entered into without witnesses or during the woman's Edit), but that Infidels are not liable to be called to an account until they embrace Islam, or until they appear to the law,—that is to say, carry the matter before the judge.—The two disciples concide with Haneefa in the first case [the defect of witnesses], but agree with Ziffer in the last [the Edit]. The argtment of Ziffer is that the word of the sacred writings extends to all men alike, and consequently to Infidels; but the parties, as being Zimmees, are not liable to molestation; but this exemption from molestation is an effect of indulgence, and does not proceed from any idea of the marriage being legal and of course, where it becomes a subject of litigation, or the parties become Mussulmans separation must ensue, the illegality of their marriage still remaining.—The arguments of the two disciples are that the illegality of Poliandry is universally admitted amongst Mussulmans, and that Infidel subjects have engaged to follow the temporal law in all such points as are universally admitted; but with respect to the illegality of marriage without witnesses there subsists a difference of opinion among the Mussulmans; and Infidels have engaged only to follow such temporal law of Islam as are universally admitted, and not such as are disputed; hence, in the case of Polianday a separation becomes necessary, but not in the case of marriage without witnesses. Haneefa argues that the marriage is not rendered illegal by the injunctions of the law, because those injunctions are not addressed to Infidels; neither does any reason exist why the Edit should be obligatory on account of the right of a husband who has no faith in the necessity of it; contrary to a case where the Infidel woman is the wife of a Mussulman, because he has faith in the necessity of Edit: and therefore the illegality of her marriage [with the Infidel] should in this case be established, on account of his [the Mussulman's] right; and the marriage being valid abinitio, on account of no illegality appearing therein, continues to exist as such, since testimony is not a condition with respect to the period of its existence: and the circumstances of appeal to the law or of conversion to the faith, take place during the existence of the marriage: neither does the circumstance of the Edit forbid the continuance of the marriage; as when a man (for instance) has carnal connexion, erroneously, with the wife of another, in which case an Edit is incumbent upon the woman, but the marriage continues to hold good.

Unless it be a marriage within the prohibited degrees—If a Majoosee wed his mother or his daughter, and they afterwards become Mussulmans, they are to be separated. This holds with the two disciples, because a marriage within the prohibited degree is universally admitted to be null, on which account the rule extends to Infidels as well as Mussulmans (as before mentioned, from them, in the case of Edit), and the parties, upon their conversion, being necessarily liable to molestation on account of such marriage, it follows that a separation must take place upon that event; and it holds also with Haneefa, because, although such marriage be deemed lawful in the Rawayet Saheeh, yet the circumstance of the wife being within the prohibited degrees forbids the continuance of it after conversion, on which account separation is to take place: contrary to the circumstance of Edit, which (according to Haneefa) does not forbid the continuance of the marriage.

But if one of them only be converted, a separation takes place.—If only one of the parties be converted to the faith, a separa-

* Book of Divorce, Chap. IX.

tion follows; but if one only appeal, Haneefa holds that separation does not take place: contrary to the opinion of the two doctors, according to whom separation takes place in this case also.—The reason, with Haneefa, for making this distinction between these two cases is, that the right of one party is not invalidated by the appeal of the other, as the faith of the one is not altered by the appeal of the other: but where one of the parties becomes a Mussulman, although the faith of the other be not altered by that event, yet the faith of an Infidel is not sufficient to controvert or oppose the Islam of a Mussulman, as Islam is the subjector and cannot be subjected.—But where both the parties enter into a litigation, it is universally agreed that separation takes place, because this mutual litigation amounts to both authorizing any third person to effect a separation between them, which if they were to do, the separation so effected would be legal.

Apostates are incapacitated from marrying.—IT is not lawful that an appostate marry any woman, whether she be a believer, an Infidel, or an apostate, because an apostate is liable to be put to death; moreover, his three days of grace are granted in order that he may reflect upon the errors which occasion his apostacy; and as marriage would interfere with such reflection, the law does not permit it to him.

In like manner, it is not lawful that a female apostate marry any man, whether Mussulman or Infidel, because she is imprisoned for the purpose of reflection (as above), and her attention to her husband would interfere therewith; moreover, this circumstance of her imprisonment necessarily prevents the matrimonial intercourse;—now marriage is lawful, not in respect to itself, but to its ends, and consequently, where these are defeated, it cannot be deemed in any respect legal.

If either the father or mother be Mussulman, their children are Mussulmans.—WHENEVER either the husband or the wife is a Mussulman, their children are to be educated in the Mussulman faith. And if either one or other [of an Infidel couple] become a Mussulman, and they have infant children, those are to be considered as Mussulmans in virtue of the Islam of one of their parents, because this is tenderness to the children.

Or where one is of a superior order of Infidels, and the other of an inferior, their children are of the superior order.—IF one of a married couple be a Kitabee, and the other a Majoosee, their children are to be regarded as Kitabees, because, in this also there is a degree of tenderness with respect to the children, as a Majoosee is worse than a Kitabee. This is contrary to the doctrine of Shafei, who holds the infidelity of a Majoosee, and that of a Kitabee, to be equal: but with our doctors a Kitabee is held superior to a Majoosee.

Upon the conversion of one of the parties, the magistrate is to require the other to embrace the faith, and must separate them, in case of recusancy.—WHEN the wife becomes a convert to the faith and her husband is an Infidel, the magistrate is to call upon the husband to embrace the faith also; if he accede, the woman continues his wife; but if he refuse, the magistrate must separate them; and this separation, with Haneefa and Mohammed, is a divorce.—In like manner, if the husband become a Mussulman and his wife be a Majoosee, the magistrate is to call upon her to embrace the faith also; if she accede, she remains his wife; but if she refuse, the magistrate must separate them; but this separation is not divorce.—Aboo Yoosaf has said that the separation is not divorce in either case.—What is here advanced of the magistrate calling upon the party to embrace the faith, is an opinion of our doctors,—Shafei maintains that the magistrate is not to make any such requisition because this is molestation and we have engaged not to molest Zimmees, as they have entered into a contract of subjection to us.

OBJECTION.—It would hence appear that the matrimonial right of possession should not terminate in this case; whereas Shafei also holds that it is terminated.

REPLY.—The matrimonial intercourse is not admissible between a Mussulman and an Infidel; for which reason it is that the matrimonial right of possession is terminated on the instant of conversion, where either party embraces the faith, before consummation, because in this case the right has not been confirmed; but, on the other hand, if conversion take place after consummation, the termination is delayed until the end of three menstruations, because the right has on this occasion been confimed; as holds in divorce.—The argument of our doctors is, that, upon either party embracing the faith, the ends of marriage are defeated, on account of difference of religion; hence it is absolutely necessary that recourse be had to some means by which a separation may be effected;—now Islam, as an act of piety, is incapable of being rendered a cause of separation; the Infidel party is therefore to be called upon to embrace the faith, in order that the ends of marriage may be answered by conversion, or that a cause of separation may be established in case of refusal. The reason upon which Aboo Yoosaf founds his opinion is that the occasion of separation, to wit, refusing the faith, may proceed from either the man or the woman; a separation, therefore, on account of such refusal, is not divorce, any more than on account of a right of property;—that is to say, if, of husband and wife, either become the owner of the other, a separation ensues; but this separation is not divorce; and so also in the present case.—In reply to this, Haneefa and Mohammed argue that the husband, when he refuses the faith, wilfully withholds the customary benevolence from his wife, where he has it still in his power to continue it to her, by becoming a Mussulman; and such being the case, the magistrate acts merely as his substitute, in effecting the separation; in the same manner as where a husband is impotent, or deprived of his penis; but a woman is not empowered to divorce, for which reason the magistrate cannot be regarded as her substitute in effecting the sparation when she has refused the faith.

It is to be observed, that where the separation takes place on account of the woman's refusal of the faith, she is still entitled to her dower, provided her husband has consummated the marriage, as in this case her right has been confirmed by the carnal act; but if the marriage should not have been consummated she cannot, receive any dower, because the separation has proceeded from her, and her right to the dower is not confirmed; thus the case here is the same as where a woman apostatizes or admits the son of her husband to carnal connexion.

And if the conversion of either happen in a foreign country, separation takes place upon the lapse of the woman's term of probation. —If the wife embrace the faith in a foreign country, and her husband be an Infidel,—or, if a foreigner there becomes Mussulman, and his wife be a Majooseea,—the separation between them does not take place until the lapse of three terms of the wife's courses, when she becomes completely repudiated.—The reason of this is, that Islam cannot be made an occasion of separation (as has been before observed): and requiring the other party to embrace the faith is impracticable, as the authority of the magistrate does not extend to a foreign land, nor is it acknowledged there; yet separation is indispensable for the removal of evil; the condition, therefore, of separation (to wit, the lapse of three terms of the woman's courses), must stand in the place of separation effected by the magistrate; and in this rule no distinction is made between a woman enjoyed, and one unenjoyed.—Shafei makes a distinction, on this occasion, between a woman enjoyed and one unenjoyed, in the same manner as he distinguishes between them when they reside in a Mussulman territory, and one of them embraces the faith; as has been before explained.

If the wife be an alien, she is not to observe an Edit, from separation, in csnsequence of her husband's conversion.—When a separation takes place between husband and wife, in consequence of the conversion of the former, and the latter is an alien, she is not subject to any observance of Edit, according to all the doctors.—Haneefa holds the rule to be the same, where the woman becomes a convert and her husband is an alien; that is, that the woman, in this case also, is not subject to any observance of Edit but the two disciples maintain that she must here observe an Edit the same as would be incumbent upon her if she were to come into the Mussulman territory; as shall be hereafter demonstrated.

The conversion of the husband of a Kitabeea does not occasion separation.—If the husband of a Kitabeea become a Mussulman, their marriage still endures, because the marriage of a Mussulman with a Kitabeea being legal ab initio, its continuance is so a fortiori.

Case of a convert removing from a foreign land into a Mussulman territory.—If either husband or wife become a convert to the faith in a foreign country, and afterwards remove thence into the Mussulman territory, a separation takes place between them:—this is contradicted by Shafei:—but if either party be brought, as a captive, out of the foreign country, separation takes place between them, according to all the doctors; if, however, both the parties be brought captives together we hold that there is no separation; whereas Shafei says that separation takes place.—Hence it may be collected that the circumstance of the parties residing apart in different countries is held to be a cause of separation by our doctors, but not that of their capture; and that Shafei maintains the reverse of this opinion.—The argument of the latter is that separation of country is a cause of termination of authority, but has no effect in occasioning an absolute separation in this case, any more than where an alien resides under protection in a Mussulman territory, whilst his wife remains in her own country; or where a Mussulman goes under protection into a foreign land, leaving his wife in the Mussulman territory; in neither of which cases would separation take place, and so in this instance likewise:—capture, on the other hand, leads to this, that the captive is the sole and exclusive property of the captor, which cannot be established without a termination of the former's marriage, as it is on the same principle that a captive stands virtually released from all his debts.—Our doctors, in support of their opinion, argue that by operation of country all matrimonial intercourse between the parties, whethe actual or consequential, is entirely broker off, and thus this separation resembles illengality by affinity; capture, on the otheh hand, occasions property in the person, whica does not forbid marriage at first, for if man contract his slave in marriage, it is lawful; and so, also, it does not forbid the continuance of the marriage; as in the case of purchase, where if a person should perchas a female slave, the wife of another, the mar riage does not, on that account, become null, —And in reply to what Shafei has advanced with respect to capture,—it is admitted that this makes the captive the exclusive property of the captor, in respect to substance, but the object of marriage (to wit, the use of the woman's person), is not substance, and therefore capture does not annul the marriage: moreover, between a protected foreigner and his wife separation of abode does not virtually take place, as his ultimate intention is to reurn home, whence he may be regarded, virtually, as in a foreign country, during his residence in the Mussulman territory.

A woman, retiring from a foreign to a Mussulman country, is at liberty to marry.—If a woman come out of a foreign country into the Mussulman territory, and there become either a Zimmee, or a convert to the faith, it is lawful for her to marry;* and Haneefa holds that she is not under any obligation to observe an Edit. The two disciples say that she must observe an Edit, because separation takes place upon her entering the Mussulman territory and she then becomes subject to the Mussulman laws. The argument of Haneefa is that the Edit is a consequence of an antecedent marriage, enjoined on account of the importance of the matrimonial tie; but this tie is of no importance whatever with respect to foreigners, for which reason it is that Edit is not enjoined upon a woman who is a captive.

But if pregnant, she must wait until her delivery.—If the woman in question be pregnant, she must not marry until she be delivered. This is the doctrine of the Zahir Zawayet. It is recorded from Haneefa that her marriage is approved; but her husband must not have carnal connexion with her until after her delivery, as is the rule with women pregnant by fornication. The ground of the former opinion is that the parentage of the fœtus is ascertained [as from some alien] and therefore the former matrimonial tie is regarded, with respect to the establishment of parentage, and must consequently be so, with respect to forbidding her marriage likewise, on a principle of caution.

In a case of apostacy separation takes place without divorce.—If either husband or wife apostatize from the faith, a separation takes place without divorce, according to Haneefa and Aboo Yoosaf. Mohammed alleges that if the apostacy be on the part of the husband, the separation is a divorce, because he conceives an analogy between this case and that of the husband refusing the faith; for as, in the latter instance, he by his refusal appears wilfully to withhold the customary benevolsence from his wife, where he has it still in his power to continue it to her, so likewise in the former, by his apostacy. Aboo Yoosaf holds here to his opinion as before recited in the case of refusal. Haneefa makes a distinction between refusal of the faith and apostacy from it; and his reason for this distinction is that apostacy annuls marriage, because the blood of an apostate no longer remains under the protection of the law, and his life is Mobah [free to any one to take; now divorce is used for the purpose of dissolving a marriage which actually exists; and hence apostacy cannot possibly be considered as divorce: contrary to the case of refusal of the faith, because it is on account of the ends of matrimony being thereby defeated that separation is enjoined, in that instance, as has been already said; and for this reason it is that the separation is there suspended upon a decree of the magistrate, whereas in apostacy it takes place without any such decree. It is to be observed, however, that if the apostacy be on the part of the husband, his wife is entitled to her whole dower where he has had carnal connexion with her or to half her dower in defect of this; and where the apostacy is on the part of the wife, she is in like manner entitled to her whole dower, if her husband has had carnal connexion with her; but if not, she has no claim whatever either to dower or alimony, because the separation is in this case a consequence of her own act.

But if a man and wife apostatize together, their marriage still continues.—If the husband and wife should both apostatize together, and afterwards return to the faith at the same time, their marriage is by a favourable construction of the law, permitted to endure. Ziffer says that it is annulled, because the apostacy of any one of them forbids the duration of it, and where that appears in both, it is found in one of them: but our doctors, in support of their opinion, cite an instance recorded to have happend in the time of the blessed companions [of the Prophet], when the tribe of Binney Haneefa, after having apostatized, returned to the faith, and the companions did not direct them to renew their marriage; and their apostacies were all considered as having taken place at the same time, because of the uncertainty of the dates. But if after their joint apostacy, either the husband or wife were singly to reurn to the faith, their marriage is dissolved, because here one of them persists in apostacy, and that forbids the continuance of marriage, the same as it does the matrimonial engagement at first.

CHAPTER VI.

OF KISSM OR PARTITION.*

A man must cohabit equally with all his wives.—If a man have two or more wives, being all free women, it is incumbent upon him to make an equal partition of his cohabitation among them, whether he may have married them as virgins or as Siyeebas, or whether some of them be of the former description, and others of the latter; because the Prophet has said, "The man who hath two wives, and who, in partiton, inclines particularly to ONE of them, shall in

*Although she be already married in the foreign country.

*By Kissm is understood that equal partition of cohabitation which a husband is required, by aw, to make among his wives, where he has a plurality of them.

the day of judgment incline to one side" (that is to say, shall be paralytic); and it is recorded by Aysha that he made such equal partition of cohabitation among his wives,—saying, "O God, I thus make an equal partition as to what is in my power: do not therefore bring me to account for that which is not in my power" (by which he means the affections, these not being optional).

The wife of a prior marriage, and a new wife, are alike in this point, because the tradition above cited is general in its application, and also, because partition is one of the rights of marriage, and in these both descriptions of wives are equal.

But the mode of partition is left to himself.—It is left to the husband to determine the measure of partition; that is to say, if he choose, he may fix it at one day of cohabitation with each of his wives, successively, or more; and it is also to be remarked that by the equality of partition incumbent upon the husband is to be understood simply residence, but not coition, as the latter must depend upon the erection of the virile member, which is not a matter of option, and therefore, like the affections, not always in the husband's power.

Partition, where the wives are of different rank or degree, must be adjusted accordingly.—If a man be married to two wives, one of them a free woman, and the other a slave, he must divide his time into three portions, cohabiting two portions with the former and one with the latter, because the same is recorded of Alee: and also, because, as it is lawful to marry a free woman upon a slave, but not a slave upon a free woman,* it hence appears that the rights of the former in marriage are short of those of the latter.—And a Mokatiba, Modabbira, or Am-Walid, are, with respect to their right of partition, the same as slaves.

Partition is not incumbent whilst the husband is on a journey.—Women have no right to partition whilst their husband is upon a journey, and hence, during that period, it is at his option to carry along with him whomsoever he pleases; but it is preferable that he cause them to draw lots, and take with him on the journey her upon whom the lot may happen to fall.—Shafei says that the determination of this point by lots is incumbent upon the husband, because it is recorded of the Prophet, that whenever he intended a journey he caused his wives thus to draw lots.—Our doctors, however, allege that the Prophet's reason for this was only that he might satisfy the minds of his wives; wherefore drawing lots is laudable merely, because a man's wives have no claim whatsoever to partition during the period of their husband being on a journey, since he is at liberty not to carry any of them along with him, and consequently it is lawful for him to take any one of them.

The time of a journey is not to be counted against a husband;—that is to say, he is under no obligation, on his return, to make up for the partition lost within that time, by a proportionable cohabitation with the wife or wives whom he may have left at home, they having no claim whatever to his cohabitation with them during such period.

If one wife bestow her turn [of cohabitation] upon another, it is lawful; because Soolah the daughter of Zooma gave up her turn to Aysha: but if a woman give up her turn, she is not at liberty to resume it, because she drops a right which is not as yet established in her, and absolute dereliction cannot take place unless it be of a right already established,—wherefore her resumption here is as if she were to withhold from bestowing her turn upon the other.

* By marrying one woman upon another is to be understood a man marrying a woman when he is already possessed of a wife; the expression is merely idiomatical.

BOOK III.

OF RIZA, OR FOSTERAGE.

Definition of the term.—Riza, in its legal sense, means a child sucking milk from the breast of a woman for a certain time, which is termed the period of fosterage.*

Degree of fosterage which occasions prohibition.—Prohibition is attached to fosterage in whatever degree, if it be found within the usual period of infants subsisting at the breast.—Shafei says that prohibition is not established unless the child have sucked the breast at least five different times, insomuch that if an infant were to suck for any particular space of time, whether a day or an hour, uninterruptedly, this would not occasion prohibition, because the Prophet has said, "Sucking, or giving suck, for once or twice, does not render prohibited."—Our doctors support their opinion upon the authority of the sacred text, God saying, in the Koran, "Your mothers who have suckled you are prohibited unto you;"—and also upon a precept of the Prophet, that "whatever is prohibited by consanguinity, is also prohibited by fosterage,"—where no distinction whatever is made between a smaller and a greater degree of it.

* Fosterage, with respect to the prohibitions occasion by it, is of two kinds; First, where a woman takes a strange child to nurse, by which all future matrimonial connexion between that child and the woman or her relations with the prohibited degrees, is rendered illegal; Secondly, where a woman nurses two children, male and female, upon the same milk, which prohibits any future matrimonial connexion between them.

Objection.—A greater degree of fosterage is essential to the establishment of prohibition, because the latter is here founded solely in an apprehension of a participation of blood,* on account of the growth and increasing bulk of the body, which cannot take place without fosterage, in a considerable degree; moreover, it occurs in the traditions that fosterage is the source of a child's growth.

Reply.—Although prohibition be founded in an apprehension of a participation or blood, on account of growth, yet that is a point which is incapable of being absolutely ascertained, and hence prohibition by fosterage is attached, not to the degree, but to the more act of fosterage, which is the occasion of such increase of growth: and with respect to the saying of the Prophet, as mentioned by Shafei, our doctors reply that if the date of descent† of the text [of the Koran] before quoted was posterior to that of this saying, its authority is thereby superseded, and if it was prior thereto, yet the saying is rejected, because it contradicts the text.

Length of the period of fosterage.—The period of fosterage is thirty months, according to Haneefa. The two disciples hold it to be two years, and of the same opinion is Shafei. Ziffer maintains that it is three years, because something in addition to two years is absolutely requisite (according to what shall be hereafter shown), and such addition is fixed at one year, because that space admits of the child's state undergoing a complete alteration. The argument of the two disciples is the word of God, to wit, "His [the child's] time in the womb‡, and [until] his weaning is thirty months:" now the smallest space of pregnancy is six months, and hence two years remain for fosterage; moreover, the Prophet has said that "after two years there is no fosterage." The arguments of Haneefa are twofold; First the text already quoted, where it appears that God makes mention of two things, one the Hamal [or time of gestation], and the other the Fisal [or weaning], for both of which he indiscriminately mentions one period, namely, thirty months, wherefore it applies to each in two; the same as in a case of two debts; that is to say, if a man (for example) were to make a declaration that he owed such a person "one thousand Dirms, and five bushels of wheat, payable within two months," this period of two months applies to each debt equally, and so in this case likewise. It may indeed be objected that, admitting this, it would follow that the time of being in the womb is also thirty months, whereas it is otherwise,—pregnancy being by law restricted to two years; but to this we reply, that there is a cause of restriction short of that period operating upon Hamal (as being recorded in the traditions that a child does not remain in the womb of the mother above two years), whereas there is none upon Fisal, which of course stands as it appears to be: moreover, as a sucking child is nourished at the breast for two years, so is it also after the expiration of that term; for the weaning is not precisely determined to any particular period, but is effected by degrees, as the child insensibly forgets the breast and inclines to other food: it is therefore necessary that some space for fosterage be allowed in addition to the two years, and this additional space is fixed at six months, being the shortest term of pregnancy, as the lapse of that period affords reason for altering the manner of the child's subsistence, because the subsistence of a foetus is irreconcilable with that of a suckling;* and with respect to the traditionary saying of the Prophet, as cited by the two discipes, it has reference solely to the period of the claim of fosterage; that is to say, it only goes to show that no obligation arises from fosterage; so as to render payment or hire of the same obligatory upon the [child's] father, beyond the space of two years; and the text of the Koran, which says, "Mothers should suckle their childern for two years," has also reference to the period of the claim of fosterage.

Sucking beyond the term of fosterage is not an occasion of prohibition.—If a child continue to suck after the proper period of fosterage is elapsed, prohibition is not hereby established;† because the Prophet has declared that there is no fosterage after the expiration of the proper period; and also, because prohibition is not established by any fosterage, except such as is a cause of growth and increase, which are obtained only by

---

*Arab. Jazeeyat, a term which has no sense in our dictionaries in any manner applicable to the present case. It appears, from the context, to signify a participation of bodily substance, causing two persons to partake of one common nature.

†The Koran was declared by Mohammed to have been delivered down to him in different portions at various times, and those he termed the Noozools, or descents.

‡Arab. Hamal. By this is generally understood pregnancy; but as the text here quoted has reference to the child, and not to the mother, the translator is under the necessity of rendering it in a phrase applicable to the former.

*That is to say, it is to be supposed that within the last six months the woman may have conceived, and may, at the end thereof, produce a child; and a woman cannot, without injuring the foetus, give suck to another, either during or after her pregnancy.

†That is to say, if, after the expiration of the proper period of fosterage, another child be brought to the breast, and the former nursling still continue to suck, these two are not hereby prohibited to each other in marriage, although they would have been so if they sucked together during the fosterage of the first child.

the fosterage within its proper period, since grown up persons would not find any effectual nourishment from sucking.

A CHILD's forsaking the breast before the expiration of the period of fosterage is not regarded; that is to say, if a child withhold from taking its milk before the period of fosterage has elapsed, and there be still milk in the mother's breast, and any other infant suck the milk before the expiration of that period, in this case prohibition by fosterage is established between those children,—This is the Zahir Rawayat.—Hasan has recorded it as an opinion of Haneefa, that this is the case only where the first child has not as yet become attached to another species of food, so as to be capable of subsisting altogether without milk; but if the child have adopted entirely another species of food, this circumstance is to be considered as a weaning, and prohibition by fosterage cannot in this case be established, because where the child is arrived at such a state as that other food suffices, the manner of its subsistence is altered, and that growth and increase which the child derived from sucking is at an end, wherefore the property of participation of blood, which is the occasion of prohibition, is not afterwards found.

Is the sucking of a child, after the expiration of the period of fosterage, allowable or not?—Upon this point there are various opinions; some have said that it is not so, because the act of suckling at all is permitted solely out of necessity, the milk being a constituent part of the woman's frame, the use of any portion of which, except as a matter of necessity, is prohibited; and this necessity ceases upon the expiration of the period of fosterage.

Exceptions from the general rule of prohibition by fosterage.—"WHATEVER is prohibited by CONSANGUINITY is so likewise by FOSTERAGE" (according to the saying of the Prophet already quoted), except a sister's mother by fosterage,* whom it is lawful for a man to marry, although he cannot lawfully marry his sister's mother by blood, as she must either be his own mother, or the enjoyed of his father, both of whom are prohibited to him; contrary to her mother by fosterage. —A sister's mother by fosterage may be conceived in three different ways; FIRST, where a man has a sister by blood, who has a foster-mother, whom he may lawfully marry:—SECONDLY, where a man has a foster-sister, who has a mother by blood, whom he may likewise lawfully marry;—and THIRDLY, where a male and female infant, between whom there is no affinity, suck at the breast of one woman, and the female infant also sucks at the breast of another woman, in which case the male infant may lawfully marry the last woman, who is the foster-mother of the female infant) that is to say, of his foster-sister.)

A MAN may also lawfully marry the sister of his foster-son, although it be not lawful for him to marry the sister of his son by blood, as she must be either his own daughter, or the daughter of his enjoyed wife, both of whom are prohibited to him.

Case of illegality induced by fosterage.—IT is not lawful for a man to marry the wife of his foster-father, or of his foster-son (in the same manner as he is prohibited from marrying the wife of his natural father or son), because of the tradition before quoted.

OBJECTION.—It has been declared, in the sacred writings, that it is lawful for man to marry the wives of their sons by blood should this particular restriction to blood should seem to imply that marriage with the wives of foster-sons was lawful; whereas it is otherwise.

REPLY.—The restriction above mentioned refers to the exclusion of the wives of children by descent, and not to the exclusion of the wives of foster-sons, for the reasons already mentioned.

PROHIBITION is attached to the milk of the man (that is to say, to the milk of which he is the cause); if, for example, a woman nurse a female child, the latter is prohibited to her husband, and to his father and son, because the husband, through whom the woman's breasts have been filled with milk, is as a father to that child.—It is recorded, as an opinion of Shafei, that prohibition is not attached to the milk of man; because this prohibition arises from an apprehension of participation of blood; and the milk is a secretion from the blood of the woman, and not of the man.—The arguments of our doctors in this case are threefold; FIRST, the saying of the Prophet, as before quoted, "Whatsoever is prohibited by consanguinity is also prohibited by fosterage,"—and prohibition by consanguinity being found in both father and mother, it follows that it is found in both these relations by fosterage;—SECONDLY, the Prophet once said to Aysha (who had complained to him of Afla, the brother of Aboo Keis, appearing before her whilst she had only a single cloth upon her), "The act of AFLA, in thus approaching you, is of no consequence, as he is your paternal uncle by fosterage;" which proves that affinity by fosterage is established on the paternal side, and that as the woman who suckles is the child's mother, so is her husband its father, by fosterage;—THIRDLY, the man is the cause of the entrance of the milk into the woman's breasts, and therefore the milk is, out of caution, to be regarded (with respect to the point of prohibition) as deriving its existence from him.—

A MAN may lawfully marry the sister of his foster-brother, it being allowed to him to marry the sister of his brother by blood (that is, the maternal sister of his paternal brother).

*This is a very equivocal and vague expression, as appears by the succeeding definition of the various descriptions to which it applies.

It is to be observed as a rule that when a male and female infant suck from one breast, they are prohibited to each other in marriage, because they have one common mother, and are therefore as brother and sister.

It is not lawful for a female to marry any of the sons of the woman who has suckled her, because they are her brothers, —nor the sons of those sons, because they are her nephews.

It is not lawful for a male to marry the husband's sister of the woman who has suckled him, as she is his paternal aunt by fosterage.

Cases of admixture of the milk with any foreign substance.—If the milk be drawn from the nurse's breast, and mixed with water, prohibition is still attached to it, provided the former exceed the latter in quantity; but if the water exceed, prohibition is not attached.—Shafei maintains that prohibition is attached, in the latter case also, because there is actually some of the milk in that water, and therefore it is indispensable to be regarded, especially in a point of prohibition, that being a matter of caution.—To this our doctors reply that anything less in quantity than that with which it is mixed is regarded as virtually non-existent, as in the case of a vow, for instance, where, if a man swear that "he will not drink milk," and he afterwards drink it mixed with a greater proportion of water, he is not forsworn.

If the milk be mixed with other food, prohibition is not attached to it, although the former exceed the latter in quantity. This is according to Haneefa. The two disciples say that if the milk exceed, prohibition is attached. The compiler of the Hedaya remarks that this opinion of the two disciples proceeds upon a supposition that the milk and victuals do not undergo any culinary preparation after admixture; but that, if they be boiled, or otherwise prepared by fire, all the doctors admit that prohibition is not then occasioned.—The two disciples argue that regard is to be had to that which exceeds (as in the case of mixing milk with water), provided it have not undergone any change by boiling or other cause.—The argument of Haneefa is that the food is the subject, and the milk only a dependent, with respect to the end it is intended for, to wit, sustenance; the case is therefore the same as if the proportion of the food (exceeded that of the milk.

If the milk be mixed with medicine in a proportion exceeding the latter in quantity, prohibition is attached to it, because the milk is designed for sustenance, which is the end, and the purpose of the medicine is only to strengthen the child's stomach, or to forward digestion.

If the milk of the nurse be mixed with that of an animal, in a proportion exceeding the latter in quantity, prohibition is attached to it; but not if the milk of the animal exceed the other; regard being here had to that which exceeds, as in the admixture of milk with water.

Or with the milk of another woman.—If the milk of one woman be mixed with that of another, in this case Aboo Yoosaf holds that regard should be had to the excess.—that is to say, that prohibition is attached to that woman's milk which exceeds the milk of the other in quantity,—because here the two milks, when mixed together, become as one substance, and hence the smaller quantity is to be considered (in the effect produced) as a dependant on the greater quantity,—Muhammed and Ziffer contend that prohibition is attached to both milks equally, as both are of the same nature and a thing cannot be said to exceed a homogeneous thing, because the admixture with any article of a homogeneous nature adds to the sum, but does not occasion any destruction or change in the matter; and the end intended is the same in both. There are two opinions recorded from Haneefa upon this subject, one coinciding with Aboo Yoosaf, and the other with Mohammed.

Prohibition is occasioned by the milk of a virgin.—If the breasts of a virgin should happen to produce milk, prohibition is attached to it,—that is to say, if a male child were to subsist upon it, the virgin becomes his mother by fosterage, and his marriage with her is prohibited, according to the word of God in the Koran, "Your mothers who have suckled you are prohibited unto you," which text being generally expressed, applies to all women alike:—moreover, the milk of the virgin is a cause of growth in the child, which induces an apprehension of participation of blood.

Or of a corpse—If milk be drawn from the breasts of a deceased woman, prohibition is attached to it.—This is contrary to the opinion of Shafei, who says that in the establishment of prohibition by fosterage, the primary subject of such prohibition is the woman whose milk has been sucked by the child, the prohibition pervading through the medium of that woman to others (her relatives], but. by her decease, the original subject of prohibition is removed, she being then a dead substance; whence it is that if a man were then to commit the carnal act with her, he would not be subject to the punishment of fornication, nor would prohibition by affinity be by that act established. The argument of our doctors is that prohibirion by fosterage arises from an apprehension of participation of blood, which appear in the increasing growth of the [child's] body, and this last ts occasioned by milk; as in the present case.

Cases in which milk does not occasion prohibition.—If a woman's milk be administered to a child in a glyster, prohibition by fosterage is not attached to it.—It is recorded from Mohammed that prohibition is thereby established, in the same manner as fast would be vitiated by it :—but the reason of this apparent inconsistency (according to the Zahir Rawayet) is that the cause of violating the fast is the restoration of the body, which is effected by the glyster : whereas the cause of prohibition by fosterage is the increase of the body's growth, which is not thereby effected, nothing being sustenance to men except what is administered by the mouth.

IF a man's breasts should happen to produce milk, prohibition is not attached to it, because the substance thus produced is not, in fact, milk, and consequently increase of growth is not obtained by means of it.—The principle upon which this proceeds is that milk cannot be secreted in the breasts of any person but one who is capable of child-bearing.

PROHIBITION by fosterage is not attached to the milk of a goat (or other animal) that is to say, if two infants, a male and a female, were to subsist together, upon the milk of one goat, prohibition by fosterage is not established between them, because between mankind and brutes there can be no participation of blood (that is to say, such participation as would occasion, affinity) and prohibition by fosterage arises from participation of blood.

Case of one of two wives suckling the other.—IF a man marry an infant and an adult, and the latter should give milk to the former, both wives become prohibited with respect to that man [their husband], because if they were to continue united in marriage to him, it would imply the propriety of joint cohabitation with the foster-mother and her foster-daughter, which is prohibited, in the same manner as joint cohabitation with a natural mother and daughter.—It is to be observed on this occasion, that if the husband should not have had carnal connexion with the adult wife, she is not entitled to any dower whatever because the separation has proceeded from her, before consummation :—but the infant has a claim to her half dower, the separation not having proceeded from her.

OBJECTION.—The separation proceeds from her, because sucking the milk from the breast was her act.

REPLY.—Although the sucking was certainly her act, yet the act of such an one is not considered as destructive of her right, for which reason it is that if she should happen to kill her inheritee, this would not set aside her right of inheritance.—If, moreover, it should appear that the adult had acted with any sinister view of dissolving the marriage, the husband is in this case empowered to take from her the half dower which he pays to the infant ; but not unless she have acted with such a view, even though she were aware of the infant being the wife of her husband. It is recorded from Mohammed, that the husband is authorized to take the infant's half dower from the adult, in either case,—that is to say, whether a dissolution of the marriage may have been her intention or not ; but the former (which is the Zahir Rawayet) is the more orthodox opinion, because although the adult has by her act fixed and rendered binding upon the husband the half dower aforesaid (which had before stood within the possibility of dropping*), and her so doing amounts to a damage, yet she here stands (not as the actual perpetrator, but) as the cause of the damage, since the act of giving her milk to the infant is not the occasion of dissolving the marriage any further than as it induces a consequence of joint cohabitation with a step-mother and step-daughter:— moreover, the annulling of a marriage is not what renders a dower obligatory, but is rather the occasion of its dropping ; but the half dower is incumbent, in the manner of a Matat, or present, in compliance with established custom ; and the annulling of the marriage is the condition of its becoming incumbent ; and in this view the adult is the cause of the damage ; and as being the cause only, and not the actual perpetrator, transgression is made a condition of her responsibility, the same as in the case of digging a well,—that is to say, if a person were to transgress, in digging a well, by sinking it in another person's ground, or in the highway, he is responsible for the Deeyat of any one who might happen to fall into it, whereas, if the well were sunk in his own ground, he would not be responsible:—now this transgression is not found in the adult, unless where she is aware of the infant being the wife of her husband, and that her view is sucking it is a dissolution of the marriage; but where she is not aware of that circumstance, or being so, yet gives her milk, not with any view of dissolving the marriage, but rather of preserving the infant from perishing, in neither of these cases is transgression supposed to exist ; and, in the same manner, it does not exist, if she knew that the infant is the wife of her husband, but be not aware that her sucking it will occasion a dissolution of the marriage.

OBJECTION.—No regard is paid to ignorance of the law in a Mussulman territory ; how, therefore, can ignorance be pleaded in her excuse in the present case ?

REPLY.—Regard is here paid to her ignorance, not in order to avert the sentence of the law (which induces responsibility upon her), but solely to avert the construction of intent of dissolution, or of wilful transgression, to which her act might otherwise be liable, and which being thus disproved, she is exonerated from responsibility as these are the only causes thereof, and neither of them can apply to her.

Evidence to fosterage requires the full-

*That is to say, the obligation of which might possibly have been annulled or cancelled by the occurrence of some accident previous to the payment of it, such as the decease of the infant before consummation of the marriage &c

number of witnesses.—The evidence of woman alone is not sufficient to establish fosterage; nor can it be established but on the testimony of two men, or of one man and two women.—Imam Malik has said that it may be established on the evidence of one woman, provided she be an Adil, because prohibition is one of the rights of the law, and may therefore be established upon a single information,—as, for instance, where a person purchases flesh meat, and any one bears testimony to its being part of a Majoosee sacrifice, in which case prohibition is established with respect to it.—The argument of our doctors is that the establishment of prohibition in marriage is in no respect different from the extinction of a right of possession; and the annulling of a right of possession cannot take place but upon the evidence of two men, or of one man and two women:—contrary to the case of flesh meat, as the prohibition to the eating may be established without affecting the proprietor's right of possession, it still remaining his property under that prohibition:—the prohibition of this article, therefore, appears to be merely a matter of religion, and in which, consequently, a single evidence suffices.

BOOK IV.

OF TALAK, OR DIVORCE.

Definition of the term.—Talak, in its primitive sense, means dismission;—in law it signifies the dissolution of a marriage, or the annulment of its legality, by certain words.

CHAPTER I.

OF TALAK-AL-SONNA, OR REGULAR DIVORCE*.

Distinctions of divorce.—Divorce is of three kinds;—First, the Aksan, or most laudable:—Second, the Hoosn, or laudable (which are the distinctions of the Talak-al-Sonna); and Third, the Biddat, or irregular.

Talak Ahsan.—The Talak Ahsan, or most laudable divorce, is where the husband repudiates his wife by a single sentence, within a Tohr (or term of purity),* during which he has not had carnal connexion with her, and then leaves her to the observance of her Edit, or prescribed term of probation. This mode of divorce is termed the most laudable, for two reasons:—First, because the companions of the Prophet chiefly esteemed those who gave no more than one divorce until the expiration of the Edit, as holding this to be a more excellent method than that of giving three divorces, by repeating the sentence on each of the two succeeding Tohrs:—Secondly, because in pursuing this method the husband leaves it still in his power, without any shame, to recover his wife, if he so inclined, by a reversal os the divorce during her Edit: this method is, moreover, the least injurious to the woman, as she thus remains a lawful subject of marriage to her husband even after the expiration of her Edit† which leaves a latitude in her favour unreprobated by any of the learned

Talak Hoosn.—The Talak Hoosn or laudable divorce, is where a husband repudiates an enjoyed wife be three sentences of divorce, in three Tohrs. Imam Malik asserts that this method elasses with the Biddat, or irregular, and that no more than one divorce is admitted as unexceptionable, because, as being in itself a dangerous and disapproved procedure, it is only the urgency of relese from an unsuitable woman that can give a sanction to divorce; and this urgency is fully answered by a single Tohr. The arguments of our doctors on this topic are twofold:—First, a precept of the Prophet delivered to Ebn Amir, "One thing required by the Sonna is that ye wait for the Tohr and pronounce a divorce in each Tohr;"—Secondly, the propriety of a divorce rests merely upon the establishment of the actual urgency itself; that being a matter concealed and unascertained [but by virtual proof.] and the act of proceeding to divorce at a time when the desire of coition with the woman is fresh renewed (to wit, at the recommencement of her Tohr), is a proof of the urgency; opposition to Talak Biddat, which signifies a novel, unauthorized or heterodox mode of divorce: the terms regular and irregular are here adopted as being the most familiar.

---

*Talak-al-Sonna literally means "divorce according to the rules of the Sonna," in

*Meaning the space which intervenes between the menstrual fluxes.

†Contrary to any other mode of divorce, as a wife repudiated in any other way cannot be again married to her first husband, unless she be previously married to, and divorced by, another man.

and the repetition of divorce at the two subsequent returns of the Tohr amounts to no more than a repetition of the proof, and is therefore allowed of. Some of the learned have said that, in this species of divorce, it is most advisable that the husband delay pronouncing the first sentence of it until towards the termination of the Tohr, so as that the Edit may not be too much protracted : but it is evident that the husband should rather pronounce the divorce at the commencement of the Tohr, because, if he were to delay it, he might probably be tempted to have carnal connexion with the woman in the interim, under an intention of divorcing her, and then divorce her after such carnal connexion, which is forbidden.

Talak Biddat.—The Talak Biddat, or irregular divorce, is where a husband repudiates his wife by three divorces at once,—(that is, included in one sentence), or where he repeats the sentence separately, thrice within one Tohr ; and if a husband give three divorces in either of those ways, the three hold good but yet the divorcer is an offender against the law.

Shafei has said that all these three descriptions of divorce are equally unexceptionable and legal, because divorce is in itself a lawful act, whence it is that certain laws have been instituted respecting it ; and this legality prevents any idea of danger being annexed to it : moreover, divorce is not prohibited, even during the woman's courses, the prohibition there applying to the protraction of the Edit, and not to divorce.—Our doctors, on the other hand, say that divorce is in itself a dangerous and disapproved procedure, as it dissolves marriage, an institution which involves many circumstances as well of a temporal as of a spiritual nature; nor is its propriety at all admitted, but on the ground of urgency of release from an unsuitable wife : and there is no occasion, in order to procure this release, to give three divorces at once, whereas there is an excuse for giving three divorces separately in three Tohrs, as this exhibits repeated proofs of the urgency of it :—and with respect to what Shafei advances, that "the legality of divorce prevents any idea of danger being annexed to it," we answer that the legality of divorce, in one respect (that is to say, inasmuch as it is a destroyer of subjection), does not admit the idea of its being dangerous, but that, in another respect (to wit, its occasioning the dissolution of marriage, which involves concerns both of a spiritual and temporal nature), it must be considered as attended with danger.

The pronouncing for two divorces within one Tohr comes under the description of Biddat, or irregular, the same as that of three divorces, as already intimated.

A question has arisen among the learned, whether the pronouncing of a single divorce irreversible within one Tohr be of the description of Biddat or not ?—Mohammed, in the Mabsoot, has said,—"Whoever gives an irreversible divorce, although it be within the Tohr, forsakes the Sonna, as there is no urgent necessity for such a sentence to effect release from the wife, since by the lapse of the Edit that end is obtained ;" but again, in the Zeeadat, he says that this method is not to be reprobated, on account of the occasional urgency of immediate release, which by an irreversible divorce is obtained, it not being then suspended upon the lapse of the Edit.

Points to be attended to in adhering to the Sonna divorce.—Sonna [that is, attention to the mode prescribed by the Soona] in divorce appears in two shapes, adherence to number, and to time ; to the former, by restricting the sentence to that of a single divorce reversible, in which the enjoyed and the unenjoyed wife are the same ;—and to the latter (in which the enjoyed wife is solely considered), by pronouncing the divorce in a Tohr during which the husband has not had carnal connexion with her,—because it is the proof of urgency that is regarded ; and the act of proceeding to a divorce at a time when the desire of coition with the woman is fresh renewed (as at the recommencement of her Tohr), is the best proof of such urgency : for during the actual time of the courses the woman is not an object of desire, and in a Tohr where she has been enjoyed, desire is lessened towards her. With respect to an unenjoyed wife, the Tohr and the courses are equal,—that is to say, the pronouncing of divorce upon her whilst she is in the latter situation is not irregular, nor reprobated, any more than whilst in the former. This is contrary to the opinion of Ziffer, he considering an unenjoyed wife in the same point of view as one enjoyed :—but our doctors observe that the desire of coition, with respect to an unenjoyed woman, is ever fresh, and is not lessened by the circumstance of her courses, so long as the husband's object (namely, coition), remains unobtained ; whereas, with respect to an enjoyed wife, desire is renewed upon the Tohr.

Mode of adherence to the Sonna in repudiating a wife not subject to the courses.—If the wife be a person who, from extreme youth or age, is not subject to the courses, and her husband be desirous to repudiate her by three divorces in the regular way, he is first to pronounce a single sentence of divorce upon her, and at the expiration of one month another, and in like manner a third at the expiration of the next succeeding month ; because the term of one month corresponds with a return of the courses, as is mentioned in the Koran.—It is here to be observed that if the first divorce be given in the beginning of the month, the three months from that period are to be counted by the lunar calendar, and if in the middle of it, by the number of days, with respect both to the completion of divorce and of the Edit.—This is the rule with Haneefa.—The two disciples maintain that the second and third months are to be invariably counted by the lunar calendar.

the deficiency of the first month to be taken from the fourth succeeding month, so as to complete it. And it is also to be observed that it is lawful for the husband to divorce this wife immediately after carnal connexion, without the intervention of any time between the embrace and the divorce.—Ziffer says that the husband ought to allow the intervention of a month, because the term corresponds with a return of the courses, and also, because in consequence of the embrace desire becomes languid, and is not renewed until after the lapse of some time —Our doctors argue that there can be no apprehension of pregnancy with respect to the woman in question; and divorce, after the carnal embrace, in the case of a woman who is subject to the courses, is not reprobated on any other account than as it induces a possibility of pregnancy, which renders the duration of her Edit dubious, that of a pregnant woman being determined by her delivery, and, of one not pregnant, by courses; and as to what Ziffer alleges, that "desire becomes languid in consequence of the embrace," it may be replied, that although this be admitted, yet in the present instance desire is greater than in common cases, as the husband can indulge his carnal appetite with such a wife without any apprehension of her producing children, the support of whom might fall upon him; she therefore is an object of desire to him at all times equally, so that this state [of a woman not being subject to the courses] is the same as the state of actual pregnancy; now it is lawful to divorce a pregnant wife immediately after carnal connexion with her, because no doubt is induced with respect to the duration of her Edit, and the time of pregnancy is a time of desire, as a husband feels desire towards a pregnant wife, either because she produces a child to him, or because the embrace with her does not occasion pregnancy; his desire, therefore, is not lessened towards such a wife by enjoyment.

Or one who is pregnant.—IF a man be desirous of repudiating his pregnant wife by three divorces in the regular way [that is, according to the Sonna], he is first to pronounce a single sentence of divorce upon her, and at the expiration of one month another, and in the same manner a third at the expiration of the next succeeding month. This is according to Haneefa and Aboo Yoosaf.—Mohammed and Ziffer say that the Talak-al-Sonna, with respect to a pregnant woman, consists in giving her a single divorce only, because divorce is in itself a dangerous and disapproved procedure; moreover, the only rule instituted by the law in effecting a triplicate divorce is, that the husband first pronounces one divorce, and at the expiration of a month, or the passing of the next courses, another and in the same manner a third at the expiration of the following month or the passing of the next succeeding courses; now the courses do not occur to a pregnant woman, nor does the lapse of a month stand in place of a return of her courses (as with a woman whose youth or age prevents her having them), her whole period of pregnancy being as one long Tohr; and hence it follows that it is improper to pronounce more than a single sentence, the rule of the Sonna being restrictive to one divorce in one Tohr.—To this Haneefa and Aboo Yoosaf reply that, although divorce be in itself a dangerous and disapproved procedure, yet it is admitted on the ground of urgency, and the lapse of a month is the proof of that urgency, and is therefore to be regarded here, the same as in the case of a woman whose youth or age prevents her having the courses: the foundation of this is that the period in question is such a time as affords a renewal of desire to persons in health and vigour, and therefore the act of divorce being proceeded in at such a season affords proof of the urgency of it, with respect to a pregnant woman, the same as to any other; contrary to a woman whose Tohr is long [that is, by constitution or accident protracted to any unusual length], as the lapse of a month is not a proof of necessity with respect to such an one; this proof of necessity being found in her only on the renewal of the Tohr after the courses, the recurrence of which, with regard to her, is at all times possible, whereas, with regard to a pregnant woman, it is impossible.

Case of divorce pronounced during menstruation.—IF a man repudiate his wife during her courses, it is valid; because, although divorce within the term of the courses be disapproved, yet it is lawful, nevertheless, as the disapproval is not on account of any thing essential, but merely because a divorce given during the courses occasions a protraction of the Edit.—This kind of disapproval, or interdict, is termed Nihee-le-ghirehee,* and does not forbid legality, whence a divorce given during the courses is valid; but yet it is laudable that the husband reverse it as it is recorded that the son of Omar having divorced his wife during her courses, the Prophet desired Omar to command his son to take her back again; which tradition shows that divorce during the courses is valid, but that reversal is in this case laudable.—This doctrine of the laudability of reversal is maintained by many of our modern doctors; but it is certain that, in this case, reversal is not only laudable, but incumbent, for three reasons; FIRST, in the tradition above quoted, the Prophet desires Omar positively "to command his son," and command is always injunctive;—SECONDLY, the pronouncing of divorce during the courses is an offence, which it is incumbent upon a man to expiate by every means within his power; and this may be effected, in the present instance, by doing away its consequence, namely, the Edit;—THIRDLY, the protraction of the Edit

*This may be rendered prohibition for another reason.

is injurious to the woman, wherefore reversal is incumbent, the order that she may not be subjected to injury :—thus it is indispensably incumbent upon the husband to reverse the divorce, when given during the courses ; after which, when she has become purified from her courses, and has again had them, he may then either divorce her on the commencement of her second succeeding Tohr, or suffer her to remain The compiler of the Hedaya observes that this last is what is said in the Mabsoot. Tehavee has said that, if the husband choose he may regularly divorce his wife on the commencement of the Tohr immediately succeeding the courses in which he had given divorce, and reversed it, as above, Koorokhee says that what is thus mentioned by Tehavee is the doctrine of Haneefa. That which is taken from the Mabsoot is the opinion of the two disciples : and the ground of it is that the regularity of divorce depends upon the intervention of a complete menstrual discharge between every two sentences ; and the first of these is defective, on account of divorce having been pronounced in the middle of it, so that as part had previously elapsed, whence it would appear necessary to complete it from the next following return ; but it is not lawful to have regard to one part only of the courses, and not to the other ; consequently, regard must be had to the next returning courses in toto. —The ground of Tehavee's opinion is that the divorce, with its effects, having been annulled entirely by the reversal, it is the same as if no divorce whatever had taken place during the woman's courses ; and hence it is perfectly regular to pronounce divorce in the Tohr next immediately succeeding.

If a man were to address his wife, saying, "You are divorced thrice, according to the Sonna,"—and he have no particular intention in so doing, then supposing the wife to be one with whom he has had carnal connexion, and also subject to the courses, she becomes once divorced in that and each of the two succeeding wohrs : and if the husband intended in so saying, either that three divorces should take place collectively upon the instant, or, that a single divorce should take effect at the end of each succeeding month, the divorce, in each instance, takes effect according to his intention, whether she be in her courses or her Tohr at the period of its thus taking effect upon her.—And if she be one whose Edit is calculated by months (such as a woman, for instance, whose courses are stopt through age), and the husband have no particular intention in thus addressing her, in this case a single divorce takes effect upon the instant, another at the expiration of a month, and a third at the expiration of the next succeeding month : because the term of a month corresponds, in such an one, with the Tohr of a woman who is subject to the courses, as was formerly observed ; or if he intended that three divorces should take place collectively upon the instant, the three take place accordingly, in the manner already stated. But if the husband were only to say, "You are divorced according to the Sonna," comitting the word "thrice,"—in this case the intention of three divorces collectively is not efficient. The proofs and arguments upon this passage are all drawn from the Arabic, and derive their weight from certain peculiarities in that idiom.

Section

Of the persons who are competent to pronounce divorce —The divorce of every husband is effective, if he be of sound understanding, and mature age ; but that of a boy, or a lunatic or one talking in his sleep, is not effective, for two reasons :—First, because the Prophet has said "Every divorce is lawful, excepting that of a boy or a lunatic ;"—Secondly, because a man's competency to act depends upon his possession of a sound judgment, which is not the case with infants, or lunatics :—and one talking in his sleep is the same, in this point, as a boy or a lunaeic, since his words in this case are not the result of a deliberate option.

A divorce pronounced by compulsion, is effective—The divorce of one acting upon compulsion, from threats, is effective, according to our doctors.—Shafei maintains that it is not effective, because a person who is compelled has no option, and no formal act of law is worthy of regard unless it be purely optional ; contrary to the case of a jester, who in mentioning divoree, acts from option which is the cause of its validity.—Our doctors, on the other hand, allege that the person here mentioned pronounces divorce under circumstances of complete competency [maturity of age and sanity of intellect], the result of which is that divorce takes effect equally with that of a person uncompelled for with him necessity* is the reason of its efficiency ; and the same reason applies to the divorce of a compelled person, as he is also under necessity of divorce, in order that he may be released from the apprehension of that with with which he was threatened by the compeller.—The foundation of this is that the man alluded to has the choice of two evils ; one, the thing with which he is threatened or compelled ; and the other, divorce upon compulsion ; and viewing both, he makes choice of that which appears to him the easiest, namely, divorce ; and this proves that he has an option, though he be not desirous that its effect should be established, or, in other words, that divorce should take place upon it ; nor does this circumstance forbid the efficiency of his sentence : as in the case of a jester ; that is to say, if a man pronounce a divorce in jest, it takes effect, although he be not desirous that it should ; and so likewise the divorce of one who is complled.

*Namely, the necessity of separation from a wife, who may be odious or disagreable to him.

Or in a state of inebriety, is valid.—If a man pronounce a divorce whilst he is in a state of inebriety from drinking any fermented liquor, such as wine, the divorce takes place. Koorokhee and Tehavee hold that divorce ought not to take place in this case; and there is also an opinion recorded from Shafei to the same effect. The argument upon which they maintain this doctrine is that reality of intention is connected with the exercise of reason, which is suspended during intoxication from wine; in the same manner as where a person has taken any allowed but inebriating medicine, such as laudanum, in which case a divorce pronounced would not take effect, and so in this case also. But to this our doctors reply that, in the case now under consideration, the suspension of reason being occasioned by an offence, the reason of the speaker is supposed still to remain, whence it is that his sentence of divorce effect, in order to deter him from drinking fermented liquors, which are prohibited. But yet if a man were to drink wine to so great a degree as to produce a delirium or inflammation of the brain, thereby suspending his reason, and he in that situation pronounce divorce, it will not take effect.

And so also that of a dumb person.—The divorce of a dumb person is effectual, if it be expressed by positive and intelligible signs, because signs of the dumb are authorized by custom, and are therefore admitted to stand in the place of speech, in the present instance in order to answer the necessity of him who makes them. The various species of signs used by the dumb in divorce shall be set forth hereafter.

Number of divorces in respect to free women and slaves.—The utmost number of divorces, with respect to a female slave, is two, whether her husband be a slave or free: and the same with respect to a free woman is three.—Shafei has said that, in the number of divorces, respect is to be had to the state of the man; that is to say, if the husband be free he is empowered to pronounce three divorces, although his wife be a slave; whereas, if he be a slave, he is not authorized to give more than two divorces, although his wife should be a free woman, the Prophet having said "In divorce the state of the husband is to be regarded, and in the Edit that of the wife:"—moreover, personal consequence is an essential circumstance in all points of authority, and that appertains to a freeman in a higher degree than to a slave, whence his authority, is most extensive.—The arguments of our doctors are twofold upon this topic;—First, a precept of the Prophet, declaring, "The divorce of a female slave are two, and her Edit is two courses;—Secondly, it is the woman who is the subject of legality, and this legality entitles her to benefits; but slavery entitles only to half of these benefits; hence it follows that the divorce of a female slave should not exceed one and a half, but such subdivision of it being impossible, her divorces extend to two —As to the saying of the Prophet quoted by Shafei, that "in divorce the state of the husband is to be regarded," it means no more than that the effciency to divorce proceeds from him.

A master cannot divorce the wife of his slave.—The divorce of a slave upon his wife takes place; but that of a master upon the wife of his slave is of no effect, because the matrimonial propriety being a right of the slave, the relinquishment of it rests with the slave, not with his master.

CHAPTER II.

OF THE EXECUTION OF DIVORCE.

Distinctions.—Divorce (in respect to the execution of it) is of two kinds; Sareeh or express, and Kinayat, or by implication:—and first of express divorce.

The manner of express divorce.—Talak Sareeh, or express divorce, is where a husband delivers the sentence in direct and simple terms, as if he were to say, "I have divorced you," or "you are divorced" which effects a Talak Rijai, or divorce reversible,—that is to say, a divorce such as leaves it in the husband's power lawfully to take back his wife at any time before the expiration of the Edit: and these forms are termed Sareeh, or express, as not being used in any sense but divorce; and it appears in the sacred writings that reversal after an express divorce is lawful.—The intention is not a condition of divorce taking place from these forms, for the same reason as was already assigned, to wit because they directly express divorce, as not being used in any other sense —And it is to be observed that a reversible divorce only is effected by these forms, although the intention of the husband be a complete divorce, because his intention is here to effect that upon the instant which the law suspends upon the lapse of the Edit, and is therefore unworthy of regard: and if his intention should be merely to express a delivery from bondage (which the term Talak is occasionally used to imply), and he make a declaration to this effect before the Kazee, it is not admitted, as it disagrees with his apparent design: but yet it is admitted before God, because he intended in those words a meaning which they are capable of bearing: and if his intention be to express a release from bodily labours, his declaration to this effect is not at all admitted, either before the Kazee, or before God, as the word Talak does not bear the construction of release with respect to bodily labour, although it may occasionally bear that construction with respect to bondage: and it is also to be remarked that no more than a single divorce can be effected by these forms, although the intention be more.—Shafei alleges that divorce takes place according to whatever the intentio may be —The proofs on each side are drawn from the Arabic.

Different formulas of express divorce.—If a man say to his wife, "You are [under] divorce," or "You are divorced by divorce," or, "You are divorced according to divorce,*" without any particular intention, or intending thereby one divorce, or two divorces, a single divorce reversible takes place; and if his intention be three divorces a triple divorce takes place accordingly.—The proofs are drawn on this occasion from the Arabic.

If a man were to say to his wife (as above), "You are divorced by divorcement," and declare that by the word "divorced" he meant one divorce, and by the word "divorcement" a second divorce, his declaration is credited, because each of these words are capable of being construed into an intention of effecting divorce, and hence two reversible divorces take place, provided the woman has been enjoyed by him.

If a man apply divorce to the whole woman, by saying (for instance), "You are divorced," in this case divorce takes place, on account of its application to its proper subject, namely, the woman, the relative "You" implying the woman's person in too; and the rule is the same where he applies it to any particular part or member, from which the whole person is necessarily understood, as if he were to say, "your neck," or "your trunk," or "your head," or "your body," or "your vulva,"—"is divorced,"—for by such words the whole person is implied, the terms trunk and body bearing that sense evidently, and the others in common use: and they moreover occur, both in the tradition, and also in the Koran; and, according to one tradition, the term blood may also be used in the same sense. Divorce takes place also where it is applied to any general portion of the wife, as if the husband were to say to her, "your half," or "your third, is divorced,"—because any general portion is a proper subject of all acts, such as sale, purchase, and so forth, and is therefore equally so of divorce; but the subject in question (to wit, the woman) is incapable of division, and hence divorce is established upon her in too, and is not restricted to the portion mentioned.

Divorce when applied to any specific part or member of the body such as does not (in common use) imply the whole person, is of no effect.—If the husband say to his wife, "your hand," or "your foot, is divorced," divorce does not take place.—Ziffer and Shafei maintain that it does: and the same difference of opinion subsists where the divorce is applied to any other specific member, or organ such as does not imply the whole person, as the ear or the nose, &c. —The argument of Ziffer and Shafei is, that those members contribute to the matrimonial enjoyments, such as kissing, touching, and so forth, and whatever is of this description, as being a subject of the laws of marriage, is a proper subject of divorce, and as such; when divorce is applied to it, it takes place upon it, and consequenly extends to the whole person, in the same manner as where it is applied to any general portion such as an half, and so forth; contrary to the application of marriage, to any specific member, such as the hand or the foot, in which case the marriage is not valid, because it is not conceivable that legality should be established in that particular member, and extend, in consequence, to the whole person, as the illegality existing in the other members exceeds the legality in that particular member, —whereas, the reverse holds in divorce.—To this our doctors reply, that a specific member, such as the hand or foot; not being in itself a proper subject of divorce, the application of that too is null, the same as to a woman's spittle, or to her nails, the ground of which is that the subject of divorce must be something upon which a bond or connexion may exist (as divorce implies the dissolution of a bond or connexion), and there is no bond upon the hand: for which reason it is that the application of marriage to that part is invalid; contrary to a general portion of the body, which being (with our doctors) a proper subject of marriage, the application of that too is valid, and it is consequently a proper subject of divorce also. There is a similar difference of opinion where the divorce is applied to the belly or the back; but it is evident that here divorce does not take place, as these parts are never used to imply the whole person.

A partial divorce is complete in its effect—If a man pronounce upon his wife an half divorce, one divorce takes place, because divorce is not capable of division, and the mention of any portion of a thing of an indivisible nature stands as a mention of the whole; and the fourth, or fifth, or any other proportion of divorce, is analogous to the half, in what is now said, for the same reason.

Equivocal.—If a husband say to his wife, "you are under three moieties of two divorces," three divorces take place, because the half of two is one, and consequently three moieties of two divorces amount to three.—And if he were to say, "you are under three moieties of one divorce," some are of opinion that two divorces take place, this amounting to one and a half; but others allege that it produces three divorces, because every moiety, amounts to one complete divorce, on the principle already stated: various doctors agree in approving the former opinion.

And indefinite form.—If a man say to his wife, "you are under divorce, from one to two," or "between one and two," in this case one divorce takes place; and if he were to say,—"from one to three," or "between

*These and the succeeding forms of divorce, literally rendered, are most of them apparently unintelligible, or absurd; they are each, however, to be considered as having some peculiar force or effect, which it is impossible to express, or to convey an idea of, in translation.

one and three," two divorces take place,—This is the doctrine of Haneefa —The two disciples assert that by the first form two divorces take place and by the last three—Ziffer, on the other hand, maintains that by the first form no divorce takes place, and by the second one divorce only, this being conformable to analogy, because the boundaries of a thing are not included in the contents ; as for example, where a man says, "I have sold such a piece of ground, from this wall to that wall," in which case neither wall is included in the saie.—The ground of opinion of the two disciples is that, in such a mode of speaking, the whole is by custom understood, as for example, where one man says to another, "take of my property, from one Dirm to a hundred," which implies the whole hundred."...The argument of Haneefa is that, in this indefinite mode of expression, no particular number is implied, any more than where a man in discourse, says, "my age is from sixty to seventy years," or "between sixty and seventy," by which he means some indefinite term between these two : and in reply to the argument of the two disciples, it is sufficient to observe that the whole is to be understood only where the expression relates to a thing of an indifferent nature, as in the instance cited by them ; but divorce is in itself a dangerous and disapproved procedure ; and to what is advanced by Ziffer it may be answered, that it is necessary that the first boundary be in existence, so as that the second may bear a relation to it ; but in the present case the first boundary (to wit divorce), is not in being, nor can be so, unless by divorce taking place, which it accordingly does of this necessity : contrary to the case of sale, cited by Ziffer as apposite to this because there both boundaries (understood by the two walls) do actually exist previous to the sale. It is to be observed on this occasion, that if the husband, speaking in the second form, intend only a single divorce, it is admitted withGod, as he may be allowed to intend whatever construction the words will bear, but it is not admitted with the magistrate as being contrary to apparent circumstances.

If a man say to his wife, "you are ivorced once by twice," intending the multiple or multiplied product thereof, or not having any particular intention, a single divorce reversible takes place. Ziffer says that two divorces take place, such being the number understood from this mode of speaking in arithmetic ; and this opinion is adopted by Hasn-Bin-Zeead. But if, in speaking as above, he intend to say, "you are divorced once and twice," three divorces take place accordingly, because this way of speaking is capable of that construction, as the word fee [by] has also [in the Arabic] the sense of and : if, however, the woman be unenjoyed, no more than one divorce takes place, as in the case where a man says to his unenjoyed wife, "you are divorced once and twice," but if he intend to say, "you are divorced once with twice," three divorces take place, although she should be unenjoyed ;—and if he mean to express himself in a sense which implies that the one is contained in the other as if he were to say, "you are divorced once in twice," and divorce takes place, the superadded words in twice being held to be redundant, because divorce is incapable of bei g a container.*

If a husband say to his wife, "you are divorced twice by twice," intending the multiple ; yet no more than two divorces take place. With Ziffer three divorces take place, because from this multiplying mode of expression is to be understood four divorces, and three consequently take place, as being the greatest lawful number.

Divorce with a reference to place.—If a man say to his wife, "you are divorced from this place to Syria," a single divorce reversible takes place. Ziffer says that it occasions a complete or irreversible divorce, because, where he thus gives the divorce a description of length, it is the same as if he were to say, "you are under a long divorce," and if he were to say so, a complete divorce would take place, and consequently the same in the present instance. Our doctors, on the other hand, allege that the sentence does not affix any description of length to the divorce, but rather the reverse, because when divorce takes effect in any one place it does so in all.

If a man were to say, "you are under divorce in Mecca," divorce takes place upon her immediately in every country ; and so also if he were to say, "you are divorced in this house," because divorce is not restricted to any particular place,—and [if he were to intend, by thus speaking, that "she shall become divorced if over she should enter Mecca, or that house," his declaration to this effect is admitted with God but not with the Kawzee, as the tenor of his words apparently contradict this construction.

If a man say to his wife, "you are under divorce when you enter Mecca," in this case no divorce takes place until she enter Mecca, he having suspended the divorce upon that circumstance.—And if he say, "you are divorced in entering the house," this means "if you enter the house," because the containing particle frequently stands expressive of a condition, and not being applicable here in its containing sense, it necessarily assumes the meaning of a condition.

Section.

Of Divorce with a Reference to Time.

If a man say so to his wife, "you are divorced this day to-morrow, or "you are

*The words in the original are, "Ante Talikoon wahdetoon fee Sinnatinee," which is an indefinite or equivocal mode of expression, as the word fee (among various other senses) bears those of by, with, or and, as well as in, which accounts for the distinction here made, and the latitude permitted.

divorced to-morrow this day," in the first instance divorce takes place on the instant, and, in the second, on the beginning of the morrow; and the second word is in both cases redundant; because, where he first says "this day," divorce takes place immediately ou the present day, and consequently is not procrastinated to the morrow,—and, on the other hand, where the first says "to-morrow," the divorce is procrastinated to the morrow, and does not take place immediately on the present day; the second word is therefore redundant in both cases.

Where a man says to his wife, "you are divorced to-morrow," the divorce takes place on the dawn of the next morning: and if he should intend by the word "to-morrow" the end of the morrow, it is so admitted with God, but not with the Kazee, because this contradicts appearances: but if he were to say, "you are divorced in to-morrow," declaring his intention therein to be "at the end of the morrow," it is admitted with the Kazee, according to Hane fa. The two disciples say that it is not admitted with the Kazee, although it be so with God, because the words to morrow and in to-morrow are one and the same thing, as the word to-morrow is mentioned in an inclusive sense* in both cases, whence it is that, from the expression "to-morrow," divorce takes place on the first instance of the ensuing day, where the husband has no particular intention.—The argument of Haneefa on this subject is that the husband may be allowed to have intended some such meaning from his expression, because the word in is introduced as a Zirf; or particle of containance, which does not require that the whole of the container should be understood from it; and the reason why divorce takes place, in the present instance, from the beginning of the ensuing day, where the husband had no particular intention, is, that as nothing appears to the contrary, its commencement is necessarily determined to that period; and regard being thus had to necessity in the determination of it, follows that if that speaker fix it at the end of the day, this determination must be regarded, a fortiori: contrary to his saying, "you are under divorce to-morrow," (omitting the word in), in which case, if he should have intended the end of to-morrow his declaration to that effect is not admitted with the Kazee, because the word to-morrow without in, occasions the woman to fall under the description of being divorced for the whole of to-morrow, which cannot be effected but by the divorce taking place upon her in the beginning of the day: and consequently the end of the day, in this case, contradicts appearances.

If a man say to his wife, "you are under divorce yesterday," and it should so be that he was married as this day, divorce does not take place at all, because he has here referred divorce to a period in which he was not competent to pronounce it, and therefore his divorce is nugatory, the same as if he were to say, "you are under divorce before my existence."—But, in the present case, if he had married her before the time of which he speaks, divorce takes place at the time of his speaking; because, if a man signify a divorce in the preterite form, it is an indication in the present, and hence the divorce takes place accordingly, this expression being an indication of what is new, and not a relation of what is past, as it does not appear that he pronounced any divorce yesterday, so as that he should now give intelligence thereof.*

If a man say to his wife, "you are under divorce previous to your marriage with me," —divorce does not take place, because he applies the divorce to a period which forbids it, the same as if he were to say, "you are under divorce in my infancy," or in" my sleep."

If a man say to his wife, "you are under divorce upon my not divorcing you," or "when I do not divorce you," and then remain silent, divorce takes place, because he has here applied it to a time which appears the moment he ceases to speak.—But, if he were to say, "you are under divorce if I do not divorce you," divorce does not take palce until near the period of his decease, because here the condition does not become established until life be despaired of.

If a man say to his wife, "you are under divorce, whilst I do not divorce you, you are divorced,"† she becomes divorced on account of the last repudiation, to wit, "you are divorced."—This is where the last words of the sentence are uninterruptedly connected with the first part of it, and proceeds upon a favourable construction, for analogy would suggest that the first divorce takes place also (to wit, "you are divorced whilst I do not divorce you") and thus both divorces would take place, provided the woman be enjoyed; and such is the opinion of Ziffer; but the reason for the more favourable construction here, is that it is the intention of the vower to fulfil his vow, in such a manner that he may not be forsworn, which is impossible in the present case, unless that portion of time which may enable him to pronounce the divorce be excepted from his speech, "you are divorced whilst I do not divorce you;" and being thus excepted, divorce takes place, on account of the words which follow. Cases

* This is an Arabic mode of expression, implying no more than that here the particle in is understood.

* The reasoning here turns solely upon certain idiomatical pecularities in the construction of the Arabic language, in which the preterite is frequently adopted, by the law, in a creative sence. (See book II., Chap. I.)

† This is one of the forms under which divorce by vow is conceived.

correspondent to this occur in the Book of Eiman.

If a man say to a strange woman, "you are under divorce the day upon which I marry you," and he afterwards marry her in the night, she is divorced; because by day is sometime meant the day time, and this sense alone it bears where it relates to a matter, of continuance (such as fasting, for instance), and sometimes it is meant to express time in general, which sense it bears where it relates to a transient or momentary transaction and of this nature is the act of divorce; and consequently by the word day in the present case, is to be understood time generally, applying equally to day and night both—But if the husband were to say that by day he meant the daytime, and not time generally, his declaration is admitted with the Kazee, as he may be allowed to have intended that constriction which is applicable to the word day, since, according to custom, day applies to the daylight, and night to darkness.

Section.

If a husband say to his wife, "I am divorced from you," by this nothing is established, although divorce be the intention: but if he were to say, "I am separated from you," or "I am prohibited to you," intending divorce, becomes divorced.—Shafei holds that divorce takes place in the former instance also, where such is the intention because the matrimonial right of possession is equally participated by the husband and the wife insomuch that the latter is entitled to demand coition of the former, and the former to demand admission to coition from the latter, and the legality of the carnal enjoyment also appertains equally to both; and divorce being used for the purpose of dissolving the right, and the legality, the application of it to the husband holds good, as well as to the wife, and consequently divorce takes place under the first of the above froms, as well as under the second or third.—The argument of our doctors is that divorce is used for the removal of restraint and this is found in the woman, but not in the man (whence it is that a married woman cannot go out of the house); and admitting that divorce were used for the purpose of dissolving the matrimonial right of possession (as advanced by Shafei, it may be replied that the husband is the possessor of the wife and the wife possessed of the husband [whence the woman is called the married, and the man the marrier), and consequently possession applies to woman; contrary to separation or prohibition, the first of these being a total dissolution of connexion, and the second of legality, both of which equally appertain to each of the parties: and hence the application of them to either is equally forcible, whereas that of divorce is of no force except when applied to the wife.

If a man say to his wife, "you are divorced once or not," divorce does not take place. The compiler of the Hedaya observes that the same is said in the Jama-Sagheer; nor is any difference of opinion recorded there. This is what is said by Haneefa, and in one place by Aboo Yoosaf. According to Mohammed (with whom Aboo Yoosaf in another place coincides) a single divorce reversible takes place; and in the book of divorce in the Mobsoot it is recorded that, where the husband says to his wife, "you are divorced once or nothing" a single divorce reversible takes place, according to Mohammed; now between this and the preceding form there is no sort of difference, and consequently, if the case cited in the Jama-Sagheer be the opinion of all the doctors, it follows that there are two opinions recorded from Mohammed upon the point, —The argument of the latter is that the number is rendered dubious on account of the particle of doubt "or" intervening between the word "once" and the negative "not," wherefore regard to the former drops, and his words remain; "you are divorced:" contrary to a case where he says, "you are divorced or not," in which instance divorce does not take place, since in this last case the doubt exists with respect to divorce itself.—The arguments of Haneefa are drawn from the Arabic idiom.

If a man say to his wife, "you are divorced after my death," or "after your death;" no consequence whatever ensues from this expression, because, in the first instance, he has applied the divorce to a time which forbids it, since a husband is not competent to the execution of divorce after death; and, in the second, the woman no longer remains a fit subject of it; and both these circumstances are essential to a legal divorce.

Separation takes place upon either party becoming possessed of the other as a slave—If a husband become the proprietor of his wife [as a slave] either wholly or in part, or a wife the proprietor of her husband, separation takes place between them, possession by bondage and, possession by matrimony being irreconcilable;—in the latter instance, because, if separation were not to take place, it would follow that the wife is at once the possessor and the possessed (she falling under the latter description by virtue of marriage):—and, in the fomer instance, because possession by matrimony is established of necessity, and when the husband becomes actual possessor of his wife's person, this necessity ceases, and consequently possession by matrimony also.

Or upon a husband purchasing his wife.—If a man purchase his own wife [as a slave], and afterwards divorce her, divorce does not take place, because without the continuance of marriage it cannot exist, and in the present case the marriage has ceased in every shape whatever, since it does not continue even with respect to Edit; and in the same manner, when a wife becomes possessor of her husband, either wholly or in part, if the latter were to divorce her, his divorce does not take effect, because in this case also the marriage has ceased, for the resons before assigned —Mohammad says that in the latter case divorce holds good, because the woman is enjoined an Edit, and hence the marriage continues in one shape: contrary to a case where the husband purchases his wife, for then the marriage totally ceases, because she is not under any obligation of Edit with respect to her husband, who is now her proprietor, and has a right to continue carnal cohabitation with her in that capacity.

The divorce of a wife (being a slave) when suspended upon the emancipation of her owner, takes place upon the occurrence of that condition —IF a man marry the female slave of another, and say to her, "you are divorced twice upon the manumission of your owner," and her owner afterwards emancipate her, the divorce takes place; but it is still in the husband's power to reverse it, because he has suspended the divorce upon the manumission of the master, and that is the condition of it (as a condition is a thing not existing at present, but the occurrence of which is probable, and this case actually takes place on manumission, wherefore that is the condition, and divorce is suspended upon it); and divorce taking place after the occurrence of the condition, it follows that it takes place upon her as a free woman, and hence she is not, by two divorces, rendered prohibited* by a rigorous prohibition.

IF the person in question were to say to the female slave, his wife, "when to-morrow arrives you are free," in this case it is not lawful for the husband to marry her again, until such time as she has been married to another man, and repudiated by him, and her Edit (which is three terms of her courses) has elapsed.—This is the doctrine of the two Elders.—Mohammed says that the husband is at liberty to reverse the divorce, since the execution of the divorce is connected with the master's manumission, because the husband has suspended his repudiation upon the same circumstance on which the master has suspended his manumission; hence the repudiation is (as it were) associated with the emancipation; and freedom being also associated with the emancipation, it follows that the execution of divorce is, of course, associated with freedom, and the divorce takes place upon the slave after freedom (whence it is that the Edit of the woman here treated of is fixed at three terms of her courses, whereas if she were a slave, her Edit would be two terms only), and such being the case, reversal is approved, in this, as well as in the preceding example. The argument of the two Elders is that the husband has suspended divorce on the some circumstance upon which the master has suspended freedom; and as that takes place upon the woman whilst she is yet a slave, so does divorce likewise; now the slave becomes forbidden [in marriage to her husband], in consequence of two divorces, by the rigorous prohibition, wherefore reversal is not approved; nor does it become lawful to him to marry her till such time as she shall have been possessed by another husband; but this reason does not apply to the Edit, since that is a matter of caution, which is evident from fixing its duration to three terms of the courses, so that the complete fulfilment of it may be indubitable: and with respect to what Mohammed says, that, "as repudiation is connected with freedom, divorce takes place after freedom," it is of no weight, because, if freedom be connected with manumission, on account of the one being the cause of the other, and if the repudiation and manumission be associated together in such a manner that repudiation and freedom must take place at the same time, we reply that divorce is also associated with repudiation, on account of the latter being the cause of the former; whence it follows, that freedom is associated with divorce, and not that divorce takes place subsequent to freedom.

Section.

Of Divorce by Comparison and the several descriptions of it.

The number of divorces may be determined by signs made with the fingers.—IF a man say to his wife, "you are under divorce thus," holding up his thumb and fore and middle finger, three divorces take place, because from the holding up of the fingers number is customarily understood, where the sign is associated with a relative to number; and the word "thus" is of this kind; and the fingers held up are three in number, whence three divorces are to be understood:—and if the sign be given with one finger, a single divorce takes place; if with two fingers, two divorces.—It is to be observed thas the sign is to be understood from the fingers which are extended, and not from those which are clenched. Some of our modern doctors, however say that, if it be made with the back of the fingers, it is understood from those which are clenched.—And if the divorcer were to say, "I have given the signal with the two clenched fingers," whilst at the same time he had actually given it with the extended fingers, his declaration is credited with GOD, but not with the Kazee; and so also where he says, "I have intended the signal by the palm of my hand, and not by the fingers;" insomuch that two divorces take place [in the first instance, and one in the last, in a religious view; because signs are made with the shut fingers, or the palm of the hand, as well as with the extended fingers, and hence he may be allowed to have intended to express the

*Three divorces being the utmost number to a free woman, and two to a slave, it follows that if two divorces take place upon a woman as a slave, becomes irreversibly divorced. (See Chap. I).

number of divorce by signs capable of that construction: but it contradicts appearances.

But not unless it to be expressed with a relation to number.—And in the case now under consideration, if the word "thus" be omitted, and the sign be made with the thumb and fore and middle finger, yet one divorce only takes place, because the sign is not associated with the relative, and hence the words only remain, to wit, "you are divorced" from which one divorce only results.

Divorce pronounced with an expression of vehemence is irreversible in its effect.—If a man give to the divorce which he is pronouncing a description of particular vehemence or amplification, as if he were to say, "you are divorced irreversibly" or "you are divorced to a certainty," an irreversible divorce takes place, whether the wife whom he so addresses may have been enjoyed or not.—Shafei says that the divorce is reversible where she has been enjoyed, because reversal during Edit, after divorce from a wife already enjoyed, is sanctioned by the precepts of the law, and bringing it under the description of irreversibility is contrary to them; thus a husband is not at liberty to pronounce, upon an unenjoyed wife: a divorce irreversible; the word "irreversibly," therefore, is nugatory on this occasion, as much as if he were to say, "you are divorced, with this condition, that no right of reversal remains to me." The argument of our doctors on this point is, that the man has pronounced the divorce under a description which it is capable of bearing because divorce takes place irreversibly upon a wife unenjoyed (and also upon any other, at the expiration of the Edit); and such being the case, the divorce takes place in this case irreversibly upon an enjoyed wife, the same as upon one unenjoyed, the husband having, by his description, specified a circumstance which is really applicable to divorce. And with respect to the case of reversal being mentioned as an additional condition (as cited by Shafei in support of his doctrine), it is not admitted; because there also a divorce irreversible takes place, where it is pronounced either without intention, or with the intention, of two divorces; but where three divorces are intended, that number must take place, as irreversibility bears the construction of three divorces.

If a man say to his wife, "you are divorced irreversible," or "you are divorced to a certainty, and intend by his words "you are divorced," to express one divorce, and by the additional words "irreversibly," or "to a certainty," another divorce, two divorces irreversible take place, as these expressions are of themselves capable of effecting divorce.

If a husband say to his wife, "you are under a most enormous divorce," a divorce irreversible takes place, because divorce is thus described only with a view to its effect in the immediate dissolution of the marriage and hence the description of it by enormity is the same as by irreversibility. And it is the same if he were to say, "a most base divorce," or "the worst kind of divorce;" and so also if he were to say, "a diabolical divorce, or "an irregular divorce;" because reversible divorce is restricted to those of the regular description [or Talak-al-Sonna], and consequently all others are of an irreversible nature.—It is recorded as an opinion of Aboo Yoosaf, that, where the husband says "an irregular divorce," a divorce irreversible does not follow, unless such be the intention, because irregularity [Biddat] in divorce is of two kinds,—one originating in the circumstance under which divorce is executed (as where it is pronounced upon the wife during her courses),—the other, in the nature of the sentence (as where the husband pronounces the divorce irreversible in direct terms), and hence it is indispensably requisite that the intention be regarded. It is also recorded as an opinion of Mohammed, that from the use of the descriptions irregular or diabolical, a divorce reversible takes place, any divorce may be thus described, not with a view to irreversibility, but merely to the irregularity of the circumstances under which it is pronounced (as where it is pronounced upon the woman during her courses), and hence the divorce is not irreversible, unless such be the intention.

If a man say to his wife, "you are under a divorce like a mountain," a divorce irreversible takes place, according to Haneefa and Mohammed.—Aboo Yoosaf holds that the divorce is reversible, because a mountain is a single thing, and hence the comparison of divorce with a mountain gives the former a descripition of unity. The argument of the other two sages is, that simile, in divorce, is always used in an amplifying sense; and amplification implies irreversibility; whence a divorce irreversible is the effect.

If a man say to his wife, "you are under a most vehement divorce," or "you are divorced like a thousand," or "a houseful," one divorce irreversibie takes place, unless his intention be three divorces, in which case three take place accordingly. The divorce is irreversible from the first of these forms, because it is there mentioned under a description of vehemence, which occasions irreversibility, as applying something in its nature decisive, and incapable of recall,—whereas, divorce reversible is capable of recall, and therefore the description of vehement does not apply to it; and it is irreversible from the second form, because this simile sometimes expresses force, and sometimes number (as it is said, for instance, that such a man is like a thousand, by which it is to be understood that he is possessed of uncommon strength), and hence the intention applies with equal propriety to either sense; and where no intention exists, the least extensive meaning of the two is adopted, to wit, one divorce irreversible; and from the third form, because a house may be filled either by the magnitude of its contents, or by the number, and hence the intention applies with equal propriety to either circumstance; and where no intention exists the least extensive sense is adopted, as above.

Divorces when pronounced with a simile, is always irreversible.—It is a rule, with Haneefa, that whenever divorce is thus pronounced with a simile, it produces a divorce irreversible, whatever the thing may be with which it is compared, and whether the magnitude of that thing be mentioned or not; it having been before remarked the simile in divorce is always used in an amplifying sense; and amplification implies irreversibility.—Aboo Yoosaf, on the other hand, holds, that if the magnitude of the subject of simile be mentioned, the divorce is irreversible, but not otherwise, whatever that may be, because a simile may sometimes be introduced merely to express unity; wherefore indefinte comparison is not to be taken in an amplifying sense; but where the magnitude is mentioned that undoubtedly is to be construed amplification; and hence irreversibility is established.—Again, Ziffer maintains that if the subject of simile be of such a nature as conveys an idea of magnitude, the divorce is irreversible, but otherwise not. Some commentators allege that Mohammed coincides with Haneefa on this point; others, that he agrees with Aboo Yoosaf. The nature of these diversities of opinion is exemplified in a case where a man says to his wife, "you are under a divorce like a needle," or "like the size of a needle's eye," or "like a mountain," or "like the size of a mountain;" for under the first of these forms the divorce is held to be irreversible by Haneefa alone: under the second it is so with Haneefa and Aboo Yoosaf, and not with Ziffer; and under the third it is so with Haneefa and Ziffer, and not with Aboo Yoosaf; but under the fourth form it is irreversible with them all.

If a man say to his wife, "you are repudiated by a heavy divorce," or "by a broad," or "by a long divorce," one divorce irreversible takes place; because a thing of which the reparation is impraticable is called heavy, and an irreversible divorce is of this kind, inasmuch as the reparation of it is difficult; and with respect to those things of which the reparation is difficult, it is common to say, "they are long and broad"—It is recorded from Aboo Yoosaf that the divorce thus occasioned is reversible, because the descriptions of difficulty, length or breadth, do not apply to divorce, and are therefore nugatory. And if the man should, by any of these sentences, intend three divorces, it is approved because separation is divided into two kinds, the light and heavy, so that when the heavy (which is three divorces) in particularly specified, it is held to be efficient.

Section.

*Of Divorce before Cohabitation.**

Three divorces take place upon an unenjoyed wife when they are pronounced together, but only the first when they are pronounced separately.—When a man divorces a woman before cohabitation, by saying to her, "you are divorced thrice," three divorces take place upon her, because he has here given three collectively; but if he pronounce the three separarely, saying, "you are divorced,—divorced,—divorced," one divorce irreversible takes place from the first, but nothing from the second or third, because each repetition of the word "divorce" is a separate execution of divorce; and the first of them having already rendered the woman decisively and irreversibly divorced, it follows that the second and third cannot take effect upon her. And it is the same where he says, "you are divorced once and again" (where a single divorce takes place), because the woman becomes completely divorced by the first part of the sentence.

If a man say to his unenjoyed wife, "you are divorced once," and the woman should happen to die before the word "once" be pronounced, in this case divorce does not take place, because he has here associated the number with the divorce, which consequently ought to take place accordingly; but the woman dying before the number is mentioned, no subject of divorce remains at the time when it should take place, and hence the execution of it is null; and so also, where he says, "you are divorced twice" or "thrice."

If a man say to his unenjoyed wife, "you are divorced once before once," or once, and, after that, again," a single divorce takes place; but if he were to say, "you are divorced once, and previous thereto once," two divorces take place; and so also if he were to say, "you are divorced once after once." The proofs are all drawn, in this case, from the Arabic idiom. And if the man say, "you are divorced once with once," or "once along with once," two divorces take place, because of the associating particle *with*, which makes the sentence appear as of two divorces collectively. Aboo Yoosaf says that, under the second form, one divorce only takes place; his proof is drawn from the Arabic idiom. In all these instances it is to be remarked, that two divorces would take place upon an enjoyed wife.

If a man say to his unenjoyed wife, "if you enter the house you are divorced once and again," and she afterwards enter the house, a single divorce only takes place upon her, according to Haneefa. The two disciples say that two divorces take place. But if he were to say, "you are divorced once and again, if you enter the house," and she afterwards enter it, two divorces take place upon her, according to all. And if he declare the same sentence, with a variation in the construction of it, thus, "you are di-

*Divorce pronounced upon a woman before cohabitation is in all cases complete and irreversible. An attention to this rule is necessary to the understanding of several cases in this section.

vorced once,—and again if you enter the house," Koorokhee has said that here also there is a difference of opinion, one divorce only taking place with Haneefa, and two with the two disciples. Aboo Lays, however, observes that here one divorce only takes place, according to all the doctors, as under this construction the last member of the sentence is utterly distinct and separate from the first, and this is approved.

In implied divorce.—The second kind of divorce, namely Talak-Kinayat, or divorce by implication, is where a man repudiates his wife (not in express terms), but by the mention of something from which divorce is understood; and divorce does not take place from this but intention or circumstantial proof, because the implication is not used to express divorce alone, since it may mean divorce, and also something else, and hence intention or circumstantial proof are requisite to determine the construction in which it is to be taken.

In implied divorce are three forms which effect a reversible divorce.—The compiler of the Hedaya observes that implication is of two kinds. The First is that form which a single divorce reversible takes place; and this consists of three forms of words, to wit,——"Count!"—"Seek the purification of your womb!"—"You are single!"—of the First, because to count means enumeration, and hence the word "count!" bears two constructions, one, "count!" (the courses that are incumbent upon you)," and the other, "count! (the blessings of Almighty God);" and if the speaker intend the former meaning divorce is the ascertained construction of the word, in virtue of such his intention; and here the divorce takes place, of necessity, from his having desired her to count her courses, which other is of no force except where he has divorced her, because previous to the divorce, the counting of her courses was not incumbent upon her, and hence it is the same as if he had said, "you are divorced, and count!" And as this necessity is sufficiently answered by a reversible divorce, a reversible divorce accordingly takes place. And of the Second, because "seek the purification of your womb!" may either mean, "see that your womb be free from progeny, in order to your getting another husband" (since this expressly applies to the same thing as is designed by the preceding word "count," and therefore may, in the present case, stand intsead of it), or it may mean, "see that your womb be free from progeny, in order that I may divorce you; and where the husband intends the former meaning, a divorce reversible takes place, the same as in the preceding case. And of the Third, because "you are single!" may either mean, "you are repudiated by a single divorce" (and where such is the intention, a single divorce reversible takes place, as by this form such a divorce is effected), or it may mean, "you are single (having no other along with you);" or "you are single (among women, in beauty, and so forth"). Thus, these words bearing a variety of constructions, intention is essentially requisite to their effect; and it is to be observed that those forms occasion no more than a single divorce, because such forms amount to "you are divorced;" and as where the words "you are divorced" are expressly mentioned, no more than a single divorce takes place, so also, in this case, a single divorce only takes place a fortiori, because mere implication is weaker in its effect than the express mention of anything.*

Seventeen which effect an irreversible divorce.—And from all other implications of divorce, besides those three, where divorce is the husband's intention, a single complete (or irreversible) divorce takes place; or if he intend three divorces, three divorces take place: or, if two, two divorces; and these expressions of implication of divorce are as follow:—"You are separated!"—"you are cut off!"—"you are prohibited!"—"the reins are thrown upon your own neck!"—"be united unto your people!"—"you are devoid!"—"I give you to your family!"—"I set you loose!"—"your business is in your own hands!"—you are free!"—"veil yourself!"—"be clean!"—"so forth!"—"go to!"—"go!"—"arise!"—"seek for a mate!"—all which expressions are implicative of divorce, as each of them bears a construction either of divorce or otherwise; since "you are separated!" may either mean "you are separated (from me in marriage"), or "you are separated (from your family"). In the same manner, "you are cut off!" may either mean "you are cut off (from marriage") or "you are cut off (from your family and friends"): and so also "you are prohibited!" may either mean "you are prohibited (in marriage"), or "you are prohibited (to me as a companion because of your evil disposition"). In the same manner, "the reins are thrown upon your own neck!" may either mean "you are at liberty to go where you please (as I have divorced you)," or "you may go to visit your parents," and so forth); and so also, "be united unto your people!" may either mean "return to your family (as I have divorced you,") or ("as you are unfit for society on account of the badness of your disposition"). You are devoid," may, in the same manner either mean "you are devoid (of marriage)," or "you are devoid (of virtue and religion); and so also, I give you to your family!" may either mean, "I return you to your family (as I have divorced you), or, "I return you to your family (on account of your evil disposition, in order that you may remain there"); agreeably to the same mode of reasoning, I set you loose!" may either mean "I set you loose (from the restraint

*An observation is here introduced in the text, which, as it turns upon a point of grammatical criticism, is incapable of translation, and is therefore necessarily omitted.

of marriage, as having divorsed you)," or "I set you loose (to go where you please) ;" so also, "your business is in your own hands," may either have respect to divorce, or in any other circumstance ; and "you are free !" may either imply "you are free (from the bond of marriage)," or, "you are free (as not being a slave)," and as also; "veil yourself !" may either mean "veil yourself (from me as I have divorced you)," or, "veil yourself (that you may not be seen by a stranger) ;" in the same manner, "be clean !" may either mean, "ascertain whether your womb be free from seed, that you may be enabled to marry with another man," or, "that the descent of a child begotten upon you may be known ;" and so also, "go forth !" may either mean, "go forth (as I have divorced you)," or, "go forth (to visit your parents) ;" and, "go to !"—"go !"—"arise !"—may either signify, "go to (and so forth) as I have divorced you," or, "go to (and so forth) and do not provoke me to divorce you ;" so also, "seek for a mate !" may either mean, "seek for a husband, as I have divorced you," or, "seek for a proper companion to sit with you :" since, therefore, all those expressions admit the construction either of divorce or otherwise, the intention is essential to their effect, except where the husband uses them in reply to a requisition of divorce made by his wife, in which case the Kazee is to decree a divorce, but yet it does not exist as a divorce between the husband and God, unless such was his intention.*

THE compiler of the Hedaya observes that Kadooree has not made any distinction whatever between these expressions in divorce : on the contrary, he has said, "from all those expressions, when used in reply to a requisition of divorce, a divorce takes place, independent of the intention, in a legal view, but not in a religious view," whereas it is not so, this rule being confined to such expressions as are incapable of being construed into a denial of the requisition of divorce.

IT is to be observed as a rule, that there are three possible situations in which the person making use of these expressions may stand ; FIRST, a general situation, that is, where he is neither swayed by anger, nor by any requisition of divorce, but acts from an unbiased volition ; SECONDLY, where divorce is the subject of discourse at the time of speaking (as, for instance, where it is demanded of him by his wife) ; THIRDLY, where he is under the impulse of anger. The expressions of implication are also of three kinds :— FIRST, those which equally bear a construction either of denial or assent ;—SECONDLY, those which can be construed into assent only :—and, THIRDLY, those which may be construed either into assent, or into exclamations of contumely and reproach ; and, in the first of these situation, divorce does not take place from any of those expressions, but by intention ; and if the husband declare that he had no such intentions, his declaration is to be credited, because they all bear a double construction, and hence the intention is necessary to establish the effect ; and, in the second situation, divorce takes place independent of the intention in a legal view, and the declaration of the husband is not to be credited, where he has used expressions bearing a construction of assent only ; which are as follow :—

"You are disengaged !"
"You are separated !"
"You are cut off !"
"You are prohibited !"
"Count !"
"Your business is in your own hands !"
"Choose !"

The reason of which is, that the evident meaning of the husband, in using them in reply to a requisition of divorce is divorce, as they do not bear a construction of denial ; but if, in this situation, the husband use any of these expressions which may be construed equally into denial or assent, divorce does not take place but by intention ; and the declaration of the husband, with respect to his intention is to be credited. The expressions alluded to are as follow :—

"Go !"
"Got up !"
"Veil yourself !"
"Get out !" and so forth ;

because these words may all be construed into denial of the request : and as the denial of a request is a circumstance less forcible than the act of divorce, they are rather to be taken in the former sence : but yet, as they also bear a construction of assent they occasion divorce, where such is the intention. Those expressions may be construed into a denial of the request, on account that, "Go!" may mean, "quit thus speaking ;" Be gone ! and do not talk thus ;" and the same of "Veil yourself !" as a direction to put on the veil sometimes implies an order to go away ; wherefore it may imply on this occasion, "go away, and leave off speaking in this manner ;" and the same also of, "get out !"—but, in the third situation, divorce does not take place without the intention of the speaker, from the use of any expression of implication, except such as may be equally construed into assent, and into exclamations of contumely and reproach ; and those are the three following :—

"Count !"
"Choose !"
"Your business is in your own hands !"

from all of which, when used in anger, divorce takes place in point of law, independent of intention ; and the declaration of the

*That is to say, although divorce take place in point of law from the judicial decree, yet in foro conscientiae the man must continue to hold himself married, insomuch that he cannot, without sin, marry another woman, in lieu of her who is thus divorced. This is the distinction between law and religion in divorce throughout.

husband, denying such intention, is not to be credited, because the circumstance of anger proves the intention to be divorce.—It is recorded from Aboo Yoosaf that if the husband were, in anger, to say, "I have no property in you!" or, "I have no control over you!" or, "I give you your own way!" or, "I have separated from you!" or "join yourself to your people!" His declaration is credited, even where he denies having intended divorce, because these expressions may all be construed into exclamations of contumely or reproach, as well as of divorce; as his words, "I have no property in you!" may mean, "because you are so base that you are incapable of being considered as a property;" and, in the same manner, his words, "I have no control over you!" may mean, "because of the wickedness and stubbornness of your disposition;" and so also, "I give you your own way!" may mean, "because I cannot direct you;" and, in like manner, "I have separated from you!" may mean, "because of your vicious disposition."

What has just been stated, viz., that "where the husband says, you are separated! or, you are cut off! divorce irreversible takes place," is the opinion of our doctors.—Shafei has said that the divorce occasioned by these words is reversible, because the reason why those expressions occasion divorce is, that they are implication of divorce; whence it is that the intention is a condition of their effect, and also, that the divorce occasioned by them is complete in part of number, the same as in an express divorce, where the husband is authorized to pronounce three divorces, and having given one, his authority remains with respect to two other;—and also, that if he intend three divorces, three take place accordingly; and such being the case, reversal is lawful here in the same manner as in an express divorce, the thing which is implied. The argument of our doctors on this point is, that the act of irreversible divorce has proceeded in this case from a competent person, and is exercised upon a fit subject of it, according to the power by law established over the wife, which enables her husband to put her away in such a manner as that she shall be decisively and irreversibly separated from him; and here the husband is competent to the act of irreversible divorce, as being of sound mind and mature age; and the wife is a fit subject of it, as being lawfully liable to irreversible divorce before cohabitation (and also after it where for husband pronounces it for a compensation); and this power, like many others, is instituted by the law with a view so the convenience of the individual, which sometimes requires a decisive separation to be effected slowly and deliberately (as in divorce reversible), whereas, at other times, it requires that such a separation should take place on the instant, without any continuance of connexion with the subject of it (as in the triple form of divorce), and at other times it also requires separation to be completely effected on the instant admitting a continuance of connexion with the subject; and it is indispensably necessary that this last species of irreversible separation be also countenanced by the law, in order that the door of reparation may not be closed against the husband if he should repent (that is to say, that it may remain in his power again to marry his wife, without her being previously married to another); and also, in order that the woman's delicacy may be preserved from the effect of a divorce, by the man taking her back without the intervention of marriage with another; and such being the case, divorce irreversibly ensues from those expressions. In reply to the assertion of Shafei, we observe that those expressions are not positively implications, since each of them may be used in its own literal sense;—and as to what he further alleges, that "the intention is a condition of their effect" (thence inferring that they are undoubtedly implications of divorce), the inference is not admitted, because the intention is made a condition for the purpose of ascertaining one of two species of separation, and it is thus made a condition for the purpose of ascertaining one of two sorts of a separation which is a separation from marriage, and not for the purpose of divorce taking place: with respect to what Shafei further advances, that "the divorce occasioned by any of those expressions is incomplete in point of number" (thence inferring that they are implications of divorce), we reply that the paucity of the number of divorces is not on account of those expressions being implications of divorce, but because divorce is established on account of the connexion of marriage becoming dissolved; that is to say, on account of those expressions the tie is dissolved, and divorce signifies the dissolution of a tie, wherefore divorce is necessarily established; the inference, therefore, is that the taking place of divorce, is involved; but not that the aforesaid expressions are implications of divorce:—and with respect to what he further says, that "if the husband intend three divorces from the use of any of those expressions, three take place accordingly" (infering that they are implications of divorce), we reply that the intention of three divorces from those expressions is approved only as three divorces is one species of separation (for separation is of two species,—the mild and the rigorous*), and, where there is no inten-

*By the mild separation is meant that species of complete divorce which admits of the husband re-marrying his repudiated wife without the necessity of her intermediate marriage with another. By the rigorous separation is meant that sort of complete divorce which does not admit of the man re-marrying his repudiated wife until she shall have been married to, enjoyed, and repudiated by another man. They have been already fully explained.

tion, the least forcible is established. It is to be observed that an intention of two divorces is not approved with our doctors; contrary to the opinion of Ziffer: but this has already been treated of.

If a man say to his wife, "count!—count!—count!" and afterwards declare that by the first of these words he meant divorce, and by the others the repetition of the woman's courses [requisite to its completion] his declaration is credited in point of law, as he appears to have intended these last words in their true sense, it being customary for a husband, where he divorces his wife to desire her to count the course necessary to the completion of her Edit; and hence apparent circumstances bear evidence to his intention; but if he were to confess that in these last words he had no particular intention, three divorces take place, because, from his intending divorce by the first word, it follows that he repeated it a second and third time, in a situation where divorce is the subject of discourse, and this situation proves his intention in these repetitions to be divorce also; wherefore if he were to deny this intention, yet he is not credited, circumstances bearing evidence against him; contrary to where he declares that he had no intention of divorce in any of the three words, for there divorce does not take place at all, because circumstances do not tend to disprove his declaration; and contrary, also to where he declares divorce to be his intention in the third word, but not in either of the two preceding, in which case no more than one divorce takes place, because, as he does not put the construction of divorce upon the two preceding words, it does not appear that divorce was the subject of discourse at the period of his speaking the last. It is to be observed that the declaration of the speaker in denial of his intention is not to be credited, unless it be given upon oath, because he relates what, having passed solely in his own mind, cannot be known to any other person,—and hence he is the Ameen, or inquisitor, with respect to the intelligence he gives; and the declaration of an inquisitor is credited upon oath.

CHAPTER III.

OF DELEGATION OF DIVORCE

Definition of the phrase.—Tafweez al Talak, or delegation of divorce, is where the husband delegates or commits the pronouncing of divorce to his wife, desiring her to give the effective sentence, and it is comprehended under three different deeds, termed Option, Liberty and Will.

Section 1.

Of Ikhtiyar or Option.

Delegation by Option confers on the wife a power of divorcing herself; but this right of option is restricted to the precise place or situation in which she receives, it.—If a man say to his wife "choose!" (thereby meaning divorce), or "divorce yourself!" the woman has a power to divorce herself so long as she remains in the precise situation* in which she received it; but if she remove, or turn her attention to anything else, the power thus vested in her is done away, and her option no longer remains, because the exerise of the optional power thus committed to the woman is held, by all the companions, to be restricted to the precise situation in which it is received: and also, because this species of delegation is a transfer of power, not a commission of agency, and to give effect to the former, the reply is required on the spot of declaration, the same as in sale, since all the moments of one situation are accounted as a single moment: but a situation may be altered, sometimes by change of place, at other times by chance of employment, because a situation of eating and drinking (for instance) is not that of disputation; and a situation of business, on the other hand, is neither a situation of eating or drinking, nor of disputation.

And is annulled by her removal.—The right of option of the woman is annulled, upon the instant of her rising from her seat, as that circumstance proves her rejection of it: contrary to the case of Sillim or a Sirf sale, which does not become null upon the instant of rising or removing, the cause of in validity there being removal without seisin.

Intention on the part of the husband, is requisite to constitute a delegation.—And where the husband thus addresses his wife, an intention of divorce is a condition requisite to the effect (as mentioned in the preceding chapter) because the word "choose!" is one of the implications of divorce, as it is capable of two constructions, by one it desires the woman to choose herself, and by another to choose her clothes, and so forth: and if she choose herself,† and divorce irreversible takes place. Analogy would suggest, in this case, that from choosing herself nothing whatever should ensue, although divorce be the intention of the husband, because he cannot himself effect divorce by the use of such words; that is to say, if he were to say to his wife, "I have choosen myself from you," nothing whatever would follow, and consequently how can he give a delegation of this nature?—But here divorce takes place upon a more favourable construction, for two reasons:—First, all the companions agree that divorce takes place from the use of this expression;—Secondly, the husband has it at his option either to continue the marriage with his wife or to put her away and hence it follows that he may constitute her his substitute with respect to that

*Arab Majlis—This term is treated of at large elsewhere.

†This is an idiomatical phrase in the Arabic, signifying that she chooses her liberty from the matrimonial tie.

rule: and where the woman is thus left it her option, and says "I choose mayself," a divorce irreversible takes place, because the woman's choosing of herself cannot be established but by her becoming sole and independent, which can only be the case in irreversible divorce, as, where it is reversible, the husband is at liberty to take her back without her consent at any time during the continuance of her Edit, and thus she would not become sole and independent on the instant, which the nature of the case requires.

Under this form a single divorce only takes place, whatever may be the intention.—It is to be observed that, in the case at present under consideration, one divorce only can take place, and not three although the husband should actually have intended the latter option not being of different descriptions:—contrary to complete separation, for if the husband were to say, "you are completely separated," intending three divorces, the three take place accordingly, where such is his intention, because this complete separation is of two descriptions, the mild and the rigorous, and it follows that intention with respect to and of these holds good.

And, to effect divorce, it is requisite that the personal pronoun be mentioned by one or other of the parties.—It is also to be observed that, where the husband uses the expression "choose!" it is requisite that the personal pronoun self be mentioned either by the husband or the wife, insomuch that if the husband were to say, "choose!" and the wife answer, "I have chosen," divorce does not take place, because the effect of divorce is established by all the doctors upon the condition of the mention of the personal pronoun by one of the parties; and also, because the pronoun cannot be understood under any circumstances of ambiguity, and these words of the woman bear two constructions; one, that she chooses her husband (which would not occasion divorce); and another, that she chooses her self (which would occasion irreversible divorce); divorce therefore, does not take place in defect of the pronoun, on account of its ambiguity.

That is, either by the husband, in his declaration.—If a man say to wife, "choose yourself," and she answer, "I have chosen," a divorce irreversible takes place, because the word self here occurs in the words of the husband, and the words of the woman are in reply to him; and hence her words virtually comprehend herself. And, in the same manner, if the husband were to say, "choose an option," and she reply, "I have chosen," a divorce irreversible takes place: the proofs here are drawn from the Arabic.

Or by the wife in her reply.—If a man say to his wife: "choose!" and she reply, "I have chosen myself," divorce takes place, where such was the husband's intention because the word *self* here occurs, in the reply given by the woman, and the expression of the husband bears the construction of that which he intended.

And divorce takes place, although her option of it be expressed in the Mozaree or common tense.—If a husband say to his wife, "choose!" and she reply to him in the Mozaree tense [which, in the Arabic, is common to the present and future], saying "I do (or will) choose myself," divorce takes place, on a favourable construction.—Analogy would suggest in this case that no divorce takes place, because, if the woman's reply be taken only in the future, it stands as a promise, and bears that construction also, if taken in the present; and hence divorce does not take place, from her answer amounting only to a promise in the former sense, and from its ambiguity in the latter; as if a man were to say to his wife, "divorce yourself," and she were to reply, Atliko Nafsee ["I do (or will) divorce myself"], in which case divorce does not take place, and so in this case likewise: but the reasons for the more favourable construction are twofold;—First, it is recorded that, upon the descent of the passage of the Koran relating to option, viz. O my son! say to your wives, If you desire the life of this world" (to the end),—the Prophet said to Aysha, "I have something to mention to you, but do not reply to it until such time as you consult your parents," after which he read to her the above passage, and then gave her an option: and Aysha said, "in such a matter as this I shall not consult my father or mother, but will (or do) choose God and his Prophet," which words the Prophet considered as a reply, importing, "I do choose;"—Secondly, the word Akhtarto ["I do (or will) choose myself"], express the present literally, and the future figuratively, the same as the word Ashado [I do (or will) testify], in giving evidence before a magistrate; contrarty to where a woman answers Atliko Nafsee [I do (or will) divorce myself], for here it is impossible to receive her words in a present sense, as they do not relate to a thing now existing; whereas the expression Akhtarto [I do (or will) choose myself], on the contrary, relates to a thing now present, to wit, the woman choosing herself.

Where the husband gives a power of option thrice repeated, and the wife make only a single reply, yet three divorces take place from it, independent of the husband's intention.—If a man say to his wife, "choose!"—choose!—choose!" and she reply, "I have chosen the first," or "the second" or "the third," three divorces take place, according to the doctrine of Haneefa, and the intention of the husband is not requisite although the word here used be an implied expression, because his repetition of the word "choose!" proves his intention to be divorce, as the option given to the woman is repeated only with that view.*—The two disciples say that only one divorce takes

*Some grammatical reasoning, incapable of translation, is omitted in this part.

place in either case ; but they agree with Haneefa, that the intention is not essential, for the reasons above assigned.—And, in the same manner, if the woman were only to reply, "I have chosen," it is effective of three divorces. And so also, if she were to reply, "I have chosen a choice."—This is admitted by all the doctors ; because, where she only says, "I have chosen," it is productive of three divorces ; and, consequently, when she speaks in a way to give this additional force, it produces the same a fortiori. —And if she were to reply, "I have divorced myself," or "I have chosen myself with respect to one divorce," one divorce reversible takes place.

Where the word divorce is mentioned by the husband, the divorce which follows is reversible.—IF a man say to his wife, "one divorce is at your option," or "choose with respect to a single divorce," and she reply, "I have chosen myself," one divorce reversible takes place, because the man has given the woman an option so far as one divorce, and expressing it in direct terms (as above)* the divorce proceeding from it is reversible.

Section II.

Of Amir-ba-Yed, or Liberty.†

In a delegation of liberty, divorce takes place according to the number mentioned by the wife : independent of the husband's intention : and the divorce which follows is irreversible—IF a man say to his wife, "your business is in your own hands," intending three divorces, and the woman answer, "I have chosen myself with one choice," three divorces take place. The proof of this is drawn from the nature of these expressions in their original idiom.

BUT if the woman were to reply, "I have divorced myself with one divorce," or "I have chosen myself by one divorce," one divorce only takes place ; and this divorce is irreversible, although the reply be delivered in express and not in ambiguous terms, because it bears relation to the words of the husband, which being an implication, amount to a delegation of irreversible divorce, and not of reversible.—The reason why an intention of three divorces is admitted in the present instance, is that the words, "your business is in your own hands," are capable of both a restrictive and an extensive construction, and hence may imply three divorces, as well as one ; an intention to that effect therefore holds good, since that is one of the senses in which the words may be taken : contrary to the expression considered in the preceding section, to wit, "choose !" that being incapable of bearing an extensive construction, as was there demonstrated.

Delegation of liberty may be restricted to a particular time, or to several different specified periods of time.—IF a man say to his wife, "your business is in your own hands this day, and after to-morrow," the night is not included :—and if the woman reject the liberty thus given to her for this day, it is, with respect to this day, annulled ; but it still remains to her for the day after the morrow, because the husband has expressly specified two particular periods, with the intervention of a similar periods to which the liberty does not extend (to wit : to-morrow) ; and hence it appears that those are two distinct liberties, and the rejection of one does not amount to a rejection of the other. Ziffer says that both amount only to a single liberty, this being analigous to a case where a man says to his wife, "you are divorced this day and the day after to-morrow," which implies one divorce only, and not two (on the idea of one taking place this day, and the other the day after the morrow) ; and hence, in like manner, one liberty only is implied.—But to this it may be replied, that divorce is not of a nature to admit restriction to any particular time, whereas liberty is capable of such restriction ; and hence that which regards the first period mentioned is restricted to that period, and that which regards the second period commences de novo.

IF a man say to his wife, "Your business is in your own hands to-day and to-morrow," the night is comprehended in it : and, if the woman should reject the liberty on the instant, it is totally annulled, and does not return on the morrow (according to the Zahir Rawayet), as this amounts only to one liberty, because that between the two periods specified no similar period intervenes to which the liberty does not extend.

OBJECTION.—Although a period similar to the two specified does not intevene, yet night intervenes, from which it would follow that the liberty given for to-day and to-morrow is not a single liberty.

REPLY.—Two distinct liberties are not occasioned by this circumstance, because the intervention of night, althoughit may interrupt or suspend a matter, does not divide or terminate it, as in a public court, for instance, which may, on account of the night coming on, be adjourned, without any actual breach in the series of its proceedings ; thus it is the same as if the man were to say, "your business is in your own hands for two days," in which case a single liberty only is understood.

And it is not annulled by the wife's rejection of it until the time or times mentioned be fully expired.—IT is recorded, from Aboo Haneefa, that although the woman should reject the liberty on the instant, yet it still remains with her for the following day, as she is not empowered to reject it (that is to s.., she cannot refuse her assent to receiving

*Because an express divorce is uniformly reversible unless otherwise specified.

†This is a contraction of Amir-ke-ba-Yed-ke, literally, "your business is in your own hands, *i.e.*, "you are at liberty to do as you please."—The word liberty is adopted singly, for the sake of brevity.

it), it becoming established in her upon the husband saying. "your business is in your own hands," independent of her consent (as in the direct execution of divorce, for instance, where, if the husband were to say, "you are divorced," divorce takes place independent of the consent of the wife); and such being the case, liberty remains still with her for the morrow, when she may lawfully make use of it by chosing divorce. The ground upon which Zahir Rawayet proceeds, is that as, if she were to choose divorce as this day, no liberty remains with her for to-morrow, so if she reject the liberty this day, no right of choice remains with her for to-morrow, because a person who has a choice of two things is not authorized to choose more than one of them.

It is recorded, from Aboo Yoosaf, that if a husband say to his wife," your business is in your own hands for this day, and the same for to morrow," this amounts to two liberties because here the delegation applies to two portions of time, distinctly and separately expressed: contrary to the preceding case, where the times are not thus discriminated, but are both mentioned, under one head.

The time of it may be fixed for the occurrence of any specified event.—If a man say to his wife, "your business is in your own hands on "the day on which such an one arrives," and the person mentioned arrive, but his arrival be not known to the wife until night, her right of choice no longer remains, because liberty is a thing of continuance, and hence the word day, with which it is associated, is restricted to the day time, and that having passed away, it discontinues.

It is not annulled by delay (where there is no specification of time), nor until the wife rises from her seat, &c.—If a man say to his wife, "your business is in your own hands," or "choose !" and she delay answering the whole day, and do not rise from her seat, her right of option remains to her so long as she does not employ herself in any other matter, because a delegation of divorce by the forms of liberty or option is a transfer of power to execute divorce (that is, the husband by that delegation empowers his wife to give divorce, as persons are termed empowered who act for themselves, and the act of the woman here is pronouncing divorce upon herself, wherefore this property is supposed to reside in her),—and in transfer of power a privilege of reply continues to the end of the situation of declaration, as has been demonstrated in the beginning of this chapter. And if the woman hear the declaration, respect is had to the situation in which she hears it; but if she should not hear it, respect is, in that case, had to the situation in which she is informed of it, because, although Amir-ba-Yed, or liberty, be a transfer of power to execute divorce, yet the property of suspension is also allowed to exist in it, as it is a suspension of the event of divorce upon the act of the wife in pronouncing it, and hence it comprehends two things, a transfer of power, and a suspension;—in the sense of a suspension, it continues in force beyond the Majlis, or continuance of the situation of declaration, to the Majlis or situation in which the woman understands or is informed of it, where she is absent, or in the sense of a transfer of power, it is annulled, on her rising from her seat, where she is present; but the situation of the husband is not regarded, because the suspension, is absolute with respect to him; contrary to a case of sale, as in that the declaration of sale does not remain in force beyond the Majlis of declaration, since in a sale the Majlis or situation of the seller is regarded as well as that of the purchase: and the retraction of the seller, at any time previous to the consent of the purchaser is admitted, as sale, is merely of a transfer of property, in which suspension is not of all understood; now since it appears that the situation of the wife alone is regarded, and not that of her husband, we must recollect that her situation may be altered in various ways sometimes by removal from one place, to another, and sometimes by her employing herself in any other matter, as was previously stated.

But it is annulled on the instant of her rising from her seat.—The option of a woman who is left at liberty to choose is annulled on the instant of her rising from her seat, as this act proves rejection, because by getting up the attention is deranged and withdrawn from the present subject: contrary to a case where she delays answering for a whole day, for instance, and does not rise from her seat, nor employ herself in anything else: for here her option remains to her, as a Majlis or situation is sometimes of a short and sometimes of a long duration, wherefore her right of option continues until such time as something appears sufficient to terminate the Majlis, or to prove rejection. And here it is to be observed, that by employing herself in anything else is to be understood such a thing as is, in its nature, terminative of her situation, and not any general thing.

It is not annulled by a change of posture from a mere active to a mere quiescent position.—If the woman be standing, at the period of receiving the liberty of option from her husband, and afterwards sit down, her option remains, and is not annulled, as her sitting does not imply rejection, but rather the contrary, since her attention is thereby more collected.—And the rule is the same where the woman, being seated, leans upon a pillow, or having leaned upon her pillow (at the time the husband speaks), sits up without a pillow, because these are no more than changes from one mode of sitting to another, and do not import rejection any more than where a person sitting upon one part changes and sits upon another. —Our author remarks that this is the doctrine of the Jama Sagheer, and is most approved.—It is elsewhere said, that where the woman is sitting up without a pillow, and then leans upon a pillow, option no longer remains, as this shows an indifference respecting it amounting to a rejection.

A wife may signify her wish to consult her friends, without prejudice to her right of option.—If the woman, on receiving a liberty of opinion, say that she wishes to see her father in order to consult him, or to get witnesses, in order to have their evidence, her option remains, because counsel is expedient in every business, and witnesses are requisite to controvert the husband's denial of the fact; and hence neither of these wishes expressed on her part is a proof of rejection.

If the woman be riding upon a quadruped or in a camel-litter, and stop the animal on her husband's offer of liberty, still the right of option is not annulled; but if she proceed upon her journey, it is annulled because the going on or stopping of the animal is the same with those acts in the woman, since its motions depend upon the rider.

A boat or ship is the same as a house, as by the going on of the vessel the woman's option is not annulled; because its motion does not always depend upon the person whom it carries.

Section III.

Of Masheeat or Will

Where a man empowers his wife to divoce herself in express terms, the divorce which follows is reversible.—If a man say to his wife, "divorce yourself," not having any particular intention, or intending one divorce, and the woman reply, "I have divorced myself," a single divorce reversible takes place; and if she were to say, "I have given three divorces," three accordingly take place; where such is the intention of the husband: the reason of this is that divorce, being a general expression, takes place in the lowest species; but as, like other generic nouns, it also applies to the whole, an intention of three divorces is admitted: and, where there is no particular intention, a single divorce reversible takes place, because the power of divorce is delegated to the wife in express terms, and express divorce occasions a divorce reversible.—If the husband should in this case intend two divorces it is not admitted, because a generic noun does not bear that construction, where the woman is free; but, if she be a slave, an intention of two divorces is admitted, that being considered as the whole, with respect to her.

Although her reply be expressed in the form of an irreversible divorce.—If a man say to his wife, "divorce yourself,"—and she reply, "I have separated myself," a divorce reversible takes place, because separation is of the same nature with divorce, since, if a husband were to say to his wife, "I have irreversibly separated you [from me], intending divorce, a divorce irreversible takes place;—and, in the same manner, if the woman were (as here) to say, "I have separated myself," and her husband reply. "I have consented thereto," she becomes irreversibly divorced; and hence the expression of the woman, "I have irreversibly separated myself," stands the same as the husband's delegation, which is of simple divorce; but here the description of irreversibility which the woman has added to the simple divorce is held to be nugatory: and the simple divorce only takes place; no if she had replied, "I have repudiated myself by one irreversible divorce," in which case a divorce reversible only would take place; contrary to a reply of option, for if she were to answer, "I have chosen myself," no divorce whatever would take place, as these words are not of the same nature with divorce, for which reason it is that if a man were to say to his wife, "I have chosen you," or "choise!" intending divorce, no divorce whatever takes place; and in like manner, if the woman were to speak first, saying, "I have chosen myself," and her husband reply, "I have consented," no divorce whatever takes place; yet it is an universally received doctrine, that if the woman say, "I have chosen myself," in reply to a delegation of option, divorce takes place; but the words of the husband in the present case, namely, "divorce yourself," is not a delegation of option, and hence the reply of the woman, as above stated, "I have chosen myself," is nugatory.

It is recorded, as an opinion of Haneefa, that in the present case divorce does not take place from the reply of the wife, "I have separated myself," because the woman acts contrary to the power vested in her, by taking upon her to pronounce a thing different from that delegated to her by her husband, as the expression "separated" is different from divorce, the one being implicative and the other express; and the husband delegated express divorce only.

The power, when thus granted, cannot be retracted.—If a husband say to his wife, "divorce yourself," he is not at liberty to retract, as his expression involves a vow,* because he has, in this instance, suspended divorce upon the execution of it by his wife, and a vow is an obligatory act, for which reason a man is not allowed to recede from it. If, however, the woman rise from her seat, or remove from the place, the words of the husband, as above, transferring the power of divorce to her, are annulled, their force being confined to the situation where the offer is made:—contrary to where he says to her, "divorce your Zirra [fellow-wife]," as

*Literally, "his words express (or amount to (a Yameen," that is to say, suspend the matter spoken of upon the occurrence of some condition on the event of which that matter takes place, independent of any further volition on the part of the speaker; and it is therefore, with respect to him, absolute and unretractable. Yameen is here translated vow, as the above is one definition of vow.

this is a commission of agency, which is not restricted to place, and may be therefore retracted to the constituent whenever he pleases.

The power may be granted generally.—If a husband say to his wife, "divorce yourself when you please," she is at liberty to divorce herself either upon the spot or at any future period, because the word *when* extends to all times; and hence it is the same as if he were to say, "divorce yourself at whatever time you like."

If a man say to another, "divorce my wife," the person thus addressed may divorce her either upon the spot at any other time, and the husband may also retract, because this is a commission of agency, and therefore is not absolute, nor restricted in point of place; contrary to where he says to his wife, "divorce yourself," this being a transfer of power, not a commission of agency,* as the woman thus addressed acts from herself and not from another. But if a man say to another, "divorce such an one my wife," (adding) "If you please," the man is empowered to divorce the wife upon the spot only: and here the husband cannot retract. —Ziffer says that this and the proceeding case are alike, the addition of "if you please" in the one instance, or the omission of it in the other, making no difference, because the person so commissioned afterwards acts from his own will, like an agent in sale, to whom it may have been said, "sell this thing if you please." The argument of our doctors is that the words of the husband are a transfer of power, as he suspends the divorce upon the will of the person whom he addresses, and he is the principal who acts from his own will; divorce, moreover, admits of suspension, whereas sale does not.

A wife empowered to give herself three divorces may give herself one divorce.—If a man say to his wife, "give yourself three divorces," and she give herself one divorce only, it takes place accordingly, because, having been empowered so far as three divorces, it necessarily follows that she is enabled to give a single one.

But, when empowered to give herself one divorce only, she cannot give herself three.—If a man say to his wife, "divorce yourself once," and she give herself three divorces, nothing whatever takes place, according to Haneefa. The two disciples say that a single divorce takes place, because the woman has done that to which she was empowered, together with that to which she was not empowered; and hence it is analogous to a case in which a husband says to his wife, "I repudiate you by a thousand divorces" where three divorces take place, because he has pronounced that to which he is empowered along with that to which he is not empowered; consequently the former takes effect, but the latter is nugatory; and so likewise in the present case —The argument of Haneefa is that the wife has, in this case, attempted to do an act, the power of doing which has not been delegated to her by her husband, and hence she appears to divorce herself, first, and not in reply to the desire expressed by him, as he has empowered her so far as one divorce only, and between three divorces and one there is contradiction, the word three expressing a compound number, and one a single unit; contrary to where a man pronounces a thousand divorces upon his wife, as here three take place, because he acts in consequence of the desire of another; and contrary also to the preceding case (viz. where the husband desires his wife to repudiate herself by three divorces, and she declares one only), for here one divorce takes place on account of her being empowered so far as three: whereas, in the present case, she is not empowered so far as three, and having acted contrary to the power vested in her, what she does is nugatory.

Where the wife's reply disagrees with the husband's declaration in respect to the nature of the divorce, it takes place according to his declaration, not according to her reply.—If a man desire his wife to repudiate herself by a reversible divorce, and she divorce herself irreversibly, or the contrary, that mode of divorce takes place which was desired by the husband: thus, if a man say to his wife, "give yourself one divorce reversible," and she reply, "I have given myself a divorce irreversible," a divorce reversible takes place, because the woman has declared a divorce in express terms, but with an additional description, and the latter is nugatory, as being contrary to the desire expressed by the husband; but the former (which is in its nature reversible) takes place, as being in conformity to the husband's desire:—and, on the other hand, if the husband say to his wife, "give yourself one divorce irreversible," and she reply. "I have given myself" a divorce reversible," a divorce irreversible takes place, because the description of reversibility attached to the divorce by the wife is nugatory, since the husband, having himself affixed a description to it, does not require more of his wife than simply divorce, without any description; hence it is the same as if she had pronounced the divorce itself in a defective way: thus the divorce takes place under whatever description may have been affixed to it by the husbad, whether reversible or irreversible.

Where the power is conditional upon the pleasure of the wife, it is annulled by her reply disaccording with the husband's declaration.—If a man say to his wife, divorce yourself thrice, if you please," and she give herself one divorce, no effect whatever follows, because the meaning of his words is

*That is to say, after being thus empowered, she stands as a principal in the execution of divorce, and not as an agent: and a commission of agency may be annulled at pleasure, whereas the power devolved to another to act as a principal cannot be so.

"if you desire three divorces, repudiate yourself," and the woman giving one only, it appears that she does not desire three, and hence, the condition not being fulfilled, the divorce does not take place.

If a man say to his wife, "divorce yourself once, if you please," and she give herself three, no divorce whatever ensues, according to Haneefa, because a desire of one divorce only is essentially different from a desire of three, this being analogous to a case of execution as before mentioned, that is to say, as the execution of three divorces in that instance was demonstrated to be a sensible contradiction to that of one; so, in the present instance, a wish for three is contradictory to a wish for one; and, from the woman pronouncing upon herself three divorces, it appears that she was not desirous of one; and hence the condition is not fulfilled.—The two disciples say that one divorce takes place on this occasion, because a desire for one divorce is comprehended in a desire for three, on the same principles as the execution of three divorces comprehends that of one (agreeably to their doctrine before mentioned); and hence the condition is virtually fulfilled.

And so also, by her suspending her will upon that of her husband.—If a man make a delegation of divorce to his wife, by saying to her, "you are divorced if you be desirous of it," and she reply, "I am desirous, if you desire it," and he reply, in return, "I am desirous" (intending divorce), the delegation is void, because the husband has suspended the divorce upon the will of the women where that is unrestricted, that is to say, independent of anything else; but, from the conversation, it appears that she suspends her will upon that of her husband, and hence the condition of divorce, namely, the independent will of the woman, is not fulfilled; thus she does not act from option; and the delegation is void of course.—The words of the husband, in the last reply, namely, "I am desirous," are not effective of divorce, although such be his intention, because there is no mention whatever of divorce in the words of the woman, from which the husband's wish to that effect might be inferred in his answer, and the intention alone does not suffice, as it has no operation with respect to a thing not mentioned; whereas, if he were to say, "I am desirous of your divorce," it takes place if he so intend it, because he in this case appears to give divorce de novo, as a desire expressed with respect to any thing implies the existence of that thing, and hence his expression, "I am desirous of your divorce," is as if he were to say, "I cause your divorce," which accordingly takes place: contrary to what would follow, if he were to say, "I intend your divorce," in which case divorce would not take place, because an intention expressed does not imply the existence of the thing intended.—If, moreover, in the case now recited, the woman were to reply, "I am desirous if my father be so," or, "if such a circumstance happen" (meaning a circumstance which does not yet exist), and the father afterwards signify his desire, or the circumstance upon which she has suspended the divorce come to pass, yet divorce does not take place, and the delegation is void:—but if she in saying, "if such a thing happen," mean a thing which has already passed, divorce takes place, because suspension upon a condition already fulfilled amounts to immediate or unsuspended divorce.

When the power is expressed with an unrestricted particle (in respect to time), it is perpetual, extending to all times, and places.—If a man say to his wife, "you are divorced when you please," or, "whenever you please," and she reject his offer, saying, "I am not desirous of it" her rejection is not final, for here the power vested in her is not confined to the place or situation where it is delegated, on which account she is at liberty to use it either there or elsewhere, because the terms when and whenever are used with reference to all times, and extend to every time indiscriminately, and hence the sense of the expressions, "when you please," and "whenever you please," is "at whatever time you please," and they are, therefore, not confined to place. And if the woman reject at present, still it is not a final rejection, because her husband has empowered her to divorce herself at whatever time she pleases, wherefore the power does not apply to the time when she does not please.—But it is to be observed that the woman is not it this case authorized to pronounce upon herself more than one divorce, because the words when and whenever apply to all times, but not to more than a single divorce; thus she is authorized to divorce herself at whatever time she pleases, but not to pronounce divorce as often as she pleases.

If a man say to his wife, "you are divorced as often as you please," she is at liberty to divorce herself time after time, until three divorces, because the expression "as often" admits a repetition of the act:—but it is to be observed that this suspension of divorce upon the woman's will is restricted solely to the marriage at present existing, and does not exend to that which may afterwards occur; and hence, if the woman give herself three divorces, and be again married to the same man, after being rendered lawful to him, and then pronounce divorce upon herself, it does not take place, because a marriage has then occurred de novo;—and it is also to be remarked that the woman is not at liberty to pronounce the three divorces upon herself in one sentence, because the expression "as often as," implies unity, and does not admit of the circumstances to which it relates being taken collectively, and hence it is lawful for the woman to pronounce three divorces upon herself at three separate times, but not at once.

But not when it is expressed with an unrestricted particle in respect to place.—If a man say to his wife, "you are divorced wherever you please," yet the woman cannot divorce herself but in that place; and if she rise from her place before she pronounce it, her will is not regarded afterwards, because the words wherever, or whatsoever, are adverbs of place, and divorce has no connexion with place; the word wherever is therefore nugatory, and the will only remains, which is confined to the precise place, contrary to the case of time (that is, where the husband says, "when you please"), to which divorce has a relation, as it may take place at one time and not at another, and hence the mention of time in divorce is regarded, whether it be particular, as "you are divorced to-morrow;" or general, as "you are divorced when you please."

If a man say to his wife, "you are divorced how you please," and she remain silent, a divorce reversible takes place, whether she be desirous or not: or, if she break silence, and say, "I am desirous of one divorce reversible," and the husband reply, "such also is my desire," divorce takes place accordingly, because a conformity is established between the will of the wife and the intention of the husband; but where the wife desires three divorces, and the husband only one divorce irreversible, or the contrary, a divorce reversible takes place, because her act is rendered nugatory by the non-conformity of her will with that of her husband, and his words (viz. "you are divorced"), remain, which are effective of a divorce reversible: but if the husband have no particular intention, the will of the wife alone is regarded, insomuch that, whether she desire three divorces, or only one irreversible divorce, it takes place accordingly, in the opinion of our modern doctors, as this is what a right of option requires.—The compiler of the Hedaya observes that Mohammed, in the Mabsoot, says that the taking place of one divorce independent of the will of the wife, as above, is the doctrine of Haneefa; but that, with the two disciples, divorce does not take place so long as the woman does not divorce herself; thus she has her option of either one divorce reversible or irreversible, or of three divorces: and the same difference of opinion subsists with respect to manumission; that is to say, if a master say to his slave, "you are emancipated how you please," the slave is free upon the instant, according to Haneefa; whereas, according to the two disciples, he is not free, so long as he is not desirous of being so.—The argument of the latter is that the husband has delegated to his wife a power to effect divorce upon herself under whatever description she pleases, whether a single divorce reversible or irreversible, or three divorces; and hence it is indispensibly requisite that the divorce itself be also suspended upon her will, so that a will shall be confimed to her in all circumstances that is, both before carnal connexion and after it; for, if the divorce itself were not suspended upon the will of the wife, it would follow that the wife could have no will with respect to the description of the divorce before carnal connexion, as before consummation she cannot give herself three divorces, since in such case the wife becomes irreversibly repudiated by a single divorce before the passing of her Edit, and no longer remains a subject of divorce.—The argument of Haneefa is that the word "how" implies a requisition of description; now delegation of the description of a thing requires the existence of the subject of it, and divorce cannot have existence but by taking place.

If a man say to his wife, "you are divorced by as many as you please," or 'by what you please," she is empowered to divorce herself by whatever number she pleases, as the expression as many as and what are used with relation to number; and hence the husband appears to have delegated a power to the woman with respect to whatever number she may approve. If, however, she rise from her place before pronouncing any divorce the delegation is void; or, if she reject, her rejection is final, because this sort of singular delegation does not argue or admit a repetition of the act; and the address implying a thing required to be immediately determined upon, consequently demands an immediate answer.

If a man say to his wife, "divorce yourself what you please, out of three," she is empowered to give herself one or two divorces, but not three, according to Haneefa.—The two disciples, on the contrary, maintain that she may give herself three divorces, if so inclined.—The arguments on both sides are drawn from the Arabic.

CHAPTER IV.

OF DIVORCE BY YAMEEN OR CONDITIONAL VOW.

Definition of the term Yameen with respect to divorce.—By Yameen is here understood the suspension of divorce upon a circumstance which bears the property of a condition, and this suspension is termed Yameen, because Yameen, in its primitive sense, signifies strength or power; and the suspension is a motive to the suspender to be strong in the avoidance of the condition in such a manner that he may not be subjected to the consequence or penalty, which is divorce or manumission.

Divorce pronounced with a reference to a future marriage, takes place upon the occurrence of such marriage.—Where a man refers of annexes divorce to marriage (that is, suspends it upon marriage), by saying to any strange woman, "if I marry you, you are divorced," or by declaring "any woman whom I may marry is divorced," in this case divorce takes place on the event of such marriage.—Shafei maintains that divorce does not take place, the Prophet having said that there is no divorce antecedent to marriage.—The argument of our doctors is that the annexing of divorce to marriage is a Yameen, or suspension, as appears from its containing a condition and a consequence, and present authority is not requisite to its propriety, because the divorce does not take place until the occurrence of the condition, at which time the authority necessarily takes place; and the end which it answers, before the occurrence of the condition, is, that it restrains the vower from marrying that woman, as his meaning in the expression is, "I will not marry you, or, if I do, you are divorced." With respect to the saying of the Prophet cited by Shafei, it goes to the prohibition of immediate divorce only, and not of that which is suspended upon the occurrence of a future possible event.

Or upon the occurrence of any other circumstance on which it may be conditionally suspended.—If a man annex divorce to a condition specified, by saying to his wife, "if you enter this house you are under divorce," the divoce takes place upon the occurrence of the condition. This is universally admitted by the learned, because of the existence of the matrimonial authority, at the time of the husband's declaration; and it is evident that this declaration remains in force until the condition be accomplished.

Provided it be pronounced during an actual, or with reference to an eventual, possession of authority.—But the annexing of divorce to marriage is not lawful, unless the vower be either authorized at the time, or annex divorce to a future possession of authority; as it is indispensably requisite that the penalty be a thing of probable occurrence, in order that the apprehension of it may operate upon the fears of the vower, and that thus the property of Yameen (viz. restraint from the apprehension of penalty), do really exist at the time of declaring the condition, in virtue either of present authority, or of a reference to a future authority.

Objection.—What is now said appears to contradict the doctrine advanced in the preceding case, of a man annexing divorce to marriage, by saying to a strange woman, "if I marry you, you are divorced," for in that case he is neither in present authority, nor does he annex divorce to the future possession of it.

Reply.—Although he does not annex the divorce to an existing right, yet he annexes it to the cause of a right which may exist, (namely, marriage*), and annexation to the cause is the same as to the right itself, because in the former the latter is involved.—But if a man say to a strange woman, "if you enter such an house you are divorced," and he afterwards marry her, and she then enter the said house, divorce does not take place, because in this case, he is neither invested with any present right, nor does he annex the divorce either or a future right or to the cause thereof.

Five conditional particles of various effect.—The coditional particles are as follows, viz.: "if," "when," "whenever," "whensoever," and "as often as."—Of these the particle "if" is solely conditional; in the use of the others condition is implied.—And under the four first of these expressions, upon the condition being fulfilled, the Yameen, or vow, is completed, and no longer exists; that is to say, if the condition should again occur, the penalty is not incurred a second time, because the words above mentioned do not involve all future acts of the kind expressed in the condition, nor do they demand a repetition of the penalty; and hence, where the act which constitutes the condition is once found to occur, the condition is fulfilled, and no longer remains; and the vow does not continue in force without the condition; but from this rule must be excepted the expression "as often as," which applies universally, and such being the case, it is requisite that the penalty be repeatedly incurred:—in every case, therefore, where divorce is the penalty derived from the use of "as often as," it repeatedly takes place upon the recurrence of the condition.

If a man say to his wife, "you are divorced as often as you enter, the house," and she enter it three times, and then marry another man, and afterwards again marry her first husband, and the condition should then occur, divorce does not take place, as no penalty remains on account of its having been completely incurred in the three divorces which followed the repetition of this act in the first marriage; and as the continuance of a Yameen, or conditional vow, depends upon the continuance of the condition and the penalty, when these no longer remain the vow discontinues also.

If the words "as often as" be introduced "in reference to marriage, by a man saying, "as often as I marry any woman she is divorced," divorce takes place upon every instance of his marrying afterwards, though he should marry the woman a second time, after her having been in the interim married to another, because here the penalty is referred to the power he possesses of divorce, which is a consequence of marriage; and as this power is not restricted to any particular instance, but invariably accompanies every marriage, it follows that the penalty must take place upon every occurrence of the condition.

A conditional vow of divorce is not annulled by the extinction of property.—A conditional vow of divorce is not annulled by the extinction of the right; that is, if a man say to his wife, "you are divorced, when you enter this house," and the afterwards give her one or two divorces, and her Edit be completed, the force of the vow still continues under the extinction of right occasioned by such divorce; because the condition specified, namely, her entrance into

*Marriage being the cause of the right to divorce.

the house, has not yet been accomplished, and therefore still continues to exist; and the penalty remains, because of the continuance of its subject; wherefore the vow also continues: thus, if the condition take place during the existence of right, the vow is accomplished and divorce takes place, because of the occurrence of the condition, and because the subject is liable to the penalty; and if it occur under the extinction of right, as above, the vow is done away, on account of the condition having occurred: but no divorce takes place, because in this case the woman is not a subject of divorce; for a subject of divorce is a woman who is a property according to the right of marriage.

Case of a dispute between the parties concerning the occurrence of the condition.—If a husband and wife differ concerning the condition, the former asserting that it had not yet occurred, and the latter that it had, the declaration of the husband is to be credited, unless the woman produce proof in support of her allegation, because the husband is as the defendant, denying the existence of divorce, and the consequent extinction of his right; whereas the wife is as the plaintiff, affirming it. This relates to a case where the condition is of such a nature that its occurrence may be ascertained by other means than by the testimony of the wife herself; but if it be of such nature that no evidence but her own is competent to the ascertaining of the condition, her declaration is to be credited in preference to that of her husband. This, however, holds with respect to herself only, and not with respect to any other woman; for if a man say to his wife, "upon the coming on of your courses you are divorced, and also such an one my other wife," and the woman afterwards declare her menstruation to have commenced, divorce takes place upon her only, and not upon the other wife. This proceeds upon a favourable construction. Analogy would suggest that divorce does not take place upon her either, because she is in this case in the character of plaintiff, affirming the occurrence of the condition, and the consequent divorce, and the husband is as the defendant, denying; and the declaration of a plaintiff is not to be credited but upon proof; but the reason for the more favourable construction of the law in this instance is that the woman is inquisitor with respect to herself, as occurrence of her courses cannot be known but through her; and hence her declaration is credited on this occasion as well as in cases of Edit, or carnal conjunction; that is to say, if a woman, having been divorced, should declare that "her Edit having passed, she had then been married to a man, who having duly consummated, had then divorced her, and that her Edit from that husband had also elapsed," this her declaration is credited, so as to render her lawful in marriage to her first husband; and in the same manner the declaration of the wife is credited with respect to herself in the present instance; but it is not so with respect to the other wife because this one is only in the character of a witness with respect to the other, and the declaration of a single witness is not to be credited, especially where she is liable to suspicion, which must be the case in the present instance, on account of the enmity subsisting between her and the other, from the latter being her Zirra, or fellow wife; whence her declaration respecting such an one is not credited.

In the same manner, if a man say to his wife, "if you be desirous that God should torment you with hell fire, you are divorced, and this my slave to free," and she reply, "I am desirous of such torment," or if he should say, "if you love me you are under divorce, and this my other wife along with you," and she reply, "I love you," in both cases divorce takes place upon the woman who is addressed in these terms; but the slave is not emancipated in the former instance, nor is the fellow-wife repudiated in the latter, for the reasons mentioned in the preceding case.

Objection.—It would appear that divorce ought not to take place in the former of these instances, as the falsehood of the woman's reply is evident, since no one can be supposed desirous of hell fire.

Reply.—The falsehood is not certain, as it is possible that her hatred of her husband may be sufficiently violent to induce her to wish for a release from him at the expense even of infernat torments. But notwithstanding that the penalty (to wit, divorce) be annexed to her reply, with respect to this woman, although she speak falsely, yet with respect to the other person who is named, divorce or manumission are not so annexed, and consequently that person is unaffected by it.

Rule in case of divorce suspended upon the courses.—If a husband suspend divorce upon the coming of his wife's courses, saying, "upon the coming of your courses you are divorced," and she afterwards perceive the signs of the menstrual discharge, the divorce does not take place until the discharge shall have continued for three days, as that which terminate within a less time is not a regular discharge; but where the discharge has continued for three days, divorce is decreed from the period of its commencement.

But if a man say to his wife, "you are divorced upon one term of your courses," she is not repudiated until she become clean from her next succeeding courses, and her Tohr, or term of purity, arrive; because by one term of the courses is to be understood a complete menstruation, and menstruation is not complete until and return of the term of purity.

And if he say to her, "you are divorced when you fast a day," she becomes divorced on the sunset of the first day on which are fasts: but if he only say, "you are divorced when you fast," her divorce takes place from the first time that she begins a fast. The proofs are drawn on this occasion from the term of those expressions in the original idiom.

IF a man say to his pregnant wife, "if you bring forth a male child you are divorced once, and if a female, twice," and she should happen to produce twins, a son and a daughter, and it be unknown which of them was first born, the Kazee is here to decree a single divorce; but caution dictates that it be regarded as two divorces.—In this case the woman's Edit, or term of probation, is accomplished by her delivery; for if she brought forth the son first, a single divorce would take place, and her Edit would be accomplished by the birth of the daughter, after which no other divorce could take place on account of the birth of the latter, as the accomplishment of the mother's Edit includes a complete dissolution of her marriage, under which divorce cannot take place; and, on the other hand, if she brought forth the daughter first, two divorces take place, and her Edit is accomplished by the birth of the son, after which no other divorce could take place, for the same reason; hence, in the first instance, one divorce only would take place, and in the second two divorces; but in the present case the second divorce is not decreed, on account of the doubt in which the matter is involved; yet (as was already observed) caution dictates that this be considered as amounting to two divorces.

Cases of divorce suspended upon acts which admit of frequent repetition.—* IF a man say to his wife, "if you converse with Zeyd and Amroo, you are under three divorces," and he afterwards give her a single divorce, and she become separated by the accomplishment of her Edit, and she then converse with Zeyd, and afterwards again marry her former husband, and then converse again with Amroo, she falls under two divorces together with the first.—In all three divorces, Ziffer maintains that on this occasion no divorce whatever takes place.—This case may be considered in four different views:—FIRST, where both the conditions appear, to wit, converse with both Zeyd and Amroo within marriage, in which case divorce would follow evidently;—SECONDLY, where both conditions appear without marriage, in which case divorce does not take place, the reason of which is also evident;—THIRDLY, where the first condition exists within marriage and the second without,* in which case likewise divorce does not take place, as that penalty cannot follow without the existence of the marriage;—and, FOURTHLY, where the first condition exists without the marriage, and the second within it†;—and this is the case concerning which Ziffer differs from our doctors.—The argument of Ziffer is, that as the existence of marriage is conditional to the divorce taking place at the time of the occurrence of the last condition, so it is in the same manner conditional at the time of the occurrence of the first condition, because they are both (with respect to the rule of divorce) as one thing, since that divorce cannot possibly take place without the concurrence of both of them. To this our doctors reply that the case now under consideration is a vow, which, being an act affecting the maker of it, rests upon his competency; now the existence of marriage, at the period of suspension (that is, of making the vow), is made conditional, in order that the penalty may to a certainty ensue at the period of the conditions specified taking place: and, in the present case, marriage actually existing at the period of suspension, the vow holds good: and the existence of marriage is also rendered conditional at the time of the condition being completely fulfilled, in order that the penalty may take place within marriage; because this penalty is divorce, which cannot take place but within marriage: but, in the present case, the time of the occurrence of the first condition is neither a period within which the vow has any force, nor in which the penalty can take place; wherefore that interval is considered merely as the time of the continuance of the vow, to which the existence of marriage is not absolutely necessary, as it depends upon the vower, a vow being an act peculiarly affecting the maker of it, as was already remarked.

Case of a man first procuring a conditional divorces, and then repudiating his wife by two express divorces.—‡ If a man say to his wife, "if you enter this house you are under three divorces," and he afterwards repudiate her by two express divorces; and her Edit be fulfilled, and she be afterwards married to another man, and he have carnal connexion with her, and divorce her, and she be then

*In this and the succeeding passages a matter must be adverted to which it is necessary to understand, in order that their sense may be fully comprehended. When a man pronounces two or three conditional divorces, these remain so far in force that they recur upon the recurrence of the condition, even after an intervening marriage; but any divorce by which that marriage may have been dissolved is then counted in with that which thus recurs upon the recurrence of the condition

*That is to say, where the first occurs within the first marriage and the second intermediately between the dissolution of that and the commencement of the second marriage.

†That is to say, where the first occurs intermediately between the dissolution of the first marriage, and the commencement of the second, and the second within the second marriage.

‡This and the following are termed cases of obliteration. They are more fully treated of under the article Aila.

married to her first husband, and after that enter the said house, three divorces take place upon her, according to the two Elders.*—Mohammed says that no more can take effect upon her than the one divorce remaining after the two which she had already received, as above; and such also is the opinion of Ziffer. The foundation of this difference, in point of doctrine, is that the two divorces are held, by the Elders, to have been entirely annihilated by the circumstances of the intervening marriage, and hence the first husband still continues empowered with respect to the three divorces [conditionally declared as above] upon the woman returning to him; contrary to Mohammed and Ziffer, who hold that they are not annihilated, and therefore that in such event he continues empowered only with respect to the remainder of the three (as shall be hereafter explained). The effect of this difference of opinion appears in a case where a husband, having suspended one divorce upon the circumstance of his wife's entering a certain house, afterwads repudiates her by two divorces, and the woman, after having married another man, returns to her first husband, and then enters the house, in which case she falls under the rigorous prohibition, according to Mohammed, the two former divorces not having been annihilated by the intermediate marriage; but, in the opinion of the two Elders, she does not fall under the rigorous prohibition, as they conceive the two former divorces to have been annihilated.

Or by three express divorces.—If a man say to his wife, "you are under three divorces if you enter this house," and he afterwards repudiate her by three express divorces and she marry another man upon the expiration of her Edit, and after being divorced by him, be again married to her former husband, and then enter the said house, no effect whatever ensues—Ziffer says that three divorces take place, because three divorecs are suspended generally upon the condition, whether in virtue of the right from the present existing marriage, or of that which recurs after the intervening marriage with another; and the expression is general, and not restrictive; hence, therefore, the occurrence of the three suspended divorces may still be conceived possible after the three divorces before given; for which reason the vow also continues in force, as the permanence of that is implied in the possiblity of such occurrence. The argument of our doctors is that the penalty does not consist of three divorces generally, but of the three suspended divorces, with respect to which the husband is authorized, in virtue of the present existence of marriage, because he has imposed the vow upon himself for the purpose of determent, and it is only the three divorces therein mentioned which can operate in that way, not those with respect to which he may be authorized by a subsequent marriage, an event the occurrence of which is not probable, the chances being so much against it; and the penalty consisting of those three particular divorces being done away by the three divorces (in consequence of which the subject of divorce no longer remains), the vow is also done away: but it would be otherwise if, after a vow expressed as above, the husband were to repudiate his wife by a single irreversible divorce, for there the vow remains in force, because of the permanence of its subject.*

Case of divorce suspended upon carnal connexion with the wife.—If a man say to his wife, "when I have carnal connexion with you, you are under three divorces," and he afterwards have carnal kowledge of her, divorce takes place upon the instant of such carnal connexion taking place; and here, although he should not immediately cease such connexion, yet he does not become liable for either a fine† or a proper dower; but the fine or dower becomes obligatory upon him if, after the shortest cessation, he should again have carnal connexion with her. This is analogous to a vow made with respect to a female slave; for if a master say to his female slave, "when I have carnal connexion with you, you are free," and he afterwards have carnal knowledge of her, she is emancipated on the instant of such connexion; yet she has no claim to a fine, although he should not immediately cease; but if, after a cessation, he again renew the connexion, she has then a claim to a fine. This is the doctrine of the Zahir Rawayet—It is recorded from Aboo Yoosaf that a fine is due where he delays, although he should not entirely retreat and again renew the connexion, because this amounts to carnal conjunction after divorce or emancipation, on account of his continuing the act; but punishment is not due, since the whole is only one act, in which, as the commencement affords no cause for punishment, so neither is punishment incurred by the accomplishment of it; but yet the fine is incumbent, as the commission of the carnal act upon a prohibited subject cannot be free from both punishment and fine. The grounds on which the Zahir Rawayet determines in this case, is that by Jama [the carnal act] is understood the commencement of the act: and continuation is not commencement; wherefore carnal connexion de novo is not implied; contrary to a case of cessation and renewal, because in that case the connexion takes place after divorce; but yet, even in this instance, punishment is not incurred; on account of the doubt occasioned by the unity of place and of passion; but such

*Haneefa and Aboo Yoosaf.

*The subject still remains, because, after a single divorce, a wife continues a legal subject of two other divorces. until the expiration of her Edit.

†Meaning the Akir, or fine of trespass.

being the case, the fine is incumbent, as the commission of the carnal act upon a prohibited subject cannot be free both from punishment and fine.

IF moreover, in the case now recited, the husband had suspended a reversible decree upon his commission of the carnal act, the divorce is virtually reversed by his d lay, agreeably to Aboo Yoosif; but if he cease and again renew, it is then reversed, according to all the doctors.

Section

Of Istisna: that is, Reservation or Exception

Divorce, with a reservation of the will of God does not take place.—IF a man say to his wife, you are divorced (adding) if it please God" without any stop between, divorce does not take place, because the Prophet has said, "where a man makes a vow of divorce or manumission, saying, IF IT PLEASE GOD, he cannot be forsworn;" and also, because the husband has here introduced the words "if it please GOD," in the form of a condition, and hence the divorce is suspended upon the will of GOD, and does not take place until the occurrence of the condition: but the will of GOD, not being known, nothing can be decreed which is suspended upon it.—And here, as the suspension destroys the effect of the preceding words, it is a condition that the same follow then connectedly, and without pause, as in other similar cases: and the words "if it please GOD," are here said to be introduced in the form of a condition, because they are not actually conditional, as by a condition is understood a thing not at present existing, but the future occurrence of which is conceivable; wherefore a thing now existing cannot be termed a condition; nor a thing the existence of which is impossible; and the will of GOD is of one or other of these descriptions.

Unless it be pronounced with a pause between the divorce and the reservation.—WHAT is here said proceeds upon a supposition that the words, "if it please GOD," follow the preceding words immediately, and without separation, by a pause; but if the man should first say, "you are divorced." and remain a moment or two silent, and then say, "if it please GOD," the virtue of the former words is established, because in that case the additional words come in as a retraction from the first words which is not held legal.

IF a man say to his wife, "you are divorced, if it please GOD," and she die before the utterance of the latter words, divorce does not take place, because on account of the reservation, "if it please GOD," the words preceding do not stand or operate as a desire expressed.

OBJECTION.—As death prevents divorce, that is to say, as it is on account of death that divorce cannot take place, it follows that the same circumstance in the present case precludes the words, "if it please GOD," and thereby prevents them from operating to annul the first words in their effect, and thus it would appear that on account of the woman's dying as above, the divorce should take place upon her, she not having expired until after the words, "you are divorced," and before the utterance of the reservation, "if it please GOD.

REPLY.—Death operates to the prevention of divorce on account of its cutting off the subject of it; but it does not prevent the effect of the reservation in the present case, as the validity of reservation depends upon that of the declaration, which rests upon the husband, who is still living: but it would be otherwise if he should die before having uttered the reservation, as in that case it is not added to the preceding words.

Divorce pronounced with an exception in point of number takes place accordingly.—IF a man say to his wife, "you are under three divorces all but one," two divorces, take place; and if he say, "all but two," one divorce takes place; for it is a rule that this figure of speech termed Istisna, is expressive of a remainder from the whole of a given number from which an exception is made; and this is approved, because there is no difference whatever between a man's saying (for example), "I owe such an one nine Dirms," or, "I owe such an one ten Dirms all but one;" wherefore this mode of speaking by the exception of a part from the whole is approved, because it amounts to a mention, simply, of what remains after the exception is made, as in the present instance.

BUT the exception of the whole from the whole is disapproved, since, after exception of the whole, nothing whatever remains the mention of which might be established; and hence, if a man say to his wife," you are under three divorces all but three, the three divorces take place upon her, because the exception of a whole from a whole is nugatory, and therefore not admitted to have any effect.

AND here, as in the preceding cases, the exeception is of no effect, unless it be immediately connected with what goes before namely, the sentence of divorce.

CHAPTER V.

OF THE DIVORCE OF THE SICK.*

A wife divorced by a dying husband inherits if he die before the expiration of her Edit.—IF a man lying on his death-bed, re-

*By the Mussulman law, a woman, on the death of her husband, is entitled to an inheritance from his estate; but it is possible that the husband may sometimes be induced, from personal dislike, or other motive, where he finds himself dying, to repudiate his wife, in order to exclude her from her right of inheritance, in the event of his death; an injustice which the rules and cautions laid

pudiate his wife either by one irreversible divorce, or by three divorces, and die before the expiration of her Edit, she is still entitled to her inheritance from his estate: but if he should not die until after the accomplishment of her Edit, she has no claim. Shafei maintains that she is not an inheritress in either case, as the matrimonial connexion, which was the cause of her inheritance, is dissolved by the divorce; whence it is that if this man were to repudiate his wife by an irreversible divorce, and she were to die within her Edit, before the decease of her husband, the husband does not inherit of her, the matrimonial connexion which was the cause of that relationship which entitled to inheritance no longer remaining. To this our doctors reply that the matrimonial connexion at a time of a mortal illness is a cause of inheritance with respect to the wife: but where the husband is desirous of defeating this right by giving an irreversible divorce, his intention is resisted, by postponing the effect of his sentence of divorce to the expiration of his wife's Edit, in order to shield her from injury; and such procrastination is possible, as a marriage is accounted still to subsist during the Edit, with respect to various of its effects, such as the obligations of alimony, residence, and so forth: and hence it may lawfully be accounted to continue in force with respect to the woman's inheritance; but, as soon as the Edit is accomplished, a further procrastination is impossible, because the marriage does not then continue in any shape whatever. The case, however, is very different where the wife happens to die before her husband (as mentioned by Shafei), for in this instance the connubial connexion is not a cause of inheritance in the husband (in virtue of his right as connected with her property), because she was not sick but in health at the time of his pronouncing divorce and the connexion is dissolved with respect to his right; especially where he himself manifests his desire that it should be so, by pronouncing upon her an irreversible divorce: since as the connexion would be dissolved though he were not desirous of the annulment of his right, it follows that it is so where he is desirous, a fortiori. The mode in which the connexion may be dissolved without the consent of the husband is by the wife, upon her death-bed, admitting the son of her husband to carnal connexion and dying within her Edit, in which case the husband would not inherit of her, the matrimonial connexion with respect to him becoming null, notwithstanding he does not consent to such annulment.

Unless she be divorced at her own request, or by her own option, or for a compensation.—If a woman require her husband, who is sick, to repudiate her by an irreversible divorce, and he accordingly pronounce the same upon her,—or, if he desire her to choose, and she choose herself,—or, if she procure divorce of him in the manner of Khoola, that is, for a compensation, and he afterwards die before the expiration of her Edit,—she does not inherit of him, because the only reason for postponing the effect of the divorce is a regard for her right, to the destruction of which she in this case consents. But if she require him to repudiate her by a reversible divorce, and he pronounce three divorces upon her, she inherits, because a reversible divorce does not dissolve the marriage; and hence her requisition of such a divorce does not imply her consent to the destruction of her right.

In case of any possible collusion between the parties, by the husband, after a declared divorce, acknowledging himself indebted to her, or bequeathing her a legacy, she receives whatever may be of least value, inheritance, debt, or legacy.—If a man, upon his death-bed, declare that he had repudiated his wife by three divorces, at such a time, during health, that her Edit had passed, and she confirm this, and he afterwards make an acknowledgment of his being indebted to her in a certain sum, or bequeath her a legacy, she will, in the event of his decease, be entitled to that sum of the three which is the least, the legacy, the debt, or her proper inheritance: that is to say, if her heritance be of smaller amount than the debt or the legacy, it goes to her, and so of the others. This is the doctrine of Haneefa. The two disciples say that the acknowledgment or bequest are either of them legal, and therefore that the woman is entitled either to the whole of the acknowledged debt, or to the entire legacy (provided that does not exceed the third, or devisable proportion of his property‡), as the case may be. And if the husband, in conformity with the requisition of his wife, pronounce three divorces upon her on his death-bed, and afterward acknowledge himself indebted to her in a certain sum, or bequeath her a legacy, she is in this case entitled to whatever is of least value, the debt, the legacy, or the inheritance, according to all, except Ziffer, who says that she is entitled to the whole bequest (not exceeding the third of property), or to the whole of the debt acknowledged, because her right to inheritance being annulled by her requisition of divorce, the obstruction to the legality of the acknowledgment or bequest (namely, the matrimonial connexion), is removed. The argument of the disciples, with respect to the former case, is that when the husband and wife agree respecting his having divorced her, and her

down in this chapter are intended to counteract and guard against; some of them are also designed to counteract any fraudulent collusion between the wife and her dying dusbanh, to the prejudice of his heirs.

*This, which is termed Sils Mal, is fully explained in the Book of Wills, Vol. IV.

Edit having passed, she from that period becomes a stranger to him, and he no longer remains liable to suspicion (that is to say, in the present case, suspicion of his preferring her before his other heirs, and giving her more than her right, which is inheritance), whence it is that his evidence to her advantage is credited : and it is also lawful for him to pay her his Zakat, or to marry her sister, or for her to marry another man : contrary to the second case, as there the Edit still remains unaccomplished, and the continuance of that affords ground for such suspicion : now the subject of suspicion is a circumstance as yet concealed and unknown. wherefore the ground for suspicion is regarded, and not the actual fact suspected or apprehended ; and as the continuance of the Edit affords ground of suspicion, the effect of suspicion is established, namely, the invalidity of acknowledgment, or bequest ; and hence also is established the incredibility of the evidence of husband or wife respecting each other : as well as the incredibility of evidence, in respect to relations either by blood or by marriage ; since marriage and affinity are grounds of suspicion. The agrument of Haneefa is that suspicion exists in either instance ; in the second, because a woman may choose divorce, in order to open to her the door of acknowledgment, or bequest, so that she may receive more than her proper inheritance : and in the first, because it may happen that the husband and wife may form a collusion, and agree to hold forth their separation and the completion of her Edit, in order that he may be enabled to favour her, by giving her more than her just inheritance ; and the suspicion is confirmed where the subsequent acknowledgment or bequest appears to be of more value than the inheritance, on which account it is that such excess is rejected, and the rule dictates that she shall receive the smallest of the three, the debt, the bequest, or the inheritance.—It is here to be observed that no suspicion exists respecting the proper amount of the woman's inheritance, that being adjusted in proportion to the whole property inherited, according to established rules.—Neither are Zakat or evidence subjects of suspicion, as a husband and wife are never known to from a collusion for the purpose of enabling him to give her the Zakat upon his property, to be bear evidence in and matter affecting her.

Divorce pronounced in a situation of danger cuts off the wife from her inheritance, unless the danger be imminent or certain.—IF a husband being in a besieged town, or in an army, repudiate his wife by three divorces, she does not inherit of him in the event of his death, although that should happen within her Edit .—but if a man engaged in fight, or a cirminal carrying to execution, were in such situation to pronounce three divorces upon his wife, she inherits where he dies in that way, or is slain ; for it is a rule that the wife of a Faar (or Evader*), inherits of him, upon a favourable construction of the law ; and his evasion cannot be established but where her right is inseparable connected with his property, which is not the case, unless he be [at the time of pronouncing divorce] sick of a dangeorus illness (appearing from his being confined to his bed, and other symptoms), or in such other situation as affords room to apprehend his death : but it is not established where he pronounces divorce in a situation in which his safety is more probable than his destruction :—thus, a man who is in a fort or town besieged, or one who resides in an army, cannot be said to be in any imminent danger, the former of these situations being designed for security against the enemy, and the latter to repel his attacks ; —whereas one engaged in fight, or carrying to execution, is in circumstances of imminent danger : and consequently the evasion is established in the latter circumstance, but not in the former.—There are various cases recorded corresponding with these at present recited, and which proceed upon the same rules.—It is to be observed however, that what is here said, viz ; "where he dies that way, or is slain," shows that there is no essential difference between the two cases where he dies in the way mentioned, or in any other way, the same as a husband confined to a sick bed, who happens to be slain.

A conditioned divorce pronounced in sickness, does not cut off the wife from her inheritance, unless the condition be her own act.—IF a man, being in health, say to his wife "when the first of such a month arrives" —(or)—"when your enter this house"—(or)— "when such an one repeats evening prayers" —(or)—"when such an one enter this house,"—"you are under divorce," and the thing mentioned take place at a time when he is sick, she does not inherit of him :— but if he were to make such a condition upon his death-bed she inherits in all these cases except one, namely, "when you enter this house."—It is to be observed that the suspension now treated of are of four different kinds :—FIRST, where divorce is suspended upon the arrival of a specified time; —SECONDLY, where it is suspended upon the act of a stranger ;—THIRDLY, where it is suspended upon the act of the husband himself ;—and FOURTHLY, where it is suspended upon the act of the woman : and each of these again are of two descriptions ; one, where the suspension is declared in health, and the condition occurs in sickness ; the other, where both take place in sickness. In the two first instances, namely where the

*Meaning one who endeavours unjustly to defraud his wife of her right, or by some means to deprive her of it, that is (accommodating the explanation to the term used in the text), one who flies from or evades rendering his wife her right.

husband suspends the divorce upon the arrival of a specified time, by saying, "when the first of such a month arrives you are under divorce," or where he suspends it upon the act of a stranger, by saying, "when such an one enters the house," (or) "when such an one repeats evening prayers," if the suspension and the condition both occur in sickness, the woman is entitled to inherit of her husband, because his intention here appears to be evasion, from the circumstance of his suspending divorce at a time when the wife's right is inseparably connected with his property; but if the suspension take place in health, and the condition in sickness, the woman does not inherit of him.—Ziffer says, that in this last case also she inherits because whatever is suspended upon a condition takes place on the occurrence of that condition, and is than like the fulfilment of a promise; and also, because in this case divorce occurs during sickness.—The argument of our doctors is that the antecedent suspension induces divorce at the time of the occurrence of the condition consequentially, but not designedly, and injury is not established but from design; the act of the husband, therefore, is not to be set aside by the annulment of its effect, namely, non inheritance.—And, in the third instance (that is where the husband suspends the divorce upon his own act), he is considered as an Evader, and the woman inherits of him, whether, the suspension take place in health, and the condition in sickness, or both occur in sickness; and also, whether the act be of an avoidable or an unavoidable nature: the reason of which is, that the husband on this occasion evidently designs to defeat his wife's right, whether by the suspension, or by producing the condition during a mortal illness.

OBJECTION.—It would seem that the husband is not an evader where the condition is an act of an unavoidable nature.

REPLY.—In the case now under consideration, although the act of condition be unavoidable by him, yet it is in his power to avoid the suspension of divorce upon that act, and hence his act is set aside, in order that the woman may not be injured.

Provided that act be of an avoidable nature.—AND in the fourth instance (that is, where the husband suspends divorce upon an act of the wife), if the suspension and condition both occur in sickness, and the act be of such a nature as may be avoided by the woman (such as speaking to Zeyd, for instance), she does not inherit, as she in this case consents to divorce: but if the act be of a nature unavoidable by her (such as eating and drinking, or prayer, or conversing with her parents), she is entitled to inherit of her husband, as she is compelled to performance of such acts. since, if she were not to perform them there is fear of her perishing either in this world or the next; and the consent cannot exist where she acts from unavoidable necessity; but if the suspension take place in health, and the condition in sickness, and the act be of a nature avoidable by the woman, she does not inherit, for evident reasons. And where the act is of an unavoidable nature, the rule is the same. with Mohammed and Ziffer (that is, she does not inherit), because, on this occasion, no act appears on the part of the husband, after the conexion of the wife's right with his property.—With the two Elders, on the contrary, she does inherit, because the husband in this case obliges her to the commission of that act, and for that reason the act becomes his own, she being only as his instrument; as in a case of compulsion, a compellee being one who is straitened between two things; in which predicament the wife here stands, since, if she perform the act of condition, she sustains the injury of divorce, and if she refrain she is in danger of perishing either here of hereafter.

Where recovery intervenes between a sick-bed divorce and the death of the husband, the wife is cut off from inheritance.—IF a man pronounce upon his wife three divorces in sickness, and afterwards recover his health, but happen to die before the expiration of her Edit, she does not inherit.—Ziffer says that she inherits, because the husband in this case appears to have intended evasions but to this our doctors reply that the sickness in which divorce was pronounced having been removed by the intermediate recovery of health, the last sickness which follows, is the same as health, whence it appears that her right is not connected with his property- and therefore the husband is not an evader in divorcing her.

And so also where her apostacy intervenes.—IF a sick person pronounce three divorces upon his wife. and she afterwards apostatize from the faith, and again return to it, and the husband then die before the expiration of her Edit; she does not inherit of him.

But not where her incest intervenes.—IF, however, she were not to apostatize, but should admit the son of her husband to carnal connexion, she inherits.—The difference between those two cases is, that by apostacy her capacity of inheritance is destroyed; whereas, by admitting the son of her husband to the commission of the carnal act it is not so, for although this renders her prohibited to her husband, yet it does forbid her competency of inheritance, since prohibition and inheritance may be united in the same person (as, for instance, in a mother or a sister), wherefore she inherits in this case: but it would be different is she were to admit the son of her husband to carnal connexion during the existence of marriage, because separation is the consequence, whence it appears that she consents to the destruction of the matrimonial connexion, which is the occasion of her inheritance, whereas, if she admit the son of her husband, to carnal connexion after the latter having pronounced three divorces upon her, prohibition is not established by that act as it had been already established by divorce.

Divorce occasioned by the the slander of a dying husband does not cut off his wife from her inheritance.—If a man, being in health, slander his wife, that is, accuse her of adultery, and afterwards make asseveration respecting the same on his death-bed, she inherits of him.—Mohammed says that she does not inherit: but if the slander be also declared upon his death-bed, she inherits, according to all our doctors.—The reason of this is that the slander amounts to the suspension of divorce upon a thing unavoidable by the woman, as it constrains her to opposition,* that she may remove from herself the scandal of the imputation.

And so also of a death bed divorce occasioned by an Aila.—If a man make an Aila,† or vow of abstinence, from his wife, during health, and she become divorced, in consequence of it when he is upon his death-bed, she does not inherit of him; because Aila is a vow of abstinence from carnal connexion with her for the space of four months, which at the end of that period occasions divorce, and hence it amounts to a suspension of divorce upon the arrival of a specified time, being the same as if he had said to her, "upon the lapse of four months, if I have not carnal connexion with you within that period, you are divorced;" which was already explained.

Where a death-bed divorce is reversible, the wife inherits in every case.—If a man upon his death-bed repudiate his wife by a reversible divorce, she inherits of him in all the cases here recited, because the marriage is not finally dissolved, since it continues lawful for him to have carnal connexion with her; and such being the case, the principle upon which she inherits stands still unimpeached.

Note—In all these cases where it is said that the wife inherits, it means, "in case of the decease of the husband, before the expiration of her Edit,"—the reason of which has been already mentioned.

CHAPTER VI.

OF RIJAAT, OR RETURNING TO A DIVORCED WIFE.

Definition of Rijaat.—Rijaat in its primitive sense means restitution; in law it signifies a husband returning to, or receiving back, his wife after divorce, and restoring her to her former situation, in which she was not liable to separation from the passing of her courses, or of the space of time corresponding with their periods, and which she recovers by Rijaat; this is the definition of it in the Jama Ramooz; from what occurs respecting is in the present work, it appears simply to mean the continuance of marriage.

A man may return to a wife repudiated by one or two reversible divorces—If a man give his wife one or two divorces reversible, he may take her back any time before the expiration of her Edit, whether she be desirous or not, God having said in the Koran, "YE MAY RETAIN THEM WITH HUMANITY," where no distinction is made with respect to the wife's pleasure, or otherwise; and by the word retain is here understood Rijaat, or returning to, according to all the commentators.

Provided he do so before the expiration of her Edit.—The existence of the Edit is a condition of Rijaat, because by Rijaat is understood a continuance of the marriage (whence the term retain is applied to it), and this cannot be established but during the Edit since after that is past the marriage no longer remains.

Rijaat is of two kinds, express and implied.—Rijat is of two species: the First is termed express, where the husband says, for example, "I have returned to (or taken back) my wife, or addresses the same to her personally: and the Second implied, where he has carnal connexion, or takes conjugal liberties with her, such as viewing those parts of her which are usually concealed, and so forth. This second description of Rijaat is according to our doctors. Shafei says that the Rijaat is not approved, or regular, but where it is expressly pronounced by the husband (provided he be able to speak), because Rijaat stands as a marriage de novo, and (according to him) carnal connexion with the wife is in this case prohibited, on account of its legality having been annulled by the divorce, which is a dissolver of marriage, for it would appear that the marriage is itself dissolved by a divorce, although it be of the reversible kind, were it not that the law there leaves to the husband an option of Rijaat, which is the sole reason why he confines its effect to the prohibition of carnal connexion, and does not extend it to a dissolution of the marriage itself. The argument of our doctors is that that by Rijaat is understood a continuance of the marriage, as was before explained; and this may be shown by an act, as well as by words, for acts sometimes evince continuance, as in the case of abolishing the option of a seller; that is to say, in the same manner as the abolition of the option of a seller (which is the continuance of property) is proved by an act, so also in the present case; now acts peculiar to marriage are signs of the continuance of it; and the carnal connexion, or other acts, as before stated, are

---

*That is to say, forces her to require her husband to verify his accusation by a Laan, or solemn asseveration, before the magistrate, which, if he does so, occasions divorce, —For a full explanation of this, see Chap. X. treating of Laan.

†See Chap. VII.

peculiar to marriage, especially in the case of free women, since, with respect to them, they cannot be lawful but through marriage, and, with respect to female slaves, they are sometimes lawful by right of marriage, and sometimes by right of possession: contrary to touching, or looking at the pudenda of a woman, without lust, because that is sometimes lawful without marriage, as in the case of a physician or midwife; and the sight of other parts than the pudenda sometimes happens to people who reside together and if a wife resides with her husband during her Edit, if such an accident were to imply Rijaat, he might then give her another divorce to her injury, as it would protract her Edit.

The evidence of witness to Rijaat laudable, but not incumbent.—IT is laudable that the husband have two witnesses to bear evidence to his Rijaat; yet if he have no witnesses the Rijaat is nevertheless legal, according to one opinion of Shafei.—Malik holds that it is not lawful without witnesses, GOD having so commanded, saying, in the Koran, "RETAIN THEM WITH HUMANITY, OR DISMISS THEM WITH KINDNESS, AND TAKE THE EVIDENCE OF TWO WITNESSES OF YOUR OWN PEOPLE, AND SUCH AS ARE OF JUST REPUTE;" where, the imperative being of injunctive import: the taking of evidence appears to be incumbent. To this our doctors reply, that in all the texts which occur concerning Rijaat, it is mentioned generally, and not under any restriction of being witnessed; moreover, by Rijaat is to be understood (as was before stated) the continuance of marriage, to which evidence is not a necessary condition; as in a case of Aila, for instance, where it (the Aila or vow of abstinence) is done away by the carnal act, to which there are no witnesses: but yet the taking evidence to Rijaat is laudable, for the greater caution, so as to put it out of the power of any person to contradict it. With respect to the sacred text quoted by Malik, the imperative is to be taken not in an injunctive, but in a recommendatory sense; for in this instance retaining them, and separating from them, are connected by the intermediate particle "OR," the text saying "RETAIN THEM, OR DISMISS THEM, AND TAKE TWO WITNESSES," &c., from which it appears that the calling witnesses is laudable only, and not injunctive, in the present case, because, in separation, it is held to be laudable only by all the doctors.

The wife, should have due notice of it.—IT is also laudable that the husband give his wife previous information of his intention of Rijaat, lest she fall into sin; for, if she be not aware of his intention, it is possible that she may marry another husband after the accomplishment of her Edit, and that he may have carnal connexion with her by an invalid marriage, which is prohibited.

A declaration of previous Rijaat, made after the expiration of the Edit, is to be credited where both parties agree in it.—IF, after the accomplishment of the woman's Edit, her husband were to declare that he had taken her back before the expiration of it, and she confirm this, Rijaat is established; but if she deny the fact, her declaration is credited, because the husband in this case pretends to have performed an act which is not at present in his power, and his declaration is therefore liable to suspicion, and is not to be credited unless that be removed by the woman's confirmation. It is to be observed that the oath of the woman (according to Haneefa) is not necessary. This is one of the six cases of Isthillaf,* which are discussed at large in the Book of Marriage.

But not when they disagree.—IF a man, having repudiated his wife by a reversible divorce, afterwards say to her "I take you back," and she reply, "my Edit, is past," the Rijaat is not valid, according to Haneefa. The two disciples say that it is valid, because it occurs within the Edit, that being accounted to continue until the woman gives notice of its completion; and in this case the Rijjat takes place before such notice; hence also it is that if the husband say to her, "I have divorced you," and she reply, "my Edit is passed," still divorce takes place. The argument of Haneefa is that that the Rijjat appears to occur after the completion of the Edit bacause the wife is trustee with respect to her declaration of her Edit being completed: and as to the case of divorce cited by the two disciples, it is not admitted by Haneefa; for divorce in such a circumstance, according to his opinion, would not take place: admitting, however, that it did take place, it may be replied that divorce takes place from the declaration of the husband, after the completion of the Edit (by his saying "that he had divorced her during her Edit"), because this a severity† upon himself, and may therefore be allowed credit, contrary to returning to a wife, as that cannot be established by a declaration made after the expiration of the Edit, since such declaration affects another person.

The declaration of wife who is a slave must be credited respecting the termination of her Edit.—IF the husband of a female slave, after her Edit is past, declare that he had taken her back during her Edit, and her owner confirm his declaration, but she herself deny it, she is to be credited, according to Heneefa. The two disciples say that the confirmation of her owner is to be credited, because her person is his property, and hence he makes a declaration in favour of the husband, respecting a thing which is his particular right; this, therefore, is analogous to a case where a master makes a

*Cases treating of the necessity of a wife's confirming any question respecting her marriage by oath.

† Because (if she had been before under two sentences of divorce) this is a third sentence, which repudiates her from him by the rigorous prohibition

declaration concerning his slave's marriage; that is to say, if a man assert that he had married the female slave of such an one after the expiration of her Edit, she denying and her master confirming his assertion, the declaration of the master is to be credited in preference to that of the slave; and so likewise in the case in question. To this our doctors reply that the efficiency of Rijaat is founded upon the Edit, because, if that still exist, the former is good and valid, but not otherwise; and as the declaration of the female slave is to be regarded concerning her Edit, it must in the same manner be regarded with respect to what is founded upon it. But if the above case be reversed,—that is, if the slave confirm and the owner deny the husband's assertion,—the denial of the owner is to be credited, according to the two disciples (and also according to Haneefa, in the Rawayet Saheeh), because her Edit no longer remains, and the right to the Matat, or present,* rests with her owner; wherefore her assertion is not to be credited to the prejudice of her master's right, as she is in this case liable to suspicion; contrary to the former case, in which the owner by confirming the assertion of the husband, acknowledges the continuance of Edit at the period of Rijaat; and supposing this to be the case, his [the owner's] authority disappears; his right, therefore, is not injured by her denial, and hence that is to be credited. If, however, in this case the female slave assert that her Edit is past, and the husband and owner unite in saying that it is not past, her assertion is to be credited, she being trustee with respect to that she says, as having sole information upon the point in dispute.

At what time the power of Rijaat terminates.—WHEN the menstrual discharge, in the third courses after divorce, continues for ten days, or upwards, the power of Rijaat terminates upon the stoppage, although the woman should not yet have performed her customary ablutions: but if it stop within less than ten days, the power of Rijaat does not terminate till such time as the ablutions are performed, or the hour of prayer is past. The reason of this is that a menstruation is not accounted to exceed the space of ten days, and hence the woman's purification is understood on the instant of the stoppage, at any time beyond that period; and the power of Rijaat consequently terminates; whereas, when it stops within that period, it is possible that it may still return, and hence her purification cannot be finally determined until the customary ceremonies of ablution, &c., are performed. What is now advanced applies to the case of Mussulman women only; but with Kitabees the power of Rijaat terminates on the instant of stoppage of the menstrual discharge in the third courses after divorce, although it should happen within ten days, because with such women no other sign is requisite to establish purification than the simple cessation, as they are not held, by our doctors, to be subject to the injunction of the law in this particular

THE power of Rijaat terminates where the woman performs the teyummim,* and repeats the usual prayers, according to Haneefa and Aboo Yoosaf. This proceeds upon a favourable construction of the law. Mohammed says that it terminates immediately upon the performance of teyummim; and this opinion is conformable to analogy, because the teyummim, where water is not to be had, stands as a purification, having the same virtue with ablution, as being a substitute for it.—The argument of Haneefa and Aboo Yoosaf is that sand or dust is rather a defiler than a purifier, as it soils the body, and the latter even adheres to it; and rubbing the body therewith is admitted to be a purification from necessity only; but this necessity does not absolutely exist until the proper hour of prayer arrives; and that which is established through necessity is restricted in its virtue to the particular point which occasions the necessity; and hence the teyummim is regarded with respect to prayer only, and not with respect to the termination of the Edit. Some doctors have delivered it as the opinion of the two Elders, that the power of Rijaat terminates upon the commencement of prayer; other say that it does not terminate until the conclusion, in order that the rule respecting the repetition of prayer may by fulfilled.

WHERE the woman, in performing ablution, omits any part of her person, if it be a complete limb (such as the hand or foot, for instance), or more, the power of Rijaat does not terminate:† but if the part omitted be less than a limb (a finger, for instance) it terminates The compiler of the Hedaya observes that this rule proceeds upon a favourable construction of the law; for analogy would dictate, in this case, that if a

*See Book II. Chap. III

*According to the Mussulman law, no religious act can be performed without a previous purification, by ablution, where water is to be had, or, in defect of water, by teyummim, that is, rubbing the hands, face, and other parts of the body, with sand or dust. A woman; while in a state of impurity, is incapable of any religious act; and hence this formal purification is requisite upon the stoppage of the menstrual discharge. The point upon which the case here considered turns is whether, as the teyummim is only a substitute for ablution, the power of Rijaat continues until her repetition of prayer, or whether it terminates immediately upon the performance of that act.

†That is, as the ablution is in this case incomplete, the power of Rijaat does not terminate until prayer; but when that is repeated, it terminates of course,—the woman's purification being then fully ascertained.

complete limb be through forgetfulness omitted, the power of Rijaat discontinues, because the woman has performed the ablution upon the greatest number of her limbs, and the rule of the whole applies to the greatest number; whereas, on the other hand, in the omission of any part short of a complete limb, it would suggest that the power of Rijaat still remains, because the laws respecting Janayat and the courses do not admit of division, and hence, where the power of Rijaat remains with respect to a part, it continues with respect to the whole, as in the liberty of prayer, for instance; in short, analogy requires that the rule be the same in both cases; but the reason for a more favourable construction is that there is an essential difference in the two cases, because any part short of a complete limb soon becomes dry, especially in hot weather; and hence it is not certain but that part may have undergone ablution together with the rest, for which reason it is here said that the Rijaat terminates: whereas a complete limb does not quickly become dry; neither can the omission of so large a portion of the person, in ablution, be ascribed to forgetfulness. It is recorded from Aboo Yoosaf that the omission of ablution with respect to the mouth or nostrils is the same, as with respect to a complete limb; but it is elsewhere recorded from him that these stand the same as any part short of a complete limb (and of this opinion is Mohammed), because there is a difference of opinion concerning the divine injunction directing the ablution of those parts.

*A husband may take back an enenjoyed divorced wife, provided she be delivered of a child within such a time as establishes its parentage in him.**—If a man divorce a wife who is pregnant, or who has brought forth a child, and declare that he has never had carnal connexion with her, he is nevertheless at liberty to take her back, because where the pregnancy appears within such time as renders it possible to be derived from him, to him it is to be ascribed; and this circumstance proves his connexion with her, whence a right of Rijaat is established in him, as the divorce thus appears to be reversible, and in the same manner where the parentage of the child born of her is established in him, his connexion with her is also established; and it thus appearing that she has been enjoyed by him, the divorce is consequently reversible; and his declaration is in either case null, as the law denies it, because, by ascribing the woman's pregnancy, or the birth of the child, to the carnal act of the husband, it establishes her marriage, and consequently his right of Rijaat, a fortiori. It is to be observed that by the husband divorcing a wife who has brought forth a child is here meant divorce after delivery; for if the child were born after the divorce, the Edit would be thereby accomplished and the power of Rijaat would terminate of course.

A man acknowleding that he had never consummated with his divorced wife has no power of Rijaat, although he have been in retirement with her.—If a man retire with his wife in such a way as amounts to a Khalwat Sáheeh, and afterwards divorce her, declaring that he has not had carnal connexion, he has no power of Rijaat, because that would have been confirmed to him by his commission of the carnal act; but he acknowledges that this has not taken place, and hence his declaration is credited, as it operates to the prejudice of his right; and the law does not on this occasion deny his declaration, because a woman's right to her stipulated dower is founded upon her making delivery of her person, and not upon her husband's seisin of it: contrary to the former case, as there the law is repugnant to the husband's declaration.

If a man divorce his wife after a retirement, and again take her back, and afterwards assert that he has not had carnal connexion with her, and she should be delivered of a child within a day short of two years after divorce, the Rijaat is valid notwithstanding his assertion, because the parent age of the child is established in him, as the woman had not declared the completion to her Edit, and a child may be supposed to continue so long in the womb, whence the husband is considered as having had carnal connexion with her before divorce, because if her pregnancy were ascribed to such connexion after divorce, the marriage stands dissolved on the instant of divorce, on account of its not having been then consummated: and of course the subsequent carnal connexion is unlawful; and Mussulmans are not supposed to commit any unlawful acts.

Rijaat may be established by the birth of a child.—If a man suspend the divorce of his wife upon the cirumstance of her producing a child, and she be delivered of a child, and again of another within not less than six months after, although it were more than two years, Rijaat is established,* provided the woman have not declared the completion of her Edit, because divorce taking place upon the woman in consequence of her first delivery, Edit was incumbent upon her; and her second child must be supposed to pro-

*To understand the scope of this case, it is requisite to advert to one of the fundamental laws of divorce,—that a divorce pronounced upon a woman with whom the husband has not had carnal connexion is, in all cases, irreversible. The case here considered supposes the husband to have repudiated his wife by a sentence of divorce undefined, that is, without specifying whether it is reversible or irreversible: for if he were to declare it under the latter description, it holds so at all events.

*That is to say, the man is considered as having taken back his wife. (See the beginning of this chapter.)

ceed from an embrace of the husband during the Edit, which act on his part amounts to a formal reversal of the divorce.

IF a man say to his wife, "every time that you produce a child you are under divorce," and she be delivered of three children at three separate births, that is, within not less than six months of each other, Rijaat is established by the birth of the second child and in the same manner by that of the third, because, upon the birth of the first, divorce takes place, and Edit is incumbent, and upon that of the second Rijaat is established, for the reason before observed, that it must be supposed to proceed from an embrace of the husband during the Edit; and a second divorce takes place, because the husband has suspended divorce upon child birth with the expression, "every time that," and Edit is incumbent in consequence of this divorce; and by the birth of the third, Rijaat is again established, for the same reason as above, and a third divorce takes place in the same manner as the second; and in this case the Edit is to be counted by the courses, because the woman is not pregnant, but subject to courses, at the period of each divorce taking place upon her.

A woman under reversible divorce may adorn herself.—IT is allowed to a woman under reversible divorce to adorn herself as she is lawful to her husband on account of their marriage still holding: and as Rijaat is laudable, and her adorning of her person may excite him to it, the action is therefore permitted by the law.

A man must not approach a reversible divorced wife without giving her intimation.—IT is not proper for a man, having a wife under reversible divorce, to approach her without previous intimation, or letting her hear his footsteps:—this is where he has no intention of Rijaat; because a woman is sometimes undressed, and it might happen that if he were to come upon her unawares he would see parts of her, the sight of which occasions Rijaat; and this not being his intention, he would give her another divorce, which would protract her Edit.

A divorced wife cannot be carried upon a journey until Rijaat be established.—A MAN cannot carry with him, upon a journey, a wife whom he has repudiated by a reversible divorce, until he have called witnesses to bear evidence to his Rijaat.—Ziffer says that the husband has such a power, because their marriage still holds; which is the reason why he may lawfully have carnal connexion with her, according to Haneefa.—The arguments of our doctors are twofold:—FIRST the word of GOD, who has said, "TAKE THEM NOT FORTH FROM THEIR DWELLINGS," where the text applies to the woman under reversible divorce, the carrying of whom upon a journey is the removal of them from their dwellings, and is therefore illegal:—SECONDLY, the only reason why the effect of a sentence of reversible divorce is postponed to the accomplishment of the Edit is, the possible intention or wish of the husband to take back his wife; but where he does not do so before the Edit is accomplished, it appears that he had no such wish or intention, in which case it would be evident that the sentence took effect upon the instant of his pronouncing it and that the wife was consequently separated from that period; for if the effect of the sentence were in reality restricted to the completion of the Edit, another Edit would then always be requisite after the first: and hence, as it appears that the wife is, in effect as a stranger to her husband, from the time of the sentence of divorce, it follows that he has no authority to carry her forth; whence it is here said that he cannot carry her upon a journey until he has called witnesses to bear evidence to his Rijaat:—in which case the Edit is annulled, and his authority re-established.

Cohabitation is not made illegal by a reversible divorce. CARNAL connexion with a wife is not rendered illegal by a reversible divorce, according to our doctors. Shafei maintains that it is rendered illegal thereby, since the connubial connexion is dissolved because of the appearance of that which terminates marriage, namely, his sentence of divorce. The argument of our doctors is that the connubial tie still continues, insomuch that the husband is at liberty to take back his wife, even against her will, because a right of Rajaat is reserved to him out of tenderness, in order that he may be enabled to recover his wife when he becomes ashamed of having divorced her: and this necessarily implying that he is empowered to recover her, his being so proves that Rijaat is a continuance of the marriage, and not a marriage de novo, as a man cannot marry a woman against her will. With respect to what Shafei advances, that "the connubial connexion is dissolved on account of the appearance of that which terminates marriage," namely, his sentence of divorce, it may be replied that the effect of the terminator is postponed to the completion of the Edit, according to all the doctors, out of tenderness the husband, as above.

Section.

Of Circumstances which render a divorced Wife lawful to her Husband.

A man may marry a wife repudiated from him by one or two irreversible divorces.—IN a case of irreversible divorce, short of three divorces, the husband is at liberty to marry his wife again, either during her Edit, or after its completion, as the legality of the subject still continues, since the utter extinction of such legality depends upon a third divorce; and accordingly until a third divorce take place, the legality of the subject continues

OBJECTION.—IF the legality of the subject continue, it follows that it is lawful for any other person besides the husband to marry the wife during her Edit.

REPLY.—Her marriage with any other during her Edit is forbidden, on account of its inducing a doubtful parentage; but if the husband marry her, this objection cannot exist.

But if by three divorces he cannot marry her until she be previously married to another man.—IF a man pronounce three divorces upon a wife who is free, or two upon one who is a slave, she is not lawful to him until she shall first have been regularly espoused by another man; who, having duly consummated, afterwards divorces her or dies, and her Edit from him be accomplished, because GOD has said "IF HE DIVORCE HER, SHE IS NOT, AFTER THAT, LAWFUL TO HIM" (that is after a third divorce) "UNTIL SHE MARRY ANOTHER HUSBAND." And here two divorces to a slave are the same as three to a free woman, because the legality of the subject has only half its force in a slave, on account of her state of bondage; and hence it would follow that, to such an one, a divorce and a half stands the same three divorces to a free woman, but as divorce is incapable of subdivision; two divorces are allowed. As to what is said, that the second husband duly consummating is a condition, it is founded on the text here quoted, in which the word Nikah [marriage] implies carnal connexion, as it bears two meanings, by one of which it signifies carnal conjunction, and by the other the legal union of the sexes and it is on this occasion taken in the former sense; but ever admitting that the word Nikah, in the text, meant simply the marriage contract, yet the condition is established upon a well-known tradition of the Prophet who being questioned concerning person a power of marrying again a wife who, after he had repudiated her by three divorces, had been married to another man, and whom, after retiring with her, and lifting her veil, that man had divorced, replied "the woman is not lawful to her first husband until she has tasted the embrace of the other;" but the condition requires only the entrance of the penis into the vagina, and not the emission of seed, as the above tradition implies the entrance generally, whence that only is understood.

Nature of the consummation in the second marriage which renders a divorced wife again lawful to her first husband.—A YOUTH under puberty is the same as a full grown man with respect to legalizing; that is to say, if a man give his wife three divorces, and she after her Edit, marry with a youth under maturity, and he perform the carnal act with her, she then [in case of his decease or divorce] becomes lawful to her first husband because the condition, namely, entrance, in virtue of a regular marriage, is necessarily supposed to be fulfilled. Malik says that the carnal act of a full-grown man is the condition, because unless he be arrived at maturity the woman's testing (that is enjoying pleasure from) his embrace, which is the condition, is not fulfilled: but the cases before recited in the book of marriage disprove this distinction of Malik. It is to be observed, that it is recorded in the Jama Sagheer, that a boy under puberty but who is such as to be able to perform the carnal embrace is termed a Moorahick; and where such an one has carnal knowledge of his wife, ablution is incumbent upon her, and she is thereby rendered lawful to a former husband, if he should have repudiated her by three divorces; and the carnal embrace of such an one is implied from the circumstance of his having a priapism and desire. It is also to be observed that ablution is made incumbent upon the woman, in the present case, only on account of the entrance of the boy's penis into her vagina exciting an emissio seminis on her part, the necessity thereof with respect to her being soley in consequence of her full puberty; but it is not incumbent upon the boy, he not being subject to the necessity of such observance; but yet it required of him, that he may be habituated to a laudable custom.

A FEMALE slave, whom her husband has repudiated by two divorces, is not rendered lawful to him by the carnal embrace of her master, because that which is essential to her legatity (namely, marriage) does not exist herel.

The second marriage; when contracted under a legalizing condition, is disapproved but yet the woman is rendered legal by it to her first husband.—IF a man marry a woman whose husband had repudiated her by three divorces, under a condition of rendering her lawful to her former husband, as if he were to declare to her—"I marry you under a condition of rendering you lawful to your former husband, or, as if she were to say to him—"I marry with you under the condition of my becoming lawful to my former husband,"—this is an abominable marriage, because the second husband is here termed a Mohullil, or legalizer, and the Prophet has said, "let the curse of GOD fall upon the Mohullil and the Mohallal-le-hoo: * but nevertheless, if the parties contract a marriage under this condition, and the man divorce the woman after carnal connexion, she, upon the completion of her Edit, becomes lawful to her former husband, as there undoubtedly exists a consummation in a regular marriage, which is the cause of legality, and the marriage is not invalidated by the condition. It is recorded from Aboo Yoosaf that such a marriage is null, as it falls under the description of a Nikkah Mowokket, or temporary marriage, because the words of the husband, "I marry you under a condition of rendering you lawful to your former husband," imply, "I marry you until the time of our having carnal connexion, and not for an indefinite time, and is therefore the same as where a man says to a woman, "I marry you for a month." and so forth; and the marriage being invalid, the

* The thing rendered legal. It means, on this occassion, a thing rendered legal by some indirect and unapproved expedient.

woman cannot by that means be rendered lawful to her former husband; but in reply to this our doctors urge that the restriction of the marriage to any specified time is not expressly mentioned by the parties, nor does the man here marry the woman under any other condition than that of doing by her any marriage requires; and hence it does not come under the description of a temporary marriage. It is recorded from Mohammed that the marriage is legal and valid, for the reasons before mentioned; but yet the woman is not thereby made lawful to her first husband, because the second huaband here endevours to precipitate a thing which the law postpones (for the law postpones her legality to her former husband to the death of her present), and therefore meets a due return in the defeat of his design (to wit, legalizing the woman to her former husband); in the same manner as in the murder of an inheritee; that is to say, if any person slay his inheritee, he is thereby cut off from inheritance, as having attempted to precipitate that which the law has postponed, and thus meets his punishment in the defeat of his design (to wit, immediate inheritance); and so also in the present case.

The first husband, recovering his wife by an intervenient marriage, recovers his full power of divorce over her.—If a man repudiate his wife by one or by two divorces, and; her Edit being completed, she be married to another man, and afterwards return to her former husband, he becomes again authorized so far as three divorces, the one or the two divorces formerly pronounced upon her by him having been cancelled and obliterated by her marriage with the second husband, in the same manner as three divorces would have been.* This is the doctrine of the two Elders, Mohammed says that marriage with a second husband does not obliterate any thing short of three divorces. The proofs on either side are drawn from the Arabic.

The wife's declaration of her having been legalized is to be credited.—If a man pronounce three divorces upon his wife, and she afterwards declare that "her Edit having been duly accomplished, she has been married to another man, and enjoyed and divorced by him, and that her Edit from him is elapsed,"—her former husband may lawfully admit her asservation, and marry her, provided that from the period of his divorcing her such a space of time have elapsed as affords a possibility of this having been the case, and that he actually believe her assertion to be true: because the substance of the woman's assertion is either a matter of mere temporal concern (as not comprehending) any merit or demerit before God), or it is a matter of religion (on account of legality being suspended upon it), and the declaration of a single person, either in matters of a temporal or spiritual nature, is worthy of credit; and the confirmation of her assertion is not forbidden or reprobated, where the space of time which has intervened admits the possibility of its truth.—The learned differ concerning the shortest period which admits of this possibility, as shall be fully explained in treating of Edit.

*That is to say, one or two divorces are obliterated, the same as three would be, had that been the number formerly pronounced by him. It is necessary to observe that this case involves a principle in divorce which is nowhere expressly mentioned: namely, that the same woman is not a legal subject of more than three divorces to any one man, and consequently, that a man who repudiates his wife by two divorces (for instance), if he marry her again, unless the intervention of another husband obliterate these two, has no power beyond one divorce in the escond marriage.

CHAPTER VII.

OF AILA.

Definition of the term.—Aila, in its primitive sense, signifies a vow. In law, it implies a husband swearing to abstain from carnal knowledge of his wife for any time above four months, if she be a free woman. or two months, if she be a slave.

The mode in which Aila is established.—If a man swear that he will not have carnal connexion with his wife,—or, that he will not have such connexion with her within four months,—an Aila is established; because God has said, "Where a man makes a vow [Aila] with respect to his wife, he must stay four months,"—to the end of the verse.

In breach of Aila expiation is incumbent.—If a man, in a case of Aila, have carnal knowledge of his wife within four months after, he is forsworn in his vow, and expiation is incumbent upon him, this being incurred by the breach of his vow; and the Aila drops, as his vow is cancelled by the breach of it.

But if it be observed, a divorce irreversible ensues at its termination.—But if he have not carnal knowledge of her for the space of four months, a divorce irreversible takes place, independent of any decree of separation from the magistrate,—Shafei says that a decree of the magistrate is requisite, because the husband here withholds her right (namely carnal connexion) from his wife, and hence the magistrate acts as his substitute, in effecting a separation; as in the case of ennuchs and impotent persons, in short, according to Shafei, a right to demand separation rests with the woman, in the same manner as in the case of her marriage to one who is impotent or an ennuch; and in consequence of a decree of the magistrate she becomes repudiated by a divorce irreversible.—The arguments of our doctors are twofold:—First, the husband, in abstaining from carnal connexion for the space of four months, acts unjustly towards his wife, by withholding from her that which is her right, for which the law makes him a due return, in depriving him of the benefit of marriage upon the expiration of that term; and this is an opinion recorded from Othman, and Alee, and Abdoola-Ibn-Mussaood, and Abdoola-Ibn-Abbass, and Abdoola-Ibn-Aumroo, and Zeyd-Ibn-Sabit:—Secondly, in times of ignorance* an Aila stood as a divorce, and the law afterwards constituted it a divorce postponed to the period of four months:—Now, if a man swear to abstain for four months, his vow drops at the expiration of that term; that is, if the same man should afterwards marry and cohabit with the same woman he is not forsworn, because the vow was temporary; but if he should have sworn to abstain for ever, his vow continues in force, because it is general (that is to say, is not restricted to four months), and no violation appears by which it might be cancelled yet divorce does not take place upon it repeatedly, unless where marriage is repeated, because, after separation, the withholding of the woman's right cannot be supposed to exist: but if, after separation, the vower were to marry her again, the Aila returns; and consequently, upon carnal cohabitation in this marriage, he would be forsworn; or if he abstain, an irreversible divorce again takes place upon her, at the expiration of four months, as before, because the obligation of the vow continues, on account of its being general, and in consequence of the man marrying her again her right to carnal connexion is established, and of course his injustice in withholding it from her.—And here it is to be observed that the recommencement of the Aila is to be counted from the date of the second marriage; and if this man were again a third time to marry her, the Aila returns, and occasions an irreversible divorce at the expiration of four months, in case of the husband refraining from carnal connexion for that term, for the reasons already stated.—What is now advanced proceeds upon a supposition of the vower marrying the woman again without the intervention of her marriage with another man; but if, in the interim, she had been married to another man, divorce would not take place in consequence of the vower abstaining from carnal connexion for the space of four months, in the second marriage, because the vow is confined in its effect, to divorce in the first or original propriety,† the Aila in the present case, being the same if the husband were to suspend divorce upon his abstaining from carnal cohabitation for the space of four months, where the effect is restricted to the propriety then existing, and so in this case likewise.—This case is grafted on the case of obliteration, concerning which there is a difference of opinion between Ziffer and our doctors: and that case is where a man, having said to his wife, "if you enter this house you are under three divorces," afterwards repudiates her by an express sentence of three divorces, and she is again married to him, and then enters the said house, from which no divorce takes place, according to our doctors, whereas Ziffer holds that divorce takes place: as was recited at large in a former chapter.—But observe that, in the case now under consideration, although divorce do not take place, yet the obligation of the vow remains, as it was general, and continues uncancelled by any breach of it: and hence, if the man should ever have carnal connexion with the wife at any subsequent period, expiation is incumbent upon him; on account of this breach of his vow.

A vow of abstinence for a term short of four months does not constitute Aila.—If a man make a vow to abstain from carnal knowledge of his wife for less than four months (as if he were to restrict it to two or to three months), it is not an Aila, because Ibn Abbas has said that Aila is not occasioned by a vow of abstinence from carnal connexion with a wife for a period short of four months; and also, because a husband who abstains from the embrace of his wife for the space of four months or upwards; has no obstruction to plead, that being the longest space during which any obstruction is supposed to exist;* but an obstruction

*That is, before the establishment of the Mussulman faith.

† When a man marries a woman, his milk (which is here and elsewhere rendered propriety, or right; that is, peculiarity of possession) continues with respect to her, notwithstanding divorce, until it be abrogated by her marriage with another. In short, the propriety, or peculiar right, of a husband is a priciple which is alive in the actual existence of marriage, and is not annihilated, but remains dormant, or quiescent, under a termination of it by divorce; and hence it is that, where a man marries a woman, after having repudiated her, he is said to attain a revival of propriety, not a propriety de novo. Many of the most important and (apparently) unaccountable laws of divorce are to be traced to this source. In the present case the Aila is said to have been restricted in its effect to the vower's original propriety, and consequently, in its effect, recurs upon every revival of that propriety by marriage; but it being abrogated by the woman's intervening marriage with another, the vower's subsequent marriage with her is an attainment of propriety de novo, in which the vow cannot operate.

*By the obstruction here mentioned is to be understood pregnancy for the last four months, during which it is not deemed lawful for a husband to have carnal connexion with his wife.

may continue for a time short of four months and consequently divorce will not take place from a vow of abstinence for that time.

IF a man make a vow, saying to his wife, "by GOD I will not have carnal connexion with you for two months, nor for two months after that," Aila is established. The proofs of this are drawn from the Arabic. But if a man swear that "he will not have carnal connexion with his wife for two months," and then remain silent for a day, and the next day again swear that "he will not have carnal connexion with her for two months, after the other two," Aila is not established, because the second vow is distinct and separate from the former, the husband, upon his making his first vow, being prohibited from carnal connexion for two months, and upon making the second, four months, excepting the day on which he remained silent, whence the term of four months complete (being the space of time requisite to constitute Aila) is not included in this vow.

IF a man vow that "he will not have carnal connexion with his wife for a year, excepting a day," Aila is not established. This is contrary to the opinion of Ziffer, who places the excepted day at the end of the year, conceiving this to be analogous to a case or hire; that is to say, if a man agree to let or hire a house to another for a year excepting a day, the day e cepted is transferred to the end of the year, and so in this case likewise; and the exception being transferred to the end of the four months the complete term of an Aila is involved in the vow. The argument of our doctors is that the term Mawalee [maker of an Aila] is applied only to one who cannot have carnal connexion with his wife for the space of four months without incurring a penalty, such as expiation for instance; but in the present case the husband may have carnal connexion with his wife without incurring any penalty, because the day excepted is not particularly specified, contrary to a case of hire, where the excepted day is transferred to the end of the year, from necessity, as the contract, or engagement of hire, would without that be void, on account of ignorance; whereas this is not the case in a vow. But if, after this vow, the man were on any particular day to have carnal connexion with his wife, and four months or upwards of the year still remain, Aila is established, as the exception then drops.

IF a man, being in Basra, and his wife in Koofa, swear that he will not go to Koofa, Aila is not established, because he can still have carnal connexion with his wife, without incurring any penalty,* by bringing her from Koofa to the place of his residence, and there enjoying her.

A vow of abstinence, under a penalty annexed, constitutes an Aila.—IF a man make a vow, annexing to his breach of it pilgrimage, fast, alms-gift, manumission, or divorce, by saying to his wife, "If I have carnal connexion with you, I am under an obligation to fast,"—or "to give alms,"—or "to perform a pilgrimage,"—or "such an one, my slave, is free,"—or "you are divorced,"—or "such and one, my wife, is divorced,"—Aila is established, as in this case an obstacle is opposed to the commission of the carnal act from the terms of the vow, in the mention of the condition and the penalty, the several penalties above mentioned amounting to prohibition, as the incurring of any of them is attended with trouble or injury. Aboo Yoosaf objects that suspending the manumission of a slave upon the commission of the carnal act does not amount to an Aila, as it is possible for the husband to evade the penalty, by first selling the slave, in which case he might commit the act without incurring any penalty. To this Haneefa and Mohammed reply that the sale of the slave is not a matter of certainty, as a purchaser is not always found, and hence this objection is of no weight.

Aila holds respecting a wife under reversible divorce.—IF a man make an Aila with respect to a wife under reversible divorce, the Aila is established; but if with respect to one under irreversible divorce, it is not established, because the connubial union still subsists in the former case, but not in the latter; and in the sacred writings she alone is declared to be a subject of a vow of abstinence who is the wife of the vower.

But drops on the accomplishment of her Edit.—IF a man make an Aila with respect to a wife under reversible divorce, and her Edit be accomplished before the expiration of the term of Aila, the Aila then drops, as the woman (becoming totally separated by the completion of her Edit) no longer remains a subject of it.

An Aila made respecting a woman before marriage, is nugatory.—IF a man say to a strange woman, "By GOD I will never have carnal coxnexion with you,"—or "you are to me like the back of my mother,"* and he afterwards marry her, neither Aila nor Zihar are established, as these expressions are ipso facto null, the woman, at the time of his addressing her in these terms, not being a subject of either one or the other, since none are so but wives; but yet if a man marry a woman after having vowed in this manner, and have carnal knowledge of her, he must perform expiation on account of breach of his vow, which is still binding upon him.

*That is, without subjecting himself to any obligation of performing expiation for the breach of his vow.

*A species of abuse, by which, in times of ignorance, the wife stood virtually divorced. Since the propagation of the faith, it only occasions the wife to be prohibited to her husband until such time as he shall perform an expiation. See article Zihar.

The term of Aila, with respect to slave, is two months, this being the space of time fixed for her final separation; thus the term of Aila of a slave is half that of a free woman, as well as her Edit.

An Aila made respecting a wife at a distance may be orally rescinded.—If, at the time of making an Aila vow, there should exist any natural or accidental impediment to generation on the part of either the man or the woman (such as the former being sick, or the latter being impervia coeunti, or an infant incapable of the carnal act—or their being at such a distance from each other as does not admit of their meeting during its term), it is, in this case, in the man's power to rescind his Aila, by saying "I have returned to that woman," upon which the Aila drops.—Shafei says that Aila, cannot be rescinded but by the carnal act (and such is likewise the opinion of Tehavee), because, if the above declaration of the husband amounted to a rescindment, it would follow that a breach of the vow is therein established, and consequently that expiation is incumbent:—whereas this is not the case.—The argument of our doctors is that, the Mawalee, having wronged his wife by a vow prohibiting his carnal connexion with her, it remains with him to make her such satisfaction as circumstances admit of, by a verbal acknowledgment: and the wrong being thereby removed, he is no longer subject to the penalty annexed to it, namely, divorce.—It is to be observed that if the obstruction to generation, in the case under consideration, be removed during Aila, and after the Mawalee's oral rescindment as above such rescindment is null, and his commission of the carnal act is then requisite to rescind it, as he is here enabled to employ the actual means, whilst the end remains as yet unattained.

An equivocal expression of divorce, takes effect according to the husband's interpretation of his intention.—If a man say to his wife, "you are prohibited to me," let him be asked concerning the intention of these words: and if he say, "my design, in those words, was to express a falsehood," his declaration is to be credited, as his intention coincides with their actual tenor. (Some have said that his declaration is not to be credited before the Kazee,* as his speech is apparently a vow, since the rendering prohibited that which is lawful amounts to a vow.) And if he say, "I intended divorce," and single divorce irreversible takes place, except where he designed three divorces in which case three divorces take place, as was stated in treating of Talak Kinayat, or divorced by implication; and if he say, "I intended Zihar," Zihar is accordingly established with the two Elders. Mohammed says that this is not Zihar; because it is essential to Zihar that the husband compare his wife to his own relation within the prohibited degrees, which is not the case in this instance.—The argument of the two Elders is that he has declared prohibition generally; and Zihar also involves a sort of prohibition (namely, the prohibition of carnal connexion, until after expiation), and a circumstance generally expressed is capable of bearing a restricted construction,—And if he say, "I intended prohibition,"—or "I had no particular intention," his speech amounts to a vow, and consequently an Aila is established from it, because a vow is the original thing (with our doctors) in rendering prohibited that which is lawful, as shall be demonstrated in treating of vows. Some doctors construe any expression of prohibition into a divorce, where there is no particular intention, as being agreeable to custom.

*That is, in point of law.

CHAPTER VIII.

OF KHOOLA.

Definition of the term.—Khoola, in its primitive sense, means to draw off or dig up. In law it signifies an agreement entered into for the purpose of dissolving a connubial connexion, in lieu of a compensation paid by the wife to her husband out of her property.—This is the definition of it in the Jama Ramooz.

Reasons which justify Khoola, or divorce for a compensation.—Whenever enmity takes place between husband and wife, and they both see reason to apprehend that the ends of marriage are not likely to be answered by a continuance of their union, the woman need not scruple to release herself from the power of her husband, by offering such a compensation as may induce him to liberate her, because the word of God says "No crime is imputed to the wife or her husband respecting the matter in lieu of which she hath released herself;" that is to say, there is no crime in the husband's accepting such compensation, nor in the wife's giving it.

Which occasions a single irreversible divorce.—And where the compensation is thus offered and accepted, a single divorce irreversible takes place, in virtue of Khoola; and the woman is answerable for the amount of it, because the Prophet has said that Khoola effects an irreversible divorce: and also, because the word Khoola bears the sense of divorce, whence it is that it is classed with the implied expressions of it, and from an implied divorce a divorce irreversible takes place;—but intention is not essential to Khoola, because by the mention of a compensation, the act is made independent of it:—and also, because it is not to be imagined that the woman would relinquish any part of her property but with a view to her own safety and ease, which is not to be obtained but by a total separation. What is now advanced proceeds upon a supposi on of the aversion being on the part of the wife, and not on that of the husband; but if it be on the part of the husband, it would be abominable in him to take any thing from her, because the sacred text days: "IF YE BE DESIROUS OF CHANGING (that is, repudiating one wife and marrying another), TAKE NOT FROM HER ANY THING:"—and also because a man, by divorcing his wife from such a desire, of change, involves her in distress; and it behoves him not to increase that distress by taking her property. If, moreover, the aversion be on the part of the woman, it is abominable on the husband to take from her more than what he had given or settled upon her namely, her dower. (According to the Jama Sagheer, if the husband take from her more than the dower, it is strictly legal, as the text of the Koran already quoted is expressed generally, but the former opinion is founded on a tradition of the Prophet, to whom a woman having mentioned her hatred of her husband, he advised her to give up her dower, as a compensation, to induce the husband to divorce her, to which she replied, "I will give that and more!" but the Prophet answered "not more!"—and here the aversion was on the part of the woman).—But yet if the husband should take more than the dower, it is approved in point of law;—and so also, if he were to take any compensation, where the eversion is on his part, because the sacred text, goes to establish two points; one, the lawfulness of Khoola in a judicial view; and the other, its admissibility between the parties and GOD Almighty; now from the tradition which has been recited, appears that where the aversion is on the part of the wife, a Khoola for more than the dower is disapproved; and, on the other hand, the text before quoted shows that if the aversion be on the part of the husband, he should not take any thing, and consequently not more than the dower a fortiori; wherefore the ground of admissibility is abandoned, on account of the contradiction between the tradition and the text; and practice is established upon the other remaining ground, namely the lawfulness of Khoola in a judicial view.

The wife is responsible for the compensation.—IF a husband offer to divorce his wife for a compensation, and she consent, divorce takes place, and she becomes answerable for the compensation, ; because the husband is empowered, of himself, to pronounce either an immediate or a suspended divorce, and he here suspends the divorce upon the assent of the woman, who is at liberty to agree to the compensation, as she has authority over her own person, and the matrimonial authority, like retaliation, is one of those things for which a compensation is lawful although it do not consist of property; and the divorce is irreversible for the reason already assigned, and also because Khoola is understood to be an exchange of property for the person; and upon the husband being vasted with a right in the property, the woman; in return, is vested with a right in her own person, in order that an equality may be established.

Difference between a wife requiring Khoola in lieu of an unlawful article and requiring divorce in lieu of the same in express terms.—IF the thing offered to the husband in return for Khoola be not lawful property (as if the woman were to desire him to grant her Khoola in lieu of wine or a hog, and he consent, saying, "I agree to a Khoola in lieu of such wine," or so forth; a divorce irreversible takes place, but nothing is due to th husband: but if a compensation for divorce consist of a thing not lawful property (as if the woman were to desire her husband to divorce her for a cask of wine, and he consent, saying "I divorce you in consideration of such wine," and so forth), a reversible divorce takes place.—The reason, or divorce taking place in both instances : that the husband has suspended it upon the consent of the woman, which is already testified; and the difference between the case of Khoola and that of divorce is that, in the former, the compensation being null, the word used by the husband [Khoola] remains, and that, as being a Kinayat, or implied sentence, is effective of irreversible divorce; whereas, in the latter the word divorce is express, and consequently occasions reversible divorce only.—And the husband has here no claim upon his wife, because she has not named any appreciable article, which might be the means of deceiving him; and also, because if the thing named be particularly specified by her, it cannot be lawfully made incumbent upon her in favour of her husband, on account of his being a Mussulman; and in the same manner, it cannot be made incumbent if it be not particularly specified, as in that case she does not charge herself with it:—but it is otherwise where she specifies a thing under a false denomination (as if, for instance, she were to make a proposal of Khoola to her husband, by saying, "divorce me for this cask of vinegar," and he agree, and the cask afterwards appear to contain wine), for in this case he had a claim upon her for an equal quantity of vinegar of the medium standard, because her naming an appreciable article has been the means of deceiving him, —and it is also countrary to a case in which a master emancipates his slave, or constitutes him a Mokatib, in return for a cask of wine, for then the emancipated person is responsible to his emancipator for the amount of his estimated value as a slave, because the owner's property in his slave is a thing which bear a certain estimable value, and which he therefore cannot be supposed willing to relinquish gratuitously; whereas the property in the wife's person is not to any estimable value in the circumstance of the dissolution of the connubial right, as the only reason for its being so, in the attainment of such rights, is its importance, and consequent title to respect, when it is that the attainment of that right without a return is not countenanced by the law; but the relinquishment of that right being in itself a manifestation of such respect, there is then no occasion to impose upon any one an obligation of property for the purpose of manifesting it.

The compensation for Khoola may consist of anything which is lawful in dower.—WHATEVER is capable of being accepted as a dower, is also capable of being accepted as a compensation for Khoolá since whatever is capable of being a proper return for that which is appreciable (namely), the woman's person at the time of its coming into propriety), must, in a superior degree, be capable of being a compensation for a thing not appreciable (namely, the woman's person at the time of the destruction of propriety).

Case of Khoola required in lieu of property unspecified.—IF a woman say to her husband, "Grant me Khoola for what is in my hand," and he agree, and it should afterwards appear that she had nothing in her hands divorce, takes place; but nothing remains incumbent upon the woman, as she has not deceived her husband by any specific mention of property: but if she were to say "grant me Khoola for the property in my hand," and he agree accordingly, and it should appear that she had nothing in her hand, she must in this case return to him her dower, because she has deceived him by a specification of property which did not exist; and hence he does not appear to consent to a relinquishment of the connubial propriety without a return, and the woman cannot be legally bound to give the thing specified, or its value, as its kind or species is unknown; neither can she be laid under any legal obligation to render the estimated value of her person, that is, her proper dower, because, in the circumstance of the destruction of the connubial propriety, that is not appreciable; it is therefore fixed that there remain incumbent upon her whatever the husband may have given in lieu of his attainment of the propriety, in order that thus he may be shielded from injury.—If, moreover, a woman say to her husband, "grant me Khoola for the Dirms in my hand," and he agree and it afterwards appear that she had nothing in her hand, he has a claim upon her for three Dirms.—The proofs are here taken from the Arabic.

Case of Khoola in lieu of an absconded slave.—IF a man enter into an agreement of Khoola with his wife, in lieu of an absconded slave, on the condition that, if the slave be recovered, she shall make him over to the husband, but if not, she shall not be answerable; yet she is not released from responsibility, and it remains incumbent upon her either to make delivery of the slave or of his value, because an agreement of Khoola is of a reciprocal nature (whence it is requisite that the recompence be received on the part of the husband); and the condition of release from responsibility agreed to by the parties is disapproved, and consequently void; but yet the Khoola is not so, as it is not rendered void by involving an invalid condition. Analogous to this is a case of marriage;—for if a man marry a woman, agreeing to give, as her dower, an absconded slave on the condition that if he be recovered he shall be made over to her—but if not, that the husband is not to be answerable: yet the husband is not released from responsibility, and it remains incumbent upon him either to deliver to his wife the slave specified when able so to do, or to pay her his price.

Cases of Khoola granted for a specified sum.—IF a woman say to her husband, "divorce me thrice for one thousand Dirms," and he pronounce a single divorce, there remains incumbent upon her* one third of the thousand Dirms, because, in requiring three divorces for the whole sum, she has required each divorce, separately, for the third of that sum.—It is however to be observed that the single divorce pronounced in this case is irreversible, as being given in lieu of property.

IF a woman say to her husband, "divorce me thrice, upon my paying you one thousand Dirms," and the husband give her one divorce, nothing is incumbent upon the woman, according to Haneefa, and the husband is at liberty to take her back. The two disciples say that a divorce irreversible, takes place in return for one third of the thousand Dirms because the expression "upon payment of" is the same as the word, "for" in contracts of exchange. The argument of Haneefa is that the expression "upon payment" is a condition, and the thing conditioned cannot be divided according to the parts of the condition itself: contrary to the word "for" as that is used to express a return, and as the property is not due, divorce express (and consequently reversible) remains.

IF a man say to his wife, "divorce yourself thrice, for (or upon payment of) one thousand Dirms," and she pronounce upon herself one divorce, no effect whatever takes place, because the husband is not desirous that she should become separated for any thing short of the whole sum specified; contrary to a case where the proposal comes from the wife (as in the preceding instance), because, as she there appears to be desirous of procuring separation from her husband at the whole expense specified, it follows that she is willing to procure it, at the third of that expense only, a fortiori.

IF a man say to his wife, "you are divorced upon payment of one thousand Dirms," and she agree, divorce takes place upon her, and the husband has a claim upon her for the thousand Dirms, in the same manner as where a man says, "you are divorced for a thousand Dirms," and the wife consents, in which case divorce takes place, and one thousand Dirms are incumbent upon her:—but it is to be observed that in both cases the woman's assent is a condition, because the words of the husband, "you are divorced for one thousand Dirms," mean, "you are under divorce in return for one thousand Dirms due from you to me,"—and his words, "you are divorced upon payment of one thousand Dirms," mean "you are under divorce on condition that one thousand Dirms be due from you to me," and the return cannot be made incumbent upon her without her assent; moreover, a circumstance suspended upon a condition cannot take place until the condition be previously fulfilled, wherefore the effect in this case depends upon her agreeing to what is proposed. And here the divorce is irreversible, for the reason already stated.

If a man say to his wife, "you are divorced, and there is against you a thousand Dirms," and she consent,—or, if a man say to his slave, "you are free and there is against you a thousand Dirms," and the slave assent,—the slave is free, and divorce takes place upon the wife, but nothing remains incumbent upon either, according to Haneefa:—the rule is also the same if they were not to assent.—The two disciples say that the sum specified is incumbent upon them, where they assent; but that, if they do not assent, neither divorce nor emancipation take place; for they argue that the latter part of the husband's address is such as is used in bargains of exchange; and a contract of Khoola, or of Kitabat, being a contract of exchange, is therefore to be considered as such;—as in hire, for instance, where if a man say to another, "carry this burthen, and there is a Dirm for you," it is the same as if he were to say, "carry this burthen for a Dirm."—To this Haneefa replies that the latter part of the sentence has a separate and detached sense; and therefore is not be connected with the preceding part, unless there be something to show that it is so;—but here nothing exists to evince such connexion, because divorce and manumission are frequently produced without any substantial return:—contrary to cases of sale, or of hire, as neither of these are to be conceived without a substantial compensation.

A proposal of Khoola made to the wife, with a reserve of option to the husband, is invalid.—If a man say to his wife, "you are divorced for a thousand Dirms, on a condition of option to me (or, to you) for three days," and she consent, the option is invalid, where it is reserved to him, but valid where it is reserved to her; and if she rejects his proposal within the three days, the Khoola is null: but if she do not reject it within that time, the divorce takes place, and the sum specified by the husband becomes incumbent upon her.—This is the doctrine of Haneefa. The two disciples say that the option is null in either case, and that divorce takes place upon the woman, and the sum specified becomes incumbent upon her, because option is used for the purpose of dissolving a contract, or other agreement, after it has been concluded, and not for preventing the execution of it; and the act of the man, or of the woman, implying proposal on the part of the former, and acceptance on that of the latter, does not carry with it dissolution on either part; his proposal does not, as it is a Yameen, or suspending vow, on account of its involving a condition and a consequence (namely, the suspension of divorce upon the woman's consent); and a vow is in itself incapable of effecting dissolution; nor does her acceptance, as that is the condition of the vow and as the vow is in itself incapable of effecting dissolution, so is the condition; and such being the case, the reserve of option on either part null.—The argument of Haneefa is that Khoola on the part of the woman stands as a sale, since it is a transfer of property for a return, and accordingly, if it proceed first from the wife, by her saying to her husband, "divorce me in return for one thousand Dirms, on a condition of option to me (or, to you) for three days," and she afterwards retract before her husband signifies his consent, her retraction is approved, on which account it is restricted to that Majlis, or situation, and does not extend beyond it,—that is, if she rise from her seat before her husband signifies his assent, it becomes null; the condition of option in it therefore, when proceeding from the wife, is approved; but when it proceeds from the husband, the condition of option is not approved, because it is then a vow, wherefore his retraction of it is not approved, and it continues in force beyond the Majlis; and as it is a vow on the part of the husband, he can have no option, since a vow does not admit of option. Let it be also observed that the case of a slave, with respect to manumission, is the same as that of a wife, with respect to divorce;—that is to say, manumission for a consideration is an exchange, on the part of a slave, that same as divorce for a return, on the part of a wife.

The assertion of the husband respecting Khoola is to be credited.—If a man say to his wife, "I yesterday divorced you for a thousand Dirms, but you did not consent,"—and the woman reply that she did consent, the assertion of the husband is to be credited: but if a man say to another, 'I yesterday sold you this slave for a thousand Dirms, but you did not consent," and the other reply that he did consent, the assertion of the purchaser is to be credited.—The reason of the difference between these two cases is that divorce for a compensation is a vow, when proceeding from the husband, and his acknowledgment of his having made the proposal does not necessarily imply an acknowledgment of the condition having taken place, as the vow holds good independent of that circumstance, whereas sale cannot be effected without the consent of the purchaser, and hence an acknowledgment of sale necessarily implies an acknowledgment of that circumstance without which sale cannot exist, namely, consent, and the seller's denial of that circumstance is a contradiction to his previous acknowledgment, and consequently not to be credited.

A mutual discharge leaves each party without any claim upon the other.—A Mobarat, or mutual discharge (signified by a man saying to his wife, "I am discharged from the marriage between you and me," and her consenting to it), is the same as Khoola,—that is to say, in consequence of the declaration of both, every claim which each had upon the other drops, so far as those claims are connected with their marriage. This is the doctrine of Haneefa. Mohammed says that nothing is done away by either except what is particularly mentioned by both the husband and the wife. Aboo Yoosaf unites with Mohammed, as to the Khoola, but with Haneefa as to the mutual discharge.—The argument of Mohammed is that mutual discharge and Khoola are contracts of exchange, in which the circumstances specifically stipulated are also regarded, and not those which are not stipulated. The argument of Aboo Yoosaf is that the word Mobarat, from its grammatical form bears a reciprocal sense, and therefore requires that the discharge be equally established on both sides; and this is general; yet the discharge is in this case restricted to those rights connected with marriage, as the design proves it to be so; but Khoola only requires that the woman be freed from the restraint of her husband; and as that is obtained by the dissolution of the marriage, it does not require that all its effects be terminated. The argument of Haneefa is that Khoola bears the sense of separation, and that is general, the same as a mutual discharge, and consequently marriage is thereby terminated, together with all its rights and effects, the same as by a mutual discharge.

Khoola entered into by a father on behalf of his infant daughter is invalid.—If a father transact a Khoola with the husband of his infant daughter, agreeing to pay the consideration out of her property, the Khoola is not valid with respect to her, because this exhibits no regard for her interest, as her person is not appreciable in the dissolution of a marriage, whereas the consideration is so: contrary to marrige (as where a man contracts his infant daughter to another) for that is valid, because the woman's person, on entering into a marriage, is appreciable:—and the woman's person not being appreciable in the dissolution of a marriage, the Khoola of a wife sick of a mortal illness is considered as proceeding from third of her property: but being appreciable upon entrance into a marriage, if, a man sick of a mortal illness were to marry a woman on a proper dower, it is considered as coming from the whole of his property.—The Khoola, therefore, being illegal, the dower of the infant does not drop, nor does the husband acquire any right to her property.—There are two traditions with respect to the act of the father occasioning divorce in this instance; according to one, divorce does take place; according to the other it does not; the former, however, is the better opinion, because the Khoola is a suspension of divorce upon the consent of the father, which is the same as upon any other condition.

Unless he engage to hold himself responsible for the compensation.—If a father transact a Khoola on the part of his infant daughter for a certain sum, engaging to hold himself responsible for the payment, the Khoola is valid, and the sum specified bacomes incumbent upon him, because the engagement even of a stranger for the consideration of Khoola is valid, and consequently that of a father in superior degree: in this instance also the infant's dower does not drop, as the father has no authority with respect to the relinsquishment of it.

Or refer it to his daughter's consent.—And if the father were to stipulate that his daughter is to be responsible for the sum specified, this will depend upon her consent where she is competent (that is, capable of comprehending the nature of her situation and that of the present transaction, and pronouncing upon them); and if she consent, divorce takes place, on account of the condition being fulfilled upon which it is suspended: but the sum specified (or consideration) is not incumbent upon her, as an infant is incapable of undertaking the discharge of any pecuniary obligation: and if the father consent on his daughter's behalf, there are two traditions concerning it;—according to one, divorce does not take place until she shall exentually express her consent; and according to another, divorce takes place independent of it; but here the compensation agreed for is not incumbent upon her at all events.—And in the same manner, if a father, transacting a Khoola on the part of his infant daughter, agree that the compensation shall consist of her dower, and he happen not to be surety for the same,* the validity of the Khoola depends upon the daughter's consent, which if she declare, divorce takes place; but yet her dower does not drop: and also, if the father consent on his daughter's behalf, there are two traditions concerning it, as already stated: if however, he be surety for the dower, amounting to one thousand Dirms (for instance), divorce takes place, because the condition (namely consent) is existing; and five hundred Dirms only are incumbent upon him, according to a favourable construction of the law. Analogy would suggest that he is liable for the whole thousand, upon this ground, that where an adult woman transacts Khoola on her own behalf, before consummation of marriage, for any specified sum (say one thousand Dirms), and her dower be also one thousand, the whole sum is incumbent upon her, and is discharged by five hundred dropping from her dower, and her paying the

* See Book of Marriage, Chap. III.

other five hundred out of her own property:—but according to the more favourable construction of the law, nothing whatever is incumbent upon her, because the intent of the husband, in the transaction, is merely to free himself from the obligation of her dower; and this end being obtained, nothing beyond that remains incumbent upon her.

CHAPTER IX.

OF ZIHAR

Definition of the terms.—The word Zihar is drived from Zihr, the back.—In the language of the law it signifies a man comparing his wife to any of his female relation, within such prohibited degree of kindred, whether by blood, by fosterage, or by marriage, as renders marriage with them invariably unlawful,—as if he were to say to her [by a peculiarity in the Arabic idiom], "you are to me like the back' [Zihr] of my mother." It is essential to Zihar that the person compared be the wife of the speaker, insomuch that Zihar does not apply to a female slave; and competency to pronounce Zihar appertains only to one who is a Mussulman, of sound mind, and mature age, that pronounced by a Zimmee or an infant being nugatory; and its effect is to prohibit the person who pronounces it from carnal connexion with his wife, until he shall have performed an expiation.

Zihar prohibits carnal connexion until expiation.—If a man say to his wife, "you are to me like the back of my mother," she [the wife] becomes prohibited to him, and his carnal connexion with her is unlawful, as well as every other conjugal familiarity, until he perform expiation for the same as is enjoined in the sacred writings.

Nature and duration of Zihar.—In times of ignorance (that is, before the establishment of the Mussulman faith), Zihar stood as a divorce; and the law afterwards preserved its nature (which is prohibition), but altered its effect to a temporary prohibition, which holds until the performance of expiation, but without dissolving the marriage.—The reason for this is that Zihar is an offence, as being a declaration founded upon a falsehood, and which amounts to a disowning or denying of the wife; and therefore finds its proper punishment in her being rendered unlawful to him who pronounces it, by a prohibition which cannot be removed but by his performing expiation: and as carnal connexion becomes prohibited by Zihar, so do all its accompanying privileges, such as kissing, touching, and other familiarity, lest the husband be tempted to the commission of the carnal act; in the same manner as is the rule with respect to relations within the prohibited degrees, with whom not only the carnal act itself, but also every familiarity which leads to the commiseion of it, are prohibited: contrary to that respecting women fasting, or in their courses, with whom although the commission of the carnal act itself be prohibited, yet other liberties are not so, as those situations are perpetually recurring to them and if such a rule were to hold, it would operate as an almost continual restraint upon them; whereas, with respect to women under Zihar, or within the prohibited degrees, this is not the case.

If the prohibition occasioned by Zihar be violated, yet no additional penalty is incurred.—If a man, having produced Zihar upon his wife, have carnal connexion with her before he make expiation, it behoves him to respect and pray forgiveness from God; but nothing is incumbent upon him, except the expiation on account of his Zihar, as before, and that he refrain from any repetition of the carnal act with her until he perform such expiation, because it is related of the Prophet that he thus commanded one who had committed the carnal act with his wife after Zihar, and before expiation from which tradition it appears that nothing more is incumbent (in consequence of the commission of the carnal act before expiation), for if it were so, the Prophet would somewhere have mentioned it.

Zihar cannot occassion divorce.—Let it be observed that from the words of the husband, "you are to me like the back of my mother," nothing but Zihar is established, because the term employed expressly signifies Zihar; and if he should intend divorce by it, yet that does not take place, as the law of divorce is broken through in this particular.* and consequently Zihar does not admit of divorce being intended by it.

Zihar is established by a comparison with any part of the body which implies the whole person.—If a man say to his wife, "you are to me like the belly of my mother," or "the thigh," or "the pudendum,"—Zihar is thereby established, as Zihar signifies the likening of a woman to a kinswoman within the prohibited degrees, which interpretation is found in the comparison being applied to any of the parts or members improper to be seen.—And Zihar is in the same manner established, by the likening of the wife to any other kinswoman within such prohibited degree as that marriage with them is at all times unlawful, such as sisters, and aunts, and foster-mothers, who are invariably prohibited, as well as a natural mother. And so also if a man say to his wife, "your head is to me like the back of my mother," or "your pudendum," or "your waist,"—because by these the whole person is figuratively expressed; and so also if he were to say, "your half or your third," because in this case the effect is established in a

*That is to say, Zihar has been made, by the law, a thing distinct and separate from divorce, and subject to a rule peculiarly applicable to itself.

diffusive portion* and consequently extends to the whole person, because, as the diffusive portion of any thing is a proper subject of all other acts such as purchase, sale and so forth, so is it of divorce; but divorce being incapable of division, is necessarily established in the whole person: and as Zihar resembles divorce it therefore, like divorce, extends to the whole also.

A general comparison takes effect according to the husband's explanation.—Where a man says to his wife, "you are to me like my mother," it is requisite that his intension be examined into, so as to discover the true predicament in which the wife stands; and if he declare that his meaning was only to show respect to his wife, it is to be received according to his explanation, because in speech respect may be expressed by a general comparison; or, if he declare his intention, to have been Zihar, that is accordingly established, for here appears a comparison with the whole person of his mother, in which her back is included: but as that is not expressly mentioned, the speaker's intention is requisite to establish it; and if he declare his intention to be divorced, a divorce irreversible takes place, as his comparing his wife with his mother is likening her to one who is prohibited to him, and is therefore the same as if he were to say, "you are prohibited to me," thereby intending divorce;—but if he declare that he had no positive intention neither Zihar nor divorce are established (according to Haneefa and Aboo Yoosaf), because the address bearing the construction of respect, must here be taken in that sense, as being of less importance than any other. Mohammed says that Zihar is established independent of intention, because a comparison of the wife with a limb or member of the mother occasioning Zihar, it follows that, where it is made with the whole, Zihar, is established a fortiori.—With Aboo Yoosaf if the intention of the husband be merely prohibition, an Aila only is established, because the prohibition by Aila is less rigorous than by Zihar.—With Mohammed, on the contrary, Zihar is established: his argument is taken from the Arabic.

And the same of a comparison in point of prohibition.—If a man say to his wife, "you are to me prohibited, like my mother," intending either Zihar or divorce, it takes effect according to his intention, as this address may be taken in either sense,—in that of Zihar, as being a comparison,—and in that of divorce, as expressing prohibition; strengthened by the comparison. In this case; however, if he have no intention, according to Aboo Yoosaf, Aila is established,—and, according to Mohammed, Zihar,—as in the preceding case.—And if he say, "you are to me prohibited like the back of my mother," and thereby intend divorce or Aila, yet nothing but Zihar is established, according to Haneefa.—The two disciples say that whatever he may intend is established, as prohibition equally implies either Aila or divorce; according to Mohammed, however where divorce is the intention, no Zihar is established; whereas, according to Aboo Yoosaf, divorce and Zihar are both established together (that is, divorce is established on account of the intention, and Zihar on account of the term Zihr [back] being expressly mentioned, as was stated in its proper place)—The argument of Haneefa is that the words above recited expressly signify Zihar, and therefore do not bear any other sense; and the word prohibited, which is introduced there, relates solely to the prohibition by Zihar, as prohibition is of various kinds of which that by Zihar is one, and is on this occasion preferred, on account of the accompanying comparison with the back of the mother, and all other kinds of prohibition being only constructive, and that by Zihar positive, the prohibition to which the word "prohibited" alludes, is to be taken as relating to the Zihar only.

Zihar has no effect upon any but a wife.—Zihar is not established with respect to any but the wife of the speaker, insomuch that if a man pronounce a Zihar upon his female slave, it has no effect for various reasons.—First, God has said,—"Men who pronounce Zihar upon their women,"—where, by women is understood wives; secondly, the legality of a female slave is of a secondary or dependent nature and that of a wife of a primary or original nature, and hence those two persons must not be confounded; Thirdly, Zihar is an imitation of divorce, and divorce does not take place upon a slave.

If a man marry a woman without her consent, and pronounce a Zihar upon her before that be obtained, and she afterwards signify her consent, the Zihar is void, because the husband, in making the comparison, said no more than what was at that time strictly true, and hence what he says does not amount to a disowning or denying of her.

Objection.—It would here appear that the validity of the Zihar remains suspended upon the woman's consent to the marriage, in the same manner as the manumission of the purchaser of a slave from an usurper rests upon the consent of the proprietor (that is to say, where a person purchases a slave of the usurper of him, and emancipates him, the validity of his emancipation depends upon the proprietor's assenting to the sale), because Zihar is a right of possession by marriage, in the same manner as manumission is a right of possession by right of property.

Reply.—The validity of the Zihar is not suspended upon her consent of the marriage, because Zihar is not one of the rights of marriage, as it has no place in the ordinances

*Joozoo Shae is here rendered a diffusive portion, in opposition to Joozoo Mayeen a particular or specified portion.

of the law,* whereas matrimony has a place in them, and that which is not of the law is incapable of appertaining as a right to that which is one of its ordinances; contrary to the case of manumission proceeding from the purchaser of a slave out of the hands of his usurper, as manumission is a right of property.

Zihar collectively pronounced takes place upon every individual to whom it is addressed.—WHERE a man addresses all his wives collectively, saying, "ye are to me as the back of my mother," Zihar is established with respect to every one of them, he having on this occassion applied the Zihar to them all indiscriminately, as in divorce, where if a man direct a sentence of divorce to the whole of his wives collectively, it takes place upon the whole. And here an expiation is incumbent upon him, on account of each wife respectively, because prohibition has been established with respect to each; and expiation is ordained for the purpose of terminating and abolishing the probibition; and where that is numerous the expiation must be so likewise, according to the number of prohibition; contrary to a case where a man, pronounce an Aila (or vow of four months' abstinence from carnal connexion) upon all his wives collectively, and break his vow by having carnal knowledge of them within the four months, for here a single expiation only is incumbent upon him, because in this case expiation is incumbent upon him, out of respect to the honour and greatness of the name of GOD; and his name, in a vow of Ali, is mentioned once only, as it is pronounced by the man saying to all his wives, "by GOD I will not have carnal connexion with you."

Section.

Of Expiation.

A Zihar may by expiated by the emancipation of a slave, &c.—THE expiation of a Zihar may be effected by the emancipation of a slave; or if, from not being possessed of such slave, this mode be impracticable, it may be effected by a fast of two months successively;† or if the state of the health do not admit of such fast, by the distribution of victuals to sixty poor men: because a passage which occurs in the Koran, respecting expiation, demonstrates the obligation of performing it in one or other of those ways: but the expiation is supposed to precede a man's touching his wife, after having pronounced a Zihar upon:—in expiation by manumission or fasting this is evident, because the text relates to that; and so also in expiation by the distribution of victuals to the poor;—because by expiation prohibition is terminated, wherefore it is necessary that the expiation be first made in order that carnal connexion may be lawful.

The emancipation of a slave of any description suffices.—IT suffices for an expiation that a slave be released, whether that slave be an infindel or a Mussulman, an infant or an adult a male or a female, because the word Rakba, in the Koran, applies equally to all of these, as it signifies one who is possessed, in right of property, by another, under any description whatever.—Shafei says that the emancipation, of an infidel does not suffice as an expiation, because this is a right of GOD, which cannot lawfully be expended upon one who, as being an infidel, is his enemy; like Zakat, which is a right of GOD, and the disbursement of which upon infidels, as being the enemies of GOD, is therefore illegal.—To this our doctors reply, that the emancipation of a slave [Rakba] is what is mentioned in the text, and that is fulfilled by the manumission of an infidel: and as to what Shafei advances, of expiation being a right of GOD, and therefore not to be expended upon his enemies, it may be replied that the intention of the expiation is to render the slave equal to the fulfilment of such duties as relate to GOD, that is to say, of Zakat, pilgrimage, bearing evidence, fighting for the faith, magistracy, and so forth; and if the slave be not a Mussulman, and continue an infidel after manumission, thereby enhancing his crime of infidelity, and precluding himself from receiving those advantages which he was qualified to enjoy through his freedom, it is to be attributed to the error of his choice, and not to any defect in the act of the expiator.

Unless such slave be defective in one of his faculties.—IT is not sufficient, as an expiation, to emancipate a slave who is blind, or maimed of both the fellow-members, whether hands or feet, because here such a slave is utterly deprived of one of his bodily endowments either of seeing, carrying, or walking, and the privation of any one advantage in a slave renders the manumission of him insufficient as an expiation, since a person in such a state is accounted dead: but where the privation is not entire it does not forbid the validity of the expiation, and hence it suffices for that purpose to emancipate a slave who is blind of one eye or maimed of one hand or foot, or of a hand and foot, from opposite sides, as this amounts not to an absolute privation of one of the advantages, but only to a defect: the case, however is otherwise where he is maimed of a hand and foot upon the same side, for in this case his emancipation would not suffice, as this amounts to a privation of the advantage of walking, since, without the assistance of the hand upon the lame side, that is impracticable.

The emancipation of a deaf slave suffices.—IT suffices, as an expiation, to emancipate a deaf slave. Analogy would suggest that this

*That is there are no particular rules instituted for it in the Koran, the laws respecting it being taken from the Sonna.

† By Sawm, or fasting is here and elsewhere understood an abstinence from food and every carnal enjoyment from the rising to the setting sun of each day, within the prescribed term.

is not sufficient, as the slave is here deprived of one faculty; but it is admitted as sufficient, upon a favourable construction of the law, as the radical faculty still continues, since one who is considered as deaf may yet be capable of hearing what is spoken aloud: if, however, he cannot hear at all (as where a person is born perfectly deaf), his emancipation does not suffice.

But not that of one who has lost both his thumbs.—IT does not suffice, as an expiation, to emancipate a slave who has lost both his thumbs, as his power of carrying, which is one of his bodily endowments, is in that case destroyed.

Or who is insane.—NEITHER does it suffice to emancipate a slave who is insane, because no use is to be derived from the members of the body unless they be informed with reason, and therefore a privation of reason amounts to a privation of all the corporal endowments.

Unless it be an occasional insanity only.—BUT if the slave be one who is insane only at intervals, his freedom suffices for an expiation, as this circumstance is not an utter privation of the faculty, but only a defect in it, which does not prevent the sufficiency.

Nor of a Modabbir, or Am-Walid or Mokatib, who has paid part of his ransom.—IT does not suffice, as an expiation, to emancipate a Moddabir, or Am-Walid, as such are eventually entitled to their freedom, and hence their bondage is incomplete;—and so also of a Mokatib who has fulfilled his contract of Kitabat in part, because in this case his freedom must be accounted as in return for the part of his ransom already received, and consequently does not suffice for an expiation, as that is an act of piety, in which speciality is essential.—It is recorded as an opinion of Haneefa that the release of this Mokatib is sufficient, as bondage is found to exist in him in every shape, and accordingly the contract of Kitabat admits of being annulled; contrary to Am-Walids and Modabbirs, as a Tadbeer or Isteelad cannot be cancelled.

IF a person who pronounces Zihar emancipate, for expiation, a Mokatib who has not paid any part of his ransom, it suffices.—Shafei says that it does not suffice, because the Mokatib is a claimant of freedom, in virtue of the contract of Kitabat, and is therefore the same as a Modabbir.—The argument of our doctors is that bondage exists in a Mokatib in every shape, because the contract of Kitabat is capable of annulment; and also, because the Prophet has declared "a MOKATIB is a slave as long as a single DIRM remains due from him."

That procured for a parent or child suffices.—IF a man purchase his father or his son intending expiation thereby, it suffices.—Shafei says that it does not suffice;—the same difference of opinion subsists in the case of expiation of a Yameen, as shall be recited at large in treating of vows.

But not that of a share in a coparcenary slave.—IF a man, being rich, emancipate his half of a coparcenary slave, and then indemnify his partner for the value of the remainder, this does not suffice for an expiation with Haneefa.—The two disciples hold that it suffices, because the expiator, becoming possessed of his partner's share by indemnifying him, does in effect emancipate a slave who is entirely his own property:—but it were otherwise if the expiator be poor, as in this case it is incumbent upon the slave to perform Siayet, or emancipatory labour, for the partner's share; and hence the emancipation is, so far, for a return. The argument of Haneefa is that in this case the emancipation is defective in the proportion of the partner's share, until the transition of the property is it to the emancipator be effected by his indemnifying the other partner, and this circumstance forbids its sufficiency for an expiation.

The partial emancipation of a sole slave (when followed by the emancipation of the remainder) suffices.—IF a man emancipate half of his own slave, as an expiation, and afterwards emancipate the remainder for the same purpose, it suffices, as this amounts to no more than emancipating him by two sentences instead of one; and the defect which appears in the second half on account of the first half being already free is not regarded, since this defect has been induced upon the expiator's property, in consequence of his emancipating it on account of expiation: and a defect like this is not regarded; but is considered in the same light as when a man having thrown a goat on its side for the purpose of sacrifice, happens to direct his knife in the animal's eye, so as to render it defective, which is not regarded, the sacrifice of the goat being still lawful, as the defect has befallen the property on account of sacrifice: contrary to the preceding case, because there the defect appears in the property of the other partner.—This proceeds upon the tenets of Haneefa.—With the two disciples manumission is indivisible, and consequently the emancipation of an half is, in effect, the emancipation of the whole slave, so that it is not considered in that instance as proceeding from two sentences.

But not if carnal connexion take place between the two emancipations.—IF a man emancipate half his slave, as an expiation of Zihar, and then have carnal connexion with the wife upon whom he had pronounced the Zihar, and afterwards emancipate the other half, it is not valid as an expiation, according to Haneefa, because he holds that manumission admits of division, and the condition of its sufficiency, in the sacred writings, is that it be performed before the man touch his wife; but here the emancipation of one half takes place after touching.—With the two disciples, on the contrary, the emancipation of an half amounts to an emancipation of the whole, wherefore the emancipation, in this case appears to take place upon the whole; before touching.

Zihar may be expiated by fasting two month

—IF the person pronouncing a Zihar be not possessed of a slave, his expiation may be made by fasting for two successive months, provided those do not include the Ramzan, nor the festival of Fittir,* nor the days of Nihr† or Tashreek.‡ The fast must be successive (that is, uninterrupted), because it is thus expressed in the text; and it is a condition that the Ramzan be not included, because the abstinence observed in that period is not counted in expiation; for if it were to be so counted, this would in effect induce the annulment of a thing ordained by GOD; and it is also a condition that the festival of Fittir, and the days of Nihr and Tashreek, be not included, as (these being ordained festivals) any extraordinary abstinence in them is forbidden.

But if carnal connexion take place during the fast, it must be commenced de novo.—IF the expiator, either wilfully or through forgetfulness, in the night, or, from the latter cause, in the day time, should during the term of expiation have carnal connexion with the wife upon whom he had pronounced the Zihar, he must again begin the fast anew, according to Haneefa and Mohammed. Aboo Yoosaf says that it is not incumbent upon him to begin it again, as his connexion with the wife does not amount to an interruption of the fast, since that is not broken by it; and if it be said that one condition of the fast is that it precede touching, it may be replied that a compliance with that injunction is here rendered impossible; he therefore holds that it must in this case suffice that a part of it precede touching, for if the fast be commenced anew (as in the doctrine of Haneefa and Mohammed), if follows that the whole would be subsequent to touching.—The argument of Haneefa and Mohammed is that the conditions of making expiation by fast are twofold;—one, that the fast precede touching;—another, that the two months be exempt from touching; and the second of these being violated by the connexion, the circumstance with respect to which the condition was made is not fulfilled, and therefore the fast must be commenced anew, because though the observance of the first condition be now rendered impossible, yet still it remains in his power to perform the expiation in such a way as may fulfil the second condition of it.

IF the expiator wilfully break his fast in the day time, within the two months, either with or without excuse, he must commence it anew, according to all the doctors, as this is an interruption of the fast, a condition of which is that it be for two months successively; and this being still in his power it is therefore incumbent upon him.

Fasting the only mode in which a slave can expiate Zihar.—IF a slave pronounce a Zihar upon his wife, a fast of two months successively is the only mode of expiation which is allowed him, because he is incapable of possessing any thing in his own right as a proprietor, and consequently cannot expiate in any other way.—And here, if the owner of this person were to release another of his slaves, or to distribute victuals to sixty poor men, on his behalf, yet it does not suffice, as a slave, being incapable of possessing property, cannot be regarded as a proprietor, from his master's consignment or transfer of it.

Zihar may be expiated by the distribution of alms.—IF the person pronouncing a Zihar be incapable of observing a fast (from the ill state of his health or other cause), it is incumbent upon him to give victuals to sixty poor men, GOD having said, "WHERE A MAN CANNOT FAST, LET HIS EXPIATION BE MADE BY DISTRIBUTING VICTUALS TO SIXTY POOR MEN."—By the term victuals is here understood half a Saa* of wheat, or one Saa† of barley or dates, or the value thereof in money; because the Prophet has said, "for each pauper there is half a SAA OF WHEAT;"—and also, because regard is here had to the removal of want from each for one day, and consequently the proportion to each is determined by the Sadka Fitter, or alms given on the festival breaking Lent.—Observe that what is here said, "or the value thereof in money," is the opinion of our doctors, as has been related at large in the book of Zakat. And if the expiator bestow one Man ‡ of wheat, or two Mans of Barley, or dates upon the poor, it suffices, since this fulfils the design, as wheat and barley are of one and the same genus or nature, in respect to food, and consequently to compensate the defect in one grain by an addition of the other is lawful: contrary to a case where a man fasts, and at the end of a month becomes incapable of continuing the fast, on account of sickness, for here the expiation would not be effected by giving victuals to thirty paupers, because fasting and victuals are not homogeneous, and consequently the completion of one by means of the other is insufficient.

IF the person pronouncing a Zihar desire another person to distribute the victuals for him as an expiation, and the latter do so, it suffices, as this amounts to borrowing so much; and the pauper to whom the person so commissioned gives the victuals appears first to make seisin of them in behalf of the expiator, and then to receive them on his own account; thus the expiator is first

*The day of breaking Lent.

†The day of sacrifice, being the tenth of the month Zooal Hidjee when the pilgrims assemble at Mecca.

‡The true sense of Tashreek (as here applied) the translator has not been able to discover.

*About four pounds.

†About eight pounds.

‡About eighty pounds.

seised of the property, and then makes it over to the pauper.

If the pronouncer of a Zihar feed sixty paupers morning and evening it suffices, where they are filled, whether they eat more or less.—Shafei says that this does not suffice, as it is requisite that the victuals be regularly consigned to sixty poor men, the same as in Zakat and Sadka Fitter, because in consigning, their wants are more effectually relieved than by feeding, which is only an act of permission, and consequently cannot stand for consignment.—The argument of our doctors is that the word Itaam, or feeding is what is mentioned in the text, and the literal meaning of that is to give a power over food, which is found in permitting to eat, the same as in consignment: but in Zakat and Sadka Fitter; consignment is essentially requisite, and mere permission does not suffice, because there the gift is incumbent, and by gift, consignment is understood.—In short, with respect to whatever is mentioned in the sacred ordinances of the law under the term victuals, permission is sufficient; but in what is mentioned under the terms of gift or payment. consignment is a condition.

If among the sixty paupers thus fed morning and evening there by an infant newly weaned from the breast, it does not suffice, as the expiation is not in that case completely performed, a child of this description not being yet able to eat a full proportion of victuals.

With barley-bread it is requisite that some provision be bestowed such as it is usual to eat with bread, as the appetite cannot be satisfied with that alone; but with wheaten-bread this is unnecessary.

If victuals be given to one pauper for sixty days, it suffices, because the relief of want is what is required, and want recurs every day, wherefore giving it to the same person a second day amounts to giving it to a second pauper.—But if the victuals for sixty be given at once to a single pauper, it does not suffice:—yet if they be given to him at sixty separate times within the day it suffices, according to some; but others allege that it does not suffice.

Carnal connexion during expiation by alms does not require that the alms be distributed anew.—If the person pronouncing a Zahir have carnal connexion with his wife within the time of his performance of expiation by alms, as above, still it is not necessary that he should recommence, as it is not set forth aa a condition in the word of God that this species of expiation should precede touching; but it nevertheless behoves him not to touch her until he shall have made expiation, as it is possible that in the interim he may be enabled to perform that by the manumission of a slave, or by fasting for two months, in which case this would induce expiation by those methods after touching, contrary to the injunction of the text.

If a man, as an expiation for two Zihars, distribute to each of sixty paupers a double proportion of victuals (suppose one Saa of wheat to each), yet this does not suffice for more than one Zihar, according to the two Elders.—Mohammed says it suffices for both.—But if the victuals be bestowed in this way upon sixty paupers, as an expiation for the breach of a fast, and for Zihar, it suffices for both.—The argument of Mohammed is that what is bestowed upon the paupers aforesaid suffices for the performance of both expiations, and the persons upon whom it is bestowed are also proper subjects of both expiations, and consequently the act is effectual for two expiations, in the same manner as where the occasions of expiation are different (as in the case of expiation for a breach of fast and a Zihar),—or where the expiations are separately performed. The argument of the two Elders is that the intention, where things are of one and the same nature, is nugatory: but regard is had to it, when things are different in nature, because a respect to intention is ordained, for the sake of distinguishing between different things; and hence, if antonement were due from a person for the neglect or omission of two days' fast, in the month of Ramzan (a Thursday and a Friday for instance), and the person by fasting afterwards two days intend atonement, it suffices although the days on which he thus fasts be not the same with the days of omission, because the thing is essentially the same; contrary to where a person owes one day's fast for atonement, and another day's fast in pursuance of a vow,—for then a distinction is necessary, because of the difference between the things; now as the intention, where the things are of the same nature, is nugatory, and as the thing bestowed is capable of constituting a single expiation only (because half a Saa of wheat to each pauper is ordained as the smallest amount sufficient towards expiation, wherefore the expiation is vitiated by being under, but not by exceeding, the prescribed quantity), it follows that the distribution of victuals as aforesaid is effectual towards one expiation only, the same as where a single expiation only is intended:—contrary to where the victuals are bestowed at separate times, because giving a second time is the same as giving to another pauper.

If the man upon whom two expiations of two Zihars are thus incumbent emancipate two of his slaves, it suffices, although he have no specific intention as to either the slaves or the Zihars, respectively;—and in like manner, if he fast for four months, or distribute victuals to one hundred and twenty paupers, it suffices, because, as the thing is the same, specifie intention is not requisite.

If moreover, this man emancipate a single slave in part of expiation of two Zihars, it rests with him to specify to which of the two he intends the manumission of that slave to apply; but if he were thus to emancipate a slave in part of expiation of a Zihar, and of a Murder, it is invalid with respect to either.

Ziffer says, that the emancipation of a single slave is totally ineffectual in either case.—Shafei, on the other hand, maintains that it is equally efficient in both cases, the specification resting with the expiators, because all expiations are of one and the same nature with respect to their end, which is the covering of criminality, but as intention with respect to things similar in nature, is unavailable, the simple intention remains; and as (if that were expiation) the expiator is at liberty to specify to which expiation the act is to apply, so here also—The argument of Ziffer is that the expiator in this case appears to have emancipated half his slaves on account of one Zihar, and the other half on account of the other Zihar, and consequently, that he is not at liberty afterwards to specify his emancipation as applying to either Zihar in particular, after having granted it as applying to both, since he then possesses no further option.—Our doctors argue (with Shafei) that specification, with respect to things similar in nature, is unavailable, and consequently nugatory, wherefore simple intention remains; but where things are different in nature (such as the emancipation of a slave, as an expiation for Zihar, and also for homicide), the specification of intention is available; and the intention being approved, the emancipation of the slave does not apply wholly either to the expiation for Zihar or to the expiation for homicide.—As to what Shafei advances, that all expiations are of one and the same nature, in regard to their end, it may be replied that a difference of nature between the expiations, in the present case, subsists in regard to the different occasion of them, although in respect to their end they be of one and same nature.

CHAPTER X.

OF LAAN, OR IMPRECATION

Definition of the term.—LAAN, in the language of the law, signifies testimonies confirmed by oath, on the part of a husband and wife (where the testimony is strengthened by an imprecation of the curse of GOD, on the part of the husband, and of the wrath of GOD on the part of the wife), in case of the former accusing the latter of adultery.

A man accusing his wife of whoredom must verify his charge by an imprecation.—IF a man slander his wife (that is to say, accuse her of whoredom), or deny the descent of a child born of her by saying, "this is not my child," and she require him to produce the ground of his accusation, imprecation is incumbent upon him, provided both parties be competent in evidence—(that is, of sound mind, adults free, and Mussulmans,) and that the woman be of a description to subjects her slanderer to punishment (that is, married,*) for if she be not such (as if she have been for instance, enjoyed under an invalid marriage, or delivered of a child whose father is unknown), the man is not under any obligation to make an imprecation, although she be a person competent in evidence.

Conditions under which the imprecation is incumbent.—LAAN, according to the tenets of our doctors, is a testimony confirmed by oath, as was before observed; and it involves, on the part of the husband, if his accusation be false, the CURSE of GOD, which stands as a substitute of punishment for slander;—or, on the part of the woman, the wrath of GOD, which stands in the place of punishment for whoredom, if it be true:—it is therefore requisite that the parties be both competent in evidence, as the ground thereof is testimony; and it is also requisite that she be of a description to subject her slanderer to punishment, as the Laan, with respect to the husband, stands as a substitute of punishment for slander (whence the necessity of her being a married woman): and Laan is incumbet on account of the denial of a child, because the husband, in denying the child's descent, accuses his wife by implication.

OBJECTION.—The denial of the child's descent does not positively imply an accusation of the wife, as it is possible that the child may not have been begotten by the husband, and yet that the wife is not an adultress (as where a man, for instance, has had carnal connexion with her erroneously, and a child is produced from it, in which case the child is the undoubted progeny of another), and hence, in his denial of its descent from him, the husband speaks truly, without any accusation of adultery against the wife being implied.

REPLY.—This possibility is of no weight, because a stranger, if he were to deny the descent of child from the known and reputed father, is held to be a slanderer notwithstanding this possibility; and so in this case only.—It is also a condition of imprecation that the wife require her husband to produce the ground of his accusation, as this is her right, the demand of which is necessary; as well as that of all other matters of right: and if he decline it, the magistrate must imprison him until he either make an imprecation, or acknowledge the falsity of his change, by saying, "I falsely attributed adultery to her,"—as this is a right due from him to his wife, and which it is in his power to render her, wherefore he is to be imprisoned till such time as he does what is incumbent, or acknowledges his falsity, so as that the occasion for the imprecation may be removed (that is, the condition of imprecation, namely, the mutual change of falsehood), because imprecation is not incumbent except where each changes the plea of the

---

*Arab.—Mahsana. For a full definition of this term, see SLANDER.

other with falsehood, after the husband having produced against his wife an accusation of adultery. And the husband having made an imprecation, the same is then incumbent upon the wife, it being so ordained in the Koran (but Imprecation commences with the husband, as he in this case appears as the plaintiff); and if she decline making imprecation, the magistrate is to imprison her till such time as she either agrees to make it, or to acknowledge her husband's veracity, this being his right incumbent upon her, and which she is able to render, wherefore she is to be imprisoned until she renders it

Not incumbent upon slaves or infidels—IF a slave, or an infidel, or one who has suffered punishment as a slanderer, accuse his wife of whoredom, punishment for slander is due upon him, because here imprecation is impossible,* and consequently its original is due, and this punishment for slander, that being, the original ordinance in this case, according to the word of GOD,—"IF MEN ACCUSE MARRIED WOMEN OF WHOREDOM, AND PRODUCE NOT FOUR WITNESSES, SCOURGE THEM WITH EIGHTY STRIPES;" no imprecation is the substitute of punishment for slander; and where the substitute cannot be had, the original is due.

Nor, where the wife is a slave, an infidel, or a convicted slanderer.—IF the accuser be a person competent in evidence, and his wife be a slave, or an infidel, or a Kitabeea, or one who has suffered punishment as a slanderer, or of the description of those whose accusers are not liable to punishment, as being an infant, or idiot, or adultress, punishment is not due, nor is imprecation incumbent upon him, as in this instance neither competency in evidence nor marriage (in the sense which induces punishment) are attached to the accused.

OBJECTION.—It would appear that in this case punishment for slander is due upon the husband, as imprecation is a substitute for that, and where the substitute cannot be had, it follows that the original is due.

REPLY.—Punishment is not due upon the husband, as he is capable of imprecation, the obstacle to which exists in this case on the part of the wife, and this circumstance precludes punishment, in the same manner as where she acknowledges the truth of the accusation.—The foundation of this is a saying of the Prophet, namely, "There are four descriptions of women with respect to whom imprecation is not incumbent, Jews and Christians married to MUSSULMANS, and slaves married to freeman, and free women married to slaves."

Nor where both parties are convicted slanderers.—IF the accuser and his wife be persons who have both already suffered punishment for slander, punishment is due upon the former, because in this case a reason is found against imprecation the part of the accuser, he being incapable of making it.

Form of imprecation and the manner of making it—THE manner of imprecation is as follows:—The Kazee first applies to the husband, who is to give evidence four several times, by saying, "I call GOD to witness to the truth of my testimony concerning the adultery with which I charge this woman;" and again, a fifth time, "may the curse of GOD fall upon me if I have spoken falsely concerning the adultery with which I charge this woman,"—after which the Kazee requires the woman to give evidence, four separate times, by saying, "I call GOD to witness that my husband's words are altogether false, respecting the adultery with which he charges me," and again, a fifth time, "may the wrath of GOD light upon me if my husband is just, in bringing a charge of adultery against me,"—Hasan records it as an opinion of Haneefa that the husband should, in making the imprecation, address himself in the second person, saying "by GOD I speak truly concerning the adultery with which I charge you," because the use of the second person does not admit the possibility of the address affecting any other. The reason for the form, as above stated, is that the relative, when joined to the third person, removes doubt.

When both parties have made imprecation a separation takes place.—AND on both making imprecation in this manner, a separation takes place between them; but not until the Kazee pronounces a decree to that effect.—Ziffer says that separation takes place upon the imprecation, independent of any judicial decree, because a perpetual prohibition is established by it, the Prophet having said, "the two who make imprecation can never come together,"—which proves their separation, as the Prophet's forbidding their ever coming together after imprecation expressly declares this. The argument of our doctors is that as, in consequence of the establishment of a prohibition between them, the retaining of the woman with humanity* is impossible, it is incumbent upon the husband to divorce her on a principle of benevolence; but if he decline so doing, it then behoves the Kazee to issue a decree of divorce, as the Kazee is the substitute of the husband in this matter for the purpose of removing injustice: and a proof of this is that Aweemar divorced his wife after imprecation, in the presence of the Prophet, which shows that the marriage still continued, and was not virtually dissolved by the imprecation, otherwise the Prophet would have prevented him from pronouncing divorce.—Observe that the separation here

*As infidels and slaves, not being competent to give evidence, are incapable of imprecation.

*Alluding to the words of Koran,—"RETAIN THEM WITH HUMANITY, OR DISMISS THEM WITH KINDNESS. (See Rijat.)

mentioned is an irreversible divorre, according to Haneefa and Mohammed, because the act of the Kazee must be referred to the husband, as in cases of impotence.

The husband, on receding from his imprecation, may again marry his wife.—IF, after imprecation, the husband should acknowledge that his accusation was false, by saying, "I falsely laid adultery to her charge," he becomes privileged with respect to her, that is to say, it is lawful for him to marry her as well as any other person.* This is according to Haneefa and Mohammed. Aboo Yousaf says that she is for ever prohibited to him, and that he cannot marry her,—the Prophet having said, "two who make imprecation can never come together," which shows the separation established between them to be perpetual: wherefor his marriage with her is illegal.—The argument of Haneefa and Mohammed is that the husband's acknowledgment is a retraction from his evidence (that is, from has imprecation), and evidence is by subsequent retraction rendered null and of no effect: and as to the saying of the Prophet above cited, it means that the parties cannot come together as long as they both persevere in their imprecation; but after the husband's acknowledgment, the imprecation no longer remains either in substance or in effect, and consequently they may then come together.

Imprecation occasions a decree of bastardy.—IF a husband accuse his wife, by denying her child, it is requisite that the Kazee issue a decree denying the descent of the child from him and affixing it upon the mother;† and the manner of the imprecation here is that the Kazee first makes the husband give evidence saying, "I testify in the sight of God that I speak truly concerning the matter I have brought against her, in denying the child;" after which he makes the wife give evidence in the same manner, saying, "I call God to witness that he speaks falsely concerning the matter he has brought against me, in denying the child."

IF a husband accuse his wife both by bringing a charge of adultery against her, and also by denying a child born of her, it is necessary that both these circumstances be mentioned in the imprecation, after which the Kazee is to issue a decree, denying the descent of the child from the husband, and fixing it upon the mother, because the Prophet, once so decreed upon such an occasion, and also, because the design of the imprecation in this case is to bastardize the child, wherefore a decree must be passed agreeably to the design of it.

A DECREE of separation between the parties comprehends a decree of bastardy in respect to child.—It is recorded as an opinion of Aboo Yoosaf that, in a decree of separation, a decree of bastardy is not comprehended, but that it is requisite that the magistrate first effect the separation, and then say, "I throw the child upon the mother, and remove it from the father's house;" because separation may sometimes take place without affecting the descent of children, as where a man accuses of adultery a wife who has children,* in which case a separation is established by imprecation, but bastardy is not induced upon the children; the Kazee's mention of bastardy is therefore requisite.

A husband receding from imprecation must be punished for slander.—IF a husband, after imprecation, contradict himself, by acknowledging that he had accused his wife falsely let the magistrate punish him, because he then acknowledges himself liable to punishment*; and it is afterwards lawful for the husband to marry her again (according to Haneefa and Mohammed), because having once suffered punishment for slander, competency to make imprecation no longer appertains to him; and the prohibition which is the effect of the imprecation is removed. In the same manner, if the husband and wife make imprecation, and the husband afterwards accuse of adultery a strange woman, who is married, and suffer punishment on that account, it then becomes lawful for him to marry his wife again for the reason aforesaid. And so also, if the wife, after divorce in consequence of imprecation, be found in adultery, and suffer correction from the Kazee on that account, it then becomes lawful for the husband to marry her again, as a competency to make imprecation no longer appertains to her.

Imprecation not incumbent where the husband or wife is an infant, or an idiot.—IF a man accuse his wife, she being an infant or an idiot, imprecation is not incumbent upon the parties, because the accuser of such a person is not liable to punishment for slander unless he be a stranger: imprecation, therefore, is not incumbent in the accusation of such wives by their husbands, as it is the substitute of punishment for slander. And the rule is the same where the husband is insane, or an idiot, because such an one is not competent in evidence.

Or where the husband is dumb.—IF a dumb person accuse his wife, imprecation is not incumbent, because imprecation is not incumbent unless the accusation be expressed in terms, as is the case in slander, where punishment is not incurred unless the accusation has been expressly made.—Shafei opposes this; for he holds that punishment is due upon the accusation of a dumb person, and consequently, that imprecation is incumbent, because his signs are the same as the words of one who has the power of speech; but the argument of our doctors is that the signs of a dumb person are not altogether free from doubt, and punishment is removed by any circumstance of doubt.

*That is, without her being previously married to another.

†That is, bastardizing it.

*Meaning, children already born, before the period of the husband's accusation.

Or where the accusation is indirectly insinuated.—If a man say to his wife, "your pregnancy is not of me," imprecation is not incumbent.—This is the opinion of Haneefa and Ziffer : and the reason upon which they found it is, that the circumstance of pregnancy does not admit of being positively ceritified, wherefore the husband's words do not convey an immediate accusation.—The two disciples say that imprecation is incumbent in this case, provided the woman be delivered of a child within six months ; and it is this which is meant by what is said in the Mabsoot that "the existence of pregnancy at the time of accusation may be certified ;" but to this we reply that where the accusation cannot be immediately established, it must remain suspended upon a condition, in the same manner as if the husband were to say to his wife, "if you produce a child it is not mine ;" and the suspension of accusation upon a condition is nugatory.

But if he were to say to her, "you are an adulteress, and your pregnancy proceed from adultery," imprecation is incumbent upon both parties, as accusation is here established in the mention of adultery. Yet the Kazee is not in this case to issue any decree affecting the descent of the fœtus.—Shafei says that a decree of bastardy must be pronounced, because the Prophet decreed a bastardy in the instance of Hillall, who had accused his pregnant wife.—The argument of our doctors is that the effect of a decree of bastardy cannot take place until after delivery, since before delivery there is a possibility of doubt respecting the pregnancy ; the Kazee, therefore, is not to decree a bastardy.—As to the decree of the Prophet quoted by Shafei, it is possible that the Prophet may have been certified of the woman's pregnancy by inspiration.

Imprecation made posterior to the birth of a child does not affect that child's descent —If a husband deny the descent of the child upon the near approach of birth, or at the time when it is usual to receive congratulations, and to purchase clothes and make preparation for it, his denial holds good, and imprecation is incumbent upon him on account of it : but if he do not deny it until afterwards although imprecation be here also incumbent, yet the descent of the child remains established in him.—This is the doctrine of Haneefa.—The two disciples say that the denial is admitted during labour, as it is admitted within a little time, but not within a long time, and hence a distinction is made between the shorter period and the longer, by the time of labour, as the pains of labour are among the effects of breeding.—The argument of Haneefa is, that it is impossible to fix any time, because time is fixed for the purpose of consideration, and mankind vary in the length of time necessary for that purpose ; wherefore regard is had to a thing which shows the child to be his, namely, his receiving the usual congratulations, or remaining silent at the time of such congratulations, or purchasing things to prepare for the birth, or letting that time pass without denying it —This is where he is present ; but if he be absent, and ignorant of the birth of the child, and afterwards come, the time aforesaid is regarded, according to both authorities ; that is to say, with Haneefa, it remains to him to deny the child within such space of time as congratulations are admitted—and with the two disciples, within the space of time which corresponds with a woman's labour.

If two children be produced at one birth, and the husband deny the descent of the first-born, and admit that of the second, in this case the parentage of both is established in him, because they are both supposed to be begotten from one seed ; and punishment is due upon the husband, because he has contradicted himself in acknowledging the second child ; and if he admit the first, and deny the second, the parentage of both is established in him for the same reason : and imprecation is here incumbent because his denial of the second child implies an accusation from which he does not afterwards retract (as in the former instance), since his virtual declaration of his wife's chastity, in acknowledging the parentage of one of the children, here precedes the accusation, being the same as if he were first to say, "she is chaste," and then to say, "she is an adulteress" in which case imprecation would be incumbent, and so here likewise.

CHAPTER XI.

OF IMPOTENCE

An impotent husband must be allowed a year's probation after which separation takes place —If a husband be Inneen [impotent], it is requisite that the Kazee appoint the term of one year from the period of litigation, within which if the accused have carnal connexion with his wife it is well ; but if not, the Kazee must pronounce a separation, provided such be the desire of the wife, because the same is recorded from Alee, and Omar, and Ebu Musood,—and also, because the woman is entitled to the carnal enjoyment, and it is possible that the husband may be incapacitated from the performance of that act, not only by a radical infirmity, but also by some supervenient and accidental cause, whence it is necessary that some certain term be appointed, in order that the true reason of his inability may be ascertained ; and this term is fixed at one year because that contains four seasons, and diseases are principally occasioned by an excess either of heat, cold, dryness, or humidity, qualities which are peculiar to each season respectively ; and it is probable that one of these four may particularly agree with the man's condition, [so as by its influence to dissipate his disease; thus it may be ascertained, when a year has completely elapsed, whether his inability proceeded from any radical infirmity, in which case, it is impossible to retain the wife with humanity,* and hence it is incumbent upon the husband to separate from her, upon a principal of benevolence: but if he should not do so, the Kazee is in that case to pronounce a separation, as his substitute; yet it is requisite that the woman desire such separation, as is her right.—The separation here mentioned amounts to the execution of a single divorce irreversible, because the act of the Kazee is attributed to the husband, whence it is the same as if he had himself pronounced such a sentence upon her. Shafei alleges that this separation is an annulment of the marriage: but with our doctors marriage is held to be incapable of being annulled of itself, although it may be annulled by effect, in the same manner as in the case of a husband's apostacy. And this separation amounts to an irreversible divorce, not a reversible, because the intent of it is the woman's relief from a hardship, which cannot be effected but by complete divorce: for if it were not so, it would still remain in the husband's power to reverse it, which would defeat the design.

And the wife retains her whole dower, if the husband should ever have been in retirement with her.—The wife, in the case here mentioned, is entitled to her whole dower, if the husband should ever have in retirement with her, because retirement with an Inneen is accounted a Khalwat Saheeh, or complete retirement, as well as with any other person; and an Edit is incumbent upon her, as was mentioned in a former place. What is here advanced proceeds upon a supposition of the husband acknowledging that he has not performed the carnal act with his wife.

But the wife's claim of separation may be here defeated by the husband swearing that he had enjoyed her.—BUT if he controvert her plea, asserting that he has copulated with her, and she have been married as a Siyeeba, his affirmation upon oath is to be credited, because he is the defendant against her claim of separation, and the affirmation of a defendant must be credited when given upon oath: moreover, the instrument of generation is originally created free from inability or disease, and it is natural that he should perform the carnal act where no obstruction exists: and the declaration of a person is to be credited when apparent circumstances bear testimony to his veracity, and where he rests his cause upon the nature of things. If, therefore, the husband thus make oath, the wife's right of separation is thereby defeated; but if he decline this, the term of a year is then to be appointed as aforesaid. Where she was married as a virgin, she is to be examined by some of her own sex, and if they declare her to be still a virgin, the term of a year is to be appointed, as above, because the husband's falsehood is then evident: but if they declare her muliebrity,* the Kazee is in that case to require the husband to make oath, which if he do, her right to separation is defeated; but if he decline, decision is to be delayed for a year as above.—All that has here been said supposes the husband to be merely Inneen, or impotent: but if he be a Majboob, or complete eunuch (that is, one deprived both of yard and testicles, or of the former only), the Kazee is to pronounce an immediate separation (where such is the woman's desire), because in this case the delay of a year can be attended with no advantage: if, however, he be only a Khasee, or simple eunuch (that is, castrated), decision is to be deferred for a year, as in a case of impotency, because there the yard still remains with which it is possible that he may perform the act.

Rules to be observed at the expiration of the year of probation.—WHERE the term of a year is appointed for the trial of a man charged with impotence by a wife whom he had married as a virgin, and he declares, at the expiration thereof, that he has had carnal connexion with her within that interval, and she denies this, she is then to be examined by some of her own sex: if they pronounce her to be still a virgin, she has it at her option either to separate from her husband, or to continue with him, because the testimony of the examiners is confirmed by her virginity, that being the original state of every woman; but should they declare her muliebrity, the husband is then to be required on the other hand to make oath which if he decline, she has an option, as, above, her plea being strengthened by the circumstance of his declining to swear; but if he swear, she has no option. If, moreover, she was a Siyeeba originally (that is at the time of marriage), and the husband declare that he has had carnal connextion with her within the year of probation, and she deny this, his declaration upon oath is to be credited.—that is to say, the oath is to be tendered to him, which if he take, she has no option; but if he decline it, she has then an option as already stated. And here, if she choose to continue with him, she has no subsequent option, as by so doing she manifests an assent to the relinquishment of her right.

The year of probation to be calculated by the lunar calendar.—THE year of probation appointed by the Kazee in cases of impotence is to be counted by the lunar calendar; this is approved; and the days of the courses, and of religious fasts (such as Ramzan), are

*Alluding to the words of the Koran before mentioned.

*Meaning womanhood, as opposed to virginity.

therein included, as these occur in all years alike, nor can a year pass without them; but the days of sickness of either party are not included, as a year may pass exempt from such an occurrence.

A husband cannot annul the marriage, where the defect is on the part of the wife.—If the defect be on the part of the woman, the husband has no *right to annul the marriage* - Shafei maintains that he may annul it, and put her away, on account of any of the five following defects namely, leprosy, scrophula, madness, Ritk,† or Karrn,‡ because some of these (such as the two latter) are obstructive of generation; and others (such as the three former) are causes of natural and insuperable aversion, as is confirmed by a tradition of the Prophet, who has said, "flee from LEPERS as ye would from a WILD BEAST."—The argument of our doctors is that if the enjoyment of the wife's person were to be totally precluded by any circumstance (such as death, for instance, before retirement), yet the marriage is not annulled, but is rather established and confimed, insomuch that the whole dower remains due; and hence, where such privation of the connubial enjoyment is merely dubious, on account of its being occasioned only by a defect in the subject, it remains unannulled, a fortiori-upon this ground, that the design of matrimony is to legalize generation, and the connubial enjoyment is the advantage proposed in it; and the ability to perform the act, where any natural obstruction exists, may be obtained, as in a case of Ritk or Karrn (for instance) which are to be remedied by chirurgical operations; and in all other cases the ability is evident.

A wife cannot sue for a separation on the ground of her husband being leprous, scrophulous, or insane.—If the husband be lunatic, leprous, or scrophulous, yet his wife has no option, as in cases where he is an eunuch, or impotent. This is according to Haneefa and Abou Yoosaf. Mohammad says that she is entitled to an option, in order that she may remove an evil from herself; contrary to the case of a husband, he having it in his power, in similar circumstances, to relieve himself by divorce.—The argument of the two Elders is that in marriage no right of option originally exists, for if this were allowed, it would operate to the destruction of the husband's right; and it is admitted in the case of eunuchs, or of persons naturally impotent, only because the circumstance of natural or accidental infirmity tends to defeat the end for which marriage was instituted; but with persons of the descriptions now under consideration this reason does not hold, as the husband who laboures under any of those defects is still capable of generation, whence an evident difference appears between the two cases.

CHAPTER XII.

OF THE EDIT.

Definition of the term.—By Edit is understood the term of probation incumbent a woman in consequence of the dissolution of marriage after carnal connexion: the most approved definition of Edit is, the term by the completion of which a new marriage is rendered lawful.

The Edit of a divorce of a free woman is three menstruations.—When a man repudiates his wife, being a free woman, either by a reversible or an irreversible divorce, or when separation takes place between a husband and wife, without divorce, after carnal connexion, the Edit, or woman's term of probation, consists of three terms of her courses, provided she be one who is subject to the menstrual discharge, God having so commanded in the Koran.—The separation which takes place between a married couple, independent of divorce, bears the same construction as divorce, because the Edit is made incumbent in a case of divorce for the purpose of ascertaining whether the woman be pregnant, and the same necessity occurs where separation takes place between a husband and an enjoyed wife without divorce.—The separation without divorce may be occasioned either by a woman admitting the son of her husband to carnal connexion, or by her apostatizing from the faith.

And of one not subject to courses, three months: and of one who is pregnant, the term of her travail.—The Edit of a woman who, on account of extreme youth or age, is not subject to the menstrual discharge, is three months, because God has so ordained in the sacred writing.—The Edit of a pregnant woman is accomplished by her delivery, whether she be a slave or free, because God, in the sacred writings, has so ordained respecting woman in that situation.

That of a slave is two menstruation—The Edit of a female slave is two terms of her courses, because it is thus mentioned in the traditions, and also, because bondage is restrictive to the half, whence it would appear that the Edit of a slave should be only one term and a half of her courses, but the menstrual discharge being incapable of subdievision, the half is, of necessity, made a whole term, and hence the Edit of such an one is two terms; and it is to this that Omar advert, where he says, "I would if possble fix the Edit of a female slave at one and an half of her courses."

And of one not subject to courses a month and an half.—Where the famale slave is one who from extreme youth or age is not

*That is, to break it off so as to destroy the woman's claim to her dower, which could not be done by divorce.

†Vulva impervia coeunti.

‡A bone, or other unnatural excrescence, vulva anteriore parte enascens.

subject to the menstrual discharge, her Edit is one month and an half, because time being capable of subdivision, the term is fixed at the half on account of her bondage.

Edit of widowhood.—The Edit of a free woman upon the decease of her husband is four months and ten days. Such being the term mentioned in the Koran:—and that of a female slave in the like circumstance is two months and five days, bondage being restrictive to the half.

Case of Edit of widowhood after divorce.—If a man divorce his wife upon his deathbed, so as that she still inherits of him,* Haneefa and Mohammad say that her Edit, in consequence of his decease, is four months and ten days, if she complete three terms of her courses within that period; but if the three terms be not accomplished, as requiring a longer time (five months for instance), her Edit is in that case three terms of her courses, whatever time those may require. In short, here are two terms; one, that of four months and ten days; and the other, that of three menstruation; and whichever of these is the longest, the same is the term of Edit.—Aboo Yoosaf says that the Edit of this woman is three menstruations.—This difference of doctrine obtains where the sick person has repudiated his wife by one divorce irreversible, or by three divorces:—but where the divorce is reversible, the Edit is four months and ten days, according to all the doctors. The argument of Aboo Yoosaf, in support of this doctrine, as above, is that the marriage had been dissolved and terminated by the divorce, previous to the decease of the husband, and the Edit of divorce is three terms of the courses, whence such is the Edit incumbent in the present case, as that of four months and ten days (being the Edit of widowhood), is required only where the marriage was dissolved by the husband's decease; but in the present case it was dissolved before his death, by divorce. To this indeed it may be objected that, if the marriage be dissolved before the husband's decease, it would follow that the wife cannot inherit:—but the marriage is accounted to hold, in respect to inheritance only, and not so as to alter or affect the Edit:—contrary to where a dying husband repudiates his wife by a reversible divorce; her Edit in that case being universally held to be strictly an Edit of widowhood, since the marriage then actually continues in every shape,—The argument of Haneefa and Mohammed is that the marriage being here accounted to continue with respect to inheritance, is also accounted to continue with respect to Edit; and hence the longest of the two is regarded.—If a man be put to death for apostasy, so as that his wife inherits of him, the same difference of opinion obtains respecting her Edit as is above recited.—Some commentators allege that her Edit is held to be three terms of her courses by all the doctors, as her marriage is not accounted to continue to the time of her husband's decease with respect to inheritance, since a Mussulman woman cannot inherit of an infidel; but yet the wife does here inherit, because her claim to inheritance is established upon the instant of her husband's apostasy;—her Edit, therefore, is three terms of her course.

A female slave, emancipated during Edit, must observe the Edit of a free woman.—If a master emancipate his female slave, whilst in her Edit from a reversible divorce, she is in that case under Edit as a free woman, and must count it accordingly: because, in reversible divorce, so long as the Edit is unaccomplished, marriage continues in every shape:—but if a master emancipate his female slave, whilst in her Edit from a divorce irreversible, or from the deceased of her husband, her Edit is not affected or altered by such emancipation:—that is, it does not become the Edit of a free woman, because her marriage has been completely dissolved by the irreversible divorce, or by the husband's death.

Rule of Edit of a woman past bearing.—If an Ayeesa* be in her Edit, counting it by months, and the menstrual discharge should chance to appear upon her, in this case all regard to that portion of the Edit which has been counted by months drops, and her Edit commences de novo, to be counted by the terms of her courses.—The compiler of this work observes that this is where the Ayeesa had been subject to the courses before she became hopeless of children, as in this case her despair is done away; and this is approved, because it is evident that months, with respect to such a woman, are not the absolute substitutes of Edit: but if an Ayeesa be one to whom the menstrual discharge had never occurred before, and be in her Edit, counting it by months, and see the appearance of the sanguinary discharge, regard to the term of the Edit which has been counted by months does not drop, because the counting by months is the original rule with respect to such a woman, and not merely the substitute for her courses.

If a woman be in her Edit counting it by the term of her courses and after two of those they should stop, and she become an Ayeesa, her Edit commences de novo, to be counted by months, and all regard to the courses drops, so as that the substitute (which is months) and the original (which is the courses) may not be confounded.

Rule of Edit in an invalid marriage.—The Edit of a woman wedded by an invalid marriage is counted by her courses, both in case of her husband's death, and also of a separation taking place between them; and so likewise that of a woman with whom a man has had carnal connexion erroneously; because in those cases, the Edit is incumbent

*See Chap. IX

*Literally, a despairer, that is, a woman whose courses are stopped, and who is consequently supposed to be past child-bearing.

merely for the purpose of ascertaining whether the woman be pregnant, and not as a right of marriage; and as the courses are the means of ascertaining the state of the womb, the Edit of those women is to be counted by their returns.

Edit of an Am-Walid.—If the master of an Am-Walid should die, or emancipate her, her Edit is three terms of her courses.—Shafei says that her Edit is only one term, as it is incumbent upon her on account only of the extinction of the owner's propriety, and consequently no more is requisite to effect it than what may suffice to cleanse her womb.—The argument of our doctors is, that Edit is incumbent upon her on account of the extinction of Firash* (for she is the partner of her master's bed), and is, therefore, the same as that used in the dissolution of marriage:—moreover, Omar has said, "the Edit of an Am-Walid is three terms of her courses."—If the Am-Walld be not subject to the menstrual discharge, her Edit is three months, the same as that of a married woman.

Edit of the widow of an infant.—If an infant die; leaving a wife pregnant, her Edit is accomplished by her delivery, according to Haneefa and Mohammad. Aboo Yoosaf says that it is four months and ten days (and such also is the opinion of Shafei), because the pregnancy cannot be attributed to the infant, and is, therefore, with respect to him, the same as if it had taken place posterior to his decease.—The arguments of Haneefa and Mohammed herein are twofold; First, the word of God, who has said in the Koran, "a woman, if he be pregnant, must wait until her delivery,"—which is generally expressed, and therefore applies to the woman here treated of: Secondly, the Edit of a woman whose husband dies is (in case of her pregnancy) fixed at the remaining term of her travail, whether that be short or long: now the Edit of a widow is not designed for the purpose of ascertaining the state of her womb; for if it were so, it would not be determined by the lapse of time (supposing her to be one who is subject to the menstrual discharge), but by three terms of her courses: whereas we see that the law fixes it at four months and ten days, although she be a woman of that description; but it is made incumbent merely as a fulfilment of one of the rights of marriage; and the same reasoning applies to the wife of the infant in question, although her pregnancy be not attributed to him: contrary to where pregnancy takes place, subsequent to the infant's decease; for here her Edit of four months and ten days having commenced, is not afterwards to be altered by her subsequent pregnancy; but in the case now under consideration, the Edit of the term of travail was due from instant that Edit become incumbent; hence there is an evident difference between the two cases; and consequently there is no analogy between them. The pregnancy is determined to have taken place after the death of the husband, where the woman is not delivered within less than six months from the date of the husband's decease.—This is the approved rule. Some have said that it is so judged only where she is delivered within not less than two years. But if a husband, being adult, should die, and his wife be delivered of a child at any time between six months and two years from the period of his decease, her Edit is accomlished by her delivery, because the pregnancy is in this case attributed to the husband, and hence is accounted the same as if it had existed at the period of his decease.—Observe that the parentage of a child born of the wife of an infant cannot be established in the infant, whether her pregnancy had appeared during his life, or not until after his decease, because an infant, not being possessed of seed, cannot be conceived capable of impregnating a woman; and marriage is not held to be a substitute for seed,* excepting where the existence of seed on the part of the man may be supposed.

Edit of divorce of a menstruous woman.—If a man divorce his wife whilst in her courses, that term is not to be counted in her Edit, because the Edit is fixed at three complete menstruations, and if the above were to be counted, it would induce a deficiency, as part of that had passed previous to divorce, and therefore cannot be included.

Edit of a divorced woman who has connexion with a man during the term of her Edit of divorce.—If a man have erroneous carnal connexion with a woman who is in her Edit from divorce, another Edit becomes incumbent upon her, and the two are blended together,—that is to say, her ensuing courses are accounted in both Edits; and if the former Edit should be accomplished before the latter, the accomplishment of that still remains incumbent upon her. This is the opinion of our doctors.—Shafei mainains that two Edits cannot be blended together, because the Edit is an act of piety (as it restrains from taking another husband, and so forth) and two acts of piety are not permitted to be united in one account; as in fasting for instance, where no part of the abstinence of one day can be put to the account of another.—The argument of our doctors is that the design of the Edit is to ascertain the state of the womb, and as that is answered by a single Edit, the two Edits may be counted together; and piety is not the design of the Edit, but rather a dependant on it;

---

*Firash literally means a bed, whence it is metaphorically used to express a right of cohabitation or concubinage: it is so used in the sense of a wife or a concubine, whence it is here and elsewhere translated partner of his bed.

*That is, cannot be held to amount to a virtual establishment of parentage.

whence it is that the Edit may be accomplished, even without the knowledge of the woman, merely by her refraining from going abroad, or from marrying another husband, or from consummating her marriage with him during the term of it.

Edit of a widow who admits a man during her Edit of widowhood.—If a man have carnal connexion with a woman who is in her Edit from the death of her husband, she is to complete that of four months and ten days, being the Edit of widowhood; at the same time counting such terms of her courses as may occur within the remainder of that time, so as that the two Edits may be counted together as far as is possible.

The Edit of a widow, or a divorced wife, may be accomplished without her knowledge.—The Edit of divorce commences immediately upon divorce, and that of widowhood upon the decease of the husband; if, therefore, a woman be not informed of her widowhood or divorce until such time as the term of Edit be passed, her Edit is then accomplished, because the occasion of Edit being incumbent is widowhood or divorce, and it is therefore held to commence upon the occurrence of the occasion.—Our modern doctors have decreed that the Edit of divorce should not be held to commence until the divorce be publicly declared, in order to guard against collusion between the parties; as it is possible that a husband and wife might privately agree to declare a divorce, and pretend that Edit had already past, so as that, by this means, the marriage being dissolved, he might be enabled to acknowledge a debt in her favour, or make her a bequest of more than her proper inheritance.

Edit from an invalid marriage.—In an invalid marriage the Edit commences immediately upon the Kazee's decree of separation, or upon the determination of the husband. expressly signified, to refrain from carnal connexion.—Ziffer says it commence from the date of the last carnal connexion from parties because, in an invalid marriage, it is the carnal connexion which gives occasion for it, and not the marriage.—The arguments of our doctors are twofold;—First, every instance of carnal connexion occurring in an invalid marriage stands only as one single act, as they all proceed from, and originate in; one contract (whence it is that one dower suffices for the whole): wherefore, until the actual separation, or determination signified, as above, Edit cannot be established, for in every previous instance of carnal connexion it is possible that the same may be repeated; and hence, so long as the separation or determination do not exist, no particular instance of the carnal act can be positively termed the last:—Secondly, the last instance of carnal connexion cannot be ascertained to be the last, but by the husband's signified determination to refrain for the future, since permission on the part of the woman, and ability on that of the man, in a matter of so concealed and doubtful a nature as carnal connexion, stand as a continuance of it, and any other man who may be desirous to marry the woman will require to know the effect of the Edit; it is therefore requisite that something known and visible be substituted for that which is concealed, so as that such visible circumstance may afford a standard whereby to determine.

A woman's oath confirms the accomplishment of her Edit.—If a woman under Edit should declare that it is accomplished, and her husband deny this, her declaration upon oath is to be credited, because she is confided in this point and he has thrown an imputation upon her veracity; she is therefore to swear in the manner of a plaintiff.

Case of a woman re-married after divorce and again repudiated.—When a man having, repudiated his wife by an irreversible divorce, marries her again during her Edit, and afterwards divorces her before consummation, a complete dower is in this case incumbent upon him, and upon the woman an Edit *de novo*, according to Haneefa and Aboo Yoosaf, -Mohammed says that no more is incumbent upon the man than an half dower, nor upon the woman that the accomplishment of her first Edit, because the second divorce is a divorce before consummation, and, therefore does not require either that he should pay a complete dower, or that he should observe a new Edit; nor does anything remain with respect to her, but that she complete the first Edit incumbent in consequence of the first divorce: for the obligation upon the woman to complete her first Edit disappeared upon the husband marrying her again; but this last marriage being done away by his divorcing her a second time, her obligation to the completion of her first Edit recurs. The argument of Haneefa and Aboo Yoosaf is that the second divorce is, in fact, given after carnal connexion, since the woman is still actually within the seisin of the man in consequence of such connexion formerly had with her, the effect of which remains, namely, the Edit; and where he marries her again during her Edit, she being still within his seisin, such possession is the substitute of that which appertains to him in virtue of the second marriage; as in the case of an usurper. who if he make purchase of the article usurped whilst it is within his seisin, is held to be seised of the purchase on the instant of the execution of the contract of sale; it is therefore evident that the second divorce is a divorce after carnal connexion.—Ziffer says that no Edit whatever is incumbent upon the woman, because, the former Edit dropt in consequence of the second marriage and therefore cannot recur; and no Edit is due on account of the second divorce, as that is a divorce before consummation: but the arguements of the two Elders, as above recited, are a sufficient reply to this.

If a Zimmee, or infidel subject, repudiate his wife who is also an infidel subject, no Edit is incumbent upon her: and the same rule applies to an alien woman who having been converted to the faith, comes from the foreign into the Mussulman territory:* it is therefore lawful for such women to marry before the expiration of the term of Edit, unless they be pregnant. This is the opinion of Haneefa with respect to such infidel subjects as do not hold or believe in the obligation of Edit. The two disciples say that Edit is incumbent upon women of either description;—upon infidel subjects, because they have bound themselves to the observance of all such things as appertain to the temporal law; and upon aliens who, having embraced the faith, come into the Mussûlman territory, because it is so upon such women on other accounts, such as the death of their husbands, or the in admitting the son of the husband to carnal connexion, and is therefore equally obligatory on account of separation of country;—contrary to the case where a man, being converted to the faith, comes from a foreign into a Mussulman territory, and his wife remains in the foreign country, for upon her no Edit is incumbent, as the obligation of it cannot reach or effect her in a foreign land.—The argument of Haneefa with respect to infidel subjects is that they not being under any obligation in respect to the ordinances of the law, the obligation of the Edit, as a right of the law, cannot be conceived to affect them; nor can it be supposed to do so on account of the right of the husband, as he does not hold or believe in the obligation of it, and his arguments with respect to alien woman are twofold;—First, God has commanded Mussulmans, saying, "ye may marry foreign women, who being converted to the faith, come into the territory of the believers;" Secondly wherever the Edit is incumbent, the right of man is connected with it; but a Hirbee, or alien, is not considered as man, but as mere matter (whence it is that he is made a property or slave).—But where the woman is pregnant the Edit is incumbent, on account that the foetus of which she is pregnant is of established descent.—It is recorded from Haneefa that it is lawful to marry such women, being pregnant, but that the husband must refrain from carnal connexion until after delivery, in like manner as in the case of women pregnant and by whoredom.—The former, however, is the better opinion.

Section.

Of Hidad, or Mourning.

Definition.—By Hidad is understood a woman abstaining from the use of perfumes, such as scented or other oils; or of ornaments, such as dying the edge of the eyelids with antimony, and so forth, except on account of some particular pretext, or (as is said in the Jama Sagheer on account of aches or pains which those application may remedy.

Mourning is incumbent on the death of a husband—Hidad, or mourning, is incumbent upon a woman whose husband dies, where she is of mature age and a Musslima, because the Prophet has said, "It is not lawful for a woman who believes in God, and a future state, to observe Hidad for more than three days on account of the death of any one except her husband; but for him it is incumbent upon her to observe Hidad for the space of four months and ten days.

Although he die during the wife's Edit from irreversible divorce—Our doctors say that it is equally incumbent upon a woman whose husband dies whilst she is under repudiation by irreversible divorce.—Shafei asserts that it is not incumbent upon her, because the sole intention of its institution is to signify grief for the decease of a husband who has faithfully adhered to the marriage contract until death; but there is no cause of grief for the demise of one who had, during life, thrown his wife into difficulty and perplexity by divorce. The arguments of our doctors, in support of their opinion upon this point, are twofold, First, the Prophet forbade women under Edit dyeing their hands with Hinna,* as it is a species of perfume; Secondly, mourning is incumbent as a sign of grief for the loss of the blessings of matrimony, which is not only the means of her support, but also of the preservation of her chastity; and an irreversible divorce is a more complete termination of those blessings than even death itself, since it is lawful for a woman to perform the last offices of ablution, and so forth, to the corpse of a deeeased husband from whom she is not irreversibly divorced, whereas it is not lawful for her to perform those offices to the corpse of one from whom she is completely divorced; wherefore in this case also a mourning is incumbent.—It may here be observed that mourning is incumbent for two reasons: First, as it is a manifestation of grief (as was mentioned above. Secondly, because ornamenting or setting off the person by the use of the above articles is a means of exciting the desires of men, and to a woman under Edit marriage is forbidden, wherefore she must refrain from the use of such things, lest she fall into that which is prohibited.—It is recorded, in the Nakl Saheeh, that the Prophet would not permit women under Edit to use antimony upon their eyelids, or to apoint themselves, as the former is an ornament, and the latter is one way of using perfume.—By what is said in the definition of Hidad, in the beginning of this section, viz., "abstaining from perfumes, and so forth, except on account of some particular pretext," is to be understood the use of those is lawful, where there is any sufficient

*This supposes a woman who, having been converted to the faith in a foreign land, deserts her infidel husband there, and comes into the Mussulman territory.

*A sort of herb, the juice of which dyes the palms of the hands and soles of the feet of a reddish colour. The herb cyprus, or privet.

reason for it, as they are then used of necessity; but it is requisite that the intention [of the mourner] in the use of them be medicine, and not ornament.

If a woman be accustomed to the use of unctions, in such a manner that there might be an apprehension of her health suffering from the disuse, in this case, provided the cause for apprehension be in her conception apparent and evident, it is lawful to continue the use of them, because things of which occurrence is strongly apprehended by her are considered as actually existing and established, and in the same manner, she may wear warm furred or velvet garments, where there is a necessity: but it is in no way lawful for her to use Hinna, because of the precept of the Prophet before recited: nor to wear cloth dyed with saffron, before that gives a perfume.

Mounding not incumbent upon infidel women or infants (but it is incumbent upon slaves).—Mourning is not incumbent upon an infidel woman, as she is not bound to the observances required by the law; neither is it incumbent upon infants or girls under age, for the same reason; but it is incumbent upon female slaves, they being bound to the observances of the law in all such points as do not affect the right of their owner, which is the case with mourning; it is to be observed, however, that the mourning, with respect to female slaves does not include a prohibition from going abroad, since this would be an infringement upon the proprietor's right, which precedes the right of God, as the individual is necessitous, whereas God, is not so.

Nor upon Am-Walid, nor upon widows from invalid marriage.—Mourning is not incumbent upon an Am-Walid under Edit from the decease of her proprietor; nor upon a woman under Edit who has been contracted in an invalid marriage, because, with respect to such women, the blessings of marriage cannot be said to perish so as to afford a reason for the manifestation of grief, moreover, ornaments and the use of perfumes, and so forth, are in their original nature allowable: and where no special reason appears for the prohibition of them, they necessarily continue to be so.

Proposing for a woman during her Edit is disapproved.—It is not decent in any person publicly or expressly to solicit or seek connexion with a woman under Edit; but it matters not if this be done in an indirect and ambiguous manner: yet they should not pass any secret promise of marriage to each other, this being forbidden in the Koran.—The ambiguous mode of proposal above mentioned is described by Ebn Abbas to be, that the man in the woman's presence may declare his wish to marry, in general terms without any particular application.

Rules for the behaviour of women during Edit.—It is not not lawful for a woman under divorce to go abroad, either in the night or day, whether the divorce be reversible or irreversible, because the word of God in the Koran forbids them from appearing abroad: but a widow is at liberty to go forth during the whole day, and for a short eason of the night also; yet she must not pass the night anywhere but in her own apartments. The reason of this indulgence is that as a widow has no provision from her husband's property, it may be necessary that she should go forth to seek for a subsistence, and it may sometimes happen that she is detained abroad a considerable time, perhaps till after nightfall, whence the extension of the liberty to a part of the night; but it is otherwise with a woman under divorce, as she is entitled [during Edit] to a subsistence from the husband. Yet if a woman were to enter into an engagement of Khoola with her husband, making the consideration for Khoola to consist of her subsistence during her Edit, some say that she is at liberty to go during the day, while others maintain that she has no liberty of going forth whatever, as the loss of alimony during Edit is a consequence of her own voluntary act, wherefore the prohibition, which is right of the law, still continues in force.

It is incumbent upon a woman under Edit that she observe and accomplish the same in the place where she was resident at the period of divorce taking place, or of the husband's decease, whether that be her own accustomed dwelling, or a house where she may be upon a visit (that of her parents, for instance), because this is so ordered in the Koran; and it also appears in the traditionary precepts of the Prophet that he said to a woman whose husband was slain, "stay in your own house until your Edit be a accomplished.

A widow may remove from her husband's house, if inconveniently situated there.—If the apartment allotted to a widow, in the house of her deceased husband, be not sufficiently spacious for her accommodation, and it should happen that the heirs of the defunct exclude her from the other parts of the house, it is then lawful for her to remove elsewhere, because she has here an excuse, and any good pretext suffices in all matters appertaining to the spiritual law, of which description is Edit; the case is therefore the same here as where the woman has reason to fear thieves in her own house, or where there is an apprehension of its falling, or where she holds it by hire, and is unable to pay the rent: all which circumstances are a sufficient case of removal as well as in the present case.

A wife under irreversible divorce must be accommodated with a separate apartment—Where a husband and wife are separated by irreversible or triplicate divorce, it is requisite that there be a curtain or partition between them; and there is no objection to their continuing to reside in the same house, provided this be attended to, as the husband has himself declared her to be prohibited to him: but if he be a dissolute person, one who has no command of his passions, and of whom it may be apprehended that he will commit with her that which is unlawful, it is in this case expedient that she remove to another house (since there it evidently a sufficient excuse), and that she continue there until the accomplishment of her Edit; it is better, however, that the dissolute husband leave her in his house, and remove to another himself.—It is laudable in the parties, whether the husband be dissolute or otherwise, to engage a female friend to reside in the house with them, who may be able to prevent any improper connexion.—If the dwelling house be so small as not to admit of their residing in it under these precautions, it is then necessary that the wife remove elsewhere; but it is better that the husband remove, and leave her to reside in the house. All this proceeds upon a supposition of the busband's having no more than one house.

Rule respecting a wife divorced upon a journey.—If a woman accompany her hus band upon a journey, or on a pilgrimage to Mecca, and he give her three divorces upon the way, or die, leaving her in an uninhabited place, she must return to her own city, provided the distance be within three days' journey, because this is not to be considered as going abroad, but rather as a cosequence of her having before gone abroad; but if the distance exceed three days' journey, she is then at liberty either to return home, or to proceed upon the pilgrimage, whether her guardian be with her or not.—The compiler of this work observes that this is only where she is left within three days' journey from Mecca, where her stay would be more dangerous than her proceeding; but her return to her own city is preferable, in order that she may there accomplish her Edit in the house of her husband.—But if, in the case under consideration, the divorce or death occur in a city, or other inhabited place, the woman must not go forth from that place until her Edit be accomplished, after which she may leave it, provided she be accompanied by any male relation within the prohibited degrees.—What is here advanced is the doctrine of Haneefa.—The two disciples say that, if the woman be accompanied by a relation within the prohibited degrees, she may leave the place before her Edit be past; for they argue that she ought to be allowed to return home, in order that she may relieve herself from the disagreeable circumstance attending her residence in a strange place, and also from the derangement and trouble of a journey, because these are sufficient pretexts, and the impropriety of her travelling is removed by the circumstance of her relation accompanying her.—To this Haneefa replies that Edit affords a stronger reason against removal than even the want of a relation's protection, as a woman may lawfully go to any distance within a day's journey, without being accompanied by a relation, whereas this is not lawful for a woman under Edit: and where it is unlawful for a woman to go to any greater distance, unaccompanied by a relation, it is for one under Edit, a fortiori.

CHAPTER XIII.

OF THE ESTABLISHMENT OF PARENTAGE.

A child born after six months from the date of a marriage upon which is suspended a conditional divorce, is the lawful offspring of such marriage.—If a man make a declaration, saying, "if I marry such a woman she is divorced," and he afterwards marry her, and she produce a child after six months from the day of the marriage,* the parentage of the child is established in him, and the dower is incumbent upon him; the former is established, because the wife is in this case considered as a partner of his bed at the period of conception, as having brought forth a child at the expiration of six complete months from the date of the marriage, a time considerably posterior to the divorce, since that takes place immediately after the marriage, wherefore the conception must be considered as having taken place prior to the divorce, that is, within the marriage.

Objection.—It is not to be imagined that conception should take place at the time of marriage, as it is a consequence of the carnal act, which happens posterior to it; how therefore, can it be established that the conception took place before divorce, since the latter occurs upon the instant of the marriage?

Reply.—Conception may be imagined upon the instant of the marriage, as it is possible that the man may marry the woman whilst in the commission of the carnal act, and consequently, that marriage and conception may have taken place at the same instance; and as genealogy is a matter, the establishment of which is of great moment, this supposition has therefore been adopted: and the dower is incumbent, because the descent of the child being established in him, he is virtually held to have cohabited with his wife; and it is due on account of consummation.

The parentage of a child born two years after reversible divorce is established in the divorce.—If a man repudiate his wife by a divorce reversible, and she bring forth a child at the end of two years, or more, from the time of the divorce, the parentage of the child is established in him, and the divorce is reversed, provided she had not before declared the accomplishment of her Edit, because it is possible that her pregnancy may have taken place during Edit, as the Tohar (or term of purity) of some women

---

* This means any time between six months and two years from the date of the marriage as the former of these is held to be the shortest, and the latter the longest possible term of pregnancy.

is much longer than that of others, which circumstance may have protracted its continuance: but if she be delivered of a child within less than two years from the divorce, she becomes completely separated from her husband, on account of the completion of her Edit by delivery; and in this case also the parentage of the child is established in the husband, because it is as possible that the conception may have taken place previous to divorce (that is, within the marriage), as it is that it may have taken place after divorce (that is, within the Edit): but yet reversal is not established, because, as it is possible that conception took place after divorce, so it is also possible that it took place before divorce: wherefore reversal cannot be established, on account of the doubt which exists on this point: but where the woman is not delivered until after two years, reversal is established, as the conception is posterior to divorce, and must be attributed to the husband, since no charge of adultery has been advanced against the wife, wherefore it is evident that he has had connexion with her during Edit, a circumstance by which reversal is established.

And so also of the child born within two years after triplicate or irreversible divorce.—If a man repudiate his wife either by three divorces, or by an irreversible divorce, and she be delivered of a child within less than two years from the period of the divorce, the parentage is established in him, as it is possible that the pregnancy may have existed at that time; and the right of cohabitation does not positively appear to have been dissolved previous to pregnancy, whence the parentage is established in this manner for the sake of caution.—But if the delivery were not to take place until after the expiration of two years from the period of separation, the parentage of the child is not established, as pregnancy in that case evidently appears to have taken place posterior to divorce, and consequently the child cannot be supposed to be begotten by the man in question, since to him carnal connexion with the woman is unlawful: yet if he claim the child as his own, the parentage is established in him, as he here takes it upon himself, and it may be accounted for by supposing him to have had connexion with the woman, erroneously, during her Edit.

And so likewise of a child born of a wife under age within nine months after either irreversible or reversible divorce.—If a man repudiate, by an irreversible divorce, a wife who is under the age of puberty, but yet such an one as may admit of carnal connexion, and she bring forth a child after the expiration of nine months from the time of divorce, the parentage of the child is not established in him; but if the delivery be within less than nine months, it is established.—This is according to Haneefa and Mohammed,—Aboo Yoosaf says that the parentage is established in the man, although the child, should not be born within less than two years from the period of divorce, because she was under Edit, and it is possible that the pregnancy may have existed at the time of the divorce, and she not have declared the accomplishment of her Edit, wherefore this infant wife is the same as a full-grown woman.—The agrument of Haneefa and Mohammed is that the Edit, of the wife is in the case appointed to be counted by months, therefore it is accomplished at the expiration of three months, by the rule of the law, independent of any declaration on her part;—if, therefore, she be delivered of a child within less than six months from the end of that term which completes her Edit, the parentage of the child is established; but, if she bring not forth until after that time, the parentage is not established, as it appears to have been begotten at the time when she was not a partner of the husband's bed, for the case treats of a girl irreversibly divorced under puberty, and consequently not subject to the menstrual discharge, and whose Edit is therfore completed by the lapse of time, namely, three months, wherefore it is not possible that pregnancy should have existed at the time of divorce; and the right of cohabitation appears to have undoubtedly expired before pregnancy, so that the descent cannot be established. And if the wife under these circumstances be repudiated by a reversible divorce, the rule is the same (with Haneefa and Mohammed) as before recited. Aboo Yoosaf says that the parentage of the child is established in the husband if it be born within twenty-seven months from the time of divorce, as it must be allowed that he may have had connexion with her at the latter end of the term of three months, which constitutes her Edit, and she be delivered within the longest term of pregnancy admitted by the law, namely two years. But if the infant wife declare her pregnancy to have taken place during Edit, the rule is then the same as with respect to grown women; that is to say, the parentage of the child is established in the husband, as her puberty is proved by her own affirmation.

The parentage of a child born of a widow within two years after the decease of her husband is established in him.—If a widow bring forth a child, the parentage is established in her husband, provided the delivery happen within two years from the time of his decease.—Ziffer says that if she be not delivered until after six months from the time of the completion of the Edit of widowhood, in this case the parentage cannot be established, because her Edit, upon the lapse of four months and ten days, is completed by the ordinance of the law, as the Edit is, by the law, fixed to that time, and is therefore the same as if she were to declare the accomplishment of her Edit, as in the case of the infant before mentioned.—Our doctors, on the other hand, say that the Edit of the woman in question is not absolutely fixed at four months and ten days, but has also another mode of completion, namely, delivery since marriage with an adult woman is considered as a cause of pregnancy ; contrary to the case of a girl under puberty, because the natural state of such an one is an incapacity to bear children, as an infant is not a subject of impregnation until she attain maturity, and concerning the maturity of the infant there is a doubt.

And so also of a child born within six months after the wife declaring her Edit to have expired.—If a woman under Edit declare the same to be accomplished, and be afterwards delivered of a child within less than six months from the time of her declaration, the parentage of the child is established, as it is evident that her declaration was unfounded, and is consequently null : but if she be delivered after six months from the time of her declaration, the parentage is not established, because nothing appears in this case to annul her declaration, as it is possible that her pregnancy may have occurred after that.

Whatever be the occasion of the Edit.—This reasoning applies to every woman under Edit, whatever the occasion may be, whether divorce reversible or irreversible, or the decease of her husband ; or of whatever description or nature, whether it be counted by months, or by the return of the courses.

The birth must be proved by evidence.—When a woman under Edit is delivered of a child, the parentage is not established, (according to Haneefa), unless the birth be proved by the evidence of two male witnesses or of one male and two females.—This is a rule where there is no apparent pregnancy, or where the same is not acknowledged by the husband ; but if the pregnancy be apparent, or the husband have acknowledged it, the parentage is established independent of the testimony of witness. The two disciples maintain that, in all cases, the parentage is established upon the testimony of one woman,—because the husband's right of cohabitation still continues during Edit, and it is this right which occasions the fixing of the parentage of a child upon the husband, wherefore nothing more is required that some person prove the birth, and the identity, by testifying "This is the child of which such a woman was delivered,"—and thus much may be sufficiently proved by the testimony of a single woman, in the same manner as it is during marriage, in a case where the husband disputes the child's identity.—Haneefa, on the other hand, argues that the Edit is accomplished by the woman's declaration of delivery ; but the mere completion of Edit is not proof, and the descent still remains to be first established, for which reason it is that complete proof (that is, the testimony of two men, or of one man and two women) is made a condition ; but it would be otherwise if the pregnancy were apparent, or acknowledged by the husband, as in this case the parentage is established prior to the birth : and the child's identity is there ascertained by the identity of one woman,—the midwife, for instance.

The parentage of child born of a widow, when uncontroverted, is established, in her deceased husband, independent of evidence.—If a man under Edit from the death of her husband bring forth a child and declare it to be his, and the heirs confirm her assertion, though no person hear evidence to the birth, the child is held to be descended of the husband, according to all our doctors.* This, with respect to inheritance, is evident, as inheritance is a sole right of the heirs, and consequently their testimony or acknowledgment is to be credited in every matter which affects it.—A question, however, may arise in the case whether the parentage of the child be by such testimony established with respect to others than those heirs : and upon this the learned in the law observe, that if those heirs be persons of a description capable of being admitted as witness, the parentage is established with respect to all others as well as themselves, because their testimony amounts to proof, for which reason some doctors require that their confirmation of the woman's assertion be delivered in the form of evidence, but the necessity of this is denied by others, because the establishment of parentage, with respect to the rest of mankind, is a necessary consequence of its establishment with respect to the immediate heirs of the deceased by their confirmation ; and where a matter is once fully established upon any particular ground, no necessity exists for any further conditions with respect to its establishment.

A child born within less than six months after marriage is not the offspring of that marriage ; but if after six months it is so, independent of the husband's acknowledgment ; or upon the evidence of one witness the birth where he denies it : and Lean is incumbent, if he persist in his denial ; and the wife's testimony is to be credited in respect to the date of the marriage.—If a man marry a woman, and she bring forth a child within less than six months after the marriage, the parentage of the child is not established in the husband, as pregnancy in that case appears to have existed previous to the marriage, and consequently cannot be derived from him ; but if she be delivered after six months, it is established, whether he acknowledge it or not, because then the marriage appears to have existed at the time of impregnation, and the term of pregnancy is complete. If, moreover, the husband deny the birth, it may be proved by the evidence of one woman, after which the parentage is established in virtue of the marriage ; and such being the case, if he persist in denying the child, imprecation becomes incumbent, because his denial then amounts to an imputation on his wife's chastity, since it implies a charge of adultery against her. And if, upon the birth of a child, a dispute were to arise between the husband and wife, he

---

*This means, at whatever time the child be born, after the husband's decease.

asserting that he had married her only four months before, and she maintaining that they had been married six months, the declaration of the wife is to be credited, and the child belongs to the husband, because apparent circumstances testify for the wife, as it appears that her pregnancy has been a consequence of marriage and not of whoredom.—A question has arisen among our doctors whether the woman's assertion is to be credited without being confirmed by oath? The two disciples hold that it requires her oath; but Haneefa maintains the contrary opinion.

Divorce suspended upon the birth of a child cannot take place on the evidence of one woman to the birth.—If a man suspend divorce upon the circumstance of his wife's bearing a child, by saying to her, "upon being delivered of this child you are divorced,"—and a woman afterwards give testimony to her being delivered, yet divorce does not take place according to Haneefa. The two disciples maintain that divorce takes place, because the evidence of a single woman suffices in all such matters as are improper to be held by men; and the evidence of one woman to a birth being admitted, it is also to be admitted with respect to whatever proceeds from the birth, which in the present instance is divorce.—The argument of Haneefa is that the woman, in this case, stands as a plaintiff for penalty against her husband, and he appears as the defendant, wherefore her claim cannot be established but by complete proof.—The foundation of this is that the evidence of a woman is admitted with respect to child-birth from necessity only, and has therefore no effect with respect to divorce, since that is a matter altogether distinct from child-birth, and unconnected with it, although such connection appear to exist from the peculiar circumstances of the present case But if the husband acknowledge the pregnancy, divorce takes place upon the woman independent of the evidence of others, according to Haneefa.—The two disciples hold that in this case also the testimony of the midwife is necessary, because proof is indispensable to the establishment of a Dawee Hins, or claim of penalty, and the evidence of the midwife amounts to proof, according to what was before said.—The arguments of Haneefa are twofold;—First, the acknowledgment of pregnancy amounts to an acknowlegment of that which pregnancy induces, and extends thereto, and that thing is child-birth; Secondly, the husband, in acknowledging the pregnancy, declares his wife a trustee, as the child is a deposit in her possession, and consequently her word is to be credited in the surrender of the deposit, as much as that of any other trustee.

The term of pregnancy is from six months to two years.—The longest term of pregnancy is two years, because of the declaration of Aysha, "the child does not remain in the mother's womb beyond two years:" and the shortest term is six months, because the sacred text says, "the whole term of pregnancy and weaning is thirty months;" and Ibn Abbas has said that the term of suckling is two years, wherefore six months remain for the pregnancy.—Shafei has said that the longest term of pregnancy extends to four years; but the text here quoted, and the opinion of Ibn Abbas as above, testify against him.—It is probable that Shafei may have delivered this opinion upon hearsay, as this is a matter which does not admit of reasoning.

Case of a man divorcing a wife who is a slave, and then purchasing her.—If a man marry a female slave, and afterwards divorce her, and then purchase her, and she be delivered of a child within less than six months from the day of purchase, the parentage is established in him; but if she be delivered after six months, the parentage is not established; because, in the first instance, the child is considered as born of a woman under Edit, conception appearing to have taken place before purchase; but in the second instance, it is regarded as slave-born, as the length of the term of pregnancy here admits of conception being referred to a time subsequent to purchase; and the child thus appearing to be born (not of a wife, but) of a slave, his acknowledgment requisite to the establishment of its parentage.—What is not advanced proceeds upon the supposition of the slave being repudiated by a single divorce, reversible or irreversible, or by Khoola: but if she be repudiated by two divorces, the parentage of the child is established, if it be born within two years from the date of the divorce, because in this case she is rendered uulawful to her husband by the rigorous prohibition, whence the pregnancy can be referred only to a time previous to divorce, since, under such a circumstance she is not rendered lawful to the man by his subsequent purchase of her.

Miscellaneous cases.—If a man say to his female slave, "if there be a child in your womb it is mine," upon a woman afterwards bearing testimony to the birth, the slave becomes Am-Walid to that man, because here all that is requisite is to prove the child's indentity, by showing that "such a woman has been delivered of such a child,"—and this is sufficiently ascertained by the testimony of the midwife, according to all our doctors.

If a man say of a boy, "this is my son," and afterwards die, and the mother come declaring herself to be the wife of the deceased, she must be considered as such, and the boy as his child, and they both inherit of him. It is recorded in the Nawadir that this rule proceeds upon a favourable construction of the law, for analogy requires that the woman should not inherit, since descent is established not only in virtue of a valid marriage, but also of an invalid marriage, or of erroneous carnal connexion, or of possession by right of property, and therefore the main's declaration that "this is his son" does not amount to an acknowledgment of his having married the mother: but the reason for a more favourable construction of the law here is, that the case supposes the woman to be one whose freedom and materal right in the child are matters of public notoriety, and the validity of a marriage is ascertained by circumstances. But if the woman be not known to be free, and the heirs of the husband maintain that she is only an Am-Walid, she is not entitled to any inheritance, because the mere appearance of freedom (supposing the case to occur in a Mussulman territory), although it defend the party from slavery, is not sufficient to establish a claim of inheritance.

CHAPTER XIV.

OF HIZANIT, OR THE CARE OF INFANT CHILDREN

In case of separation, the care of the infant children belongs to the wife.—IF a separation take place between a husband and wife, who are possessed of an infant child, the right of nursing and keeping it rests with the mother, because it is recorded that a woman once applied to the Prophet; saying "O Prophet of GOD! this is my son, the fruit of my womb, cherished in my bosom and suckled at my breast, and his father is desirous of taking him away from me into his own care;"—to which the Prophet replied, "thou hast a right in the child prior to that of thy husband, so long as thou dost not marry with a stranger:"—moreover, a mother is naturally not only more tender, but also better qualified to cherish a child during infancy, so that committing the care to her is of advantage to the child; and Siddeek alluded to this, when he addressed Omar on a similar occasion, saying, "the spittle of the mother is better for thy child than honey, O OMAR!" which was said at a time when separation had taken place between Omar and his wife, the mother of Assim, the latter being then an infant at the breast, and Omar desirous of taking him from the mother; and these words were spoken in the presence of many of the companions, none of whom contradicted him:—but the Nifka or subsistence of the child is incumbent upon the father, as shall be hereafter explained. It is to be observed, however, that if the mother refuse to keep the child, there is no constraint upon her, as a variety of causes may operate to render her incapable of the charge.

Order of precedence in Hizanit, after the mother.—IF the mother of an infant die, the right of Hizanit (or infant education) rests with the maternal grandmother, in preference to the paternal, because it originates in, and is derived from, the mother; but if she be not living, the paternal grandmother has then a right prior to any other relation she being as one of the child's mothers (whence it is that she is entitled to a sixth of the effects of a child of her son, which is the mother's share*); and she must, moreover, be considered as having a more tender interest in her own offspring than any collateral relation. If there be no grandmother living, in this case a sister is preferable to either a maternal or paternal aunt, as she is the daughter of the father and mother, or of one of them, whence it is that she would take place of the aunts in inheritance—(according to one tradition, the maternal aunt is preferable to a half-sister by the father side, the Prophet having said, "the maternal aunt is as a mother").—A full sister, also, has preference to an half-sister, maternal or paternal; and a maternal sister to a paternal sister; because the right of Hizanit is derived to them through the mother. The maternal aunt has preference to the paternal, because precedence is given, in this point, to the maternal relation. The same distinction also prevails among the aunt as among the sisters;—that is, she who is doubly related has a preference to her who is singly related; thus the maternal aunt, who is full sister to the mother precedes an half sister, maternal or paternal: and, in the same manner, a maternal sister precedes a paternal sister; and so also of the paternal aunts. If, however, any of these women, having the right of Hizanit, should marry a stranger, her right is thereby annulled, an account of the tradition before quoted, and also because, where the husband is a stranger, it is to be apprehended that he may treat the child unkindly: where the woman, therefore, who has charge of an infant marries, it is neither advantageous nor advisable that the infant remain with her, unless the person she marries be a relation,—as where the mother, for instance, having charge, marries the child's paternal uncle, or the maternal grandmother marries the paternal grandfather,—because these men, being as parents, it is to be expected that they will behave with tenderness:—and so also of any other relation within the prohibited degrees, for the same reason.

ANY woman whose right of Hizanit is annulled by her marrying a stranger recovers the right by the dissolution of the marriage, the objection to her exercise of it being thereby removed.

In defeat of the maternal, it rests with the nearest paternal relation.—IF there be no woman to whom the right of Hizanit appertains, and the men of the family dispute it, in this case the nearest paternal relation has the preference, he being the one to whom the authority of guardian belongs (the de-

*This must mean, in case of the mother's death.

grees of paternal relationship are treated of in their proper place): but it is to be observed that the child must not be entrusted to any relation beyond the prohibited degrees, such as the Mawla or emancipator of a slave, or the son of the paternal uncle, as in this there may be apprehension of treachery.

Length of the term of Hizanit.—The right of Hizanit, with respect to a male child, appertains to the mother; grandmother, or so forth, until he become independent of it himself, that is to say, become capable of shifting, eating, drinking, and performing the other natural functions without assistance; after which the charge devolves upon the father, or next paternal relation entitled to the office of guardian, because, when thus far advanced, it then becomes necessary to attend to his education in all branches of useful and ornamental science, and to initiate him into a knowledge of men and manners, to effect which the father or paternal relations are best qualified—(Kasaf says that the Hizanit, with respect to a boy, ceases at the end of seven years. as in general a child at that age is capable of performing all the necessary offices for himself, without assistance).—But the right of Hizanit with respect to a girl appertains to the mother, grandmother, and so forth, until the first appearance of the menstrual discharge (that is to say, until she attain the age of puberty), because a girl has occasion to learn such manners and accomplishments as are proper to women, to the teaching of which the female relations are most competent; but after that period the charge of her properly belongs to the father, because a girl, after maturity, requires some person to superintend her conduct, and to this the father is most completely qualified. It is recorded from Mohammed that the care of a female child devolves upon the father as soon as she begins to feel the carnal appetite,* as she then requires a superintendence over her conduct; and it is universally admitted that the right of Hizanit of girls is restricted to that period, with respect to all the female relations except the mother and grandmother. It is written in the Jama Sagheer, that the right of Hizanit, with any except the mother or grandmother, discontinues upon the girl becoming capable of performing natural offices without assistance, because no other is entitled to require any service of her (whence it is that they cannot hire her as a servant to others), and such being the case the end (namely, the girl's education) cannot be obtained: but it is otherwise with the mother or grandmother, as they are invested with a legal right to require her services.

A slave has the right upon obtaining her freedom.—If a man contract his female slave or Am-Walid, in marriage to any person, and she bear a child to her husband, and the master afterwards emancipate her, she then becomes (with respect to the child) as a free woman; that is, upon becoming free she obtains her right of Hizanit which had not existed while she was a slave, because her service, as a slave, would necessarily interfere with the proper discharge of the duties of Hizanit.

And also an infidel mother the wife of a Mussulman.—A Zimmeea, or female infidel subject, married to a Mussulman, is entitled to the Hizanit of her child, although he be a Mussulman like the father; but this only so long as the child is incapable of forming any judgment with respect to religion, and whilst there is no apprehension of his imbibing an attachment to infidelity; but when this is the case, he must be taken from the mother, because, although it be for the child's advantage to be under her care until that period, his remaining longer with her might prove injurious.

Children after the term of Hizanit, remain solely under the care of the father.—A boy or girl, having passed the period of Hizanit have no option to be with one parent in preference to the other, but must necessarily thenceforth remain in charge of the father. Shafei maintains that they have an option to remain with either parent, because of a tradition of the Prophet to this effect. The argument of our doctors is, that young persons, from want of judgment, will naturally wish to stay with the parent who treats them with most indulgence, and lays them under least restraint, wherefore giving them a choice in this matter would not be tenderness, but rather the reverse, as being contrary to their true interest; and it appears in the Nakl Saheeh that the companions withheld this option from children. With respect to the tradition cited by Shafei, it may be observed that, in the instance there alluded to, where the Prophet gave a boy his choice, he first prayed to God to direct him therein, and the boy then chose, under the influence of the Prophet's prayer.

Section

A mother cannot remove with her child to a strange place.—If a divorced woman be desirous of removing with her child out of a city, she is not at liberty to do it: but yet if she remove with her child out of a city, and go to her native place, where the contract of her marriage, was executed, in this case her removal is lawful, because the father is considered as having also undertaken to reside in that place, both in the eye of the law. and according to common usage, for the Prophet has said, "Whoever marries a woman of any city is thereby rendered a Denizen of that city;" and hence it is, that if an alien woman were to come into the Mussulman territory, and there to marry an infidel subject, she also becomes an infidel subject; it is to observed, however, that

*This is supposed by the Mussulmans to commence some time before the appearance of the menstrual discharge, at between eleven and twelve years of age.

this rule does not apply to an alien man, that is to say, if an alien man were to come into the Mussulman territory, and there to marry a female subject, he is not thereby rendered a subject; for if he choose, he may divorce this wife and return to his own country.

IF a divorced woman be desirous of removing with her child to a place which is not the place of her nativity, but in which her marriage contract was executed, she is not at liberty to do it. This demonstrated by Kadooree in his compendium, and also accords with what is related in the Mabsoot. The Jama Sagheer says that she may take her child thither, because where a marriage contract is executed in any place, it occasions all the ordinances thereof to exist and have force in that place, in the same manner as sale amounts to a delivery of the article sold in the place of sale; and a woman's right to the care of her children is one of the ordinances of marriage, wherefore she is entitled to keep her child in the place where she was married,, although she be not a native of that place. The principle upon which the Mabsoot proceeds in this case is, that the execution of a contract of marriage in a place merely of casual residence (such as the stage of a journey, does not constitute it a home, according to general usage, and this is the better opinion. In short, to the propriety of the woman carrying her child from one place to another, two points are essentially requisite one. that she be a native of the place to which she goes; and the other, that her marriage contract has been there executed; this, however, means only where the places are considerably distant; but if they be so near that the father may go to see his child and return the same night,' there is no objection to the wife going to the other place with the child, and there remaining; and this, whatever be the size or degree of the places, whether cities or villages; nor is there any objection to her removing from the village to the city or chief town of a district, as this is in no respect injurious to the father, and is advantageous to the child, since he will thereby become known and acquainted with the people of the place; but the reverse [that is, her removal from the city to a village], would be injurious to the child, as he would thereby be liable to acquire the low manners and mean sentiments of villagers; wherefore a woman is not at liberty to carry her child from a city to a village.

CHAPTER XV.

OF NIFKA, OR MAINTENANCE

Definition of the term.—NIFKA, in the language of the law, signifies all those things which are necessary to the support of life, such as food, clothes, and lodging: many confine it solely to food.

Section I

Of the Nifka of the Wife.

The subsistence of wife is incumbent upon her husband.—WHEN a woman surrenders herself into the custody of her husband, it is incumbent upon him thenceforth to supply her with food, clothing, and lodging, whether she be a Mussulman or an infidel, because such is the precept both in the Koran and in the traditions; and also, because maintenance is a recompense for the matrimonial restraint: whence it is that where a person is in custody of another on account of any demand, or so forth, his subsistence is incumbent upon that other,—as when a public magistrate, for instance, is imprisoned on account of any mal-administration in his office, in which case his subsistance must be provided from the public treasury; and as the authorities upon which this proceeds make no distinctions between a Mussulman and an infidel, the rule holds the same with respect to either in the present case.

In proportion to the rank and circumstances of the parties.—IN adjusting the obligation of the Nifka, or maintenance of a wife, regard is to be had to the rank and condition both of her and her husband: thus if the parties be both wealthy, he must support her in an opulent manner: if they be both poor, he is required only to provide for her accordingly: and if he be rich, and she poor, he is to afford her a moderate subsistence, such as is below the former and above the latter.—The compiler of this work says that this is the opinion adopted by Khasaf; and that decrees pass accordingly. Koorokhee is of opinion that the rank and condition of the husband alone is to be regarded (and such also is the doctrine of Shafei), because the sacred text says, "LET HIM SUPPORT HER ACCORDING TO HIS ABILITY."—The ground of Khasaf's opinion is a tradition respecting the Prophet, who, on a woman applying to him for his judgment upon this point, said to her, "take from the property of your husband whatever may suffice for the subsistence of yourself and your child in the customary way;" for which it appears that the circumstances of the woman are to be regarded as well as those of the man, for maintenance is incumbent only so far as may suffice for the purpose intended by it, and as a womam in mean circumstances has no occasion for the same subsistence as one who is accustomed to live in affluence, such is (with respect to her) unnecessary; and as to the text above quoted by Shafei, it means no more than that if the woman be in affluent circumstances, and her husband otherwise, he shall suppose her according to his ability, and the remainder, or difference, shall be a debt upon him. By the expression "customary way," in the tradition quoted by Shafei, is to be understood a middling or moderate way, that is, a medium between the circumstances of the wife and those of the husband where the former happens to be rich and the latter poor; and as the Prophet in his decision left this to the judgment of the parties themselves, the proportion is not specifically determined by the law.—Shafei has so determined it, saying that the Nifka or maintenance incumbent upon a husband in behalf of his wife, if he be opulent, is two Mids, or about one thousand Dirms* annually,—if he be poor, one Mid: and if in middling circumstances, one and a half: this, however, is not admitted, because a thing declared to be incumbent "so far as may suffice" cannot be legally fixed at any specific rate, as the proportion must necessarily vary according to circumstances.

And this, although she withhold herself on account of her dower.—If a woman refuse to surrender herself to her husband, on account of her dower (that is, on account of its not having been paid to her), her maintenance does not drop, but is incumbent upon the husband, although she be not yet within his custody, since her refusal is only in pursuance of her right, and consequently the objection to the matrimonial custody originates with the husband.

But not if she be refractory.—If a wife be disobedient or refractory, and go abroad without her husband's consent, she is not entitled to any support from him, until she return and make submission, because the rejection of the matrimonial restraint in this instance originates with her; but when she returns home, she is then subject to it, for which reason she again becomes entitled to her support as before. It is otherwise where a woman, residing in the house of her husband, refuses to admit him to the conjugal embrace, as she is entitled to maintenance, notwithstanding her opposition, because being then in his power, he may, if he please, enjoy her by force.

Or an infant incapable of generation.—If a man's wife be so young as to be incapable of generation, her maintenance is not incumbent upon him, because although she should be within his custody, yet as an obstacle exists in her to the carnal embrace, this is not the custody which entitles to maintenance, that being described "custody, for the purpose of enjoyment," which does not apply to the case of one incapable of the act:—contrary to the case of the sick woman, to whom maintenance is due, although she be incapable, as shall be hereafter demonstrated.—Shafei says that maintenance is due to an infant wife, because he holds it to be a return for the matrimonial propriety, in the same manner as it is with respect to a slave for the propriety in his personal service. To this however, our doctors reply that the dower is the return for the matrimonial propriety, and one thing does not legally admit of two returns; wherefore, in the case of an infant wife, the dower is due but not maintenance.

But it is due to an adult wife from an infant husband.—But if the husband be an infant incapable of generation, and the wife an adult, she is entitled to her maintenance at his expense, because, in this case delivery of the person has been performed on her part, and the obstacle to the matrimonial enjoyment exists on the part of the husband.

It is not due where the wife is imprisoned for debt.—If a woman be imprisoned for debt, her husband is not required to support her, because the objection to the matrimonial custody does not in this case originate with him, whether her imprisonment be owing to herself (as in a case of wilful delay and contumacy) or otherwise (as where she is poor and unable to discharge the debt).

Or forcibly carried off.—And, in the same manner, if a woman be forcibly seized and carried off by any person, she has no claim to maintenance from her husband; and so also, if a woman go upon a pilgrimage, under charge of a relation within the prohibited degrees,—because she is not then in custody of her husband, and her not being so is occasioned by her own voluntary act.

Or goes upon a pilgrimage.—It is recorded from Aboo Yoosaf that a woman upon a pilgrimage is entitled to a maintenance from her husband, as her undertaking the indispensable pilgrimage* is a sufficient pretext for her leaving him; but he allows her only a Nifka-Hizr, or support as in a settled place; and not a Nifka-Sifr, or support as upon a journey; as the former only incumbent upon the nusband, not the latter.

Unless she be accompanied by the husband.—But if the husband accompany his wife upon her pilgrimage, her maintenance is then incumbent upon him according to all our doctors, because in this case she continues in his custody; but she is entitled to Nifka-Hizr only, not to a Nifka-Sifr, as he is not the occasion of her travelling, whence it is that he is not obliged to furnish her with a conveyance.

It continues during her sickness.—If a woman fall sick in her husband's house, she is still entitled to a maintenance. This is upon a principle of benevolence, as analogy would suggest that she is not entitled to maintenance where she falls sick so far as to be incapable of admitting her husband to the conjugal embrace, since in this case she cannot be deemed in custody for the purpose of enjoyment; but the reason for a more favourable construction of the law in this case is, that she still remains in custody, as her husband may associate and indulge in dalliance with her, and she may continue to superinted his domestic concerns, and the obstacle to carnal enjoyment is (like the men-

*Dirms have varied in their value at different times, from twenty to twenty-five passing current for a Deenar. The sum here mentioned is from about eighteen to twenty-two pounds sterling.

*Arab Hidj-Farz.—It is incumbent upon all Moslamites to perform at least one pilgrimage to Mecca, and this one is reckoned among the Firayez, or sacred ordinarces, whence the above epithet.

strual discharge) an accidental occurrence.—It is recorded from Aboo Yoosaf that if a woman deliver herself into the custody of her husband, and then fall sick, she is still entitled to maintenance; but if she fall sick first, and then deliver herself to him, she has no claim to maintenance until her recovery, as the surrender of her person is not in this case complete; and the learned in the law admit this to be a proper distinction.

A husband must maintain his wife's servants.—The maintenance of the wife's servants is incumbent upon her husband, as well as that of the wife herself, provided he be in opulent circumstances, because he is obliged to provide his wife's maintenance, "so far as may suffice" (as aforesaid), and it is not sufficient, unless her servants also be supported, they being essential to her case and comfort; but it is not absolutely incumbent upon him to provide a maintenance for more than one servant, according to Haneefa and Mohammad. Aboo Yoosaf says he must provide maintenance for two servants, as one is required for service within the house, and the other out of doors.—The arguments of Haneefa and Mohammed on this point are twofold:—First, one servant may answer both purposes, whence two are unnecessary; Secondly, if the husband were himself to undertake all the services required by the wife, it would suffice, and a servant would be unnecessary; and, in the same manner, it suffices if he constitute any single servant his substitute therein; wherefore a second servant is not requisite. The learned in the law say that the rate of maintenance due from an opulent busband to his wife's servants is the same as that due from a poor husband to his wife,—namely, the lowest that can be admitted as sufficient.—Haneefa says that a husband who is poor is not required to find maintenance for his wife's servants; and this is an approved doctrine, as it is to be supposed that the wife of a poor man will serve herself. Mohammed holds that it is due from a poor husband, in the same manner as from one more opulent.

If the husband be poor, the magistrate must empower the wife to raise subsistence upon his credit.—If a husband become poor, to such a degree as to be unable to provide his wife her maintenance, still they are not to be separated on this account, but the Kazee shall direct the woman to procure necessaries for herself upon her husband's credit, the amount remaining a debt upon him.—Shafei says that they must be separated, because whenever the husband becomes incapable of providing his wife's maintenance, he cannot "retain her with humanity" (as is required in the sacred writings), and such being the case, it behoves him to divorce her; and if he decline so to do, the Kazee is then to effect the separation as his substitute, in the same manner as in cases of emasculation or impotence: nay, the necessity for this is more urgent in the present instance than in either of those cases, as the maintenance is indispensable. To this our doctors reply that if a separation take place the right of the husband is destroyed in toto, which is a grievous injury to him; whereas, if the wife be desired to procure maintenance for herself upon his credit, his right is by this means preserved with the smallest possible injury; wherefore they are not to be separated, but the wife shall be directed to take up the articles necessary for her subsistence upon his credit, as was already stated:—but the wife is in this case restricted in her expenses to a rate which must be determined by the Kazee.

At a certain specified rate.—The Kazee cannot act as the substitute of the husband in effecting a separation here, as in cases of emasculation or impotence, because property in marriage is only a dependant, or secondary consideration, the primary object being procreation, and that which is a dependant merely cannot be put in competition with the original intent, upon which principle it is that the Kazee is empowered to effect a separation in either of the other two instances, as there the original intent is defeated; but it is not so in the present case. The advantage of the Kazee desiring the woman to procure a maintenance upon her husband's credit, and of his fixing the rate thereof, is that she is thereby enabled to make her husband responsible for the amount; for if she contract any debt without this authority, the creditors claim lies against her, and not against her husband.

To be varied according to any change in his circumstances.—If the husband were in indigent circumstances at the time of the Kazee authorizing the wife as aforesaid, and he have consequently determined her maintenance at the rate of poverty, and the husband afterwards become rich and she sue for a proportionable addition to her maintenance, a decree must be given in her favour, as the rate of the maintenance differs according to the poverty or opulence of the husband.

Arrears of maintenance not due unless the maintenance have been decreed by the Kazee or the rate of it previously determined on between the parties.—If a length of time should elapse during which the wife has not received any maintenance from her husband, she is not entitled to demand any for that time, except when the Kazee had before determined and decreed it to her, or where she had entered into a composition with the husband respecting it, in either of which cases she is to be decreed her maintenance for the time past, because maintenance is an obligation in the manner of a gratuity,* as by a gratuity is understood a thing due without a return, and maintenance is of this description, it not being held (according to our doctors) to be as a return for the matrimonial

* Arab, Sillit. By this is to be here understood a present or gratuity promised but not yet paid.

propriety ; and the obligation of it is not valid but through a decree of the Kazee, like a gift, which does not convey a right to possession but through seisin, which establishes possession : but a composition is of equal effect with a decree of the Kazee, in the present case, as the husband, by such composition, makes himself responsible, and his power over his own person is superior to that of the magistrate—This reasoning does not apply to the case of dower, as that is considered to be a return for the use of the wife's person.

Arrears of a decreed maintenance drop in case of the death of either party.—IF the Kazee decree a wife her maintenance, and a length of time elapse without her receiving any and the husband should die, her maintenance drops ; and the rule is the same if she should die ; because maintenance is a gratuity, respecting which the rule is that it drops in consequence of death, like a gift, which is annulled by the decease of either the donor or donee before seisin being made by the latter.—Shafei says that the maintenance is in all circumstances to be considered as a debt upon the husband, in conformity with his tenet, that it is not a gratuity but a return, wherefore it cannot drop like demands of the former description.—This was before replied to.

Advances of maintenance cannot be reclaimed.—IF a man give his wife one year's maintenance in advance, and then die before the expiration of the year, no claim lies against the woman for restitution of any part of it.—This is the doctrine of Haneefa and Aboo Yoosaf.—Mohammed says that she is entitled only to the proportion due for the term past, from beginning of the year till the husband's decease, the remainder being the right of his heirs ; if, therefore, the difference remain with her in substance, she must restore it ; or, if it do not remain, she is responsible for the value (and this also is the doctrine of Shafei, and the same difference of opinion obtains in respect to clothes and apparel), because the wife in this case has received in advance the return for the matrimonial confinement, to which she has a claim, in virtue of such confinement, but her claim is annulled by the husband's decease, since she no longer remains confined, and consequently the return is annulled in proportion to the annulment of her claim, in the same manner as the stipend of a Kazee:—The argument of the two Elders is that the maintenance is a gratuity, of which the claimant has already taken possession ; and restitution of a gratuity cannot be demanded after death, the virtue of it being completed by that event, as in a case of gift ; whence it is that if the maintenance were to perish in the woman's possession, without her consuming it, no part of it can be demanded of her, according to all the doctors, whereas, if it were a return, it might be demanded in a case of destruction, as well as in one of consumption, nor would there be any difference between the two.—It is recorded from Mohammed that if the proportion advanced do not exceed that of one month ; no restitution is required, as this proportion is inconsiderable, and stands as an allowance for present use.

A slave may be sold for the maintenance of his wife, if the latter be free.—IF a slave marry a free woman, her maintenance is a debt upon him, for the discharge of which he may be sold ; but this is only provided the marriage was with his owner's consent, as her maintenance being due from the slave the obligation to it must ultimately affect his owner ; the debt is therefore charged to the slave, in the same manner as one contracted in trade by a Mazoon, or privileged slave ; but his owner is at liberty to redeem him by discharging the debt, because the woman's right extends to her maintenance only, not to the slave's person : and if the slave die, her right to any arrear of maintenance drops (and so also where he is killed), since it is a gratuity, as was already stated,

A husband must maintain his wife, being a slave, were she resides with him.—IF a man marry the female slave of another, and her owner give her permission to reside in her husband's house, her maintenance is incumbent upon the husband, because she is then within his custody : but if she have not permission to reside with her husband, he is not responsible for her maintenance, as in this case her custody is not established.—The term here applied to the permission granted by the master [taboweeat] means not only liberty to reside in the husband's habitation, but also an exemption from all service ; wherefore, if any service be afterwards required of her, the maintenance from the husband drops, as custody which is the ground of her right to maintenance from him, necessarily ceases on such an occasion —It is lawful for the master to require the service of his female slave, although he have granted her leave to reside with her husband, because such leave is not binding upon him, as is demonstrated in its proper place, —But it is to be observed that if the female slave voluntarily perform her master's service, without his calling upon her, her right to maintenance from her husband does not drop.

And the same of Am-Walids.—THESE rules apply equally to Am-Walids as to absolute slaves.

Section II.

A wife must be accommodated with a separate apartment.—IT is incumbent upon a husband to provide a separate apartment for his wife's habitation, to be solely and exclusively appropriated to her use, so as that none of the husband's family, or others. may enter without her permission and desire, because this is essentially necessary to her, and is therefore her due the same as maintenance, for the word of God appoints her a dwellings-house as well as a subsistence ; and as it is incumbent upon a husband to provide a habitation for his wife, so he is not at liberty to admit any person to a share in it, as this would be injurious to her by endangering her property, and obstructing her enjoyment of his society ; but if she desire it, the husband may then lawfully admit a partner in the habitation, as she by such a request voluntarily relinquishes her right ; neither is the husband at liberty to intrude upon his wife his child by another woman, for the same reason.

If the husband appoint his wife an apartment within his own house, giving her the lock and key, it is sufficient, as the end is by this means fully obtained.

But under the control of her husband, with respect to visitors, &c—A husband is at liberty to prevent his wife's parents, or other relations, or her children by a former marriage, from coming in* to her, as her apartment or habitation is his property, which he may lawfully prevent any person from entering ; but he cannot prohibit them from seeing and conversing with her whenever they please, for if he were to do so, it would induce Katta Rihm, or a breach of the ties of kindred, and their seeing or conversing with her is in no respect injurious to him. Some have said that he cannot prohibit them from coming in to her, any more than from conversing with or seeing her, but he may prevent them from residing with her, as this might cause disturbance and inconvenience. Others have said that he cannot prohibit his wife from going to visit her parents, nor prevent the parents from visiting her every Friday ; neither can he forbid her other relations from visiting her once a year ; and this is approved.

Maintenance to the wife of an absentee is decreed out of his substance.—If a woman's husband absent himself, leaving effects in the hands of any person, and that person acknowledge the deposit, and admit the woman to be the wife of the absentee, the Kazee must decree a maintenance to her out of the said effects ; and the same to the infant children of the absentee, and also to his parents. And the rule is the same if the Kazee himself be acquainted with the above two circumstances, where the trustee denies both or either of them.—The argument upon which this proceeds is that where the above person acknowledges the woman to be the wife of the absentee, and also, that he has property of the latter in his hands, such acknowledgment amounts to an avowal of her being entitled to receive her right out of the said property, without the husband's consent, as a woman is authorized to it by law.

Objection,—If a woman be decreed her maintenance out of the effects of her absent husband, in consequence of the trustee's acknowledgment, this admits the judgment of a magistrate against an absentee, which is illegal.

Reply.—The order of the Kazee is not in this case directly against an absentee, but only virtually, and by implication, because the above person is the Zoo-al-Yed, or immediate possessor of the property, and the acknowledgment of such an one is to be credited in anything affecting his trust, but more especially in the present case, since if he were to deny either the marriage or the deposit it would not be in the woman's power to sue him, for if she do so, and produce witnesses in support of her plea, their evidence could not be received, as a trustee cannot be sued on a plea of marriage ; nor can the woman appear as plaintiff against him with respect to the property in his hands, since she is not the husband's agent : and the trustee's acknowledgment being credited, the Kazee, in consequence of it, issues a decree for the wife's maintenance, which must affect the husband of course ; and the decree of a Kazee, affecting an absentee in this way, is approved.—If, moreover, the property of the absentee be in the hands of the person aforesaid in the way of Mozaribat, or as a debt, the rule holds the same as if it were a deposit.

Unless that be of a nature different from what is necessary to her support —What is now said supposes the property to be of the same nature with the woman's right, such as money, grain or cloth : but where it is otherwise, a maintenance must not be decreed out of it, because, in this case, it cannot be furnished from it but by selling a part, and defraying the expense of it out of the amount ; and all our doctors agree that the property of an absentee cannot be sold —Haneefa is of this opinion, because the Kazee cannot sell the effects even of a person on the spot, but must require him to sell them, and discharge the maintenance with the amount ; and consequently he is prohibited from selling the property of an absentee, a fortiori. The two disciples also are of the same opinion, because, although they hold that the Kazee may dispose of the property of a person on the spot, for the discharge of his wife's maintenance, without his consent, yet this is only where he refuses to do so ; but the property of an absentee cannot be thus disposed of, as his refusal is not known.

But she must give security that she has not already received anything in advance.—When the Kazee decrees a woman her maintenance out of the effects of her absent husband, it behoves him to take security from her for whatever she receives for the indemnity of the absentee, as it is possible that she may already have received her maintenance in advance, or that she may have been divorced, and her Edit be passed ; and the Kazee must

*Although, by the customs of the east, men are not permitted to enter into the women's apartments without especial permission, yet it is not uncommon to converse with a woman through a curtain, or (as some part of this passage seems to imply) through a gate.

also require her to make oath that she has not received any part of her maintenance in advance: contrary to a case where the Kazee makes a distribution of inheritance among present heirs, according to evidence, and they do not deny any knowledge of another heir, for in this case he does not require a similar security from them on behalf of another heir, who may hereafter appear, because the Makfool-le-hoo, or surety, is there unknown and undefined; but in the present case the surety is known, being the absent husband.

It can be decreed only to the wife, infant children, or parents of the absentee.—A KAZEE cannot decree maintenance, out of the effects of an absentee, in behalf of any but those already mentioned (namely, the wife, infant children, and parents of the absentee), as they alone are authorized to receive a maintenance independent of any decree of the Kazee (that, in the present case, being only in aid of their right), whereas the other relations within the prohibited degrees are not entitled to any maintenance without a decree of the Kazee previously obtained for that purpose, as the obligation of it with respect to them varies according to circumstances, wherefore the Kazee decreeing it to them would amount to a judgment against an absentee, which is not allowed.

No decree can be issued against an absentee's property upon the bare testimony of his wife.—IF the Kazee himself be not assured that the woman is the wife of the absentee and the trustee factor, or debtor, do not acknowledge her to be so, and she should offer to produce witnesses to prove that she is so,—or, if the absentee should not have left any effects, and she offer to prove her marriage by evidence, with a view to obtain a decree authorizing her to procure a maintenance upon the absentee's credit, still the Kazee cannot issue a decree accordingly, because this would be a judgment against an absentee, which is inadmissible.—Ziffer says that it is the duty of the Kazee to hear the proofs, and (although he cannot decree the marriage to be thereby established) to order her a maintenance, as this is a tenderness due to her, and no injury to the absentee, becaus if he should afterwards appear and confirm her assertion, she has only taken what was her right,—or, if he should deny the marriage, an oath will be tendered to her (in case of her having no witnesses), and if she decline swearing, his assertion remains established; but if she prove her assertion by evidence, her right is established; and if she cannot produce any proof, and he swear she or her bail then remain responsible.—The author of this work says that it is the duty of the Kazee, in the present instance, to decree maintenance to the absentee's wife, from necessity.

Section III

A divorced wife is entitled to maintenance during her Edit.—WHERE a man divorces his wife, her subsistence and lodging are incumbent upon him during the term of her Edit, whether the divorce be of the reversible or irreversible kind.—Shafei says that no maintenance is due to a woman repudiated by irreversible divorce, unless she be pregnant.—The reason for maintenance being due to a woman under reversible divorce is that the marriage in such a case is still held to continue in force, especially according to our doctors, who on this principle maintain that it is lawful for a man to have carnal connexion with a wife so repudiated.—With respect to a case of irreversible divorce, the arguments of Shafei are twofold; FIRST, Kattima Bint Kays has said, "My husband repudiated me by three divorces, and the Prophet did not appoint to me either a place of residence or a subsistence;"—SECONDLY, the matrimonial propriety is thereby terminated, and the maintenance is held, by Shafei, to be a return for such propriety (whence it is that a woman's right to maintenance drops upon the death of her husband, as the matrimonial propriety is dissolved by that event);—but it would be otherwise if a woman repudiated by irreversible divorce be pregnant at the time of divorce, as in this case the obligation of maintenance appears, in the sacred writings, which expressly direct it to a woman under such a circumstance. The argument of our doctors is that maintenance is a return for custody (as was before observed), and custody still continues, on account of that which is the chief end of marriage, namely, offspring (as the intent of Edit is to ascertain whether the woman be pregnant or not), wherefore subsistence is due to her, as well as lodging, which last is admitted by all to be her right; thus the case is the same as if she were actually pregnant; moreover, Omar has recorded a precept of the Prophet, to the effect that "maintenance is due to a WOMAN "divorced thrice during her Edit:"—there are also a variety of traditions to the same purpose.

No maintenance due to a widow.—MAINTENANCE is not due to a woman after her husband's decease, because her subsequent confinement [during the term of Edit, in consequence of that event] is not on account of the right of her husband, but of the law, the Edit of widowhood being merely a religious observance, whence it is that the design of ascertaining the state of her womb is not in this instance regarded, and accordingly the Edit is not counted by the menstrual terms, but by time; maintenance is moreover due to a woman from day to day, and the husband's right in his property ceasing upon his decease, it is impossible that any maintenance should be made due from what is, after that event, the property of his heirs.

Nor to a wife in whom the separation originates.—WHEN the separation originates with the woman, from anything which can be imputed to her as a crime, such as apostatizing from the faith, or having carnal connexion or dalliance with the son of her husband, she has no claim to maintenance during Edit, since she has deprived her husband of her person unrighteously, in the same manner as if she were to go out of his house without permission.

Unless it originate in a circumstance not criminal.—BUT it is otherwise where the separation originates with the woman from a circumstance which cannot be imputed to her as a crime, as in a case of option of puberty or manumission, or of a separation demanded by her on account of inequality, in all which cases she remains entitled to maintenance during Edit, as she has here legally withdrawn herself from her husband, in the same manner as where she keeps herself from him on account of non-payment of her dower.

A wife who apostatize has no right to maintenance.—IF a woman under triplicate divorce apostatize from the faith, her maintenance drops; but if one in the same circumstance admit the son of her husband to carnal connexion, still her right to maintenance continues because here the divorce has not been caused by the apostasy or the incest of the woman: but the apostate is imprisoned until such time as she may repent; and a husband is not under any obligation to provide a maintenance for his wife if she be a prisoner whereas a woman who admits the son of her husband to carnal connexion is not liable to imprisonment on that account; which makes an essential difference between the two cases.

Section IV.

A father must provide for the maintenance of his infant children.—THE maintenance of infant children rests upon their father; and no person can be his associate or partner in furnishing it (in the same manner as no person is admitted to be associated with a husband in providing for the maintenance of his wife), because the word of GOD, in the Koran, says, "THE MAINTENANCE OF THE WOMAN WHO SUCKLES AN INFANT RESTS UPON HIM TO WHOM THE INFANT IS BORN" (that is upon the father), from which it appears that the maintenance of an infant child also rests upon the father, because, as maintenance is decreed to the nurse on account of her sustaining the child with her milk, it follows that the same is due to the child himself a fortiori.

A mother is not required to suckle her infant.—IF the child be an infant at the breast, there is no obligation upon the mother to suckle it, because the infant's maintenance rests upon the father, and in the same manner the hire of a nurse; it is possible, moreover, that the mother may not be able to suckle it, from want of health or other sufficient excuse, in which case any constraint upon her for that purpose would be an act of injustice.

Except where a nurse cannot be procured.—WHAT is here advanced proceeds upon a supposition of a nurse being easily procured; but where this is not the case, the mother may be constrained to take that office upon herself, lest the infant perish.

The father must provide a nurse.—IT is the part of a father to hire a woman to suckle his infant child, as this is a duty incumbent upon him; and it is necessary that the nurse so hired stay with or near the mother, if the latter desire it, as the child must be with its mother, she having the right of Hizanit.

But he cannot hire the child's mother in that capacity.—BUT it is not lawful for the father to hire the mother of the child as its nurse, if she be his wife, or divorced from him; and in her Edit,—because, although suckling her child be not incumbent upon a mother in point of law, yet it is so in point of religion, the word of GOD in the Koran saying, "IT BEHOVES MOTHERS TO SUCKLE THEIR CHILDREN;"—and a mother is excused from this duty only on the supposition of incapacity; but if she agree to perform it for a compensation, this is an acknowledgment of her capacity, making the duty incumbent upon her without any consideration whatever. This rule obtains (as above observed) where the mother is either actually the wife of the father, or reversibly divorced from him, and in her Edit, in which case the marriage still continues in force; and (according to one tradition) this also is the rule where the mother was in her Edit from irreversible divorce; but another tradition says that such a person may be lawfully hired by the father as a nurse, because her marriage no longer remains in force.—The argument in favour of the former tradition is that the marriage still continues in force with respect to some of its obligations, such as the provision of food, lodging, and so forth.

Yet he may hire any other of his wives for that purpose.—BUT a father may lawfully hire, to suckle his child, one of his wives, who is not the child's mother, as suckling it is not a duty incumbent upon her.

Or the child's mother, after the expiration of her Edit.—HE may also lawfully hire the mother of the child herself for this office, where her Edit from divorce has been completed, because when that is past the marriage no longer remains in force in any respect, and the woman may then be hired as well as any indifferent person.—In this case, however, if the father offer to hire any strange woman to suckle his child, and the mother offer to perform that office either for the same hire, or gratis, she has the prior right, as it is to be supposed that she feels a tenderness for the child beyond any other person, wherefore regard for the child dictates that it should be committed to her in preference to any other. But if the mother require higher wages than the stranger, the father cannot be compelled to give her a preference, as this would be injurious to him.

Difference of religion makes no difference as to the obligations of furnishing maintenance to a wife or child.—THE maintenance of an infant child is incumbent upon the father, although he be of a different religion: and, in the same manner, the maintenance of a wife is incumbent upon her husband, notwithstanding this circumstance;—the first, because the word offspring, in the sacred text (as before quoted) is of general application, and also because the child is a partaker of the father's flesh and blood, and consequently is a part of him;—and the second; because the occasion of the obligation of maintenance (namely, a valid marriage) may exist between a Mussulman and an infidel woman.

The maintenance of children incumbent upon the father only where they possess no independent property.—IT is to be observed that what has been asserted respecting the maintenance of infant children being incumbent upon the father, obtains only where the child is not possessed of any property;—but where the child is possessed of property, the maintenance is provided from that, as it is a rule that every person's maintenance must be furnished from his own substance, whether he be an infant or an adult.

Section V.

A man must provide a maintenance for his indigent parents.—IT is incumbent upon a man to provide maintenance for his father, mother, grandfathers, and grandmothers if they should happen to be in necessitous circumstances, although they be of a different religion:—for his father and mother, because the text of the Koran, upon this point, was revealed respecting the father and mother of a Mussulman. who were infidels:—and for his grandfathers and grandmothers because a grandfather is as a father, and a grandmother as a mother; the former being vested with the authority of a father, in all points of guardianship and inheritance, in defect of the father, and the grandmother being the mother's substitute, in defect of her, with respect to Hizanit, and so forth: but their poverty is made a condition of the obligation, because, they be possessed of property, their maintenance must be provided from that, rather than from the property of any other person:—and difference of religion is no objection, with respect to grandparents, because of the text above mentioned.

Difference of religion forbids the obligation to the maintenance of any relations except a wife, parents, or children.—IT is to be observed, however, that in the case of difference of religion, a man is under no obligation to provide maintenance for any except his wife, his parents, grandparents, children, and grandchildren. to all of whom it is due, notwithstanding this circumstance:—to the wife because (as was already stated) the cause of the obligation of maintenance to her is custody for the purpose of enjoyment under a valid contract, and the establishment of this cause does not depend upon unity of sect or religion, as it perfectly exists where the wife is a Christian (for instance) and her husband a Mussulman;—and to the parents and others, as enumerated above, because, between the child and parent exists a common participation of blood, and he who participates of another's blood is, in fact, the same as the participatee himself; and as a man's infidelity is no objection to his providing his own maintenance out of his own property, it follows that the same circumstance can be no objection with respect to one who is a part of him.

And to those also it is not due if they be aliens.—BUT if those relations be aliens, their maintenance is in no degree incumbent upon a Mussulman, although they be Moostamins,* because the lawgiver has forbidden us from showing kindness to those with whom we are at war on account of religion.

Christian and Mussulman brothers are not obliged to maintain each other.—THERE is no obligation upon a Christian to provide maintenance to his brother, being a Mussulman; neither is a Mussulman under any obligation to provide for the maintenance of his brother, being a Christian; because (according to what appears in the sacred text) maintnance is connected with inheritance; and as a Mussulman and infidel cannot inherit of each other, it follows that the maintenance of either is not incumbent upon the other:—it is to be remarked, however, that this rule does not obtain with respect to the other effects of consanguinity; for if a Mussulman become possessed of his Christian brother, as a slave, the latter is virtually emancipated, on account of nearness of kindred, notwithstanding the difference of religion.

The maintenance of a parent is exclusively incumbent on the child.—THE maintenance of a father and mother is incumbent upon their child alone, wherefore no man can be his partner or associate in furnishing it to them, because parents have a right in the property of their child (according to various well-known traditions), which they do not possess with respect to that of any other person; and also, because the child is more nearly related to his parents than to any other person whatever. The maintenance to parents is equally incumbent upon a daughter as upon a son, according to the Zahir-Rawayet; and this is approved, because the principle upon which the obligation of it is founded applies equally to both.

Maintenance to other relations, besides the wife, parents, or children.—IT is a man's duty to provide maintenance for all his infant male relations within the prohibited degrees, who are in poverty; and also to all female relations within the same degrees, whether infants or adults, where they are in necessity; and also to all adult male relations, within the same degrees, who are poor, and disabled, or blind: but the obligation does not extend beyond those relations, because the duties of consanguinity are not

* That is, residing in the Mussulman state under a protection.

absolutely incumbent towards any, excepting the nearer (or Karreebat) degrees of kindred, and do not extend to the more distant degrees, as this would be impracticable: on this occasion, moreover, the necessity is made a condition of the obligation; and tenderness of sex, or extreme youth, or debility, or blindness, are evidences of this necessity, since persons from these circumstances are rendered incapable of earning their subsistence by labour; but this rule does not apply to parents, for if they were to labour for a subsistence, it would subject them to pain and fatigue, from which it is the express duty of their child to relieve them; and hence it is that maintenance to parents is incumbent upon the child, although they should be able to subsist by their own industry.

MAINTENANCE is due to a relation within the prohibited degrees, in proportion to inheritance; in other words, upon him who has the greatest right of inheritance in the said relation's estate, the largest proportion of maintenance is incumbent: and upon him who has the smallest right, the smallest proportion, and so of the others, because it is said in the Koran, "THE MAINTENANCE OF A RELATION WITHIN THE PROHIBITED DEGREES RESTS UPON HIS HEIR,' and the word heir, shows that in adjusting the rate of maintenance the proportion of inheritance is to be regarded.

A father and mother must provide a maintenance to their adult daughters (and also to their adult sons who are disabled), in proportion to their respective claims of inheritance.—THE maintenance to an adult daughter, or to an adult son who is disabled, rests upon the parents in three equal parts, two-thirds being furnished by the father, and one-third by the mother, because the inheritance of a father from the estate of his son or daughter is two-thirds, and that of a mother one-third. The compiler of the Hedaya remarks that this is the doctrine of Khasaf and Hasan. According to the Zahir-Rawayet, the whole of the maintenance to these rests upon the father, the word of GOD being thus expressed, "THE SUBSISTENCE OF CHILDREN RESTS UPON THOSE TO WHOM THEY ARE BORN" (as was before mentioned), and the person to whom they are born is the father, wherefore their maintenance rests upon him, in the same manner as that of his infant children: but the former doctrine proceeds upon the idea of there being two points which make an essential distinction between infant children and adults, with respect to the father; FIRST, a father is invested with the authority of guardianship over his infant child;—SECONDLY, the maintenance to his infant child is expressly declared to rest solely and exclusively upon him: but with adults it is otherwise, as a father has no right of guardianship over them, wherefore the mother is to assist him in furnishing their maintenance in case of necessity; and as, in the maintenance of other relations, the proportion of inheritance is regarded, so in the present case, in conformity with that rule

Sisters must furnish maintenance to an indigent brother in the same proportion.—THE maintenance of a brother, in poverty, rests upon his full paternal and maternal sisters, in five shares, according to their degree of inheritance; that is to say, three-fifths must be furnished by the full sisters, one-fifth by the paternal sisters, and one-fifth by the maternal. It is to be observed, however, that to the obligation of furnishing maintenance to a poor relation, the capability of inheritance only is a condition, and not the prior or more immediate right: thus if a poor man have a rich maternal aunt, and also a rich paternal uncle's son his maintenance rests upon the former in preference to the latter, although the latter would inherit of him in preference to the former, for this reason, that a maternal aunt is within the prohibited degrees, whereas a cousin-german is not.

THE miantenance of a relation within the prohibited degrees is not incumbent upon his heirs, if they be of a different religion because in this case, they are incapable of inheriting from him, which is the condition of the obligation.

A poor man is not required to support any of his relations except his wife or infant children.—THE maintenance of relations within the prohibited degrees is not incumbent upon a person in poverty, because it is an obligation (like the other duties of consaguinity) which cannot be fulfilled by one who, on account of his situation, has a claim to that very assistance from others. But this argument does not hold with respect to a wife or infant child, for whom it is incumbent upon a man to provide subsistence notwithstanding his poverty, because in marrying he subjects himself to the expense of maintaining his wife, as otherwise the ends of marriage would be defeated, and his child from participation of blood, is a part of himself (as was before observed), for whom it is therefore his duty to find support as much as for himself.

Definition of the term rich, as here used.—ABOO YOOSAF defines the term rich, as used in this chapter, to apply to a person possessed of property to the amount of a single Nisab. Mohammed says that it means a person possessed of property above what may suffice to support himself and family one month: or whose superfluity from his daily earnings enables him to afford it,—because the obligation, in acts of piety, depends upon the ability generally, and not upon any specific degree of it, Nisab being a proportion invented merely for convenience; decrees, however, pass according to the former opinion. By the Nisab here mentioned is understood that which is so small as to prohibit almsgiving: for instance, two hundred DIRMS: and Hawlan-Hawl, or possession for a year, is not a condition of it: whence, if a man were, from a state of poverty, to become possessed of two hundred Dirms as this day, the maintenance of his poor relations becomes immediately incumbeat upon him.

Maintenance to the parents of an absentee may be decreed out of his effects.—IF an absent son be possessed of property, a maintenance to his parents is to be decreed out of it, for the reason already mentioned; and if a father were to sell his absent son's effects, for the purpose of providing his maintenance, it is held by Haneefa to be lawful, on a principle of benevolence; but he cannot lawfully sell his lands. The two disciples say that the sale of his effects is also illegal; and this is conformable to analogy, because a father has no absolute authority over his adult son, and therefore is not empowered to sell his effects in his presence on any pretence, nor to do so in his absence, but for the discharge of debts which do not include maintenance; and the same reasoning applies to the mother. The reason for the more favourable construction, as adopted by Haneefa, is that a father is authorized to take charge of his absent son's effects; for as the conservation of an absentee's property is allowed to devolve upon his executor, it must be admitted that it appertains to his father in a superior degree, as he is more immediately interested; and the sale of moveable property is one part of conservation; wherefore the father is at liberty to sell his absent son's moveable property; but this reasoning does not apply to lands, these not being subject to conservation, as they do not require it; neither does it apply to any other than a parent, as the more distant relations are not endowed with any absolute authority whatever over an infant, nor with any power of conservation over the effects of an adult. And where a father thus sells the property of his absent son, if the price he receives for it be of the same nature with his right (namely, maintenance), he is at liberty to take his right therefrom: and in the same manner, if a father dispose of the effects or lands of his infant son, he is at liberty to take his maintenance out of the price, that being of the same nature with his right.

The parents of an absentee may take their maintenance out of his effects; but a trustee cannot provide it in that manner without a decree.—IF the effects of an absent son be in the hands of his parents, and they take their maintenance from them, they are not responsible, as what they take in this manner is their right, a maintenance being their due, independent of any decree from the Kazee but if the effects be in the hands of a stranger, and he furnish the maintenance to the parents therefrom, without a decree from the Kazee, he is responsible, as he in that case takes upon him to dispose of the property of another without authority, since he is no more than merely the absentee's agent for conservation (contrary to where he acts under the Kazee's orders, in which case he is not responsible, as those are absolute and indispensable); and being thus responsible, he has no right to seek indemnification from the parents, because in assuming the responsibility, he, in fact, becomes proprietor, and then appears to have given the property to the parents gratuitously.

Arrear not due in a decreed maintenance.—IF the Kazee decree a maintenance to children, or to parents, or to relations within the prohibited degrees, and some time should elapse without their receiving any, their right to maintenance ceases, because it is due only so far as may suffice, according to their necessity (whence it is not so to those who are opulent), and they being able to suffer a considerable portion of time to pass without demanding or receiving it, it is evident that they have a sufficiency, and are under no necessity of seeking a maintenance from others: contrary to where the Kazee decrees a maintenance to a wife, and a space of time elapses without her receiving any, for her right to maintenance does not cease on account of her independence, because it is her due, whether she be rich or poor.

Unless where it is decreed to be provided upon the absentee's credit.—WHAT has been observed on this occasion applies to cases only in which the Kazee has not authorized the parties to provide themselves a maintenance upon the absentee's credit: but where he has so authorized them, their right to maintenance does not cease in consequence of a length of time passing without their receiving any, because the authority of the Kazee is universal, and hence his order to provide a maintenance upon credit is equal to that of the absentee himself, wherefore the proportion of maintenance for the time so elapsed is a debt upon the absentee, and does not cease from that ciscumstance.—The time here meant is any term beyond a month; and if the time elapsed be short of that term, maintenance does not cease.

Section VI.

Maintenance of slaves incumbent upon their owner.—THE maintenance of male and female slaves is incumbent upon their owner, because the Prophet has said concerning them "they are your brethren, whom GOD has placed in your hands, wherefore give them such food as ye yourselves eat, and such raiment as ye yourselves are clothed with, and afflict not the servants of your GOD:" if, therefore, the owner do not provide their maintenance, and they be capable of labour, they must be permitted to work for their own subsistence, as this is tenderness not only to the slaves, but also to his master, being equally advantageous to both; since the life of the slave is thereby preserved, at the same time that the owner's property in him continues unaffected.—But if the slave be incapable of labour (as where a male slave, for instance, is deprived of the use of his limbs, or where a female is unfit to hire on account of extreme youth or tender habit), the owner must then be compelled either to provide their maintenance, or to sell them, because slaves are claimants of right notwithstanding their bondage, and by sale their right is obtained, at the same time that the ower's right is also preserved to him by his acquisition of an equivalent in the price for which he disposes of them.—This rule does not hold with respect to other living property (such as horses, and so forth), because cattle are not claimants of right, and consequently the owner is not compelled to an alternative with respect to them, as in the case of slaves: but yet men are directed to furnish their cattle with subsistence on a principle of piety, as the neglect of this is cruelty towards the creature, and at the same time destructive of property, which is forbidden by the Prophet.—Aboo Yoosaf is of opinion that the owner of cattle may be compelled to furnish them a proper and sufficient subsistence: but it is the more approved doctrine that he is not liable to any compulsion on that head.

BOOK V.

OF ITTAK, OR THE MANUMISSION OF SLAVES.

[*This book has been omitted, in consequence of the abolition of slavery by Act V, of 1843, so that the learning upon the subject has become obsolete, and of no utility except to the antiquarian, who can consult the early Edition.*]

BOOK VI.

OF EIMAN, OR VOWS.

Definition of Eiman.—EIMAN is the plural of Yameen.—Yameen, in its primitive sense, means strength or power; also the right hand:—in the language of the law it signifies an obligation by means of which the resolution of a vower is strengthened in the performance or the avoidance of any thing; and the man who swears or vows is termed the Haliff, and the thing sworn to or vowed the Mahloof-ali-hee.

CHAPTER I.

Oath [of a sinful nature] are the three kinds.—OATHS are of three different kinds:—FIRST, Ghamoos;—SECOND, Moonakid (which is also termed Makoodat);—and THIRD, Lighoo.

Perjury—A YAMEEN GHAMOOS * signifies an oath taken concerning a thing already past, in which is conveyed an intentional falsehood on the part of the swearer:—and such an oath is highly sinful; the Prophet having declared—"whosoever sweareth falsely, the same shall GOD condemn to hell."

KAFARA, or expiation, is not incumbent (that is to say, is of no avail) in a Yameen Ghamoos; but a repentance and deprecation of the anger of heaven are incumbent.—Shafei alleges that expiation is incumbent, because that was ordained for the purpose of doing away any disrespect shown to the name of GOD, which is sinful; and this disrespect is evident in a Yameen Ghamoos, as it is calling GOD to witness to a falsehood; a Yameen Ghamoos is therefore the same as a Yameen Moonakid; and as, in that, expiation is incumbent, so in this likewise The argument of our doctors is that a Yameen Ghamoos is a crime of great magnitude (or deadly sin),—and expiation is an act of piety (whence it may be fulfilled by fasting and intention is a condition of it); but there is no expiation for a deadly sin, and consequently there is none for a Yameen Ghamoos: contrary to the case of a Yameen Moonakid, as that falls under the class of Mobah, or things indifferent.

OBJECTION.—The description of Mobah, or indifferent, applies to things in which there

* Literally, a false oath, or perjury.—It is here proper to observe that the distinctions explained in this chapter relate solely to such oaths or vows as, being false or broken, are sinful, and consequently supposed to excite the divine anger, which must be appeased by expiation: contrary to true oaths, or to vows duly fulfilled; as the former of these are frequently required for the sake of justice, and the latter are permitted, whence neither an oath nor vow, simply as such, can be supposed to require expiation.

is no offence: now as a Yameen Moonakid is of an offensive nature, how can it be Mobah?

REPLY.—The offence, in a Yameen Moonakid, occurs subsequently to the declaration of it, and is occasioned by a disrespect shown by the vower to the name of GOD,* of his own free option; whereas the offence, in a Yameen Ghamoos, exists from the first: and such being the case, a Yameen Ghamoos is not to be confounded with a Yameen Moonakid.

Contracted vows (when not fulfilled).—A YAMEEN MOONAKID* signifies an oath taken concerning a matter which is to come.—Thus a man swears that he will do such a thing, or he will not do such a thing;—and where the pronouncer fails in this—(that is, where he does not act according to the obligation of his oath)—expiation is incumbent upon him: and this is established upon the authority of the sacred writings.

And inconsiderate oaths.—A YAMEEN LIGHOO† is an oath taken concerning as incident or transaction already past, where the swearer believes that the matter to which he thus bears testimony accords with what he swears, and it should happen to be actually otherwise: and from the divine mercy it may be hoped that the swearer will not be condemned for such an oath, since GOD has declared, in the Koran, "I WILL NOT CALL YOU TO ACCOUNT FOR AN INCONSIDERATE OATH." An instance of Yameen Lighoo is where a person sees Amroo passing at a distance, and supposing him to be Zeyd, says, "by GOD that is Zeyd!"

Expiation is incumbent, whether the vow be wilful or compulsatory, or although the oath be taken under a deception of the memory.—A WILFUL vow, and a compulsatory vow, and an oath taken under a deception of the memory, are all the same, and on account of each expiation is incumbent,‡ because the Prophet has said, "there are three points of serious import, the sporting with which is also serious, to wit. MARRIAGE, DIVORCE, and a vow."—Shafei, controverts this doctrine.—His arguments will be hereafter recited at large under the head of Ikrah, or compulsatory process.

The violation of a vow, whether by compulsion or through forgetfulness, requires expulsion.—IF a man do a thing which breaks his vow, either by compulsion, or through forgetfulness, these are both the same, and expiation is incumbent upon him in either case, because the specified act which is the condition of expiation is not made void by the circumstances of compulsion or forgetfulness:—and so also, if the thing should be done by a maniac or an idiot,—because there likewise the condition is actually fulfilled.

OBJECTION.—Expiation is not incumbent but for the purpose of obliterating a sin now no sin can be imputed to maniacs or idiots, as such are not made answerable; it would therefore follow that expiation is not incumbent upon them.

REPLY.—Although expiation be intended for the purpose of expunging sin, yet the obligation of in this case rests upon the argument of a sin (namely, the breach of a vow), and not upon the actual sin itself, so that, wherever the breach of a vow appears, expiation is incumbent.

*Literally, a contracted oath, or vow.

†Literally, a nugatory oath, or (some times) a rash oath.

‡That is, if the thing sworn to be false, or the vow be violated.

CHAPTER II.

OF WHAT CONSTITUTES AN OATH OR VOW, AND WHAT DOES NOT CONSTITUTE IT.

An oath may be expressed by using the name of God, or any of his customary attributes.—YAMEEN (that is, an oath or vow) is constituted by the use of the name of Almighty GOD, or of any of those appellations by which the Deity is generally known and understood, such as Rihman and Riheem.* An oath may also be expressed by such attributes of the Deity as are commonly used in swearing. such as the power, or the glory, or the might of GOD, because an oath is usually expressed under one or other of those qualities; and the sense of Yameen, namely, strength, is by this means obtained, since as the swearer believes in the power, glory, might, and other attributes of the Deity, it follows that the mention of these attributes only is sufficient to strengthen the resolution in the performance of the act vowed, or the avoidance thereof.

Excepting his knowledge, wrath, or mercy.—IF a man swear "by the knowledge of GOD," it does not constitute an oath, because an oath expressed by the knowledge of GOD is not in use: moreover, by knowledge is frequently implied merely that which is known; and in this sense the word knowledge is not expressive either of the name of GOD, or of any of his attributes.—In the same manner, should a person swear "by the wrath of GOD," or "by the mercy of GOD," it does not constitute an oath, because an oath is not commonly expressed by any of these attributes: moreover, by the word Rihmat [mercy] is sometimes understood rain, and heaven is also occasionally expressed by that term; and by the word Ghazb [wrath] is understood punishment; and none of these are either appellations or attributes of the Deity.

It is not constituted by using any other name.—IF a person swear by any other name than that of GOD,—such as the Prophet, or the holy temple, this does not constitute an

*Anglice, the merciful and the beneficent. Those attributes are affixed to the name of the Deity, at the beginning of the Koran, and (in imitation thereof) at the beginning of every Mussulman book.

oath,—as the Prophet has said, "if any man among ye take an oath, he must swear by the name of GOD, or else his oath is void." If a person also swear by the Koran, it does not constitute an oath, although the Koran be the word of GOD, because men do not swear by the Koran. The compiler of the Hedaya observes that this is where the swearer only says "by the Prophet," or "by the temple," or "by the Koran;" but if the swearer say, "if I act contrary to what I now say, may I be deprived of the Prophet," or "of the temple," or "of the Koran;" this constitutes an oath, because such privation would reduce the swearer to the state of an infidel, and the suspension of infidelity upon a condition amounts to Yameen.

Particles of swearing.—AN oath is confirmed by the use of the particles of swearing; and these (in the Arabic) are three, namely, the letters, waw, and be, and te,* as oaths are commonly repeated and understood under this form; and in this sense these particles occur in the Koran. Let it be also observed that the particles of swearing are sometimes understood, though not expressed, that is, are omitted in the expression, although impl ed in the sense; and this constitutes an oath; as if a man were to say, "GOD, I will not do this:" because [in the Arabic] it is common to reject the particle for the sake of brevity: sometimes indeed the letter lam is used for the swearing particle, as it is capable according to Mooktar†) of being substituted for be.

Swearing by the truth of God is not an oath.—HANEEFA alleges that if a man should swear "by the truth of GOD," this does not constitute an oath, and in this Imam Mohammed coincides. There are two opinions of Aboo Yoosaf recorded of this point: according to one it is not an oath; but according to the other it is an oath, because truth is one of the attributes of the Deity, signifying the certainty of the divine existence, and hence it is the same as if the swearer were to say, "by GOD, truth!" and as oaths are common under this mode of expression, so an oath is here constituted. The argument of Mohammed and Haneefa is that the term "the truth," as here expressed, relates merely to the identity of the godhead as the object of obedience, and hence an oath thus expressed appears to be taken by that which is neither an appellation nor an attribute of GOD. The learned, however, say, that if a person express himself thus, "by the truth, I will do so and so," this constitutes an oath, because the truth is one of the appellatives or proper names of GOD. But, if a person were to say "I will do this truly," it does not amount to an oath, because the word truly can only be taken, in this case, as a corroboration of confirmation of the promise contained in the speech, being the same as if he were to say "I shall do this indeed."

The expressions "I swear," "I vow" or "I testify," contitute an oath, without the name of God.—IF a man say, "I swear," or "I vow," or "testify," whether the words "by GOD" be superadded or not, it constitutes an oath, because such words are commonly used in swearing: the use of them in the present tense is undisputed; and they are also sometimes used in the future tense, where the context admits of a construction in the present; and attestation amounts to an oath, as in that sense it occurs in the sacred writings: now swearing by the name of GOD is both customary and conformable to the divine ordinances, but without the name of GOD it is forbidden; when it so occurs, therefore, it must be construed into a lawful oath;* hence, some say, that intention is not requisite in it; others, however, allege that the intention is essential, because the words here recited bear the construction of a promise,—that is, they admit of being received as applying to the future, and also of being taken as a vow without the name of GOD.

IF a person, speaking in the Persian language, were to say, "I swear by GOD," it amounts to an oath, because here the idiom confines the expression solely to the present; but, if he were to say simply, "I swear" some allege that this does not constitute an oath. If he were to say, "I swear by the divorce of my wife," this is not an oath as an oath is not so expressed in practice.

Swearing by the existence of God makes an oath.—IF a man, in swearing, say, "by the age," or "the existence" (of GOD), it constitutes an oath because the age or existence of GOD signifies His eternity; which is one of His attributes. [Several] other forms of swearing are here recited, but of no consequence, as their validity or nullity depends altogether upon certain peculiarities in the Arabic idiom.]

A vow may be contracted by the imprecation of a conditional penalty.—IF a person should say, "if I do this may I be a Jew," or "a Christian," or "an infidel," it constitutes an oath; because, as the swearer has made the condition a sign of infidelity, it follows that he is conscious of his obligation to avoid the condition; and this obligation is possible, by his making it an oath, in such a way as to render unlawful to himself that which is lawful.—And if the oath relate to any thing which he has done in the time past, as if he were to say, "if I have done so

*Each of these letters, prefixed to the name of GOD, is expressive of the English by.

†A celebrated Arabic grammarian and rhetorician.

*That is, the superaddition of the expression, "by GOD," must be understood in it, so as to make it appear an oath made conformably to the divine ordinance, lest the speaker, by swearing in a way that is forbidden, be found guilty of an offence.

may I be a Jew," or "an infidel," and so forth, this is a Yameen Ghamoos, or perjury. The swearer is not, however, in this case made a Jew or an infidel, because the words, "may I be an infidel" (and so forth), relate to some future indefinite period.—Some, on the contrary, have alleged that he becomes actually as an infidel,* because the penalty which the swearer imprecates upon himself relates to the present instant of his testimony, being the same as if he were to say, "I am a Jew, &c.—But the fact is, the swearer does not become a Jew or infidel in either of the case before us (that is, in that of a vow with respect to the future, or an oath regarding the past), provided he sonsider this merely as a form of swearing: † but if he believe that by thus swearing he fully subjects himself to the penalty expressed, he suffers accordingly, in either instance, because he appears consenting to infidelity, on account of having ventured upon a thing by the commission of which he conceives that he may be rendered an infidel.‡

If a person say, "if I do thus, may the anger of God fall upon me," this does not constitute a vow, as not being a customary mode of expression for that purpose. And so, also, if a person were to say, "may I be an adulterer," or "a drunkard," or "an usurer," because these are not generally understood or received as form, of swearing.

CHAPTER III.

OF KAFARA. OR EXPIATION. §

A vow may be expiated by the emancipation of a slave; the distribution of alms.—The expiation of a vow is effected by the emancipation of a slave; and the emancipation of such a slave as suffices in Zihar, suffices also in the case of a vow:—or if the swearer choose, let him clothe ten paupers, giving to each one piece of cloth, or more (the smallest quantity to each is as much as is necessary in prayer*;—or if he please, let him distribute victuals among ten paupers, the same as in the expiation of Zihar.—All these modes of effecting the expiation of a vow are authorized in the Koran, according to the words in the text,—"THE EXPIATION THEREOF MAY BE EFFECTED BY FEEDING TEN POOR PERSONS WITH SUCH FOOD AS IS USUALLY CONSUMED IN YOUR FAMILIES, OR BY CLOTHING TEN POOR PERSONS, OR BY THE RELEASE OF A SLAVE.—It is manifest, therefore, that, in the present instance, one of these three modes is indispensable.

Or fasting.—But if the delinquent (from his poverty, or other cause) should not be able to effect his expiation in any of these three modes, he may do it by fasting three days successively.—Shafei says that he has an option; if he think proper, he may fast for three days successively, or for any three separate days,—because the words of the Koran are, "IF HE BE UNABLE TO DO THIS, LET HIM FAST FOR THREE DAYS," which expression is general.—The Haneefite doctors, in support of their opinion upon this point, quote the authority of the reading of Abdoola Ibn Massaood, who expounds the text to mean three days successively; and this accords with what occurs in the Hadees Mashhoor †—With respect to what has been said of the smallest quantity of cloth sufficient in expiation it is recorded from Imam Mohammed.—Haneefa and Aboo' Yoosaf assert that the smallest quantity of cloth proper upon this occassion is as much as may be sufficient to clothe nearly the whole body: for a mere Shilwar ‡ is not sufficient; and this is the more authentic doctrine; because one who is only thus clothed is regarded as naked.—That portion of cloth, however, which may not suffice in regard to clothing, may be sufficient in eating, according to its value: that is, if a person were to bestow, as an expiation, such a quantity of cloth as, although it may not suffice for the proper clothing, yet is equal in value to the feeding of ten poor men. it suffices as a feeding expiation, whether such may have been the intention or not.—Thus, if the person to make expiation were to give to each poor person the half of a proper dress (for instance), this would not be sufficient for an expiation by clothing; but if the value of the cloth thus distributed to each be equal to the price of three pounds of wheat, it suffices as an expiation by feeding.

Previous expiation does not suffice.—If a person perform the expiation before the violation of his vow, it does not suffice.—Shafei maintains that it suffices, where the expiation

---

*That is, becomes subjected to the penalties of actual apostasy from the faith.

† Where no other penalty than that of expiation can be incurred.

‡ All these cases suppose the thing sworn to be false.

§ The term Kafara means not only an expiatory atonement for the breach of an absolute vow, but also the substitution of an expiatory act for the penalty imposed by a vower upon himself in the case of a vow suspended upon a condition, by which he had designed to restrain himself from the commission of any particular act:

Meaning expiation for the breach or violation of a vow,—or for any other description of Yameen which admits of expiation, such as a Yameen Lighoo, &c.

* Mussulmans must be clothed in prayer at least from the waist downwards.

† A collection of traditions so called.

‡ A species of drawers which are a sufficient clothing for prayer.

is effected by means of property, and not by fasting, because the expiator makes his atonement posterior to the occasion of it, (namely, his vow), and hence the case is the same as that of a pilgrim performing expiation for wounding game,*—that is, if the pilgrim perform expiation after the act of wounding, it suffices; and so also in the present case. The argument of our doctors is that expiation is ordained as an atonement for offence: but in the case before us no offence has yet appeared.—In reply to what is advanced by Shafei, they observe that the vow is not the occasion of the offence, as nothing can be considered in any degree the occasion of an offence, but what necessarily leads thereto, and a vow does not necessarily leads to its own violation, but is rather prohibitory of it; hence the vow is not the cause of the offence in the present instance: contrary to the case of the pilgrim, adduced by Shafei, in which the wound inflicted upon the deer leads to its destruction, by ultimately occasioning its death; these therefore are not analogous cases.—It is to be observed that whatever the expiator may have given to the poor before the violation of his vow, he must not take back again, because this is alms, and it is not lawful for a man to take back his alms.

A sinful vow must be broken and expiated.—If a man bind himself, by a vow, to the commission of a sin, as if he were to swear, "by God I will not pray," or "I will not converse with my father," or "I will murder such an one in such a month." it is incumbent upon him to violate his vow, and perform an expiation, because it is recorded in the traditions that if a man vow a thing, knowing that the neglect is preferable to the fulfilment, he ought to act accordingly, performing an expiation for the breach of his vow.

The vows of infidels, being nugatory, cannot be held as violated.—If an infidel should make a vow, and afterwards violate the same, either as an infidel or as a Mussulman, (supposing him to have been converted to the faith in the interim), still he is not forsworn, because he was not competent to make a vow; as a vow is contracted (that is, is made binding) by a reverence for the name of God, and the vower, whilst he was an infidel, cannot be supposed to have entertained any reverence for the name of God:—an infidel, moreover, is not competent to the performance of expiation, as that is an act of piety.

Vows of abstinence.—If a man make certain articles unlawful to him, † which are in their own nature lawful, as if he were to say, "I have made this cloth (or, this provision) unlawful to me," yet such article does not actually become unlawful to him, but he must perform expiation when he happens to put on that cloth, or to eat that provision.—Shafei says that expiation is not incumbent upon him, because rendering unlawful that which is lawful does not amount to a vow, as a vow is an act authorized by the law.—The argument of our doctors is that the words, "I have made unlawful," evince the establishment of illegality in the thing: now there is a possibility of establishing illegality in a thing that is really otherwise, by supposing that the speaker had taken an oath that he would not wear the clothes, or eat the provisions; and this supposition is adopted, in order to establish the illegality declared by the speaker; and it follows that whenever he does that thing which he has rendered illegal to himself, he becomes forsworn, whether the matter be great or small, because when unlawfulness is once established in a thing, the illegality pervades every part of it.

If a man were to say, 'every thing lawful is unlawful to me," every species of food and drink forthwith becomes unlawful to him, unless where the intention or design of the vow has regarded something else.—This proceeds upon a favourable construction. Analogy would suggest that the vower, as soon as he has uttered his vow, must become forsworn, as being unavoidably and continually placed in the performance of some lawful act, such as breathing, moving, resting, or so forth; and such is the opinion of Ziffer upon it; but the more favourable construction is that the design of the vow is to establish something, the commission of which shall be a crime; and as this cannot be effected where the intention, from the words of the vow, appears to be general, regard to its universality drops, and such being the case, the vow will be construed as respecting meat and drink, for the sake of general application, as it is in practice commonly applied to the articles of customary subsistence. A vow of this nature does not include the use of women, unless by the intention of the vower: but in this case it constitutes an Aila, because the form of words here recited is a vow, bearing the interpretation of "by God, I will not have carnal connexion with my wife:" and it is to be observed that, where the vower, by the words, "every thing lawful," intends woman, yet meat and drink are not excluded from the vow, but still remain and are to be considered as constituting a part of it.—What is now advanced is taken from the Zahir Rawayet.—Our modern doctors have said that divorce follows a vow of this form, independent of the intention, as the aforesaid words are frequently used in divorce;

* Pilgrims are forbidden to destroy game of any kind within a certain distance of Mecca, termed the Ihram [forbidden ground] of pilgrimage.

† This is a phrase by which is understood a vow of abstinence from the thing expressed.

* In reciting these forms of vows the address ["by God," or "I swear" &c] is for the sake of brevity, omitted; it is always however, to be understood.

and there are decrees upon record to this effect. It is also proper that the same rule should hold where the vow is pronounced in the Persian tongue, for the sake of general application. Let it be observed, however, that if a man were to say, "whatsoever I have in my right hand is unlawful to me," there is a difference among casuists concerning the effect of it; some doctors say that the intention is a condition, whilst others maintain that it is not so; it is evident, however, that divorce takes place from it, independent of the intention, on account of custom.

A vow is binding without any condition annexed.—If a person express a vow in general terms, that is, not suspended upon a condition as if he were to say, "I shall fast upon such a day for the sake of God," he is bound to the observance thereof, because it is said, in the traditions, "whoever makes a vow, and specifies it, he is bound to the observance of what he has so specified."

If a person suspend a vow on a condition, and the condition afterwards occur, he is bound to the performance of what he has vowed; and expiation is here of no avail, because the tradition above recited is general —that is, applies to a suspended as well as an unsuspended vow; and also, because a vow suspended upon a condition becomes, upon the condition taking place, the same as one of immediate performance.—It is recorded of Haneefa, that he receded from this doctrine, alleging that if a man were to say (for instance), "if I do so, I am under obligation to perform a pilgrimage," or "to fast a year," or "to bestow all my property in alms," and then perform an expiation for his vow, it suffices; and such is the opinion of Mohammed. If, however, the vower should not make an expiation, but perform the thing which he had specified, he is discharged from the obligation of that also, provided the condition be of such a nature as that the vower had no intention it should ever take place. The reason of this is that, where the condition is of the description now mentioned, the speech of the vower, as aforesaid, bears the sense of a Yameen, or suspended vow; and also of a Nuzr, or absolute vow:—evidently of a Nuzr, because such a form of words is commonly used to express a Nuzr; and also of a Yameen, because the design of the person, in so speaking, is to restrain himself from doing the act which constitutes the condition; and such being the case, it remains at his option either to perform expiation, regarding his words in the light of a Yameen, or to perform the condition specified, regarding them in the light of a Nuzr: it is otherwise, however, where the thing conditioned is not of the above-mentioned description, but is actually intended by the speaker.—as where a man (for instance) says, "if God grant me a recovery from this illness, I am under an obligation to perform a pilgrimage," for here expiation does not suffice, but it is incumbent upon him to perform the actual thing specified, because in this case the words do not bear the sense merely of Yameen, but also of an absolute vow of performance:—and this distinction is approved.

A vow pronounced with a reservation of the will of God, is null.—If a person make a vow of any thing, adding, "if it please God," as if he were to say, "by God I will do this, God, willing," he cannot be forsworn, because the Prophet has said, "he who vows any thing, adding, 'if it please God, cannot be forsworn."—It is to be observed, however, that it is a condition that the words "God willing," do follow in immediate connexion with the words preceding, because if they be pronounced separately, after having uttered the vow, it is a retraction; and a retractation in Yameen is not lawful,

CHAPTER IV.

OF VOWS WITH RESPECT TO ENTRANCE INTO, OR RESIDENCE IN A PARTICULAR PLACE.

A vow against entering a house is not violated by entering a mosque, church &c.—If a person make a vow, that "he will not enter any house," and he should afterwards enter a mosque, or synagogue; or church, he is not forsworn, because a house is a place built for the purpose of dwelling in (that is of sleeping, &c.), and buildings of the above description are not designed for this purpose:—the rule is also the same, if the swearer should enter a porch or portion before the door of a house for the same reason. Some have asserted that if the portico be inclosed, in such a manner, that when the front door is shut, a person may be said to be in the house, the swearer by entering such portion violates his vow, it being customary for persons to reside and sleep in such a place, If the swearer also enter an Iwan* he is forsworn, because that is designed as an occasional residence in the hot weather, and is a species of dwelling as much as a summer or winter residence. Some have conceived that this is the case only where the Iwan has four walls [that is, where it is a complete quadrangle]: this distinction is made, because those buildings in Koofa, and other parts of Arabia, are generally so constructed: whereas, with us [that is, in Hindostan and Persia] they have commonly three walls only, being quite open in front, and therefore are not to be considered as a house,—Others, however, say that entering a lawn is a violation of the vow, whether it be constructed of three walls or of four; and this is approved.

* An Iwan is an open gallery or balcony, on the top of or adjoining to, an house, the roof of which is generally supported by piers or pillars, for the benefit of the air in the hot season.

A vow against entering a Serai is not violated by entering a ruin.—IF a person swear that "he will not enter into a place" that is, into a Serai, and he afterwards enter a place which is desolate and in ruins, he is not forsworn: but if a person swear that "he will not enter such a place," the place being then in a good and habitable state, and he should enter it after it had fallen to ruin, and been laid level with the plain, he is forsworn, because the term Daar, among both the Arabs and Persians, means any particular place, as with them it is common to say, "such a Daar is peopled,"—or, "such a Daar is desolate (that is, abandoned);" now an edifice is the description of the term Daar, and this description is regarded in the first of the above cases, but not in the last.

IF a man take an oath saying, "I will not enter into this Daar;" and the said place should afterwards become ruined and desolate, and should again be rebuilt, or repaired, and the swearer should after that enter it, he is forsworn, according to what was before observed, that the appellation Daar still continues to be applied to the place, after the destruction of the edifice which stood upon it.—but if this place, after having been ruined and desolate, should be rebuilt as a mosque; bath, or dwelling-house, and the swearer should, after that, enter it he is not forsworn because in any of these cases the term Daar is no longer applied to the place, as it is then called by another name. such as mosque, and so forth: and the same rule holds where this person enters that place after the destruction of such mosque, bath, or other public building, as may in the interim have been erected there, because the place will not recover its original name after such destruction.

A vow against entering any particular house is not broken by entering it when in ruins.—IF a man swear "he will not enter such a dwelling-house," and he should enter therein after it has been destroyed or become desolate, he is not forsworn; because the term dwelling-house is abrogated, as no person then dwells in it; whereas, if the roof only should have fallen in, and the walls remain, and he were then to enter it, he would be forsworn, because it is still considered as habitable, and the place does not lose its appellation of a dwelling house [Bait] from that circumstance. In the same manner he is not forsworn where, the house having been destroyed and laid level with the plain, another house is built upon the same spot, and he then enters this house—because the term dwelling-house, as applied to the former house, was rendered inapplicable by the circumstance of its ruin.

A vow against entering a house is not violated by going upon the roof, or entering the portico, &c.—IF a man swear that "he will not enter a certain house," and he afterwards go on the top of the house, from the outside, he is forsworn, because the roof is a part of the house. Some have said that, with us, he is not forsworn.—In the same manner, he is forsworn if he enter the portico only of the house specified in the vow. The compiler of the Hedaya observes that this case admits of a distinction; thus, if the portico be such as that, if the door be shut, it forms a part of the house, and it be covered in, he is forsworn, but if otherwise, he is not forsworn.—If he stand under the arch of the doorway he is also forsworn, provided the arch be so constructed as that when the door is shut it becomes included as a part of the house; but if the arch be so situated as that, after shutting the door, it is not included as a part of the dwelling, he is not forsworn, because the door is designed as a protection to the house; so that whenever the archway is not, by shutting the door, included as a part of the house, but is without the door, it is evident that it is not included in the house.

Case of vows respecting abstinence from a thing in which the vower is at present engaged.—IF a man should swear "I will not enter into this house," and it should so be that he is in the said house at the time of swearing thus, he is not forsworn by sitting down in that house, nor unless he go out of the house, and again enter it. This is upon a favourable construction.—Analogy would suggest that the vower is forsworn, because the effect of the commencement of the act and of its continuance is one and the same; and as he would be forsworn by the commencement of the act, so he is by its continuance: but the more favourable construction is that, admitting the effect of the commencement and the continuance to be the same, yet this can only be where the act is of such a nature as to be capable of continuance, which the entrance into a place does not allow, as the word entrance simply implies passing from without to within

IF a person swear that "he will not put on a particular garment," and should happen to have the said garment upon him at the very time of his so swearing, and should forthwith take it off, he is not forsworn. And so also a person riding upon a mule [or other beast] if he takes an oath, saying, "I will not ride upon this animal," and should forthwith alight, he is not forsworn. In the same manner, a person residing in a house, if he swear that "he will not live in this house," and thereupon begin to remove out of it, he is not forsworn,—Ziffer maintains, however, that the swearer, in the last of these instances, is forsworn, as the circumstance upon which the violation of his vow is suspended (namely, his residence in the house), does already exist, however short the time may be. Our doctors argue that a vow is imposed with a view to the fulfilment of it, and therefore, that in the present instance, such a space of time as admits of the fulfilment must be excepted from the vow; and hence, if the swearer make any delay he is forsworn, because such acts as are here mentioned are capable of continuance, as a man may, with propriety, say, "I rode a whole day," or "I wore such a robe for a day:" contrary to the act of entrance: as a man could not say, "I entered for a day:" and the possibility of continuance in such acts being thus proved, it follows that the effect of the commencement and the continuance is one and the same:—but if the swearer should here purely intend the commencement of the act, and say that his design was to vow that "he would not ride again" (for instance), his declaration is to be credited, as his words admit of that construction.

If a man make a vow, saying, "I will not reside in this house," and he should himself leave the house, his family and effects still remaining in it, although he may have no intention of returning to reside there, yet he is forsworn, because he is still supposed to be an inhabitant of that house, from the circumstance of his family and effects continuing therein; as merchants, who reside in the Bazaars [that is, have shops there], say, notwithstanding. "they reside in such a street," meaning the residence of their families.

A vow against residing in a city is not broken by the vower's family continuing there.—If a man make a vow, saying, "I will not reside in this city," and he go forth from it resolving not to return thither, although his family should still continue to reside there, yet he is not forsworn, and his observance of the vow does not depend upon his carrying his family and effects out of that city according to what is recorded from Aboo Yoosaf, because (contrary to the preceding case) he is then no longer considered as an inhabitant thereof in the customary acceptation:—and a village is (in the Rawayet Saheeh) declared to be the same as a city, with respect to this rule.—Haneefa observes, upon the preceding case, that the removal of the whole of the effects from the house is necessary, insomuch that if even a single nail of the vower's property be left therein, he is forsworn,—because, as his residence in that house was understood from the whole of his effects being there, so will it still be understood whilst any part of them remains therein.—Aboo Yoosaf alleges that the removal of a principal part of them is sufficient, because the removal of the whole is sometimes impracticable. Mohammed says that the removal of such quantity only is necessary, as might be sufficient for housekeeping, because any thing beyond that is not of a residentiary nature; and the learned have agreed that this is the most laudable distinction.—It is here requisite that the swearer remove to another house, without delay, in order that he may observe his vow; for if he should not remove into another house, but into the street or a mosque, the learned in the law say that he does not fulfil his vow; the reason of which is that if a person were to remove out of a city with his family, so long as he does not fix upon another place of abode, his first residence remains with respect to prayer:* whence, if he return to his former abode, he is still accounted an inhabitant; and the same holds good in the present case.

CHAPTER V.

OF VOWS RESPECTING VARIOUS ACTIONS; SUCH AS COMING, GOING, RIDING, AND SO FORTH.

An evasion of a vow is a violation of it:—If a man swear that he will not go out of the mosque, and afterwards desire another to carry him forth from it, and the other do so, he is forsworn, because an act performed by the direction or any person is attributed to the director, and it is here, therefore, the same as if he had mounted a beast, and rode out upon it: but if another person were to carry him out of the mosque by compulsion he is not forsworn, because the act of a person compelling cannot be attributed to the person who is forcibly compelled, as he gave no direction in it.—*If,* moreover, a person should carry out the swearer with his will, but without his direction, he is not forsworn (according to the Rawayet Saheeh), because his removal cannot here be established, as it can only be so by the the circumstance of his directing or desiring it, and not by his will alone; and his desire or direction do not appear.

If a man swear that he will not go forth [from his house] except to a funeral and he afterwards go to attend the funeral, and some other business should then occur to him, and he go upon that business, he is not forsworn, because the act of going to the funeral was excepted from his vow, and his motions after that are not forthgoings, as by going forth is understood removing from the inside of a house to the outside.

If a man swear, saying, "I will not go forth towards Mecca," and he afterwards go forth with a design of going to Mecca, and return, he is forsworn; because his going forth with a design of going to Mecca (which is the condition) is here found, since, by going forth is understood removal from the inside of the house to without, which has here occurred But if he should have sworn, saying, "I will not come to Mecca," and he afterwards go towards Mecca, and return, he is not forsworn, nor until such time as he actually enters Mecca, because coming implies arriving, and that has not taken place. If a man swear also, "that he will not go

---

*That is, he is supposed to be included in the public prayers offered up in the mosques for the welfare of that city and its inhabitants.

towards Mecca," some lawyers say that the case will be the same as this last recited, whilst others assert that it corresponds with the preceding case; this last however, is the more approved doctrine, because going implies removal, and arrival is not necessary to constitute removal

An undermined vow of performance is not violated until the death of the vower.—IF a man make a vow that "he will go to Mecca," and he should not go to Mecca during his life, he is forsworn: but he will not be accounted forsworn until after his death, because whilst life remains there is a hope of his fulfilling his vow.

Vows made with vow of prevention.—IF a man make a vow, saying to his wife, "if you go out unless by my permission, you are divorced,". and he should afterwards once grant such permission, and the woman go out accordingly, and she should again go out without her husband's permission, the consequence of his vow is incurred (that is the woman becomes divorced), because permission is requisite each time that she goes out, as he excepted from his vow the act of her going out with his permission, and any other act of going out beyond that is included in the inhibition, wherefore the consequence is induced by her going forth without his permission.—If the vower explain, saying. "I intended one permission only," his declaration is to be credited in a religious view, but not in point of law, because although his words, as above, are capable of this construction, yet it is contrary to their apparent tendency.

Case of a vow express generally, but restricted, in its sense, to some particular occasion.—IF a woman be desirous of going out, and her husband say, "if you go out, you are divorced," and she thereupon sit down, and afterwards go out, the consequence is not induced,—that is, divorce does not take place:—and so also, if a man be desirous of beating his slave, and another vow, "if you beat him, such an one my slave is free," and the man, desisting only for a momentary space, beat his slave, the slave of the other person does not become free. The reason of this is that the design of the speaker in what he vows is to prevent that going forth of the woman, or that which (according to what then appears) the woman or the master is intent upon doing, and of course the vow is restricted to that beating, or that going forth, as the foundation of the vow rests upon what appears at the particular crisis.—This species of vow is termed Yameen Fowr, or a sudden vow. and Haneefa is the first who makes any mention of this kind of vow: for previously vows were described as of two species, one general (as where a man says, "I will not do so")—and the other restricted (as where a man says, "I will not do so this day")—but Haneefa deduced from these a third, saying, "the third sort is that which is general with respect to the words, but restricted with respect to the sense.

IF a man invite another to sit down and eat breakfast with him, and the other make a vow, saying, "if I eat breakfast my slave is free," and he should then proceed to his own house, and there eat his breakfast, he does not incur the penaly of his vow, because what he said, as being an answer, relates solely to the speech of the other person, and is therefore construed as regarding that breakfast to which the other had invited him. But if the person thus invited were to answer, "if I eat breakfast this day my slave is free,"—upon his breakfasting either there or elsewhere at any time during that day the penalty is incurred, because here he has superadded to his reply the expression "this day," and hence what he has said is rendered a separate sentence and not a reply.

IF a man swear that he will not ride upon the beast of any other person, and he should afterwards ride upon a house, the property of one of his slaves, who is a Mazoon, he is not forsworn (according to Haneefa), whether such Mazoon be involved in debt or not.*—If the Mazoon, however, should be very much involved in debt, the vower is forsworn, although he should not intend it, as the master, in such case, is not held (by Haneefa) to be possessed of any property in the animal. If, on the contrary, the debts of the Mazoon be of trifling consequence only, or if he should not be in debt at all, the master is not forsworn, where he does not intend it, because in either case, he is himself the virtual proprietor of the animal.—but the animal is held to belong to the Mazoon, both in the eye of the law, and also by common usage, and hence concerning his belonging to the master there is no doubt; wherefore his intention in the act is requisite. Aboo Yoosaf says that he is not forsworn in any of those cases, unless he be so intentionally, because whether the animal be the property of the master or not is dubious. Mohammad, on the other hand, says that he is forsworn, although he be so unintentionally, since the animal is his property, as the two disciples hold that debt is in no respect repugnant to a slave being the property of his master.

CHAPTER VI.

OF VOWS WITH RESPECT TO EATING OR DRINKING.

Vows with respect to eating dates.—IF a person swear that "he will not eat of such a date-tree," his vow relates to the fruit of that tree only, because he has referred his

*Because all the effects of his slave are virtually his own property, provided the slave be not involved in debt.

vow to a thing which is not eatable, namely, the tree: wherefore his vow is metaphorically taken to regard the article which is the product of the tree, namely, the dates; and the subject admits the metaphor, as the date-tree is the cause as that article existing. But it is a condition that the dates do not undergo any change by a new operation; for if he were to drink a Nabbeeza (or infusion) prepared from these dates, or juice expressed from them, yet he would not be forsworn.

A vow of abstinence from anything is not broken by eating that thing when it has acquired a new description.—IF a man swear that "he will not eat of those Boosrs" (half-ripe dates), and should afterwards eat of them when they have become ripe, he is not forsworn; and so also, if he should swear that "he will not eat of those Ritbs" (ripe dates), "nor drink of this milk," and he afterwards eat of these mixed together, after the Ritbs shall have become mellow and the milk coagulated, because the description of half-ride or of ripe is the motive for the vow, and those descriptions are no longer applicable; end in the same manner, the milk being in the state of milk is the motive of the vow, wherefore the vow is taken respecting it in that state; milk, moreover, is ranked among eatables, wherefore by milk is not understood anything which may be produced from it. It is otherwise where a man vows that "he will not converse with such an infant," or "with such a youth," and he converses with the infant after he becomes a man, or with the youth after he has become aged,—for here he is forsworn; because refraining from converse with a Mussulman is forbidden by the law, whether such Mussulman be an infant or a youth; hence the descriptions of infancy or adolescence are not regarded, in the eye of the law, as motives of the vow; consequently the vowis understood to respect such a person; and the vower is accordingly forsworm if he converse with that person after he arrives at years of maturity.

Or denomination.—IF a person swear that "he will not eat of such a kid," and he should eat thereof after the said kid shall have become a goat, he is forsworn, because the description of kid, in such an animal, is not the motive of the vow, since a person who avoids eating the flesh of kids, still more avoids eating the flesh of goats.

IF a man make a vow that "he will not eat Boosrs (unripe dates), and should afterwards eat Ritbs (ripe dates), he will not be forsworn, because Ritbs are not Boosrs.

IF a person make a vow that "he will not eat Ritbs or Boosrs," and he should afterwards eat Mozennibs (dates which are beginning to ripen), he is forsworn, according to Haneefa. The two disciples say that he is not forsworn by eating Boosr-Mozennibs, in a case where he may have sworn not to eat Ritbs; neither does he violate his vow by eating Ritb-Mozennibs, in a case where he has made a vow against eating Boosrs; because Ritb-Mozennibs are termed Ritbs, and Boosr-Mozennibs are termed Boosrs. Thus it is the same as if a man were to make a vow with respect to buying:—that is, if a man were to swear that he will not this day buy Ritbs (or ripe dates), and he should afterwards on that same day purchase Mozennibs (or half-ripe dates), he is not forsworn; and so in this case likewise. The argument of Haneefa on this point is that Ritb-Mozennibs are such as rather incline to Boosrs and Boosr-Mozennibs are the reverse—(that is, such as rather approach to Ritbs), wherefore eating either of those is eating Boosrs or Ritbs, and the vow regards one or other of them:—contrary to the case of buying, as the buying relates to every species, wherefore the inferior species is a dependant of the superior.

IF a man vow that "he will not buy any ripe dates," and he should afterwards purchase a cluster of unripe dates, among which there may chance to be some ripe, he is not forsworn, because the purchase relates to the whole, and the smaller quantity is a dependant of the greater; but, if the vow were made with respect to eating, he is forsworn, because the eating of them relates to from time to time, wherefore the vow regards every one of them. This case is therefore the same as if a man were to vow that he would not purchase any barley, and he should afterwards buy wheat, having among it some grains of barley, in which case he is not forsworn; but if he should vow that he would not eat any barley, and he should afterwards eat wheat, among which are some grains of barley, he is forsworn, for the reason here stated.

IF a man vow that "he will not eat flesh" and he should afterwards eat the flesh of fish, he is not forsworn, on a favourable construction of the law. Analogy would suggest that he is forsworn, because the meat of fish is termed flesh, and so it is denominated in the Koran; but the reason for the more favourable construction of the law is that the meat of fish is only termed flesh metaphorically, as flesh is produced from blood, and there is no blood in fish, on account of their inhabiting the water. If the vower, on the contrary, were to eat of the flesh of a hog or a man, he would be forsworn, because that is actually flesh, although the use of it be forbidden, and a vow is sometimes made with respect to forbidden things; and in like manner he is forsworn if he were to eat of the liver or the paunch of any animal, because that is in reality flesh, as being produced from blood, and is, moreover, used in the same manner as flesh. Some say that, in our times, the vower is not forsworn by eating of liver or paunch, as these articles are not among us accounted flesh.

IF a person swear that "he will not eat or buy fat" (that is tallow), he is not forsworn by eating or purchasing fat, unless it be the fat or tallow of the belly. The two disciples allege that the swearer would violate his vow by purchasing or eating the fat of the back, because the peculiar quality of tallow, which is melting in the fire, exists in this species, as well as in that of the belly. The argument of Haneefa is that the fat of the back is in reality flesh, as being produced from blood; and it is, moreover, used as flesh, and thence the flesh derives its value and goodness; for which reason a person eating it would violate his vow, where he had sworn not to eat flesh, and is not forsworn by selling the fat of the back, where he had sworn that "he would not sell fat." Some allege that this difference subsists only where the vower hast sworn concerning fat, but not where he has sworn concerning tallow, as that is never used in the way of flesh

If a man makes a vow that "he will neither eat nor buy flesh or fat," and he should afterwards either eat or purchase the fat tail of a sheep, yet he is not forsworn, because this part is altogether distinct from both flesh and fat, as not being used for the same purpose as either of them.

If a man swear that "he will not eat of this wheat," he does not violate his vow, unless he chew it; and if he should eat bread made of the wheat, he is not forsworn, according to Haneefa.—The two disciples maintain that by eating the said bread he is forsworn, since by the terms of the vow is also understood wheaten bread, according to common usage.—The argument of Haneefa is that, the eating of wheat is a thing actually practised, as men eat wheat boiled and dressed in other modes, and the literal acception must (according to its tenets) always be preferred to the metaphorical, although that be sanctioned by custom.—If the swearer should chew the wheat, the two disciples coincide in opinion with our doctors, that he is forsworn; and this is approved, since the eating of the wheat comprehends the chewing of it, in the common form of Metonymy, as where a man vows that he will not set his foot in the house of such a person, and afterwards enters that house, in which case he is forsworn, whether he rides into the house, or goes in on foot.

If a man make a vow, saying, "I will not eat of this flour," and he should afterwards eat bread made thereof, he is forsworn: because flour is not eaten in its simple state, and hence it is construed to mean such articles of food as are prepared from it.—If, on the contrary, he were to eat the actual flour, he is not forsworn; and this is approved; because here it is certain that the words were intended in their metonymical sense, and with that sense the eating of flour in its simple state does not accord.

If a person swear that "he will not eat bread," by this is to be understood, such bread as is commonly eaten in that place; and this is, in general, either wheaten or barley bread, one or other of which is almost universally used. If, also, the swearer should eat walnut or almond bread in Irak* he is not forsworn; because such bread is not common in that region; whereas, if he were to eat such bread in Tabristan †, or any other place where it is the usual diet, he would violate his vow.

If a person swear that "he will not eat Shawa" (or stew), then the oath relates to the flesh of the stew, and not to the vegetables or eggs that may be mixed with it; because the term Shawa means the meat of the stew, and is therefore to be construed in its literal meaning, unless where the swearer may have intended by the word Shawa to express and include the above mentioned articles also, when the abstinence ought to be conformable to the intention.

If a person swear that "he will not eat Tabbeekh" (or boiled meat), his vow respects boiled flesh. ‡ This proceeds upon a favourable construction of the law, according to general usage; and the ground of it is, that the unrestricted sense of Tabbeekh cannot be admitted on account that this would preclude the vower from the use both of food and of medicine, which is not his design. The term Tabbeekh, therefore, is here construed to mean the particular thing usually understood by it (namely, flesh cooked in water), unless where the intention of the vower may have extended farther, as if he were to declare that he meant thereby every species of boiled provisions,—for here this declaration is to be credited, since this is a violence to himself, and a man is empowered to inflict penalties upon himself. If, moreover, in this case, the vower were to sup of the broth of flesh-meat he is forsworn, because it partakes of the quality of flesh, and broth is also termed Tabbeekh, wherefore he would be forsworn, "as having eaten Tabbeekh."

If a person vow that "he will not eat any Ras" [head], by this is to be understood the head of an animal, as usually prepared for cookery, and exposed to sale.—It is written in the Jama Sagheer, that if a person swear that he will not eat Ras, by this is understood the heads of cows, bullocks, and goats, according to Haneefa;—but that the two disciples hold it restricted to the heads of goats.—This diversity of opinion, however, arises solely from the difference of times; for in the time of Haneefa the words Ras was used to express the heads of both kinds; but in the time of the two disciples, the heads of

* A division of Persia: the ancient Chaldea.

† A province in upper Persia: the ancient Hyrcania.

‡ Tabbeekh literally means boiled; in common usage it signifies boiled flesh; but according to its literal meaning, the term might equally well be applied to any other food.—This whole case turns upon the express and generally accepted meaning of the word.

goats only; and in our times, decrees are issued according to whatever may be customary in conformity with general usage, as is mentioned in the abridgment of Kadooree.

IF a person vow that "he will not eat Fakiha,"* and he should afterwards eat of oranges, citrons, dates, pomegranates, or cucumbers, he is not forsworn; but if he should eat apples, melons, or apricots, he violates his vow.—This is according to Haneefa.—This two disciples say that he is also forsworn if he eat oranges, dates, or citrons. In short, Fakiha is a term used to express things introduced as a delicacy before or after meals (that is, such things as are indulged in as a delicacy over and above the common food); and it is the same whether the fruit of which it is composed be dried, or in the natural state, provided it be thus indulged in, in both ways (for the vower would not be forsworn by eating dried melons, which it is not common to use as a superfluous delicacy), and this is the case with apples, melons, and apricots wherefore he would be forsworn by eating them: but it is not the case with cucumbers and citrons; as these are considered merely as vegetables in buying and selling, and also in eating;—in buying and selling, as they are sold by green-sellers;—and in eating, as they are, at the time of meals, set along with other vegetables; wherefore the vower is not forsworn by eating cucumbers or citrons. With respect, however, to oranges, dates, and citrons, there is a difference of opinion, as above mentioned;—for the two disciples maintain that by eating of those the vower is forsworn, as the description of Fakiha is applicable to them, since they are the most rare of all delicacies and a higher treat than any other: but he is not forsworn, according to Haneefa, because oranges and dates are eaten as food, and men eat citrons also as a medicine; wherefore the description of Fakiha is incomplete, since they are used for the support of life; and hence it is that when dried they are used in cookery.

IF a person vow that "he will not eat Idam," by this is to be understood anything which is usually eaten in bread; thus Kabobs are not considered as Idam, whereas salt is supposed to come under the denomination.—This is according to Haneefa and Aboo Yoosaf: but Imam Mohammed says that whatever is most commonly eaten along with bread is to be recorded as Idam (and there is also an opinion regarded from Aboo Yoos.f to this effect), because Idam is derived from Mowademit, or congeniality, and such articles are usually eaten with bread as are agreeable and congenial thereto, such as simple flesh, fowls, and so forth,—The argument of Haneefa herein is that Idam implies that which is eaten as a dependant, and dependancy is actually found in a case of admixture where it stands in the place of bread; and it virtually exists where the article used is of such a nature as never to be eaten alone. With respect to what Aboo Yoosaf alleges of Idam being derived from Mowademit, or congeniality, it may be replied that such congeniality is completely found in admixture:—and vinegar, or other similar fluids, are never eaten alone, but mixed with bread or other food; and salt, also, is not usually eaten alone; and it, moreover, is liable to melt; wherefore it is a dependant (contrary to the case of flesh, and other corresponding substances, which are frequently eaten alone):—and hence by eating these, the vower is not forsworn, unless where he intends such articles in his vow, for this is a violence to himself, and a man is empowered to inflict penalties upon himself. It is to be observed that oranges and dates are not considered as Idam: this is approved.

IF a person make a vow that "he will not eat Ghadd" [dinner], by this is understood eating at any time from daybreak till noon; as by Asha [supper], is understood what is eaten between meridian prayer and midnight, because any time after the sun's daclination from the meridian is the time of Asha. Some assert that this was the distinction among the ancients; but that with the moderns the time of Asha is from afternoon prayer; and the morning meal is that which may be eaten between midnight and day, break, because the morning is from midnight until daybreak.—It is to be observed that where a person makes a vow against eating dinner or supper, a full and entire meal is to be understood of either, such as is customary: this will, of course, be regulated by the usual quantity of those meals in different countries respectively; but, to violate the vow, more than half the usual quantity must be eaten,

IF a man make a vow, saying, "if I clothe myself, or eat, or drink, my slave is free," and he should explain his intention, in the first of these articles, to regard a particular kind of cloth only, his declaration is not to be credited either with respect to a decree of the Kazee, or in a religious view (and the same is to be observed with respect to the two other articles of eating and drinking); because intention is not approved unless it be expressed, and the cloth, or so forth, are not mentioned in the vow.—If a man, also, were to make a vow, saying, "if I put on a robe," or "eat food," or "drink wine,—my slave is free," and he afterwards say that he meant this robe and not that robe, or so forth his declaration is not to be credited in point of law: but it is credited in a religious view, because the words robe, food, and wine, are here mentioned; but yet an intention of discrimination with respect to them contradicts appearances, wherefore his declaration

*Fakiha is said, in the lexicons, to mean fruit; it in reality means any superfluous delicacy which does not come under the denomination of food, and this generally consists of fruit.

is not to be credited as far as regards a decree of the Kazee.*

Vows respecting drinking out of a fountain or vessel.—If a person were to make a vow that "he would not drink out of such a fountain," and afterwards lift water out of the fountain in a cup, and drink, he is not forsworn,—nor unless he lift it with his mouth [that is, drink it without a vessel], in which case he would be forsworn.—The two disciples say he is forsworn if he drink it out of a cup, as this is the usual mode of drinking. Haneefa's arguments are deduced from the Arabic.

If a man make a vow, saying, "I will not drink of the water of such a fountain," and afterwards drink the water of the fountain out of a vessel, he is forsworn, because the water of the fountain, after being taken up and drank, is still referred to the fountain, which is the condition; he is therefore forsworn as much as if he were to drink water out of a stream which runs from the fountain.

If a man make a vow, saying, "if I do not drink, this day, of the water which is in this vessel, my wife is divorced" and it should so happen that there is no water in it, he is not forsworn; and so also (according to Haneefa and Muhammed) if there be water in the vessel, and it should chance to be spilled before the night of that day, Aboo Yoosaf says that he is forsworn, in either case, upon the close of that day;—and the same difference of opinion subsists where a man makes a vow to God (that is, where he says, "by God I will drink of the water which is in this cup this day); for it is a rule with Aboo Yoosaf that the possibility of fulfilling the vow is not a condition, either of the obligation of the vow, or of its continuance;—whereas, according to Haneefa and Mohammed, the possibility of fulfilment is a condition of the obligation of the vow, and also of its continuance, because a vow is taken with a view to its accomplishment, and it is therefore requisite that the accomplishment be possible and conceivable, so as to be obligatory.—The argument of Aboo Yoosaf is, that although the accomplishment of the vow be impossible, yet its substitute (namely, expiation) is possible, wherefore such a vow may be lawfully taken, insomuch as it is the occasion of expiation: but to this we reply that it is requisite that the original act be practicable, so as to render the taking of the vow valid, since, if the original act be practicable, how can the vow be taken so as to give occasion for a substitute?—and hence it is that a Yameen Ghamoos (or false oath made respecting a thing already past) cannot be taken in such a manner as to occasion expiation.—If, moreover, in the case now under consideration, the words "this day" should not have been mentioned, but the vow be general, as if the man had said, "if I drink not of the water in this vessel, my wife is divorced," and there should happen to be no water in the vessel, he is not forsworn, according to Haneefa and Mohammed: but with Aboo Yoosaf he is forsworn, upon the instant.—But if there be water in the cup at the time of speaking, and it be spilled before night, the vower is forsworn, according to all our doctors.—Aboo Yoosaf makes a distinction between an unrestricted and a restricted case; for he says that, in the restricted case, the vower is forsworn after the day is closed; but, in the unrestricted case, he is forsworn the instant he ceases from speaking: the reason of which distinction is that, as the specification of a time is made for the purpose of extention, the act does not become absolutely incumbent until the last instant of the time; and hence the vower is not forsworn until then; but in the unrestricted case, the fulfilment is incumbent on the instant the person ceases from speaking, which, being impossible, the vower is forsworn on the instant.—Haneefa and Imam Mohammed also make a distinction between the restricted and the unrestricted case; for they say that where the vow is general, and there is water in the vessel, and it happens to be spilled, the vower is forsworn; but not where the vow is restricted; the reason of which distinction is that, in the unrestricted case, the fulfilment is incumbent on the instant the person cease from speaking; and the fulfilment being defeated, by the thing no longer remaining, respecting which the vow was taken, the vower is forsworn, because the thing vowed is in this case defeated subsequently to the time when fulfilment was incumbent; in the same manner as if the vower should happen to die, and the water remain in the cup, in which case he would be forsworn:—but, where the vow is restricted, the accomplishment is not absolutely incumbent, until the last instant of the time specified; but the accomplishment is then impossible, because the water, which was the subject of it, no longer remains: and where the accomplishment is no longer possible, it is not incumbent; wherefore the vow becomes null, as much as if there were no water whatever in the vessel.

A vow made respecting an absolute impossibility is held as violated upon the instant.—If a person make a vow, saying, "I will, by some means or other, ascend to heaven," or, "I will, somehow, convert this stone into gold," this constitutes a vow,* and the vower

---

*That is, if a man, having made such a vow, were afterwards to perform any of the acts therein specified, pleading that he made his vow under a restrictive intention, and that the articles he has eaten or drank, or the robe he has put on, were meant as exceptions therefrom, the possibility of the truth of this declaration is to be admitted; but yet the Kazee (who can judge only from appearances) must decree the emancipation of the slave.

*Arab. Yoonakido-al-Yameeno, the vow

is forthwith forsworn.—Ziffer says that this does not constitute a vow, since ascending to heaven, or turning stone into gold, are impracticable, in the usual nature of things, and therefore are the same as things actually impossible.—The argument of our doctors is. that the fulfilment is here actually practicable, because it certainly is possible to ascend to heaven, as we know that the angels of GOD ascend the skies; and in the same manner it is possible that a stone may be converted into gold by the Almighty exerting his power for that purpose: now the thing vowed being possible, the vow is contracted so far as to give occasion for expiation; and the vower is forthwith forsworn, because of his inability, in the ordinary nature of things, to execute the thing which he has undertaken; in the same manner as if a vower were to die before the accomplishment of his vow, in which case he would be forsworn, although it be possible that he may yet be restored to life: contrary to the case of the vessel of water, because the drinking of the water undertaken to be drank is not possible in either of those cases, and therefore the vow is null.

CHAPTER VII,

OF VOWS WITH RESPECT TO SPEAKING AND CONVERSING.

A vow against speaking to such a person is violated by speaking to him within hearing distance, although he be asleep.—IF a person make a vow, saying, "I will not speak to such an one," and he should afterwards speak to that person while asleep, from such a distance as may be within his hearing, he is forsworn; because he has spoken to that person, and the words have reached his ears; although, in consequence of being asleep, he may not have heard them, and it is therefore the same as if he had called to that person from a place within his hearing, and the person be not sensible of his addressing him through inattention. In some passages of the Mabsoot it is said that it is conditional to the violation of the vow that the person sleeping be awaked by the words spoken (and in this opinion our doctors coincide): because, if he be not awakened, it is the same as if the speaker had called to him from a place so distant as not to be within hearing. in which case he would not be forsworn, and so here likewise.

Case in which the violation of the vow depends upon the meaning of the terms used in it.—IF a man make a vow that, "he will not speak to such an one without his permission," and the person mentioned should permit him to speak accordingly, but the vower be not certified thereof until after he shall have spoken to him, he is forsworn; because the term Izn [permission] is devied from the word Azan, which signifies indication; or if it signifies a thing received by the ears, which can only be done by hearing, Aboo Yoosaf says that he is not forsworn, because Izn signifies licence, which is fully understood by tacit consent alone; that is (like the will), it does not depend upon anything else: for instance, if one were to swear that "he would not speak to such a person without his will," and the person should will his speaking to him, but the vower be not certified thereof until after he has spoken, yet he is not forsworn, because the will is fully established by the person being merely willing, and does not depend upon anything else. But to this we reply that the will is merely an act of the mind, whereas Izn is not merely so, for the reasons above stated.

Case of a vow against conversing with a person for a specified time—IF a person make a vow, saying, "I will not speak to such an one for a month," it is to be understood from the time of making such vow, because if he were not to mention the words for a month, the vow would take place as a perpetual relinquishment of converse with the person mentioned; the mention of month, therefore, is for the purpose of excluding from the vow anything beyond one month, and hence that which is connected with the vow must be included in the vow, from the argument of the state in which it is pronounced, as being a state of anger, since the reason for the observance of the vow is the anger which occurs to the vower at the instant, for which reason converse with the person mentioned is prevented from that instant. It would be otherwise if a man should say, "by GOD I will fast for a month," because, if the words "for a month," were not mentioned, yet the vow would not take place as inducing a perpetual fast; the mention of a month, therefore, is merely for the purpose of restriciting the fast to a month; and as the month is indefinite, and not specified, the specification of it is left to the vower.

Repetition of prayer, &c., at the stated seasons, does not violate a vow of silence.—IF a man make a vow that "he will not speak," and he afterwards read the Koran at the stated periods of devotion, he is not forsworn; but if he should, at any other time, read the Koran, he is forsworn. The same rule also holds with respect to the Tasbeeh,* Tahleel † and Takbeer ,‡—that is

---

is contracted; that is to say, is valid in its effect, and binding upon the vower. The expression, as above, is preferred by the translator. ..s being more familiar to an English reader.

*Calling upon the name of GOD in prayer by saying, "BEESM ALLAH! in the name of GOD."

†Repeating the Kalma, or creed, "THERE IS NO GOD BUT GOD, &c."

‡Magnifying GOD (in prayer) by saying "ALLAHOO AKBERO!" [GOD is greatest

to say, he repeat any of these at the stated time of prayer, he is not forsworn; but if he should repeat them at any other time, he violates his vow. This proceeds upon a favourable construction.—Analogy would suggest that the vower is forsworn in either case (and such is the opinion of Shafei), because reading the Koran, or repeating the Tasbeeh, and so forth, are all actual exertions of the speaking faculty.—The argument of our doctors is that prayer does not come under the description of speech, either generally, or in the construction of the law the Prophet having said, "these prayers which I teach are not capable of being construed as containing any of the words of men."—Some have said that in our days the vower would not be forsworn, even at any other time than the stated periods of prayer, because the person who repeats those things is not said to be speaking, but reciting; and decrees pass accordingly.

A vow made respecting the day extends to the night also.—IF a man were to say, 'on the day [Yawm] upon which I speak to such an one, his wife is divorced,"* this extends both to the day and the night, because the word day where it comes in context with a thing which is not a matter of continuance, means time generally; and as speaking to a person is not a matter of continuance, by the word day, is to be here understood time in general.—But if the swearer should declare that his intention in the vow was confined to the daytime in particular, his declaration must be credited with the Kazee, because the term Yawm is used also in this sense.—It is recorded from Aboo Yoosaf that his declaration not to be credited with the Kazee as it is contradictory to general usage.—But if the vower should, in the place of the word day, use the word night, by saying, "on the night [Lail] on which I converse" (and so forth, by this is to be understood night only, because the positive meaning of the term Lail is night, in the same manner as the positive meaning of the term Nihar is day; but no instance is known of Lail being used to express time generally.

Case of a vow of inhibition restricted to a particular occurrence.—IF a person say, "if I speak to Zeyd, unless a certain person come, his wife is divorced," and he should afterwards converse with Zeyd, before the coming of the other person, he is forsworn,—but, if after, he is not forsworn.—In the same manner, if the swearer were to express himself, "if I speak to Zeyd until such an one shall have arrived" or "unless by permission of such an one," or "until the permission of such an one,"—his wife is divorced," and he should afterwards converse with Zeyd, before the arrival or before permission obtained, of the other person, he is forsworn;—but, if after, he is not forsworn; because the arrival or permission is the termination of the vow, which remains in force until the termination, but discontinues upon that taking place; and he cannot be forsworn after the vow is completed.—In the case here stated, if the person named should happen to die, the vow ceases: contrary to the opinion of Aboo Yoosaf, for with him the vow does not drop, but the vower is forsworn if ever he should speak to Zeyd.—The argument of Haneefa and Mohammed is that the thing prohibited by the tenor of the oath is conversation with Zeyd; and this, by his death, being rendered impossible, the vow drops of course: but with Aboo Yoosaf the possibility is not a condition, whence, upon the death of Zeyd the vow becomes perpetual.

A vow against conversing with a person described is (in relation to another) not violated by conversing with that person after the description (with respect to the other) is done away.—IF a man make a vow, saying "I will not speak to the slave of such a person," without intending any particular slave,—or, if he should express his vow, "I will not speak to the wife," or "the friend of such a person," and the person should sell his slave, or repudiate his wife, or fall at enmity with his friend, and the vower afterwards converse with either of these, he is not forsworn, because his vow is taken as regarding a circumstance which has its existence in a matter relative to the person named, whether that matter be relation by right of property, as in the case of the slave; or relation by connexion, as in the case of the wife, or the friend; and when that matter no longer remains, the vower cannot be forsworn.—The compiler of this work observes that what is here said is taken from the Jama Sagheer; and other authorities agree with it, in respect to the relation by right of property: but in respect to the relation by connexion the vower would be forsworn, according to Mohammed, because such relation is purely of an indicative nature, and is not to be taken in a restrictive sense, since the case admits the design of the vower to be a renunciation of conversation with those persons, as either of them is capable of being held an enemy from injuries received but not because of the relation in which they stand to the person named; the continuance of that relation, therefore, is not a condition; and hence the effect is connected with the identical person of either, as in a case of pointed reference;—that is, if a person say, "I will not converse with this friend, or with this wife, of such a person," and he should converse with them after the falling out with

*It is to be observed, in this and other similar modes of expression, that the vow is by no means efficient of divorce to the woman mentioned in it, but is considered, with respect to her, as a vague and idle speech, and in itself void, inducing nothing more than an expiation on the part of the person speaking.

the friend, or the divorce of the wife, he is not forsworn: and so here also.—The reason for what is recited in the Jama Sagheer is that it is possible that the design of the vower may be to quit conversing with those person on account of the relation in which they stand to the person named (whence he has not mentioned them with any pointed reference), and it is also possible that the design may be merely to quit conversing with those persons; thus a doubt exists, whether the relation be the motive to the vow or not; and such being the case, the vower is not forsworn by conversing with any of those persons after the dissolution of the relation in which they stood to the person named.—If, moreover, the man should have made his vow with respect to a person paticularly specified, by saying, "I will not converse with this slave of such an one," or "this wife," or "this friend" (and so forth), and he should converse with them after the slave shall have been sold, or the wife divorced, or the friend at enmity, he is not forsworn in the case of the slave, but he would be so in the case of the wife or the friend.—This is the doctrine of Haneefa and Aboo Yoosaf.—Mohammad says that he is forsworn in the case of the slave likewise; and such also is the opinion of Ziffer. And if a man were to make a vow, saying, "I will not enter into this house of such an one," or "I will not ride upon this beast of such an one," and he should enter the house, or ride upon the beast, after the owner has disposed of them, the same difference of opinion prevails among the doctors as is above stated.—The argument of Mohammad and Ziffer is, that the mention of the relation of the slave to his owner is for the purpose of indication; but pointed reference is more forcible, in indication, than the relation which a thing bears to another, as that altogether obviates doubt: wherefore regard is had to pointed reference alone, and the mention of the relation is nugatory, in the same manner as in the case of the wife or the friend.—The argument of Haneefa and Aboo Yoosaf is that the moving cause of the vow, in the case of the slave, the house, or the animal, is some property which is to be found in the person to whom they have reference; because the house or the animal are incapable of being of themselves held in enmity; and so also the slave, as he does not stand in a rank sufficiently respectable to admit his being an object of enmity; wherefore the quitting from converse from those is on account of a property which is to be found in the proprietor of them; and hence the vow is restricted to the continuance of the right of the owner: contrary to a case of relation by connexion, such as the relation of the wife or the friend; as enmity and separation from them may be the design, for which reason the mention of the relation in which they stand to the person named is merely for the purpose of indication; and it is evident that the moving cause of the vow, with respect to them, is some property which is to be found in themselves, and not in the person to whom they have reference; because they are mentioned with a pointed reference: contrary to the case of the slave, the house, or the animal, as in those cases the thing mentioned is incapable of being of itself held in enmity, unless on account of some property to be found in the person in reference to whom it is mentioned, namely, the proprietor.

If a man make a vow, saying, "I will not speak to the owner of this turban," and the owner of the turban should afterwards sell it, and the vower should thereafter converse with the said person, he is forsworn; because here the mention of the relation of the thing to the person is purely for the purpose of indication, since men do not fall at variance with turbans; and hence it is the same as if he had spoken with a pointed reference to the owner of it, by saying, "I will not speak to this owner of the turban:" in which case he would be forsworn; and so here likewise.

A vow against conversing with such a youth is violated by conversing with him after manhood.—If a person make a vow, saying "I will not converse with this youth," and he should afterwards converse with him when he has arrived at an advanced age, he is forsworn; because the effect is connected with the person mentioned; as a descriptive expression is not necessary to specify a person who is presene, and the description of youth cannot be considered as the motive to the vow.

Section.

Vows respecting converse with a reference to it man.—If a person make a vow, saying, "I will not converse with such an one for a time" [Hyne]—or "for a space of time" [Ziman], by these modes of expressing time is to be understood six months; because Hyne sometimes means a short space of time, and sometimes forty years; and it also is sometimes used to express a few months;—and the space of six months is a medium between these extremes; wherefore, by the term Hyne is here to be understood six months. The principle upon which this proceeds is that a very small space of time cannot be designed for the prevention of conversation, as prevention may apply to a little space of time, in common usage, wherefore in such a case a vow s unneccessary for prevention: and a very long space of time is not designed for prevention, as that stands as a perpetuity: moreover, if he had omitted all mention of time, by not introducing the word Hyne, his vow would be taken as meaning to quit converse with the person named for ever; but as he mentioned time, it appears that his design is not perpetual: since if it were so, he would have omitted the word Hyne, or have used the word Abid [for ever]; and such being the case, it is ascertained that his intention in the word Hyne is six months:—and so also of the word

Ziman, as that is used in the same sense with Hyne.—What is here advanced proceeds upon a supposition that the vower had no particular intention: but if he should have intended to express any particular space of time, it is to be understood according to his intention, because that is the literal meaning of the words aforesaid.*

If a person make a vow in the following terms, saying, "I will not speak to such an one for days" [Ayam]—by the word Ayam is to be understood three days: but if he should use the restricting article, saying, "I will not converse with such an one for the days" [Al-Ayam], by this is understood ten days, according to Haneefa, and a week according to the two disciples. If the vower, also, were to express himself, "I will not speak to such an one for months" [Shoohoor], by this is understood ten months, according to Haneefa,—and a year according to the two disciples:—and if he should vow, saying, "I will not converse with him for weeks" [Jooma] or "for years" [Soonatine],—by Jooma (according to Haneefa) is understood ten weeks,—and by Soonatine ten years; but the two disciples understand by either of these the whole life of the swearer. The arguments here, on both sides, are deduced from certain grammatical points in the Arabic.

If a man make a vow with respect to his slave, saying, "if you serve me for many days [Ayamoon Kaseeritoon], you shall become free,"—by many days (according to Haneefa) is understood ten days, because ten is the greatest number comprehended in the term Ayam, which is the plural of Yawm.—The two disciples, on the other hand, say that by the words many days are to be undersrood seven days only, because anything beyond is an excess. Some have asserted that if a man were to make this vow in the Persian tongue, by many days is understood seven with all our doctors; because in the Persian language there is no difference between more than ten days and less than ten, for men say, "ten days or more," without expressing day in the plural.†

CHAPTER VIII.

OF VOWS IN MANUMISSION AND DIVORCE.

Divorce vowed on condition of the birth of a child takes place although the child be stillborn.—If a man say to his wife,* "whenever you bring forth a child you shall become divorced," of a dead child, divorce takes place upon her; and in the same manner, if a man say to his female, "whenever you bring forth a child, you shall become free," and she should afterwards be delivered of a dead child, she becomes free;—because the condition (namely, childbearing) is fulfilled, as an infant, though stillborn, is yet actually a child, and it is also termed a child by general usage. Regard is moreover had, in law, to such a birth, whence it is that the Edit is accomplished by it: and the discharge which follows the birth of a dead child is termed Niffas, as well as that which follows the birth of a living child: and in the same manner the mother of such a child, where she happens to be a slave, and her owner acknowledges the child, becomes an Am-Walid.

Freedom vowed in favour of a child that may be born of a female slave, takes place on her first live-born child.—If a man say to his female slave, "whenever you bring forth a child, that child is free," and she be afterwards delivered, first of one child dead, and again of another child living, in this case the living child alone is free,—that is to say, that one is free, but no other who may be born afterwards.—This is the doctring of Haneefa,—The two disciples say that no child whatever is emancipated, because the condition of the vow has already taken place in the birth of the dead child, for the reasons stated in the preceding case; and hence the vow is dissolved, without its consequence (that is, the vow is accomplished and done away, without its consequence taking place),—as the dissolution of a vow does not depend upon the induction of its consequence: thus if a man were to say to his wife, "if you go into such a house you are divorced," and she enter that house after having been repudiated by a complete divorce, and her Edit be past, the vow is dissolved without its consequence: and so also in the present instance, as a dead child is not a proper subject of manumission.—The argument of Haneefa is that the term Walid [a child] as expressed in the vow, although it be applicable to one born dead, yet in the present case is restricted to the description of living, because the design of the vewer is to bestow freedom upon a child, and as this is a power by virtue of which the despotic authority of others over

* Some grammatical controversy here follows respecting the word Dehr, which does not admit of an intelligible translation.

† This and the preceding case turn upon certain points of grammar. In the Arabic language are four sort- of plurals, which are termed plurals of paucity: some of the commentators suppose (with Haneefa) that this species of plural expresses any number up to ten, whilst others maintain (with Mohammed) that the utmost number which can be expressed by it is seven. In the Persian language a noun is always expressed in the singular when preceded by a plural nameral, although it consequently has a plural signification.

*In this and all the corresponding cases, the form of the vow, although omitted here for the sake of brevity, is always to be understood as preecding the sentence, thus, "BY GOD, whenever you bring forth, &c.," or, "I vow, whenever, &c."

the person endowed with it is removed, cannot possibly be established to one who is dead. The term Walid, therefore, expressed in the vow, is restricted to the living description; in the same manner as where a master says to his female slave, "whenever you are delivered of a living child, such child is free," and the slave is delivered of a dead child, and afterwards produces a living one;—in which case this living one is free; and so here likewise.—It is otherwise where divorce or manumission has been suspended upon the birth of a child, for there the divorce or manumission so suspended takes place; as in this instance it is not requisite that the birth be restricted to the living description, since the life of the child is not necessary to the divorce of the wife, or the manumission of the slave.

Case of a vow of freedom to the first purchased slave.—IF a man say, "the first slave that I purchase is free," and he should afterwards buy a slave, such slave is free, because the word first points to the prior single slave, which applies in this instance:—but if the vower, in such a case, were to purchase two slaves together, and afterwards a third, none of these slaves is free, because singularity does not apply to the third slave, wherefore he is not the first. If, however, this man had said, "the first slave that I purchase singly is free," the third slave would be liberated, because here the vower has intended singularity at the time of purchase, and this one is the first with respect to such singularity.

Case of a vow of freedom to a last purchased slave.—IF a man say, "the last slave that I buy is free," and he should purchase a slave, and then die, yet the slave so purchased is not free; because the term the last applies to the individual adjunct,* and as no other has preceded this one, he cannot be considered as adjunct; but if the vower were to die after having purchased another slave, this slave is free, as being the individual adjunct. It is to be observed that this second slave is free (according to Haneefa) from the day of purchase; and being free from the date of the purchase, the same is regarded as from the whole of the property of the deceased, on account of his having released him during health.—The two disciples say that he is emancipated upon the death of that person, and hence it is regarded as from the third of his property only, on account of the deceased having emancipated him upon his deathbed: for they argue that the posteriority of that slave cannot be fully established, until such time as it becomes certain that no other can be purchased after him; and this cannot possibly be determined but by death; hence the condition is found upon the master's decease, and the freedom of the slave is therefore also established upon that event. The argument of Haneefa is that the posteriority of the slave is ascertained by the master's decease, but the description of posteriority applies to him from the period of the purchase.—The suspension of a triplicate divorce upon posteriority is also subject to the same difference of opinion;—in other words, if a man vow, "the last woman I marry shall be thrice divorced," and he first marry one woman, and afterwards another, and then die, three divorces take place upon the second wife according to Haneefa insomuch that she cannot inherit the deceased; but according to the two disciples the three divorces take place upon her from the day of her husband's decease, and consequently she does inherit of him.

Case of a vow of freedom to whoever of his slaves shall congratulate the vower on the birth of a child.—IF a man say, "whoever of my slaves congratulates me upon the delivery of my wife shall be free," and afterwards several of his slaves successively should inform him of his wife's delivery, the one who first brought him the intelligence only is free; because by Bisharit [which is here rendered congratulation] is meant any intelligence which works a change upon the countenance, whether that intelligence be agreeable or otherwise (but yet in common usage, it is requisite that the intelligence be agreeable), and this description is fully found only in the first intelligence,—not in the second, or third, because no change is by that wrought upon the countenance.—If, however, the slaves all bring him news together, they are all free, as the Bisharit then proceeds equally from all.

The emancipation of a slave, in consequence of a vow, does not suffice for expiation.—IF a man were to say, "If I purchase a slave he shall be free," and he afterwards purchase a slave, with a view, by his release to effect the expiation of a vow, this does not suffice for expiation; because it is requisite that the intention of expiation be associated with the occasion of manumission, which is not the case here, as the vow is the cause of manumission in the present case, and at the time of making it expiation was not the intention of the vower; and as to the purchase of the slave, that is not the occasion of the manumission, but rather the condition of it.

But the emancipation of a father, in consequence of purchase, suffices.—IF a man purchase, as a slave, his own father, with a view to the expiation of a vow, it suffices, with our doctors. This is contrary to the opinion of Ziffer and Shafei, who contend that the act of purchasing a father is the condition of manumission, and not the occasion of it, as the occasion of it is relationship (for purchase is an establishment of right of property, and manumission is a destruction of that right, and each of these is repugnant to the other, wherefore it is impossible that purchase should be the occasion of manumission); and it thus appearing that the

*Arab. Fard Lahik.—It is a term used solely in grammar.

cause of the manumission is relationship and not purchase, the intention of the manumission is not associated with the cause of it.—The argument of our doctors is that the purchase is blended with the manumission, as the Prophet has said, "no child makes so effectual a return to his parent as one who, finding his parent the slave of another, purchases, and thereby emancipates him,"—which proves that the Prophet constituted the purchase itself a manumission, as there is here no other condition of manumission except purchase, according to all the doctors.

The emancipation (by purchase), of a female slave, by a person to whom she stands in the relation of an Am Walid does not suffice.—IF a man purchase, as a slave, a woman who has borne him a child, with a view to the expiation of a vow, it does not suffice.—The nature of this case is thus. A man marries the female slave of another, and she produces a child to him, and he says to her, "if I at any time hereafter purchase you, you shall become free, as an expiation of my vow," and he afterwards purchase her, when the woman becomes forthwith released,' because of the occurrence of the condition upon which her emancipation was suspended; but this does not suffice for the expiation of a vow, because the slave is a claimant of freedom in virtue of Isteclad,* and hence her freedom is not purely in consequence of the vow, and therefore does not suffice for the expiation of a vow.—This case is contrary to one where a man says to a female slave, who has not borne a child to him, "If I purchase you, you shall become free as an expiation for my vow," and he afterwards purchase her; for in this case the slave becomes free, and her freedom suffices for an expiation of his vow, because the slave is not in this instance a claimant of freedom on any other ground, she being emancipated purely, in consequence of the vow, and not of anything else; and the intention of expiation is found associated with the occasion of the manumission;—she is therefore emancipated; and it suffices for an expiation

Case a vow of freedom to a female slave on condition of concubinage.—IF a man say "If I make a concubine of a female slave, she shall be free," and he should afterwards make a concubine of any female slave, his own property, she is free accordingly: because the vow has been taken with respect to that slave, she being the property of the vower.—The principle upon which this proceeds is founded on the grammatical construction of the vower's words in the original Arabic; and it is accounted for thus:—the expression "a female slave," in the case in question, is indefinite, and an indefinite noun is comprehended, in an instance of prohibition, in the way of general individuality;* now here this expression stands in the place of a prohibition, with regard to the design (as the design of the vower is to prohibit himself from concubinage), and such being the case, the expression "a female slave" applies to every slave individually.—If, however, the vower were to purchase a slave, and make her his concubine, she does not become free.—This is contrary to the opinion of Ziffer, for he maintains that she also becomes emancipated; because, as it is not allowed to a man to make a concubine of any woman who is not his property, it follows that the mention of concubinage is equivalent to the mention of a right of property; being the same as if a man were to say to the wife of another, "if I divorce you, my slave is free," which is equivalent to his saying: "if I marry you, and afterwards divorce you,"—and so forth;—because, as divorce cannot take place without property by marriage, the mention of divorce may be said to amount to a mention of marriage:—and so also in the present case.—The arguments of our doctors on this point are, that a vow of manumission is not of any effect, excepting in a case of actual right of property, or where it is referred, either to the right of property itself, or to the cause of the right; and not one of these is found in the present case. There is do actual right of property, evidently; nor is there any reference to the right of property, as the vower did not say, "if I become possessed of a female slave, and make that slave my concubine:" nor is there any reference to a cause of right. as the vower has referred only to concubinage, and that is not a cause of right of property in a slave, because Haneefa and Mohammed define concubinage [Tesirree] to signify merely "a man's keeping his slave up, and providing a dwelling for her, and preventing her from going abroad, and having carnal connexion with her, whether he claim the children born of her or not;" (Aboo Yoosaf holds that the claim of children is also a condition, as a concubine is, in general usage, one whose children are claimed);—and no one of these particulars is a cause of right of property.—Yet a right of property being requisite to concubinage, must, in the present instance, be taken for granted, as an essential, from the necessity of the concubinage (which is the condition) being legal: this right of property (however, is taken for granted only so far as is necessary, and does not appear with respect to the consequence (namely, emancipation), because whatever is established merely from necessity, does not pervade beyond the point of necessity. With respect to the example of divorce, cited by Ziffer, it may be re-

*Her master claiming the child born of her as his own, [See Claim of Offspring.)

*Literally, "in the way of universality of singularity:"—this is a technical phrase, the sense of which is best explained by the context.

plied that the consequence induce (namely, emancipation) is there admitted only on account of the vow being made with respect to actual property (for the vower); and the marriage, which is there taken for granted, as a necessary inference, is so only with respect to the condition (namely, divorce), but not with respect to the consequence; insomuch that if the man were to say to the strange woman, "if I divorce you, you are divorced thrice," and he afterwards marry her, and divorce her, yet three divorces do not take place, as the condition had not been declared either under an actual right of property, or in reference to such right, as to the cause of it:—this case, therefore, is analogous to the case, in question, for this reason, that in both of them the establishment of the condition is merely for the purpose of admitting that, but does not pervade to the admission of the consequence.

A general vow of freedom to slaves includes every description of them.—If a man say, "every person my property is free," his Am-Walid, and Modabbirs, and Abids, all become free accordingly, because the reference to a right of property with respect to them is complete, as all these are the actual property of the swearer: but his Mokatibs do not become free, unless such be the intention, because absolute possession does not apply to a Mokatib, whence it is that his master is not the proprietor of his acquisitions, and also that it is not lawful for a master to have carnal connexion with his Mokatiba: contrary to a Modabbira, or Am-Walid:—reference to a right of property, therefore, with respect to a Mokatib, is incomplete and deficient, for which reason intention is requisite.

Case of a vow of divorce indefinitely expressed.—If a man having three wives, say of them, "this one is divorced, or this, or this," divorce takes place upon the last wife; and it remains in the choice of the husband to declare and specify which one of the other two should become divorced, whether the first, or the second: because the vow, as above expressed, is the same as if he had said, "one of you two is divorced,—and also this one."—The ground of this is found in the grammatical construction of those words in the Arabic.—In the same manner, if a master should say, with respect to three slaves, "this one is free,—or this one,—or this one,"—the last becomes free, and it remains at the option of the master to specify which of the others shall be free, the first or the second.

CHAPTER IX

OF VOWS IN BUYING, SELLING, MARRIAGE, AND SO FORTH.

A vow against the performance of certain acts is not violated by procuring an agent to perform those acts.—If a man make a vow, saying, "I will not sell, or purchase, or hire or let out at rent," and he should afterwards appoint any person his agent, to buy, or sell, or so forth, he is not forsworn; because the agent is the contractor, and not his constituent, insomuch that all the rights of the contract appertain to the agent, not to his constituent (whence, if the vower himself were a party to the contract he would be forsworn); and such being the case, the condition of violation, namely, the contract of the principal, is non-existent, nothing attaching to him, excepting only the effect of the contract, not the contract itself. He is, therefore, not forsworn, excepting where he so intends (as this is injurious to himself), or where the principal is a person of high rank, and consequently is not accustomed himself to make contracts, in which case he would be forsworn by directing another to act for him; because a vow is made for the purpose of restraining from the commission of some customary act; and it is usual for such a person to transact all concerns of purchase or sale by commission; hence where he gives his orders to another respecting such transactions, and the other executes those orders, he is forsworn.

Except in a case of marriage, manumission, or divorce.—If a man make a vow saying, "I will not marry," or "divorce my wife," or "liberate my slave," and he should afterwards commission another person to perform any of these acts for him by a power of agency, and the said agent do so accordingly, the vower is forsworn; because the agent in such concerns acts merely as the negotiator, or in the manner of a messenger, whence it is that he does not refer such acts to himself, but to his employer, to whom the rights thereof appertain, and not to the agent. Here, however, if the vower were to declare that his intention in the vow was restricted to such marriage, divorce, or manumission, as might be executed by himself alone, yet his declaration is not to be credited with the Kazee: but it is credited with God.—The reason of this shall be explained in a subsequent case.

Or any act, the rights of which solely appertain to the vower.—If a man make a vow saying, "I will not beat my slave," or "I will not kill my sheep," and he should afterwards order another to do either of these, and the other act accordingly, the vower is forsworn; because a master has authority to beat his own slave, or to slay his own sheep, and is therefore entitled to authorize another to do so; and the advantage thereof results to him; whence he may be said to be himself the executor of either of these acts, because the rights of them do not in any respect appertain to the person so ordered.—But if the vower should explain that his intention was to restrain himself from the performance of such acts as executed by himself, his declaration is to be admitted by the Kazee: contrary to the preceding case of divorce, &c, where the declaration is not credited by the Kazee. The reason of this difference is that divorce merely signifies a speech which goes to the repudiation of a wife, and a commission to effect divorce resembles such a speech; as the vow therefore extends to both of these, where the vower's intention was that he would not pronounce a divorce himself, he must have intended a particular restraint only, from a thing which was general in its application [his vow], and hence his declaration, although it be admitted with God, is not to be credited by the Kazee, as it contradicts appearances:—but the beating of the slave, or the slaying of the sheep, on the other hand, are perceptible acts, visible in their effects, and are immediately referable to the director of them in the way of an efficient cause (since he is the cause of the beating or slaying) and such being the case, where he intended, by his vow, to restrain himself from the commission of those acts with his own hands, he intended what is the literal meaning of the words of his vow; his declaration, therefore, is credited with God, and with the Kazee also.

Nor by employing another to do thing, where the advantage results solely to the subject of the vow.—If a man make a vow saying, "I will not beat my child," and he should afterwards order another to beat the child, and the other should beat it accordingly, the vower is not forsworn; because the advantage of the beating, namely, instruction, results to the child, and hence the act of the person directed must not be referred to the director. It is otherwise where a person directs another to beat his slave, for there the advantage (namely obedience) results to the director, in consequence of his order, and hence the act of the person directed may be said to be the act of the director.*

A vow of freedom conditioned upon the sale of a slave takes place on the instant of sale, and the sale is null.—If a person make a vow saying, "if I sell this slave he is free," and he afterwards sell that slave under a condition of option,† he [the slave] is free, because the conditions of his freedom (namely, sale and possession) being both accomplished, the consequence, which is emancipation, takes place; and the sale is null.‡ Thus also, if a person, bargaining for a slave make a vow saying, "if I buy this slave he shall be free," and he should afterwards buy that slave under a condition of option, the slave is free: because the condition of his freedom, namely, purchase and possession, are both accomplished.—This, according to the tenets of the two disciples, is evident, because the freedom of the slave is suspended upon the act of purchase, and the condition of option on behalf of the purchaser does not with them prevent the establishment of the purchaser's possession;—and so also, according to the tenets of Haneefa, because the freedom in the case in question is suspended by the suspension of the vower, and a thing suspended becomes the same as a thing prompt, upon the condition being found; and, as if, after purchase, under a condition of option, the buyer were to emancipate his slave promptly, the slave would become free by possession being first established in the purchaser as an essential, so also in the present case.

Divorce suspended upon the not selling of a slave takes place on emancipation or Tadbeer.—If a man make a vow, saying, "if I do not sell this slave (or this bondmaid) my wife is divorced," and he should afterwards emancipate the slave or the bondmaid, or should grant to either a Tadbeer, divorce takes place upon his wife, because the condition, namely, his not selling them, is fully accomplished, as sale cannot now possibly take place, since the slave or bondmaid mentioned, in consequence of the act of manumission or Tadbeer, remain no longer subjects of sale.

A vow of general divorce in reply to a wife charging her husband with bigamy, takes place upon her in the same manner as upon the rest.—If a woman say to her husband, "you have married another woman, in addition to me," and the husband, in reply, make a vow saying, "every wife I have is divorced," a divorce takes place (on the decree of the Kazee) upon the wife who has asserted as above.—This is the Zahir-Rawayet.—It is recorded from Aboo Yoosaf that the wife here mentioned does not become divorced, because the words of the husband, as above recited, are to be considered merely as a reply to the woman, and must be received as such: moreover, the design of the husband in so speaking, may be merely to please and soothe his wife; and as this would be effected by the divorce of his other wives, the divorce is restricted to the other wives only.—The ground upon which the Zahir-Rawayet proceeds is that the husband's expression is general, as he has introduced the word "every" (which argues generality), in addition to the simple reply, whence it appears that his intention is generally, and not speciality: and it follows that the sentence must be received as a speech de novo, and not as a reply.—In reply to the arguments of Aboo Yoosaf, it is to be observed that the words of the husband admit of being construed into a design of terrifying and frightening the woman, on account of her having upbraided him with that which it is

---

* A long case is here omitted, as it is purely of a grammatical nature, turning entirely upon the different effects of the Arabic particle Lam, according to its different position in construction, and consequently does not admit of an intelligible translation.

† That is, upon a condition, if not approved within a trial of three days, of being returned by the purchaser.

‡ Consequently the master has no claim for the price stipulated in the sale.

lawful for him to do: and, under such a construction, the restriction to the other wives is not admissible.—If the husband were to declare that his intention respected only the other wives, he is to be credited with God, but not with the Kazee: because he has intended a particular thing by a general expression, and his words admit of being taken in this sense; but it contradicts appearances; his declaration, therefore, is to be credited in a religious view, but not in point of law.

CHAPTER X.

OUR VOWS RESPECTING PILGRIMAGE, FASTING, AND PRAYER.

Case of a vow of Masha.—If a man make a vow "to perform a Masha [pedestrian pilgrimage] to the temple of God," it is incumbent upon him to perform a pilgrimage to the Kaba on foot,—or that he make the visitation termed Amrit; and if he choose he may ride on his pilgrimage, or Amrit;—but he must in this case perform a sacrifice. This is on a favourable construction of the law. Analogy would suggest that neither pilgrimage nor Amrit are rendered incumbent upon him, he having engaged no farther than to walk to the temple "on foot," which is not incumbent as an act of piety, but is merely an indifferent act; neither is going on foot the original design, that being simply the performance of pilgrimage or Amrit.—The reasons for the more favourable construction here are twofold;—First, Alee has declared that, in a vow of this nature, either pilgrimage or Amrit are incumbent upon the swearer:—Secondly, from the expression aforesaid either pilgrimage or Amrit are universally understood; and hence it is the same as if he had said, "I owe a visitation to the temple on foot;" wherefore it is incumbent upon him to perform his pilgrimage or Amrit on foot, or that, if he choose to perform it on horseback, he also perform a sacrifice.*

Case of a vow of manumission suspended upon the non-performance of pilgrimage.—If a man make a vow saying "if I do not perform a pilgrimage this year, such an one my slave, is free,"—and after the lapse of that year a dispute should arise between the master and the slave,—the slave alleging that the master had not performed the pilgrimage, and the master alleging that he had performed it, and the slave's witnesses bear testimony in this manner,—"that the master had performed, within that year, a sacrifice at Koofa," the slave (according to Haneefa and Aboo Yoosaf) is not emancipated.—Imam Mohammad says that the slave is emancipated, because the witnesses have testified to the master having performed sacrifice at Koofa, which is a well-known act, and which necessarily implies that he has not performed pilgrimage, and hence the condition of the penalty (namely, non-performance of pilgrimage) is fulfilled.

Case of a vow against fasting—If a man make a vow that he will not fast, and he should afterwards intend a fast, and keep the same a short time, and then break his fast within the same day, he is forsworn on account of the condition of violation being fulfilled; because the word Sawm [fast] signifies abstinence from those things the use of which breaks a fast kept with a pious intent, which in this case is evident.

Case of a vow against fasting for a day.—If a man make a vow that "he will not fast a day," and he afterwards intend a fast, and observe the same for a few hours (for instance), and then break his fast, he is not forsworn, because he intended such a fast as is regarded in the law, and that is not completed until it be accomplished by the ending of the day; moreover, the full time of a day is expressly mentioned in his words, "I will not fast a day," and therefore it is to be so understood.

Case of a vow against praying.—If a man make a vow that "he will not pray," and he should after that stand up and perform Kiraat [reading the Koran], or Rookoo] a submissive posture used in prayer], he is not forsworn: but if he perform the Soojda along with those other ceremonies, he is forsworn. This proceeds upon a favourable construction.—The suggestion of analogy is that he would be forsworn in consequence of beginning to pray, from the correspondence of this with a case of fasting; that is, if a man make a vow that "he will not fast," and he should afterwards keep a religious fast, he would be forswon upon the commencement of it; and so also in the present case. The reason of this is that a person, upon beginning to pray, is termed a Moosillee, or praying person, in the same manner as one beginning a religious fast is termed a Sayim, or faster; but the reason for a more favourable construction is that a prayer implies and includes a variety of ceremonies, such as standing, kneeling, and prostration;—and hence, until the whole of these be performed, it is not termed prayer: contrary to fasting, as that consists of only one single observance, namely, abstinence.

If a man vow that "he will not perform prayer according to the ordinance of the law," he will not be forsworn upon praying, until he come to that part of the ceremony which requires the second genuflection; because, by the above mode of expression he appears to mean that kind of prayer which is regarded in the law; and the

---

*Most of the expressions here treated of are to be fully understood only in the original idiom; hence much of the reasoning upon them is lost in a translation. Two other cases are here omitted for the same reason, and also because the rights of individuals are no way concerned in them.

smallest degree which constitutes that is two genuflections, as the Prophet has forbidden short or interrupted prayer.

CHAPTER XI.

OF VOWS RESPECTING CLOTHING AND ORNAMENTS.

Vow of a husband against wearing cloth of his wife's manufacture.—IF a man make a vow, saying to his wife, "if I put on any of your work (that is, cloth made of thread of your spinning), such cloth is Hiddee (that is, an offering at the shrine of the Prophet)," and that man should afterwards buy cotton, and his wife spin it into thread, and of that thread cloth be woven, and the man put on the same, it is incumbent on him (according to Haneefa) to make an offering thereof at Mecca. The two disciples have asserted that it is not incumbent upon the vower, in the case in question, to make an offering of his cloth, unless where the thread has been spun of cotton which was his [the vower's] property at the time of his making the vow; for they contend that a Noozr, or devoting vow, is not valid, unless it respect actual property, or be pronounced in a way which has reference to the cause of a right of property; and neither of these are existent in this case, as the vower putting on the cloth, or the woman spinning the thread of which it is composed, are not causes of a right of property to the vower. The argument of Haneefa is that it is customary for a wife to spin her husband's cotton, and whatever is customary, the same is meant and intended; and the act of the wife, in spinning the cloth, is a cause of the husband's right in it;* here therefore, appears a reference of the Noozr, or devoting vow, to the cause of a right of property, wherefore the vow is valid; and hence the vower is forsworn upon the wife spinning cotton which was his property at the time of the vow.†

IF a man make a vow that "he will not sleep on such a bed," and he should afterwards sleep thereon, it having a sheet, blanket, quilt, or so forth, spread over it, he is forsworn; because such covering is also an appertainence to the bed, and hence sleeping on the covering may be said to be sleeping on such bed. But if another bed be laid upon the bed which is the subject of the vow, and the swearer sleep thereupon, he is forsworn, because a thing cannot be an appertainence to a similar thing, and hence sleeping upon this bed is not to be accounted sleeping upon the other.

IF a person swear that "he will not sit upon the ground," and he should afterwards sit upon a carpet or mat spread thereon, he is not forsworn; because a person in such case is not said to be sitting on the ground. It is otherwise where the skirts of his garment only are between the ground and him, as his garment is merely an appertainence to himself, and hence is not to be considered as the thing upon which he sits.

IF a man vow that "he will not sit upon such a seat," and he should afterwards sit thereupon when there is a covering spread upon it, he is forsworn; because the person who sits upon that covering is considered as the occupier of that seat, in common usage, as this is the usual way of sitting upon a bench, or other raised seat. It is otherwise where the seat which is the subject of the vow has another seat set over it, and the vower sits upon the upper seat, for then he is not forsworn, because the second seat is a fellow to the first, and a thing cannot be an appertainence to a similar thing (as has been already observed); sitting upon the second seat, therefore, is not to be accounted the same as sitting upon the first which was the subject of the vow.

CHAPTER XII.

OF VOWS CONCERNING STRIKING, KILLING, AND SO FORTH

A vow made against striking a person is not violated by striking that person when dead; and the same of a vow against clothing.—IF a person make a vow, saying [to another], "if I strike you, my slave is free," and the vower should strike that man after his death, he is not forsworn; because striking is restricted to life, as being the name of an action which gives pain, and excites the feelings of the person struck, which is not possible with the dead. So also, if a man were to say to another, "if I clothe you, my slave is free," and he should after his death clothe him, he is not forsworn; because by clothing, when it is indefinitely expressed, is meant a complete transfer of property in the article of clothing, and this transfer cannot be made to a defunct; unless when the vower by clothing simply meant covering, in which case he would be forsworn, for here he intends his words in a sense which they are capable of bearing.). Some doctors say that, if a person were to make a vow in the Persian tongue, saying to another, "if I clothe you,

* According to the Mussulman law, any change brought in the descriptive quality of goods (such as turning cotton into thread), causes in itself a transfer of the property from the former proprietor to the person who makes or effects such change in it, independent of any previous contract of purchase, the person to whom such transfer of property is made remaining responsible to the original proprietor for the value of the goods in their former state. (See usurpation of Property.)

† Here follows a long but very frivolous case of vows against wearing Hoolea [superfluous ornaments] omitted in the translation, as it turns entirely upon the acceptation of the term Hoolea, which has been held to consist of different articles at different times.

my slave is free," and he should clothe that person after his death, he is forsworn; because by this, in the vulgar idiom, is meant simply covering.)

Speaking to, going to.—IN the same manner, if a man were to make a vow, saying to another, "if I speak to you," my slave is free," or "if I come to you," and so forth, and he should speak to, or go to, that person after his death, yet he is not forsworn; because the intent of speaking is to impart ideas, which death prevents the possibility of; and "coming to the dead" implies a Zeearit, or visitation, which is not to the dead, but to the shrine or mausoleum of the dead.

Or washing a person.—IF a man make a vow, saying to another, "if I wash you, my slave is free," and he should wash that person after his death, he is forsworn; because to wash simply signifies to ablute with a wish to purification, which takes place in the ablution of the dead.

A vow against beating is violated by any act which causes pain, unless that act be committed in sport.—IF a man make a vow that "he will not beat his wife," and he afterwards pull her hair, or seize her by the throat, or bite her with his teeth, he is forsworn; because beating is the term for an act which causes pain, and pain is excited by the acts in question. Some have asserted that if these acts are done in the course of mutual playing and dalliance, that vower is not forsworn, because under such circumstances these bear the construction of jests, and not of beating.

Vow of slaying a person who is already dead incurs the penalty.—IF a man say, "if I do not slay such an one, my wife is divorced," and the person mentioned be not living, and the vower himself know this, he is forsworn: because he here makes his vow respecting that life with which GOD may inspire the deceased anew; and as this is possible, his vow stands valid: and he is then forsworn, because the slaying of that person is in the common course of things impossible. If, however, the vower be not aware of that person's being already deceased, he is not forsworn, because he has here made his vow respecting that life which he supposes to be existing in such a person, but which, in the common course of things, is no longer conceivable. There is a diversity of opinion between Haneefa and Aboo Yoosaf concerning this case, from the analogy it bears to the case of the vessel of water; that is, if a man were to vow, "if I do not drink out of this cup my wife is divorced," and there should happen to be no water in the cup, he is not forsworn, according to Haneefa and Mohammed, on account of the invalidity of the vow, from the impossibility of fulfilling it: but according to Aboo Yoosaf he is forsworn; because he does not hold the possibility of fulfilment to be a condition of the validity of the vow; and so also in the present case. In the case of the vessel of water, however, there is no distinction made with respect to knowledge; that is the vower (according to Haneefa and Mohammed) is not forsworn, whether he be aware of the cup having no water in it or not; and this is approved. It is otherwise in the case in question, for there a distinction made, as has been already mentioned.

CHAPTER XIII.

OF VOWS RESPECTING THE PAYMENT OF MONEY

Difference, in a vow, between the terms shortly, and in a length of time.—IF a man make a vow, saying, "I will discharge my debt to such an one shortly," this means within less than one month; and if he say, "I will discharge my debt due to such an one in a length of time," this means more than a month; because any space within a month is accounted a short time, and a month or any term beyond it is accounted a long time; and hence it is that where two friends meet after a long separation, one will say to the other "I have not seen you this month!" and so forth.

A vow to discharge a debt is fulfilled by discharging it in light or base money, or in money belonging to another.—IF a man make a vow, saying, "I will discharge my debt, owing to such an one, this day," and he pay the debt upon that day accordingly, and some of the money in which he has paid it should afterwards prove light, or base, or the right of another person, yet the vower is not forsworn; because lightness is only a defect, which does not destroy the specie (whence it is that if one of the parties, in a contract of Sirf sale, should, through negligence, receive base metal in return for pure metal, the exchange is completely fulfilled—and so also, the seller is fully paid his price, in a contract of Sillim sale, where he receives base coin in place of pure coin)—and such being the case, the condition of fulfilment (namely the payment of the debt) is accomplished: the vower, therefore, is not forsworn: the receipt of the money, also, where it is the right of a third person, is valid nevertheless, and the fulfilment thus established is not afterwards affected by the restoration of the same to that third person. (If, however, any of the money, after payment, should appear to be composed of pewter, or tin, the vower is forsworn; because those metals are not regarded as specie, whence, if through negligence they should be accepted in a Sillim or Sirf, contract it is not a lawful payment.)

Or by means of liquidation.—IF, also, the vower should sell his slave to his creditor, within the course of the day, in lieu of the debt, and the creditor accept of the same, the fulfilment of the vow is accomplished; because liquidation is one mode of discharging debts;—that is, the debt due to one party ceases in lieu of the debt due to the other (for the creditor is responsible for whatever he receives, as he received it on its own account by becoming proprietor of it, and thus the same obligation rests upon the creditor in behalf of his debtor as already rests upon the debtor in behalf of the, creditor); a mutual liquidation, therefore, takes place between them, and the debt of each is remitted in lieu of the debt of the other. (This mode of discharging the debt by liquidation is because the actual discharge is inconceivable, as the debtor does not here offer anything but substance, and the right of the creditors is not to substance, but is merely to the debt which has been incurred by the other; and hence the learned in the law say, "a debt must be discharged with its like)." Liquidation, therefor, being one mode of discharging debt, the fulfilment of the vow, in the case in question, is established, because the liquidation is established upon the instant of the sale of the slave.

OBJECTION.—The liquidation being established upon the instant of sale, why is the purchaser's seisin of the slave made a condition?

REPLY.—Seisin is made a condition in order that the debt due to the seller, namely, the price of the slave, may be fully confirmed and established, because although it be incumbent upon the purchaser from the instant of slave, yet it stands within the possibility of ceasing, as it is possible that the article sold may perish before seisin; but by seisin the debt is fully confirmed and established upon the purchaser.

But not by the gift of the creditor.—IF the creditor make a gift of the debt to the debtor within the course of the day, the fulfilment of the vow is not established; because repayment has not taken place; and also, because the discharge of the debt is an act of the debtor alone, and the gift of the debt implies that the creditor relinquishes his right to it, which is an act of the creditor, and not of the debtor, wherefore the condition of fulfilment (namely, the act of the debtor) is not accomplished. It is here to be observed, however, that although the fulfilment be not accomplished, yet the vower is not forsworn, but the vow becomes void: because the vow was restricted to that day, and the creditor having remitted the debt within that day, the swearer is thereby effectually precluded from the fulfilment of his vow before the expiration of its term, which does not take place until the end of the day, whence the vow become void, in the same manner as in the case of the vessel of water.*

A vow not to accept reimbursement of a debt in partial payments is not violated until the whole debt shall have been so received.—IF a debtor were to make an offer, saying to his creditor, "I will discharge my debt to you, by partial payments," and the creditor should reply, with an oath, saying, "I will not thus receive my due by accepting part, and not the whole," and he should afterwards take a part of the debt, yet he is not forsworn so long as he receives not the whole debt thus by partial payments; because here the point which produces a violation of the vow is the receiving the whole debt, but in partial sums, and that has not taken place.—If the debt consists of articles computable by weight, and the vower accept payment by two or more weighings thereof, in such a manner as not to be employed in any other concern between these two weighings, he is not forsworn, although this be a partial mode of receiving payment, because the receipt of the whole at once is sometimes in any common way impossible, and hence any debt of this description is an exception from the present case.

IF a creditor make requisition from his debtor of a part of what is due to him, suppose two hundred Dirms, and the debtor reply that "he has not so much money," and the creditor disbelieves him, and he answer, "if I possess more than one hundred Dirms, my wife is divorced," and it should happen that he is, at the time of saying this, possessed of fifty Dirms only, he is not forsworn; because his design, in this declaration, is merely to express, his denial of being possessed of more than one hundred Dirms; and also, because his exception of one hundred Dirms, involves an exception of every component part or proportion of one hundred; and fifty is one of these proportions; wherefore fifty also are excepted, and hence he is not forsworn, And the rule is the same if instead of "more than one hundred Dirms," he should say, "other than one hundred Dirms," or "beyond one hundred Dirms,"—because all these terms equally express exception.

CHAPTER XIV.

OF MISCELLANEOUS CASES

A vow against doing a thing, unrestrictively pronounced, operates as a perpetual inhibition—IF a man making a vow, saying, "I will not do so and so," it is necessary that he for ever abstain from the commission of that act, because he has expressed the negative of the act generally, and hence the prohibition is general, in consequence of the negative being unrestrictively expressed.

A vow of performance is fulfilled by a single instance of performance.—IF a man, make a vow that "he will do such a thing," and he should once do it, his vow is fulfilled, as he has not undertaken more than the commission of that act in one single instance unspecified, because such is to be understood from the words by which he binds himself, fulfilment is therefore established, upon his once performing a single instance of the act

*See Chap. VI., ante p. 162.

in question, whatever instance that may be, and whether such performance by voluntary or compulsive. In a case of this nature, moreover, the vower is never considered as forsworn, unless where he may be utterly excluded from a possibility of performing the act, which can only be by his death, or by the destruction of the subject of the act.

An oath imposed by a supreme magistrate continues in force only during the existence of that magistrate's authority.—IF a sultan, or other supreme governor, or magistrate of a kingdom or province, should require an oath of a person that "he will inform him of the dwelling of every evil-doer, who shall enter that territory," and the person swear accordingly, such oath binds him to convey such information to the magistrate aforesaid, during the existence of his authority only, and no longer; because the intention of the magistrate, in imposing such an oath, is to repel the wickedness of evil-doers, or to prevent such wickedness in others by the punishment of those evil-doers; conveying this information, therefore, after the expiration of the magistrate's government and authority, is no manner of use; and the expiration of the magistrate's authority takes place either on his death, or his removal from office.

A vow of gift is fulfilled by the offer of the gift, although it be not accepted of.—IF a master make a vow "that he will bestow such a slave upon such a person," and he should bestow that slave accordingly, and the person refuse such gift, yet the vow is fulfilled.—This is contrary to the doctrine of Ziffer, who considers gift to be the same as sale, being equally a transfer of property; and as, if a man swear that "he will sell his slave to such a person," and that person refuse to buy the said slave, the vow remains unfulfilled, so in this case likewise.—The arguments of our doctors on this point are twofold:—FIRST, gift is a voluntary or gratuitous deed, and hence is executed on the part of the giver alone, independent of the receiver: thus we say, "such a person presented so-and-so to such a person," although the other may not have accepted it:—SECONDLY, the design of the swearer, in making such a vow as the above; is to exhibit his own generosity and liberality; and that is effected by means of the deed of gift; but a contract of sale is a mutual engagement, which can be executed only by the act of both the parties concerned in it.

Vows in respect to odoriferous herbs or flowers have force according to the sense in which the denomination of them is generally taken—IF a man make a vow that "he will not smell Reehan," and he should afterwards smell to the rose or the jessamin, he is not forsworn, because Reehan is that species of flowers which have no stalk, and the rose and jessamin have stalks or branches from which they depend.

IF a man were to make a vow, saying, that "he would not purchase violets," and have no particular intention therein, the vow is construed to mean oil of violets, from general custom, according to which, a person dealing in that article is termed a violet-seller; and as purchase is founded upon sale, a person purchasing oil of violets is termed a buyer of violets.—(Some doctors maintain that, with us, by the term violets, is understood the flower only, and not the oil.)—If the vower were to say that "he would not purchase flowers" by this is to be understood the leaves only, and not the oil, as such is the literal meaning of his expression; and custom also accords with this, because by flowers is usually understood the leaves of the flowers. In the case of violets custom has established it otherwise, as the word violets is commonly used to express oil of violets,

END OF THE FIRST VOLUME.

VOL. II.

BOOK VII,

OF HOODOOD, OR PUNISHMENTS.*

Definition of Hidd.—HOODOOD is the plural of Hidd; and Hidd in its primitive sense signifies obstruction; whence a porter or gatekeeper is termed the Hiddad, or obstructor, from his office of prohibiting people from entering. In law it expresses the correction appointed and specified by the law on account of the right of God, and hence the extension of the term Hidd to retaliation is not approved, since retaliation is due as a right of man, and not as a right of GOD; and in the same manner, the extension of it to Tazeer (or discretionary chastisement) is not approved, as Tazeer is a species of correction not specified or determined by any fixed rules of law, but committed to the discretion of the Kazee, The original

* These are here confined solely to whoredom, drunkenness, slander. The punishments for theft, &c., are treated of under their proper heads.

design in the institution of Hidd is determent, that is, warning people from the commission of offensive actions; and the absolution of the person punished is not the original design of it, as is evident from its being awarded to Infidels in the same manner as to Mussulmans.

CHAPTER I.

OF ZINNA, OR WHOREDOM,

Whoredom may be established by proof or by confession.—Whoredom is established before the Kazee, in two different modes—by proof and by confession —by proof, because that is a demonstration founded on the appearance of facts; and by confession, because probability is most in favour of the truth in such acknowledgment, especially where it is to be the occasion of suffering and shame to the person confessing; and whoredom being', an act the nature of which most frequently excludes the possibility of positive proof, it is necessary that circumstantial evidence be admitted as sufficient to establish it, lest the door of correction might be shut.

To establish it upon proof four witnesses are required.—The manner of giving evidence to whoredom is by four persons bearing witness against a man and a woman that they have committed whoredom together, because God has commanded in the Koran, saying, "PRODUCE FOUR WITNESSES FROM AMONG YOU AGAINST THEM;" and also, "IF ANY PERSON ADVANCE A CHARGE OF WHOREDOM AGAINST OTHERS OF CHASTE REPUTE, AND CANNOT PRODUCE FOUR WITNESSES IN SUPPORT OF HIS ACCUSATION, LET HIM BE PUNISHED WITH EIGHTY STRIPES," Moreover, the Prophet once said to a man who brought before him an accusation against his own wife, "Bring four men who may bear testimony to the truth of your allegation;" and this degree of proof is also required, because it is laudable to conceal and cover infirmity, and the contrary is prohibited; and by requiring no fewer than four witnesses to a charge of whoredom both these ends are obtained.

Who must be particularly examined in respect to all the circumstances of the fact.—When witnesses come forward to bear evidence in a case of whoredom, it is necessary that the Kazee examine them particularly concerning the nature of the offence; that is, that he ask of each witness respectively, "What is whoredom?" and "in what manner have the parties committed it?" and "where?" and "at what time?" and "with whom?"—because the Prophet interrogated Maaz as to the manner of the fact, and the nature of the offence: and also, because examination in all these particulars is a necessary caution, since it is possible that the witnesses, by the term Zinna, may mean something not directly amounting to carnal conjunction (such as seeing and touching), Zinna being a phrase occasionally applied to these also. It is possibe, moreover, that the whoredom may have been committed in a foreign country, and therefore that it is not cognizable; or it may have been committed at a distant period, prior to the charge, which is therefore inadmissible; it may happen, too, that the fact may have been committed under an erroneous conception of the parties with respect to its legality, such as would occasion remission of punishment, and such as neither the parties themselves, nor the evidences against them are aware of (as in a case where a man has connexion with the female slave of his son): it is therefore requisite that the judge examine the evidence minutely with respect to all these particulars, since, some circumstance may appear, in the course of such investigation, sufficient to exempt from punishment.

Upon the evidence being duly given, sentence of punishment is passed.—And when the witnesses shall thus have borne testimony completely, declaring that "they have see the parties in the very act of carnal connjunction" (describing the same), and the integrity of such evidence is also known to the Kazee from both an open and a secret purgation, let him then pass sentence of punishment for whoredom, according to such evidence. The apparent probity of the witness does not suffice in the present case, but it is necessary that the magistrate ascertain their probity, both by an open and a secret purgation, in such a manner, that (possibly) some circumstance may appear sufficient to prevent the punishment, because the Prophet has said, "Seek a pretext to prevent punishment according to your ability;" contrary to all other cases, in which the apparent integrity of the witnesses is (according to Haneefa) held sufficient. The mode of open and secret purgation is fully set forth under the head of Evidence.

Mohammed has said, in the Mabsoot, that the Kazee may imprison the accused, until he make a purgation, of the witnesses, because the person against whom the testimony is given stands charged with whoredom upon the evidence of witnesses; and also, because the Prophet once ordered a person charged with whoredom to be imprisoned: contrary to a case of debt, since a debtor

* Meaning either adultery or fornication.

cannot be imprisoned upon a charge of debt exhibited against him by witnesses, until their probity be fully proved. The nature of this distinction shall be treated of at large in another place.

Confession must be repeated four different times.—The confession which establishes whoredom is made by a person of sound mind and mature age acknowledging himself (or herself) guilty of whoredom four times, at four different appearances, in the presence of the Kazee, he [the Kazee] declining to receive the confession, and sending the person away the first second, and third time. The maturity and sanity of the person confessing are conditions, because the declaration of an infant or an idiot is not worthy of any credit, or because the acknowledgment of such is not sufficient to induce a sentence of punishment. The condition of the confession being made four times at four different appearances is agreeable to our doctors According to Shafei, a single confession, in a case of whoredom, is sufficient, because he considers the law to be the same here as in all other cases, the confession or acknowledgment of any circumstance being the means of disclosing or discovering that which is so confessed or acknowledged ; and a single confession is fully adequate to this purpose, a repetition being of no manner of use, since the disclosure or discovery is not in any degree increased or amplified by it : contrary to plurality of witnesses, as the abundance of witnesses is a means of removing all doubt with respect to their veracity, and of affording fuller satisfaction to the mind ; whereas, by the repetition of the declaration of a single person (as in case of confession), no such additional satisfaction is obtained. The arguments of our doctors in opposition to what is here advanced by Shafei are twofold : First, the case of Maaz, on whom the Prophet would not decree any punishment until he should have made confession of his offence four different times at four different appearances, where it is to be concluded that if a single confession had sufficed, and it had been proper to proceed to punishment upon the force of it alone the Prophet would not have delayed to inflict it until the confession should be four times repeated as above ;—Secondly, as in evidence to whoredom four witnesses are requisite, so also in the confession thereof four repititions are requisite, and for the same reason, namely, that it is laudable to conceal infirmity ; and this condition of the repetition of confession has a tendency to conceal infirmity. The reasons for establishing four appearances of the person confessing as a condition are twofold ;—First, the tradition of Maaz, as already related ;—Secondly, a plurality of confessions is made a condition, and that cannot be obtained without a plurality of appearances on the part of the confessor, since one effect of an unity of place or appearance is to render the separate declaration of the same thing as one declaration ; and hence four confessions, in a single appearance,* amount only to a single confession ; and as confession relates only to the person confessing, the unity, or otherwise, of his appearance, is regarded, and not that of the Kazee's assembly ; and this appearance is made four separate times. by the Kazee repelling the person's first confession, and saying, to him, "Thou art mad !" and such other words, the person, upon the Kazee thus repelling his confession, going forth, so as to be out of the Kazee's sight, and returning again, and repeating his confession :—and so on to the fourth time. This is recorded from Aboo Haneefa, on the authority of the conduct of the Prophet in the instance of Maaz, whom he thus sent out of his sight three different times.

The person confessing must be particularly examined.—When confession shall have been made in this manner four different times, the Kazee must then proceed to examine the person so confessing, asking him, "What is whoredom ?"—and "where, and in what manner, and with whom—have you committed this whoredom ?"—All which duly observed, the person confessing becomes then properly obnoxious to punishment, as the proof is complete. The advantages attending the examination of the confessing person have been already explained under the head of witnesses bearing evidence to whoredom ; but it is to be observed that although it be directed there that the Kazee examine the witnesses with respect to the time of the perpetration of the fact, yet it is not requisite to put a similar question to a person who confesses, because that delay which would impeach the credibility of a witness does not in any respect impugn the credibility of a person who makes a voluntary confession : some, however, have said that if the Kazee interrogate such a person with respect to the time of the fact, it is lawful.

* The term Majlis, which for the sake of perspicuity, is in this place translated appearance, literally signifies a seat or place of sitting ; and it may admit of various explanations, according to the circumstance under which it is applied, or the person to whom it relates. When it is mentioned as the Majlis of the Kazee, it means the public assembly or court of that magistrate : when it applies solely to the parties who come to make any declaration before the Kazee, it may be rendered the appearance of that party in court. It also frequently refers to a private company, and sometimes merely to the posture of the party (as in the case of divorce left at the option of the wife). In short, to define the true and precise application of the term Majlis in the present case, regard must be had to the Mussulman usages, it being customary for the Kazee to admit people to deliver the substance of their testimony in a sitting posture, and hence every time the party arises and again resumes his seat may be rendered a new appearance of that party in court.

since it is possible that it may have been committed during infancy.

A person may retract from his confession.—IF the person confessing should deny the fact, and retract from his confession, either before or during the infliction of punishment, his retraction must be credited, and he must forthwith be released.—Shafei and Ibn Lailee have said that retractation after confession is not to be credited, but that the punishment must be inflicted, since as it has been already incurred by the confession, it cannot be done away in consequence of denial; as in a case where whoredom is established against a person upon the testimony of witnesses;—or as in a case of retaliation, or of punishment for slander;—that is to say, when retaliation or punishment for slander are once established upon the confession of the offender, they do not drop in consequence of his subsequent denial of the fact; and so in this case likewise. The argument of our doctors is that denial after confession is an intimation, which (like the confession) may be either false or true; and there is no person to disprove such denial; and hence, from the inconsistency between the confession and the denial, a doubt arises concerning the confession; and punishment drops in consequence of any doubt: contrary to intimations which involve the rights of individuals (such as retaliation, and punishment for slander), as the claimant of the right, in those cases, is the disprover of the person who has confessed, when he afterwards denies, which is not the case in any matter involving merely a right of the law.

IT is laudable in the Kazee, or Imam, before whom confession of whoredom may be made, to instruct the person confessing to deny it, by saying to him, "Perhaps you have only kissed or touched her," because the Prophet spoke so to Maaz;—and Mohammed, in the Mabsoot, adds that the judge may also examine the confessing person with respect to such circumstance as, if made to appear, would tend to his entire exculpation, such as, "whether the fact confessed may not have been committed in marriage," or "under an erroneous misconception of its legality?"

Section.

Of the Manner of Punishment, and the Infliction thereof.

A married person convicted of whoredom is to be stoned.—WHEN a person is fully convicted of whoredom; if he be married, let him undergo the pûnishment of Rajim, that is, lapidation, or stoning to death, because the Prophet condemned Maaz to be thus stoned to death, who was married; and he has also declared, "It is unlawful to spill the blood of a Mussulman, excepting only for three causes, namely, APOSTACY, WHOREDOM after marriage, and MURDER"—and in this all the companions likewise unite.

Mode of executing lapidation.—IT is necessary, when a whoremonger is to be stoned to death, that he should be carried to some barren place, void of houses or cultivation; and it is requisite that the stoning be executed—first by the witnesses, and after them by the Imam or Kazee, and after those by the rest of the by-standers, because it is so recorded from Alee, and also, because in the circumstance of the execution being begun by the witness there is a precaution, since a person may be very bold in delivering his evidence against a criminal, but afterwards, when directed himself to commence the infliction of that punishment which is a consequence of it, may from compunction retract his testimony; thus causing the witnesses to begin the punishment may be a means of entirely preventing it. Shafei has said that the witnesses beginning the punishment is not a requisite, in a case of lapidation any more than in a case of scourging. To this our doctors reply that reasoning upon a case of lapidation from a case of scourging is supposing an analogy between things which are essentially different, because all persons are not acquainted with the proper method of inflicting flagellation, and hence, if a witness thus ignorant were to attempt it, it might prove fatal to the sufferer, and he would die where death is not his due: contrary to a case of lapidation, as that is of a destructive nature, and what every person is equally capable of executing, wherefore if the witnesses shrink back from the commencement of lapidation, the punishment drops, because their reluctance argues their retractation. In the same manner punishment is remitted when the witnesses happen to die or to disappear, as in this case the condition, namely the commencement of it by the witnesses, is defeated. This is when the whoredom is established upon the testimony of witnesses: but when it is established upon the confession of the offender, it is then requisite that the lapidation be executed first by the Imam or the Kazee, and after them by the rest of the multitude, because it is so recorded from Alee; moreover, the Prophet threw a small stone like a bean at Ghamdeea, who had confessed whoredom. What is said on the subject is taken from the Zahir-Rawayet.

THE corpse of a person executed by lapidation for whoredom is entitled to the usual ablutions, and to all other funeral ceremonies, because of the declaration of the Prophet with respect to Maaz, "Do by the body as ye do by those of other believers;"—and also, because the offender thus put to death is slain in vindication of the laws of GOD, wherefore ablution is not refused, as in the case of one put to death by a sentence of retaliation: moreover, the Prophet allowed the prayers for the death to Ghamdeea, after lapidation.

An unmarried free person is to be scourged with one hundred stripes.—IF the person convicted of whoredom be free, but unmarried, the punishment with respect to him is one hundred stripes, according to what is said in the Koran, "THE WHORE AND WHOREMONGER SHALL YE SCOURGE WITH AN HUNDRED STRIPES;"—for although this text be cancelled with respect to married persons, yet in regard to all other than those who are married the law must be executed in conformity to it.

Mode of executing scourging.—OBSERVE that the hundred stripes inflicted by the decree of the magistrate must be administered with a rod which has no knots upon it; and that the stripes must be applied in moderation, that is to say, neither with severity nor yet with too much lenity: because Alee, when he was about to inflict correction, used to smooth off from the rod any knots which might happen to be upon it: and as too much severity on the one hand tends to destruction, on the other hand too much lenity is inadequate to the design of correction. And when punishment is to be inflicted on any person, it is necessary that he be stripped naked; that is to say, that all the clothes be taken off, except the girdle;—because Alee directed so in this matter; and also, because the punishment is in this way administered with the greatest effect: but as the removal of the girdle from the body would expose nakedness, it is therefore to be left.

The stripes must not all be given on one part of the body.—IT is requisite that the hundred stripes be given not all upon the same part or member* of the person upon whom punishment is inflicted, but upon different parts, as it might otherwise be attended with danger to life; and none of the stripes must be inflicted on the face, the head, or the privities, because the Prophet once said to an executioner, "In inflicting the punishment, take care not to strike the FACE, the HEAD, or the PRIVITIES;" and also, because the first of those is the seat of expression and likewise of beauty; and the second is the central seat of the senses; and the third is a part which cannot be wounded without danger to life: and it is to be apprehended that in the first and second instance the appearance and the faculties might sustain material injury, and the injuring of those is a species of destruction to the man; and that in the last life might be endangered: it is unlawful therefore to strike on any of those parts, the design of correction being amendment and not destruction. Aboo Yoosaf has said that one or two strokes may be given on the head as Aboo Bikr once said to an executioner, "Strike on the head, because there the devil resides:" in reply to this, however, we remark that Aboo Bikr gave this direction with respect to an infidel alien, who had been used to seduce believers from the faith, and whose life of course had been forfeited.

*In the original, Azoo, a limb, which would make this species of correction more properly to apply to the bastinado.

Scourging must be inflicted upon a man standing, and upon a woman sitting.—WHEN a man is to be scourged for whoredom he is to receive his punishment in a standing posture, because Alee has said, "Correction is to be inflicted upon men standing, and upon women sitting;" and also, because the proper infliction of punishment depends upon its being open and public, which is best effected by its being received in a standing posture; but yet as a woman is nakedness,* in thus administering the correction to her there might be an apprehension of the exposure of nakedness. It is to be observed that in administering punishment it must not be inflicted in the way of Mid.† Concerning the meaning of the term Mid there are various opinions:—some say that it signifies laying a person on his face upon the ground, and stretching out his limbs;—some, that it signfies the executioner drawing the rod over his own head; others, that it signifies the executioner drawing back the rod, after giving the blow; but the correction must not be inflicted in the way of Mid, according to any of these acceptations, as it is more than what is due.

A slave to receive fifty stripes.—IF the person convicted of whoredom be a slave, male or female, the punishment of such is fifty stripes, because the Almighty has said [in the Koran], speaking of female slaves, "THEY SHALL BE SUBJECT TO HALF THE PUNISHMENT OF FREE MARRIED PEOPLE;"—and the term slave in the text extends to males as well as females. Moreover, as bondage occasions the participation of only half the blessings of life, it also occasions the suffering of only half the punishments, because an offence increases in maganitude in proportion to the magnitude of the blessings under the enjoyment of which it is committed.

A woman is not to be stripped.—THE punishment of whoredom is the same with respect to both sexes, as all the texts which occur in the sacred writings upon this subject extend equally to both; but yet a woman is not to be stripped, neither is her veil to be taken off, but only her robe, or other outward garment, as the removal of any other part of her dress would be offensive to modesty; but as the robe or outward garment would prevent the effect of the correction, and the removal of such is not indecent, she is to be stripped of these.

A WOMAN is to receive her punishment in a sitting posture, according to the direction of Alee before recited, and also, because in this a regard is shown to decency, which it is incumbent to preserve: and for the same reason, where a woman is to be stoned, a hole or excavation should be dug to receive

*"A woman is nakedness;" that is to say, every part of a woman's person is equally indecent to be seen.

† Literally lengthth; it admits of various applications.

her, as deep as her waist, because the Prophet ordered such a hole to be dug for Ghamdeea before mentioned, and Alee also ordered a hole to be dug for Shooraha Hamdeeanee: it is however immaterial whether a hole be dug or not, because the Prophet did not issue any particular ordinance respecting this; and the nakedness of a woman is sufficiently covered by her garments; but yet it is laudable to dig a hole for her, as decency is thus must effectually preserved. There is no manner of necessity to dig a hole for a man, because the Prophet did not do so, in the case of Maaz. And observe it is not lawful to bind a person in order to execute punishment upon him in this case, unless it appear that it cannot otherwise be inflicted.

Slaves cannot be punished for whoredom but by authority.—A MASTER cannot inflict correction upon his male or female slave [for Whoredom] but by permission of the Kazee. Shafei has said that it belongs to a master to inflict correction upon his slave, in this as well as in any other case, because a man's authority over his slaves is general and absolute even preferably to that of the Kazee, as a master is empowered to perform acts with respect to his slaves in which the Kazee is not empowered; this, therefore, is the same as Tazeer, or discretionary correction; that is to say, the master is at liberty to inflict stated punishment for whoredom upon his slaves in the same manner as discretionary correction The arguments of our doctors are twofold:—FIRST, the Prophet has declared that there are four things committed to magistrates, and that one of these is Hidd, or stated punishment, which is here treated of; SECONDLY, Hidd, or stated punishment is a right of GOD, as the design of it is to purify the world from sin; and as it is a right of GOD, hence it cannot be done away by the act of any individual, wherefore this right is to be exacted by the prince, as the deputy of the law, or by the Kazee, as the deputy of the prince: contrary to Tazeer or discretionary correction, because that is a right of the individual, whence it is that infants are subject to Tazeer, although they be not liable to Hidd.

Definition of the state of marriage which subject an adulterer to lapidation.—THE state of marriage necessary to induce lapidation requires that the whoremonger be of sound understanding and mature age, and a Mussulman, free, and who has consummated in a lawful marriage with a woman at a time when she also is sane, free, adult, and a Musslima. This is the definition of Haneefa and Aboo Yoosaf. According to Mohammed and Shafei the state of marriage in question requires simply that the whoremonger be free, and a Mussulman, and one who has consummated in a lawful marriage with a woman of the same description. It is to be considered, however, that sanity of intellect and maturity of age are conditional to the receiving of punishment, since, without these, men are incapable of reading or understanding the ordinances of the law; and the other requisites, besides these two, are made conditions in order that the sin may appear in its greatest magnitude, from the consideration of the magnitude of those blessings under which it is committed, as ingratitude for the blessings of Providence, is greatest, and most atrocious, when those blessings are enjoyed in the highest degree; now the particulars aforesaid, namely, the Mussulman faith, and freedom, and the enjoyment of a woman in a lawful marriage, are among the greatest blessings of life; wherefore lapidation on account of whoredom is ordained in cases where all these circumstances exist; and hence lapidation is enjoined when these conditions exist; contrary to the superiority derived from the other gifts of nature or of fortune, such as family, learning, capacity, beauty, and wealth, which are not conditions, because the law has no regard to those circumstances, and also, because those which have been stated are alone sufficient to constitute the magnitude of the sin of whoredom, so as to subject the offender to lapidation, since, by virtue of freedom, a man is enabled to contract himself in a lawful marriage, and by virtue of a lawful marriage he is enabled lawfully to indulge his carnal appetite, and by such indulgence to allay his passions; and, by virtue of being a Mussulman, he is enabled to marry a Musslima, which fixes and confirms the belief of the prohibition of whoredom to him; all these things, therefore, particularly forbid and inhabit a man from the commission of whoredom; and a sin is great in proportion to the force of the inhibitions under which it is committed. The sect of Shafei differ from our doctors with respect to that part of the proposition which asserts that the profession of the Mussulman faith is a requisite condition; and there is also a record from Aboo Yoosaf to the same effect. Their argument is, that in the time of the Prophet a Jew committed whoredom with a Jewess, and the Prophet ordered them both to be stoned; but to this our doctors reply that the Prophet passed that sentence in conformity to the Tawreet, or Jewish law, which has since been superseded by the Mussulman law; and the declaration of the Prophet, "Whosoever is not a true believer shall not be regarded as married" * is a confirmation of this The consummation now mentioned as a condition is understood in the conjunction having taken place so far as to require the prescribed ablutions; and as it is a condition essential to such marriage as induces lapidation, that the woman, at the time of consummation, be of the same description with the man, in the points of sanity, maturity, freedom, and profession of the faith, it follows that if a man were to consummate with a wife who is an idiot, an infant, a slave, or

*Arab Mahsan; that is, married, under the circumstances requisite to induce lapidation

an infidel, he is not considered as married in this sense,' since, on account of these circumstances, the advantages of the matrimonial enjoyment are incomplete, because a man has a natural aversion to consummate with a lunatic woman: and he can have but little gratification with one under age, where desire is not reciprocal; and, in the same manner, he has not a strong desire to consummate with a slave, as in that case his children are slave-born; and so also the enjoyment of a wife who is an infidel affords the less satisfaction, because of the difference of religious principles. In all these cases, therefore, the advantage of the carnal enjoyment is defective, whence the husband of such woman does not, by consummation, become a Mahsan, or married man, in that sense which induces lapidation And the rule is the same where the husband is an idiot an infant, a slave, or an infidel, and his wife sane, adult, and a Musslima. Aboo Yoosaf has said that where the wife is an infidel, her husband, being a Mussulman by consummating his marriage with her, becomes as a married man: but, in reply to this, besides what has been above advanced, it is to be remarked that the Prophet has declared, "A MUSSULMAN is not rendered a married man by connexion with a CHRISTIAN, nor is a FREEMAN rendered married by connexion with a wife who is a SLAVE: nor a SLAVE by connexion with a wife who is FREE."

Stoning and scourging cannot be united.—IT is not lawful to unite the punishments of stoning and scourging in the same person, because the Prophet has left no precedent of this kind; and also, because if they were to be united, the scourging would be useless, since the design of correction is a warning from vice, and this warning is effected by lapidation in respect only to others than the person so punished; for a warning cannot be effected, with respect to the person punished, after his destruction.

Nor (with respect to a woman) scourging and banishment.—IF a woman guilty of whoredom be of mature age, in her punishment scourging and banishment cannot be united. According to Shafei, these two may be united with respect to her by way of punishment,—that is, banishment may also be included in her punishment,—because the Prophet has declared, "If a man, being unmarried, commit whoredom with a woman who is of age, the punishment of such is one hundred stripes; and he shall be excluded from the city for the space of one year, as by his banishment the door is shut against whoredom, because in an unsettled situation a man meets with few female companions to tempt him to commit it" The arguments of our doctors are twofold;—FIRST, GOD has declared, "THE WHORE AND THE WHOREMONGER SHALL YE SCOURGE WITH AN HUNDRED STRIPES." from which it is evident that the sole punishment of such is one hundred stripes, for if it were more it would be there mentioned, and one hundred stripes alone would not have been declared sufficient; SECONDLY, her banishment is opening the way to the further commission of her crime, because people are under less restraint when removed from the eye of their friends and relations, as those are the persons whose censures they are most in dread of; moreover, in an unsettled situation, and among strangers, the necessaries of life are with difficulty procured, whence she might be induced voluntarily to prostitute herself for a supply, which of all kinds of whoredom is the most abominable; and the saying of Alee, that "Banishment is a means of reduction," is founded on this second season. As to the saying of the Prophet quoted by Shafei, it is superseded, as well as the remainder of that saying, "if a SIYEEB (meaning a man who has consummated a marriage) afterwards commit adultery with a SIYEEBA, their punishment is one hundred stripes and lapidation." The way in which this is superseded is explained in its proper place, In short, banishment with respect to a loose woman, in the way of punishment, is not lawful; but yet if the magistrate should find it advisable, he may banish her for the space of one year, or less, but this banishment is in the way of Tazeer, or discretionary correction, as banishment may in some cases operate as a warning, wherefore it is committed to the Kazee or the Imam; and what is recorded concerning the companions, of their having banished people, is to be regarded in the way of Tazeer.

The execution of stoning is not suspended on account of sickness.—IF a sick person, being one whose proper punishment is lapidation, commit whoredom, he is to be stoned because his destruction is due, and is therefore not to be suspended on account of his illness: but if he be one whose punishment is scourging, the execution of it must be deferred until his recovery, lest life should be endangered, for the same reason as the limb of a sick thief is not cut off until he be in a proper habit of body to endure the amputation without risk of life.

But it is so on account of pregnancy.—IF a pregnant woman commit whoredom, and her punishment be lapidation, the execution must be delayed until her delivery, for if she were to be stoned whilst pregnant, the child would be destroyed in her womb, and its blood is not to be taken; and if her punishment be scourging, the execution must be deferred until she shall have recovered from her labour, as that is a species of sickness, wherefore a delay must be made until her health be perfectly restored; contrary to a case of stoning; where the punishment need not be delayed until a perfect recovery, since the delay in this case is only with a view to the preservation of the child in her womb, which is separated from her upon the instance of its birth. It is recorded from Haneefa that in stoning also the execution must be delayed until the child become independent of her care, in case there should be no other person to foster it in her stead; because by this delay the child is preserved from destruction; and it is moreover related that when Ghamdeea, after her delivery, came before the Prophet, that he might execute punishment upon her, he said to her, "Go and remain until such time as your child is independent of you.

A pregnant woman, convicted upon evidence, must be imprisoned.—AND OBSERVE —If a pregnant woman be convicted of whoredom upon evidence she must be confined in prison until she be delivered, lest she should abscond: contrary to a case where a pregnant woman is convicted upon her own confession: for in this case she is not to be confined, as her denial after confession must be credited (for which reason punishment is remitted in case of her denial), wherefore to imprison her would be useless.

CHAPTER II.

OF THE CARNAL CONJUNCTION WHICH OCCASIONS PUNISHMENT, AND OF THAT WHICH DOES NOT OCCASION IT.

Definition of the term Zinna.—THE carnal conjunction which occasion punishment is Zinna, or whoredom; and this, both in its primitive sense, and also in its legal acceptation, signifies the carnal conjunction of a man with a woman who is not his property either by right of marriage or of bondage, and in whom he has no erroneous property, because Zinna is the denomination of an unlawful conjunction of the sexes, and this illegality is universally understood where such conjunction takes place devoid of property, either actual or erroneously supposed. What is here said is the definition of whoredom with respect to a man:—as to the whoredom of a woman, it simply signifies her admitting the man to commit the fact.

Definition of erroneous carnal conjunction.—ERROR in carnal conjunction is of two kinds.—the first, error in respect to the act, which is termed Shoobha-Ishtibah, or error of misconception: the second, error in respect to the subject, which is termed Shoobha-Hookmee [error by effect].—or Shaba-Milk [erroneous property].—The first of these distinctions of error is not established, nor understood, but with respect to a man who mistakes an illegal carnal conjunction for legal, because Ishtibah signifies the man having carnal intercourse with a woman, under the supposition of the same being lawful to him; in consequence of his supposing something other than that which is necessary to constitute legality as affording an argument of such legality; it is therefore necessary that this mistake should have operated in his mind in order to establish Ishtibah, or misconception; and hence this species of error is not understood, except in the case of a person who is under such misapprehension.—The second species of error is established, where the argument of the legality of carnal conjunction exists in itself, but yet practice cannot take place upon it. because of some obstacle; and this does not depend upon the apprehension or belief of the person who commits the unlawful act: whence this species of error is regarded in respect to all men, that is to say, men who so conceive, and also those who do not.—And punishment drops in consequence of the existence of either of these two species of error, on account of a well-known tradition.

Parentage is established in a case of error with respect to the subject, but not in a case of error with respect to the act.—IN a case of error of the second species, the parentage of the child is established in the man who has had such connexion, if he claim such child; but in a case of error of the first species the parentage of the child is not to be established in the man, notwithstanding his claim,—because, in a case where the error is of the first species, the act of generation is positive wheredom, although punishment be not incurred, on account of a circumstance which has reference to the man committing such act (namely, that of the illegality of the act being misconceived by him, according to his apprehension of it): but the act of generation, in a case of error of the second species, is not positive whoredom.

ERROR in respect to the act exists in eight several situations; namely, with—

I.—The female slave of a man's mother.
II.—The female slave of his father.
III.—The female slave of his wife.
IV.—A wife repudiated by three divorces, who is in her Edit.
V.—A wife completely divorced for a compensation and is in her Edit.
VI.—An Am-Walid, who is in her Edit after emancipation with respect to her master.
VII.—The female slave of a master, with respect to his male slave.
VIII.—A female slave, delivered as a pledge, with respect to the receiver of such pledge (according to the Rawayet-Saheeh in treating of punishment);—and it is to be observed, that a borrower, in this point, stand in the same, predicament with the receiver of a pledge.

And there is no punishment in either case.—AND in all those situations the person who has carnal conjunction does not incur punishment, provided he declare—"I conceived that this woman was lawful to me;"—but if he should acknowledge his consciouness that the woman was unlawful to him, he incur punishments.

ERROR in respect to the subject exists in six situations namely, with—

I.—The female slave of a man's son.
II.—A wife completely repudiated by an implied divorce.
III.—A female slave sold, with respect to the seller, before the delivery of her to the purchaser.
IV.—A female slave Mamhoora—(that is, a slave stipulated to be given in dower to a wife)—with respect to the husband, before seisin of her being made by the wife.
V.—A female slave held in partnership, with respect to any of the partners.
VI.—A female slave delivered in pledge, with respect to the receiver of such pledge, according to the Book of Pawnage.

And in all those situations a person who has carnal connexion does not incur punishment, even though he should confess his consciousness of such woman being unlawful to him.

A contract of marriage prevents punishment, although avowedly illegal.—ACCORDING to Haneefa, a contract of marriage is a sufficient ground of error, although the illegality of such marriage be universally allowed, and the man entering into such contract be sensible of this illegality. With our other doctors, on the contrary, a contract of marriage is not admitted as a legal ground of error, if the man be sensible of the illegality. —The effect of this difference of opinion appears in a case where a man marries a woman related to him within the prohibite degrees, as shall be hereafter explained.

Connexion with a wife thrice divorced (before the expiration of her Edit), occasions punishment.—IF a man pronounce three divorces upon his wife, and afterwards have carnal connexion with her during her Edit, and acknowledge his consciousness of her being unlawful to him, punishment is incurred, because here possession by marriage, which legalizes generation, has been totally annihilated, and hence there can be no error, as the text in the Koran shows that legality is destroyed in this case; and all the doctors coincide in this opinion. But if he were to declare that "he conceived, or supposed, she was still lawful to him," punishment is not incurred, because his apprehension is to be regarded, since the effects of marriage still remain, with respect to the establishment of the parentage of children, and the matrimonial restraint, and alimony (for if the woman should bear a child, at any period within two years from the date of divorce, the parentage of such child is established in the husband; and she remains under the restraint to which she is subject in marriage, and her alimony also remains incumbent upon her husband); his apprehension, as above pleaded, is therefore of force to prevent punishment, on account of error by misconception. And an Am-Walid, after manumission, and a woman in a state of repudiation by Khoola, or one divorced for a compensation (who are in their Edit), stand in the same predicament with a woman repudiated by three divorces, as their illegality is universally admitted, and certain effects of marriage continue during their Edit, as well as in a case of a wife under three divorces.

Connexion with a wife divorced by implication does not induce punishment.—IF a man divorce his wife by implification, saying, "You are divested," or "you are at your own disposal," and she choose divorce—and he afterwards have carnal knowledge of her within the term of her Edit, and should acknowledge that he knows her to be unlawful to him, yet punishment is not incurred; because concerning this case there is a difference among the companions; for Omar holds that the forms above mentioned are effective of only a single divorce reversible: and the same in all expressions of divorce by implication; he also holds the rule to be the same, where the husband intends three divorces, as he maintains that here likewise a single divorce reversible only takes place, and that the intention of three divorces is not regarded.

Nor that with the female slave of a son or a grandson.—PUNISHMENT is not incurred by a man having carnal connexion with the female slave of his son, or of his grandson, although he should acknowledge his consciousness of such female slave being unlawful to him, for in this case the error is by effect, since it proceeds from an argument founded upon the words of the Prophet, who said to one with whom he was conversing, 'THOU and THINE are thy FATHER'S;"— and the grandfather is subject to the same rule with the father, as he is also a parent. The parentage also of the child begotten in such carnal conjunction is established in the father aforesaid, who remains responsible to his son for the value of the female slave.

Or of a father, mother, or wife (where misconception is pleaded.)—IF a person have carnal connexion with the female slave of his father, or his mother, or his wife, and plead his conception that such slave was lawful to him, he does not incur punishment; neither is his accuser liable to punishment—(but if he should acknowledge his consciousness of the illegality, punishment is to be inflicted upon him,—and the same rule obtains where a slave has connexion with the bondmaid of his master):—because between these there is a community of interests in the acquisition of profit; and hence the man who commits the act may in those cases have conceived, with respect to the enjoyment, that this species of usufruct is also lawful to him,— wherefore error by misconception is applicable to him; but nevertheless this is actual whoredom, for which reason punishment is not incurred by the accuser. The law is the same (according to the Zahir Rawayet), if the female slave, in either of these cases, were to plead her supposing that the act was lawful, without any such plea on the part of the man,—because the carnal conjunction of a man and a woman being one act, it follows that a plea of supposed legality, made by either party, establishes error with respect to both, and hence the punishment of both is abrogated.

Punishment is incurred by connexion with the slave of a brother.—IF a man have carnal connexion with the bondmaid of his brother or of his uncle, he incurs punishment, although he should plead that he had conceived her to be lawful to him, because between such relations no community of interest exists. And the law is the same with respect to the female slaves of all other relations within the prohibited degrees excepting those who are related to the man within the parental degree (such as his father or his son), because between him and those prohibited relations no community of interest exists.

Connexion with a woman married by mistake does not occasion punishment.—IF a man engage in a contract of marriage with a woman, and another woman be sent to him,* the female relations declaring her to be the woman married to him by such contract, and he have carnal communication with that woman, he does not incur any punishment; but yet he must pay the woman her dower, because Alee once passed a decree to this effect;—and he also subjoined, in his decree that the woman should observe an Edit:—moreover the man has proceeded upon apparent proof namely, the information of the woman's female relations, with respect to the subject of his error, since men can have no personal knowledge of or acquaintance with their wives prior to the matrimonial engagement; and hence the man in this case is the same as a person acting under a deception. And the accuser of this person does not incur the punishment of slander, because possession by marriage, requisite to legalize generation, is in no respect established. There is an opinion recorded by Aboo Yoosaf; that the accuser is liable to punishment; because the carnal conjunction is to all appearance legal, with respect to the man, according to the information of the woman's female relations, and of course his accuser becomes liable to punishment, as a decree must be founded upon what is apparent

IF a man have carnal connexion with a woman whom he finds in his own bed, punishment is incurred by him, because there can be no error where he passes any length of time in the company of his wife, and thence his apprehension of this woman being his wife, from the circumstance of his finding her in bed, is not regarded, so as to prevent punishment:—the reason of this is that sometimes a relation of the wife, residing in the house with her, may sleep upon her bed. And the law is the same where the man is blind, because it is always in his power to ask and discover this by the sound of her voice. But yet if he invite the woman to the act, and she consent, signifying that "she is his wife,"—and he copulate with her, in this case he does not incur punishment, as he is deceived by the woman's declaration and behaviour.

Connexion with a woman under an unlawful marriage does not induce punishment.—IF a man marry a woman whom it is not lawful for him to marry, and afterwards have carnal connexion with her, he does not incur punishment, according to Haneefa; but if he be at the time aware of illegality, he is to be corrected by a Tazeer, or discretionary correction. The two disciples and Shafei have said that he is liable to punishment, when he marries the woman, being aware of the illegality: because, as the contract has not been executed in regard to its proper subject, it is of course void; for here the woman is not a proper subject of marriage, because the proper subject of marriage; or of any other deed, is a thing which is a proper subject of the effects of such deed: now one of the effects of marriage is the legalizing of generation; but as the woman is among those who are prohibited to the man, the contract of marrige with her is consequently nugatory, in the same manner as a contract of marriage between man and man. The argument of Haneefa is that the contract has taken place in regard to its proper subject as the woman is a proper subject of marriage, because the proper subject of any deed is a thing which admits of the ends intended being obtained from it; now the end of marriage is the procreation of children, and to this every daughter of Adam is competent; the case therefore admits of the contract being engaged in with respect to all its effects, and of all its effects being obtained from it; but on account of the prohibition in the sacred text, the legalization of generation is not obtained; and such being the case error is occasioned, as error is a thing which is the appearance of a proof, and not the substance of one; and as, in the present case, the man has perpetrated an offence for which the stated punishment, or Hidd, is not appointed, Tazeer, or discretionary correction, must be inflicted.

Acts of lasciviousness are to be corrected by Tazeer.—IF a man commit any act of lasciviousness with a strange woman, such as Takhfeez,* he is to be corrected by Tazeer, since such acts are illegal and forbidden by

* It is almost unnecessary to remark that, from the nature of the Mussulman customs, a man can never be supposed to have seen his wife until after marriage,—the woman being utterly excluded from the sight of all men except her relations within the prohibited degrees.

* Penem fricens inter femora.

the word of GOD; but a stated punishment is not appointed for them; Tazeer must therefore be inflicted upon that person.

And so likewise sodomy, committed with a strange woman.—IF a man copulate with a strange woman in ano—(that is, commit the act of sodomy with her), there is no stated punishment for him, according to Haneefa; but he is to be corrected by Tazeer. The Jama Sagheer directs an aggravation of the Tazeer or correction in this case, and says that the offender must be kept in a place of confinement until he declare his repentance. The two disciples have said that as this act resembles whoredom, the person committing it is subject to the stated punishment for whoredom; and there is one opinion of Shafei to his effect: but another opinion of his is that the parties should be put to death, of whatever description they may be—that is, whether they be married or not—because the Prophet has said. "Slay both the ACTIVE and the PASSIVE" (or, according to another tradition, "Stone both the AGENT and the SUBJECT)"—The argument of the two disciples is that the act in question has the property of whoredom, as that is defined to be "an act of lust committed in that which is the subject of the passion, completely and under such circumstances as to be purely unlawful, and where the design is the injection of Semen." Haneefa, on the other hand, argues that his conjunction is not actual whoredom, because the companions of the Prophet have disagreed concerning their decrees upon it, for some of them have said that offenders of this kind should be burnt, some that they should be buried alive, others, that they should be cast headlong from some high place, such as the top of a house, and then be stoned to death—and so forth; moreover, the conjunction in question has not the property of whoredom, as it is not the means of producing, offspring so as (like whoredom) to occasion any default in birth or confusion in genealogy;—besides, this species of carnal intercourse is of less frequent occurrence than whoredom, because the deire for it exists only on the part of the active and not of the passive, whereas in whoredom the desire exists equally on both sides. As to the tradition cited by Shafei, it probably relates to a case where an extraordinary and exemplary punishment is requisite; or where the perpetrator inculcates and insists upon the lawfulness of the act.

And bestiality.—IF a man commit bestiality he does not incur Hidd or stated punishment, as this act has not the properties of whoredom, for whoredom is a heinous offence, as being a complete act of lust, to which men feel a natural propensity; but this definition does not apply to copulation with beasts, which is abhorred by an undepraved mind (whence it is not held incumbent to cover or conceal the genitals of brutes); and men can have no reason for desiring carnal connexion with brutes, but from the most vitiated appetite, and the utmost depravity of sentiment:—Hidd therefore is not incurred by this person; but he is to be punished by a discretionary correction, for the reasons already specified. It is recorded, also, that the beast should be slain and burnt: this, however, is only where the animal is not of an eatable species; but if it be of the eatable species, it is to be eaten (according to Aboo Haneefa), and not burnt. Aboo Yoosaf holds that it should be consumed with fire in both cases, the prepetrater (where it belongs to another person) remaining responsible to the owner for the value; but yet the burning of it is not absolutely incumbent: nor is it to be burnt for any other reason than as, by this means, all recollection of so vile a fact may be obliterated, and the perpetrator shielded from the disgrace which would attach to him in case of the animal remaining alive.

Punishment is not incurred by committing whoredom in a foregin county.—IF a Mussulman be guilty of whoredom in a foreign country, or in the territory of the rebels, and afterwards return into a Mussulman state, punishment is not to be inflicted upon him, on the plea that a man, in embracing the Mussulman faith, binds himself to all the obligations therof, wherever he may be, The arguments of our doctors on this occasion are twofold;—FIRST, the Prophet has said, "punishment is not to be inflicted in a foreign land;"—SECONDLY, the design of the institution of punishment is that it may operate as a prevention or warning; now the Mussulman magistrate has no authority in a foreign country, wherefore if punishment were instituted upon a person committing whoredom in a foreign country, yet the institution would be useless: for the use of the institution is that punishment may be executed; and as the magistrate has no authority in a foreign country, the execution is impossible; whence it appears that the commission of whoredom in a foreign country does not occasion punishment there: and if this person should afterwards come from the foreign territory into a Mussulman state, punishment cannot be executed upon him; because as his whoredom did not occasion punishment at the time of its being committed, it will not afterwards occasion.

Punishment may be inflicted by the chief magistrate within his camp.—THE person to whom the authority of inflicting punishment officially appertains (such as the Khalif, for the time being or the governor of Egypt), when he carries forth his troops upon an expedition, is at liberty to inflict punishment upon any person who may be guilty of whoredom within his camp, since the prepetrator of the offence is under his immediate authority; but chief or commanders of an inferior degree are not at liberty to inflict punishment upon a persons guilty of whordom within their camp, because they are not invested with authority to inflict punishment.*

Case of whoredom committed between infidel subjects and aliens.—IF an alien come into a Mussulman state under a protection, and there commit whoredom with a Zimmeea, or female infidel subject; or if a Zimmee, or male infidel subject, so commit whoredom with a female alien, punishment is to be inflicted upon the infidel subject (according to Haneefa), but not upon the alien. This also is the opinion of Mohammed with respect to an infidel subject, where he is guilty of whoredom with a female alien; but if an alien be guilty of whoredom with a female infidel subject, in this case he holds that there is no punishment for either party. There is also an opinion recorded from Aboo Yoosaf to this effect: but he afterwards delivered another opinion, that punishment is incurred by all the parties concerned, both by the alien and the female infidel subject, and also by the male infidel subject, and the female alien, for he argues that an alien under protection, during the time that he continues in a Mussulman territory, subjects himself to all the ordinances of the temporal law, in the same manner as an infidel subject does for life, whence it is that punishment for slander may be inflicted on an alien under protection, and that he may also be put to death in retaliation: contrary to punishment for drinking wine, as in his belief the use of wine is allowable. The argument of Haneefa, and Mohammed is that a protected alien does not come into a Mussulman state as a resident, but is only brought there occasionally, for some particular motive, such as commerce, and the like, and therefore is not to be considered as one of the inhabitants of a Mussulman country (whence it is that he is at liberty to return into the foreign country, and also that if a Mussulman or an infidel subject were to murder a protected alien, no retaliation would be exacted of them); now a protected alien subject himself to such of the ordinances of the law only as he himself derives an advantage from; and those are all such as respect the rights of individuals; for where he is desirous of obtaining justice for himself from others, he also subjects himself to justice being exacted on him in behalf of others; and retaliation† and punishment for slander are among the rights of individuals, but punishment for whoredom is a right of the law. The argument of Mohammed is that in whoredom the man is the principal, and the woman only the accessary, according to what was before stated: now the prevention of punishment in respect to the principal occasions the prevention of it in respect to the accessary, but the prevention of punishment with respect to the accessary does not occasion the prevention of it with respect to the principal; as in a case, therefore, where a protected alien commits whoredom with a female infidel subject, there is no punishment for the alien, so neither is there any for the infidel subject: but where an infidel subject commits whoredom with a female protected alien, punishment is to be inflicted on the subject, but not upon the alien; and the remission of punishment in respect to the alien does not occasion its remission with respect to the infidel subject, because the woman is only an accessary. Correspondent to this is the case of a man committing whoredom with a girl who is an infant, or with a woman who is insane, where punishment is inflicted upon the man, but not upon the infant or the lunatic; whereas, if a woman admit a boy or an idiot to commit whoredom with her, neither of the parties is liable to punishment. The argument of Haneefa is that the act of the protected alien is whoredom, because he is equally with Mussulmans called to the observance of certain commands and prohibitions, on account of the torments and chastisements of a future state (according to the Moozhab-Saheeh), although he be not called to the religious observances of the LAW: but the woman's admitting him to commit the fact is the occasion of punishment to her; contrary to the case of the boy or the idiot, for they are not called, nor under any constraint. A difference similar to this obtains in the case of a man, who being possessed, or under the influence of magic, commits adultery with a woman not under such influence; that is to say, according to Haneefa, punishment is inflicted: but according to Mohammed it is not inflicted on either of the parties.

Whoredom committed by an infant or an idiot does not induce punishment.—IF a boy or an idiot commit whoredom with a woman who is of mature age and sound judgment she consenting thereto, in this case there is no punishment, neither to the boy, to the idiot, nor the woman. Ziffer and Shafei maintain that in this case the woman incurs punishment; and there is also one tradition of Aboo Yoosaf to the same effect. But if a man who is of mature age and sound judgment commit whoredom with a girl who is a idiot or an infant, capable of copulation, in such case punishment is incurred by the man alone, according to all the doctors. The argument of Ziffer is that a plea on the part of the woman does not occasion the remission of punishment with respect to the man: and in the same manner, a plea on

*Meaning Hidd, which being a right of the law, is a thing of too much importance to be committed to inferior persons: but every person who acts as a commander or magistrate is entitled to inflict Tazeer, or discretionary correction.

† This is an apparent contradiction, as it is said above that there is no retaliation for the murder of an alien: it is to be considered, however, that although a Mussulman, or an infidel subject, be not liable to retaliation for the murder of an alien, yet the alien would be so for the murder of a Mussulman, or an infidel subject.

the part of the man does not occasion punishment to be remitted with respect to the woman; because each party is responsible only for their own act. The argument of our doctors is that the act of whoredom proceeds from the man, the woman being no more than merely the subject of it, and hence it is that the man is denominated by the active term in copulation or whoredom and the woman by the passive.*

Objection – The woman is also termed Zaneea,† as appears in the Koran

Reply —The woman is termed Zaneea by a metonymical figure, which sometimes uses the active participle for the passive; or it may on this occasion be employed because the woman is the primary cause of the act of whoredom, by her admitting the man to the commission of it. Punishment, with respect to a woman, therefore, depends upon the circumstance of her admitting a man to commit the act of whoredom with her; but the act of a boy is not whoredom, as whoredom is an act proceeding from a person who has been called upon to refrain from it, and the perpetrator of which is an offender, by his commission of it; and as the act of a boy is not of this nature, it follows that punishment is not incurred by his act.

Whoredom committed upon compulsion does not subject to punishment —If a sovereign prince should compel a man to commit whoredom, there is no punishment incurred by that man. Aboo Haneefa had held a prior opinion, that the man is liable to punishment (and such is the doctrine of Ziffer)—because a man cannot commit the act of whoredom unless the virile member be properly distended, which distension is a token of desire on his part: compulsion, therefore, cannot be proved with respect to him. The reason for the more recent opinion is that the means of compulsion (namely, the power of the sovereign), exists both actually and apparently; and the distension of the virile member is no certain proof of desire, since it sometimes occurs independent of any operation of the mind, as in sleep, for instance; this circumstance, therefore, is of no weight in competition with a fact which admits of actual proof, namely, the compulsion. But if any other person than the sovereign should compel a man to commit whoredom, the man thereby incurs punishment according to Haneefa. The two disciples have said that no punishment is incurred in this case, because the compulsion, which is the obstruction to the punishment in the former cases may also proceed from others than the sovereign: but Haneefa argues that this species of compulsion cannot be supposed to proceed from any except the sovereign; because no other person is possessed of the means of such compulsion since the sovereign is enabled to repel it in all inferior persons, as the sovereign authority is instituted by the law for the purpose of repelling tyranny: and also, because all others stand in awe of the sovereign, and hence no such compulsion can proceed from them. It is to be remarked that the learned in the law impute this difference of opinion between Haneefa and the two disciples to the difference of the times in which they lived; for in the time of Haneefa others than the sovereign were not possessed of any power which it was not in the sovereign's power to repel; but in the time of the two disciples every petty ruler possessed a power independent of the sovereign, and hence the compulsion of others than the sovereign afforded (in those times) a ground of doubt sufficient to prevent punishment.

Case of one of the parties confessing whoredom, and the other pleading marriage.—If a man make a confession four times, at four different appearances before the Kazee, "that he has committed whoredom with such a woman," and the woman should thereupon declare, "that he had married her,"—or, if a woman should thus make confession that "such a man had committed whoredom with her," and the man should plead that "he had been already married to her,"—in this case no punishment falls upon either party, because the plea of marriage is possibly true, and therefore occasions a demur; but the man owes the woman a dower, since the enjoyment of the woman's person cannot be admitted gratuitously, as a woman's person is an object of respect

Case of whoredom with the female slave of another, who dies in consequence.—If a man commit whoredom with the female slave of another, to such a degree as that the said female slave dies, the man incurs two penalties,—one, the punishment of whoredom, and the other, the payment of the value of such slave to her owner,—because he has here committed two offences, whoredom and murder, and hence the law is to be carried into execution with respect to both. It is recorded from Aboo Yoosaf that punishment is not incurred by the man, because the obligation of responsibility, which lies upon him, is a cause of his property in the slave; and the occurrence of a cause of property, before punishment has taken place, prevents the infliction of it (as where a thief, for instance, purchases the property stolen of the proprietor before his hand is struck off), and is the same as if a man were first to commit whoredom with a female slave, and then to purchase her of her master, in which case he incurs punishment, according to Haneefa, but not according to Aboo Yoosaf, and so in this case likewise. Haneefa and

* [In the original] "The man is denominated the Watee, or Zanee, and the woman tho Mowtooa, or Moozneea." The two first are the active participles meaning the copulator, and the whoremonger; the two second are these terms expressed in the feminine participle passive. It is not easy to convey the full force and meaning of such passages in any translation.

† The fem. act. part. from Zinna.

Mohammed say that the responsibility, in this case, is a responsibility for murder (in the manner of the Deeyat, or fine of blood), which does not occasion a right of property [over the slain].

Or who goes blind.—If a man commit whoredom with the female slave of another, to such a degree that she loses her sight, he owes the price of the said slave to her owner and punishment drops, because the slave, by the man being thus responsible for her value, becomes his property, and she is still actually existing, wherefore the circumstance of his thus obtaining a property in her occasions a demur sufficient to prevent the punishment.

The sovereign is not punishable, but is responsible for property, and liable to retaliation —If a supreme ruler (such as the Khalif, for the time being) commit any offence punishable by law, such as whoredom, theft, or drunkenness, he is not subject to any punishment (but yet if he commit murder he is subject to the law of retaliation, and he is also accountable in matters of property),—because punishment is a right of God, the infliction of which is committed to the Khalif [or the supreme magistrate], and to none else; and he cannot inflict punishment upon himself, as in this there is no advantage, because the God proposed in punishment is that it may operate as a warning to deter mankind from sin, and this is not obtained by a person's inflicting punishment upon himself: contrary to the rights of the individual, such as the laws of retaliation, and of property, the penalties of which may be exacted of the Khalif, as the claimant of right may obtain satisfaction either by the Khalif empowering him to exact his right from himself, or by the claimant appealing for assistance, to the collective body of the Mussulmans. And punishment for slander, (although it be in some shape a right of the individual), is subject to the same rule with other punishments which are a right of God, as the learned have declared that in the punishment for slander the right of God is chiefly considered.

CHAPTER III.

OF EVIDENCE IN WHOREDOM, AND OF RETRACTION THEREFROM

Delay in giving evidence destroys the validity of it, except in cases of slander.—If witnesses bear evidence at a distant period* [after the perpetration of the alleged offence], where there had existed no obstruction (such as their distance from the magistrate, and so forth), their testimony is not to be credited, except in a case of slander. It is recorded in the Jama Sagheer,—"If witnesses bear evidence against any person, with respect to theft, or wine-drinking, or whoredom, after a certain period of time shall have elapsed, such testimony it not to be received; but yet the person so accused of theft is responsible for the value of the goods alleged to have been stolen." The principle upon which this case proceeds is that all evidence, with respect to such punishments as are purely a right of God, is vitiated and rendered void by such a delay in the production of it amounts to Takadim: but with Shafei it is not rendered void, for he considers those punishments as a right of the individual, and supposes evidence under the circumstance to be the same as confession inducing punishment; that is to say, as distance of time [Takadim] does not affect the validity of confession, inducing a distant punishment, so in the same manner distance of time does not forbid the reception of evidence respecting the rights of the individual, because it is apparent that the evidences speak truly; and the same reason holds in such punishments as are purely a right of God.—The argument of our doctors is that a witness in a penal cause has two things at his option, both equally laudable; the first, evidence to an offence committed against the laws;—the second, the veiling and concealment of infirmity:—now if it be admitted that the delay in giving in the evidence arose from the charitable motive last mentioned, it follows that any subsequent evidence could only arise from motives of malice, or of private interest, exciting the witness thereto, in which case the witness incurs a suspicious destructive of the validity of his evidence: if, on the other hand, the delay should not have arisen from a wish to cover infirmity, the person giving evidence after such delay must be held unworthy of attention, as having for so long a time neglected that which was incumbent upon him, namely, the giving of evidence;—from all which it follows that, after such a lapse of time as amounts to Takadim, the witnesses are clearly liable to suspicion, either from their falsity, or their unworthiness: and this suspicion impugns the credibilty of their testimony. This case is contrary to a case of confession, as men do not bear malice against themselves: and punishment for whoredom, or wine-drinking, or theft, are purely a right of God, whence the retractation of a person who makes a confession inducing such punishments is approved; and for this reason, distance of time in those instances forbids the reception of evidence: but punishment for slander is a right of the individual, as by it the scandal is removed from the person accused by the slanderer; (whence the retractation of a person acknowledging his having slandered another, is not admitted):—and distance of timer

* Arab, Mootkadim: this is the participle from Takadim; by which is understood such a distance of time as suffices to prevent punishment. It operates in a way somewhat similar to our statutary limitations.

in a case which regards the the rights of the individual, does not impugn the credibility of the evidence, as the witnesses here do not fall under any suspicion of sinister motives from delay in their testimony, since the claim of the plaintiff is conditional to the admission of evidence concerning the rights of the individual, and therefore their delay in giving evidence is to be attributed to the plaintiff not having called for it. All this is contrary to a case of punishment for theft, in which the evidence of witnesses is invalidated by delay, because the witnesses, by their delay in bearing testimony, become subject to suspicion of sinister motives, as here the claim is not a condition of punishment, since the punishment is purely a right of GOD, the claim being a condition only in matters of property: and also, because theft is chiefly committed during the night, at a time when the owner of the property is asleep and unwatchful, wherefore it is incumbent upon the witnesses to apprise the proprietor of the theft, and to bear testimony to it; but as, in a case of distance of time, or Takadim, they have not so borne evidence, they become criminal and unworthy of credit from their neglect.

Delay also prevents punishment, after the Kazee's decree of it.—TAKADIM, or distance of time, as it prohibits the admission of evidence in the first instance, so it prohibits (according to our doctors) the infliction of punishment after the decree of the Kazee: if, therefore, the convicted person were to abscond, after having received a part of his punishment, and after the lapse of a period sufficient to constitute Takadim, be taken and brought back, the remainder of the correction cannot then be inflicted upon him, because the infliction of the whole punishment is included in the Kazee's decree; and a part of it stands in the same predicament with the whole: and as the Kazee, because of distance of the time, could not decree punishment, so neither can he in the same circumstance, decree the infliction of the remainder of the punishment.

Limitation of the delay in question.—THERE are various opinions among the learned respecting the limitation of the Takadim, or distance of time, now under consideration. In the Jama Sagheer the limitation of it appears to be six months: and the same is mentioned by Tahavee. Haneefa does not prescribe any limitation, but leaves it to the discretion of the magistrate, to be determined according to the customs of each respective age or country. It is recorded from Mohammed that he fixed the limitation of it to one month, as any less space of time falls within the description of Ajil* (and there is a record from Haneefa and Abbo Yoosaf to the same effect); and this last is the most approved doctrine, where the witnesses are not at the distance of a month a journey from the Kazee; but where there is a distance of a month's journey between them, their testimony must be credited, because there appears on this occasion an obstruction to their giving evidence, namely, their distance from the Kazee; and hence they are not in such a case liable to suspicion. The limitation of Takadim in respect to the punishment of wine-drinking, is also the same, according to Mohammed. According to the two Elders the limitation of it is confined to the going off of the smell of the liquor, as shall be hereafter demonstrated.

The evidence of the witnesses is valid against one of the parties, although the others be absent.—IF witnesses bear evidence against a person "that he has committed whoredom with a certain woman, and the woman be absent, yet punishment must be inflicted on the man: but if witnesses bear evidence against a man that he has committed theft, and the owner of the property stolen be absent, the hand of the accused cannot be cut off. The difference between these two cases is that in theft the previous claim of the plantiff is a necessary condition to the admission of evidence, but not in whoredom: and the owner of the property stolen being absent, no claim can be instituted.

OBJECTION.—It would appear that, in the case of whoredom also, punishment ought not to be inflicted on the man, because it is possible that if the woman were present she might advance some plea productive of a demur.

REPLY.—This is a conclusion founded on mere conjecture, and therefore of no weight.

Unless the other be unknown.—IF witnesses give evidence against a man "that he has committed whoredom with a woman whom they do not know," punishment is not to be inflicted upon the man, because it is possible that the woman may be his wife, or his slave, and this, with respect to a Mussulman, is most probable. But if a man make confession that "he has committed whoredom with a woman unknown," punishment must be inflicted on him since, if the woman with whom he committed the fact had been either his wife or his slave, she could not have been unknown to him.

Case of a contradiction in the evidence.—IF two witnesses give evidence against a man, that "he has committed whoredom with such a woman, and forced here thereto," and two other witnesses give evidence to the same fact, but, with this variation, that "the woman was consenting."—In this case (according to Haneefa and Ziffer), punishment drops with respect to both the parties; and such also is the opinion of Shafei.—The two disciples say that punishment is in this case to be inflicted on the man alone; because the varying witnesses

* By Ajil is meant a space of time so short as not to admit of its taking the description of delay,—Thus the payment of a debt is termed Moajil [prompt] where it takes place at any time within a month after it is due.

do yet agree in this that the man has committed whoredom, which is the occasion of punishment to him, for the only difference between the witnesses is that one party of them testifies to an additional offence (namely, his having forced the woman), which does not occasion the remission of punishment with respect to him: contrary to the case of a woman, with respect to whom punishment drops, because her consent is the condition on which her being liable to punishment depends, and this consent is not proved, because of the contradiction among the witnesses. The arguments of Haneefa on this point are twofold:—First, the evidence is contradictory with respect to the man, because whoredom is one act, committed by two persons, the man and the woman,—and as the evidence is contradictory with respect to the woman, it must be held so with regard to the man likewise;—Secondly, the two witnesses who bore testimony to the consent of the woman are slanderers, and consequently their testimony is unworty of any credit.

Objection.—From this it would appear that punishment for slander is incurred by them, whereas it is not so

Reply—Punishment for slander cannot be inflicted on them, on account of the evidence of the other two witnesses, who have deposed to force having been used by the man; for the woman can no longer be considered as married, in the sense which induces punishment for slander, since the description of married (in this sense) is not applicable to a woman after she has been enjoyed unlawfully, although she be forced.

Contradiction among the witnesses, in regard to the place, prevents punishment.—If two witnesses bear evidence against a man, that "he has committed whoredom with such a woman in Koofa," and two others, "that he had committed such whoredom with that woman in Basra," in this case punishment drops with respect to both the man and the woman, because the circumstance alleged is the act of whoredom, and that is contradicted by the contradiction with respect to the place. The evidence to the fact is here in both instances defective, but yet the witnesses are not liable t punishment for slander, because of a demur, as the fact of whoredom, to which they bear testimony, is one single whoredom with respect to the perpetration of it, since the whoremonger is the same person, and the whore is also the same person, in the evidence of the contradictory witnesses on both sides, and there is no difference except with respect to the place in which the fact was committed. But if witnesses contradict each other, by two persons bearing evidence that such a man has committed whoredom with such a woman in such a spot of such a house, and by two other persons giving evidence that the man had committed the whoredom with that woman in another spot of the house, in this case punishment is to be inflicted upon that man. This is upon a favourable construction.* Analogy would suggest that punishment is not incurred, since there is also in this case a positive contradiction with respect to the place in which the fact was committed. But the reason for a more favourable construction is that a coincidence between the testimonies may by conceived, by supposing the act to have been begun in one corner of the house, and completed in another corner, in consequence of the motions of the parties: and it is also possible that the act may have been committed in the middle of the house, and a person seeing it from the front may conceive it to be performed in the fore part of the house, and another viewing it from the back part may conceive it to be performed in the back part of the house; and each bears evidence according to his own conception.

Evidence, agreeing in point of time, but contradictory in point of place, does not occasion punishment.—If four witnesses bear evidence against a man "that he has been guilty of whoredom with such a woman at sunrise in Hind" (a place near Koofa, which is also called the place of Abdal-Rihman), and four other witnesses give evidence against the man that "he has been guilty of whoredom with such a woman at sunrise in Nookhla" (which is also a place near Koofa), in this case neither the man nor the woman are liable to punishment for whoredom, nor are their accusers liable to punishment for slander. The accused are not liable to punishment for whoredom, because the testimony of the contradicting witnesses must, on one part, be false, although it be impossible to ascertain on which side of the evidence the falsehood lies; and the accusers are not liable to punishment for slander, because it is possible that the evidence on one side may be true; and this possibility applies equally to both parties, punishment for slander cannot be inflicted upon either.

Evidence against a woman who is afterwards proved to be virgin is void.—If four witnesses bear testimony against a woman, that "she has committed whoredom with such a man," and it should appear, upon examination made by females employed for that purpose, that the woman is still a virgin, in such case neither of the persons thus accused are liable to punishment for whoredom; nor are the accusers liable to punishment for slander, because the evidence of the females employed to examine the woman accused is a proof which suffices to prevent the infliction of punishment for whoredom upon the parties accused; but it is not a proof sufficient to subject the accusers to

* That is to say, with respect to the witnesses: for if the evidence be not sufficient to subject the parties to punishment, the witnesses are liable to punishment for slander.

punishment for slander;* punishment for whoredom, therefore, is not inflicted on the accused; nor are the accusers liable to punishment for slander.

Incompetent witnesses, by bearing testimony to whoredom, incur punishment for slander.—IF four witnesses give evidence against a man that "he has committed whoredom with such a woman," and it should happen that these witnesses are blind, or have ever been punished for slander; or that one of them is a slave, or has been punished for slander; in this case the witnesses are all liable to punishment for slander; but the accused does not incur punishment for whoredom; because, as a matter of property cannot be determined by the evidence of such wi n sses, it is impossible that punis'ment should be established by it; and the witnesses, where they are all blind, or have all before suffered punishment for slander, are incapable of bearing evidence; and where one of them is a slave, he is totally incapable of bearing evidence; and so also of one of them who has before suffered punishment for slander. By their evidence, therefore, even a doubtful whoredom is not established; and hence their testimony becomes converted into slander; wherefore they are slanderers, and punishment for slander is consequently incurred upon them.

The evidence of reprobate person is neither attended with punishment for whoredom to the accused nor with punishment for slander to the accusers.—IF four witnesses bear evidence to whoredom at a time when they are reprobate,† or if this character should be affixed upon them by competent proof after they have given evidence, they are not liable to punishment for slander; because, although the evidence of a reprobate person be defective, from his veracity being liable to suspicion on account of the badness of his character, yet he is a competent witness, insomuch that if a Kazee issue a decree upon the evidence of a reprobate person, his decree is valid, according to our doctors. The evidence of reprobate persons, therefore, goes to establish a doubtful whoredom, and they are consequently not exposed to punishment for slander; and since, moreover, from the defect in their testimony, on account of their being reprobate, a doubt appears that whoredom has not been committed, the accused are therefore not liable to punishment for whoredom. Shafei dissents from our opinion concerning this case, as he holds a reprobate person to be incapable of being an evidence, and, consequently, that he stands in the same predicament as a slave.

Witnesses defective in point of number incur punishment for slander.—IF fewer than four persons bear evidence to whoredom, punishment for slander is applicable to them. This effect is induced because, although their testimony be good, yet testimony to whoredom is so accounted only where it amounts to evidence; and the testimony of fewer than four persons, in a case of whoredom, is not evidence so as to be accounted good; wherefore it is slander.

And so also, of the complete number of witnesses, where one of them afterwards proves incompetent; but no fine is due in this case, except the accused suffer lapidation, when a deyit is due from the public treasury.—IF four person bear evidence against a man, that "he has been guilty of whoredom" and the Kazee should inflict punishment for whoredom upon the parties accordingly, and it should afterwards appear that one of the witnesses is a slave, or has at any time been punished for slander, punishment is incurred by all the witnesses as the witnesses are on this occasion only three in number. Observe, however, that in this case no A ish, or fine of damage is due on account of such flagellation, either from the witnesses or from the public treasury; but if in consequence of the evidence the person accused should have been stoned to death by a sentence of lapidation, the Deyit, or fine of blood, is due from the public treasury. This is the doctrine of Haneefa. The two disciples say that the fine of damage is also due from the public treasury in the former case. The compiler of the Hedaya remarks that this difference of opinion obtains where the accused happens to be cut by the stripes he has received. The two disciples also hold that if the accused should chance to die in consequence of the correction by scourging, the fine of blood is due from the public treasury—in opposition to Haneefa; and likewise, that if the witnesses should retract from their evidence after the accused has been cut by scourging, or died in consequence thereof, they [the witnesses] become responsible for the fine of damage in the first instance, or the fine of blood in the second. The argument of the two disciples is that, in consequence of the testimony of the witnesses, stripes are to be inflicted generally,* whether they be of a cutting nature or otherwise, since to avoid cutting is not always in the executioner's power; the scourging, therefore, which is due in consequence of the testimony of the witnesses, comprehends both cutting stripes and also stripes which do not cut, and con-

* Because it is, notwithstanding, possible that the act may have been performed upon the woman, although not to such a degree as to destroy the appearances of virginity.

† Arab. Fasik. It is elsewhere rendered unjust; but the term here adopted approaches, perhaps, nearer to the real meaning. Fasik signifies a person who neglects decorum in his dress and behaviour, and whose evidence, therefore, is not held to be admissible.

* That is, not restricted to any particular description of stripes.

sequently the cutting is to be referred to the testimony of the evidences, whence they are responsible for the same, where they retract from their testimony. But where the witnesses do not retract (that is, where their evidence is set at nought, not by retractation, but by one of them being afterwards discovered to be incompetent), the fine of blood is due from the public treasury, because the act of the executioner is to be referred to the Kazee, and the Kazee acts on behalf of a community of Mussulmans wherefore, the atonement for the act falls upon that which is the property of all the Mussulmans, namely, the public treasury, in the same manner as in a case of wounds or retaliation. The argument of Haneefa is, that as nothing is due in consequence of the testimony of the witnesses, further than punishment (by which is understood such a scourging as excites pain, but such as evidently cannot prove destructive, except through the fault of the flagellator, proceeding from his carelessness or incapacity), the cutting, therefore, is to be referred to him alone, and not to the testimony of the witnesses ; but yet (according to the Rawayet-Saheeh) the scourger is not made responsible, lest men should be deterred from the infliction of punishment, by an apprehension of being made answerable for the consequences of it.

The testimony of secondary witnesses invalidates that of primary witnesses.—If four witnesses bear testimony to an evidence given by four other witnesses, against a man, of his having committed whoredom punishment is not to be inflicted upon the person so accused, because evidence in support of evidence introduces an increase of doubt, since wherever, in the recital of a fact, the channels of communication are multiplied, the doubt of its truth increases in proportion ; and there is in this case no necessity for considering the secondary witnesses in the light of original witnesses. And if the four original witnesses should afterwards come and bear testimony of themselves to the whoredom, in the place where the secondary witnesses had before given their evidence, here also no punishment is to be inflicted on the accused, because their testimony has already been rejected in one shape, in consequence of the rejection of the testimony of the secondary witnesses, respecting the same fact, as the secondary witnesses are the substitutes of the primary witnesses, from the circumstance of those having directed them, and thrown the matter upon them. But here punishment for slander is not to be inflicted on either the original or the secondary witnesses, because both are complete in point of number, although punishment for whoredom be not inflicted, on account of a doubt, which is such as suffices in bar of punishment for whoredom, but is not sufficient to subject the witness to punishment for slander.

One of four witnesses retracting, after lapidation upon the accused, incurs punishment for slander, and is responsible for one-fourth of the fine of blood.—If four witnesses give evidence against a man, that he has committed whoredom, and he suffer lapidation, and one of the witnesses afterwards retract, punishment for slander is to be inflicted upon him alone, and he is also responsible for one-forth of the fine of blood. The reason for one-fourth only of the fine of blood being due from him is that three-fourths of the veracity of the evidence remain, in consequence of the evidence of the three remaining witnesses still continuing ; by the evidence, therefore, of the witness who retracts, only one-fourth of the varacity is affected —(Shafei says that the death of the retracting witness is incurred, and not a fine upon his property, according to his tenets concerning witnesses in retaliation, as shall be hereafter shown in treating of Deyit).—That punishment for slander is incurred by the witness is the opinion of our three doctors. Ziffer says that punishment for slander is not due, because, if the slanderer be considered as the slanderer of a living person, his slander is rendered void by the death of that person : or if he be considered as the slandered of a defunct, the said defunct has suffered lapidation under a sentence of the Kazee, whence originates a demur respecting the propriety of punishment for slander. The argument of our doctors is that evidence to whoredom does not become slander, in consequence of retractation, on any other account than as the evidence is thereby cancelled ; the evidence, therefore, at the time of retractation, is rendered slander with respect to the dead ; and a person who slanders a married person defunct is liable to punishment for slander. With respect to what Ziffer advances (that the defunct has suffered lapidation under a sentence of the Kazee, which gives rise to a demur respecting the propriety of punishment for slander), we reply, that upon the evidence, which is the proof, being cancelled by retractation, the decree of the Kazee, sentencing lapidation, does not give rise to any demur in bar of punishment for slander ; wherefore punishment for slander is to be inflicted upon him who retracts from his testimony : contrary to what would be the case if any other than the retracting person were to slander him who had suffered lapidation, as the latter is not a Mahsan in respect to any other person, since the sentence of the Kazee against the deceased is, with regard to that other, proper and just.

But if he retract before lapidation, all the witnesses are liable to punishment.—What is now advanced regards a case where one of the witnesses retracts, after lapidation : but if one of them were to retract before the execution of lapidation, after sentence has been passed by the Kazee, in this case punishment for slander is to be inflicted on all the witnesses: and the unishment of the accused is remitted. This is the doctrine of the two Elders. Mohammed says that,* in this case also, punishment for slander is to be inflicted on the retracting witness alone, because the evidence of the witnesses has been corroborated by the Kazee's sentence, and therefore is not cancelled except with respect to the respector alone,—in the same manner as where the witness retracts after the execution of the sentence.—The argument of the two Elders is, that the infliction of punishment is only a supplement to the sentence of the Kazee; the retractation in the present instance; therefore, is the same in effect as if one of the witnesses were to retract before the sentence had been passed (for which reason punishment drops with respect to the accused); and if one of the witnesses were to retract previous to the Kazee's sentence of lapidation, punishment for slander would be inflicted upon all of them. Ziffer says that in this case also punishment for slander would be inflicted on the retracting witness alone, because his retractation is not of account with regard to any except himself The argument of our doctors is that the declaration of the witnesses is radically slander, and does not become evidence until it be so rendered by a sentence of the Kazee, passed in conformity to it: and where this sentence has not been passed, such declaration countinues to be slander; as it radically was; wherefore punishment for slander is to be inflicted upon all of them.

One of five witnesses retracting, does not incur either punishment or fine.—IF five persons bear evidence [to whoredom], and one of the five retract after lapidation, no penalty whatsoever is incurred by the witness so retracting—because, four witnesses still remaining, the evidence remains complete. But if, afterwards, one of the remaining four witnesses should retract, punishment for slander is then due upon both retractors, and each is indebted in one-fourth of the fine of blood. Punishment for slander is due upon them, because evidence to whoredom is rendered slander by subsequent retractation, as before explained; and they are each indebted one fourth of the fine of blood, because by the three persevering witnesses still remaining, three-fourths of the validity of the body of evidence continues unimpeached, as the perseverance of those who remain is regarded. and not the retractation of those who draw back (according to what is said upon that head in its proper place); and as only one-fourth of the veracity is destroyed by the retractation of these two witnesses, it follows that they remain responsible for one-fourth only of the fine of blood.

Where justified witnesses prove afterwards defective, the fine of blood is due from the purgators of these witnesses.—IF four witnesses give evidence of whoredom against a man, and these witnesses be justified by Tazkeeat,* and the accused suffer lapidation, and it should afterwards appear that those witnesses were idolaters, or slaves (by the purgators retracting their evidence of justification, and declaring them to be slaves, or idolaters), in this case the fine of blood is due from the purgators, according to Haneefa. The two disciples say that in this case the fine of blood falls upon the public treasury. Some hold that this difference exists only where the purgators, in their retractation, declare that their justification of the witnesses had been according to the best of their knowledge and belief at that time. The argument of the two disciples is that the purgators have done nothing more than merely speaking in commendation of the witnesses, in the same manner as if they were to speak in commendation of the accused, by testifying to his being within the description of Ihsan,† in which case nothing is due from them, and so here likewise. The argument of Haneefa is, that testimony of the witnesses is not proof, nor worthy of any regard, but through the justification of the purgators; wherefore the justification is, in reality, the efficient cause of the sentence; whence the sentence must be referred and attributed thereto: contrary to their bearing testimony to the Ihsan of the accused as that state is conditional to a person being considered a Mahsan.—that is, married, under such circumstances as (in case of whoredom) subject him to lapidation. It is also to be remarked that, whether the before-mentioned justifier should pronounce the justification in the proper and formal terms of evidence,—(thus, "We testify that these witnesses are freemen and believers") or not in the formal terms of evidence—(as thus, "These are freemen and believers,") the effect is in both cases the same, and there is no difference whatever between them; this, however, holds only where the purgators restrict their justification to the freedom or faith of the evidences, as above; but if they should say, "These witnesses are "adils," ‡ and it should afterwards appear that they are slaves, in this case the purgators are not responsible for the fine of blood; because slaves are, in some instances, of the descriptions of adils:—neither are the witnesses, in this case, responsible for the fine of blood, as their declaration does

*That is, by a certain number of other witnesses bearing testimony to the competency, &c. of witnesses who are giving evidence in any cause, the former being denominated the Moozkees, or purgators; the nature of this mode of justification is exhibited at large in treating of Evidence.

† That is, by testifying that the accused is married, under such circumstances of freedom, and so forth, as (in case of whoredom) subjects a person to lapidation.

‡ Persons of respectable character, in opposition to reprobates.

not amount to evidence;* nor are they subject to punishment for slander, because their accusation was made against a living person, but that person is now dead, and his heirs cannot procure punishment for slander to be inflicted on them, as it is not inheritable. If the purgators persevere in their justification, or have unknowingly borne testimony therein, and it should afterwards appear that the witnesses are of an incompetent description, nothing whatever falls on the purgators:—but in this case the fine of blood falls upon the public treasury.

Case in which the fine of blood falls upon the slayer.—If four persons bear testimony of whoredom against a man, and the Kazee sentence him to be stoned, and any person should slay him, and it should afterwards appear that the above witnesses were incompetent, in such case the fine of blood falls upon the slayer, according to a favourable construction of the law.—Analogy would suggest, in this case, that retaliation is incurred, as the slayer has killed an innocent person without cause: but the reasons for a more favourable construction of the law are twofold; First, the Kazee's sentence of lapidation was, in appearance, regular and valid, at the period of slaying, and hence was established an erroneous admissibility of slaughter: contrary to a case in which the accused is slain before the Kazee issues his decree of lapidation, as the testimony of the witness is not proof until then:—Secondly, the slayer has acted under a conception that the slaying of that man became allowable, he having a confidence in the argument of such permission, namely, the Kazee's sentence of lapidation; and hence it is the same as where a person slays another, supposing him, from former circumstances, to be an enemy, in which case the fine of blood is incumbent upon that person, and so here likewise.—It is to be observed that the fine of blood thus incurred is a charge upon the estate of the slayer, and does not fall upon his tribe, because it is wilful homicide, for which the tribe is not responsible: and this fine of blood must be discharged within three years [after the perpetration of the fact], as being due on account of homicide. But if no person were in this manner to slay the accused, and he suffer lapidation by the sentence of the Kazee and it should afterwards appear that the witnesses were incompetent, the fine of blood in this case falls upon the public treasury because the persons who stone the accused act in conformity with the order of the Kazee and hence their act must be referred to the Kazee; and as, if the Kazee were to execute the sentence upon the accused with his own hands, the fine of blood would fall upon the public treasury, so also it falls upon the same, where any other person executes such sentence under the Kazee's authority. This case is evidently contrary to one where the Kazee passes a sentence of lapidation, and another person slays the accused in a different manner, and not by stoning; for in so doing he has not acted in conformity to the order of the magistrate.

Evidence to whoredom is valid, although the knowledge of the fact be unlawfully obtained.—If witnesses bear evidence of whoredom against a man, declaring that "they had come to the knowledge of it by wilfully looking into the person's private apartment at the time of the fact," yet such evidence is to be credited, nor is it to be rejected on account of the manner in which the knowledge of the witnesses was obtained, as their looking was allowable, in order that they might be enabled to bear evidence; they are therefore the same as physicians or midwives.*

The accused's plea of celibacy, if unfounded, does not prevent lapidation.—If four witnesses bear evidence of whoredom against a man, and the accused should plead that "he is not a married man," and it should happen that he has a wife who has brought forth a child to him—(in other words, should deny the consummation of his marriage, after the establishment of all the conditions of it), he is to be stoned, because the effect of the establishment of the child's parentage † is a consequence of his having had carnal communication with his wife (whence it is that if he were to pronounce a divorce upon her, a divorce reversible takes place);—and his being a married man is established, on account of the aforesaid effect: and if the wife should not have borne a child, yet if one man and two women, as witnesses, bear testimony to the marriage of the accused, in this case lapidation is to be inflicted upon him, Shafei says that the accused, in this case, does not suffer lapidation; and this his opinion is founded on his doctrine in the laws of evidence, that "the testimony of women is not admissible, excepting in cases of property."—Ziffer remarks that the circumstance of the accused being a married man, although it appear to be only the condition of the sentence, yet is in reality the cause, as rendering the offence more atrocious; wherefore the sentence must be referred to that circumstance; and this condition being, in reality, the occasion therof the evidence of women cannot be admitted in it, any more than with respect to the original offence, namely, the whoredom. Thus it is the same as where two infidel subjects of the Mussulman government testify concerning a Mussulman

* Because they afterwards appear (from the retractation of the purgators) to be incompetent evidences.

*To explain this it may be proper to remark that a person's looking into the private apartment of another is an unlawful act, which, if it was not justified by the motive, would invalidate his testimony.

† Established in him in virtue of his marriage.

slave, who has committed whoredom, that "his master had emancipated him before the perpetration of the fact," which testimony would not be admitted, because the Ihsan of the slave [that is, his being a free married man] is so far a condition of the sentence as to be, in reality, a cause of it. The argument of our doctors is that marriage in a state of freedom is an honourable state, and is repugnant to the commission of whoredom (as was already stated), wherefore this circumstance cannot be, in reality, a cause of the sentence. The testimony, therefore, of the witnesses to the Ihsan of the accused is the same as their testimony in any other case than whoredom; and as their testimony to his Ihsan would in other cases be credited, so also in a case of whoredom: contrary to the case of the two infidel subjects and the slave, as cited by Ziffer; because there the freedom of the slave is proved by the testimony of those two witnesses: but it is not thereby proved that the date of the slave's freedom was antecedent to the commission of whoredom, either because a Mussulman denies such date, or because that circumstance would be injurious to a Mussulman. If the witnesses who testify to Ihsan retract, yet they are not responsible for the fine of blood: contrary to the doctrine of Ziffer, according to what was before observed.

CHAPTER IV.

OF HIDD SHIRRUB, OR THE PUNISHMENT FOR DRINKING WINE.

General rule.—IF a Mussulman drink wine, and be seized whilst his breath yet smells of the wine, or be brought before the Kazee whilst he is yet intoxicated therewith, and witnesses give evidence, that "he has drunk wine," punishment for wine-drinking is to be inflicted upon him; and in the same manner, punishment incurred by him when he makes confession of having drunk wine, whilst his breath yet retains the smell; because the offence of wine-drinking is proved upon him, and Takadim, or distance of time,* does not appear, since the flavour of the wine still remains. This doctrine is originally founded upon a precept of the Prophet, "Whoever drinks of wine, let him suffer correction by scourging, as often as he drinks thereof."

Punishment is not inflicted in a case of confession or accusation made after the smell is gone off.—IF a man make confession of having drank wine, after the smell has ceased, in this case punishment is not to be inflicted upon him, according to the two Elders. Imam Mohammed maintains that it is to be inflicted. The same difference of opinion obtains in a case where witnesses bear evidence against a man that "he has drank wine" after the smell has ceased. The reason of this diversity of opinion is that Takadim, or lapse of time, forbids the reception of evidence in a case of wine-drinking, according to all the doctors: but Mohammed fixes the limitation of Takadim, in wine-drinking, to a certain time, namely, one month (according to the most approved authorities), he conceiving an analogy between this, and a case of whoredom, because delay is established by lapse of time, and not by the ceasing of a smell; and the existence or non-existence of a smell is of no weight, as there are other things the flavour of which resembles that of wine. According to the two Elders, on the contrary, Takadim is established by the non-existence or departure of the smell, for two reasons;—FIRST, a decree of Abdoola Ibn Massaod, who, when certain persons brought before him a man charged with drinking wine, directed that "they should examine his breath, and that if any flavour of wine were discovered, punishment should then be inflicted upon him;" SECONDLY, the existence of the effect (namely the smell), is an irrefragable proof of wine having been lately drunk. And as to what Mohammed advances, that "there are other things the flavour of which resembles that of wine," it may be replied that the difference between the smell of wine, and other articles, may be easily distinguished by one who is possessed of judgment and discernment, nor can any but ignorant persons be doubtful concerning it. Thus, according to Mohammad, confession of wine-drinking is not rendered ineffectual by distance of time, in the same manner as (according to him) confession of whoredom is not rendered ineffectual by distance of time, agreeably to what was before advanced:—with the two Elders, on the contrary, punishment for wine-drinking is not to be inflicted but on the condition that the smell still remain, because Ibn Massaod stipulated that condition, as before stated.

Unless this be owing to an unavoidable delay in bringing the accused to the seat of justice.—IF witnesses seize a drinker of wine* at a time when he is intoxicated, or whilst he still retains the smell of the liquor, and carry him to a city where there is a Kazee, and in the mean time the flavour or the intoxication should cease, before they arrive at the seat of justice, yet in this case punishment for wine-drinking is to be inflicted upon that person, according to all our doctors, because there is an excuse for the delay, analogous to that which is created by distance of place in a charge of whoredom; and the witnesses are not suspected where such excuse exists.

Punishment is incurred by drinking Nabeez.—IF a person be intoxicated by drinking

---

* See the preceding Chapter; p. 188.

* This case supposes his being seized in some remote place, at a distance from the seat of justice.

Nabeez,* punishment is incurred by him, because it is related of Omar that he decreed punishment for wine-drinking upon a wild Arab, who was intoxicated by drinking that liquor.—(The punishment for drunkenness, and the degree of scourging in the punishment for wine-drinking, shall be hereafter explained.)

The smell alone does not suffice for conviction, without evidence.—If the smell of wine be discovered upon a person, or he should vomit wine, yet if witnesses have not actually seen him drinking it, punishment is not incurred, because the smell alone leads but to a very uncertain conclusion, as this appearance may proceed either from the person having drank wine, or from his having sat among wine-drinkers, from whom he may have contracted the smell;—and it is also possible that wine may have been administered to him by force, or menaces, in which case no punishment is incurred.

Nor intoxication, unless it be known to proceed from wine.—Punishment for wine-drinking is not incurred by intoxication alone, unless it be known that the person has been intoxicated by the voluntary drinking of wine, or of Nabeez, because men are sometimes inebriated by the use of articles which are permitted, such as the juice of Henbane, or mare's milk; and men may also be sometimes compelled to drink wine, which is not a punishable offence, when thus committed by compulsion.

Punishment not to be inflicted during intoxication.—Punishment is not to be inflicted upon a wine-drinker, whilst he is intoxicated, nor until his intoxication shall have ceased, in order that the end therefore (namely determent) may be obtained.

Punishment for wine-drinking to a free-person is eighty stripes.—The punishment of a free person, for drinking wine or other intoxicating liquor, is eighty stripes, on the authority of all the companions; and those eighty stripes are to be inflicted in every respect under the same rules and restrictions as in the case of whoredom, according to what is mentioned under that head: and (according to the Rawayet Mashhoor), the wine-drinker must be stripped naked to receive his punishment. It is recorded from Mohammed that the offender must not be stripped, as nothing concerning the punishment for wine-drinking occurs in the sacred writings, wherefore it is expedient, for the sake of lenity, that a wine-drinker be not stripped to receive correction. The reason for what is recorded in the Rawayet Mashhoor is that one kind of lenity is already shown in the number of stripes prescribed, those in whoredom being one hundred, whereas in wine-drinking there are only eighty; hence it is not requisite that a second sort of lenity be shown in the mode of infliction.

And, to a slave, forty stripes.—If the drinker of wine be a slave, male or female, the punishment for wine-drinking, with respect to such, is forty stripes only, because the state of bondage induces only half punishment, as has been repeatedly mentioned.

Confession may be retracted.—If a person make confession to the drinking of wine, or any other intoxicating liquor, and afterwards retract from such confession punishment is not to be inflicted upon him, as the punishment of wine-drinking is purely a right of God.

The offence is proved by two witneses, or, by one confession.—Wine-drinking is proved on the testimony of two witnesses; and also by confession once made. It is recorded from Aboo Yoousaf, that two confessions are requisite. But it is to be observed that the evidence of women against men is not admissible in wine-drinking, because the evidence of females is liable to variation, and they may be also suspected of absence of mind, or forgetfulness.

Degree of intoxication required to induce punishment.—The degree of intoxication which occasions punishment amounts to this,—that the person so intoxicated be not able to distinguish what is said to him in any shape;—nor to know a man from a woman. The compiler of the Hedaya observes that this is the doctrine of Haneefa The two disciples have said that the degree of drunkenness which induces punishment is sufficiently found in the intoxicated person speaking confusedly and indistinctly, as it is from this that drunkenness is generally understood. Many doctors agree with the two disciples in this point. The argument of Haneefa is that the drinking of wine is among the causes of punishment, wherefore it is to be noticed only in the excess; for in acts which are causes of punishment the excess of them only is regarded, on account of seeking a pretext for the purpose of averting punishment; and excess of drunkennes appears in the intoxication so far overpowering the reason as not to leave the person a capacity of distinguishing one object from another.—(In ascertaining the illegality of intoxication produced by drinking any other liquor than wine, regard is had to what the two disciples maintain concerning the punishment for drunkenness produced by wine-drinking.)—Shafei, in the punishment for drunkenness, has regard to the appearance of the effect produced by the wine, in the intoxicated person's walking, or other actions, by his staggering or turning giddy when he attempts to walk; but our doctors say that such effect may proceed from different causes, as they sometimes do not attend drunkenness, and sometimes occur in other cases (such as weakness for instance), wherefore this species of effect is not regarded.

Confession of any offence, made during intoxication, is not regarded.—If a person, during a fit of intoxication, should make confession of anything which occasions

* A fermented liquor made by steeping dates, raisins, &c., in hot water. It is described particularly in another place.

punishment (such as whoredom for instance), no punishment is to be inflicted upon him, as in such a confession, there is apprehension of falsehood, and this apprehension is to be regarded so far as to avert punishment, since punishment [Hidd] is purely a right of God:—it is otherwise, however, in punishment for slander; for if a man in a state of intoxication were to make confession of slander, punishment for slander must be decreed upon him, because this is not purely a right of GOD, but is also a right of the individual, and therefore a state of drunkenness is here the same as a state of sobriety, for the sake of inflicting a penalty, in the same manner as in all other matters, such as divorce, manumission, and so forth.

Nor apostacy.—IF a man, during intoxication, should apostatize from the faith, his wife is not thereby divorced from him because infidelity depends upon what may be a person's belief, and that cannot be ascertained during drunkenness.

CHAPTER V.

OF HIDD KAZAF, OR THE PUNISHMENT FOR SLANDER.

Definition of Kazaf.—KAZAF, in its primitive sense, simply means accusation, By Kazaf, in the language of the law, is understood a man insinuating a charge of whoredom against a married man or woman: the person so acting being termed the Kazif, or slanderer; and the man or woman so scandalized the Makzoof, or slandered.

Punishment for slander to be ordered by the magistrate.—IF any person expressly accuse of whoredom a man or woman who is married,* in such case, if the accused require the magistrate to pass sentence of punishment for slander upon that person, the magistrate is bound to order its infliction.

The punishment, to a freeman, is eighty stripes.—THE punishment for slander is eighty stripes, if the slandered be free, because GOD has so commanded in the Koran, saying,—"BUT AS TO THOSE WHO ACCUSE MARRIED PERSONS OF WHOREDOM, AND PRODUCE NOT FOUR WITNESSES, THEM SHALL YE SCOURGE WITH FOURSCORE STRIPES." And the conditions upon which this punishment is to be inflicted are twofold;—FIRST, That the accused make requistion thereof, because of his right being involved in it, inasmuch as scandal is by that means removed from him;—SECONDLY, That the accused be a married man, this being particularly specified in the text already quoted.

IT is necessary that the eighty stripes [or strokes] be inflicted on different parts [or limbs] of the offender, in conformity to what has been already advanced upon that subject with respect to the punishment for whoredom; but it is to be observed that the person suffering this correction is not to be stripped naked, because the occasion of the punishment is not absolutely certified, since it is possible that the accuser may have spoken truly, for which reason it must not be inflicted with severity, as in punishment for whoredom. The outer garment or robe, however, together with any clothes which are stuffed or quilted, must be removed, because such a covering would prevent a person from feeling his punishment.

And to a slave forty stripes.—IF the accused be a slave, the punishment for slander with respect to him is forty stripes; as bondage induces only half punishment,—according to what has been before repeatedly observed upon that head.

Description of a person the slandering of whom induces punishment.—THE state of marriage of the slandered person [which is a requsite condition or punishment to the slanderer] acquires that he or she be free, of sound judgment, of mature age, and a Mussulman; and also of chaste repute; that is to say,—free form any suspicion of adultery; there are, therefore, five conditions required in it; FIRST,—The freedom of the accused, because the word of GOD says, "UPON THEM" (that is upon female slaves) "IS DUE HALF THE PUNISHMENT THAT IS DUE UPON Mahsanas,"—Where the word Mahsamas, by the context, implies free women, in opposition to slaves, whence it appears that the term married [Mahsan] here applies only to free people;—SECONDLY, Sanity of intellect, and, THIRDLY; Maturity of age,—because infants and idiots are not liable to be scandalized as whoredom cannot be proved upon such;—FOURTHLY, Islam, because the Prophet declared, "A Polytheist is not a Mahsan :" and FIFTHLY,—Chastity, because no scandal attaches to any other persons than those who are of chaste repute, and the accuser of an unchaste person, moreover, speaks truly.

Cases which constitute slander.—IF a person deny another's parentage: as if he were to say to him, "Thou art not the son of thy [reputed] father !" such person thereby incurs punishment for slander ; this, however, is only where the mother of the person thus addressed is a married woman; because such denial is a positive accusation with respect to the mother of that person, since the legitimacy of a child cannot be denied unless it be begotten in whoredom.

IF one person, in the heat of passion, say to another, "Thou art not the son of such-a-one," and the person mentioned be his father, and his descent be established as from him, in this case the person so speaking incurs punishment for slander. But if these words be spoken in any other circumstance than the heat of passion, punishment for slander is not incurred by the speaker, because such words, if spoken in wrath, imply malicious and wanton abuse, whereas, if uttered in a calm

---

*Without producing the number of witnesses requisite to prove the charge.

and deliberate moment, they may mean no more than on upbraiding, by denying any likeness between the person spoken to and his father, in point of goodness of disposition, such as benevolence and so forth.

IF a man say to another, "Thou art not the son of such a-one," and it should happen that the person named is the grandfather of him who is thus addressed, the speaker does not incur punishment for slander, because his assertion is literally true. And, in the same manner, if a man should declare another to be the son of one who is his grandfather, he does not thereby incur punishment for slander, because the child's child is metaphorically referred to the grandfather, and is called his child.

Case of a claim of punishment for slandering a defunct.—IF a man call another "a son of a whore," and it should happen that the mother of him who is thus addressed is dead, and had been a married woman, in such a case, if he [the son] require punishment for slander to be inflicted upon the speaker, the same must be inflicted accordingly, because the speaker has slandered a married woman after her death. It is to be observed, however, that a right to demand punishment for slander, in behalf of a deceased person belongs only to one in whose parentage a flaw is created by the imputation, and this is either the parent or the child, because scandal attaches to the child of the accused, and hence the slander applies to the child also in effect. According to Shafei, any heir may demand punishment for slander in behalf of a person deceased, because punishment for slander is held by him to be a matter of inheritance, as shall be hereafter demonstrated. According to our doctors, on the other hand, the power of demanding punishment for slander in behalf a person deceased is not in the way of an inheritance, but for a reason already intimated, that the scandal arising from the slander attaches to the deceased;—whence it is that the right to demand punishment for slander on behalf of a defunct appertains to one who may be excluded from inheritance by the murder of the person from whom he inherits; and that it also appertains to the child of the daughter, in the same manner as to the child of the son (contrary to the opinion of Mohammed); and also, that it appertains to the child's child during the lifetime of the former (contrary to the opinion of Ziffer);—and so also, that if the deceased person who was slandered were married, it is lawful for that person's child to demand the punishment for slander, although such child should be an infidel or a slave. This last is also contrary to the opinion of Ziffer, who argues that if the right of demanding punishment for slander, in behalf of a defunct, were to rest with the child, being an infidel, it must so appertain, either in the manner of an inheritance, or on account of his being a party, because of the slander extending to him by effect (since the scandal arising from it attaches to him); and both these inferences are unsupported ; the first, because punishment for slander is not a matter of inheritance: and the second, because, as an express accusation of whoredom made against the child does not induce punishment for slander (since an infidel cannot be a married person in the sense which subjects the accuser to punishment), so, in a case where the slander is established with respect to him by effect only, it does not induce punishment a fortiori. —Our doctors, on the other hand, argue that, in the case in question, the slanderer, by accusing a married person, has fixed a stain upon the child, for which he will seek satisfaction by punishment for slander:—the principle upon which this proceeds is that the circumstance of the accused being a married person is made a condition [of punishment upon a slanderer], in order that, in the charge of whoredom, the imputation of a stain upon him may be completely established, after which such imputation of a stain descends to his child ; and such is the case in the present instance : and although the child be an infidel, yet infidelity does not prevent a claim of right : contrary to a case where an express accusation is advanced against the child himself; for in this case punishment for slander is not incurred because here the imputation of a stain does not completely exist, as marriage (in the sense which would induce punishment for slander), does not exist with respect to the accused, on account of his being an infidel.

A slave cannot demand punishment upon his master ; nor a son upon his father.—A SLAVE is not permitted to demand punishment for slander upon his master,—where the latter has slandered his mother, being a married woman;—neither does it belong to a son to demand punishment for slander upon his father,—where the latter has slandered his mother, being a married woman;—because a master is not liable to any chastisement on account of his slave, nor a father on account of his son; whence it is that retaliation is not executed upon a father on account of his son, nor upon a master on account of his slave. But if the mother should have another son by another father, that son may demand punishment for slander to be inflicted, on behalf of his mother, upon the father aforesaid, because the occasion for punishment (namely, slander) is in that case fully established, and the obstacle to the demand of it does not exist in the person who demands it.

The decease of the slandered party prevents punishment.—IF any person accuse another of whoredom, and the person so slandered die, punishment for slander is not incurred. Shafei maintains that punishment is not to be remitted. And in the same manner, if the slandered person should die after the infliction of a part of the punishment upon the slanderer, the remaining part thereof ceases according to our doctors,—Shafei alleges that it does not cease. This difference of opinion obtains because punishment for slander is a matter of inheritance, according to Shafei, whereas according to our doctors it is not so. It is to be observed that there is no difference of opinion concerning the punishment for slander being a right of God and also a right of the INDIVIDUAL;—because the punishment for slander has been ordained by the LAW for the purpose of removing scandal from the person slandered, and the advantage results solely to the slanderer, on which account, punishment for slander is a right of the individual;—and it has also been ordained for the purpose of determent (whence punishment for slander is termed Hidd*), and the design of the institution is to purify the world from sin, and this demonstrates that punishment for slander is a right of God;—some of the rules in it, moreover, prove punishment for slander to be a right of the individual, such as that "it cannot be decreed but where some person sues for it," which is a right of an individual;—and, on the other hand, some of its rules prove punishment for slander to be a right of God, such as, that 'the exaction of it is committed to the magistrate, and not to the person slandered,"—In short, in the punishment for slander there are two contending principles; and such being the case, Shafei gives the first principle the preference, namely, the right of the individual, considering that as superior to the right of God, the right of the individual being preferable, because of his being necessitous, whereas God is not necessitous; our doctors, on the other hand, give the second principle the preference, and hold it to be the superior, because in whatever degree the right of the creature may be concerned, the Creator is the surety, and the guarantee thereof: and hence the conversation of the rights of the individual is therein obtained: but the case is not the same in the reverse of this proposition, because there is no authority to exact the right of God, but but in the way of a vicarious delegation. These different tenets, as held by each party, are notorious; and from them proceeds a contradiction of opinion respecting a variety of cases in punishment for slander Thus, according to Shafei, punishment for slander is an inheritance; but in the opinion of our doctors it is not so, as inheritance obtains only in the rights of the individual, and not in the rights of God.—Again, the remission of it is not approved by our doctors; but, according to Shafei, it is approved: and again, it is not lawful to accept of anything in lieu of punishment, according to our doctors; but, according to Shafei, this is lawful. It is recorded that the opinion of Aboo Yoosaf respecting remission is the same with that of Shafei.

Confession of slander cannot be retracted.—If a person make confession of slander, and afterwards retract from such confession, his retractation is not to be credited, because, as the right of the slandered person is therein concerned, it is to be supposed that he will falsify the retractation:—contrary to such punishments as are purely a right of God, where the retractation must be admitted, as there is no person concerned to oppose the veracity of it.

A term of abuse does not constitute slander.—If a man were to call an Arab a Nabathean;* punishment for slander is not incurred by him, because he is here supposed only to speak comparatively—implying merely that the person he addresses is a Nabathean in badness of disposition, or in want of virus; and in the same manner, if a man were to say to an Arab "Thou art not an Arab," no punishment would follow for the same reason.

If a man say to another. "O son of the rain," he is not a slanderer, because these words may be considered as implying purity and softness of manners, as rain is distinguished by the qualities of purity and softness.

If a man, in speaking to another, should declare him to be the son of any of his parental relations other than his father, such as his maternal or paternal uncle, or his stepfather, he is not a slanderer, because it is common to bestow the appellation of father upon each of these relations, in the same manner as upon the natural parent.

Equivocal accusation of whoredom incurs punishment for slander:—If a man, being in anger, say to another Zinte-feeal-Jiblee,† and should plead that he thereby meant "you climbed up the hill," yet punishment for slander is to be inflicted on him, according to the two Elders. Mohammed maintains that punishment is not to be inflicted on him, because the word Zinte means ascending, in its literal sense, and the mention of a mountain proves that such is intended by it. The argument of the two Elders is that Zinte is used to express whoredom also; and the circumstance of anger proves that by the word Zinte whoredom is intended; wherefore punishment is to be inflicted, in the same manner as if the term Zinte had been used without any mention of a mountain, and he were to say that by Zinte he meant ascent.

If one man were to say to another Zinte ali-al Jiblee,‡ according to some doctors

*See the definition of Hidd in the beginning of this bock.

*The Nabatheans are a tribe upon the confines of Joak, remarkable for the barbarity and ferocity of their manners.

†This may be either translated "you committed whoredom in the mountain," or "you ascended the mountain," as the term Zinna signifies not only whoredom, but also "climbing, or ascending."

‡Literally, "You ascended upon the mountain," or, "You have committed whoredom upon the mountain." The word Alee [upon] is the only difference between this and the preceding case.

punishment for slander is not incurred by him, because the mention of a mountain, in this place, demonstrates that by Zinte he meant accending; but according to others, punishment for slander is incurred, because a situation of passion and abuse proves the meaning of the speaker to be whoredom.

And so also mutual recrimination.—If one man should say to another "Thou art a whoremonger," and the other should answer "Nay, but thou,"—they both incur punishment for slander, as attempting each to fix an imputation of whoredom upon the other.

Recrimination between a husband and wife induces punishment for slander upon the wife.—If a man should sav to his wife "Thou adulteress !" and she should answer saying, "Nay; bur thou !" punishment for slander is incurred by the woman : and there is no Laan in this case; because the husband and wife are both equally accusers : but the accusation advanced by a husband against his wife induces Laan : and that by a wife against her husband induces punishment for slander ; and punishment for slander is here first inflicted upon the woman in order to prevent Laan, as a person who has suffered punishment for slander is incapable of making Laan; for if this arrangement were reversed (that is to say, if the Laan were previously required of the woman), neither the Laan nor the punishment would drop; the punishment, therefore, is to be first inflicted, in order that Laan may be prevented ; for it is laudable to seek remedy by which Laan may be avoided, because that is also punishment in effect.* But if the wife, in the example here recited, were to reply to her husband, "I have committed adultery with you," in this case there is neither punishment for slander, nor Laan; for there is a doubt concerning both punishment and Laan, as it is possible that the woman may allude to a fact of whoredom committed before marriage, in which case punishment for whoredom would be incurred by the woman, and not Laan, she having, by her reply, confirmed the assertion of her husband, in this imputing whoredom to him; but by the husband nothing would be incurred, as he does not confirm here assertion: and, on the other hand, it is also possible that she may allude to carnal connexion after marriage, as if she were to say [in explanation],—"My adultery consisted in your having connexion with me, after our marriage, against my will" (and this, in such a situation,* is the most probable meaning of her words), in which case Laan would be incumbent upon the woman, and punishment for slander would not be incurred by her, as the accusation is made by the husband, and not by the wife : and in consequence of these two contradictory possibilities, a doubt exists equally with respect to Laan and punishment for slander ; wherefore neither is to be insisted on.

Case of acknowledgment of a child, and subsequent denial.—If a man should have acknowledged a child born of his wife, and should afterwards deny it, in this case Laan is incumbent, because the parentage of the child has been established in him by his previous acknowlegment, and by his subsequent denial an accusation is implied with respect to his wife, who is the mother of the child; he must therefore make Laan. But if he should first deny the child, and afterwards acknowledge it, in this case punishment for slander is to be inflicted upon him, because when he thus falsifies, Laan is prevented, as Laan is a sort of punishment imposed from the necessity of the case, owing to a mutual falsification,† in which punishment for slander is the original thing, and hence, in a case where the mutual falsification is done away,‡ that which is the original must be put in force. The parentage also of the child is established in this man, in both these cases, since he has acknowledged it, whether such acknowledgment be made before denial, as in the former instance, or after denial, as in the latter.

Objection.—In the former instance, upon Laan becoming incumbent, it should follow that the parentage of the child is not established.

Reply.—Bastardy is not a necessary consequence of Laan, for Laan may be imposed without bastardizing the child, in the same manner as where a man denies a child after a long lapse of time from the period of the birth, in which case Laan is incumben, and the child is not bastardized, but its parentage remains established ;—as, on the contrary a child may be bastardized in a case in which Laan is not incumbent ; as where a husband denies a child born of his wife, who is a slave, in which case the child is bastardized, but Laan is not incumbent.§

If a man were to say to his wife "This is neither my child, nor yet yours." in this case Laan is not incumbent, nor is punishment for slander due, as the husband here merely denies the child being born of his wife and

*And if the wife were first required to make Laan, and the punishment for slander (which the Laan would not prevent), were afterwards inflicted on both parties, she would (by this mode of proceeding) suffer, on effect, two punishments, which is unlawful. To understand this rightly it is necessary to remark that the imposition of an oath is considered as a violence or hardship mounting to punishment.

*Of recrimination and scolding.

†Where the wife denies the husband's assertion; and the husband denies the chastity of his wife.

‡By one of the parties confessing the other to be in the right ; as the husband here does, by acknowledging the child after having denied it.

§Owing to the wife being a slave.

a husand is not a slanderer by such denial.

Accusation of a woman who has children destitute of any acknowledged father is not slander.—If a man accuse of whoredom a woman who has children, the father of whom is unknown, or if he should so accuse a woman who has made Laan, in consequence of any of her children having been denied [by her husband], whether such children be living or not,—in neither of these cases is punishment for slander incurred, because the signs of whoredom are found with the woman, namely, her children, who are without any acknowledged father: the reputation of this woman is therefore questionable, on account of these signs; and perfect chastity of repute in the accused is one condition of punishment for slander being incurred by the accuser. But if a man were to accuse of whoredom a woman who has made Laan in consequence of an imputation of adultery made against her by her husband, and not on account of his denial of her children, in this case punishment for slander is to be inflicted upon the accuser, since here no signs of whoredom are found with the woman.

Accusation against a person who has unlawful commerce with a woman is not slander.—If a man have unlawful commerce with woman in whom he has no right of cohabitation.* punishment for slander is not to be inflicted upon this accuser, because chastity of repute is not applicable to the accused (and this is conditional to his being married, in the sense which induces punishment for slander upon the accuser), and also, because the accuser in this instance speaks truly.

Under certain restrictions..—It is to be observed as a rule, that punishment for slander is not incurred by the accusation of any person guilty of such a carnal conjunction as is in its own nature unlawful, because the term whoredom [Zinna] signifies a carnal conjunction of this description : but where a person forms such a carnal connexion as is unlawful on some other account, punishment for slander is incurred by the accusation of him, as a carnal conjunction of this description is not whoredom. The connexion of a man with a woman who is not his property in any shape whatever (such as a strange woman), or with one in whom he has no property in some one shape (as in a partnership slave, for instance), is unlawful in its own nature ; so also is his connexion with a woman who is his slave, but who is one with whom cohabitation is unlawful to him by a perpetual illegality (such as his foster-sister); but his connexion with a slave with whom cohabitation is unlawful to him by such an illegallty as is not of a perpetual nature (as in the case of one with whose sister he cohabits, either as his wife, or as his slave), is unlawful, on another account.* Aboo Haneefa (in the case of illegal cohabitation under a perpetual illegality) makes it a condition† that the perpetual illegality be universally admitted and established upon the authority of the most generally accepted traditions, so as to be determined and known beyond all doubt or dispute : for example, if a man were to accuse another, who had carnal connexion with a partnership female slave, in this case punishment for slander is not to be inflicted upon the accuser, because the accused appears to have committed the act with one who is his property in one shape, but not in another. But if a man were to accuse a person who has cohabited with his female slave, being a Pagan, or with his own wife during her courses; or with his Mokatiba, punishment for slander is incurred by the accuser, because here the illegality (supposing the existence of the right of property) is merely of a temporary nature, continuing only until the removal of those obstacles (namely, Paganism, or the courses, or the contract of Kitabut) ; this illegality, therefore, is illegality on another account, and hence the act is not whoredom. It is recorded from Aboo Yoosaf that the carnai conjunction of a man with his Mokatiba occasions the destruction of Ihsan in him ; and such is also the opinion of Ziffer, because a Mokatiba is not her owner's property in respect to carnal enjoyment (whence it is that if a master commit that act with his Mokatiba, he becomes responsible for her Akir‡) ; our doctors, on the other hand, observe that the person of the Mokatiba is the property of her master, but that the enjoyment thereof (with respect to the master) is illegal on another account§ since it is an illegality which continues only until such time as the Mokatiba appears unable to pay her ransom or the contract of Kitabat be broken. If a man accuse a person who has had carnal connexion with his female slave, being his foster-sister, punishment for slander is not due upon the accuser, because carnal connexion with this slave is prohibited to the master by a perpetual illegality ; and this is approved doctrine.

---

*There are many cases of this description which do not amount to whoredom, as may be seen under the head of Erroneous Connexion, &c.

*That is to say, although it be not unlawful in its own nature, yet it is made so by circumstances: but this is not a perpetual illegality, as the prhibition (in the instance here cited) would be removed by the death or other means of removal of the sister : contrary to perpetual iilegality, which, existing in the subject herself, can by no means be removed.

† Of the act amounting to whoredom,

‡ Meaning the portion which is to be paid to her in the manner of a dower.

§ That is, not in its own nature, but occasioned by circumstances.

Punishment is not due for slandering a deceased Mokatib.—IF a person accuse a deceased Mokatib who may have left effects sufficient to discharge his ransom, yet punishment for slander is not due upon the accuser, because here is a doubt with respect to the pefect freedom of the Mokatib, the companions differing in opinion upon this point.

Or a convert before his conversion.—IF a person accuse a Mussulman convert, who, whilst yet a Pagan, had married his mother, punishment for slander is to be inflicted upon the accuser, according to Haneefa; but the two disciples allege that it is not due. The foundation of this difference of opinion is that the marriage of a Pagan with his own mother is approved among the Pagans, according to Haneefa ; but the disciples hold that it is not approved, as was explained at large in the book of Marriage.

Punishment is incurred by an Infidel who slanders a Mussulman.—IF an infidel, residing under protection in a Mussulman state, should accuse a Mussulman, punishment for slander is incurred by him, because, in punishment for slander, the rights of the individual are concerned, and the protected infidel has undertaken to pay a due observance to the rights of individuals, since, as he himself desires to be screened from injury, it follows that he undertakes that he will not offer injury to others ; and also, that he subjects himself to the consequence, if he should do so.

A Mussulman suffering punishment for slander, is incapacitated from being a witness.—IF punishment for slander be inflicted upon a Mussulman; his evidence cannot afterwards be received, although he should repent. Shafei alleges that, in case of repentance, the credibility of his evidence is restored. This point will be further explained in treating of Evidence.

And an infidel also (with respect to Zimmees).—IF an infidel suffer punishment for slander, his evidence becomes inadmissible, not only with respect to Mussulmans, but also with respect to Zimmees, because competency in evidence appertained to him with respect to all of his own description (namely, Zimmees), but his evidence is thenceforth to be rejected,—rejection of evidence being one of the consequences of punishment for slander, But if this infidel should be afterwards converted to the faith, his evidence then becomes admissible with respect to both classes (that is, both Mussulmans and Zimmees), because, upon his embracing the faith, he obtains, de novo, a competency in evidence which did not before exist,* and the rejection of which, therefore, is not a consequence of the punishment for slander: contrary to where a slave suffers punishment for slander and is afterwards emancipated : for here his evidence still continues inadmissible, since, as he was not competent to appear at all as a witness, during his slavery, so as that the rejection* of his evidence might be the consequence of his having suffered punishment for slandar, this circumstance will operate to that effect after his emancipation.

Case of an infidel embracing the faith during infliction of punishment.—IF a single stroke be inflicted on an infidel on account of slander, and he should then embrace the faith, and the remainder of the punishment be afterwards inflicted, in such case his evidence is admissible, because the rejection of evidence is the means of rendering punishment entire and complete, and is therefore a manner of punishment ; but as the degree of punishment inflicted after his having embraced the faith is only a partial correction and not what can be properly termed punishment, the rejection of evidence is not to be considered as a manner of it †—It is recorded from Aboo Yoosaf that his evidence must for the future be rejected, because the degree of punishment inflicted subsequent to his conversion is the greater proportion of it, and the smaller is a dependent of the greater. But the former is the more approved doctrine.

A single punishment answers to all the previous repetitions of whoredom or wine-drinking.—IF a man commit whoredom at several different times, or repeatedly drink wine, and the punishment for either be afterwards inflicted, the single punishment, in either instance, is considered as answering to all repetitions of offence ; and so also, if a person were repeatedly guilty of slander, and punishment for slander be afterwards inflicted on him. The ground of this, in the case of whoredom and wine-drinking, is that the punishment in both these instances is purely a right of GOD, and the design, in the infliction of it, is to deter people from the perpetration of such offences; and a probability of this end being obtained is established by a single infliction of punishment, wherefore the obtaining of it by another infliction of punishment is dubious :‡ and hence punishment cannot be inflicted a second time, because of this doubt : contrary to where a person commits whoredom, and is also guilty of slander, and of wine-drinking for in this case a punishment is to be inflicted separately for every distinct species of offence, because each of these acts is of a nature different from either of the other two, and the design of each of them is different, wherefore, in the punishment of such acts there cannot be any coalescence.

* Namely, with respect to Mussulmans.

*Meaning the inadmissibility.

† This strange sophistry turns entirely upon the meaning of the term Hidd, which is defined to be a certain stated correction competely executed, any thing short of this not being Hidd [punishment], but only chastisement.

‡ Because having been, probably, already obtained, it is (in that case) impossible that it should be obtained a second time.

Or slander.—And with respect to slander, in the punishment of it the right of God is held by our doctors to be predominant, whence the same arguments apply to it as to whoredom and wine-drinking. Shafei maintains that, in the case of repetition of slander, if the slandered person be different (as if the first person slandered were Zeyd and the second Amar), or, if the person with whom the slandered is accused be different (as if a man were to accuse Zeyd of whoredom first with one woman and afterwards with another) in this case there is no coalescence of punishment, but for each slander a separate punishment must be inflicted; for according to Shafei, in the punishment for slander, the right of the individual is predominant.

CHAPTER VI.

OF TAZEER* OR CHASTISEMENT.*

Definition of the term.—Tazeer, in its primitive sense, means prohibition, and also instruction; in law it signifies an infliction undetermined in its degree by the law, on account of the right either of God, or of the individual; and the occasion of it is any offence for which Hidd (or stated punishment) has not been appointed; whether that offence consist in word or deed.

Chatisement is ordained by the law—Chastisement is ordained by the law, the institution of it being established on the authority of the Koran, where God enjoins men to chastise their wives, for the purpose of correction and amendment: and the same also occurs in the traditions. It is moreover recorded that the Prophet chastised a person who had called another perjured; and all the companions agree concerning this. Reason and analogy moreover both evince that chastisement ought to be inflicted for acts of an offensive nature,† in such a manner that men may not become habituated to the commission of such acts; for if they were, they might by degrees be led into the perpetuation of others more atrocious. It is also written in the Fatave Timoor-Tashee of Imam Sirukhsh, that in Tazeer, or chastisement, nothing is fixed or determined, but that the degree of it is left to the discretion of the Kazee, because the design of it is correction, and the dispositions of men with respect to it are different, some being sufficiently corrected by reprimands, whilst others, more obstinate, require confinement, and even blows.

And is of four orders, or degrees.—In the Fatavee Shafee it is said that there are four orders or degrees of chastisement:—First, the chastisement proper to the most noble of the noble (or, in other words, princes, and men of learning), which consists merely in admonition, as if the Kazee were to say to one of them, "I understand that you have done thus, or thus" so as to make him ashamed;—Secondly, the chastisement proper to the noble (namely, commanders of armies, and chiefs of districts), which may be performed in two ways, either by admonition (as above), or by Jirr, that is by dragging the offender to the door and exposing him to scorn:—Thirdly, the chastisement proper to the middle order (consisting of merchants and shopkeepers), which may be performed by Jirr (as above): and also by imprisonment; and Fourthly, the chastisement proper to the lowest order in the community, which may be performed by Jirr, or by imprisonment, and also by blows.

Chastisement may be inflicted by the imposition of a fine.—It is recorded from Aboo Yoosaf that the sultan may inflict chastisement by means of property,—that is, by the exaction of a small sum in the manner of a fine, proportioned to the offence; but this doctrine is rejected by many of the learned.

Chastisement may be inflicted by any person.—Imam Timoor-Tashee says that chastisement, where it is incurred purely as the right of God,* may be inflicted by any person whatever: for Aboo Jafir Hindooanee, being asked whether a man, finding another in the act of adultery with his wife, might slay him, replied, "if the husband know that expostulation and beating will be sufficient to deter the adulterer from a future repetition of his offence, he must not slay him; but if he see reason to suppose that nothing but death will prevent a repetition of the offence, in such case it is allowed to the husband to slay that man: and if the woman were consenting to his act, it is allowed to her husband to slay her also;"—from which it appears that any man is empowered to chastise another by blows, even though there be no magistrate present. He has demonstrated this fully in the Moontaffee; and the reason of it is that the chastisement in question is of the class of the removal of evil with the hand, and the Prophet has authorized every person to remove evil with the hand, as he has said, "Whosoever among ye see the evil, let him remedy it with his own hands: but if he be unable so to do, let him forbid it with his tongue"—(to the end of the speech).—Chastisement, therefore, is evidently con-

---

*It is difficult to separate the ideas of chastisement and punishment.—The law, however, considers them as being essentially distinct, since the degree of Hidd (or punishment) is specified by the law itself, whereas, Tazeer (which for distinction's sake we render chastisement) is committed to the discretion of the magistrate, and for this reason it is elsewhere rendered discretionary correction.

† Meaning petty offences.

*That is, where it is incurred by an offence committed merely against the law, and not affecting an individual.

trary to punishment, since authority to inflict the latter does not appertain to any but a magistrate or a judge.—This species of chastisement is also contrary to the chastisement which is incurred on account of the right of the individual (such as in cases of slander, and so forth), since that depends upon the complaint of the injured party, whence no person can inflict it but the magistrate, even under a private arbitration, where the plaintiff and defendant may have referred the decision of the matter to any third person.

It is to be inflicted wherever it is authorized.—CHASTISEMENT, in any instance in which it is authorized by the LAW, is to be inflicted where the Imam sees it advisable.

Chastisement is due for slandering a slave or an infidel.—IF a person accuse of whoredom a male or female slave, an Am-Walid, or an infidel, he is to be chastised, because this accusation is an offensive accusation, and punishment for slander is not incurred by it, as the condition, namely, Ihsan (or marriage in the sense which induces punishment for slander), is not attached to the accused: chastisement therefore is to be inflicted. And in the same manner, if any person accuse a Mussulman of any other thing than whoredom (that is, abuse him, by calling him a reprobate, or a villain, or an infidel, or a thief), chastisement is incurred, because he injures a Mussulman, and defames him; and punishment [Hidd] cannot be considered as due from analogy, since analogy has no concern with the necessity of punishment: chastisement therefore is to be inflicted. Where the aggrieved party is a slave, or so forth, the chastisement must be inflicted to the extremity of it: but in the case of abuse of a Mussulman, the measure of the chastisement is left to the discretion of the magistrate, be it more or less; and whatever he sees proper let him inflict.

It is not incurred by calling a Mussulman an ass, or a hog.—IF a person abuse a Mussulman, by calling him an ass, or a hog, in this case chastisement is not incurred, because these expressions are in no respect defamatory of the person towards whom they are used, it being evident that he is neither an ass nor a hog. Some allege that, in our times, chastisement is inflicted, since, in the modern acceptation, calling a man an ass or a hog is held to be abuse.—Others again allege that it is esteemed such only where the person towards whom such expressions are used happens to be of dignified rank (such as a prince, or a man of letters), in which case chastisement must be inflicted upon the abuser, as by so speaking he exposes that person of rank to contempt; but if he be only a common person, chastisement is not incurred: and our author remarks that this is the most approved doctrine.

The degree of it is from three stripes to thirty-nine.—THE greatest number of stripes, in chastisement, is thirty-nine; and the smallest number is three. This is according to Haneefa and Mohammed. Aboo Yoosaf says that the greatest number of stripes, in chastisement, is seventy-five. The restriction to thirty-five stripes is founded on a saying of the Prophet, "The man who shall inflict scourging to the amount of PUNISHMENT, in a case where PUNISHMENT is not established, shall be accounted an AGGRAVATOR" (meaning, a wanton aggravator of punishment), from which saying it is to be inferred that the infliction of a number of stripes, in chastisement, to the same amount as in punishment, is unlawful; and this being admitted, Haneefa and Mohammed, in order to determine the utmost extent of chastisement, consider what is the smallest punishment: and this punishment for slander with respect to a slave, which is forty stripes: they therefore deduct therefrom one stripe, and establish thirty-nine as the greatest number to be inflicted in chastisement. Aboo Yoosaf, on the other hand, has regard to the smallest punishment with respect to freemen (as freedom is the original state of man), which is eighty stripes: he therefore deducts five, and establishes seventy-five as the greatest number to be inflicted in chastisement as aforesaid, because the same is recorded of Alee, whose example Aboo Yoosaf follows in this instance. It is in one place recorded of Aboo Yoosaf that he deducted only one stripe, and declared the utmost number of stripes, in chastisement, to be seventy-nine. Such, also, is the opinion of Ziffer; and this is agreeable to analogy.*—Mohammed, in his book,† has determined the smallest number of stripes in chastisement to three, because in fewer there is no chastisement. Our modern doctors assert that the smallest degree of chastisement must be left to the judgment of the Imam, or Kazee, who is to inflict whatever he may deem sufficient for chastisement, which is different with respect to different men. It is recorded of Aboo Yoosaf that he has alleged that the degree thereof is in proportion to the degree of the offence: and it is also recorded from him that the chastisement for petty offences should be inflicted to a degree approaching to the punishment allotted for offences of a similar nature; thus the chastisement for libidinous acts (such as kissing and touching), is to be inflicted to a degree approaching to punishment for whoredom; and the chastisement for abusive language, to a degree approaching to punishment for slander.

Imprisonment may be added to scourging.—IF the Kazee deem it fit, in chastisement, to unite imprisonment with scourging, it is lawful for him to do both, since imprisonment is of itself capable of constituting chas-

* Because, in all other cases the deduction of one from the whole number is sufficient to reduce the thing from a higher to a lower class.

†Meaning the Mabsoot.

tisement, and has been so employed, for the Prophet once imprisoned a person by way of chastising him. But as imprisonment is thus capable of constituting chastisement, in offences where chastisement is incurred by their being established, imprisonment is not lawful before the offence be proved, merely upon suspicion, since imprisonment is in itself a chastisement: contrary to offences which induce punishment, for there the accused may be lawfully imprisoned upon suspicion, as chastisement is short of punishment (whence the sufficiency of imprisonment alone in chastisement); and such being the case, it is lawful to unite imprisonment with blows.

The blows or stripes may be inflicted from the most lenient to the severest degree.—THE severest blows or stripes may be used in chastisement, because, as, regard is had to lenity with respect to the number of the stripes, lenity is not to be regarded with respect to the nature of them, for otherwise the design would be defeated; and hence, lenity is not shown, in chastisement, by inflicting the blows or stripes upon different parts or members of the body. And next to chastisement, the severest blows or stripes are to be inflicted in punishment for whoredom, as that is instituted by the word of GOD in the Koran. Whoredom, moreover, is a deadly sin, insomuch that lapidation for it has been ordained by the LAW. And next to punishment for whoredom, the severest blows or stripes are to be inflicted in punishment for wine-drinking, as the occasion of punishment is there fully certified; and next to punishment for wine-drinking, the severity of the blows or stripes is to be attended to in punishment for slander, because there is a doubt in respect to the occasion of the punishment (namely, the accusation), as an accusation may be either false or true: and also, because severity is here observed, in disqualifying the slanderer from appearing as an evidence: wherefore severity is not also to be observed in the nature of the blows or stripes

If a person die in consequence of chastisement there is no fine.—IF the magistrate inflict either punishment or chastisement upon a person, and the sufferer should die in consequence of such punishment or chastisement, his blood is Hiddir; that is to say, nothing whatever is due upon it: because the magistrate is authorized therein, and what he does is done by decree of the LAW; and an act which is decreed is not restricted to the condition of safety. This is analogous to a case of phlebotomy; that is to say, if any person desire to be let blood, and should die, the operator is in no respect responsible for his death, and so here also. It is contrary, however, to the case of a husband inflicting chastisement upon his wife; for his act is restricted to safety, as it is only allowed to a husband to chastise his wife: and an act which is only allowed is restricted to the condition of safety, like walking upon the highway. Shafei maintains that, in this case, the fine of blood is due from the public treasury; because, although where chastisement or punishment prove destructive, it is Kattl Khota, or homicide by misadventure (as the intention is not the destruction, but the amendment of the sufferer), yet a fine is due from the public treasury, since the advantage of the act of the magistrate extends to the public at large, wherefore the atonement is due from their property, namely, from the public treasury. Our doctors, on the other hand, say that whenever the magistrate inflicts a right of GOD upon any person, by the decree of GOD, and that person dies, it is the same as if he had died by the visitation of GOD, without any visible cause; wherefore there is no responsibility for it.

BOOK VIII.

OF SARAKA, OR LARCENY.

CHAPTER I.

Definition of Saraka.—SARAKA literally means the secretly taking away of another's property. In the language of the law it signifies the taking away the property of another in a secret manner, at a time when such property is in custody,—that is, when the effects are in supposed security from the hands of other people; and where the value is not less than ten dirms, and the effects taken the undoubted property of some other than of him who takes them.

[*This subject is omitted, as larceny is now dealt with under the Penal Code.*]

BOOK IX.

AL SEYIR, OR THE INSTITUTES

Definition of Seyir.—SEYIR is the plural of Seerit, which, in its primitive sense, signifies regulation, in matters spiritual and temporal.—Seyir, in the language of the LAW, more especially applies to the institutes of the Prophet in his wars.

[*This subject is omitted, as it is inapplicable to India.*]

BOOK X.

OF THE LAWS RESPECTING LAKEETS, OR FOUNDLINGS.

Definition of Lakeet.—LAKEET, in its primitive sense signifies any thing lifted from the ground :—the term is chiefly used to denote an infant abondoned by some person in the highway :—in the language of the LAW it signifies a child abandoned by those to whom it properly belongs, from a fear of poverty, or in order to avoid detection in whoredom.—The child is termed Lakeet, for this reason, that it is eventually lifted from the ground, wherefore this term is figuratively applied, even to the property which may happen to be found upon it. The person who takes up the foundling is termed the Mooltakit or taker-up.

The taking up of a foundling is laudable, and (in some cases) incumbent.—THE taking up of a foundling is laudable and generous, as it may tend to preserve his life. This is where the finder sees no immediate reason to suppose that if the child be not taken up it may perish :—but where he sees reason to apprehend that it may otherwise perish, the taking of it up is incumbent.

A foundling is free.—A FOUNDLING is free ; because freedom is a quality originally inherent in MAN ; and the Mussulman territory, in which the infant is found, is a territory of freemen, whence it is also free : moreover, freeman, in a Mussulman territory, abound more than slaves, whence the foundling is free; as the smaller number is a dependant of the greater.

And is maintained by the State.—THE maintenance of a foundling is to be defrayed from the public treasury ; because it is so recorded from Omar ; and also, because, where the foundling dies without heirs, his estate goes to the public treasury : and as that is the property of the Mussulman community, his maintenance must be furnished from this property, since as the advantage results to the community, the loss also falls upon the community ;—whence it is that the Deyit, or fine of blood, is due from the public treasury, where a foundling commits manslaughter.

A foundling owes nothing to his Mooltakit for subsistence unless he furnish it by order of the magistrate.—THE Mooltakit is not to exact any return from the foundling on account of his maintenance, since in maintaining him he acts gratuitously, as he has no authority over him :—he therefore cannot exact any return from the foundling,—except where he has furnished him maintenance by order of the magistrate, in which case this maintenance is a debt upon the foundling, because, the magistrate's authority being absolute, he is empowered to exact the return from the foundling.

No person can take a foundling from his Mooltakit but by virtue of a claim of parentage.—IF any person take up a foundling, no other person is at liberty to take the foundling from him, because the right of charge of the foundling is established in him, as he first laid hands upon it.—If, however, any person claim the foundling, saying, "This is my child," the claimant's declaration is credited on a principle of benevolence. This is where the Mooltakit does not advance any claim of parentage : but if the Mooltakit also make a claim, saying, "This is my child," he has the preference, because both parties are upon an equal footing with respect to their claim, but one of them, namely, the Mooltakit, is in immediate possession, and is therefore preferred to the other. Analogy would require that the declaration of the claimant be not credited, because in consequence of it the right of the Mooltakit is destroyed : but the reason for a more favourable construction of the law in this particular is that the claim of the plaintiff is a declaration upon a point which is advantageous to the infant, as he thereby obtains the honour of an avowed parentage, and the disgrace of a want of parentage is by the claim removed from him. Some have asserted that the declaration in question is valid only with respect to the establishment of parentage, but not with respect to the destruction of the Mooltakit's right of possession ;—and some, again, say that upon the parentage being established, the Mooltakit's right of possession is destroyed, because one consequence of an establishment of parentage is that the father has a preference, in the charge of his child, over all others.

A Mooltakit's claim of parentage with respect to his foundling is admitted.—IF a Mooltakit declare his foundling to be his own child, after having already declared it to be a foundling, some say that his declaration is valid, both from analogy, and also on a principle of benevolence, because his claim respects a thing already in his hands, and is uncontroverted.—nor is any other person's right thereby destroyed. The better opinion.

however, is that his claim is valid only on a principle of benevolence, and not from analogy, because the Mooltakit contradicts himself, as he at first declared the child to be a foundling, and afterwards avers it to be his own child;—and the reason for a more favourable construction is that the contradiction respects a thing of a concealed nature, since it is possible that this child may have been born of his wife, without his knowledge, and that he afterwards comes to a knowledge of the circumstance.

Case of a claim of parentage made by two persons.—If two persons advance a claim together, each asserting—"the foundling in the hands of such a person is my child," and one of them point out a particular mark upon the foundling's body, and not the other, the foundling is adjudged to him, because apparent circumstances bear testimony in his favour, as the mark corresponds with his declaration. But if neither of them point out any particular mark, the foundling is adjudged to both of them, because they are both upon a footing with respect to the ground of their claim. If one of them, however, lay his claim first [that is, before the other], the foundling is adjudged to him because his right is established at a time when no person controverted it;—except where the other brings evidence, as evidence is more powerful than a simple claim.

A foundling discovered by a Zimmee in a Mussulman territory is a Mussulman.—If a foundling be taken up in a Mussulman city or village, and a Zimmee claim it as his child, the parentage is established in the Zimmee, but the child is a Mussulman. This proceeds upon a favourable construction; because the claim of the Zimmee involves two points, I.—a declaration of parentage, which is advantageous to the child,—II. a destruction of the Islamism established from the circumstance of the child being found in a Mussulman territory, which is injurious to the child; and his claim is admitted so far as it is advantageous to the child, but not so for as to be injurious to him.

And if in a Zimmee territory, he is a Zimmee.—If, however, the child be found in a city or village of the Zimmees, or in a church or synagogue, it is a Zimmee. This last opinion is universal (that is to say, is unanimously admitted) where the foundling is taken up, in those places, by a Zimmee:—but if a foundling be taken up in any of those places by a Mussulman, or if a Zimmee take up a foundling in any Mussulman place, there is a difference of opinion: for it is said in the Mabsoot, treating of foundlings, that in this case the place is regarded, and not the Mooltakit or taker-up of the foundling;—that is, if it be found in a Mussulman place, the foundling is a Mussulman, and if not, it is a Zimmee, whether it be taken up by a Mussulman or an infidel: and the reason is this, that the foundling has been first discovered in that place. In some copies of the book of claims from the Mabsoot it is said that in this case regard is had to the Mooltakit;—that is, if a Mussulman have taken up the foundling, it is a Mussulman, and if a Zimmee have taken it up it is a Zimmee—(and the same is mentioned by Ibn Simaia from Mohammed): and the reason is this that possession is more powerful than place; because, if parents were brought as captives, with their infant child from a foreign country into the Mussulman territory, the infant is an infidel in conformity with the state of the parents, from which it is evident that possession is more powerful than place. In other copies of the book of claims it is said that, out of tenderness to the child, regard must be invariably had to Islam;—in other words, if the child be found in a place belonging to Zimmees, and be there taken up by a Mussulman, it is a Mussulman; and if it be taken up by a Zimmee in a Mussulman place, it is in this case also a Mussulman.

A foundling cannot be claimed as a slave.—If any person lay claim to a foundling, as being his slave, his claim is not admitted, because as it is apparent that the foundling is free, it cannot be supposed a slave unless the claimant produce evidence to prove that it belongs to him as such.

A slave's claim of parentage with respect to a foundling is admitted; but the foundling is free.—Observe, also, that if a slave were to claim a foundling, saying, "this is my child," the parentage is established in him, because this is advantageous: the foundling, however, is free, because the child of a man who is slave is free when born of a free woman, and it is a slave when born of a woman who is a slave; concerning the child being a slave, therefore, there is a doubt; and hence its freedom, which is shown by apparent circumstances, cannot be destoryed because of the doubt. A freeman, in claiming a foundling, has preference to a slave, and a Mussulman has preference to a Zimmee, because the claim of a freeman or of a Mussulman is most advantageous to the infant.

The property discovered upon a foundling is his; and may be applied to his use upon the authority of the Kazee.—If there be any property upon a foundling (such as bracelets, and so forth), such property belongs to the foundling, because apparent circumstances argue this; and in the same manner, and for the same reason, if there be any property fastened on the animal upon which a foundling is exposed, such property also belongs to the foundling. The Moo takit, moreover, must expend this property in supplying the wants of his founding, upon an order from the Kazee, because no person is known as proprietor of it, and the Kazee has authority to expend property of this nature upon such an object. Some say that the Mooltakit is at liberty to expend the property in supplying the wants of his foundling, without any order from the Kazee, because it appears that the property in question belongs to the foundling: and a Mooltakit is authorized to provide subsistence for his foundling, and to purchase such articles as are requisite and necessary for him, such as victuals and clothing.

A Mooltakit cannot contract his foundling in marriage.—IT is not lawful for a Mooltakit to contract his foundling in marriage, because he has no authority for so doing, since the reason for such authority (namely, relationship, proprietorship, or sovereignty) do not exist in him.

Nor perform any acts in respect to his property (without authority).—IN the same manner, it is not lawful for a Mooltakit to perform any acts respecting the property of his foundling, analogous to the restriction upon a mother;—that is, a mother has a right to the charge of her infant child, but yet is not at liberty to perform any acts respecting his property; and a Mooltakit stands in the same predicament. The principle upon which this proceeds is that authority to act with respect to the property of an infant is established with a view to the increase of that property; and this is assured only by two circumstances, perfect discretion, and complete affection; now in each of the persons in question, only one of these qualities exists; for a mother, although she entertain a complete affection for her child, is deficient in point of discretion; and a Mooltakit, although he be possessed of perfect discretion, is deficient in affection.

But he may take possession of gifts.—IT is lawful for a Mooltakit to take possession of any thing presented to his foundling as a gift, because this is of singular advantage to the foundling and for this reason it is that an infant is at liberty to take possession of a gift, where he has attained discretion: and in the same manner the mother of an infant, or her executor, are at liberty to take possession of any gift presented to the infant.

And send him to school.—A MOOLTAKIT is at liberty to send his foundling to school for the purpose of education, because this comes under the head of tuition and instruction, and attention to his welfare.

He cannot let him out to hire.—A MOOLTAKIT is at liberty to hire out his foundling. Our author remarks that this is recorded by Kadooree in his compendium. In the Jama Sagheee it is said that it is not lawful for a Mooltakit to hire out his foundling;—and this is approved. The ground upon which the report of Kadooree proceeds is that letting out to hire is one mode of instruction. The reason for the opposite doctrine, as stated in the Jama Sagheer, is that a Mooltakit is not at liberty to turn the faculties of his foundling to his own advantage; he is therefor in the same situation as an uncle: contrary to the case of a mother, since she is at liberty to turn the faculties of her child to her own advantage, as shall be hereafter demonstrated in treating of Abominations.

BOOK XI.

OF LOOKTAS, OR TROVES.

Definition of Lookta.—LOOKTA signifies property which a person finds lying upon the ground, and takes away for the purpose of preserving it, in the manner of a trust. It is proper to observe that the terms Lakeet and Lookta have an affinity with respect to their sense: the difference between them being merely this, that Lakeet is used with regard to the human species, and Lookta with regard to any thing else.

A trove property is as a trust in the hands of the finder.—A LOOKTA, or Trove property, is considered as a trust in the hands of the Mooltakit or finder, where he has called persons to witness that "he takes such property in order to preserve it, and that he will restore it to the proprietor,"—because this mode of taking it is authorized by the LAW, and is even the most eligible conduct,* according to many of our doctors. This is where there is no apprehension of the property being damaged or destroyed;†—but where that is to be apprehended; the taking of it up is incumbent, according to what the learned in the law have remarked upon this point.

Who is not responsible for any damage it may sustain in his hands—Now such being the case, the property is not a subject of responsibility: that is, indemnification for the trove property is not incumbent upon the finder, where it happens to perish in his hands; and in the same manner, the finder is not responsible in a case where himself and the proprietor both agree that he had taken the property avowedly "for the owner;" because their agreement in this point is a proof with respect to both; and hence the declaration of the proprietor that "he [the finder] had taken them from the owner," amounts to the same as if the finder were to produce evidence that he had taken them for the owner.

Unless he avow that he took the property with a view to convert it to his own use.—IF, however, the finder declare, "I took them for myself," responsibility is incumbent upon him according to all authorities, because he here appears to have taken the property of another without that other's consent, and without the permission of the LAW.

The finder is responsible for the trove, if he have not witnesses to testify that he took it for the owner.—IF the finder should not have called any person to witness, at the time of his taking the property, that "he took it for the owner," and he and the owner afterwards differ upon this point, the finder

* That is to say, the taking up of the property is permitted by the LAW, and is even more eligible than suffering it to remain where it is found.

† Meaning—"in case of its not being taken up.

saying, "I took it for the owner,"—and the owner denying this,—indemnification is due, according to Haneefa and Mohammed. Aboo Yoosaf says that indemnification is not due, and that the finder's declaration is to be credited, as appearances testify in his behalf, because it is probable that his intention was virtuous, and not criminal. The argument of Haneefa and Mohammed is that the finder has already acknowledged the fact which occasions responsibility (namely, his taking the property of another), and afterwards pleads a circumstance in consequence of which he is discharged from responsibility, by declaring that he had taken the property for the owner: but as this is a doubtful plea, he is not discharged from responsibility: and with respect to what is urged by Aboo Yoosaf, that "appearances testify in the finder's behalf," they reply that in the same manner as appearances argue that the finder took the property for the owner, so do they likewise argue that he has taken them for himself, as it is probable that a person who performs acts with respect to property does so for himself, and not for another; and hence, as appearances on both sides lead to opposite conclusions, they are on both sides dropped.

The trove is sufficiently witnessed by the finder's notification of it to the bystanders — In calling people to witness it suffices that the finder say to the bystanders "If ye hear of any one seeking for this trove property, direct him to me;"—and this, whether the trove property consist of a single article, or of numerous articles, because, as the term Lookta is a generic noun, it applies either to a single article, or to several different articles

A trove under ten dirms must be advertised for some days, and one above ten dirms, for a year—If the trove property be of less value than ten dirms, it behoves the finder to advertise it for some days—that is, for so long as he deems expedient,—but if it exceed ten dirms in value, he must advertise it for the space of a year. The compiler of the Hedaya remarks that this is one opinion from Haneefa. Mohammed, in the Mabsoot, maintains that the finder should advertise it for the space of a year, whether the value be great or small (and such is also the opinion of Shafei), as the Prophet has said "the person who takes up a trove property must advertise it for a year,"—without making any distinction between a small property and a great property. The reason for the former opinion is that the fixing it at the space of a year occurred respecting a trove property of the value of one hundred deenars, which are equal to a thousand dirms; now ten dirms, or anything above that sum, are the same as a thousand dirms with respect to the amputation of a thief's hand, or the legalizing of generation,* whence it is enjoined to advertise a trove property for a year, out of caution; but anything short of ten dirms oes not resemble a thousand dirms with respect to any of those particulars, whence this point is left to the discretion of the finder of a property of that value. Some allege that the approved opinion is that there is no particular space of time, this being left entirely to the discretion of the finder, who must advertise the trove property until he see reason to conclude that it will never be called for by the owner, and must then bestow it in alms. All that is here advanced proceeds upon a supposition that the trove property is of a lasting and unperishable nature: but if it be of a perishable nature, and unfit to keep it must be advertised until it is in danger of perishing and must then be bestowed in alms. It is proper to remark that the finder must make advertisement of the trove property in the place where he found it, and also in other places of public resort, as by advertising it in such places it is most probable that the owner may recover it

A trove of an insignificant nature may be converted by the finder to his own use.—If the trove property be of such a nature as that it is known that the owner will not call for it (such as date-stones, or pomegranate skins), it is the same as if the owner had thrown it away, insomuch that it is lawful to use it without advertisement: but yet it still continues the property of the owner,* as transfer to a person unknown is not valid.

If the owner do not in due time appear, the finder may either bestow the property in alms, or keep it for the owner.—If the finder duly advertise the trove property, and discover the proprietor, it is well:—but if he cannot discover him, he has two things at his option;—if he choose; he may bestow it in alms, because it is incumbent to restore the property to the owner as far as may be possible, and this is to be effected either by giving the actual property to the owner, where he is discovered or by bestowing it in alms, so as that a return for it (namely, the merit) may reach the owner, as he will assent, upon hearing of its having been so bestowed: or if the finder choose, he may continue to keep the property, in hopes of discovering the owner and restoring it to him.

Where the trove has been bestowed in alms, the owner may either ratify the alms-gift.—If the finder of a trove property discover the owner, after having bestowed it in alms, the owner has two things at his option:—if he choose, he may approve of and confirm the charity, in which case he has the merit of it; because, although the finder has bestowed it in alms by permission of the LAW, yet as the owner has not consented to his so doing, the alms-gift remains suspended upon his consent to it: as the pauper, however, becomes

*Ten dirms is the smallest dower admitted in marriage.

* That is to say, although it be lawful for the finder to use it, yet the owner has a claim upon him for the value.

endowed with the property in question previous to his consent, it does not remain suspended upon the continuence of the subject* (contrary to a case of sale by an unauthorized person ; in other words, if an unauthorized person execute a sale, the validity of it depends upon the continuance of the subject,† that is, of the articles sold, because the purchaser does not become endowed with it until after consent) :

Or take indemnification from the finder.—OR, if the owner choose, he may take an indemnification from the finder, because he has bestowed a property upon the poor without consent of the proprietor.

OBJECTION —It would appear that indemnification is not in umbent upon the finder, as he has bestowed the property in alms, with the consent of the LAW.

REPLY.—His bestowing it in alms, with the consent of the LAW, does not oppose the obligation of responsibility, in behalf of the right of the owner ; in the same manner as where a person eats the property of another when perishing with famine ; for in this case he owes indemnification, although he be permitted by the LAW to eat another's property in such a situation ; and so also in the case in question.

Or from the pauper upon whom it has been so bestowed.—OR, if the owner choose, he may take indemnification from the pauper, where the trove property has perished in his hands,—because he has taken possession of the property of another person without his consent.

Or, if still existing, may claim restitution of it.—OR, if the property be remaining in the hands of the pauper, the owner may take it from him, as he thus recovers his actual property.

OBJECTION.—It has been already stated that the pauper becomes endowed with the property previous to the owner's consent ; whence it would appear that the owner has no right to restitution.

REPLY.—Establishment of property does not oppose a right to restitution ; in the same manner as a donor is at liberty to resume his gift, although the donee have become proprietor upon taking possession of it.

Stray animals ought to be secured and taken care of for the owner.—IT is laudable to secure and take care of strayed cattle ; such as oxen, goats, or camels. Malik and Shafei maintain that where a person finds strayed camels or oxen in the desert,‡ it is most eligible to leave them, the seizing of them being abominable :—and concerning the securing of strayed horses there is the same difference of opinion. The argument of Malik and Shafei is that illegality is orginally connected with taking the property of another, which is not allowable except where there is apprehension of its perishing if it be not taken ; but where a trove property is of such a nature as to be capable of repelling beasts of prey (such as oxen, who may repel them with their horns, or camels and horses, who may repel them with their hoofs or their teeth), there is little apprehension of its perishing : it is still however to be suspected that it will perish, and hence it is declared abominable to secure it, and most laudable to leave it.* The argument of our doctors is that the animals in question are trove property, and there is reason to apprehend their perishing, whence it is laudable to secure and adverties them, in order that the property may be preserved, in the same manner as the securing of strayed goats is laudable according to all.

But he is not responsible to the finder for the subsistence, unless it be furnished by order of the magistrate.—IF, moreover, the finder give subsistence to troves of this description without authority from the magistrate, it is a gratuitous act, because of his not possessing any authority : but if he give subsistence by order of the magistrate, it is a debt upon the owner, because the magistrate is endowed with authority over the property of an absentee for the purpose of enabling him to act with kindness† to the absentee ; and the giving of subsistence is a kindness on some occasions as shall be demonstrated elsewhere.

Who, if they be fit for hire, must direct them to be hired out for that purpose.—IF the question respecting the subsistence of the troves be brought before the magistrate, he must inquire into the particulars ; and if the troves be capable of hire (such as horses, camels or oxen), he must order them to be hired out, and subsisted from their hire, because in this case the animals continue the property of the owner without subjecting him to any debt (and a similar judgment must be passed with respect to fugitive slaves) :

Or, if unfit, to be sold and the price retained for the owner—BUT if the troves be unfit for hire (such as goats or sheep), and it be apprehended that, if the finder were to subsist them, the subsistence would equal their value, the magistrate must direct them to be sold, and the price to be kept in such a manner that the troves may be virtually pre-

* " Upon the continuance of the subject." That is, upon the continuance of the property in the hands of either the donor or the proprietor.

† That is, upon the continuance of the property, which is the subject of the sale, in the hands of the owner.

‡ Arab. Sihra. This is the term applied in general to the extensive and barren deserts of Arabia ; it also means any waste or unenclosed land.

* This is strange reasoning ; it may perhaps have some reference to predestination ; *i.e.* as those animals seem destined to perish, it is impious to attempt to prevent this destiny.

† By the term kindness is here and elsewhere meant a due attention to the interest of the party concerned.

served, in their value, because the preservation of them in substance is impracticable.

Unless he think fit to order them a subsistence, which is in that case a debt upon the owner.—If, however, the magistrate deem it fit to give subsistence; he must adjudge subsistence to be given, making the same a debt upon the owner of the animals,—because the magistrate is appointed for the purpose of exercising humanity and kindness; and the giving of subsistence is a kindness both to the owner and to the finder:—to the owner, because his property is thus preserved to him in subsistance: and to the finder, because the subsistence he furnishes is thus made a debt upon the owner.

But subsistence must not be ordered for more than a few days.—The learned in the law, however, have said that the magistrate is to issue the order for subsistence only for the term of two or three days, in hopes that the owner may appear; and that if the owner do not appear, he must then order the troves to be sold, because to afford subsistence to them for a continuance would be to eradicate the property, whence there would be no kindness in affording them subsistence for a long term (that is, for a term beyond three days).

Nor unless the finder produce evidence in proof of the trove.—It is observed, in the Mabsoot, that the production of evidence is requisite,—that is, the magistrate is not to give an order for subsisting the animal, except where the finder produces evidence to prove that "such an animal is a trove;" and this is approved, because it is possible that he may have obtained possession of the animal by usurpation, and in a case of usurpation the magistrate does not give an order for subsistence, but directs the thing usurped to be restored to the owner, except in a case of deposit, which cannot be proved without evidence; the production of evidence, therefore, is essentially requisite, in order that the actual state of the case may be ascertained.

Objection.—Evidence is not admissible without an adversary; and in the case in question there is no adversary:—how, therefore, can evidence be admitted?

Reply.—The evidence, in the present case, is not required for the purpose of a judicial decree, so as to make the existence of an adversary a necessary condition.

If the finder have no evidence, the order for subsistence must be conditioned upon the veracity of his declaration.—If the finder say: "I have no evidence of the animal being with me as a trove" still as it is apparent that it is a trove, the magistrate must say, "Subsist this animal, provided your declaration be true!" and then, if the finder's declaration be true, he will have a claim upon the owner for the subsistence but not if he be an usurper.

The finder has no claim upon the owner for the subsistence, unless the magistrate expressly declare, in his order, that the owner is responsible for the same;—It is here necessary to remark that what is advanced above, that "the magistrate must adjudge subsistence to be given, making the same a debt upon the owner of the animals," plainly implies that the finder will have no claim upon the owner for such subsistence, upon his appearing at a time when the trove has not yet been sold, unless the magistrate, in his decree, direct that "he shall have such a claim upon him;"—but if the magistrate should not thus have rendered the subsistence a debt upon the owner, the finder would have no claim upon him for it:—this is approved doctrine. Some say that the finder has a claim upon the owner for the subsistence, where he furnishes it by order of the magistrate whether the magistrate may have explicity declared the same to be a debt upon the owner or not.

But he may detain the trove from the owner until he be paid for the subsistence;—Upon the owner appearing, the finder is at liberty to detain the trove, until he pay him for the subsistence; because the finder has preserved the trove, and kept it alive by subsisting it. The case is therefore the same as if the owner had obtained his right of property through the finder; and consequently the trove resembles an article of sale; that is, in the same manner as the seller is entitled to detain the article sold until the purchaser produce the price, so also, the finder is entitled to detain the trove until the owner produce an equivalent for the subsistence. The finder, moreover, resembles a person who apprehends and brings back a fugitive slave, that is, in the same manner as that person is entitled to detain the slave on account of a recompense (since it may be said that he has preserved him), so also, the finder is a liberty to detain the trove on account of the subsistence to be afforded to it, since he has thus preserved it alive.

If, however, the trove perish in the finder's possession after detention, he has no claim.—It is to be observed that the debt for subsistence is not extinguished by the circumstance of the trove perishing in the hands of the finder, before his detention of it: but it is extinguished by the trove perishing in his hands after detention, because by detention it is placed in the same state as a pledge, and as debt is extinguished by the destruction of the pledge, so in the same manner the debt for subsistence is extinguished by the trove perishing after detention.

Troves of unlawful articles are to be advertised and diposed of in the same manner as those of lawful articles.—Troves of lawful articles and of unlawful are the same, in this respect, that the finder is to advertise them for a year. Shafei contends that an unlawful article is to be advertised until the owner appear, because the Prophet has declared "A trove of a FORBIDDEN thing is not lawful to any but the MOONSHID" (that is, the claimant or the owner): and it thus appearing that the trove is unlawful to any except the owner, it is indispensable that the finder advertise it until the owner appear; and he restore it to him; for it must not be bestowed in alms. The arguments of our doctors upon this point are twofold:—FIRST, the Prophet has said, "Advertise the trove by its marks,* and then continue to advertise it for a year," in which no distinction is made between a lawful article and an unlawful:—SECONDLY: the unlawful article in question is a trove: and if, after the expiration of the term of advertisement, it be bestowed in alms, the owner's right of property in it still continues in force; † and such being the case, the finder may bestow it in alms, after the expiration of the term aforesaid, in the same manner as any other troves.—With respect to the saying quoted by Shafei, the explanation of it, that a trove of a forbidden thing is lawful only to the Moonshid (that is, to the advertiser, or person who makes notification of it), and that it is not lawful for any person to take it for his own use.‡ A trove of a forbidden thing is particularly adverted to in this saying, because such a trove must be advertised, although it appear to be the property of strangers (who are continually passing through the country), and if it were not for such an injunction, people might apprehend that, as being the property of strangers who will probably never return to demand it, the advertising is useless.

The claimant of a trove must prove his right by evidence; but it may be delivered to him upon his describing the tokens of it: in this case, however, the magistrate cannot compel a surrender.—IF a person appear, and lay claim to a trove, it is not to be given to him until he produce evidence. If however, the claimant describe the tokens of the trove, by mentioning the weight of the dirms (for instance), or the purse in which they are contained, and its tying, it may be lawfully given to him: but the magistrate is not to use any compulsion upon this point. Malik and Shafei allege that the magistrate may compel the finder to give up the trove; because he merely disputes with the claimant the possession of the trove, and not the right of property in it; and such being the case, a description of the tokens is made a condition as the parties dispute concerning the possession, but the production of evidence is not made a condition, as they do not dispute concerning the right of property. The argument of our doctors is that possession or seisin is a right which may be desirable, in the same manner as actual property in a thing, wherefore no person is entitled to claim the possession of it but through proof, that is, through evidence, in the same manner as no one is entitled to claim the property in it, but through evidence:—but yet it is lawful for the finder to surrender the trove to the claimant, upon his describing the tokens, because the Prophet has said, "If the owner appear, and describe the thing which contains the trove, and the quantity of the contents, let the finder surrender it to him:"—that is, it is allowable to surrender it to him; for the ordinance here is merely of a permissive nature, since it appears, in the Hadees Mashhoor, that the claimant must produce evidence, and the defendant must swear,—which evinces that the command contained in this saying is of a permissive and not of an injunctive nature, otherwise it would not be incumbent upon the claimant to produce evidence.

The finder surrendering a trove upon description of the tokens, without evidence, must take security from the claimant.—WHEN the claimant describes the tokens of the trove, without producing evidence, and the finder surrenders it to him, it is incumbent on the finder to take security from him out of caution; * and concerning this point there is no difference of opinion (according to the Rawayet Saheeh) because here the finder requires the security for himself.† This is contrary to the case of security required in behalf of an absentee heir;—that is, where the Kazee distributes the effects of a person deceased among such of his heirs as are present,—in this case there is a difference of opinion concerning his requiring security of the present heirs, in behalf of an absent heir, provided such should hereafter appear—for, according to Haneefa, security is not required in behalf of the absentee heir, but according to the two disciples security is so required.

The finder is not to be compelled to surrender the trove, although he acknowledge the right of the claimant.—IF any person claim a trove and the finder verify his claim, yet some say that the Kazee must not compel him to surrender the trove:—similar to the case of an agent empowered to take possession of a deposit; in other words, if any person plead that "he is an agent empowered to take possession of a deposit from such a person." and the trustee verify his declaration, yet he is not compelled to surrender the deposit to the agent; and so here likewise. Some, on the contrary, say that compulsion

* Literally, "advertise the BAG OR PURSE containing the trove, and its tying and then advertise the TROVE for a YEAR."

† As he still has a claim of restitution, (See p. 210).

‡ The difference here turns solely upon the sense in which the term Moonshid is to be taken. Moonshid literally signifies a person who points to the place where any thing is lost,—a description which applies equally to the loser or the finder. Shafei takes it in the former sense, and Haneefa in the latter.

* Lest another person should afterwards appear, and prove the trove to belong to him, by evidence.

† He takes the security in his own behalf, and not in behalf of any future possible claimant, who, if he should appear, has recourse to him for restitution.

may be used, because in the case in question, the owner is a person unknown, whereas, in the case of a deposit, the owner of the deposit is a person who is known, whence the possessor cannot be compelled to surrender it to the agent, he not being the owner.

A trove cannot be bestowed in alms upon a rich person.—The finder must not bestow the trove in alms upon a rich person, because the Prophet has said, "If no owner of a trove property appear, BESTOW IT IN ALMS;"—and it is not lawful to bestow alms upon an opulent person; a trove, therefore, resembles Zakat.

Nor can the finder (if rich) lawfully convert it to his own use.—If the finder be in opulent circumstances, it is not lawful for him to derive any advantage from the trove. Shafei affirms that this is lawful, because the Prophet said to Yawabee, who had found an hundred deenars, "If the owner come, surrender the trove to him; but if not, make use of it;"—and yet Yawabee was in opulent circumstances. Moreover, the use of the trove is allowed to the finder, where he happens to be in indigent circumstances, only in order that this permission may be a motive to him to take up the trove, in such a manner that it may be preserved; in other words, the finder, in hope of this advantage, will take up the trove from the ground, and it will thus be preserved from perishing. Now, the poor and the rich are both alike in this particular; and consequently, the finder who is rich may lawfully convert it to his own use, in the same manner as one who is poor. The argument of our doctors is that a trove is the property of another, and hence it is not allowable to derive an advantage from it without his permission, because the passages in the sacred writings which prohibit the enjoyment of another's property are generally expressed.—The use, moreover, is permitted to the poor (contrary to what analogy would suggest), in consequence of the saying of the Prophet already mentioned, and of the opinion of all the doctors; and therefore, any others than those remain under the original predicament, which is an inhibition of the use.—With respect to what Shafei urges (that "the use of the trove is allowed to the finder where he happens to be in indigent circumstances, only in order that this permission may be a motive to him to take up the trove, so that it may be preserved, in which particular the rich and the poor are both alike)," we reply that this reasoning is not admitted; because a rich person may sometimes take up a trove from the ground under the idea that he may himself possibly become a pauper within the term prescribed for advertisement and a poor person, on the other hand may sometimes neglect to take up a trove, under the idea that he may, possibly become rich within that term; what Shafei urges, therefore, under this idea, is no ground of argument. With respect to the instance adduced of Yewabee, it is to be considered that he converted the trove to his own use by permission of the Imam; and the use of a trove, by permission of the Imam, is lawful.

The finder, if poor, may convert the trove to his own use, or, if rich, may bestow it upon his poor relation.—If the finder of a trove be poor, he need not hesitate to make use of the trove, since* in such a disposal of it a kindness is performed both to the owner and to the finder.† Upon the same principle, also, it is lawful to bestow it upon any other poor person; thus if the finder be rich, and his parents, children, or wives poor, he may bestow the trove in alms upon them, for the reason above alleged.

BOOK XII

OF IBBAK, OR THE ABSCONDING OF SLAVES.

[*Slavery being abolished, this subject has been omitted.*]

BOOK XIII.

OF MAFKOODS, OR MISSING PERSONS.

Definition of Mafkood.—MAFKOOD, in its literal sense, means lost and sought after. In the language of the LAW it signifies a person who disappears, and of whom it is not known whether he be living or dead, or where he resides.

When a person disappears, the Kazee must appoint a trustee to manage his affairs.—If a person disappear, and it be not known whether he be dead or alive, or where he resides, the Kazee must appoint some person to look after his property; and to manage his affairs, and maintain his rights: because the Kazee is appointed for the purpose of attending to the interests of all such as are unable to attend to their own concerns; and as a missing person is of this description (whence he stands in the same predicament with an infant or an idiot), it is for his interest to appoint a person to look after his property and manage his affairs.

Who is empowered to take possession of all acquisitions arising to him.—By what is above stated, that "the person appointed by the Kazee shall maintain the rights of the missing person," is meant that this person shall take possession of all acquisitions arising to the missing person from his tenenents, lands, or effects, and also of such debts as are acknowledged by his debtors;—and that he shall also prosecute for debts owing in consequence of

---

*After having duly advertised it, as before directed.

†Because the finder thus obtains a relief from his wants, and the owner has the merit of the charity.

contracts entered into by himself* and which are disputed by the debtor, as the rights of the contract appertain to him, he being the contractor.

But cannot prosecute for disputed debts, or deposits.—BUT he is not to prosecute on account of debts owing in consequence of any contract entered into by the missing person, and which are disputed by the debtors; nor can he prosecute for the missing person's share in lands or effects, in the hands of a third person, who disputes the same: because he is neither the principal, nor the deputy of the principal, being no more than merely an agent for seisin on the part of the Kazee, who is not empowered to prosecute, according to the united opinion of our three doctors;—for their only difference of opinion is with respect to an agent for seisin appointed by the proprietor himself, in a case of debt whom Haneefa holds to be empowered to prosecute, whereas the two disciples deny him this power.—The reason of this is that if it were lawful for the Kazee's agent for seisin to prosecute, and he were to prosecute accordingly, and the debtor to produce evidence proving that the missing person had already received the debt, or discharged it, the Kazee must necessarily pass a decree accordingly, and this would be a decree against an absentee, which is unlawful.—It is not lawful for him, therefore, to prosecute, except where the Kazee is of opinion (with the sect of Shafei), that it is lawful to pass a decree against an absentee, and he directs accordingly, in which case it is lawful, because a decree is of where it is passed in any case concerning which there is a difference of opinion.†

OBJECTION.—The point upon which the difference of opinion rests, on the present occasion, is the decree itself; and hence the case requires that the validity of the decree be suspended upon the warranty of another Kazee.‡

REPLY.—The decree itself is not what the difference of opinion rests upon in the present instance, but the cause of the decree, namely, the evidence, the point of difference being, merely, whether evidence, where there is no actual prosecutor, amounts to proof?—and where the Kazee is of opinion that the evidence amounts to proof, and directs accordingly, his decree is legal and valid.

The missing person's perishable effect must be told.—It is to be observed that if there be, among the effects of the missing person, articles, of a perishable nature (such as fruit, and so forth) the Kazee must sell them: because, as the preservation of them both in substance and in effect is impracticable, they are to be preserved in effect.'

But not those which are unperishable.—BUT he is not to sell any articles not liable to perish, either on account of subsistence, or for any other purpose, because the Kazee is invested with authority, with respect to an absentee, for the conservation of his property and hence it is incumbent upon him to preserve it in substance where that is practicable.

Subsistence must be afforded, out of the effects, to the parents and children of the missing person; and to all others who; without a decree, were entitled to it during his presence.—THE KAZEE is to give subsistence to the wife and children of a missing person out of his property. This rule is not restricted to his immediate children, but extends to all related to him in the time of paternity, such as the father, the grandfather, the son's son, and so forth; for it is a rule that every person entitled to a subsistence from the property of the missing person whilst he was present, independent of an order from the Kazee (such as his infant children, and adult daughters, or adult sons who are disabled) must in his absence be furnished with a subsistence, out of his property, by the Kazee:—but to those who, whilst the missing person was present, had no right to subsistence independent of an order from the Kazee (such as brothers, sisters, or maternal uncles or aunts), no subsistence is, in his absence, to be furnished by the Kazee, because these are entitled to a subsistence only through a decree, and a decree against an absentee is illegal. By the property of the missing person, as here mentioned, is meant money, because the right of the above persons is meat and clothing, and where those are not to be found among the missing person's effects, there is a necessity for the Kazee to decree the value; and the value consists of cash. Bullion (that is, uncoined gold and silver) is in this respect subject to the same rule with cash, since that also admits of being given as value, in the same manner as cash. This is where the Kazee has money in his hand.

Where there are no effects in the Kazee's hands, he may furnish the subsistence from debts or deposits, the property of the missing person—IF, however, there be no money in his hands, but there happen to be some in trust, in the hands of another persons,—or a debt owing from some other person, the Kazee is in that case to provide the subsistence from such deposit or debt, where the

*On behalf of the Mafkood or missing person.

†That is, where the Kazee may happen to dissent in opinion from the Haneefite doctors. The Arabic copy simply says "in which case it is lawful, because the KAZEE is a person supposed to be possessed of judgement and learned in the LAW." What is here advanced affords a striking instance of the power of a Kazee, and the latitude allowed to him in passing his decrees.

‡Because this Kazee being himself a representative of the Mafkood, or missing person, and consequently a part concerned in the decree, cannot carry it into effect, without such authority.

trustee or debtor acknowledges the deposit or debt, and also the marriage or parentage, This acknowledgment. however, is necessary only where these points are not fully known to the Kazee; for if they be fully known to him, the acknowledgment is not requisite.—If, on the other hand, some of these points be known (such as the debt and the deposit), and others unknown (such as the marriage or the parentage), or vice versa, in this case the acknowledgment is requisite with respect to that which is unknown: this is approved. If the trustee or debtor furnish the subsistence without an order from the Kazee, the trustee is responsible for such disbursement, and the debtor is not discharged from his debt, because in so doing they have not paid anything either to the owner or to his representative: contrary to where they furnish subsistence by order of the Kazee, because he appears as representative of the owner.

If the trustee or debtor deny the deposit or debt, together with the marriage and parentage, or if they deny the marriage and parentage only, in this case the persons entitled to subsistence cannot be admitted, as plaintiffs, to prove and establish those points which the trustee or debtor denies; because a claim is not admitted, unless it be laid against either the principal, or his representative; and the principal, in the present instance, is absent; and the debtor or trustee are not either actually or virtually his representative?—they evidently are not actually so, because he has not constituted any person his agent; nor are they virtually so, because, in the prosecution of the plaintiff's claim against the absentee, the specification of the occasion* of the claim is no good plea for the establishment of his right (namely, subsistence from the property in the debtor's or trustee's hands),—since, in the same manner as subsistence is due from that property, it is also due from any other property belonging to the missing person:—the debtor or trustee are therefore not virtually the missing person's representatives.

The Kazee cannot effect a separation between a missing person and his wife.—The Kazee is not empowered to effect a separation between a missing person and his wife. Malik maintains that, at the expiration of four years the Kazee may pronounce a separation, after which the wife is to observe an edit of four months and ten days, such being the edit of widowhood.—and she may then marry whoever she pleases; becauses Omar thus decreed with respect to a person who disappeared from Medina; and also, because a missing person, by his absence, obstructs the woman's right:—the Kazee, therefore must pronounce a separation between the parties after the lapse of a certain time, because of the analogy this case bears to that of Aila, or of impotence;—that is to say, in the same manner as, in a case of Aila, an irreversible divorce takes place at the end of four months,* on account of the husband, by Aila, obstructing his wife's right,—and in the same manner also as in a case of impotence, the Kazee pronounces a separation † at the end of the year, on account of the husband thus obstructing his wife's right,—so likewise, in the case in question, the Kazee must pronounce a separation, for the same reason:—and the case of absence being equally analogous to a case of Aila and of impotence, the length of the term is adjusted with a regard to both, by adopting the number four from Aila, and the term year from impotence, so as to make practice in this particular accord in the same manner with the other two. The arguments of our doctors upon this point are twofold.—First, the PROPHET once declared, with respect to the wife of a missing person, "She is his wife until such time as his DEATH or DIVORCE shall appear:" and Alee also said, with respect to the wife of a Mafkood. "She is a mourner, wherefore she must be patient, until she be perfectly informed of his death, or of his having divorced her."—Secondly, the existence of the marriage is notorious; and as the mere disappearance of the husband is not a sufficient cause of separation, and his death be a matter of uncertainty, it follows that the marriage cannot be dissolved, because of the doubt. With respect to the authority of Omar, as cited by Malik, we reply that he afterwards adopted the opinion of Alee—As to what he farther urges respecting the analogy between the case in question, and a case of Aila, it is not admitted; because Aila, in times of ignorance, was an immediate divorce, but the law afterwards constituted it a deliberate divorce‡ and hence it is that Aila occasions a separation.§—In the same manner also the analogy urged by him between the case in question and a case of impotence is not admitted; becauee where a husband disappears, it is possible that he may reappear, whereas it is not possible that an impotent person should recover his virility, after his impotence has continued for above a year.

The missing person is to be declared a defunct:—When one hundred and twenty years shall have elapsed, from the day of the missing person's birth, he is to be declared

*Meaning, the circumstance of "the trustee or debtor having property belonging to the missing person in his hands," which is not admitted as a plea on behalf of the plaintiff, since his subsistence is equally due from any other part of the missing person's property,

*See vol. I. p. 109.

†See vol I. p. 126.

‡Arab. Talak Mowjil, meaning a divorce which is to take place within a certain time.

§ That is to say, it is for this reason, and not because of the husband obstructing his wife's right, as supposed by Malik.

defunct.*—The compiler of Hedaya remarks that Hassan has related this as an opinion of Haneefa. According to the Zahir Rawayet, this point is to be determined by the decease of the co-evals of the missing person, or of his equals—that is, those who are known to resemble him in health and habits of body. It is recorded from Aboo Yoosaf that the term is one hundred years.—Some of the learned, again, fix it at ninety years. Analogy requires that the term should not be fixed at any particular period, such as one hundred years, or ninety years, since to fix a time merely from judgment or opinion is illegal: but yet it is requisite that it be fixed by some specific standard, such as the demise of the missing person's co-evals, because, if no criterion whatever were established, his decease could never be declared.

At the end of ninety years from his birth.—THE benevolence of the law, however, suggests that the term be fixed at ninety years, as this is the shortest fixed term mentioned,† and it is difficult to ascertain anything respecting the circumstances of the missing person's co-evals or equals.

When his wife is to observe an edit of widowhood.—UPON the death of the missing person being duly declared, his wife must observe her edit for four months and ten days from the date of the declaration, such being the edit of widowhood.

And his property is divided among his living heirs.—AND his property is to be divided among such of his heirs as are then living; the case, therefore, is the same as if he had actually died upon the instant of the declaration, and hence any person who died previous to the declaration does not inherit of him.

A missing person's right of inheritance from a relation cannot be established during his disapperance.—IF the relation of a missing person die during his disappearance, the missing person is not an heir, because his existence at the time is established merely from circumstances, as having been once known, and consequently accounted to continue so long as nothing appears to the contrary. Now mere circumstantial evidence is but weak, and therefore incapable of constituting proof to a claim (that is, to the establishment of a thing as yet unestablished): although it constitute proof sufficient for repulsion (that is to say, to prove the continuance of a thing already established).

But his portion is held in suspense.—WITH respect to the expression "the missing person is not an heir," it means that, whatever may be his portion of inheritance, he does not obtain a property in it, but it is held in suspense; because his being in life is doubtful; and this is a sufficient cause of suspense.

And at the end of the ninty years (if he do not appear in the interim), is divided among the other heirs.—IF, therefore, he afterwards appear to be living, it goes to him; but if there be no evidence of his being in life when ninety years have elapsed, his portion, which has been so suspended, is then to be distributed among those who were heirs to the original proprietor at the period of his demise, as in the case of embryos in the womb. In the same manner, also, if a person make a bequest to a missing person, and the testator die, the bequest does not take place, but is held in suspense, because bequest, stands upon a similar footing with inheritance.

Disposal of inheritance in case of a coheir.—IT is a rule that if there be another heir beside the missing person who is not entirely precluded by the missing person, but whose right is diminished by his intervention, this heir is to receive that which is the least of the two portions of inheritance and the remainder is held in suspense. If, on the other hand, there be an ther heir, who is entirely precluded by the missing person, no part of the inheritance is to be paid to him, but the whole portion of inheritance must be held in suspense. An example, in illustration of this case, is as follows:—A person dies, leaving two daughters, and a son who has disappeared; and also a son's son, and a son's daughter; and his estate is in the hands of a stranger: and the above heirs and the stranger, all agree that the son of the deceased is a missing person; and the two daughters demand their inheritance; in which case they are paid their moiety out of the deceased's estate, as this is their undoubted share: but the other moiety, which is the portion of the missing person, is held in suspense, and no part of it paid to the son's children, because they are entirely precluded by the missing person if he be living, and are therefore not entitled to receive the inheritance, because of the doubt; and this remaining moiety is not to be taken out of the hands of the stranger, unless he be discovered in some dishonest practices—Opposite to the example of the missing person is the case of a foetus in the womb, for whom a child's inheritance is reserved, according to an opinion upon which decrees are passed. If, also, there be another heir beside the foetus, who is not in any circumstance precluded, nor his portion altered by the intervention of the foetus, his complete portion is paid to him: but if this heir be such as is entirely precluded by the intervention of the foetus, nothing whatever is paid to him. Thus, if a man die, leaving a maternal sister and a pregnant wife, nothing whatever is paid to the sister, as she is entirely precluded from inheritance by the intervention of a child whether male or female. If, on the other hand, the heir be one whose share is altered by the interven-

*This is the rule in the Soona. The compiler of the Hedaya, however, has fixed it at ninety years, as appears a little below.

† By any of the law doctors or commentators.

tion of the fœtus, in this case the smaller of the two portions is paid to him, as this smaller share is his undoubted right, in the same manner as in the case of a missing person. For instance, a man dies, and leaves a pregnant wife, and a mother who acknowledges the pregnancy, in which case the wife is paid an eighth and the mother a sixth; because, if the fœtus be born alive, the wife would receive an eighth, and the mother a sixth; but if it be not born alive, the wife would receive a fourth, and the mother a third. A sixth and an eighth are therefore paid immediately, as these are their portions at all events.

BOOK XIV

OF SHIRKAT, OR PARTNERSHIP

Definition of Shirkat.—SHIRKAT, in its primitive sense, signifies the conjunction of two or more estates, in such a manner, that one of them is not distinguishable from the other. The term Shirkat, however, is extended to contracts, although there be no actual conjunction of estates, because a contract is the cause of such conjunction. In the language of the LAW it signifies the union of two or more persons in one concern.

Partnership is Lawful:—PARTNERSHIP is lawful, because in the time of the Prophet men were accustomed to have transactions in partnership, and the Prophet confirmed them therein.

And of two kinds; by right of property and by contract.—PARTNERSHIP is of two kinds, shirkat Milk, or partnership by the right of property, and Shirkat Akid, or partnership by contract.

Partnership by right of property is either optional, or compulsive; and does not admit of either partner acting with respect to the other's share.—SHIRKAT MILK applies where two or more persons are proprietors of one thing;—and it is of two different natures, optional and compulsive:—optional, where two persons make a joint purchase of one specific article: or where it is presented to them as a gift, and they accept of it; or where it is left to them, jointly, by bequest, and they accept of it;—or where they both obtain possession, by conquest, of one specific article in an enemy's country;—or where they unite their respective properties in such a way is that one is not distinguishable from the other (such as the mixture of wheat with wheat).—or where it may be difficult to distinguish them (as in a mixture of wheat with barley):—and compulsive, where the properties of two persons become united without their act, under such circumstances as render it difficult or impossible to distinguish between them; or: where two persons inherit one property. In this species of partnership, therefore, it is not lawful for one partner to perform any act with respect to the other's share, without his permission each being as a stranger with respect to the other's share. It is, however, lawful for either partner to sell his own share to the other partner, in all the cases here stated:—and he may also sell his share to others without his partner's consent, excepting only in cases of association or a mixture of property, for in both these instances one partner cannot lawfully sell the share of the other to a third person without his partner's permission. The distinctions upon this point are related in the Kafayat-al-Moontihee.

Partnership of contract.—SHIRKAT AKID or partnership by contract, is effected by proposal and consent,—that is, by one person saying to another, "I have made you my partner in such a property," &c. and the other replying "I consent:" and it is a condition of the contract that the concern respecting which it is made be of such a nature as to admit of delegation, in order that the acquisition arising from it may be participated in by both parties, and that thus the effect or design may be established,—in other words, that the acquisition may become equally the property of both.

Is of four descriptions, by reciprocity, in traffic, in arts. and upon personal credit.—PARTNERSHIP by compact is of four kinds, viz:

I.—Shirkat-Mofawizat, or partnership by resiprocity.

II.—Shirkat-Aiman, or partnership in traffic.

III.—Shirkat-Sinnaia- or partnership in arts.

IV.—Shirkat-Woodjooh, or partnership upon personal credit.

Description of partnership by reciprocity.—Shirkat-Mofawizat, or partnership by reciprocity, is where two men, being the equals of each other, in point of property privileges, and religious persuasion, enter into a contract of co-partnership:—because this species of partnership is an universal partnership in all transactions, where each partner reciprocally commits the business of the partnership to the other, without limitation or restriction: for the term Mofawizat, in its literal sense, means equality.

It requires equality in point of capital:—IT is therefore indispensable that a perfect equality exist throughout, in the property, that is, in the partnership capital, such as dirms and deenars.—(No regard, however, is paid to an excess in anything beyond the partnership capital, such as goods or effects, lands, or debts.)

And of privileges;—In the same manner, it

*The commentators define it partnership in purchase and sale. The term does not admit of any literal translation.

is indispensable that an equality exist with respect to privileges ;* because, if either partner were endowed with privileges not vested in the other, there could be no perfect equality.

And similarity of religion and of sect.—In the same manner also, equality is indispensable in point of religion and of sect, as shall be hereafter demonstrated. Partnership by reciprocity is lawful, upon a favourable construction ;—but, according to analogy, it is unlawful. This, also, is one opinion of Shafei. Malik says, "I know not what Mofawizat is !"—Analogy would suggest that a partnership of this description is unlawful,—because it includes a power of agency with respect to an unknown subject, and also an obligation of security with respect to a thing underfined ; and as each of these, individully, is illegal: it follows that, when un ted, they are illegal a fortiori. The reason for a more favourable construction upon this point is that the Prophet has said, "Enter into partnerships by reciprocity, for in that there is great advantage." In this manner, also, men had transactions together, no person forbidding them Analogy, therefore, is abandoned. Ignorance; moreover, in the contract in question, is lawful as a dependant of another circumstance,—that is, as a dependant of equality ;—in the same manner as in a contract of Mozaribat, where the contract comprehends a commission of agency for the purchase and sale of article unknown, which commission is in itself illegal, but is nevertheless legal in a contract of Mozaribat, as a dependant of the contract ; and so also in the case in question.

The term reciprocity must also be expressed in the contract.—A contract of reciprocity is not complete unless reciprocity be expressly mentioned in it, by the parties declaring "we are partners, in a partnership by reciprocity,"—because the conditions of it cannot otherwise be known. If however, in entering into such a contract, they declare all the conditions of it, the contract is lawful, although the term reciprocity be not particularly expressed in it, because regard is had to the sense, and not to the letter.

It is lawful between free adults, whether Mussulmans or Zimmees.—A contract of reciprocity is lawful between to adults who are free, whether they be both Mussulmans, or both Zimees, since, in either case, an equality exists between the parties. If one of them, also, be a scriptural Zimmee,† and the other a Pagan, the contract is lawful, because infidelity is one general description with respect to faith, and hence equality in point of religion exists in this instance.

It is not lawful between a slave and a free man or an infant and an adult—A contract of reciprocity is not lawful between a slave and a freeman or between an infant and an adult ; because equality does not exist in those instances ;—as an adult freeman is competent to transact buisness, and to give bail whereas a slave is not competent in either of those points but by consent of his master ; and an infant is not at all competent to give bail, nor to transact business, but by permission of his guardian.

Or a Mussulman and an infidel.—A contract of reciprocity is not lawful between a Mussulman and an infidel, according to Haneefa and Mohammad Aboo Yoosaf alleges that it is lawful, because equality exists between those in point of agency and bail, since in the same manner as it is lawful for a Mussulman to be an agent or a surety, so is it also for an infidel : and with respect to those particular transactions which are lawful to one of those, and not to the other (such, for instance, as dealings in wine or pork), they are not regarded, in the same manner as a similar difference is not regarded where a Haneefite enters into a contract of reciprocity with a follower of Shafei, for here the contract is lawful, notwithstanding the different tenets of those sects respecting wilful dealings in the offspring of Tasmeeas,* which are held to be lawful by the followers of Shafei ; but which are deemed illegal by the Haneefites, as being (according to them) forbidden. Such a contract, however between a Mussulman and a Zimmee is nevertheless abominable (according to Aboo Yoosaf) ; as Zimmees frequently enter into engagements of an unlawful nature, in consequence of which a Mussulman might fall into what is prohibited. The argument of Haneefa and Muhammed is that the two persons in question are not upon an equality in point of power of action,—because, if a Zimmee purchase wine or pork with the capital stock, the purchase is valid, whereas, if a Mussulman were to purcha e these articles it is invalid : hence the parties are not upon an equal footing in point of transaction.

Nor between two slave, two infants, or two Mokatibs—A contract of reciprocity is not valid between two slaves, two infants, or two Mokatibs, because a contract of reciprocity is founded upon each party being surety for the other, and the bail of such persons is invalid. It is to be observed, however, that on all occasions where a contract of reciprocity proves invalid from the non-existence of some of its conditions, and those conditions are not requisite in Ainan (or partnership in traffic), the contract of reciprocity) becomes a contract of partnership in traffic because of the existence of all the conditions requisite in such a contract.

It comprehends both agency and bail.—A contract of reciprocity comprehends the

*Arab. Tissirraf ; that is, power of action.

†A Jewish or Christian subject of the Mussulman government.

*Tasmeeas are camels turned loose and suffered to pasture at large without a herdsman, as being dedicated to God.

properties both of agency and bail. It comprehends the property of agency, because if each of the contracting parties were not the agent of the other, the end (namely, a mutual participation of property), would be defeated. It also comprehends the property of bail, because if each party were not surety for the other, the equality, in certain particulars essential to traffic (such as the demand of payment from either of them for purchases made by the other), could not exist.

A purchase made by either partner is participated between both; except in articles of subsistence.—Whatever is purchased by either of two partners under a contract of reciprocity is participated of by both, except the food and clothing purchased by the partner for himself and his family:—because a contract of reciprocity requires that both parties be upon a perfect equality: and as each is the other's subsitute in all dealings, is follows that a purchase made by one is equivalent to a purchase by both. This, however, is exclusive of such articles as are here excepted (which exception proceeds upon a favourable construction), as the articles in question must be excluded from a contract of reciprocity, necessarily, because there is perpetual occasion for them: for one partner cannot be made answerable for the other's wants; neither can one of them expend the property of the other in the supply of his own wants; yet the purchase of these articles is indispensable; and, on account of this indispensable necessity, the food and other articles mentioned appertain solely to the purchaser. (Analogy would suggest that those articles also are participated in by both partners, in conformity with what was before advanced, that "a contract of reciprocity requires that both parties be upon a perfect equality.") The seller of the food or clothing is, however, at liberty to take the price of his commodity from either partner, as he pleases; from the purchaser, evidently, since it was he who bought the article; and also from the other partner, since he is surety for the purchaser; and in this last case the other partner takes from the purchaser a moiety of what he has paid to the seller, as having discharged a debt of the purchaser out of property common to both.

A debt incurred by either partner is obligatory upon the other.—Whatever debt is incurred by either of two partners in reciprocity, for a thing in which partnership holds, the other partner is responsible for the same, in order that equality may be established. Of those things in which partnership holds are sale, purchase, and receipt of hire or wages:—and of those in which partnership does not hold are marriage, and divorce for a compensation, composition for blood wilfully shed, and composition for a subsistence, and offences against the person.

Bail for property, engaged in by either partner, is binding upon the other;—If a partner in resiprocity become, in behalf of a third person, surety for property to a stranger, it is binding upon the other partner likewise, according to Haneefa. The two disciples allege that it is not binding upon the other partner; because a person's becoming surety for another is a gratuitous act* (whence it is that the bail of an infant, a Mazoon, or Mokatib, is invalid,—and also; that if a person give bail upon his deathbed it is valid with respect to a third of his property only):—and as becoming surety is a gratuitous act, it is equivalent to the act of granting a loan, or giving bail for the personal appearance of any one; † in other words, if one of two partners in reciprocity were to grant a loan to a stranger out of the partnership stock, it does not affect the other partner, insomuch that the right of exacting repayment rests solely with the lender, as lending is a gratuitous act;—and in the same manner, if one of two partners in reciprocity become bail for the personal appearance of any one, a requisition for the production of the person bailed cannot be made to the other partner;—and so likewise in the case in question. The argument of Haneefa is that bail for property is gratuitous in its principle, but in its consequence induces a kind of obligation or contract; because in consequence of the bail, the surety is entitled to exact of the person bailed whatever he pays to his creditors, provided the bail had been given with his concurrence. It is therefore comprehended in a contract of reciprocity, with regard to its continuance (and the circumstance of its continuance is the point in question, as we say "it becomes binding upon his partner after becoming so upon himself)." With respect to what the two disciples urge, that "a person's becoming sufety for another is a gratuitous act, whence the bail of an infant, a Mazoon, of Mokatib, is invalid; and consequently, that it is not comprehended in a contract of reciprocity," we reply that a contract of bail entered into by incompetent persons is invalid in its principle; but in the case in question it is binding upon the other partner in the circumstance of its continuance only. Bail, therefore, with regard to its continuance, as being an act of exchange, bears a relation to traffic; and traffic is comprehended in a contract of receiprocity. If a dying person, on the other hand, enter into a contract of bail, it is valid with respect to a third of his property, in regard to its execution, as well as its continuance. Thus bail for property is not of a gratuitous nature in its continuance, whereas bail for

* All concessions, or acts of a gratuitous description, are admitted in law to affect only the actor himself.

† There is a material difference between bail for property, and bail for the person; as is shown at large elsewhere. (See Bail),

the person, on the contrary, is gratuitous, both in its execution and its continuance. Hence bail for property is in no respect analogous to bail for the person. As to what the two disciples further urge, that "if one of two partners in reciprocity were to grant a loan to a stranger out of the partnership stock, it does not affect the other partner, as lending is a gratuitous act"—it is not admitted: because it is recorded from Haneefa, that the act of lending does affect the partner: if, however, it even were admitted by Haneefa, as not affecting the other partner, we reply that a loan in money is equivalent to the act of lending any article of goods or effects; and hence the property paid to the lender by the borrower may be said to be the same identical property which he had borrowed, and not a compensation for it (whence a stipulated time or place of repayment are not valid in it), and therefore, that lending does not bear the property of exchange.

Unless it be engaged in without consent of the suretee.—All which is here advanced proceeds upon a supposition of the bail for property having been contracted with the concurrence of the person bailed. If, however, it be entered into without his concurrence, it is not binding upon the other partner (according to the Rawayet Saheeh of Haneefa), because in a bail so contracted the property of mutual obligation or exchange does not exist in its continuance. Let it be observed also, that indemnification for usurped property, or indemnification for damages, stand on the same ground as bail for property, as these are of retributive nature in their principle.

An accession of property to either partner by gift or inheritance resolves a partnership by reciprocity into a partnership in traffic.—IF a property* of such a nature as that partnership in it is valid, should fall to one of two partners in reciprocity, by inheritance,—or, if any person present him with such property, by gift, and he take possession of it,—the contract of reciprocity is null, and the partnership becomes a Shirkat Ainan, because equality in point of property (such as is capable of constituting capital stock) is a condition essential to a contract of reciprocity throughout, and this does not exist in the present case, as the other partner is not a participator in the property so acquired by gift or inheritance, no principle of partnership therein appearing with respect to him. The partnership by reciprocity, however, is resolved into a Shirkat Ainan, or partnership in traffic, as the case admits of such a partnership, equality not being essential thereto; in reciprocity, on the other hand, it is essential, and consequently reciprocity no longer continues. The reason of this is that a contract of reciprocity is not of an absolute nature: now, in a contract which is not of an absolute nature, the rules with respect to its continuance and its commencement are one and the same: hence an increase of the capital stock [of either parties] during its continuance is equivalent to an inequality in its commencement; and as an inequality of capital, in the commencement of a partnership of reciprocity, is prohibitory to contracting it, so, in the same manner, such inequality taking place during its continuance prohibits it;—the contract of reciprocity, therefore, teminates.

Unless the property be of a nature incapable of continuing stock.—If one of two partners in reciprocity inherit goods or effects,* these are his sole property; but the contract of reciprocity does not become null (and the same rule also obtains if one of them inherit land): because, as those articles are incapable of constituting capital stock, equality with respect to them is not a condition.

Section.

Partnership by reciprocity cannot be contracted but in cash.—PARTNERSHIP by reciprocity cannot be contracted but in dirms, deenars, or fluctuating faloos.† Malik alleges that such a partnership is lawful in goods and effects, and also in all articles estimable by weight (or measurement of capacity, where the species is the same, because a partnership so contracted respects a known and specified capital whence those articles are equivalent to money. It is otherwise in a contract of Mozaribat: for that is restricted solely to cash, the legality of it being contrary to analogy, since under this species of engagement a profit is acquired on property concerning which there is no responsibility (as the manager is not responsible for the Mozaribat stock): and the Prophet has forbidden the acquisition of gain upon property in which there is no responsibility; the contract, therefore, must not go beyond what is prescribed by the LAW; and the only thing in which the LAW declares Mozaribat to be lawful is cash. The arguments of our doctors upon this point are twofold.—FIRST, if a contract of reciprocity, in goods and effects, were held to be legal (as maintained by Malik), it would necessarily induce a profit upon a property concerning which there is no responsibility; because, upon each partner in reciprocity selling his own particular capital (consisting of goods and effects), if the goods of one

* Arab Mal. Meaning property in cash, bullion, or other article capable of constituting capital stock; in opposition to Raht and Matta, that is, specific goods and effects.

* Arab. Rakht wa Matta. In opposition to Mal.

† Arab. Faloos - Rabiha. Faloos is a copper coin of uncertain value. Faloos-Rabiha means copper coin on which an advantage may be gained (owing to the fluctuation in its value), and hence the term Rabiha is here rendered fluctuating.

partner produce a greater price than the goods of the other, the excess of profit upon the goods of the former would be due to the latter; and this would be a profit from property for which the person who gains by it is not responsible, and in which he has no right; because in this instance the contract is connected with actual goods, and not with the semblance of them, such as debts; and the goods are a trust in the hands of each partner respectively:—whence it is evident that a profit is induced upon property concerning which there is no responsibility. It is otherwise with cash, because whatever either partner may purchase with the capital stock, consisting of cash, the purchase thereof is not connected with the actual capital, but with its semblance, namely, debt (since the price of it is a debt);—now the purchase being connected with the semblance of the capital (namely, debt, and the other partner also being liable to be called upon for it (as a contract of reciprocity involves mutual bail), it follows that the consequence objected (of profit upon property concerning which there is no responsibility) is not induced, since his is a property in which there is responsibility. SECONDLY, The first transaction in goods and effects is the sale of them; and the first transaction in cash is purchase made with it:—now a person selling his property under the condition of another being his partner in the proceeds is unlawful, since this is endowing, with a right of property in the debt, and an endowment of right in a debt, made to any other than the debtor himself, is illegal: on the other hand, his making a purchase with his own property, under the condition of another being his partner in the article purchased, is lawful, since this is endowing with a right of property in an actual substance, and not in a debt.

And copper coinage is comprehended under the head of cash.—FALOOS-RABIHA, or fluctuating copper coins, are connected with dirms and deenars [cash], as they pass current, in the same manner as gold and silver coin. Mohammed is of this opinion, because he holds that faloos are cash, insomuch that they cannot be particularized by specification; whence it is that if any person were to purchase an article, for certain faloos, he is at liberty to give any other faloos in place of them; and also, that two specified faloos cannot be sold for one faloos, according to what is established. According to the two elders, partnership, or Mozaribat, are not lawful in faloos, although they be current, as the valuation of them fluctuates from time to time, and they at length become the same as goods or effects.* Aboo Yoosaf is elsewhere said to entertain the same opinion with Mohammed upon this point. It is also recorded, from Haneefa that a contract of Mozaribat is lawful in current faloos; but not a contract of reciprocity. Thus partnership by reciprocity is not lawful in any thing beyond dirms, deenars, and current faloos*

Or in gold or silver bullion, where that passes in currency.—IT is to be observed, however, that if gold or silver bullion, by general usage, pass current for value,† in this case partnership by reciprocity is lawful in it. This is also related in the Kadooree. It is asserted, in the Jama Sagheer, that partnership by reciprocity is not lawful in gold or silver bullion; for according to that authority, uncoined gold and silver are the same as household stuff, distinguishable by identic specification, and therefore incapable of constituting capital in either partnership or Mozaribat. It is said in the Mabsoot, treating of exchange, that gold or silver cannot be indentified by specification, insomuch that a contract of sale is not broken in consequence of any accident to the bullion before delivery (that is, if a person purchase any article, agreeing to give for it certain gold or silver uncoined, and it be lost before delivery, the contract of sale is not broken, because the gold or silver cannot be particularly specified).—Now such being the case, it follows (according to this statement) that uncoined gold or silver are capable of constituting capital stock, in either Mozaribat or partnership, on this ground, that the precious metals were originally introduced for the purpose of valuation‡. The opinion delivered in the Jama Sagheer, however, is the most approved; because, although the precious metals were orginally introduced for the purposes of traffic, yet their capacity to represent property depends upon their being coined, as when once coined, they are no longer liable to be used for any other purpose (such as making ornaments for the person, and so forth): uncoined gold or silver, therefore, does not constitute value, except where the use of it in that way is customary, in which case it is the same as coin, and consequently a representative of property, and as such capable of constituting capital stock. It is to be observed that what was before advanced, that "partnership by reciprocity is not lawful in anything beyond dirms, deenars, and current faloos," applies to all articles of weight and measurement of capacity, or which are of a heterogeneous nature.§ The illegality of reciprocal partnership in these articles is admitted by all our doctors, pro-

*That is, are no longer current.

*That is, such as have not yet become depreciated below the current standard.

†Arab. Simn (or Thimn); meaning a representative of property, and therefore used (in purchase and sale) to express price.

‡ Arab. Sil-Simneeat; that is, for the purpose of constituting price, or (in other words) of representing property.

§ Arab. Adwee Mootkatib, that is, resembling in appearance, but differing in species.

vided the partnership be contracted previous to the union or admixture of stocks, in which case it is illegal, and each partner receives the profit arising from his own particular commodity, and the loss upon it also falls on him. If, also, two persons mix homogeneous stocks, and then enter into a contract of partnership, Aboo Yoosaf holds the rule to be the same, and that a partnership by right of property is here established, not a partnership by reciprocity. Such, also, is the doctrine of the Zahir Rawayet. According to Mohammad, the contract of partnership, in this instance, holds good.

Or (according to Mahammed) in homogeneous stocks, after admixture.—THE result of this difference of opinion appears where the property of both partners is equal, and they stipulate a larger profit to one, and a smaller profit to the other :—for in this case. according to Aboo Yoosaf, each is to receive in proportion to his property, and he in whose favour the larger profit hnd been stipulated is not on that account entitled to receive any excess ; but, according to Mohammed, each is to receive agreeably to what was stipulated. The ground upon which the Zahir Rawayet proceeds is that articles of weight and measurement of capacity,* and so forth, are distinguishable by specification after admixture, in the same manner as before. The argument of Mohammed is that the articles in question are, in one shape, value ; for if a person where to sell goods for such articles, so that the price of the goods (consisting of those articles), is a debt upon the purchaser, it is lawful ; and, in another shape, they are subjects of sale, as admitting of specification ; attention. therefore, is paid to both these circumstances, with respect to situations both of admixture and of non-admixture : in other words, partnership in them, before admixture, is unlawful, as they are then subjects of sale ; but after admixture it is lawful, as they then constitute value : contrary to the case of goods and effects of any other decription, since these are not value in any shape.

It cannot be contracted respecting heterngenerous stocks—IF the stocks [of the respective parties] be of two different species, such as barley and wheat, or olives and pepper, and the proprietor unite them, and then enter into a contract of partnersnip, it is unlawful according to all our doctors. The reason for this distinction, according to Mohammad, is that whatever is mixed, of one species, is Zooatal Imsal ; † and whatever is mixed, of two different species, is Zooatal Keem :* now as things of different species, when mixed together, are Zooatal Keem, ignorance exists with respect to them (because, it is requisite that appraisers fix the value of them), † and they are therefore incapable of constituting capital stock, in the same manner as any other goods or effects :—a partnership in them is consequently invalid ; and such being the case, they become subject to the rules in admixture of property, as treated of under the head of Decrees, in the Jama Sagheer and which shall be fully set forth (in this work when we treat of deposits.‡

Partnership by right of property is effected by each partner selling one half of his stock to the other.—WHERE two persons are desirous of entering into a contract of partnership in goods and effects, each must sell one half of his own goods in lieu of one half of the goods of the other, so that a Shirkat-Milk, or partnership by right of property may be established between them : and then let them enter into partnership by compact.—(Our author remarks that in this instance a partnership in right of property is established, but that a partnership by reciprocity is not lawful, as goods and effects are incapable of constituting stock in such a partnership) With respect to what is advanced above, that "each partner must sell one half of his own goods in lieu of one half of the goods of the other." it means, that each is thus to sell a moiety of his goods to the other, provided the value of the goods of each be equal. If, however, the value of the goods of each be different it is requisite that he whose goods are of least value sell such a portion as may suffice to establish a partnership ; for instance, if the value of

---

*Meaning always grain, or liquids, such as are capable of admixture ; in opposition to Rakot and Matta, that is goods and effects.

†Things compensable by an equal quantity of their own species (such as wheat, for wheat. barely for barley, &c.)

*Things compensable only by an equivalent in money,

† Before the respective proportion of each partner, in the capital stock, can be ascertained.

‡ The arguments throughout this and the preceding passages are so much involved in subtle distinction and perplexing casuistry, and are in many places so little capable of an intelligible translation (from the impossibility of rendering clearly the technical terms which so frequently occur in them), as greatly to obscure the matter. The principle upon which the whole turns is that 'a partnership by reciprocity cannot be entered into with respect to any articles which are not standards of value ," and the question is "what articles they are which may be considered as standards ?"—which some of the doctors confine solely to cash in the precious metals : others extend it to bullion ; and others, again, to copper coins [faloos] ; whilst some include grain, contending that this is a standard of value, and may therefore be used to represent property, in the same manner as cash.

the goods of one be four hundred dirms, and that of those of the other be one hundred dirms, then let the latter sell four fifths of his goods to the former, in lieu of one-fifth of his goods, so that the whole of the goods may be held in partnership between the parties in five lost, or shares. With respect to what is advanced by our author, as above, that "a partnership in right of property is established, but a partnership by reciprocity is not lawful," it is of no weight; for rendering goods and effects capital stock in a contract of reciprocity is, illegal, only, because this would induce a profit upon property concerning which there is no responsibility, or, because the respective capital of each would be unknown at the time of division: but neither of these reasons exist in the case in question:—the first reason does not exist, because upon each selling a moiety of his estate to the other, the half of each partner, respectively, is a subject of responsibility to the other, with respect to its value, and hence the profit which accrues from the property of both is a profit from property which is a subject of responsibility: and the second reason does not exist evidently, because there is no occasion for specifying the respective capital of each partner at the time of division, so as to require the valuation of appraisers thence inferring ignorance respecting at, because the property of both is equal, and they are both partners in that property, and consequently, whatever price the property may bring must necessarily be divided between them in equal shares.

Description of partnership in traffic.—SHIRKAT-AINAN, or partnership in traffic, is contracted by each party respectively becoming the agent of the other, but not his bail. This species of partnership is where two persons become partners in any particular traffic, such as in clothes or wheat (for instance), or where they become partners in all manner of commerce indifferently.

It does not admit mutual bail, but it requires mutual agency.—No mention, however, is to be made concerning bail, in their agreement, as bail is not a condition in a partnership of this nature:—but it is indispensable requisite that each act as agent on behalf of the other; since, without this, the design (namely, partnership in property), cannot be obtained; as acts done on behalf of another are performed either in virtue of some avowed authority, or of agency; and no authority existing, agency is constituted in order that each may act for the other, so that the property may be held in partnership between them.

It admits of inequality in point of stock.—IF the stock of one of these partners exceed that of the other, it is lawful, because there is occasion for this equality (as shall be hereafter demonstrated), and the terms in which such a partnership is contraced do not require equality.

And also of a disproportionate profit.—In partnership in traffic, it is lawful that the stock of each partner be equal, and yet the profit unequally shared,—that is, that it be stipulated that the profit to one partner exceed the profit to the other. Ziffer and Shafei maintain that this is not lawful; for if, with equality of stocks, an inequality of profit be admitted, it induces a profit upon property concerning which there is no responsibility; because, if the capital appertain to the two in equal shares, and the profit be divided into three lots (for instance), the shar r in the larger proportion of profit is entitled to a superior profit without any responsibility, since the responsibility is in proportion to the capital;—and also, because a paranership in the profit exists in virtue of partnership in the capital (according to their tenets, whence they likewise hold the admixture of the property to be condition);—the profit upon the property, therefore, is the same as increase of living stock; and each is consequently entitled thereto, in proportion to his original right of property in the capital. The arguments of our doctors upon this point are twofold.—FIRST, the Prophet has said, "The profit between them is according to their agreement, and their loss in proportion to the property of each respectively;" where no distinction is made between the equality or inequality of their properties.—SECONDLY, in the same manner as a person is entitled to profit in virtue of property, he is also entitled to it in virtue of labour (as in a case of Mozari at for instance): it may also sometimes happen that one of the partners is more skilful and expert in business than the other, and consequently, that he will not agree to the other sharing equally in the profit whence it is requisite that one have a larger share than the other. It would be otherwise if the whole profit were restricted to one of the partners, because in this instance the contract is not a contract of partnership: neither is it a contract of Mozaribat, for if, in Mozaribat, the whole profit be assigned to the manager, it is a loan; or if to the proprietor of the stock, it is a Bazat. With respect to what is object by Ziffer and Shafei, that "if, with equality of stocks, an inequality of profit be admitted it induces a profit upon property concerning which there is no responsibility,"—we reply that a contract of partnership in traffic resemble a contract of Mozáribat, in this particular, that each party respectively manages with the stock of his partner; and it also resembles partnership by reciprocity, both with regard to its name (as being a partnership), and likewise with regard to the conduct of it, because both partners act in it. In consideration, therefore, of its resemblance to Mozaribat, we determine that it is lawful to stipulate a profit upon property concerning which there is no responsibility; and, in consideration of its resemblance to partnership by reciprocity, we determine that, if it be stipulated that both partners shall act alike,* yet the contract of partnership in actual stock is not invalidated

A person may engage a part only of his property in it.—It is lawful for either party, in partnership in traffic, to engage in the contract with respect to a part of his property only, and not the whole, because an equality in point of stocks is not essential to it, since the term Ainan does not require it.

The stock can only be such as is lawful in reciprocal partnership.—Partnership in traffic is not valid except in such property as is lawful in partnership by reciprocity.

But the respective stocks may be heterogeneous.—It is lawful for two men to engage in a partnership in traffic, where the stock of one party consists of dirms, and that of the other party of deenars, or where on one side it consists of white dirms, and on the other of black dirms.† Ziffer and Shafei allege that this is illegal. This difference of opinion founded on a difference of sentiments respecting the admixture of stocks; for, according to those two doctors, a coalescence of the capital is essential to the partnership; and that cannot take place where the two stocks are heterogeneous. This point will be more fully treated of hereafter.

Debts can only be claimed from the partner who incurs them.—Where one of two partners in traffic makes a purchase, the demand for the price lies against him, and not against the other partner (because, as has been already demonstrated, the contract of partnership in question comprehends agency, but not bail, and the agent is the original with respect to rights).‡

And this partner, on making payment has recourse to the other for his proportion.—And on making payment, the purchaser is to take from the other partner his proportion of the price (provided he has satisfied the demand out of his own particular property, and not out of the partnership stock), because he is the other's agent with respect to his share. If, however, it be not known whether he has paid the price out of the partnership stock, or out of his own property, except from the declaration of the purchaser himself, it is in this case incumbent upon him to produce proof; because the purchaser here advances a claim for property against his partner; and the partner resists his claim: and the declaration of a defendant (delivered upon oath), is to be credited.

The contract is annulled by the loss of the whole capital; or of the stock of either partner in particular.—If the whole partnership stock or the stock of either partner in particular, perish before any purchase be made, the contract of partnership is annulled: because, in a contract of partnership, in the subject of the contract is property (that being specified in a contract of partnership, in the same manner as in a deed of gift, or a will), and, in consequence of the destruction of the subject the contract is dissolved, in the same manner as in sale. It is otherwise in Mozaribat, and singular agency,* because in those the dirms or deenars cannot be identified by specification,† or in any other mode than by actual seisin. The agency herein mentioned is restricted to the singular description, for the purpose of distinguishing it from the agency implicated in a contract of partnership or of pawnage, because that is annulled by the dissolution of the partnership or the pawnage, as a thing which is comprehended is annulled by the dissolution of that which comprehended in. An example of singular agency is where a person commissions another to purchase him a slave (for instance), in which case, if he give the agent money for that purpose, and the money perish in the agent's hands, yet the agency is not annulled. "It is otherwise." (says Fakr-al-Islam, in his commentary on the Zeeadat), "in cases of Mozaribat and partnership, because the dirms and deenars are in both identified by specification, insomuch that if the money be lost before delivery, the Mozaribat is annulled." This is contradictory to what our author has above advanced, that, "in Mozaribat and singular agency, the dirms and deenars cannot be identified by specification, nor in any other way than by actual seisin." It is, however, probable that there are two opinions recorded on the point. What is above said, that "if the whole partnership stock, or the stock of either partner in particular, perish before any purchases be made, the contract of partnership is annulled,"—is evident, where the whole stock of both partners perishes; and where the stock of one of the partners perishes the contract in sale annulled, because the partner whose property has not perished had agreed to the other participating in his property for no other reason than that he should also participate in the other's property; but, upon this being rendered impossible, he will not agree that the other should participate in his property.

And (in the last case) the loss falls entirely upon the partner to whom such stock had belonged.—The contract, therefore, is void, as its continuance is useless: and, to whomsoever the destroyed property belonged, the loss affects him only, and not the other, whether it perish in his own hands, or in the hands of his partner;—if in his own hands evidently: and also, if in the hands of his

* Although a greater share of the profit be conditioned to one of the partners.

† The translator has not been able to discover the difference between black dirms and white dirms: it is probably some local distinction, known in Persia and Arabia.

‡ That is, he is the person upon whom all demands are to be made.

* Arab. Wikalit-Moofradit; meaning, agency with respect to some particular act.

† That is, by the mention of them in the contract.

partner, because it is a trust in the hands of that person.*

Unless it had perished after admixture.—It is otherwise, however, where the stock perishes after admixture: for in this case the loss falls upon the partnership stock generally, since, as the property of each is no longer distinguishable, it follows that the loss must after both.

A purchase made by one partner, where the stock of the other afterwards perishes, is participated in by both; and the partnership continues in force, agreeably to the contract.—If one of the partners in question make a purchase with his own stock, and the stock of the other afterwards perish before he has made any purchase with it, in this case the thing purchased by the first partner is in partnership between the two, agreeably to stipulation, because, as partnership subsisted between them at the time of the purchase, the article purchased become a subject of partnership between them at that time; and the effect is not altered by the destruction of the other's property after the purchase. This partnership in the purchase is a partnership by contract † (according to Mohammed), insomuch that, whoever of the two sells it, the sale is lawful. Hassan-Ibn-Zeeyad alleges that the partnership is merely a partnership by right of property,‡ insomuch that it is not lawful for either pattner to sell more than his own share, because the contract of partnership was dissolved in the present instance, in consequence of the destruction of stock, in the same manner as where the destruction takes place before any purchase being made; nothing, therefore, remains, except the effect of the purchase, namely, right of property [in the thing purchased], and hence it is a partnership by right of property. The argument of Mohammed is that the contract has been completely fulfilled with respect to the article purchased, and consequently cannot be rendered void by the destruction of property after such completion. It is to be observed that, in the case now under consideration, the purchaser is to take from his partner his proportion of the price [of the article purchased], because he bought a moiety of it by agency, and paid the price out of his own substance, as was before mentioned.—What is now advanced proceeds upon a supposition of the purchase made by one partner having been effected before the destruction of the other's stock.

But if it perish before the other's purchase, that continues between them under a partnership by right or property.—If, however, the stock of one partner first perish, and the other partner then make a purchase with his own substance; and it should have been expressly agreed, in the contract, that each is to act as an agent on behalf of the other, in this case whatever the purchaser may have bought is divided between the two, according to their previous stipulation; because, although the contract of partnership be annulled, yet the agency, which was expressly mentioned in it, continues in force; the purchase is therefore participated in by both, in virtue of the agency; the connexion continues a partnership by right of property; and the purchaser is accordingly to take from his partner his proportion of the price, for the reason before stated.

Unless there be no mention of mutual agency in the contract; for in this case it belongs solely to the purchaser.—If, on the other hand, the partnership only be mentioned in the contract, and nothing expressed in it respecting each partner acting as an agent on the other's behalf, the article purchased by one partner appertains solely to him; because, if the article were participated between the two, it could be so only in virtue of the mutual agency implicated in the contract; but, that being annulled, the power of agency implicated in it is also annulled. It is otherwise where the parties have expressly mentioned a mutual power of agency; because in this case the agency is not annulled by the annulment of the partnership, as agency is here one especial design of the contract, and is not merely implicated in it.

Partnership holds without admixture of stocks.—A PARTNERSHIP is legal, although the parties should not have mixed stocks. Ziffer and Shafei maintain that it is illegal, because the profit is a branch of the stock, and the branch is not to be participated in except where the original stock itself is also participated, which cannot be so but by coalescence or admixture. The ground upon which they proceed is that, in a contract of partnership, the stock is the subject of the contract (whence it is that the partnership is referred to the stock, by each partner saying to the other, "I make you my partner in such stock,"—and also, that the specification of the capital is an essential),—and, such being the case, it is indispensably requisite that the stock be participated in by both. It is otherwise in Mozaribat, as that is not partnership, since it implies nothing more than that, as the manager is to act for the proprietor of the stock, he is consequently entitled to a share in the profit, as wages on account of his labour, which is different from the case in question, where the profit is a branch of the stock, and not wages for labour. This is a grand leading principle with Ziffer and Shafei, insomuch that (arguing upon this ground) they allege it to be indispensable, in a contract of partnership, that the stock of both partners be of the same species; for, if otherwise (as where

* A trustee is not responsible for his trust in cases of loss or destruction. (See Deposits.)

† Meaning, that the partnership (with respect to the purchase) continues in force under the original contract.

‡ That is, existing merely in virtue of a mutual right of property and not of the contract.

one is possessed of dirms and the other of deenars), they hold that the contract is invalid because of the capital not being participated in by both; and they also allege (upon the same principle) that mixture is an essential: and likewise, that it is unlawful to stipulate an excess of profit to either partner, where their stocks are equal, as the profit is a branch of the stock:—and also, that partnership in arts* and trades † is illegal, as in those there is no stock (as shall be hereafter explained).—The arguments of our doctors upon this point are twofold,—FIRST, partnership in profit is referred to the contract and not to the stock; because as the contract is termed "a contract of partnership," it is indispensable that the property of the term partnership exist in it; and, such being the case, it follows that the admixture is not essential.—SECONDLY, as the money [of which the stock consists] is not specified, the profit is not derived from the capital, nor indeed from anything else than the transactions [which are had with the stock]; because each party is a principal, with respect to one half of the stock and an agent with respect to the other half; and, as it hence appears that partnership may be established, in point of transaction, without admixture of stocks, it follows that it may also be established in the thing which accrues from transaction (namely the profit), without such admixture: and, as the contract of partnership thus becomes similar to a contract of Mozaribat, a similarity of species in the stocks and an equality of profit, are not essentials, although the stock of each be equal. A partnership in arts is also lawful on the same principle.

Partnership does not admit a specification of profit in behalf of either partners—A CONTRACT of partnership, which stipulates any particular sum out of the profit for one of the partners, is unlawful, as this condition is a means of destroying partnership, since it is possible that no more profit may be acquired altogether, than the sum so stipulated. Correspondent to this is a case of cultivation; that is to say, where the parties, in a compact of cultivation, stipulate a particular quantity of produce to one of them (that is, to the cultivator or to the landlord), the compact is invalid; because such a stipulation is a means of destroying partnership; and in cultivation it is essential that the produce of the land be equally participated between those persons

Either partner may make over his stock, in the manner of a Bazat.—EACH of the partners, in a contract either of reciprocal partnership or of partnership in actual stock, is at liberty to give his stock in the manner of a Bazat: because it is customary so to do in contracts of partnership; and also, because either partner is at liberty to hire any person to work for the acquisition of profit; and as the acquisition of profit without any return is still less objectionable than hiring with the same view, he is consequently authorized to adopt the other mode a fortiori.

Or lodge it as a deposit.—In the same manner, also, either of them is at liberty to lodge this capital as a deposit, as this is customary, and sometimes necessary, among merchants.

Or entrust it to the care of a manner, by Mozaribat—EACH of them is also at liberty to give his capisal in the way of Mozaribat, because, as Mozaribat is subordinate to partnership either by reciprocity or in traffic, it follows that a contract of partnership comprehends Mozaribat. It is recorded from Haneefa that a partner has not this in his power, because Mozaribat is also a mode of partnership. The former opinion, however, is according to the Mabsoot, and is the most approved, because partnership is not the design of a contract of Mozaribat, the only view in it being the acquisition of profit. It is therefore lawful to give the capital in the way of Mozaribat, in the same manner as it is lawful for the proprietor of the stock to hire a labourer with wages. It is lawful, indeed, in a superior degree, because, where the Mozarib manages, and no profit is acquired, there are no wages owing to him from the proprietor of the stock, whereas, in a case of hire, where the hired person manages the stock and no profit is acquired, wages are nevertheless due to him from the hirer. It is otherwise with respect to a contract of partnership, for neither party is at liberty to engage in such a contract with a third person, with regard to the capital, because a thing cannot be a dependant of a similar thing.

Either partner may also appoint an agent on his own behalf.—EITHER of two partners, by reciprocity, or in traffic, is at liberty to constitute a person his agent to transact for him, because the appointment of an agent for purchase and sale is a dependency of traffic: and contracts of partnership are formed for the purpose of traffic. It is otherwise with an agent for purchase, for he is not at liberty to constitute another person his agent, to make the purchase on his behalf, as the appointment of an agent for purchase is a particular contract, the end of which is the acquisition of some specified and existent article, and a thing cannot be the dependant of its similar.

Each partner holds the stock in the manner of a trust.—THE possession of each of two partners, by reciprocity or in traffic, over the partnership stock, is considered as the possession of a trust, since each possesses the property with consent of the proprietor, for this reason, that he is to give something in lieu of it, in the same manner as where a person takes possession of a thing with a view to purchase it (not because it is a

* Arab. Shirkat Takabbal (synonymous with Shirkat Sinnai).

† Arab. Shirkat Ammal.

pledge, as in pawnage) ; the stock is therefore a deposit.

Description of partnership in arts.—SHIRKAT SINNAI, or partnership in arts (which is also termed Shirkat Takabbal*), signifies where two tailors, or two dyers (for instance), become partners, by agreeing to work and to share their earnings in partnership ; which is lawful according to our doctors Ziffer and Shafei allege that this is unlawful ; because the design of partnership is a participation of gain between the parties, and the partnership in question is not calculated to answer this end, since a capital is indispensable, as partnership in profit is founded on partnership in stock (according to their tenets, as before set forth), and in the case in question there is no capital The argument of our doctors is that the design of the contract in question is the acquisition of property, which is attainable by each party constituting the other his agent ; because upon each becoming agent on the part of the other with respect to one half, and a principal with respect to the other half, a partnership is established in the property to be acquired

It is not requisite that the parties both follow the same trade or reside in the same place.—Unity of trade and of dwelling place are not essentials in this species of partnership. Malik and Ziffer controvert this ; for according to them unity of trade and of residence are essentials.

OBJECTION —It was before mentioned that, according to Ziffer, partnership in arts is unlawful ; but here it appears that he holds it to be lawful ; which is a contradiction,

REPLY.—There are two reports of the opinion of Ziffer upon this point. That before recited is confirmable to one report ; and what is now mentioned is according to another report.

THE argument of Ziffer in support of his latter opinion is that if the parties be of different trades (such as where a dyer and a bleacher become partners), each will be at a loss with respect to the business undertaken by the other, as that is not his trade ; the end of partnership, therefore, cannot be obtained : in the same manner, also, if their places of residence be different, each is at a loss with respect to the business of the other. The argument of our doctors is that the cause of the legality of the partnership (namely, the acquisition of property) is in no way affected by unity of trade and place of residence, or the reverse :—it is not affected by unity of trade, or the reverse, because an appointment of agency made by agreement, with respect to any business, is approved, whether the person who undertakes it be able to execute it in a good and sufficient manner or not at all, since the person who so agrees is not under any obligation to perform the business himself, but is at liberty to appoint any other person to perform it ; and as each party has it in his power thus to appoint a person to perform the business in question, the contract is consequently valid : neither is it affected by unity of place, or the reverse, because, if one of the two partners work in one shop, and the other in another shop, yet it is evident that no difference whatever is thereby created in essential circumstances.

It admits an inequality of profit.—It is to be remarked that if, in the case now under consideration, the partners stipulate to perform equal labour, and to divide the acquisition arising from it in three lots,* the same is lawful, upon a favourable construction. Analogy would suggest that this is unlawful, because the responsibility is in proportion to the labour, whence, if this stipulation were admitted, it would induce a profit from a matter concerning which there is no responsibility : any excess to either party, therefore, is unlawful in the present instance, in the same manner as it is unlawful in a Shirkat Wodjooh, or partnership upon credit (as shall be hereafter demonstrated), The reason for a more favourable construction is that what each of the partners takes he does not take in the manner of profit ; as gain does not bear the denomination of profit except where the stock and the gain are of the same nature ; but they are not of the same nature in the case in question, because the capital, in this instance, is industry, and the profit substance the property so acquired, therefore, is not profit, but merely a return for industry ; now industry is appreciable by means of estimation ; and consequently, where both partners agree to receive a certain specific proportion, such proportion is an estimate of the industry of each respectively : the excess, therefore, is not unlawful with respect to him in whose behalf it is stipulated. It is otherwise in a partnership upon credit, because in that instance the gain is of the same species with the capital (as both consist of substance) ; and profit is established where the capital and the gain are of the same nature : and as profit on property concerning which there is no responsibility is unlawful, except in a contract of Mozaribat, it follows that it is unlawful in a contract of partnership upon credit : the case in question, therefore, is in no respect analogous to a case of partnership upon credit,

The work agreed for by either partner is binding upon the other ; and either is at liberty to call upon the employer for payment.—IN a partnership in arts, whatever work one partner agrees to is incumbent upon him, and also upon the other partner, insomuch that the employer may require the perform-

*Literally "a partnership by mutual agreement."

*Two lots for one partner, and one lot for the other.

ance of it from either; and each is entitled to demand payment from the employer for the business performed. Upon the employer, also, thus paying either, he is thereby discharged of all demands. This is evident where the partnership in arts is of a reciprocal nature (by both partners being upon an equality with respect to those particulars in which equality is requisite in a contract of reciprocity);—and where the partnership in question is not of a reciprocal nature, but in the manner of a partnership in traffic, the same is admitted, on a favourable construction. Analogy would suggest otherwise: because the partnership has been contracted in general terms, without any mention of hail; and hail is not one of the articles of a partnership in traffic: it would therefore follow that the employer is not empowered to require the performance of the business from either of them indifferently; and also, that they are not both empowered to require payment from the employer:—and likewise, that the employer is not discharged from all demands; by paying either indifferently. The reason for a more favourable construction is that the partnership is an occasion of responsibility; that is, in consequence of the partnership, the performance of work is incumbent upon the parties; whence any business engaged in by either is incumbent upon the other also; and the other is accordingly entitled to the payment, as one of them engaging to perform any work equally affects the other: for if the other also were not subject to this obligation, he would not be entitled to payment: the partnership in question, therefore, is equivalent to a partnership by reciprocity, with respect to the obligation of work, and the taking possession of the payment for it.

Description of partnership upon credit.—SHIRKAS WADJOOH, or partnership upon credit, is where two persons, not being possessed of any property, become partners by agreeing to purchase goods jointly, upon their personal credit* (without immediately paying the price), and to sell them on their joint account. This species of partnership is termed Wadjoob, for this reason, that no person can purchase articles upon credit but one possessed of personal notoriety [Wijahit] among mankind.

It may include reciprocity—IT may lawfully constitute a partnership by reciprocity; because each partner may become both bail and agent for the other. Where, therefore, two persons, capable of bail, make a purchase of any article, on condition that it shall be held between them in equal shares, introducing the term "by reciprocity" into their agreement, it is a contract of reciprocity, If on the other hand, they express their agreement merely in general terms, it is a Shirkat Ainan, or partnership in traffic, because, when thus generally expressed, it is conducted in the manner of such a partnership. The legality of the partnership in question is according to our doctors. Shafei alleges that it is illegal. The arguments on both sides have been already recited.

Each partner is agent for the other.—IN partnership upon credit, each partner is agent on behalf of the other, with respect to what he purchases;—because any act which affects another is unlawful, except it be performed in virtue either of agency or of authority;* and as authority does not exist in the present instance, agency is certified.

The profit of each partner must be in proportion to the share of each in the adventure.—IF the partners agree that what they purchase shall be held between them in equal shares, and that the profit also shall be equally divided, it is lawful: but it is not lawful, in such a case, to stipulate an excess of profit to one of them. If, however, they agree that what they purchase shall be held between them in three lots, and that the profit also shall be divided into three lots,† it is lawful. In short, if the profit be in proportion to the right of property it is lawful, but otherwise not. The reason of this is that men are entitled to profit only on account of stock, management, or responsibility; thus the proprietor, of a stock is entitled to profit in virtue of the stock; a manager in virtue of his management; and a master artisan, who employes a scholar or apprentice at half wages or third wages (for instance) is entitled to the profit arising from his work in virtue of his responsibility for such work (whence it is that if a person say to another. "Transact with your own stock on condition that the profit be mine," it is unlawful, because in such a case, no one of the above particulars exists). As men, therefore, are entitled to profit only on some one of these three principles, and as, in a partnership of credit, the title to profit is in virtue of responsibility (as aforesaid), and as also, responsibility attaches in proportion to the right of property in the thing purchased, it follows that whatever exceeds the proportion of such right of property is a profit upon a thing concerning which there is no responsibility. Now the stipulation of profit from a thing concerning which there is no responsibility is not valid except in a contract of Mozaribat; and a partnership upon credit has not the property of a contract of Mozaribat. It is otherwise in a partnership in traffic, as that has the property of a contract of Mozaribat, inasmuch as each partner in traffic transacts business with the stock of the other partner, in the same manner as a manager transacts with the stock of the proprietor, whence a partnership in traffic is, in effect, a Mozaribat.

*Arab, Wijahit. Literally, personal presence, or notoriety.

*Arab, Willayat Meaning the authority derived from natural or personal sight, such as that of a guardian or a proprietor.

†That is, two lots to one, and one lot to the other.

Section.

Of Invalid Partnerships,

Partnership does not hold in articles of a neutral nature.—PARTNERSHIP is not lawful in wood, grass, or game. If, therefore, two persons enter into a contract of partnership with respect to such articles, and afterward collect wood, or grass, or kill game in hunting, the wood or grass so collected, or the game so killed, by either of them, belongs to him solely, and not to the other partner. The same rule holds in cases where two persons enter into a contract of partnership. with respect to any other articles of a neutral nature (such as fruit collected from the trees of the forest, which are common property), because a contract of partnership comprehends a commission of agency: and the appointment of an agent for procuring things of a neutral description is null, because the instructions of a constituent to this effect are invalid, since an appointment of agency signifies an endowing with authority to transact concerning a matter originally subject to the acts of the constituent only, and not of the agent; but it is otherwise in the case in question as the agent is here at liberty himself to take the neutral article without the instruction of his constituent. and consequently is incapable of appearing as his deputy concerning it. In short, a right of property in a neutral article is established only by the acts of taking and putting it in custody.

Unless they be taken possession of jointly.—IF, therefore, both partners take it jointly, it is equally in partnership between them, as they are both equally entitled to it. But if one of them only exert himself in taking it, the other doing nothing, it belongs wholly to the one who acts: if, on the other hand, one be the chief actor, and the other only an assistant (as where one plucks the fruit, and the other collects it,—or, where one both plucks and gathers it, and the other carries it away), in this case the assistant is to receive wages in proportion to his labour—This is according to Mohammed. (Aboo Yoosaf alleges that this rule holds only where the wages do not exceed half the value of the article in question; but that, if the wages exceed this, one half of the value only is paid to the assistant, because, as he had agreed to accept one half of the article specified, his right fails with respect to any larger proportion.)

Nor in this instance, where the means of acquiring them are different.—IF one man possess a mule, and another a Mashack (or leather bucket, such as is used in drawing water) and they enter into a contract of partnership in drawing water,* by agreeing that whatever may be acquired thereby shall be in partnership between them, such partnership is invalid, the whole acquisition going to the person who actually draws the water; and if this be the owner of the mule, he owes the other the adequate hire for the bucket; or, if it be the owner of the bucket, he owes the other an adequate hire for the mule. The reason of the partnership being invalid is that it is contracted with respect to an article of a neutral nature (namely, water), and is therefore unlawful. The hire of a mule or the bucket is due, because the neutral article (namely, the water) becomes the property of the person who drew it; and as he derives an advantage, under an invalid contract, from the property of another person (namely, from his mule or his bucket), it follows that he owes n hire for the same.

The profit to each partner must be in proportion to the stock.—IN all cases of invalid partnership, the profit is in proportion to the stock; any stipulation. therefore, of an excess of profit to either partner is null. Accordingly, if the stock be between the partners in equal shares, and they agree to their profit being in three lots, such agreement is null, and the profit must be equally divided; because, as the profit which accrues is a dependant of the stock, the degree of it must be in proportion to the stock, in the same manner as, in a contract of cultivation, the grain which is reaped is a dependant of the seed The reason of this is that a claim to an excess profit can exist only in virtue of a previous specific agreement: but in the case in question this agreement has become invalid in consequence of the invalidity of the contract of partnership itsef: the claim, therefore, remains in force only in proportion to the capital stock.

A contract of partnership is annulled by the death or apostasy of either partner.—IF one of two partners die, or apostatize, and be united to a foreign country, * the contract of partnership is annulled; because a contract of partnership comprehends an appointment of agency, which is essential to the existence of partnership, for the reasons already assigned: now agency is annulled by death; and it is also annulled by the circumstance of desertion to a foreign country during apostasy, where the Kazee issues a decree in consequence of such

* Water is in many parts of Asia procured from draw-wells, sunk to a considerable depth. From the edge of such wells a road is constructed or cut, going off from twenty to thirty yards, in an inclined plain; and over the well is erected a frame or cross price, furnished with a pulley, through which a line runs, having suspended at one end a large leather bucket [Mashack]; the other end is fastened to traces, in which a mule, bullock, or other animal, moving to and fro on the inclined road, by this means draws the water.

* That is, be expatriated by a decree of the Kazee, issued in consequence of his apostasy and desertion.

desertion, because that is equivalent to death: upon the agency, therefore, being annulled, the contract of partnership is also annulled.

Whether the survivor be aware of that event or not.—IT is also to be observed that the surviving partner being aware of the decease of his fellow, or otherwise, makes no difference whatever with respect to the dissolution of the partnership; because as, in the case in question, the survivor is virtually discharged from the agency by the decease of his partner, it is not essential that he be informed of that event. It is otherwise where one of two partners breaks the contract of partnership, for the effect of such a breach depends upon the knowledge of the other partner, as the breach is a designed dissolution of the contract.

Section.

A person cannot pay Zakat upon his partner's property without his permission.—IT is not lawful for either partner to pay the Zakat upon the other's property without his permission, as the payment of Zakat is not a branch of traffic.

Case of mutual permission to pay Zakat.—IF each of the partners give a general permission to the other to pay the Zakat upon his property, and each should afterwards first pay the Zakat upon his own particular share in the stock, and then pay Zakat upon his partner's share, in this case he who last paid the Zakat is responsible, whether he be aware of the other having already paid it or not. This is according to Haneefa. The two disciples allege that he is not responsible, where he is not aware of that circumstance. What is here advanced proceeds upon a supposition of each partner having paid the Zakat upon their respective shares of stock successively, and not altogether; for where they have paid it altogether, each is responsible for the other's proportion of it. A correspondent difference of opinion obtains where any indifferent person directs another to pay the Zakat upon his property, and the other accordingly pays the Zakat upon his property after the person who so directed him had already paid it: for, according to Haneefa, the person acting under such direction is responsible, whether he pay the Zakat with a knowledge of the above circumstance, or otherwise. The two disciples, on the other hand, maintain that he is not responsible unless he pay it, having a knowledge of that circumstance, as he has acted by direction, and consequently cannot be held answerable. They admit, indeed, that it may be objected that what the person acting under with direction pays is not Zakat,* and consequently he ought to be responsible:—but to this they reply the order which the person in question received was not in fact an order to pay so much Zakat, but rather, merely, an order to transfer so much to the POOR, since the payment of actual Zakat is not within his province, as this is connected with the intention of the principal, and no more can be required of the person so directed than what is within his province and ability:—the person in question, therefore, stands in the same predicament with one who is directed to perform sacrifice on behalf of another, in a case of detention; thus, if a person engaged in the ceremonies of pilgrimage were to fall into the hands of an enemy, and to direct any other person to preform sacrifice at the temple on his behalf, and the other perform sacrifice accordingly, after the principal had been released from the enemy, and had completed his pilgrimage, yet he does not bear the loss,* whether he be aware of the detention having ceased, or otherwise. The argument of Haneefa is that the person in question has been directed "to pay ZAKAT;" and as what he pays is not in fact Zakat, it is evident he has acted contrary to the orders of his principal, whose design in giving such orders was to discharge himself from an obligation incumbent upon him (for it is evident that his sole view in subjecting himself to such an expense is to ward off the divine anger attending the neglect of Zakat);—now as (in the case in question) this design has been fully answered by the payment of the principal himself, it can no longer be so by the payment of his substitute, and hence it follows that the substitute is discharged from his commission, whether he be aware or not, because this is a virtual discharge, and to that knowledge is not essential. With respect to the case of sacrifice under a circumstance of detention, as adduced by the two disciples, some in reply to it allege that the principle there advanced is not generally admitted, as concerning that also there is a difference of opinion. Others, again, maintain that there is an essential difference between that case, and the case under consideration. The reason they give for this difference is, that sacrifice is not incumbent upon the detained person, as he is permitted to delay it until his detention shall cease. The payment of Zakat, on the other hand, is incumbent, whence the design in appointing an agent to pay it is to discharge an obligation; and as this design is not fulfilled,† it follows that the agent has no credit for his payment, and that what he pays is a waste and destruction of the property of his

* Because Zakat has been already paid by the principal, and hence what this person pays is not properly Zakat, but rather gratuity or alms-gift.

*That is to say, the expense attending the sacrifice (although it be insufficient and nugatory under such a circumstance), nevertheless falls upon the director, not upon the person directed.

†As it has been already fulfilled by the payment of the principal himself.

principal, for which he is consequently responsible. The case of sacrifice under a circumstance of detention, therefore, is not analogous to the case now under consideration, as sacrifice in such a circumstance is merely lawful but not incumbent, and hence the sacrifice performed by the delegate is not to be regarded as a waste and destruction of the property of his principal, for which reason he is not responsible.

A female slave, purchased under a contract of reciprocity, becomes the property of that partner who with permission of the other, has carnal connexion with her.—If one of two partners by reciprocity permit the other partner to purchase a female slave with the partnership stock, and to have carnal connexion with her, and the other act accordingly, in this case the slave appertains to the purchaser, and he is not responsible for anything. This is according to Haneefa. The two disciples allege that the other partner is entitled to take half the price of the slave; because the purchaser has paid for the slave out of the partnership stock, and consequently his partner has a right to be repaid his share in the same manner as in the purchase of victuals or clothing (that is, as, where one of two partners by reciprocity purchases victuals or clothing, paying the price out of the partnership stock, the other partner is entitled to take half the price from the purchaser, so also in the case in question), The ground upon which this proceeds is that the slave in question has become the sole and exclusive property of the purchaser because of the necessity of legalizing generation; and as the price is due in proportion to the right of property, it follows that the price of the slave is solely and exclusively due from the purchaser. The argument of Haneefa is that the slave has fallen into the possession of both partners, a certiorari, according to what partnership requires (for they cannot alter the requisites of partnership): the slave therefore, is the property of both, in the same manner as if no permission had been given: now the permission implies that the person who grants it makes a gift of his share to the purchaser: for carnal connexion is lawful only in virtue of right of property: and there is no mode of establishing that in the present case but by gift: because sale cannot be supposed on this occasion,* as the establishment of a right of property by sale would be repugnant to the requisites of a contract of partnership; for if the partner were to sell his share to the purchaser, still that share is in partnership between the two, and does not belong exclusively to the purchaser His share, therefore, is made the property of the purchaser by gift implied in the permission granted to the purchaser to have carnal connexion with the slave. It is otherwise with respect to victuals and clothing, becauss, as these are excepted from the contract of necessity, they are the sole property of the purchaser in virtue of the spirit of a con ract of purchase and sale; he, therefore, must pay half the price th reof to his partner, because he has discharged a debt due from himself [for the above articles] out of the partnership stock, whereas, in the case ur der consideration the purchaser discharged a partnership debt, which was equally due from both partners, for the reasons already alleged.

But the seller may take the price from either.—It is to be observed that, in the case in question, the seller of the slave is at liberty to take the price from either partner, according to all our doctors, because this price is a debt incurrred by an act of traffic. A contract of reciprocity, moreover, comprehends bail: and hence the price of the slave resembles (in this respect) the price of victuals or clothing.

* Meaning a complete sale from one partner to the other.

BOOK XV,

OF WAKF. OR APPROPRIATIONS.*

Definition of Wakf; and various opinions respecting it—Wakf, in its primitive sense, means detention. In the language of the law (according to Haneefa), it signifies the appropriation of any particular thing in such a way that the appropriator's right in it shall still continue, and the advantage of it go to some charitable purpose, in the manner of a loan. Some give it as the opinion of Haneefa that, as the advantage of a thing is a nonentity, and as the alms-gift of a nonentity is invalid, it follows that appropriation is utterly illegal. † It is, moreover, recorded in the Mabsoot that Haneefa held appropriation to be invalid. The most approved authorities, however, declare it to be valid according to him: but since (like a loan) it is not of an absolute nature, ‡ the appropriator is held to be at liberty to resume it, and the sale or gift of it is consequently lawful. According to the two disciples. Wakf signifies the appropriation of a particular article, in such a manner as subjects it to the rules of divine property, whence the appropriator's right in it is extinguished, and it becomes a property of God by the advantage of it resulting to his creatures.—The two disciples, therefore, hold appropriation to be absolute; and, consequently, that it cannot be resumed, or disposed of by gift or sale; and that inheritance also does not obtain with respect to it. (There is, indeed. one point upon which the disciples differ in opinion: for, according to Aboo Yoosaf, the sppropriation is absolute from

* Meaning always of a pious or charitable nature.

† That is, has no force in law.

‡ That is, it is not irrevocable.

the instant of its execution: whereas Mohammed holds it to become absolute only on the delivery of it to a Mootwalee, or procurator:*—as will hereafter appear,) Thus the term Wakf, in its literal sense; comprehends all that is mentioned both by Haneefa and by the two disciples. Now, such being the case, no preference can be given to the tenets of one party over that of the other, as drawn from the meaning of the term: this preference. therefore, must be given as drawn from arguments. The arguments of the two disciples upon this subject are twofold. FIRST, when Omar was desirous of bestowing in charity the lands of Simag, the Prophet said to him, "You must bestow the ACTUAL LAND ITSELF, in order that it may not remain liable to be either SOLD or BESTOWED, and that INHERITANCE may not hold in it—SECONDLY, there is a necessity for the appropriation being absolute, in order that the merit of it may result for ever to the appropriator; and this necessity is to be answered only by the appropriator relinquishing his right in what he appropriates, and dedicating it solely to GOD; which dedication, as being agreeable to the LAW, in the same manner as that of a mosque, must therefore be made in the same mode. The arguments of Haneefa concerning it are various. FIRST, the Prophet has said, "Property cannot, after the decease of the proprietor, be detained from division among his heirs" (in other words. appropriations are not ABSOLUTE, but INHERITABLE), Shirrah moreover says, "the Prophet determined the sale of an appropriation to be lawful,"—which is as much as to say, that "before the promulgation of the LAW by the holy Mohammed (on whom be the blessing and peace of GOD) appropriations were absolute; but our LAW has rendered them otherwise." —SECONDLY, the appropriator's right in the article appropriated must still continue in force, for this reason, that it is lawful for the creatures of GOD to derive an advantage from it, either by tillage (if it consist of land). or by residence (if it consist of dwelling-houses): for if no one had any right in it, any acts with respect to it would be unlawful, in the same manner as with respect to a mosque. It is, therefore, evident that a right of property in it still continues: and it is also evident that this right of property must rest with the appropriator, and not with any other person, as he alone is entitled to expend the revenue arising from it upon the objects of the appropriation, and to appoint a procurator over it: but yet, as the term Wakf implies giving in charity, the use of it resembles that of a loan. THIRDLY, the appropriator wishes to apply the revenue arising from what he appropriates to some charitable purpose in perpetuity which is impossible, unless his right of property in it continue. FOURTHLY, it is impossible that the appropriator's right of property in the Wakf should be extinguished, during its existence; without its becoming the property of some other person, as the LAW does not admit the idea of a thing, during its existence, going out of the possession of one proprietor without falling into the possession of another proprietor Wakf, therefore, in this particular resembles a Sayeeba. (A Sayeeba is a female camel, set at liberty in pursuance of a vow (as where a man says, "if I return home from this journey," or, "recover from this disorder a certain female camel of mine is Sayeeba,"*) which the owner prohibits himself from any further use of; in the same manner as a Baheera, or female camel, which after producing ten colts, it was customary, in times of ignorance, then to set at liberty, rendering it unlawful to be used or eaten.) Appropriation, in short, resembles the Pagan act of setting a camel at liberty, in this respect, that the thing appropriated does not go out of the right of property of the proprietor: —in other words, if a man constitute his quadruped a Sayeeba, still it continues his property; and so also, if a person appropriate his lands or quadruped. It is otherwise in a case of manumission, as that is a dereliction of property. It is otherwise also in the case of a mosque, as that is dedicated purely to GOD (whence it is unlawful to derive any advantage from a mosque), whereas in a case of appropriation, the right of the individual still continues in force, and that, consequently, is not dedicated purely to GOD,

Alienation of the article appropriated is completed by a decree of the magistrate, and the declaration of the appropriator, or the consignment of it to a procurator.—IT is reported by Kadooree, from Haneefa, that the appropriator's right of property is not extinguished, except where the magistrate so decrees, or where the appropriator himself suspends it upon his decease, by declaring "When I die, this house is appropriated to such a purpose" (and so forth). Aboo Yoosaf alleges that his right of property is extinguished upon the instant of his saying "I have appropriated"—(and such also is the opinion of Shafei); because that is a dereliction of property, in the same manner as manumission. Mohammed says that it is not extinguished until he appoint a procurator, and deliver it over to him; and decrees are passed upon this principle. The reason of this is that the right of God cannot be established in an appropriated article but by implication, in the consignment of it to

*Literally, a person endowed with authority; the term procurator is adopted by the translator, as being peculiar to the management of a religious foundation, and as distinguishing this office from that of a common agent.

* Literally, running about at liberty. An may be used towards a female slave as for formula of manumission.

his creature (as a transfer to the Almighty, who is himself the proprietor of all things, although it cannot be effected actually and expressly, yet may be so dependantly) ;—it therefore becomes subject to the rules of divine property dependantly, and consequently resembles Zakat and alms-gift. With respect to what is reported from Haneefa, that "the appropriators's right of property is extinguished by a decree of the magistrate,"—our author remarks that this is approved doctrine, as such a decree removes all difference of opinion. With respect, however, to what is further reported from him, that "the appropriator's right of property is extinguished in consequence of his suspending that upon his decease, it is altogether unfounded, as his right of property cannot be extinguished but by his bestowing the use of the article for charitable purposes in perpetuity, in which case it is the same as a bequest of perpetual usufruct :—in this instance, therefore, his right of property becomes extinct, and the appropriation is absolute.

A decree of the magistrate fixes an appropriation ; but the decision of a referee does not fix it.—It is related, in the Fatavee Kazee Khan, that judicial decrees are issued on the subject of appropriations only in cases where a person having appropriated a particular article, and delivered it over to a Mootwalee or procurator, is afterwards desirous of resuming it ; and the latter disputes the resumption, on the plea of the appropriation being absolute ; and they carry the matter before a Kazee, who decrees it to be absolute —Concerning a case where the parties authorize any third person to decide upon this point, and he decides the appropriation to be absolute, there is a difference of opinion ; it is certain, however, that such a decision is not binding upon parties.

Case of an appropriation made upon a death bed.—If a person make an appropriation upon his death-bed. Tehavee reports that, according to Haneefa, it stands in the same predicament with a bequest after death —(that is to say, is absolute) : contrary to an appropriation made during health, which is held by Haneefa not to be an absolute nature. The true statement, however, is that the appropriation in question is not absolute, according to Haneefa ; but it is absolute, according to the two disciples ; with this distinction, however, that the appropriation here treated of is regarded as from the third of the appropriator's estate, whereas an appropriation made during health is regarded as from the whole of the appropriator's property.

The appropriator's right of property is destroyed : but without a transfer of that right to any other person.—Upon an appropriation becoming valid (that is, absolute, according to the various opinions of our doctors, as here stated, —according to Haneefa, in consequence of the appropriator's declaration, and the magistrate's subsequent decree —and according to Aboo Yoosaf, by his simple declaration,—and according to Mohammed, by his declaration and delivery to a procurator),—it passes out of the possession of the appropriator ; but yet it does not become the property of any other person ; because, if this were the case, it would follow that it is not a state of detention, but may be sold in the same manner as other property ; and also, because if the person or persons to whom it is assigned were to become the proprietor of it, it, it would follow that it could not afterwards pass out of his possession in consequence of any condition stipulated by the former proprietor,—whereas it is not so, for if a person were to appropriate a dwelling-house (for instance) to the poor of a particular tribe, and the property of any one of these were afterwards removed, the right in it passes to the others, which it could not do if this person were a proprietor.

Any undefined part of a thing may be appropriated.—The appropriation of an undefined part or portion of any thing* is lawful, according to Aboo Yoosaf. Mohammed alleges that an appropriation of this nature is unlawful ; because as actual possession is held by him to be an essential (by the procurator taking possession of the article appropriated), so, in the same manner that without which possession cannot take place is also an essential, namely, division ; and this can only be in a thing capable of division. (With respect, however, to a thing incapable of division, the appropriation of an indefinite portion of it is held to be legal by Mohammad also as he conceives an analogy between this and a gift, or charitable ...tion). The ground upon which the opinion of Aboo Yoosaf, procee s is, that the separation of an indefinite part of any thing is indispensable to the taking possession of it ; but as the taking possession is not (according to him) essential in a case of appropriation (whence the means of taking possession is also unessential) it follows that the appropriation of an indefinite part of any thing is held by him to be lawful. From this rule, however, he excepts a mosque, or burying-ground, the appropriation of any undefined portion of which is unlawful, although it be of an indivisible nature ; because the continuance of a participation in any thing is repugnant to its becoming the exclusive right of God ; and also, because the present discussion supposes, the place in question to be incapable of division, as being narrow and confined, whence it cannot be divided but by an alternate application of it to different purposes, such as its being applied one year to the interment of the dead, and the next year to tillage, or, at one time to prayer, and at another time to the keeping of horses which would be singularly abominable. It is otherwise with regard to the appropriation of anything else than a mosque

*Such as the half, or the fourth, of a field, house, &c.

or burying ground; because the appropriation of an undefined portion of any other matter, where it is of an indivisible nature, is decreed to be lawful by all our doctors, as it may be hired (for instance), and the parties may divide the rent.

Case of appropriation of land, where an indefinite portion of it afterwards appears to be the property of another person.—If a person appropriate land,* and it should afterwards appear that an indefinite portion of the land (such as the fourth) was the property of another person, the appropriation is void with respect to the remainder also, according to Mohammed: because, in this instance, the separation into indefinite divisions is associated with the appropriation, which is consequently invalid, in the same manner as a gift. It is otherwise where a donor resumes a part of his gift; or where the heirs of a donor who had made the gift upon his death-bed resume two-thirds of his gift after his decease: for if a person, upon his death-bed, make a gift or appropriation of the whole of his property, and the heirs resume two-thirds, still the gift or appropriation are not rendered void, because, in this instance, the separation into indefinite divisions is supervenient, and not associated: that is, at the time of the gift or appropriation, the article was not divided into undefined portions, but became so afterwards. If, however it, should appear that another is entitled to a portion of the land, of a specific and not an undefined nature, in this case the appropriation is not void with respect to the remainder, because of no in definite division existing in this instance: and gifts and charitable donations are also subject to the same analogy.

The objects of an appropriation must be of a perpetual nature.—An appropriation is not complete, according to Haneefa and Mohammed, unless the appropriator destine its ultimate application to objects not liable to become extinct; as where, for instance, a man destines its application ultimately to the use of the poor (by saying, "I appropriate this to such a person, and after him to the poor)."—because these never become extinct. Aboo Yoosaf maintains that where the appropriator names an object liable to termination (as if he were to say, "I have appropriated this to Zeyd), it is valid, and after the death of Zeyd it passes, as an appropriation, to the poor, although the appropriator had not named them. The argument of Haneefa and Mohammed upon this point is that appropriation requires an extinction of right of property. Without a transfer of it; and as this, like manumission, is of a perpetual nature, it follows that if a thing be appropriated to a finite object, the appropriation is imperfect; whence it is that an appropriation is rendered void by making it temporary, in the same manner as a sale is made void by limiting its duration.

Objection.—This argument of Haneefa, that the right of property becomes extinct without "a transfer of it," contradicts what was formerly said, that, "according to Haneefa, in appropriation, the right of property is not extinguished."

Reply.—There are two reports from Haneefa upon this subject. One of them is that which was before stated. Another makes the opinion of Haneefa to agree with that of Mohammed. Some also allege, in reply to this objection, that what is here advanced from him proceeds from a supposition of the magistrate having decreed the appropriation to be absolute, under which circumstance it passes out of the possession of the appropriator according to all our doctors.

The argument of Aboo Yoosaf is that the design of the appropriator is to perform an act of piety acceptable to God; and this is fully answered in either case; because piety on some occassions may consist in the appropriation of an article to a terminable object, —and it may at other times consist in the appropriation of a thing to an interminable object:—The appropriation, therefore is equally valid in both instances; Now some say that perpetuity, is essential to it. Aboo Yoosaf, however, does not consider the mention of perpetuity as an essential, as the terms appropriation or charity do clearly argue thus much, according to what was before advanced, that "Appropriation, like manumission, signifies an extinction of a right of property without a transfer of that right." According to Mohammad, on the other hand, the mention of perpetuity is an essential; because appropriation is a charitable donation of the use of a thing, or of actual product: and as those are sometimes temporary and sometimes perpetual, the general mention of it cannot be understood as a perpetuation: it is therefore indispensable that perpetuity be expressly mentioned.

Appropriation of immoveable and of movable property.—The appropriation of land is lawful; because several of the Prophet's companions appropriated their lands; but the appropriation of movable property is altogether unlawful, whether purposely, or as a dependant. This is the opinion of Haneefa. Aboo Yoosaf alleges that if a person appropriate lands, together with the cattle and slaves attached to them, it is lawful; and the same of all instruments of husbandry; because those are all dependants of the soil in the fulfilment of the design; the appropriation of these, therefore, as dependants of the land, is lawful; for many things are admissible dependantly, which are not so positively; thus the sale of wine (for instance) by itself is unlawful; whereas, along with land it is lawful,—and in the same man-

*Arab, Akkar: meaning any immoveable property whatever, whether lands or tenements. Zimeen is the term in the Persian version and the translator therefore renders it land throughout.

nor the appropriation of the beam of a house is unlawful, whereas along with the house it is clearly legal. The opinion of Mohammed, also, accords with that of Aboo Yoosaf in this point, because as he holds the appropriation of moveables to be lawful merely in virtue of the appropriator's declaration, it follows that he admits the appropriation of them as a dependant to be legal a fortiori. Mohammed is also of opinion that if a person appropriate horses, camels, or arms, to carry on war against infidels, it is lawful ;—in which opinion (as lawyers report), Aboo Yoosaf coincides with him. This proceeds upon a favourable construction ; for analogy would suggest that such an appropriation is unlawful, for the reasons already alleged. The reason for a more favourable construction, however, is that the Prophet once said, "KHALID has appropriated his HORSE and ARMOUR in the way of GOD ; and TELLIHA has appropriated his HORSE in the way of GOD."*—According to Mohammed, the appropriation is lawful of all moveables, the appropriation of which is commonly practised, such as spades, shovels, axes, saws, planks, coffins (and their appendages) stone or brazen vessels, and books : but according to Aboo Yoosaf it is unlawful ; because analogy cannot be abandoned but on the express authority of the sacred writings : and as horses and armour only are there mentioned, the admission must be restricted accordingly. Mohammed says that analogy may be abandoned on account of utility, (as in arts or manufactures, for instance) ; and utility exists in the articles in question. It is, moreover, recorded of Nasseer Ibn Yehee, that he appropriated his books, as conceiving that to be analogous to the appropriation of a KORAN (in other words, as the appropriation of a KORAN is lawful, so also is the appropriation of any other book) : and this is approved, because other books as well as KORANS are kept for the purpose of reading and instruction. Most lawyers have passed decrees according to the opinion of Mohammed in this particular. It is written in the Fatavee-Kazee-Khan that there is a difference of opinion between the Elders concerning the appropriation of books.—Fikkea-Aboo-al-Seyb, however, holds it to be lawful ; and decrees pass accordingly.

The appopriation of articles in which it is not customary is unlawful.—IT is not lawful to appropriate moveables, the appropriation of which is unusual or uncommon, according to our doctors. Shafei alleges that the appropriation is lawful of everything which admits of the use without a destruction of the subject, or of everything lawfully saleable, because such articles as admit usufruct resemble land, horses, or arms. The argument of our doctors is that appropriation requires propetuity, according to what has been already stated ; and this cannot exist in moveables, since these are not of a lasting nature ; analogy therefore suggests that the appropriation of moveables in general is unlawful :—it is admitted, however, in some articles (although contrary to analogy), because of the traditions already recorded,—and in other articles (such as axes, saws and so forth), because of utility : but the appropriation of furniture, clothes, and salves, is unlawful, as being contrary to the suggestions of analogy, because they have neither tradition nor utility to support the legality, and therefore resemble dirms and deenars. With respect to what Shafei has advanced that "those articles are analogous to lands, horses, and armour," we reply that no analogy can be admitted between them ; because land endures perpetually ; and horses and armour are instruments of war against infidels, which is among the highest religious obligations, whence the property of piety exists in the appropriation of these articles in a much stronger degree than in the appropriation of other moveables ;—the analogy, therefore, is not allowed.

An appropriation cannot be sold or transferred.—UPON an appropriation becoming valid and absolute, the sale or transfer of the thing appropriated is unlawful, according to all lawyers : the transfer is unlawful, because of a saying of the Prophet, "Bestow the ACTUAL LAND ITSEF in charity, in such a manner that it." An appropriation, therefore, is incapable of sale or transfer, upon becoming valid and absolute

But it may be divided off, where it consists of an undefined part of anything.—IF, however, the appropriation consist of an undefined part of anything, and (in conformity with the doctrine of Aboo Yoosaf) become absolute, and the partner require it to be divided off, such division is lawful ; because division implies separation and distinction. In all things, indeed, except those which are computable by weight or measure, exchange chiefly prevails : in appropriation, however, a superior regard is had to separation and distinction, in order that the appropriation may be valid : the dividing it off, therefore, is not to be regarded in the light of a sale or transfer, and is consequently legal.

IF a person appropriate his share in partnership lands, he must divide it off and detach it from those of his partner ; because he alone has authority to do this during his life, or his executor, after his decease. If on the other hand, a person appropriate the half (for instance) of his own land, in this case the Kazee is to divide it off, and alienate it from the appropriator—(or the appropriator may sell one half (for instance) of his land to any other person, and then divide off the portion appropriated and alienate it from that person, and afterwards re-purchase the remainder from the purchaser*) ;—for the

*This is, in waging war against the infidels.

*This is merely a device, for the purpose of obviating legal objections.

appropriator is not at liberty himself to divide off the portion of land which he has appropriated, or to separate it from that portion which he has not appropriated, because one person is incapable of himself making a division, and thus giving to himself, since division can take place only between two.

In case of dividing it off, the payment of a balance made by the appropriator is lawful; but if made to the appropriator, it invalidates the appropriation.—If, in dividing off appropriated land, any balance occurs (as where a person appropriates his share in partnership land, and he and his partner accordingly make a division of the land, and the share of one of them proves defective, and the other makes up the difference by a payment in money), it is unlawful, where this balance is paid to the appropriator, as the sale of an appropriated article is unlawful: but if it is the appropriator who pays the balance, it is lawful and what he gets in return is his property;—if, therefore, he be desirous of having it divided off from the part he has appropriated, he must refer the matter to the Kazee, in order that he may separate the portion appropriated from what he [the appropriator] gets in return for the balance.

The income of an appropriation must be expended (in the first instance) upon keeping it in repair.—It is incumbent that the income of an appropriation be in the first instance expended in the repairs* of it, whether the appropriator may have stipulated this or not; because his design was that the income should serve as a perpetual fund, and as a perpetual income cannot be drawn from the article appropriated unless it be preserved in continual repair, that is a necessary attendant upon it; and also, because all acquisition must be attended with expense—(in other words, he who enjoys the profit must also bear the loss),—In short, upon the person to whom the advantage of a thing accrues, must rest the inconveniences attending it; and such being the case, it follows that the repair of an appropiation resembles the subsistence of a slave whose service has been bequeathed to any one, for the subsistence of such slave rests upon the legatee of usufruct. If, therefore, the appropriation be to the poor, and the requisition of repairs from them be impossible (because of the appropriation itself being their sole dependence) the repairs must be afforded out of the income arising from it.

Unless the appropriatee be rich, in which case he is answerable for the repairs—If, however, the appropriation be to some particular person, in the first instance, and after him to the poor, the repairs are in this case due out of that person's property (but he is at liberty to furnish the means out of whatever part of his property he chooses), during his life: and in this case no part of the income is laid out in repairs because the requisition from the person who enjoys the benefit is in such instance possible, since he is specified and known.

But in such a degree only, as may suffice to preserve it in its original state.—It is to be understood, however, that the repairs are to be made out of the property, only in such a degree as may be requisite to preserve it in the state in which it was appropriated: if, also, it fall to ruin [or run waste] it is to be restored to the state in which it was appropriated, because the income of it was made over to others, and was to be derived from it as in THAT state, and not as in any superior state; and as such income is the right of him to whose use it is appropriated, it is not lawful, without his permission, to expend it in repairs to a degree beyond the original state of the appropriation. Some are also of opinion that the same rule obtains where the appropriation is to the poor at large, and not to any particular individual, —that is to say, the income is not to be expended in repairs beyond the original state of the appropriation. Others allege that this is lawful. The former, however, is the better opinion; because the income arising from an appropriation is expended in the repairs of it only from the necessity of preserving it as it was originally and there is no necessity for repairs beyond what may suffice for this purpose.

The repairs of a house are incumbent upon the individual occupant pro tempore.—If a person appropriate a house, with this condition, that his son or any other person shall reside therein during life, the repairs are incumbent upon him who has the right to inhabit it, because he who enjoys the profit must also bear the loss (as has been already stated), and the case consequently resembles the subsistence of a slave whose service has been bequeathed to any person by his master.

Or if he neglect this, the magistrate must let the house, and furnish the repairs out of the rent—If, therefore, the person in question refuse or neglect to repair the house, or be incapable of so doing, from poverty, the magistrate must in this case let it, and provide for the repairs out of the rent; and must return it to him upon the repairs being completed: because by this means attention is paid to the rights both of the appropriator and of the person to whose use it is appropriated, if it were not duly repaired, the tenement would be lost, and the rights of both would be consequently destroyed; the repair must therefore be provided out of the rent, in order that the rights of the parties may be secured.

But the occupant is not liable to any compulsion—It is to be observed, however, that where the person to whom the article is appropriated refuses to make the repairs, he is

*Arab. Tameer; meaning, the rendering a place habitable, by cultivation, if it be land, or by rebuilding, &c., if it be houses.

not to be compelled, because the repairs would be at his loss, his case being the same as that of the proprietor of the seed, in a contract of cultivation, who, if he refuse to cultivate the land, is not liable to any compulsion, as the cultivation cannot be effected without the loss of his property, namely, the seed.

Objection.—Upon the occupant refusing to make the repairs, it would appear that the magistrate should not return the house to him after the repairs are completed : because, as he thus assented to the destruction of his right, and attention to that is unnecessary.

Reply.—The refusal of the occupant to repair the house does not argue his assent to the destruction of his right as there is a doubt with respect to the motive of his refusal, since it is possible, that he has refused merely on account of the expense to his property ; his right, therefore, is not destroyed because of the doubt.

And none can let the house but the magistrate—It is proper to observe that it is not lawful for the occupant to let the house, since he is not proprietor. The magistrate, on the contrary, possesses a general power, as being the agent of the community.

Decayed materials are to be used for repairs.—Such buildings or materials of an appropriation as become damaged or useless must be employed by the magistrate in the repairs of it, where necessary ; and if these be not immediately necessary, he must keep the articles in question until such time as occasion offers when he must employ them in making the necessary repairs ; as repairs are required from time to time, in order that the appropriation may be continually preserved; and the design of the appropriator answered. If the materials of the decayed place be damaged so much as to render it impracticable to employ them in the repairs (by the timbers being broken, for instance), it is incumbent on the magistrate to sell them, and expend the price in such repairs : but it is not lawful for him to give them to the occupants, because the timbers, and so forth, are constituent parts of the actual appropriation, in which no person has any right,—their right being merely to the use, and not to the thing itself.

Case of appropriation, with a reserve of the use to the appropriator during life.—If a person appropriate a house (for instance), with a reserve of the income to his own use during life, and after his death to go to the poor; this is lawful, according to Aboo Yoosaf. Our author remarks that this is deemed lawful by Aboo Yoosaf ; but that, juding from the opinion of Mohammed, it is unlawful :—and such is the opinion of Hillal Kazee and Shafei respecting it. Some allege that the difference between Aboo Yoosaf and Mohammed upon this point is occasioned by their difference of opinion concerning the neeessity of consignment ; for, according to Mohammed, the consignment of the appropriation to the Mootwalee, or procurator, is an essential, and consequently it is unlawful for the appropriator to reserve the income to himself : according to Aboo Yoosaf, on the contrary, this is lawful, as he does not hold the consignment to a procurator to be an essential. Others, again, allege that their difference upon this point is not occasioned by their difference upon any other point, but is merely an original difference of opinion with respect to the present case itself. This difference of opinion between disciples subsists in every case that is, whether the appropriator reserve the whole or a part only of the income to himself during life, and after his death to go to the poor. If, also, the appropriator reserve the whole or part of the income from his appropriation to the use of his Am-Walids, or his Modabbirs, during their lives, and after their deaths destine it to the poor, some say that this is lawful according to all our doctors. Others, however, maintain that, in this instance also, the above difference of opinion obtains ; and this is approved, because his reserving the income to their use for their lives is equivalent to his reserving it to his own use The argument in favour of Mohammed's opinion is that appropriation is a gratuitous act, effected in the transfer of a property to God; by delivering over the thing appropriated to a Mootwalee or procurator (for a transfer to the Almighty, who is himself the proprietor of all things, although it cannot be effected actually and expressly, yet may be so dependently : and the reserving of the whole or part of the income arising from it to his own use is repugnant to this, because, the delivery cannot be made to himself —The case, therefore, resembles the reserve of an alms-gift,—and also the reserve of a part of a mosque :—in other words, if a person were to assign certain property to the poor, stipulating at the same time, that his right in part of it should continue, the alms under such a condition are unlawful ;—or, if the founder of a mosque stipulate that his right in a part of the mosque shall continue, this opposes the legality of the whole foundation :—and so also in the case in question. The arguments of Aboo Yoosaf upon this point are threefold, First, the Prophet was accustomed himself to consume the revenue arising from what he had appropriated. Now the use would not at any rate be lawful, unless the appropriator had previously stipulated it for himself at the time of appropriation : the Prophet consuming the revenue therefore, argues that it is lawful for an appropriator to reserve that to his own use. Secondly, appropriation implies the owner of a property destroying his right in that property by a transfer of it to God, under some pious intention (as was formerly stated ; and such being the case, where an appropriator reserves a part or the whole of the revenue arising from what he appropriates to his own use, it follows that; in so doing ; he reserves to himself a thing which is the property of God (not that he reserves to himself what is his own), and a person's reserving to himself a thing which is the property of GOD is lawful; thus, if a man build a caravansera, or construct a reservoir, or give ground for a burial-place, reserving to himself the right of residing in the caravansera, or of drinking water out of the reservoir, or of interment in the burial-place, it is lawful; and so likewise in the case in question. THIRDLY, the design, in appropriation, is the performance of an act of piety; and piety is consistent with the circumstance of a person reserving the revenue to his own use, as the Prophet has said, "A man giving a subsistence to HIMSELF is giving ALMS."*

Or, with a reserve of a liberty to change the subject.—IF the appropriator reserve to himself a right of changing the lands he appropriates for any other lands, at pleasure, it is lawful, according to Aboo Yoosaf, Mohammed maintains that the appropriation itself is valid, but that the condition reserved is void; because the condition does not prevent an extinction of right of property; and the appropriation is consequently complete, because of the extinction of this right; but not the condition, as being invalid, is void, in the same manner as the reserve of a right of change, in the foundation of a mosque, is void.

Or, with a reserve of a right of option.—IF the appropriator reserve to himself a right of option with respect to his appropriation, for three days, by saying (for instance) "I appropriate this house to such and such purposes, with this condition, that I shall have a right of option for three days; according to Aboo Yoosaf, both the appropriation and the condition are lawful. According to Mohammed, on the contrary, the appropriation is null. Their difference of opinion upon this point originates in the difference of their doctrine respecting a reserve of the revenue of an appropriation to the use of the appropriator: for as, according to Aboo Yoosaf, an appropriator may lawfully reserve to his own use, during life, the revenue arising from what he appropriates, it follows that he deems it lawful that the appropriator reserve a right of option for three days, for the purpose of consideration Mohammed, on the other hand, holds that the possession of a Mootwalee, or procurator, is an essential, and as a reserve of option prevents possession from being completely taken, it follows that, according to him, the appropriation is void. An appropriation, moreover, is not complete without the will of the appropriator; and as, where he makes a reserve of option, this cannot be ascertained, it follows that the appropriation is void; had being once void, its validity cannot afterwards be restored by the condition ceasing to operate.

Or with a respect of authority—IF a person appropriate land, with a reserve of his authority over it, it is lawful, according to Aboo Yoosaf.—Our author remarks that Kadooree has expressly declared this. Such also is the doctrine of Hillal; and it is, indeed, the generally received opinion. Hillal particularly mentions it in treating of appropriations. Some doctors allege, that if the appropriator particularly stipulate a reservation of authority over the lands, this authority remains to him accordingly; but not unless it be particularly stipulated by him. Our modern doctors, however, consider it as very doubtful whether this be an opinion of Mohammed, because it is a tenet of his that delivery into the hands of a procurator is essential to the validity of an appropriation; and where such delivery takes place the appropriator can no longer possess any authority over it. According to the tenets of Aboo Yoosaf, on the other hand, the delivery to a procurator is not an essential, and consequently the authority remains with the appropriator, although he should not have so stipulated. What was mentioned above, concerning the opinion of Mohammed, that "where the delivery to a procurator takes place, the appropriator can no longer retain any authority over the appropriation," applies to a case where the appropriator had not stipulated any reservation of authority to himself at the first:—for if he had stipulated this at the time of making the appropriation, his authority is not rendered void by delivery to a procurator, because as his authority continues where he stipulates a right of authority in behalf of another, it follows that, where he stipulates it in behalf of himself, it continues a fortiori.—The arguments in support of the opinion of Aboo Yoosaf (which is the most generally received doctrine), are twofold. FIRST, the procurator enjoys his authority, only on behalf of the appropriator, in consequence of his reservation; and it is impossible that the appropriator himself should not be possessed of any authority, at the same time that another person enjoys an authority held on his behalf —SECONDLY, the appropriator stands in a nearer relaions to what he appropriates than any other person, and it is consequently proper that he possess an authority over it; in the same manner as where a person builds mosque, in which case the business of repairing it, as well as the appointment of all the officers, &c, appertain solely to him; or as where a person emancipates a slave, in which case the Willa appertains solely to him, as he stands in a nearer relation to the slave than any other person.

IF, however, the appropriator who makes this condition (namely, a reservation of authority to himself), be a person of infamous character and unworthy of confidence, the magistrate may take the appropriation

*As where (for instance) a man appropriates the whole of his property, thus reducing himself to poverty; in which case the charity is as effectual with respect to him (where he necessarily reserves a sufficiency from the product for his own sustenance) as with respect to any other pauper.

out of his hands, from a regard to the intere t of the poor ; in the same manner as he is at liberty to suspend the powers of an executor, where he happens to be a person of bad character, from a regard to the interest of the orphans. If, also, an appropriator constitute another the Mootwalee or procurator, declaring that "the sovereign or magistrate shall not take the appropriation out of his charge," yet these are at liberty to take it from him, where he happens to be a person of bad character ; – because, as such a declaration is repugnant to the precepts of the LAW, it it consequently void.

Section

A mosque is not alienated from the founder otherwise than by the preformance of public worship in it.—IF a person build a mosque, his right of property in it is not extinguished so long as he does not separate it from the rest of his property, or give general admission to people to come and worship in it : but as soon as the people in general, or a single person, say their prayers in it, his right of property is extiguished, according to Haneefa. The utter separation of it from the rest of the appropriator's property is indispensable, for this reason that the mosque cannot become dedicated solely to GOD until that be effected : and the performance of prayer in it is a condition ; because, as a consignment (according to Haneefa and Mohammed) is indispensable, it follows that consignment is requisite in this way, since in whatever way may be proper to the nature of the appropriation and the mode of consignment proper to a mosque is public worship ; or, the performance of prayer is a condition, because as it cannot be conceived that GOD himself should take possession of a mosque, it follows that that which is the design must stand as a substitute for the taking possession of it. It is proper in this place to observe that if a single person say his prayers in the mosque it suffices (according to one report from Haneefa and Mohammed); because, as it is impossible that all men should perform their prayers in it, the circumstance of a single individual performing his prayers is the condition. It is also reported, from Haneefa and Mohammed, that the performance of prayer by a whole congregation is a necessary condition, because a mosque is founded with a view to public worship. Aboo Yoosaf maintains that the founder's right of property is destroyed immediately upon his saying, "I constitute this a mosque !"—because he does not hold consignment to be a condition, since according to him, appropriation signifies a relinquishment of right on the part of the individual ; the thing appropriated, therefore, appertains solely to GOD merely in consequence of the right of the individual ceasing,—as was before demonstrated.

Cases of a mosque, as connected with a dwelling-place.—IF a person erect a building of two stories, making the under storey a mosque, and the upper storey a dwelling, or vice versa,—with the door of the mosque towards the public road, and detach the mosque from his own property [in the manner before described], he is nevertheless at liberty to sell it;—or, if he die, the mosque is an inheritance ;—as the mosque does not in this instance, appertain solely to GOD, because of the individual's right in it still subsisting. This, however, is only where the dwelling has not been constructed merely for the purposes of the mosque : for if it have been constructed for the purposes of the mosque (as in the great mosque at Jerusalem), the appropriation is absolute, Hasan reports from Haneefa, that if the lower storey be a mosque, and the upper story a dwelling, the former continues for ever a mosque ; because a mosque is one of those things which are designed to continue in perpetuity, and an under storey answers this purpose better than an upper storey. The reverse of this is reported from Mohammed, because reverence is indispensably due to a mosque and where an upper storey is constructed over a mosque, for the purpose either of dwelling in or of letting out to hire: this reverence cannot be observed. It is recorded, also, that when Aboo Yoosaf went to Bagdad and beheld the narrow and crowded condition of the place, he held the appropriation to be lawful and absolute in either case,—that is, whether the mosque be in the lower storey and the dwelling in the upper, or vice versa:—but this he admitted out of necessity. The same is recorded of Mohammed, when he went to Rai,* and for the same reason.

IF a person convert the centre hall of his house into a mosque, giving general admission into it, still it does not stand as a mosque but remains saleable and inheritable : because a mosque is a place in which no person possesses any right of obstruction ; and wherever a man has such a right with respect to the surrounding parts, the same must necessarily affect the place inclosed in them. This place, therefore, cannot be a mosque : besides, it is necessarily a thoroughfare for the family, and consequently does not appertain solely to GOD. It is reported from Mohammed that the centre hall of a house, thus constituted a mosque, cannot afterwards be given away, sold, or inherited. He consequently considers it to stand as a mosque ; and Aboo Yoosaf is of the same opinion, because, as the person in question was desirous, that this pl ce should become a mosque, and as it cannot become so without a road, or entrance into it, the road is included without specification, in the same manner as in a case of hire.

Ground appropriated to building a mosque cannot be sold or inherited.—IF a person appropriate ground for the purpose of erect-

*The capital of Irak (the ancient Chaldea).

ing a mosque, he cannot afterwards resume or sell it, neither can it be inherited, because this ground is altogether alienated from the right of the individual, and appertains solely to God. The reason of this is that all things whatever are originally the property of the Almighty. When, therefore, the individual relinquishes his right in the ground, it reverts to its originrl state, and his power over it terminates, in the same manner as a master's power over a slave terminates in consequence of manumission, and cannot be resumed.

A mosque cannot, in any instance, revert into the property of the founder.—If the place in which a mosque is situated should become deserted or uninhabited, insomuch that there is no farther use for the mosque, no person coming to worship therein, still it continues to stand as a mosque (according to Aboo Yoosaf), and does not revert to the founder; because as he had put it out of his own possession, it connot again become his property. Mohammed alleges that the mosque again becomes the property of the founder, or of his heirs, in case of his decease: because he had erected it for the purpose of public worship: and as that has ceased, the mosque is in the same predicament with the materials for building a mosque. In other words, if there be no farther occasion for materials (such as bricks and so forth) designed for the erection of a mosque, they revert to the founder, and so also in the case in question. This, however, is a conclusion which does not accord with the doctrine of Aboo Yoosaf for he holds that where there is no farther occasion for those materials in the construction of this mosque, they must be carried to another.

Cases of appropriations made to the use of the community at large:—If a person construct a reservoir for public use, or a caravansera for travellers, or erect a house upon the infidel frontiers for the accommodation of the Mussulman warriors in their excursions (which is termed a Ribat), or dedicate ground as a burying place, his right of property therein is not extinguished until the magistrate issue a decree to that effect; because no termination of the proprietor's right takes place in this instance, insomuch that he may still lawfully continue to use those things (by residing in the house or Ribat, or drinking water out of the reservoir, or interring in the burial-place). It is therefore requisite either that the magistrate issue a decree, in order to complete the alienation, or that the founder himself refer the appropriation to his decease, in order that it may stand as a bequest, and become absolute upon that event, in the same manner as in the case of an appropriation made to the use of the poor. It is otherwise in the case of a mosque, because in that instance no right of usufruct remains to the founder, as the mosque appertains solely to God independent of any magisterial decree. All that is here advanced is according to Haneefa. Aboo Yoosaf is of opinion that the person's right of property ceases on the instant of his saying, "I have made this for such and such purposes" (of residence, interment, or so forth), because with him it is a rule that appropriation is absolute, and that consignment is not a condition of it. Mohammed maintains that as soon as people drink water out of the reservoir, or enter the caravansera, or warriors take up their residence in the Ribat, or interment takes place in the burying-ground, the proprietor's right is extinguished; because consignment (which he holds to be a condition) is established by such acts, as the consignment of any thing must be made in the mode proper to that thing. It is sufficient also (according to him) if these acts be performed by, or with respect to only a single individual; because as the whole community cannot engage in those acts, regard must necessarily be had to them as performed in any single instance. Wells and fountains are also subject to the same rule.

They may be consigned to a procurator.—If, in the cases last recited, the founder consign the article to a Mootwalee or procurator, such consignment is approved, because the procurator is in the character of a deputy, and the act of the deputy is the act of the principal. With respect to a mosque, indeed some allege that the delivery of it to a procurator is not a complete consignment, because there is no business for a procurator in a mosque. Others again say that consignment is established, as it is necessary, in a mosque, that there be some person to keep it in order, and lock up the doors; the consignment of a mosque, therefore, to a procurator is approved. Some also assert that a burying-ground is considered in the same light as a mosque in this particular, because the procurator of a burying-ground is an office not in use. Others, again, maintain that it resembles a reservoir, or caravansera; if, therefore, it be delivered to a procurator, consignment is established; because such an appointment is valid, although it be contrary to general usage.

Appropriations may be consigned to the prince of chief magistrate—If a man, having a house in Mecca, appropriate it to the accommodation of pilgrims, or if a person, having a house in any other place, appropriate it to the accommodation of the poor, or mendicants, or, having a house upon the frontiers, dedicate it to the accommodation of the Mussulman warriors and their cattle, or dedicate the revenue from his lands to the support of the warriors in the way of God,* and make over or consign those houses or lands to the prince (who is empowered to act in those particulars) such consignment is lawful. If, therefore, the person in ques-

* That is engaged in war against the infidels.

tion be afterwards desirous of revoking his appropriation, he cannot lawfully do so, for the reasons before alleged. The revenue arising from the lands, however, is lawful to the poor only, and not to the rich; but the use of any of the other articles (such as residing in the caravansera, or drinking water from the well, fountain, or reservoir) are lawful to rich and poor alike The reasons of this distinction are twofold. First, people in general, in the appropriation of a revenue, intend only the relief of the needy, whereas, in that of the other articles, the accommodation of rich and poor is equally indended. Secondly, the articles of drink and lodging are requisite equally to the rich and to the poor; but in the article of pecuniary assistance, the rich are not necessitous, on account of their wealth, whereas the poor are necessitous.

BOOK XVI

OF SALE.

Definition of the terms used in sale—Beeya, or sale, in the language of the law, signifies an exchange of property for property with the mutual consent of the parties. Shirra signifies purchaser. The seller is termed Bayee: the purchasee Mooshterree: the thing sold Moobea: and the price Simmin.

Sale is contracted by declaration and acceptance.—Sale is completed by declaration and acceptance, the speech of the first speaker, of the contracting parties, being termed the declaration, and that of the last speaker the acceptance. Thus, if Zeid should first say to Omer, "I have sold to you a particular article belonging to me for ten dirms," and Omar should then say, "I have bought that article belonging to you for the said price," the speech of Zeid is in that case termed the declaration, and that of Omar the acceptance. If, on the contrary, Omar should first say to Zeid, "I have purchased a particular article belonging to you for ten dirms," and Zeid should then say, "I have sold the same to you for the said price," the speech of Omar is in this case termed the declaration and that of Zeid the acceptance.

Expressed either in the preterite or the present—It is a necessary condition that the declaration and acceptance be expressed (in the present or preterite tense indicative; for if either be expressed in the imperative or future the contract is incomplete. Thus, if the seller should say to the purchaser. "Buy this article belong to me for ten dirms," and the purchaser reply, "I have bought the said article for ten dirms,"—or if the seller should say "I have sold this article to you for ten dirms," and the purchaser reply, "I will purchase the said article for ten dirms;"—in neither case would the sale be binding.

Or by any expressions calculated to convey the same meaning.—It is to be observed that in the same manner as a sale is established by the words "I have bought," or "I have sold: so also is it established by any other words expressive of the same meaning;—as if either of the parties, for instance, should say, "I am contended with this price," or "I have given you this article for a certain price:" or "take this article for a certain price;" because, in sale, regard is had to the spirit of the contract, and the particular use of the words bought and sold is not required; whenc it is that sale may be contracted simply be a Taata or mutual surrender, where they seller gives the article sold to the purchaser, and the purchaser in return gives the price to the seller, without the interposition of speech. Some have alleged that this mode of sale by a mutual surrender is valid with relation to things of small value; but not otherwise It is, however, certain that sale by a mutual surrender is valid in every case, as it establishes the mutual consent of the parties.

Objection.—It would appear that the sale, as recited above, to be rendered complete by the words "Take this," &c. is not valid, as it was before declared to be a necessary condition that both declaration and acceptance should be expressed in the present or preterite tense indicative, and neither of them in the imperative.

Reply.—In this case the words "Take," &c., are not of themselves declaration, but merely indicate the existence of a declaration in the preterite tense;—as if the seller had first said, "I have sold this thing," and were then to add, "Take this," &c, for the command is consequent to the declaration.

The acceptance may be deferred until the breaking up of the meeting; whether the declaration be made personally.—If either of the parties make a declaration, it is in the power of the other to withhold his acceptance or refusel until the breaking up of the meeting; and this power is termed the option of acceptance.* The reason of this is that if such a power did not rest in

---

* Arab, Khair-al-Kabool.

one of the parties, it must necessarily follow that the sale would take effect without his consent. It is to be observed, in this instance, that as the declaration is not of itself efficient to complete the contract, the person making the declaration is at liberty to recede from it.

Or by letter. or message.—If either the buyer or seller should send a letter or a message to the other, that other has the power of suspending his acceptance or refusal until he leave the place or meeting where he received such message or letter.

An offer made by the purchaser cannot be restricted by the seller, to any particular part of the goods.—If the purchaser make a declaration of his purchase of merchandise at a particular price, the seller is not in that case entitled to construe his acceptance as limited to a part of the merchandise only at a rate proportionate to the declaration for the whole;—and, in the same manner, if a seller should make a similar declaration, the purchaser is not at liberty to construe his purchase after that manner;—because this is a deviation from the terms proffered; and also because the declarer has not expressed his assent thereto.

Unless he oppose a particular rate or price to particular parts or portions.—If, however, the person who makes the declaration should specify a particular rate, opposed to particular parts of the merchandise, the acceptance may be limited. Thus if a person should say, "I will sell this heap of grain for ten dirms," the purchaser, if he declare his acceptance, is not in that case at liberty to limit his purchase to half the grain for five dirms; whereas, if the seller should say, "I will sell this grain at the rate of one man for a dirm," the purchaser after declaring his acceptance, may limit his purchase to what quantity he pleases.

If the acceptance be not expressed in due time, the declaration is null—If either a seller or purchaser make a declaration, and one of the parties quit the place before any acceptance be expressed, the declaration so made is void.

Declaration and acceptance, absolutely expressed, render the sale binding.—When the declaration and acceptance are absolutely expressed, without any stipulations, the sale becomes binding, and neither party has the power of retracting unless in a case of a defect in the goods, or their not having been inspected. According to Shafei, each of the parties possesses the option of the meeting* (that is, they are each at liberty to retract until the meeting break up and a separation take place),—because of a saying recorded of the Prophet "The buyer and seller has each an option until they separate." Our doctors argue that the dissolution of the contract, after being confirmed by declaration and acceptance, is an injury to right of one of the parties; and that the tradition quoted by Shafei alludes to option of acceptance, as already explained.

Where the article and the price are both produced, the sale is complete, without any specification of quantity or amount.—If, at the time of concluding a contract of sale, either the merchandise, or the price, or both be present and alluded to in it (as if the seller should say, "I have sold this wheat to you for these dirms," or the purchaser, "With these dirms now present I have purchased such an article belonging to you"), in this case the sale is valid, although neither the quantity of wheat (such as "so many loads," for instance), nor the amount of the money (such as "so many dirms"), be mentioned; for the reference made to them is sufficient to ascertain the subjects of the contract, and does not leave room for any dispute.

But a mention of money: without a specification of the sum (unless it be produced upon the spot), is not valid.—If, at the time of concluding the contract, the dirms or deenars be not present, so as to admit of being referred to; in this case the general mention of them, without a specification of the numbers or of the quality, is not valid; because the delivery of them on the part of the purchaser is requisite; and as the general mention of them would occasion a contention between the purchaser and seller (the one wishing to give a few and of a bad quality, the other insisting on a greater number and a better quality), the delivery would therefore become impracticable. (It is here proper to observe, that every species of uncertainty which may prove an occassion of contention is invalid, in a contract of sale.)

A sale may be entered into either for ready money, or with specification of a promised time of payment.—A SALE is valid either for ready money or for a future payment: provided the period be fixed; because of the words of the Koran, "ABSOLUTE SALE IS LAWFUL;" and also, because there is a tradition of the Prophet having purchased a garment from a Jew, and promising to pay the price at a fixed future period, pledging his coat of mail for the performance of it. It is indispensably requisite, however, that the perior of payment be fixed as an uncertainty in this respect might occasion a contention, and be preventive of its execution, since the seller would naturally demand the payment of the price soon, and the buyer would desire to defer it.

The price must be stipulated at some known and determinate rate.—A SALE, stipulating a payment of dirms in an absolute manner (as if a person should say, "I have sold this for ten dirms") is valid: provided, however, that all the different species of dirms be of the same value: and in that case the purchaser is entitled to pay the price in any of the species he pleases.—If the different species of dirms be of different value, the sate then rests upon that which is most generally in use. If, however, the different species be of different

* Arab. Khair-al-Majlis.

values, and it be impossible to ascertain the one of most common use, the absolute expression of dirms in this case renders the sale void, because the price being thereby rendered uncertain, a contention must necessarily ensue : still, however, if the parties choose to remove the cause of contention by voluntarily fixing the rate, the sale is valid.

Grain may be sold for other grain of a different species.—It is lawful to sell wheat, or other kinds of grain either by means of measures of capacity, or by conjecture,* provided it be in exchange for a different kind of grain ; because the Prophet has said, "Sell any thing that is in exchange for a different kind, in whatsoever manner you please and without regard to the equality :" and also, because the uncertainty in this case proves no bar to its delivery. It is not lawful, however, to sell grain in exchange for the same kind, by conjecture, because this is of an usurious nature.

Goods may be sold by a weight or measurement which is not of any particular standard.—It is lawful, in sale, to use the measure of a particular vessel of which the exact capacity may not be ascertained,—or the weight of a particular stone, the exact weight of which is not ascertained,—because the uncertainty in this case cannot be productive of contention, since either of these instruments of estimation may be used and the delivery take place immediately after ; and it is not probable that the vessel or stone should be lost or destroyed in the interval between the measurement and the delivery, the only case in which a contention could arise.

Except in a case of Sillim sale.—A measurement of this kind, however, is not allowed in Sillim sales (that is, where the price is advanced, and the merchandise delivered afterwards), because in such case there is a probability of the vessel or stone being lost or destroyed during the long interval that takes place between the conclusion of the contract and the delivery of the goods ; in which case, as the parties had no other criterion (during the existence of the stone or vessel) than their eyesight to judge from, a contention might afterwards arise as to the size or weight of the stone or vessel.

A sale fixing a particular price to each particular part or portion of goods, in the gross, extends only to one such part.—If a person sell a heap of grain, by declaring, "I have sold this heap at the rate of one dirm for every Kafeez," † in this case (according to Haneefa) the sale takes place in one Kafeez only : nor can it extend beyond that quantity, unless the seller should explain, in the same meeting, the sum of the Kafeez's. The two disciples are of opinion that the sale of the whole is valid in both cases. The reasoning of Haneefa is that it is impracticable to extend the sale to the whole of the heap, because both the goods to be delivered and the price to be received are in this case uncertain : it must therefore be construed as existing in one Kafeez, the only ascertained quantity. It is rendered vaild, however, with respect to the whole quantity, by the removal of the uncertainty,—that is, by the seller either explaining the total, or ascertaining it by measurement during the meeting. The argument of the two disciples is, that the power of removing the uncertainty rests with the parties : and that the uncertainty, in this case, ought not to be deemed a bar to the validity of the sale ; in the same manner as it is not a bar where a person sells one slave out of two, leaving it in the option of the purchaser to fix one either of them.

And a sale expressing the whole quantity, in this way, is altogether void, unless the amount of the whole be particularly specified.—If a person say, "I have sold my flock of goats at the rate of one dirm for each," the sale in that case is altogether invalid,—in other words, it is not extended even to one goat,—according to Haneefa ; and in the same manner, the sale is altogether invalid if a person sell cloth at the rate of one dirm the yard, without explaining the number of yards ; and the same of every other article, such as wood, pots, or the like. The two disciples are of opinion that, in all these cases, the sale is valid with respect to the whole quantity ; because the removal of the uncertainty is in the power of the parties ; and also, because such uncertainty does not prevent the validity of the sale, as is demonstarted in the preceding case. The arguments of Haneefa in support of his opinion are also the same as those advanced by him in the preceding case ;—in which, however, he has admitted the validity of the sale with respect to one Kafeez of wheat, because all Kafeez's of wheat being the same, no contention can arise in the delivery of it,—whereas, in the case in question, the different articles, comprehending in themselves unequal unities the delivery could not be made without contention.

If the quantity agreed for fall short, the purchaser may either take it, or undo the contract.—If a person purchase a heap of grain for one hundred dirms, on the condition of the heap amounting to one hundred Kafeez's; and it be afterwards discovered to fall short of that amount, in this case the purchaser has the option of either taking the actual amount, at a rate proportioned to the terms of the contract, or of undoing the contract entirely ; because a branch of the terms takes place before the deed is rendered complete since, in order to render the deed complete, it is necessary that the actual quantity stipulated be taken possession of.

But, if it exceed, the sale is valid to the amount of the quantity bargained for.—If, on the other hand, the heap be afterwards

*Meaning, by Estimate.

†A measure containing about sixty-four pounds weight.

found to contain an excess beyond the stipulated amount; the sale is valid with respect to the amount of the one hundred Kafeez's, and the excess continues the property of the seller; because the sale is restricted to a specific quantity; and the excess is not included in the description, so as to be a dependant thereof, and not a separate article.

If the quantity be of a nature capable of specification and fall short, the purchaser may either take it, or undo the bargain.—If a person sell a piece of cloth for ten dirms, on the condition of its contents amounting to ten yards,—or a piece of ground for one hundred dirms, on condition of its measuring one hundred yards,—and a deficiency afterwards appear, the purchaser has in that case the option either of cancelling the bargain entirely, or of taking the ground, or cloth thus defective, at the stipulated price; for the specification of yards is a mere description of the length and breadth; and no part of the price is opposed to the description of the wares;—in the same manner as in cases with respect to animals;—in other words; if a person purchase a goat, which afterwards appears to want an ear, he would have the option of taking the defective goat for the price stipulated, or of undoing the bargain: but he would have no right to diminish the price on account of such defect, because no part of the price is opposed to the ear in particular, so as to admit of any fixed diminution on account of its deficiency;—and so also in the case in question. It is otherwise in the preceding case, relative to wheat; because there the deficiency comes under the head of the quantity and not the description of the wheat; and the price being opposed to quantity, a proportionate diminution is accordingly made from it. Still, however, the purchaser has the option of undoing the contract if he please, on account of the difference from the terms; his consent having been given to the purchase of one hundred Kafeez's.

But if it exceed, the sale is binding to the amount agreed for.—If however, the ground or the cloth should prove larger than the description, in this case the excess becomes the property of the purchaser, and no option remains to the seller, because (as has been already explained) the specification of yards relates merely to description and not to substance. The case, in short, becomes the same as if he had sold a slave on the supposition of his being defective, but who afterwards proves to be perfect.

If the quantity be so expressed as to relate both to description and to substance, the purchaser may either stand to or undo the bargain, whether it exceed or fall short of the amount specified.—If a person sell a piece of cloth, by declaring, "I have sold this piece of cloth, which measures one hundred yards, at the rate of one dirm for each yard," and a deficiency should afterwards appear, in this case the purchaser has the option, either of taking it, with a proportional deduction from the price, or of dissolving the contract entirely; because, although the specification of yards comes under the head of description, yet in this case the yards are considered as relating to the substance, the seller having opposed the price to each of them, which renders each (as it were) a separate piece of cloth. Besides, if the seller should take the defective quantity at the rate proposed for the whole, it would follow that the terms of the contract (namely, the payment of one dirm per yard) did not take place:—if, on the other hand, the amount of the cloth exceed one hundred yards, the purchaser has the option, either of taking the whole, at the rate of one dirm for each yard, or of dissolving the bargain: for although he has an advantage in the receipt of more cloth than he had contracted for, yet this being tempered with a loss, in the necessity it lays him under of paying an additional sum, he is therefore left at liberty either to abide by the contract on these conditions, or to undo it.

The sale of a specific number of yards of a tenement is null; but not the sale of a share—If a person purchase ten yards of a house or bath measuring one hundred yards, such purchase is invalid, according to Haneefa, whether the buyer may or may not have known the measurement of the whole house. The two disciples maintain that it is valid. If, on the contrary, a person purchase ten shares of a house or bath containing one hundred shares, it is valid, in the opinion of all our doctors The argument adduced by the two disciples in support of their opinion is, that ten yards of house of an hundred yards in capacity are in fact the same as ten shares out of an hundred shares. Haneefa, in support of his doctrine, argues that a yard, in its original meaning, is a stick applied to the purpose of measurement; but it is also used to denote the thing measured, and the thing so measured must be relative and not an abstract idea of the mind, such as a share: now it is impossible, in this case, to render such yards relative, since there exists an uncertainty, as no mention is made of the particular side of the house from which they have been measured: and such uncertainty would occasion contention between the parties. It is otherwise with respect to shares, for these are abstract ideas of the mind and not undefined relatives: and although, of consequence, an uncertainty exist with respect to them also, yet such uncertainty cannot occasion a contention, since the possessor of ten shares of the house may either enjoy them indefinitely, or may receive his share according to the mode prescribed in the division of joint property.

The purchase of a package of cloth is null, if it contain more or less than the quantity of pieces agreed for.—If a person purchase of package containing cloth, on condition of there being ten pieces in it, and it afterwards appear that there are nine or eleven pieces in it, the sale is invalid, because of the uncertatinty, with regard to the price, in the one case, and to the merchandise in the other; for in case of there being nine pieces, as the price of the piece wanting is unknown, that of the remaining nine is of consequence also unknown; and where, on the other hand, there is one too many, it is unknown which are the specific ten that ought to be delivered.

Unless the seller previously specify the price of each particular piece.—If, however, the seller should explain the price of each piece of cloth, and there be too few, the sale is valid; but the purchaser has the option of undoing it if he please; whereas, if there be too many, it is invalid, because of the uncertainty with respect to the goods, as it would be impossible to ascertain the particular ten that are included in the sale.—Some have said that in case of deficiency also the sale is invalid, according to Haneefa. But this is unfounded.

A sale is null in toto, if the description of the goods be at all fallacious.—If a person sell two pieces of cloth, on the condition of their being Heratee, and one of them afterwards prove to be Murwal'ee.* in that case the sale is completely invalid, that is, does not hold good even with respect to the true one, although the seller should have specified the prices of both; for when the seller joined together both pieces in the declaration of a sale of Heratee pieces, he, as it were, established a condition that the purchaser should accept a piece of Murwallee which being a false condition, the sale is therefore annulled.

Case of the purchase of a piece of a cloth at so much per yard.—If a person purchase a piece of cloth, on the condition of its measuring ten yards, and at the rate of one dirm for each yard, and the measurement afterwards prove to be ten yards and a half, or nine yards and a half, in this case the purchaser (according to Haneefa) must pay ten dirms in the first instance, and nine in the second; still having the option to undoing the contract if he please. Aboo Yoosaf alleges that if the purchaser choose to abide by the contract, he must pay eleven dirms in the first instance, and ten in the second. The opinion of Mohammed is, that in case the purchaser chooses to abide by the contract, he must pay ten and a half dirms in the first instance. and nine and a halt in the second; because the measurement of a yard having been fixed at one dirm, it necessarily follows that half a yard must be rated at half a dirm. The reasoning of Aboo Yoosaf is that as the price of each yard was fixed at one dirm, it follows that each yard becomes virtually a distinct piece of cloth; and as one of these proves defective, it follows that the purchaser has the option either of undoing the bargain, or of taking the goods according to the terms of the contract. The arguments adduced by Haneefa in support of his opinion are, that the specification of yards is considered as referring to the description, and not the real quantity of the thing, excepting only where the price of each given measurement is specifically stipulated as a condition of the contract. Now, as in the case in queation, the rate is opposed to each completed yard, but not to any smaller quantity, it follows that such smaller quantity must be considered as remaining in its original form,—that is, as applying merely to description, and therefore cannot involve an additional payment Some have observed that in coarse cotton cloths, of which the extreme and interior parts are of a similar texture, it is not lawful for the purchaser to take any excess beyond the terms of the contract; as it may be cut off and restored to the seller without any injury to the piece, in the manner of things estimable by weight; and hence the learned deem it lawful to sell even a single yard of it.

In the sale of a house, the foundation and superstructure are both included.—If a person sell the place of his abode (in other words, his house), the foundation and superstructure are both included in such sale, although they may not have been specified by the seller; because they are comprehended in the common acceptation of the term; and also, because, being joined to the ground in the nature of fixtures, they are considered as dependant parts of it.

In the sale of land, the trees upon it are included.—In a sale of land, the trees upon it are included, although they be not specified, because they are joined to it, in the same manner as foundation and superstructure in the preceding case.

But not the corn.—In a sale of ground, the grain then growing on it is not included, unless particularly specified by the seller; because it is joined to the ground, not as a fixture, but for the purpose of being cut away from it, in the same manner as goods of any kind which may have been placed upon it.

Nor, in the sale of a tree, is the fruit then upon it included.—So also, if a person should sell a tree on which fruit is growing, the fruit belongs to the seller, unless it had been specifically included in the sale; because the Prophet has said, "If a person sell a DATE tree with fruit upon it, the fruit belongs to the seller, unless the purchaser should have stipulated its delivery to him as a condition of sale." Besides, although the fruit be, in fact, a part of the tree, yet as it is intended to be plucked and gathered, and not to be suffered to hang on the tree, it is therefore the same as grain.

But the purchaser must immediately clear these away.—It is to be observed, however, that in the sale of a tree with fruit, or of ground with grain upon it, the seller must be immediately desired to clear them away, and deliver the property to the purchaser; because, in these cases, the property of the

*Of the manufacture of the provinces of Herat and Murwa.

purchaser and seller being implicated together, it becomes incumbent on the seller to clear away what belongs to him; in the same manner as if he had placed any of his goods upon the ground in which case the clearance of them would have been requisite. Shafei maintains that in both these cases the grain and the fruit must be suffered to remain until they become ripe, because there ought to be a period stipulated for the delivery of the things sold, and that period ought to be extended to the complete growth and maturity of these vegetables; in the same manner as in the case of a lease of ground, where if, at the expiration of the lease, the grain on the ground be green, it is suffered to remain until it ripen. Our doctors, on the other hand, argue that the obligation is the same on a lessee; and if he be permitted to extend the lease on account of the unripeness of the grain, he must, however, pay additional rent for it, which is a substitute for the delivery; and the substitute is in effect the same as the thing itself. It is to be observed that in the sale of a tree, the fruit is not included, whether it be of an appreciable nature or otherwise, unless it be specifically mentioned.

In the sale of ground, the seed sown in it is not included.—IF a person sell a piece of ground in which seed has been sown, but of which the growth has not appeared above ground, in this case the seed is not included in the sale. If the apparent growth should have taken place though not in such a degree as to render the vegetable of any value, in this case there is a difference of opinion Some allege that the vegetation is not included in the sale: and others, that it is. This difference of opinion has its foundation in the different sentiments which the parties entertain with regard to the validity of the sale of vegetation, prior to its being fit to be cut down by the hook, or used by animals in the way of forage: for those who consider the separate sale of such vegetation to be valid. are of opinion that is not included; whilst those who consider the sale of it as invalid, are of opinion that it is included in the sale of the ground.

The time-product is not included, in the sale of land or trees, although the rights and appendages be expressed in the contract.—GRAIN and fruit are not included in a sale of ground, or of a tree, although the purchaser and seller specify the rights and appendages (in other words, although the seller declare, "I have sold this ground, in this tree, with all its rights and appendages"), because grain and fruit do not fall under these descriptions. (The rights of a thing are those without which it cannot be enjoyed, and which form the principal object of possession, such as a watercourse or a road: the appendages are things from which we derive use; but which are more particularly considered as dependant parts; such as a cook-room, or a house for keeping water.) In the same manner, if the seller should say, "I have sold this tree, or this piece of ground, with every thing small and great of its rights and appendages which I possess in it" still neither the fruit nor the grain is included in it.

Nor unless all its dependencies be generally expressed.—IF however, he should say, in a general manner, "I have sold this tree (or this piece of ground), with every thing great and small which I possess in it," in this case the grain and the fruit are necessarily included in it.

Nor can any product be included after being gathered or cut down.—IT is to observed that grain which has been cut, or fruit which has been plucked, cannot by any construction whatever be included in the sale, unless expressly mentioned as such

Fruit may be sold upon the tree in every state of growth.—THE sale of fruit upon a tree is valid, whether the strength of the fruit be ascertained or not; that is, whether it may or may not have reached such a degree of strength as may preserve it from common accidents; because fruit is a property of certain value, either immediately, in case of its being ripe, or hereafter, in case of its being in an unripe state (some have said that the sale of fruit in a weak state is invalid: the first doctrine is however, the most authentic): and the sale of fruit in an absolute manner being valid, the purchaser must immediately take it from the tree, wheather this be particularly expressed as a condition in the sale or otherwise.

But if the contract involve any condition not properly appertaining to sale, it is null.—IF, however, the condition of suffering the fruit to remain on the tree be stipulated, the sale is null. because such a condition is illegal, since it implicates together the right of property of the two parties, which is repugnant to the nature of sale; and every condition of this kind invalidates the sale. Besides, in this case, it must necessarily follow that one deed is interwoven with another; in other words, that either a loan or a lease is implicated with the sale, which is unlawful. In the same manner, the sale of grain, with a stipulation of leaving it on the seller's ground, is unlawful, and for the same reason. The same rule also obtains (according to Haneefa and Aboo Yoosaf) where the fruit or corn has attained its full growth, as this implicates the right of property of two parties. Mohammad is of opinion that, in this instance, such a condition is lawful, because of the existence of the whole of the thing in question; whereas, in the former case, the part of the property which afterwards vegetated was not in being at the time of the conclusion of the deed; and the stipulation of a condition with regard to a nonentity being illegal, the sale is therefore null.

The additional growth of fruit purchased on the tree, if suffered to continue upon it, by consent of the seller, is the property of the purchaser.—IF a person purchase fruit upon the tree before it had reached its full growth, in an absolute manner (that is without stipulating the condition of its remaining upon the tree until it become ripe), and afterwards, with the permission of the seller, suffer it to hang on the tree, in this case the additional growth becomes his lawful property. If, however, he act in this manner without the consent of the seller; he must then bestow the difference in charity, as being the produce of the property of another without the consent of that other. If, on the other hand, the sale should have taken place when the fruit had attained its full growth, and the purchaser suffer it to remain until it become ripe, he is not on that account required to bestow any thing in charity, because in this instance a change from one state to another takes place without any increase being made to the substance.

And so also if the purchaser take a lease of the tree.—IF a person, having in an absolute manner purchased fruit which had not attained its full growth, should afterwards suffer it to remain on the tree till it become ripe, by taking a lease of the tree till that period, in this case the increase of substance is lawful to him, because the lease is null, on account of a want of precise knowledge with respect to the period of it,—and also, on account of its not having been warranted by absolute necessity, since it was in the power of the leases to have purchased the tree itself:—and the lease being null, there remains only the consent of the seller, to which regard must be had.

But this rule does not hold with respect to grain purchased upon the ground.—IT is otherwise where a person purchases grain upon the ground, and having then taken a lease of the ground until the grain be capable of being cut down, suffers it to remain until that time: for the increase of substance is not in such case lawful to him, since the lease so made is invalid, and an invalid lease is the occasion of baseness and abomination

Any new fruit which may grow in the interim is the property of the seller and purchaser.—IF a person, in an unconditional manner, purchase fruit upon a tree which had not completely vegetated, and afterwards, before he had received a formal seisin of it, new fruit should grow, in this case the sale is invalid, because of the impracticability of delivery on the part of the seller, from the impossibility of distinguishing between what was the subject of the sale and what was not. But if new fruit should appear after the seisin of the purchaser, such fruit is in an equal degree the right of both, because of its intermixture with the property of both. The assertion of the purchaser, however, with regard to the quantity, is credited, because the fruit is in his possession. (The sale of artichokes or melons which are growing is subject to the same law as that of fruit growing upon trees).

Rule in the purchase of vegetable sold on a tree.—IF a person wish to purchase fruit, artichokes, or melons, and afterwards to have it in his power to let them remain until they become ripe, or until they shall yield a new crop, so as to have a lawful claim to the property, the expedient to be practised, in order to render such conduct legal, is to purchase the tree or bed itself, and after clearing it of the fruit when ripe, to undo the contract of sale with regard to the tree or bed.*

IF a person should sell fruit, with a reservation of a specific number of Ratls of it, the sale is invalid, whether the fruit be upon the tree or off it; because although the reservation be itself specific and known, yet the residue is unknown. It is otherwise where a reservation is made of a specific tree; because there the remainder is known, being obvious to the eye.—Our author remarks that this doctrine is conformable to a tradition of Hasan, adopted by Tahavee: but that such a sale is valid, according to the Zahir Rawayet, and also in the opinion of Shafei, because it is a rule that whatever may be lawfully sold, separately, may also be lawfully excepted from a deed of sale. Thus the sale of one Kafeez from a heap of grain being lawful, the exception of it is also a lawful act.—It is otherwise with respect to a fœtus in the womb, or any particular member of an animal: because as the separate sale of such subjects is illegal, so also is the reservation of them.

Grain may be sold in the ear, or pulse in the husk.—THE sale of wheat in the ear, or of beans in the husk, is valid: and the law is the same with respect to rice or rape seed in the husk. Shafei is of opinion that the sale of green beans in the husk, or of walnuts, almonds, or Fistachio nuts in the shell, is not valid; but with respect to wheat in the ear, he has given two opposite opinions. All these sales are, however, valid in the opinion of all our doctors. The reasoning of Shafei is that the subject of the sale, in these cases, is hidden within a thing of no value in itself namely, the husk, and that therefore the case becomes the same as if a goldsmith should sell a heap of earth mixed with particles of gold, in exchange for another heap of a similar nature, which is invalid. The arguments of our doctors upon this point are twofold, FIRST, the Prophet has said, "The sale of fruit upon the tree, or of grain in the ear, is invalid, unless it approach to a state of ripeness,† SECONDLY, wheat is an article capable of yielding advantage; and hence the sale of it in the ear is valid in the same manner as that of barley, the one being an appreciable article as well as the other. It is otherwise with gold dust, for the sale of

* The consent of the seller is here presupposed: for neither of the parties can undo a sale without the consent of the other. This expedient is therefore suggested on a supposition of the future undoing of the sale being equally agreeable to both parties.

† Whence it may be inferred that the sale, in the ear, or upon the tree, is admissible.

that, mixed with earth, is lawful from the possibility of its being usurious.

The sale of a house includes the fixtures and their appendages.—If a person sell a house, of which the locks are not of the hanging but of the fixed kind, in this case, the keys of such locks are considered as included in the sale ; because the locks themselves are included in the house, in consequence of their being fixtures ; and the sale of a lock includes the key, without its being expressly stipulated, because it is considered as a constituent part of it, since a lock without a key is of no use.

The seller must defray the expense of weighers, tellers, measurers, and money-essayers—The wages of the measurer* of the goods, or of the essayer of the money, must be paid by the seller :—the wages of the measurer, because, as measurement is essential to enable the seller to deliver over the goods the payment of the expense attending that falls properly upon him (and so also, the wages of weighers or tellers) :—and the wages of the essayer, because of a tradition, delivered by Ibn Roostim, that such is the doctrine of Mohammed ; and also for this reason, that the essay of the money takes place after the delivery, when it becomes the business of the seller to have it essayed, in order that he may distinguish what is his right and what is not ; and that he may ascertain the bad coin in order to reject them. Ibn Soomai relates it as the opinion of Mohammed that the purchaser should defray the wages of the essayer, because he stands in need of ascertaining the good dirms which he has stipulated to deliver, and the good dirms are known by means of an essayer, in the same manner as quantity by means of a measurer.

But the charge of weighing the price must be defrayed by the purchaser.—The charge of weighing the price is due by the purchaser, because he is under the necessity of delivering it to the seller, and the delivery is completed after ascertainment of the weight.' In a sale stipulating immediate payment, the purchaser must first deliver the price to the seller, because his right (namely, the goods sold) is of a fixed and determinate nature, whereas the price is not so ; and it is therefore incumbent on him, in order that both parties may be on a part to deliver the price to the seller, which fixes and determines it : for it cannot be determined but by delivery.†

In barter or exchange, the mutual delivery must be made by both parties at the same time.—In a sale of goods for goods, or of money for money, it is necessary that both parties make the delivery at the same time ; because being on a par in point of certainty and uncertainty, there is no necessity for a prior delivery.

CHAPTER II.

OF OPTIONAL CONDITIONS.

Definition of the term—An optional condition is where one of the parties stipulates it as a condition that he may have the option, for a period of two or three days, of annulling the contract if he please.

A condition of option may be lawfully stipualted by eithe party.—The stipulation of a condition of option, on the part either of the seller or purchaser, is lawful ; and it may be stipulated to continue for three days or less ; but it must not be extended, beyond that term ; because it is related that Hooban having been defrauded in several of his bargains, the Prophet addressed him thus, "Hooban, when you make a purchase bar deceit, and stipulate a condition of option."

Provided it exceed not the term of three days.—An optional condition, stipulated to remain in force for a period exceeding three days, is unlawful according to Haneefa ; and Ziffer and Shafei are of the same opinion. The two disciples, on the contrary, maintain that it may be stipulated to continue to any length of time whatever : because it is related that Ibn Omar extended it to two

* Meaning properly, some person who is employed as a sworn or professed measurer.

† Thus if the price stipulated be ten dirms, and the purchaser be in possession of a thousand dirms (for example) in this case, although the number ten be determinate, yet the units to compose that number and to be taken from a great number, are not specific and determinate, until actually delivered. This doctrine is frequently and particularly enlarged upon in the sequel of this book.

* Arab. Khiar-al-Shirt. In contracts of sale there are five different options: These are, 1st. Option of acceptance. 2. Optional conditions. 3 Option of determination. 4. Option of inspection, and 5. Option from defect. An option of acceptance is a liberty which either of the parties: in a contract of sale, has of withholding his acceptance, after the tender of the other, until the breaking up of the meeting. An optional condition is where one of the parties stipulates a period of three days before he gives his final assent to the contract. An option of determination is where a person, having purchased one out of two or three homogeneous things, stipulates a period to enable him to fix his choice. Option of inspection, is the power which the purchaser of an unseen thing has of rejecting it after sight. Option from defect is the power which a purchaser has of dissolving the contract on the discovery of a defect on the merchandise. The translator has thought it proper, in this note, to bring into one point of view an explanation of the several kinds of option, as it may possibly tend to give a clearer idea of them than what could be collected from the scattered definitions of them as they occur in the course of the work.

months; and also because it is ordained, by the LAW, for the purpose of answering the necessities of man, in enabling him to consider and set aside what is bad; and as a period of three days may not be sufficient for this purpose, the indulgence is therefore extended with respect to the merchandise, in the same manner as with respect to the price. The argument of Haneefa is that an optional condition is repugnant to the nature of the act, which fixes an immediate obligation on the parties, and is allowed only because of the saying of the Prophet already quoted; whence it cannot be extended to a period beyond what has been there specified

If it exceed three days, and the stipulating party declare his acceptance before the expiration of the third day, the sale is lawful—ALTHOUGH a conditional option beyond three days be not permitted, still if such a condition be stipulated, and the person making such stipulation, before the lapse of the three days, declare his acceptance of the contract, the sale is in that case valid, according to Haneefa. Ziffer, however, is of different opinion; for he argues that the sale being invalid from the beginning, on account of the illegality of the condition, it cannot be afterwards rendered valid by the removal of such condition. The arguments of Haneefa on this point are twofold. FIRST as the acceptance of the sale was declared before the lapse of the three days, the cause of its invalidity has not begun to operate. SECONDLY, the invalidity takes place on the fourth day; and as the acceptance is declared before that period, the sale is consequently kept free from any cause of invalidity From this second argument some have considered that the invalidity of the sale does not take place until the commencement of the fourth day;—whilst others (founding their opinion on the first argument), hold that the contract was invalid from the beginning: but is afterwards rendered valid by the removal of the cause of its invalidity previous to its operation.

The payment of the price may be substituted as the condition.—IT is lawful for a person to make a purchase on this condition, that "if in the course of three days he do not pay th price, the sale shall be null and void". If, however, instead of three days he stipulate four, the sale is not valid, according to Haneefa and Aboo Yoosaf. Mohammed is of opinion that it is valid, whether he stipulate four days or more. All our doctors, however, agree, that in case of such a stipulation having been made, if the purchaser in the mean time pay the price, previous to the lapse of the third day, the sale is valid. The reason of this is that a condition of this nature is of the same nature with an optional condition, because in case the purchaser cannot furnish the price, the seller stands in need of a power to annul the act. As, moreover, Haneefa holds that a sale is invalid, where the condition of option extends beyond three days, but may afterwards be rendered valid by a formal confirmation previous to the lapse of the third day, so also in the case in question. As Mohammed, on the contrary, holds that the extension of the condition of option beyond the third day is lawful, so also in the present instance. Aboo Yoosaf, on the other hand, although (contrary to analogy) he holds the extending of a condition of option beyond three days to be lawful, because of a tradition which he quotes to this effect, yet is of opinion that the same extention is unlawful in the present instance (arguing from analogy), as there is no tradition in support of it. There is another explanation, from analogy, with respect to this case, which has been adopted by Ziffer, to the following effect, that, in the sale in question, an invalid dissolution has been stipulated (for the dissolution is invalid, as it depends upon a condition); and as a sale is rendered void by the stipulation of a valid dissolution, it follows that by the stipulation of an invalid dissolution it is rendered void a fortiori. The reason, however, for a more liberal construction in this particular is, that the condition here stipulated is considered as an equivalent to a condition of option, as has already been explained.

The seller, by stipulating a condition of option, does not relinquish his property in the article sold.—IF the seller stipulate a condition of option, the right of property over the goods does not in that case shift from him, because the completion of the sale depends on the mutual consent of the parties, and the condition of option evinces that the seller has not completely consented. If, therefore, under these circumstances, the seller should emancipate a slave whom he had in that manner sold, the emancipation would hold good.—Neither is the purchaser in such a case entitled to use or employ the goods, although he should have taken possession of them with consent of the seller.—If, after the purchaser had possessed himself of the goods, they should perish or be destroyed previous to the expiration of the period of optional condition, he becomes in that case responsible for the value; because by the destruction of the goods the sale is annulled (for the execution of it rested only on the consent of the seller; and where the subject of it is lost, the execution of it becomes impracticable; and it is null of course); and as the goods were in possession of the purchaser with a view to purchase (which circumstance renders a purchaser responsible for the value), he is responsible accordingly. If, on the other hand, the goods be lost in the possession of the seller, the deed is annulled; and no payment is incumbent on the purchaser, in the same manner as in the case of an absolute sale, that is, a sale where no condition is stipulated.

But the property in it devolves upon the purchaser where the stipulation is made on his part; and he is consequently responsible

for the loss of the goods.—IF the condition of option be stipulated by the purchaser, the right of property over the goods shifts from the seller, because the sale is rendered complete on his part The right of property, however, although it shift from the seller, does not vest in the purchaser, according to Haneefa. The two disciples have said that the purchaser becomes the proprietor; for, if this were not the case, it must necessarily follow that, after it moved from the seller, it would remain subject to no person; and this is a state not supposed by the LAW. The arguments of Haneefa on this point are twofold. FIRST as the right of property with respect to the price has not shifted from the purchaser, it follows that if the right of property with respect to the goods also vest in him, the property with respect both to the thing purchased and the return for it is concerned in one person, which is absolutely illegal. SECONDLY, if the right of property with respect to the goods were to vest in the purchaser, it might frequently happen that the goods would, in the interval, before the completion of the sale, be made away without any intention on the part of the purchaser (as if the purchaser had bought a slave related to himself within the prohibited degrees)* ; and as the sole object of the reserve of option is the benefit of the purchaser, in allowing him time for consideration, it follows that if the right of property were to vest immediately in him he might be deprived of the advantage which is the object of the reserve of option.

If the purchaser have the option, and the goods be injured or destroyed in the interim, he is responsible for the price.—IF the merchandise, where the stipulation of option is on the part of the purchaser, perish or be destroyed, the purchaser is in that case answerable for the price, in the same manner also, if the goods receive an injury, the purchaser is responsible for the price; because the goods, after sustaining an injury, cannot be returned, and the sale consequently becomes binding. The purchaser, therefore, is responsible for the price in either instance; for destruction necessarily implies previous injury: and hence in a case where the purchaser is utterly destroyed, the sale first becomes binding and complete, and the destruction takes place afterwards

But if it rest with the seller, the purchaser is responsible for the value only.—AND as, in a case of injury, the payment of the price becomes obligatory, so also in a case of destruction. It is otherwise where the merchandise perishes in the possession of the purchaser when the option had been stipulated by the seller; for in this case the purchaser is answerable only for the value ;† because the circumstance of the injury does not render the restitution impracticable, since the seller, in that case, had the option either of taking the merchandise thus injured, or of rejecting it, if he place; as the optional condition remains with him: and hence, as the sale does not become binding on the occurrence of the injury, if the seller choose to confirm it, the purchaser in that case only pays the value of the injured merchandise.

Right of option, in the purchase of a wife, is not affected by cohabitation with her in the interim of option.—IF a person purchase his own wife, with a reserve of option for three days, in this case the marriage subsists during that interval, as the right of property does not take place because of the optional condition: and if he have carnal connexion with her during that interval, the condition of option is not thereby annulled; because he has it is still in his power, after such connexion, to undo the sale, since his cohabitation with her is the exercise of a right in virtue of his marriage, and not of his right of property. If, however, his wife be a virgin, his cohabitation with her annuls the condition of option, and establishes the sale, as it is a damage to her, and a diminution of her value. This is the doctrine of Haneefa. The two disciples are of opinion that the husband becomes immediate property of his wife by the optional purchase, whence the marriage is immediately annulled. If therefore, he should have cohabitation with her, he cannot afterwards reject her, although she may have been a woman;* because the marriage being null, the cohabitation was not in virtue of marriage, but of property. This difference of opinion between Haneefa and the two disciples, respecting the property vesting immediately in a conditional purchaser, has given rise to opposite decisions in a variety of different cases. Of this number are the following :-

Case of optional purchase of a slave related to the purchaser—IF a person make an optional purchase of a slave related to him within the prohibited degrees, the emancipation, in the opinion of the two disciples, takes place immediately; whereas according to Haneefa, it does not take place until after the confirmation of the contract.

And of a slave optionally purchased under a vow of emancipation.—IF, also, a person make a vow to emancipate a slave whenever he becomes proprietor of one, then, according to the two disciples, if he make a conditional purchase of one, the emancipation takes place immediately: whereas, according to Haneefa, it does not take place till after the confirmation.

Or of a menstruous female slave—IF, also, a person make an optional purchase of a female slave, and her monthly courses happen during the term of option, these courses are included in the prescribed term

*In which case the slave would become immediately free.

†And not for the price set upon it in the contract.

*That is to say, not a virgin.

of abstinence,* according to the two disciples; whereas, according to Haneefa, they are not included. And if the purchaser, availing himself of his optional condition, should return her to the seller, the seller need not observe the prescribed term of abstinence, according to Haneefa: whereas, the two disciples hold that such observance is incumbent on him.

Or of a pregnant wife.—IF, on the other hand, a person make an optional purchase of his own wife, and if she, during the interval of option, bring forth a child, she is not an Am-Walid to the purchaser, according to Haneefa; whereas, according to the two disciples, she is so. If also, a person make an optional purchase, of merchandise, and having with the consent of the seller, received possession of it, afterwards give it in deposit to the seller, and it be lost in the interval, in this case, according to Haneefa, the trust is null and void, as the deposit was not the property of the purchaser, and therefore he is of opinion that the loss results to the seller; whereas the two disciples, holding the said deposit to be valid, are of opinion that the loss results to the purchaser, agreeably to the law of deposits.

Optional purchase made by a privileged slave.—IF, on the other hand, a privileged slave make an optional purchase, and the seller, during the interval of option, exempt him from the payment, in this case, according to Haneefa, the condition of option remains in force: because if he should return the merchandise, it follows that he does not choose to accept of the property, and a privileged slave has the power of accepting or rejecting as he please: but, according to the two disciples, the condition of option is annulled by the exemption of payment; because (in their opinion) the property having vested from the beginning, it follows that if he were to return the merchandise to the seller, it would be in effect a gift to him, and a privileged slave has not the power of making a gift.

Case of optional purchase of wine by a Zimmee, who in the interim embraces the faith.—IF, moreover, a Zimmee purchase spirituous liquors from a Zimmee, on a condition of option, and the purchaser in the interval, become a Mussulman, in this case, according to the two disciples, the condition of option remains no longer in force, because the purchaser having (agreeably to their tenets) become proprietor of the liquor, it follows that if he were permitted to reject it, he would create in another a right of property with respect to liquors, which no Mussulman is allowed to use. According to Haneefa, on the contrary the sale becomes void, because the purchaser (agreeably, to his tenets), not being then the proprietor and the circumstance of becoming a Mussulman putting it out of his power to become the proprietor by removing the condition, the sale is of necessity annulled.

The possessor of option may annul the sale with the knowledge of the other party, or confirm it without his knowledge.—In case of a sale on a condition of option, it is lawful, according to Haneefa and Mohammed, for the party possessing the option to annul the contract within the stipulated period, or to confirm it: which latter he may do without, the knowledge of the other party: but it is not lawful for him to annul it without the knowledge of the other Aboo Yousaf alleges that the parties possessing the option may annul the contract without the knowledge of the other: and such, also, is the opinion of Shafei. The argument of Aboo Yoosaf is that the party possessing the option is empowered, on the part of the other, to annul the contract: and that therefore, such annulment cannot rest upon that other's knowledge of it: in the same manner as his knowledge of it is unnecessary in case the possessor of the option confirm the contract; as in the case of an agent for sale (for instance), who may lawfully act in every matter to which his agency extends, without the knowledge of his constituent, in virtue of the powers given to him on his behalf. The arguments of Haneefa and Mohammed are, that a contract of sale involves the rights of both parties, and that the annulment of the sale by one party only is an exercise of a right partly belonging to the other, whilst at the same time such exercise may eventually be attended with a loss to the other: for supposing the possessor of the option to be the seller, and that he annul the sale without the knowledge of the purchaser, and the purchaser, in the mean time, in the confidence of the sale being complete, take possession of the merchandise, then, in case of its destruction, he must of consequence be responsible for it: or, supposing the purchaser to be the possessor of the option, and that he annul the sale without the knowledge of the seller, then an eventual loss may result to the seller, as it is possible that, on the presumption of his goods being already sold, he may enquire out another purchaser. Hence as such an exercise, on the part of either, of the right of the other, may be attended with an eventual injury, the annulment of an optional sale is therefore made to rest upon the knowledge of the other party. This case, in short, resembles the dismission of an agent: for if a person, having appointed an agent, should afterwards dismiss him without his knowledge, it would not be valid until the agent was himself informed of it; and so also in the case in question. It is otherwise with the confirmation o..

*The purchaser of a female slave is required to abstain from carnal connexion with her until she shall have had three different courses from the period of her becoming his property, that it may be ascertained whether she be pregnant or not. (See Edit.)

sale; as the exercise of such a right by one party only does not entail an injury. The assertion of Aboo Yoosaf that "the possessor of the option is empowered to make such annulment on the part of the other," is not admitted; for how can the other, who does not himself possess such power, bestow it upon the possessor of the option?

And even if he annul it without the other's knowledge, and the other be informed before the expiration of the term, it is valid.—If the person possessing the option annul the sale without informing the other party, and such knowledge, nevertheless, reach him before the expiration of the stipulated period, then, because of his acquirement of such knowledge, the annulment is rendered complete. If, on the other hand, it should not have reached him until the expiration of the stipulated period, then the annulment is rendered complete, because of the expiration of the stipulated period

A right of option, in sale, cannot descend to an heir.—If a person possessing the right of option in a sale should die, the sale is then complete, and the right of option becomes void, and does not descend to his heirs.—Shafei maintains that the option descends to the heirs, because, being a fixed and established right in sale, it may be inherited, in the same manner as an option in case of defect, or an option of determination. The arguments of our doctors are that an option is in reality nothing but desire, or disposition, which is not capable of being transferred from one to another; and nothing but what is capable of devolving from one person to another can be inherited.—It is otherwise with respect to option in case of defect, as that is granted to the heir, because of his right to obtain possession of a thing whole and complete, in the same manner as the deceased, and not because of his right of inheritance, since option is incapable of being a subject of inheritance. It is otherwise, also, with respect to an option of determination, as the heir becomes the proprietor in that instance, because of the mixture of property, and not because of his right of inheritance.

A right of option may be referred to a third person.—If a person, in purchasing any article, stipulate the option of another person, in this case, provided either the purchaser or the possessor of the option confirm the sale, it is valid; or, if either of them annul it, it becomes void. The reason of this is, that the stipulation of the option of another is admitted, upon a favourable construction. Analogy would suggest that it is inadmissible, and such is the opinion of Ziffer, because option being one of the articles of the contract, it follows that the stipulation of it for another who is not one of the contraction parties, is illegal, in the same manner as if it were stipulated that some other than the purchaser should pay the price.—The arguments of our doctors are, that the establishment of the right of option in one who is not a party to the contract is by way of appointment from him to act as his substitute. In this case, therefore, the option is vested both in the party and in his substitute: and consequently it is lawful for either of them to confirm or annul the contract.—If one of them should confirm, and the other annul the contract, in this case the first of these acts which may have been performed becomes valid. If both should have been performed at the same time, then (according to one tradition) the act of the contracting party is valid;—or (according to another) the validity of the annulment is preferred to that of the confirmation. The principle on which the first tradition proceeds is that the act of the contracting party is of superior force to that of a substitute who derives his authority from him; and the principle on which the second tradition is founded is that annulment is of superior force to confirmation, because annulment may take place after confirmation, but confirmation cannot take place after annulment. Some have asserted that the first tradition is conformable to the doctrine of Mohammed, and the second to that of Aboo Yoosaf;—arguing from their different decisions in the case of an agent of sale and his constituent: for if both of them should at the same time sell the same thing to different persons the sale of the constituent is valid, according to Mohammed;—whereas, according to Aboo Yoosaf, both sales are valid; but the article sold must be divided between the two purchasers.

Case of selling two slaves, with a condition of option with respect to one of them.—If a person sell two slaves for a thousand dirms, stipulating an optional condition with respect to one of them, the case admits of four different statements.—I. Where the seller does not oppose a specific price to each of the slaves, nor specify the one respecting whom the optional condition is to operate: and this is illegal, because of the uncertainty both as to the subject of the sale and the price: for as the slave, concerning whom the condition of option is stipulated, is not (as it were) included in the sale and as he is not specified, it follows that the other, who is the subject to the sale, is also unknown—II. Where the seller sets a particular price upon each of the slaves, and also specifies to which the condition of option relates; and this is valid, because of the certainty with respect to the subject of the sale and the price.

Objection.—It would appear that the sale is in this case illegal; because the slave who is the subject of the condition is not, in effect, included in the sale; and, as both are joined together in one declaration, it follows that the acceptance of the sale with relation to what is not the subject of it, becomes a condition of the validity of the sale with regard to what is: it being the same, in short, as if a person should join a freeman and a slave in one declaration of sale, which is illegal, because the acceptance of the sale with regard to what is not capable of being the subject of it (namely, the free man) is here made a condition of the validity of the sale with respect to the slave; and this condition is the cause of annulling the sale: it therefore follows that the sale is in the same manner invalid in the case in question, as the same condition (which occasions an annulment of the sale) is equally induced in this instance.

REPLY—The sale, in the case in question, is lawful; because, although the acceptance of the sale, with respect to the slave concerning whom the option is stipulated, be a condition of the validity of the sale with respect to the other slave also, still such condition does not annul the sale, since the optional slave is a fit subject for sale: it is therefore, in fact, the same as if a person were to join a Modabbir and an absolute slave in one declaration; and as the sale is in that instance valid, so also in the case in question:—contrary to where a seller joins a slave and a freeman in one declaration: because a freeman is not a fit subject of sale. —III Where the seller opposes a particular price to each slave, but does not specify to which of them the condition of option relates.—IV Where the seller specifies the slave to whom the condition of option relates, but does not oppose a specific price to each of them.—In both these cases the slave is invalid, because of the uncertainty of the subject of the sale in the one instance, and of the price in the other.

Option of determination.—IF a person purchase one of two pieces of cloth for ten dirms, on the condition of his being at liberty for three days to determine on the particular piece which he may approve, such sale is valid; and the condition so stipulated is called an option of determination.*

It extends to a choice out of three, but not out of more.—A SALE is in the same manner valid, where a person purchases, with a reserve of option, one out of three pieces; but it is not lawful to purchase, in that manner, one out of four pieces.—What is here advanced proceeds upon a favourable construction.—Analogy would suggest that the sale is not lawful in either of these three cases, because the subject of sale is uncertain;—and such, also, is the opinion of Ziffer and Shafei—The reason for a more favourable construction is, that optional conditions have been ordained for the benefit of man, in order that he may thereby be enabled to set aside the bad, and to choose the good for himself:—it is, moreover, evident that man stands in need of contracts of this nature, in order that he may be enabled to show the merchandise to some person in whose judgment he confides; or if an agent be employed that he may show it to his constituent; and this the seller would not permit him to do unless such a condition were stipulated.—This species of sale therefore, being in effect the same as an optional one, it follows that it is in a similar manner lawful.—This necessity on the part of man, however, is fully answered by means of three pieces, as this number comprehends the three qualities of good, bad, and medium; and there can be no uncertainty with respect to the subject of the sale, in this species of contract, to occasion contention, as regard is had solely to price on which the purchaser determines.

OBJECTION.—Why then is it not lawful with respect to four pieces, as in that case also no contention would take place?

REPLY—Although, in this case also, there would be no uncertainty with regard to the subject of the sale, to occasion contention, still the efficient cause of the legality (namely, the necessity of MAN) does not here exist, and it is therefore unlawful.

An option of determination may involve a condition of option.—SOME have observed that, in a case of option of determination, a condition of option is also indispensable; and that is recorded in the Jama Sagheer. Others, again (following the Jama Kabeer), say that the condition of option is not requisite; and hence it is inferred that what has been recorded in the Jama Sagheer is that such a condition often takes place; not that it is absolutely necessary

But the term for making the determination must not at all events, exceed three days,—IT is to be observed, however; that if, in a sale stipulating an option of determination, it should not be thought necessary to insert a condition of option, the period for determining the choice must in that case, according to Haneefa, be limited to three days: but according to the two disciples it may be fixed to whatever period they please.

Of the articles referred to the purchaser's choice, one is the subject of the sale, and the others are as deposits—IT is also to be observed that in case of option of determination, the subject of the sale is one piece of cloth (for example), and the other piece is a deposit in the hands of the purchaser.* If, therefore, one of the pieces be lost or spoiled the sale takes place with respect to it in exchange for the stipulated price; and the other price is as a deposit; because it is impossible to reject the piece which is lost or spoiled. If, on the other hand, both pieces be lost at the same time, the purchaser must in that case pay the half of the price of each, because the determination of purchase not having been made with respect to either of the pieces, it follows that sale and trust operate indefinitely with respect to each.

And both may be returned in case of a condition of option.—IF besides the option of determination, a conditional option be also

*Arab. Khiar-al-tayeen

*And consequently (according to the laws of deposit) he is responsible in case of accidents, for one piece only.

stipulated, the purchaser is in that case at liberty to ret rn both pieces.

The heir of the person endowed with an option of determination may return one of the two articles referred to the purchaser's option, in case of his death.—If a person possessing an option of determination should die, his heir is empowered to return one of the articles; for an option of determination (as has been before explained) necessarily descends to an heir, because of the implication of his property with that of another; whence he is not, in his option of determination, restricted to three days —If, on the contrary, a person recently possessed of a power of option die, his heir has no option, as was before ex laine ..*

Option is declared and the sale made binding by any act of the purchaser in relation to the article sold—If a person purchase a house under a condition of option and the adjoining house be afterwards sold before the expiration of the period of option, and the purchaser under the condition of option claim the right of Shaffa, in this case his assent to the first sale is thereby virtually given, and his right of option exists no longer;—because his claim of Shaffa presupposes him to be confirmed in the adjoining property, otherwise he would have no right to make such a claim; and it is therefore inferred, that he first tacitly annuls his condition of option, and then urges his claim. It is to be observed that the necessity of this explanation arises from the doctrine of Haneefa; for by his tenets, a purchaser under a condition of option does not become proprietor of the article of sale during the interim of option The two disciples hold, on the contrary, that he becomes immediate proprietor under the condition of option; whence this explanation is, with regard to their doctrine unnecessary.

An option of determination, vested jointly in two persons, is determined by the subsequent consent of either to the purchase.—If two persons purchase a slave, on this condition, that both purchasers shall have the option of rejecting him, and one of them afterwards express his consent, the other cannot reject him, according to Haneefa. The two disciples allege that if the other choose, he may reject his share in the slave. The same disagreement subsists with respect to two purchasers in a case of option of inspection or option from defect. The argument of the two disciples is that as the power of rejection was vested in both the purchasers, it consequently operated in each of them; and the rejection of the cannot abrogate the right of option with respect to the other, as that would be a destruction of his right, which is not lawful. The argument of Haneefa is that the subject of the seller, when it issued from the tenure of the seller, was not injured by the defect of participation; but it one of the purchasers have the liberty of rejecting his portion singly, it necessarily follows that upon the rejection the seller holds the article in partnership with one of the purchasers; and this is a defect in the tenure, to which he was not before subject.

Objection.—It would appear that the rejection of one of the purchasers is valid although attended with an injury to the seller, since the seller has himself virtually assented to it, because in giving such power to two persons, it is evident that he assents to a possible rejection by one of them.

Reply.—The consent of the seller to the injury is inferred from a supposition of his having consented that one might reject where the power of rejection was given to two. This, however, is not the case in the present instance; for it is to be supposed that the seller understood that both should declare their rejection together; and on this supposition his consent was given, not on the other.

If an article purchased under one description prove to be of another description the purchaser may either confirm or annul the contract.—If a person purchase a slave on account of his being a scribe, or a baker, and he prove to be neither of these, the purchaser is in that case at liberty either to abide by the bargain, or to undo it, as he pleases; because the descriptive quality being the object he had in view, and being specified as a condition in the contract, is therefore his right, and the want of it gives him the power of dissolution if he please, because his assent signified was on this condition, and not otherwise.

Objection.—It would appear that the sale is in this case invalid, in the same manner as in the case of purchasing a male slave who afterwards proves to be a female.

Reply.—The sale in the case quoted is invalid because of difference of sex, which does not exist in the case in question. Thus a person that is a baker or not a baker is of the same sex and differs only in the quality; and hence the analogous application of the one case to the other is unfounded. It is to be observed, that a difference of the sex does not invalidate the sale, unless it defeat the purchaser's object. Thus the object in the purchase of a man (for instance) is different from that in the purchase of a woman, and therefore the sale is invalid in case of a difference: if. on the contrary, a man should purchase a he-goat on the supposition of its being a female, the sale would not be invalid, but it would remain with the purchaser to abide by it or not, as he pleases. It is to be observed however, that, in the case in question, if the purchaser choose to abide by the bargain he must pay the whole of the priee; as no diminution is admitted on account of the defect of quality, which (as has been before explained) is of a dependant nature.

*Because a condition of option is not inheritable.

CHAPTER III

OF OPTION OF INSPECTION.*

A purchaser may reject an article upon inspection after purchase.—If a person purchase an article without having seen it, the sale of such article is valid, and the purchaser after seeing it has the option of accepting or rejecting it as he pleases, Shafei maintains that a sale of this nature is wholly invalid, because of the uncertainty with regard to the object of it. The arguments of our doctors are.—First, a saying of the Prophet, that "whosoever purchases a thing without seeing it, has the liberty of rejection after sight of it. Secondly, the uncertainty with respect to the object cannot occasion litigation, since, if it be not agreeable, the purchaser is at liberty to reject it.

Although, before seeing it, he should have signified his satisfaction.—If a person, having purchased an article unseen, should say, "I am satisfied with it," in this case also he is at liberty, after, sight of it, to reject it if he please, for two reasons. First, as the option of inspection (according to the tradition already quoted) rests entirely upon inspection, it follows that it becomes established by the inspection, whereas before that it was not established; and as the acquiesence signified previous to the inspection is not repugnant to this, it consequently remains established.

Objection:—If the right of option do not exist previous to the actual sight of the article of sale, it would follow that the purchaser, before inspection, has not the power of annulling the contract;—whereas we find, on the contrary, that he is actually possessed of this power before inspection.

Reply.—His right to dissolve the contract previous to this inspection, proceeds from the contract not being then binding; and not from any reference to the tradition above quoted

Secondly, the purchaser's acquiescence in the article before he attains an actual knowledge of its qualities, is perfectly nugatory; and hence no regard is paid to his acquiescence previously signified:—contrary to his rejection, which is regarded, because the contract has not as yet become binding.

A seller has no option of inspection after sale.—If a person sell a thing which he himself has not seen, he has no option of inspection;† because the tradition before cited limits this option entirely to the purchaser: moreover, it is related that Osman sold a piece of ground belonging to him at Basra to Tilha-Bin-Abeedoola; when a person said to Tilha, "you have been injured in this matter:" but he replied, "I possess the liberty of rejection, having purchased a thing unseen:—after which another said to Osman, "You have been injured in this sale," and he replied, "I have the liberty of retractation, having sold a thing which I had not seen:" upon which Mazim was appointed arbitrator between them: and he decreed that the right of option rested only with Tilha; and this decree was given in the presence of all the companions of the Prophet, none of whom objected to it.

The option of inspection continues in force to any distance of time after the contract, unless destroyed by circumstances.—The right to option of inspection is not, like an optional condition, confined, to a particular period: on the contrary, it continues in force until something take place repugnant to the nature of it.—It is also to be observed that whatever circumstance occasions the annulment of an optional conditions (such as a defect in the merchandise, or an exercise of right on the part of the purchaser, in the same manner occasions an annulment of the option of inspection.

Such as would have annulled a condition of option.—If, therefore, the exercise of right be such as cannot afterwards be retracted (such as the emancipation of a slave, or the creating him a Modabbir),—or, if it be such as to involve the rights of others (such as absolute sale, mortgage, or hire,)—the option of inspection is immediately annulled, whether the thing have been seen or not; because these acts render the sale binding, and the existence of the option is incompatible with the obligation of the sale. If, on the contrary, the exercise of right be not such as to involve the right of others (such as a sale with an optional condition, a simple tender to purchase, or a gift without delivery),—the option of inspection is not annulled previous to the actual sight of the article sold, because acts of this description are not of a stronger nature than the purchaser's acquiescence; and as the purchaser's express acquiescence to inspecting is not the cause of annulling the option of inspection (as has been already demonstrated), it follows that the acts above described do not annul it, a fortiori;—whereas those acts after inspection annul the option of inspection, as they indicate an acquiescence, and an acquiescence after the sight of the thing occasions the annulment of the option.

Option of inspection is destroyed by the sight of a part of the article, where that suffices as a sample of the whole.—If a person should look at a heap of grain, or at the outward appearance of cloth which is folded up, or at the face a female slave, or at the face and posteriors of an animal, and then make purchase of the same, he has no option of inspection. In short, it is a rule that the sight of all the parts of the merchandise is not a necessary condition, because it is often impracticable to obtain it. and therefore it is sufficient to view that part whence it may be known how far the object of the purchaser will be obtained. In the purchase, therefore, of articles of which the parts are simila-

*Arab. Khiar-al-Rooyat.

†That is, he has no power of retraction. if, upon inspection of the article sold, he should happen to repent of the sale.

(such as articles sold by weight or o- m. surement of capacity, and the mode of ascertaining the goodness of which is by presenting a sample to the purchaser) the sight of a part is sufficient; that is, no option of inspection can afterwards be claimed unless the other parts of the article should prove inferior to the part which has been seen In the purchase, on the other hand, of things of which the individuals are not similar (such as cloths or animals), the sight of one does no suffice;—on the contrary, the purchaser must see each individual article. Of this kind are eggs and walnuts, according to Koorokhee. (The compiler of this work observe how ever, that these are of the nature of wheat and barley, since their individuals are nearly alike.)—Now such being the stablished rule, it follows that the sight of a heap of wheat is sufficient, as the quality of what is hidden may be inferred from what is seen, wheat being an article sold by measurement of capacity, and the equality of which may consequently be ascertained by means of a sample: and in the same manner, the sight of the outside of a piece of cloth suffices, unless there be a particular part within the folds necessary to be known, such as (in stamped cloths) the pattern, in which case the option of inspection is not annulled until the purchaser see the inside of the piece In the case of a man * on the other hand, a sight of the face is sufficient; and in animals a sight of the face and posteriors—Some allege that in animals a sight of the four and hinder legs is necessary. What was first related is on the authority of Aboo Yoosaf In goats purchased on account of their flesh it is necessary to squeeze and press the flesh in the hands, as that ascertains the goodness of it. But if purchased for breed, or for giving milk, it is necessary to look at their dugs. In purchasing victuals ready dressed, it is necessary to taste them, to ascertain their goodness.

Option of inspection in the purchase of a house.—If a person look at the front of a house, and then purchase it, he has no option of inspection, although he should not have seen the apartments:—and so also, if a person view the back parts of a house, or the trees of a garden from without. Ziffer has said that it is requisite that the purchaser inspect the apartments of the house. Our author also remarks that what is here advanced with respect to a sight of the front or back part of a house being sufficient, is founded on the customs of former times, when, all their building being of a uniform nature, the sight of the front or back parts sufficed to ascertain the interior parts; but that in the present time it is very necessary to enter, in, as buildings are in these days variously contructed, whence a view of the outside is no standard by which to judge of the inside; and this is approved.

As agent for seisin may inspect in the same manner as the purchaser.—The inspection of an agent appointed to take possession of an article purchased is equivalent to the inspection of the purchaser, and consequently after the inspection of such agent, the purchaser has no power of rejecting the article purchased, unless in a case of a defect. The inspection, however, of a messenger on the part of the purchaser is not equivalent to his own inspection. This is the doctrine of Haneefa The two disciples hold that an agent and a massenger are in effect the same (that is, the inspection of neither is equivalent to that of the purchaser, and the liberty consequently, that the purchaser has afterward of rejection in both instances. The argument they adduce in support of their opinion is, that as the constituent has appointed the agent merely to take possession, and not to annul his option, it follows that such annulment does not belong to him;—in the same manner as holds with respect to option from defect: in other words, if an agent should knowingly take possession of a defective article, the option of the purchaser is not thereby annulled:—and in the same manner also, as holds with respect to a condition of option; that is, if a person should purchase any article, with a reserve of option, and his agent, in the interval, take possession of the article, the purchaser's right of option is not annulled;—and in the same manner also, as holds in the wilful annulment of an option of inspection; as if an agent should take possession of an article concealed, and after inspection expressly declare the option to be null; in which case the purchaser's right of option would nevertheless still continue in force.—Haneefa, on the other hand, argues that seisin, or to act of taking possession, is of two kinds.—I. Perfect, which is the seisin of the article with sight and knowledge, II. Imperfect, which is the seisin of it without sight, that is, whilst it is concealed. The first is termed perfect, and the second imperfect, because the completeness of seisin depends upon the completeness of the bargain.* which cannot be complete whils an option of inspection remains; and as, in the former instance, this option has been done away, it follows that the bargain is in that instance complete and perfect; but as in the latter instance, on the contrary, it still continues in force; it follows that the bargain is in that instance imperfect.—Now as the constituent is empowered to take possession in either of these modes, it follows that the agent is equally empowered, since his constituent has appointed him, in an absolute manner, his agent for seisin. Where, however, an agent takes possession of an article without seeing it, his power is terminated by such imperfect seisin, and he consequently cannot afterwards exert an option of inspec-

*Meaning a slave set up to sale.

*Arab. Safka, literally, the act of striking hands, in making a bargain.

tion so as to destroy that privilege on the part of his constituent by any express declaration. It is otherwise in the case of an option from defect, because, as that is no bar to the completeness of the bargain, the seisin is in that instance perfect, notwithstanding the continuance of the option of defect —Concerning the case of condition of option there is a difference of opinion.—Admitting, however, that the agent has not the power of annulling such option, it is because the constituent himself is not in this case empowered to make a perfect seisin, inasmuch as the object of such conditional option is experience and trial which can only be acquired after seisin; and as the constituent himself is not empowered to make a perfect seisin, it follows that his agent cannot be so.—With respect to a messanger, he possesses no power, being barely commissioned to deliver a message, and cannot therefore be capable of taking formal possession of any thing.

The inspection of a blind person may be made by touch, smell, or taste.—Sale or purchase, made by a blind person, is valid: and after purchase, he has still an option as having purchased an article without seeing it; which option is determined by the touch of the article, provided it be of such a nature that the touch may lead to a knowledge of it: or by the smell, if it be of a nature to be known by the smell; or by the taste, if the article be of an esculent nature;—in the same manner as all these modes determine the option of a person possessed of sight.

Or (in a purchase of and) by description —The option of a blind person, in the purchase of land, is not determined until a description of the qualities of it be given to him: because such a description is equivalent to a sight of the object, as in the case of Sillim sales.—It is recorded from Aboo Yoosaf, that if a blind person, in purchasing land, should stand on a spot whence, if he possessed his sight, he might inspect the whole, and should then declare, "I am content with this ground which I have purchased," the right of option is annulled; because the standing on the spot in this manner is analogous to the actual view of it; and the semblance is equivalent to the reality where the reality is unattainable; as in the case of a dumb person, the motion of whose lips is deemed equivalent to the reading of the Koran; or, as in the case of a bald person, with respect to whom the motion of the razor to and from over his head is deemed equivalent (in case of his making a pilgrimage to Mecca) to actual shaving.—Hoosn-Bin-Zeeyad has said that a blind person must appoint an agent for seisin, who may inspect and take possession of the article on his behalf; and this is conformable to the doctrine of Haneefa, who is of opinion (as has been already explained) that the inspection of an agent is equivalent to that of his constituent.

A sight of one of two articles, such as do not admit of samples, still leaves a power of rejecting both.—If a person, having seen one of two garments, should purchase both, and should afterwards see the other, he has then the option of rejecting both; because, as garments differ essentially from one another, a sight of one is not equivalent to a sight of both; and therefore his right of option remains with respect to the one he had not seen. He has it not in his power, however, to reject that one singly; for in such case an alteration in the bargain would take place before the completion of it,* as a bargain is not complete whilst an option of inspection remains: and hence it is that the purchaser may reject the article, independent of an order from the Kazee, or the consent of the seller; and such rejection is a dissolution of the sale from the beginning,—in other words, it becomes the same as if the contract had never existed,

The option is destroyed by the decease of the person with whom it rested.—If a person possessing the option of inspection should die, the option in such case becomes null: for (according to our doctors) it is not a hereditament, as has already been explained in treating of optional conditions.

Cases of inspection previous to purchase —If a person, having once seen an article, should afterwards, at a distant period, purchase it, and the article, at the time of purchase, exist in the form and description in which he first saw it, he has not in this case any option, because he is possessed of a knowledge of the qualities from his former inspection; and an option is allowed only in defect of such knowledge.—If, however, the purchaser should not recognize or know it to be the same article, he has in that case an option; because under such circumstances his consent cannot be implied; or if, on the other hand, the nature of the article be changed, he has an option; because the qualities being changed, it becomes in fact the same as if he had never seen it.

If a purchaser and seller dispute concerning any recent† change in the nature of the

---

* A contract of sale, when settled by the parties, does not become complete until the execution of it; yet it cannot admit of any alteration of the terms of it in the interval. Thus, if two bushels of wheat be sold for two dirms, and the parties, before the execution of the contract mutually agree to reduce the sale to one bushel for one dirm, this agreement, as being an alteration of the terms previous to their fulfilment, would be unlawful. In short, it is requisite, in this instance, either that the parties previously dissolve the first contract, and then enter into a new contract of sale of one bushel for one dirm; or that they formally complete the first contract by mutual seisin, and that the purchaser then sell one of the bushels to the seller for one dirm.

†Arab Hadis [or Hadith], meaning, supervenient upon the contract.

article,—the purchaser asserting this circumstance, and the seller denying it,—in this case the allegation of the seller, confirmed by an oath, must be credited; because the interval between the sight and the purchase being short, the probability is in favour of the assertion of the seller, that such change did not happen till after the purchase had taken place. If, however, a long period should intervene between the sight and the purchase, our doctors are in this case of opinion that the allegation of the purchaser is to be credited; because, as it is the nature of everything to decay in course of time, it follows that his assertion is supported by probability.

If the parties dispute concerning the period when the article was inspected, the seller asserting that the purchaser had first seen and then purchased the article, and the purchaser denying this,—in that case the allegation of the purchaser, upon oath, is to be credited.

A person, after disposing of a part of his purchase, has no option with respect to the remainder.—If a person purchase a bundle of clothes of a Zoota* without seeing them, and afterwards sell or give away part of them; in this case he has not the power of rejecting any of those that remain unless they should prove defective. In the same manner, if he purchase a bundle of clothes of a Zoota, stipulating a condition of option, and afterwards sell or bestow in gift part of them, his right of option is annulled; because it is not in his power to reject what he has no longer any property in; if, therefore, he were to reject the remainder, it would induce a deviation from the bargain before the completion of it (for the existence of an option of inspection, or of a condition of option, is a bar to the completeness of the bargain). It is otherwise in an option from defect; as the bargain, notwithstanding the existence of such option, is completed upon seizing the article sold, although it be not complete before seisin;—but the present case proceeds on the supposition of possession having been taken. If, however, the supervenient deeds of sale or gift, on the part of the purchaser, be rendered null (as if the secondary purchaser should undo the bargain on account of the discovery of a defect,—or, as if the purchaser himself should recede from his gift), in this case the option of inspection still remains—This is from Shimsh-al-Ayma. It is related, as an opinion of Aboo Yoosaf, that an option of inspection once annulled cannot again revive, any more than a conditional option; and Kadoore has adopted this doctrine.

*(A tribe of black Arabs.—"Zoot.—A tribe of Arabs who formerly inhabited the fenny region lying between Wadis and Basra; they were defeated and reduced to servitude by Mootasim, the eighth Khalif."—(De Herbelot.)

CHAPTER IV.

OF OPTION FROM DEFECT

A purchaser discovering a defect in the article purchased, is at liberty to return it to the seller.—If a person purchase and take possession of an article, and should afterwards discover it to have been defective at the time of sale, it is at his option either to take it for the full price, or to reject it; because one requisite, in an unconditional contract [of sale], is that the subject of it be free from defect;—when, therefore, it proves otherwise, the purchaser has no option; for if the contract were obligatory upon him, without his will, it would be injurious to him. He is not, however, at liberty to retain the article, and exact a compensation, on account of the defect, from the seller; because, in a contract of sale, no part of the price is opposed to the quality of the article—and also, because the seller does not consent to be divested of the property for a less price than that which he stipulates:—if, therefore, the purchaser were to retain the defective article and exact a compensation from the seller on account of the defect, it would be injurious to the latter:—but it is possible to obviate the injury to the purchaser without entailing an injury on the seller, by permitting him either to retain the article, if he approve of it with the defect, or to reject it.

Unless he was aware of the defect beforehand.—If, however, the purchaser, at the time of sale, or of taking possession, be aware of the defect, and nevertheless knowingly and wilfully make the purchase, or take possession, no option remains to him; because when he thus purchases or takes possession of the article, it is evident that he assents to the defect.

Whatever tends to depreciate an article is a defect.—WHATEVER may be a cause of diminishing the price amongst merchants is considered as a defect; because injury is occasioned by deficiency in point of value; and deficiency in point of value occasions deficiency in price; and the mode of ascertaining this is by consulting merchants who are practised in estimating the value of articles.

Defects incident to children affect the sale of a slave during infancy, but not after maturity.—A DISPOSITION to abscond, or to make urine upon carpets, or to commit theft, are defects in children during their nonage, but not after they attain to the age of maturity. If, therefore, any of these defects appear in an infant slave during childhood whilst in the hands of the seller, and afterwards appear in him during childhood whilst in the hands of the purchaser, he [the purchaser] is in that case at liberty to return him to the seller, in virtue of option from defect; because this is the same defect that existed whilst in the possession of the seller. If, on the other hand, any of these defects should occur in him, in the purchaser's hands, after he attains to maturity, the purchaser is not at liberty to return him by option from defect; because this defect is different from that which appeared during childhood in the hands of the seller, since these effects proceed from different causes in the periods of childhood and maturity; for the making of urine upon a carpet (for instance) during the time of childhood, is owing to a weakness in the bladder,—whereas, after maturity, it arises from a disease in the interior parts; and, in the same manner, the running away of a child is from a desire of play; and the commission of theft from thoughtlessness; but these, where they occur after maturity, are the effect of innate wickedness By a child is here meant one in its perfect senses; for a child not in its perfect senses is incapable of running away; whence it is that the term used in that case is lost or strayed, not absconded:—the running away, therefore, of such a one is not a defect.

Lunacy operates as a perpetual defect, provided it ever occurs after the sale.—MADNESS during infancy operates as a perpetual defect;—in other words, if an infant slave be subject to lunacy in the hands of the seller and the lunacy recur whilst in the hands of the purchaser, whether during childhood or after maturity, the purchaser is at liberty to return him to the seller; because this madness is in effect the same as had originally existed whilst the slave was yet in the seller's hands, as being occasioned by the same cause, namely, an internal malady—It is not, however, to be understood (as some have imagined that the return of the madness is not required as a condition to enable the purchaser to dissolve the bargain; for GOD Almighty, as being all powerful, may remove the madness, although that seldom happen. Hence it is necessary that the madness return, to enable the purchaser to dissolve the bargain, for, unless it actually return, he has not this privilege.

Defects which operate in the sale of female slaves, but not of males—A BAD smell, from the breath or armpits, is a defect in regard to female slaves, because in many instances the object is to sleep with them; and the existence of such defects is a bar to the accomplishment of that object.—These, however, are not defects with regard to male slaves: because the object, in purchasing them, is merely to use their services: and to this these defects are not obstacles, since it is possible for a slave to serve his master without the necessity of the master's sitting down with him, so as to receive annoyance from these defects—If, however, they proceed from disease, they are considered as defects with regard to male slaves also.

WHOREDOM and bastardy are defects with regard to a female slave, but not with regard to a male; because the object in the purchase of a female slave is cohabitation and the generation of children, which must be affected by either of the above circumstances: whereas, the object in the purchase of a male slave is the use of his services, the value of which is not depreciated by his committing whoredom.—If, however, a male slave be much addicted to whoredom, our lawyers are of opinion that it is a defect because in the pursuit of women he neglects the service of his master.

Infidelity is a defect in both male and female slaves.—INFIDELITY is a defect in both a male and female slave* because the disposition of a Mussulman is averse to the society of infidels; and also, because as, in the expiation of murder, the emancipation of an infidel slave does not suffice, it follows that the possession of such a slave is not what is desired, since a part of the object is thus defeated. If, on the contrary, a person should purchase a slave, on condition of his being an infidel, and he afterwards prove a Mussulman, the purchaser has no power of dissolving the bargain, since the exemption from infidelity is no defect.

Constitutional infirmities are defects in a female slave.—A TOTAL suppression of the courses, or an excessive evacuation of them, are defects with respect to a female slave, as they proceed from internal maladies. It is to be observed, however, that the wants of the courses is not considered as a defect until the extreme period of maturity be elapsed, which in females (according to Haneefa) is seventeen years; and this knowledge must be had from the information of the slave herself.—If, therefore, a person purchase a female slave arrived at full maturity (that is, seventeen years of age), and learn from herself that her courses have not appeared, he is then entitled to return her to the seller before taking possession; and even after taking possession, provided the seller simply deny the circumstance, and refuse to confirm it with an oath. If, however, the seller deny the circumstance upon oath, the purchaser is not entitled to return her.

A purchaser is entitled to compensation for a defect in an article where it has sustained a further blemish in his hands; but he cannot, in this case, return it to the seller.—IF an article, after being sold, should receive a blemish in the hands of the purchaser, and the purchaser should afterwards learn that it had also a blemish at the time of sale, he is, in that case, entitled to receive from the seller a compensation for the defect; but he is not permitted to return it to him, as that would be attended with an injury to the seller, since it would necessiate him to receive again into his property a thing with two blemishes which, in issuing from him, had only one. As, therefore, the return of the article is in this case impracticable, and

* That is, supposing the slave to be purchased as a Mussulman and he prove to have been an infidel at the time of purchase.

as it is necessary to remove injury from the purchaser, the expedient of entitling him to a compensation from the seller for the defect has been devised: unless, however, the seller should consent to receive it with the two blemishes, and voluntarily acquiesce in his own loss.—By the phrase compensation for defect, is to be understood, throughout this work, the difference between the value of an article in its perfect state, and the value it afterwards bears in its defective state.

A purchaser is entitled to compensation for a defect discovered after the article has been cut up.—If a person purchase cloth, and cut it up, and then, before he had begun to sew it discover it to be defective he is in this case entitled to a compensation for the defect from the seller; because although, in consequence of the cloth being cut, a bar be opposed to the returning of it to the seller (as the cutting is a defect which the purchaser himself is the occasion of), yet the return is eventually possible, by the seller's acquiescing in it, which he may do if he please, since the bar is opposed only in tenderness to his right; and this right it is in his power to forego.

Unless, after cutting, he put it out of his power to restore it to the sellers.—If, however, after cutting the cloth, the purchaser should sell it to another, he is not then entitled to any compensation for the defect; for although, after cutting the cloth, the bar to his returning it to the seller, may be eventually removed, by his [the seller's] acquiescence, yet when the purchaser afterwards disposes of it to another, he himself fixes a bar to the possibility of its being returned to the seller, for which reason he is not entitled to a compensation for the defect.

Or, if the return be rendered impracticable by any change wrought upon the subject prior to the sale he is entitled to a compensation for defect, notwithstanding the sale of it.—If a person purchase cloth, and, after cutting either dye it or sew it, or purchase flour and mix it up with oil, and afterwards discover the article to be defective, he is in that case entitled to a compensation for the defect: because the return of the article to the seller is in either of those instances impracticable, as it has become implicated with a thing which cannot be separated; it is therefore impossible to return the article simply by itself; nor can it be returned with the addition, since the addition was not in any respect a subject of the sale; and the seller, moreover, is not at liberty to receive it back with such addition, because the obstacle to the return, in these instances, is not in right of the seller, but in right of the LAW*. If the purchaser, therefore, in any of these instances, should sell the article, after discovering it to be defective, he is still entitled to a compensation from the seller: because, as the bar to his returning the article to him existed previous to the sale of it on his part, he cannot by such sale be considered as the cause of detaining it from the seller.

Appropriation of a purchase to the use of an infant (implied in any act concerning it which has a reference to the infant) by precluding a return to the seller, leaves the purchaser no right to compensation for a defect.—If a person purchase cloth, and cut it out for clothing on account of an infant son, and after having sewn it up discover a defect in it, he is not entitled to a compensation for the defect from the seller. If, however, the son in this instance be an adult, the purchaser is entitled to such compensation.—The reason of this distinction is that, in the former instance, the right of property, with regard to the infant, takes place immediately on the cutting of the cloth, and previous to its being sewn; and consequently, as the purchaser by this act invests the infant with a right of property immediately upon cutting the cloth, he becomes the cause of the detention of it from the seller previous to its being sewn, and is therefore not entitled to the compensation:—in the latter instance, on the contrary, the right of property with regard to the adult does not take place upon the sewing, nor until he actually take possession of the garment; and hence, as it is by the sewing, and not by the investiture in the adult, that the return of the cloth to the seller becomes impracticable, it follows that the purchaser, by making this investiture, does not detain the cloth from the seller, and consequently, that he is entitled to a compensation.*

The purchaser of a slave is entitled to a compensation for defect, after the death or emancipation of the slave.—If a a person purchase a slave, and afterwards emancipate him,—or the slave die in his hands, and purchaser then become acquainted with his having been defective, he is in either case entitled to a compensation from the seller:—in case of the slave dying, because death renders his property in the slave complete and perfect, and the impracticability of returning him does not arise from any act of the purchaser, but from an unavoidable calamity;—and also in case of his emancipating the slave, upon a favourable construc-

*Because the LAW (meaning the text of the Koran) forbids usury, under which head this transaction falls, as being the receipt of an addition, with the original.

*As an infant is incapable of taking possession in a case of gift, the property vests in him immediately on the declaration of the donor, or on his [the donor's] performing some act which manifests his intention as in the cutting of the cloth by the purchaser in the above case: in the case of an adult person, on the contrary, actual seisin is requisite to an investiture with right of property.

tion of the law.—Analogy would suggest that in this last case the purchaser is not entitled to a compensation, because the obstacle to the return proceeds, in this instance, from the act of the purchaser: the case, therefore, is the same as if he had killed the slave; and as, in that case, he would not have been entitled to any compensation for defect, so in this instance likewise. He is, however, so entiled, upon a favourable construction, because by the emancipation his property attains to its height and completion; for MAN is not, in his original nature, a subject of property, all men being originally created free; nor can any right of property exist with respect to him but under restriction, and of limited duration, continuing in force no longer than until he be made free: emancipation, therefore, like death, occasions a completion of right of property, and it may consequently be said that a right of property still, remains in the subject of the sale, notwithstanding the impossibility of returning it, as a thing is rendered fixed and unalterable by its completion.—It is to be observed that constituting the slave a Modabbir or an Am-Walid is, in this particular, equivalent to emancipation.

But not after the emanicipation, where it has been granted in return for property.—IF a person purchase a slave, and afterwards emancipate him in return for property,* and then discover him to have been defective, he is not entitled to a compensation from the seller, as the detention of the return is, in effect, a detention of the consideration.—It is recorded, from Haneefa, that the purchaser is in this case also entitled to a compensation; because an emancipation, whether it be gratuitously made or otherwise, occasions the completion of the right of property.

Nor after his death, where he has been slain by the purchaser.—IF a person purchase a slave, and afterwards put him to death, and then discover him to have been defective, he is not entitled to a compensation for the defect, according to Haneefa.—This also is agreeable to the Zahir-Rawayet.—It is reported, from Aboo Yoosaf, that the purchaser is entiled to a compensation; because the law annexes no wordly punishment to the murder of a slave by his master.† and the case is therefore the same as if he had died a natural death. The principle on which the Zahir-Rawayet proceeds is that murder, wherever it takes place, occasions responsibility; and as, in the case of a master killing his slave, the responsibility is remitted only on account of the master's right of property, the master consequently, as it were, takes the responsibility* in return for his right of property: the case is therefore the same as if he had sold the slave. It is otherwise where he emancipates him without any return, as that act does not occasion reponsibility, any more than where a poor person emancipates his portion in a partnership slave.

A purchaser of food is not entitled to a compensation for defect after having eaten it.—IF a person purchase any articles of food, and eat them, in that case, according to Haneefa, he is not entitled to any compensation from the seller.—According to the two disciples he is entitled to a compensation. The same difference of opinion subsists with respect to the case of a person who, having purchased garments, and worn them. until they had become ragged, then discovers that a defect had formerly existed in them. —The arguments of the two disciples are, that the purchaser having performed no act with respect to the subject of the sale but what is agreeable to the object of the purchase, and what is customary, the case is therefore the same as if he had emancipated a slave.—The argument of Haneefa is that the return of the food to the seller is impracticable, because of the purchaser having performed an act with regard to it which induces responsibility; and the case is therefore the same as that of sale or of murder. The act of a purchaser, moreover, although it be the object of the purchase, is nevertheless disregarded: whence it is that the purchaser is entitled to no compensation for a defect, after having sold the goods notwithstanding sale be one of the objects of purchase.

And so also, after having eaten only a part of the food.—IF a person purchase certain articles of food, and eat part of them, and then discover them to be defective, he is not, according to Haneefa, entitled to return to the seller what remains, and to demand from him a compensation for the defect in what he had eaten; because provisions are in the nature of an unity; and the case is therefore the same as if a person were to sell part of goods purchased by him, and then to discover a defect in them; in which case he would not be entitled to return the remainder to the seller, and demand a compensation for the defect; and so also in the case in question. There are two opinions of the two disciples on this case. According to one opinion, the purchaser may retain the remaining part of the provisions, and receive from the seller a compensation for the defect of the whole: and, according to the other, he may return the remaining part to the seller and receive a proportionable compensation for the defect of what he had eaten.

Case of defect in very perishable commodities.—IF a person purchase eggs, musk

*See Manumission for a Compensation.

†That is, it only subjects the murderer to explation by charity, fasting, or other religious penances.

*In other words, "bears the loss."

melons, cucumbers, walnuts, or the like, and after opening them discover them to be of bad quality; in that case, if they be altogether unfit for use, the purchaser is entitled to complete restitution of the price from the seller, as the sale is invalid, because of the subject of it not being in reality property. If, on the other hand, notwithstanding their badness; they be still fit for use, the purchaser is not entitled to return them to the seller, because the opening of them is an additional defect of his own creation: he is, however, entitled to a compensation for the defect; as by this means the injury he would otherwise sustain is remedied to the greatest possible extent. Shafei has said, that he is entitled to return them after opening them; because that is the exercise of a power committed to him by the seller. In reply to this our doctors argue, that the seller has empowered him to open them in virtue of his becoming the proprietor. Hence the case is the same as where a person purchases a garment, and, having cut it discovers a defect in it; in which case the purchaser is not entitled to return the garment upon the seller's hands, although he [the seller] had authorized him to cut it down. In short, if the articles prove defective only in a small part, the sale is valid, upon a favourable construction, because it is incident to walnuts, and such other articles, to be bad in a small part (by a small part is meant what is commonly the case, such as one or two in a hundred); but if, on the other hand, a great part prove bad, the sale is invalid, and the purchaser is entitled to a complete restitution of the purchase money: because in this case the seller has united together entities and non-entities with regard to value; and the case is therefore the same as if a person were to sell together freemen and slaves.

Case of a purchaser selling what he has purchased, which is afterwards returned to him in consequence of a defect.—IF a person, having purchased a slave, should sell him to another, and that other return the slave to him on discovering him to be defective, and he agree to receive him back, on the Kazee's issuing a decree to that effect, founded on the proof of the defect by witnesses, or on the refusal of the first purchaser to confirm his denial upon oath, in that case the first purchaser is entitled to return the slave to the seller, because, although it be not lawful for a purchaser, after the sale of the article on his part, to return it to the seller, still, in this case, the second sale having been annulled by the Kazee, it becomes the same as if no such sale had ever existed.

OBJECTION.—As the first purchaser denied the defect, and obliged the second purchaser to establish the fact by witnesses, it would appear that he is not entitled to return the slave; because, if he ground his right on the defect, he is guilty of prevarication, since he first denies the defect, and then asserts it.

REPLY.—The disproof of the denial by the Kazee's decree, founded on the proof of the fact by witnesses, renders such denial of no validity in law, hence the apparent contrariety of his denial and assertion is reconciled, and as the first sale continues in force, and the defect is at the same time proved, it follows that he is entitled to return the slave to the seller. If therefore, he choose to return him, it is a valid rejection; but if he should rather choose to keep him, the sale continues in force. It is otherwise where an agent for sale disposes of an article, and the purchaser returns it to the agent in consequence of a defect; for this is in reality a return to the constituent; and the agent is not required to return the article to his constituent, because, in this case, there is only one sale, whereas in the case in question there are two, whence the dissolution of the second sale does not dissolve the first. In short, if the second purchaser, on the discovery of a defect return the slave, and the first purchaser receive him back, in consequence of a decree of the Kazee, he [the first purchaser] is in that case entitled to return him to the original seller. If, on the other hand, the first purchaser agree to receive him back without a decree of the Kazee, he in that case is not entitled to return him to the original seller, because, although the second sale be annulled with regard to himself and the second purchaser, still it is equivalent to a sale de novo with regard to all other persons; and the original seller is another person.—It is recorded, in the Jama Sagheer, that when the subject of the sale is returned to the first purchaser, without a decree of the Kazee, on account of such a defect as very rarely happens (such as an additional finger, for instance), the first purchaser has not the power of returning it to the original seller: and this (as our author remarks) is a direct proof that the effect is the same in both cases; that is, whether the defect be of such a nature as may have recently happened, or such as never recently happens. In some traditions it is mentioned, that in the latter case the purchaser may return the subject of sale to the original seller, as there is then a certainty that such defect did exist whilst in the hands of the original seller.

Conduct to be observed by the magistrate, in case of a purchaser, after taking possession, alleging a defect in the article.—IF a person purchase a slave, and take possession of him, and then assert a defect in him, the Kazee in such case must not enforce the payment of the price on the part of the purchaser until he shall have investigated his assertion, either by the declaration of the seller, upon oath, that the slave had no defect, or by the proof of the fact on the part of the purchaser by witnesses. The suspension of the Kazee's decree with regard to the payment of the price is requisite, lest such decree should be rendered vain and useless by the subsequent proof of the defect ; and also, because the tenor of such decree is that the purchaser shall pay the complete price in fulfilment of the specific claim of the seller,—whereas the purchaser, by asserting a defect, denies the obligation on him to pay the complete price. The Kazee, therefore, must first proceed to examine into the circumstance of the defect ; and if the purchaser should say that his witnesses are in Syria,* he must then exact from the seller his denial upon oath. If the seller should take the oath accordingly, the Kazee must then decree the payment of the price ; because in suspending the price till the arrival of the witnesses, an injury would result to the seller ; and the immediate enforcement of the payment does not in so great a degree injure the purchaser, because after the return of the witnesses from Syria, if he should establish his proof, the purchase money will be returned to him on his returning the slave to the seller. If, however, the seller should refuse to take an oath in support of his denial, the assertion of the purchaser is then established, as such refusal is an argument in favour of the existence of the defect

Case of a purchaser alleging the existence of a defective property before he had made the purchase ; and the forms of deposition to be required of the seller in this instance.—IF a person, having purchased a slave, should afterward assert that "he had run away from him, and had also run away whilst in the possession of the seller," and the seller offer to take an oath that "he had never run away from him" [the purchaser], the Kazee must in that case refuse to receive his deposition until the purchaser first prove by witnesses that "he had run away from him" [the seller], after which the Kazee must tender an oath to the seller to this purport, "by GOD, I have sold the said slave and delivered him to the purchaser, and he never ran away whilst he belonged to me" (as is mentioned by Mohammed in the Jama) ; or to this purport, "by GOD, the purchaser has no right to return to me such slave, on account of the defect which he asserts :" or in this manner, "by GOD, such slave never ran away whilst he belonged to me." He must not, however, tender an oath to him to this purport, "by GOD, I sold the said slave at a period when he had not the said defect :" nor in this manner, "by GOD, I sold the said slave and delivered him to the purchaser at a period when he had not the said defect ;" because, in taking such oaths, the meaning of the seller may be, that "although he had such a defect formerly, yet he had it not at the identical period of sale or delivery ;" and thus, without any deviation from truth, he may defraud the purchaser of his right If the purchaser should not be able to prove, by witnesses, that the slave had run away from him [the purchaser], the oath, in that case also (according to the two disciples) must be tendered to the seller. Our modern doctors have differed concerning the opinion of Haneefa upon this point ; as some of them say that, according to him, an oath is not to be administered to the seller in this instance. The argument of the two disciples is, that as the assertion of the plaintiff is worthy of regard, and such as would be attended to in case of its being proved by witnesses, it follows that in default of such witnesses the seller must be required to deny the assertion upon oath. The reasoning of Haneefa (as recorded by those who have said that, according to him, an oath is not to be administered to the seller) is that the form of swearing a defendant has been ordained by the LAW for the purpose of removing any litigation that may happen to arise,—not for the purpose of exciting litigation. Now, in the present case, the exaction of an oath from the seller will only give birth to a new litigation : because, in case he should refuse to take it, and the proof of the fact be thence established, it will become a new subject of contention whether the said defect did exist or not during his being in the seller's possession, and there will be a necessity for tendering to him another oath, upon this point for the purpose of removing this fresh case of dispute.

IF a person purchase a female slave, and having received from the seller, should, on the discovery of a defect, desire to return her, and the seller assert that "he had sold two female slaves to purchaser of which he only produced one," and the purchaser maintain, on the other hand, that "he had only sold one,"—in that case the declaration of the purchaser, upon oath, is to be credited; for, as the disagreement here relates to the quantity taken possession of, the person who took possession must be credited, as being the most competent judge ;—in the same manner as holds in a case of usurpation ;—that is if the person whose property is usurped assert the usurpation of a particular quantity, and the usurper deny the quantity, his declaration upon oath is to be credited ; and so also in the case in question. If, on the other hand, the purchaser and seller agree in the extent of the sale, but differ with respect to that of the seisin (as if both should allow the two female slaves to have been the subject of the sale,—the seller asserting that "the purchaser had received both," and the purchaser on the other hand, maintaining that "he had only received one")—in that case also the declaration of the purchaser, upon oath, is to be credited, for the reason already explained.

Case of a person purchasing two slaves, one of whom proves defective.—IF a person purchase two slaves by one contract, and take possession of one, and then discover the other to be defective, he is not in that case permitted to attain the one he had

*That is, at such a distance as renders their appearance in court impracticable.

taken possession of, and to relinquish the other; but he has the option of either retaining or relinquishing both; because until both be taken possession of the terms of the contract are not fulfilled: and hence, if he should retain one and relinquish the other, it would induce a deviation from the bargain previous to its fulfilment, which (as was before explained) is unlawful. If the defect should lie in the slave of which possession had been taken, in that case there is a disagreement among our doctors. It is recorded, from Aboo Yoosaf, that the purchaser is in such case entitled to return the defective slave only. The more approved doctrine, however, is that he must retain both or relinquish both; because the fulfilment of the bargain rests upon a complete possession of the subject of the sale, namely, the two slaves. This case, therefore, resembles a case of detention of the article sold, in satisfaction for the price; that is, if the seller should detain the goods in satisfaction for the price. such detention cannot be abrogated until he actually receive complete possession of the price; and in the same manner, in the case in question, the bargain is not perfected until the purchaser receive complete possession of the articles sold. If, however, in the case in question, the purchaser should have made seisin of both, and should afterwards discover a defect in one of them, he is then entitled to return the defective one singly. Ziffer has given a different opinion; because in this case a deviation from the bargain takes place; and it is not free from injury, since it is an established custom, in sales, to unite good and bad things together; the case is therefore the same as if he had rejected one before the seisin of the whole,—or as if he had made the purchase under a condition of option, or with an option of inspection. Our doctors, on the other hand, allege that in this case the deviation from the bargain takes place after the fulfilment of the contract; because the seisin of the goods renders the contract complete; and the existence of the option of defect does not operate against the completion of the contract after seizin. A deviation, moreover, from the bargain, after the fulfilment of it, is lawful, as has been already demonstrated, whence it is that if, after taking possession of both slaves, one of them should be found to be the property of another, the purchaser is not in that case at liberty to return both to the seller; but must retain one, and receive from the seller a deduction of the price, on account of the one belonging to another, notwithstanding this be a deviation from the bargain,—contrary to conditional options, or options of inspection, for the existence of such conditions is a bar to the fulfilment of the bargain, notwithstanding seisin may have taken place.

In the purchase of articles of weight, or measurement of capacity, the part which proves defective may be returned to the seller.—If a person purchase articles estimable by weight, or by measure of capacity (such as silver or wheat, for instance), and he afterwards discover the article to be in part defective, he is entitled, in that case, either to return the whole to the seller, or to retain the whole; but he has not the power of returning the defective part only, because the unities of articles estimable by weight or by measure of capacity are considered as forming one individual, provided they be all of the same species. Some have alleged that this proceeds on a supposition of the articles in question being contained in one vessel; but that, if they be contained in two, the one containing the defective article may be returned, and the other retained.

If a part of such articles prove the property of another, still the purchaser is not at liberty to return the remainder.—If, after the purchase of articles estimable by weight, or measurement of capacity, a part of them should prove to be the property of another, the purchaser is not in that case allowed to return the remainder to the seller; because no injury can result to him from his being obliged to keep them, as article of this nature may be separated and divided without sustaining any blemish, and the proof of part of the subject of the sale having been the property of another is no impediment to the completion of the contract since that depends on the consent of the seller and purchaser, and not of the person who is discovered to be the proprietor of a part. This is where possession has been taken by the purchaser, before a part of the subject is discovered to be the right of another;—for if the right of property of the other be discovered previous to the purchaser taking possession, he is, in that case, entitled to return the remainder, since a deviation from the contract takes place previous to the completion of the bargain. If the articles be not such as are estimable by weight, or measurement of capacity, but cloth, for instance then the purchaser is entitled to return the remainder to the seller at all events, as division and separation of the article would, in this instance, prove an injury to it.

A purchaser, by applying a remedy to the defective article, or making of it, deprives himself of the power of returning it to the seller.—If a person purchase a female slave, and discover that she has an ulcer or some other such ailment, and apply a remedy to it,—or, if a person purchase an animal, and discover it to be defective, and ride upon it on some business of his own,—the application of a remedy in the one case, or the act of riding in the other, indicate an acquiescence in the defect on the part of the purchaser, and he is therefore not entitled to return either the slave or the animal on the plea of an option from the discovery of a defect. It would be otherwise if he had purchased the animal on a condition of option; for the object of such condition is an experimental knowledge, which cannot be obtained but by a trial. If, moreover, he were to ride upon the animal, not on his own business, but merely with an intention of restoring it to the seller, no inference could be drawn of his acquiescence in the defect;—and so also, if he were to ride upon the animal with an intention of giving it water or forage; provided, however, the riding for these purposes be unavoidable, either because of the animal being unruly and ungovernable, if not mounted, or because of the purchaser himself being incapable of walking

If a purchased slave suffer amputation for a theft committed with the seller, the purchaser may return him, and receive back the price.—If a person purchase and take possession of a slave, not knowing that he had formerly, whilst in the possession of the seller, been guilty of theft, and the theft be afterwards proved, and the slave suffer amputation for it in the seller's hands, the purchaser is, in that case, entitled, according to Haneefa to return him to the seller, and receive back the whole of the price. According to the two disciples, the purchaser is still to keep possession of the slave, and to receive from the seller the difference between the value whilst in his perfect state, and that which he bears after his hand is cut off.

And so also, if he suffer death for a crime committed with the seller.—The same disagreement subsists in case of a slave suffering death whilst in the possession of the purchaser, for a crime he had committed whilst in the possession of the seller; Haneefa being of opinion that the purchaser is entitled to the restitution of the whole of the price; and the two disciples, that he is entitled only to the difference between the value of the slave before his blood has become neutral, and that which he bears after it has been neutral.* In short, according to Haneefa, the existence of a cause of mutilation or death is equivalent to a claim of right,†—whereas, according to the two disciples, it is equivalent to a defect. The reasoning of the two disciples is that the cause only of multilation or death occurred with the seller, but not the actual death or mutilation itself;—now the existence of a cause of death or mutilation is not repugnant to the subject being property; the slave, therefore, notwithstanding the existence of the cause of mutilation or death, is nevertheless property, and capable of being the subject of a sale; as, however, a slave in whom exists a cause of death or mutilation is defective, it follows that the purchaser is entitled to receive from the seller a compensation for the deficiency, where the return has become impracticable; and in either of these instances the return is impracticable;—where he suffers death, evidently; and also, where he suffers mutilation, because such mutilation is a defect that has taken place in the hands of the purchaser;—in the same manner as where a person purchases a pregnant female slave, being ignorant of the circumstance, and the slave dies in labour, in which case the purchaser is entitled only to a compensation for the difference between the price which she bore when not pregnant, and that which she bore when pregnant. The reasoning of Haneefa is, that the cause of mutilation and death occurred with the seller: and as a cause induces its effects, the death or mutilation must be referred to the period of the cause. The case is, therefore, the same as if a person were to usurp a slave, and the slave, whilst in his possession, were to commit a crime inducing mutilation or death, and the usurper then restore him to his proper owner, and the slave then suffer death or mutilation; for in that case the usurper would be responsible for the whole of the value to the owner; in the same manner as he would have been in case of the slave's having been put to death whilst in his own possession, as the cause, in either instance, occurred with him. With respect to the case of pregnancy, adduced by the two disciples, it is not admitted by Haneefa. If, however, it were admitted, still there is no analogy between it and the case in question, since pregnancy is the cause of delivery, and not of death, except in a few instances.

Case of a slave suffering amputation for two thefts, one committed with the seller, and the other with the purchaser.—If a slave first commit theft with the seller, and then, after being sold, commit theft with the purchaser, and afterwards suffer amputation for both thefts, in that case, according to the two disciples, the purchaser is entitled to the difference of relative value of the slave at the time of sale, and after the commission of the second theft. According to Haneefa on the other hand, the purchaser is not entitled to return him, unless the seller should of his own accord consent to receive him: but he is entitled to a compensation for the fourth of his value; and if the seller should himself agree to receive him, in that case he must restore to the purchaser three fourths of his price; because the hand of a man is esteemed equal to half his person; and as, in this case, the hand is forfeited for the commission of two thefts, it follows that a deduction of one quarter ought to be made on account of the theft committed whilst in the possession of the purchaser.

Case of a slave, after being three sold, suffering amputation for a theft committed with the first seller.—If a slave, having been severally sold, and delivered to three different person, should then suffer amputation for a theft which he had committed whilst in

*That is, has become forfeited to the LAW, and consequently liable to be shed without responsibility.

†In other words, is the same, in effect, as if the slave, after the purchase, should prove to be the property of another person.

the possession of the first seller, and of which the different purchasers were not apprised at the period of concluding their respective contracts,—in that case, according to Haneefa, the last purchaser has a right to return him for a full retribution of the price to the person from whom he bought him ; and he again is entitled to return him, on the same condition, to the person from whom he bought him ; and in this manner the return may be made throught the different gradations of purchasers to their immediate sellers, until at length the slave be returned to the seller in whose hands he committed the theft ;—in the same manner as in a case of claim of right ; for the existence of a cause of amputation is (according to Haneefa) equivalent to a claim of right, as was before explained. According to the two disciples, on the other hand, the last purchaser is entitled to a compensation from the immediate seller ; but he again is not entitled to any compensation from his immediate seller ; in the same manner as in a case of defect ; for the existence of a cause of amputation is (according to them) equivalent to a defect, as was before explained*—(It is to be observed that the mention of the purchaser being ignorant of the theft committed by the slave is insisted on in the two preceding examples, on account of the particular tenets of the two disciples ; for as in their opinion, the existence of a cause of mutilation is equivalent to a defect, it follows that if the purchaser had previous knowledge of the existence of such cause, he would appear to have acquiesced in the defect, and consequently have relinquished any right to a compensation. As Haneefa, on the contrary, holds the existence of a cause of mutilation to be equivalent to a claim of right ; and as the knowledge or ignorance of this circumstance makes no difference with respect to the purchaser, it follows that such specification, with regard to his tenets, is perfectly immaterial.)

Where the purchaser grants the seller an exemption from defects, he cannot afterwards return the article, whatever the defects in it may be—If a person should sell a slave, stipulating an exemption to himself of all responsibility for his defects, as if he should say, "I have sold this slave with all his defects,"—in that case, if the purchaser acquiesce in such condition, and exempt him from any responsibility, he is not afterwards permitted to return him to the seller on account of any defect, notwithstanding the condition of the seller may have been general, this is, without specifying the particular names of the defects from the responsibility of which he exempted himself.—Shafei is of opinion that such exemption is not valid, unless that name of every defect to which it refers be specified ;—for it is a rule, with him, that exemption from undefined claims is invalid : because exemption has some of the properties of investiture (whence it is that it may be rejected), and investiture of an undefined nature is invalid. The argument of our doctors is that the grant of such exemption is in fact a voluntary surrender of one's own right, the uncertainty with respect to which can be no cause of contention, since delivery is not requisite. It is to be observed that Aboo Yoosaf is of opinion that the exemption, in this case, includes all defects actually existing at the time of sale, and also all which may happen in the interval between that and their delivery. Mohammed and Ziffer, on the contrary, are of opinion that the defect which may happen in the interval ought not to be included. The argument of Aboo Yoosaf is that the probable object of such surrender on the part of the purchaser is to render the sale binding and conclusive, which would not be the case unless the defects that may happen in the interval between the sale and the seisin were also included.

CHAPTER V.

OF INVALID, NULL, AND* ABOMINABLE SALES.

A SALE IS INVALID where it is lawful with respect of its ESSENCE but not with respect of its QUALITY, and NULL, where the subject is not of an appreciable nature ; and the terms INVALID and NULL, are often indiscriminately used.—An ABOMINABLE sale is such as is lawful both in its ESSENCE and QUALITY, but attended with some circumstance of ABOMINATION.

Distinctions between a null and an invalid sale.—A SALE in exchange for carrion, blood, or the person of a freeman, is null, because none of these cases bears the characteristic of sale (namely, an exchange of property for property), since these articles do not consitute property with any person. A sale in exchange for wine or pork (on the other hand) is merely invalid ; because the characteristic of sale does exist in these instances, as these articles are considered as property with some descriptions of people, such as Christians and Jews ; but they do not constitute property with Mussulmans, and a contract comprehending these articles is therefore invalid.

*The word in the original is Makrooh, which the translator (following its literal and common acceptation) has rendered abominable. The term, however, in this work, is not to be understood in the ill sense in which it is generally employed in the English language ; the cases to which it relates being such as are in every respect legal, but which being attended with circumstances of impropriety, an abstinence from them is recommended.

The property purchased under a null sale is merely a trust in the purchaser's hands.—IN a sale that is null, the purchaser is not empowered to perform any act with respect to the subject of the sale, but it remains as a trust in his hands, according to some of our modern doctors; because, as the contract of sale, in such an instance, is totally disregarded, there remains only the seisin of the purchaser with the consent of the seller: and accordingly, if the article were to perish in the purchaser's hands, in this instance, he is not responsible for it. Others are of opinion that the subject of the sale, in this case, is not a deposit, but that the purchaser is not responsible for it (in other words. If it perish in the purchaser's hands, he is answerable);—because the article is as much in his possession, in this instance, as an article detained in a person's hands with an intention of purchase, and for which he is responsible. Some allege that Heneefa is of the first opinion, and the two disciples of the second. The reasons of this difference of doctrine will be explained in treating of the decease of an Am-Walid or Modabbir, in the hands of a purchaser.

But that purchased under an invalid sale becomes his property.—IN a case of invalid sale, the purchaser becomes proprietor of the article upon taking possession of it; and is responsible for it [if it be lost in his hands]. Shafei is of a different opinion, as will be hereafter explained.

THE sale of carrion, blood, or the person of a freeman, is null, in the same manner as a sale in return for those articles as null; because as those articles do not constitute property, they are unsaleable.

A sale of forbidden things, if for money, is null; but if in the way of barter, is invalid.—A SALE of wine or pork, if in return for money, is null; and if in return for any other article (as cloth, for instance), it is invalid,—whence it is that the seller of pork or wine, for cloth, becomes the proprietor of such cloth, although the actual pork or wine do not become the property of the purchaser The distinction in these cases is, that wine and pork are held by Zimmees to be property, where Mussulmans consider them as articles from which no use can be derived, because the LAW has commanded the contempt of them, and prohibited all regard to them among Mussulmans. Now, a Mussulman's purchasing either of these for specie implies a regard to them, because it is not money (which constitutes the price) that is the object of the sale, as it is merely the instrument of acquiring the object: for in fact it is only the wine or pork that is the object; and as these articles are not appreciable with respect to Mussulmans, it follows that the sale of them is null. It is otherwise if a Mussulman purchase cloth for pork or wine, because that can admit of no other construction than that he regards the cloth as the object of the transaction, considering the pork or the wine only as the means of attaining such object, and not (as in the other case) as the object itself. The specification of the pork or wine, therefore, is regarded merely that the purchaser may become the proprietor of the cloth, and not in order that the seller may become proprietor of the wine or pork; and hence the mention of those articles is invalid, and the payment of the price of the cloth, and not the delivery of the flesh or liquor, is incumbent on the purchaser (and so also, where a person sells wine or pork for cloth);—for, as cloth is a saleable article, the cloth must, in this instance, be considered as the subject of the sale; for which reason this is an invalid and not a null sale; becuase where, in a contract of sale, the subject on both sides consists of something else than money, either may with equal propriety be considered as the subject of the sale. (This species of sale is termed a Beeya Mookaveza, or barter.)

The sale of a Modabbir, an Am-Walid, or a Makatib is null.—THE sale of an Am-Walid, a Madabbir, or Mokatib, is null;—because an Am-Walid has a claim to freedom, as the Prophet has said, "Her child hath set her free" (that is, her child is a cause of freedom to her);—and the cause of freedom, with respect to a Modabbir, is not established upon the decease of his owner. but must be considered as actually extant in him at present, as the owner is incapable of emancipating him after his decease;—and a Mokatib, on the other hand, is possessed of his own person as a right established in him, and binding upon his owner, insomuch that the owner cannot of himself break or infringe upon it:—if, therefore, the sale of any of these were valid, that which is established in them would be rendered null;—hence the sale of them is null.—Respecting a case where a Mokatib himself acquiesces in being sold, there are two opinions recorded. According to the Zahir Rawayet, the sale in such case is valid. It is to be observed that by a Modabbir is here meant such as is absolutely so, and not one whose condition of freedom is restricted to the non-recovery of his master from the illness under which he laboured at the time of granting the tadbeer.

And the purchaser is not responsible if they die in his hands.—IF, after the sale of an Am-Walid or Modabbir, and the seisin of the purchaser, one or other should die, in this case, according to Haneefa, the purchaser is not responsible,* According to the two disciples he is responsible for the value (and there is one tradition which reports that Haneefa coincides with them on this point).—The reasoning of the two disciples is, that as the purchaser took possession of the Modabbir or Am-Walid in virtue of a sale, he is therefore responsible for the loss; in the same manner as for the loss of any other property after purchase and seisin;—for this

* That is, the loss is considered as falling upon the seller, and not upon the purchaser

reason. that an Am-Walid or Modabbir may be included* in a contract of sale : whence it is that aay article united with them in a contract of sale becomes the actual property of the purchaser. It is otherwiser with re-responsible for the loss of him, because, being possessed of his own person, the purchaser's seisin of him is not fully established ; and the responsibility attaches in virtue of the seisin. The argument of Haneefa is, that actual sale cannot operate with respect to what is not in reality a fit subject of it: and as a Modabbir or Am-Walid re not in reality fit subjects of sale, they are therefore considered in the same light with a Mokatib. In reply to what the two disciples urge it may be observed, that an Am-Walid or Modabbir are not included in a sale for the sake of their persons, but only in order that the effect of sale may be established with respect to such articles as may have been united with them in the contract ; in the same manner as where property of the purchaser happens to be involved in the contract ;—in other words, if a person purchase two salves by one contract, and one of those slaves happens to be his property, such slave is nevertheless included in the contract,—not indeed for the sake of his person, but merely in order that the effect of the sale may extend to the other slave, who is united with him in it.

The sale is null of fish in the water.—The sale of fish which is not yet caught is null as it is not in the state property ;—In the same manner also, the sale of a fish which the vender may have caught and afterwards thrown into a large fountain from which it cannot be taken without difficulty, is null, because there the delivery is impracticable. (It is lawful, however, in case the fountain be so small as to admit its being caught with ease,)—If fish should of themselves come into a fouhtain without the proprietor's having taken any means, by the erection of a dam, or a like, to prevent their egress, they are not considered as property, and the sale of them is therefore null

Or of a bird in the air,—The sale of a bird in the air, or of one which after having been caught is again set at liberty, is null ; because in the one case it is not property, and in other the delivery is rendered impracticable.

Or of a foetus in the womb (or its off-spring),—The sale of a foetus in the womb, or of the offspring of that foetus, is null ; because the Prophet has prohibited it ; and also, because there is a probability of fraud, from there being a want of certainty in the case.

Or of milk in the udder.—The sale of milk in the udder is null : because there is a possibility of fraud, in the udder's being perhaps void of milk, and full of wind ; or because there might arise a contention with respect to the mode of extracting the milk : or because it might happen that the udder contained more milk at the time of extracting it than at the time of sale ; and hence there migh be implicated in the sale something not properly the subject of it.

Or of their (or wool) upon an animal.—The sale of wool or hair growing upon an animal is null ; because, whilst joined to the animal, it is considered as a constituent part of it ; and also, because it cannot be exactly cut away from the animal, without either leaving a part of it or taking away part of the skin, since it is not practicable to pull it out. It is, moreover, recorded in the Nakl Saheeh, that "the Prophet prohibited the sale of wool upon the animal, of milk in the udder, and of butter in the milk."* It is recorded of Aboo Yoosaf, that he admitted the legality of the sale of growing wool ; but to this the above tradition is an answer.

The sale is invalid of any article which cannot be separated from its situation without injury.—It is. not lawful † to sell a piece ef wood sustaining a weight, such as a pillar or a beam, although the piece of wood he specified and determinate. Neither is it lawful to sell a yard from a piece of cloth which is sewed, whether the parties specify that the yard shall be cut off from it or not ; because in this case a delivery without injury is impracticable. It is otherwise where a person agrees to sell ten drams (for instance) from an ingot of silver of these may be cut off from the ingot without injury to it. It is to be observed, however, that if the seller, before the dissolution of the contract, should cut off the yard of cloth, or pull away and separate the piece of wood, the sale in that case becomes complete, since the cause of its invalidity is removed.

Or of which the quality or existence cannot be ascertained.—It is otherwise with respect to the sale of the kernels of dates, because that continue null, although the stones be afterwards opened and the kernels taken out ; since (contrary to the case of the yard of cloth, or the piece of wood) the existence of them was originally uncertain.

It is not lawful for a game-catcher to sell "what he may catch at one pull of his net :" because the subject of the sale is uncertain ; and also because the purchaser may be deceived, as it is possible that none may be caught.

Or the quantity of which can only be judged of by conjecture.—It is not lawful to sell dates growing upon a tree in exchange for dates which have been plucked, and which are computed, from conjecture to be

*That is, "may be joined with other articles."

* That is, before it has been extracted by churning.

† By the phrase "it is not lawful," is here (and in the following examples) to be understood, "it is invalid."

equal in point of measurement to those that are upon the tree. This species of sale is termed Mozabinat * and has been prohibited by the Prophet, as well as the sale termed Mohakila, which is the sale of wheat in the ear, in exchange for a like quantity of wheat by conjecture. The law is the same with respect to the sale of grapes on the vine in exchange for raisins. Shafei holds these sales to be lawful, provided they be not extended to a quantity exceeding five Wusks;† because, although the Prophet has prohibited a sale by Mozabinat, yet he has permitted what is termed Oraya: which he explains to be a sale of dates upon a tree, provided the quantity be less than five Wusks, in exchange for a quantity which have been plucked, and which are similar, in point of measurement, according to computation. Our doctors on the other hand, explain Oraya in its literal sense to mean a gift: and the nature of it is this. A person makes a gift of the dates of his orchard to another, who thereupon comes and enters the orchard. This gives disgust to the pso-prietor, as his family reside in the orchard: but being, at the same time, unwilling to violate his agreement, he prohibits the other from entering into the orchard, and gives him a quantity of dates which have been pulled in exchange for those which were growing in the orchard. This is the proper interpretation of the traditional saying of the Prophet, quoted by Shafei; and this mode of sale, which is termed Moojar, is valid in the opinion of our doctors. It is not, however, in reality a sale, because the right of property had not vested in the donee, on account of his not having made seisin of the dates, and therefore the dry dates which were afterwards given to him is considered as a new gift.

Or where the bargain is determined by the purchaser touching the goods, &c.—It is not lawful to sell goods by the way of Molamisa, Monazibee, or Alka Hidgir;—that is, the touch of the goods, the throwing of the goods; or the casting of a stone:—as where, for instance, a person having exhibited his goods to another, and specified the price, the parties agree between themselves that the contract shall be binding either on the purchaser's touching the goods, or the seller's throwing them towards him, or the purchaser's casting a stone at them. These modes of sale were common in the days of ignorance; but were inhibited by the Prophet.

The sale is invalid, of grass upon a common.—It is not lawful to sell grass growing on a common, because it is not the property of the seller: for it is declared in the traditions that "in grass all men are alike sharers"—(that is, it is common to all). Neither is it lawful to let it out on lease; because, as it is not permitted to farm anything, where the object is the destruction of it, even though it be the property of the lessor, it is consequently in a superior degree unlawful to let in lease an article of which the property is common to all, where the object of the lesses is the destruction of it.*

Or of bees (unless in a hive, or with the comb)—The sale of bees is not lawful according to the two Elders. Mohammed is of opinion that it is lawful, provided the bees be in a place of custody,† and not wild:‡ and such is also the opinion of Shafei; because a bee is an animal yielding good; and as we are permitted by the law to enjoy the good which that creature yields, it follows that the sale of the animal is permitted. The reasoning of the two Elders is that, the animal being of an offensive nature, the sale of it is therefore unlawful, in the same manner as in the case of wasps. Besides, the good is derived from its produce, not from its substance, whence no advantage can be derived from it until the honey be produced. If, however the comb be sold, with the honey in it, and the bees, the sale of the bees is in this case lawful, as a dependant. Koorokhee is also of this opinion.

Or of silk-worms—It is not lawful to sell silk worms, according to Haneefa, as they are animals of an offensive nature. Aboo Yoosaf thinks that if the silk have appeared they may than lawfully be sold, as a dependant. Mohammed is of opinion that the sale of them is lawful in any case, as being an animal whence an advantage is derived. Haneefa is of opinion, also, that the sale of their eggs is unlawful. The two disciples, on the contrary, are of opinion that such sale is lawful of necessity.

---

* Properly, a sale without weight of measure.

† Wusk literally means a camel's burthen, which is computed to be sixty saas.

* The object of a lease is usufruct, or (in the language of the Mussulman lawyers) a destruction of the produce of the thing, but not of the thing itself: thus if a person should take a lease of a piece of ground, or a fruit tree, he would be entitled to appropriate to himself the produce of the ground, whether grain or grass, or the fruit that might grow upon the tree; but he would have no right to use the ground or the tree (the immediate subjects of the lease) so as to occasion any destruction of their substance. Hence proceeds the illegality of a lease of a field of grass, of grain of the fruit of a tree or the like; for the lease in any of these cases would be entirely useless, since the lessee, being entitled only to the use of the produce of the subject of the lease, would not be entitled to the use of any of these which are themselves the immediate subject of the lease.

† Such as a hive, or bee-house.

‡ Literall, "not in the air."

The sale of tame pigeons is valid.—THE sale of pigeons, of which the number is ascertained, and the delivery practicable is lawful, as in such circumstances they constitute property.

The sale of an absconded slave is invalid (unless he be in the hands of the purchaser).—IT is not lawful to sell an absconded slave, because the Prophet has prohibited this; and also, because the delivery is impracticable. If, however, the purchaser should declare that "the fugitive is in his possession," the sale is lawful, because the obstacle on which the prohibition is founded is in this case removed.—It is to be observed that if the purchaser, in this instance, should have declared, before witnesses, that "he had taken possession of this slave with intent to restore him to his owner," he is not held, on the conclusion of the contract, to become seised of him in virtue thereof: because the former seisin, being in the nature of a trust, cannot stand in the room of that made on account of purchase. If, on the other hand, he should have made no such declaration, in that case he is held to be seised of the slave. in virtue of the sale, immediately on the conclusion of the contract; because the former seisin, being in the nature of an usurpation, may therefore stand in the room of a seisin for sale; for both are the same in effect, as they both equally induce responsibility. If the slave should have eloped to some other person. and the purchaser say to the proprietor, "sell me your slave who has run away to such an one," and the seller accordingly agree, the sale is in that case also unlawful, because of the impracticability of the delivery.

Although the seller should afterwards recover and deliver him to the purchaser.—IF a person, having sold a fugitive slave, should after the sale recover him, and deliver him to the purchaser, the sale is nevertheless unlawful, because it was originally null, in the same manner as if it had related to a bird in the air. It is recorded, as an opinion of Haneefa, that the sale in this case is, valid, provided it was not undone previous to the delivery, because it was founded on property, and there was no bar to its effect except the impracticability of the delivery, which is removed by the recovery of the slave (and such is also related as the opinion of Mohammed);—in the same manner as if a slave, after having been sold, should run away previous to the seisin of the purchaser, in which case, if the seller should afterwards recover him, and deliver him to the purchaser, the sale is binding, provided it was not dissolved in the interval.

The sale is invalid of a woman's milk.—THE sale of a woman's milk is unlawful, although it be in a vessel. Shafei is of opinion that if it be in a vessel the sale of it is lawful, because it is a pure beverage. The argument of our doctors is that, as being part of a human creature, it ought to be respected; and the exposure of it to sale is an act of disrespect. In the Zahir-Rawayet there is a distinction between the milk of a female slave and a free woman, It is related, as an opinion of Aboo Yoosaf, that the sale of the milk of a female slave is lawful, because the sale of the slave herself is lawsful. The answer to this is that the sale of the female is legal, because of the bondage, which is a quality of her person; but such quality does not relate to the milk; the one being alive, and the other dead.

Or the bristles of a hog.—The sale of the bristles of a hog is unlawful, because the animal is essentially filth, and because the exposure of this article to sale is a degree of respect, which is reprobated and forbidden. It is lawful, however, to apply it to use, such as stitching leather, for instance, in the room of a needle. as this is warranted by necessity.

OBJECTION.—It would appear that the sale of it is warranted from necessity, in the same manner as the use of it.

REPLY.—There is no necessity for the sale of it, since any quantity of it may be had gratuitously and without purchase.—It is to be observed that hogs' bristles falling into a little water* renders it impure, according to Aboo Yoosaf.—Mohammed is of a different opinion, because the legality of the use of the article in question is (according to him) an argument of its purity Aboo Yoosaf, on the other hand, argues that the legality of the use of it is founded on necessity, and not od its purity; and there exists no necessity in the case of its falling into water.

Or human hair.—THE sale of human hair is unlawful, in the same manner as is the use of it: because, being a part of the human body, it is necessary to preserve it from the disgrace to which an exposure of it to sale necessarily subjects it. It is moreover recorded, in the Hadees Shareef, that "God denounced a curse upon a Wasila and a Moostwasila."—(The first of these is a woman whose employment it is to unite the shorn hair of one woman to the head of another, to make her hair appear long: and the second means the woman to whose head such hair is united.) Besides, as it has been allowed to women to increase their locks by means of the wool of a camel, it may thence be inferred that the use of human hair is unlawful.

Or undressed hides.—THE sale of the hides of animals is not lawful until they be dressed, because the use of them, until then, is prohibited in the traditions of the Prophet. It is lawful, however, to sell dressed hides.

But animal substances of all descriptions (excepting those of men or hogs) may be either sold or converted to use—It is permitted either to sell or apply to use the

*By a little water (say the commentators) is here meant such a quantity as may be contained in a cup or other vessel.

bones, sinews, wool, horns, or hair, of all animals which are dead, excepting those of men and hogs. The reason of this is that these articles are pure, and are not considered as carrion. besides, death does not affect them as it does the animal, as these articles are not possessed of life.—it is to be observed that Mohammed considering an elephant as essential filth, like a hog, holds the sale of it be unlawful :—but the two disciples, considering it in the nature of a wild animal, regard the sale of it, or of the bones of it, as lawful

A right cannot be sold, unless it involve property—If in a house, of which the upper and under apartments belong to different persons, the whole, or the upper storey only, should fall down, in that case the proprietor of the upper storey is not permitted to sell his right (namely, the right of building another upper storey), because this, as being only a right, is not property.

Objection—It would hence appear that the sale of a right to water* (that is, of a share in water used in tillage) is not lawful, as it is not the seller's property, but merely his right : whereas such a sale is allowed, if made along with the land, according to all authorities ; and according to one tradition (which has been adopted by the Sheikhs of Balkh) the sale of the right to water by itself is lawful

Reply.—The sale of a right to water is valid, because the term Shirb means a share in water : and that is an existent article, and in the nature of property ;—whence it is that if a person, in a case where it is enjoyed by rotation, should destroy it during the term of his right he is responsible for the value of it ;—and also, that, when it is sold along with the ground, a part of the price is opposed to the right to water

Anything may be sold which admits of a precise ascertainment : but not otherwise.—If a person bestow or sell a road† it is lawful : but neither the sale nor the gift of a water-course is valid. These cases admit of two suppositions.—I. The sale may be of the absolute right to the road or water-course, without defining the length or breadth of either.—II. It may be of the right of passing upon the road, or receiving the benefit of the water. ‡—Upon the first supposition, the difference between the two cases is that the road is certain and ascertained, because the known breadth of it is equal to that of a door-way ;—but in the case of a water-course there is an uncertainty because it is not known how much ground the water covers.—Upon the second supposition. there are two traditions with respect to a sale of a right of passage on the road :—according to one tradition the sale is lawful ; and according to another it is invalid :—The difference between the sale of a right of passage on the road and a right of benefit from the water (as inferred from the first tradition), is that a right of passage is a point which admits of being precisely ascertained, as it is connected with a known object, namely, the road ; whereas the right of benefit from the water is of a nature which cannot admit of being precisely ascertained,—and this, whether the water be conveyed in a trough supported upon a wooden frame, or in a trench cut in the ground.

A deception with respect to the sex invalidates the sale in slaves, but not in brutes.—If a person sell a slave as a female, who afterwards proves to be a male, in that case the sale is utterly null—It is otherwise where a person sells a goat (for instance) as a male, and it afterwards proves to be a female ; for in that case the contract of sale is complete : the purchaser, however, has the option of keeping the animal, or rejecting it. The difference between these two cases is founded on this general rule,—that wherever denomination and pointed reference are united, by the seller pointing to the subject of the sale, and mentioning its name (as if a person should say, "I have sold this goat, for instance),—in this case, if the article refered to prove essentially different from what was mentioned, the sale is supposed to relate to the article named ; and therefore if the article referred to prove of a different species from what was named, the sale is null.—If, on the other hand, the article referred to prove of the same species with the article named, but of a different quality, in this case the sale relates to the article referred to ; and where the article referred to is found, the sale is complete : the purchaser, however, has in this instance an option, because of the quality mentioned not existing in the article ;—as where, for instance, a person sells a slave as a baker, and he proves to be a scribe —Now it is to be observed that a male and a female slave are not of the same, but of two different sexes, which is accounted, in this instance, as acquivalent to being of different species, because of their different uses ; whereas in goats the object for purchase (namely, to eat their flesh), is the same, with respect both to the male and the female, and therefore they are not held to be of two different species.—It is proper to remark, in this place, that, amongst lawyers, the unity or difference of the object, and not the unity or difference of the essence, determines the unity or difference of the species. Thus vinegar of the grape is held to be of a different species from the sweet juice of the grape.

A re-slave to the seller for a sum short of

*Arab. Shirb.—This term properly signifies draw-wells dug for the purpose of watering lands, and the right to the use of which is transferable. in the same manner as any other property.

†By a road is here meant a lane or narrow passage leading into a street or high-road.

‡Literally, causing the water to run (by opening sluice; or so forth).

the original price, before payment of that price, is invalid.—If a person purchase a female slave for a thousand dirms, stipulating either a future or immediate payment and having taken possession of her, should sell her to the person from whom he had purchased her, for five hundred dirms, previous to his having made payment of the thousand dirms, this second sale is invalid. Shafei is of opinion that as the right of property in the slave had vested in the purchaser; because of his having taken possession of her, such sale, on the part of the purchaser to the seller, is valid, in the same manner as it would have been valid to any other person,—or as it would have been valid to the seller in case the second price had been equal to or greater than the first,—or in case it had been in exchange for other goods, although these should have been of a less value.—The arguments of our doctors are,—First, a tradition that Ayeesha, having heard of a woman who, having purchased a female slave from Zeyd Bin Rakim for eight hundred dirms, had afterwards sold her to the said Zeyd for six hundred dirms spoke to her thus : "This purchase and sale on your part is bad ; inform Zeyd, that certainly God will render null his pilgrimages and enterprises achieved along with the Prophet unless he repent of such conduct."—Secondly, if the sale in question be valid, it follows that the first seller remains indebted to the purchaser for five hundred dirms, and the purchaser to him for one thousand dirms. Now if their account should be balanced, and five hundred dirms be struck off from the debt of the purchaser, in liquidation of his claim upon the seller, there remains five hundred due by the purchaser for which he has received no return, and this is unlawful. It is otherwise where the seller, in the second sale, gives the purchaser goods in return ; because there the difference is not obvious ; being apparent only with respect or articles of the same kind.

But the contract is not invalid with respect to any other subjects which may be joined to the original in the re-sale.—If a person, having purchased a female slave for five hundred dirms, and taken possession of her should afterwards, before he had discharged he price, sell her, in conjunction with another, for five hundred dirms to the person from whom he had purchased her, in that case the sale is valid with respect to the female slave whom he had not formerly purchased from that person, but null with respect to the other. The reason of this is that, as a part of the price is necessarily opposed to the new slave, it follows that he purchases a slave, and sells her again to the same person for a less price than he had purchased her for, which is not lawful, as has been already shown.—No such reason of illegality, however, existing with regard to the sale of the other slave, it is therefore valid. in a price proportioned to her value.

Objection.—It would appear that the sale of the other slave is also invalid, because the person has sold both by one contract, and as the sale of the one is invalid, it would follow that the sale of the other is also invalid (according to the tenets of Haneefa), in the same manner as where a freeman and a slave are sold by one contract, the sale of the slave being in that case invalid as well as that of the freeman

Reply.—The sale of the other slave is valid ; and the invalidity of sale with respect to one does not affect the sale of the other ; because the invalidity, in this instance, is weak, as there is a difference of opinion regarding it amongst our doctors ; and also, because it is founded on a suspicion of usury, the effect of which suspicion cannot extend beyond the subject of suspicion, namely, the first slave.

The stipulation of specific tare invalidates a sale.—If a person purchase oil, on this condition, that it be weighed with the vessel in which it is contained, and that a deduction of fifty ratls shall be made on account of the weight of the vessel, such sale is not valid ; whereas, if the condition be in general terms, thrt "a deduction shall be made for the weight of the vessel," it is valid ;—because the former condition is not essential to the contract, whereas the letter is essential.

Case of dispute concerning the tare of a vessel which contained the commodity.—If a person, having purchased oil in a leathern bag, should carry it away with him, and afterwards return a bag the seller weighing ten ratls, and the seller assert that "this is not the bag he had carried away with him. as that only weighed five ratls ;" In this case the averment of the purchaser is to be credited, whether the question of disagreement be considered as relating to the bag being different,—or to the consequent difference it creates with respect to the quantity of oil ; because, if the difference be considered as relating to the indentity of the bag of which the purchaser had taken possession, his assertion must be credited, since the word of the possessor is to be credited, whether he be responsible for the article (as in the case of an usurper) or merely a confident (as in the case of a trustee) ;—or if, on the other hand, the difference be considered as relating to the quantity of oil this resolves itself into a difference with respect to the amount of the price, the seller claming more, and the purchaser acknowledging less : the purchaser is therefore the defendant ; and the assertion of a defendant, upon oath, must be credited.

A Mussulman may commission a Christian to sell or purchase unlawful articles on his account ; and such sale or purchase, made by the agent, is valid.—If a Mussulman desire a Christian either to purchase or sell wine or a hog on his account, and the Christian act accordingly, in that case (according to Haneefa) such sale or purchase is valid ; but an order of a Mussulman to this effect being in the highest degree abominable, he is therefore enjoined (where it respects the sale of those articles) to devote the price obtained for them to the poor.—The two disciples maintain that the purchase or sale of wine or a hog by a Christian, on account of a Mussulman, is invalid (and the same) difference of opinion also obtains which respect to the case of a Mohrim appointing an agent for the sale of the game he may have caught, when it became unlawful for him to make such sale). The argument of the two disciples is that the constituent, as not having himself the power of selling or purchasing these articles, cannot of consequence invest others with such power; besides, as all the acts of an agent revert to the constituent on whose behalf they are performed, it is therefore the same as if the Mussulman were himself to sell or purchase these articles, which would be illegal. The argument of Haneefa is that the contractor (that is, the purchaser or the seller) is, in this instance, no other than the agent; for this reason, that he is fully empowered to perform these acts: the reverting, moreover, of the property to the constituent is a necessary and unavoidable effect, and therefore is not prevented by his Islam:—in the same manner as the articles in question may descend to a Mussulman by inheritance (in other words, if a Christian, whose heir is a Mussulman, should himself embrace the religion of Islam, and afterwards die, before releasing his hog, or converting his liquor into vinegar, in that case they would descend to his Mussulman heir). It is to be observed, however, that although Haneefa admits the validity of the purchase of these articles by a Christian agent, on behalf of a Mussulman, still he holds it incumbent on the Mussulman to convert the liquor into vinegar, and to set free the hog.

A sale is rendered invalid by the insertion of any condition advantageous to either party, or repugnant to the requisites of the contract; or which may occasion contention, by involving an advantage to the subject of the sale—IF a person sell a male slave, on condition that the purchaser shall emancipate him, or make him a Mudabbir, or a Mokatib; or if a person sell a female slave, on condition that the purchaser shall make her an Am-Walid, such sale is invalid; because this is sale suspended on a condition: and such sales are condemned by the Prophet. The rule, in this particular, is founded on a tenet of our doctors, that the insertion of any condition which is a necessary result of the contract (such as where the seller bargains that "the purchaser shall become proprietor of the article sold"), can no away effect the validity of the contract, since that would be established independent of any stipulation; and, on the other hand, that the insertion of any condition which is not a necessary result of the contract, and in which there is an advantage either to the qu;er or the seller, or to the subject of the sale, of capable of enjoying an advantage (such as where the seller bargains that "the purchaser shall emancipate the slave he sells to him"), renders the contract invalid; because an additional and extraneous act is, in this instance, required from the purchaser, without stipulating a recompence to him, and which of consequence is of an usurious nature: and also' because as there is an advantage in this condition to the subject of the sale, who is capable of claiming it, it follows that a contention must necessarily ensue and hence the object of sale (namely, the prevention of srife) is frustrated. Conditions of this nature are therefore unlawful, excepting where custom and precedent prevail over analogy; as where a person purchases unsewed shoes on condition of the seller's sewing, or causing them to be sewed for him. The insertion, on the, other hand, of any condition which is not a necessary result of the contract, and which, moreover, is not attended with advantage to any particular person, does not invalidate the contract. An example of this occurs where a person sells an animal, on condition that "the purchaser shall sell it again;" which condition is lawful, because there is no particular person whose right it is to claim the performance of it (since the animal is incapable of so doing), and hence neither usury nor strife can attend such a stipulation. Now, having explained the tenets of our doctors, it is proper to remark that the conditions recited in the cases in question are repugnant to the nature of the contract, as they tend to deprive the purchaser of every right to which the sale entitles him; and they also involve an advantage to the subject of the sale, who is capable of claiming it: they, therefore invalidate the contract. Shafei dissents from our doctors, as he holds the sale of a slave, on condition of his emancipation, to be valid.

But such sale recovers its validity, by the purchaser performing the condition with the article purchased.—IF a person should emancipate a slave whom he had purchased on that condition, then the sale, which, because of such condition, was previously illegal, becomes valid, according to Haneefa; and the purchaser is responsible to the seller for the price. The two disciples are of opinion that the emancipation does not render the sale valid; and that therefore the payment of the value, and not of the price, is incumbent on the purchaser; because, as the sale was originally invalid, in consequence of the condition, it cannot afterwards be rendered valid by means of the emancipating. any more than by the purchaser's murdering or selling the slave. The reasoning of Haneefa is, that although the condition of emancipating the slave be not, in itself, agreeable to the requisites of a contract of sale (as was before explained), still it is so in effect; because it completes the right of property on the part of the purchaser; and a thing becomes established and confirmed by its completion; whence it is that the emancipation of a purchased slave is no bar to a right of compensation from the seller in case of a defect.

Sale is rendered invalid, by a reservation of any advantage to the seller from the article sold.—If a person sell a slave, on condition that "he shall serve him for the space of two months after the sale;" or a house, on condition that "he shall reside in it for the space of two months after the sale;" or if a person sell any other article, on condition of the purchaser's lending him a dirm (for instance), or making him some present, the sale so suspended on any of these conditions in invalid:—First, because these conditions are not agreeable to the nature of a sale, and are attended with an advantage to the seller. Secondly, because the Prophet has prohibited a sale on condition of a loan: and, Thirdly, because, if any diminution be made in the price, on account of the sevices of the slave, or the residence in the house, it follows that a contract of rent is interwoven in that of sale or if on the other hand, no diminution be made in the price on these accounts, it follows that a deed of loan is interwoven in the sale; and both of these are illegal.

Or, by the stipulation of a delay in the delivery of it.—If a person sell goods on condition of his being permitted to suspend the delivery for a month, the sale is in such case invalid, because a suspension with respect to the delivery of goods which are extant and specific is an unlawful condition. The reason of this is that a suspension in point of time has been ordained by the law, merely for the purpose of ease, and is therefore only applicable to a debt, in order that the debtor may have time to collect the sum within the prescribed period and pay it accordingly; but with respect to a thing actually extant (such as cloth, for in tanc), there can be no occasion for such suspensi n.

Or, by the insertion of an invalid condition.—The sale of a pregnant slave, with a reservation of the foetus in her womb, is invalid; because it is a general rule that nothing, the sale of which by itself is illegal. can be made an exception to a contract of sale; and of this nature is a foetus. The sale, therefore, is invalid, because of the invalidity of the condition. It is to be observed that a contract of Kitabat, of hire or of pawnage, are the same with a contract of sale, in this respect, that an invalid condition is a means of invalidating the deed. In the case of Kitabat, however, the invalid condition must actually exist in the deed; as when a person enters into covenant with his slave to emancipate him on condition of his giving him wine, or a hog. It is also to be observed that in the cases of gift, alms, marriage, Khoola, and composition for wilful murder, the exception of the foetus does not invalidate the deed; on the contrary, the deed takes place in full; but the condition is invalid. In the same manner, an exception of the foetus does not invalidate a legacy, for in this case the exception is a valid condition.

Or of a condition which implicates the subject of another contract.—If a person purchase cloth. on condition that the seller sew it into the form of a vest on his account, the sale is in such case invalid; since this condition, besides being attended with an advantage to the purchaser, is not a requisite of the contract of sale. Moreover this necessarily supposes the implication of terms of two different contracts; that is, either of sale and loan, or of sale and hire.

If a person purchase one shoe from another on condition that the seller prepare a fellow to it on his account,—or purchase a pair of shoes on condition of the seller making straps to them, for the purpose of tying them, the sale in either case is invalid.—(The compiler of the Hedaya remarks that this is according to analogy; for a more favourable construction would suggest that such sale is lawful, on account of its being customary amongst men).

Or by a stipulation of the payment of the price, at a period not precisely known to both parties.—If a person should purchase an article, and stipulate the payment of the price on the day of the new year, or on the Mihrjan,* or on the fast of the Christians, † or the day of breaking lent amongst the Jews, the sale, under such conditions, is invalid, provided both parties be not informed with certainty respecting those periods. The sale, however, is lawful, if these periods be ascertained within the knowledge of both parties.

Or the date of the occurrence of which is uncertain.—A sale is not valid where the price is stipulated to be paid on the return of the pilgrims, or, on the cutting of the grain, or on the gathering of the grapes, or on the shearing of the sheep,—because in none of these cases is the period absolutely determinate: contrary to the act of giving bail; for the giving of bail, until, any of these periods, is lawful; because a small degree of uncertainty does not invalidate a bail-bond, in the same manner as it does a contract of sale.

But it is valid where the time of payment is fixed by a subsequent agreement.—If, however, a sale be made in an absolute manner, and the seller afterwards agree to receive the price at any of the periods in question, it is lawful, because, this stipulation not being included in the contract of sale, it becomes a stipulation with regard to payment of debt (not the price), which admits of a small degree of uncertainty.

A sale, invalid in consequence of stipulating an uncertain time of payment, recovers its

* This is also termed Mirhkan. A festival observed by the ancient Persians on the day of the autumnal equinox.

† Easter.

validity by removal of the uncertainty.—IF a sale be made, stipulating payment of the price at any of the periods above stated, and afterwards the purchaser and seller jointly, or the purchaser alone, remove the obstacle of uncertainty,* price to the actual occurrence of the period stipulated the sale then becomes valid. Ziffer maintains that, the sale being originally invalid, the subsequent removal of the obstacle cannot render it valid; in the same manner as a marriage originally contracted for a fixed period would not become valid by rendering it perpetual. The argument of our doctors is, that the invalidity of the sale, in this case, is merely because of the apprehension of the litigation, to which the uncertainty may give rise; and of course, when this uncertainty is removed, the sale remains valid. Moreover, as the uncertainty, in this case, relates only to an accidental circumstance, that is, to the period when the price is to be paid, and not to the price itself, which is one of the essentials of sale, the uncertainty is capable of being removed. It is otherwise where a person sells one dirm for two dirms, and afterwards relinquishes the additional dirm; for the sale does not in consequence of such relinquishment become valid, since the invalidity related to the price itself, which is an essential of the sale. It is also otherwise in a case of marriage for a particular period, because this, in fact, is not a marriage, but a separate deed called Matat; and by no subsequent acts can one deed be transmitted into another deed.

The sale of a saleable with an unsaleable subject is invalid.—IF a person expose to sale a freeman and a slave, and sell them both in one contract,—or, in the same manner, sell a carrion goat,† and one that has been slain by the prescribed from of Zibby,—such sale according to Haneefa, is utterly invalid with respect both to the freeman and the slave, as in the first case, and the carrion, and slain goat (as in the second;—and this: whether the seller have opposed a specific price to each or not (the two disciples are of opinion that if a specific price be opposed to each, the sale is valid with respect to the slave, or the slain goat).

But if the unsaleable subject be property, the sale holds good with respect to the saleable subject.—IF, on the contrary, a person unite in sale, an absolute slave and a Modabbir, or a slave that is his property, and another that is not, the sale is in either case lawful, with respect to the absolute slave, or the slave which is his absolute property, in return for a proportion from the whole price stipulated. This is, according to our doctors, (namely, Haneefa and the two disciples).—Ziffer is of opinion that the sale is not lawful in either case, with respect to either subject. The two disciples argue, that where a specific price is opposed to each particular subject, the invalidity of the sale extends only to that subject which contains a cause of invalidity (namely, the freeman or the carrion) but does not reach to the other subjects (namely, the slave or the slain goat);—in the same manner as where a person marries a stranger woman and his own sister by one contract, in which case the marriage is valid with respect to the stranger, although it be invalid with respect to his sister,—for that invalidity does not extend to the stranger;—and so also in the case in question. It is otherwise where the price of each particular subject has not been specified; for in that case the invalidity extends to the whole. Haneefa argues that there is a material difference between the two cases;—namely, the case of joining in sale a freeman with a slave, and that of joining a Modabbir with a slave; because a freeman, as not being property, is utterly incapable of being included in a contract of sale; and as the comprehension of him in the sale necessarily establishes the condition of the acceptance of the sale with respect to him, it follows that the sale is invalid, because of the invalidity of the condition: contrary to marriage, as that is not rendered invalid by an invalid condition. The sale, on the other hand, of a slave the property of another, or of a Makatib, Modabbir, or Am-Walid, is merely suspended for these may be included in a contract of sale, as they are property.—whence it is that the sale of them may be carried into execution, in the case of the stranger's slave, by the consent of the proprietor,—in the case of a Mokatib by his own consent,—and in the case of a Modabbir or Am-Walid (in the opinion of the Elders) by a decree of the Kazee to this effect;—but as it is to supposed that the proprietor of the slave, on account of his right to the subject of the sale, and the Mokatib, Modabbir, or Am-Walid, because of the claims established in their persons, will repel the sale, the sale therefore is executed only with relation to the absolute slave; in the same manner as where a person purchases two slaves, of whom one dies, previous to the purchaser taking possession of them; in which case the sale holds good with respect to the other.

Section

Of the Laws of Invalid Sales.

In an invalid sale, the purchaser is responsible, not for the price, but for the value, of the article, in case of its perishing in his hands, where he has taken possession of it by content of the seller.—WHEREVER the purchaser, in an invalid sale, takes possession of the goods, with the consent of the seller then, provided both the goods and the price

*By paying the price, or fixing the time of payment to some specific period, such as forty days for instance.

†Meaning any dead goat, not slain according to LAW.

be property,* the purchaser becomes proprietor of the article sold, and remains responsiblo, not for the price, but for the value of the goods, in case they be destroyed in his possession. Shafei maintains that the purchaser does not become proprietor, although he take possession of the article, because an invalid sale is forbidden, and therefore cannot substantiate a right of property; besides, anything which is forbidden is not sanctioned by the LAW, since prohibition is repugnant to ordinance; an invalid sale, therefore, is in no respect sanctioned by the LAW (whence it is that the purchaser of goods does not become proprietor before seisin); and the case is consequently the same as if a person should sell something in exchange for carrion, or should sell wine in exchange for money. Our doctors, on the other hand, argue that, in this case, the essential of sale (namely, an exchange of property for property), exists. The subject of the sale, moreover, is property, and is therefore a fit subject. The buyer and seller also are both competent to the act:—and where all these circumstances exist, the sale is duly contracted. Besides, the prohibition is no way repugnant to the legality of the sale itself, because the prohibition relates only to an accessary circumstance, namely an invalid condition; the right of property, therefore, after seisin, accrues to the purchaser in virtue of the sale itself, which is legal, and not in virtue of any matter which is prohibited, or contrary to the LAW. The purchaser, moreover, does not become proprietor of the goods before seisin, for two reasons:—FIRST, because, although an invalid sale be a cause of right of property, yet it is a weak cause, and therefore stands in need of the aid of seisin to give it effect; SECONDLY, because, if the purchaser become proprietor previous to the seisin, it would necessarily follow that a sanction is given by LAW to the invalidity, whereas it is incumbent to remove the invalidity. With respect to the cases of a sale of any thing in exchange for carrion, or of wine in exchange for money, the essentials of sale do not exist in either of these, as has been already demonstrated. It is established as a condition, in this instance, that the seisin be made with the consent of the SELLER: it is sufficient, however (according to a favourable construction of the LAW), if this consent be by implication; as if the purchaser should make the seisin in the place of sale, and in presence of the seller. The reason for a favourable contruction of the law, in this particular, is, that as the seller, by the contract of sale, virtually empowers the purchaser to make seisin, and as the purchaser does so in his presence, without his making any objection thereto, it is therefore construed to have been made with his consent: in the same manner as the seisin of a gift, in the place where the deed of gift is executed, is valid according to a favourable construction of the law. It is also a condition, that both the goods and the return be property, in order that an exchange of property for property (which is one of the pillars of sale) be established: for if this were not the case, the sale would be null, in the same manner as a sale in return for carrion, blood, the person of a freeman, air, or the like; and hence if in these cases, the purchaser should take possession of the goods with the consent of the seller still he is not responsible for them.

And the value must be paid in money, or in a similar according to the nature of the article.—With respect to what was stated, that the seller "remains responsible, not for the price, but for the value of the goods," it relates only to such goods as are of a nature to be compensated for by money; for with respect to such as ere compensable by similars, the purchaser, is responsible for a similar; because that which is a similar both in appearance and in effect, is a more equitable compensation than that which is similar in effect only.

Either party may annul the contract befor seisin.—IN an invalid sale, either of the parties, previous to the seisin, has the power of annulling the contract, in order that the invalidity of it may be removed. The law is also the same after seisin, provided the invalidity exist in the body of the contract. If, however, the invalidity be occasioned by the addition of an invalid condition, the person stipulating the condition is allowed to annul it, but not the other party.

A purchaser under an invalid sale may validly sell the article, in which case his right of annulling the sale expires.—IF the purchaser, in an invalid sale, take possession of the article, and then sell it, in that case the second sale is valid,—as the first purchaser, having become proprietor in virtue of seisin, is fully competent to sell the article; and, upon his so doing, the right of returning the article to the first seller expires:—FIRST, Because the right of the individual (namely, the second purchaser) is connected with the second sale; and the annulment of the first sale, in consequence of its invalidity is on account of the right of GOD* but the right of the individual has preference to the right of GOD, as the individual is necessitous, whereas GOD is not so; SECONDLY, Because the first sale is legal in its essence, but invalid in its quality,—whereas the second sale is legal in point of both; and it follows that the latter cannot be obstructed in its operation by the former; and, THIRDLY, because the second sale is made with the virtual assent of the first seller, as the power to that effect was by him bestowed on the

*That is, be of such a nature as to constitute property.

*In other words,—the right of the LAW.

first purchaser. It is otherwise where the purchaser of a house, in which there is a right of Shaffa, sells it to another; for there the person entitled to the right of Shaffa has nevertheless just title to it; because it is the right of the individual, in the same manner as that of the second purchaser; is equal to it in point of legality; and has not been forfeited by any power given by him to the purchaser to make the sale.

The purchaser of a lawful article in return for one which is unlawful, may after possession dispose of it as he sees fit; remaining responsible only for the value.—If a person purchase and take possession of a slave, in exchange for wine, or a hog, and afterwards either emancipate him, sell him, or bestow him in gift, all of these acts are valid, because of the purchaser, in virtue of the seisin, having become proprietor; and he is responsible to the seller for the value of the slave. In the case of emancipation, as the property immediately ceases, the slave becomes (as it were) destroyed, and hence proceeds the responsibility of the purchaser for the value. In the case of sale or gift, the responsibility arises from the right of returning him to the seller being annulled in consequence of these deeds, as has been already explained. It is to be observed that pawnage, or the making a slave a Mokatib, is equivalent to sale, and therefore annuls the right of return to the seller. The redemption of the pledge, however, or the inability of the Mokatib to perform his covenant, restores the right, because the bar to its operation is removed.

The seller cannot resume the article until he return the purchase-money; and if the seller die, the purchaser is entitled to set up the article to sale, to indemnify himself for the price he has paid.—In an invalid sale, the seller is not allowed to resume the goods from the purchase, until he shall have first restored the purchase-money; because the goods, being opposed to the purchase-money, are retained in the nature of a pledge until the restitution of it. If the seller should die then the purchaser has a prior claim to the subject of sale; that is, he is permitted to take payment of the price from the sale of the goods, giving the remainder (if there be any) to the other claimants; because, as he has a right in the goods superior to any other person, during the lifetime of the seller, he consequently has right preferably to the seller's heirs or creditors after his decease; in the same manner as the holder of a pawn. It is to be observed, that if the price was paid in dirms, the purchaser has a right to exact from the seller the indentical dirms he paid him; since the purchase-money: in the case of an invalid sale, remains in the hands of the seller in the nature of an usurpation. If, however, the identical dirms be not in his possession, then the purchaser is entitled to an equivalent.

Case of an immoveable property, in which a change is wrought by a purchaser under an invalid contract.—If a person purchase a house by an invalid sale, and afterwards convert it into a mosque, he is in that case responsible, according to Haneefa, for the value of house. This is also related by Aboo Yoosaf, in the Jama Sagheer, as the opinion of Haneefa; but he afterwards entertained doubts respecting it. The two disciples maintain that the house must be restored to its original state, and then returned to the seller. The same difference of opinion obtains, if the purchaser should plant trees in the court-yard of the house. The argument of the two disciples is that the right of the neighbour is of weaker consideration than the right of the seller (whence it is that the right of a neighbour requires to be supported by decree of the Kazee, and also, that it becomes null, by any delay in the demand of it,—neither of which is the case with respect to a seller's right); and as the right of the neighbour, which is the weaker right, would not be annulled by the conversion of the house into a mosque, it follows that the right of the seller, which is the stronger, is not thereby annulled a fortiori. The argument of Haneefa is, that the act of building or planting proceeds on an idea of perpetual possession; that the purchaser in so doing acts in virtue of a power to that effect which he holds from the seller; and that therefore the same has no right to the restitution, in the same manner as in the case of its being resold by the purchaser. It is otherwise with the right of a neighbour, as he does not give power to the purchaser to build or plant on the place over which his right extends; whence it is that if the purchaser had either bestowed it in a gift, or sold it, his right to neighbourhood would nevertheless still have remained in force. Aboo Yoosaf, who reported what is here advanced as the opinion of Haneefa on this subject, afterwards distrusted his memory, as has been already observed. Mohammed, however, in treating of Shaffa,† expressly infers the difference of opinion here recited;—for, he says, "where a purchaser, under an invalid sale, builds upon the ground he has purchased, the neighbour has no right of Shaffa therein, according to the two disciples, any more than previous to the purchase." Now as Haneefa, on the other hand, has maintained that in such case the neighbour is entitled to take the place, upon paying the value, in virtue of his right of Shaffa, it clearly follows that in his opinion the right of the seller is annulled; because it is on this circumstance that he founds his opinion of the existence of the right of Shaffa, since, so long as the right of the seller remains in force, that of the neighbour cannot take place;—whereas, according to the two dis-

*Arab. Shaffee; meaning the person entitled to the right of pre-emption in virtue of Shaffa.

† In the Mabsoot.

ciples, the right of the seller is not destroyed by the building of the purchaser, and therefore the claim of Shaffa does not take place.

The profit acquired by the purchaser, upon a definite article, purchased under an invalid contract, must be bestowed in charity.—If a person purchase a female slave (for instance) by an invalid contract, and take possession of her, and the seller take possession of the purchase-money, and the purchaser then dispose of her, by sale, to another person at a profit, it is in that case incumbent on him [the purchaser] to bestow in charity the profit so acquired :—but if the first seller should have acquired a profit upon, or by means of, the purchase-money, he is not required to bestow such profit in charity. The reason of this distinction is that as the female slave (for instance) is a definite article, the second contract of sale relates identically to her, and the profit acquired by the sale of her is accordingly base.—Dirms and deenars, on the other hand, are not definite in valid contracts; and as the second contract is of a valid nature. it consequently does not relate to them identically, and accordingly the profit acquired by them is not case. This distinction however, obtains only where the baseness is founded on the invalidity of the right ; for where it is founded on the absolute non-existence of right of property.

And so also, profit acquired upon any article in which no right of property exists.—(As where, for instance, a usurper acquires a profit upon the property he has usurped),—there is no difference whatever ;—that is, from whichever subject the profit is obtained, it is unlawful and must be bestowed in charity ;* because, where a person sells an article, the identical property of another (such as any article of household goods), the contract of sale relates to that actual article, and the profit acquired by it is accordingly unlawful ; where, on the other hand, a person purchases a thing with money belonging to another, although the contract do not relate to that actual money (since, if other money were given instead of it, the contract nevertheless holds good), still, however, there is a semblance of the contract relating to that particular money ; for if he were to give that actual money to the seller, the article purchased in return would remain appropriated to him) : or if, on the contrary, he were only to point to that money, and then give other money instead of it, the amount of the price of the article is. virtually, in that money ;—for this reason, therefore, there is a semblance of the contract relating to that money, and consequently that the profit is acquired by means of the property of another person. Now, as the baseness occasioned by an invalidity of right is of less moment than that occasioned by the absolute non-existence of right, it follows that the baseness occasioned by the invalidity in the right of property occasions a semblance of baseness in anything in which the absolute non-existence of right occasions actual baseness (and that is anything of a definite nature, such as a slave girl, for instance, as in the case in question) ;—and, on the other hand ; that it occasions an apprehension of a semblance of baseness in anything in which the absolute non-existence of right occasions only a semblance of baseness ;—and regard is had to a semblance of baseness, but not to an apprehens on of a semblance.—It is to be observed that if a person claim a debt from another of a thousand dirms, and obtain payment of the same, and both parties afterwards agree that the debt was not due,—in that case the profit which the claimant may in the meantime have acquired by possession of the money is lawful to him ; because the baseness, in this instance, is occasioned by invalidity of right : for this reason, that the debt had been owing in consequence of the demand of the claimant, and the defendant's acknowledgment of it ; and it afterwards appears that this debt is not the right of the claimant, but of the other (namely, the defendant) : still however, the thousand dirms which the claimant took in satisfaction for his demand have become his property. as the satisfaction for a claim becomes the property of the claimant, although it be under an invalid right :—and as the baseness, in this instance, is occasioned by the mere invalidity of right of property, and not by the absolute non-existence of that right, it consequently cannot operate, nor have any effect with respect to a thing of an indefinite nature, such as money, for instance.

Section.

Of Sales and Purchases which are Abominable.

It is abominable to enhance the price of merchandise by a fictitious tender of a high price.—The Prophet has prohibited the practice of Najish,—that is, the enhancement of the price of goods, by making a tender for them, without any intention to purchase them, but merely to incite others to the offer of a higher price The Prophet has also prohibited the purchase of a thing which has already been bargained for by another ; but this prohibition supposes that both parties had before come to a mutual agreement ; for otherwise there is no impropriety in such subsequent purchase.

Or, to anticipate or forestall the market.—The Prophet has also prohibited an anticipation of the market,—as where people meet the caravan, at a distance from the city, with a view of purchasing the grain brought by the merchants, in order to sell it to the people of the city at an enhanced price. This prohibition, however, proceeds on a supposition that the forestallers deceive the merchants with respect to the price of grain in the city;

*For an explanation of the principle on which this proceeds, see Partnership, where it is declared that "profit cannot be lawfully acquired upon a property concerning which there is no responsibility."

for otherwise there is no impropriety in this practice.

Or to enhance the price of grain, in towns, by a citizen selling for the farmer.—The Prophet has also prohibited a citizen from selling for a countryman; as where, for instance, a countryman brings grain or other goods into a city, and one of the citizens takes care of it, and acts as his agent, in order that he may sell it at a high price to the people of the city. Some have given a different explanation of this prohibition, by supposing it to allude to a citizens selling anything at a high price to a countryman: but in the Fattahal Kadeer of Moojtibba the former is mentioned as the most authentic explanation, It is to be observed, however, that this prohibition supposes that a scarcity of grain prevails in the city, as otherwise such conduct is not improper.

Or to buy or sell on a Friday.—It is abominable to buy or sell on a Friday,* after the crier proclaims the hour of prayer, because God has said, in the Koran, "When ye are called to prayer, on the day of the assembly, hasten to the commemoration of God, and leave merchandising." Moreover, if at such time purchase and sale were allowed, an absolute duty (namely, attendance at prayers) would necessarily be omitted. It is to be observed, however, that although such purchases and sales be abominable, still they are not invalid; for the invalidity, in such instances, exists with respect merely to points that are extraneous and additional, and not with respect to the essentials of the contract nor with respect to the establishment of any condition essential to its obligation.

Merchandise may be set up for sale to the highest bidder.—A sale to the highest bidder is not abominable. Thus, if a merchant, for instance, having shown his wares to a purchase, should receive from him a tender for them but, before he had expressed his acquiescence, should receive a higher tender from another, in that case it is not abominable in him to sell them to the latter; because the Prophet sold a cup and a sheet to a higher bidder; and also, because sales of this kind are for the interest of the poor.

It is abominable to separate two infant slaves (or an infant and an adult), related within the prohibited degrees, by a sale of one of them.—It is abominable for a person possessing two infant slaves, related to each other within the prohibited degrees, to separate them from each other; and the rule is the same where one of them is an infant and the other an adult. This decision is founded on a declaration of the Prophet, "Whosoever causes a separation between a mother and her children, shall himself, on the day of judgment, be separated from his friends by God." It is, moreover, related that the Prophet gave two infant brothers to Alee, and afterwards inquired of Alee concerning them, and being answered by him, that "he ead sold one of them," the Prophet then said "take heed! take heed!" and repeatedly enjoined him to take him back. Besides, one infant naturally conceives an attachment to another, and an aduld person participates in the sorrow of an infant, and hence the separation of them in either case argues a want of tenderness to a child, which has been reprobated in the traditions, where it is declared, "Whosoever does not show tenderness to a child, and respect to an elder, is not of may people," A separation, therefore, either between two infants, or between an adult and an infant, is prohibited. It it to be observed that the cause of the prohibition, in this instance, is affinity within such a degree only as prohibits marriage between the slaves in question, and not general affinity, for which reason any distant relation, such as a step-mother, or one prohibited by fosterage, or by affinity with the fosterer, are not included; nor the son of the uncle; nor any one that is not within the prohibited degrees Neither are a husband and a wife included in this prohibition, notwithstanding they be both infants, and they may consequently be separated, because the tradition which contains the prohibition, as being contrary to analogy, must therefore be observed in its literal sense; that is, it must be applied to such only as are within the prohibited degrees. Moreover, in the aforersaid tradition, both relation are required to be the property of one master: if, therefore, one infant brother belong to Zeyd, and another infant brother to Omar, each is at liberty to sell his respective property.

Unless in the pursuance of an indispensable duty, or in cases of unavoidable necessity.—It is allowed, likewise, to esparate two infant slaves related to each other, if with a view to fulfil an incumbent duty, as where one of the two commits a crime, and is given up, as a compensation for such crime, to the avenger of the offence. In the same manner, also, one of the two may be sold, for the payment of a debt incurred by him in the course of purchase and sale, in consequence of his being a privileged slave,—or, by the destruction of the property of another,—in either of which cases that slave may be sold alone, in discharge of the debt, although this induce a separation, So also, it is lawfut to return one of the two to the seller of them, in case he should prove defective. The adjudication, in all these cases, proceeds on this principle, that the object of the Prophet in this prohibition was to prevent an injury to the infants without detriment to the proprietor; an object which, if the prohibition were extended to these cases, must necessarily be defeated.

But such sale is nertheless valid.—It is to be observed, however, that if a person separate one infant from another, or an infant from an adult, by selling one of them, such sale is valid: yet still the act of separation is abominable. It is recorded, from

* Friday is the Mussulman Sabbath.

Aboo Yoosaf, that a sale of this nature is invalid only where the relation of patrernity (such as mother and son, for instance) exists between the parties; but that in all other cases it is valid. Another report, from Aboo Yoosaf, mentions that sales of this nature are invalid in all cases where the separation is abominable, because of the tradition already mentioned with respect to Alee; for the Prophet positively enjoined him to take back the salve he had sold, whence it may be inferred that he considered the sale as invalid, since a return of the commodity is not admitted but in an invalid sale. The reasoning of Haneefa and Mohammed is that, in the case in question, the sale is transacted by a competent person, and with respect to a fit subject: it is therefore valid; and the abomination does not apply to anything except what is merely a concomitant, or immediate effect of the sale, namely, the distress occasioned to the two infants, which is a degree of abomination exactly equivalent to that of a person purchasing a thing over the head of another, from whence no invalidity arises. Moreover, the order of the Prophet to Alee to take back the slave must be construed either into a dissolution of the sale, or a repurchase of the slave from the person to whom he had sold him.

Adult slaves may be separated without offence.—It is not abominable to separate two slaves that are adults, notwithstanding they be related within the prohibited degrees; for this case falls not under the ordinance before mentioned; and there is an authentic tradition of the Prophet having occasioned a separation between Maria and Sireen, two female slaves that were sisters.

CHAPTER VI

OF AKALA, OR THE DISSOLUTION OF SALES.

Definition of Akala —Akala literally signifies to cancel.—In the language of the law it means the cancelling or disolution of a sale.

A sale may be dissolved in consideration of an equivalent to the price.—The dissolution of a sale is lawful, provided it be for an equivalent to the original price, because the Prophet has said "whosoever makes an Akala with one who has repented of his bargain, shall receive an Akala of his sins from God, on the day of judgment;"—and also, because, as the contract of sale comprehends the rights of both parties, namely, the buyer and the seller, they have therefore the power of dissolving such contract, to answer their own purposes.

But not for anything greater or less.—If, however, either a greater or less sum than the original price be stipulated as the condition of the dissolution, such condition is null, and the dissolution holds good; and the seller must return to the purchaser a sum equal to the original price.—It is a rule with Haneefa, that a dissolution is a breaking off of the contract with respect to both the parties, but a sale de novo with respect to others. If, therefore, the breaking off be impracticable, the dissolution is null.—According to Aboo Yoosaf, on the other hand, it is a sale de novo: but if a new sale should from any cause be impecable, then it must be considered as a breaking off: and in case of that also being impracticable, the dissolution then becomes null.—The opinion of Mohammed is that it is a breaking off; and in failure of this, from impracticability, a sale de novo; and in case of that also being impracticable, it is null.—The argument of Mohammed is that Akala, in its literal sense, signifies dissolution; and, in its constructive sense, sale (whence it is a sale de novo with relation to all others than the parties): it is therefore regarded as a dissolution or breaking off, agreeably to the literal meaning of the term; or, if the breaking off be impracticable, it is regarded as a sale, agreeably to the constructive meaning.—The argument of Aboo Yoosaf is that Akala means an exchange of property for property with the mutual consent of the parties, which corresponds with the definition of sale, and is also subject to the same rules; whence it is that, in case of the loss of the wares in the possestion of the purchaser after the conclusion of the Akala, or dissolution, it [the Akala] is null; and also, that the sell is allowed so return the wares to the purchaser in cafe of their having been blemised or become defective whilst in the hands of the purchaser; and that the right of Shaffa is also established by it.—Haneefa, on the other hand, argues that Akala means a dissolution, or breaking off, and cannot, by any construction of it, supposed to mean sale, although the breaking off should be impracticable; because sale and dissolution are terms of opposite import, which no one word can be supposed to bear:—if, therefore, the breaking off be impracticable, the Akala is null. With regard to its being a sale de novo, in relation to others, this is a mere matter of necessity, as to them it exhibits similar effects with sale: that is to say, the seller, in virtue of the Akala, becomes again proprietor of the wares; and it is accordingly a sale with respect to all others than the seller and purchaser, for this reason, and not because of the meaning of the word, which in reality is the opposite of sale—Such are the opinions and arguments of our three doctors with regard to Akala—Hence it appears that in a stipulation be made, that the seller shall return to the purchaser a sum greater than the original price, the dissolution, agreeably to the tenets of Haneefa, would hold good to the amount of the original price; because (according to his tenets) Akala is a dissolution; and a dissolution cannot possibly relate to the excess, as there is no sale which might be opposed to such excess; and it is impossible to dissolve what does not exist:—the condition, therefore, is invalid, but not the dissolution, as that is not rendered null by involving an invalid condition.—It is otherwise with respect to sale (that is, the sale of one DIRM for two DIRMS, for instance),—for if a person should sell one dirm for two dirms, such sale would be invalid; nor could it be construed as existing with respect to one dirm, and as null with respect to the additional one, so as to render such sale lawful; because the establishment of an excess in sale is possible, as that is an establishment to a matter as yet unestablished, and it is no way difficult to establish an unestablished point: but if the excess dirm were established, it would induce usury:—a sale of this nature, therefore, is invalid.—The conclusion therefore is. that the dissolution in question is valid, but the condition is otherwise. The law is also the same where a stipulation of smaller amount than the original price is made; that is to say, the dissolution holds good, but the condition is void; because the sale being established with regard to the original price, and the deficiency not then existing, it follows that the dissolution can apply only to what does exist,—namely, the original price,—since it is impossible to dissolve what does not exist.—If, however, this deficiency be stipulated on account of a defect which had taken place in the wares, it is lawful.—In the opinion of the two disciples, the stipulation of a sum exceeding the original price, in a dissolution, amounts to a sale.—according to Aboo Yusaf, because (as has been already explained) he considers Akala as a sale:—and also according to Mohammed because, although he be of opinion that a dissolution is a breaking off, yet he has said that, in case of the impracticability of a breaking off, it must be considered as a sale; and as the dissolution in question is of that nature, he is therefore of opinion it is a sale;—With respect to a dissolution in which is stipulated an amount less than the original price Aboo Yoosaf (proceeding on his general opinion concerning dissolutions), considers it as a sale: but in the opinion of Mohammed it is a dissolution with respect to the whole of the original price; because he considers the deficiency to be a silence maintained with respect to a part of the price; and as the dissolution would have been valid if a silence had been maintained with respect to the whole, so it is in a superior degree valid when the silence is mantained only with respect to a part. A dissolution, stipulating a smaller sum than the original price, in a case where the wares have been blemished in the hands of the purchaser, is considered by Mohammed as a dissolution; the deficiency being opposed to the blemish.

Dissolution, in consideration of an equivalent of a different kind, is a breaking of.—IF a dissolution be agreed upon, stipulating, in lieu of the original price, an equivalent of a different kind, it is a breaking off,* according to Haneefa, for the original price; and the stipulation of a different kind is nugatory. The two disciples consider this dissolution as a sale, founding their opinion on their ideas of the natute of dissolution, as already explained.

The sale of a female slave cannot be annulled after she has borne a child.—IF a dissolution of sale take place with respect to a female slave who had borne a child whilst in the possession of the purchaser, it is null, according to Haneefa, because (agreeably to his tenets) a dissolution is a breaking off; and the birth of the child is preventive of a dissolution, as this is a supervenient addition of a separate thing; and such addition after seisin, prevents a dissolution of the bargain.—This dissolution, however, is considered as a sale by the two disciples.

A sale may be dissolved previous to delivery and seisin of the article.—THE dissolution of a sale previous to taking possession or the aricle sold, whether of a moveable or immoveable description, is a breaking off, according to Haneefa. According to Aboo Yoosaf, it is a breaking off with regard to moveable property only, because a sale of moveable property, previous to taking possession of it, is not lawful, and hence a dissolution with respect to moveable property, previous to the seisin of it, cannot be considered as a sale, and is consequently a breaking off. A dissolution with respect to immoveable property, on the contrary, previous to the taking possession of it, is a sale (according to Aboo Yoosaf), as he holds that the sale of immoveable property, previous to the seisin of it, is lawful.

THE loss or destruction of the wares is a bar to the legality of a dissolution, but not the destruction of the price; because a dissolution is the breaking off of sale; and the breaking off of a sale rests upon the existence of the sale; and this again relates to the wares, not to the price.

Barter may be dissolved, after a destruction of one of the subject.—IN cases of Mookayeza, or a sale of goods for goods,* a dissolution agreed upon after the destruction of one of the two subjects is valid; because each of them falls under the description of the subject of the sale; and applying this term, therefore, to the one that remains, it follows that the dissolution is lawful, because of the existence of the subject of the sale.

CHAPTER VII.

OF MOORABIHAT, AND TAWLEEAT, THAT IS, SALES OF PROFIT AND OF FRIENDSHIP.†

Definition of Moorabihat and Tawleeat. MOORABIHAT, or a sale of profit, means

*And consequently valid, as it completely annuls the contract.

*That is, barter:—the term by which Mookayeza will be hereafter always expressed.

†Moorabihat and Tawleat are technical terms, which (like many others in this work)

the sale of anything for the price at which it was before purchased by the seller, with the superaddition of a particular sum by way of profit. Tawleeat, or a friendly sale, is where one person sells any thing to another for the exact price which he himself paid for it. Both these modes of sale are lawful; because the conditions essential to the validity of a sale exist in them; and also, because mankind stand in need of them. For example, a man who has himself no skill in making purchases is necessitated to confide in a purchase from a person skilled in such matters; in other words, he will purchase the article from this person at the same rate at which he had purchased it, without allowing him any profit upon it, as in a sase of Tawleeat, or friendly sale,—or, he will purchase it from him at the same rate at which he had purchased it, allowing him an addition, by way of profit, as in a case of Moorabihat, or profitable sale; and this will leave him satisfied and at ease in his mind; since a person destitute of skill is by either of these modes secured from fraud, whereas, following any other mode, he would be exposed to great imposture. Mankind, therefore, having occasion for both these modes, they are both permitted:—and as, in both instances, the purchaser is under a necessity of placing an absolute confidence in the word of the seller, who is skilled in the business of traffic, it is therefore incumbent on the seller to be just and true to his word and to abstain from fraud, or from the semblance of fraud. Fraud is where a person avers that he had purchased a certain thing for twelve dirms, when, in fact, he had only paid ten dirms; and the semblance of fraud is where a person sells any thing by a profitable sale, stipulating prompt payment, when, in reality, he had himself purchased the same thing on credit.

They require that the price consist of similars; or, if otherwise, that the person who enters into the agreement with the purchaser should have obtained possession of the price in the interim: but the profit agreed for must be in money or specific articles of weight, or measurement of capacity, and must be stipulated upon the whole price, generally, and not proportionably upon its parts.—Profitable and friendly salves are lawful only where the price of the wares is of the description of similar such as dirms and deenars, for instance; because, if the price stipulated be an article of which the unities are not similar (such as a slave, for example), if follows that the purchaser becomes proprietor of the the purchaser becomes proprietor of the wares for a price of which the value is unknown, a circumstacce which induces illegality in a sale. If, however, the purchaser* should, in the mean time, have acquired possession of the price (as if, for instance, the price be a slave, and that identical slave be then the property of the purchaser), in such case a sale of friendship is lawful; and also a sale of profit,—provided the profit be stipulated in money, or in articles estimable by weight, or measurement of capacity, which are described and ascertained;—because the purchaser is in this case enabled to make delivery of the thing which he has rendered obligatory on himself. It is not lawful, in a sale of this nature, to stipulate a profit proportionate to part of the price (such as a profit of one dirm upon ten, two upon twenty, and so forth), because the particular value of the price [the slave] not being ascertained, this could not be carried into practice:—it is necessary, therefore, to stipulate a general profit upon the whole price.

All intervening expenses which enhance the value of the article may be added to the prime cost.—It is lawful for the sellers,† in a profitable or friendly sale, to add to the capital sum‡ the wages of the bleacher, the dyer, or the figurer (of cloths), the spinner (of cotton or wool), or the porter (of wheat, and so forth)—because it is a custom amongst merchants to add such expenses to the capital sum; and also, because whatever is the cause of an increase either to the substance of the thing puschased, or to the value of it, is an addition to the capital: this, moreover, is a general rule, apdlying to all the articles here mentioned; for the dyeing, figuring, or spinning is an increase to the substance of the article; and the bleaching of linen, or the porterage of wheat, and so forth, is an increase to their value because cloths are rendered more valuable by being bleached and the price of wheat various in different places. It is requisite that the seller, in making or ineluding such addition, should

do not admit of a literal translation. Neither is the definition of them, as here given (according to the Persian version of the Hedaya) completed satisfactory. In the Arabic copy, a Moorabihat is defined to mean "a transfer, made by the proprietor, under the original contract, at the original price, with the addition of a profit,"—and Tawleeat "a transfer, by the proprietor, under the original contract, at the original price, without an addition of profit." Hence it would appear that in a case of Moorabihat, the contract [of Moorabihat] refers itself merely to the profit agreed for, and not (as in other sales) to the whole price to be paid, since that (exclusive of the profit alone) is determined by the nature of the contract, without specification; and that, in a case of Tawleeat, on the other hand, the contract [of Tawleeat] refers itself to the original price, since that is fixed at the prime cost, from the nature of the contract.

*Meaning the person who enters into the Tawleeat or Moorabihat agreement with the first purchaser.

†Meaning the party who first purchased the article, and then agrees to transfer it by Tawleeat or a Moorabihat. (The terms seller and purchaser are thus to be understood throughout this section.)

‡Arab. Ras Mal: meaning (in this place) the prime cost or original price of the article.

say, "this article has cost me so much," and not, "I have purchased this at such a rate," because the letter assertion would be false. It is to be observed that the driving of goats from city to city is equivalent to the porterage of wheat: but neither the wages of the shepherd, nor the rent of the house in which the wares are kept, is to be included, as no increase with respect either to the substance or the value arises from these circumstances: neither are the wages of a teacher of the Koran, or the like, to be included.* because the increase of value obtained by instruction is acquired through the wisdom and ability naturally existing in the scholar, which last is the immediate cause of an increase of value:—the charge, therefore, must be placed to the head of the wisdom, or natural ability, which is the immediate cause and not to the teaching, which is a remote cause.

In case of an over-statement of the price the purchaser may undo the bargain.—If, in a sale of profit, the purchaser should discover that the seller had practised a fraud in stating the price of the wares, in such case, according to Haneefa, the purchaser is at liberty either to adhere to or undo the bargain, as he pleases.

Or (in Tawleeat) deduct the excess—And in case such fraud should be practised in a sale of friendship, the purchaser is at liberty to deduct the amount of the fraud from the price. Aboo Yoosaf is of opinion that a deduction proportionate to the fraud must be made in either case; but that, in the sale of friendship the deduction is made from the price; and in a sale of profit, from both the price and the profit. Mohammed maintains that in both cases the purchaser has the option of adhering to or relinquishing the contract as he pleases:—for he argues that the mention of the price is to be regarded, as that is known; and the mention of friendship or profit, is made with a view to incite desire, and is therefore to be considered as the inducement, in the same manner as the inducement of security against a blemish or defect: and consequently, if the inducement fail, the purchaser is at liberty with respect to the contract. The argument of Aboo Yoosaf is that, in cases where friendship or profit are mentioned, it is an essential that friendship or profit be established:—whence it is that the sale in question is concluded, if the seller say to the purchaser, "I have sold this thing to you, by way of friendship, for its original price,"—or, "I have sold this thing to you for a profit on its original price," provided its original price in both cases be known and ascertained: Now, such being the case, it necessarily follows that a deduction must be made in proportion to the fraud of the purchaser, in order that Tawleeat or Moorabihat may be established:—in a case of Tawleeat the deduction is made from the price; and in a case of Moorabihat from the price and the profit. The argument of Haneefa is that if, in a sale of friendship no deduction be made for a fraud, the description of Towleeat no longer appertains to it, since the price, in such a case, must otherwise exceed the original price and consequently the transaction, which is supposed a transaction of friendship, would be altered in its nature; a deduction is therefore adjudged:—if, on the other hand, no deduction were made in a profitable sale, yet the sale would still retain its original nature of a profitable sale, with the difference only of the extent of it; for which reason the purchaser is at liberty to abide by or undo the contract as he pleases. Hence if, in a profitable sale, after the purchaser had become acquainted with the fraud, the wares should be lost or destroyed in his possession,—or, if they should have contracted some blemish preventive of a dissolution of the sale, the purchaser is responsible, according to all the most authentic traditions, for the whole price,—since in such a case no proportion whatever of the original price is opposed to the option of the purchaser so that he might deduct such proportion, because of the destruction of his option:—as holds in cases of option of inspection or condition of option. It is otherwise in cases of option of defect; for there the claim which the purchaser has on the seller relates to a loss with respect to the wares, arising from a defect; and a deduction is accordingly made from the price on account of such loss, provided it be not in the power of the seller in any other way to repair such loss arising from defect.

A profit be a Moorabihat sale cannot be twice obtained upon the same article,—If a person purchase cloth (for instance), and afterwards dispose of it to another by Moorabihat, and then repurchase it from that other at the price for which he had originally purchased it, in that case, if he should again wish to sell it by Moorabihat, it is necessary that he deduct from the price fixed in the last sale (calculating that at the rate of price in the first sale) the sums of the profit he acquired in the intermediate sale:—but if after such deduction nothing remains, he is not allowed to sell it by Moorabihat. This is according to Haneefa. The two disciples maintain that it is lawful for him to sell it with an addition of profit grounded on the last sale. To exemplify this case:—suppose that a person purchases cloth at ten dirms, afterwards sells it to another for fifteen dirms, and again purchases it from that other for ten dirms, in this case, if he should wish to resell it by way of profit, he must fix the price at five dirms, being what in reality the cloth has cost him, and what he ought therefore to found a profit upon:—suppose, on the other hand, that a person purchases a piece of cloth for ten dirms, and having sold it to another for twenty dirms afterwards repurchases it from that other for the original price, namely, ten dirms; in this

*In the sale of a slave.

case he is not entitled to sell it again with an addition of profit. The two disciples maintain that he is in both cases entitled to sell it for a profit on the last price, namely, ten dirms, and their reasons are, that he repurchase is a new contract, and has no connexion with the effects of the former sale ; and that therefore a profit may be imposed, founded on the second contract ; in the same manner as if the second purchaser should sell it to a third purchaser, and the first purchaser repurchase it from the third one, in which case it would be lawful for the first purchaser to sell it at a profit on the last price, and so also in the case in question. The argument of Haneefa is, that in the case in question, there is an apprehension of the first profit being obtained by means of the second contract. since until the person repurchased the cloth there was a possibility that he might return it upon the seller's hands in consequence of a defect, and that his [the seller's] profit might thereby have been lost, although upon his repurchasing it from the purchaser, this possibility vanishes, and the profit remains confirmed and established. The apprehension, however, had existed ; and in Moorabihat sales apprehension is regarded as equivalent to certainty, out of caution (whence it is that a profit of this nature is not allowed upon anything given in composition ; in other words, if a person be indebted to another to the amount of ten dirms, for instance, and he compound the debt with his creditor by a piece of cloth, it is not lawful for the creditor to sell this cloth at a profit of this nature over and above ten dirms, because in the composition it is to be apprehended that the value of the cloth was short of ten dirms, as composition is founded upon remission of a part).—In the case in question, therefore, the seller, because of the apprehension above stated, appears, in consequence of the second contract, to have purchased five dirms, together with the cloth, for ten dirms ; he must therefore deduct five dirms from the whole and declare that "the cloth has fallen to him for five dirms ;" and take his profit upon those five, It is otherwise where the second purchaser sells the cloth to a third person, and the first seller then repurchases it from this person : for in this case the acquisition of the first profit is confirmed and established by means of the second purchaser's having sold it into the hands of another, and not by means of the first seller repurchasing it from the third person so as to leave any room for apprehension in this case also. There is therefore a material difference between this case, and the case under consideration, and consequently it is evident that the analogy adduced by the two disciples is unfounded.

Case of Moorabihat transacted by a privileged slave with his owner.—If a privileged slave, involved in debt, should purchase a piece of cloth for ten dirms, and afterwards sell it to his master for fifteen dirms, and the master wish to sell the said cloth in the manner of Moorabihat, he must set his profit upon ten dirms. In the same manner, if a master purchase a piece of cloth for ten dirms, and sell it to his privileged slave for fffteen dirms, the slave is not entitled to dispose of it at a profit upon more than ten dirms. The reason of this is that, in both cases, there is a semblance of illegality in the sale ; because the property of the slave being as it were, the property of his master, it appears that the master, in the first case, purchases his own property : and that, in the second case, he sells his own property to himself.

Case of Moorabihat transacted between the manager of a stock and the proprietor.—If a person give to another ten dirms, in the way of Mozaribat, (stipulating that the profit acquired therefrom shall be equally divided between them, and the Mozarib, or manager so constituted, purchase with the said money a piece of cloth. and then sell it to his constituent for fifteen dirms, and the constituent afterwards wish to dispose of it by a profitable sale. he is not allowed to fix the price at more than twelve and a half dirms. The reason of this is, that although the purchase made by the proprietor of a Moorabihat stock from his manager be, in fact, the purchasing of his own property with his own property, yet, such purchase is held to be lawful by our doctors : because the proprietor of the stock has no power over it whilst in the hands of the manager : and as this power, which is a desirable object, resulted to him from the purchase, the said purchase, because of its being the means of procuring to him an object of desire, is therefore lawful ; nevertheless, as there is in this case an appearance of invalidity of sale (since the constituent did as it were purchase his own property with his own property, by which means a mutual exchange of respective property did not take place), the purchase is therefore reckoned null so far as regards the half of the profit ; and accordingly, in the case in question, the profit must be imposed upon twelve and a half dirms.

An article may be disposed of by Moorabihat, where a defect has intervened not proceeding from the seller, or where the seller has used the article, in the interim, without injury to it.—If a person purchase a female slave, and she afterwards, without any appearance of violence, but merely from a natural cause, become blind of an eye,—or if, being a woman * he cohabit with her, without harm accruing,—it is in either case lawful for him to dispose of her by Moorabihat, without giving any explanation of either of these circumstances ; for neither in consequence of the blindness or the cohabi-

*Arab. Sayeeba in opposition to a virgin. The reason for restricting the case to muliebrity, in this instance, is that cohabitation with a woman is not considered as a depreciation of her value :—contrary to the case of deflowering a virgin.

tation does any thing remain to him in opposition to which a deduction might be made from the price; because no part of the price is opposed to the quality of the article (whence it is that if the quality be destroyed previous to seisin by the purchaser, no deduction from the price would on that account be allowed); and in the same manner, no part of the price is opposed to the use of a woman's person. It is reported, from Aboo Yoosaf, that in the first case the slave must not be disposed of in the manner of Moorabihat, without an explanation being given of the blindness, any more than where blindness occasioned by violence: and this opinion has been adopted be Shafei.

But if the defect be occasioned by, or compensated to, the seller, a proportionable deduction must be made from the price.—It to be observed, that if the purchaser himself had occasioned the blindness, or if it had been occasioned by another from whom the purchaser either had or had not received an amercement, he is not in either of these cases entitled to dispose of the slave by Moorabihat, without giving an explanation of the blindness; because here the purchaser (or another) did with design or intention destroy the eye; and it is consequently repuisite that a proportionable deduction be made for a defect so occasioned. The same rule also obtains where a purchaser has cohabitation with a female slave who is a virgin; because virginity, being merely a t nde- membrane, is a constituent part of the ve, and this the purchaser has destroyed.

it the article be damaged by an accident not preceding from the seller, still it is a proper subject of Moorabihat.—If cloth which a person had purchased be burnt by fire, or damaged by vermin, in that case it is lawful for the purchaser to dispose of it by Moorabihat without explaining either of these circumstances? but if the cloth be torn in the folding and opening of it, it is not lawful for the purchaser thus to dispose of it without noticing the same to the party, because the damage, in this case, is occasioned by his own deed.

A misstatement of a prompt payment instead of a suspended payment, leaves it in power of the purchaser to undo the bargain in a sale either of profit—If a person, having purchased a slave (for instance) for one thousand dirms, payable at a future period, should afterwards sell him for one thousand dirms, payable immediately, with a profit of one hundred dirms without noticing to the other the respite of payment he himself has obtained,—in that case the other, if he should afterwards discover this circumstance, is at liberty either to abide by or undo the bargain at his option; because the suspension of the payment resembles an addition to the substance of the wares; and hence it is custom amongst merchants, in granting a respite of payment, to increase the price of the merchandise. Now a semblance, in a sale by profit, is deemed equivalent to reality; and hence it follows that the said person did, as it were, purchase two things for one thousand dirms, namely a slave and a suspension of payment; and afterwards sold only one of these things by way of profit, grounded on the price which he paid for both: a fraud from which an abstinence is particularly enjoined in cases of Moorabihat—the purchaser, therefore, has an option of adhering to or undoing the bargain as he pleases, as in the option from defect. If, however, the purchaser should destroy the wares, and then receive notice of the fraud which had been practised upon him, he is not in such case entitled to make any deduction on that account from the price, because no part of the price is in reality opposed to the suspension of payment.

Or of friendship.—If a person, having purchased a slave (for instance) for a thousand dirms payable at a future period, should afterwards dispose of him to another, by a Tawleeat, for a thousand dirms ready money, without intimating the respite of payment, in that case the other, on discovery of this circumstance, is at liberty either to abide by or annual the contract, as he pleases: because an abstinence from a fraud of this nature is equally enjoined in friendly as in profitable sales.—If, however, in this case the purchaser, having destroyed the slave, should then become acquainted with the suspension of payment that had been granted to the seller, it is incumbent on him to make a prompt payment according to the agreement; nor is he entitled to make any deduction from the price on the score of suspension of payment, as before explained.—It is related, as an opinion of Aboo Yoosaf, that the purchaser is in this case to pay the value to the seller, and to receive from him the whole of the price, in the same manner as holds (according to him) in a case where a creditor, having received payment of the debt due to him in a bad specie, discovers this circumstance after having expended them;—in which case he has a right to return to the deptor a similar number of the specie he had received, and to demand from him a like number of good specie.—Some have said that an appraisement ought to be made of the value in the case of prompt payment, and also in the case of a distant payment; and that the difference should be given by the seller to the purchaser.—All that has been here advanced proceeds on a supposition of the suspension of the payment being included in the contract of sale; for if, without such stipulation, it should happen that the payment be made at a distant period (as is often the case amongst merchants), there subsists, in such case, a difference of opinion upon this point, whether, under these circumstances, in a subsequent sale of profit or of friendship, it be incumbent upon him to make known this matter.—Some have said that such notification is incumbent upon him, since an establishad custom is equivalent to a condition.—Others, again, allege, that he is under no necessity of giving such notification, since it is evsdent that, as no condition was stipulated the sale was therefore for prompt payment.

In a sale of friendship the rate must be specified; and the purchaser has a right of option until after the specification.—IF a person dispose of a thing to another by a sale of friendship, declaring that "he sells it to him at the rate it had stood him in,"—and the purchaser be not acquainted with that rate, the sale is invalid, from the uncertainty with regard to the price;—if, however, the seller should afterwards inform the purchaser of the rate, at the same meeting, the sale then becomes valid, but it still remains in the option of the purchaser to abide by or recede from the contract as he pleases, since the acquiescence he had before expressed was not fully established, from his ignorance of the price and after the knowledge of it he has an option, in the same manner as in the case of an option of inspection. The reason of the validity of this sale is that the invalidity does not become firmly established until the departure of the parties from the meeting.—When, therefore, the purchater, in the meeting, is informed of the price, it becomes the same as if a new contract had taken place after the purchrser had acquired this knowledge; and it is for him to withhold his acquiescence until the end of the meeting.—If, however, the parties should separate, the invalidity then becomes fixed; nor can it be removed by any knowledge which the purchaser may afterwards obtain of the amount of the price.—Similar to this is the case where a person sells cloth for the value which is marked upon it, but of which the purchaser is ignorant; for such sale is invalid, but may be rendered otherwise by the explanation of the seller, before the breaking up of the meeting.

Section

Moveable property cannot be re-sold before seisin.—IT is not lawful for a person to sell moveable property, which he may have purchased, until he receive possession of the same: because the Prophet has prohibited the sale of a thing prior to the seisin of it on the part of the seller: and also, because there is an unfairness in it, since, if the merchandise should be lost or destroyed before the seisin, the first sale becomes null, and the property reverts to the former proprietor, in which case it must necessarily appear that the person in question has sold the property of another without his consent.

But land may be re-sold previous to seisin by the first purchaser.—THE sale of land,* previous to seisin, is lawful, according to Haneefa and Aboo Yoosaf. Mohammed maintains that it is unlawful; because the traditional saying of the Prophet before quoted is absolute, and not particularly confined to moveable property; and also, because of its analogy to moveable property. Besides, the sale of land is similar to the hire of it; in other words, as it is unlawful to let land before seisin so is it likewise to sell land before seisin. The reasoning fo the two disciples is that, in the case in question, the sale is effected by competent parties with respect to a fit subject;—that there is no unfairness in it, since the destruction of ground is rate, whereas that of moveable property is probable;—and that the prohibition of the Prophet is founded on the possibility of the unfairness already explained, which does not exist in the case of land, the destruction of it being rare.—Some have asserted that a lease of land before seisin, as adduced by Mohammed, is lawful in the option of the two disciples.—Admitting, however, that it were unlawful according to all our doctors, it proceeds evidently on his principle, that a lease is made with a view to the produce, the destruction of which not being uncommon, the unfairness already explained (with respect to the sale of moveable property before seisin) may consequently take place in it. This, however, cannot happen with respect to the sale of ground, the destruction of which is rare, and consequently the one case is not analogous to the other.

In the re-sale of articles of weight, and measurement of capacity, it is requisite that the article be weighed or measured again by the second purchased—IF a person purchase articles estimable by a measure of capacity, such as wheat,—or articles of weight, such as butter,—as if he should say, "I have purchased this wheat, on condition of its being equal to ten bushels,"—or "this butter, on condition of its weighing ten mans,"—and if, having measured or weighed these articles accordingly, he should then take them and sell them to another, on the same condition of measure or weight, in that case it is not lawful for that other to sell or use these articles, until he has measured or weighed them on his own account; because the Prophet has prohibited the sale of wheat until it be measured both by the buyer and the seller: and also, because there is a possibility of these articles exceeding the warranted quantity; in which case the excess, as being the property of the seller, would not be lawful to the purchaser; and an abstinence in the case of this possibility is necessary.—It is otherwise where the sale is made by conjecture, without any condition of measurement; for the excess, in that case, is the right of the purchaser; and it is also otherwise in the sale of cloth by yards, for there likewise the excess is the right of the purchaser; since yards (as has been already explained) are a description of the cloth, and not a quantity, as in the case of articles of weight or measure of capacity.—It is to be observed that the measurement of the cloth

*Arab Akkar; meaning any species of immoveable property. Zimeen is the term used in the Persic version, whence the translator renders it land.

by the seller, previous to the sale, is not valid, although it should have been done in the presence of the purchaser, because the measurement of both the seller and purchaser is required, and these terms are not applicable to the parties until after the sale takes place. So also, the measurement made by the seller after the sale is invalid, unless it be in the presence of the purchaser, because the object of measurement is delivery, and delivery without the presence of the purchaser is impracticable.

It suffices, however, that the article be weighed or measured by the seller, in the purchaser's presence.—IF the seller only should measure the merchandise after the sale, in presence of the purchaser, a question has arisen, whether this be sufficient?—or, whether it be not necessary that the purchaser should also examine it by his own measure?—Some have said that the measurement of it by the seller only, is not sufficient, according to the plain sense of the tradition already quoted. The more approved doctrine, however, is that it is sufficient, since by the measurement of the seller the quantity is ascertained, and delivery completely established. The tradition before quoted alludes to the junction of two contracts; as where, for instance, a person having purchased, measured, and taken possession of a thing afterwards sell it to another: in which case it is necessary that the second purchaser himself measure it; and the measurement of the first purchaser, who stands in the relation of seller to him, is not sufficient, as will hereafter be more fully explained in the chapter of Sillim sales.

In the re-sale of articles of tale or longitudinal measurement, the telling or measuring by the second purchaser is not requisite.—IT is related as an opinion of the two disciples, that articles of tale are analogous to those of longitudinal measurement; that is, if a person having purchased and received articles of this nature on condition of their amounting to a particular number, should afterwards sell them to another on the same condition, there is, in that case, no obligation on that other to enumerate them on his own account, because such articles are not susceptible of ususy.—It is related, also, as an opinion of Haneefa, that articles of tale are similar to those of weight, because in regard to them the receipt of any excess beyond the stipulated number is unlawful to the purchaser; articles of tale are therefore analogous to articles of weight.

A seller may dispose of the price of his goods without having taken possession of it.—ANY deeds of the seller with regard to the price of the merchandise, prior to the actual receipt of it, such as gift, sale, hire, or bequest, is lawful, whether the price be stipulated in money or goods;—because the cause of legality, namely, right of property, is established in the seller; and the act is attended with no unfairness (such as has been shown to exist in the case of selling moveable property prior to the receipt of it), because the price, if expressed in dirms and deenars, is indeterminate, and is therefore incapable of being destroyed; and if it consist of any thing else, still the sale is not invalidated by a destruction, since the value remains due from the seller.—It is otherwise with respect to the article purchased, as the sale of that before receipt of it induces fraud, as was before explained.

The parties are at liberty to make any subsequent addition or abatement, with respect either to the goods or the price; and such addition or abatement are incorporated in the contract.—IT is lawful for the purchaser to make an increase of the price in favour of the seller: and for the seller to make an increase in the merchandise in favour of the purchaser;—and it is also lawful for the seller to make abatement from the price in favour to the purchaser; and this increase or abatement is incorporated in the original contract (that is to say, in case of an increase, the original and additional from the price or the article; and in case of an abatement, what remains after the deduction is the price of the article). Hence, in the first case, the seller possesses a right to the original price, together with the increase superadded to it; and, in the second case, the purchaser has a right to the original merchandise with the increase superadded. Shafei and Ziffer are both of opinion that such increase is a mere act of favour, and therefore cannot be incorporated in the original sale; for, if so, it must necessarily follow that a person gives his own property in exchange for his own property, since, previous to the increase of the price, the article was the property of the purchaser in exchange for the original price; and; consequently, if the increase be made in the price, the property of the purchaser is given in exchange for what was before his property; in the same manner, also, in the second case, as the price, previous to the increase, was the property of the seller, it follows that in increasing the wares; he gives his own property in exchange for his own property.—Neither can an abatement from the price, by the seller, be incorporated with the original contract: but it must rather be considered as an act of favour; because; prior to the abatement, an exchange of the merchandise for the whole of the price had taken place; and it is impossible to set aside any part of the price, since in such case it must follow that a part of the merchandise had no correspondent exchange opposed to it; and this is unlawful

OBJECTION.—This consequence does not follow; because the remaining sum, after the deduction of the abatement is considered as an exchange for the whole of the merchandise.

REPLY.—It is impossible to consider the remainder as an exchange for the whole, because no new contract has taken place with regard to the diminished price, and the old contract relates only to the full price.

The reasoning of our doctors is, that the buyer and seller, by means of the increase and abatement, do only alter the contract from one lawful accident to another lawful accident; and that, as the parties possess the power of annulling the contract, they are, a superiori, entitled to make an alteration in the non-essential properties of it. The case is therefore the same as if the parties should annul an optional power, or stipulate one after the conclusion of the contract.—Now, since it is lawful for the parties to alter the accident of the contract by means of increase or abatement, it follows that such increase or abatement is incorporated with the original contract; because the accident of a thing adheres to that thing, and does not exist abstractedly of itself. It is otherwise where a seller abates the whole price; for such abatement could not be incorporated with the original contract, since in that case a change would take place in regard to what is an essential property, and not an accident of the contract.—It is also to be observed, that from the increase and abatement being incorporated with the original contract, it does not necessarily follow that a person gives his own property in exchange for his own property, because the original contract does as it were related to such increase or abatement.—The advantage of the incorporation of the increase and the abatement in the original contract is evident, in a case of friendly or profitable sale: for if a person sell something by a profitable sale to a purchaser who increases the price in the seller's favour, in that case it is lawful for him [the seller] to charge his profit on the original and the increase united, as, in case of an abatement, on the other hand, his profit must be charged on the residue after the deduction.—The advantage arising from this is also evident in a case of Shaffa: for the person possessing the right of Shaffa is entitled to the subject of the sale, in case of an abatement in exchange for the diminished price.

Objection.—Since the abatement and increase are incorporated with the original contract, it would follow that, in a case of increase: the person possessing the right of Shaffa is to take the subject of the sale at the aggregate amount of the original price, and its increase,—instead of taking it (as is the case) at the original price only.

Reply.—In case of an increase of the price, the proprietor of the right of Shaffa takes the subject of the sale at the original price only, because his right relates to the original price, and it is not in the power of the buyer and seller, by any act of theirs, to annual such right.

The price cannot be increased after the destruction of the goods in the purchaser's hands.—Any increase of the price, after the destruction of the wares in the possession of the purchaser, is not valid (according to the Zahir-Rawayet), because of the wares not having been in a state that admitted of the lawful opposition of an exchange for them.

Objection.—It would appear that the increase of the price remains in force after the destruction of the goods; for although the goods be not then in a state to admit any exchange being opposed to them, yet the increase incorporates with the original contract, which was concluded at a time when the goods being extant, it was lawful to oppose an addition to the exchange for them.

Reply.—If the wares had remained in a condition to admit of an exchange of property for them immediately, then such exchange might have been immediately established, and referred afterwards to the period of forming the contract; for a thing is first established on the instant, and is then referred to the formation of the contract:—but as, in the present instance, the immediate exchange, of the property cannot be established, the wares no longer existing, the reference back is impossible: and hence any increase of the price is evidently invalid—It is otherwise with respect to an abatement of the price after the destruction of the wares, because these, after their destruction, are in a state which admits of a diminution of the price: which is therefore referred to the formation of the contract.

A prompt payment may be commuted for a distant payment.—If a person, having sold something on condition of prompt payment, should afterwards agree to receive the price at a future fixed period, it is lawful, because the price is solely the right of the seller; and as it is in his power, if he choose to forego it altogether, he is consequently entitled, for the convenience and ease of the purchaser, to take a future payment instead of a prompt one, a fortiori.—If the period stipulated be not certain, and the uncertainty be very great (as if he should stipulate payment when the wind blows, for instance), it is not lawful. If the period, on the contrary, be only in a small degree uncertain (as if he should stipulate the payment at the cutting of the corn, or the threshing of it), it is lawful, in the same manner as in the case of bail, of which an explanation has already been given.

In all debts except those incurred by a loan.—Every debt immediately due may be suspended, in its obligation, to a future period, by the creditor, on the principles laid down in the preceding case.—excepting a loan,* the suspension of the obligation of

* Arab, Karz; signifying a loan of money, in opposition to Areeat, which means a loan of anything but money. These deeds are considered, by Mussulmans, to be of a distinct and separate nature. In the one the intention is to destroy the substance of what is borrowed, that is, to spend the identical money received, and afterwards return an equal number of similars. In the other, the intention is to enjoy the usufruct without injuring the substance, which is to be returned in its identical state.

which is not approved.—The reason of this is that the lending of money is, in the immediate act, equivalent to a loan of any other thing,* and an act of benevolence (whence it is that if a person should tender a loan of money to another, expressing his intention by the word Areeat—as if he should say, "I deliver these ten dirms as an Areeat,—it is valid; and also, that no person who is incapable of any gratuitous act, such as an infant or a lunatic, is competent to this deed): but in the end it operates as an exchange, since the borrower gives to the lender an equal sum, but no the identical specie he received —In consideration, therefore, of the immediate act a respite is not binding upon the lender, as there can be no constraint in an act purely gratuitous; and, in consideration of the end, the respite is not approved, for in this case the transaction would resolve itself into a sale of money for money. which is usury,—It is otherwise in the bequest of a loan for a fixed period; for if a person bequeath the loan of one thousand dirms to another, for a year (for instance), the performance of this is incumbent on the executor; nor is he entitled to make any demand on the legatee until the expiration of the term, since this bequest is of a gratuitous nature, and resembles the bequest of the services of a slave, or the use of a house.

CHAPTER VIII.

OF RIBBA, OR USURY.

Definition of the term.—RIBBA, in the language of the LAW, signifies an excess, according to a legal standard of measurement or weight in one of two homogeneous articles [of weight or measurement of capacity] opposed to each other in a contract of exchange, and in which such excess is stipulated as an obligatory condition on one of the parties, without any return,—that is, without anything being opposed to it. The sale, therefore, of two loads of barley (for instance) in exchange for one load of wheat does not constitute usury, since these articles are not homogeneous:—and, on the other hand, the sale of ten yards of Herat cloth in exchange for five yards of Herat cloth is not usury, since, although these articles be homogeneous, still they are not estimable by weight or measurement of capacity.

Usury (occasioned by rate united with species) is unlawful.—USURY is unlawful; and (according to our doctors) is occasioned by rate†, united with species.—Shafei maintains that usury takes place only in things of an esculent nature, or in money.—It is necessary, in order to the operation of the illegality, that the articles be homogeneous; but an equality in point of weight or measurement of capacity annihilates the usury. —It is to be observed that a superiority or inferiority in the quality has no effect in the establishment of the usury; and hence it is lawful to sell a quantity of the better sort of any article in exchange for an equal quanitity of an inferior sort.

It consists in the sale of an article (of weight or measurement of capacity) in exchange for an unequal quantity of the same article.—THE sale, at an unequal rate, of articles of weight or measurement of capacity, in exchange for homogeneous articles, is usurious, according to our doctors, although the articles be of a description not esculent (such as loam or iron, for instance); —because they hold that the cause of usury exists, in articles of weight and measurement of capacity, although they be not of an esculent nature. Shafei maintains that such sale is lawful, agreeably to his tenets with respect to usury. Supposing, however, the equality of the rate, such sale is lawful in the opinion of all the doctors.—(It is to be observed that loam is an article of measurement by capacity, and iron of weight.)

But does not exist where the quantities are not ascertained by some known standard of measurement.—THE sale of anything not measured out according to the legal standard, at an unequal rate, is lawful. Thus it is lawful to sell one handful of wheat in exchange for two handfuls: or two handfuls in exchange for four:—and also, one apple in exchange for two apples; because, in such case, the measurement not having been made according to a legal standard, it follows that a superiority of measurement (which is essential to the establishment of usury) has not according to the rules of measurement, taken place. Shafei maintains that such sale is unlawful; because the article is, in this instance, of an esculent nature, which (according to his tenets) is the efficient cause of usury; and also because the equality destructive of usury does not here exist. (It is to be observed that whatever is less than half of a Saa is considered equivalent to an handful, since the law has fixed no standard of measure beneath that quantity.)

It is occasioned either by an inequality in point of quantity, or by a suspension of repayment; unless the consideration and the return be heterogeneous.—WHERE the quality of being weighable or measurable by capacity, and correspondence of species (being the causes of usury) both exist, the stipulation of inequality, or of a suspension of payment to a future period, are both usurious. Thus it is nsurious to sell either one measure

---

*Literally, "a KARZ is, in its immediate occurrence, equivalent to an AREEAT."

†It may be necessary here to observe that rate, amongst the Mussulmans, applies only to articles of weight or measurement of capacity, and not to articles of longitudinal measurement, such as cloth, or the like.—The phrase here used implies an inequality of RATE with a similarity of SPECIES.

of wheat in exchange for two measures,—or one measure of wheat for one measure deliverable at a future period. If, on the contrary, neither of these circumstances exist (as in the sale of wheat for money), it is lawful either to stipulate a superiority of rate, or the payment at a future period. If, on the other hand, one of these circumstances only exist (as in the sale of wheat for barley, or the sale of one slave for another), then a superiority in the rate may legally be stipulated, but not a suspension in the payment. Thus one measure of wheat may lawfully be sold for two measures of barley, or one slave for two slaves: but it is not lawful to sell one measure of wheat for one measure of barley payable at a future period: nor one slave for another, deliverable at a future period. Shafei is of opinion that correspondence of species alone does not render illegal a suspension of delivery; because where, in an exchange, a prompt delivery is opposed to a future delivery, there is only a semblance of a superiority of rate, founded on the preference given to prompt payment. Now if a superiority of rate, in reality, be not preventive of the legality of the sale (as in the case of one slave for two slaves), it follows that the semblance only of a superiority is not preventive of such legality, a fortiori. The arguments of our doctors are, that wherever either correspondence of species, or the quality of being weighable or measurable exists, the wares are, in one shape, of that description in which usury takes place; and accordingly, a semblance of usury takes place in them, which is repugnant to the legality of the sale in the same manner as actual usury. The ground of this is what is written in the Hadees Shireef, that "articles of different species may be sold in any manner the parties please, provided the bargain be from hand to hand."

Objection.—Since correspondence or species, or the quality of being weighable or measurable does either of them singly prevent the legality of a suspension of delivery, it would follow that a contract of Sillim sale stipulating an exchange of saffron for dirms or deenars, is invalid, as both are articles of weight:—whereas such a sale is valid.

Reply.—The contract is lawful, notwithstanding saffron and deenars be both articles of weight, because they do not agree in the quality of the weight, as saffron is weighed by Mans, and being a subject of sale only, is therefore definite by specification; whereas dirms and deenars are weighed by stones, being only price and not a subject of sale; and therefore do not become definite by specification. In the same manner, also, if a person should sell saffron to another for one hundred dirms, ready money, that other may lawfully employ the said dirms either in purchase or in any other mode without reweighing them:—whereas if a person sell saffron, on condition of its being two Mans, the purchaser is not afterwards at liberty to dispose of it by sale or by any other mode without reweighing it; as holds with respect to all articles of weight or measurement of capacity. Now it being thus demonstrated that the weight of saffron and other articles is different from the weight of dirms and deenars, in appearance, substance, and effect it follows that they do not unite in any circumstance with respect to the quality of the weight; and consequently, that the semblance of usury, in this case, is only an apprehension of a semblance, which is not regarded.

All articles ordained by the Prophet to be articles of measurement, continue so, notwithstanding any alterations of custom;—and the same of all ordained by him to be articles of weight.—Every thing in which the usuriousness of an excess has been established by the Prophet on the ground of measurement of capacity (such as wheat, barley, dates, and salt), is for ever to be considered as of that nature, although mankind should forsake this mode of estimation;—and in the same manner, everything in which the usuriousness of the excess has been established by the Prophet on the ground of weight, continues for ever to be considered as an article of weight, like gold or silver; because the custom of mankind, which regulates the mode of measurement, is of inferior force to the declaration of the Prophet; and a superior cannot yield to an inferior. (Aboo Yoosaf is of opinion that in all things practice or custom ought to prevail, although in opposition to the ordinance of the Prophet; for the ordinance of the Prophet was founded on usage and practice, of his own time:—in ordinances, therefore the prevalant customs among mankind are to be regarded; and as these are liable to alter, they must be attended to, rather than the letter of an ordinance.) If, therefore, a person should sell wheat in exchange for an equal quantity, by weight, or gold in exchange for an equal quantity, by a measurement of capacity, neither of these sales would be lawful (according to Haneefa and Mohammed), although these modes of weighing wheat and measuring gold should become sanctified by the custom of mankind.

All articles referred to any known standard of weight are considered as articles of weight.—Whatever is referred to Ratls is considered as an article of weight, This the compiler of the Hedaya explains to mean that whatever is sold by the Awkiyat* must be considered as an article of weight; for an Awkiyat is a fixed standard of weight in opposition to all other measures of capacity, as none else are standards of weight. Now as everything sold by the Awkiyat comes under the description of an article of weight, it follows that if this thing be sold

*This term has been formerly mentioned to signify an ounce, (See Vol, I. p. 9.) From the context, however, it would appear that it also signifies a measure of capacity.

by the measurement of any other vessel not of a fixed standard of weight, opposed to a similar vessel, such sale is unlawful, because of the probability of a disparity of weight, notwithstanding the equality in point of measurement of capacity: for this, in fact, is the same as if one person should sell one article of weight in exchange for another of the same kind and adjust the quantity by conjecture.

Note concerning Sirf sale.—IT is to be observed that a Sirf sale means the sale of price in exchange for price: and price implies dirms and deenars. In this mode of sale it is a necessary condition that the intercharge of properties take place at the meeting, because the Prophet has ordained the sale of silver in exchange for silver, from hand to hand,—as shall be explained at large in treating of Sillim sale: but in every other article, provided it be of that kind in which ususy takes place (such as wheat in exchange for wheat, for instance) the interchange upon the spot is not a condition, it being only required that the article be specific. Shafei maintains that in the sale of wheat for wheat mutual seisin is a condition, because of the ordinance of the Prophet, "Sell it from hand to hand;" and also because, if one party should make seisin, and not the other, it follows that an appearance of usury takes place inasmuch as prompt payment is superior to future payment. Our doctors argue that wheat, as being a determinate subject of sale, does not, like cloth, stand in need of seisin, since the object of the contract is the attainment of a power over the article, which is fully established by its being determinate. It is otherwise with respect to Sirf sales, for there the seisin is made a condition in order that the price and subject of the sale may be rendered determinate, which is only to be effected by means of seisin. With respect to the ordinance of the Prophet, enjoining the sale from hand to hand, Obadah Bin Samat has explained it to mean the sale of one determinate thing in exchange for another. Besides, on the postponement of the seisin, no loss is reckoned to result, in the opinion of mankind:—contrary to where a prompt and future payment is stipulated: because the latter in the opinion of mankind is a detriment.

Similiar may be sold for each other, without inducing usury.—THE sale of one egg in exchange for two eggs, from hand to hand, is lawful; and the same with respect to dates and walnuts; because these articles are neither subject to measurement of capacity or weight, with regard to which only usury relates. Shafei, in this case, differs from our doctors; because usury, according to his opinion, relates to articles of an esculent nature, of which kind these are.

Usury cannot take place with respect to Faloos, as they are articles of sale.—THE sale of one specific Faloos,* in exchange for two other specific Faloos, is valid, according to Haneefa. Muhammad maintains it to be unlawful; because, as the fitness to constitute price is established in Faloos, with the consent of mankind, it cannot be annulled by any agreement of a seller and purchaser counter thereto, and as the fitness to constitute price still continues the Faloos cannot be rendered determinate by means of a stipulation to that effect in the contract. The case, therefore, becomes the same as if a person should sell one underminate Faloos in exchange for two underminate.—or, as if a person should sell one dirm in exchange for two. The reasoning of the two disciples is that this fitness to constitute price in Faloos cannot subsist with relation to a buyer and seller, unless by their mutual agreement to that effect;* and, consequently, where they agree to the contrary, the fitness to represent price is, with respect to them, null; nor can the general consent of others, to admit Faloos as a representative of price, operate as an argument with respect to them, since in this matter others have no power over them. Hence it follows that, as the fitness to constitute price is, with respect to them, null, the Faloos may be identified by their specification

OBJECTION.—Upon the fitness to constitute price being done away by the agreement of the parties, the Faloos will of consequence revert to their primary nature, namely, weight (for the Faloos was originally a weight).—It would therefore follow that the sale of one Faloos for two Faloos is not valid although the fitness to constitute price be done away by the agreement of the contracting parties.

REPLY.—The Faloos do not revert to their original nature, because, by the agreement of mankind, they are considered as articles of tale, and this agreement remains in force. Hence they stand in the same predicament as walnuts or other articles of tale, and the unequal sale of them is of consequence in the same manner lawful.—It is otherwise with respect to dirms and deenars, because these naturally constitute price.—It is also otherwise with respect to the sale of one undeterminate Faloos in exchange for two undeterminate Faloos; for this is, in fact, a stipulation of future payment and future delivery, a species of sale which has been forbidden by the Prophet.—It is also otherwise where the stipulation of one of the parties relates to undeterminate Faloos, for this is equivalent to a postponement of payment, and such postponement is rendered unlawful by homogeneity alone.

Flour of meal cannot be sold for wheat.—THE sale of wheat in exehange for the flour or meal of wheat is unlawful, because wheat, and the meal and flour of it, are all of one

* A copper coin. (See Vol. II. p 220.)

*That is to say, copper coins are not to be considered as price but by a previous agreement of the parties.

species.—It is impossible, moreover, to ascertain the equality between those articles by measurement, since flour and meal are of a close and compact nature, and what is not. Hence this kind of sale is essentially invalid, even in the exchange of one measure of the one for one measure of the other.

Flour may be sold for flour.—The sale of flour in exchange for flour is valid, provided the quantities be equal by measurement, because the condition of legality (namely, equality) is here established.

But not for meal.—The sale of flour in exchange for meal* is not valid, according to Haneefa, in any mode; neither at an equal, nor at an unequal rate; for as it is not lawful to sell flour in exchange for parched wheat, or meal in exchange for raw wheat, so also it is not lawful to sell either of those articles for the other, because of their homogeneity.—According to the two disciples the sale in question is lawful; because flour and meal are of different species, inasmuch as the object to be derived from each is different; for the object of flour is bread and that of meal is a culinary preparation, mixed up with water or oil.—But the answer to this is that the original object of both is the same, nemely, food; which is not affected in its nature by the modification of it, since raw wheat and parched wheat are considered as of the same species, and likewise wheat affected by vermin and wheat that is whole and preserved,—although, in answering particular objects, these kinds be different.

The sale of flesh for a living animal is not usurious.—The sale of flest in exchange for a living animal is lawful, according to Haneefa and Aboo Yoosaf. Mohammed is of opinion that the sale of flesh in exchange for a living animal of the same species is unlawful, unless the quantity of the dead flesh exceed that of the living flesh, in order that the excess may be opposed in exchange to the other parts of the living animal, independent of flesh; and the remaining part of the slain flesh remain opposed in an equal degree to the living flesh; because otherwise usury must necessarily take place, since, if the quantities of flesh were exactly equal, it must necessarily follow that the other parts of the living animal had no exchange opposed to them;—or if, the quantities of flesh being equal, a deduction be made from the dead flesh, in opposition to the other parts of the living animal, it would necessarily create an inequality in the exchange of flesh for flesh. The sale in question, therefore, resembles a sale of sesame seed in exchange for sesame of, which is unlawful. The arguments of the two disciples in support of their opinion is, that the case in question is in fact the sale of an article of weight for what is not an article of weight; since it is not customary to weigh living animals, it being indeed impracticable to ascertain their weight as they are not at all times of equal weight, an animal being lighter when hungry, and heavier, when filled with food.—It is otherwise with oil-seeds, as by weighing those may at once be ascertained the quantity of oil contained in them when separated from the dregs or refuse.

Nor the sale of fresh dates for dried dates.—The sale of fresh dates in exchange for dried ones is lawful, according to Haneefa. The two disciples hold a different opinion, because of a tradition, in which it is mentioned that a person having interrogated the Prophet regarding the legality of such sale, the Prophet, in return, desired to know whether fresh dates did not diminish in drying?—and upon that person answering in the affirmative, he declared that, such being the case the sale of fresh dates in exchange for dry ones was not lawful. The arguments of Haneefa in support of his opinion are twofold:—First, the word Tammir, expressive of dry dates, is also applicable to fresh dates, because there is a tradition that a person brought some fresh dates from Kheebir to the Prophet, who, on their being presented to him, inquired if all the Tammir of Kheebir were of that kind? and as fresh and dry dates are from this circumstance held to be of the same kind, it follows that the sale of the one in exchange for the other, on condition of an equality in the rate, is lawful, since the Prophet has said, "Sell Tammirs in exchange for Tammirs, at an equal rate."—Secondly, if it be not admitted that fresh dates fall under the appellation of Tammir, still the sale is lawful, because of another saying of the Prophet, "When two things are of different species, then let them be sold in whatever manner the parties please," In regard to the saying quoted by the two disciples, it rests entirely on the authority of Zeyd Ibn Abbas, which is considered weak among the traditionists.—It is to be observed that the same disagreement subsists with respect to the sale of dried and fresh grapes, founded on the same arguments as those already cited. Some have asserted that the sale of dried grapes in exchange for fresh is unlawful, according to all our doctors, grounding this assertion on the analogy which subsists between this case and that of parched and raw wheat, the sale of which in exchange for each other is universally declared to be invalid.

The sale of fresh dates in exchange for fresh dates, at an equal rate in point of measurement of capacity, is lawful, in the opinion of all our doctors.*

---

*Arab. Saveek. A sort of coarse meal prepared either from wheat or barley.—Also, what remains after sifiting off the fine flour,

*The remainder of this case, which is of considerable length, as well as the complete succeeding case, has been omitted in the translation, because the disputations contained in them are founded entirely on verbal criticisms, which do not admit of an intelligible translation.

The sale of the manufactured produce of an article in exchange for a similar article, is usurious, unless it exceed that article in quantity—The sale of olives in exchange for oil of olives is unlawful, excepting when the actual oil is greater in quantity than the oil contained within the olives, in which case the excess being opposed to the dregs that will necessarily remain after the expression of the oil prevents the establishment of usury.—The law is the same with respect to the sale of walnuts for the oil of walnuts, of sesame seeds for the oil of sesame, of milk for butter, or of the juice of the grape or dates in exchange for grapes or dates. With respect to the sale of cotton in exchange for the thread of it there is a difference of opinion. The sale of cotton, however, in exchange for calico is universally allowed to be legal.

One species of flesh may be sold for another species.—It is lawful to sell one species of flesh, in any manner, in exchange for another species of flesh, (such as the flesh of a cow for that of a camel or a goat). It is to be observed that the flesh of a cow and of a buffalo are of the same species, as is also the flesh of a sheep and that of a goat.

The sale of the milk of one animal for an unequal quantity of milk of another species of animal does not induce usury—The milk of a cow and of a goat are of different kinds, and may therefore be lawfully sold in exchange for each other at unequal rates. It is related, as an opinion of Shafei, that these are of the same kind, because the object to be derived from each is the same. But our doctors argue that the flesh of these animals is evidently of a different kind, since it would not be lawful for a person, on whom the gift of a cow in alms was enjoined, to substitute a goat in lieu of a cow if it prove defective; the milk of these animals, therefore, differs in point of species in the same manner as their flesh. It is to be observed that the vinegar of dates is of a different kind from the vinegar of grapes, because of the difference of their oringals. So also, the wool of a sheep is of a different kind from that of a goat, because they answer different objects.

Bread may be sold for flour at an unequal rate—It is lawful to sell bread made of wheat in exchange for wheat, or the flour of wheat, at an unequal weight, because bread is considered either as an article of tale or of weight, and consequently is of a different kind from wheat or flour, which are subject to measurement of capacity—It is related as an opinion of Haneefa, that such sale is utterly invalid: but decrees pass according to the first adjudication, and this, whether the delivery of either the wheat or the bread be stipulated to take place at a future period. According to Haneefa the borrowing of bread is utterly unlawful,—that is whether it be considered as an article of tale or weight,—because there is great difference with respect to cakes of bread; either in respect to themselves, or the workmanship of the baker. According to Mohammed it is absolutely legal; that is, whether the bread be considered as an article of tale or weight. According to Aboo Yoosaf it is lawful, if considered as an article of weight; but not if considered as an article of tale, because of the difference of the unities.

Usury cannot take place between a master and his slave.—Usury cannot take place between a master and his slave, because whatever is in the possession of the slave is the property of the master, so that no sale can possibly take place between them, and hence the impossibility of usury.

Unless the slave be an insolvent Mazoon.—This proceeds upon a supposition of the slave being privileged and free from debt; for in the case of a privileged slave who is insolvent, usury, may take place between him and his master, according to Haneefa, because (agreeably to his tenets) the possessions of such slave do not belong to the master;—and according to the two disciples, because although (agreeably to their tenets, the possessions of such slave be the property of his master, still as the claims of the creditors are connected with them, the slave stands in the same relation to his master as a stranger, and consequently usury may exist in their dealings.

Nor between a Mussulman and infidel in a hostile country.—Usury cannot take place between a Mussulman and a hostile infidel in a hostile country.—This is contrary to the opinion of Aboo Yoosaf and Shafei, who conceive an analogy between the case in question and that of a protected alien within the Mussulman territory. The arguments of our doctors upon this point are twofold. First, the Prophet has said, "There is no usury between a Mussulman and a hostile infidel, in a foreign land.'—Secondly, the property of a hostile infidel being free to the Mussulmans, it follows that it is lawful to take it by whatever mode may be possible, provided there be no deceit used.

It may take place between a protected alien and a Mussulman.—It is otherwise with respect to a protected alien, as his property is not of a neutral nature, but sacred, because of the protection that has been afforded to him.

CHAPTER IX.

OF RIGHTS AND APPENDIX

Definition of rights and appendages, as connected with sale.—The rights of a sale are things essentially necessary to the use of the subject of the sale, such as, in the purchase of a house, the right of passing through the road that leads to it; or, in the purchase of a well, the right of drawing water from it.—Appendages imply things from which an advantage is derived, but in a subordinate degree, such as cook-room, or a drain.

Difference of rights in a purchase, with respect to a Manzil, a Dar, and a Bait.—IF a person purchase a Manzil above which there is another Manzil, he is not entitled to the upper Manzil, unless he have stipulated the purchase of the Manzil "with all its rights, and all its appendages,"—or "with everything great and small upon it, in it, or of it."—If, on the other hand, a person purchase a Bait above which there is another Bait, with a stipulation of all its rights, still he is not entitled to the upper Bait. But if a person purchase a Dar (that is, a serai) with its enclosure, he is entitled to the upper storeys and the offices; because the term Dar signifies a place comprehended within an enclosure, which is considered as the original subject, and of which the upper storey is a dependant part. Bait, on the contrary, simply signifies any place of residence; and as the upper storey of a house is of this nature as well as the under, it cannot be included in the purchase of a Bait, unless by an express specification, since a thing cannot be a dependant of its fellow. A Manzil, on the other hand, is a mean;—that is, it is greater than a Bait, and smaller than a Dar;—for although it comprehends everything necessary to a dwelling-place, still it is deficient in having no place for cattle: a Manzil, therefore is in one respect similar to a Dar, and in another respect similar to a Bait; and hence, from its similarity to a Dar, the upper house is included in virtue of its being a suborhinate part, whenever a specification of the rights is made; and, from its similarity to a Bait, the upper house is not included in the sale, unless a specification of the rights be made.—Some have said that, in the practice of the present age, the upper house is necessarily included in all the above cases; because a Bait (which means a house in the Persian language) does necessarily include the upper storey.

A porch over a road, connected with a house, is not included in the sale of it, unless it be expressly specified.—A PORCH over a road, of which the beams in one end are laid upon a Dar [or house] which is the subject of a sale, and in the other end upon the opposite house, or upon a pillar, is not included in the sale of the house, unless a specification of rights be made in the sale; because the porch covering the road is held to be of the same nature as a road.—The two disciples have observed that if the said porch should form the entrance into the house, it is then virtually included in the sale.

The avenue is not included in the purchase of an apartment of a house—nor wells or drains in the purchase of lands, unless the appendages be expressed in the contract.—IF a person purchase a room [Bait] in the house [Dar] or dwelling-place [Manzil], he is not entitled to the use of the road, unless he have stipulated the rights and appendages, or the great and small belonging to it.—In the same manner, in the sale of land, a well or drain is not included, unless by a specification of the rights or appendages; because they are not considered as a part of the ground: but as a dependant on it.—It is otherwise with respect to a lease, for that virtually includes the well and road without any specification, because the object of a lease is an usufruct, which is not to be obtained but by the use of the road and well; and it is not a custom amongst farmers to rent a road or a well. But the object of a sale may be answered without the necessity of including the road or well, since it is customary, amongst purchasers, to sell and trade with the subjects of their purchase, and to dispose of them into the hands of another; whence an advantage is derived from the transaction, without the road or other appendage being included.

CHAPTER X

OF CLAIM OF RIGHT (RREFERRED BY OTHERS TO THE SUBJECT OF SALE)

A female slave claimed after having produced a child whilst in the purchaser's possession, is, together with her child, the property of the claimant, provided the claim be established by evidence:—but if the claim be supported by the purchaser's acknowledgment only the child is not his property.—IF a female slave, being sold, bring forth a child whilst in the purchaser's possession, and another person afterwards establish, by witnesses, that she was originally his property, and had not belonged to the seller such person is entitled to the female slave, and also to the child.—IF, however, the proof be established by the acknowledgment of the purchaser, the claimant is in this case entitled to the female only, unless he also specifically include the child in the claim, in which case the acknowldgment of the purchaser entitles him to both. The distinction between a case of evidence and a case of acknowledgment is, that testimony is absolute proof, being adapted for the elucidation of the fact. By evidence, therefore, it is manifested that the slave belonged to the claimant ab initio, that is to say, from a time prior to the purchase of her; and as, at that period, the child was a dependant part of her (since it had not issued from the womb), it follows that the claimant has a right to it as well as the mother.—Acknowledgment, on the contrary, is defective proof, since it establishes the right of property of the thing claimed in the claimant, purely from the necessity of veriyfying acknowledgment; because an acknowledgment is a declaration; and if the establishment of the right of poperty did not in any degree take place, the declaration must of course be false.—Now this consequence mav be prevented by the establishment of the right of property at the time of the acknowledgment ; and the child, at that period, not being a dependant part as having issued from the womb, is therefore not included in the property of the claimant.—Some have said that, in case of the establishment by testimony, when the Kazee issues his decree for the claimant to take the slave, the child, from its dependance, is virtually included ; and that there is no necessity for a specification of it in the decree.—Others, again, have said that the specification of the child is an absolutely necessary condition, of which the adjudication in several analogous cases is a clear proof. Thus Mohammed has declared that where the Kazee decrees the original to any person, without having any subordinate parts are not comprehended in the decree. Where, also, in a case of a claim of right to a female slave, purchased by another, the Kazee decrees the slave to the claimant, and it so happens that the child she has brought forth is in the hands of some other person than the purchaser, such child is not comprehended in the decree.

A person selling another as as slave, who afterwards proves to be free, must restore the purchase-money :—or if the alleged slave have excited the purchaser to the bargain, he must restore it in defect of the seller.—If a person purchase a slave, and the slave afterwards prove by witnesses that he is tree notwithstanding that, at the time of concluding the contract, he had said to the purchaser, "purchase me, for I am a slave," —and the seller be present, or absent at a place that is known, the purchaser is entitled to recover the price from him ; but if the seller be absent, and the place of his sojournment unknown, the purchaser is in that case entitled to take the price from the slave, who is to recover the same from the seller whenever it may be in his power.—If on the contrary a person accept of a slave in pawn, on the ground of the slave saying to him, "accept of me in pawn, for I am a slave," and it afterwards appear that he is free, the pawnee is not in that case at liberty to take payment from the slave of the sum due to him, whether the pawner be absent or present but must at all events seek it from the pawner, Aboo Yoosaf holds that the same rule also obtains in the case of sale,—that is, that the purchaser has no right, under any circumstances, to an indemnification from the slave, because he has no right to take the price from any but the seller, or his security,—and the slave is neither of these but merely a liar, which does not superinduce responsibility.—The argument of the two disciples is that, in the case in question, the purchaser engaged in the contract on the sole ground of confiding in the slave's declaration, "purchase me, for I am a slave ;" and hence it follows, that where a slave has been guilty of a deceit, he is liable for the price, in case the recovery from the seller be impracticable, in order that the injury occasioned by his deceit may be removed from the purchaser. The recovery from the seller, however, is impracticable only in case of his being absent at a place which is not known, --As, moreover, sale is a contract of exchange, it is possibie to render the director of it responsible for the consideration (namely, the price), when the subject is lost or destroyed to the purchaser, this being what a contract of sale requires. It is otherwise with respect to pawn, as that is not a contract of exchange, but merely a contract of security for the receipt of the substance of the pawnee's right ; for which reason it is lawful to give a pawn as security for the price, in a Sirf sale, or for the goods, in a Sillim sale, although an exchange with respect to either of these be unlawful ;—in other words, if a pledge should be destroyed whilst in the possession of the pawnee, the pawnee is in that case held to have received the substance of his right ;—whereas, if a contract of pawn were in the nature of a contract of exchange. It would follow that in these cases an exchange for the price in a Sirf sale, or for the goods in a Sillim sale, had been made previous to the seisin and this is unlawful. The person, therefore, who directs others to enter into a contract of pawn cannot be rendered responsible for the debts to which the pawn is opposed, Analogous to this is a case where the master of a slave says to merchants, "trade with this slave of mine, for I have privileged him to trade ;" and the merchants having traded with him accordingly, it becomes afterwards known that the said slave is the property of another ; for in this case the creditors have a right to receive payment of their debts from the master.—It is to be observed that the difficulty, in this case, arises from the tenets of Haneefa, for, according to him, a claim is a necessary condition for the establishment of freedom ; and here a claim is out of the question, since, if the slave, after the acknowledgment of his slavery, should assert a claim to his freedom, he would be guilty of prevarication ; and prevarication is destructive of the validity of a claim. It is therefore impossible that after his own declaration, his freedom should be made apparent ; and hence the statement of this case, according to the tenets of Haneefa, is erroneous.—But, in reply to this objection, some have observed that the proper statement of this case is,—that a person purchases a slave at a time when the slave himself said, "purchase, me for I am a slave," and if afterwards appears that the person so purchased was originally free ; for this statement is strictly agreeable to the tenets of Haneefa, since (according to him) the claim of freedom is required as a condition only in the case of a freedman, and not in that of a person originally free—Others again maintain that the claim o freedom, in this statement of the case also is a necessary condition; and that the prevarication so occasioned is not destructive of the validity of the claim; for generation is a concealed circumstance; and the person not knowing that his mother was free at the time of his generation, he on that account declared himself a slave; but afterwards, attaining a knowledge of his mother's freedom at that period, he therefore claims his freedom —If it be thus stated that, a person having purchased a slave, it afterwards appears that the person so purchased was free, as having been emancipated by his master such statement is correct, as it does not involve prevarication, since the master is empowered to emancipate his slave.—This case is therefore, in fact, the same as if a woman should purchase her divorce from her husband, and should afterwards establish, by witnesses, that previous to such bargain he had divorced her three times; or as if a Mokatib should establish, by witnesses, that previous to the contract of Kitabat his master had emancipated him;—for in both these cases the claim and the evidences are admitted, notwithstanding the prevarication: and so also in the preceding case. The ground of this is that the master being competent to emancipate his slave, he may have done it during his absence, and the slave may afterwards have preferred his claim immediately on its coming to his knowledge; and on this supposition the prevarication is not held to be destructive.

Case of claim to an immoveable property after a composition with respect to it.—If a person claim a right in a house, in an indefinite manner and then compound his claim with the possessor of the house for an hundred dirms, and a third person afterwards prove a right to the whole of the house excepting the quantity of a cubit, for instance, in that case the possessor of the house has no right to any restitution from the person with whom he entered into the composition; because that person, having before made an indefinite claim without explaining the extent of it, may now lawfully declare it to have been the quantity excepted by third person.—If, on the other hand, a person, having claimed the whole of a house, should then compound with the possessor for an hundred dirms, and another person should afterwards lay claim to part of the house, in that case the possessor of the house is entitled to a restitution of a part of the sum he had paid in composition, proportionate to the amount of the second claim.—It is to be observed that a composition of an undefined right for defined property is lawful, because the annulment of an undefined right cannot occasion contention.

Section

Of Fazoolee Beea, or the Sale of the Property of another without his Consent.

A sale contracted without authority may be dissolved by the proprietor of the subject.—If a person sell the property of another without his order, the contract is complete, but it remains with the proprietor either to confirm or dissolve the sale as he pleases Shafei is of opinion that the contract, in this case, is not complete; because it has not issued from a lawful authority; for that is constituted only by property or permission, neither of which exist in this case. The arguments of our doctors are, that such a sale is a transaction of transfer, performed by a competent person with respect to a fit subject: it is therefore indispensable that the contract be regarded as complete; for, besides that there is no injury in this to the proprietor (as he has the prower of dissolving it), it is attended with a great advantage to him, inasmuch as it frees him from the trouble of seeking for a purchaser, settling the price with him, and other matter.—Moreover, it is attended with an advantage to the seller, whose word it preserves sacred, and to the purchaser, to whom it confirms a bargain, with which, as having voluntarily concluded it, he may be supposed to be pleased.—In order, therefore, to obtain these advantages, a legal power is established in the seller of another's property, more especially as the consent of that other has been given by implication, since a wise man naturally assents to a deed attended with advantage to himself.—It is to be observed that if is requisite that the proprietor give his consent on the condition of the subject of the sale, and the buyer and seller being extant; because, as his assent is a deed relative to the contract; it is necessary, of consequence, when he gives it that the contract be in existence; and the existence of the contract depends on the existence of the parties, and of the subject of the sale.

If assented to, the price is the property of the proprietor, and a deposit with the Fazolee seller.—When the proprietor of an article, in a Fazoolee sale, gives his assent to it, the price becomes his property, and remains in the hands of the Fazoolee seller as a deposit, in the same manner as if he had been an agent for sale; because the assent is equivalent to a previous appointment of agency.

Who is at liberty to dissolve the contract without his concurrence.—It is in the power of the Fazoolee, or person who sells the property of another without authority to dissolve the contract without having obtained the consent of the proprietor. It is otherwise in the case of a marriage contracted by a Fazoolee, as that cannot be dissolved without the consent of the person on whose account he concluded it.

It is to be observed that the existence of the parties, and of the subject of the sale, is sufficient towards the consent of the proprietor only in case of the price being in money; for, if it be stipulated in goods, then the existence of the price also is a necessary condition —In this case, however the consent of the proprietor is not an assent to the contract of sale (because the sale is, in this instance, a sort of purchase and a Fazoolee purchase does not rest upon the assent of the person on whose account the Fazoolee made the purchase, inasmuch as the purchase is considered in law to have been made for himself), but merely an assent to the Fazoolee purchaser making over the property he has agreed to give in return for the property which has been constituted the price of it This price, therefore, consisting of goods, becomes the property of the Fazoolee, who remains responsible for the subject of the sale, payable in a similar, if it be of a nature that admits of similars,—or, if otherwise, for the value of it.

If the proprietor should die; then the consent of the heirs is of no efficacy in the confirmation of the Fazoolee sale, in either case; that is, whether the price have been stipulated in money or in goods; because the contract rested entirely on the personal assent of the deceased.

If the proprietor die, and the subject be not specified, the sale is invalid.—If a person, having given his assent to a Fazoolee sale, should afterwards die, and it be not known whether the subject of the sale was extant or not when he gave his assent, in that case (according to one opinion of Aboo Yoosaf, which has been adopted by Mohammed), the sale is valid, because of the probability of the existence of the subject of the sale at the period of assent. Aboo Yoosaf, however, afterwards receded from this opinion, and declared this sale to be unlawful, because of the doubt with regard to the existence of the subject of the sale, which in his opinion is destructive of its legality.

The emancipation, by the original proprietor, of a slave usurped and sold by the usurper, is valid.—If a person usurp a slave, and sell him to another and, that other having emancipated him the original proprietor afterwards confirm the sale, in this case the emancipation, according to Haneefa and Yoosaf, is valid, upon a favourable construction. Mohammed maintains that it is not valid, since an emancipation cannot be made except with relation to property, in conformity with a tradition of the Prophet to that effect; and the purchaser was not proprietor of the slave at the time of the emancipation, because the validity of the sale then rested on the assent of the proprietor; and a suspended sale does not endow with a right of property. Where, moreover, the right of property is confirmed by the master's assent to the sale, it becomes confirmed, first in the usurper and then in the emancipator, by a retrospect and devolution; and a right of property thus confirmed is established in one shape but not in another shape; and manumission is not valid except where the right of property exists in every shape, in conformity with the tradition above cited. Upon this principle it is that emancipation is not lawful where a person, having suurped a slave, gives him his liberty and afterwards makes a retribution to the proprietor;—or, where a person, having purchased a slave, allowing an option to the seller, emancipates him, and afterwards receives from the seller a confirmation of the sale. On the same principle also the sale is unlawful, where a person, having purchased a slave from an usurper, sells him again to another, and the proprietor afterwards confirms the sale of the usurper;—and emancipation is likewise invalid, where a person, having purchased a slave from an usurper, gives him his liberty, and the usurper afterwards makes a retribution to the proprietor. The argument of the two Elders is that, in the case in question, a suspended right of property is established in the purchaser in virtue of an absolute deed instituted for the purpose of enjoyment of property, namely an absolute sale without any stipulation of option; and as, in the establishment of this right of property, no injury results to any one, it follows that the emancipation of the purchaser (which rests upon his right of property), is also established in suspense, in the same manner as the right of property. When, therefore, in virtue of the assent of the proprietor, the right of property operates, it follows that the suspended emancipation also operates;—in the same manner as where a person purchases a slave in pawn from the pawner, and afterwards emancipates him,—in which case the emancipation remains suspended in its operation, as well as the right of property of the purchaser, until the consent of the pawnee be obtained, or the pawn be redeemed by the pawner:—or, as where an heir emancipates a slave belonging to the deceased, at a time when the estate was encumbered with debt,—in which case the emancipation remains suspended in its operation until the debts be liquidated when it immediately takes place. It is otherwise where an usurper, having emancipated the slave he had usurped; afterwards makes a composition with the proprietor; because usurpation does not entitle to the enjoyment of property:—or, where a purchaser of a slave, under a sale stipulating a condition of option to the seller, emancipates the said slave; because in that case the sale is not absolute, and the existence of the option is preventive of the operation of the right of property in the purchaser:—or, lastly, where a person, having purchased a slave from an usurper, sells him to another, and afterwards the original proprietor gives his assent to the sale of the usurper; because in virtue of the assent of the proprietor the right of property vests in the purchase, upon such assent being signified but not before: the right of property, moreover, of the second purchaser was suspended; and consequently, as the right of property vests in the first purchaser now (and not before), it necessarily follows that such suspended right of property becomes null.

The fine incurred for maiming a slave sold under a usurpation goes to the purchaser, if the former proprietor assent to such sale.—

If a person purchase a slave from one who had usurped him, and the slave be maimed* by any person whils in the possession of the purchaser, and he [the purchaser] exact the fine of trespass from the maimer, and the original proprietor then give his assent to the sale,—in this case the fine is the property of the purchaser; because the slave is in such case considered as the property of the purchaser, from the period of the purchase, whence it is evident that he was so at the time of the maiming and this is an argument against he doctrine of Mohammed, exhibited in the preceding case, since as the fine is, in this instance, the right of the purchaser solely in virtue of the establishment of right of property in him from the period of the purchase, it follows that the emancipation of the purchaser would be valid for the same reason. The reply of Mohammed to this is, that a right of property established in one shape only (that is, in an incomplete manner) is sufficient to entitle to a fine, but not to the performance of emancipation, which requires that the right of property be perfect and complete. It is to be observed that although the fine, in this case, be the right of the purchaser, still if it exceed the half of the price, it is requisite that he bestow the excess in charity; because the fine for the destruction of the limb cannot exceed half the price, as the fine of trespass for maiming a freeman is one half of the fine of blood, and consequently, the fine for maining a slave is one half of his value. Now nothing can be included in the responsibility beyond what may be opposed to the price, and implicate in it. Any excess, therefore, over half the price, is an acquisition to which the proprietor is not entitled, or to which his claim is doubtful and is therefore not perfectly lawful to him.

The resale of a slave purchased from a usurper is rendered invalid by the proprietor signifying his assent to the first sale: but if the slave perish in the interim the assent is of no account.—If a person purchase an usurped slave, and sell him to another, and the proprietor afterwards give his assent to the first sale, in that case the second sale is invalid; because the right of property then established in the first purchaser destroys the suspended right of property of the second purchaser, as has been already explained; and also, because there is an unfairness in it, since it is possible that the proprietor may not give his assent to the sale. But if, after the sale of the slave by the purchaser, he should then either die or be killed, and the proprietor afterwards give his assent to the sale, such assent is not valid; because the existence of the subject of the sale is requisite to the assent, and that no longer exists in either instance.

Objection.—The reason here alleged is a valid one where the slave dies a natural death; but it is not so where he is slain, because in that case the slave, in virtue of the existence of the amercement, is considered, as it were, to be himself in existence,—for if a slave, having been sold by a valid contract, should afterwards be murdered whilst in the possession of the seller, still the sale is not null, since the consideration for the subject of the sale (namely the amercement) is extant,—whereas, if he die a natural death in the hands of the seller, the sale is null. It would therefore appear that the assent in case of the murder of the slave, is of no effect.

Reply.—In the case in question it is not possible to consider the fine as the right of the purchaser, since not having been the proprietor of the slave at the period of the murder, he can have no right to the amercement, nor can the slave, in virtue of the existence of the amercement, be considered as extant with respect to him. The slave, therefore, is not extant with relation to him, either actually or virtually. It is otherwise in the case of a valid sale, because there the purchaser had acquired a right of property to the slave which may be transferred to the consideration for him; and consequently the slave may be considered as extant with respect to him.

An article purchased through the medium of an unauthorized person cannot be returned to the proprietor, although the purchaser prove the want of authority, or the proprietor's assent to the sale:—but if the seller avow his not being authorized, the sale is null.—If a person sell a slave, the property of another, and the purchaser establish by witnesses that the seller had acknowledged that he had sold him without the assent of the proprietor,—or, that the proprietor had declared that he had not given his assent to the sale and the purchaser wish to return the slave, the evidence adduced by him is not to be admitted; because there is a prevarication in his plea, since his act of purchasing the slave amounts to a declaration of the validity of the sale, and the plea he afterwards prefers is contradictory of this: his plea, therefore, is not valid; and testimony is to be taken only where the plea it tends to establish of a valid nature. If, however, the seller should declare before a magistrate that he had made the sale without the authority of the proprietor, the sale in that case becomes null, provided the purchaser desire the dissolution of it, because the inconsistency of the purchaser is no bar to the validity of the declaration of the seller, and when the parties both concur in the same wish the sale is rendered null of course:—but the concurrence of the purchaser is a necessary condition. What is here advanced, that "the evidence adduced by the purchaser is not to be admitted," is the doctrine of the Jama Sagheer. The compiler of the Hedaya observes that it is mentioned in the Zeedat, that if a person purchase a female slave (for instance) for one thousand dirms, and take

*By dismemberment of a limb, such as the hand.

possession and pay the price, and afterwards, in consequen e of another person claiming her as his property, and asserting his right to her, surrender her to him,—and he [the purchaser] establish, by witnesses, that the seller had acknowledged that the salve was the porperty of the said claimant, the testimony so given is inadmissible. Between these two cases, therefore, there is an evident contradiction which, however, our modern doctors thus account for, In the case alluded to in the Jama Sagheer, the slave was in the possession of the purchaser when he produced the witnesses ; but in that from the Zeeadat the slave was in the possession of the claimant and not of the purchaser ; and the condition on which a restitution of the purchase-money from the seller is warranted (namely, non-existence of the subject of the sale with relation to the purchaser) not existing in the first case, but existing in the second, the evidence in the first case is therefore rejected, and in the second it is admitted.

In the sale of immovcabe property by an unauthorized person, the seller is not responsible.—If a person sell a house belonging to another, without his permission ; and make delivery of it to the purchaser, and afterwards declare that he had sold it without the permission of the owner, then (according to Haneefa and the last opinion of Aboo Yoosaf) the seller is not responsible* The first opinion of Aboo Yoosaf was that the seller is responsible, and this opinion has been adopted by Mohammed. This case is one of the examples of usurpation over immoveable property, concerning which there is a difference of opinion, as will be fully explained under the head of Usurpations.

CHAPTER XI

OF SILLIM SALES

Definition of Sillim—Kadooree explains Sillim literally to signify, a contract involving a prompt delivery in return for a distant delivery. In the language of the law it means a contract of sale, causing an immediate payment of the price, and admitting a delay in the delivery of the wares. In this kind of sale, the wares are denominated Mooslim-fee-hee,† the price Rasal-Mal,‡ the seller Mooslim-ali-he,§ and the purchaser Rubul Sillim.¶

A Sillim sale is lawful.—A sillim sale is authorized and rendered legal by a particular passage in the Koran, and also by an express declaration of the Prophet prohibiting any one from the sale of what is not in his possession, but authorizing a Sillim sale. It is to be observed that Sillim sale is contrary to analogy, because of the non-existence of the subject of it, since it is a sale of a non-existent article, as the subject, in a Sillim sale, is merely the thing for which the advance is made, and that does not appear, Analogy, however, is abandoned in this instance, because of the text and tradition above cited.

In all articles of weight (except dirms and deenars), measurement of capacity.—A sillim sale, with relation to articles of weight, or measurement of capacity, is lawful; because the Prophet has said : "Whosover enters into a sillim sale with you, let him stipulate a determinate weight and measurement, and a determinate period of delivery." Dirms and deenars, however, are not included in the description of articles of weight, because both of these are representatives of price, and in a Sillim sale it is requisite that the subject of it be otherwise than a representatives of price. Hence if a person should enter into a Sillim sale, stipulating the immediate payment of ten yards of cloth to the seller in lieu of ten dirms to be delivered to him by the seller at a future period, the Sillim sale so contracted is invalid. Some have said that this sale is absolutely null. Others, again, have said that although: considering it as a Sillim sale, it is certainly invalid, still it is not null, since it may be executed so as to answer the views of the parties as far as possible, by considering it simply as a sale of cloth for a price payable hereafter : more especially since, in all contracts, the spirit is what is to be attended to. The former, however, is the better opinion; because, although sales may lawfully be rendered valid in every possible degree, with relation to the things concerned which the parties have contracted, yet as, in the case in question, the things so contracted for are dirms and deenars, which from an express prohibition are incapable of being made the subject of a Sillim sale the contract with relation to them cannot in any degree be rendered valid.

Longitudinal measurement and tale.—A sillim sale with respect to articles of longitudinal measurement, such as cloth, or the like, is lawful, because is it possible to define them exactly by specification of the number of yards in respect to the length and breadth, and the duality and workmanship of it. (By the quality is meant the fineness or coarseness: and by the workmanship the looseness or closeness of the texture.) The specification by a recital of these particulars, moreover, is requisite, in order that ignorance may be avoided : it is therefore essential to the validity of the contract. In the same manner also, a Sillim sale is lawful with respect to all articles of tale, which do not essentially differ in their unities, such as eggs and walnuts; because, in all articles of tale between the unities of which the difference

*Meaning that the proprietor is not to look to the seller for the price of his house, but to the purchaser ;—or, that the seller is not security for the purchaser.

†Literally, the advanced on account of.

‡The capital stock.

§Literally, the advanced to.

¶Literally, the advancer.

is trifling, the rate is ascertainable, the quality definable, and the delivery to the purchaser practicable: a contract of Sillim, therefore; with respect to such articles is lawful: In articles of this nature, also, the great and the small are considered as the same, because mankind have agreed in making no account of the difference. It is otherwise with respect to melons and pomegranates, because the difference in them is considerable. It is to be observed, that where there is a difference in the individuals of any kind it may be known whether such difference be of any accouns or not by the effect it has no the price. Thus articles of which the individuals of the same kind bear a diff rent price are considered as different; but where the price is the same with respect to the individuals they are considered as similar. It is related, as an opinion of Haneefa, that ostrich eggs are not similars, as they bear different prices.

It is to be observed that in the same manner as a Sillim contract is lawful with respect to similars of tale according to number, so is it lawful with respect to them according to a measurement of capacity. Ziffer has said that it is not lawful according to a measurement of capacity, as that does not apply to articles of tale; and it is also a tenet of his, that a Sillim sale with respect to articles of tale is unlawful because of the difference between the individuals of the kind. The reasoning of our doctors is, that quantity is sometimes ascertained by number and sometimes by measurement of capacity; and that similars of the same species being considered as articles of tale only because of the consent and practice of mankind, they may for the same reason be subjected to a measurement of capacity by the consent of the parties. A Sillim sale is likewise lawful with respect to Faloos. Some have said that this is the opinion of the two disciples: but that Mohammed is of a different opinion, since, according to his doctrine, Faloos are representatives of price. The doctrine of the two disciples on this head has been already explained in treating of Usury.

It is not lawful with respect to animals.—A SILLIM sale with respect to animals is unlawful. Shafei deems it lawful, as the article may be ascertained by an explanation of the genus, the age, the species, and the quality: after which only a small difference can take place, in the same manner as in the case of cloth. Our doctors, on the other hand, argue that after such explanations the difference may still be great with respect to various qualities and hidden circumstances, which must occasion a contention: in opposition to the case of cloth, because, as being the workmanship of man, there is rarely any material difference in two pieces of the same kind. Besides, it is recorded in the Nakl Saheeh that the Prophet forbade the Sillim sale of animals: and this prohibition extends to every species of animals, even to sparrows.

Or the parts of animals, or skins, firewood or hay, unless the quality be ascertained.—SILLIM sale is not lawful with respect to the parts of an animal, such as the head, or the feet, because those are not similars of tale, nor is there any measure by which the size of them might be ascertained. In the same manner also, a Sillim sale is unlawful with respect to skins; according to number, or firewood according to bundles, or hay according to packages, except the quantity be ascertained by specifying the length of the string that ties them: for then the Sillim sale with respect to them is lawful, provided the mode of binding be not such as to create a difference.

Nor unless the subject be in continued existence until the time of delivery.—A SILLIM sale is not lawful, unless the subject of it be in existence, from the conclusion of the contract, until the stipulated period of its delivery. Hence the sale is not lawful if the subject be not in existence at the formation of the contract but be extant at the period stipulated for its delivey: or vice versa;—or if, being extant at the formation of the contract, and the time of delivery, it should have been non-existent at some period of the intervening time. Shafei maintains that the existence at the period of delivery is sufficient whether the articles have been extant before or not; because in this case the seller is capable of delivery at the period on which delivery is required. The arguments of our doctors upon this point are twofold.—FIRST, a saying of the Prophet, "Ye shall not sell fruit by way of SILLIM until their ripeness be apparent," which evidently implies that the capability of the delivery from the formation of the contract is necessary. SECONDLY, the capability of delivery is founded on the article being fit to be taken possession of by the puchaser, and it is therefore indispensable that it be in uninterrupted existence from the formation of the contract to the instant of delivery.

If, at the promised period of delivery, the subject of the Sillim be lost or disappear, the purchaser has in that case the option of dissolving the contract, and receiving back the price from the seller,—or of waiting until the subject of the sale may be recovered. This is analogous to the absconding of a slave after the sale of him but before the delivery, in which case the purchaser has the power of either dissolving the contract or waiting unil the slave may be recovered.

It is lawful with respect to articles which although perishable in their nature, are kept in a state of preservation, or in situations where the article may always be had.—A SILLIM sale is lawful with respect to dried and salted fish, provided it be according to a standard weight, and the species be known; because in this case the subject of the sale is of an ascertained nature, the quality is defined, and the delivery is practicable, since such fish is always fit to be taken possession of. This species, of sale, however, is not allowed according to tale, since the individuals amongst fish are not similar:—nor is it allowed with respect to fresh fish,—unless at such a particular period of the year as renders the procurement of them certain, in which a Sillim sale with respect to them, according to a fixed weight, is lawful, provided the species be defined. The reason of this is that fresh fish is not always to be had, being sometimes withheld, in the winter season, in consequence of the water being frozen. In any city however, where fresh fish are always to be procured, a Sillim sale with respect to them is perfectly lawful provided it be according to weight and not by tale.—It is related, as an option of Haneefa, that it is not lawful to make a Sillim sale with regard to the flesh of fish of so large a nature as to occasion their flesh to be cut in the same manner as that of oxen or goats, for instance, because, being illegal with respect to all other animals, it follows that it is likewise so with respect to fish, of which the flesh is equivalent to that of any other creature.

It is not lawful with respect to flesh-meat.—A SILLIM sale of fish is utterly unlawful, according to Haneefa. The two disciples maintain that it is lawful with respect to the flesh of quadrupeds, provided a notification be made of the flesh of known and determinate part (such as the haunch, for instance), and that a description be given of the qualities (such as fatness or leanness, for instance); because in this case the weight of the flesh is determined and the qualities are ascertained,—whence it is that, in case of its destruction, a compensation of a similar is given, and also that it is lawful to borrow it according to weight, and that usury takes place with regard to it. It is otherwise with respect to the flesh of birds, for a Sillim sale of that is unlawful, since it is impossible to specify the flesh of a particular part inasmuch as it is not a custom to separate the parts of birds in sale, because of their smallness. The agrument of Haneefa is that the quantity or flesh is uncertain, because of the difference occasioned by the bones, in regard either to their number or grossness; and also, because of the difference which takes place with respect to the fatness or leanness, as animals are fat or lean according to the seasons; and as this uncertainly is a cause of contention, such sale is therefore inadmissible;—and for the same reason, the Sillim sale of flesh without bones is not lawful. This is approved. With respect to the cases quoted by the two disciples of a compensation of a similar being made for flesh in case of its destruction, and of it being lawful to borrow it, the legality of such compensation, &c., is not admitted: but admitting the legality, still the principle on which the compensation of a similar proceeds is evidently because the retribution of a similar is more equitable than that of money, since money answers only to the object, whereas the similar answers both object and appearance; and the legality of borrowing flesh is because a seisin made by borrowing is an obvious and perceptible one: in opposition to that of a Sillim sale, which rests upon description.

The period of delivery must be specified.—A SILLIM sale is not lawful unless the period for the delivery of the wares be fixed.—Shafei has said that it is lawful in either case (that is whether the period of delivery be fixed or not); since it is recorded in the traditions that the Prophet authorized Sillim sales in an absolute manner, without any restrictions regarding the limitation of the period. The arguments of our doctors upon this point are twofold.—FIRST, the Prophet has ordained that all Sillim sales shall be made with a stipulation of a fixed period for delivery.—SECONDLY, the Prophet has prohibited man from selling what is not in his possession, but has nevertheless authorized and rendered legal Sillim sales, on this principle, that poor people stand in need of such engagements, in order that, by means of the money they receive in advance, they may acquire the subject of the sale, and deliver it to the purchaser. It is therefore requisite that a fixed period be stipulated, because if the seller were liable to an instantaneous delivery on demand, the principle on which the legality of such sale is founded would not be answered. Moreover, an indefinite period is unlawful, because of the uncertainly; in the same manner as in a sale, where the price settled is to be paid at a future period without defining it. It is to be observed that the smallest term that can be fixed for a delivery, in a Sillim sale, is one month.—Some allege the smallest to be three days; others again fixed it any term exceeding half a day. The first opinion is authentic; and decrees are passed accordingly.

Private standards of measurement cannot be used in it.—THE stipulation of a private measure of capacity or longitude is not lawful in a Sillim sale, because of the uncertainty, founded on the possibility of the criterion being lost in the interval between the conclusion of the contract and the delivery; as has been already explained. It is necessary also that the instrument of measurement be of a substance not liable either to contract or expand, but that it be of a fixed nature, such as a large cup. Leathern bags, however (such as those in which [illegible]ter is contained), are allowable for this purpose, according to Aboo Yoosaf, because of the practice of mankind.

It is not lawful under a restriction of the subject to the produce of a particular place.—A SILLIM sale, with respect to the grain of a specific village, or the fruit of a specific orchard, is not lawful; for if any accident should happen to these particular places, the delivery becomes impracticable; such practice has moreover been prohibited by the Prophet.—T[illegible] specification is, however, lawful, acco[illegible]g to some doctors, provided it be to define the quality, as where a specification is made of the grain of Kishmaran in Bokhara, or of Boshakee in Fargana.

And requires that the genus be specified, and that the species, quality quantity, period of delivery, rate and place of delivery, be all determined.—A SILLIM sale is not lawful, according to Haneefa, except on seven conditions. I. That the genus of the subject of the sale be specified, such as wheat or barley. II. That the species of it be fixed, such as wheat of a soil that is watered by means of a canal, or order artificial mode, or wheat of a soil watered by rain. III. That the quality of it be fixed, such as of the best or worst kind. IV. That the quantity of it be fixed according to a standard of weight, or measurement of capacity. V. That the period of the delivery be fixed, according to ordinances in the traditions; VI. That the rate of the capital advanced be fixed, provided it be of a nature definable by a rate, as where it is an article of weight, of measurement of capacity, or of tale,—And, VII. That the place of delivery be fixed, provided the subject of the sale on account of its weight, require porterage.—The two disciples have said, that if the capital to be advanced be present, and exhibited, there is then no need of any mention of the rate; and also, that there is no need of explaining the place of delivery, since the delivery must be made in the place where the contract is concluded. Thus there is a disagreement of opinion with respect to these two conditions between Haneefa and the two disciples.—The argument of the two disciples in support of their former position, is that as the price is present and exhibited the object may be obtained by a reference to it, the case being, in fact, the same as that of cloth stipulated as the price, in a Sillim sale of which specification is not a requisite condition, provided it be produced to view and capable of a reference The arguments of Haneefa are twofold FIRST, as it often happens that many of the dirms and deenars are of a bad kind, and that the purchaser during the meeting is incapable of exchanging them, the seller therefore returns them; and a proportionate deduction being made from the wares, the sale remains extant in a degree proportionate to the sum received by the seller. Now, in this case, and under such circumstance, if the amount of the dirms be not known; it follows that it cannot be known in what extent the Sillim sale exists. SECONDLY, as it sometimes happens that the seller being incapable of acquiring the subject of the sale, is under the necessity of restoring the price, it follows that if this should not have been explained, it is imposible to judge what sum he ought to return.

OBJECTION.—These two suppositions are merely imaginary, and therefore of no weight.

REPLY.—Imaginations, with respect to Sillim sales, are equivalent to realities; because such sales are of but a weak nature, being authorized (as has been already explained) in opposition to analogy. Hence imaginations with respect to them are of weight; and it is necessary that the price be definite with respect to the rate, provided it be of a such a kind as that the contract may relate to rate; but if it be cloth, the specification of a number of a yards is not required as a condition, since these are not considered as a rate, but the description.

As, also (according to Haneefa), an explanation of the rate of the price is an essential condition to the Sillim sale, it follows that (agreeably to his tenets) a sale of this nature is not lawful where the wares, being of different kinds (such as wheat and barley) are opposed to any specific sum (one hundred dirms, for instance), without a separate price being specified in opposition to each of the kinds, because the amount being here opposed generally to both, the particular price of each remains unknown.—In the same manner also, it is not lawful where, the price being of different kinds (such as dirms and deenars), an explanation is given of the quantity of one of these kinds and not of the other; for in this case the contract of Sillim is not lawful in the degree to which an unknown quantity is opposed to it; and consequently, it is also invalid with respect to the degree in which it is opposed to a known quantity, since one contract relates to both. According to the two disciples both these modes of Sillim are lawful, since in their opinion an exhibition of the price without any explanation of the rate is valid.—The argument of the two disciples in support of their second position is, that the place of the contract is fixed for the delivery, because the contract, which is the cause of the delivery, did there take place; the case is therefore the same as that of a borrower or usurper, on each of whom it is incumbent to deliver what he may have borrowed or usurped at the place in which these deeds took place.—The reasoning of Haneefa is, that as the delivery of the subject of a Sillim sale is not immediately incumbent, the place in which the contract is concluded is not absolutely fixed as the place of delivery.—(It is otherwise in cases of loan or usurpation, since the repayment of the loan and the restitution of the usurped article are incumbent upon the instant).—Now as the place of concluding the contract is not necessarily fixed as the place of delivery, it is requisite that some place be specified, as the uncertainty in this particular may otherwise produce a contention, since the price of goods varies in different places: it is therefore indispensable that a place of delivery be specified by the parties Ignorance, moreover, with respect to the place of delivery, is equivalent to uncertainty with respect to the quality of the goods or the quality of the price: and accordingly, some of our modern doctors have said that if a contention arise between the parties with respect to the place of delivery, then, agreeably to the tenets of Heneefa, their oaths must be severally taken: as in the case of a contention regarding the quality of the price:—whereas, agreeably to the tenets of the two disciples, their oaths are not to be taken Others, again, have said that, agreeably to the tenets of Haneefa, their oaths are not to be taken; whereas agreeably to the tenets of the two disciples, their oaths are to be taken because, according to them, the place of delivery is virtually involved in the contract itself, and consequently a contention with respect to it induce the necessity of the oaths of both parties, in the same manner as if it related to the goods of price:—and that the delivery, in the opinion of Haneefa, not being involved in the contract, but existing only as a condition, is therefore equivalent to a condition of option, or a determination of the period of the payment of the price;—and a contention regarding these does not induce the necessity of the oaths of the parties, but is determined by the affirmation of the seller.

It is to be observed that, in the same manner as Haneefa and the two disciples disagree regarding the specification of the place of delivery in a Sillim sale, so also they disagree regarding the specification of a place for the payment of the price (where it is stipulated at a future period),—the specification of a place for the payment of rent,—and also, the specification of a place for the payment of a sum due from a partner in a division of stock An example, with respect to payment of the price, appears where a person purchases anything in exchange for articles of weight or measurement of capacity,—or for some definite price,—in which case, according to Haneefa, it is requisite that the place of payment be specified, provided the price be payable at a future period:—whereas, according to the two disciples, such condition is unnecessary, as the place of concluding the contract is absolutely fixed for the payment.—(Some have said that Haneefa, in this particular coincides with the two disciples. This, however, is erroneous, since it is certain that a difference of opinion obtains, as has been already stated; and such, also, it the opinion of Shimsal-Ayma).—An example, with respect to rent, appears where a person rents a house, a quadruped, or the like, stipulating the price to consist of some article of weight or measurement of capacity, or of some specific article such as is capable of being a debt upon the person,—in which case, according to Haneefa, it is requisite that the place of payment of such rent be particularly mentioned,—whereas, according to the two disciples the mention of it is not requisite, but the house itself is fixed as the place of payment,—or (in case of hire of an animal), the place where the hirer returns the animal to its owner.—An example with respect to a division of property, appears where two persons, jointly possessing a house, agree to divide off their shares, and one of them, having obtained a larger portion than he is entitled to, agrees to compound with the other by the payment of of a particular sum,—in which case, according to Haneefa, the specification of the place of payment is a necessary condition,—whereas, according to the two disciples, this is unnecessary, as the place of concluding the agreement determines the place of payment.

The place of delivery, however, need not be determined with respect to articles which are not of expensive carriage.—If the article for which the advance is made be of such a nature as does not require any expense of porterage, such as musk, camphire, saffron, or small pearls, there is no necessity, according to all our doctors, for fixing the place of delivery: because the difference of place occasions no difference of price; and in this case the delivery must be made where the contract is concluded.—The compiler of the Hedaya remarks that this is the doctrine laid down in the Jama Sagheer, and also in the Mabsoot treating of sales:—but that in the Mabsoot treating of hire it is said that the seller may deliver the goods wherever he pleases,—and this is approved; because the delivery is not immediately due; and also, because, all places in this case being similar, there is no necessity for the particular determination of any. Now, the question is, if the parties agree upon a place of delivery, whether it be absolutely fixed thereby or not.—Some are of opinion that it is not fixed, because in so determining it there is no advantage.—Others, again, maintain that it is fixed thereby, as its being so is advantageous, since the danger of the roads is thereby avoided.

Nor, if a city be mentioned, need the particular street be specified.—If, in case of the goods requiring porterage, a city be fixed on for the delivery, there is then no necessity for specifying the particular street of lane, because a city notwithstanding the variety of its parts, is considered as one place.—Some have said that this proceeds on a supposition of the city not being large;—but that, if its extent be a Farasang,* the specification of a particular part is, in that case, a necessary condition.

The pice must be received at the meeting.—A SILLIM sale is not valid unless the seller receive the price in the meeting, prior to a separation from the purchaser; because if the price be stipulated in money, it would otherwise follow that one bebt is opposed to another debt; a practice which has been prohibited by the Prophet;—or, if the price be stipulated in wares, it is invalid, because the characteristic of Sillim is "a prompt receipt of something in lieu of something to be given," which would not be established if a prompt delivery of the price did not take place. Besidos, the payment of the price is necessary to enable the seller to acquire the goods, that he may become capable of delivery:—and hence lawyers have said that a Sillim sale, containing a condition of option in favour of both or one of the parties, is invalid, because a condition of option is

* A league, about 18,000 feet, of 31/2 miles in length,

a bar to the completion of the seisin, inasmuch as it prevents the conclusion of the contract in regard to its effect, namely, the establishment of right of property:—and also, that the purchaser has no option of inspection, because it is vain and useless: since the goods are a debt due from the seller, and consequently undetermined; whereas a thing seen becomes determined.—It is otherwise with respect to an option of defect; because that is no bar to seisin;—and hence, if such a stipulation be made, and the parties annul it before the close of the meeting, and the seller be in possession of the price, such Sillim sale is valid; in opposition to the opinion of Ziffer.

Whence, if a debt owing from the seller to the purchaser be considered as part of it, the sale is invalid in that proportion.—If a person purchase a Koor* of wheat, by a Sillim contract, for two hundred dirms, and, the seller being indebted to him one hundred dirms, he [the purchaser] make the advance by immediately paying to him [the seller] one hundred dirms, and opposing the debt of one hundred dirms to the remainder,—in that case the contract is invalid in the amount of the debt of one hundred dirms,—because a present seisin is not made of them; but it is valid in the amount of the one hundred dirms paid down, because of the observance of the conditions of legality with respect to that proportion, and because it is not affected by the invalidity of the other proportion, as such invalidity is supervenient, the sale being valid originally; and hence, if the purchaser in this case, should pay down one hundred dirms on account of the debt before the end of the meeting, the sale becomes valid; but as, in the present instance, the purchaser does not pay off his debt, but merely opposes a clearance of his debt in lieu of ready payment of one hundred dirms, and the contracting parties separate from the meeting, the sale is therefore invalid in that degree.—The reason of this is, that if a debt be established as the price, in a contract of sale, still that is not absolutely fixed as the price (whence if a person purchase goods in exchange for a debt due to him by the seller of the goods, and both parties afterwards agree that the debt was not due, yet the sale does not become null); and since the debt is not absolutely fixed as the price, so as to be capable of constituting capital stock, it follows that the contract, in such case, does originally take place, and afterwards becomes invalid from that circumstance.

But it cannot be disposed of by the seller until he take possession of it.—It is not lawful for the seller to convert to use, or, by deed, to dispose of the price advanced, in a Sillim sale (as if he should sell it, for instance), prior to his seisin of it, because in this case the seisin of the price, which is an essential condition in a Sillim sale, would be defeated.

Nor can the purchaser perform any act with respect to the goods, until he receive them.—In the same manner, also, it is unlawful for a purchaser, in a Sillim sale, to perform any act with respect to the goods, previous to the receipt of them; because an act with relation to the subject of a sale previous to the seisin is unlawful.—For the same reason, also, it is unlawful for the purchaser, prior to seisin, to admit another to a share in the goods, or to dispose of them at prime cost.

In a dissolution of Sillim the stock cannot be applied to the purchase of any thing from the seller until it be first received back.—If both parties agree to dissolve a contract of Sillim, the purchaser is not, in that case, entitled to accept or purchase any thing from the seller in exchange for the stock he has advanced, until he has first received it back complete; because the Prophet has said, "Where ye dissolve a contract of sale upon which an advance has been made, take not from him to whom ye have paid the advance any thing except that which ye have advanced to him;"—and also, because, as the capital advanced, in this instance, is resembling and like unto the subject of the sale, it follows that any act with respect to it, previous to seisin, is invalid.—The reason why the capital advanced resembles the subject of the sale is, that a dissolution is equivalent to a new sale with relation to a third person (that is, to any other than the parties themselves) and it is therefore necessary that the subject of the sale be extant. Now it is impossible that the goods contracted to be provided can be considered as the subject of the sale, since they are not extant; it is therefore necessary to consider the price in that light; and this consequently becomes as debt due by the seller, in the same manner as the goods were.

Objection.—Since a dissolution is equivalent to a new contract, similar to the first, it would follow that it is indispensable that the advanced capital be received back by the purchaser at the meeting in which the dissolution is determined on, in the same manner as it is requisite that it be advanced to the seller at the time of concluding the contract; whereas it is otherwise.

Reply.—It is not indispensable that this be received back at the interview of dissolution, because the dissolution is not in all respects similar to the first contract.

Concerning the case in question Ziffer has given a different opinion, for, according to him, any deed relating to the price, previous to the seisin, is lawful:—but the reasoning above stated is a sufficient refutation of this opinion.

An article subsequently purchased, and made over in fulfilment of a Sillin sale, is not held to be delivered.—If a person sell a Koor of wheat by a Sillim sale, and after-

* A dry Babylonish measure of 7,10) lib—(See Richardson's Dictionary.)

wards, when the period of delivery arrives purchase the same from another, and then desire the purchaser to receive it from that other in discharge of his claim upon him: and the purchaser accordingly take possession of the same, still he is not considered to have made seisin of the subject of the Sillim sale, and consequently, if the wheat be lost or destroyed whilst in his possession, the seller is responsible for the same.

Unless the purchaser receive it first on behalf of the seller, and then make seisin of it on his own account, by two distinct measurements.—But if the seller should have desired him to receive it first on his [the seller's] account, and afterwards on his own account, and the purchaser accordingly, first measure it out and receive it on account of the seller, and afterwards measure it out and receive it on his own account, the subject of the Sillim sale is in that case delivered, and the purchaser becomes completely seised of the same. The reason of this is, that there is here a conjunction of two contracts: first, the Sillim sale: and, secondly, the sale between the seller of the Sillim sale and the third person: and it is a necessary condition that the measurement take place in both, because the Prophet has prohibited the sale of wheat until the measure both of the purchaser and the seller shall have been applied to it; and this prohibition (as has been already explained) evidently alludes to the conjunction of two contracts, such as in the case in question.

Objection.—As the Sillim sale is previous to the purchase of wheat made by the Sillim seller, it follows that the two contracts are not conjoined.

Reply.—The Sillim contract is antecedent, but the seisin of the subject of it is posterior;—and the seision here is equivalent to a sale de novo; because; although the subject of the Sillim sale was a debt incumbent on the seller, and what the purchaser had received was determinate thing, and consequently, in reality, different from a debt yet they are in this ease considered as one and the same thing, lest it should follow that the exchange of the subject of a Sillim sale has been made previous to the seisin of it; for if they were to be considered as two things, it would follow that the subject of the Sillim sale prior to the seisin of it was given in exchange for what the purchaser made seisin of namely, a determinate thing and not a debt.—Now since the seisin is proved to be in the nature of sale de novo, it follows that two contracts are conjoined, namely, the purchase of the wheat by the Sillim seller, and the seisin of it by the Sillim purchaser, which is equivalent to a sale de novo, that is, the case is the same as if the Sillim seller, having purchased it from the purchaser, were to re-sell it to the Sillim purchaser.

A second measurement is not required in a similar receipt of article by a lender.—If a person, indebted to another in a Koor of wheat, not on account of a Sillim sale,* but on account of a loan, should purchase a Koor of wheat from another, and then desire his creditor to receive the same from the other, in lieu of what he had borrowed, and the creditor, having measured out the same, should accordingly take possession of it such seisin is valid, and a re-payment of the loan is established; because a loan of indefinite property [Karz] is equivalent to a loan of specific property [Areaat],—and hence the Koor of wheat so measured and received by the lender may be said to be his actual right, for which reason the transaction is not regarded as a conjunction of two contracts [with respect to one subject], and it is consequently not requisite that the wheat be measured a second time.

If the seller measure the article, on behalf of the purchaser, in his absence, it is not a delivery—although it be measured into the purchaser's sack.—If a person, having purchased a Koor of wheat by a Sillim sale, should order the seller to measure it and put it into his (the purchaser's) sack, and the seller having accordingly measured it out should put it into the sack at a time when the purchaser is not himself present, in this case a delivery of the goods is not held to have taken place (insomuch that if the wheat should in that situation be destroyed, the loss falls entirely on the seller); because the purchaser, in a Sillim sale, does not become proprietor of the article, for which he makes the advance, until actual seisin, as his rigt is of an indefinite nature and not determinate: now the wheat, in the case in question, is a determinate article, and hence the order given to the seller by the purchaser to measure it out was not valid—since the order of a director is of no account except with respect to his own property.—Thus the seller, as it were, borrowed the sack of the purchser, and put wheat which was his own property into it;—in the same manner as if a person, having a debt of some dirms due to him by another, should give his purse to the debtor and desire him to weigh the dirms and put them into it; in which case if the debtor act accordingly, still the creditor does not by the performance of this act become seised of those dirms.—If, on the contray, a person, having purchased wheat that is determinate and present, should direct the seller to measure it, and put it into his [the purchaser's] sack, and the seller act accordingly, at a time when the purchaser is absent, the purchaser is nevertheless seised of the same in virtue of that act, because his directions to the seller were efficient, as the property of the wheat had vested in him in consequence of his purchase of it.—Hence it appears that in a common sale the purchaser becomes proprietor of the article previous to the seisin,—

* That is, as an article for which he had received an advance.]

whereas, in a Sillim sale, the right of property does not vest until after the seisin.—Hence, also, in a Sillim sale, if the purchaser desire the seller to grind the wheat, put in the manner above recited into his bag, the flour is the property of the seller;—whereas, if the same were to be done in case of a common sale, it would be the property of the purchaser. In the same manner, also. if the purchaser should desire the seller to throw the wheat into the river, and he act accordingly, then, in a Sillim sale, the loss would result to the seller,—whereas, in a common sale it would fall upon the purchaser, and he would remain responsible for the price, since his order was efficient. Hence, in the Rawayet-Saheeh, it is declared to be sufficient that the seller, by the direction of the purchaser, measure out the article and put it into the purchaser's sack; and there is no necessity for another measurement, since in this case the seller acts as agent for measurement to the purchaser; and the seision is completely established, because of the falling of the wheat into the purchaser's sack.

And so also if it be measured by the seller into his own sack, at the purchaser's instance. although the purchaser be present.—If a person purchase wheat, and direct the seller to measure it out and put it into his own sack, and the seller act accordingly, the purchaser is not seised of it, inasmuch as he borrowed the sack of the seller without taking possession of it, and consequently does not become seised of its contents.—The case is therefore the sams as if the purchaser had directed the seller to measure out the wheat and place it in a particular corner of his own house, which being completely in the possession of the seller, the purchaser cannot consequently be seised of anything in it.

Case of delivery of a determinate article in the same parcel with an undeterminate article.—If sn undeterminate and a specific thing be joined together, by a person (for instance) purchasing a specific Koor of wheat, and also entering into a Sillim contract for another Koor of the same (the former of which is specific and the latter undeterminate), and then directing the seller to measure out both into his own sack, in that case, if the seller first measure the specific wheat into the sack, and afterwards the undeterminate wheat. the purchaser is seised of both the measures of wheat;—of the determinate wheat because his directions to the seller with respect to it were efficient, as it was his undoubted property;—and of the undeterminate wheat because, upon the seller measuring it out, and placing it in the bag, it then becomes implicated with the property of the purchaser, and on account of such implication the purchaser becomes seised of it.—The case therefore is analogous to where a person, having solicited the loan of some wheat, desires the lender to scatter it on his (the borrower's) ground,—or, where a person consigns his ring to a jeweller with directions to add to it more gold, to the weight of half a deenar;—for in both these cases the seisin takes place immediately on the implication with the property.—If, on the contrary, in the case in question, the seller first measure out the undeterminate wheat, and place it in the purchaser's sack. and afterwards the specific wheat, the purchaser does not become seised of either; because his directions to measure out the undeterminate wheat were not efficient, and consepuently the property of it remained with the seller, as before:—and having afterwards mixed the determinate wheat with his own property, he thereby destroys and annuls the right of property of the other.—This is founded on the doctrine of Haneefa, according to whom the implication of the property of another with one's own is destructive of the right of property of that other: and on this principle he holds the sale with respect to the determinate wheat to be dissolved.

Rejection.—The above implication is with the consent of the purchaser, since it was by the order that seller made the measurement, and hence the sale ought not in this case to be dissolved.

Reply.—The implication is not made with the consent of the purchaser, since there is a probability that his object was that the specific wheat should first be measured out.

What is here advanced is founded on the doctrine of Haneefa, as above stated. The two disciples are of opinion that the purchaser has the option of either dissolving the sale or sharing with the seller in the mixed property: because, according to them, the implication of the property of another with one's own is not in all cases destructive of the right of property of that other.

If the contract be dissolved, and the article advanced perish before restitution, the seller is responsible.—If a person purchase a Koor of wheat by a Sillim contract, making a female slave the price advanced, and after the seller taking possession of the slave the parties dissolve the contract, and the slave afterwards die whilst yet in the possession of the seller, in this case the seller is responsible for the value she bore on the day of seisin.—If, also, the dissolution be made after the death of the female slave, it is valid, and the seller in the same manner remains responsible for the value at the period of seisin.—The reason of this is that the validity of a dissolution rests upon the existence of the contract, and that, again, rests upon the existence of the subject of it: now in a contract of Sillim, the article advanced for is the subject of the contract; and as that, in the case in question, still continues in existence, it follows that the dissolution is valid:—and the dissolution being valid, and the contract of Sillim consequently cancelled with respect to the article advanced for, it follows that it is also cancelled with respect to the slave (being the price paid in advance), as a dependant of the article advanced for, although it be not valid with respect to the slave, orginally, because of her non-existence, since there are many things which; although not valid originally, are yet so dependantly.—The contract, therefore, being cancelled with respect to the slave, it becomes incumbent upon the seller to return her; but as this is impracticable, he must pay her value

The dissolution of a sale is rendered invalid by the article perishing before restitution.—If a person, having purchased a slave, should agree with the seller to dissolve the bargain, and the slave afterwards die in his possession, the dissolution is invalid;—or, if the slave die first, and the parties then agree to dissolve the contract, in this case also the dissolution is invalid;—because, the slave being the subject of the sale, and his death of consequence destroying the existence of the contract, the dissolution is therefore invalid from the beginning in the second case, and becomes invalid in the end in the first case,—as the subject no longer remains. It is otherwise in a case of Beea Mookayeza, or barter; because a dissolution in that case is valid after the decay or destruction of one of the articles; since either of them being capable of becoming the subject of the sale, the existing one is therefore considered as such.

In a dispute with respect to the value of the subject, the assertion of the seller (upon oath) must be credited.—If a person enter into a contract of Sillim for a Koor of wheat, at the rate of ten dirms and the seller afterwards assert that "he had agreed for wheat of an inferior sort," and the purchaser deny this, asserting "the stipulation of wheat was made in an absolute manner, and therefore the contract is invalid," in such case the assertion of the seller, corroborated by an oath, must be credited, since he pleads the validity of the contract, by virtue of the declaration of a condition of it; and the assertion of the purchaser, notwithstanding his denial of validity of the contract, is not credited, because it tends to a destruction of his own right, since it is a custom, in Sillim sales, that the goods advanced for the superior to the sum advanced.—If a vice versa disagreement take place between the parties, the learned say that agreeably to the doctrine of Haneefa, the assertion of the purchaser is credited, since he claims the validity of the contract.—According to the two disciples, the assertion of the seller is credited in both cases, as he is the defendant in both, notwithstanding that, in the latter, he deny the validity of the contract. This will be more fully explained hereafter.

If the seller deny the appointment of a period of delivery, the assertion of the purchaser, fixing that period, must be credited. If a disagreement take place between the parties to a Sillim sale, by the seller asserting that a period of delivery had not been determined in the contract, and the purchaser asserting that it had, the assertion of the purchaser must be credited, because a determination of a period for delivery is a right of the seller, and his denial is therefore wilful injury to himself.

Objection.—The seller denies the determination of a period for delivery from a view to his own advantage; since such denial is the cause of annulling the contract, by which means he obtains the property of the goods he had engaged to deliver. Hence his denial is advantageous and not injurious to himself.

Reply.—The invalidity of a Sillim contract, because of the period of delivery being underminate, is not certain, since our doctors have disagreed on this point. The advantage, therefore, in this view, is of no account;—whereas the advantage to the seller, from the determination of such period, being obvious, his denial of it thereupon is an injury to himself,—It is otherwise in the case of a disagreement between the parties with regard to the existence of a condition concerning the quality of the article; because in that instance the invalidity of the contract, from a want of a definition of the quality, is certain

If on the other hand, the seller assert that the period had been determined, and the purchaser deny this, in that case, according to the two disciples, the assertion of the purchaser must be credited, because he denies the right which the seller claim from him, although, at the same time, he deny the validity of the contract;—in the same manner as holds with respect to the proprietor of the stock in a contract of Mozaribat;—that is to say, if the proprietor of the stock were to say to his Mozarib, or manager, "I stipulated that a half of the profit shall go to you excepting ten dirms;" and the manager deny this, and assert that he had stipulated a half of the profit in his favour, in this case the assertion of the proprietor of the stock is credited, since he denies the claim of right of the agent, notwithstanding he thereby at the same time deny the validity of the contract between them.—Haneefa says that, in the case in question, the assertion of the seller is to be credited, because he claims the validity of the contract. Besides, the purchaser and seller both agree in their having made a Sillim contract, and consequently they both apparently agree in the validity of it:—but, again, the purchaser, in denying the assertion of the seller, denies the validity of the contract, which is the denial of a thing he at the same time admits, and is consequently not worthy of credit.—It is otherwise in the case of Mozaribat, because a contract of Mozaribat is not binding upon either the manager or the owner of the stock, since the manager may refuse the execution of the Mozaribat at any time, and the constituent may dismiss him when he pleases. such a disagreement, therefore, in the case of Mozaribat, is of no consequence, the plea of invalidity, in this instance, amounting, in fact, to nothing more than a refusal to carry the contract into execution, which it is lawful for either party to do. There remains, therefore only the claim to profit on the part of the manager; and as this is opposed by the proprietor of the stock, his declaration must consequently be credited.—A Sillim contract, on the contrary, is absolute, and therefore of a different nature.

From the above discussion it appears to be a general rule that the assertion of a person who denies his own right, and not the right of another upon him, is not credited in the opinion of all our doctors:—and that whoever pleads the validity of a contract must be credited in his assertion, according to Haneefa, provided both parties be agreed in the uniformity of the contract, such as that of Sillim, which, whether valid or invalid, is of an uniform nature; in opposition to Mozaribat, which, in case of its validity, is a contract of participated profit, and in case of its invalidity is merely a contract of hire.—The two scholars are of opinion that, in the case in question, the assertion of the defendant must be credited, notwithstanding he thereby deny the validity of the contract.

In Sillim sales of price goods all the qualities must be particularly specified.—If a person enter into a Sillim contract with respect to cloth, describing its length, breadth, and quality of fineness or coarseness, such sale is valid, because it is a contract of Sillim which relates to a known thing, and of which the delivery is practicable. If the subject of the sale be a piece of silk stuff, it is necessary, in addition, to settle the weight that also being an object in this instance.

Sillim sale is not valid in shells, or jewels; but it is valid in small pearls sold by weight.—A sillim sale of jewels or marine shells is not lawful, because the unities of these vary in their value.

A sillim sale of small pearls that are sold according to weight is lawful, as the weight ascertains the subject of the sale.

In bricks.—There is no impropriety in a sale of bricks, whether they be in a wet or dry state, provided a description be given of the mould in which they are formed, because bricks, in their unities, are of a similar nature, more especially where their mould is described.

And (in short) in all articles which admit a general description of quality, and ascertainment of quantity.—In short, everything of which it is possible to comprise a description of the qualities, and a knowledge of the quantity, is a fit subject of Sillim sale, as it cannot occasion contention; on the other hand, a Sillim sale is not lawful with respect to things incapable of being defined by a description of quality or quantity; because the subject of a Sillim sale is a debt due by the seller; and if its quality be not known there consequently exists a degree of uncertainty, from which a contention must arise.

Or which are particularly defined.—There is no impropriety in a Sillim sale of pots or vessels for boiling water, or of boots, or the like, provided these articles be particularly defined, because the conditions essential to the validity of a Sillim sale are here observed:—but if the articles be not defined, the sale is absolutely invalid, the subject of the sale being in such case an undefined debt. It is also lawful to bespeak any of these articles from the workman without fixing the period of delivery.—Thus if a person should desire a boot-maker to make boots on his account, of a particular size and quality, such agreement is lawful, on a favourable construction, founded on the usage and practice of mankind, although it be unlawful by analogy, as being the sale of a nonentity, which is prohibited.

Articles bespoke from the manufacture, in a contract of Sillim are considered as entities—It is to be observed that a contract for workmanship is a sale and not merely a promise. This is approved. The subject of the sale moreover, in such case, although in reality a nonentity, is yet considered, in effect, as an entity; and the thing upon which the contract rests is considered as a substance (that is, as boots, for instance), and not as the work of a manufacturer in an abstracted manner;—and accordingly, if the manufacturer bring boots that had been worked by another, or boots which he had himself worked prior to the contract, and the person who had bespoke them should approve of the same, the contract is legally fulfilled—Besides, articles that are bespoken are not determined for the person who bespoke them until he approve of them: and hence, if the workman should sell them to another before he had shown them to this person, it is lawful.—All this is approved.

And may be rejected, if dissaproved, upon delivery.—Whosoever bespeaks goods of a workman has the option of taking or rejecting them, because of his having purchased articles which he has not seen—The workman, however, has no option, insomuch that the person who bespoke them may, if he please, take them from him by force.—This is recorded by Mohammed, in the Mabsoot, and is the most authentic doctrine.—It is related, however, as an opinion of Haneefa, that the workman also has an option, inasmuch as it is impossible for him to furnish the articles bespoken without detriment, since, in order to make boots (for instance), it is necessary to purchase hides, and instruments to cut them, and this is not free from loss.—It is related, as an opinion of Aboo Yoosaf, that neither party possesses an option; for the workman, as being the seller, is not entitled to an option,—in the same manner as, in a sale of goods unseen, the seller hath no option; and with regard to the person who bespeaks the goods, if an option were given to him it would be an injury to the seller, since if he rejected the goods other people might not choose to purchase them for the value; as where, for instance, a commander of high rank bespeaks goods, and the workman accordingly makes them in a style suitable to his rank and he afterwards rejects them; in which case the common rank of people would not purchase them for their value.

An engagement with a manufacturer to furnish goods which it is not customary to bespeak is not valid.—A CONTRACT with a workman for the furnishing of goods is not lawful with respect to such articles as it is not customary among mankind to bespeak,—as cloth (for instance), because the bespeaking of goods is in itself unlawful, and is therefore admitted by the law only so far as it is authorized by the custom of mankind, which is considered as a necessary instrument of its legality.—It is also requisite, in bespeaking articles authorized by the custom of mankind, to discribe their quality, in order to enable the workman to furnish them accordingly; and unless such description be given the contract is unlawful.—It is to be observed that the prohibition of a stipulation of period for delivery, as recited in the first of these cases relative to contracts of this kind, proceeds upon this ground, that if a period were stipulated in a contract for the supply of work of articles authorized by custom, and the price paid immediately to the workman, it would then become a Sillim sale in the opinion of Aboo Yoosaf: in opposition to that, however, of the two disciples, who hold that it would still remain merely a contract for the supply of work:—but if the period should be stipulated in the case of articles not authorized by custom it then becomes a Sillim sale in the opinions of all our doctors.—The reasoning of the two disciples in support of their opinion in the first case, is that the word Istsina literally means a requisition of workmanship, and ought of consequence to be used in that sence, so long as the context does not determinate it to some other sense.

OBJECTION.—The stipulation of a period is a context which clearly indicates that Istsina is to be taken in a sense different from its literal meaning; and that is to be understood as implying a Sillim agreement; otherwise what need for the stipulation of a period?—It would therefore appear that in such a case it amounts to a Sillim.

REPLY.—The stipulation of a period, as in the first case, is not a convincing argument that the word Istsina is not to be taken in its literal sense, but ought to be understood as implying an agreement of Sillim; because the stipulation of a period may be supposed to have been made with a view to expedition—and it may be supposed that the object of the bespeaker, in fixing a period, was to prevent delays: in opposition to the case of things not authorized by custom, for there a contract for a supply of workmanship, as being invalid is construed to mean a Sillim sale, which is lawful.

The reasoning of Huneefa is that, when a period is stipulated, it fixes the subject of the sale to be debt, because periods are not fixed except with regard to debts; and the subject being proved to be a debt, the construction of the contract into a Sillim sale is easy and natural. It is therefore construed to be a Sillim sale, which is lawful, in the opinion of all our doctors, beyond a doubt: whereas, there is a doubt with respect to the other, since practice means the deeds of all people of all countries, and this can never be known with certainty: as therefore, the legality of a sillim sale is certain, and practice is not free from doubt, it follows that it is preferable to construe acontract for a supply of work to mean a contract of Sillim.

Section

Miscellaneous Cases.

It is lawful to sell dogs or hawks.—IT is lawful to sell a dog or a hawk, whether trained or otherwise It is related, as an opnion of Aboo Yoosaf, that the sale of a dog that bites is not lawful,—and Shafei has said that the sale of a dog is absolutely illegal; because the Prophet has declared "the wages of whoredom, and the price of a dog, are in the number of prohibited things;" and also, because a dog is actual filth, and therefore deserving of abhorrence; whereas the legality of sale entitles the subject of it to respect; and is consequently incompatible with the nature of a dog. The arguments of our doctors upon this point are twofold FIRST the Prophet has prohibited the sale of dogs, excepting such as are trained to hunt or to watch'—SECONDLY, dogs are a species of property, inasmuch as they are capable of yielding profit by means of hunting and watching; and being property, they are therefore fit subjects of sale; in opposition to the case of noxious animals, such as snakes or scorpions, which are not capable of yielding use. With respect to the tradition quoted by Shafei, it applies to the infancy of Islam, at which period the Prophet prohibited every one from eating the price of a dog, in order to restrain men from a fondness for dogs, as it was then a custom to keep dogs of breed, and to suffer them to sleep on the same carpet But when this custom fell into disuse, and men abstained from a fondness for dogs, the Prophet ordained the sale of them. With respect to the assertion of Shafei, that dogs are actual filth, it is not admitted; but admitting this, still it follows that the eating, and not the selling of them is unlawful.

It is not lawful to sell wine or pork.—THE sale of wine or pork is not lawful; because, in the same manner as the Prophet has prohibited the eating or drinking of these, so also has he prohibited the sale of them, or the eating of the price of them; and also, because these are not substantial property with regard to Mussulmans, as has been before frequently explained.

Rules with respect to Zimmees in sale.

Zimmees, in purchase and sale, are the same as Mussulmans :—because the Prophet has said "Be regardful of Zimmees, for they are entitled to the same right, and subject to the same rules with Mussulmans !"—and also because, being under the same necessities, in the transaction of their concerns, as Mussulmans, they stand in need of the same immunities. They are therefore the same as Mussulman, with respect to purchase and sale,—excepting, however, in the sale of wine and pork, which is lawful to them, as the sale of wine, by them, is considered in the same light with that of the crude juice of the grape by the Mussulmans : and the sale of pork by them is equivalent to that of the flesh of a goat by Mussulmans ; because these things are lawful in their belief, and we are commanded to suffer them to pursue their own tenets. Moreover, Omar commanded his agents to empower the Zimmees to sell wine, taking from them a tenth part of the price : a proof that the sale of wine is lawful among them.

A person inciting another to sell his property to a third person, by offering an addition over and above the price, is responsible for such addition ; but not unless this addition be expressed as forming a part of the price.—If a person say to another, "sell your slave to a particular person for one thousand dirms, on condition that I be responsible to you for five hundred dirms, of the price, independent of the one thousand dirms," and the said person act accordingly, it is valid and he is entitled to one thousand dirms from the purchaser, and to five hundred dirms from the security ; whereas if he were simply to say, "I will be responsible for five hundred dirms," without mentioning the words "of the price," the seller is, in that case, entitled only to the one thousand dirms from the purchaser, and has no claim on the surety.—The reason of this is that an increase in the price, or in the wares, is lawful, according to all our doctors, and is joined to the original contract (as has been already explained), being only an alteration of the contract from one lawful quality to another lawful quality ;—and as it is lawful for the purchaser to make an alteration in the price, although he be no gainer in other respects by it (as if he should increase the price, notwithstanding it be adequate to the value of the goods before the increase), so also it is lawful for a stranger to lay himself under an obligation for an increase of price, although he have no advantage in other respects ;—in the same manner as the consideration for Khoola becomes incumbent upon a wife in virtue of her assent to the Khoola, although she receive nothing in exchange, for woman is originally free, and the procurement of a divorce adds nothing to her original freedom. It is essential, therefore, to the validity of the seller's claim upon this person, that the increase be opposed to the goods by the specification of the words "of the price," because if these words be omitted, the declaration or stipulation is of no account.

A female slave may be contracted in marriage by the purchaser without his taking possession of her.—If a person, having purchased a female slave, make her over in marriage to another before seisin, and that other cohabit with her, such marriage is lawful, as having been concinded in virtue of the authority of the proprietor :—and it also determines the seisin of the purchaser. If, however, the husband should not cohabit with her, the marriage does not, in that case, determine the seisin according to a favourable construction of the law.—Analogy, indeed would suggest that the purchaser becomes seised of the slave on the instant of the marriage-contract, since, in consequence thereof, the right of property over the slave is rendered virtually defective !—it would therefore follow that the seisin becomes established as an effect of the contract, in the same manner as in the case of an actual defect occasioned by any act of a purchase.—The reason for a more favourable construction, on this occasion, is that any act by which an actual defect is occasioned infers an exertion of power over the subject, which consequently established a seisin of the subject ; but an act which merely induces a virtual defect does not admit of this inference, so as to establish seisin.

Case of the purchaser disappearing, without taking possession of his purchase, or paying the price.—If a person, having purchase a slave, should afterwards absent himself without taking possession, or paying the price, and the seller prove by witnesses that he had sold the slave to the absentee, in that case, provided the place of his retirement be known and ascertained, the slave cannot be re-sold on account of the exigencies of the seller, for these may be otherwise answered, and such sale would destroy the right of the first purchaser :—but if the absentee's place of retirement be not known, the slave may be rersold, and the debt of the purchaser to the seller paid by means of the price ; for the seller has proved, by witnesses, that the slave is the property of the purchaser, and that he has a claim upon him ; and consequently, when the place of retirement of the purchaser is unknown, it is incumbent on the magistrate to direct the slave to be sold for the satisfaction of the seller ; which could not otherwise be obtained ;—in the same manner as where a pawner dies before having released his pledge, in which case it is sold for the discharge of his debt to the pawnholder.—It is otherwise where the purchaser disappears after seisin, for in this case the slave cannot be sold to answer the right of the seller, since his right is not particularly connected with the salve, as he, in such a circumstance, stands in the same predicament with the other creditors.—It is to be observed that, in case of the slave being sold an account of the seller, if anything remain after the discharge of his claim by means o the price the seller must keep such remainder in behalf of the purchaser, to whom it is due as an exchange for his property :—but if the price should not suffice to answer his claim, he is in that case entitled afterwards to the remainder, from the purchaser.

Or of one of two purchasers disappearing under the same circumstance.—Supposing there be two purchasers, and only one of them disappear, the one of that is present is entitled to pay the whole of the price of the slave, and to take complete possession of him ; and if, in this case, the other purchaser afterward appear, he is not entitled to receive his share until he shall have paid to his partner the price of it This is the adjudication of Haneefa and Mohammed. Aboo Yoosaf has said that, if the present purchaser pay the whole of the price, still he is only entitled to take possession of his own share, and that, as the payment of the debt of the absentee was a gratuitous and unsolicited act in his favour, he is not entitled to receive it from him, since he paid it without his authority Besides, as the present purchaser is, as it were, a stranger with respect to the absentee, he is not entitled to take possession of his share. The reasoning of Haneefa is that the present purchaser, in making payment on behalf of the absentee, acted from necessity, and not from choice ; because it was not otherwise possible for him to enjoy his own share, since, having purchased the slave jointly with the other by one contract, it was impossible for him to detain him in his possession whilst there existed the claim of another with respect to part of him. Now whosoever pays the debt of another from necessity is entitled to repayment, notwithstanding his having acted without authority ; as in the case of the loan of pledge ; for if a person lend to another something in order that he may pledge it, and that other having pledged it accordingly, the lender afterwards, from a necessary want of the said thing, redeem it from the pawnee, he is, in such case, entitled to repayment from the borrower, although he have redeemed the pledge without authority from him —Since therefore the present purchaser, in the case in question, has a right to repayment from the absentee, it follows that he has also a right to detain in his possession the share of the absentee until he receive payment of the sum due to him ; in the same manner as an agent for purchase, who pays from his own property the price of the goods purchased on behalf of his constituent, is entitled to retain possession of them until he receive payment of the price from his constituent.

Case of gold and silver being indefinitely mentioned in the offer of a price.—If a person purchase a female slave in exchange for one thousand miskals of gold and silver,—saying, "I purchase this slave for one thousand miskals of gold and silver," in that case it is incumbent on him to pay five hundred miskals of gold, and five hundred miskals of silver ; for the reference of the miskals to the gold and silver having been in an equal degree applicable to each, an equal proportion in the payment is of consequence incumbent.—If, on the other hand the purchaser should say, "I have purchased this slave in exchange for one thousand of gold and silver, in this case he must pay five hundred miskals of gold, and five hundred dirms of silver (of the septemal weight): for the terms one thousand having been referred to the gold and silver in a general manner, it is therefore construed to apply to the weight in common use with respect to each in particular.

The receipt of base money instead of good money, if it be lost or expended, is a complete discharge.—If a person indebted to another in the amount of ten dirms of a good sort, afterwards pay him this amount in an inferior species, and the other, being ignorant of this circumstance, receive them, and afterwards expend them, or lose them, in this case the debt is completely discharged, and the creditor is not entitled to any compensation for the difference of quality.—This is according to Haneefa and Mohammed.—Aboo Yoosaf has said, that in this case the creditor is entitled to return to the debtor a tantamount of dirms of the sort be receivedt and o demand from him ten dirms of a superior sort, to which he has a right ; because, in the same manner as his right relates to the substance of the dirms, so also is it established in the quality. A conservation of each right is therefore indispensable ; but as the conservation of the second right, by means of an allowance in exchange for the difference of quality, is impracticable (since quality in homogenous articles is of no relative value), this mode must necessarily be adopted. The reasoning of Haneefa and Mohammed is, that the bad dirms are of the same species with the good ; and that after the receipt and expenditure, or destruction of them, the debt is discharged ; because the claim which remains relates to quality, and this is impossible to satisfy by the granting of a compensation, inasmuch as quality in itself bears no value.

Articles of a neutral nature do not become property but by actual seisin.—If a bird incubate its eggs in the land of a particular person, the right of property over broad does not, in virtue of such incubation, vest in the proprietor of the ground ; on the contrary, they remain free to the person who shall first seize them.—The law is also the same with respect to eggs which a bird, lays upon any particular ground.—So also, if a deer should sleep for a night in a field, it does not by that act become the property of the proprietor of that field ; on the countrary, it remains free to whatsoever it may be caught by. The reason of this is that both the young onces and the deer are considered in the nature of game, and as such are free to the person who catches them, although no stratagem be used for that purpose ;—and the same, also, of eggs; whence, if a Moharim should either break or broil them, he is subject to make expiation.—Moreover, the proprietor did not purposely prepare his land that the bird should lay or incubate her eggs, or that the deer should sleep upon it.—It is therefore the same as if a person should spread out his net for the purpose of drying it, in which case, if any game should fall into it, it would not become immediately the property of the proprietor of the net, but would continue netural until some one seize it;—or, as if game should come into a house, in which case it does not become the immediate property of the proprietor of the house. —or, as if a person, scattering sugar or dirms (for instance) among the people, should chance to throw these into to clothes of some one: in which case the property does not immediately vest in that person, until he warp it up or prepare to seize it.—It is otherwise with respect to honey, for the property of it vests in the proprietor of the ground in which it is gathered together; because honey is considered as the produce of the ground, and hence the proprietor of the ground obtains a property in it as a dependant of the soil, in the same manner as in the trees which grow in his land, or in which water flows through it.

BOOK XVII

OF SIRF SALE

Definition of Sirf sale.——BEEYA SIRF means a pure sale; of which the articles opposed in exchange to each other are both representatives of price. This is termed Sirf, because Sirf means a removal, and in this mode of sale it is necessary to remove the articles opposed to each other in exchange from the hands of each of the parties, respectively, into those of the other. Sirf also means a superiority; and in this kind of sale a superiority is the only object; that is, a superiority of quality, fashion, or workmanship; for gold or silver being, with respect to their substance, of no use, are only desirable from such superiority.

The articles opposed must be exactly equal in point of weight: but may differ in quality.—THE sale of gold for gold, or silver for silver, is permitted only when they are exactly equal in point of weight: but the one may be of a superior quality to the other; or the one may be bullion, and the other may be wought; because the Prophet has said "Sell GOLD for GOLD, from hand to hand, at an equal rate according to weight: for any inequality in point of weight is USURY." And he has also declared "the GOODNESS and BANDNESS of quality is the same" (as has been already explained in the preceding book treating of sale).

The exchange must take place upon the spot.—MUTUAL seisin is an indispensable requisite in a Sirf sale;—that is, it is indispensable that each of the parties, prior to their departure from the meeting, take possession of the article respectively given in exchange; because of the tradition above quoted; and also, because Omar and to one of the parties in a Sirf sale. "If the other party require leave to go to his house, yet you must not grant it."—Besides, the seisin of one of the parties is an indispensable requisite, lest the contract prove to be an exchange of a debt for a debt:—and as the seisin of one of the parties is requisite, it follows that, in order to establish an equality the seisin of the other is also requisite, since usury would otherwise be induced. In a sale of this nature, moreover, neither subject has a priority with respect to the other; and hence a mutual seisin is requisite, whether both the subjects be of a determinate nature (as in the sale of one silver vessel for another silver vessel), or of a nature not determinate (as in the sale of dirms and deenars in exchange for dirms and deenars), or one of them determinate and the other not (as in the sale of a silver vessel in exchange for dirms and deenars); because the tradition enjoining a mutual seisin is absolute, and makes no discrimination of these circumstances.—Besides, although a silver vessel be determinate, still there subsists a doubt with respect to its determination, inasmuch as silver is considered in its nature as a representative of price; and, in a case of this nature, a doubt is a sufficient cause for the necessity of seisin, because a doubt, in matter relative to usury, is equivalent to a reality.—It is to be observed that what is meant by mutual seisin, is that both parties make seisin prior to their separation; whence if the parties walk aside together, or sleep in the place of meting, or become insensible, the Sirf sale is not thereby rendered null, because Omar has said "If the seller, in SIRF sale should leap from the top of the house, do you leap after him.

Gold may be sold for silver, at an unequal rate provided the exchange take place upon the spot.—THE sale of gold in exchange for silver, at an unequal rate, is permitted, because these articles are of a different genus. Still, however, in such case, mutual seisin is indispensable, because the Prophet has said, "The sale of gold for silver is usury unless it be from hand to hand." If, therefore, the parties separate before both or one of them make seisin, the sale is invalid; and hence it is not lawful to stipulate an optional condition, or an optional period, because such stipulations are preventive of mutual seisin, which is an indispensable condition. If, however, a Sirf sale be contracted with an optional condition, and the condition be afterwards removed previous to the separation of the parties, the Sirf sale is in that case valid, because of the cause of its invalidity being destroyed previous to its complete establishment.

No act can be performed with relation to

he return until it be received.—Any deed with respect to the return in a Sirf sale, previous to seisin of it, is unlawful. If, therefore, a person, having sold a deenar for ten dirms, should, previous to the seisin of them, purchase a piece of cloth for them, in that case the sale of the cloth is invalid, on this principle, that the seisin of the ten dirms was absolutely incumbent; because otherwise the Sirf sale would be usurious; and as God has prohibited usury, it follows that if the sale of the cloth were licensed, an absolute commandment of God would thereby be defeated.—It is related, as an opinion of Ziffer, that the sale of the cloth is capable of being rendered valid; because dirms being undeterminate, it follows that the price of the cloth relates to ten dirms in an absolute manner, and not to the ten dirms of the Sirf sale in a specific manner. Our doctors on the other hand, argue that price, in a Sirf sale, is also a subject of the sale: because, as every sale must have a subject, and as the articles, in a Sirf sale, are both representatives of price, without any of them having a preference over the other, it follows that either of them is the subject; and the sale of the subject previous to the seisin is unlawful.

Objection.—The consideration, in a Sirf sale, is a representative of price, and therefore of an undeterminate nature: whence it would follow that it cannot be considered as the subject, since the subject of a sale is required to be determinate.

Reply.—The subject of a sale is not required to be determinate; for, in a Sillim sale the thing on account of which the advance is made is the subject of the sale; but still it is undeterminate.

Gold may be sold for silver, by conjectute: but not gold for gold. nor silver for silver.—The sale of gold for silver, by conjecture,* is lawful, because equality, in a sale or this nature, is not required—It is unlawful, however, to sell gold, for gold, silver for silver, by conjecture, because in such sale there is a suspicion of usury.

In the sale of an article having any gold or silver upon it, the price paid down is opposed to the gold or silver—If a person sell, for two thousand Miskals of silver, a female slave whose real value is one thousand Miskals, and on whose neck there is a collar of silver equivalent to one thousand Miskals of silver, and the purchaser having paid a thousand Miskals of silver, ready money, the parties then separate from the meeting. such payment is considered to be the price of the collar, because the seisin of so much of the price of the whole was a necessary condition. as the sale in that proportion was a Sirf sale; and hence it is reasonable to conclude that the seller paid the exact amount of which he knew the seisin to be indispensibly necessary. In the same manner, also, if he purchaser the said slave with the collar, for two thousand Miskals of silver, of which one thousand is prompt and the other thousand postponed, the prompt payment is considered as the price of the collar, because the stipulation of payment at a future period not being lawful in a Sirf sale, and being permitted in the sale of a slave, it is reasonable to suppose that the parties in contracting the sale, and stipulating the distant period, intended to proceed according to law—If, also, a person sell, for one hundred dirms, a sword, of which the silver ornaments amount to fifty dirms, and the purchaser pay immediately fifty dirms of the price in prompt payment, such sale is lawful, and the payment made is considered to be for the price of the ornaments, although the purchaser may not have specified this.—The same rule, also, holds if the purchaser say to the seller, "Take this: fifty dirms in part of the price of both" (that is, of the ornaments and sword), because two things are sometimes mentioned where only one is intended, and this supposition is here adopted from the probability of it. If, however, the parties separate without a mutual seisin, the eale is null with respect to the silver ornaments because of its being in that degree a Sirf sale, to the validity of which mutual seisin is essential:—or, if the sword be so framed as not to admit a separation of the ornaments without sustaining detriment, the sale of it is in this case also null, because so situated the separate sale of it is not permitted. in the same manner as it is not permitted to sell the beam of a roof.—If, on the other hand, the sword admit of a separation of the ornaments, without detriment, the sale, in the manner above mentioned, is valid with respect to the sword; but with respect to the ornament it is null.—It is to be observed that the sale of a sword with silver ornaments in exchange for dirms is lawful only where the silver of the dirms exceeds that of the ornaments; and that, if the silver of the dirms be either barely equal to, or less than, that of the ornaments,—or if it be not known wheather it be more or less, the sale is invalid. The reason of the invalidity in case of its not being known whether it be more or less is, that the probability is in favour of its being invalid; since there are two causes of invalidity, namely, equality and inferiority; whereas there is only one cause of validity, viz., superiority.

In the purchase of plate, if the parties separate before payment of the full price, the sale is valid only in the proportion paid.—If a person, having sold to another a silver vessel, should receive payment in part, and both parties then separate, in that case the sale is null with repsect to the amont remaining to be paid, but valid in the amount taken possession of; and the parties have each a share in the property of the vessel;—because this sale is Sirf, or pure, with regard to the whole of the subject, and consequently

*That is, by a loose undeterminate estimate.

valid in that degree in which the conditions of a pure sale have been observed, and invalid in the degree in which they have been omitted; for the invalidity, in this case, is not essential, but accidental, inasmuch as the sale was valid in its formation, and afterwards, in consequence of the separation of the parties after the receipt of a part, became invalid with relation to part of the subject: and hence the validity, which is accidental, does not operate upon the part in which all the conditions of the sale have been observed.

Or, if it be discovered to be in part the property of another, the purchaser may relinquish the bargain.—IF a person sell a silver vessel which afterwards appears to be in part the property of another, in that case the purchaser has the option either of retaining a right of property in the remaining part of the vessel, or of cancelling the bargain entirely: bacause partnership in a vessel is equivalent to a blemish in it.

But this does not hold with respect to an ingot.—IF a person sell an ingot of silver, and part of it afterwards appears to be the property of another, the purchaser is in that case constrained to take the remaining part at a proportionate price:—and he is not allowed an option, in this instance, b cause the division of an ingot of silver does not in any shape injure it.

Where the article, on each side, consists of two species of money, the sale at an unequal rate is lawful.—THE sale of two dirms and one deenar, in exchange for two deenars and one dirm, is valid; because in this case the dirms are considered as opposed to the deenars; and as they are of a different genus, an inequality in the proportion is therefore admitted. Shafei and Ziffer maintain that this sale is unlawful; and they have disagreed in the same manner with respect to the legality of the sale of one Koor of barley and one Koor of wheat in exchange for two Koors of wheat end two Koors of barley. Their reasoning in support of their opinion is that the seller and buyer have opposed one total to another total; and this requires that every separate part of the one be opposed to every separate part of the other (in an indefinite and not a definite manner):—now in the opposing of each genus respectively, to a different genus, a modification is induced in this particular, which is not lawful, notwithstanding such a construction of the sale be the means of rendering it valid.—In the same manner as where a person, for ten dirms, purchases a silver bracelet weighing ten dirms, and again, for other ten dirms, purchases a piece of cloth, and then disposes of both articles together, by a Moorabihat contract (suppose) for thirty dirms, in which case the Moorabihat sale is invalid, although it be possible, by supposing the whole of the profit to be exacted on the cloth, to render it valid:—or, where a person purchases a slave for one thousand dirms, and previous to the payment of the price, sells him, along with another, for fifteen hundred dirms, to the person from whom he had bought the slave for one thousand dirms: for in this case the sale is invalid in relation to the slave of a thousand dirms because there is a possibility that the other slave may have been worth more than five hundred dirms; and supposing this, it necessarily follows that the seller has purchased the slave for a smaller price than that for which he formerly sold him; although in this case it be possible to render the sale valid by supposing the one slave to be opposed to one thousand dirms, in a specific manner, and the other to five hundred dirms, so as to remove the possibility of the seller having received him at a smaller price than that for which he had sold him;—or, where a seller, having exhibited two slaves, of which one only is his property, says to the purchaser, "I have sold to you one of these slaves," in which case the sale is invalid, notwithstanding it be possible to render it valid by supposing that the seller meant his own slave:—or, where a person sells a dirm and a piece of cloth for a dirm and a piece of cloth, and both parties then separate without making seisin,—in which case the sale is invalid, although it be possible to render it valid by supposing the dirms on each side to have been opposed to the cloth of the other:—for, in all these cases, although there be a possibility of rendering the sales valid, still they remain invalid, for the reason already alleged. The arguments of our doctors are, that the opposition of a total to a total, provided it be in an absolute manner (that is, without any particular specification), admits of this supposition, that the separate parts are opposed to the separate parts;—as in the case of an homogeneous sale, for instance, such as a sale of two dirms for two dirms, in which the unities on each side are opposed to those on the other respectively; whence it each of the contracting parties respectively take one dirm, and they then separate from the meeting, the sale is valid to the amount seised;—whereas, if the separate parts of the subject of the sale, instead of being opposed to each other in a definite manner, should be opposed to each other in an indefinite manner, the sale in the amount seised would not be lawful, since it must necessarily follow that the amount seised by each of the parties would stand opposed indefinitely, to what was seised and what was not seised.—It is therefore evident that the opposition of a total to a total infers the opposition of the unities respectively; and as this, to give validity to the contract in question, must be in a definite manner, it is presumed to be so, in order that the contract may be valid.—With respect to what Ziffer and Shafei urge, that "a modification is induced with regard to the requisites of the contract," we reply, that a modification is induced with respect to the quality of the contract, but not with respect to the orgina requisites of it, because the original requisite of the contract is that a total shall be transferred in exchange for a total, and this contumes unaltered.—Analogous to this is a case where a person sells the half of a slave, shared in an equal degree between him and another; for in that case the law supposes the sale to apply to his own share, in order to its validity. The cases enumerated by Ziffer and Shafei, on the contrary, are not analogous to this in question.—The first case (namely, that of a Moorabihat sale) is not analogous, as it is not possible to suppose that the whole of the profit is exacted on the cloth, for, if so, the sale of the bracelet would be rendered a sale of friendship, and hence an alteration would take place in the essence of the contract. The second case, also, is not analogous, because the mode there proposed for legalizing the sale is not determinate, since in the same manner as it is possible to construe the sum opposed to the slave to be one thousand dirms, so also is it possible to construe it to be more than one thousand, in every different gradation, untit it amount to one thousand four hundred and ninety-nine dirms; in opposition to the case in question; where the mode proposed is determinate The third instance, also, is not analogous, because the force of the sale there rests upon an indefinite object, which is incapable of being the subject of sale; and as indefinity and specification are of opposite import, it is impossible to construe the sale as applicable to any specific article. In the last instance, on the other hand, the sale is originally valid, and becomes otherwise from an accident namely, the separation of the meeting: but the present question relates to a contract in its original formation, and not to any adventitious circumstances.

And so also, where the article, on one side consists of a certain number of coins of one species, and, on the other, of an equal number, of the species.—A SALE of eleven dirms in exchange for ten dirms and one deenar, is valid:—and in this case ten dirms are considered as opposed to ten dirms and the remaining dirm to the single deenar; because in a sale of dirms for dirms equality is indispensible and it is therefore reasonable to suppose that such was the intention of the parties; and with respect to the remaining part of the sale, namely, the opposition of one dirm to one deenar, equality is not requisite, as they are not homogeneous

A deficiency of value, on one side, in point of weight, may be made up by the addition of any other article of proportionable value.—IF, in a sale of gold for gold, or silver for silver, the subject, on one part, be inferior in point of weight to the other, and there be joined to the inferior something equal in value to the deficiency arising from the difference of weight, in this case the sale is valid, without being abominable. If, on the other hand, the value of the thing so added be not equal to the difference, still the sale is valid, but abominable. But if, on the contrary, the additional thing bear no value (such as dust, for instance), the sale is not valid, because of its being usurious, inasmuch as nothing is opposed to the difference of the weight.

A debt may be commuted in the course of a Sirf sale.—IF a person, indebted to another to the amount of ten dirms, sell to his creditor one deenar for ten dirms, and having delivered the deenar to him, the parties then commute the ten dirms which they reciprocally owe to each other, it is lawful. This case, however, supposes the sale of the deenar to relate to ten dirms in an absolute manner, and not to the debt.

One pure and two base dirms may be sold for two base and one pure.—THE sale of one pure dirm and two base ones in exchange for two pure dirms and one base one, is lawful.—By a base dirms is to be understood, such as passes amongst merchants, but is rejected at the public treasury.—The reason of the legality, in this instance, is that an equality according to weight is established, and the quality of purity is of no account.

Description of, and rules respecting, base coinage.—DIRMS in which the silver is predominant are considered as silver, and deenars in which the gold is predominant are considered as gold; and a difference in the proportion with respect to them in a sale is consequently inlawful, in the same manner as in the case of pure dirms or deenars. Hence it is unlawful either to sell base money in exchange for pure, or base in exchange for base, unless upon a footing of equality in regard to weight.—In the same manner, also, it is unlawful to borrow base money except according to weight: for dirms and deenars, in common, are not free from a mixture of base metal; because gold and silver do not receive the impression well without a mixture of it, and it is sometimes innate in them,

IF, however in dirms and deenars, the base metal predominate, they are not, in effect, dirms and deenars, because the law adverts to the predominancy. Hence if a person should purchase pure silver in exchange for dirms of that nature, the law is the same as has been already stated in the case of a sword with silver ornaments. It is lawful, moreover, to sell dirms and deenars of this nature in exchange for others of the same kind, at an unequal proportion; for as these consist of two different materials (namely, gold and base metal, or silver and base metal), one genus may therefore be opposed to another.—This, however, is nevertheless a Sirf sale, because of there being an opposition of gold or silver on each side; and hence mutual seisin in the meeting is necessary: and in the same manner as seisin of the silver or gold is necessary in the meeting, so also is that of the base metal, because a separation cannot be effected without detriment.—The compiler of the Hedaya observes, that the modern lawyers of his country* do not pass decrees agreeably to this doctrine; for as base money is there much in use, it follows that if the sale of it at an unequal proportion were permitted, the door of usury would thereby be opened.

With respect to mone in which the base metal predominates, it is to be remarked that, if it pass current by weight, purchase, sale, and loans are transacted in it by weight. If, on the other hand, it pass current by tale, all matters are transacted in it by tale.—If, however, both modes prevail, it is in that case permitted to follow either; for custom is decisive with respect to matters of this kind, provided they be not otherwise determined by the ordinances of the LAW.—It is also to be observed, that money of this kind, whilst it continues in use, is a representative of price, and is therefore incapable of being rendered determinate: but if it should not be in use, it is considered as other wares or articles of merchandize, and is therefore capable of being rendered determinate.

If dirms be adulterated to such a degree at to pass current with some but not with others, they are equivalent to Zeyf or base dirms. Hence, if a person enter into a contract for something in exchange for a hundred specific dirms of this description, the contract does not relate to those specific dirms in particular, but to a similar amount of base dirms, provided the seller were aware of the circumstance;—but if otherwise, it relates to a similar number of pure dirms;—because in the first case the assent of the seller to receive the base species is established by his knowledge of the baseness,—whereas in the second case his assent is unestablished because of his ignorance of the baseness

A sale for base dirms is null, if they lose their currency before the period of payment.—If a person purchase wares in exchange for base dirms, and, previous to the payment of them, they should fall into general disuse, in that case the sale, according to Haneefa, is null. Aboo Yoosaf maintains that it is incumbent on the purchaser to pay the value which these dirms bore on the day of sale. Mohammed, on the other hand, alleges that it is incumbent on him to pay the value which they bore on the last day of their currency. The arguments of the two disciples are that the contract in itself is valid; but the delivery of the dirms becomes impracticable from the disuse of them; a circumstance, however, which does not induce invalidity;—any more than where a person purchases an article for fresh dates, and the season for those passes away;—in which case the sale is not invalid; and so also in the case in question.—As, therefore, the contract is not invalid, but still endures, it follows that, according to Aboo Yoosaf the value the dirms bore at the time of the sale is due, because from that period responsibility for them takes place; in the same manner as in a case of usurpation;—and that, according to Mohammed (on the other hand) the value they bore on the last day of their currency is due, since at that period the right of the seller shifted from them to their value—The argument of Haneefa, is that the price is destroyed by the disuse; for money is the representative of price solely from custom, and hence this property is annulled from disuse. The sale, therefore, remains without any price being involved in it; and is consequently null; and as the sale is null, it is of course incumbent on the purchaser to restore the goods to the seller, provided they be extant; or, if otherwise, the value which they bore on the day he obtained possession of them; in the same manner as in an invalid sale.

Rules with respect to copper coinage.—A SALE in exchange for Faloos is valid, because they are considered as durable property. If, therefore, the Faloos pass in currency, the sale is lawful, although they may not have been specified,—because Faloos are, from custom, representatives of price and consequently stand not in need of specification. If, however, they should not pass in currency, it is in that case requisite that they be particular specified, in the same manner as other articles of merchandize.

If a person purchase wares for Faloos, which at that time passed in currency, but which previous to the payment of them fall into disuse, the sale is in that case null, according to Haneefa: contrary, however, to the opinion of the two disciples.—The difference of opinion upon this point is analogous to what has been already mentioned in treating of dirms in which the alloy is predominant.

If a person borrow Faloos, and their currency should afterwards cease, then, according to Haneefa, the borrower must make repayment in similars;* because Karz [a loan of money] is equivalent to Areeat [a loan of substance], and therefore requires the restoration of the actual article with respect to its nature, that is, its value.—The property of representing price, moreover, is merely an adventitious property, in copper coin, to which no regard is had in the borrowing of them; on the contrary, they are borrowed on the principle of their being similars; and this quality they tetain after the disuse of them as money, whence it is that a loan in them is valid after they have lost their currency—According to the two disciples, on the contrary, the borrower must in this case pay to the lender the value of the Faloos; for their quality of representation of price being annulled by the disuse.

*Mawur al Nihr.

*By similars is always understood any articles compensable by an equal number of the same description, such as eggs for eggs, Faloos for Faloos. &c. It is treated of at large in various other parts of the work.

it is therefore impracticable for the borrower to restore them with the qualities they possessed when he received them; and hence, as the payment of similars would be an injury, it is required that he pay the value. in the same manner as holds where a person borrows any articles of which the unities are similar, and the whole genus of which afterwards becomes extinct. According to Aboo Yoosaf, their value must be fixed from the day of seisin; and according to Mohammed, from the last day of their currency, in conformity with what has been already explained. This difference of opinion originates in a difference of doctrine respecting a case where a person usurps an article of the class of similars, and of which the similars afterwards become extinct,* when, according to Aboo Yoosaf, the usurper is responsible for the value the article bore on the day of usurpation; and according to Mohammed, for the value it bore on the last day of its existence. It is to be observed that the opinion of Mohammad is founded upon tenderness to mankind, and that of Aboo Yoosaf on conveniency

It is lawful for a person to purchase any thing in exchange for a half dirm of Faloos;† and in this case he required to pay the number of Faloos adequate to the price of half a dirm In the same manner, it is lawful to purchase any thing for the Faloos of a drink ‡ of silver, or a Kerat § of silver. In all these cases, Ziffer is of opinion that the bargain is unlawful, because Faloos being an article of tale, estimated by number and not by their relation to dirms or daniks, a specification of the number ought therefore to have been made. The reasoning of our doctors is, that the exact number of Faloos adequate to the price of a half dirm, or danik, is known (for the case question proceeds on the supposition of such a knowledge), and that a specification of the number is therefore unnecessary. If the purchaser were to say, "I have bought this thing for the Faloos of one dirm, or two dirms," the bargain in that case also valid, according to Aboo Yoosaf; for this expression means the number of Faloos to which the price of one or two dirms is adequate, and not the weight. It is related as an opinion of Mohammed, that a sale for the Faloos of one dirm is not lawful; but that a sale for the Faloos of any thing under a dirm is lawful, as it is customary to purchase things for Faloos, where the value is not adequate to a dirm, but not otherwise. Lawyers have observed, that the opinion of Aboo Yoosaf is the most approved, especially in countries where the practise of selling and purchasing for Faloos is common, and where, of course, the rate they bear, with respect to dirms, is known and ascertained.

If a person, having delivered a dirm to a Sirraf, or money changer, should say to him, "Give me Faloos in exchange for one half of this, and a half dirm wanting one grain of silver in exchange for the other half," in this case the sale, according to the two disciples, is valid with respect to the one half in exchange for Faloos, and invalid with respect to the other; because the sale of a half dirm in exchange for Faloos is lawful (as has been already explained); but the exchange of a half dirm in exchange for a half dirm wanting one grain of silver, is usurious, and, consequently, unlawful. Agreeably to the tenets of Haneefa, the sale is in this case completely null, because the whole is comprehended under one contract, and the invalidity being strong, with respect to a part, does therefore communicate itself to the whole If, however, the word "Give" be repeated, by the person saying "Give me Faloos in exchange for one half, and give me a half dirm wanting one grain in exchange for the other half," the opinion of Haneefa, in such case, accords with that of the two disciples, because here exist two separate sales, one valid, and the other invalid. If the purchaser, without opposing the halves of the dirm, were to say, "Give me, in exchange for this dirm, the Faloos of half a dirm, and a half dirm wanting one grain;" the sale is valid in full, because, in this case, it is construed to be an opposition, on the one hand, of one half dirm wanting a grain in exchange for one half dirm wanting a grain; and on the other, of a half dirm with the superaddition of a grain for the Faloos of a half dirm; and this is lawful.

*Such as fruits, or other articles which are to be had only at particular seasons of the year.

†That is, for Faloos to the value of half a dirm.—(The distinction, in this instance, turns entirely upon the nature of the phrase in the original idiom)

‡ A small silver coin, the sixth part of a dirm.

§ A Carat, the twenty-fourth part of an ounce.

BOOK XVIII.

OF KAFALIT, OR BAIL.

Definition of the terms used in bail.—KAFALIT, literally, means junction. In the language of the LAW it signifies the junction of one person to another in relation to a claim (some have said, in relation to a debt only; but the first is the most approved definition).—The person who renders obligatory on himself, the claim of another, whether it relate to person or property, in termed the Kafeel, or surety:—the claim itself in favour of which bail is given, whether it relate to the person or property, is termed Makfool-be-hee;—the claimant is termed Makfool-le hoo; and the principal or person who gives bail, is termed Makfool-an-hoo.—In cases of bail for the person, however, the terms Makfool-be hee and Makfool-an-hoo relate to the same thing.

Chap, I.—Introductory.
Chap. II —Of Bail in which two are concerned.
Chap. III.—Of Bail by Freemen in behalf of Slaves, and by Slaves in behalf of Freemen.-

CHAPTER I.

Distinction.—Bail is of two descriptions. I. Bail for the person, which is termed Hazir-Zaminee. II. Bail for property, which is termed Mal-Zaminee.

Bail for the person.—Bail for the person is valid; and in virtue of it the surety is bound to produce the principal, or person whom he has bailed.—Shafei is of opinion that bail for the person is not valid, because the surety undertakes and renders obligatory on himself a delivery which he is not capable of performing, inasmuch as he possesses no power or authority over the person of the principal: contrary to bail for property, as in that case the surety possessing power and authority over his own property is thereby enabled to discharge the obligation he has contracted,—The arguments of our doctors upon this point are twofold. First, the Prophet has said, "The surety is responsible," which is a proof that both modes of bail are lawful. Secondly, the surety is in a degree capable of delivering the person for whom he is bail, as he may inform the claimant of his place of abode, and thus remove the bar between them, since, after obtaining such knowledge, the claimant may demand the aid of the officers of the Kazee, by whose means he may secure his presence. There is, moreover, a necessity amongst mankind for this kind of bail; and the characteristic of bail, namely, a junction of one person to another in relation to a claim, is observed in it.

Under what formis contracted.—Bail for the person is contracted, where any one says: "I have become bail for the person of a particular man," or, "for his neck," or, "for his soul," for his body," or, "for his head," or "for his face;" because some of these words really mean, in their common acceptation, the whole of the person, and others bear that sense metaphorically, as has been already explained under the head of divorce.—The effect is also the same when a person says, "I have become bail for the half of a certain person," or "for a third of him," or "for a part of him;" because the person, in the case of bail, being incapable of division of dismemberment, the mention of a part indefinitely is therefore equivalent to the mention of the whole. It is otherwise where a person says, "I have become bail for the hand" (or" the foot'), because neither of these parts are ever used to denote the whole of the person, and the bail so given is therefore invalid.

If a person say, "I am responsible [Zamin for such a person," it is a valid bail: because this is an express declaration of the intention of bail. It is also a valid bail, if a person say, "This is upon me," or, 'This is towards me," because both these expressions indicate an obligatory engagement. In the same manner, also, bail is contracted by the words Zeyim and Kabeel, for both of these signify bail, and hence it is that bail-bonds and other instruments of obligation are termed Kabala. If, on the contrary, a person say, "I am responsible for the notoriety of a certain person," bail is not contracted, since the responsibility, in such case, relates merely to the notoriety and not to the claim. Hence, if a person should say, in the Persian language, "His acquaintance is upon me," he does not thereby become bail—If however, he should say, "He is my acquaintance," lawyers are of opinion that he becomes bail because of ancient custom

The surety must deliver up the person for whom he is bail at the stipulated period; and in failure of this. is liable to imprisonment.—If, in a contract of bail, it be stipulated that "the surety shall, at a fixed period, deliver over the principal or person bailed to the claimant," it is in that case necessary that he be delivered to the claimant if it be required, either at the fixed period, or at any time afterwards, in order that the surety may acquit himself of the engagement into which he has entered. If, therefore, he deliver the person bailed on the demand of the claimant, he then becomes released from his engagement: but if he refuse to deliver him, the magistrate must in that case imprison him for failure in the performance of his engagement. He is not, however, to be imprisoned on the first summons, as he may not then know for what reason the Kazee had summoned him.

If the principal disappear, the surely must be indulged with time to search for him; and the contract is fulfilled by delivering up the principal at any place which admits of litigation.—If, in a case of bail for the person, the principal should disappear, it is in that case incumbent on the Kazee to afford the surety a sufficient period to go and come in search of him; and afterwards to imprison him, in case of his not producing the principal, because he is then proved to have failed in his engagement.—If, however, he produce the principal and deliver him to the claimant, in such a place as may enable him to litigate his suit with him, the surety is then released from his engagement of bail, because of his performance of the obligation he had contracted; and the end of the contract is likewise answered, as it only requires that he deliver him once ff he should have agreed to deliver him "in the assembly of the Kazee," and afterwards deliver him in the market-place, still he is released from his enagement, because the object of the bail is answered. (Many have observed that in the present age the surety would not in such case be released from his obligation; because, as the probability in this age is that the people would aid the defendant in preventing his appearance in the assembly of the Kazee, and that they would not assist the claimant in enforcing it, such a clause is therefore beneficial.)—If, however, the surety deliver over the principal in a desert, he is not released from his engagement. bacause the claimant could not in such place litigate his suit with him, and the object of bail remains therefore unaccomplished In the same manner, he is not released from his obligarion in case he deliver him up in a village where there is no Kazee; because, where there is no Kazee, the claimant can obtain the decree. If he should deliver him up in another city than that in which he had entered into the contract of bail, he is then (according to Haneefa) exempted from any further obligation.—The two disciples are of a different opinion, because it may often happen that the witnesses are in the city in which the contract was formed—If, moreover, he deliver over the principal in the prison, where he has been previously confined by another for a different cause, he is not released from his engagement because the claimant has no power, in such situation, to litigate his suit with him.

The death of the principal releases the surety.—IF, in a case of bail for the person, the principal should die, the surety is then released from his engagement; first, because of the impracticability of producing the person; and, secondly, because in the same manner as the appearance of the principal is by such event defeated, so also is the enforcement of it on the part of the surety.

And the death of the surety annuls the contract.—THE same rule also holds in case of the death of the surety; because it then becomes impracticable for him to deliver up his principal; and, also, because his property is not of an analogous nature, so as to admit a discharge of the obligation by means of it. It is otherwise in the case of bail for property, for if the surety for property die, the obligation of bail does not then cease, since it is necessary to discharge it by means of his property, to whatever amount he may have rendered himself liable,

If the claimant die, the heirs or executors may demand the fulfilment.—IF the claimant should die, his executor (if there be any), or otherwise his heirs, are entitled to claim the fulfilment from the surety; because heirs and executors represent the dead.

The surety is released by delivering up his suretee.—IF, in a case of bail for the person, the surety should not stipulate his release from the bail on the delivery of the person, he is nevertheless released on such delivery, because this being the intention of the contract, it is consequently established independent of an express declaration. It is to be observed, likewise, that the surety becomes exempt from his obligation on the delivery of the person, without the acceptance of the claimant being required as a condition, in the same manner as in the payment of a debt.

Or, by delivering himself up.—THE effect is also the same, in case the principal should of himself present his person, as if he should say, "I have presented myself on account of the bail of a particular person who has become surety for me." This is approved because the surety being entitled to contend with him, in order that he may deliver himself up, it is therefore permitted to him to deliver himself up voluntarily to prevent contention.

Or, by his being delivered up by a messenger.—IT is also lawful for the agent or messenger of the surety to deliver the person, as these are the representatives of the surety himself.

The payment of the claim may be suspended upon the non-production of the principal.—IF a person become bail for the appearance of another, on this condition, that, if he do not deliver him within a particular period, he shall then be responsible for the claim upon him (a thousand dirms, for instance, and he afterwards fail of producing him within the fixed period, he is then bound to make good the claim upon the suretee; because, in this case a bail for property is suspended on the condition, namely, the failure in producing the person within a fixed period; and such suspension is valid, because of the custom of mankind.

But still the bail for the person remains in force—HENCE, when the condition is not fulfilled, the surety becomes responsible for the claim; and he is not, nevertbeless, released from the bail for the person; because bail for the person and bail for the property are not incompatible.—Shafei maintains that the bail in this instance is not valid; because bail for property induces a responsibility for property in the same manner as sale: and hence it is unlawful to suspend it on a matter of doubt and uncertainty; in the same manner as in the case of sale.—The reasoning of our doctors is that bail for property is ultimately like sale, inasmuch as it entitles the surety to repayment from the principal of what he advanced to the claimant on his account,—and that in the beginning it resembles a gift, being an acquiescence in responsibility without any exchange.—In due observance: therefore, of both these circumstances, it is declared that the suspension of it, on an uncertain condition (such as the blowing of the wind, the falling of the rain, and the like), is invalid; but that it is valid if suspended on a certain condition, such as in the case in question,

If the time be fixed, and the suretee die in

the interim, the surety becomes responsible.—If a person be bail for the appearance of another "on the morrow," under a condition of answering the claim upon the other himself, in case of failure, and the principal die before the morrow, he is in that case surety for the property; because here the condition on which he agreed to the responsibility clearly takes place,

Case of bail for property, connected with bail for the person.—If a person claim one hundred deenars from another, either with or without an explanation of their quality, and a third person become bail for the person of the debtor, under a condition that "if he do not deliver him on the morrow, he shall be responsible for an hundred deenars," and he fail in the delivery of him on the next day, he is in that case responsible, according to Haneefa and Aboo Yoosaf, for the one hundred deenars.—Mohammed maintains that if the quality of the deenars be not explained previous to the acceptance of the bail, the claimant has no right afterwards to explain their quality and demand them from the surety.—His arguments in support of this opinion are twofold. First, the surety has reated indefinite money upon a matter of doubt and uncertainty, inasmuch as he has not specifically referred the one hundred deenars to those which were claimed (for which reason the bail is invalid, even if a definition of the quality have been previously given) —Secondly, the claim of an hundred deenars, without a definition of their quality, is invalid; whence no obligation lies on the surety to produce the debtor; and as, where the production of the debtor is not obligatory on the surety, the bail for the person is of consequence invalid, it follows that the bail for the property is also invalid, since this rests upon the other.—(From what is here advanced it appears that the bail in question is valid if the quality of the deenars be specified.)—The argument of the two elders is that the deenars, mentioned by the surety do evidently, from the circumstance of the case, relate to those claimed.—It is, moreover, a frequent practice to keep a claim in a state of doubt and uncertainty.—The claim in question, therefore is, valid, in this way, that the claimant will (it is to be expected) explain the quality, and such explanation will be applied to the original claim:—and upon the claim becoming valid, the first bail (namely, bail for the person) becomes valid; and in consequence thereof the second bail (namely, bail for the property) also becomes valid.

Bail for the person cannot be exacted in cases of punishment or setaliation.—Bail for the person is not lawful in cases of punishment and retaliation, according to Haneefa;—that is, the Kazee has no power to exact it by compulsion.

But may be taken if offored by the accused.—If, however, the person upon when punishment or retaliation is claimed, should in a voluntary manner give bail of himself, it is admissible in the opinion of all our doctors; because that which is the end of bail for the person is in this case also answered, since the production of the person of the accused is hereby secured.—It is to be observed that the person upon whom punishment or retaliation is claimed, must not be imprisoned until evidence be given, either by two people of unknown character (that is, of whom it is not known whether they by just or unjust), or by one just man who is known to the Kazee; because the imprisonment, in this case, is founded on suspicion, and suspicion cannot be confirmed but by the evidence of two men of unknown character, or of one just man. It is otherwise in imprisonment on account of property; because the defendant, in that instance, cannot be imprisoned but upon the evidence of two just men; for imprisonment on such an account is a grievous oppression, and therefore requires to be grounded on complete proof.—In the Mabsoot, under the head of duties of the Kazee, it is mentioned that, according to the two disciples, the defendant, in a case of punishment for slander, or of retaliation, is not to be imprisoned on the evidence of one just man, because, as the exaction of bail is in such case (in their opinion) lawful, bail is therefore to be taken from him.

A pledge or bail may be accepted for the payment of any fixed tribute.—It is lawful to take a pledge or accept of bail for the payment of any fixed tribute, because tribute being a debt of which the payment is demanded, it may be discharged by means of the pledge or the bail, and hence the objects of these contracts is unswered.

If bail for the person be first taken from one and afterwards from another, the bail in that case holds with respect to both; for the design of bail is to fix the obligation of a claim, and this may be extended to may, so as to render them severally responsible. Besides, as the object of bail is security, this is increased by the taking of bail from another; and hence there is no incongruity in the existence of both at the same time.

Bail for property is lawful, if founded upon a just debt whether the extent be known ar uncertain.—All that has been here advanced relates to bail for the person.—With respect to bail for the property, it is lawful whether the extent of the property be known or uncertain, provided it be founded on a just debt,—that is, a debt which cannot be annulled but by payment or exemption; in opposition to a claim of person which is a debt due by a Mokatib to his master,—because that may possibly become null without payment or exemption, by an inability in the Mokatib to discharge it. Property known in the extent is (for instance) where a person says to a claiman "I have become bail for a person who owes you a thousand new dirms." The nature of uncertain property may also be explained by any axample; as for instance, where a person says, "I have become bail for the debt which a particular person owes of you;" or, "I have become bail in this sale for whatever claim may hereafter be made on the subject of it"—which bail is termed Kafalit-be'l-dirk, or bail for accidents, that is for whatever may happen. In short, bail for certain or uncertain property is lawful, because bail rests upon a broad foundation, and a small degree of uncertainty in it is therefore of no consequence. Besides, all our doctors are agreed in the legality of Kafalit-be'l-dirk, or bail for what may happen: what is a convincing argument of the legality of bail for uncertain property. Moreover, bail is lawful in the case of unintentional Shoodja [a wound occasioned by the throwing of a stone] although there be in it a great degree of uncertainty; because it is possible that death may ensue, which induces retaliation: and it is also possible that a recovery may take place in which case a fine of property only is required. Now if, notwithstanding this degree of uncertainty, the bail be lawful, it follows that it is in the same manner lawful in the case of uncertain property.

In a case of bail, the claimant is at liberty to make his demand either from the surety or the principal.—The person to whom the bail is given is at liberty to demand payment either from his debtor, who is the principal, or from his surety, because bail signifies a junction of personal responsibility to the personal responsibility of the debtor, in a claim; and this does not imply an exemption to the debtor from the claim: on the contrary, it marks the continuance of his responsibility;—unless such exemption should have been specified as a condition in the contract of bail, in which case the contract of bail becomes a contract of transfer, in the same manner as a transfer becomes bail if a condition of exemption to the debtor be not specified: because regard must be had to the spirit of the contract; and in the former instance the contract bears the sense of a transfer, in the same manner as, in the latter, it bears the sense of bail.

Any may call upon either or both.—If the person to whom the bail is given call upon one of the two parties,—that is, upon either the debtor or the surety,—he is entitled also to call upon the other; and he may, if he please, call upon both.—It is otherwise where the proprietor demands compensation for his property from one of two usurpers (that is, from the original usurper, or from another who has usurped it again from him; for he cannot then demand it from the other; because upon his agreeing to accept compensation for the usurped property from one of them, he thereby constitutes him proprietor, since option of compensation involves investiture with right of property; and hence the impossibility of his afterwards constituting the other proprietor. A claim in virtue of bail, on the contrary, does not involve an investiture with right of property.—There is therefore a difference between these cases.

Bail may be suspended upon any fit and proper condition.—The suspension of bail upon a condition is lawful.—Thus is a person say to another. "If you sell your goods to Zeyd, the price is upon me,"—or, "If anything be due to you from a certain person, that is upon me,"—or, "if a certain article be usurped from you, the damage is upon me,"—in all these cases the bail is lawful, because all our doctors have agreed upon the legality of Kafalit-be'l-dirk, when suspended on a condition. It is to be observed, however, that although conditional bail be lawful, still it is requisite that the condition on which it is suspended be of a nature adopted to the contract of bail,—either by resting upon the obligation of a right, (as if the surety should say. "If the subject of the sale be not claimed by another, I hold myself responsible for the price),"—or, by resting upon the possibility of the exaction of a debt (as if he were to say, "upon Zeyd [meaning the principal] arriving," &c.), or, by resting upon the impossibility of the exaction of a debt (as if he were to say, "upon such a person [meaning the principal] disappearing, &c.), for the suspension upon a condition not of a fit nature (such as, upon the falling of rain, or the blowing of wind), is unlawful.—In the same manner also, it is unlawful to stipulate these events as the period for payment of debt;—as if a person should say, "I have become bail for the debt due to you by a certain person until the rain fall, or the wind blow" in which case the bail is valid, but the condition is invalid, and therefore an immediate payment of the money is required; because the suspension of bail on a condition is valid, and it does not become invalid from the invalidity of the condition, being similar to the case divorce and emancipation.

Where the bail is given in an unlimited manner, the amount is ascertained by testimony, or, that failing by the, declaration of the surety.—If the surety say to the claimant "I am bail for the debt due to you by a particular person," and it be afterwards proved, by witnesses, that the debt amounts to one thousand dirms, in that case the surety is answerable for that sum, because proof by testimony is equivalent to that by actual sight. But if the amount of the debt should not be proved by witnesses, the averment of the surety is in that case to be credited in the amount which he may acknowled: for with respect to whatever sum may be alleged beyond his own acknowledgment, he is considered as the defendant.—Hence if the principal acknowledged a greater amount than that acknowledged by the surety, it cannot be admitted to operate against him; because, considered as an acknowledgment or declaration with regard to another, it is invalid as an acknowledger has no power over another.

with relation to himself; for he has power over his own person.

Bail may be contracted with or without the consent of the principal.—It is lawful to become bail either with or without the desire of the principal; because the tradition with respect to it is absolute; and does not restrict it to the desire of the principal. Bail, moreover, being an obligatory engagement, is a deed relative to the surety himself, in which there is an advantage to the claimant and no detriment to the principal: for if he should have become bail without the desire of the principal, then he has no right to apply to him for what he may pay on his account; or if, on the other hand, the bail was contracted by his desire, then the principal has expressed his acquiescence in his claim of repayment from him, to which he is entitled because of his having made the payment in virtue of authority from him,—whereas he has no right to repayment in case of having become bail without the desire of the principal, as the payment so made was a gratuitous deed.

Circumstances under which a surety has or has not a right to demand compensation from his principal.—It is to be observed that the surety has a right to a repayment, from the principal, of the sum which he may have advanced on his account in virtue of the responsibility he contracted by his desire.—As for instance, if the debt be one thousand good dirms, and he pay the claimant one thousand good dirms, he is then entitled to the repayment of one thousand good dirms.—But if he should make a payment of a nature different from his engagement,—as, if, having become bail for one thousand good dirms, he should pay the claimant one thousand bad, or vice versa,—he is in that case entitled to receive from the principal the full amount for which, by his desire, he had become responsible; because the surety, from the payment of the debt, becomes proprietor of it, and stands therefore in the place of the creditor:—in the same manner as if he had become proprietor of it by virtue of a gift, or of inheritance (that is, as if the claimant had bestowed on him a gift of the debt due to him by the principal, and permitted him to take possession of it,—or, as if the surety had succeeded to the debt in right of heritage;—or, in the same manner as where the person to whom a debt has been transferred acquires a property in the debt by either of these modes).—It is otherwise in the case of a person instructed to pay a debt; for if a person be desired by another to pay a debt on his account, and pay it accordingly, he is in that case entitled to receive from the other the exact sum he has paid on his account, although the debt relate to bad dirms, and he pay it in good; because a person so instructed, having incurred no responsibility, has therefore no right to become proprietor of the debt in virtue of is having paid it,—It is otherwise, also, if a person, having become bail for a debt one thousand dirms, should compound with the claimant for the payment of five hundred dirms;—for in this case he is entitled to receive only five hundred dirms from the debtor, because composition is similar to annulment of part of the debt, and the case is therefore the same as if the claimant had remitted part of the debt to the surety: and as, in case of remission of the debt by the claimant, the surety has no right to receive anything from the debtor,—it follows that, in the case of composition also, he has no right to receive more than he has actually paid

He cannot claim reimbursement until he has actually discharged the claim upon the principal.—A SURETY has no right to advance any claim on the principal until he make payment on his account, because he does not become proprietor of the debt until he pays it. It is otherwise with respect to an agent for purchase; as he is entitled to receive from his constituent the price of the merchandise previous to the payment of it on his part. The reason of is this is that there virtually subsists a contract of exchange between the constituent and his agent; because the right of property is first established in the agent, and afterwards shifts to the constituent;—and hence they stand to each other in the relation of buyer and seller:—when it is permitted to the agent to detain the merchandize from his constituent until he receive the price from him

But he may proceed as the claimant proceeds.—If the claimant importune the surety in pursuit of his claim, then the surety may in the same manner importune the principal or suretee. If, also the surety be imprisoned by the claimant, he is in the same manner entitled to imprison the principal.

He is released by a discharge to the principal; but the principal is not released by an exemption to him.—If the claimant remit the debt to the suretee, or receive payment of it from him, the surety is in that case released from his engagement, because the debt, in reality, is due by the suretee:—but if he exempt the surety, the suretee (or principal) does not thereby become exempted from his debt: because the surety is merely a dependant; and, also, because he is liable only to a claim, whereas the debt exists in the principal independent of such claim.

And the same of a suspension of the claim—If the claimant allow the principal a respite from his claim, or suspend his claim upon him to a more distant period, such respite or suspension of claim operates also in favour of the surety;—but if he grant a respite of his claim to the surety it does not operate in favour of the principal;—because respite or suspension, as being a temporary remission, is therefore analogous to an absolute remission.—It is otherwise where, the debt being immediately due, the creditor accepts bail for the payment at the period of a month afterwards; for this suspension of his claim for a month operates also in favour of the principal, because here the period of suspension agreed upon is a circumstance annexed to the debt, which, at the time of contracting the bail, was immediately due,

A surety, compounding the debt of the princ pal with the claimant, discharges both from any further demands.—If a surety, in a debt of one thousand dirms, compound with the creditor for a payment of five hundred dirms in that case both the principal and the surely become exempted from their respective obligations for the remaining five hunored dirms ;—because the surety having referred the composition to the thousand dirms due by the principal, the principal becomes thereby released from his obligation by the payment of five hundred dirms ; for composition is a cancelling of part of the debt ;—and the release of the debtor from his obligation occasions the release of the surety.

And has a claim upon the surety for what he pays in composition.—He is also in this case entitled to five hundred dirms from the surety, provided he entered into the bail with his consent,—It were otherwise if the surety should compound the debt for some thing of a different species (as if, instead of the dirms, he should agree to pay a particular number of deenars, or any article of merchandise) ; for in such case he is entitled to a full payment of the debt, since such composition is in the nature of a contract of exchange, and the sure y becomes proprietor of the debt in virtue of his having given a consideration for it.

A surety compounding for an exemption on his own behalf does not discharge the principal.—If the surety compound with the creditor for an exemption from the obligation contracted by him in virtue of the bail, the principal is not thereby exempted, because the said composition is merely an exemption granted to the surety from a claim upon him. —Thus, for instance, if the surety for one thousand dirms compound with the creditor for one hundred dirms—in other words, if the creditor agree that, on condition of his paying one hundred dirms, he will exempt him from the rest of his obligation,—in that case he becomes exempted from responsibility ; and, provided he had become bail by desire of the principal he is entitled to receive one hundred dirms from him, whilst the creditor retains his claim on the principal for the remaining nine hundred dirms.

Cases in which the surety's right against the principal depends upon the terms of his exemption or discharge.—If a claimant say to the surety, who had become bail by desire of the principal, "You are enlarged from the claim towards me," in that case the surety is entitled to receive the amount in question from the principal ; because, according to the rules of grammar, this sentence, in which the preposition from with respect to the object, and that of towards with respect to the claimant of such object, are used means that the claim has been discharged—Hence the claimant in this case, is held to have made an acknowledgment of the discharge of the claim ; and for this reason the surety is entitled to receive the payment of it from the principal.—But if he should merely say, "I have enlarged you," the surety is not entitled to anything from the principal ; because his enlargement being here expressed without by mention made of its operation towards another, is considered as an annulment, and not as a declaration of discharged.—If he should only say, "you are enlarged," without adding, 'towards me" in that case there is a disagreement amongst our doctors,—Mohammed alleges that it is similar to the second instance—"I have enlarged you" Aboo Yoosaf, on the other hand, is of opinion that it is similar to the first instance—"You are enlarged from the claim towards me." Some, again, have said that, in all these cases, if the claimant be present, it is requisite to demand an explanation from him, since he has used a dubious expression,

An enlargement from bail cannot be suspended upon a condition.—The suspension of enlargement from bail on a condition is not lawful ; because an enlargement of this kind, as well as that of other description, involves an endowment with right of property, and the suspension of an endowment with right of property is not lawful.*—There is a tradition that such suspension is lawful ; because, in fact, a surety is responsible for a claim, and not for a debt, whence such enlargement is, like divorce, a mere annulment,† and therefore cannot be undone by the rejection of the surety :‡—and the enlargement

*An endowment with a right of property (such as a gift, for instance) must operate immediately, otherwise it is not valid.

†This doctrine is founded on the metaphysical distinction which the Mussulmans draw betwixt a debt and a claim Thus where a person remits to another a debt contracted by borrowing, purchase, or the like, he, as it were. conveys or makes over so much property to that other :—but where he remits an obligatory claim upon another to answer the debt of a third person, he then merely annuls a right of his own ; for as that other had not in reality received any property from him. he cennot by such remaission be said to have made over so much property to him.

‡ A gift, or any deed vesting property in another, cannot operate without the consent of that other. On this principle a gift is not held to take place until the seisin of the donee, as, until then, it is in his power to render it void by a rejection. But it is not in the power of the surety to prevent the operation of the exemption in his favour by the rejection of it, as it as held to it be an annulment of a right on the part of the claimant, and not a deed conveying property to him.

from bail being a mere annulment, it follows that the suspension of it upon a condition is lawful, in the same manner as the suspension of divorce of emancipation; in opposition to the enlargement of the principal; as that is an endowment with right of property, and may therefore be rejected by him.

Bail, in cases of punishment or retaliation, is valid only for the perso .—BAIL is not valid with respect to any right of which the fulfilment is impracticable by means of bail, as in cases of punishment or retaliation,—because proxies are not admitted in case of corporal punishment. But bail for the persons of criminals under the sentence of such punishments is lawful.

Bail may be given for the price, but not for the goods, in a sale.—A PERSON may lawfully become bail, on the part of a purchaser, on the payment of the price, because price is a debt: but it is not lawful to become bail, on the part of the seller, for the merchandise; for that is substance, of which the compensation, in a case of destruction is insured, by means of something of a different kind namely, the price; and although bail for insured substance be lawful in the opinion of all our doctors, still it is required that the substance be insured for a similar in kind: such as the subject of an invalid sale, an article seized in virtue of an intention to purchase, or an article usurped; but not for any substance which is insured for something of a different kind such as the subject of a valid sale, or a pawn; nor for any substance held in the nature of trust, such as a deposit, a subject of rent, a loan, Mozaribat stock, or partnership stock.—If, after the purchaser, in a case of sale, had paid the price, a person become bail for the delivery of the goods to him.—or if, in a case of pawnage, a person become bail for the pawnee restitution of the pledge,—or, in a case of hire, for the renter's restoring the article hired,—in all these cases the bail is valid, because of the surety having engaged for the performance of what was due and incumbent.

Bail for the performance of work by a specific animal is not valid.—IF a person hire a quadruped for the carriage of a burthen, and another be bail for the animal carrying the said burthen, it is not valid, because of the animal being the property of another.—This, however, proceeds on a supposition of the hire having related to a specific animal; for, if the animal be not specific, the bail is valid, as in that case it is in the power of the surety to supply an animal of his own for the carriage of the burthe . In the same manner, in case of a peson hiring a slave for service, bail given for his performance of the service is invalid, as the slave is not the property of the surety, and he has consequently no power of enforcing what he has undertaken.

A contract of bail must be formed with the consent of the claimant.—A CONTRACT of bail is not valid unless it be formed with the consent of the claimant.—This is according to Haneefa and Mohammed.—Aboo Yoosaf alleges that a contract of bail is valid, if, having been formed without the knowledge of the claimant, it receive his assent on its being notified to him: and (according to several copies of the Mabsoot) his assent is not a condition.—This disagreement relates equally to bail for the person, and bail for property.—The reasoning of Aboo Yoosaf, in support of the opinion, is, that as bail signifies an obligatory engagement, it is therefore binding on the person who undertakes it; and hence it would appear that it does not depend on the assent of the claimant: but the reason for suspending it upon his concurrence is the same as occurs under the head of marriage, treating of Fazoolee marriage: "The d cla ration of the surety that he has become bail for a particular thing, on the part of a particular person, renders the contract complete; but as it is a deed affecting the claimant (inasmuch as it invests him with a right to a claim), it is therefore suspended upon his assent."—The reasoning of the other two doctors is that bail creates a right; in other words, the surety constitute the claimant proprietor of claim upon him, which he accordingly demands from him after the completion of the contract,—Hence it follows] that two points are necessary to the completion of the contract, namely the speech of the surety (which is equivalent to a declartion with respect to the claimant), and the speech of the claimant (which is equivalent to acceptance)—No in the case in question there exists only one of these two requisites the contract, therefore is not suspended beyond the meeting; and consequently a contract of bail is not valid but through the consent of the claimant at the meeting

Except where the debtor is dying.—EXCEPTING only in one instance.—namely, where a sick* person says to his heir, "be you bail for whatever debts I may owe," and the heir becomes bail accordingly in the absence of the creditors; for in this ca e the bail is effectual, notwithstanding the absence of the creditors, upon a favourable construction.—for two reasons: FIRST, the ba l so co tracted is, in effect, a will, and is therefore valid without the intervention of the claimant (and hence lawyers have remarked that this species of bail is not lawful unless when the sick person is in possession of property; because a will would not otherwise be lawful; SECONDLY, the sick person is the representative of his creditors, because he stands in need of being so, in order that he may divest himself of his obligation; and also, because this is attended with an advantage to the creditors—The case is therefore the same as if creditors had themselves been present.

OBJECTION.—If the sick person represent his creditors, it follows that his acquiescence is a necessary condition, in the same manner

* Arab Mareez.—Always meaning a person sick of a mortal illness.

as that of the creditors, had they been present; and that the expression of "Be you bail on my part for whatever I owe," is not conclusive of the contract; whereas this renders it conclusive.

REPLY.—The bail founded on this speech of the sick person is valid, and his acquiescence is not required as a condition; because the meaning to be deduced from the speech is, evidently, a desire on the part of the sick man that the bail be concluded, and not merely a consultation respecting it: and his speech therefore resembles an order for the conclusion of a marriage, as already explained under the head of marriage.—(It is to be observed that if the speech of the sick person be addressed to a stranger, there is in that case a disagreement with respect to the validity of the bail.

Case of bail gratuitously entered into on behalf of an insolvent defunct.—IF a debtor die without leaving any property, and another become bail to his creditors, such bail is not valid, according to Haneefa.—The two disciples allege that it is valid; because it is undertaken on account of a bebt, established as the right of the creditors, and which is still extant, since no person has discharged it, whence it still exists, so far as relates to the laws of futurity; that is to say, the debtor, if it be not discharged, becomes a criminal before God Almighty.—As, also, if the surety were actually to discharged the debt, such discharge would be valid being a gratuitous act o justice, in the same manner bail for it is consequently valid.—The argument of Haneefa in support of his opinion is, that the bail is in this case given for a debt which is annulled with relation to the laws of this world; and the validity of bail being founded on the laws of this world, it cannot be legally given for what no longer legally exists.

A debtor paying his surety the sum for which bail has been given, before the surety has satisfied the creditor cannot reclaim it.—IF a person, by desire of another, should become his bail for one thousand dirms which he owes, and the debtor give the surety one thousand dirms by way of payment prior to his [the surety's] having paid the creditor, he [the debtor] is not in that case permitted to take from the surety the money he has advanced to him, for two reasons. FIRST the right of the possessor (namely, the surety) is connected with the one thousand dirms on the probability of his having occasion to pay them to the creditor, and therefore whilst such probability exists the principal surety has no right to take them from him; similar to a case where a person hastily (that is, before the stated time) pays Zakat to the collector, in which case he would not be entitled to take it back from him. SECONDLY the surety becomes proprietor of the said sum in virtue of the seisin; on a principle which shall be presently explained.—It is otherwise where the debtor gives the sum to the surety be way of commission (as if he were to say to him "Take this sum and deliver it to the debtor") ; because the surety does not become proprietor in virtue of such a seisin; on the contrary, he is in such case merely a trustee.—It is to be observed that where the surety thus receives the thousand dirms, and becomes proprietor in virtue of such receipt, he is not required to devote in charity whatever profit he may acquire from it;* because in his instance the property vests in him immediately on the receipt. Where he receives it after having himself paid the debt, the reason of the property then vesting in him is evident; and where he receives it before he has paid the debt, he becomes proprietor immediately on the receipt.—The reason of this is, that the surety has a claim on the debtor for an article similar to that for which the creditor has a claim upon him; but the claim of the surety upon the debtor is suspended until he pay the debt to the creditor. —The claim of the surety, therefore, is in the nature of a debt to become due hereafter (whence it is that if the surety should previous to his having discharged the debt to the creditor, exempt the debtor from the claim he had upon him such exemption would be valid).—Now as an article similar to that for which the surety is responsible to the creditor is due to him by the debtor, it follows that on his receiving payment from the debtor he becomes proprietor in virtue of such receipt.—The degree of baseness, moreover, which obtains in such a transaction (as shall be hereafter set forth), does not take effect, where a right of property exists, with respect to indefinite thing; as has been already explained in treating of invalid sales.

Case of a delivery of substance by the principal, to guard his surety against loss.—IF bail be given for a Koor of wheat, and the principal deliver a Koor of wheat to the surety, and he sel and acquire profit by the same, in that case the profit so acquired is, in the eye of the LAW, the right of the surety, on the principle already explained, of the property having vested in him in virtue of the receipt.—The author of the work observes, that in his opinion it is most laudable that the surety give the said profit to the debtor, although, in the eye of the law this be not incumbent upon him: and such (according to one passage in the Jama Sagheer) is the opinion of Haneefa upon this point.—The two disciples maintain that as such profit is the right of the surety, he ought not therefore to give it to the debtor:—and this also is related as an opinion of Haneefa, as well as another, namely, that the surety ought to bestow it in charity.—The argument of the two disciples is that the profit, as having resulted from the property of the surety, becomes of consequence his right.—Haneefa, on the other hand, argues that, notwithstanding the existence of the

---

*That is to say, whatever profit may arise from it between the period of his receiving it, and that of gratifying the claimant.

property, there is still a degree of baseness in it, because it was in the power of the debtor to retake the Koor of wheat from the surety, and deliver it himself to the creditor; or, because, in delivering it to the surety, it is probable that he did it with a view that he should deliver it to the creditor.—No the baseness here operates in consequence of the thing to which it relates being definite; and the mode of purging such baseness is (according to one tradition) by devoting the profit in charity, or (according to another) by giving it to the debtor, as the baseness is occasioned by his right, and not by the right of the LAW.—This latter is the most authentic doctrine; but it prescribes only a laudable, and not an incumbent duty; for the right of the surety is clear.

Case of bail discharged by an aynit sale.—If a person become bail, by desire of the principal, for a debt of one thousand dirms, and the principal afterwards desire him first to purchase on his account silks to the value of one thousand five hundred dirms, in the manner of an aynit, and then to resell the same, and discharge the debt by means of the price, and the surety act accordingly, the purchase so made is considered as on his own account, not on account of the principal, and he must, of consequence, sustain the loss arising from the aynit sale.—An aynit sale is where a merchant, for instance, having been solicited by a person for a loan of money, refuse the same, but offers to sell goods to the other on credit at an advanced price; as if he should charge fifteen dirms for what is worth only ten, and the other person agree to the same. This is termed an aynit or substantial sale, because it is a recession from a loan to a specific substance (in other words, the merchant declines granting the loan required of him by the borrower, but agrees in lieu thereof, to sell him the cloth, which is a specific substance);—and it is abominable, as being a recession from a loan of money, which is a laudable action, on a principle of avarice, which as a sordid quality.—With respect to the nature of the case in question, our doctors have disagreed. —Some have asserted, that the direction, given by the principal to the surety infers his [the principal's] being responsible for any loss that may be sustained by the purchaser in consequence of the aynit sale; and that his direction in this particular is not a commission of agency; for this reason, that the order of the principal ("purchase silks on my account") implies this assumption of responsibility;—but a responsibility of this nature is invalid, since responsibility cannot hold except in an article in which the person who is responsible has some interest; and no person has any interest in the loss on the present occasion. Others again say, that the direction in question amounts to a commission of agency; but that it is an invalid commission, as the silk to which it relates are not definite, neither is the price of them definite from an ignorance of how much it may exceed the amount of the debt.—The purchase of the silks is, in fact, considered as having been made on account of the surety, and the loss resulting from it falls entirely upon him (not upon the principal), since it was contracted by him.

Evidence cannot be heard in support of any claim against a surety which does not come within the description in the contract of bail.—If a person become bail on the part of another, for whatever may be proved to be due by him, or for whatever the Kazee may decree against him, and the debtor afterwards disappear, and a claimant offer to prove, by evidence, that the sum due to him is one thousand dirms, such evidence is not to be admitted: because here the bail is limited to whatever the Kazee may decree, as it is evident from the expression "Whatever the Kazee may decree, and likewise from that of "Whatever may be proved to be due by him," since nothing can be proved but by the decree of the Kazee, and the claim in question has not this limitation;—it is therefore invalid, and accordingly the evidence in support of it cannot be heard.

A decree passed against a surety in the absence of the principal cannot affect the latter unless the bail were entered into by his desire.—If a person prefer a claim before the Kazee to this effect, "That an absentee owes him a thousand dirms, and that a particular person present is by desire of the debtor, bail for the same" and establish his assertion by testimony, in that case the Kazee must pass a decree against both the debtor and the surety.—If, however, the bail have been given without the desire of the debtor, the Kazee must in that case decree the debt solely against the surety; and in this instance the evidence adduced by the claimant is admitted as sufficient, because the bail is absolute, and not qualified, as in the preceding case.—It is to be observed that the different decrees which the Kazee gives in the case of bail with, and without, the desire of the debtor (that is, the decree against both, in the one case, and against the surety only in the other), is founded on the difference which obtains in the nature of these two modes of bail:—for bail by desire of the debtor is a gratuitous deed in the origin, and a contract of exchange in the end; but bail without the desire of the debtor is a gratuitous deed both in its origin and its consequences.—Now where the claim relates to one only, the decree cannot be extended to the other. But if a decree should be passed relative to a surety by desire, it must necessarily include the principal, since the desire he expressed is a virtual acknowledgment of the existence of the debt.—It is otherwise with respect to a voluntary surety; for as the existence of the debt in that case is proved by his belief of it, in having undertaken the bail with regard to it, and not by any virtual acknowledgment of the debtor, the decree is therefore solely referred to him.—In the former case (namely, that of bail by desire), the surety is authorized to receive from the seller what he may have been obliged to pay on his account —Ziffer maintains that he is not entitled to such compensation; because, having himself refused to pay, and having been compelled to it, he is of consequence in his own opinion oppressed; and it is not permitted to such as are opposed to oppress others.—Our doctors, on the other hand, argue that whenever a refusal is undone by law, the opinion founded upon it becomes of consequence null.

Case of Kafeel-bell dirk.—If a person sell a house, and another become Kafeel-be'l dirk or security against accident,* on his behalf, the security so given is a direct declaration of the house being the property of the seller.—If, therefore, the surety should afterwards prefer a claim of right to the house, such claim is inadmissible.—The reason of this is, that if the security be a condition of the sale (as if the purchaser should have said, "I will buy the said house, provided a particular person will be security against any future claim to it"), in that case the completion of the sale rests upon the agreement of the surety; and afterwards, when he prefers a claim of right to the house, he endeavours to destroy that which he had himself rendered complete;—if, on the other hand, the security should not be a condition of the sale, the surety, in that case, by agreeing to the bail, did, as it were, incite the buyer to the bargain (since his desire of purchase was founded on the procurements of bail).—The bail so given, therefore, is equivalent to a declaration of the right of property of the seller.

An attestation to a contract of sale is not equivalent to Kafeel-be'l-dirk.—If, in the sale of house, a person should attest the bill of sale, and put his seal to it, without giving any security, such testimony and affixture of seal is not an acknowledgment of the seller's right of property, and hence the witness may, if he please, afterwards claim the house, because attestation is neither a condition of sale nor a declaration of the property of the seller, as it sometimes happens that men sell their own property, and sometimes that of others —Besides, the witness may have made this attestation merely as a memorandum of the transaction; a supposition which the case of bail could not admit of,—Lawyers have remarked that if it be expressed, in the bill of sale, that "a certain person had sold such a house, which is his property, by a complete and valid sale," and the person attest the writing to this effect, "Witness thereto," this is an acknowledgment and declaration of the seller's right of property —If, on the other hand, he attest it thus, "Witness to the agreement of the buyer and seller," this is not a declaration of the seller's right of property.

Section
Of Zamins or Guarantees.

The guarantee of agents to their employere is null.—If an agent sell the cloths of his constituent, and hold himself responsible for the payment of the price to his constituent,—or, it a Mozarib sill the goods of his employer and hold himself responsible for the payment of the price.—the responsibility in either case is null: First, because surety or bail is an engagement compelling the undertaker to answer a claim; and as, in these cases, the agent and Mozarib are themselves the claimant for the price of the goods, it follows that if they were responsible for the same, they would be security on their own behalf, which is absurd:—and, Secondly, because the goods remain in their hands in the nature of a trust; and trustees are not held by the law to be liable to responsibility.—If, therefore, they were held responsible, it would be contrary to the precepts of the law.—Hence the taking of security from them is null, in the same manner as a condition of respontibility is null with respect to a trustee or a borrower

The guarantee of partners, in a purchase ana sale to each other, is null—If two shares in a slave sell him by one contract, and each of them be security to the other, on behalf of the buyer, for his payment of the proportion of the price due to that other, such security is null: because if the security were valid under a general copartnership in the price, it necessarily follows that each is in part security on behalf of himself, since every member of the slave is indefinitely shared between them;—or if, on the other hand, the security of each were valid with respect to the other's share in particular, this induces a division of a debt before the receipt of it, which is unlawful.—It is others wise whers two partners in a slave sell their shares by different contracts; as their security to eaeh other, for the prices respectively due, is valid, since there is no partnership in this instance, because whatever is owing to each, respectively, in virtue of his perticular contract, appertains solely to him, without any participation of the other;—whence it is that the parchaser is at liberty to accept the share of them only and to take possession of it, after the payment of the price; and also that he may take possession of the share of one of them only after paying to him his proportion, notwithstanding he may have purchased both shares.

Guarantee for land-tax, and all other regular or justifiable imposts, is valid.—If a person become security in behalf of another

---

*Dirk signifies, properly, any possible contingency. Kafeel-be'l-dirk, therefore, means bail for what may happen —In the present instance it alludes to the possibility of a claim being afterwards set up to the house by some other person, which, if substantiated, would annul the sale,

for tribute due by him or for a nawayeeb* levied upon him for his kissmat, all such securities are valid.—Security for tribute is valid, because tribute is in the nature of a debt (and may be a lawful subject of claim as has been already explained (in opposition to Zakat, as that is a matter solely affecting him who pays it, in the manner of a gift, and of which his property alone can be the subject; whence, after his death, it cannot be discherged our of his effects, unless prescribed in his will):—and with respect to nawayeeb, if it extend only to what is just (such as exactions for digging a canal, for the wages of safe guards, for the equipment of an army to fight against the Indfidels, for the release of Mussulman captives, or for the digging of a ditch, the mending of a fort, or the construction of bridge) the security is lawful in the opinion of the whole of our doctors.—But if nawayeeb extend to exactions wrongfully imposed, that is, to such as tyrants extort from their subjects (as in the peesent age), in that case, concerning the validity of security for it, there's a difference of opinion amongst our modern doctors.—Sheikh Iman Alee is of the number of those who hold the security in this instance to be valid.—With respect to kissmat, there is a difference of opinion concerning the meaning of the word.—Some allege that it signifies the same with nawayeeb, whilst others define it to be same with Mowzifa Ratiba that is fixed imposts which ar exacted at stated periods such as once in the month, or onee in every two or three months.—Now nawayeeb means the casual exactions made by the sovereign, which have no fixed or stated period. The law, however, is as above explained, with respect to both, If, therefore, the exaction be right, then the security for it is lawful, according to all our doctors; or if wrong, there is a disagreement with respect to the validity the security.

Difference between a suspended debt and suspended bail.—If a person say to another, "I owe you a debt of one hundred dirm, payable a month hence," and the other assert that the debt is immediately due, his assertion, as claimant, is to be credited—But if a person should declare to another, "I am security to you, in behaif of another, for a debt of one hundred dirms, payable a month hence," and the other assert that the debt is due immediately, the declaration of the surety is to be credited.—The difference between these two cases is, that in the former case the debtor makes an acknowledgment of the debt, and then claims his right to a suspension of payment for one month: whereas in the latter case the surety makes no acknowledgment of the debt, inasmuch as the obligation of the debt does not rest upon the bail or surety, as has been often before explained—In fact, he has simply acknowledged a claim to which he is responsible after the lapse of a month, which the claimant denies, asserting that he is answerable for such claim immediately:—and regard is paid, in LAW, to the affirmation of the defendant.—A clause of suspension, moreover, is merely an accidental property of a debt, and not an essential, whence it is that it cannot be proved unless it has been express'y stipulated.—The affimation, therefore, of the person who denies the stipulation of such condition is credi'able,—in the same manner as in the case pf a condition of option, in sale,—Bail under a suspension, on the contrary, is one species of bail, in which the being susp nded in its operation is an inherent quality, and not an accident; whence this species of suspension may be proved without having been stipulated; as where for instance, the debt due by the principal is a suspended debt. According to Shafei, the affirmation of the claimant is to be credited in either case; and the same is related as an opinion of Aboo Yoosaf.

Bail against accident, in the sale of a slave—If a person purchase a female slave, and another warrant her to be the property of the seller,* and she afterwards prove to be the property of some other person, the purchaser is not entitled to exact the price from the surety, until the Kazee shall have first passed a decree against the seller for the restitution of the price because, according to the Zahir Rawayat, the sale does not become null immediately on the proof of the subject of it being the property of another but endures until the Kazee pass a decree in favour of the purchaser, directing the seller to return the price. Since, therefore, previous to issuing the said decree, it is not incumbent on the principal [that is the seller) to make restitution of the purchase-money, so neither is it incumbent on the surety It would be otherwise if the slave were proved to be free, and the Kazee pass a decree to that effect, for in such case the sale becomes null immediately on the issuing of such decree, since freedom is incapable of being the subject of sale, and the buyer would, therefore, be entitled to exact the purchase-money either from the surety or from the seller, without waiting for a deeree of restitution from the Kazee.—It is related as an opinion of Aboo Yoosaf, that sale becomes null immediately on the proof of the subject of it being the property of another; and that, consequently, the buyer has in such case a right to exact the price either from the surety or the seller, without waiting for the decree of the Kazee to that effect.

Security for fulfilment is null.—If a person purchase a slave, and another be security for the fulfilment of the bargain,† such security

*Nawayeeb are all extraordinary aids beyond the established contributions, levied at the discretion of government to answer any particular emergency of the state.

*Literally, "and another be bail against accident."

† Arab. Zamin ba Ohda,

is null; because the word Ohda [fulfilment] is of a comprehensive nature, as having a variety of meanings. I It relates to the former bail of sale which the seller received from the person who sold the slave to him; and this being the property of the seller, any security with respect to it is invalid. II. It relates to the contract and its rights. III. It relates to a warrant or security against accidents. And, IV. To option.—As, therefore, the term comprises so many things the particular application of it is dubious; and hence practice cannot take place upon it.—It is different with respect to the term dirk, for although that signify whatever may happen, yet the custom of mankind has restrained the application of it to one particular sense, namely, a security against any future claim; and Ziman-be'l-dirk, or security against accident, is therefore valid.

Security for a surrender of the article to the purchaser is invalid.—If a person sell an article, and another be security to the purchaser for the release* of that article, such security is invalid, according to Haneefa, as the intention of it is the release of the article, and the delivery of it to the purchaser, which the security is not competent to perform.—The two disciples held this of be valid, as in their opinion it is equivalent to a security against accident;—in other words, it imports an obligation to deliver to the purchaser either the article sold, the value, or the price;—and such being the case, it is valid of course.

CHAPTER II.

OF BAIL IN WHICH TWO ARE CONCERNED

Case of two persons who are joint principals in a debt, and bail fot each other.—If two men owe a debt in an equal degree, and each be security on behalf of the other,—as where, for instance, two persons purchase a slave, jointly, and each is security on behalf of the other.—in this case, if either of them pay off a part, he has no right to make any claim on the other:—unless, however, the payment so made exceed a half of the whole debt, in which case he has a right to exact such excess from the other.—The reason of this is, that each of them is a principal with respect to one half of the debt, and a security with respect to the other half;—for what each owe in virtue of his being a principal is no bar to the obligation upon him as a security, the one being founded on debt, and the other on a claim, which is subordinate thereto,—Whatever payments, therefore, either of them may make are held to be in virtue of the former, namely, the debt, as far as that extends: and any excess is referred to the latter, namely, the security.

Case of two persons who are bail for a third, to the amount of the whole claim, and also, reciprocally, bail for each other's security.—If two persons be bail for property in behalf of another,—in this way, that each surety, respectivey, holds himself responsible for the other surety,—in this case, whatever either surety may pay [in virtue of the bail]. whether the sum be great or small, he is entitled to exact the half of it from the other surety.—This proceeds upon a supposition that each of these two sureties, respectively. is bail for the whole property on the part of the principal, and likewise for the whole obligation on the part of his co-surety. Hence in each of the two sureties two bails are united: one on behalf of the principal, and one on behalf of the co surety; and bail on behalf of a surety is lawful, in the same maner as on behalf of a principal, or as a transfer on behalf of a transferee: because the intention of a contract of bail is undertaking the obligatton of a CLAIM; and this end is answered by bail on behalf of a surety.—As, therefore, two bails are in this case united in each of the sureties, it follows that whatever payments are made by either of them are made, in an indefinite manner, on account of both; for the payment so made was purely in virtue of the bail; and each, with respect to the bail, stands in the same predicament; that is to say, neither has a superiority over the other.—(It is otherwise where each surety is a principal with respset to part of the debt, as in the first example: for in this case neither has a right to exact any thing from the other on account of the payments he may make, unless such payments exceed the sum for which he is a principal, because the principal has a superiority.)—Now since. in the case in question, whatever payments either of the two may make are made indefinitely, on account of both, it follows that the person making such payments is entitled to exact the half of them from the other. And this induces no unnecessary revolution, because the intention of the contract, in the present instance, is that the parties be on a footing of perfect equality with respect to the bail, which can only be answered by the one party taking from the other the half of what ahe may have paid The other, therefore, is not entitled to retake it again from the person who has first paid, because this, if permitted, would destroy the equality already established.—(It is otherwise in the preceding case, for there each of the parties is a principal with respect to a portion of the debt, and consequently they are not on a footing of perfect equality with respect to the bail.)—When, however, one of the parties shall have taken the half from the other, then they are jointly entitled to exact the whole of what has been paid from the principal; since they paid the same on his behalf; the one making the payment immediately from him-

* Arab. Khilas: meaning, the surrender of the article, by the seller, to the purchaser.

self. and the other doing it, as it were, by his substitute :—or the surety who paid is at liberty, if he please, to exact the whole of what he paid from the principal, because he was bail for the whole of the property by his desire.—If, in this instance, the creditor exempt one of the two sureties, he has a right to claim the whole from the other. because the exemption of a surety does not operate as an exemption in favour of the principal, and therefore the whole of the debt remains due by the latter ; and the remaining surety being still bail for the whole of the property, it is consequently lawful to claim the whole from him.

In the dissolution of a reciprocity partnership, each partner is responsible for any debts contracted under their partnership.—If two partners by reciprocity dissolve their copartnership and separate, whilst some of heir bebts still remain due, the creditors have in that case a right to claim the whole from whichever of them they please; because each of these partners is surety for the other, as has been already explained in treating of partnership.—Neither of the partners, moreover, has a right to make any claim upon the other for whatever payment he may have made to the creditors. unless such payment exceed the half of the debt, in which case he has a right to exact from him the payment of such excess, for the reason already explained. in discussing the case of reciprocal bail by two.

Case of two Mokatibs, bail on each other's behalf, for their ransom—If a master constitute two of his slaves Mokatibs, by one contract, for a thousand dirms (for instance), and each of them become bail for the other, in that case, whatever sum, from the whole amount covenanted to be paid by the master, is discharged by either. the half of that sum may be exacted from the other.—Analogy would suggest that the bail, in this instance, is not valid ; because bail is valid only when opposed to a valid debt : and the consideration of Kitabat, or the degree of freedom bestowed upon a Mokatib, is not a valid debt, as has been already explained.—It is lawful, however, upon a favourable construction, by considering each of the slaves as a principal with respect to the obligation of the whole consideration of Kitabat, namely, a thousand dirms :—in other words, by considering each of them, respectively, as being responsible to the master for the payment of the whole : and, consequently, that upon his making payment of the whole, the other obtains his freedom as a dependant,—in this way, that the freedom, of both is suspended on their payment of one thousand dirms, and the master is at liberty to claim the said thousand from each of them respectively, as a principal, not as a surety Each, however, is considered as surety on behalf of the other, with respect to exacting a moiety of what he pays on account of the consideration of Kitabant (a particular explanation of this will hereafter be given in treating of Mokatibs),—From the explanation of the law in this case it appears that both slaves are equal with respect to the payment of the thousand dirms, which is the consideration of their Kitabat ; and hence each is respectively entitled to take from the other a moiety of whatever part of the said thousand dirms he may pay.—If the master, in this case, should emancipate one of the slaves prior to his having made any payment on account of his Kitalat, in that case he becomes free; because his master, whose property he then was, chose to emancipate him.—He becomes likewise exempted from any obligation to pay his half of the consideration of Kitabat, because he acquiesced in that obligation merely as a means to obtain his freedom ; but upon his becoming free in consequence of the emancipation of his master it exists no longer as a mean and therefore ceases altogether.—The obligation, however, for the payment of an half still continues incumbent upon the other, who remains a slave ; because the whole amount of the consideration was opposed to the bondage of both ; and the whole was considered as due from each, respectively, merely as a device, in order to render the bail of each in behalf of the other valid, and thereby to enable each to take from the other a moiety of what he pays.—But when the master emancipates one of them, there exists no further necessity for this devise ; whence the debt is then considered as opposed to them both, jointly (not, in toto, to each respectively), and is accordingly divided into two separrate parts, of which one still continues due from him who remains a slave, —In taking this portion, the master is at liberty either to exact it from the freedman, in virtue of his being security, or from the slave, because of his being the principal.—If he take it from the freedman, the freedman is then entitled to retake it from the slave, because of his having paid it by his desire ; but if he take it from the slave, he [the slave] is not entitled to take anything from the freedman, because he merely pays a debt which he justly owes.

CHAPTER III

OF BAIL BY FREEMEN IN BEHALF OF SLAVES, AND BY SLAVES IN BEHALF OF FREEMEN.

A person becoming surety on behalf of a slave for a claim, to which the slave is not liable until after emancipation, must discharge it immediately.—If a person be surety in behalf of a slave, for some thing not claimable from the slave until after he recover his freedom, without specifying whether the thing in question is claimable immediately, or hereafter, in that case it is to be considered as immediately due ;—that is to say, it is claimable immediately from the surety.—For instance, if an inhibited slave acknowledge his destruction of the property of any person,—or that he owes a bebt which his master disavows,—or if, having married without the consent of his master, he should have had carnal connexion with the women on the supposition of such marriage being valid (in all which cases nothing could be exacted from the slave immediately, nor until he become free), and a person be a surety for the compensation eventually claimable from the slave, he is liable to an immediate claim for it. The reason of this is, that the slave ought immediately to discharge the compensation, because there exists an evident cause of its obligation upon him, and a slave, in virtue of his being a MAN, is capable of being subject to obligation. He is, however, exempted from an immediate claim for the compensation, because of his property, since everything he possess is the property of his mastes, and his master is not assenting to the obligation. *The surety, on the contrary, is not poor, and is therefore liable to the claim immediately, in the same manner as a person who becomes surety for an absentee or a pauper.—It is otherwise where a person becomes bail for a debt not immediately due, for there the surety also is not liable to an immediate claim, any more than the debtor, since the debt is suspended in its obligation to a future period by the consent of the creditor.—It is, however, to be observed, that in the case in question, the surety, on discharging the claim upon the slave, is not entitled to demand it from the slave until he shall have obtained his freedom; because the creditor had no right to demand it until that event: and the surety stands in the place of the creditor.

Bail for the person of a slave is cancelled by his death.—IF a person advance a claim on an unprivileged slave, and another become surety for his person, and the slave afterwards die the surety is in that case released from his engagement, because of the principal being released.—(The law is the same where the slave, in whose behalf bail for the person is given, is emancipated.)

Bail to a claim of right in a slave subjects the surety to responsiblity in the event of the slave's decease.—IF a person claim the right of property in a slave, and another become surety in behalf of the possessor of him, and the slave then die, and the claimant establish his right by witnesses, the surety is in that case responsible for the price.—because it was incumbent on the possessor to repel the claim, or, if he failed in so doing, to give the value for which the surety became answerable; and as the obligation, after the slave's death, rests upon the principal, so also it now rests upon the surety,—it is otherwise in the preceding case; for there the obligation was merely to produce the person of the slave, which is cancelled by his death.

Bail by a slave in behalf of his master, or by a master in behalf of his slave, does not afford any ground of claim by the surety upon the principal.—IF a slave, who is not in debt, be surety for property in behalf of his master, or any other man, and he afterwards made free, and then pay the amount for which he was surety,—or, if a master become surety for property in behalf of his slave, whether he be indebted or not, and after emancipating him, pay the amount for which he stood security, in neither of these cases is either of the parties entitled to take any thing from the other.—Ziffer maintains that in both these cases the parties have a right to recur to each other: that is, each is entitled to take from the other what he may have paid.—(It is here proper to remark, that the reason for restricting the slave, in the first case, to one that is free from debt is, that if he were otherwise, he could not be surety for property in behalf of his master, since this would affect the right of his creditors.—The argument of Ziffer is that a ground of claim (namely, bail by desire of the principal) exists in both cases; and the bar to its operation (namely, slavery) is removed and done away.—The argument of our doctors is that the bail in these cases is not in the beginning a ground of claim, since neither can the master nave a debt due to him by his slave, nor can the slave have a claim of debt upon his master.—Hence as no ground of claim existed in the beginning, it does not afterwards take place, in consequence of the removal of the bar to it (namely, slavery); for the law here is the same as where a person becomes susety for another without his desire, in which case the subsequent assent of the surety is of no effect.

The consideration of Kitabat is not a subject of bail.—BAIL for the consideration of Kitabat, whether the surety be a slave or a freeman, is not valid; because the consideration of Kitabat is allowed to exist as an obligation merely from necessaity, it being repugnant to reason, inasmuch as a master cannot have a claim of debt upon his slave; and in the case in question the Mokatib, or person who owes the consideration of Kitabat, is supposed the slave of the claimant.—Hence the consideration of Kitabat is not so fully established as to admit of bail for it—because wherever a thing is established from necessity, it is restricted entirely to the point of necessity. Besides, the debt of Kitabat ceases entirely in case of the inability of the slave to discharge it; nor is it possible to revive it, by claiming it from the surety, because the meaning of bail is "the junction of one person to another person in relation to a claim.—As therefore; the claim does not operate upon the principal, it of consequence ceases with regard to the surety; because it is rule that a principal and his surety are both equally liable for the same claim.

Nor a consideration in lieu of emancipatory labour.—A CONSIDERATION, in lieu o emancipatory labour, resembles the consideration of Kitabat, in the opinion of Haneefa, because (according to him) a slave that works out his freedom by labour is in the same predicament with Mokatib.

BOOK XIX

OF HAWALIT, OR THE TRANSFER OF DEBTS.

Definition of terms.—HAWALIT, in its literal sense, means a removal: and is derived from Tahool, which imports the removal of a thing from one place to another.—In the language of the LAW it signifies the removal or transfer of a debt, by way of security and corroboration, from the faith or the original debtor, to that of the person on whom it is transferred. The debtor or person who transfers the debt is termed Moheel: the transferee or person upon whom the debt is transferred, Mohtal-ali hee, and the creditor, or transfer receiver, Mohtal

The transfer of a debt.—THE transfer of a debt is lawful; because the Prophet has said, "Whenever a person transfers his debt upon a rich man, and the creditor assents to the same, then let the claim be made upon the rich man;" and also because the person upon whom the debt is transferred undertakes a thing which he is capable of performing; whence it is valid, in the same manner as bail. It is to be observed, however, that transfer is restricted to debt; because it means an ideal removal; and an ideal removal, in LAW, applies to debt, and not to substance, which requires a sensible removal.

Is rendered valid by the consent of the creditor and transferee.—A CONTRACT of transfer is rendered valid by the consent of the creditor and transferee. The consent of the creditor is requisite, because the debt (the thing transferred) is his due; and mankind being of different dispositions with respect to the payment of debts, is therefore necessary to obtain his consent. The consent of the transferee is also requisite, because by the contract of transfer an obligation of debt is imposed upon him, and such abligation cannot be imposed without his consent. The consent of the principal, on the contrary, is not requisite, because (as Mohammed observes in the Zeadat) the engagement of the transferee to pay the debt is an act relative to himself, which is attended with a benefit to the principal, and is no way injurious to him, inasmuch as the transferee has no power of reverting to him, in case of having accepted the obligation without his desire.

It exempts the debtor from any demand.—WHEN a contract of transfer is completed, the Moheel, or person who makes the transfer is exempted from the obligation of the debt, because of the acquisscence of the transferee Ziffer has said that he is not exempted, because of the analogy which subsists between this case and that of bail; for they are both contracts of security or corroboration; and as, in the case of bail, the person who is bailed does not become exempted from the debt so neither ought the transferrer in this case. Our doctors, on the other hand, agree that Hawalit literally means removal; and when a debt is removed from the faith of one person, it cannot afterwards remain upon it Bail on the contrary, means a junction; and the intendment of it is, that the bailer unites his faith to that of the suretee with respect to the claim. Now the decrees of the law proceed according to the literal meaning; and the object of transfer, namely, corroboration, is obtained when a person that is rich and a fair dealer acquiesces in the obligation of the debt, as it is to be supposed that he will readily fulfil his obligation.

OBJECTION.—If the debt shift from the faith of the debtor to that of the transferee, it would follow that there can be no conpulsion on the creditor to receive payment from the debtor, where he offers to discharge the debt; in the same manner as a creditor is not compellable to receive payment of his debt from a stranger in a gratuitous manner.

REPLY.—The creditor is compenable to receive payment of the debt from the debtor, if he offer to make payment, because the claim may eventually revert upon him, in case of the destruction of the debt, since if the transferee were to die insolvent, without having paid the debt, the claim would revert upon the transferer, for reasons that will be shown in the next case. Hence, the payment of the transferrer cannot in every respect be considered as gratuitous; like that of a stranger.

Unless the transferee deny, or become unable to fulfil, his engagement.—THE creditor is not entitled to make any claim upon the transferrer excepting where, his right on the transferee being destroyed, he cannot otherwise obtain it: in which case the debt reverts upon the transferrer. Shafei alleges that the creditor has no right to make any claim for his due upon the transferrer, although his right be destroyed; because, in consequence of the transfer, the transferrer becomes exempted from the debt; and this exemption a absolute, and not restricted to the condition of payment from the transferee. Hence the debt cannot revert upon the transferrer, except on account of some new cause; and none such is to be found in this case. The argument of our doctors is that, although the exemption be absolute, in the terms of the contract, yet it is restricted, in the sense, to the conditien of the right being rendered to the creditor. The transfer is therefore dissolved in case of his right being destroyed; because the contract is capable of dissolution, and may be dissolved by the agreement of the parties. The condition, moreover, of the safe delivery of the debt to the creditor, is equivalent to that of warranting the subject of a sale to be free from blemish; that is to say, such a warranty implicitly exists, as a condition, in every sale, although it be not specifically mentioned; and, in the same manner, the security of the debt exists, as a condition, in a contract of transfer; although not specified in it. The destruction of the debt due to the creditor in a case of transfer is established, according to Haneefa, by one of two circumstances. I. Where the transferee denies the existence of the contract, upon oath, and the creditor cannot produce witnesses to prove it. II. Where the transferee dies poor. In the event of either of these circumstances the debt is destroyed; since in neither case it is practicable for the creditor to receive payment from the transferee. This is the true meaning of a destruction of the debt in a case of transfer. The two disciples maintain that a destruction of the debt is occassioned by one of three circumstances. Of these, two are the same with those above recited; and the third is,—a declaration, by the magistrate, of the poverty of the tsansferee during his lifetime. This third circumstance is not admitted by Haneefa: because, according to his doctrine, poverty cannot be established by the decree of the magistrate, since property comes in the morning and goes in the evening; but, according to the two disciples, the decree of the magistrate establishes poverty.

The transferee has a claim upon the doctor for what he transfers upon him.—If the transferee should demand, from the transferrer, the amount of what he has paid in virtue of the transfer made upon him, and the transferrer affirm that "he had made such transfer upon him, in exchange for a debt of the same amount which he owed him." the affirmation of the transferrer is not admissible, and he is bound to pay the demand of the transferee, because the reason of such demand (namely, the actual payment of it by his desire) is established.—The transferrer moreover, asserts a claim which the other denies; and the affirmation of the defendant is creditable.

Objection.—It would appear that the affirmation of the transferee is not to be credited although he be the defendant; because he has acknowledged what he afterwards denies, inasmuch as his acceptance of the transfer is a virtual acknowledgment of the debt he owes to the transferrer.

Reply.—The acceptance of the transfer is not an acknowledgment of bebt due to the transferrer, because contracts of transfer are sometimes made without the transferee's owing any thing to the transferrer.

A debtor may transfer his debt upon a property in the hands of another person.—If a person, having deposited a thousand dirms with another, should afterwards make a transfer on it (as if he were to desire his creditors to receive payment of his debt, from a deposit placed by him with such a person), such transfer is valid, because the trustee is capable of discharging the debt from the deposit. If, however, the deposit be destroyed, the transferee (who is otherwise a trustee) is in such case released from the engagement of transfer; because the transfer was restricted to the deposit, since the trustee engaged on further than the payment of the debt from the amount of the actual deposit. It is otherwise with respect to a transfer restricted to usurped property: for if a person were to make a transfer on an usurper, on account of specific property usurped by him, and the said property be afterwards destroyed, the transfer so made does not become null: on the contrary, it is incumbent on the usurper to pay the creditor a similar,—or the value, in case the property in question had not been an article of which the unities were similar;—because, as a similar or the value is a representative of the thing itself, the property in this case is not held to have been destroyed.

A transfer may be restricted to what is due from the transferee to the debtor.—It is to be observed that transfers are sometimes restricted to debts due by the transferee to the transferrer;—and in all cases of such restricted transfers, the law invariably is that the transferrer has no right to make any claim upon the transferee, for the substance or the debt upon which he has made such transfer because the right of the creditor is connected with it, in the same manner as that of e pawnholder is connected with the pawn: and also, because, if such a right remained with the transferrer, the act of transfer (which is the right of the creditor) would be rendered null. It is otherwise with respect to an absolute transfer (that is, where a person simply says to his creditor "I have transferred the debt I owe you upon a particular person" without making any mention of debt being due to him, or of specific property of his being in the possession of that person whether from deposit or usurpation); for in this case the right of the creditor does not relate to the property of the transferrer, but rests entirely upon the faith of the transferee; and hence if the transferrer should receive payment of the substance or debt due to him from the transferee, still the transfer does not become null.

The loan of money in the manner of Sifitja is disapproved.—Sifitja is abominable;* that is to say, the giving of a loan of any thing in such a manner as to exempt the lender from the danger of the road; as, for instance, where a person gives something by way of loan, instead of a deposit, to a merchant, in order that he may forward it to his friend at

* That is to say, it is disapproved, although not absolutely illegal. (See the meaning of the term Abominable, p. 206.)

a distance. The abomination in this case is founded on the loan being attended with profit, inasmuch as it exempts the lender from the danger of the road: and the Prophet has prohibited our acquiring profit upon a loan.

BOOK XX

OF THE DUTIES OF THE KAZEE

CHAPTER I

A Kazee must possess the qualifications of a witness.—THE authority of a Kazee is not valid, unless he possess the qualifications necessary to a witness; that is, unless he be free, sane, adult, a Mussulman, and unconvicted of slander; because the rules with respect to jurisdiction are taken from those with respect to evidence, since both are analogous to authority; for authority signifies the passing or giving effect to a sentence or speech affecting another, either with or without his consent; and evidence and jurisdiction are both of this nature. (The rules with respect to jurisdiction are here said to be "taken from those with respect to evidence," because, as the sentence of the Kazee is in conformity with the testimony of the witness, it follows that the evidence is, as it were, the principal, and the decree of the Kazee the consequent) As therefore, jurisdiction, like evidence is analogous to authority, it follows that whoever possesses competency to be a witness is also competent to be a Kazee; and also, that the qualifications requisite to a witness are in the same manner requisite to a Kazee—and likewise, that an unjust* man is qualified to be a Kazee; whence if such a person be created a Kazee, it is valid, but still it is not advisable: in the same manner as holds with respect to evidence;—that is. if a Kazee accept the evidence of an unjust man, it is valid, in the opinion of all our doctors; but still it is not advisable to admit the testimony of such a person, since an unjust man is not deserving of credit.

He does not forfeit his office by misconduct.—IF a Kazee be a just man at the time of his appointment, and afterwards, by taking of bribes, prove himself an unjust man, he does not by such conduct become discharged from his office,—but he is, nevertheless, deserving of a dismission. This is the doctrine of the Zahir Rawayet; and it has been adopted by modern lawyers.—Shafei maintains that an unjust man is incapable of the office of Kazee, in the same manner as (in his opinion) he is incompetent to give evidence. It is related in the Nawadir, as an opinion of our three doctors, that an unjust man is incapable of dischargeing the duties of a Kazee. Some of the moderns have also given it as their opinion that the appointment of a man, originally unjust to the office of Kazee, is valid; but that if, having been just at the time of his appointment, he afterwards become unjust; he stands discharged from his office; because as the Sultan appointed him from a confidence in his integrity, is to be presumed that he will not acquiesce in his discharge of the duty without integrity.

A Mooftee must be a person of good character.—A QUESTION has arisen, whether an unjust man be capable of being a Mooftee;* and on this subject different opinions have given, Some have said that he is incapable of being a Mooftee, because the giving of a Fitwa (or statement of the law applicable to any case) is connected with religion, and the word of an unjust man is not creditable in matters relative to religion. Others again have said, that an unjust man is capable of being a Mooftee, because of the probability that he will toil and labour in the discharge of his duty, lest the people charge him with his faults. The former, however, is the better opinion. Some have established it as a condition, that a Kazee be a Moojtahid:† the more approved doctrine is, however, that this is merely preferable, but not indispensable.

An ignorant person may be appointed a Kazee,—THE appointment of an ignorant man to the office of Kazee is valid. according to our doctors.—Shafei maintains that is it not valid; for he argues that such appoints

---

* Arab. Fasik.—In some instances the term applies merely to a person of loose character and indecorous behaviour, (See Vol. I. p. 26) In the present instance; however, the character also includes want of integrity, as appears a little lower down.

* Anglice, an expounder of the LAW.—As the offices of Kazee and Mooftee are frequently confounded by European writers, it may not be improper to remark, in this place that the word Kazee (or Cadi) is derived from Kaza, signifying jurisdiction, and Mooftee from Fitwa, meaning an application or statement of the LAW. The Mooftee, therefore, the officer who expounds and applies the law to cases, and the Kazee the officer who gives it operation and effect.

†Moojtahid is the highest degree to which the learned in the law can attain, and was formerly conferred by the Madrissas (or colleges); of which one of the first instances occurs in the life of Haneefa, whom all the leaned acknowledge as their superior.

ment supposes a capability of issuing decrees, and of deciding between right and wrong; and these acts cannot be performed without knowledge. Our doctors, on the other hand, argue that a Kazee's business may be to pass decrees merely on the opinions of others. The object of his appointment, moreover, is to render to every subject his just rights; and this object is accomplished by passing decrees on the opinions of others

It is the duty of the sovereign to appoint fit persons to that office.—It is incumbent on the Sultan to select for the office of Kazee a person who is capable of discharging the duties of it, and passing decrees; and who is also in a superlative degree just and virtuous; for the Prophet has said, "Whoever appoints a person to the discharge of any office, whilst there is another amongst his subjects more qualified for the same than the person so appointed, does surely commit an injury with respect to the rights of GOD, the PROPHET, and the MUSSULMAN." It is to be observed that a Moojtahid means either a person who is in a high degree conversant with the Hadees or actions and traditional sayings of the Prophet, and who has also a knowledge of the application of the law to cases; or one who has a deep knowledge of the application of the law to cases and also some acquaintance with the Handees. Some have said that he ought also to have a knowledge of the customs of mankind, as many of the laws are founded upon them.

A person may be appointed who has a confidence in his own abilities.—THERE is no impropriety in selecting for the office of Kazee a person who has a thorough confidence in his ability to discharge the duties of it: because the companions of the Prophet accepted this appointment; and also, because the acceptance of it is a duty incumbent on mankind.

But not one who is dubious of himself.—IT is abominable to select a person for the office of Kazee who suspects that he is incapable of fulfilling the duties of it, and who is not confident of being able to act with a strict regard to justice because the selection of such a person is a cause of the propagation of evil. Several of our doctors, however, have said that the acceptance of the office of Kazee without compulsion is abominable, because the Prophet has said, "Whoever is appointed Kazee suffers the same torture with an animal, whose throat is mangled, instead of being cut by a sharp knife." Many of the companions, moreover, declined this appointment; and Haneefa persisted in refusing it, until the Sultan caused him to be beaten in order to enforce his acceptance of it; but he suffered with patience rather than accept the appointment. Many others, in former times, have also declined this office. Mohammed remained thirty and odd days, or forty and odd days, in imprisonment, and then accepted the appointment. In fact, the acceptance of the office of Kazee, with an intention to maintain justice, is approved, although it be more laudable to decline it: because it is a great undertaking, and notwithstanding a person may have accepted it from an opinion that he should have been able to maintain justice, yet he may have erred in this opinion, and afterwards stand in need of the assistance of others when such assistance is not to be had. Hence it is most laudable to decline it;—unless, however, there be no other person so capable of discharging the duties of it, in which case the acceptance of it is an incumbent duty as it tends to preserve the rights of mankind, and to purge the world of injustice.

The appointment must not be solicited or coveted.—IT becomes Mussulmans neither to covet the appointment of Kazee in their hearts, nor to desire it with their tongues because the Prophet has said, Whosoever seeks the appointment of Kazee shall be left to himself; but to him who accepts it on compulsion, an angel shall descend and give directions; and also, because whatsoever desires this appointment shows a confidence in himself, which will preclude him from instruction: and whoever, on the other hand, puts his trust in GOD, will be secretly inspired with a knowledge of what is right in the discharge of his office.

IT is lawful to accept the office of Kazee from a tyrannical Sultan, in the same manner as from a just Sultan; because some of the companions accepted this office from Moaviah,† notwithstanding the right of government during his time remained with Alee: and also, because some of the followers‡ accepted it from Hijaj,§ who was a tyrant Hence the acceptance of the office of Kazee from a tyrant is lawful;—provided, however the tyrant do not put it out of the power of the Kazee to render right to the people; for otherwise the acceptance of it would not be

---

*The term tyrannical, when applied to a sovereign, generally signifies his being an usurper.

†Moaviah, the son of Abee Sifwan. He had been originally appointed, by Othman, to the government of Syria; and suspecting Alee to be instrumental to the death of his patron Othman (who was some time after slain in an insurrection) refused to acknowledge him on his being elected to succeed Othman, and in the end obtained the Khalifat for himself, being the first Khalif of the house of Ommiah, commonly termed the Ommiad Khalifa.

‡Arab, Tabayeen.—A title given to those doctors, &c., who succeeded the Ishab, or companions of the Prophet.

§Hijaj Bin Yoosafal Sakifee.—He had been originally appointed Governor of Arabian Irak by Abdamalik, the fifth Khalifa of the house of Ommiah, after which he defeated Abdalla bin Zabair, who had assumed he title.

lawful, as the end of the appointment could not then be answered.

A Kazee, on his appointment, must take possession of all the records, &c. appertaining to his office.—Whenever a person is appointed to the office of Kazee, it is incumbent on him to demand the Dewan of the former Kazee.—By the Dewan is meant the bags in which the records and other papers are kept; for those must be preserved to serve as vouchers on future occasions.—These bags, therefore, must always remain in the hands of the person possessing the judicial authority; and as the judicial authority rests, for the time being, with the person appointed to the office, he must therefore require them from the Kazee who has been dismissed.—It is to be observed that the papers, in which such proceedings, &c. are written, must necessarily be the property either of the public treasury, of the litigants, or of the dismissed Kazee.—Still, however, in all these cases, the new-appointed Kazee has a right to demand them from the late one:—in the first case, evidently; and in the second, because the litigants left the said papers in the hands of the late Kazee, that he might act according to them; and as his power of action afterwards devolves upon the new Kazee, he is of course entitled to receive them; and also in the third case, because the late Kazee did not preserve them as property, but merely as the instruments of justice; and hence it is the same as if he had devoted them to the public.

Through his Ameens, who must investigate the nature of them.—It is requisite that the new Kazee send two Ameens,* in order to take possession of the bags of the Dewan in the presence of the late Kazee, or in the presence of his Ameen. It is also necessary that they ask and inquire of the late Kazee, which are the papers that register his proceedings; and which are those that establish guardians for the property of orphans? and that then the late Kazee arrange the several descriptions of papers in different bags, in order that no doubt may arise to the new Kazee.—It is to be observed, however, that this investigation is merely for the sake of knowledge, and not for the purpose of impeachment.

And must inquire and decide concerning prisoners confined upon any legal claim.—It is requisite that the new-appointed Kazee examine into the state of the prisoners, because this is one of the duties of his office.—Whoever of them makes an acknowledgment of right in favour of others, the new Kazee must render it obligatory upon him, as acknowledgment induces obligation on the acknowledger.—Whoever of them, on the contrary, makes a denial, the new Kazee must not credit the affirmation of the late Kazee with respect to him unless supported by evidence, because, in consequence of his dismission, his affirmation carries no more authority than that of any of the people in general; and the evidence of one person is not proof, more especially when such evidence relates to an action of his own.—If the late Kazee should not be able, in the last instance, to produce evidence, still the new one must not immediately release such prisoner; on the contrary, he must issue proclamation and use circumspection; that is, he must cause a person to proclaim, every day, that "the Kazee directs that whatsoever has any claim against such a prisoner is appear and be confronted with him."—If any person appear accordingly, and prefer, claim against the prisoner, the Kazee must desire him to produce evidence.—but if no person appear, he must then release the prisoner, provided he see it advisable.—He must not, however, precipitate his enlargement, before these precautions have been taken; because the imprisonment of him by the former Kazee having been done apparently with reason, it is probable, if he should hastily release him, that the claimant against him might lose his right.

And also concerning deposits of contested property.—It is requisite that the new Kazee examine into the deposits,* which the dismissed Kazee may declare to be in the hands of particular persons, and also into the proceeds arising from the Wakfs [charitable appropriations] of Mussulmans,—and that he act with these according to such evidence as may be established concerning them, or according to the acknowledgment of the person in whose hands are the deposits or the proceeds of the Wakf, because evidence and acknowledgment are both proofs:—but he must not credit the affirmation of the late Kazee:—unless the person in whose hands the property lies avow that "the said property was given in charge to him by the Kazee:" in which case the new Kazee may credit the affirmation of the old one with regard to such property, as it here appears, from the trustees acknowledgment, that the psoperty in question had been in the possession of the dismissed Kazee, whence it may be said to be still in his hands:—his affirmation, therefore, with respect to such property, must, in this case, be credited.—This proceeds on a supposition that the actual possessor had from the beginning acknowledged the dismissed Kazee's consignment of the property to him; for if he should first have declared, "this property belongs to Zeyd" (for instance), and afterwards, "the dismissed Kazee deposited this

*Anglice, trustees or confidants. It is the name of an office in the Kazee's court, in the manner of a register. It also signifies an inquisitor.

*Meaning controverted property, held by the Kazee until the issue of the suit or litigation, and which he delivers over to some person to keep, in the manner of a trust.

with me." and the Kazee affirm it to be the property of some other than Zeyd, in this case he [the possessor] must give the property to Zeyd, in favour of whom he made the first acknowledgment, as his right is rendered preferable by such acknowledgment; and he must then give a compensation, also, to the dismissed Kazee, because of his having afterwards acknowledged that "the said property was in his custody:"—and the dismissed Kazee must give the compensation so received to the person in favour of whom he makes the affirmation.

He must execute his duty in a mosque—or other public place.—It is requisite that the Kazee sit openly in a mosque for the execution of his office, in order that his place may not be uncertain to travellers or to the inhabitants of the town.—The Jama mosque* is the most eligible place, if it be situated within the city, because it is the most notorious.—Shafei maintains that it is abominable for a Kazee to sit in a mosque for the execution of his duty, since polytheists are admitted into the court of the Kazee and these are declared in the Koran to be filth.—Moreover, women during their monthly courses may enter the court of the Kazee, but are not allowed admission into a mosque.—The arguments of our doctors on this point are twofold, First, the Prophet has said "mosques are intended for the praise of God and the passing of decrees;" and he moreover decided disputes between litigants in the place of his Yettekaf [a particular penance] by which must be understood a mosque: besides, the Rashedian, Khalifa sat in mosques, for the purpose of hearing and deciding causes.—Secondly, the duty of a Kazee is of a pious nature, and is therefore performed in mosques in the same manner as prayers are offered there.—In answer to Shafei, it is to be observed, that as the impurity of polytheists relatee to their faith and not to their externals, they are not therefore prohibited from entering a mosque; and with respect to menstruous women, they have it in their power to give notice of their case to the Kazee, who may then go out and meet them at the gate of the mosque, or depute some other for that purpose, as is done where the case is of a nature unfit for public discussion.

Or in his own house.—There is no impropriety in the Kazee's sitting in his own house to pass judgment; but it is requisite that he give orders for a free access to the people.

And must be accompanied by his usual associates.—It is requisite that such people sit along with the Kazee as were used to sit with him prior to his appointment to the office; because, if he were to sit alone in his house, he would thereby give rise to suspicion.

He must not accept of any present except from relations or intimate friends.—The Kazee must not accept of any presents, excepting from relations allied to him within the prohibited degrees, or those from whom he was used to receive them prior to his appointment; neither of which can be esteemed to be on account of his office, the one being in consequence of relationship, and the other of all acquaintance.—Excepting these, therefore he must not accept presents from any person as these would be considered as given to him on account of his office, and such it is unlawful for him to enjoy.—If, also his relation within the prohibited degrees, having a cause depending before him, should offer him a present, it is incumbent on him to refuse it.—So likewise, if any person accustomed to send him presents prior to his appointment should send him more than usual,—or if, having a suit before him he should send him any presents whatever; in neither case is it lawful for him to accept them, since they would be considered as given to him in consequence of his office, and hence an abstinence from such is indispensable.

Nor of any feast or entertainment—The Kazee must not accept of an invitation to any entertainment, excepting a general one; because a particular entertainment would be supposed to have been given on account of his office, and his acceptance of it would therefore render him liable to suspicion: in opposition to the case of a general one.—This ordinance, which has been adopted by the two Elders, applies equally to the feasts of relations and others.—It is related, as an opinion of Mohammed, that the Kazee may accept of an invitation to a feast from his relation, although it be a particular one, in the same manner as he is permitted to accept of presents from him.—It is to be observed that a particular entertainment means such as depends entirely on the preference of the Kazee; that is, such as would not take place in case of his absence; and a general one is the reverse.

He must attend funerals, and visit the sick.—It is fitting that the Kazee attend at funeral prayers; and also, that he visit the sick; for these are amongst the duties of a Mussulman, inasmuch as the Prophet, in enumerating six incumbent offices of the Mussulmans towards each other, mentioned funeral prayers and the visiting of the sick.—But it is requisite that, on these occasions, he make no unnecessary delay, nor permit any person to hold a coversation on the subject of his suit, lest he should thereby afford room for suspicion.

Precautions requisite in his general conduct and behaviour.—The Kazee must not give an entertainment to one of the parties in a suit without the other; because the Prophet has prohibited this; and also because it is of a suspicious nature.

* The Jama mosque is the principal mosque in a town, where public prayer is read every Friday: in opposition to a Masjid, which signifies a smaller mosque, where public prayer is not read.

WHEN the two parties meet in the assembly of the Kazee, he must behave to both (in regard to making them sit down, and the like) with an equal degree of attention; because the Prophet has said, "Let a strict equality be observed towards the parties in a suit with respect to their sitting down, or directing them, or looking towards them."

THE Kazee must not speak privately to either of the parties, or make signs towards him, to give him intructions or support his argument; for, besides giving rise to suspicion, he would thereby depress the other party, who might be induced to forego his claim, from an opinion that the Kazee was biased towards the other.

THE Kazee must not smile in the face of one of the parties, because that will give him a confidence above the other; neither must he give too much encouragement to either, as he would thereby destory the proper awe and respect due to his office.

And in his conduct towards witnesses in court, or whilst giving evidence,—IT is abominable in the Kazee to prompt or instruct a witness, by saying to him (for instance), "Is not your evidence to this or to that effect?" Because assistance is hereby, in effect, given to one of the parties; and it is therefore abominable, in the same manner, as it would be to instruct either of the parties themselves. —Aboo Yoosaf has said that instruction to a witness, on an occasion free from suspicion, is laudable;—because a witness may sometimes be at a stand from the awe with which he is struck in the assembly of the Kazee: and in such case to encourage him, in order to give life to the right of his party, is the same as the deputing of a person to compel the appearance of the defendant in court, which is lawful, notwithstanding it be an assistance to the plaintiff,—As, also, it is lawful to exact bail from the defendant, although an assistance be thereby given to the plaintiff; in the same manner it is lawful to give encouragement to a witness, to preserve his right, although assistance be thereby offered to one of the parties.

He must not give judgment at a time when his understanding is not perfectly clear and unbiased.—THE Kazee must not give judgment when he is hungry or thirsty, because such situations diminish the intellect and understanding of the person affected by them. Neither must he give judgment when he is in a passion or when he has filled his stomach with food, because the Prophet has said "Let not the magistrate decide between disputants when he is angry or full."

A YOUNG Kazee ought to satisfy his passion with his wife before he sits in the court, that he may not be attracted by the view of women that may be present there.

Section

Of Imperishment.

Rules in imprisonment for debt.—WHEN claimant establishes his right before the Kazee, and demands of him the imprisonment of his debtor, the Kazee must not precipitately comply, but must first order the debtor to render the right; after which, if he should attempt to delay, the Kazee may imprison him.—This is related in Kadooree: and it proceeds on the principle, that imprisonment is the punishment of delay;—whence it is necessary first to order him to restore the right to its owner, that his delay may be made apparent.—This is where the right is established by the debtor's acknowledgment; for in that case the non-payment on the first demand is not construed into delay, because it is possible that the debtor expects a respite, and therefore has not brought the money along with him. But if he should delay after the decree of the Kazee, he must then be imprisoned, as his delay is then evident —Where, on the other hand, the right is established by evidence, the defendant must be imprisoned immediately on the establishment of it; because his denial, which occasioned the necessity of proof by evidence, furnishes a sufficient argument of his intention to delay.

In an award of debt, the defendant must be imprisoned immediately on neglecting to comply with the decree,—provided it be incursed for an equivalent, or by a contract of marriage.—IF a defendant, after the decree of the Kazee against him delay the payment in a case where the debt due was contracted for some equivalent (as in the case of goods purchased for a price, or of money, or of goods borrowed on promise of a return), the Kazee must immediately imprison him, because the property he received is a proof of his being possessed of wealth.—In the same manner, the Kazee must imprison a refractory defendant who has undertaken an obligation in virtue of some contract, such as marriage or bail, because his voluntary engagement in an obligation is an argument of his possession of wealth, since no one is supposed to undertake what he is not competent to fulfil.—If, also, in this case, he plead poverty, this plea is nevertheless rejected, and the plaintiff's assertion (of his being possessed of wealth) credited.—It is to be observed, that the obligation contracted from marriage, as here mentioned, relates only to the Mihr Mooajal, or prompt dower, and not to the Mihr Mowjil, or deferred dower, because an engagement to pay a future debt does not argue the possession of wealth.—In cases, also, of debt of any other description (such as a compensation for usurped property, amercement for a crime, the consideration of Kitabat, compensation for the freedom of a partnership slave, the maintenance of a wife, and so forth), the Kazee must not imprison the defendant when he pleads poverty; because none of these acts indicate the possession of wealth, and therefore his declaration of poverty must be credited.

And also in every other instance, if the creditor prove his capacity to discharge it —

If, however, the plaintiff prove that he is possessed of wealth, the Kazee must in that case imprison the debtor, under any of the above circumstance.—The distinctions here stated are from the Zahir Rawayet.—It is said, by other authorities, that the assertion of the plaintiff must be credited in every case of debt: that is, whether one debt be contracted in exchange for an exquivalent, or voluntari y engaged for by the party: because poverty is the original state of man, and wealth merely supervenient, and thus the netural condition of man is an argument of the truth of the defendant's declaration of poverty.—There is also another tradition, that the defendant's declaration of poverty is creditable in every case of debt, excepting such as is contracted in exchange for an equivalent.

Case of a wife suing for her maintenance.—If a wife demand her subsistence from her husband, and he plead poverty, his declaration, corroborated by an oath, is to be credited.—In the same manner, if a person emancipate his share in a partnership slave, and his partner demand a compensation for his share, and he plead poverty, his declaration is to be credited.

Objection.—These two cases are conformable to the two last quoted traditions: but they are repugnant to the doctrine of the Zahir Rawayet; for although; in virtue of the marriage in the one case, and the emancipation of the joint slave in the other, there exists in both a voluntary engagement of responsibility, which indicates the possession of wealth, still his declaration of poverty is nevertheless declared to be creditable.

Reply.—Subsistence to a wife is not an absolute debt (that is, such as can be rendered void only by payment or exemption), for it becomes void, according to all our doctors, without payment or exemption, in case of death In the same manner also, compensation for freedom is not an absolute debt, according to Haneefa, being in his opinion the same as the consideration of Kitabat:—and the doctrine of the Zahir Rawayet alludes only to absolute debts

In a case where the defendant pleads poverty, and the plantiff proves, by evidence, his possession of wealth, the Kazee must imprison him [the defendant] for two or three months; after which it is requisite that he make an investigation into his circumstances; and if upon such investigation; the people say he is wealthy, let him be continued in confinement,—but if they say he is poor, let him be released; because he stands in need of an allowance of time to enable him to acquire which: and the continuance of his imprisonment is, in such case, an oppression.—In Kadooree's abrigement, it is related that he is to be rel ased from eonfinement, but that the plaintiff is not to be prohited from using importunity with him.—The case of importnnitv will be more fully discussed hereafter in treating of Hijr.—The period of imprisonment is fixed at two or three months for this reason, that as the imprisonment is inflicted on account of contumacy, in the debtor's withholding payment of the debt, notwithstanding the Kazee's order, the Kazee must therefore imprison him until such time as he reveal his property; in case he have any concealed; and as it is requisite that the te rm be of some duration, to the end that this advantage may be obtained from it, Mohammad has therefore fitted it at the period above mentioned.—Other authorities nx it at one month; at five months and at six months.—In fact, this is a point which must be left io the discretion of the Kazee: because to conditions of men are various in regard to their endurance of the hardships of imprisonment, some being capable of bearing it longer than others; and hence the necessity of leaving it to the Kazee to act as he may deem best.—If the debtor prove his poverty by witnesses, prior to the expiration of the prescribed period,* in that case there are two traditions. According to one, the witnesses are to be credited: but according to the other their evidence is not to be admitted.—Many of our modern doctors follow the latter opinion.

Case of aeknowledgement of debt.—It is related, in the Jama Sagheer, that if a person make an acknowledgment of debt before the Kazee, he [the Kazee] must in such case imprison him, and must then make inquiry of the people into his circumstances. If it appear that he is rich, he must in that case continue his imprisonment: but if his poverty be made apparent, he must release him.—The compiler of the Hedaya remarks that this alludes to a person who, having at one time made an acknowledgment of debt to the Kazee, or to some other, afterwards discovers an intention of delay; for otherwise it would differ from the doctrine of Kadooree, before quoted in which it is expressly declared that the Kazee ought not immediately to imprison a debtor after acknowledgment.—(The compiler gives this explanation with a view to reconile the doctrine of the Jama Sagheer with that of Kadooree.)

A husband may be imprisoned for the maintenance of his wife; but a father cannot be imprisoned at the suit of his son—A husband may be imprisoned for the maintenance of his wife, because in witholding it he is quilty of oppression: but a father cannot be imprisoned for a debt due to his son, because imprisonment is a species of severity; which a son has no right to be the cause of inflicting on his father: in the same manner as in cases of retaliation or

* This is an apparent contradiction to what immediately procedes, concerning the discretionary power of the Kazee with rospect to the period of imprisonment.—It is, hbwever, merely a continuation of the doctrine Mohammed, who has prescribed a term.

punishment —If, however, a father withhold maintenance from an infant son, who has no property of his own, he must be imprisoned; because this tends to preserve the life of the child; and also because there is no other remedy, since maintenance (in opposition to debt) is annulled by the lapse of rime, and therefore it is necessary to prevent its destruction for the future.

———

CHAPTER II.

OF LETTERS FROM ONE KAZEE TO ANOTHER

Letters authenticated by evidence are admissible in cases of property.—A LETTER from one Kazee to another is admissible relative to all rights except punishment and retaliation, provided it be authemticated by evidence exhibited before the Kazee to whom it is addressed, for which there is an absolute necessity, as will be shown hereafter

Difference between a record, and a Kazee's letter.—IF witnesses exhibit evidence, before a Kazee, against a defendant, the subject of the suit being at a distance, the Kazee may pass a decree upon such testimony, because it establishes proof. The decree so made is written down, and this writing is termed a Sidjil or record, and is not considered as the letter of one Kazee to another.*—If, however, the evidence be given in the absence of the defendants, the Kazee must not pass a decree, it being unlawful to do so in the absence of the person whom it affects, but he must take down the evidence in writing, in order that the Kazee to whom such writing shall be addressed may use it as evidence, —This writing is termed Kitab Hookmee, or the letter of one Kazee to another, and is a transcript of real evidence.

A letter is transmissible only on certain conditions—It is to be observed that the transmission of letters of one Kazee to another is restricted to several conditions, which will hereafter be explained; and the legality of it is founded on its necessity, since it may often be impossible for the plaintiff to bring the defendant and the evidences together in the same place, because of the distance of their abodes —Hence the lettler of one Kazee to another is, as it were, the evidence of evidence, as a branch from the trunk.—It also to be observed that the term rights above used; comprehends debts, and also marriage dowers, portions of heirs usurpations, contested deposits, or Mozaribat stock denied by the manager; because all these are equivalent to bebt, and are capable of ascertainment by description, without the necessity of actual exhibition.—Letters from one Kazee to another are also admissible in the case of immoveable property, because it is capable of ascertainment by a description of its boundaries:—but they are not admissible with regard to movable property, because in that case, there is a necessity for actual exhibition.—It is related as an opinion of Aboo Yoosaf, that letters from one Kazee to another are admissible wjth respect to a male slave, but not with respect to a female, because the probability of elopement is stronger in the one than the other.—It is also related as an opinion of his, that they are admissible with respect to both male and female slaves, but that particular conditions are requisite to establish their admissibility, which will be expained in their proper place—It is related as an opinion of Mohammed, that the letters of a Kazee are admissible with respect to every species of movable property, and this opinion has been adopted by our modern doctors

The testimony requisite to authenticate it.—THE letters of Kazees are not admissible unless authenticated by the testimony of two men, or of one man and two women. because there is a similarity between all letters, and it is therefore necessary to establish their authenticity by complete proof,—that is, by evidence.—The ground of this is that these letters are binding in their nature, and therefore require to be completely proved—It is otherwise with respect to the letters of Hirbees [Infidel aliens] to the Imam, soliciting protection; for these require not to be proved by evidence since they are not binding in their natute, inasmuch as it rests with the Imam to grant the protection or not at his plesure.—It is also otherwise with respect to the message of a Kazee to a Moozee [purgator of witnesses,] or with respect to the message of a purgator to the Kazee, for such a message has no force, considered as the message of a purgator but merely as being a corroboration of the testimony of witnesses.

The contents must be previously explained to the anthenticating witnesses.—IT is incumbent on the Kazee to read his letter in the presence of the witnesses who are to authenticate it, or to explain the contents of it to them, that they may have a knowledge thereof: because evidence cannot be given without knowledge. Afterwards he must close the letter, and affix his seal to it in their presence, and then consign it over to them, that they may have a security against any possibility of alteration in it.—This is according to Haneefa and Mohammed; and the reason is, that a knowledge of the subject of the letter, and an evidence of the affixture of the seal, are indispensable requisites; and in the same manner a remembrance of the contents is also requisite; whence it is that the Kazee must furnish tnem with an open copy

* This case supposes the thing in dispute to be situated in the jurisdiction of a different Kazee from him before whom the parties bring their suit; and the decree which in this case the Kazee gives being written down, is carried to the other Kazee, who is bound to see it enforced.

of the letter; with which they may refresh their memory.—It is however related, as the last opinion of Aboo Yoosaf, that no one of these particulars is requisite, it being sufficient to attest that this is the letter and this the seal of the Kazee; and it is also reported, from him, that the affixture of the seal is not necessary.—Hence it appears that, after his attaining the dignity of Kazee, he considered this matter as of little consequence; and his opinion is of great weight, since those that only hear are not so competent to determine as those that see.—Shimsal-Ayma has adopted the opinion of Aboo Yoosaf.

It must not be received but in presence of the dsfendant.—When a letter from a Kazee arrives, the Kazee to whom it is addressed ought not to receive it unless in the presence of the defendant; because as such letter is equivelent to an exhibition of devidence, the presence of the defendant is therefore indispensable.—It is otherwise with respect to the other Kazee's hearing the evidence, because that is done merely with a view to transmit it, and not to pass sentence upon it.

Forms to be observed in the reception of it.—When the witness bring the letter to the Kazee to whom it is addressed, let him first look at the seal of it and after hearing their testimony) that "this is the letter of a particular Kazee."—that "he delivered it to them in his court of judgment,"—the "he read it in their presence,"—and, that "he affixed his seal to it before them'), let him then open and read it in the presence of the defendant, and pass a decree agreeably to the contents.—This is according to Haneefa and Mohammed.—Aboo Yoosaf has said it is sufficient for the witnesses to attest that "this is the letter and seal of such a Kazee."—In the Kadooree, the proof of the integrity of the witnesses prior to the opening of the letter is not made a condition.—The better opinion, however, is that it is a necessary condition; and the same has been declared by Khasaf; for this reason, that there may eventually be a necessity to recur to other evidence, in case of a want of proof of the integrity of those that brought it; and it would be impossible for any others to give their testimony unless the seal still remained upon it: it is therefore absolutely necessary that the Kazee defer breaking the seal of the letter until the integrity of the bearers be proved.

It is rendered void by the death or dismission of the writter in the interium.—One Kazee must not accept a letter from another, unless the Kazee that wrote it be, at the time, still fixed and established in his office.—If, therefore, prior to the receipt of the letter, the Kazee that wrote it should have died, or have been dismissed from his office, or have become disqualified from the duties of it, from apostasy or insanity, or from having suffered punishment for slander.—the Kazee to whom the letter is addressed must then reject it; because the author of it being at that period reduced to the level of the people, any information from, him, independent of what relates to himself, or mutually to them both, is not admissible.

Or (unless generally addressed) by the death or dismission of him to whom it is transmitted.—So, likewise, if the Kazee to whom the letter is addressed should have died, another Kazee must not open it, unless the address run in this manner, "To the son of——. Kazee of the city of——, or to whatever Kazee it may concern this letter,"—in which case another Kazee may receive it, because he is comprehended in the address from the specification of his office and city—If the address, however, be merely, "To whatever Kazee it may concern,' he is no entitled to open it, from the uncertainty of the address.

If the defendant die previous to the arrival of the letter with the Kazee, judgment must be passed upon it in presence of his heir, as being his representative.

It is not admissible in cases of punishment or retaliation.—A letter from one Kazee to another is not valid in cases of retaliation of punishment; because as in such a letter there exists a semblance of substitution (for the letter is not itself evidence, but merely a substitute for evidence), it is therefore equivalent to evidence upon evidence; and as evidence upon evidence is not admitted in these cases, the ietter of a Kazee cannot be admitted.

Section.

A woman may executive the office of Kazee in all cases of property.—A woman may execute the duties of a Kazee in every case except punishment or retaliation, in conformity with the rule that the evidence of a woman is admissible in admissible in every cases of punishment or retaliation: for the rules of jurisdiction are derived from the rules of evidence, as was before stated.

A Kazee is not at liberty to appoint a deputy without the authority of the Imam.—It is not permitted to a Kazee to appoint a deputy. unless he have received a special power from the Imam to that effect: for although he have been himself appointed to the office of Kazee, yet he has not been empowered to confer such appointment on another.—Hence, in the same manner as it is unlawful for an agent to appoint an agent unless with the permission of his constiruent, so is it unlawful for a Kazee to appoint a deputy unles by the authority of the Imam.—It is otherwise with respect to a person appointed to read the Friday's prayers; for he may appoint a deputy to act for him, since if any delay should happen in the performance of this service, the prayers would become void and null, as the period for them is fixed: the appointment of a person to read these prayers, therefore, is virtually an argument of his being empowered to appoint a deputy to act for him, with a view to prevent the nullity of the service:—country to jurisdiction, which, not depending on a fixed period, is not therefore defeated by delay.

But the decrees of the deputy, passed in his presence, or with his approbation, are valid.—IF a Kazee, not having power to appoint a deputy, should nevertheless appoint one, and the said deputy, either in presence of the Kazee, or in his absence, but with his approbation, pass a decree, the decree so passed is valid;—in the same manner as where the agent of an agent performs any act in the presence of the agent, or with his consent, in which case such act is valid.—The ground of this is that the decree being passed in the presence of the Kazee, or with his approbation, and the act being performed in the presence of the agent, or with his approbation, the judgment and reflection of the Kazee himself is therefore exerised in the case of the decree passed by his deputy,—and the judgement and reflection of the agent in the case of the deed done by his agent,—which is what was required.

If he appoint a deputy, by authority, he cannot afterwards dismiss him.—IF the Imam give authority to the Kazee to appoint whomsoever he pleased his agent, the person whom he appoints becomes in that case the deputy of the Sultan; and the Kazee is not entitled to dismiss him.

He must maintain and enforce the equal decree of every other Kazee.—IT is incumbent upon every Kazee to maintain and enforce the decree of another Kazee, unless such decree be repugnant to the doctrine of the Kora , or of the Sonna, or of the opinions of our doctors; in other words, unless it be a decision unsupported by authority.—It is related, in the Jama Sagheer, that if a Kazee pass a decree in a meter concerning which different opinions have been given, and be afterwards succeeded by another Kazee of a different opinion with respect to that matter, the latter Kazee must nevertheless enforce the decree so made; for it is a rule that when a Kazee passes a decree in a doubtful case, the decree is executed accordingly; not is it permitted to a succeeding Kazee to rescind it because although the succeeding Kazee be equal in poin of judgment to his predecessor, still the judgment of the predecessor is in this instance allowed a superiority, because of its having been exercised in passing the decree; and therefore it cannot be affected by the judgment of his successor, which is deemed inferior from its not having been exercised.

His determination in a doubtful case is valid, although it be repugnant to the tenets of his sect.—IF a Kazee, in a doubtful case, determine country to his tenets, from having forgotten the principles of his sect, such decree must neverthless be enforced, according to Haneefa,—If, on the contrary, he pass such decree knowingly, and not through forgetfulness, there are in that case two opinions recorded.—According to one, the decree must be enforced in that instance also, because the error in is is uncertain.—In the opinion of the two disciples the decree must not be enforced in either case; that is, whether the error be wilful, or proceed from forgetfulness: and this is the approved exposition.—By a doubtful case is meant one in regard to which there is no particular ordinance, either by the word of GOD, or by the Prophet, and concerning which, consequently, different opinions have been supported by the companions and their followers.—Where a great number, however, have concurred and only a few have differed, it is not considered as a doubtful case.

An article decreed unlawful, upon evidence, continues so, although the evidence prove false.—EVERYTHING of which the illegality is decreed by the Kazee from apparent circumstances, that is to say, from the testimony of witness, although in reality such testimony be false, is nevertheless ipso facto unlawful,*—This is according to Haneefa: and he is also of the same opinion where the Kazee decrees the legality of a thing; provided, however, that the claim of the plaintiff be founded on some determinate plea, such as purchase, lease, or marriage,—as if, for instance, he should claim a female slave by asserting that he had purchased her.

A decree cannot be passed against an absentee but in presence of his representative.—THE Kazee must not pass a decree against an absentee unless in the presenee of his representative.—Shafei maintains that it is lawful for a Kazee to pass a decree against an absentee; because, upon the establishment of proof by testimony the right in the judgment of the Kazee becomes evident —The arguments of our doctors upon this point are twofold —FIRST, the passing of a decree on the testimony of witnesses is with a view to put an end to contention; and as contention supposes a refusal on the part of the defendant, it follows that as his absence precludes the possibility of his refusal, no contention can have existed. SECONDLY, the absence of the defendant admits of two suppositions, namely, that (if present) he would either have acknowledged the claim, or denied it: if the former, the Kazee must have passed a decree upon that ground; or, if the letter, upon testimony. Now decrees passed on those different grounds are of a distinct nature, since that which is founded on testimoney is binding on all men, whereas the other is not.—Where, therefore, the defendant is absent, it becomes a matter of doubt with the Kazee what kind of decree he ought to pass; and hence it is requisite that he suspend it until the arrival of the defendant,

---

*For instance, if two people declare that there is a drop of wine in a particular vessel of water, and the Kazee in consequence decree it to be unlawful, it must be considered as such, although the falsity of their declaration be afterwards proved.

when the nature of the decree he ought to pass will be ascertained.

Nor against one who first opposes the claim and then disappears.—If a defendant, having first denied the claim, should afterwards disappear in that case also the Kazee must suspend his proceeding during his absence, because is is requisite that the denial exist at the time of passing the decree, which is not the case in the present instance.—The opinion of Aboo Yoosaf, on this case, is different.—It is to be observed that the representative of an absentee is either one appointed by himself to act for him (such as an agent), or one appointed by LAW (such as an executor nominated by the Kazee), or, lastly, one who stands as virtual representative, by the claim which the plaintiff prefers against the absentee being also a cause of claim against some person present. This last may occur in various modes; aud the following may serve for an example.—A person establishes, by testimony, his right to a house in the possession of a particular person, in virtue of his having purchased it from an absentee, who was at the time the proprietor of it and from whom the present possessor has usurped it;—in which case, if the possessor deny all this, and the plaintiff establish it by evidence, the Kazee may pass a decree relating both to the absentee and the person present; nor would the denial of the sale by the absenee if he should afterwards return, be credited, because the purchase of the house from its proprietor is the cause of that which the paintiff claims from the person present, namely, the right of property in the house. In such case, therefore, the person present stands as the agent for the absentee, and his denial is consequently equivalent to that of the absentee.—The groun of this is that the plaintiff is not capable of proving his claim against the person present, unless he first establish it against the sentence. The person present is therefore considered as the resporesentative of the absentee; and hence the decree of the Kazee against the person present stands as the decree against the absentee.—Where, however, the claim of the plaintiff upon the absentee is the condition of something which he claims against the person present, the latter is not in that case considered as the representative of the absentee. A full discussion of this is to be found in the Jama.

The Kazee may lend the property of orphans.—It is lawful for Kazee to lend the property of orphans, keeping a record of it in writing because such loans is advantageous for the orphans, since it tends to preserve and secure their property; and the Kazee has the power of enforcing the restitution of it. An executor, on the contrary, is responsible for the property he lends, as is also a father, because neither of them has the power of enforcing a restitution of it.

———

CHAPTER. III.

OF ARBITRATION*

An arbitrator must possess the qualities essential to a Kazee.—If two persons a point an arbitrator,† and express theirs atisfaction with the award pronounced by him, such award is valid; because, as these persons have a power with respect to themselves, they consequently possess a right to appoint an arbitrator between them, and his award is therefore binding upon them. This is where the person so appointed possess the qualifications of a Kazee; for the stands in that relation to the other two, it is therefore requisite that he be competent to discharge the function of a Kazee.

He must not be a slave, an infidel, a slandered or an infant.—It is mot lawful to appoint a slave, or an infidel, or a person that has been punished for slander, or an infant, to act as an arbitrator; because none of these is competant to be a witness.

But he mdy be an unjust person.—If an unjust man be appointed an arbitrator, it is valid, because of the validity of his appointment to the office of Kazee, as has been already explained.

Either party may retract from the givetration before the award—If two men appoint another an arbitrator, still it is lawful for either of them to recede before he gives his award, because as the arbitrator has received his powers from them he cannot exert those powers without their consent. The award, however, when given, is binding upon them, as the power of the arbitrator over them was established by their own agreement.

On a reference to the Kazee, he must give effect to the award, if approved.—If the parties refer the award of the arbitrator to the Kazee, and it be conformable to his opinion, he must cause it to be carried into execution, because it would be useless to annul it, and then pass a similar decree,—But if it he contrary to his opinion, he must annul it, as the award of an arbitrator is not binding on the Kazee, since he did not authorize it.

Reference to an arbitrator is invalid in cases of punishment or retaliation.—The ap ointment of an arbitrator is not valid in cases where punishment or retaliation is incurred, because the party has no power over his own blood, and is therefore not capable of assignirg it to others. Lawyers have observed that the particular exception of retaliation and punishment affords an argument of the legality of arbitration in all other coutested questions, such as divorce. marriage, and the like. This is approved. Still, however, there is a necessity for ratification of the award in these cases by a decree of the Kazee, in order that a control

*Arab. Tahkeem. † Arab. Hakam.

being maintained ov'r mankind, their presumption may be restrained, for otherwise men would continually settle their differences by a private reference, without regard to the LAW.

An arbitrator's award of a fine against the tribe of an offender is of no effect.—IF, in a case of homicide from error, the slayer and the heir of the deceased appoint an arbitrator and he award a fine of blood to be paid by the tribe of the slayer, such award is of one effect ; in other words : the heir is not entitled to exact such fine from the tribe in virtue of the award, for it has no force over them, as they did not authorize the arbitrator.

Nor against the offender himself, unless he acknowledge the offence.—IF also, the arbitrator award the fine to be paid by the slayer, the Kazee must annul it, as being contrary to the LAW, which prescribes the fine to be paid by the tribe ;—excepting, however, where the fact is proved by the confession of the slayer ; for in that case the tribe are not liable to the fine.

He may examine witness.—An arbitrator is empowered to hear the witnesses of the plaintiff, and also to pass an award upon the denial or acknowledment of the parties, because this is agreeable to the LAW.

The varties, acknowledging an arbitrator's decree cannot afterwards retract from it —IF an arbitrator give information to the Kazee of the acknowledgment of one of the parties, or of the integrity of the witnesses, at a time when both the parties continue to adhere to his award, such information must be credited, and the Kazee must not afterwards credit the denial of either of the parties, as the arbitrator's authority still continues unshaken.—If, on the other hand, he give information to the Kazee related to his award (that is, if the parties dispute concerning his award,—one of them saying that "it was to such or such effect," and the other denying this, and the arbitrator inform the Kazee that "he has award so and so"),—his information must not be credited, since in such case his authority no longer endures.

Any award passed in favour of a parent, child, or wife, is null—THE determination of every person acting in the capacity of a judge (whether he be a Kazee or an arbitrator) in favour of his father, his mother, his child, or his wife, is null and void, because evidence in favour of any of these relations being unlawful on account of the suspicion which it suggests, a determination in their favour is also unlawful, for the same reason. —A determination, however, against any of these relations is valid, because evidence against them is accepted, since it is liable to no suspicion.

Joint arbitrators must act conjunctively.—IF two persons be appointed arbitrations, it is incumbent upon them to act conjunctively in giving a determination, as this is a matter which requires wisdom and judgment.

Section.

Miscellaneous Cases relative to Judicial Decssions.

No act can be performed him respect to the unaer storey of a house. which may any may affect the building—In a house of which the upper storey belongs to one man, and the under storey to another, the proprietor of the under storey is not entitled to drive in a nail, or to make a window, without the permission of the proprietor of the upper storey.—This is the doctrine of Haneefa. The two disciples hold that the proprietor of the under storey may do any act whatever with respect to it, provided injury result to the upper storey. The same disagreement also subsis' will regard to the proprietor of the upper storey building upon that foundation. Some of our lawyers remark that the doctrine ascribed to the two disciples is only an explanation of that of Haneefa, and that, in reality, there exists no disagreement between them.—Others again say that, according to the two disciples, there is a prefect freedom ;—in other words, either of the proprietors is at full liberty to do whatever act he pleases with relation to his property ; for property, in its very nature, implies a perfect freedom with regard to it, restrictions upon it being merely supervenient to another. Hence it the detriment be only doubtful, and not inevitable, the proprietor cannot lawfully be restrained from acting upon his own proparty. According to Haneefa, on the other hand, there is restriction ;—in other words, neither of the proprietors is premitted to do any acts with regard to their respective property without the permission of the other, because such acts affect a place with which the right of another is connected, and that right is sacred from any act of his, in the same manner as the right of a mortgager or a lessee.—Besides, the freedom and absoluteness of the property to its owner is here supervenient, since it depens on the consent of another : so long, therefore, as that consent is doubtful, the original restriction oparates. In these cases, moreover the detriment is not eventual but is in some degree certain ; since the driving in of a nail or wedge, or the breaking of the wall to make a window, tends to weaken the edifice, whence these acts are prohibited.

A passage cannot be made into a private lane.—IF there be a long lane, parallel to which, either on the right or left, runs another iong lane, not a thoroughfare (that is, not open at both ends), it is not permitted to any of the inhabitants of the first lane to make a door to open into the second lane ; because the object of making a door is to obtained a passage to end fro ; and the second lane in not free to the inhabitants of the first since not being a thoroughfare. the right of passage through it belongs only to the In habitants of it.—Some have said that it is perfectly lawful for any of the inhabitants of the first lane to open a door into the second; because the opening of a door is nothing more than the breaking of a wall by its proprietor, which is lawful; but that the prohibition against passing to and fro nevertheless remains in force. The authentic doctrine, however, is, that the opening of a door, in such case, is unlawful; because after the door is opened it will be difficult to prevent a continual thoroughfare; and also, because there is a possibility that after some time the right of passage might be claimed by the person who made the door, and the very circumstance of the door might be pleaded as a proof of his right. If, however, the second lane be not long, but short, the inhabitants of the first lane have a right to open doors into it: because they have a right of passage through it, since on account of its shortness it is considered as a court, in which all have a right of participating, whence it is that they have all an equal claim of Shaffa in case of the sale of any of the houses in it.

An indefinite claim may be compounded.—If a person vaguely claim something belonging to a house, and the proprietor of the house deny his right to anything, but afterwards compound with him for his claim, such composition is valid; for although the article in dispute was not known, yet a composition with a known article for one that is unknown is lawful, according to our doctors, since as the article compounded for merely drops, the uncertainty concerning it can never create strife;—for uncertainty, in a matter which drops, leaves no room for contention, as this cannot occur but in cases of uncertainty respecting things the delivery of which is required.

Case of a claim fonnded on gift and purchase.—If a person claim a house in the possession of another, on the plea that "the possessor had, at a former period, made a gift of it to him," and upon being required to produce evidence, should then say, "he denied the gift, and I therefore bought the house from him," and produce witnesses, and they attest the purchase, but state the date of it to be antecedent to the gift, such testimony is not admissible, because of its differing from the assertion of the claimant with respect to the date of the deeds;—whereas, if they were to attest the purchase as having been made posterior to the gift their testimony would, in that case, be admitted, because of its conformity to the claimant's plea. If, on the other hand, he plead a gift, and then bring witnesses to prove the purchase previous to the gift, without mentioning the denial of the gift by the donor, in this instance also the evidence is not admissible.—This is mentioned in various copies of the Jama Sagheer; and the reason of it is that the claim of the house, in virtue of a gift, is an acknowledgment of its being the property of the giver; but from which the claimant afterwards recedes by declaring that he had purchased it prior to the gift; which is a contradiction; it is otherwise in the former case; for there the purchase is declared to be posterior to the gift; and a declaration to this effect, so far from denying the property to have existed in the donor at the time of the gift, is rather a confirmation of it.

If the purchase of female slave be denied by the purchaser, the master may cohabit with her.—If a person possessed of a female slave say to another, "you purchased this slave from me, and have not paid me the price." and the other deny the sale, and the possessor of the slave determine in his own mind to drop the suit, and of consequence refrain from any further contention withe other, he may then lawfully cohabit with the, since the deniai of the purchaser annuls the sale in the same manner as where both parties deny it.

Objection.—How can the sale be annulled by the mere determination of the seller in his own mind to relinquish the suit, since no contracts can be annulled by the mere determination on annual them; whence it is that, in a sale with an option, If the possessor of the option determine to annul it, still the annulment does not take place immediately on the forming of such resolution?

Reply.—In the case in question the sale does not become null merely by the determination, but because of the determination being joined to a conduct that manifests it, such as the detention of the slave in the proprietor's possession, his carrying her away from the place of contention to his own house, and his using her as a servant.

In the receipt of money, the declaration of the receiver must be credited with respect to the quality—If a person acknowledge that he had received ten dirms from another, but afterwards assert that they were Zeyf, or bad, in that case his declaration must be credited; because bad dirms. although of an inferior value, are nevertheless of the species of dirms, whence if, in a Sirf sale, a person take possession of bad ones in exchange for good, it is valid. As, moreover, a receipt of dirms is not restricted to good ones, it does not follow, from his acknowledgment of the seisin, that the dirms were good; and such being the case, his declaration must be credited, because he denies the receipt of good dirms, which is his right.—It would be otherwise if he were to declare that "he had received ten good dirms," or that "he had received his right," or "the price of his wares," or "a discharge of his claims," and afterwards to allege that the dirms were bad; for in neither of these cases would his declaration be credited; because in the first case he expressly acknowledges the receipt of good dirms; and in the three following he makes such acknowledgment by implication, and therefore his subsequent declaration to the contrary, being considered as a prevarication, is not credited.*

A creditor denying his debtor's acknowledgement cannot afterward substantiate his claim but by proof, or the debtor's verification —If one person say to another, "I owe you one thousand dirms," and the other reply, 'you do not owe me anything," but afterwards, in the same meeting, say, "you owe me one thousand dirms;" in that case he is not entitled to anything unless he adduce proof, or the debtor verify his assertion; because the debtor's acknowlecgment was virtually annulled by his denial; and his subsequent assertion of course becomes a claim de novo, which therefore requires either to be proved, or to be, verified by the debtor. It is otherwise where a person says to another, "you bought certain goods from me," and that other denies; for he might nevertheless afterwards, without prevarication, confirm the declaration of the person in question in the same meeting; because in a contract of sale one of the parties only cannot annul it; in the same manner as one of them is incapable of making it.—The reason of this is that the acknowledgment of a contract of sale is the right of the buyer and seller jointly, and therefore the contract is not annulled by the denial of the purchaser only; the confirmation of the purchaser, therefore, after his denial, is valid, since his denial did not occasion an annulment.—A person, on the contrary, in whose favour an acknowledgment is made, may of himself annul such acknowledgment by a rejection of it; and his subsequent assertion corresponding with the acknowledgment is not a corroboration of it, because the acknowledgment did not then exist, it having been virtually done away by his rejection of it.—Hence the subsequent assertion is a claim de novo which consequently require either proof by witnesses, or the verification of the debtor.

In a claim for debt, the evidence of the debtor, proving a discharge, must be credited. —If a person make a claim upon another, and that other declare that he never owed him anything, and the plaintiff prove, by witnesses, that the defendant owes him one thousand dirms, and the defendant, on the other hand, prove by witnesses that has paid the same, in that case the evidence of the defendant must be credited; and in the same manner also, the evidence of the defendant must be credited, in case it tend to establish his having obtained a releasement or discharge of the claim.—Ziffer maintains that the evidence of the defendant must not be credited, since payment is a branch of obligation, and the defendant having denied the existence of the obligation at any period, is therefore evidently guilty of prevarication. Our doctors, on the other hand, argue that a consistency with regard to the denial and the proof is here poosible, because unjust debts are sometimes paid to avoid litigation, and releasements from them are likewise sometimes given. Sometimes, also, a defendant, after denying the validity of the claim, compounds with the plaintiff; and in such case he is bound to pay the composition, notwithstanding the debt for which it was made may have been unbest.—If the defendant declare, "I owe you nothing," in that case also his evidence, to the effect above recited, is creditable, because of its perfect conformity with the assertion that "he owes him nothing," which evidently means at that time, inasmuch as he proves that he had afterwards paid it to him.—But if he were to say, "I never owed you anything, and I do not know you,"—the evidence he might afterwards produce of his having paid the debt, or of his having obtained a releasement from it, would not be credited; because the contradiction between his assertion and the evidence cannot in this case be reconciled, since no man enters into the business of giving of receiving with one of whom he has no knowledge.—Kadooree remarks that in this case also the evidence must be credited, because the contradiction that subsist is not wholly irreconcileable. inasmuch as women who are kept concealed often transact business mediately through others, without knowing the person with whom the business is concluded; and it also often happens that men of rank, when a mob assemble at their door and make a noise, desire their agents to give them some money to pacify them.

Case of a disputed purchase of a defective slave.—If a person declare that "he has purchased a female slave from another," and that other deny that he had ever sold her to him, and the purchaser having proved his assertion by witnesses, an additional finger be discovered on the hand of the slave, and the seller prove by evidence that the purchaser had exempted him from responsibility for every defect, in that case the testimony of the seller must be rejected, since he is evidently guilty of prevarication. This is the doctrine of the Zahir Rawayet. It is related, as an opinion of Aboo Yoosaf, that the evidence of the seller must be credited, because of the analogy of this case to that of debt, as before explained, in which it was shown that there was a possibility of reconciling the contradiction; for a reconcilement of the contradiction is also possible in this case, by supposing the seller to have been an agent for another, on which supposition the declaration of the proprietor, that "he had not sold the slave," would have been true, and his subsequent plea, of having been exempted from a responsibility for defects, would also have been valid. Thus the apparent contradiction is capable of recon-

* Here follows an account of the different gradations of dirms from good to bad, which is omitted in the translation, as it will hereafter be fully explained in its proper place.

cilement. The ground on which the Zahir Rawayet proceeds is, the plea of having been exempted from a warranty against defects is an acknowledgment of the existence of the sale, which he had before denied, and hence it necessarily follows that he prevaricated. It is otherwise in the case of debt, for in that case the payment is no argument of the respondent's acknowledging the existence of it, since (as has been before explained) unjust debts are often paid to avoid strife.

A deed suspended, in its effect, upon the will of God, is null.—IF a person, having acknowledged a debt to another, should subscribe a deed to that effect, and at the conclusion of it insert the following sentence, "Whosoever produces this deed of acknowledgment, and claims the thing recited therein, is proprietor thereof, if it please GOD" or, if a person, having sold something to another, should at the end of the bill of sale insert the following sentence, "If any person shall hereafter claim the property of the subject of the sale, in that case I am answerably for the same, if it please GOD,"—in both these cases the deeds are of no effect; whence, in the first case, the acknowledgment is null, and in the second, the sale is invalid. The two disciples hold that in the former case the debt is binding, and in the later case the sale is valid; because in their opinion the condition "if it please GOD" applies, not to the general purport of the deed, but merely (in the former instance) to the expression, "Whoever produces this deed of acknowledgment," and so forty,—or (in the latter) to the expression, "If any person shall hereafter claim," and so forth; because the design, in drawing up deeds of acknowledgment and of sale is merely to corroborate and confirm the act; and if the expression in question had a reference to the whole deed, this design would be defeated. Haneefa, on the contrary, being of opinion that this condition applies to the whole of the deed, therefore holds to be invalid * It is to be observed, that if a blank be left at the end of a bill of sale or deed of acknowledgment, and the words "if it please GOD" be afterwards written, our lawyers are of opinion that the clause does not affect the bill or the deed, because the blank, in either case, marks the conclusion.

CHAPTER IV.

OF THE DECREES OF A KAZEE RELATIVE TO INHERITANCE.

Case of the widow of a Christian claming her inheritance after having embraced the faith.—IF a Christian die, and his widow appear before the Kazee as a Musslima, and declare that "she had become so since the death of her husband," and the heirs declare that she had become so before his death, their declaration must be credited. Ziffer is of opinion that the declaration of the widow must be credited; because the change of her religion, as being a supervenient circumstance, must be referred to the nearest possible period The arguments of our doctors are, that as the cause of her exclusion from inheritance, founded on difference of faith, exists in the present, it must therefore be considered an extant in the preterite, from the argument of the present;—in the same manner as an argument is derived from the present, in a case relative to the running of the watercourse of a mill;—that is to say, if a dispute arise between the lessor and lessee of a water-mill, the former asserting that the stream had run from the period of the lease till the present without interruption, and the latter denying this, in that case, if the stream be running at the period of contention, the assertion of the lessor must be credited, but if otherwise, that of the lessee. As, moreover, an argument drawn from apparent circumstances is proof sufficient to set aside the claim of a plaintiff, it follows that the argument in question suffices, on behalf of the heirs, to defeat the plea of the widow. With respect to what Ziffer objects, it is to be observed that he has regard to the argument of apparent circumstances, for establishing the claim of the wife upon her husband's estate, and an argument of this nature does not suffice as proof to establish a right although it would suffice to annul one.

Case of the Christian widow of a Mussulman claiming under the same circumstance.—IF a Mussulman, whose wife was once a Christian should die, and the widow appear before the Kazee as a Musslima and declare that she had embraced the faith prior to the death of her husband, and the heirs assert the contrary, in this case also the assertion of the heirs must be credited, for no regard is paid, in this instance, to any argument derived from present circumstances (as in the case of the water-mill), since such an argument is not capable of establishing claim, and the widow is here the claimant of her husband's property With respect to the heirs on the contrary, they are repellants of the claim; and probability is an argument in their favour, since the Islamism of the widow is supervenient, and is therefore an argument against her.

A trustee on the decease of his principal, must pay the deposit to whomsoever he acknowledges as heis.—IF a person who had deposited four thousand dirms in the hands of another should die, and the trustee acknowledge a certain person to be the son of the deceased and his true and only heir, he is bound to pay to that person the four thousand dirms which he held in trust; because in this case he makes an ackno-

*The arguments both of the two disciples and of Haneefa are more fully detailed in the original; but as they relate to principles proper to the Arabic language, the translator has given only the substance of them.

ledgment that what he retains in trust, is the right of the heir, and consequently it is the same as if, during the life of the person from whom he received the deposit, he had acknowledged that it was his right. It is otherwise where a trustee makes an acknowledgment that a certain person has been appointed an agent for seisin by the proprietor, or that such an one has purchased the deposit from the proprietor; for in that case he cou'd not be desired to deliver up the deposit, because this acknowledgment proves the actual existence of the depositor, since it shows him to be still living. His acknowledgment, therefore, of the agency or the purchase, is an acknowledgment affecting the property of another: but this cannot be objected to an acknowledgment made by a trustee after the death of the proprietor, for upon that event the property devolves upon the heirs. It is otherwise where a debtor acknowledges that a certain person has been appointed agent for seisin by his creditor; for the acknowledgment here relates to his own property, inasmuch as he pays the debt by means of his own property, and the agent receives the same; and hence, after such acknowledment, he becomes bound to pay it. If the trustee, after manking an acknowledgment in favour of the son and heir, in the manner above related, should again make an acknowledgment in favour of another son, and the one first acknowledged deny the same, in that case he [the trustee] is bound to pay the whole to that one; because after such acknowledgment became binding (in the manner already exp!a ned) his tenure of the property was no longer valid; and hence his subsequent acknowledgment in favour of the other son is an acknowledgment with respect to the absolute property of the first son, and is consequently invalid,—in the same manner as helds where the first son is notorious,—and also, because, as at the time when he [the trustee] made the acknowledgment in favour of the first son, no other son appeared to assert his right, the acknowledgment was therefore valid: but as the first son is present to deny the kacnowledgment afterwards made in favour of the second son that acknowledgment is therefore invalid.

In the division of an estate, the Kazee must not demand any security from the heirs or creditors in behalf of those who may be absent.—WHEN a division is made of the effects of a deceased person between his heirs and creditors, the Kazee must not require security either from the heirs or the creditors, as a precaution in case of the appearance of more heirs or more creditors, for this would be oppression, as being a deviation from common practice. This is according to Haneefa. The two disciples maintain that he must require security. This disagreement relates to a case where the debt of the creditors and the right of inheritance is proved by evidence, and where they severally declare that they know of no other debtors or heirs than themselves. The reasoning adduced by the two disciples in support of their opinion is, that the Kazee is the conservator of the rights of the absent; and it is most probable that some of the creditors or heirs may be absent, since death is often sudden, and may happen at a time when they are not all present; and as the taking of security is on this account an advisable precaution, the Kazee must therefore take this precaution, in the same manner as he exacts security when he delivers a trove, or a fugitive slave, to the owner, or when he awards maintenance to a wife from the estate of her absent husband. The arguments of Haneefa upon this point are twofold. FIRST, the right of those that are present is established with certainty in case of there being no absent heirs, and is apparently established in the mean time even if there be absent heirs; and as it is incumbent on the Kazee to act according to what is apparent to him, he must not suspend his proceedings in favour of those that are present, by exacting security for the rights of the absent, whose actual existence is uncertain;—in the same manner as where a person establishes t e purchase of any thing in the hands of another,—or a debt due to him by a slave; that is, if a person prove a right by purchase to a thing in the possession of another, it is the duty of the Kazee immediately to order it to be delivered to him without exacting security although another may eventually appear and claim it in virtue of a prior purchase; and in the same manner, if a person prove a debt due to him by a slave, the Kazee must order the slave to be sold, the end that payment may be made from the price, without exacting any security, although there be a possibility of another creditor afterwards appearing. SECONDLY, the principal is unknown, and security is invaiid if the principal be not clearly pointed out,—as where, for instance, a person says to several debtors, "I am bail for one of you." in which case the security is invalid, becaase the actual principal is not signified, notwithstanding there be a certainty of his existence, In the case in question, therefore, the security is invalid *a fortiori*, since even the existence of the principal is uncertain. It is otherwise in the case of decreeing maintenance to the wife of an absentee from the effects of her husband, because her right being known and established the person in favour of whom the security is given is not uncertain. With respect to the case of a fugitive slave, or a trove property, there are two traditions. Concerning those, however, there is also a difference of opinion. Some have said that if the Kazee give a trove property to the proprietor, on his describing the marks, or a fugitive slave to his master, on the acknowledgment of the slave that "the said person is his master," it is incumbent upon him, in either case; to take security. And all our doctors coincide in this opinion; because the right of the receiver is not proved, whence it is in the power of the

Kazee, if he please, to withhold the slave from the person in question altogether.

In the joint inheritance of a property held by a third person, the present heir receives his share; but not security is required in behalf of him who is absent.—If a person prove by evidence, that a house then in the possession of another had been left between him and his brother, who is absent, in that case one half of the house must be given to him and the other half left in the hands of the person who has possession; and no security must be exacted from him. This is according to Haneefa. The two disciples are of opinion, that if the possessor deny the right, the share of the absent brother must be put into the hands of a trustee until his return; but if he acknowledge the right it must then be left in his possession;—for they argue that a denier, as being an opponent, cannot be trusted with the property; whereas it may be entrusted to an acknowlndger, as he is a friend and confident. The argument of Haneefa is that the decree of the Kazee, awarding that "the deceased left the house to his heirs," is a decree merely in favour of the deceased; for inheritance cannot take place unless the property of the person through whom it devolves be proved; and as there is a probability of the deceased having constituted the possessor trustee, it follows that the house cannot be taken from him; as holds in the case of his acknowledging it. In regard to his denial, it is vistually annulled by the decree of the Kazee; and their is a probability of his not denying the right again, because the dispute in question has become known both to himself and the Kazee. If the claim, in the case in question, relate to moveable property, some have said that the article is to be taken from the possessor, according to all our doctors; because there is a necessity for the conservation of it; and this is answered in the best manner by the taking of it from the possessor, who, on account of his denial of his own use, of the other, may convert it to his own use, either from opposition, or from a belief of its being his own right: but when the Kazee takes it from him, and deposits it with a trustee, the probabity is that the trustee, from his integrity, will take care of it. The case is different with respect to immoveable property, for that is preserved in itself; whence it is that an executor, although he have power to sell the moveables of an absent heir, arrived at the age of maturity, yet cannot do so with regard to his immoveable property. Others, however have said that the same difference of opinion subsists with regard to moveable property. It is to be spect to immoveable property. It is to be observed that opinion of Haneefa, that the half ought to be left in the hands of the possessor, is the most authentic, because there is a necessity for conservation, and his is answered in the best possible manner by putting it in the hands of one who is responsible in case of its loss, since it it likely that he will be most careful of it. The possessor, moreover, is responsible in consequence of his denial, whereas a trustee is not. With respect to what is further said, that "no security must be exacted," it proceeds on this principle, that the exaction of bail is an occasion of litigation and contention; and it is the duty of the Kazee to prevent these,—not to excite them. If, in the case in question, the absentee return there is no necessity for again producing evidence, because he is entitled to the half in virtue of the Kazee's decree in favour of the heir that was present; for any one of the heirs of a deceased person stands as litigant on the part of all the others, with respect to any thing due to or by the deceased, whether it be debt or substance; since the decree of the Kazee, in such case, is in reality either in favor of or against the deceased; and any one of the heirs may stand as his representative with respect to such decree. It is otherwise with respect to taking possession of the portion due to another from the estate of a person deceased; that is to say, a part of the heirs, although they be litigants on behalf of another heir, cannot, however, take possession of his portion on his behalf, because a person, in taking possession, acts for himself, and is therefore incapable of acting in it, as agent, for another. Hence the person present is not entitled to receive any other portion than his own; in the same manner as where an heir claims a debt due to the deceased, and the Kazee passes a decree in his favour; in which case the heir, although he stood as litigant in behalf of the other heirs, is yet not entitled to receive their shares of the debt.

Objection.—If one heir be litigant in behalf of the other, it would follow that each creditor is entitled to have recourse to him for payment of his demand; whereas, according to law, each is only obliged to pay his own share

Reply.—The creditors are entitled to have recourse to one of several heirs only in a case where all the effects are in the hands of that heir. This is what is stated in the Jama Kabeer; and the reason of it is that although any one of the heirs may act as plaintiff in a cause on behalf of the others, yet he cannot act as defendant on their behalf, unless the whole of the effects be in his possession.

An alms-gift of Mal includes all property subject to Zakat.—If a person say, "I devote my property in alms to the distressed," in that case the word property, thus generally used, is construed to mean that part of his property which is subject to Zakat; whereas, if a person say, "I bequeath the third of my property," the term property is in that case construed to apply to his property of every description.—This distinction is according to a favourable construction.—Analogy would suggest, in the former instance also, that the whole property is understood; and this topinion has been followed by Ziffer; because he term property [Mal] applies to and includes property of every description, in a case of alms-gift, in the same manner as in a case of bequest. The reasons for a more favourable construction of the law in this particular are twofold.—FIRST, an obligation imposed by a person upon himself is analogous to an obligation imposed by GOD; in other words, if a person impose any obligation on himself, it is valid only with respect to those articles concerning which GOD has imposed obligations upon mankind: an obligation of alms, therefore, imposed by a person upon himself, takes effect only with respect to such property as GOD has imposed alms upon.—Bequest, on the contrary, resembles inheritance, as the legatee succeeds to the property of the deceased in the manner of an heir; and hence a bequest of property is not restricted to any particular description of property.—SECONDLY, from his mode of expression it is reasonable to suppose that he undertakes to bestow in alms that part of his property only which is superflous, and beyond the occasion of his wonts; and this is the part on which Zakat is imposed. Bequest, on the contrary, as it takes place at a time when the testator is free from want, is considered as extending to the whole of his property.—It is to be observed that the speaker's declaration, "I devote my property in alms, &c.," includes also his Ashooree lands, according to Aboo Yoosaf, because land of this description is subject to the obligation of alms, agreeably to his tends, that, in tithe, the consideration of alms is predominant.—According to Mohammed, on the contrary, his Ashooree land is not included, because, agreeably to his tenets, the consideration of support to the state is predominant in tithe.—His Khirajee, or tribute lands, are, however, not included, according to all our doctors, because tribute is designed purely as a support to the state, and alms are no consideration in it.

Case of an alms-gift of milk.—IF a person say, "I devote my possessions [Milk] in alms to the distressed," there is in that case a difference of opinion. Some have said that this must be construed to mean the whole of his property; because the term here used [Milk] is of a more general nature than the term Mal used in the former case:—the occasion, moreover, of restricting the application, in that instance, to such property as is subject to Zakat, is purely because of Mal being the term used on that occasion in the KORAN; and such being the case, the term Milk must therefore be explained in its common acceptation. Others, again, have said that the terms Milk and Mal import the same thing in effect; and this is the better opinion: since both terms imply that part of his property which exceeds his wants, as was before mentioned; and that is the part of his property subject to Zakat.—If, however, a person have no other property besides what he obliges himself to bestow in alms, he must in that case reserve a sufficiency for his own subsistence, and bestow the remainder; and afterwards, upon his acquiring more property, bestow a part of it adequate to what he had before reserved. With respect to a sufficiency for subsistence, Mohammed has not determined the quantity, because of the different conditions of men. Some have said that a person is to reserve only one day's subsistence, in case of his being an artificer or labourer: one month's subsistence, in case he possess houses and shops let out upon lease; one year's subsistance, in case he possess immoveable property of lands; and so on—in proportion to the length of time of receiving the income of his property:—and on this principle a merchant is to reserve as much as may suffice till the probable return of his property.

The acts of an executor are valid without any formal notification of his appointment.—IF a person be appointed executor to another, and he be not informed of that circumstance, but nevertheless sell some part of the effects of the deceased, the appointment becomes confirmed, and the sale is valid; whereas sale by an agent, on the contrary, is not valid, unless he be informed of his agency.—This distinction is according to the Zahir Rawayat. Aboo Yoosaf is of opinion that the sale by the executor is also invalid, because an executor is, in fact, a person appointed to act as agent after the death of the testator, and must therefore be considered in the same light with an agent before death.—The reason of the distinction as stated in the Zahir Rawayat, is that the office of an exceutor is to represent, not to act as agent; for it refers to a period when the appoinment of agency would he null. The acts of an executor, therefore, do not rest upon his knowledge of the testator's will any more than the acts of an heir;—in other words, if an heir were to sell some part of the effects of the deceased, not knowing that he was dead, the sale would be good; and so also of sale by an executor Agency, on the contrary, is merely a delegation, since in the case of agency the power and authority of the constituent still endure: the acts of an agent, therefore, rest upon his knowledge of his appointment.—The ground of this is, that in resting the acts of agents upon a knowledge of their appointments, there is no injury to the constituent, since he is himself capable of performing such acts: whereas, if the acts of an executor were suspended on his knowledge of his appointment, an injury would result to his constituent, who is himself incapable of performing such acts.

An agent's appointment may be established by any casual information.—IF a man appoint another his agent, and, a person having brought him intelligence of this,*

*By a person is here to be understood a person not deputed by the constituent, but one who having casually heared of the appointment brings information of it to the agent.

he immediately, upon the receipt of it, perform some act (such as sale, for instance), in that case the act is valid, whether the informant be free or a slave, of mature age or otherwise, an unjust or just man: because a simple information of his appointment establishes his right to act, although it be no way binding upon him.

But his dismission cannot be established unless duly attested.—The dismission of an agent is not established until it be attested to the agent by two persons of unknown character, or by one just man. This is the doctrine of Haneefa. The two disciples have said that the law, in this case, is the same as in the preceding: for as the dismission and appointment of agents are concerns of frequent occurrence, the notification of one person is therefore sufficient. The arguments of Haneefa are that the simple notification of dismission is binding, as being a cause of the agent's desisting from action, and inducing responsibility for the property in his possession. The notification in question, therefore, is in one shape evidence, and consequently requires one of the two conditions of evinence namely, number [of the witnesses] or integrity; in other words, it requires to be attested by one (just person, or by two persons of unknown cahracter. It is otherwise with respect to the ratification of an appointment of agency, since that is no way binding, as has been already mentioned.—It is also otherwise where the dismission is notified by a messenger from the constituent, because the word of a message-bearer is equivalent to that of the sender of it, from necessity, and in that case, therefore, the attestation of one just men or two unknown men is not required.—The same difference of opinion obtains tn cases of information conveyed to a master of the crime of his slave,—to the Shafee of the sale of a house,—to a virgin of her marriage,—or to Mussulman converts in a hostile country, who have not yet taken refuge in the Mussulman territory, of particular ordinances in regard to religion. Thus if an unjust [person inform a master that a particular slave belonging to him had committed a crime, and the master afterwards sell or emancipate the said slave, it is not in that case incumbent upon him to pay the atonement, unless the notification of the crime be attested by one just man; or by two men of unknown character, according to Haneefa: contrary to the opinion of the two disciples.—In the same manner also, if an unjust person notify the sale of a house to the Shafee, or person having the rigt of per-emption over it, and the Shafee should not thereupon put in his claim of Shaffa, still, according to Haneefa, his right is not avoided; whereas, according to the two disciples, it is forfeited. So also, if an unjust person notify her marriage to a virgin, and she thereupon remain silent such silence, according to Haneefa, is not an assent; but according to the two disciples it is.—So likewise, if an unjust man iafor man absent Mussulman of new ordinances in respect to religion, and he should not conform accordingly, Haneefa holds that he is not in that case guilty of any offence; whereas the two disciples are of opinion that he is.

AKazee, or his Ameen are not liable for any loss which may be incurred to the prejudice of another in selling on article to satisfy creditors.—In a Kazee, or Ameen apponinted by him, sell the slave of a certain person, in order to discharge the demands of his creditors, and the money, after the receipt, be lost or destroyed in the hands of the Kazee, or his Ameen, and the slave be then proved to have been the property of some other person, in that case neither the Kazee nor his Ameen is responsible for the loss; because if Kazees were subject to such responsibility, no one would accept of the appointment, and the rights of the people would consequently be destryed.—The Kazee, therefore, not being responsible for the loss, the purchaser is entitled to an indemnification from the creditors on whose account the sale was made, because of the impracticability of his being indemnified by the party with whom he made bargain.—In the same manner as where an incapable infant* or an inhibited slave appoints an agent for sale, who accordingly salls something on his behalf, and, the price being lost after he had received it, a right to the thing sold is proved by another; for in that case the claim is made on the constituent, and not the agent, although he be the party with whom the bargain was made.

If the loss be incurred by an executor, acting under the Kazee's orders, the executor is indemnified by the creditors.—If a Kazee command an executor, whom he himself had appointed, ro sell a slave to satisfy the creditors of a deceased person, and the executor, in obedience to this order, accordingly sell the slave, and the slave afterwards prove the right of another, or die previous to his being delivered to the purchaser, and the price in the mean time be lost after it had been received by the executor,—the purchaser must in that case receive an indemnification from the executor, not from the Kazee; because, having been appointed by the Kazee to act as executor to the deceased, he is therefore a representative of the deceased, and not the Kazee; and hence, in the same manner as the deceased would have been responsible under such circumstances, in case he had himself made the sale during his lifetime, so also is the executor for the sale made after his death. The purchaser, therefore, is entitled to exact the price from the executor; and he, again, is entitled to indemnify himself from the creditors, since he acted in the business of the sale on their behalf.—If, however, any more property of

* Meaning an infant so young as to be incapable of acting for himself.

the deceased be afterwards discovered, the creditors are entitled to receive from it the payment of their debts, which are still held to remain in force.—Lawyers have also said that the creditors are, on their part, entitled to receive an indemnification from the estate for the compensation they made through the executor, to the purchaser, since they incurred that loss in behalf of the deceased.

And an infant heir stanas in the same perdicament with a creditor in this particular.—An intant heir, on whose account any thing is sold from the estate of a deceased person, is considered in the light of acreditor; in other words, if an infant heir stand in need of selling something, and the executor accordingly make such sale for him, and the subject of the sale afterwards prove the right of another,—in that case the purchaser if entitled to a compensation from the executor, and the executor from the be r — If, on the cther hand, the Ameen of the Kazee sell any thing in behalf of an heir which afterwards proves the right of another: the proprietor is in that case entitled to receive a compensation directly from the heir, provided he be an adult: but if the heir be on infant, the Kazee must appoint a person for the discharge of the debt from his property.

Section.

Any person may execute a puniehment by the Kazee's direction.—If a Kazees say to a person, "I have sentenced a certain man to be stoned; do you thereforc stone him"—or, "I have sentenced such a man to have his hand cut off; do you therefore cut it off;"—or, "I have sentenced this person to be scourged; do you therefore scourge him:"—it is lawful for that person to act according to the Kazee's orders,—This is the doctrine of the Zahir Rawayet.—It is related of Mohammed, that he receded from this doetrine, and gave it as his opinion that the Kazee's directions, as here stated, are not to be obeyed unless his sentence be attested by one just man; because there is a possibility of his being in an error; and if that should appear after the performance of any of these acts, it would be impossible to repair the injury thereby occasioned. From this it would appear that the letter of one Kazee to another are not valid:—and our modern doctors greatly approve of this opinion, because many Kazees of the present age are loose and irregular: they; however, admit the validity of letters from one Kazee to another on the ground of necessity.—The arguments of the Zahir Rawayet upon this point are twofold.—First the Kazee here gives information of a matter which he is competent to order; because it was in his power to have ardered the execution of the sentence immediately; hence, as he is liable to no suspicion, he ought to be credited.—Secondly, obedience to a magistrate in authority, such as the Kazee, is declared to be an incumbent duty: and as obedience to him is manifested in a belief of his word, it is therefore incumbent to believe him,—Besides, Imam Aboo Mansoor Matirady has said, "If a Kazee be learned and just, believe and obey him, as there is than no reason to suspect him.—If, on the other hand, he be just but ignorant, it is then requisite to make enquiry of him concerning the case; and if, after a full investigation, it shall appear that this sentence was legally founded, in that case (and not otherwise) he must be believed.—If, on the contrary, he be learned but unjust in his conduct, or ignorant and unjust, his orders must not be obeyed, unless the person to whom he addresses himself discover the reason that prompted them."

Case of a disputed decree, after a Kazee's dismission from his office.—If a dismissed Kazee say to a person, "I have taken one thousand dirms from you, and paid it to another, according to a decree which I passed to that effect;" and the person in question deny this, and assert that the Kazee had taken it from him unjustly, still the declaration of the Kazee must be credited, and consequently he is not responsible for the said sum. In the same manner also, if a dismissed Kazee say to a person, "I passed a just sentence of amputation against you," and the other assert that it was unjust, the word of the Kazee must be credited. The law here proceeds on the supposition that in both these cases the persons acknowledge that the decrees were passed at a time when he was actually Kazee; and the reason of it is, that after such acknowledgment on their part, probability is an argument in favour of the Kazee: because the probability is that no Kazee will pass an unjust decree. Neither is it necessary to exact an oath from the Kazee in either of these cases, because an oath is never put to a Kazee, and both the persons in question acknowledge that he was actually Kazee when he passed these decrees.—It is to be observed that if the person who, in the first case, by order of the Kazee, took the money, or who, in the second case, cut off the hand,—should severally declare that they had done so by order of the Kazee, they are not responsible for the consequences, since the Kazee was in office when, he gave these orders, and the restitution of the property to its owner was an approved act on the part of the Kazee, in the same manner as if he had made the restitution in the presence of the defendant —If, on the other hand, the person assert that the Kazee had issued such orders either antecedent to his appointment or after his dismission, then also the declaration of the Kazee must be credited, because he has referred the decree to a period which exempts him from responsibility. His declaration, therefore, is credited: in the same manner as where a person subject to periodical madness at fixed and certain times, having divorced his wife or emancipated his slave, afterwards declare that "he did these during his madness;"—which is credited; whence the divorce or emancipation are rendered void.—In this case, however, if the executioner of amputation, or the receiver of the money, acknowledge these deeds, they become responsible for them, because they themselves acknowledge the performance of acts, which induce responsibility, since the authority under which they acted is doubtful; for the assertion of the Kazee is credited in these instances merely to procure an exemption to himself from responsibility, and not to procure it to others. It is otherwise in the first case, where these acts are allowed to have been performed in virtue of an order from him when he was actually Kazee.—All this proceeds on a supposition that the money no longer remains in the hands of the person who had received it in virtue of the Kazee's decree; for if the money be still in the possession of the receiver, and he coincide with the Kazee concerning the amount, it must in this case be taken from him, whether the person from whom it was originally taken confirm the Kazee's allegation, that "he had paid the money to that person whilst he was in office," or whether he plead that he [the Kazee] had taken and paid it whilst he was not in office; because as the receiver here in fact acknowledges that the money had formerly been in the possession of this person, his plea of having become proprietor of the money cannot be admitted but upon proof; and the mere allegation of the dismissed Kazee is not proof, since after dismission he becomes as a common person.

BOOK XXI.

OF SHAHADIT, OR EVIDENCE.

CHAPTER I.

Evidence is incumbent upon the requisition of the party concerned.—It is incumbent* upon witness to bear testimony, nor is it lawful for them to conceal it, when the party concerned demands it from them; because God says, in the Koran, "Let not witnesses withhold their testimony when it is demanded from them;"—and also, "Conceal not your testimony, for whoever conceals his testimony is an offender."—The requisition of the party, however, is a condition; because the delivery of testimony is the right of the party, and therefore rests upon his requisition of it, as is the case with respect to all other rights.

But it is not obligatory in a case inducing corporal punishment.—In cases inducing corporal punishment, witnesses are at liberty either to give or withhold their testimony, as they please, because in such case they are distracted between two laudable actions; namely, the establishment of the punishment, and the preservation of the criminal's character: the concealment of vice is, moreover, preferable; because the Prophet said to a person that had borne testimony, "Verily it would have been better for you, if you had concealed it"—and also, because he elsewhere said, "Whoever conceals the vices of his brother Mussulman shall have a veil drawn over his own crimes in the two worlds by God."—Besides, it has been inculcated both by the Prophet and his companions as commendable to assist in the prevention of corporal punishment; and this is an evident argument for the concealment of such evidence as tends to establish it.

Unless it involve property, when the fact must be stated in such a way as may not occasion punishment.—It is incumbent, however, in the case of theft, to bear evidence to the property, by testifying that "a certain person took such property," in order to preserve the right of the proprietor; but the word taken must be used instead of stolen, to the end that the crime may be kept concealed: besides, if the word stolen were used, the thief would be rendered liable to amputation; and as, where amputation is incurred, there is no responsibility for the property, the proprietor's right would be destroyed.

The evidence required in whoredom is that of four men. Evidence is of several kinds, is that of four men, as has been ordained in the Koran; and the testimony of a woman in such case is not admitted; because Zihra says, "in the time of the Prophet and his two immediate successors it was an invariable rule to exclude the evidence of women in all cases inducing punishment or retaliation;" and also, because the testimony of women involves a degree of doubt, as it is merely a substitute for evidence, being accepted only where the testimony of men cannot be had; and therefore it is not admitted in any matter liable to drop from the existence of a doubt.

In other criminal cases, two men.—The evidence required in other criminal cases is that of two men, according to the text of the Koran; and the testimony of women is not admitted, on the strength of the tradition of Zihra above quoted.

And in all other matters, two men, or one man and two women.—In all other cases the evidence required is that of two men, or of one man and two women, whether the case relate to property, or to other rights, such as marriage, divorce, agency, executorship, or

---

*Arab. Farz; meaning an ordained duty, and therefore indispensable.

the like Shafei has said that the evidence of one man and two women cannot be property, or its dependencies, such as hire, admitted, excepting in cases that relating to bail, and so forth; because the evidence of women is originally inadmissible on account of their defect of understanding, their want of memory, and incapacity of governing, whence it is that their evidence is not admitted in criminal cases

OBJECTION.—Since, according to Shafei, the evidence of women is originally invalid, it would follow that their evidence alone is not admissible even in a case of property; whereas the evidence of four women alone is, in his opinion, admissible in such case.

REPLY—The evidence of four alone is necessarily admissible in cases of property, because of their frequent occurrence:—contrary to the mode of proceeding with respect to marriage (for instance), which being a matter of greater importance and more rare occurrence than mere matters of property, cannot therefore be classe with them.

THE reasoning of our doctors is that the evidence of women is originally valid, because evidence is founded upon three circumstances, namely, sight, memory, and a capability of communication; for by means of the first the witness acquires knowledge; by means of the second he retains such knowledge; and by means of the third he is enabled to impart to the Kazee; and all these three circumstances exist in a woman (whence it is that her communication of a tradition or of a message is valid); and with respect to their want of memory, it is capable of remedy by the junction of another; that is, by substituting two women in the room of one man; and the defect of memory being thus supplied, there remains only the doubt of substitution; whence it is that their evidence is not admitted in any matter liable to drop from the existence of a doubt, namely, retaliation or punishment: in opposition to marriage, and so forth, as those may be proved notwithstanding a doubt, whence the evidence of women is admitted in those instances.

OBJECTION.—As the evidence of two women is admitted in the room of that of one man, it would follow that the evidence of four women alone ought to be admitted in cases of property and other rights; whereas it is otherwise

REPLY.—Such is the suggestion of analogy. The evidence of four women alone, however, is not accepted (contrary to what analogy would suggest), because if it were, there would be frequent occasions for their appearance in public, in order to give evidence; whereas their privacy is the most laudable

The evidence of women alone suffices concerning matters which do not admit the inspection of men.—THE evidence of one woman is admitted in cases of birth (as where one woman, for instance, declares that "a certain oman brought forth a certain child"). In the same manner also, the evidence of one woman is a sufficient with respect to virginity, or with respect to the defect of that part of a woman which is conceal from man.—The principle of the law, in these cases, is derived from a traditional saying of the Prophet, "The evidence of women is valid with respect to such things as it is not fitting for man to behold."—Shafei holds the evidence of four women to be a necessary condition in such cases. The foregoing tradition, however, is a proof against him; and another proof against him is that, in the cases in question, the necessity of male evidence is remitted, and female evidence credited, because the ocular examination of a woman, in these cases, is less indecent than that of a man; and hence also, as the sight of two or three persons is more indecent than that of one, the evidence of more than one woman is not insisted on as a condition in those instances. It is to be remarked, however, that if two or three women give evidence in such cases; it is a commedable caution, because the evidence may be of an obligatory tendency.—The law with respect to the evidence of women in cases of birth has been fully set forth in the book of divorce, treating of the establishment of parentage,* where it is said, that "if a man marry a woman, and she bring forth a child at a period of six months, or more, after her marriage, and the husband deny the parentage, in that case the evidence of one woman is sufficient to establish it."—and there are also other examples recited to the same effect The law with respect to the evidence of a woman in cases of virginity, is that if a woman complain of the impotency of her husband, and assert, that her virginity still exists, and another woman bear evidence of the same, in that case one year must be suffered to elapse, and then a separation must be effected between the husband and wife: † because virginity is a real entity, and the existence of it has here been attested by evidence.—The same rule also holds where a person purchases a female slave on condition of her being a virgin, and afterwards desire to return her because of her being a woman; for if, in that case, another woman should examine into her condition, and then declare her to be a virgin, her evidence must be credited, as virginity is an entity, and the existence of it is here proved by evidence; —or if, on the contrary, she declare her to be a woman, her muliebrity (which is a defect) is established in virtue of such declaration, and the plea of the purchaser holds good: whence the seller is required to take an oath that such defect did not exist when he sold her, which, if he refuse to do, he is bound to receive her back.

It is not admitted to prove that a child was live-born further than ralates to the rites of

---

*See Vol. I. p. 136.

† That is, provided he show no proof of virility in the interim. (See Vol. I. p. 126.)

burial - THE evidence of a woman with respect to Istihlal* or the noise made by a child at its birth, is not admissible, in the opinion of Haneefa, so far as relates to the establishment of the right of heritage in the child; because this noise is of a nature to be known or discovered by men: but is admissible so far as relates to the necessity of reading funeral prayers over the child: because these prayers are merely a matter of religion;—in consequence of her evidence, therefore, the funeral prayers are to be repeated over it.—The two disciples maintain that the evidence of a woman is sufficient to establish the right of heritage also; because the noise in question being made at the birth, none but women can be supposed to be present when it is made.—The evidence of a woman, therefore, to this noise, is the same as her evidence to a living birth: and as the evidence of women in the one case is admissible, so also is it in the other.

The probity of the witness, and his mention of the term evidence are essentials.—IN all rights, whether of property or otherwise, the probity of the witness, and the use of the word Shahadit [evidence] is requisite:† even in the case of the evidence of women with respect to birth, and the like; and this is approved; because Shahadit is testimoney, since it possesses the property of being binding; whence it is that it is restricted to the place of jurisdiction; and also, that the witness is required to be free, and a Mussulman.—If, therefore, a witness should say, "I know," or "I know with certainty," without making use of the word Shahadit, in that case his evidence cannot be admitted. With respect to the probity of the witness, it is indispensable, because of what is said in the KORAN, "TAKE THE EVIDENCE OF TWO JUST MEN;" and also, because the probity of the witnesses induces a probability of the truth,—whereas the want of it in the witness (indicated in his commission or prohibited actions) renders it reasonable to suppose that he will assert falsehoods, and consequently induces a probability of falsehood.—It is recorded, from Aboo Yoosaf, that an unjust* man, provided he be possessed of generosity, ought to be credited; because such a disposition renders it unlikely that he will either suffer himself to be suborned, or that he will wantonly assert a falsehood—The first opinion, however (namely, that the evidence of an unjust man is not to be credited), is the most authentic, —With respect to the use of the word Shahadit, it is indispensable, because all the passages in the KORAN, relating to evidence, use this word; and there is also a strong degree of precaution in the use of it: for as it serves to express an oath, people will be more cautious of using it falsely.

The apparent probity of the witnesses suffices, excepting in cases inducing punishment or retaliation.—HANEEFA has said that the magistrate ought to rest contented with the apparent probity of a Mussulman, and should not scrutinize into his character in such a manner as to give the opposite party an opportunity to scorn him; because the Prophet (according to a tradition related by Omar) has said, ALL MUSSULMANS are just with respect to evidence, excepting such as have been punished for slander;" and also, because the probable character of all that profess the religion of Islam is an abstinence from every thing prohibited by that religion; and here it is necessary to rest satisfied with probability, as the attainment of certainty is impracticable,—In cases however, inducing retaliation or punishment, mere probability is not sufficient; and therefore a purgation of the witnesses must be made; for punishment and retaliation are cases in which all possible pretexts of prevention are to be sought: it is therefore requisite that, in such cases, the character of the witnesses be strictly investi-

---

* If a child die immediately on its birth, without making a noise, it is then considered in law to have been brought forth dead, and it neither succeeds to a portion of its father's estate, nor are funeral prayers read over it. If, however, it make the smallest noise, it is then held to die possessed of its portion, and funeral prayers are read over it.—Thus if a person should die, leaving his wife pregnant, the division of his estate is in that case suspended till the birth of the child: if it prove a dead child (that is, one that appeared dead immediately at the birth and made no noise), the estate is divided as if no such child had been born; but if it have made a noise, its share is in that case allotted and divided amongst its heirs.—The determination of the heirs, and consequently the nature of the division of the estate must often rest upon this circumstance. For instance, if a person die without children, leaving a brother, and his wife who is at that time pregnant, and the child at its birth make a noise, and immediately after die, it is held to be an heir, and the mother, in exclusion of the uncle, succeeds to the whole; but, if it make no noise before its death, the uncle is then considered to be an heir, and no share is allowed to the child. The law is the same in the case of a grandson, whose father had before died, being left under such circumstances.

† In other words, it is requisite that the witness say (in Arabic) "Ash-hado, I testify" or (in Persian) "Shahadit meyekoonam, I bear witness."

*Arab, Fasik, This term is fully explained elsewhere, (See Vol. I. p. 26.) With respect to evidence, Fasik seems nearly to correspond with the term infamous, as used by our lawyers, in treating of incompetent witnesses. (See Blackstone Book III. chap. 23.)

gated :—moreover, doubt is preventive in those instances.

If, however, their probity be questioned, a purgation is required.—If the defendant throw a reproach on the witnesses, it is in that case incumbent on the Kazee to institute an inquiry into their character; because, in the same manner as it is probable that a Mussulman abstains from falsehood, as being a thing prohibited in the religion he professes, so also is it probable that one Mussulman will not unjustly reproach another:—here, therefore, is a conflict between two probabilities; and hence the necessity of the inquiry of the Kazee into the character of the witnesses, that he may discover which of the probabilities preponderates.—It is related as an opinion of Aboo Yoosaf and Mohammed, that a scrutiny must be made, with regard to the witnesses, both openly and privately, in all cases whatever; since the decree of the Kazee rests upon proof, and proof rests upon the integrity of the witnesses. Besides, an inquiry into the integrity of the witnesses tends to preserve the decree of the Kazee from annulment; because if he should pass a decree upon the probable character of the witnesses and their falsehood should afterwards be discovered, the said decree would be rendered null.—Several have alleged that this disagreement between Haneefa and the two disciples is founded on the difference of the times. In the present age, however, decrees are passed in this particular according to the doctrine of the two disciples.

Nature of a secret.—A secret purgation is made by a Kazee writing a letter, privately, to a Mozkee or purgator (that is, a person whose business it is to inquire into the character of others), and describing to him the family and countenance of the witnesses, and likewise their place of abode; and the purgator, in like manner, returning his answer privately to the Kazee, lest if it were known to the plaintiff, he might attempt to injure him.

And an open purgation.—In an open purgation it is requisite that the Kazee summon together the purgator and the witnesses, and hear the examination himself—During the first age (that is in the time of the Prophet and his companions) an open purgation was practised: but in the present times a secreet one is adopted, in order to avoid quarrels and contentions between the purgator and the witnesses; for it is related as an opinion of Mohammed that an open purgation tends to sedition and contention. Some have said that it is requisite that the purgator report the witness not only to be just, but also free; for a slave may be just, but his testimony is nevertheless invalid Others have said that his report of the integrity of the witness is sufficient; for his freedom is established [in probability] by his abode in a Mussulman country;—and this is approved.

Justification of a witness by the defendant.—It is to be observed that, according to that doctrine which maintains the neces... ...e Kazee's purgation of the witnesses, whether the defendant challenge their probity or not, the justification of them by the defendant is not of any weight; in other words, if he declare the witnesses of the plaintiff to be upright men, yet his word is not credited; and such is the doctrine of the Zahir Rawayet, from Aboo Yoosaf and Mohammed. It is also related, as their opinion, that the justification of the witnesses by the defendant is valid, under this condition, however (according to Muhammed), that there be also another justification for he holds that two are always required, one being in no case sufficient—The reasoning on which the doctrine of the Zahir Rawayet proceeds in this particular, is that the defendant is, in the conception of the plaintiff and his witnesses, a liar, and his denial of the claim unjust and unfounded, but in which he nevertheless perseveres. He is therefore incapable of appeasing as a purgator, since a purgator must be a person of integrity, according to all.—This proceeds on the supposition of the defendant having declared the witnesses to be just men, but that in the delivery of their testimony they had committed an error: or that they had been overpowered by forgetfulness. If, however, he declare that "they have spoken truth," or that "they are just men and true speakers," this amounts to an acknowledgment of the plaintiff's right, and the Kazee must in such case pass a decree against him,—not on account of his purgation of the witnesses, but of his acknowledgment.

One purgator suffices—One purgator is sufficient, and two are superfluous, according to Haneefa and Aboo Yoosaf. Mohammed, on the contrary, maintains that purgation is not valid unless performed by two,—A similar disgreement subsists between them, with respect both to the messenger who goes to the purgator on the part of the Kazee, and also the interpreter employed to explain and interpret the deposition of the witnesses.—The argument of Mohammed is, that as the power of the Kezee to pass a decree is founded upon the evidence of the probity of the witnesses, and as the evidence of their probity is founded upon purgation, it follows that plurality is in this instance requisite, in the same manner as probity,—or as, in cases inducing punishment, it is required that the witnesses be males.—The argument of Haneefa and Aboo Yoosaf is that purgation is not considered in the nature of evidence; whence neither the assembly of the Kazee, nor the use of the phrase Shahadit, are required as conditions with regard to it. Besides, the necessity of a plurality in evidence is a mere matter of religion.—in other words, is founded on a passage in the Koran, in opposition to analogy; for the truth of any assertion obtains an ascendancy from the declaration of one Just person, so far as relates to practice, as is evident from this circumstance, that many of the traditionary precepts which it is necessary to follow, have been delivered by one man) :—and the necessity of a plurality in evidence is contrary to analogy, the establishment of such necessity in purgation, by inference from that rule, would be absurd.

A slave may be a purgator in the secret purgation—As the qualifications requisite to a witness are not required in a purgator, a slave is capable of being a purgator in a secret purgation In an open purgation, however, the purgator must, according to all our doctors, be possessed of the qualifications necessary to a witness because of what is recorded by Khasaf, that "an open purgation is restricted to the assembly of the Kazee."—Lawyers have observed, also, that in the purgation of witnesses to whoredom four purgators are necessary, according to Mohammed.

Section

Evidence is of two kinds:—that which occasions effect in itself.—The things which witnesses retain and bear testimony of, are of two kinds.—The first are those which produce effect in themselves: such as sale, acknowledgment, usurpation, murder, and the sentence of a judge; in all of which the effect results from the things themselves; and consequently, whenever a person hears or sees anything of importance relating to these matters, he may lawfully give evidence of it, without its being demanded from him; because in these cases, immediately upon his hearing or seeing, he becomes acquainted with a circumstance which occasions effect in itself, and there is therefore no need of such evidence being demanded from him.—In such case, also, it is requisite that he deliver his testimony thus, "I give evidence that a certain person bought, &c." and not, "evidence has been demanded from me, &c." because this latter mode of delivery is false If, however, a person from without a door, or from behind a curtain, hear any thing spoken by another that is within in that case he is not entitled to give evidence of the same; and if he should attest it, the Kazee must not accept it, because it is illegal, since, as voices are often similar, they cannot be distinguished with certainty. But if, having first entered into the house, he discover that there is only one person within, and having then retired, and sat without the door, he hear that person make an acknowledgement, he may then lawfully attest the same, because in such case he acquires certain knowledge.

And that, the effect of which rests upon other evidence.—The second kind of things to which evidence relates, are those which do not occasion effect in themselves; such as testimony,* which does not occasion effect in itself: because, as it is merely information, it admits the supposition of being either true or false; and such things as are doubtful are not decisive proof.—Upon testimony being given therefore, the hearer does not immediately know that the right is proved; and consequently, if one person hear another give evidence of something, he is not empowered to give evidence of the same unless the witness desire him to attest his evidence; because evidence does not occasion effect in itself, nor until it be removed to the assembly of the Kazee.—Besides, as the attestation of the evidence of another is an overt act with respect to that other, it is requisite that the other previously appoint this person his deputy; and in the case in question this is not approved.—In the same manner, also if a person hear another desire a third person to attest his evidence, it is not lawful for him in such case to give evidence of the same, because the original witness appointed another, and not him, his deputy for that purpose.

The signature to a deed must not be attested, unless the witness recollect the circumstance of signing it—If a person see his own signature to a bill of sale, or the like he must not, merely on account of the sight of his signature, attest it, unless he otherwise recollect to have witnessed the said bill; since handwritings are often similar—Some have said that this is the doctrine of Haneefa; but that the two disciples are of a different opinion.—Others, again, have said that all are agreed in its being unlawful to give the attestation merely on the right of the signature; and that the only case of this kind in which there is a disagreement is that with respect to a Kazee; for if he should discover, in his Dewan or records, the evidence of any one, or a decree of his own, he may, in such case (according to the two disciples) pass a decree agreeably thereto, notwithstanding he have forgot the circumstance; because the records of the Kazee; being kept under his seal, are therefore secured against alterations, and consequently afford certain knowledge—It is otherwise with respect to bills of sale or the like, because those, as being kept in the hands of others are not secured against alterations.—In the same manner, also, if a person recollect the place in which his evidence had been taken, without remembering the affair to which it related, it is the same as his seeing his signature without remembering his subscription of it, and therefore he is not permitted to attest it:—and the same rule obtains where people in whom he places credit say to him, "you and we did formerly jointly attest such particular matter,"

Evidence cannot be given on hearsay. except to such matters as admit the privacy only of a few.—It is not lawful for a person to give evidence to such things as he has not actually seen, excepting in the cases of birth, death, marriage, cohabitation, and the jurisdiction of a Kazee, to all of which he may lawfully be a testimony on creditable hearsay.—This proceeds upon a favourable construction.—Analogy would suggest that it is not lawful for him to give evidence in those

*Meaning testimony to evidence given by another.

cases also; because evidence is founded entirely on sight, from which knowledge is derived; and as no certain knowledge can be acquired without sight, it follows that evidedce, in the cases above excepted, is not valid unless founded upon sight.—The reason for a more favourable construction. In this particular, is that these events are of such a nature as admit the privacy only of a few;—thus birth (for instance) is an event at which none is present but the midwife; the authority of the Kazee is founded on the appointment of the Sultan, which is seen only by the Vizier, or at most a few others; marriages and deaths are seen by but few; and cohabitation by none. All these, however, are acts from which originate many important concerns. If, therefore, the reality of these things were not admitted upon hearsay evidence, many inconveniences would result: in opposition to cases of sale, or the like, where privacy is not required.—It is to be observed that it is requisite, in these cases, that the information have been received from two just men, or from one just man and two women.—Some have advanced that in cases of death the information of one man or one woman is sufficient, because death is not seen by many, since as it occasions horror the sight of it is avoided.

And it must be given in an absolute manner.—WHEN a person, in any of the above cases, gives evidence from creditable hearsay, it is requisite that he give it in an absolute manner by saying for instance; "I bear testimony that A, is the son of B," and not "I bear testimony so and so, because I have heard it,"—for in that case the Kazee cannot accept it;—in the same manner as if a person, having seen a thing in the hands of A, were to say. "This thing is the property of A.," in which case his testimony is valid: but if he should state that "he gives evidence because he has seen the thing in the possession o A.," the Kazee could not accept his testimony.—So also, if a person see another sitting in the court of justice, deciding in a suit between plaintiff and defendant, it is lawful for him to give evidence that "that person was a Kazee:"—or, if a person see a man and woman dwelling in the same house, and conducting themselves towards one another in the manner of husband and wife, he may lawfully give evidence of their being husband and wife; in the same manner as it is lawful for a person who sees a melon in the hand of another to give evidence that it is the property of that person,

Evidence to the burial of a person amounts to evidence of his death.—IF a person say that he was present at the burial of another, or that he had read the funeral service over him this amounts to the same as an actual sight of the death, insomuch that if he should explain to the Kazee the principle on which he gives his evidence, it will still be valid.

WHAT is above advanced, that "it is not lawful for a person to give evidence to such things as he has not actually seen, excepting in the cases of birth, death, marriage, cohabitation and the jurisdiction of a Kazee," is taken from Kadooree; and from these particular exceptions it may be inferred that hearsay evidence is unlawful in every other instance, such as Wills, charitable appropriations, and so forth.—It is indeed related, as the last opinion of Aboo Yoosaf, that evidence from hearsay is lawful in a case of Willa; because Willa is equivalent to relation by consanguinity, as the Prophet has said "WILLA is a connection like consanguinity."—It is also related, as the opinion of Mohammed, that hearsay evidence is lawfull in a case of appropriations; for as appropriation continues to operate for a long period of time, the laws with respect to it would be rendered null if hearsay evidence were not admitted to prove it.—Our doctors, however, argue that Willa is founded upon a relinquishment, of right of property: and as, in bearing evidence to that, actual sight is required, it follows that it is in the same manner required with respect to a matter derived therefrom, namely Willa.—With respect to charitable appropriation, on the contrary, hearsay evidence must be admitted so far as regards the appropriation itself (such as where the witness says, "I attest this to be a wakf): but it is not admitted with respect to any conditional restrictions imposed by the appropriator; for although the appropriation itself be notorious, yet the conditions of it are not so.

A right of property may be attested from seeing an article in the possession of another.—IF a person see any article (excepting an adult male or female slave), in the hands of another, he may in such case lawfully attest its being the property of that other, because possession argues property, since in all causes of property, such as purchase, sale, or the like, possession is the argument of its existence.—For instance; if a person sell any thing, his possession is an argument of the legality of the sale; and in the same manner, also, the right of property is established in a purchase from the possession of the seller, and the right of property in an heir, from the possession of him from whom he inherits.—Hence, in giving evidence of a thing being the property of another, it is sufficient to have seen it in his possession.—It is recorded from Aboo Yoosaf, that besides the sight of the possession, it is requisite that the witness verily believe the article to be the property of the possessor, insomuch that if he do not really think so he cannot lawfully attest on the possessor's behalf.—Several of our doctors also remark that this explanation applies to the opinion of Mohammed, above related, respecting the legality of attesting marriage, birth, and cohabitation on hearsay;—that is, that it is lawful for a person to attest any of these incidents upon hearsay, provided he believe it in his own mind, but not otherwise.—Shafei has said that possession, together with transaction.* argues property (and many of the Haneefite doctors are also of this opinion): because possession being of two kinds, namely, either in virtue of trust or of right of property, does not argue right of property unless when united with the performance of acts —Our doctors, on the other hand: argue that transaction is also of two kinds; one, in virtue of delegation, and the other in virtue of original authority:—and hence the junction of transaction to possession leaves still a doubt in regard to the property.—In short, if a probable argument be adopted, possession is than sufficient; but if a certain one be required, possession, even when joined to transaction could not be sufficient.—It is to be observed that the case here treated of admits of four statements. I. Where a person sees both the proprietor and the property, and is acquainted with both,—that is with the countenance and the family of the proprietor. and with the boundaries of the property, which he sees him possess without strife; and afterwards sees the same thing in the possession of another; and the first proprietor appears to claim it;—in which case it is lawful for him to give evidenee of its being the property of the first person, because of his having seen it in his possession. II. Where he sees the property, and its limits, but not the proprietor:—and here also it is lawful for him to give evidence of the property (upon a favourable construction of the LAW), because the proprietor is known, so far as regards his family, from hearsay. III Where he neither sees the proprietor nor the property;—and, IV. Where he sees the proprietor but not the property; in both of which cases it is unlawful to give evidence with regard to the right of property.

And the right of property in a slave may also be attested on the same ground —If a person see a slave, male or female, in the possession of another, and know the said person to be a slave, he may lawfully give evidence to such slave being the property of that other;—for a slave not being his own master. and of consequence not entitled to go where he pleases, is apparently the property of that person in whose hands he remains. So also, if he should not know the person seen in the possession of another to be a slave, and being an infant, it should be incapable of explaining its own condition, he may in that case lawfully give evidence of its being the property of the possessor; for an infant is not its own master.—But if the person seen be arrived at the age of maturity,—that is to say, be capable of explaining his condition,—and he should not know whether he is a slave or not, then it is not lawfut to give evidence of his being the property of the possessor, simply on the sight of the possession.—This is the reason of the exception, in the preceding case, of a slave arrived at the age of maturity; and the ground ef it is that persons arrived at the age of maturity are in a manner in their own possession; and therefore the possession of another, which indicates the right of property of that other, is not to be discovered from the simple sight —It is related as an opinion of Haneefa, that even in this case evidence to the right of property may lawfully be given: but what has been before related is the most authentic doctrine.

* Arab, Teserrif: meaning (in this place,) any act of mastery performed with respect to the property in question, such as letting it out to hire, for instance:

CHAPTER II.

OF THE ACCEPTANCE AND REJECTION OF EVIDENCE

The evidence of a blind man is inadmissible.—The evidence of a blind man is not admissible.—Zaffer maintains that the evidence of a blind man is admissible with respect to matters in which hearsay prevails; (and there is also one report of the doctrine of Haneefa to the same effect); because in such matters hearing only is required, and in the hearing of a blind man there is no defect.—Aboo Yoosaf and Shafei have said that the evidence of a blind man in these matters is lawful, provided he was possessed of sight at the time of their occurrence; for by means of that he acquires a certain knowledge, which he is a afterwards, notwithstanding his want of sight, capable of communicating, as that depends entirely on the tongue, which in a blind man is not defective; and it is in his power to show his knowledge of the person with regard to whom he gives the evidence, by a description of his birth and family.—Our doctors, on the other hand, argue that in the delivery of evidence there is a necessity to distinguish between the person for and against whom it is given; and a blind man is incapable of doing this otherwise than by the voice; and this is attended with a doubt, which may be avoided, by the party producing a witness possessed of sight.—With respect to the assertion of Shafei and Aboo Yoosaf, that "it is in his power to show his knowledge of the person with regard to whom he gives the evidence by a description of his birth and family," it may be replied that this mode has been instituted for a definition of the absent, not of the present.—In short, in the the same manner as the evidence of a blind man is inadmissible in cases relative to retaliation or punishments, so also is it inadmissible in all other cases whatever.

And if a person give evidence, and become blind, a decree cannot issue upon it.—If a person, having given evidence, should after wards become blind previous to the passing of the decree, in that case (according to Haneefa and Mohammed), it not lawful for the Kazee to pass a decree thereupon; for the existence of the competency of the witnesses at the time of passing the dacree is a necessary condition, as the validity of the evidence, at that time, constitutes the proof; and in the case here supposed the evidence has at that period become null. This case is therefore the same as if a witness, after having given evidence, should either become insane, dumb, or unjust, in any of which cases the Kazee could not pass a decree upon the evidence so given.—It is otherwise where the witnesses, having given their evidence, either disappear or die; for in that case the Kazee may lawfully pass a decree upon it; because the competency of evidence is not annulled, but rather concluded, and rendered complete, by death; and absence does not destroy this competency.

The evidence of a slave is not admissible.—The testimony of any person who is property,—that is to say a slave, male or female.—is not admissible: because testimony is of an authoritative nature: and as a slave has no authority over his own person, it follows, that he can have no authority over others, a fortiori

Or of a slanderer.—The testimony of a person that has been punished for slander is inadmissible, even though he should, afterwards have repented; because God has said, in the Koran,—"But as to those who accuse married persons or whoredom, and produce not four witnesses of the fact, scourge them with fourscore stripes, and receive not their testimony for ever; for such are infamous prevaricators,—excepting those who shall afterwards repent."—The rejection of his evidence, moreover, is included as a part of the punishment prescribed for the crime, as this tends to prevent the commision of it in future; and as the rejection of his evidence is a part of the punishment: this effect must evidently remain after his repentance, on the same principle as the punishment itself is not remitted although he repent, If it otherwise with respect to a person punished for any other crime; for the evidence of such a person is admissible after repentance, since the rejection of it, in regard to him, proceeded from the stigma attached to his offence, which is done away by repentance.—According to Shafei, the evidence of a person punished for slander is admissible, provided he have afterwards repented. because God, in enjoining the rejection of the evidence of such, has particularly excepted penitents.—Our doctors, on the other hand, argue that the exception in the divine ordinance relates to that part of it which declares slanderers to be infamous prevaricators. and not to that part which declares them to be incompetent as witnsses. Penitence, therefore removes the stigma from the character of such a pesson, but does not restore his competency to give evidence.

But an infidel slanderer recovers his competency as a witness upon embracing the faith.—If an infidel, who had suffered punishment for slander, should afterwards become a Mussulman, his evidence is then admissible; for although, on account of the said punishment, he had lost the degree in which he was befor qualified to give evidence (that is. in all matters that related to his own sect), yet by his conversion to the Mussulman faith he acquires a new competency in regard to evidence (namely, competency to give evidence relative to Mussulmans), which he did not possess before. and which is not affected by any matter that happened prior to the circumstance which gave birth to it.—It is otherwise with respect to a slave, who, having suffered punishment for slander, afterwards becomes free; for his testimony is not admissible after emancipation; because in his former condition of slavery he did not possess, in any degree, ability to give evidence, and consequently the punishment was incomplete, since it was impossible to subject him to any greater degree of discredit than what was before imposed on him; the credit, therefore, which he would otherwise have acquired afterwards in virtue of his emancipation. if taken from him in order to complete the prescribed punishment.

Evidence is not admitted in favour of relations within the degree of paternity.—Testimony in favour of a son or grandson, or in favour of a father or grandfather, is not admissible; because the Prophet has so ordained.—Besides, as there is a kind of communion of benefits between these degrees of kindred, it follows that their testimony in matters relative to each other is in some degree a testimony in favour of themselves, and is therefore liable to suspicion.

Nor between an hnsband and wife, a master and his slave or an hirer and his hireling.—The Prophet has said, "We are not to credit the evidence of a wife concerning her husband, or of a husband concerning his wife;*

* This doctrine of the inadmissibility of the evidence of husband and wife in favour of each other prevails only amongst the Soonis [the followers of Omar], and has given rise to much contention with the Shiyas [the followers of Alee], who maintain the opposite doctrine.—The origin of their disagreement on this occasion is thus related.—The Prophet in the course of his wars having been presented with the village of Fattook by some Christians, who saw the impossibility of resisting his power, determined to have divided it amongst his companions, as was his usual practice in regard to the spoils taken in war. He was afterwards, however, induced to give it to his daughter Fatima, in consequence of a reve-

or of a slave concerning his master; or of a master concerning his slave; or, lastly, of a hirer concerning his hireling.—The author of this work observes that by the term hirer [Ajeer], as used in this place, is to be understood (according to the explanation of the lawyers) a select scholar who considers an injury to his teacher as an injury to himself —others have said that it is understood to mean a person who lets out any thing by lease for a month or a year; for as, at the time of giving evidence, he is entitled to the rent, in return for the usufruct enjoyed by the other, a suspicion arises of his having constituted this person his tenant merely with a view to procure his evidence.—With respect to the evidence of a husband and wife concerning each other. Shafei maintains that it is admissible; because the property of each is distinct and separate; and also because distinct seisins are made, by each, of their respective property: whence it is that retaliation is executed upon either for the murder of the other.—and also, that either may be imprisoned for a debt due to the other.—Besides, the benefit which they mutually derive from each other's property is of no accouut, because the existence of such benefit is of an involved nature;*—in the same manner as the evidence of a creditor in favour of his indigent debtor is admissible, notwithstanding he derive a benefit from it as this benefit is of an involved nature.—The arguments of our doctors upon this point are twofold FIRST, the traditionary precept of the Prophet above quoted SECONDLY, the benefit which from custom, the husband and wife derive from the property of each other, which occasions their testimony in favour of each other to be, in a manner, testimony in favour of themselves, and consequently liable to suspicion.—It is otherwise with respect to the testimony of a creditor in favour of his indigent debtor, because he has no power over the property of the debtor, whereas a husband and wife have such power from usage and custom.

The testimony of a master cannot be admitted in favour of his slave.—THE testimony of a master in favour of his slave is not admissible; because of the tradition above quoted; and also because, if the slave be not indebted to any person, such testimony is in every respect in favour of himself;—or if, on the other hand, he be indebted, still the testimony of the master is in some respect in favour of himself, as the matter remains in suspense; for if the master should choose to pay the debts, the testimony would be completely relative to himself, whereas it would not be so in any degree in case he should permit the slave to be sold in liquidation of the debt;—and as it is not known which mode he may follow, the testimony is therefore considered to be in some respect relative to himself.—It is to be observed that the evidence of a master in favour of his Mokatib is not admissible; for the reason here stated

Nor of one partner in favour of another (relative to their joint concern).—THE testimony of one partner in favour of another, in a matter relative to their joint property, is not admissible; because it is in some degree in favour of himself.—The testimony, however, of partners, in favour of each other, in matters not relating to their joint property, is admissible, because in it there is no room for suspicion.

Testimony in favour of an uncle or brother is admitted.—TESTIMONY in favour of a brother or an uncle is admissible, because the property and the immunities of these classes of relations are separate, and each has no power over that of the other.

The testimony is not admissible of public mourners or singers.—THE testimony of women that lament or sing is not admissible, because they are guilty of forbidden actions, inasmuch as the Prophet has prohibited these two species of noise.—(It is to be observed that this case alludes to a woman who laments for the adversity of others, not for her own, and who hires herself out for that purpose.)

Or of common drunkards; or of falconers, &c.—THE testimony of a person who is continually intoxicated is inadmissible, because of his commission of a prohibited act. —In the same manner, also, the testimony of a person who amuses himself with birds, such as pigeons or hawks, is inadmissible; because such amusement engenders forgetfulness; and also because in the practice of it, he sees the nudities of strange women, he having occasion to sit on the top of his house

---

lation he received from heaven, enjoining him not to give out of his own family what had been freely conferred upon him.—After his death it was seized upon by his successor Aboo Beker; and when Fatima claimed it in consequence of the gift of her father, and produced her husband Alee, and her two sons, as witnesses, her claim was rejected by Aboo Beker, on the grounds of the testimony of relations in that degree having been declared inadmissible by the Prophet. This tradition, thus quoted by Aboo Beker, has ever since amongst the Soonis occasioned the inadmissibility of the evidence of husband and wife in favour of each other. The Shiyas, however (who follow a contrary doctrine), maintain that this pretended precept of the Prophet was purposely forged by the Khalif to defraud Fatima of her right; and in support of his opinion they argue that if such a precept had existed, it could not have been unknown to Alee; and that if he had known of it, he never would in such case have appeared as a witness in favour of his wife.

*That is to say, is interwoven with and necessarily arises from, the particular circumstances of their relative situation.

to fly these birds.—In some copies, instead of the amusement of Teyoor, or birds, that of Tamboor.* or musical instruments, is written, which alludes to public singers; and the testimony of a public singers is not admissible, because he is the occasion of assembling a number of people to commit a prohibited action.†

Or of atrocious criminals.—THE testimony of a person who has committed a great crime, such as induces punishment, is not admissible, because in consequence of such crime he is unjust.

Or of immodest person.—THE testimony of a person who goes naked into the public bath is inadmissible, because of his committing a prohibited action, in the exposure of his nakedness.

Or of usurers or gamesters.—THE testimony of a person who receives usury is inadmissible;—and so, also, of one who plays for a stake at dice or chess,—because gaming in that manner is ranked in the number of great crime;—and in the same manner, also, the evidence of a person who omits his prayers, from an attention to these games, is not admissible —It is to be observed, however, that simple playing at chess without a stake is not destructive of credit, since such play does not induce a want of integrity because all our Imams are not agreed in its illegality, Malik and Shafei havin' declared it to be lawful —It is recorded in the Mabsoot, that the evidence of an usurer is inadmissible only in case of his being so in a notorious degree; because mankind often make invalid contracts; and these are, in some degree, usurious

Or of per ons guilty of indecorum.—THE evidence of a person guilty of base and low actions, such as making water or eating his victuals on the high road, is not admissible; because where a man is not restrained, by a sense of shame, from such actions as these, he exposes himself to a suspicion that he will not refrain from falsehood.

Or of free-thinkers, if they avow their sentiments.—THE evidence of a person who openly in veighs against the companions of the Prophet and their disciples is not admissible, because of his apparent want of integrity.—It is otherwise, however, where a person conceals his sentiments in regard to them, because in such case the want of integrity is not apparent.

The evidence of the sect of Hawa, and other heretics, admissible, but not that of the tribe of Khetabia.—THE evidence of the sect of Hawa* (that s, such as are not Soonis) is admissible; excepting, however, the tribe of Khetabia, whose evidence is inadmissible, for reasons that will be hereafter explained. —Shafei maintains that the evidence of no tribe whatever of the sect of Hawa is admissible, because the heterodox tenets they profess argue the highest degree of depravity. —Our doctors, on the other hand, argue that although their tenets be in reality wrong, yet their adherence to them implies probity, since they have been led to embrace them from an opinion of their being right; and there is, moreover, reason to think that they will abstain from falsehood, because it is prohibited in every religion. Hence the case is the same as if a person should eat of an animal which had not been slain according to the prescribed form of Zabbah, because of its being lawful amongst his sect. It is otherwise where the baseness proceeds from the actions, not from the belief.—With respect to the sect of Khetabia, it is to be observed that they are in a high degree heretics; and amongst them it is lawful to bear positive testimony to a circumstance on the grounds of another having sworn it to them. Some have said that it is an incumbent duty upon that sect to give evidence in favour of each other, whence their testimony is not free from suspicion.

Zimmees may testify concerning each other—THE testimony of Zimmees with respect to each other is admissible, notwithstanding they be of different religions.—Malik and Shafei have said that their evidence is absolutely inadmissible, because, as infidels are unjust,† it is requisite to be slow in believing any thing they may advance, GOD having said (in the KORAN). "WHEN AN UNJUST PERSON TELLS YOU ANY THING. BE SLOW IN BELIEVING HIM;"—whence it is that the evidence of an infidel is not admitted concerning a Mussulman; and consequently, that an infidel stands (in this particular) in the same predicament with an apostate.—The arguments of our doctors upon this point are twofold.—FIRST, it is related of the Prophet, that he permitted and held lawful the testimony of some Christians concerning others of their sect.—SECONDLY, an infidel having power over himself, and his minor children, is on that account qualified to be a witness with regard to his own sect; and the depravity which proceeds from his faith is not destructive of this qualification, because he is supposed to abstain from every thing prohibited in his own religion, and falsehood is prohibited in every religion. It is otherwise with respect to an apostate,

*In the Arabic and Persian, the words Teyoor and Tamboor are written exactly similar; and as they can only be distinguished from each other by the proper position of the diacritical points, they are therefore very liable to be confounded by the frequent omission of these points.

†Namely, listening to music.

*Anglice, the air; a derisive appellation given by the Soonis to the Shiyas.—Hawa, also, is used to express the sensual passions, whence the term Ahil Hawa signifies sensualists, or epictureans.

†Arab. Fasik; meaning, in this place, degenerate or depraved.

as he possesses no power, either over his own person, or over that of another; and it is also otherwise with respect to a Zimmee in relation to a Mussulman because a Zimmee has no power over the person of a Mussulman.—Besides, a Zimmee may be suspected of inventing falsehoods against a Mussulman from the hatred he bears to him on account of the superiority of the Mussulmans over him.

Objection.—In the same manner as there subsists an enemity between Mussulmans and Zimmees, so also is there an enmity between the followers of other religions, such as the Jews, the Christians, and the Magians: it would follow, therefore, that amongst these the testimony of those of one religion cannot be admitted with relation to others of a different religion; whereas it hath been declared admissible.

Reply.—Although the religions of these be different, yet none of them being under subjection to another, so as to engender reciprocal hatred; there is no cause to suspect that they will invent falsehoods against each other.

A Moostamin cannot testify concerning a Zimmee; but a Zimmee may testify concerning a Moostamin.—The testimony of an infidel Moostamin with relation to a Zimmee is not admissible, becasue he has no power over the person of a Zimmee, as the latter is a fixed resident in the Mussulman territory. The evidence of a Zimmee, however, is admissible with respect to an infidel Moostamin, in the same manner as the evidence of Mussulmans with relation to them is valid.

And Moostamins may testify concerning each other, being of the same country.—The testimony of one Moostamin is admissible with respect to another Moostamin, provided he be of the same country. If, however, they be of different countries (such as a native of Russia and of Turkey) their testimonies with respect to each other are not admissible; because this difference precludes the operation of their power over each other; whence it is that they cannot inherit of each other.

The testimony is admissible, of any one whose virtues preponderate.—The testimony of him whose virtues exceed his vices and who is not guilty of great crimes, is admissible, notwithstanding he may occasionally be guilty of venial crimes.—What is here advanced is an explanation of the degree of integrity to which regard is paid in bearing evidence: and this explanation is approved; for innocence with respect to great crimes, and a preponderance of virtue over vice, must necessarily be deemed sufficient, on this principle, that if any occasional commission of smaller crimes were destructive of testimony, the door of evidence would be shut, whilst the preservation of the rights of mankind requires that it should be kept open.

And of such as remain uncircumcised from any justifiable cause.—The testimony of an Acklif (that is, of one who has omitted circumcision on account of old age, or for some other sufficient reason) is admissible, because the omission of this ceremony is not destructive of justice;—excepting where it arises from a contempt of religion, or of the authority of the oral law by which it is enjoined, for in that case integrity no longer remains.

Or of an eunuch.—The testimony of an eunuch is admissible, because Omar accepted the testimony of Alkia, who was an eunuch; and also, because he has been deprived of one of his members by violence, and therefore stands in the same predicament with one who has been mutilated.

Or of a bastard.—The testimony of a bastard is valid, because he is innocent with respect to the immorality of his parents. Imam Malik maintains that the testimony of a bastard is not to be admitted with respect to whoredom, as it may naturally be supposed he wishes as many others as possible reduced to the same level with himself, and his testimony in a matter of this kind is therefore liable to suspicion.—Our doctors, however, argue that the present question relates merely to the point of integrity; and if a bastard be a just man, there is no reason to suspect him of such a wish.

Or of an hermaphrodite.—The testimony of a hermaphrodite is admissible, because such a person is either a man or a woman and the evidence of both is admissible.

Or of a viceroy.—The testimony of a governor on the part of a sultan is admissible, according to a majority of the Haneefite doctors, provided he do not enforce oppression; but if he act oppressively his testimony is not admissible. Some have said that in the latter case also his testimony is admissible, provided he be himself a man of generosity and character, and be not guilty of boasting and vain talk; because it is in such case natural to suppose that a regard for his reputation will prevent his asserting a falsehood; and the dignity of his character will deter any one from offering him a bribe.

Two brothers attesting their father's appointment of an executor must be credited, if the executor verify their testimony; and the same of the attestation of two legatees, two debtors or creditors, or two executors, to the same effect.—Where two brothers attest that their father had appointed a particular person to be his executor, if that person also claim the same, their testimony is valid, upon a favourable construction,—but not if he deny the appointment.—Analogy would suggest that their testimony is not valid in either case (and a case where two legatees attest that the testator had appointed a particular person his executor,—or where two debtors or creditors of the deceased essert the same,—or where two executors attest the junction of a third person with them in the executorship,—is subject to the same analogy):—because their evidence is in some degree advantageous to the witneses themselves, inasmuch as the advantage to be derived from it results to them also The reason for a more favourable construction in this particular is that as it is the duty of the Kazee to appoint an executor where it is required, and where the death of the person is notorious, the evidence in question is admissible, inasmuch as it exempts the Kazee from this trouble, and not because it establishes the proof of anything.—It is therefore a substitute for the cast of a die, which saves the trouble of election

OBJECTION.—Where there are two executors, there is no occasion for the Kazee's appointment of a third, and therefore theappointment of a third, upon such a ground, is unwarrantable.

REPLY.—The two executors having acknowledged that the deceased had joined a third person with them, the Kazee is there fore required to confirm him, since, in consequence of such acknowledgment they cannot act without him.

IT is to be observed that where the debtors of the deceased attest the executorship of a particular person, their evidence is admissible, whether the death of the other be notorious or not, because such evidence is an acknowledgment affecting themselves; and the death of the creditor is therefore established with respect to them, because of their acknowledgment.

Attestation to a person's appointment of an agent is not to be credited.—IF two brothers bear testimony that their absent father had appointed Zeyd an agent for the receipt of debts due to him at Koofa, their evidence is inadmissible, whether Zeyd claim the said agency or not;—for the Kazee has no power of himself to appoint an agent in behalf of an absentee; and the evidence is not in this instance sufficient to warrant it, since it is liable to suspicion.

A defendant's impeachment of the integrity of witnesses is not credited, unless he state their commission of some specific crime.—IF a defendant reproach a witness with a thing which would impeach his legal integrity, but which does not involve any of the rights of the spiritual or temporal LAW, and produce evidence in supports of his assertion, the Kazee must not hear them, nor pass a decree of the injustice of the witnesses; because this injustice is a thing of a nature which comes not within the jurisidiction of the Kazee, inasmuch as it is not permanent, being removable by repentance.—Besides, the evidence adduced in this case tends to lay open faults;*—now the concealment of faults is incumbent, and the manifestation of them prohibited: as, therefore, a witness, in giving evidence or this effect, is himself guilty of irregularity, his testimony cannot be heard: for the manifestation of faults is admitted only where it tends to maintain the rights of others; and that is only in such cases as fall within the jurisdiction of the Kazee;—but the case in question is not of that nature; and therefore the evidence cannot be admitted.

Or adduce evidence to the plaintiff's acknowledgment of their irregularity.—IF, however, witnesses were to give evidence that the plaintiff had himself acknowledged the irregularity of the witness, the evidence would in that case be valid: because acknowledgment is a thing which falls within the jurisdiction of the Kazee.

He is not allowed to adduce evidence to their being hired by the plaintiff—IF a defendant bring witnesses to prove that the plaintiff had hired his witnesses for ten dirms (for instance), such evidence must not be admitted: because, although it tend to prove something more than a mere irregularity, yet the defendant not being a regular adversary of the plantiff in regard to this matter, has no sight to establish it by evidence, since, with respect to this point, he is as it were a stranger.

Unless his own property be involved.—IF, however, the defendant be a regular adversary (as if, for instance, he should assert that the plaintiff had hired his witnesses to give evidence for ten dirms from property which he [the defendant] had put in his hands).—in that case the evidence he produces in support of his allegation must be admitted: because the defendant, is in this instance a regular adversary of the plaintiff in a matter of property; and the proof in regard to the property necessarily involves the proof of the reproach.—In the same manner also the evidence adduced by the defendant is admitted where he asserts that "he had compounded with the witnesses for a certain sum of money that they should withhold their testimony in support of such unfounded claim,—and that, having accordingly paid the stipulated sum, they had nevertheless given their evidence, and he therefore prefers a claim for the sum paid to them;"—for here the proof with respect to the claim would also establish the proof of the reproach. Lawyers have observed that as the testimony of witnesses is admitted with respect to any thing that falls within the jurisdiction of the Kazee, it follows that if the defendant bring witnesses to prove that the witness of the plaintiff is a slave, or that he has been punished for slander, or that he is a drunkard, or a slanderer, or a partner of the plaintiff,—in all these cases the evidence so adduced must be admitted.

A witness's immediate acknowledgment of mis-statement or omission, from apprehension, does not destroy his credit.—IF a person givs evidence, and before moving from the place or, the Kazee passing a decree upon it, declare that "he had given a part of his evidence under the influence of apprehen-

*By faults is here understood veniel trespasses, such as might destroy the legal integrity of a witness, but which do not amount to crimes.

sion," still, if he be a person of character,* the deposed matter to which he adheres must be credited.—The term apprehension,† as here used, implies that a fault has been committed, either by withholding part of the evidence which it was incumbent to have mentioned, or by reciting, from forgetfulness, something that was false.—The reason of admitting the evidence, in this case, is because the apprehension probably arose from the awe excited by the assembly of the Kazee; which is excused provided the person be just, and that he rectify his error in time.—It is otherwise where a person separates from the assembly of the Kazee, and afterwards returns and says. "I have omitted part of my evidence from apprehension;" for in that case his evidence would not be admitted; because there is reason to suspect a collusion with the plaintiff, which requires that caution be used: and also, because although any addition or diminution, after the delivery of the evidence, be accepted, and either added to, or deducted from, the original evidence, provided they be made in the same meeting, still this is not allowed in case of their being made at a different meeting. The same rule also holds with regard to the mistakes of a witness in explaining the boundaries of a house;—as if he should say (for instance) the east instead of the west; or in explaining genealogy, as if he should say (for instance) "Mohammed, the son of Ahmid," instead of "the son of Alee"—It is to be observed that the exposition of the law, in this case applies only to the addition, by the witness, of some circumstance which may be in its nature doubtful; for if it should be in no respect doubtful, then he may at any time afterwards, whether at the same meeting or not, lawfully add it to his evidence.—Thus if a witness omit the use of the word Shahadit, or the like, and afterwards declare this omission, it is in that case admitted, whether it be at the same meeting or not,—provided he be a just man.—It has been related, as an opinion of Haneefa and Aboo Yoosaf, that whatever addition or diminution a witness may make after the delivery of his evidence, shall in every case be admitted, although it be at a different meeting,—provided the witness be a just man. But the first doctrine is the most authentic, and decrees pass accordingly.

CHAPTER III.

OF THE DISAGREEMENT OF WITNESSES IN THEIR TESTIMONY.

Evidence repugnant to the claim cannot be admitted.—Where the evidence adduced by a claimant is conformable to the claim, it is worthy of credit; but not where it is repugnant to it; because, in matters concerning the rights of the individual, the priority of the claim is requisite to the admission of evidence; and this exists in the former instance, but not in the latter, since in the former the object of evidence (namely, a verification of the claim) is answered,—whereas in the latter the evidence tends to a falsification of it, and it is therefore the same as if no evidence at all were produced.*

The witnesses must perfectly agree in their testimony.—The concurrence of the witnesses, in words and meaning, is requisite, according to Haneefa.—If, therefore, one witness bear testimony to one thousand dirms being due, and the other to two thousand, no credit is to be given to either.—The two disciples are of opinion that the evidence is to be credited to the amount of one thousand dirms: and a similar disagreement also subsists in a case where one witness attests one divorce, and the other two or three divorces.—The arguments of the two disciples are that the witnesses agree in the smallest amount (such as in one thousand dirms, or in one divorce): and one of them, besides his agreement in this amount, attests an additional quantity.—Their evidence, therefore, must be admitted in the degree in which they concur; and the testimony of one, so far as it relates to the excess only, must be rejected.—The reasoning of Haneefa is that the witnesses differ in words, and consequently in meaning, since meaning is extracted from words. Thus two thousand (for instance) can never be construed to mean one thousand, as the terms are essentially different.—In the case in question, therefore, the one thousand, and the two thousand, respectively; are attested by only one witness; and the case is consequently the same as if their testimony had related to different articles,—as if one were to attest dirms and the other deenars, for instance.

The witnesses may be credited to the smallest amount in which they agree both in words and meaning.—If a person claim a debt of one thousand five hundred dirms, and one of his witnesses bear testimony to one thousand, and the other to one thousand five hundred, in that case the testimony must be credited in the amount of one thousand dirms;† for the

*Arab Adil: literally, a just person (in opposition to Fasik).

†Arab Tawaham

* To exemplify this case,—suppose a person were to claim the right of property in a house, on the plea of his having purchased it; and his witness attest the right of property from its having been given to him;—in that case the evidence so given would be rejected.

†The different between this and the preceding case turns entirely on the terms in which the testimony is delivered; for in the case here considered the witness, in mentioning one thousand five hundred, mentions the term one thousand, which so far coincide

witnesses concur in that amount, both in words and meaning, as one thousand is mentioned by both, and five hundred is an additional part of the speech, which adds force to the former part, instead of destroying it.—Analogous to this is one divorce and one divorce and an half; or one hundred dirms and one hundred and fifty dirms; that is to say, in both these cases the evidence is admitted in the least degree, namely, in the degree of one divorce, and to the amount of one hundred dirms.—It would be otherwise if one witness should attest ten dirms, and the other fifteen; because this is similar to the attestation of one thousand and two thousand, the effect of which has been before stated.

The evidence of a witness who attests a larger sum than the claim amounts to is null.—In a case where one witness attests one thousand dirms, and the other one thousand five hundred, and the claimant expressly declares that only one thousand dirms is due to him, the testimony for one thousand five hundred is null, as being falsified by the claimant.* The effect is also the same where the claimant alleges one thousand dirms, and one of the witnesses attests one thousand, and the other one thousand five hundred; for here also the claimant falsifies the testimony of one of his witnesses, inasmuch as his claim is different from it. A conformity, therefore, between the claim and the evidence is indispensably necessary: and hence, if the claimant should say, "my original claim was one thousand five hundred dirms, but I received five hundred," or "I exempted the debtor from five hundred;" in that case each of the above-mentioned testimonies would be credited, because of their conformity with the claim.

Evidence to a debt is not annulled by a subsequent declaration of part of the debt having been discharged.—If two persons give evidence to a debt of one thousand dirms, and one of them afterwards declare that the debtor had paid five hundred dirms of it, still the evidence of one thousand dirms being due must be credited, and that of the five hundred having been paid must be rejected. The reason of this is, that both witnesses agree in the debt of one thousand dirms, whereas one witness only attests the payment of five hundred dirms; and as two witnesses are requisite to establish proof, the testimony in the first instance is therefore admitted as proof; and the additional declaration (of one thousand dirms having been paid) is rejected —It is related as an opinion of Aboo Yoosaf that in this case the claimant is entitled only to five hundred dirms, because the sum of the testimony of the witness who attests the payment of five hundred dirms is, that the debt in fact amounts only to five hundred. The above explanation, however, is a full refutation of this opinion. It is to be observed that when the witness is informed of any partial discharge of the debt (as in the case, for instance, of five hundred out of the thousand), he must not bear testimony to the debt of one thousand until the creditor make an acknowledgment of the receipt of five hundred: for otherwise he would be considered as aiding the injustice of the creditors. In the Jama Sagheer it is related, that if two persons attest a debt of one thousand dirms due by Omar to Zeyd, and one of them afterwards bear testimony to Omar having paid five hundred of it, and the claimant deny the same,—in that case their evidence of the debt, in which they both agree, must be credited; and the single testimony of one, with regard to the payment, must be rejected. Tahavee reports it as an opinion of our doctors, that the evidence to the debt is not to be credited (and Ziffer has adopted this opinion); because the claimant contradicts tha testimony of the payment. To this, however, it is answered, that although the claimant do contradict this latter testimony, yet he does not contradict the first evidence, which is established in its validity by the concurrence of two.

The evidence of witnesses who agree with respect to fact and time, but differ with respect to place, must be rejected.—If two persons bear testimony that a certain person had killed Zeyd, on the festival of the sacrifice, at Mecca: and two others bear testimony that the said person had killed Zeyd, on the same day, at Koofa; in such case, if all these witnesses be assembled at the same time, in the presence of the Kazee, the whole of their testimonies must be rejected; because, of the evidence of the two parties, it is undoubtedly certain that that of one of them must be false, and there is no criterion to ascertain to which the preference belongs.—If, on the contrary, the evidence of one of these parties precede that of the other, and the Kazee in consequence pass sentence, and afterward two others exhibit evidence of a different nature, in that case the Kazee must not admit the evidence of the latter, because the first evidence, in virtue of the issue of the decree consequent upon it, acquires a superiority over the latter, which prevents its annulment.

Evidence to the theft of an animal is not annulled by a difference between the witnesses with respect to the colour, but it is so by a difference with respect to the sex.—If two persons attest the theft of a cow, but differ in regard to the colour of it, their evidence is nevertheless valid, and the hand of the thief must in consequence be cut off. If, on the contrary, one of the witnesses declare the animal to be a cow, and the other allege that it is a bull, their evidence, in such case,

---

with the testimony of the other witnesses;—whereas, in the former instance, the witnesses coincide only in the term thousand, which is not perfectly definite.

*Consequently the claimant must produce another witness, as two are required to establish his claim

it not admissible, and the hand of the thief must not be cut off.—This is the doctrine of Haneefa—The two disciples maintain that the thief is not to suffer mutilation in either case. Some have said that this disagreement proceeds on the supposition of the attested colours being in some degree similar, such as red and black, and not where they differ completely, such as black and white. Others again have said that it subsists in all cases where the witnesses differ with respect to the colour. The reasoning of the two disciples is, that the theft of a black cow is different from that of a white cow; in other words, they are two distinct animals; and hence the due quantity of evidence (namely, that of two witnesses) does not appear with respect to either allegation of theft.—It is therefore the same as if two persons were to testify that a certain person had usurped the cow of such a person, but to disagree with respect to the colour of the cow;—in which case the evidence of both would be rejected; and so also in the present instance, a fortiori, because the penalty annexed to theft (namely, amputation) is of a most grievous nature. Hence a difference of the witnesses with respect to the colour is the same as a difference with respect to the gender.—The argument of Haneefa is, that in a case of differenae between the witnesses concerning the colour of the animal, it is possible to reconcile the contradiction by supposing the witnesses to have viewed the cow from a distance, and in the night time, since thefts are most commonly perpetrated at that reason;—and colours are of a deceptious nature;—cattle, moreover, are often pye-balled; and it is therefore possible that the cow may be black on one side, which was seen by one of the witnesses, and white on the other side, which was seen by the other witness.—It is otherwise in a case of usurpation, since that most commonly happens in the day-time, and consequently the fact is most probably seen in the light, and near at hand. It is also otherwise with respect to the sex of the animal, since two sexes cannot unite in the same creature. Besides, a knowledge of the sex requires a close inspection, and hence the case does not admit of uncertainty.

Evidence to prove a contract is annulled by any difference with respect to the terms of the contract.—If one person attest that Zeyd had purchased a slave for one thousand dirms, and another that he had purchased the said slave for fifteen hundred dirms, in that case the evidence of both is null: because the object of the evidence is to establish a cause of property, namely, the contract of sale: but the mention of two prices necessarily implies the existence of two contracts; and the proof of either of these is defective, as there is only one witness to each. This case proceeds on the supposition of the buyer being the plaintiff; but the effect is the same in case of the claim having been made by the seller;—and it matters not whether, of the two sums attested, the plaintiff claim the largest or the smallest; because the proof is defective on either supposition, for the reason already explained.—The same rule also holds with respect to a contract of Kitabat: that is, where a Mokatib and his master disagree with respect to the amount of the ransom or consideration of Kitabat, and the two witnesses likewise disagree in their testimony, the evidence, in such case, is null, since the evidence, in (namely, the establishment of the contract of Kitabat) is defective, for the reasons already explained,—and this, whether the master or the slave be the plaintiff. If is also the same with respect to Khoola, manumission for a compensation, and composition for wilful murder, provided the claim be preferred by the wife, the slave, or the murderer:—because in all these cases the object of the evidence is the same (namely, the establishment of the existence of a contract), and is defeated by any disagreement of the witnesses.—But if, in any of these cases, the claim be preferred by the opposite party, it then becomes equivalent to a case of debt, and the law takes place accordingly.—Thus, if the claim be for one thousand five hundred dirms, and one of the witnesses declare it to be one thousand, and the other one thousand five hundred, in that case, according to all our doctors, a decree must be given for one thousand dirms.—If, on the contrary, the claim be for two thousand dirms, and one witness attest to one thousand, and the other two thousand, in that case nothing can be decreed, according to Haneefa; whereas, according to the two disciples, one thousand must be decreed.—The principle on which these cases resemble debt is, that the pardon for murder, the freedom of a slave, or the divorce of a wife, is established by the acknowledgment of the person to whom each of these rights appertain.—Hence, in such case, his claim of debt only remains, and there is no occasion for the proof of the contract.—In the case of a pledge, if one witness attest that it was pawned for one thousand dirms, and the other that it was pawned for one thousand five hundred, and the claim be preferred by the pawner, the evidence is in that case inadmissible; because the pawner has no advantage in preferring such a claim, since he cannot resume his pawn until he pay the debt opposed to it.—His claim, therefore, is not regarded; and such being the case, the evidence he adduces is, as it were, evidence without a claim: and evidence without a claim is inadmissible.—If, on the contrary, the claim be preferred by the pawnholder, it is the same as a claim for debt.—In a case of hire, if one witness testify to one thousand dirms, and the other to one thousand five hundred, then, provided this difference happen at the beginning of the term of hire, it is analogous to a similar difference concerning a sale; but if it happen after the expiration of the term, and the claim be preferred by the hirer, it is a claim of debt.

Except it regard a woman's dower when she is entitled to the smallest sum testified.—In a case of marriage, if one of two witnesses testify to a dower of one thousand dirms, and the other to a dower of fifteen hundred, the dower is established in the amount of one thousand dirms, according to Haneefa, whether the claim be preferred by the husband or wife, and whether it be for the smallest or greatest of the attested sums. This is according to a favourable construction. The two disciples, arguing from analogy maintain that the evidence is totally inadmissible.—(It, is however, recorded in the Amalee, that the opinion of Aboo Yoosaf in this instance, accords with that of Haneefa.)—The reasoning of the two disciples, in support of their opinion, is that the disagreement of the witnesses with regard to the amount of the portion is in fact a disagreement with regard to the marriage contract, since the object of both is the establishment of a cause, namely, the said contract;—the disagreement in this instance, therefore, is analogous to a similar disagreement with regard to sale.—The reason for a more favourable construction of the LAW in this particular, as adopted by Haneefa, is that property, in the case of marriage, is merely a subordinate point, the original object of it being to legalize generation, to unite the sexes, and to endow the man with a right in the woman's person. Now as there is no difference whatever upon these points, they are accordingly established in the first instance; and if any disagreement then occur concerning the subordinate or dependant point the smallest sum attested is decreed, since to that amount both witnesses agree.—What is here advanced, that the case is the same "whether the claim be for the smallest or for the greatest attested sum," is approved.—Some of the learned have said, that the difference of opinion between Haneefa and the two disciples proceeds only on the supposition of the claim having been preferred by the woman: for that, in case of the claim being made by the husband, they are all agreed in regard to the inadmissibility of the evidence; since his object can only be the establishment of the contract, whilst the object of the woman is the property.—Others again have said that this difference of opinion obtains in either case; and this is approved.

CHAPTER IV.

OF EVIDENCE RELATIVE TO INHERITANCE.

Evidence must be adduced to prove the death of the inheritee and the right of the heirs, before inheritance can take effect—It is a rule, if an inheritee's* right of property in any thing be proven, still a decree cannot pass in favour of the heirs, until proof be adduced of the death of the inheritee, and of their right of heritage.—This rule obtains with Haneefa and Mohammed. Aboo Yoosaf maintains that the thing must be immediately decreed to the heir; for he alleges that the property of the heir is, in fact, the property of the inheritee, and consequenty that evidence to the inheritee's right of property in any thing is, in fact, evidence to his heir's right of property in that thing.—Haneefa and Mohammed, on the contrary, allege that the right of the heir is inchoate and extant de novo, with respect to all the rules to which the inherited property is subject (whence it is that a course of abstinence is enjoined upon an heir, with regard to an inherited female slave,—and likewise, that whatever a poor inheritee may have received by way of charity is lawful to his rich heir); and the right of an heir being inchoate and extant de novo, it is indispensable, in such case, that the witnesses bear testimony to the shifting of the right from the inheritee to the heir,—in other words, that they attest the inheritee to have died, and to have left the article in question as an inheritance to his heirs.

It suffices that the witnesses attest either the property or possession of the inheritee at the time of his decease—They deem it sufficient, however, in order to prove the shifting of the right of property, that the witnesses attest that "the thing in question was the property of the inheritee at the period of his death;" for then the shifting is established from necessity;—and in the same manner, it suffices if they attest that "it was in the keeping and possession of the inheritee at the time of his death;" for although the possession of an article may have been in virtue of a deposit, or of usurpation, yet the possession at death, in either case, is in fact a possession in virtue of the right, because of the obligation of responsibility which then takes place:—in a case of usurpation evidently; and also in a case of deposit,* because of the death of the trustee without any explanation;—in other words, if a trustee should die, without explaining that a particular thing in his possession is the deposit of a particular person, it occa-

---

* Meaning, the person from whom inheritance is derived. The translator is aware that this term is not sanctioned by authority. Anecestor being the phrase generally used in our law-books.—The nature of the Mussulman laws of inheritance, however, renders it necessary to adopt some term of more general import, since, according to these, inheritance may either ascened or descend.—The translator, therefore, has adopted this term, both in order to avoid the inconvenience of a perpetual pariphrasis, and also because it literally expresses the sense of the Arabic term Mawris, signifying "inherited from."

* See Deposits.

sion's responsibility, because the trustee, in dying without explaining the case, was most certainly guilty of a want of care of the deposit; and a want of care of a deposit is a transgression with respect to the deposit, which induces responsibility.—Evidence, therefore, of a thing being in the possession of a certain person at his death, is equivalent to evidence of its being his property.

An heir may recover an article in possession of another by proving it to have been the property of his inheritee, or a loan or deposit from him.—Having thus explained the tenets of each of four doctors upon this subject it follows that if witnesses were to give evidence that a particular house was in th possession of a certain man at his death, the evidence so given must be admitted with respect to the claimant being the heir of the deceased. In the same manner also the testimony of witnesses must be admitted, where a person adduces evidence to prove that a particular house, in the possession of a certain person, was the property of his father, and that his father had lent it, or had delivered it in deposit to the person then possessing it. In this case, therefore, the said person is entitled to take the house from the present occup er, without being required to prove, by witnesses, that his father had died, and that the said house had been left to him inheritance.—This; according to the tenets of Aboo Yoosaf, is evident:—and so also according to the tenets of Haneefa and Mohammed; because, in the case in question, it has been shown, by the testimony of witnesses, that the father was in possession at the time of his death, inasmuch as the possession of a borrower or trustee is equivalent to his own possession: and on this account there is no necessity for proving the shifting of the property to the heir, since that is consequence of the proof of the possession, as has been already explained.—It is to be observed that the law is the same where, under these circumstances, the claimant asserts the possession of the other to have been in virtue of a lease: because the possession of a lessee is equivalent to the possession of the lessor.

The right to an article is not established by evidence to the former possession of it.—If a person claim a right of property to a house in the possession of another, and the testimony of the witnesses produced by him should run in this manner, "we testify that the said house was in the possession of the claimant one month ago."—such evidence must not be admitted.—This is the doctrine of the Zahir Rawayet. It is related as an opinion of Aboo Yoosaf that the evidence, in this case, is a admissible; because possession is an object in the same manner as property; and as the testimony of the witnesses would have been accepted, in case they had said that the house in question was the property of the claimant one month ago, it follows that it must be admitted in this case also — Besides, if the witnesses had deposed that the other had taken the house from the hands or possession of the claimant, their evidence would have been admitted, and the claimant would. in consequence, have been put in possession of the house. The doctrine of the Zahir Rawayat, in this particular, has been adopted by Haneefa and Mohammed; and the arguments in support of it are twofold.—First, the seisin of the present possessor is actually seen with the eye; whereas that of the claimant, which formerly existed, is only heard from the tongue of the witnesses; and knowledge from hearsay can never be put in competition with that from actual sight.—Secondly, the evidence, in this case, relates to a matter of uncertainty; since the former seisin of the claimant, not being definitely known, admits of three suppositions, as it may have existed in virtue either of right of property, of deposit, or of usurpation; and where the point is of so uncertain a nature, it is impossible to pass a decree upon the possession. It is otherwise where the witness attest the right of property, as that admits not of various suppositions;—or, where they attest that the house had been taken from the claimant; because this is a matter of certainty, of which the law is known, namely, the obligation of restitution, or of replacing the thing, as it formely stood, in the possession of the claimant.

Unless the defendant acknowledge such former possession.—If the possessors of the house should himself acknowledge the former possession of the claimant, in that case a decree must pass for restoring the claimant to his possession; for the uncertainty with regard to the subject of an acknowledgment is no bar to the validity of the acknowledgment itself.

Or two witnesses attest his having made such acknowledgment.—If two persons attest the acknowledgment of the defendant, that "the thing in his possession had formerly been in the possession of the claimant." the article in question must in that case be restored to the claimant; because, although the subject of the acknowledgment be a matter involved in uncertainty, yet the evidence here relates, not to it, but to the acknowledgment itself, which is a matter of certainty;—and the uncertainty in the subject of it is no bar to the decree of the Kazee since he may afterwards desire the acknowledger to explain the nature of the uncertaintly.

CHAPTER V.

OF THE ATTESTATION OF EVIDENCE

Attestation of evidence is admitted in all matters not liable to be affected by doubt.—An attestation of evidence is admissible in all such rights as do not drop in consequence of a doubt; because there is a necessity for this, since it may happen that a witness, from various causes (such as sickness), may not be able to give his evidence in person;

whence, if an attestation of his evidence were not admissible, the rights of mankind would often be destroyed. There is, however, a degree of doubt attending it: because the secondary witness in such case, is merely a substitute for the primary witness;—and if there be many gradations between him and the primary, the suspicion of falsehood becomes still stronger.—There is, moreover, a possibility of avoiding this expedient, by desiring the party to produce, independent of the witness whose attendance is impracticable, some other who is also a primary witness.—An attestation of evidence, therefore, is never admitted where it tends to establish a matter which is repelled by the existence of a doubt, such as punishment or retaliation.

The attestation of the same two witnesses suffices to prove the evidence of two.—The attestation of two men with regard to the evidence of two others is valid. Shafei maintains that the evidence of four men is necessary to authenticate that of two men; because, in his opinion, two secondary witnesses are equivalent to one principal, in the same manner as two women are equivalent to one man. The arguments of our doctors in support of their doctrine upon this point are twofold:—First, Alee has declared that an attestation of the evidence of one man is not admissible unless attested by two.—Secondly, the stating the evidence of a principal or original witness is included in the number of rights. If, therefore, two men testify to the evidence of a principal witness, and afterwards testify to the evidence of another principal witness, both evidences are valid. nor is it required that the evidence of each principal witness should be testified by two separate secondary witnesses.

But the evidence of each must be attested by the two respectively. The attestation of one person to the evidence of one witness is not admissible, because of the opinion of Alee, as before quoted.—Malik admits the attestation of one person to the evidence of one witness.—The precept of Alee, however, is in proof against him.—Besides, the evidence of one principal witness is included amongst the number of rights, and therefore requires to be proved by two witnesses.

The attestation must be at the desire of the primary witness, who must state the terms of his testimony to the attesting witness.—It is requisite that the principal witnees desire the secondary to bear testimony to his evidence, after the following manner:—"Bear testimony to my evidence, which is, that A. the son of B, has made an acknowledgment before me to a particular effect, and has desired me to attest the said acknowledgment."—The reason of this is that the secondary witness is a deputy of the principal, and it is therefore necessary that he appoint him his agent, and desire him to bear evidence in the manner above related.—It is also requisite that the principal give his evidence to the secondary, in the same manner as he would have done in the assembly of the Kazee, in order that he [the secondary] may report the same literally, in that assembly.—It is to be observed, however, that if the principal should not mention that "A, the son of B. had called him to witness his acknowledgment," still his attestation is valid; because whoever hears another make an acknowledgment may lawfully give evidence of the same, although the acknowledger should not have desired him to bear testimony.

Form of an attestation.—It is requisite that a secondary witness deliver his testimony in the following manner:—"Zeyd has called upon me to attest his evidence that Omar has made an acknowledgment before him to a particular effect, and that he had desired him to bear testimony to his evidence of the said acknowledgment."—All this is required, because it is necessary that a secondary witness recite the substance of the evidence of the principal, and specify that he had called upon him to bear testimony to it.

A person cannot attest the attestation of another, unless that other desire him so to do.—If Omar hear Zeyd assert that a particular person had desired him to bear testimony to some circumstance, it is not in that case lawful for Omar to attest the said evidence of Zeyd, unless Zeyd should have particularly called upon him to attest the same; because, in the attestation of evidence, that of having been called upon to attest it is a necessary condition. This is according to all our doctors:—according to Mohammed, because, in his opinion, the decree of the Kazee passes on the strength of both evidences; that is, of the principal and the secondary; and also because both of them are liable, in an equal degree, to the penalty in case of a recession from their evidence:—and according to Haneefa and Aboo Yoosaf. because, in their opinion, a repetition of the evidence of the principal witness before the Kazee is necessary for the establishment of proof; and therefore the circumstance which establishes the proof ought to be explained.

Attestation is admitted only in case of the death, absence (at a distant place), or sickness of the primary witness.—The attestation of evidence is not admissible excepting where the principal witness have died, or have departed to a distance of three days journey or upwards, or are so sick as to be unable to attend at the assembly of the Kazee.—The reason of this is that the attestation of evidence is admissible only from necessity; and this necessity exists only where the principal witnesses are unable to give their testimony personally, which inability exists in all these cases.—It is to be observed, that, in case of the absence of the principal witnesses, the distance must be estimated by the time requisite to travel it; because the incapability of appearing to give evidence is founded on the distance, which the law estimates from the length of time. It is related, as an opinion of Aboo Yoosaf, that if the absent person be at a place so situated as that, having occasion to appear in the assembly of the Kazee in the morning, he could not return to his family that day, in that case it is lawful to accept, for the preservation of the rights of mankind, an attestation of his evidence. Lawyers, however, remark that the former doctrine is the most authentic, as in this latter case there is no great inconveniency; and Aboo Leys has also given this exposition upon the point.

The attesting witnesses may appear as purgators on behalf of the primary witnesses.—The justification of the original witnesses by the secondary is admitted, because they are capable of being purgators.—In the same manner also, the justification of one witness by another witness is valid, for the like reason; and also because the effect of it is advantageous to him, since the Kazee will in consequence of it pass a decree. It is likewise to be observed, that this degree of advantage does not subject a just man to any degree of suspicion: in the same manner as he lies not under any suspicion from the delivery of his own evidence. A just man indeed cannot possibly lie under suspicion from his justification of another witness, because his testimony is credible in itself, although that of the other be rejected.

But their not doing so does not affect the evidence which they attest.—If secondary witnesses remain silent with respect to the justification of the principal witnesses, it is valid; that is to say, the testimony of the principal witnesses, as recited by them, must be admitted; and the Kazee must scrutinize into their characters from others. This is according to Aboo Yoosaf. Mohammed has said that in this case the original evidence, as recited by the secondary witnesses, must not be admitted; because the validity of evidence is founded entirely on the probity of the witnesses; and it consequently follows that unless the secondary witnesses explain the probity of the principals, their testimony repeated by them cannot be received as valid evidence. The reasoning of Aboo Yoosaf is, that the business of secondary witnesses is merely to recite the evidence of the principals, and not to exhibit a justification of them, since it may often happen that they are ignorant of the probity of the princpals. Besides, after they have recited their evidence, it is the business of the Kazee to examine into their probity, in the same manner as if they were actually present

The denial of the primary witnesses annuls the attestation.—If the principals deny the evidence recited on their part by the secondaries, the evidence of the secondaries must not be admitted, because of the want of proof, from the contradiction which subsists between them and the principals.

If the attesting witnesses have not a clear personal knowledge of the defendant. the identity must be proved by other witnesses.—If two men bear testimony to the evidence of two others, to this effect, that "a certain woman, the daughter of a native of Samarcand, has made an acknowledgment of one thousand dirms in favour of Zeyd,"—and these secondary witnesses further declare, that the principals had informed them, that they knew the person of the woman,—and the plaintiff produce a woman, and the secondary witnesses declare that "they do not know whether she is the woman in question or not,"—in that case the plaintiff must be desired to produce two witnesses to testify the woman's identity; for here the evidence of the witnesses tends to prove the claim upon an uncertain person, whereas the plaintiff claims his right from a person specific and present; and hence a doubt arises, to remove which it is requisite to ascertain the person.

And so also. with respect to the limits of the claim.—Analogous to this is a case where two witnesses bear testimony the two evidence of two others, that "a certain person sold a piece of ground circumscribed by particular boundaries, and the price is due by the purchaser;"—for here it is requisite to produce two other witnesses to attest that the said ground, circumscribed by the said boundaries, had been delivered over to the purchaser, who is the defendant;—and in the same manner also, it is requisite to produce two other witnesses, in case the defendant deny that the boundaries of the ground he had purchased are the same with those described in the evidence of the witnesses; to the end that these additional witnesses may bear evidence that those boundaries were the same with those of the ground in the possession of the purchaser.

The identity of a person affected by a Kazee's letter must be proved.—The law is exactly the same with regard to the letters of one Kazee to another:—as where one Kazee writes to another, that "two witnesses have given evidence that a debt of one thousand dirms is due to a certain person; the son of a certain person, of a certain family, by the daughter of a certain person of a certain family, and that he must pass a decree for the said daughter's payment of the said sum;" for here, if the plaintiff, after delivering the letter to the Kazee to whom it is addressed, produce a woman, the Kazee, before he passes the decree must, desire him to bring two witnesses to attest that she is the same woman as described in the lette of the other Kazee,—It is to be observed that if, in either of these cases (namely, attestation of evidence. or of the letters of one Kazee to another), in the specification of the family of the woman, the witnesses make use of the term Tameemia, it is not valid; it being necessary to specify some nearer and more particular branch to which the woman is related, in order that a particular knowledge may be acquired, which cannot be done in case of the specification of so general a branch as that of

Tameen, whose descendants are innumerable.—It is the opinion of some that the words Farghania implies a general and Auzchandia a particular family.—Some, also, think that the words Samarcandia or Bokharia are general; and some have said that the reference to a small lane is particular, and to a street or city general.—It is to be observed that, according to the Zahir Rawayet, the opinion of Haneefa and Mohammed (in opposition to that of Aboo Yoosaf) is that description is rendered complete by the specification of the grandfather; but that the specification of the particular family (which is termed Fakhiz*) is equivalent to the mention of the grandfather; since it is the name of a distant progenitor, which is equivalent to a nearer one,

Section.

A false witness must be stigmatized—HANEEFA is of opinion that a false witness must be stigmatized,† but not chastized with blows. The two disciples are of opinion that he must be scourged and confined; and this is also the opinion of Shafei. The arguments of the two disciples upon this point are twofold.—FIRST, it is related of Omar, that he caused a false witness to be scourged with forty stripes, and to have his face blackened with the soot of a pot, SECONDLY, false testimony is a great crime, of which the evil results to others: and as no stated punishment has been ordained for it in the LAW, it must therefore be punished by Tazeer, or discretionary correction. The arguments of Haneefa are also twofold.—FIRST, Shirreeh stigmatized a false witness, but did not scourge him, SECONDLY, prevention of the crime in future may be effected by stigmatizing, and it ought therefore to be adopted as sufficient; for were beating or scourging enjoined in such cases, it might operate to the concealment of the crime, and the consequent destruction of the rights of others;—in other words, as being a grievous punishment, the fear of it might deter false witnesses from a confession of their falsehood. With regard to the relation concerning Omar, it evidently alludes to the infliction of punishment on a criminal, as appears by the number of stripes (namely forty), and the blackening of the countenance.

Mode of stigmatizing a false witness.—THE mode of stigmatising a false witness, as prescribed by Shirreeh, is this.—If the witness be a sojourner in any public street or market-place, let him be sent to that street or market-place; or, if otherwise, let him be sent to his own tribe or kindred, after the evening prayers (as they are generally assembled in greater numbers at that time than any other);—and let the stigmatize inform the people that "Kazee Shirreeh salutes them, and informs them, that he has detected this person in giving false evidence; that they must therefore beware of him themselves, and likewise desire others to beware of him." Shimsal Ayma has said that a false witness ought also to be stigmatized, according to the two disciples; and that the degree of correction and imprisonment ought (according to them) to be left to the discretion of the Kazee.—(The nature of discretionary correction has been already explained under the head of Punishments) It is related in the Jama Sagheer that if two witnesses confess that they have given false evidence, they must not be scourged. The two disciples maintain that they are to be scourged at the discretion of the Kazee.

BOOK XXII.

OF RETRACTION OF EVIDENCE.

Evidence retracted before a decree is void,—IF witnesses retract their testimony prior to the Kazee passing any decree, it becomes void (that is to say, the Kazee must not pass any decree upon it); for the right of the claimant cannot be established but by the decree of the Kazee; and the Kazee cannot pass a decree upon contradictory testimony a and in this case the witnesses are not liable to make atonement, since they have not occasioned any injury to either of the parties.

But not if retracted after a decree has passed—IF on the contrary, the Kazee pass a decree, and the witnesses afterwards retract their testimony, the decree is not thereby rendered void; because, although the first allegation on which the decree passed be contradicted by the latter, and although the first and the last in point of credit stand upon an equal footing, yet the first, because of the sentence of the Kazee having passed in conformity to it, acquires a superiority which prevents its annulment.—In this case, however, the witnesses are bound to atone for the injury they may have occasioned by their false testimony; for they themselves acknowledge a thing which is the cause of responsibility; and contradiction is no bar to the validity of acknowledgment, as shall be hereafter explained.

The retraction must be made in open court.—THE retraction of evidence is not valid, unless it be made in the presence of the Kazee; because, being a destruction of evi-

---

* To understand the whole of this passage, it is proper to remark that of tribes among the Arabians there are six degrees, I Shooab, II. Kabeela, III. Fazeela, IV Omara, V. Batn, VI. Fakhiz;—in which last are included the nearest kindred. (Richardson's Dictionary.)

† Arab, Yewhashiro, from tash-heer, which literally signifies exposing in public; a mode of punishment somewhat similar to the stock or pillory.

dence, it must consequently be restricted to that place which is particularly appointed for the reception of evidence,—namely, the assembly of the Kazee (that is to say, of any Kazee whatever). Besides, retractation of false evidence resembles repentance of a crime; and repentance of a crime, if committed privately, must be performed privately, and if committed openly, must be performed openly. —As, therefore, retractation of evidence is not valid, unless made in the assembly of the Kazee, it follows that if the defendant should aver that the witnesses had retracted their testimony somewhere out of the assembly of the Kazee, and should either require that an oath to this effect be administered to them in the assembly of the Kazee, or offer to produce witnesses there to prove his assertion, yet neither would the oath be administered to those witnesses, nor would the evidence he offers to produce be accepted, since the plea on which he proceeds (namely, an invalid retractation) is of no effect. If, on the contrary, his plea be of an effecutal nature (as if he should assert that the witnesses had retracted their testimony before a certain Kazee, who had in consequence passed a decree for their making reparation), the evidence he offers must be admitted, because he in this instance grounds his plea upon a valid retractation.

Witnesses retracting their testimony after a decree has passed must make a compensation to the suffering party.—If two witnesses bear testimony that a particular sum is due by a certain person to another, and the Kazee accordingly pass a decree for the payment of it, and the witness afterwards retract their evidence they are in that case responsible to that person for the sum decreed against him; for whoever, by a transgression, performs an act destructive of another's property, becomes responsible for the same (in the same manner as the digger of a well on the high road);*—and in this case the witnesses have been guilty of a transgression in giving false evidence, which occasioned the loss of the defendant's property. Shafei maintains that they are not responsible; for they, in fact, only produce the cause of the destruction, and that is not regarded where those are present who actually worked the destruction, namely (in the present instance) the Kazee and the plaintiff. In reply to this, our doctors argue that to impose the responsibility, in the case in question, upon the actual operator of the destruction (namely, the Kazee) is impracticable; because, in passing the decree, he acted as it were from necessity; and also, because, if a Kazee were thus liable to responsibility, no one would accept the office of Kazee, from an apprehension of being subject to such penalties.—In the same manner also, it is impracticable to exact the compensation from the plaintiff, because the decree of the Kazee takes effect independent of him. In this case, therefore, regard is necessarily had to the producer of the cause.

Provided the decree had been actually enforced against him.—It is to be observed, however, that the witnesses do not become responsible unless the plaintiff obtain possession of the property in question, whether it be substance or debt; because the destruction of it is not established until after the seisin of the plaintiff, and also because the defendant is not, until then, subjected to anything except the mere obligation of debt, whereas what he is to take from the witnesses is actual substance; and it is not lawful to take substance as a compensation for the mere obligation of a debt, since compensation can only be made in a similar, and there is no similarity between debt and substance.

If one witness thus retract, he atones for a moity of the damage.—If, in the case in question, only one of the witnesses retract his evidence, he becomes responsible for a half of the property: for it is a rule that where part of the witnesses retract, the right shall remain established so far as relates to the remaining witnesses.

And the same of any number who may retract, where one witness perseveres in his testimony.—Hence if three persons give evidence concerning property, and one of them afterwards retract his testimony, he is not subject to any responsibility, because the whole of the right remains established in virtue of the two remaining witnesses The reason of this is that the right of the claimant is established because of the complete proof, namely, the testimony of two witnesses. If, however, another of those three witnesses afterwards retract his evidence, the two receding witnesses are in that case responsible for one-half of the property, since, in virtue of the existence of one witness, one-half of the right remains in force.

Cases of retractation where the witnesses consist of both males and females.—If one man and two women give evidence, and one of the women afterwards retract her testimony, she is liable for one-fourth of the right because in consequence of the existing evidence of one man and one woman, three-fourths of it still remain in force. If, also, both the women retract their testimony, they are responsible for an half, since in virtue of the existing testimony of one man an half of the right remains in force.

If one man and ten women give evidence, and eight of the women afterwards retract, those eight are not liable to any compensation, since the remaining evidence furnishes complete proof. If, on the contrary, nine of the women retract, those nine are responsible for a fourth, since the remaining evidence of one man and one woman establishes three

*If a person dig a well in the high road (where no person is entitled to dig a well, and which is of course a transgression) he is liable to a fine for any accident which may happen by people falling into it, &c. This is fully explained in treating of Fines

fourths of the right. If, in the case in question the whole of the witnesses retract, the man is in that case responsible for one-sixth of the right, and the ten woman for five-sixths, according to Haneefa. Aboo Yoosaf holds that the man is liable for an half, and the ten women for an half; because, although they greatly exceed in point of number, yet they are in fact only equivalent to one man, since their evidence is not admissible unless it be in conjunction with that of a man. Haneefa, on the other hand, argues that the evidence of every two women is equivalent to that of one man; because the Prophet, on account of the weakness of their understanding, has ordained that the evidence of two women shall be equivalent to that of one man. Hence, in the case in question, it is the same as if six men had given evidence and had afterwards retracted it.—If the ten women retract, and not the man, they, are responsible for an half of the right, according to all our doctors, in conformity with the rule before-mentioned.

If two men and one woman give evidence in a matter of property, and all of them afterwards retract, the whole of the responsibility rests on the two man, and none on the woman, because one woman is no more than half of a witness, whence the law regards not her in this case, inasmuch as no effect results from the mere part of a cause.

The retraction of evidence to a marriage and proper dower does not subject the retractors to any responsibility.—If two witnesses give evidence concerning a woman, of her being married on a Mihr Misl, or proper dower,* and afterwards retract their testimony, they are not bound to make any compensation;† and so likewise, if they testify to any thing short of the proper dower; because the advantage to be derived from the woman's person is not an article of value where it is lost to her by false evidence; for compensation, in case of the destruction of any thing; implies the return of a similar; and there is no similarity between substantial property and the connubial enjoyment

If two witnesses give evidence concerning a man, of his having married a woman on a proper dower, and afterwards retract the same, still they are not bound to make any compensation, although by their testimony they have destroyed the property of that man: because the destruction in this instance is attended with an equivalent, inasmuch as the connubial enjoyment is considered as an article of value, whenever it becomes the right of any one; and destruction attended with a consideration or equivalent, is the same, in effect, as no destruction. The ground of this is that responsibility is founded upon similarity Now there is no similarity between destruction with an exchange and destruction without an exchange. If, therefore, in the case in question,, a compensation were taken from the witnesses, it would be a destruction of their property without any thing in return—If, however, the witnesses were to testify to any amount beyond the proper dower, and afterwards retract, they are in that case responsible for the excess, as having destroyed that much without any consideration in return.

The retractation of evidence to a sale does not occasion responsibility, unless the price had been attested short of the value.—If two witnesses bear evidence to a sale for a price tantamount to, or greater than, the value of the thing sold, and afterwards retract, they are no in that case liable to any compensation; since destruction attended with an equivalent is, in effect, no destruction.—If, on the contrary, they should give evidence of the sale for a price less than the value, they are in that case responsible for the deficiency of value, because, in that amount, they have occasioned a destruction without any equivalent. The law here applies equally to sale with or without an option to the seller; because, in the case of an option, the cause of right of property is the original sale, and not the determination of the option.—The effect, therefore, is referred to the sale, upon the determination of the option; and hence the destruction is referred to the evidence of the sale.

Witnesses retracting their evidence to divorce before consummation are liable for half the dower.—If two witnesses give evidence of a man having divorced his wife prior to consummation, and afterwards retract, they are in that case responsible for a moiety of the dower; because they have established upon that man a thing which stood within the possibility of dropping (in other words, which might perhaps have been altogether concelled, by the wife apostatizing from the faith, or admitting the son of her husband to carnal connexion*);—and also, because separation prior to the consummation is equivalent to an annulment of the marriage, and therefore annuls the whole of the dower, as has been already explained † but afterwards the half of the dower is established de novo in the manner of a Matat or present,‡ and hence the said half is rendered due by the testimony of the witnesses.

Witnesses retracting their evidence to manumission are liable for the value of the slave.—If witnesses attest that a certain person had emancipated his slave, and afterwards retract their testimony, they are in that case responsible to the person in question for the value of the said slave, because of their

*This case supposes that the woman claims a stipulated dower, greater than her proper dower, and that the husband endeavours to resist her claim by evidence.

†That is, they are not to compensate for the difference.

*Vol. I. p. 66.
†Vol. I. p. 52.
‡Vol. I p. 45.

having destroyed his property in the slave without any equivalent in return:—The right of Willa, moreover, with respect to the slave rests with that person and with the witnesses; because as the emancipation of the slave is not, on account of the responsibility, ascribed to their testimony, it follows that the Willa does not go to them

Witnesses retracting in a case of retaliation are liable to a fine, but not to retaliation.—If two witnesses bear evidence against a person, in a case of retaliation for murder, and then retract their testimony after the person has been put to death, they are in that case bound to pay Deeyat, or fine of blood, but are not to suffer death by way of retaliation, Shafei maintains that they are to suffer death; since they were the efficient cause of death, inasmuch as the retaliation was executed on the strength as their evidence: and they therefore resemble a Mokrih, or compeller (in other words, they compel); the commission of murder—nay, they are still more criminal than a Mokrih, inasmuch as the avenger of blood in a case of murder, is aided in bringing the murderer to justice; whereas a person under compulsion is prohibited, by the LAW, from putting to death.* The reasoning of our doctors is, that the witnesses, in this case, cannot be considered either as actual perpetrators, or as instrumental causes of the bloodshed; for nothing can be considered as a case except such a thing as presses upon, and joins to, the agent; and the testimony of the witnesses cannot be considered in this light. since, notwithstanding they furnish legal grounds for the retaliation, yet pardon and forgiveness being benevolent acts. the probable consequence is that the avenger of blood will pardon the person against whom they bore evidence. It is otherwis in a case of compulsion; for the person compelled is induced to execute the murder with a view to save his own life, which the compeller threatens to take from him in case of his refusal; whereas, in the case in question, there is no compulsion on the avenger of blood to execute the retaliation: on the contrary, he is at free liberty either to pardon the other, or to execute the retaliation: and where a man acts from free liberty, and not from any necessity, the cause of his actions cannot be ascribed to the witnesses; at least, it must be allowed that there is a doubt with respect to their being the cause; and the existence of a doubt is preventive of retaliation. The Deeyat, or fine of blood, however, takes place; because that is a matter of property, and, as such, may be established, notwithstanding any doubt which may happen to attend it.

Secondary witnesses retracting their attestation are responsible for the damage; but the primary witnesses are not responsible if they retract or disavow—If secondary witnesses* retract their evidence, they are responsible; since the destruction of the defendant's property if referred to them, because of their giving evidence in the assembly of the Kazee. If, on the other hand, the primary witness retract, alleging that they had not authorized the secondary witnesses to attest their evidence they are not responsible, since they deny the evidence which occasioned the destruction of the property of the defendant In this case, moreover, the decree of the Kazee, occasioned by this testimony, is not rendered null, since the denial of the primary witnesses is susceptible of doubt (that is, it may either be false or true), and the decree of the Kazee cannot be reversed by a dubious circumstance; in the same manner as it cannot be reversed by the retraction of evidence, after it has passed on the strength of that evidence,—It is otherwise where the primary witnesses make the denial prior to the passing of a decree; because in that case the Kazee would not pass the decree on the strength of the evidence of the secondary witnesses—If, however, the primary witnesses avow that they had authorized the evidence of the secondary witnesses; but that they had committed an error in so doing, they are in that case responsible for the loss that may have been occasioned.—This is according to Mohammed—The two elders are of opinion that, even in this case, the primary witnesses do not become responsible; since the decree of the Kazee passed upon the evidence of the secondary witnesses, from the necessity under which the Kazee lies of proceeding on the proof before him, which in this case is the evidence of the secondary witnesses.—The reasoning of Mohammed is that the secondary witnesses do only repeat the evidence of the principals: and hence it becomes in effect the same if the principal witnesses were themselves present

Case of retractation by both primary and secondary witnesses—If both the primary and the secondary witnesses retract their evidence, the two Elders are in that case of opinion that compensation is due only by the secondary witnesses, because of the decree having passed on their evidence. Mohammed, on the contrary, is of opinion that the defendant has the option of taking the compensation either from the principal or the secondary witnesses; because (according to the doctrine of the two disciples) the decree passed on the evidence of the secondaries,—or (according to his own doctrine) it passes on the evidence of the principals: and hence the defendant has the option of taking the compensation from whomsoever of the two he pleases;—but as originality and dependancy are of different natures, it is not per-

*This will be more fully and clearly understood by a reference to the article Ikrah, or Compulsion.

*Meaning witnesses who attest the evidence of other witnesses. (See Chap. V of the preceding book.)

mitted to unite both the principals and the secondaries in the payment of the compensation, that is to say, the defendant cannot take it from both.

The secondary witnesses asserting the falsehood error of the primary witnesses is of no effect.—If, in the above case, the secondary witnesses assert that the primary witnesses had either been guilty of falsehood, or had committed an error in their evidence, the Kazee must not attend to this assertion, because his decree; as having passed and issued, cannot be affected by any assertion of theirs, And in this case the secondary witnesses are not liable to any compensation, since they teey have not retracted their own evidence, but have merely repeated the evidence of the principal witnesses, notwithstanding they had retracted it.

Purgators receding from their justification are responsible.—If purgators recede from their justification, they become responsible, according to Haneefa,—The two disciples are of opinion that they do not become responsible, because they have merely performed a generous action in behalf of the witnesses, and therefore resemble witnesses who bear evidence to the marriage of a person accused of whoredom,* and who, in case of retracting their evidence after the stoning of the person to whom it related, do not become responsible for the fine of blood The reasoning of Haneefa is that justification is the cause of credit given to witnesses, inasmuch as the Kazee proceeds not upon the evidence itself, but upon the justification of it —Hence the justification is, in effect, the moving cause of the decree —It is otherwise with witnesses to the marriage of a person accused of whoredom, because in that instance the circumstance of the accused being a married person is particulary essential to induce lapidation.

* Literally, "who bear evidence to Ibian," (See Vol. I. p. 17).

Case of retractation in suspended manumission or divorce.—If two witnesses give evidence of a Yameen (or susp nsion on a condition) of divorce or emancipation, and two other witnesses give evidence that the condition had taken place, and both parties afterwards retract their evidence, compensation is in that case due only by the witnesses who attested the deed of Yameen, which is the cause of the damage, and not by those who attested the occurrence of the event on which the divorce or emancipation was suspended. because the decree of the Kazee proceeded on the evidence to the deed, and not on the evidence to the condition.—If only the witnesses to the occurrence of the condition retract, there exists in that case a difference of opinion amongst the Haneefite doctors.—It is to be observed that by the divorce here mentioned is to be understood divorce before consummation; for in a case of divorce subsequent to coosummation neither party of the witnesses are liable to make compensation, because the wife's right to her dower is established by the consummation.*

* See Vol. I, p. 44.

END OF THE SECOND VOLUME.

VOL. III.

BOOK XXIII.

OF AGENCY

CHAPTER I.

A person may lawfully appoint another his Agent, to act on his behalf, in contracts.—It is lawful for a person to appoint another his agent, for the settlement in his behalf of every contract which he he might have lawfully concluded himself, such as as sale, marriage, and so forth; because, as an individual is sometimes prevented from acting in his own person, in consequence of accidental circumstances (such as sickness, or the like), he is therefore admitted, of neeessity, to appoint another his agent, in order that that person may expedite his wants by means of the powers which he derives from such appointment. It is, morever, related in the Nakl Saheeh, that the Prophet appointed Hakeem-Bin-Khiram his agent for purchase, in order that he might buy for him a camel to sacrifice;—and likewise, that he appcinted Amir-Bin-Aum his agent for marriage, that he might conclude a marriage betwixt his mother and the Prophet.

And for the management of suits, or criminal prosecutions; or for the payment or exaction of all rights except retaliation or punishment.—It is lawful for a person to appoint another his agent for the management of a suit relative to any rights whatever (even to corporal punishment or retaliation), for the reasons already alleged; and also, because every person is not himself capable of managing a business of this nature—It is moreover recorded, in the Nakl Saheeh, that Alee appointed Akeel his agent for the management of his suits, and that when Akeel became old he dismissed him, and appointed Abdoola Bin-Jafir.—In the same manner, also it is lawful to appoint an agent for the payment of rights, or the exaction of them: excepting, however, in cases of punishment or retaliation, the appointment of an agent in which (as if an agent were appointed to exact those in the absence of his principal) is invalid; because punishment or retaliation are remitted in the existence of a doubt; and the absence of the principal creates a doubt; nay, the forgiveness of the prosecutor is probable in such a circumstance, for this reason, that it is praiseworthy and laudable to pardon: contrary to where the witnesses only are absent [from the execution], as their non-retractation is most probable: and contrary, also, to where the prosecutor is present, as in this case there is no apprehension of his having forgiven.

Objection.—In case of the presence of the principal, what necessity exists for the appointment of an agent?

Reply.—Even in such case there may be a necessity for the appointment of an agent; because, as every person is not perfectly acquainted with the mode of exacting those rights, it follows that if the principal were debarred from the appointment of an agent, the door of exaction might be altogether closed.

What is here advanced is according to Haneefa,—Aboo Yoosaf alleges that agency for the establishment of corporal punishment or retaliation* (as if the agent should produce the witnesses) is not lawful.—The opinion of Moha med coincides with that of Haneefa.—Some, however, maintain that he agrees with Aboo Yoosaf.—Others, again, say that this disagreement subsists only in case of the absence of the constituent, and not in case of his presence: for, in this case, the agency is legal according to all; because the words of an agent in the presence of his constituent refer entirely to the latter.—The argument of Aboo Yoosaf upon this point is, that the appointment of an agent is the creation of a deputy, in which there is always room for doubt respecting the deputation: and as, in criminal prosecutions, every doubt must be avoided, it follows that the appointment of an agent for prosecution is invalid, in the same manner as for the exaction of punishment; and that it cannot be admitted; in the same manner as evidence to evidence, respecting the prosecution, is not admitted.—The argument of Haneefa is that prosecution is merely a condition of the exaction of the right; because the necessity of the punishment is founded, not upon the prosecution, but upon the criminality, which is rendered manifest by the evidence of the witnesses: and hence agency is admitted in this case, in the same manner as in that of other rights. A similar disagreement subsists with respect to the case of a man against whom an action inducing corporal punishment or retaliation lies, and who appoints an agent for the management of his defence.

A person under accusation may employ an agent to conduct his defence.—The doctrine of Haneefa, however, is preferred in this instance, because the agent may make replies and rejoinders; and the doubt with respect to deputation (as before mentioned) does not prevent this.—If, however, the agent should make a confession, it is not to be admitted against his constituent, because there exists a doubt of his having been authorized by his constituent to make such confession.

An agent cannot be appointed to manage a suit unless the constituent be sick, or absent.—It is not lawful, according to Haneefa, to appoint an agent for the management of a cause, unless with the consent of the adversary, excepting where the constituent is sick—or distant three day's journey, or further, from the place.—The two disciples maintain that such agency is lawful without the consent of the adversary; and Shafei is also of the same opinion. This disagreement does not relate to the legality of the agency itself, but to the necessity which operates upon the adversary to answer an agent to whose appointment he has not assented; Aboo Haneefa being of opinion that he is not under such necessity; and the two disciples thinking otherwise.—The argument of the two disciples is that the appointment of an agent is the act of an individual in regard to a right purely his own; and therefore ought not to depend on the consent of another in the present instance, any more than in a case of exacting payment of debt.—Haneefa, on the other hand, argues that the constituent is himself under the necessity of giving an answer, and must attend in case the magistrate should summon him: now individuals differ with respect to their capacity of managing suits;—If therefore, it were admitted that the appointment of an agent is absolute with respect to the adversary, this would be injurious to the adversary;—hence the validity of the appointment must be suspended on his consent:—in the same manner as where a partnership slave is made a Mokatib by one of the partners, in which case it remains with the other partner to confirm the contract of Kitabit, or to break it as he pleases; for, although the act of the

*In other words, for conducting a criminal prosecution.

first proprietor related purely to his own property, yet as the carrying of it into execution must have injured the right of the other, the validity of it is therefore suspended on his consent; and so also in the case in question.—It is otherwise where the person is sick or absent, for in this case his appointment of an agent is valid without the consent of the adversary, since he cannot himself be compelled to appear under such circumstances.

Or about to travel.—It is to be observed that in the same manner as Haneefa holds the appointment, in this particular, of an agent by an absent person to be valid, so also does he hold the appointment by one who is immediately about to travel.

A woman may appoint an agent for litigation in all cases.—A WOMAN who remains in privacy, and is not accustomed to go to the court of the Kazee, ought (according to Aboo Bekir) to appoint an agent for the management of her cause; and acquiescence is incumbent on her adversary.—This doctrine has been adopted by our modern lawyers; and decrees are passed accordingly.

Agency to be valid, must proceeed from a competent constituent—THE validity of agency, in any business, rests upon two conditions:—FIRST, that the constituent be himself legally empowered to perform the business for the execution of which he has appointed another (for, as the agent derives his competency from the constituent, it is necessary that the constituent should himself be competent, before he confer the capacity on another)

And must be vested in a person of understanding.—SECONDLY, that the agent be of sound understanding, in such a degree as may enable him to know and execute the business to which he has been appointed.—If, therefore, a person appoint a child or an idiot his agent, it is invalid; whereas, if a freeman, who is adult and of sound judgment, appoint his fellow* his agent,—or, if a privleged slave appoint his fellow his agent, it is valid.

A Mahjoor slave, or an infant (capable of understanding) may be appointed an agent.—IF a person appoint an infant who understands purchase and sale, or a Mahjoor (or inhibited) slave, to be his agent, it is in either case valid. The rights of the contract, however, do not appertain to them but to their constituent.—The reason of the validity of the appointment is that the infant is capable of explanation; and therefore his act is held to be valid, when done with the permission of his guardian;—and the slave is capable of acting, and is the master of his actions when they relate to himself, though not if they relate to his master; but agency for another does not relate to his master the appointment of the infant or slave, therefore, is valid

But the obligations they enter into are not binding upon them, but upon their constituent.—They are neither of them, however, capable of performing the obligations of the contract:—the infant, because of his want of competency; and the slave, because it would interfere with the rights of the master;—the performance of the contract, therefore, rests with the constituent.—It is related as an opinion of Aboo Yoosaf, that if an infant, or a slave, as above described, should make a sale, and the purchaser, being ignorant of their situation, should afterwards be informed of it, in that case it is in his option to annul the contract,—because having concluded the bargain on a supposition that they were competent to fulfil the rights of it, and being afterwards informed that the rights of the contract did not rest with them, he becomes of consequence entitled to annul it in the same manner as if he discovered a defect in the subject of it.

Contracts concluded by agents are either such as the agent refers to himself.—THE contracts concluded by agents are of two kinds:—FIRST, such as the agent refers to himself; and which do not depend, in any degree, on the constituent; as in the cases of sale or hire, which relate to the agent and not to the constituent.—Shafei maintains that the rights of slave appertain to the constituent; because the rights of a contract of sale are dependants of the effects of it; and as the effect namely, right of property, appertains to the constituent; so in the same manner its dependant also appertains to him; an agent for sale, therefore, is the same as a messenger, or an agent for marriage. The arguments of our doctors are that an agent is the contracting party, both in reality and in effect:—in reality, because the contract is formed by speech, and the speech of the agent is authentic because he is a man: and in effect, because, being himself competent, there is no necessity for the reference of the rights of the contract to the constituent; whereas, if he were merely a messenger, he would not be exempt from the necessity of referring the rights of the contract to the constituent, as is the case with a messenger,—Now since such is the nature of agency, it follows that an agent is considered as a principal in regard to the rights of the contract; and hence Kadooree, in the treatise which bears his name, says "an agent for sale delivers the goods and takes possession of the purchase-money, and is liable to be sued for any defect in the subject of the sale;"—and, on the other hand, "an agent for purchase receives the goods, and delivers the price, and may sue the seller for any defect in the goods;"—because all these are considered as the rights of sale. The constituent, moreover, is the proprietor of the thing purchased through his agent, abinitio in the same manner as when a slave accepts

*Meaning, one who resembles him in these points.

a gift, or catches game, or gathers fire-wood; in all which cases the master is proprietor of the gift, of the game, or of the fire-wood abinitio; that is to say, the property is not held first to rest in the slave, and then to shift to him.—This doctrine of the primary existence of the right of property in the constituent is approved:—contrary to Koorokhee, who maintains that, in consequence of the purchase, the right of property rests originally in the agent, and from him shifts to the constituent).

Or to his constituent.—SECONDLY, such as the agent refers the performance of to his constituent, and in which he has an immediate interest; such as marriage, Khoola; or composition for wilful murder; in all which cases, the rights appertain to the constituent and not to the agent.—Hence no demand can be made on the husband's agent for the dower: nor can the wife's agent be required to deliver over the dower to her husband; for in these cases the agent is a mere messenger, and is not exempt from the necessity of referring the performance to his constituent: for if the agent, in the case of marriage: were to refer the performance to himself, it would become his marriage, and not that of the constituent (whence the necessity for considering him as a mere messenger).—The reason of this is, that as none of these contracts are of a nature to admit of the agent first acting in them as a principal, he is therefore obliged to refer them to the constituent. and to act himself as a mere messenger.—Manumission for a compensation. contracts of Kitabat, and composition after denial, are all of the second class.—With regard to composition after akcnowledgment, it is of the first class, as partaking of the nature of sale.—An agent for the delivery of a gift, or of charity, or for the restitution of a deposit, as being a mere announcer. is the same as a messenger. The case is also the same with regard to an agent for the execution of loans or pledges; because the effect of these (namely, the right of property) is established by means of the seisin of the thing given or bestowed in charity, and so on;—and as the thing, in these cases, belonged to the constituent and shifts to the donee or the other in consequence of the seisin, the agent, being as it were a mere stranger to the thing, cannot be considered as a principal, but must be regarded merely as an explainer or a messenger.—It is otherwise in sale, because the effect of sale is established by speech, and the agent is the speaker.—In the same manner, also, as an agent in the above cases of executing gifts, &c, is a mere messenger, so is an agent appointed by the petitioner (or person to whom the gift, the charity, &c, is given). The case is the same with respect to an agent for a contract of co-partnership or Mozaribat.

An agent cannot be appointed to receive a loan.—WITH respect to an agent for the receipt of a loan, the appointment is null; insomuch that, if a person, in virtue of such appointment, should receive a loan, and take possession of it, he; and not the constituent, would be the proprietor of it. It is otherwise with respect to a messenger; for the receipt of a loan by a messenger is lawful,

A debt contracted to an agent cannot be exacted by his constituent.—IF a constituent, in the case of having sold goods through his agent, should demand payment of the price from the purahaser, the purchaser may lawfully refuse to comply; because, with respect to the contract or its rights, the constituent is as a stranger, since the rights of the contract appertain to the contracting party.

But if payment be made to the constituent, it is valid.—IF, however, the purchaser pay the price to the constituent, it is lawful; nor is the agent afterwards entitled to demand it from him, since he has paid it to the constituent, to whom it of right belonged:—but if the agent persist in demanding it from him, then let him take it back from the constituent and pay it to the agent, and let the agent give it to the constituent; a mode in which there is evidently no advantage to any.

And the debtor may (in his payment). deduct a debt owing him by the constituent—IT is to be observed that as the right belongs to the constituent, the purchaser may, in case of the constituent being indebted to him, deduct the debt from the price. If, however the constituent and agent be both indebted to him, he is only entitled to deduct from the price the debt of the constituent.

Or by the agent (when he alone is indebted to him).—If, on the other hand. the agent only be indebted to him, he is at liberty (according to Haneefa and Mohammed) to deduct it from the price; because the agent (as they hold) may, if he please exempt the purchaser entirely from the payment. In either case, however (that is, whether the purchaser make a deduction on account of the debt due by the agent, or whether the agent exempt him entirely), the agent is responsible for the whole to his constituent.

CHAPTER II.

OF AGENCY FOR PURCHASE AND SALE.

Section I.

Of Agency for Purchase.

An agent must be properly instructed with respect to what he is to purchase—WHEN a person appoints another his agent for purchasing some indefinite thing, it is necessary that he explain the kind and quality of the thing or the kind and price of it; in order that the agent may know the nature of the act for which he has been appointed, and thence become capable of executing it.

Except where his powers are general—IF, however, a person appoint another in absolute agent, by saying to him, "purchase for me whatever thing you may judge advisable." in that case the explanation of the kind, &c., is unnecessary, because the constituent, in this instance, charges the agent with a discretionary care of his interest; and whatever he may then purchase is considered as in obedience to his order.—In fact a small degree of uncertainty in agency (such as an uncertainty of the quality) is of no consequence, according to a favourable construction of the law; because agency is founded on liberal principles; and making an explanation of the quality an essential would be a restraint upon it.

An agency is invalid where the terms in which it is expressed leave a great degree of uncertainty with respect to the subject of it.—If the constituent, in the appointment of his agent, should use a word applicable to a variety of general kinds, such as animal,—or a word which serves to express a variety of meanings, such as Dar,*—in this case the appointment of agency is invalid, even although the constituent may have specified the amount of the price; for articles of each kind may be purchased for the same price; and it is not known which kind the constituent wishes.—Hence the agency in this case, on account of the great degree of uncertainty, becomes impracticable. If, also the word used be applicable to a variety of species, the agency is invalid, unless the constituent specify the price, or define the species, though he should not mention the goodness or badness of the quality. If, however, he specify the price, or define the quality, the agency is valid, because the specification of the pric leads to a knowledge of the species; and the mention of the species leaves only the uncertainty of the quality, which is considered a degree of uncertainty so trifling as not to prevent the execution of the agency. Thus, if a person constitute another his agent for the purchase of "a slave, whether male or female;" the agency is invalid, because "a slave whether male or female," applies to a variety of species. If, however he explain the particular species (such as Turkish, Abyssinian, Indian, or of a mixed decent), the appointment is valid.—In the same manner, also, the appointment is valid where the price only is specified, because in that case (as was before explained) a small degree only of uncertainty remains. It is recorded in the Jama Sagheer, that if a person desire another to purchase for him cloth, or an animal,† or a house, the agency is invalid, because of the great degree of uncertainty; as the term daba (for instance) means every animal that moves on the face of the earth, although, in common acceptation, it signify either a horse, an ass, or a mule;—in the same manner, cloth is a generic term, applicable to a variety of species from the finest silks to the coarsest sheet of cotton; and the term house is applied to things which (with respect to species) are conspicuously different from each other, from a variety of causes, such as neighbourhood, the abundance or paucity of rights and privileges, or the situation in particular lanes or cities; from the great uncertainty in all these cases, therefore, the agency is invalid.

Unless in case of subsequent explanation.—But it becomes valid in case of an explanation of the price of the house, or the species of the cloth or animal.

A power to purchase taam [food] is restricted to the purchase of wheat or flour.—If a person give another a hundred dirms, and say to him "buy for me, with these dirms, food;" in that case the word food is construed to mean wheat, or the flour of wheat, on a favourable construction.—Analogy would suggest the meaning to be any kind of food whatever; according to the real import of the word.—The reason for a more favourable construction, in this particular, is that the word taam [food], when used in purchase and sale, means (according to general custom), wheat and the flour of it; and as general custom must be preferred to mere analogy, the law, for that reason, in all cases of purchase and sale construes the word taam [food] to mean wheat, or the flour of it.—Some have said that if the constituent, in this case, give many dirms (ten, for instance), then the word food is construed to mean wheat: if, on the other hand, he give a few dirms (three, for instance), it is construed to mean bread made of wheat; and if a middle number (such as seven), it is construed to mean the flour of wheat.

An agent may return goods purchased by him to the seller on account of a defect.—If an agent, after purchase, discover a defect in the goods, he may then return them to the seller; because the rejection of the subject of sale on account of a defect is one of the rights of a contract of sale; and the agent, as being one of the contracting parties, is entitled to all the rights of the contract.

But not after having delivered them to his constituent.—This, however, is only where the agent has not delivered over the goods to his constituent; for, after that, he cannot return it to the seller unless by permission of the constituent; because, after delivering the goods bought to his constituent, his agency ceases; and also, because, if he were then permitted to return the goods to the seller without the consent of the constituent, the seisin made by the constituent in his own behalf would be set at nought.

A right of pre-emption may be enforced against an agent before delivery to his constituent; but not afterwards.—(It is to be observed that as, previous to the delivery of the goods to the constituent, the rights of the contract rest with the agent; and cease and expire after the delivery, it follows that if a

*This word signifies a house, a stake, and a variety of other meanings.

†Arab. Daba.

person claim his right of Shaffa* in a house purchased by an agent, he has a right to sue the agent previous to the delivery, of the house to his constituent; but after the delivery no action would lie against the agent.)

Agency in Sirif or Sillim is valid.—If a person appoint an agent for executing a contract of Sirf or Sillim † it is valid; because the constituent being himself competent to these contracts may lawfully (on the principles already explained) empower another to execute them on his behalf. It is to be observed, however, that the Sillim here mentioned means a purchase by way of Sillim (or advance), and not a sale by that mode; because, if a sale of that nature were allowed by agency, it would necessarily follow that the agent must himself become liable for a particular article in lieu of a price which he has not received.—It is likewise to be observed that if, in either of these cases (that is, either the contract of Sillim or Sirf), the agent (who is the buyer) be separated from the seller,—previous to his seisin of the goods, in the case of Sillim,—or, to the mutual seisin of the article of exchange in the case of Sirf;—the contract becomes null; because the agent being a party; his separation from the other party previous to the seisin is the cause of annulment of both contracts (contrary to where the constituent is separated from the seller before the seisin; because not being himself a party, his separation is of no consequence).—Since, therefore, the agent is a party, it follows that his seisin and delivery are valid, although he be one to whom the rights of a contract cannot appertain (such as an infant or an inhibited slave). It is different with regard to a messenger in a contract of Sillim or Sirf: for his seisin is not valid, as his function relates to the contract and not the seisin; because a messenger merely delivers the speech of his employer to another; and seisin is no way connected with speech. Moreover, a speech delivered by a messenger refers itself to the dictator of the message; a messenger is, therefore, not considered as a party; and hence his seisin, as being the seisin of a stranger, is not valid.

An agent, paying for goods which his own money, is entitled to repayment for his constituent.—If an agent for purchase pay the price of the goods from his own property, and obtain possession of them, he is entitled to repayment from his constituent, for two reasons.—First, he stands as a seller, and the constituent as a purchaser; because a virtual exchange is established between them (whence it is that if an agent and his constituent disagree, with respect to the price, an oath is tendered to both, as holds in all mutual exchanges of property for property; and the constituent may also return the thing purchased to the agent, on account of any defect):—when, therefore, the thing purchased is duly delivered to the constituent by the agent, the agent is entitled to take from him the price he may have given for it:—Secondly as the rights of the contract appertain to the agent, and as the constituent is informed of this, it follows that he gives his consent to the agent's payment of the price from his own property. If, therefore, the goods be lost in the hands of the agent, and he should not previously have made a detention in his own behalf of those goods from his constituent, the loss in that case falls upon the constituent, and he becomes liable for the price to the agent; because the seisin of the agent, so long as he makes no formal detention of the purchase from his constituent, stands as the seisin of the constituent; and therefore he is held to have been virtually possessed of the goods whilst the loss took place.

An agent may detain from his constituent what he purchases, until he be paid the price.—An agent is entitled to detain from his constituent any purchase he may have made on his account, until he be paid the price by him, according to what was before said, that the agent stands as the seller, and the constituent as the purchaser.—Ziffer maintains that the agent is not entitled to detain the purchase, as the constituent has already made seisin of it; because, as the seisin of the agent is, virtually, the seisin of the constituent, it is consequently the same as if the agent had actually delivered them over to him: the agent's right of detention, therefore (in satisfaction of his claim to payment of the price), ceases, in the same manner as in case of his actual delivery of them. Our doctors, on the other hand, argue that the delivery of the goods to the constituent (on the principle of the seisin of the agent being the seisin of the constituent) is a matter of necessity; but does not imply any consent on the part of the agent to the relinquishment of his right of detention.—The seisin of the agent, moreover, is not the actual seisin of the constituent; but is rather suspended.—If therefore the agent should not detain the goods from his constituent, his seisin stands as the seisin of his constituent; but if he detain them, his seisin is then considered as on his own behalf.

But if the purchase perish in the agent's hand during such detention, he is responsible.—If, in the case before stated, the agent detain the purchase from his constituent, and it perish in his hands, he is answerable, according to Aboo Yoosaf, in the same manner as for a pledge.*—Mohammed is of opinion that he is answerable in the same degree as when goods, the subject of a sale, decay, or lost, in the hands of the seller, in which case the responsibility is for the

---

*A right of neighbourhood, which gives the neighbour a privilege of pre-emption.—It is fully treated of under the head of Shaffa.

†See Sales.

*That is, not at the rate of the estimated price, but of the actual value.

price, not for the value;—that is, the purchaser is exempted from the payment of the price;—and such is also the doctrine of Haneefa.—Ziffer, on the contrary, is of opinion, that responsibility attaches in the same degree as in a case of usurpation:* as the detention has been made without any right.—The argument of Haneefa and Mohammed is that the agent stands as the seller of the article in question to the constituent, and detains it from him in order that he may exact payment for it; and consequently that the constituent stands acquitted of the price on the decay or destruction of the article in the hands of the agent.—The reasoning of Aboo Yoosaf, is that the thing in question, in the hands of the agent, was not at first a subject of responsibility, but became so inconsequence of detention with a view to satisfaction for the price; and the same is the actual property of a pledge:—contrary to a purchase; as that is a subject of responsibility in the hands of the seller from the first and not because of detention for the price. A contract of sale, moreover, is cancelled in consequence of the loss of the subject of it; but in the case in question, the original contract between the agent and seller is not annulled.—Haneefa and Mohammed, however, maintain that though the original contract of sale be not annulled, yet the contract which virtually subsists between the agent and constituent is annulled, in the same manner as if the constituent were to return the goods to the agent on the discovery of a defect.

Case of an agent purchasing, at the rate of his instruction, a larger quantity of an article than was specified in the instruction.—If a person appoint another his agent for the purchase of ten ratls† of flesh for one dirm, and the agent purchase twenty ratls, for one dirm, of that kind of flesh which is sold at the rate of ten ratls for one dirm; in that case (according to Haneefa) it is incumbent on the constituent to take only ten ratls for half a dirm. The two disciples maintain that it is incumbent on him to take the twenty ratls for one dirm. In some copies of Kadooree it is written that Mohammed coincides in opinion with Haneefa, and that his doctrine in the Mabsoot is not incompatible with it, he having only observed there, that "the constituent ought to take ten ratls for a half dirm."—The argument of Aboo Yoosaf is that the constituent ordered the agent to expend his dirm in the purchase of flesh, under a conception of the price being at the rate of ten ratls per dirm: when, therefore, the agent purchased twenty ratls for the dirm, as he appears to purchase them on account of his constituent, he is consequently entitled to take the whole; in the same manner as where a person empowers another to sell his slave for a thousand dirms, and the agent obtains two thousand; in which case the constituent is entitled to the whole of the sum so obtained.—The argument of Haneefa is that the constituent having expressly enjoined the purchase of ten ratls, it follows that the excess must be considered as having been purchased by the agent on account of himself,—and for which he must accordingly pay the price;—contrary to where an agent, being empowered to sell a slave for a thousand dirms, obtains two thousand for him; because, in this case, the excess being in exchange for the property of the constituent, is consequently his right.—If however, the agent, were to purchase for one dirm twenty ratls of flesh of that kind which is sold at the rate of twenty ratls per dirm, the purchase (in the opinion of all our doctors) is made by the agent for himself; because the object of the constituent was evidently fat meat, and that object has not been here obtained.

An agent cannot purchase for himself any specific article which he is directed to purchase for his constituent.—If a person appoint another his agent to purchase for him some specific article, in that case the agent is not entitled to purchase the article for himself; because this is a breach of the trust reposed in him by his constituent; and also, because it is a dismission of himself from his appointment, which he is not (in the opinion of some) empowered to do, unless in the presence of his constituent.

Unless he purchase it for something of a different nature from the price specified.—If, however, the constituent should have specified the price of the article, and the agent purchase it for a price of a different species from that mentioned by the constituent; or if the constituent not having specified the price, the agent purchase the article, not for dirms, but for something estimable by weight or measurement of capacity.

Or through the mediation of another agent.—Or, lastly, if the agent appoint another agent, and that secondary agent purchase the article in the absence of the primary agent; in all these cases the purchase is held to have been made on behalf of the agent himself, and not of his constituent, because of the deviation from his constituent's orders.—If, on the other hand, the secondary agent conclude the bargain in the presence of the primary agent, the purchase is in that case considered as made for the constituent, because the wisdom and judgment of the primary agent is held (in consequence of his presence) to have been exerted: and hence there is no deviation from the orders of his constituent.

Case of agency in the purchase of an indefinite slave.—If a person appoint another to purchase for him an indefinite slave, and the agent accordingly purchase a slave: in tha

*That is, at the rate of the full value, whatever that may be.

†A ratl is about one pound, Troy weight.

case the slave belongs to the agent himself,* unless he declare, "I intended the purchase for my constituent,"—or unless he make the purchase with the constituent's property.—The compiler of the Hedaya remarks that this case may occur in various shapes.

Which admits of four descriptions—FIRST, where the agent refers the contract to his constituent's money, as if he should say, "with this thousand dirms (meaning those of his constituent) I have purchased this slave:" in which case the slave goes to the constituent. (This is the case which is meant by the above expression, "or unless he make the purchase with the constituent's property;" for that does not mean "that he shall first make the purchase for a thousand dirms, generally; and then pay it from the property of his constituent,") SECONDLY, where the agent refers the contract to his own money; in which case the slave, for evident reasons, belongs to the agent himself, since he has referred the contract to his own property. THIRDLY, where the agent refers to money in general; in which case the purchase is made either for himself or his constituent, as he may have resolved in his mind at the time;—because the agent, in a case of the present description, is at full liberty either to make the purchase for himself, or for his constituent. If, therefore, the agent and constituent disagree (the agent asserting that he intended in the purchase for himself, and the constituent declaring that he intended it for him), then the payment of the price must determine; that is, the slave is adjudged to him from whose property the price is paid.—If, on the other hand, it be admitted by both that no resolution was formed, Mohammed alleges the slave, in this case, to be the property of the agent; because of his being the contracting party, and also, because of the probability there is that every one acts for himself, unless where it can be proved to the contrary, which the case in question does not admit of—Aboo Yoosaf is also of opinion that the payment of the price ought to determine the right to the purchase; because it serves as a criterion to determine the action of the agent, which otherwise admits of two suppositions; and also, because, if the purchase were to be considered as made on account of the agent, notwithstanding his having paid the price from the property of the constituent, it would follow that the agent is an usurper. This conclusion of Aboo Yousaf, however (that the agent would, under these circumstances, be an usurper), does not necessarily follow: on the contrary, he cannot otherwise be considered than as in the case where the parties disagree with respect to the intention; which we have already explained.—It is to be observed that all the several modes here described apply equally to the appointment of an agent for the management of a contract of Sillim.

Case of dispute between the agent and constituent respecting a slave who, after being purchased by the agent, dies in his hands—IF a person appoint another to purchase for him a slave for a thousand dirms, and the agent afterwards inform him that "he had accordingly purchased for him a slave for a thousand dirms, but that the slave had died in his possession,"—and the constituent, on the other hand, assert that "he had purchased the said slave for himself and not for him;"—in this case the assertion of the constituent, corroborated by an oath, must be credited.—This, however, proceeds on a supposition that the constituent had not previously delivered the said thousand dirms to his agent:—for if he should have given the thousand dirms, the declaration of the agent must be credited; because, in the former instance, the agent gives information of his performance of an act which he is not now capable of carrying into full execution (since he cannot purchase a slave who is dead), and his object is to get a thousand dirms from the constituent, who, on the other hand, denies his right; and the word of a defendant is creditable before that of a plaintiff: and, in the latter instance, the agent is a trustee, having the price in his hands as a deposit; and his object being to obtain a releasement from his trust, his assertion is therefore credited.—If, however the slave be actually alive at the time of the disagreement, the declaration of the agent must be credited (according to Haneefa and Mohammed), whether the constituent have delivered the price or not; because the agent gives information of his having performed an act which he is capable at that instant of carrying fully into execution (since it is in his power to purchase this slave as he is living), and hence his word is not liable to suspicion.—According to Haneefa, indeed, if the constituent should not have delivered the price, his assertion must be credited, as the agent is in the case liable to the suspicion of having first purchased the slave on account of himself, and asserting afterwards (on the discovery of a defect) that he has purchased him for his constituent. It is otherwise where he has already received the purchase-money, because then he is considered as a trustee of it, and his assertion is credited, as it tends to procure him a releasement from his trust:—whereas, in the other case, he cannot be considered as a trustee, since the purchase-money is not in his possession.

In a case of dispute between an agent and constituent respecting the purchase of a specific slave, the declaration of the agent must be credited.—IF a person desire his agent to purchase for him a specific slave, and they afterwards disagree during the life-time of

* That is, the agent is considered as having made the purchase on his own account, and consequently must pay the price out of his own property.

the slave (the constituent asserting that the agent had purchased him for himself, and the agent declaring that he had purch sed him for his constituent), in this case it is universally agreed that, whether the constituent may have delivered to him the price or not, the assertion of the agent must be credited: because the agent gives information of his performance of an act which he is at that moment capable of carrying fully into execution; and also, b cause he is not in this case liable to any suspicion, since an agent for the purchase of a specific thing cannot purchase that thing for himself in the absence of his constituent. for the reasons already explained; in opposition to the case of an indefinite thing (according to the doctrine of Haneefa, as exhibited above).

An agent. avowing his commission, cannot afterwards retract, unless the alleged constituent deny the commission.—IF one person say to another "sell to me this slave in behalf of Omar, who is my constituent;" and the slave be accordingly sold, and the agent afterwards deny that he had been authorized to make the purchase by Omar, and Omar then appear, and assert that he had desired the said agent to purchase the said slave for him,—in this case Omar is entitled to take the slave, because the agent has h mself acknowledged his agency on his behalf, and denial after acknowledgment is of no effect. —If, on the other hand, Omar should deny his having authorized the purchase, in that case he is not entitled to take the slave, because the acknowledgment of the agent is set aside by the denial of Omar.—But if, under these circumstances, the purchaser should deliver the slave to Omar, it becomes then a contract of sale, for which the original purchaser is responsible, seeing that Omar has purchased it from him after the mode of Taata, that is by mutual gift, as when a person buys a thing for another without his authority and then delivers the said thing to that other.—The doctrine of this case shows that the delivery of a thing according to sale. suffices to establish a sale by Taata or mutual gift, even although the giving and receiving of the price should not have taken place; and it also shows that a sale by Taata in things of great or little value is established by the mutual consent of the parties. This is the authentic doctrine in the case of such sales.

An agent is at liberty, if he choose, to purchase only one of two slaves specified.—IF a person commission another to purchase for him two specific slaves without mentioning the price, and the agent purchase one of them, it is valid: for in this instance the appointment of agency is valid. and does not restrict the agent to purchase both of the slaves by one contract, which is often impracticable, because of the objection of the proprietor to include them both in one contract.—The agent may therefore lawfully purchase one out of two slaves, unless when he does it by deceit, as his agency authorizes him only to make a just purchase, which precludes him from making a deceitful one.—The doctrine in this case is universally agreed to.

IF a person desire another to purchase him two particular slaves, without mentioning the price, and the agent purchase one of these slaves, it is valid; because the appointment of the agent, in this instance, is general (in other words, does not restrict the agency to the purchase of both slaves by one contract); and it seldom happens that two slaves are purchase l by one contract, as a master seldom sells two slaves by one contract

But not if the purchase be at an evident disadvantage.—IT is lawful for the agent, therefore, to purchase one of the two (unless, indeed, the purchase be made at an evident disadvantage, which would be contrary to the end of the appointment).

Nor if the price exceed the rate expressed in his instructions; unless the difference be trifling.—IF a person desire another to purchase for him two specific slaves (who are supposed to be equal value) for one thousand dirms, and the agent purchase one of these slaves for five hundred dirms or less, it is valid, according to Haneefa.—If, however, he should purchase him for more than five hundred dirms, the contract is not binding on his constituent. The reason of this is that the constituent, having opposed one thousand dirms to the two slaves, who are equal in value, did of consequence intend that the agent should pay five hundred dirms for each. The agent, therefor, in paying five hundred dirms, conforms exactly to the orders of his constituent: and although, in paying less for him, he does deviate from his orders, yet this being a laudable deviation, in favour of his employer, is therefore binding. In purchasing him, on the other hand, for more than five hundred dirms, whether the excess be great or small, he is guilty of a deviation from his orders unfavourable to the interests of his employer. and which is therefore not allowed; unless, indeed, the agent purchased the other slave for the sum remaining to complete the thousand dirms; before any litigation happen between him and his constituent, for the former purchase.—What is here advanced proceeds upon a favourable construction of the law. Analogy would suggest that the contract, in this case, ought not to be binding on the constituent, because of the deviation from his orders.—The reason for a more favourable construction in this particular, is that the purchase of the two slaves for one thousand dirms (which is the express object of the constituent) is here obtained; and that the limitation of their prices to five hundred each, in an equal manner, is only an implied object, since it requires to be established by reasoning; and an express object is always preferred to an implied one.—The two disciples maintain that if, in the case in question, the agent should have purchased one of the two slaves for more than five hundred dirms, by a contract disadvantageous only in a small degree (which cannot always be avoided), and the money remaining suffice for the purchase of the other slave, it is valid; because the agency is absolute (that is to say, is not restricted to the payment of five hundred dirms for one slave), although it be restricted to a just and proper contract, which that in question may be considered, as the disadvantage attending it is not great and obvious.—It is, however, absolutely necessary that the sum remaining suffice to purchase the other slave, in order that the object of the constituent (namely, the purchase of both for one thousand dirms) be obtained.

An agent may liquidate a debt due from him to his constituents by the purchase of a specific article.—If a person desire another, who owes him one thousand dirms, to purchase with it a specific slave, and the agent act accordingly, it is lawful; because a specification of the subject of sale amounts to a specification of the seller; and as a specification of the seller would have been lawful (for reasons which will hereafter appear), so, in the same manner, the specification of the subject is also lawful.

But if the article be not specified. and perish, after purchase, in the agent's hands, the debt is not liquidated.—If a person desire another, who is indebted to him one thousand dirms, to purchase with it an indefinite slave; and the debtor accordingly purchase a slave, and the slave die before the delivery of him to the constituent; in that case the slave is held to have been the property of the agent —If, on the other hand, he die after delivery to the constituent; he is then held to have been the property of the constituent.—This is the doctrine of Haneefa The two disciples allege that the property of the constituent commences on the instant of the agent obtaining possession of the slave.—A similar disagreement subsist with regard to the case of a creditor appointing his debtor to make a purchase with the debt, either by a contract of Sillim or Sirf.—The argument of the two disciples is that dirms and deenars, whether ready money or debt, are not specific when opposed to any thing in a contract of exchange (whence it is that if a person were to sell a specific and existing article, in exchange for a debt, and both parties agree that the purchaser does not owe the seller any thing, yet the contract of sale is not rendered void); it is therefore, the same whether they be a specified or not;* and consequently the contract of the agent is binding on the constituent, because his seisin is equivalent to that of his constituent.—The argument of Haneefa is that dirms and deenars admit of specification in agency (whence it is that if a person restrict his agent to the purchase of something with one thousand specific dirms, or with a debt, and the specific dirms be lost in the agent's hands, or the debt become cancelled, the agency is null); and such being the case, it follows that in the appointment of an agent for the purchase of a slave, or for making a Sillim contract, the property of a debt is vested in a person, by another who is not indebted to him, without his being appointed an agent for the seisin of the said debt, which is unlawful; in the same manner as if a person should purchase a thing in exchange for a debt due to him by some other than the seller (as if he should say to the seller "I have bought this thing from you in exchange for a debt owing to me by a certain person, and which you may take for the price"); in which case the sale would be invalid; and so also in the case in question.—In the appointment of an agent for managing a Sirf sale, on the other hand, it would follow that the constituent, before possession, commands the use of a thing of which he is not proprietor till after possession (for he is not proprietor of the debt till after the receipt of it); and the application of the thing in question to a Sirf sale, before the seisin of it, is null;—in the same manner as if a person should say, "give what you owe me to whomsoever you please."—It is otherwise if the constituent specify the seller; because then the seller is his agent for the receipt of the debt, and consequently takes possession of the same in virtue of his agency, and then becomes the proprietor of it himself. It is otherwise, also, where a creditor desires his debtor to bestow the amount of his debt in charity, because here the creditor destines his property to God, who is a known and determinate object.—It is to be observed that as, in all these cases, the agency (according to Haneefa) is not valid, the purchase make under it is of force and binding with respect to the agent himself, as being the actual purchaser:—if therefore, the subject of the sale should decay or be destroyed in his hands, he must sustain the loss; unless, however, the constituent should previously have received seisin of it; because, in that case, it would become his property, as a sale of the slave is in this instance established between the agent and constituent, by a sort of reciprocity.

Where an agent and constituent disagree respecting a purchase, a judgment must be given, according to the value.—If a person give another one thousand dirms, and desire him to purchase with it a female slave, and the agent accordingly purchase a female slave, and the parties then disagree,—the constituent asserting that he had purchased her for five hundred dirms, and the agent declaring that he had paid one thousand for her,—in this case the assertion of the agent is to be credited provided the value of the slave be estimated at one thousand dirms; because the price, according to him, [illegible]

*This is to say, it is the same thing, whether the agent, at the time of purchase, declare that "the thousand dirms he pays for the slave are those thousand which he owes to his constituent," or not.

one thousand dirms, in which exac amoutnt he is a trustee, he therefore, in this case, claims a releasement from his charge of trustee ; whilst, on the other hand, the constituent claims compensation from him, which he denies.—If, however, the value should be estimated only at five hundred dirms, then the assertion of the constituent is to be credited, because the agent departed from his orders in purchasing a female slave for five hundred dirms, when the constituent desired one for one thousand dirms ; and is therefore responsible.—Supposing (on the other hand) the constituent not to have paid the one thousand dirms to the agent, and all the other circumstances of the case to remain as above mentioned, then also, if the value of the female slave be only five hundred dirms, the assertion of the constituent must be credited, because of the agent's deviation from his orders :—but if the value be one thousand dirms, both parties must be required to make oath (because such is the law in a dispute about the price in a contract of sale ; and here the constituent and the agent stand to each other in the relation of buyer and seller) ;—after which the contract of sale (which is supposed to exist between the agent and constituent) is dissolved, and the right of property in the slave becomes vested in the agent.

Or according to the declaration of the seller.—IF a person desire another to purchase for him a specific slave, without mentioning the price, and the agent accordingly purchase the said slave, and they then disagree in regard to the price (the agent asserting that he had paid one thousand dirms, and the constituent asserting that he had only paid five hundred dirms), in this case, provided the seller authenticates the declaration of the agent. his assertion, corroborated by an oath, must be credited.—Some have said that an oath is not to be exacted in this instance, since the doubt arising from the disagreement is removed by the verification of the seller : in opposition to the preceding case, where the seller is supposed to be absent.—Others. again, have said that in this case also an oath is requisite. Mohammed alleges that as, after the receipt of the price, the seller is, as, it were, a stranger to both the agent and the constituent,—and, even before the receipt of the price, is in the relation of a stranger to the constituent,—his assertion can have no effect in regard to a disagreement between the constituent and agent ; and, consequently, that an oath is requisite. This is also the opinion of Aboo Mansoor ; and it is the most authentic doctrine.

Section II.

*Of the Appointment of Agents, by Slaves for the Purpose of purchasing their own Persons in their own Behalf.**

A slave may employ a person to purchase his freedom from his master.—IF a slave say to a person, "purchase me, in behalf of myself, from my master, for one thousand dirms"* (at the same time delivering the one thousand dirms), and the said person accordingly purchase the slave from his master, in behalf of the slave, he [the slave] becomes free ; and the right of Willa remains with the master, because the sale of the person of the slave to the slave himself is here interpreted in its metaphorical sense (that is, the liberation of the slave), as the interpretation of it in its literal sense (namely, the exchange of property for property) is here unattainable : the slave's purchase of his own person, moreover, is in fact an agreement on his part to accept his freedom in exchange for his property : and the agent stands merely as a messenger, because none of the rights of the contract rest in him :—the case is, therefore, the same as if the slave had purchased his own person : and as the sale of the slave is, in fact, an emancipation of him on the part of the master, he is therefore entitled to the right of Willa. If, however, the agent should not particularly say and explain to the master that he purchased the slave on behalf of the slave, but, on the contrary, simply say, "I have purchased a particular slave of yours," In that case the slave becomes the property of the purchaser ; because these words, in their literal sense, are used to express an exchange of property for property, which is here practicable, and consequently followed : in opposition to the former statement of the case, where the literal meaning not being practicable, the metaphorical sense was therefore adopted ; and, as the literal meaning (namely, an exchange of property for property) is here followed, the purchaser of consequence becomes the Proprietor of the slave ; and the one thousand dirms given to him by the slave for the purchase of himself are the right of the master, as being the slave's earnings ; and the purchaser must pay him another thousand dirms for the price. In short, in the case of an agent for a slave purchasing the said slave in his own behalf, it is necessary that he particularly explain the circumstances of the case ; that is, that he expressly specify the purchase of the slave 'to be made in behalf of the slave ;" for otherwise the purchase is for himself, and not for the slave. It is otherwise where a person, who is not a slave, purchases, in the capacity of an agent, a specific slave ; for it is not necessary that he should specify in whose behalf the purchase is made, since the contract of sale takes place, whether such an explanation be made or not ; and in either case the seller demands the price from the agent, who is the contracting party. In the case in question, on the contrary, the explanation is material ; for if it be not

*That is, with a view to their emancipation.

*In other words, "purchase my FREEDOM for one thousand DIRMS."

made, the transaction is a sale; or if it be made, it is an emancipation, with a reservation of the right of Wila; in which case the price is not demanded from the agent, notwithstanding he is the contracting party: it is, moreover, possible that the master may not be inclined to the emancipation, but may assent to the sale merely with a view to the exchange, in which case, also, explanation is indispensable.

A slave may act as the agent of another person in purchasing his own freedom.—If a person say to a slave, "purchase your own person on my behalf from your master;" and the slave say to his master, "sell me, on account of a particular person, for this quantity of dirms," and the master accordingly agree, in this case the slave becomes the property of the constituent; because a slave is capable of becoming an agent for the purchase of himself, since, with regard to the property involved in his person, he himself is as a stranger; and as he is property, a contract of sale operates with respect to him, although the seller (because of the property being in the hands of the slave himself) be not entitled to detain him from the constituent after the sale, as a satisfaction for the price: and as the slave is capable of agency, it follows that if, in the case in question, he refer the contract to his constituent, consequently because of its being in conformity to his orders; but if, instead of referring it to his constituent, he should refer it to himself, he then becomes free, because the contract is in that case an emancipation, to which the master agrees.

Objection.—The slave is, in this case, an agent for the purchase of a specific thing; but an agent for the purchase of a specific thing is not entitled to purchase that thing for himself.

Reply.—Although the slave, in this case, be an agent for the purchase of a specific thing, yet by purchasing, he in reality performs an act of a different nature from purchase,* and that act is therefore allowed to be expedited in his behalf.

If, also the slave simply say to his master "sell me," without mentioning the particular person, he is free: because his speech being absolute, and admitting of two interpretations, is not applied in favour of the constituent, on account of the doubt which exists, and which consequently determines the transaction to be a contract in behalf of himself.

Section III.
Of Agency for Sale

An agent for sale cannot sell to his father or grandfather.—An agent for purchase or sale is not permitted, according to Haneefa, to enter into a contract of purchase or sale with a person whose evidence would not be admitted in his [the agent's] behalf, such as his father or grandfather.—The two disciples allege that if an agent should sell a thing to any person whatever, standing in that relation to him (except his slave or his Mokatib), for an equivalent to the value of the subject of the sale, it is lawful; because agency is absolute; and an agent is not liable to suspicion from such a sale, since the property of those relations is distinct and separate from his property; and neither party is entitled to derive a benefit from the property of the other. It is otherwise where an agent sells a thing to his own slave, because that, in fact, is a sale to himself, as the possessions of a slave are the property of his master; and the right of a master extends to the earnings of his Mokatib, and becomes, in reality, his property in the event of the Mokatib's inability to discharge his ransom.—The arguments of Haneefa upon this point are twofold.—First, and transaction which begets suspicion must be excepted from agency;—and the act of sale on the part of the agent, to persons under the above description, does beget suspicion, since they are excluded from giving evidence in his behalf.—Secondly, a mutual right of usufruct and advantage subsists between the agent and such relations, * since each is entitled to derive an advantage from the property of the other; the sale of any thing to them, therefore, is in manner a sale to himself.—A similar disagreement subsists with respect to a contract of Sirf or of hire, under these circumstances.

He may sell the article committed to him at whatever rate, and in return for whatever commodity, he thinks fit.—Whoever is appointed an agent for the sale of any thing, may lawfully (according to Haneefa) sell that thing, either for a large or small price, or in exchange for any thing else, as well as for money.—The two disciples maintain that it is neither lawful to sell the thing at a great and obvious disadvantage, nor for any thing but money, for the following reasons: —First, agency, although absolute, is yet restricted to the common customs of mankind; because as all transactions (such a purchase and sale, for instance), are for the purpose of removing or remedying a want, they are therefore restricted to the measure of that want (whence it is that agency for the purchase of a stove, or of ice, or of any animal destined for sacrifice, is restricted to the period in which those things are wanted); and the common practice among mankind is to sell a thing or an adequate value, and for this value (not in anything else, but) in money.—Secondly, sale at a great and evident disadvantage is partly a sale and partly a gift; in the same manner, also, the sale of goods for other goods (which is termed Beea

*Namely, emancipation.

*Namely, his father and grandfather. (See Imbisat.)

Mokassa, or barter) is sale in one shape, and purchase in another shape;—neither of these, therefore, can be absolutely term'd a sale. The argument of Haneefa is that agency is absolute, and must therefore be permitted to operate in an absolue manner, provided it be not subject to suspicion.—The sale, moreover, of a thing at an evident disadvantage is a common practice when there is pressing occasion for the price; and, in the same manner, it is also common to sell goods in exchange for goods, when one of the proprietors losee all desire for his own goods.—With respect to the example of the sale of a stove, or of ice, or of an animal destined for sacrifice (as adduced by the two disciples in support of their opinion), the doctrine regarding them cannot be admitted, according to the tenets of Haneefa, since the contrary is related as an opinion of his upon those subjects.—Besides, sale at an evident disadvantage is, nevertheless, wholly a sale, and in no respect a gift; whence it is that if a person were to make a vow, saying, "by God I will not sell such a thing." and afterwards dispose of it to an evident loss, he is forsworn.

Objection.—If sale at an evident disadvantage be still wholly a sale, it follows that a father or executor may sell the goods of a minor at a disadvantage.—How, therefore, does it happen that they are both debarred from doing this?

Reply.—The reason is that their power is founded entirely upon their suppposed regard for the interest of the minor; and the transaction in question being of a nature which argues a want of this regard, is consequently not permitted to them.

In regard to a sale of goods for goods, it is either completely a sale, or completely a purchase; and cannot be partly a sale, and partly a purchase, since the properties of sale exist completely in it, as well as the properties of a purchase.

An agent may purchase a thing at any rate not greatly exceeding the value.—An agent for purchase may lawfully buy a thing for a price equivalent to its value; and also for more than its value, provided the difference be not very considerable; but it is not lawful for him to purchase it at a rate much beyond the value, as this gives room for suspicion, since it is possible that he may have first purchased it for himself; and that afterwards, on perceiving the loss, he had determined it for his constituent. If, however, an agent be employed for the purchase of a specific thing, and purchase it for a price much beyond its value, lawyers have observed that the bargain is nevertheless made for his constituent; since an agent for the purchase of a specific thing, as not being allowed to purchase that thing for himself, is not, of consequence, liable to suspicion.—In the same manner, also, if an agent for marriage should contract a woman in marriage to his constituent, engaging for a dower beyond her Mihr Misl or proper dower, it is lawful, according to Haneefa; because, in marriage, as the agent must necessarily refer the contract to his constituent, he is, therefore, not liable to suspicion:—but it is otherwise with an agent for purchase, as he may, if he please, settle the contract in an absolute manner without referring it to his constituent.—The term evident disadvantage, as here used, signifies a rate beyond the valuation of appraisers,—as where, for instance, if several persons make an appraisemnent of a thing, none of their appraisements equal the price given.—Some have said that this term is used in the exchange of goods for goods, where the difference is as ten to ten and an half; and in cattle, where it is as ten to eleven; and in immoveable property, where it is as ten to twelve. The reason of these proportions is that the sale of the first kind is common; of the second kind the sale is in a maan between frequency and rarity; and of the third, it is rare:—and the disadvantage increses in proportion to the rarity of the transaction.

An agent for the sale of a slave may lawfull sell any part or portion of him.—If a person, being appointed an agent for the sale of a slave, should sell the half of him, such sale is valid, according to Haneefa; because the agency is in this instance absolute, and does not restrict the sale either to one or more contracts; and as it would have been valid, under such circumstances, if he had sold him wholly for half of the price, it follows that it is valid where he sells the half for half of the price, a fortiori.—The two disciples allege that the sale of the half of the slave is not valid, as not being agreeable to custom, and because it involves the vexation of participation in the property:—the sale therefore, is invalid; unless the sale of the remainder also be completed previous to the disagreement of the parties, and their appeal to the Kazee—in which case it is valid, since the sale of one half may be necessary to facilitate the sale of the other half (as where, for instance, there is no purchaser for the whole, when it would be incumbent on the agent to make partial sales); if, therefore, he sell the remaining half prior to the delivery of the subject of first half was made with a view to facilitate the sale of the whole, and is consequently valid: but if, on the contrary, he should not sell the remaining half, it is evident that the partial sale was not adopted as a means of facilitating the sale of the whole, and is consequently invalid.—This distinction, according to the two disciples, procedes upon a favourable construction of the law.

An agent for the purchase of a slave may purchase him either wholly or in shares.—If a person be appointed an agent for the purchase of a slave, and purchase one half of him, the purchase remains suspended (that is to say, it is binding on the constituent in case the agent afterwards purchase the other half); because the purchase of a part may be the means of the purchase of the whole (as where the slave, for instance, has become the property of a number of persons, by inheritance, in which case there is a necessity for the agent purchasing one share from one heir, another from another, and so forth) ;—and where the agent purchases the remainder of the slave before his constituent rejects the first purchase, it is evident that the purchased part merely with a view to facilitate the purchase of the whole : —the contract of purchase is therefore binding upon the constituent, and affectual with respect to him.—This is universally admitted.—According to Haneefa, there is a difference between this and the preceding example ; for two reasons FIRST, in the purchase of a half of the slave there exists a suspicion, as it is possible that the agent may have made the purchase in his own behalf, and becoming afterwards sensible of the defect arising from participated property, may have then determined it for his employer : a suspicion which does not exist in the case of the sale of the half, SECONDLY, the order of a constituent to sell any thing is an order relative to his own property, and is consequently valid ; and such being the case : restriction or latitude must be attended to.—The order of a constituent to purchase any thing, on the contrary, is an order relative to the property of another, and is consequently invalid : and such being the case, restriction or latitude are not objects of attention.

An agent to whom an article of sale is returned, by a decree of the Kazee in consequence of an original defect, may return it to his constituent who must receive it back without any suit.—IF a person desire another to sell his slave, and the other sell the slave accordingly, and either take possession of the price or not, and the purchaser, in consequence of a defect of such a nature as could not have been supervenient (such, for instance, as an additional finger), return him upon the agent's hands, by a decree of the Kazee, founded either upon evidence, or on the refusal of the agent to take an oath, or on his express acknowledgment.—in this case the agent may return him to the constituent ; because the Kazee, in this instance has expressly determined the defect to have had existence during the possession of the seller, on which account he decrees the return ; and hence his decree is not, in fact, founded on any of the above circumstances, namely, evidence, refusal to take on oath, or acknowledgment.

OBJECTION.—What occasion, therefore, for the exhibition of these proofs? and why is any mention made of them in this case?

REPLY.—To remove the doubt thus stated, the author of this work observes, that the Kazee knows with certainty that a defect ; such as above described, could not happen in the course of a month ; but not knowing when the sale took place, there is therefore a necessity for these proofs, in order to ascertain the date of the sale, and that the Kazee may be enabled clearly to determine that the said defect had not happened since the sale, but had existed prior to it —The defect may also be of such a nature as required the inspection of woman or physicians ;—but although the opinion of women or physicians be sufficient to prevent contention, yet it is not a sufficient ground for a decree of restitution : there is, therefore, a necessity for the proofs aforesaid ;—unless, indeed, the Kazee himself witness the sale and perceive the defect, in which case there is no necessity whatever for those proofs.—The return to the agent is in fact, a return to the constituent ; and hence the the agent is under no necessity of entering a suit against his constituent to enforce his admission of the return.

And so also, where the defect is supervenient ; provided the Kazee's decree be not founded on the agent's acknowledgment.—THE law is similar where the purchaser returns the slave to the agent, in virtue of a decree of the Kazee, founded either on evidence or refusal to take an oath, on account of a defect of such a nature as may have taken place subsequent to the sale, because evidence is absolute proof ; and, as to the agent, he is under a necessity of declining to swear, as he had not always the possession of the slave having received him only after the appointment of agency, whence it is possible that he is unacquainted with the defect ;—when, therefore, the purchaser returns the slave on account of the agent's refusal to take an oath. the sale affects the constituent and he must take him back.—If, on the other hand, the purchaser return him to the agent, in consequence of a decree founded on his acknowledgment, the sale is absolute upon the agent, as acknowledgment is a weak proof (that is, does not affect any other than the acknowledger) : and the agent does not act from necessity, in this case, as he had it in his power either to have remained silent, or to have, refused taking an oath.

In which case the constituent is not obliged to receive it back without a suit.—THE agent, however, may afterwards litigate the matter with his constituent, and oblige him to take back the slave on his establishing proof by evidence, or on the constituent's refusal to take on oath.—It is otherwise where the purchaser returns the slave to the agent, on his acknowledgment, without a decree, for in this case he has no grounds for a suit against the constituent to compel him to retake the slave ; because this return is a sale *de novo* with respect to a third person who is neither the purchaser not seller ; and the constituent must be this third person since none but the agent can be considered as the seller.—The agent, therefore, in receiving back the slave from the purchaser to whom he had sold him, does, as it were, repurchase him ; and hence he is debarred from returning him to the constituent, or litigating the matter with him.—A return of the subject of the sale, on the other hand, in virtue of a decree of the KAZEE founded on an acknowledgment of the seller, is an annulment of the contract of sale, and not a sale *de novo*; because although the authority of the Kazee be general, yet acknowledgment is but weak proof.—In this case, therefore, as the contract of sale is annulled, the agent is entitled to sue the constituent, in order to compel him to receive back, the slave; but as his acknowledgment is insufficient proof, the constituent cannot be compelled to receive back the slave without proof by evidence.*

If the defect be original, the constituent must receive back the article from his agent without litigation, whether it be returned by the purchaser in consequence of his [the agent's acknowledgment. or not.—If, on the other hand, the defect on account of which the purchaser has returned the slave be of such a nature as cannot be supervenient (such as a superfluous finger, for instance), and the return be made to the agent in consequence of his acknowledgment of the defect, without, any decree of the Kazee,—in this case, according to one tradition, the constituent is obliged, without the necessity of establishing a suit against him, to receive back the slave; as the return is of a determinate nature, and therefore the parties did of themselves what the Kazee would have done.—According to many traditions, however, the agent has here no right to sue the constituent, in order to make him receive back the slave, for the reason already stated, that "the purchaser's returning the article to the agent, in consequence of his acknowledgment, is a sale de novo, with respect to others than the parties themselves; and the constituent is not a party."—In regard to the assertion contained in the first tradition that 'the return of the subject of the sale was a thing of a determinate nature," it is not admitted: because the right of the purchaser, at first, was that the subject of the sale should be in a complete and perfect state; and failing of this, his right then relates to a return of the subject; and afterwards it shifts, and relates to a restitution of the exact quantity of loss he may have sustained in the price.—In this case, therefore, the return of the subject of the sale is not a thing of a determinate nature.

A constituent must be credited with respect to his instruction.—If the constituent and agent disagree, the one asserting that "he had ordered the other to sell his slave in exchange for ready money, and that he had nevertheless sold him on credit,"—and the other, that "he [the constituent] had merely desired him to sell him, and that he had said nothing more,"—in this case the assertion of the constituent must be credited; because he is the person from whom the order issued; and no argument exists of this order being absolute, agency being in its original nature relative and restricted; whence it is that if one person should say to another, "I have made you agent with regard to my property; the agent would not be permitted to do as he pleased with regard to the property, but would be restricted entirely to the preservation of it.—If, on the other hand, a disagreement similar to that in question should take place between a manager* and his principal, the assertion of the manager must be credited; because Mozaribat is in its origina nature general and absolute; whence it is that if a person should say to another "I have delivered this property to you by way of Mozaribat," or, "take this property by way of Mozaribat," the other might lawfully perform acts of Mozaribat with that property.†—In Mozaribat, therefore, an argument exists of its being absolute. It would be otherwise, indeed, if the principal should declare that he had given the property to be used by one particular mode of Mozaribat, and the manager should declare that he had stipulated another mode; for in such a case, the assertion of the principal would be credited; because the parties are both agreed, in this instance, that the Mozaribat was restricted and not absolute: and Mozaribat, whenever it ceases to be absolute and is determined to be restricted, resolves itself into a mere agency.—It is to be observed that an unrestricted commission to sell anything may relate either to ready money,—or to credit, whether for a long or a short period, according to Haneefa. The two disciples maintain that the period of credit must be confined to what is customary.—The principle on which this proceeds has been already explained.

An agent for sale is not responsible for consequences.—If a person order another to sell his slave, and the other, having accordinly sold him, should take a pledge for the price, which pledge is afterwards lost or destroyed in his possession,—or, if he should take security from the purchaser for the payment of the price, and both the surety and the purchaser die insolvent, or disappear, so as to leave it unknown whether they are gone—in neither of these cases is the agent responsible: for he is the original with respect to the rights of the contract of sale; and seisin of the price is one of these rights,—and as the taking of security was with a view to add to his certainty, and the taking of a pledge was in the nature of a bond to answer the payment of the price, it follows that he was competent to these acts.—It is otherwise with respect to an agent for the receipt of debt; for he acts by way of substitution; that is to say, the creditor has substituted him to receive the debt for him, but has not

*Meaning, proof to the existence of the defect.

*Arab, Mozarib.—Meaning, an agent for trade. It is particularly treated of under the head of Mozaribat.

†That is to say, might employ it in trade according to his own discretion.

appointed him to take security or a pledge in opposition to the debt; whereas an agent for purchase, on the contrary, receives the price in virtue of his being a principal, and a party in the contract, and therefore the constituent cannot prevent him from performing these acts.

Section IV.

Miscellaneous Cases

Joint agents cannot act separately without a mutual concurrence.—IF a person appoint two agents, it is not permitted to either of them to act in any matter relative to their agency, without the concurrence of the other. This is the law with respect to all transactions which require thought and judgment (such as sale, Khoola, and so forth, because the constituent, in those transactions, may have a confidence in the joint judgment of both the persons in question, although not in the single judgment of either of them.

OBJECTION.—Where the price is fixed, there can be no need for thought and judgment; and therefore, in that case, the act of one of the parties ought to be valid; whereas it is held to be otherwise.

REPLY.—Although the price be fixed, yet there may be occasion for judgment to increase it, and also to make a proper choice of a purchaser.

Except in the management of a suit.—THE act of one of two agents without the concurrence of the other is not valid excepting in some particular cases :—as where, for instance, a person appoints two agents for the management of his suit, in which case either of these may lawfully act without the other; because their joint action is impracticable, as it would only create a noise and confusion in the assembly of the Kazee. Their judgment, moreover, is required to the exerted previous to the assembly of the Kazee: in other words, they ought previously to consult with each other, and then one of them ought to attend the meeting of the Kazee to manage the replies and interrogations; which may be more effectually executed by one than two, since in the latter case, much noise and confusion would ensue.

Gratuitous divorce of manumission, the restoration of a deposit, or the discharge of a debt.—IN the same manner it is lawful for one of two agents to act singly in case of their having been jointly appointed agents by another to execute a divorce in his behalf without a compensation;*—or to emancipate his slave without a consideration;—or to restore a deposit to the owner of it;—or, lastly, to discharge a debt due by him. The reason of this is, that in these cases there is no necessity for consultation and judgment, since in all of them explanation merely is required; and the speech of one man, in this respect, is equal to that of two.—It were otherwise if the constituent had said to the two agents, "divorce a particular wife of mine if you please," or "the business of such a wife is in your hands,"—for in this case it would not be permitted to one of the two agents to divorce the said wife; because the constituent has committed the divorce to the thought and judgment of both: and also, because he has suspended it upon a circumstance relative to both,—namely, their pleasure,—and as he has connected it with a circumstance relative to both, it becomes analogous to where a person connects the divorce with the arrival of two persons at a particular house; in which case the execution of it rests on the arrival of both these persons at the said house; and so also, in the case in question, it depends on the joint wish of both the agents.

An agent cannot appoint a secondary agent.—AN agent is not permitted to appoint another person an agent to execute a commission to which he himself was appointed, as the constituent, in committing the transaction to him, did not empower him to appoint an agent for the excution of it.—The reason of this is that althoguh the constituent be satisfied with the judgment of his own agent, yet it does not follow that he is satisfied with the judgment of another person since mankind in this respect are different

Unless by consent of his constituent; or, unless his powers be discretionary.—IT is, therefore, not lawful for an agent to appoint an agent, unless with the consent of his constituent; or unless the constituent should have desired the agent to act according to his wisdom and judgment,—in the first of which cases the consent is express; and in the second, the constituent commits his business, in an absolute manner, to the agent's discretion.—As, in this case, however, the agency of the secondary agent is valid, he is the agent of the primary constituent; and hence the primary agent has not the power of dismissing him, nor would his power of agency cease in case of the death of the primary agent. The agencies of both, however, would terminate in the event of the death of the constituent. A case which exemplifies this has been already set forth in treating of the duties of the KAZEE.

Contracts entered into by a secondary agent in the presence of the primary are, however, valid.—IF an agent appoint an agent without the consent of his constituent, and the secondary agent conclude a contract of sale in the presence of the primary agent, the contract is in that case valid, because it has had the advantage of the wisdom and judgment of the primary agent, which is the very object of the constituent.—A disagreement, however, subsists with respect to the rights of this contract.—Some have said that they appertain to the primary agent as the constituent has not acquiesced in any other's undertaking the fulfilment of the contract; whilst others maintain that they relate to

*In opposition to Khoola, or divorce for a compensation.

the secondary agent, as being the actual framer of the contract. If, on the other hand, the secondary agent conclude a contract in the absence of the primary agent, it is not valid, as it has not the advantage of the wisdom and judgment the primary agent.

And they are also valid, although made in his absence, provided he afterwards consent to them.—If, however, the primary agent, having received information of the contract, should express his acquiescence in it, it is then valid: and so also, a contract becomes valid which, having been concluded by some other than the agent, afterwards receives his assent on his hearing of it; since it has thus the benefit of his judgment.

And the same of a contract engagement in by any stranger.—If, also, the primary agent first fix a price to be observed by the secondary agent, and the secondary agent then enter into a contract of purchase or sale, such contract is valid; because the exertion of the primary agent's judgment is evidently required only for the purpose of fixing the price, which has been already done.

Or that (in a case of purchase or sale) the constituent had previously fixed the rate.—It is otherwise, however, where the constituent appoints two agents, and fixes the price himself; for, in this case, notwithstanding the constituent's settlement of the price, the conclusion of the contrract by one agent, although at the fixed price, would not be valid.

Joint agents must act together, although the constituent have fixed the rate.—Because where the constituent appoints two agents, notwithstanding his having fixed the price, it is evident that his object is a union of the judgments of both, in order either to increase the quantity of the goods (it they be agents for purchase), or to make a proper choice of purchasers (in case they be agents for sale), as was before stated: whereas, if the eonstituent should not fix the price himself, but resign the management of the contract to one person (being his immediate agent, and not the agent of his agent), in that case his object is to obtain the judgment of the agent in the grand point of the contract, namely' the amount of the price

A Mokatib, a slave, or a Zimmee cannot act on behalf of an infant daughter being a Musslima.—If a Mokatib, an absolute slave, or a Zimmee, contract a marriage in behalf of a minor daughter who is free and a Musslima,—or make a purchase or sale in behalf of a minor child under such description,—it is unlawful (and the same of every other transaction which they perform relative to the property of such a child); as a slave or an infidel are not endowed with authority, becanse of their slavery and infidelity; for as a slave has not the power to marry in his own behalf, it is evident that he cannot have that power with respect to others; and an infidel, on the other hand, has no power over Mussulmans; insomuch that his evidence with respect to them is not admitted.—Besides, the power in these cases (that is, the right of acting with regard to the property of an infant), is granted with a view to the infant's advantage, and out of regard to his interest; and hence it is necessary that this power be consigned to a person competent and affectionate, in order that the end may be answered: now competency is destroyed by slavery; and the existence of affection to a Mussuman is incompatible with infidelity; a right of action, therefore, with regard to the property of the infant in question, cannot be committed to a slave or an infidel.

And the same of an apostate, or infidel alien—Haneefa, Aboo Yoosaf and Mohammed, are of opinion that an apostate who suffers death on account of his apostacy, and an infidel alien, are with respect to an infant daughter who is a Mussalima, in the same predicament with a Zimmee (that is to say, neither of these has a right to perform any act with regard to her property, such as purchase or sale, or the contracting of her in marriage with another);—because an infidel alien is endowed with still less power over a Mussulman than a Zimmee: and with respect to an apostate, although (in the opinion of the two discipies) he possesses power with regard to his own property, yet his power over his children, or over their property, remains suspended upon his repentance and return to the faith, according to all our doctors'; because a power of action, with respect to the property of an infant, is founded on the infant's advantage, and a regard for his interest; and an apostate's regard for the interest of his child (being a Mussulman) must entirely depend on his return to the faith; now this is a circumstance of doubt: if he be put to death in his apostacy it is then evident that he has no power of action, and all such acts are consequently null:—if, on the other hand, he return to the faith, it becomes the same as if he had been always a Mussulman, and his acts of the natur in question are therefore valid.

CHAPTER III.

OF THE APPOINTMENT OF AGENTS FOR LITIGATION AND FOR SEISIN.—(KHASGOMAT, OR LITIGATION, MEANS A COVERSATION CARRIED ON BETWEEN TWO PERSONS IN THE WAY OF CONTENTION AND DISAGREEMENT.)

Agency for litigation implies and involves an agency for seisin.—If a person appoint another his agent to contend for something in his behalf, the person so appointed is held, in the opinion of all our doctors, to be also an agent for the seisin of that thing whether it be debt or substance.—Ziffer alleges that he cannot be considered as an agent for seisin, since his constituent acquiesces only in his agency for litigation in his behalf.—Litigation, moreover, is one concern, and seisin is another concern ; and the constituent expresses his acquiescence in the litigation, but not in the seisin. The argument of our doctors is that when a person becomes empowered with respect to anything, he necessarily becomes empowered with respect to the completion of that thing ; and the end and completion of a contention for any thing is the seisin of that thing.

But decrees are passed on the contrary principle in the present times.—In the present age decrees pass according to the opinion of Ziffer ; because of the apparent want of probity of agents in this age ; and also, because many men may be trustworthy in regard to the management of a cotention, and not with respect to the seisin of property.—It is to be observed that an agent for litigation is analogous to an agent for evacting the payment of a debt ; because he also is competent to the seisin, inasmuch as the seisin of a debt is in effect included in the suing for the payment of it. The common acceptation of the word, however, is different, because from Takaza [exacting by means of a suit at law] seisin is not generally understood ; and the common acceptation must be preferred to the virtual meaning,—According to the decrees in this age therefore, he is not an agent for seisin.

If there be two agents for litigation, they are in that case required jointly to receive seisin of the thing which is the object of contention ; because the constituent has expressed his acquiescence in the probity of them both jointly, and not in that of either of them singly ; and as the conjunction of both, with respect to seisin; is practicable, they must therefore take possession together.—It is otherwise with respect to the mere litigation, because their joint action is in that particular impracticable, as has been already demonstrated.

An agent empowered to take possession of a debt is also an agent for litigation.—Whoever is an agent in behalf of another for the seisin of a debt due to him, is also an agent for litigation in behalf of that person, according to Haneefa (whence it is that if the other party bring evidence to prove that the constituent had received payment of his debt; or had given the creditor an acquittal, such evidence, in the opinion of Haneefa, would be admitted).—The two disciples maintain that the agent in question is not an agent for litigation (and such also is reported, by Hasan, from Haneefa) : because seisin and litigation are different things ; and it does not follow that a person, from being trustworthy with regard to property, should also be skilled in the business of litigation. The acquiescence of the constituent therefore, in the agency for seisin, does not necessarily involve his acquiescence in the agency for litigation.—The argument of Haneefa is that an agent for the seisin of a debt is an agent for the substantiation of property (that is, he is an agent for the receipt of a consideration for a debt which is the right of the creditor, in order that such consideration may become the property of the creditor ; because it is impossible to receive the actual substance of the debt ; and hence whatever he receives in the discharge of the debt becomes the property of the creditor ; and as this is a compensation, or contract of exchange, the agent is consequently the principal, he being so with respect to all such rights as a contract of exchange requires) ;—and such being the case, he is of course the plaintiff, and is entitled to carry on the suit in the same manner as an agent for litigating a right of pre-emption, or for purchase. He most resembles, however, an agent for litigating a right of pre-emption ; because an agent for the receipt of a debt, institutes his suit prior to the seisin of it, in the same manner as an agent for maintaining a right of pre-emption institutes his suit prior to his taking the right whereas an agent for purchase cannot institute a suit, until he has completed the contract of purchase.

A commission to take possession of substance does not involve a commission to litigate.—An agent for the seisin of substance* is not an agent for litigation, according to all our doctors ; because he is a mere trustee ; and also, because the seisin of substance is not an exchange : he is, therefore, considered merely as a messenger.—Hence, if a person commission another to take possession of his slave, and the person in whose possession the slave is should prove by witnesses that the constituent had sold the slave to him, the Kazee must not decree the sale against the agent, until the constituent himself appear,—This proceeds upon a favourable construction.—Analogy would suggest that the slave should be delivered to the agent, because, as the proof has been exhibited against a person who is not the adversary (since the agent is not the adversary), it cannot therefore be admitted. The reason for a more favourable construction; in this particular, is that the evidence goes to two points ;—First; to prove the sale on the part of the constituent, and the consequent destruction of his property ;—Secondly, to prove that the said agent has no right to make seisin of the said slave.—Now, although the evidence on the first point be not against a regular adversary, yet in regard to the second point it is against a regular adversary (for the agent is the adversary on the second point):—the evidence, therefore, is

* Arab. Ain ;—meaning some actually existant property (such, for instance; as an article borrowed under an arreeat loan), in opposition to a debt in money, or to an article compensable by an equal quantity of the same article (such as grain, and the like).

admitted with respect to the second point, but not with respect to the first point; whence, if the constituent were himself to appear, it would be necessary to exhibit the evidence de novo, to prove that he had sold the slav.—It is therefore the same as if evidence had been adduced to prove that the constituent had dismissed his agent, for that would be admitted so far as to prevent the agent from the seisin: and so also in the case in question.—The effect is the same in cases of emancipation, divorce, and the like.—Thus, if a person commission another to bring his wife from her present place of residenee.—and the agent having arrived at the place of their residence, the wife should prove, by witnesses, that her husband had divorced her,—or the slave prove, by witnesses, that he or she had been emancipated such evidence must be admitted, so far as to prevent the agent from carrying them away until the constituent shall himself appear,—but not with respect to the divorce, or the emancipation.

An agent for litigation is empowered to make concessions on behalf of his constituent.—IF an agent for litigation make an acknowledgment, before the Kazee, of something affecting his constituent, such acknowledgment is valid with respect to the constituent. If, however, he should make the acknowledgment before any other than the Kazee, it is not valid (according to Haneefa and Mohammed, arguing on a favourable construction of the law);—but the agent, in consequence of making such acknowledgment before another than the Kazee, is dismissed from his appointment; and therefore, if he should afterwards claim his agency, and bring witnesses to prove his acknowledgment, it would not be admitted —Aboo Yoosaf alleges that an acknowledgment made before any other than the Kazee is likewise valid with regard to the constituent. What is here said proceeds upon a favourable construction.—Ziffer and Shafei maintain that the acknowledgment is not in either case valid with respect to the constituent: and this (which was the first opinion of Aboo Yoosaf on the subject) is conformable to analogy; because the agent was directed to litigate; and by litigation is understood contention, since this is an essential property of litigation: now acknowledgment is the reverse of contention; and a direction to perform any act cannot extend to the reverse of that act: on which principle it is that (as contention is necessary to the existence of litigation) an agent for litigation is not competent to the acts of composition or exemption;*—and also, that a commission of agency is vaid, where the agent's acknowledgment is expressly excepted from it, for if acknowledgment be comprehended under litigation, the exception of it would be invalid, in the same manner as the exception of the denial of the agent.*—A similar disagreement also subsists with respect to the case of a person appointing another his agent to give, in an absolute manner, an answer in his behalf; for this kind of agency is restricted to an answer that relates to litigation; because such is the common practice; and hence an agent to give an answer in an absolute manner is, in fact, an agent for contention.—The reason for a more favourable construction of the law, in this particular, is that agency for litigation is indisputably valid; and the validity of it extends to every point in which the constituent is competent. Now the constituent is in an absolute manner competent with respect to an answer, whether it relate to denial or acknowledgment; for his power is not confined and determined to one of these only. The agent, therefore, is also competent to either of the these. Simple litigation,† moreover figuratively signifies general reply; and as there is always an affinity between the figurative and the literal sense of a term (as will be hereafter demonstrated), the term must, in the present instance, be received in its figurative sense, so as to render the agency indisputably valid: for if the term be adopted in its literal sense (namely, contention), it would follow that the appointment is a commission to quarrel and contend: and quarrelling and contention are prohibited; and the appointment of an agent with respect to a prohibited thing is forbidden. It is therefore indispensable that the term be taken in its figurative sense (so as to render the agency valid), as this is most becoming the Mussulman character.

Case of an appointment of agency with an exception of acknowledgment.—IF a person appoint an agent for litigation, and except his acknowledgment, it is recorded from Aboo Yoosaf that the appointment is invalid, since after the exception of the acknowledgment there remains only the denial; and as the constituent is not empowered with respect to denial only, except where he knows the claim of the adversary to be unjust; he cennot limit the power of the agent to denial only. It is recorded from Mohammed (on the other hand), that this is valid; for the exception of acknowledgment by the constituent clearly indicates that he himself is empowered only with

* In other words, of agreeing to a composition, or giving a discharge, for a debt.

* "In the same manner as the exception of the denial of the agent:"—that is, in the same manner as if the agent's power of denying and rejoining, &c., were expressly excepted from his commission.

† Arab. *Khasoomat.*—The reasoning in this passage turns entirely upon the primitive sense and generally accepted meaning of the term

respect to denial because of his knowing the falsity of his adversary's plea. If, however, he should have expressed himself generally, the commission must be interpreted to convey a power of general reply, which is becoming the condition of Mussulmans. It is also related of Mohammed, that he made distinction between the plaintiff and defendant, observing that if a defendant should appoint an agent for litigation and should except his acknowledgment, it is invalid; because a defendant is compelled to make an acknowledgment when put to his oath, and therefore has not the power to establish agency for a purpose prejudicial to the plaintiff, that is, for denial, as to this he himself is not competent. The plaintiff, on the contrary, is at liberty either to acknowledge or deny, as he pleases, and hence he is entitled to appoint an agent for one of these purposes, and to except the other. Aboo Yousaf argues that an agent is the subsititute of his constituent: and as the acknowledgment of a constituent is not limited to the court of the Kazee, so neither ought that of his substitute to be so limited. Haneefa and Mohammed, on the other hand, argue that agency for litigation extends to a reply, which is termed litigation either in its literal or metaphorical sense. Now an acknowledgment in the assembly of the Kazee is metaphorically termed litigations either because it is opposed to the litigation that has issued, or because the litigation is the cause of the acknowledgment; the acknowledgment, therefore, is limited to the assembly of the Kazee. If, on the other hand, it be proved; by evidence, that such an agent had made an acknowledgment elsewhere than in the assembly of the Kazee, his agency determines: and consequently if he should make a claim with respect to the point concerning which he had before made acknowledgment and should adduce evidence to prove it, his claim would not be admitted, nor would the object of it be yielded to him, because of the prevarication of which he has been guilty. The agent, in this instance, therefore: resembles a father or an executor who makes an acknowledgment prejudicial to the infant under his charge in the assembly of the Kazee, which is of no affect; whence if they should afterwards prefer a claim to the object of it, and adduce evidence to prove their right, it would not be admitted, nor would the article in dispute be given to them.

Agency for the receipt of a debt. committed to the surety for the debt, is invalid.—If a person be surety for property in behalf of a debtor, and the creditor appoint the said surety his agent for the receipt of the debt, such agency is absolutely invalid, for two reasons:—First. the business of an agent is to act in behalf of another; and if the agency of the surety were supposed to be valid, it would necessarily follow that he acts as agent in behalf of his own person, in order to exempt himself from responsibility; and thus one of the essentials of agency (namely, action in behalf of another) would be destroyed. Secondly, if the agency be valid, it necessarily follows that in case the agent were to say "he had received the debt," his assertion is credited (since an agent is a trustee):* and this conclusion must be rejected in the present, instance as the agent's assertion cannot be credited since in it he endeavours to exempt himself from responsibility. The agency, therefore, is invalid, because of the inadmissibility of the conclusion arising from it. It is to be observed that the agent, in this instance, resembles the owner of a Mazoon, or privileged slave, involved in debt. In other words, if the master of an insolvent Mazoon were to emancipate him, so as to be himself responsible for his value to the creditors, and the creditors demand payment of the whole of the debts from the slave, appointing the master agent for the receipt of them, the agency would be invalid, because of the two reasons above recited, in treating of the agency of a surety.

Case of a plea of agency urged for the receipt of a debt in absence of the constituent.—If a person plead his being agent for the receipt of a debt due to another person who is absent, and the debtor verify his assertion in this case he [the debtor] must be directed to deliver the debt to the agent: because his verification of the claim is an acknowledgment against himself, since what the agent receive is purely the property of the debtor.—If, therefore, the absent person afterwards appear, and verify the assertion of the agent, there will be no contention whatever: but if otherwise, the debtor must again pay the debt to the absentee (who is now present), because his former payment of it is not established, as the creditor denies the agency; and his denial of agency, if confirmed by an oath must be admitted.—The former payment through the agent is therefore invalid; and the debtor is consequently entitled to retake from him what ever he had paid to him, provided it be still extant in this possession; because his object, in marking the payment, was to himself from responsibility; and as this object has not been fulfilled, he has therefore a right to retake it.—If, however, the thing be not extant in the possession of the agent, but have been destroyed, in that case the debtor is not entitled to retake any thing from the agent, since he, by his verification, acknowledged the right of the, agent to the receipt of it As the debtor however, in this instance suffers an oppression from his credulity, and it is not lawful for the oppressed to oppress others, he is not allowed to take any thing from the agent, in case of the destruction of the thing given to him;—unless, at the time of making the payment to

* Arab. Ameen;—meaning a confident: one whose word must be relied upon.

the agent, had taken the agent himself as security for the restitution, in the event of the absent person's denial of the agency; in which case it would be lawful for him to retake whatever he may have paid, as the agent became surety, and is consequently liable for it.

Objection.—The security, in this case, ought not to be valid, since it is essential to the validity of bail or security that there be a debt due by the suretee; and the suretee, in the present instance, is the constituent, who does not owe any debt.

Reply.—The security is valid; because it is referred to the period when the constituent shall have received the second payment of the debt; in which case he is responsible in the conception of both the agent and the debtor; the security is therefore valid, in the present instance, in the same manner as in all other cases.

If, on the other hand, a person should plead his being the agent of a certain absentee for the receipt of a debt due to him, and the debtor, without either verifying or falsifying his claim, remain silent, and yet pay the debt, and the proprietor of the debt afterwards appear and exact payment of it from the debtor, he (the debtor) is in this case entitled to a repayment from the agent, because he did not verify the agency; for in fact he did nothing else than make a payment in the hope that it would be acquiesced in by the constituent; and, on his being disappointed in this hope, he is consequently entitled to an indemnification from the agent.—The law is also the same where the debtor pays the debt to the agent, after falsifying his claim; as is obvious from the reasons already stated. —It is however to be observed that, in the several cases of verification, falsification, or silence, it is not permitted to the debtor to retake the article from the agent, after the delivery of it to him, until such time as the constituent appears; because the payment he has made is the right of the constituent from probability (as in the case of his verification), or from construction [as in the case or his falsification or silence), since it is possible that the absentee may afterwards give his assent to it. —It is, therefor, the same as if he had paid the debt to a Fazoolee, or unauthorized person, in the hope that the proprietor would confirm it; in which case it is not lawful to take back from the Fazoolee what he may have delivered to him; because there exists a possibility of a confirmation of it by the owner; and also, because it is a general rule that, when a person performs an act with any particular view or object he ought not to undo the same unless he be disappointed of the object which prompted it.

Case of a plea of agency urged for the receipt of a trust, in absence of the constituent.—If a person plead his being the agent of a certain person for the receipt of a deposit, and the trustee verify his assertion, yet the law does not award the delivery of the deposit by the trustee to this person, since (in opposition to the preceding case to a debtor) the trustee here makes an acknowledgment with respect to the property of another.—If, however, the person in question plead that "his father having died, the said deposit had devolved by inheritance to him, and that there were no other heirs." and the trustee verify this, he must be directed to deliver the deposit to this person; because the trust is no longer the father's property, after his decease; and the trustee and the person in question are both agreed in its being the property of the heir:—the trustee, therefore, must be directed to deliver his trust to this person as being the heir.

A person commissioned to receive a trust on the plea of having purchased it, is not entitled to receive it from the trustee,—If a person plead that he had purchased a deposit from the proprietor of it, and the trustee verify his assertion. yet the trustee is not entitled to deliver the deposit to him; because the verification of the trustee during the lifetime of the depositor is an acknowledgment with respect to the property of another: and hence their assertions (namely that of the trustee and of the person who perfers the claim) are not valid. with regard to the establishment of proof of the sale on the part of the proprietor.

A person commissioned to receive a debt is entitled to receive it. although the debtor plead his having already paid it.—If a person appoint an agent for the receipt of a debt due to him and the debtor plead that he had acquitted himself of the debt to the proprietor, yet it is incumbent on him to pay the debt to the agent; because the agency is here clearly established; but the debtor's acquittance is not established by his assertion: he is therefore not permitted to delay the payment;—but after he has made the payment, he has a claim upon the creditor and may exact an oath from him: but an oath cannot be exacted from the agent, since he is only a substitute.

The seller of an article cannot be compelled to take back the article from the purchaser's agent, on a plea of defect, until the purchaser swears to the defect.—If a person purchase a female slave, and afterwards plead a defect in her. and appoint an agent to manage the litigation with the seller, on this account, and then disappear,—and the agent accordingly institute a suit against the seller for the defect, and the seller plead that the purchaser had knowingly acquieseed in that defect,—in this case the slave is not to be returned to the seller; but a suspension must take place until the appearance of the purchaser, who will then be required to declare upon oath that he did not acquiesce in the defect If is other wise in the case of a debt (as befor recited); for there the debt must be paid to the agent for seisin, in behalf of the creditor, notwithstanding the debtor may plead his having previously acquitted himseif of it; because it is there practicable to make a reparation, by enjoining restitution from the agent of the amount he may have received, on the error being made apparent by the constituent refusing to swear; whereas, in the case in question, if an annulment of the sale were decreed in consequence of the defect, it cannot afterwards be revoked, since a decree for dissolving a sale takes full effect, and continues in force, although an error should afterwards appear with respect to the defect pleade .—This is the doctrine of Haneefa: according to whom, also, an oath cannot be tendered to the purchaser, after the annulment of the sale, and the return of the subject of it, since it is then to no purpose.—In the opinion of the two disciples, also, the sale ought in this case to be annulled, and the subject of it returned, without a suspensio of it on the oath of the purchase, since (according to them) a reparation is practicable, even in this case, because, if an error should appear in the decree of the Kazee, in consequence of the constituent's refusal to swear, then the decree becomes null, and the subject of the sale is returned to the purchaser.—Some have said that, according to Aboo Yoosaf, the most authentic doctrine is that in both cases a suspension should take place;—that is to say, in the case of the debt, the payment to the agent ought to be deferred, and in the case in question the return of the subject of the sale to the agent of the buyer ought also to be deferred;—because he direct his attention to the interest of the seller (whence it is that if the purchaser should afterwards appear, an oath is exacted from him without the necessity of the seller's preferring a formal plea for it):—the return, therefore, of the article sold, by the purchaser's agent, is suspended, until the purchaser himself appear and make oath;—out of tenderness to the right of the seller.

A person receiving money, to appropriate to a particular purpose, may pay his own money in lieu of it.—IF a person give another ten dirms, in order that he may give them to the family of this person for their maintenance, and the agent, instead of the specific dirms he had received, give ten dirms of his own, this is not a gratuitous payment; on the contrary, he is entitled to retain the specific dirms he received in lieu of those he gave; because an agent for the delivery of maintenance is like an agent for purchase; and such is the law, as has been already related, in treating of an agent for purchase.

CHAPTER IV,

OF THE DISMISSION OF AGENTS.

A constituent may dismiss his agent at pleasure; except where the right of another person is concerned—IT is lawful for a constituent to dismiss his agent, because the agency being his right, he may consequently, if he please, annul it: excepting, however, when the right of another is interwoven with it; as where the agent is an agent for litigation, appointed at the request of the plaintiff, in which case the constituent (who is the defendant) cannot dismiss the said agent, because of the connexion of the right of the plaintiff, since, if he should dismiss him, the right of the plaintiff would be set at nought. The agency in this instance, therefore, resembles agency interwoven with a contract of pawnage, by the pawner, at the time of settling the contract of pawnage, appointing a person his agent for the purpose of selling the pledge, and with the price so obtained discharging the debt due to the pawnholder; in which case, as the right of the pawn-holder is connected with the agency, it is in the power of the constituent to dismiss such an agent; and so also in the present instance

An agency continues in force, until the agent receives due notice of his dismission.—IF a constituent dismiss his agent, and the agent should not receive any intelligence of it, his agency continues in force until he be apprised of his dismission; and all his acts until then are binding, as his dismission is a detriment to him; because it annuls his power of action; and also, because the rights of contracts of purchase and sale appertain and result to him; and accordingly, an agent for purchase does himself pay the price from the estate of the constituent and an agent for sale delivers the subject of the sale to the purchaser; if, therefore, the dismission were to operate instantaneously, without his intelligence, and he should, under these circumstances, either make a payment of the price, or delivery of the goods, he must, in such case, become responsible, which is an injury to him.—It is to be observed that agents for marriage, or the like, are in this respect considered in the same light.—A question has been started whether it is requisite that the notification of the dismission of an agent be made by two men, or by one upright man: but as the law, on this head, has already been laid down in treating of the duties of the Kazee (under the head to Decrees relative to Inheritance), it is here unnecessary to repeat it

A commission of agency is annulled by the death, confirmed lunacy, or apostacy of the constituent.—IF a constituent die, or becomes an absolute idiot, or having apostatized, be united to a hostile country, in all these cases the commission of his agent becomes null; because a commission of agency is not a thing of an absolute or irrevocable nature, since it is in the power of the constituent, without the consent of the agent, to dismiss him; and such being the case, it necessarily follows that the existence of it must depend on the existence of the power which created it originally, as it is requisite that the constituent should, during every moment of its existence, continue to possess the same power or capacity with respect to its formation, as he did at the beginning;—and this power or capacity ceases in consequence of the above-mentioned accidents.—The absolute idiotism here mentioned is conditioned by Kadoore, as a small degree of it stands only as a temporary deprivation of sense.—The limit of absolute idiotism, according to Aboo Yoosaf, is fixed at one month, since by that space of lunacy the duty of fasting is remitted.—It is also related, as an opinion of Aboo Yoosaf, that its limit is more than one night and one day, since by that space of idiotism the observance of the five stated prayers is remitted,—whence it is that an idiot in that degree is considered as defunct —Mohammed has said that the limit ought to be extended to a complete year, since in that space of time idiotism occasions the omission of all the religious duties prescribed to a Mussulman; and that, therefore, from a principle of caution, it ought to be extended to that period.—With respect to the expression "or having apostatized, be united to a hostile country" (as mentioned in this case), lawyers observe that it is the doctrine of Haneefa; because, according to him, all the acts of a person who simply apostatizes remain suspended: if, therefore, he afterwards repent, and return to the faith, his acts (and consequently his commission of agency) are confirmed; but if he be either put to death on account of his apostacy; or fly to the infidels, his acts are rendered void, and his commission of agency is annulled.—In the opinion of the two disciples, on the other hand, the acts of an apostate are valid, and therefore his commission of agency is not annulled, unless in case of his dying, or being put to death, or being expatriated, by a decree of the Kazee.

But not by apostasy if the constituent be a woman.—If the constituent be a woman; and apostatize, her constitution of agency nevertheless, remains binding until her death, or until her removal to an infidel country, because it has been determined that the apostacy of a woman has no effect on her contracts, such as sale, or the like.

Cases in which an appointment of agency by a Mokatib, a Mazoon, or a copartner, are annulled.—If a Mokatib appoint an agent, and afterwards become incapable of discharging his ransom,—or, if a privileged slave appoint an agent, and afterwards be laid under restriction,—or, if one of two partners appoint an agent, and the partners should afterwards separate and dissolve their partnership, in all these cases the agency becomes null, whether the agent may or may not have received intelligence of these supervenient circumstances (such as the incapability of the Mokatib, and so forth), for the reason already assigned, that "the continuance of agency depends on the continual existence of the power and capacity of the constituent to create it;" which power discontinues in consequence of any of the above circumstances. Now this reason obtains in either case (that is, whether the agent be informed of these circumstances, or not): in either case, therefore, the agency is annulled.—The reason of this that the dismission of the agents is a dismission by effect and of necessity, and therefore does not rest upon his knowledge;—in the same manner (for instance) as an agent for sale is dismissed when the thing is sold by the constituent; in which case the agency necessarily ceases, as the subject of it no longer remains.

A commission of agency is annulled by the death or lunacy of the agent.—If an agent should die, or become an absolute idiot; the agency ceases; because the continuance of agency stands on the same ground as its commencement; and as, at the commencement, it is requisite that the agent be capable of executing the orders of his constituent, it follows that the continuance of this capacity is a condition of the continuance of the agency; and this capability ceases in the present instance, in consequence of the death or idiotism.

Or, by his apostacy and flight to a hostile country.—In the same manner also, if an agent apostatize and go to an infidel country, his acts are not binding; unless he again become a Mussulman, and return, in which case the agency reverts to him.—The author of this work observes that this is according to Mohammed; but that, according to Aboo Yoosaf, the agency does not revert, notwithstanding the agent's returning to the faith and to his country.—The argument of Mohammed is that a commission of agency is a latitude, or endowment with power of action as it is the renewal of the her to such power which would otherwise oppose itself Now the agent's power of action, so far as merely regards himself, rests upon the existence in him of certain qualities, namely rationality, freedom, and maturity of years; and he has been rendered incapable of exerting that power merely by a supervenient circumstance (namely, his desertion to a hostile country); when, therefore, the cause of this disability is removed, if the latitude still continue in force, he again becomes an agent, as before. The reasoning of Aboo Yoosaf is that a commission of agency is an investitute with a power of passing;—in other words, the agent, in virtue of his commission, is possessed of a power of passing his acts, so that they shall be binding upon another, namely, his constituent: in short, in virtue of his appointment, he is invested with the power of passing his acts, but not with the power of performing those acts, as this power he possessed in virtue of his natural competency.—Now the power of passing acts, or, in other words, agency, ceases on apostacy and desertion to a hostile territory, as these circumstances are held to be the same as the death of a Mussulman; and it does not afterwards revive on the agent's again becoming a Mussulman, and returning to the abode of the Mussulmans; in the same manner as (in such a case) the property in an Am-Walid or a Modabbir does not revive; in other words; if a master apostatize and go to the abode of the infidels, his Modabbirs and Am-Walids become free, and his property in them does not revive in case of his returning to his faith and his country.

Agency is not renewed by the repentance and return of an apostate constituent.—If a constituent become a Mussulman, and return to the country of the Mussulmans, after having apostatized and gone off to a hostile country, the power of his agent, which had been annulled, does not in that case revive, according to the Zahir Rawayet. Mohammed is of opinion that the agency revives, in the same manner as in the preceding case of the apostacy of the agent.—The reason for the distinction (according to the Zahir-Rawayet) between the case of an apostate constituent and an apostate agent is, that the foundation of agency, with respect to a constituent, is property, which becomes null in consequence of apostacy; but the foundation of it, with respect to an agent, is rationality, freedom, skill, and maturity of years, circumstances which are not extinguished by apostacy.

Agency for any particular act is annulled by the constituent himself performing that act.—If a person appoint another his agent for any particular concern, and afterwards execute that concern himself, the agency in such case becomes null.—This case admits of a variety of modes; as where, for instance, a person appoints an agent to emancipate his slave, or to make him a Mokatib, and he afterwards himself emancipates, or makes a Mokatib of, the slave,—or, where a person appoints an agent for the contracting of marriage between him and a particular woman, and he himself afterwards concludes the contract,—or, where a person appoints another his agent for the purchase of a specific article, and he himself afterwards purchases that article,—or, where a person appoints a person to divorce his wife, and he himself afterwards divorces her three times (or divorces her one time, and her edit expires),—or, where a person appoints an agent to conclude a Khoola with his wife, and he afterwards concludes the Khoola with her;—for in all these cases the agency (because of its impracticability in consequence of the anticipation of the constituent in the performance of these acts) is null; into much that, in the case of marriage, if the constituent should afterwards irrevocably divorce the woman he had so married, it would not then be lawful for the agent to contract a marriage with her in behalf of the constituent, because the object of the constituent, in the agency, had been already obtained, and the necessity of it, of consequence, no longer existed. (It is otherwise, however, where the agent contracts the woman, and afterwards divorces her in behalf of the constituent; because, in this instance, the constituent's object in the agency has not been obtained, and consequently the necessity for it still exists.)

An agency dissolved by any act of the constituent cannot afterwards revive.—If a person appoint another his agent for the sale of a slave, and afterwards sell that slave himself, and the purchaser return the slave to him, in consequence of a decree of the Kazee, founded on the proof of a defect, it is related as an opinion of Aboo Yoosaf, that the agent is not then entitled to sell the said slave, because the constituent in selling him himself, did virtually prohibit the agent from executing the deed, and it consequently becomes the same as if he had dismissed him.—Mohammed, on the other hand, alleges that the agent may in this case resell him, because the agency still exists, since (according to him) agency is the licensing of action.—It is otherwise where a person appoints an agent for executing a gift, and afterwards makes the gift himself, and again retracts it; for in this case it is not lawful for the agent to make the gift, since the voluntary retraction of it by the constituent did clearly indicate his wish that it should not take place: in opposition to the case of the return of the subject of a sale founded on a decree of the Kazee to the constituent, because there the constituent acts from necessity in the receiving of it; and there exists of course no argument to show that he does not wish the sale to take place: when, therefore, the subject of the sale, in consequence of being returned, becoms completely his property, the agent is entitled to resell it.

BOOK XXIV.

OF DAWEE OR CLAIMS,

CHAPTER I.

Distinction between plaintiff and defendant.—The Moodaa, or plaintiff, is a person who, if he should voluntarily relinquish his claim, cannot be compelled to prosecute it; and the Moodaa-ali-hee, or defendant, is a person who, if he should wish to avoid the litigation, is compellable to sustain it.—Some have defined a plaintiff, with respect to any article of property, to be a person who, from his being disseised of the said article, has no right to it but by the establishmenr of proof; and a defendant to be a person who has a plea of right to that article from his seisin or possession of it. Mohammed, in the Mabsoot, has said that a defendant is a person who denies.—This is correct: but it requires a skill and knowledge of jurisprudence to distinguish the denier in a suit; as the reality and not the appearance is efficient; and it frequently happens that a person is in appearance the plaintiff, whilst in reality he is the defendant. Thus a trustee, when he says to the owner of the deposit, "I have restored to you your deposit," appears to be plaintiff, inasmuch as he pleads the return of the deposit; yet in reality he is the defendant, since he denies the obligation of responsibility; and hence his assertion, corroborated by an oath, must be credited.

A plaintiff must particularly state the subject of his claim.—No claim is admissible unless the plaintiff explain the species and quantity of the article which is the object of it; because the end of a claim is, upon the establishment of the proof, to obtain a decree of the Kazee for rendering the matter obligatory upon the defendant: but no obligation can take place with respect to a matter of uncertainty.

Which (if, be moveable property) must be produced in court.—IF, therefore, the article be still existing, and in the possession of the defendant, he is required to produce it in the court of the Kazee, in order that the plaintiff may pointedly refer to it in the exhibition of his claim. In the same manner, the production of it is necessary at the time of the delivery of testimony, or of the administration of an oath to the defendant; because on these occasions the greatest possible degree of certainty and knowledge is requisite; and this is best answered by a pointed reference with respect to moveable property, such as may be brought into the court of the Kazee, since a pointed reference most completely ascertains and determines any thing.

The defendant must appear, to answer to a valid claim.—WHEN the claim of the plaintiff is of a valid nature, the appearance of the defendant is necessary. This practice has been followed by Kazee in all ages.—It is, moreover, incumbent on the defendant to give a reply to the plea, when he is present, in order that the object of his presence may be answered.

And must produce the subject of it.—IT is also necessary to produce the subject of the claim, for the reason already stated.—It is likewise incumbent on the defendant, in case of his denial, to take an oath, as shall be explained in the latter part of this chapter.

Or the value of it must be specified.—IF the subject of the claim be not present, a bare explanation of the quality of it is not sufficient; for it is indispensable, in this case that the value be specified, in order that the subject of the claim may be fully ascertained; because the substance of an entity is known by an explanation of its value, and not by that of its quality, since many individuals of that genus may partake of the same qualities; and as an actual sight of the article is, in this instance, unattainable, an explanation of the value is accepted in the place of a pointed reference to it.—(The lawyer Aboo Leys has said that to an explanation of the value ought to be added that of the gender.)

Or (if the object consist of land) the plaintiff must define the boundaries, &c., and must make an explicit demand of it.—IF the claim relate to land, or other immoveable property, it is requisite that the plaintiff define the boundaries, and say "that land is in the possession of the defendant, and I claim it from him;"—because such property cannot be described by a pointed reference, as it is utterly impossible to produce it in the assembly of the Kazee; a definition of the boundaries therefore suffices, as immoveable property may be ascertained by such a definition.—It is necessary to define the four boundaries, and to specify the proprietors of each, adding a description of their family, in which is required to go at least as far back as the grandfather,—since (in the opinion of Haneefa) a knowledge of the grandfather is essential to the complete description of a family: and this is approved. If, however, the proprietor of the boumdary be a person of notoriety, the simple mention of him is sufficient.—If, also, only three of the boundaries be defined, it is sufficient, according to our doctors (contrary to the opinion of Ziffer);—because a definition is in this case made of a majority of them; and the majority is equivalent, in effect, to the whole.—It is otherwise where all the four boundaries are mentioned, and there happens to be a mistake with respect to one of the four; for in this case the claim is falsified: in opposition to the case where a definition of one of them is omitted, as that does not induce a falsification of the claim.—(It is to be observed that, in the same manner as a definition of the boundaries is requisite in a claim regarding immoveable property, so is it also requisite in giving evidence.)—With respect to what was before advanced, that the plaintiff must say "that land is in the possession of the defendant, &c," this is indispensably requisite; because the defendant is not liable to the suit, unless he be possessed of the land. As, however, the assertion of the plaintiff and the verification of the defendant is not alone sufficient to prove this, it is requisite that the plaintiff prove the possession of the defendant by the evidence of witnesses, or that the Kazee be himself acquainted with the circumstance. This is approved: because in the assertion of the plaintiff and the verification of the defendant there is room for suspicion, since it is still possible that the land may be in the possession of another, and that they may have agreed in its being in the possession of the defendants, to induce the Kazee to pass a decree.—It is otherwise with respect to moveable property, because the seisin of the possessor being, in that case, determinable by sight, there is no necessity for proof by means of witnesses.—With respect to the plaintiff's saying. "I claim it from the defendant," this is also indispensably requisite; because to demand it is his right, and the demand must therefore be made; and also because it is possible that the land may be in the possession of the defendant in virtue of pawnage,—or detention after a sale of it. to answer the price,—and this apprehension is removed by the claim of it.—Lawyers have observed that because of the above possibility, it is requisite, in a case of moveable property, that the plaintiff declare that the thing is unjustly in the possession of the defendant,

A claim for debt requires only the claim.—IF the claim relate to debt, it is sufficient for the plaintiff to say, "I claim it." For as the person on whom the obligation rests is himself present, there remains only the claim of it; and this it is incumbent on the plaintiff to make, because it is his right, and also, because, until he himself claim it, the Kazee can take no notice of it.

And a description of the species and amount.—IT is, however, necessary that he explain whether it consist of dirms or deenars, and whether it be gold or silver, as such explanation defines the debt.

Process to be observed by the Kazee.—WHAT has now been mentioned is an explanation of the validity of claims. It is to be observed that where the claim of a plaintiff is valid, the Kazee must interrogate the defendant, and ask him "whether the plea be true or not ?" If he acknowledge the truth of it, then the Kazee must pass a decree. founded upon his acknowledgment, because acknowledgment does in itself produce the effect: the Kazee must, therefore, order the defendant to give up the possession of the article concerning which he has made the acknowledgment, and to deliver it to the plaintiff —If, on the other hand, the defendant deny the truth of the allegation, the Kazee must require the plaintiff to produce evidence, because the Prophet, in a case where a defendant objected to the allegation, said first to the plantiff; "have you evidence ?" and on his answering in the negative, he then said, "it belongs to you to demand an oath from the defendant" Now it appears from this tradition, that the right of demanding an oath from the defendant rests upon the defect of evidence on the part of the plaintiff; and hence it is requisite first to demand the evidence of the plaintiff and on his making known his inability to produce it, to demand an oath from the defendant.—If, therefore the plaintiff produce evidence in attestation of his claim, the Kazee must pass a decree in his favour, as in that case there cannot be any suspicion of falsify. If, on the other hand, he be unable to produce evidence, and demand the defendant to be put to his oath, in that case the Kazee (because of the tradition above quoted) must administer an oath to him, The damand of the plaintiff, however, is requisite to the exaction of the oath, as it is high right.

CHAPTER II.

OF OATHS

An oath must not be required of the defendant when the plaintiff's witnesses (although not immediately present) are within call.—IF a plaintiff declare that "his witnesses are present in the city, but not in the court of the Kazee." and should nevertheless demand an oath from the defendant, in that case (according to Haneefa) the defendant must not be required to take the oath. Aboo Yoosif alleges that an oath must, in this case, be exacted from the defendant; because it is established, by the tradition before cited. than an oath is the right of the plaintiff; and it must consequently be granted to him in case of his demanding it The reasoning of Haneefa is that that the establishment of a right in the plaintiff to exact an oath from the defendant is founded on the supposition of his inability to produce evidence, as is expressly declared in the above-mentioned tradition —Hence until his inability to produce evidence be made apparent, his right does not take place, any more than if the witnesses were present in the court of the Kazee The opinion of Mohammad (as reported by Khasaf) coincides with that of Aboo Yoosaf: according, however, to a report of Tahavee, it coincides with that of Haneefa.

An oath cannot be exacted from the plaintiff.—AN oath cannot be exacted from the plaintiff, because of the saying recorded in the traditions of the Prophet, "evidence is incumbent on the part of the APPLICANT, and an oath on that of the RESPONDENT;" from which it is evident that an oath is not in any shape incumbent on the plaintiff, otherwise the necessity of it would not have been restricted to the respondent or defendant.—(Shafei, however, dissents from this doctrine).

The evidence adduced on the part of the plaintiff must be preferred to that adduced on the part of the defendant.—IF both the actual possessor [of the property] and the plaintiff should adduce evidence in support of their absolute right of property, in this case the evidence of the person in possession must be rejected and that of the plaintiff admitted. Shafei maintains that the evidence of the possessor must be admitted, and a decree passed in his favour; because the evidence is corroborated by the possession, and is consequently strong and apparent; it ought therefore to be preferred in the same manner as evidence in favour of the possessor is preferred in cases of birth, marriage, or a claim to a slave that has been emancipated, or that has become an Am-Walid, or been constituted a Modabbir; in other words, if two persons should severally assert that a particular horse, in the possession of one of them, was the offspring of a horse belonging to him; and if each should bring evidence in support of his assertion, in that case the evidence of the possessor would be preferred; and so also in the case of a contested wife who if in the possession of one of two claimants,—or in the case of a freedman, an Am-Waild, or Modabbir, who is in the possession of one of the two persons who claims the right of property. In reply to this reasoning of Shafei, our doctors argue that it is not the evidence adduced by the possessor which proves the absolute right of property, because the possession of itself indicates the absolute right and consequently anticipates the proof, which would else have resulted from the evidence. It is otherwise with respect to the evidence adduced by the person not in possession, because by that absolute right of property is proved; * and as the evidence on the part of the person not in possession occasions proof, it is therefore admitted, since as the purpose of evidence is to establish proof, the evidence which occasions proof must be preferred: It is to be observed that possession indicates a right of property absolutely, but not relatively, as in the cases adduced by Shafei: and hence the analogy conceived by him between these cases and the case in question is not just

The defendant refusing to swear, the Kazee must forthwith pass a decree against him.—IF the defendant refuse to take an oath in a case where it is incumbent upon him the Kazee must then pass a decree against him because of his refusal, and must tender obligatory upon him the object of the claim on behalf of the plaintiff. Shafei maintains that the Kazee must not pass a decree immediately on the refusal of the defendant, but must first administer an oath to the planitiff and then pass a decree against the defendant; because the refusal to take an oath admits of three different constructions:—I. It may proceed from a desire to avoid a false oath;—II. It may proceed from an unwillingness to take an oath, although, in testimony of the truth, form an opinion of its being derogatory to the deponent's character; and III. It may proceed from a doubt and uncertainty whether the matter be true or false;—and as the refusal to take an oath is a matter of uncertainty, it cannot amount to proof (since anything of an uncertain nature is incapable of constituting proof); and as the oath of the plaintiff manifests the right, recourse must therefore be had to that. The arguments of our doctors, on the other hand, are that the refusal of the plaintiff to take an oath, indicates either a concession of the thing claimed, or an acknowledgment of the validity of the claim; since, if the case were otherwise, he could have no motive to refuse an oath when the maintenance of his right depended upon it. Besides, there are no grounds on which an oath can be tendered to a plaintiff, since the tradition before mentioned expressly evinces that an oath is restricted to the defendant,

The Kazee must give three separate notifications to the defendant.—IT is incumbent on the Kazee to give three notifications to the defendant, by three times repeating to him, "I tender you an oath; which if you take. it is well; if not, I will pass a decree in favour of the claimant,"—This threefold repetition is required because of the want of certainty in case of refusal to take an oath, since there aubsists a disagreement with regard to the validity of passing a sentence upon it.—The necessity of the repetition has been recited by Khasaf, as from a principle of caution, and to cut off the defendant from any further preference).—It is indeed, an established tenet, that if a decree be passed on one notification only, it is valid; and this is approved doctrine,—It is most laudable, however, to give three notifications.

Refusal to swear is of two kinds, real and virtual.—A REFUSAL to take an oath is of two kinds: I, real (where the defendant expressly says, "I will not take an oath"): and, II virtual (where he remains silent), —The effect in this latter case is the same as in the former, provided it be known that the person refusing is neither deaf nor dumb. This is approved doctrine.

An oath cannot be exacted from the defendant in claims respecting marriage, divorce, Aila, bondage, Willa, punishment, or Laan.—IF a man claim marriage with a woman, or a woman with a man, and the defendant in either case deny the claim, then (according to Haneefa) it is not necessary to exact an oath,—The law is the same (according to Haneefa) with respect to a claim of reversal [after divorce], or of rescindment in a case of Aila,—or a claim of servitude, or a claim of offsping, or claim of lineage, Willa, punishment, and Laan. Thus if, in a case of divorce, the wife, after the expiration of her edit, were to advance a plea of reversal against her husband, or the husband to advance a plea of reversal against his wife, and the defendant should, in either case, deny the claim,—or if, in a case of Aila, either of the parties were to plead a rescindment from the vow, and the other to deny it,—or, if a person were to claim the right of slavery to another whose condition is unknown, or he whose condition is unknown claim his being the slave of that other, and the defendant in either case deny the claim. —or, if a female slave were to plead her being an Am-Walid to a particular man, and that a certain person is their offspring, and the man himself deny it,*—or, if a

* As it is not anticipated by any other circumstance, and consequently must be admitted.

* This case does not, like all the rest, hold true when the terms of its are reversed; for in case the claim should have been made on the part of the man, it is considered as an acknowledgment, and the denial of the woman is then of no effect.

person were to plead that another of unknown birth is his son, or that other plead that this person is his father, and the defendant in either case deny the claim,—or, if a person were to plead that another of known condition had been emancipated by him and that he therefore possesses the right of Willa over him, or that other plead that he had been emancipated by him and the defendant, in either case, deny the claim,—or, if a person were to plead that another had committed whoredom, and that other deny it —or, lastly, if a wife should plead that her husband had slandered her,—in all these cases it is not necessary (according to Haneefa) to exact an oath from the defendant.—The two disciples maintain that it is requisite to exact an oath from the defendant in all these cases, excepting in the cases of punishment or of the Laan;—for they argue that a refusal to take an oath amounts to an acknowledgment, as such refusal is an argument that the party is false in his denial: a refusal to take an oath is, therefore, an acknowledgment either in reality or in effect; and acknowledgments are admitted in all the above cases. This species of acknowledgment, however, is of a doubtful nature, as it is not a perfectly valid acknowledgment; and punishment is remitted in consequence of any doubt; and as Laan is also punishment in effect, they hold that, in that instance also, an oath cannot be imposed.—The reasoning of Haneefa is that a refusal to take an oath amounts to a concession of the object to the plaintiff; after such refusal. therefore, it remains unnecessary to exact oath, because of the attainment of the object independent of it,—(it is most laudable to consider the refusal to swear in the light of a grant of concession, as it avoids the consequence of the defendant falsifying in his denial).—Now as a refusal to take an oath is shown to be a concession of the thing in dispute, it follows that such refusal can have no effect in the above cases, since they are not of such a nature as admit of concession: an oath, therefore, is not exacted from the defendant in such cases; because the advantage proposed, in exacting an oath, is to enable the Kazee to pass a decree in consequence of the refusal; and this advantage cannot be obtained in such cases.

Objection.—If a refusal to take an oath be equivalent to a concession, the refusal of a Maketib, or of a privileged slave, ought not to be admitted, since neither of these is competent to make a concession.

Reply.—A refusal to take an oath is considered as a concession, in order to remedy the evil of contention: the refusal of Mokatibs and privileged slaves is therefore admitted.

Objection.—If a refusal to take an oath be a concession, it ought not to be admitted in claims of debt, since the subject of a gift must necessarily be substance, whereas a debt relates [illegible] to quality.

Reply.—The validity of a concession of this nature, in cases of debt, is admitted in conformity with the conception of the plaintiff; for he conceives the thing he receives to be that actual thing to which he is entitled. Besides, concession, in this instance, merely means a cessation of obstruction; that is to say, the defendant does not obstruct the plaintiff from taking his property, and he accordingly takes it, as property is a matter of but light concern.—It is otherwise with respect to the particulars before mentioned, as these are not matters of light concern, and hence it is not lawful for the defendant to make a gift of them.

A thief refusing to swear, becomes liable for the properey stolen.—An oath must be exacted from a thief; and if he should refuse to take it, he becomes liable for the property, but does not subject himself to the penalty, of amputation; because his act involves two consequences, namely, responsibility for the property, and the loss of his hand; and as his refusal establishes the first consequence, but not the second, it is therefore the same as if the fact had been proved by one man and two women, in which case a responsibility for the property takes place, but not a loss of the hand.

A claim founded on divorce before consummation entitles a wife to her half dower, where the husband declines swearing.—If a wife advance a claim against her husband, by asserting that he had divorced her previous to consummation, an oath must be tendered to the husband, and if he refuse to take it, he becomes responsible for her half dower, according to all our doctors, because (according to them), oaths are admitted in cases relative to divorce, and particularly where the object is property.—In the same manner also, oaths are admitted in cases of marriage, where the wife claims her dower, as this is claim relative to property, which is established by a refusal to take an oath, though the marriage be not thereby proved.—In the same manner also, oathes are administered in claims of parentage, where the claim relates to some right, such as inheritance or maintenance (as where a disabled person claims that he is the brother of another, and that his maintenance is incumbent upon that other, who denies the same).—In cases also of invalid recessions from gifts (as where, a person wishing to retrac his gift, the grantee asserts that he is hi brother, and that, on account of such relation he has no right to retract,—and the granter denies the same),—an oath is tendered to the defendant, as the objects o them are the rights alluded to.

Please of consanguinity admit of an oatl being tendered to the defendant.—An oath i not tendered, according to the two disciple in simple cases of consanguinity, unless where the relation is of such a nature as t be established by the acknowledgment of th defendant; as where a person, for instance asserts that another person is his father, o his son,—or a woman asserts that a certain person is her father,—or a man or woman claims a right of Willa, or a man or woman claims marriage,—in which cases, if the defendant acknowledge the relationship, the Willa, or the marriage, they are established accordingly; and if the defendant refuse to make oath, this (according to the two disciples) is equivalent to acknowledgment. It is otherwise where a woman alleges that a certain person is her son, because in that case the relationship depends on another, and therefore, as the acknowledment of the defendant can have no effect, so neither will his refusal to take an oath.

Case of a claim of retaliation,—IF a person claim a right of retaliation upon another, and the defendant deny it, in this case (in the opinion of all our doctors) an oath must be administered to him.—If he refuse to take it, and the retaliation relate to the membere of the body, he must in that case suffer retaliation; but if it relate to murder, he must be imprisoned until he either confess or take an oath of exculpation,—This is according to Haneefa.—The two disciples are of opinion that in either case a fine must be imposed; because, although (according to their doctrine) a refusal to take an oath is an acknowledgment, yet it is attended with a degree of doubt (as has been already explained); and consequently cannot establish retaliation:—a fine of property is therefore due; especially where the bar to the retaliation arises from a circumstance on the part of the person who is liable to the retaliation; as when the avenger of blood claims for witful murder, and the defendant acknowledges erroneous murder. The argument of Haneefa is that the members of the body of a man are considered in the same light with property, and hence a concession with respect to them is admitted in the same manner as it is admitted in the case of property; for if a person should say to another. "cut off my hand," and that other accordingly cut it off. he would not be subject to any compensation, which clearly proves that the concession thereof is lawful, although it be not allowed to the man, in this instance, to cut off the hand,* as it is attended with no advantage to him.—In short, concessions are allowed with respect to parts of the body, but not with respect to the body itself; and as a refusal to swear, in cases of retaliation with respect to the parts of the body, is a concession of an advantageous nature (as being the means of terminating a contention), it follows that the cutting off the hand is advantageous in this instance, in the same manner as it is advantageous to amputate a limb in a case of mortification, or to draw a tooth in case of excessive pain.

Where the plaintiff's witness are within call. the defendant must give bail for his appearance for three days.—IF a plaintiff assert that "his witnesses are in the city, the defendant must, in that case, be required to give bail, answer for his appearance within the term of three days, lest he abscond; and thus the right of the plaintiff be destroyed:—and it is lawful thus to take bail for his appearance (according to our doctors), as has been already explained.—* The taking of bail from the defendant, in this instance, immediately on the preferment of the alleqation by the plaintiff, proceeds upon a favourable construction of the law, because of its being advantageous to the plaintiff, and not materially detrimental to the defendant: and the reason for taking it is that it is incumbent upon the defendant to make his appearance in court upon the instant of the claim (whence it is that a person is immediately despatched to summons him); and as this might prevent him from going on with any business in which he may be then employed, it is therefore lawful to take bail for his appearance.—The term of three days, as above mentioned, is recorded from Haneefa; and that term is approved.—In taking bail (according to the Zahir Rawayat) there is no difference between an unknown person and one of established note; nor between the claim of a large and of a small sum.

But if the witness be not within call, bail cannot be required from the defendant.—THE declaration of the plaintiff however that "his witnesses are in the city," is indispensable towards the taking of bail for appearance; and hence, if the plaintiff should say, "I have no witnesses,"—or, "my witnesses are absent from the city," bail is not in that case to be required from the defendant, as it is of no use.† If, therefore, the defendant, in this instance, upon being applied to, give bail for his appearance, it is well: but if he refuse, the Kazee must then direct the plaintiff to attend and watch over him, in order that his own right may not be destroyed: excepting, however, where the defendant may happen to be a traveller, or about to travel. for then the plaintiff is to watch over him only whilst in the court of the Kazee; and if he should take bail for his appearance under these circumstances, it must be extended only to the breaking up of the court of the Kazee; because if either the bail or the watching over him were extended to a longer period, it would occasion a detriment to the defendant, in as much as he would be prevented, during that space, from pursuing his journey: but where it is limited to the time of the sitting of the court, he is not subjected to any apparent incon-

*In other words, "to accept of the gift. or concession.,'

*See Bail, Vol. II. Book XVIII.

†Because the plaintiff, being destitute of witnesses, cannot possibly establish his claim.

venience.—The particulars of watching or attendance will be explained in treating of inhibition.

Section.

Of the Manner of Swearing, and requiring an Oath.

The oath must be taken in the name of God.—An oath is not worthy of credit unless it be taken in the name of God, because the Prophet has said "whoever takes an oath, let him take it in the name of God; otherwise let him omit the oath entirely:"—and also, because he has declared "whoever takes an oath otherwise than in the name of God is most certainly an Associator."*

And the Kazee must dictate the terms of it.—It is incumbent upon the Kazee to desire the swearer to corroborate his oath by reciting the attributes of God.—Thus he must direct him, for instance, to say, "I swear by the God than whom there is no other righteous God, who is acquainted with that is hidden and apparent, that neither by me, nor on my behalf, is the amount due to Omar which he claims, nor any part of it."—The Kazee is at liberty either to add or diminish from this oath as he pleases: but he must not so far extend his caution as to repeat the oath, because it is not necessary to swear more than once.—If a person should swear "by God, by the merciful, by the most merciful".—it is considered as three oaths: but if the two last particles of swearing be omitted it is then only one.—It is to be observed that the Kazee has the option either of adding the corroboration to the oath, or of omitting it, and simply desiring the defendant to swear "by God"—Some have said that it is improper to prescribe the corroboration to such as are known to be virtuous, but that to all others it is necessary.—Others, again, have said that the corroboration is necessary in claims to a great amount, but not where the amount is small.

Swearing by divorce or emancipation must not be admitted—A defendant mut not swear by divorce or emancipation (as if he should say, "if the claim preferred against me be just, my wife is divorced," or "my slave is emancipated"): because of the tradition before quoted.—Some, however, have said that, in our times, if the plaintiff should importunately require it, the Kazee may then administer to the defendant an oath by divorce or emancipation; since in this age there are many men who scruple not to swear by the name of God, but who are, nevertheless, averse from an oath by emancipation or divorce.

Jews must swear by the Pentateuch, and Christians by the Gospel.—The Kazee must administer an oath in a Jew, by directing him to say, "I swear by the God that revealed the Pentateuch to Moses;"—and to a Christian, by directing him to say, "I swear by the God that sent down the gospel of Jesus;"—because the Prophet, upon a certain occasion, administered an oath to a Jew, by saying to him, "I desire you to swear by the God that hath sent down the Pentateuch to Moses, that such is the law with regard to whoredom in your book;" and also, because the Jews believe in the divine mission of Moses, and the Christians in the divine mission of Jesus Christ.—In the administration of oaths to them, therefore, it is necessary to corroborate them, by a specification of the books which have been received through their respective prophets.

Pagans must swear by God.—The Kazee must administer an oath to a Majoosce by directing him to say "I swear by the God that created fire."—This is recorded, by Mohammed, in the Mabsoot; but it is related of Haneefa, in the Nawadir, that he never administered an oath otherwise than in the name of God—Khasaf, moreover, reports that Haneefa never gave an oath to any excepting Christians and Jews, otherwise than in the name of God, because in confounding fire with the name of God, a reverence is shown to it to which it is not entitled: contrary to the Old or New Testament, as these are the books of God, and therefore entitled to reverence. This doctrine has been adopted by several of our modern doctors.

An oath cannot be administered to an idolator otherwise than in the name of God, because all infidels believe in God, as is evident from this sentence of the Koran, "If ye ask of them (the infidels) who hath created you, verily they will answer, GOD ALMIGHTY."

Oaths must not be administered in an infidel place of worship.—An oath must not be administered to infidels in their place of worship, because the Kazee is prohibited from entering such a place.

The oaths of Mussulmans need not be corroborated by swearing them at a particular time, or in a particular place.—It is not necessary, in administering an oath to Mussulmans, to corroborate it by means of the time or place (such as by the administeration of it on a Friday, or in the mosque). because the object of an oath is a reverence to him in whose name it is taken, and this depends not on any particular time or placc.—Besides, if the corroboration of oaths to Mussulmans, by a restriction to time and place, were necessary, it would subject the Kazee to an inconvenience, in the necessity he would be under of attending at the particular time and place; and the law admits not of inconvenience, more especially where the fulfilment of right, or the execution of justice, does not depend upon it.

Cases in which the oath of the defendant must relate to the cause; and cases in which it must relate to the object.—If a person allege that he has bought a slave from

---

*Arab, Moosharik, meaning a Pagan, or Paolytheist.

another for a thousand dirms, and the seller deny the fact; in this case the seller must be required to swear, in the following manner, "I swear by God that there does not absolutely at present exist any contract of sale between me and the plaintiff;"—and not in this manner, "I swear by God that I have not sold, &c."—because it often happens that a sale is made, and afterwards an Akala, or dissolution of the contract, takes place.—In cases of usurpation it is necessary that the defendant swear, in the presence of the plaintiff, in this manner, "there is no part of that which you allege that I have usurped from you, due by me," and not "I have not usurped, &c,"—because an usurpation is often done away by the proprietor selling or making a gift of the thing to the usurper—In cases of marriage it is requisite that the defendant swear to this effect, no marriage does at this time subsist between me and the plaintiff;"—because a marriage is sometimes dissolved by Khoola.—In cases of divorce the husband must swear "this woman is not at present finally separated from me, by the divorce which she pleads:"—and not, in an absolute manner, that "he has not divorced her;"—because a new marriage sometimes takes place after a Talak Bayeen; or complete divorce.—Thus, in all these cases, the Kazee must swear the defendant with respect to the object of the plea, and not with respect to the cause of it; since, if he were to administer the oath with respect to the cause, it might be injurious to the defendant.—What is here advanced is conformable to the opinion of Haneefa and Mohammed.—Aboo Yoosaf is of opinion that, in all these cases, the Kazee must swear the defendant with respect to the cause (except where the defendant particularly requests the contrary); because sales, for instance, are sometimes made, and afterwards dissolved, divorces sometimes executed and afterwards succeeded by a marriage de novo; and usurpations sometimes done away by gift or sale:—in all these cases, therefore, the oath must be administered with respect to the object.—Some have said that the Kazee ought to be guided by the denial of the defendant:—in other words, if the defendant deny the cause, let the oath relate to the cause,—or, if he deny the effect, let the oath relate to the object.—It is to be observed that (according to Haneefa and Mohammed) the oath must in every instance relate to the object, where the cause is of such a nature as renders it liable to be done away by some other cause; excepting only where, in resting the oath upon the object, the tenderness due to the plaintiff is likely to be destroyed; for, in this case, the oath (according to all our doctors) must be rested upon the cause. Thus, if a wife, having been completely divorced, should prefer a claim of maintenance against her husband, and the husband should not think himself bound to comply, because of his being of the sect of Shafei,—or, if a proprietor of a house, or of land, should prefer a claim of pre-emption against the purchaser of a contiguous property on a plea of Shaffa, and the purchaser, being of the sect of Shafei, should not admit his claim,—in these cases (according to all our doctors) the oath ought to relate to the cause;—for, although the defendant could not deny, upon oath, the cause or circumstances of the case, still he might, upon oath, deny the object;—in other words, he might deny the validity of the claim as founded upon these circumstances; if, therefore, the oath were to relate to the object, it would evidently be injurious to the plaintiff.—If, on the other hand, the cause be of such a nature as canont be removed or done away by some other cause, in that case the defendant's oath (according to all our doctors) must relate to the cause.—Thus, if a Mussulman slave should plead his having been emancipated, and his master deny this, in that case (as the LAW does not admit of a Mussulman becoming a slave after having been once free) the oath tendered to the master must relate to the cause;—in other words, he must be required positively to swear "whether he has ever emancipated this slave, or not?"—It is otherwise, however, with respect to a female Mussulman slave, or an infidel male slave; because both of these may be again subjected to slavery after having been rendered free;—the female slave, by being first emancipated, and then apostatizing and being united to a hostile country;—and the male slave, by being first emancipated, and then breaking his contract of fealty, and being united to a hostile country.

In a case of inheritance, the oath of the defendant must relate to his knowledge.—If a person acquire a right to a slave by inheritance, and another prefer a claim of right to the said slave, in that case the oath of the defendant must relate to his knowledge;—that is, he must be required to swear that he does not know the slave in question to be the property of the plaintiff;—because not being acquainted with the acts of the person from whom the inheritance descends, he cannot absolutely swear that the slave is not the property of the plaintiff;—whereas, if he had acquired the slave by a gift or purchase, he could swear positively as to his right of property, since purchase and gift are both causes of a right of property.

When a defendant enters into a composition with the plaintiff, an oath cannot afterwards be exacted from him.—If a person prefer a claim against another, and the defendant deny it, but should afterwards give the plaintiff ten dirms, either as an expiation for his oath, or as a composition for it, such expiation or composition is valid; because it has been so related by Omar; and the plaintiff cannot afterwards demand an oath from the defendant, as having himself destroyed this right.

CHAPTER III.

TAHALIF ; OR THE SWEARING OF BOTH THE PLAINTIFF AND THE DEFENDANT.

A seller and purchaser are mutually to swear where they both disagree, and are destitute of evidence—If a seller and purchaser should disagree, the purchaser asserting that the price of the goods was an hundred dirms, and the seller, that it was more,—or, if the seller should acknowledge the article sold to be so much, and the purchaser assert that it was more,—in this case, if either of them adduce evidence in support of his assertion, the Kazee must pass a decree in his favour ; because attestation is stronger than simple assertion.—If, on the other hand, both of them should adduce evidence in support of their respective assertions, then the evidence of the party that attests most must be admitted ; because the object of evidence is proof ; and with respect to the excess, there is no opposition of evidence.—If the seller and purchaser should disagree with respect both to the price and the goods, then the evidence of the seller with respect to the price is preferable ; and the evidence of the purchaser is preferable with respect to the goods. If, however, both parties be destitute of evidence, then the Kazee must say to the purchaser "if you acquiesce in the price claimed by the seller, it is well : if not, I will dissolve the contract ; "—and to the seller, "if you are contented to yield the quantity of goods claimed by the purchaser, it is well ; if not, I will dissolve the contract ; "—because the object is to terminate the contention ; and it is probable that his thus addressing them may terminate the contention, since the parties may possibly be averse to breaking off the contract ; when, therefore, they perceive that if they do not agree, the contract will be broken, they may be content to make up their difference,—If, nevertheless, they should not even then agree, the Kazee must make each of them swear to his denial of the claim of the other.—This mutual swearing, before seisin of the article of sale, if conformable to analogy ; because the seller demands a large price, which the purchaser does not admit ; whilst, on the other hand, the purchaser demands from the seller the delivery of the goods at the rate of purchase money he has paid which the seller refuses to execute. Each, therefore, is a defendant ; and hence an oath must be required from each.—After the delivery of the goods to the purchaser, indeed, the mutual swearing would be contrary to analogy ; because the purchaser having received the goods has no further claim ; and as there remains only the claim of the seller for the excess of the price, an oath can only be exacted from the purchaser, who is the defendant, It appears, however, from an infallible guide, that an oath must, in this case also, be exacted from each, because the Prophet has said "Where a disagreement takes place between a buyer and seller, and the subject of the sale is extant and present, an oath must in that case be administered to each, and the purchaser must afterwards restore the goods to the seller, and the seller the price to the purchaser." It is to be observed that where it is necessary to administer an oath to both parties, the purchaser must be first sworn.—This doctrine is conformable to the most recent opinion of the two disciples ; and it is also agreeable to one report of Haneefa, It is also the most authentic doctrine ; because the denial of the purchaser is of the greatest importance, since the price is first demanded from him ; and also, because, in case of his refusal to take the oath, it would be attended with the immediate advantage of inducing the obligation upon him of the payment of the price ;—whereas, if the seller were first sworn, it would nevertheless be necessary to defer the demand upon him of a delivery of the goods until he had received payment of the price.—If the parties should disagree in a sale of goods for goods (that is to say, in a barter), or of price for price (that is, in a Sirf sale), in this case the Kazee is at liberty either to swear the seller or the purchaser first ; because in such a case the seller and purchaser are both upon an equal footing.

Formula of the oaths of a seller and purchaser —The nature of the oaths, in a disagreement between buyer and seller, is this.—The seller swears "by God, I have not sold the thing in question for a thousand dirms ;" and the purchaser swears "by God, I have not bought it for two thousand dirms. Mohammad, in the Zeedat, has said, "let the seller swear by God, I have not sold it for ONE thousand DIRMS, but for TWO thousand ;—and let the purchaser swear, by God, I have not bought it for TWO thousand DIRMS, but for ONE thousand."—In other words, the negation and affirmation ought to be coupled together for the greater caution—The most authentic doctrine, however, is that an oath of negation is sufficient ; because oaths proceed upon denial, as appears from the tradition concerning Kissamit* ; for it is related that the Prophet desired the people of Kissamit to swear that "by God, they had not committed the murder, and did not know the murderer."

Where both parties swear, the sale must be dissolved, by an order of the Kazee.—If the seller and purchaser, in a disgreement, should both take an oath, the Kazee must in that case dissolve the sale.—This is the adjudicatation of Muhammad : and it evinces that the sale is not of itself dissolved by the mutual swearing of the parties ; because, as the plea of neither party is established, a sale continues of an undefind nature ; and hence the Kazee must dissolve it, as well to terminate their contention, as because that

*The name of some Arabain district of tribe, where probably one of the Prophet's followers was murdered.

where the price is not established, a sale remains without a return; and this being an invalid sale most consequently be dissolved, since it is indispensably requisite that all invalid sales be dissolved.

A seller or purchaser, upon declining to swear, loses his cause.—IF, in a disagreement between a purchaser and a seller, one of the two decline swearing, the claim of the other is in that case established against him; because by such refusal the party concedes to the other the article claimed by him;—for as his plea is thus rendered incapable of controverting the plea of the other, it follows that he accedes to that plea.

The parties are not to be sworn where their disagreement relates to something not essential to their contract.—IF the parties should disagree with respect to the period fixed for the payment of the price, or with respect to the option of determination, or with respect to a partial payment that may have been made of the price,—in none of these cases are the parties to be sworn, because the disagreement, in this instance, relates to something not within the original scope of the contract. This disagreement, therefore, resembles a disagreement with respect to an abatement or remission of the price;—in other words, if a seller and purchaser should disagree with regard to a remission of part or the whole of the price, they would not in that case be sworn; and so also in the case in question.—The reason for what is here advanced is that the disagreement, in all of the supposed cases, relates to a thing which, if annihilated or done away, would not affect the existence of the contract of sale.—It is otherwise, however, where the disagreement relates to the species of the price (such as whether it is to consist of dirms of Bokhara or of Bagdad),—or with respect to the genus of it (such as whether it is to consist of dirms or of deenars), for such a disagreement is the same as if it related to the amount of the price,—in which case oaths are administered, for this reason, that the genus and species of the price are inseparable from the substance of it; because the price is a debt due by the purchaser; and a debt is only to be known and ascertained by a definition of its genus and species. The period fixed for the payment of the price, on the contrary, is not of this nature, as it is not a species of it, whence it is that the price continues extant and firm after the promised time of payment has elapsed.

In dispute respecting any superadded stipulation, the assertion of the respondent must be credited.—IF a disagreement take place between a seller and purchaser with respect to the condition of option, or the period of payment, the assertion of the respondent* supported by an oath, must be credited; because optional conditons, and extensions of the period of payment, are accidents in a sale;* and with regard to accidents, the assertion of the respondent must be credited in preference.

The parties are not to be sworn, where the goods perish in the hands of the purchaser.—IF, after the destruction of the subject of a sale, in the hands of the purchaser, a disagreement should take place between the purchaser and the seller respecting the amount of the price, the parties, in that case (according to Haneefa and Aboo Yoosaf), are not to be sworn; but the assertion of the purchaser must be credited.—Mohammed alleges that, in this case, the parties must be both sworn, and afterwards the sale dissolved, in return for the value of the subject of it which had been destroyed;—that is to say, the purchaser must pay the value of the goods to the seller, who must return to the purchaser the price of them.—Such, also, is the doctrine of Shafei.—The same difference of opinion obtains in cases where the subject of the sale has been removed from the property of the purchaser by gift or the like, or where it is in such a condition as would preclude the return of it in case of a defect.—The reasoning of Mohammed and Shafei, in support of their opinions, is that each party pleads the existence of a contract, different from what is claimed by the other; and each of them, consequently, denies the assertion of the other.

OBJECTION.—The advantage of administering an oath to each of the parties is that the sale is thereby dissolved, and the goods returned by the purchaser to the seller, and the price by the seller to the purchaser.—Now this object cannot be obtained after the destruction of the subject of the sale, and therefore there can be no advantage in the doctrine of Mohammed, of swearing both parties under such circumstances.

REPLY.—The advantage is that it relieves the purchaser from the excess of the price, in case the seller should refuse to take an oath,—as, in the same manner, it obliges the purchaser to pay such excess, in case he himself should refuse to take an oath.

THEY must therefore both be sworn, in the same manner as when, after the destruction of the subject of the sale, they disagree with regard to the genus of the price (that is, whether it consist of dirms or deenars: and after swearing, the purchaser must give the value of the goods to the seller, and the seller must return the price to the purchaser. The arguments of Haneefa and Aboo Yoosaf, in support of their doctrine upon this point, are twofold.—FIRST, the swearing of both parties, after delivery of the goods, is repugnant to analogy; because the purchaser has in

* Arab. Moonkir,—meaning, the person who denies.

* That is, are superadded to the contract.

this case, received whole and complete the thing which he claims : the swearing of both parties more over is ordained by the LAW in cases only where the subject of the sale is extant and complete, to the end that the sale may be dissolved , but this cannot be conceived in a case where the subject of the sale has perished ; swearing the parties, therefore, after a destruction of the property is not that mutual swearing expressed in the LAW.—SECONDLY, in the case in question the object of the sale (namely, the complete acquisition of the goods by the purchaser) is obtained ; and after the completion of the object, a disagreement with respect to the instrument (that is, the contract of sale) is of no importance.—Moreover, the advantage set forth by Mohammed is of no account ; since no advantages are attended to excepting such as are occasioned by the contract of sale ; and the advantage in question is not occasioned by the contract.—All that is here advanced proceeds on a supposition that the price is a money debt.—If, however, it consist of any specific article, such as cloth for instance, both the parties are to be sworn, according to all our doctors ; because, in this case, a subject of sale still exists (since the price, where it consists of any thing specific, may be considered as the subject) ; and upon both parties swearing, the sale must be dissolved ; and the seller must return the price to the purchaser: and the purchaser must give a similar in lieu of the subject of the sale to the seller, provided it was of that kind of thing compensable by similars ; or, if otherwise, he must pay the value.

Case of a dispute concerning the price of two slaves, where one of them dies.—IF a person purchase two slaves by one contract, and one of them be afterwards destroyed, and a dispute arise betwixt the parties concerning the amount of the price, the seller asserting that it was two thousand dirms, and the purchaser asserting that it was one thousand, in this case (according to Haneefa) the parties are not to be sworn ; on the contrary, the assertion of the purchaser must be credited. This, however, proceeds on the supposition of the seller being unwilling to receive the price of the living slave only, and to relinquish the price of the slave that is dead.—In the Jama Sagheer it is related that, according to Haneefa, the assertion of the purchaser is to be credited unless the seller be willing to accept of the price of the living slave only.—Aboo Yoosaf alleges that both parties must be sworn with regard to the living slave ;—that the sale, so far as relates to him, must be dissolved ;—that the assertion of the purchaser must be credited with respect to the dead slave ;—and that, therefore, the purchaser is responsible for the proportion of the dead slave, and not for the whole price.—Mohammed, on the other hand, maintains that both parties must be sworn with regard to both slaves ; and that afterwards the purchaser must return the living slave and the value of the dead one; because, as (in his opinion) the destruction of the whole subject of sale does not prevent the swearing of both parties, it follows that the destruction of a part only does not prevent it, a fortiori.—The reasoning of Aboo Yoosaf is that as the obstacle to the swearing of both is grounded only on the destruction of the subject of the sale, it ought of course to operate only in the degree in which it may have been destroyed.—The reasoning of Haneefa is that the swearing of both parties, although repugnant to analogy, is yet established by the LAW, in cases where the subject of the sale still completely exists: but where a part of the subject is destroyed, it does not completely exist ; because the complete existence of it supposes the existence of the whole ; and the whole cannot exist but by the preservation of all its parts.—If, on the other hand, both parties should swear with respect to the living slave only, it is evident that this cannot be effected, but by a reference to his particular value.—Now as both slaves are included under one price, the particular value of each cannot be known but by conjecture ; and hence it appears that the swearing of both parties, under such circumstances, must be referred to something uncertain ; and this is illegal.—If, however, the seller be willing to relinquish his right to the destroyed slave, and to consider him as having never existed, both parties may, in that case, be sworn as to their denial of the claim of the other, respecting the whole price of both the slaves; because the whole of the price is then opposed to the living slave, from the concession of the seller to take the living slave only in lieu of the whole of the price, and to consider the dead slave as excluded from the contract.—What is here advanced is agreeable to the exposition of several of our modern doctors. They have also explained the meaning of the sentence, in the Jama Sagheer, to be that the seller shall not absolutely receive anything for the dead slave ; and they have connected the exception with the omission of swearing of the parties.—Others of our moderm expositors however, have explained it to mean that the seller, shall agree to take, as the price of the dead slave only, what the buyer may acknowledge, and nothing more ; and they have connected the exception with the non-swearing of the buyer only.—Thus they have explained it to mean that the seller may take the living slave, without the necessity of the purchaser's taking an oath provided he be willing to take, for the dead slave, what the purchaser may of himself acknowledge to have been his value.

Mode of swearing the parties in this instance.—The mode of swearing the parties, in this instance (accroding to Mohammed) is the same as in a case of non-existence of the subject of the sale.—If, therefore, both take an oath, and differ in their assertions,—and if one or both should require the dissolution of the contract, the Kazee must, in that case, dissolve it, and command the purchaser to return the living slave, and the value of the dead one; and, in the determination of the value of the dead slave, the purchaser's assertion must be credited.—There is, however, a difference of opinion among our modern commentators, in their exposition of the doctrine of Aboo Yoosaf, with respect to the mode of swearing the parties, in this instance.—The most approved mode is, to tender an oath to the purchaser that "he had not purchased those two slaves for the price claimed by the seller;"—and in case of his refusal to take the oath, to confirm the claim of the seller: but if he swear accordingly, an oath must then be tendered to the seller, that "he did not sell these two slaves for the price claimed by the purchaser;" and if he should refuse to take it, the claim of the purchaser must be confirmed: but if he swear accordingly, the sale (so far as it relates to the living slave) must then be dissolved, and the purchaser must be responsible for the price of the living slave, —In proportioning the respective prices of the two slaves, regard must be had to the value they bore on the day in which the purchaser took possession of them. If the parties should disagree as to the value the dead slave bore on the day of delivery, the bare assertion of the seller is to be credited in preference to that of the purchaser. If, however, either of the parties produce evidence, it must be admitted in preference to the other's assertion; and if both should produce evidence, that of the seller must be admitted.—This is agreeable to the analogy set forth and exemplified in a case recited in the Mabsoot: and which is as follows:—If a person, having purchased two slaves by one contract, and taken possession of them both, should afterwards return one of them on account of a defect, and the other should then die in his possession, in that case he must pay the price of the slave that died; and he becomes exempted from the price of the other that he returned:—and, in proportioning their respective prices, regard must be had to the value of each on the day in which the purchaser obtained possession of them.—If the parties should disagree concerning the value of the dead slave, the assertion of the seller must be credited, as he is the defendant or respondent, since both parties admit that a price is due, and the purchaser, proceeding on his assertion of the inferior value of the slave that is dead, pleads that he has only a small sum to pay, which the seller, asserting the superior value of the dead slave, denies.—If both parties adduce evidence, the evidence of the seller must be credited, as it proves most, since it proves the superior value of the dead slave. —The reason of this is that, in oaths, regard is had to the reality; because, as the oath of each opposes that of the other, and as they both know the real state of the case, it follows that the foundation of the oath rests upon the real state of the case; and as the seller is the real defendant, his oath must therefore be credited. In evidence, on the other hand, regard is had to appearance; because, as the witnesses are not acquainted with the real state of the case, with respect to them, that must be credited which is apparent; and the seller is apparently the plaintiff in this instance, since he claims a greater quantity of price for the dead slave. The evidence, therefore, produced by him must also be admitted in preference, since it has a superiority, because of its excess of probability.—From this explanation we may collect the principle on which Aboo Yoosaf has grounded his doctrine, that "the assertion of the seller is to be admitted with respect to the amount of the price of the dead slave, and the evidence adduced by him must be preferred, in case of the parties continuing to disagree with respect to the price of the said slave after they have both been sworn."

Case of a disagreement concerning the price, in the dissolution of a contract of sale, after delivery of the subject of it.—If a person purchase a female slave, and take possession of her, and the parties afterwards agree to dissolve the sale, but disagree concerning the price in this case they must be both sworn; and after the swearing of them both, the original sale reverts, and the dissolution becomes void.—It is to be observed that the swearing of both parties, in the dissolution of a sale, is not founded on the sacred writings, since the ordinance there respects a case of absolute sale, and sale ceases to exist, in case of a dissolution, for the dissolution is a breaking off of the sale with respect to the parties.—The swearing of the parties, therefore, in this instance, proceeds upon analogy; because the example under consideration proceeds upon a supposition of the seller not having received back the article after the dissolution, in which case the swearing of the parties is not repugnant to analogy; but rather agreeable to it.—It is on this ground that we determine upon a case of hire, from its analogy to a case of sale before seisin (as where, for instance, a lessor and lessee disagree with regard to the object of their contract prior to the expiration of the lease:—in which case both parties are sworn, because of the analogy this bears to a case of sale, prior to the receipt of the goods by the purchaser):—and also, that we determine with respect to the heir of a contracting party from the analogy his situation bears to that of the contracting party himself (as where the heir of a purchaser and the heir of a seller disagree—in which case they must both be sworn, in the same manner as the purchaser and the seller would have been).—It is upon the same ground, also, that we determine the value of an article to be analogous to the substance of it, in case of the destruction of the subject of the sale whilst in the possession of the seller by some other person than the purchaser (as where, for instance, another person kills the subject of the sale,* whilst yet in the hands of the seller, delivery not having been made to the purchaser ;—in which case the slayer must pay the value, which then stands as a substitute for the substance of the articles sold) ;—whence, if the seller and the purchaser disagree concerning the price they must both be sworn, and the sale dissolved : and the value of the slave given to the seller ; in the same manner as the substance would have been given, had it been extant.—It is to be observed, however, that if the seller receive the goods after a dissolution of the contract, and the parties then disagree concerning the price, they are not to be sworn, according to Haneefa and Aboo Yoosaf.—Mohammed maintains that in this case also a Tahalif, or mutual oath, is tendered to the parties, because here also (according to his tenets) the swearing is agreeable to analogy.

Where the price has been paid in advance, and the parties agree to dissolve the contract, but disagree concerning the same advanced, the assertion of the seller must be credited.—IF a person sell a Koort† of wheat, by a Sillim contract, for ten dirms, and the parties afterwards agree to a dissolution of the contract of Sillim, but disagree concerning the price, in this case the assertion of the seller who has received the advance‡ must be credited : and Sillim contract does not in this instance revert, the dissolution still continuing in force ; because dissolution, in a case of Silliam sale, is not merely a breach of the contract, but an abrogation of it, whence the Sillim contract cannot revert ; (contrary to a dissolution of a simple contract of sale).—Hence, if the price advanced consist of goods, and the person who has received the advance wish to return them to the purchaser on account of a defect, and the Kazee pass a decree to that effect, with the consent of both parties,—in that case, if the goods be destroyed prior to the return of them to the purchaser, the contract of Sillim does not revert. A contract of actual sale would however revert under such circumstances : and this case plainly shows that there is a difference between contracts of sale and contracts of Sillim.

Cases of disagreement between a husband and wife respecting the dower.—IF a husband and wife disagree concerning the dower or marriage settlement, the husband asserting that it was one thousand dirms, and the wife that it was two thousand, in this case the party that brings evidence must be credited, as this establishes the plea of that party upon proof : and if both bring evidence, that adduced by the woman must be preferred, as it proves most.—This is where the woman's Mihr Misl, or proportionable dower, falls short of what she claims—If however, neither of the parties produce evidence, they are to be sworn (according to Haneefa) : but the contract is not dissolved ; because the only effect of the swearing in this instance, is that it annuls the bargain with respect to the dower, in the same manner as if no bargain had ever existed ; but this does not engender any doubt with respect to the marriage itself, since the dower is not an essential, but merely a dependant of the marriage :*—It is otherwise in a case of sale for there the annulment of the bargain, with respect to the price, destroys the contract (as was before observed), and the sale is consequently dissolved.—In the case in question, after the parties swearing, a proportionable dower must be adjudged to the woman.—If, on the other hand, the woman's proportionable dower, and the sum acknowledged by the husband, be equal, if her proportionable dower fall short of what he acknowledges, the Kazee must, in that case, pass a decree in favour of the husband, as apparent circumstances are on his side.—If the wife's proportionable dower be equal to what she claims or if exceed her claim, the Kazee must, in that case, pass a decree in favour of her claim.—If the propertionable dower be greater than what is acknowledged by the husband, and less than what is claimed by the wife, the Kazee must, in that case, adjudge a proportionable dower to the wife ; because, after the swearing of both parties, nothing is established either greater or less than the proportionate dower, which is therefore a mean.—The compiler of the Hedaya observes that the doctrine here advanced, of first swearing both parties, and then adjudging the proportionable dower, is the doctrine of Kooroknee : and it proceeds on this principle, that under the existence of a stipulated dower, no attention is paid to a proper or proportionable dower ;—and as the mutual swearing of the parties is the means by which that is to be set aside, the oaths are therefore tendered to the parties, in the first instance, in all the above cases ; that is, whether the proportionable dower be equal to, or greater than, the claim of the wife ; or whether it be equal to, or less than, that of the husband.—In the opinion of Haneefa and Mohammed, the oath is first, to be administered to the husband, in order that the advantage arising from his declining to swear may be quickly obtained : for, as it is his business first to advance the dower, he must be first sworn,—in the same manner as, in a case of seller and purchaser, the purchaser is first sworn.—The exposition of Razee is, however, different ; but as that as well as the disagreement of Aboo Yoosaf, have been particularly explained under the

*Supposing it to consist of a slave or animal.

†About 7,100 lb. weight, or twelve camel-loads.

‡Arab. Mooslim-ali-bee, meaning the seller, or person to whom the price has been advanced.

*See vol. I p. 44.

head of marriage, it is not necessasy to repeat them.

If a husband and wife di agree concerning the dower,—the husband asserting that he had agreed to give a particular male slave, and the wife asserting that he had assigned a particular female slave,—in this case the rule holds the same as in that immediately preceding; that is, if the woman's proper dower be equal to or greater than, the value of the male slave, the Kazee must adjudge in favour of the husband; but if it be equal to, or greater than, the value of the female slave, the Kazee must decree in favour of the wife.—The only difference between this case and the preceding, is that if the female slave and proportionable dower be equal in point of value, the wife is, in that case, entitled to the value, and not to the slave substantially; because she cannot possess the slave without the consent of her husband, which she is not, in the instance, supposed to have obtained

Case of a dispute between a lessor and lessee, concerning the rent, or the extent of the lease, before delivery of the subject.—If a lessor and lessee, before enjoyment of the object of the contract (that is, before the usufruct of it), disagree concerning the amount of the rent, or the extent of the lease, they must in that case be both sworn; and after swearing, the contract must be dissolved, and each party must return to the other whatever he may have received —The reason of this is that the swearing of both parties, with regard to sale, in case of a dis agreement prior to the purchaser's seisin of the goods, is conformable to analogy, as has been already demonstrated —Now a lease prior to the enjoyment of the usufruct, is similar to a sale prior to seisin of the subject (and such is the case here considered) —If, therefore, the parties disagree concerning the amount of the rent, the oath must be first administered to the lessee, as he denies the obligation of the rent.—If, on the other hand, they disagree concerning the extent of the subject of the lease, the oath must be first administered to the lessor.—If either of them refuse to take the oath, the claim of the other is thereby established.—If one of them produce evidence, his claim is established; but if both bring evidence, that adduced by the lessor must be preferred, in case of the disagreement relating to the quantity of the rent; and that of the lessee, in case of its relating to the extent of the lease.—If they disagree in both points, the evidence of each is in that case to be credited. in the excess which it may prove.—For instance, the lessor claims the lease to have been made for a period of one month, in exchange for ten dirms, and the lessee claims a period of two months in exchange for five dirms; in which case the Kazee must adjudge it to be for a period of two months in exchange for five dirms.

Case of the same nature. after delivery of he subject.—If a lessor and lessee disagree, after the receipt of the object of the lease the parties are not to be sworn, but the assertion of the lessee must be credited, according to all our doctors:—according to Haneefa and Aboo Yoosaf, evidently, because (in their opinion) the destruction of the object of the contract is a bar to the swearing of the parties:—and, in the same manner, according to Mohammed, because his tenet, that the destruction of the object is not a bar to the swearing of both parties, relates only to the object of a sale, and is founded on a principle that the object of a sale may be considered as price, and the swearing of both parties (that is, of the buyer and the seller) is with relation to the price;—if, therefore, the rule of swearing both parties were admitted in the case in question, and the contract were afterwards to be annulled, it must necessarily follow that the object of the lease could not be considered as price; because the object of the lease is usufruct or advantage; and advantage is not in itself price, and cannot be considered as such but from the contract; and, in the case in question, it becomes evident that there is no contract.—Now since in this case it is impracticable to swear both parties the assertion of the lessee is therefore redited as he is the defendant and denier —If, on the other hand, the lessor and lessee dispute after the receipt of part of the object of the lease, they must be both sworn, and the contract dissolved with regard to what remains.—With respect to what is past, in this instance, the assertion of the lessee must be credited; because a lease is contracted anew every moment, in proportion to the progress of the usufruct, —Thus a new contract is opposed to every individual particle of advantage or usufruct. —It is otherwise in a case of sale, as a contract of sale is opposed to the whole of the subject of it: for which reason a sale, whenever it becomes obstructed or impracticable in part, is held to be impracticable in the whole.

Case of a dispute concerning ransom.—If a master and his Mokatib disagree concerning the amount of the ransom, according to Haneefa they must not be sworn.—The two disciples are of opinion that they must be sworn, and that the contract of Kitabat must be afterwards dissolved (and such also is the opinion of Shafei); because the contract of Kitabat is a contract of mutual exchange, and is capable of dissolution,—the case in question, therefore, resembles as case of sale, since the master claims an excess of ransom, which the Mokatib denies: whilst, on the other hand, the Mokatib claims his title to freedom, on his payment of the ransom agreeable to his settlement of it; and this the master denies:—they are both therefore, in some measure plaintiffs, and also both defendants, as in a case of sale; and hence they must both be sworn, in the same manner as a purchaser and seller are both sworn when they differ concerning the price.—The argument of Haneefa is that the ransom is opposed to the removal of a restriction which operates instantaneously with respect to the slave; but that it is not considered as opposed to the freedom until the Mokatib actually pay it.—Nothing remains, therefore, but a disagreement with respect to the amount of the ransom; and with respect to that the master is a plaintiff only, and the Mokatib only a defendant (the plea and the defence not existing alike in both parties, as in some of the cases before recited):—the parties, therefore, are not sworn; but the assertion of the Mokatib, upon oath, must be credited.

In a dispute between a husband and wife concerning furniture, the article in dispute is adjudged to the party to whose use it is adapted.—IF a husband and wife disagree concerning any article of furniture, each claiming a right in it in that case, if the furniture in question be particularly adapted to the use of men, it is adjudged to the husband: and if particularly adapted for the use of women, is adjudged to the wife; because, in the former instance, probability is an argument in favour of the husband; and in the latter, in favour of the wife. If, however, the article be of such a nature as is common to the service of both (such as a pot, or other vessel), it is in that case adjudged to the husband; because the wife herself, and everything belonging to her, is in the possession of the husband; and, in claims, the assertion of the possessor is preferred: This rule, indeed, does not hold good where the article in dispute is peculiarly adapted to the service of women, for, although such articles also are in the possession of the husband, yet the probability of their being the property of the wife, from the particular nature of them, is stronger than the argument derived from possession; and therefore supersedes it.—What is here advanced proceeds upon a supposition of the actual existence of the marriage; or of a separation between the parties, in which case the law is exactly the same.

If the dispute be between the survivor and the heirs of the deceased, the article must be adjudged to the survivor.—IF, on the other hand, one of the parties should die, and the heirs of the deceased enter into a contention with the survivor concerning the family goods, in that case the goods in question are adjudged to the survivor, whether they be of a nature adapted to the service of a man or woman; since possession is clearly established in favour of the living party.—This is according to Haneefa—Aboo Yoosaf maintains that every thing which partakes of the nature of paraphernalia,* whether it be restricted to the use of a man or woman, must be adjudged to the wife; and that all the rest must be adjudged to the husband upon his swearing to the property;—because, as every woman is supposed to have brought a paraphernalia along with her, there is a probability that the specified articles may have been included in it; and this probability destroys the argument in favour of the husband from possession; but with respect to the rest of the family goods, the husband's claim, from possession, holds good as there is nothing preventive or destructive of it.—Mohammed alleges that whatever is only fit for the use of a man ought to be adjudged to the husband; that whatever is only fit for women ought to be adjudged to the wife; and, that whatever is, in point of use, common to both, ought to be adjudged to the husband or his heirs, for the reason alleged by Haneefa.

If one of the parties be a slave, it must be adjudged to the party who is free.—IF, in the case in question, one of the parties be a slave, and the contention concerning the property happen during the life of both, it must be adjudged in favour of the party who is free; because the seisin of a free person is in a superior degree valid;—but in case of the death of either, it must be adjudged to the living party, as the possession of the deceased exists no longer, and the possession of the living then remains unopposed,—This is according to Haneefa,—The two disciples maintain that a privileged slave and a Mokatib are equivalent to freemen in this point, as their possession is valid in contested cases.

Section.

Of Persons who are not liable to Claims.

A person is not liable to a claim, who sets up a plea of deposit, pledge, or usurpation (in the article claimed), supported by the testimony of witnesses, unless he be a person of notoriously bad character.—IF a defendant plead that "a certain absent person had deposited with him the article in dispute," or "had pledged it to him," or that "he himself had usurped it from a particular absent person," and bring witnesses to prove his allegation, in that case no room for suit or contention exists between him and the plaintiff; and so also, if he plead that "a certein absent person had let the said thing to him in lease," and produce evidence in proof of it;—because in all these cases it is clearly established by the evidence of the witnesses of the defendant that his tenure is not the subject of contention, since he is seised of the thing in the manner of a trust,—Ibn Shabirma maintains that the defendant is not exonerated from the suit in consequence of proving, by witnesses, the deposit the pledge, the usurpation, or the lease; because the proof of the absentee's right of property is impracticable, since there is no person in his behalf to appear as a party in the suit; and the exeneration of the defendant from the suit of the plaintiff depends on the proof of the absentee's right

*Arab. Jaheez.—Meaning vestments or furniture of any kind which a bride brings to her husband's house.

of property. Our doctors, on the other hand, argue that the evidence here adduced has two objects in view :—First, the establishment of the absentee's right of property, concerning which there is no suitor on his behalf; and which consequently cannot be proved :—Secondly, a repulsion of the claim of the plaintiff; a d as he is the immediate adversary in this concern, the repulsion is consequently established. The plaintiff in this instance, therefore, resembles a person commissioned by a husband to remove his wife :—that is to say, if a person appoint another his agent for the removing and conducting of his wife to him, and the wife prove, by witnesses, that her husband had divorced her, in this case the testimony of these witnesses must be admitted: merely so far, however, as to restrain the removal of her by the agent; but not with respect to the establi hment of the proof of the divorce [as was formerely mentioned) ;* and so also in the case in question.—It is to be observed that the defendant, in this case, is not exonerated from the claim of the plaintiff upon his bare allegation of the deposit of the absentee, or of his pawn. &c., nor until he produce evidence in support of his assertion; because the defendant is himself apparently an adversary † in contemplation of his being possessed of the subject of the claim; and is opposed by the suit of the plaintiff, which he means to repel by the declaration above mentioned ;—his declaration, therefore, cannot be admitted, unless he adduce evidence in support of it; in the same manner as where a person says to his creditor, "I have transferred the debt I owe you upon another person," in which case his assertion is not believed unless supported by evidence.—Ibn Abee Leilee is of opinion that the defendant is exempted from the plea immediately upon his assertion The last recorded opinion of Aboo Yoosaf is that if the defendant be virtuous and not noted for fraud, the rule obtains as above laid down. If, however, he be noted for fraud, he in that case is not exonerated from the claim, even on producing evidence in support of his allegation; for a fraudulent person sometimes gives property that he has usurped to a traveller (for instance) in order that the traveller may afterwards, in the presence of witnesses, resign it to him in trust; and this he does with a view of defrauding the original proprietor of his right.—Where the defendant, therefore, is open to a suspicion of such frauds as these, the Kazee must not accept of his evidence.

Or, that his witnesses bear defective testimony.—If the defendant's witness should say, "a person whom we do not know did resign this article to him in trust;" in that case the defendant is not released from the suit, for two reasons.—First, there is a possibility that that person may be the plaintiff himself—Secondly, if they had specific the person, the plaintiff would then have had it in his power to have traced him, and to have entered a suit against him; but as they have not specified him, he is deprived of the power of tracing him; and if, under such circumstances, the defendant were released from the claim, an injury is thereby occasioned to the plaintiff.—If, again, the witnesses should say, "we know the face of the man in question, but we are ignorant of his name and family," in that case the same rule obtains (according to Mohammed), because of the second reason.—According to Haneefa, on the contrary the defendant in this case is released from the claim, as having proved that the thing in question came to him from another in trust; since, as the witnesses know the countenance of the man (contrary to the preceding case), the defendant's possession is consequently no longer a subject of litigation.—In reply, also, to what is urged by Mohammed, it may be observed that either the plaintiff has been himself the occasion of the injury he sustains, in forgetting the defendant; or, the injury has been occasioned by the witnesses of the defendant; but not by the defendant himself.—(This case is termed the Makhmsa, of quinqual, of the book of plea e; because it has given rise to five different opinions, as here stated.)

He is liable, if he set up a plea of right of property.—If a defendant plead that he had purchased the article in dispute from a certain absentee, he is in that case a party, and liable to answer to the claim of the plaintiff; for in declaring that he was seised of the thing in virtue of a right of property, he acknowledged himself to be subject to the suit of the plaintiff.

Or, if the plaintiff sue him on a plea of theft, or usurpation, although he produce evidence to prove a trust.—If, in a suit, the plaintiff should say to the defendant "you have usurped this thing from me," or "you have stolen thing from me," in this case the defendant is not released from the claim, although he produce witnesses in proof of the article in question having been committed to him by an absentee in trust; because here the plaintiff asserts the action of usurpation or of the theft against him, and in this respect (and not because he is seised of the property) he is subject to the plea.—It is different where the plaintiff asserts absolutely his right of property; because in that case the defendant cannot be subjected to the claim otherwise than from his possession of the thing; whence it is that an absolute claim of property in an article is not admitted against any except the actual possessor of the article; whereas a plea for the act [of acquisition, such as usurpation, and so forth] lies against any other person

And so also, if the plaintiff sue upon a plea of theft, without specifiying the thief.—If

*Under the head of Divorce.

†That is, he may himself be regarded (in one view in the light of a plaintiff.

in a suit, the plaintiff should say to the defendant, who is seised of the thing in dispute, "this thing which is in your possession is my property, and has been taken from me by theft;" and the defendant say "a certain absentee deposited this thing with me;" and bring evidence to prove his assertion, still he is not released from the claim.— This is the opinion of Haneefa and Aboo Yoosaf; and proceeds upon a favourable construction of the law. Mohammed holds the defendant, in this case, to be exempted from the claim, as the plaintiff has not exhibited the claim of theft against him, but against an unknown person; and as a claim of this nature against an unknown person is nugatory, it follows that the claim, with respect to the act, cannot stand:—nothing, therefore, remains except a claim with respect to the right of property; and as, in a claim concerning a right of property, the suit is set aside, by the defendant proving the article in dispute to have been committed to him in trust, the case is therefore the same as if the plaintiff had declared the thing to have been taken from him by usurpation, without naming the usurper.—The reasoning of Haneefa and Aboo Yoosaf is that the mention of the act involves a plea against the agent; and the presumption is that the possessor is the agent, but that the plaintiff, from motives of tenderness, may not have specified him, in order to screen him from punishment. The case is, therefore, the same as if the plaintiff had said "you have stolen this thing."—It is otherwise where the plaintiff charges the defendant with usurpation, for in this case, although he make the charge in direct terms, still punishment is not incurred, notwithstanding it be evident that his design is to prove the usurpation.

But not if the plaintiff sue him on a plea of purchase.—If the plaintiff should say to the defendant "I have bought this thing from a certain person," and the defendant reply "that person consigned the thing to me in trust," In this case the defendant is exempted from the claim without the necessity of producing evidence; because both the plaintiff and the defendant are agreed that the thing is, originally, the property of another man; and consequently the tenure of the person seised of it is not a matter of dispute between them.—If, however, the plaintiff say that "a certain person had appointed him an agent for seisin of the said thing," and produce evidence in proof of this, he is entitled to prosecute his suit against the possessor, as having established, by witnesses, a superior right to the possession of the article in question.

CHAPTER IV

OF THINGS CLAIMED BY TWO PLAINTIFFS.

If the claim be laid to a thing of a divisible nature, and the proofs on each part be equal, the thing must be adjudged equally between both claimants.—If two men separately claim the property of an article in the possession of another, and each bring evidence in support of his claim, the Kazee must, in that case, adjudge the article to be the joint property of both in an equal degree,—One opinion of Shafei, in this case, if that, as the evidence respectively adduced by the parties is contradictory of each other, they must both be rejected —Another opinion of his is that the Kazee ought to throw the die to determine to whom the property belongs.— His reasoning in support of these opinions is that as it is an impossibility that two men can each have separately a complete right of property to one and the same thing, it follows that the evidence of one of the parties must be false; but as there is no criterion by which the truth can be determined, it is therefore proper either to reject both, or to have recourse to the die; more especially as the Prophet in a similar case caused the die to be thrown, and gave judgment accordingly. The arguments of our doctors on this point are twofold. First, a tradition reported by Tameem Bin Tirfa, that the Prophet, in a cause which was brought before him regarding a camel, in which both parties brought evidence in support of their claim, adjudged it to be the joint property of both (for, with respect to the tradition quoted by Shafei, it alludes to a decision of the Prophet in the infancy of the Mussulman religion which was afterwards disapproved of) —Secondly, it is possible to reconcile the evidence of both the parties, by supposing the evidence of the one party to allude to the cause of right of property in the possessor, and that of the other to the right of possession: and as, by this hypothesis, the evidence of each of the parties is reconcileable to truth, it is therefore incumbent to act according to it in the greatest possible degree,—namely, by adjudging each of them to have a right to the half of the property.

If it be to a wife the right must be adjudged according to her declaration.—If two men, severally, claim marriage with one woman, and each adduce evidence in support of his claim. Kazee must not, in that case, pass a decree upon these evidences; because, as the subject of dispute does not admit of divided property, it is consequently impracticable to adjudge the half to each.—He must therefore have recourse to the declaration of the wife, and adjudge her in marriage to that party whose claim she verifies.

Or (if the witnesses specify dates) according to the prior date—This, however, proceeds upon a supposition of the witnesses not having mentioned any date; for if they should specify dates to the marriage, the evidence of that party which specifies the most ancient date must be preferred.—If, on the other hand, previous to the adduction of evidence by either party, the woman should make an acknowledgment in favour of one of the plaintiffs, she is judged to be the wife of the acknowledged :—but if the other party should afterwards produce evidence in support of his claim, the Kazee must adjudge her to be his wife, as evidence is stronger than acknowledgment.

A decree adjudging a wife to a single claimant cannot be reversed in favour of a subsequent claimant, unless his witnesses prove a priority of date.—If only one man claim marriage with a woman, and she deny it, and he produce evidence in support of his claim, and the Kazee having in consequence passed a decree in his favour, another person then appear and claim his marriage with the same woman, in this case the Kazee must not reverse his decree : because, having been passed on good grounds, it cannot afterwards be affected by a circumstance of equal, and far less by one of inferior force.—If, however, the witnesses of the second plaintiff should attest the date of the marriage to have been prior to that mentioned by the witnesses of the first plaintiff, the evidence brought by the second plaintiff must in that case be preferred, as the error of the first witnesses has thereby been made apparent.—The law is the same in a case where a husband and wife living together, and their marriage being notorious, another person claims marriage with the woman, and brings evidence in support of his plea ; for in this case his evidence is not admitted unless it prove a marriage prior to that of the husband with whom the wife then lives.

Two claimants to a slave, on a plea of purchase, upon his being adjudged between them, are severally at liberty to pay half the price, or to relinquish the bargain.—If two men severally claim a right of property in a slave in the possession of another (as if each were to assert that he had purchased him from that other), and each bring evidence in support of his claim, in that case (as the Kazee must adjudge him to be the joint property of both), they are severally at liberty either to take the half of the slave at the half of the price or relinquish the bargain.—The case is therefore the same as where two unauthorized persons sell the same article belonging to a third person to two different men, and the proprietor confirms both sales, in which case each purchaser is at liberty either to take the half of the article for half the stipulated price, or to reject the sale entirely and receive back his money; because, as he had before assented to the bargain, on the supposition of its extending to the whole of the article, it cannot be inferred that he assented to the partial bargain ; he is therefore at liberty either to accept or reject it as he pleases. If, however, in the case in question, after the Kazee adjudging the half to each, one of the parties should reject it, the other cannot take the whole, because that half was adjudged to the other in consequence of evidence he produced, and on his rejecting it the sale becomes, in that half, null and void.—It were otherwise, however, if one of the parties should intimate his rejection of the half prior to the adjudication of the Kazee, for in that case he would be entitled to take the whole, because his claim went to a right to the whole from purchase, and as the bar to his obtainment of the whole (namely, the plea of the other) is removed by the relinquishment of the co-plaintiff, prior to the virtual annulment of any part of the sale by the decree of the Kazee; he is consequently entitled to the whole of his claim. (Analogous to this is the resignation made, by one of two Shafees, of his right of pre-emption, prior to the determination of the Kazee in favour of both.—Analogous, also, to the first statement is that of the resignation made by one of two Shafees of his right of pre-emption subsequent to the decree of the Kazee in favour of both.)*

But if they specify and prove dates, the slave must be adjudged to the prior purchaser.—It is to be observed that if, in the case in question, the two plaintiffs should specify the dates of their purchase, the sale must be adjudged in favour of the prior purchaser ; because it appears that he had established his right at a time when he had no opponent ; and on this account the subsequent claim of the other is invalid.—If one of the parties should mention a date and not the other, the sale must in that case be adjudged in favour of the one who specifies the date ; because he clearly establishes his claim at a particular time; and as the other does not specify any period, it becomes, of consequence, doubtful whether he purchased it prior or posterior to the particular time mentioned by the other; and the Kazee (because of this doubt) cannot pass a decree in his favour.—If neither of the parties specify a date, and one of them be in possession of the thing the claim of the possessor is preferable ; because it is probable that his right of possession was derived from prior purchase ; and also, because both of their claims being established in an equal degree the possession, which is undisputed, cannot be affected by a matter of doubt. The same rule obtains when one of the plaintiffs is seised of the thing and the witnesses of the other specify the date of his purchase.—But it is to be observed that if the witnesses should expressly attest his purchase to have been prior to that of the purchase of the possessor, the sale must in this case be adjudged in his favour ; as a certain knowledge of prior purchase establishes a positive right, whereas possession establishes only an implied right.

Where one party pleads purchase, and the other gift and seisin (without sepecifying dates), the article must be adjudged to the purchaser.—If two men claim a particular article, one in virtue of purchase, and the

* This is fully explained under the article Shaffa.

other in virtue of gift and seisin, and each produce evidence in support of his claim, without, however, mentioning dates, in this case the evidence to the purchase must be admitted in preference; because purchase is stronger in its nature than gift, as it involves a mutual exchange; and also, because purchase is in itself a cause of a right of property; whereas the right of property in a gift rests upon the acceptance.—If the claim of the one be founded upon purchase, and that of the other upon charity and seisin, and all the other circumstances be the same as above stated, the same rule holds, because of the reasons aforesaid. If, however, the claim of one be founded upon gift and seisin, and that of the other upon charity and seisin, the Kazee must in this case decree the thing to be in an equal degree the joint property of both; seeing that their claims are equal, and that neither has a preference over the other.

Objection.—A preference ought to be given to the claim of charity over that of gift; because a gift is not binding, since the giver may retract the gift: whereas charity is binding, and cannot be retracted.

Reply.—No preference if given excepting for some effect immediately operating; and the legality of retracting a gift, and the illegality of retracting charity, relate to the future: but at the moment they are on a foot of equality.—It is to be observed that this doctrine of the equality of claims of gift and of charity, and of the necessity for decreeing jointly to both, is when the thing in question is capable of division. But if the thing be incapable of division, there is a difference of opinion; some maintaining that the law in this case is the same; and others maintaining that the law in this case is different, as it induces a gift with respect to indefinite property, which is unlawful.

A claimant on a plea of purchase, and a claimant on a plea of marriage are upon an equal footing,—If two persons lay claim to the same thing, one of them in virtue of purchase, and the other (being a woman) in virtue of the possessor's having married her, and having settled that article as her dower,—in this case both plaintiffs are upon an equal footing; because the claim of each in point of strength is equal, since a contract of purchase, and of marriage, are both contracts of exchange, and both equally occasion a right of property.—This is according to Haneefa and Aboo Yoosaf. Mohammed maintains that the plea of purchase is to be preferred, and that the husband must be made responsible to the woman for the value of the article in dispute; as by this means a preference is given to the plea of purchase, whilst at the same time the claims of both are attended to.

A plea of pawnage and seisin is preferable to a plea of gift and seisin,—If one of two plaintiffs plead pawnage and seisin: and the other plead gift and seisin. and each produce evidence in support of his plea, in this case the plea of pawnage must be preferred,—This proceeds upon a favourable construction.—Analogy would suggest that the plea of gift ought to be preferred, because gifts occasion a right of property, whereas pawnage does not.—The reason for a more favourable construction in this instance is that seisin in virtue of pawnage occasions responsibility, which is not the case with respect to seisin in consequence of gift; and a contract which occasions responsibility is strong than one which does not occasion it,—It is different whence, the gift is made in exchange for some other thing; because such a gift is ultimately a sale; and sale is stronger than pawnage.

Two claims, equally supported, must be determined by the priority of date.—If two men claim an absolute right of property in the same article, which is in the possession of a third person, and each mention the date of commencement of his right, it must in that case be adjudged in favour of him who pleads the oldest date;—because having established his prior right of property, it follows that no other can afterwards obtain that but from him; and the othere plaintiff in this instance, has not obtained the right of property from him.

Two pleas of purchase, preferred against one person, must also be determined by his oldest date.—If two men prefer a claim of purchase against another who is not the possessor of the article in dispute, and each bring evidence of his purchase, specifying different dates, the person who proves the prior date must be preferred, as he prove his right at a period when he had no opponent.

If, against two different persons, the article is adjudged equally between both claimants.—If two claimants prefer an allegation of purchase, the one bringing evidence in proof of his having bought the article in dispute from Zeyd, and the other bringing evidence in proof of his having bought it from Omar, and the witnesses of each specify the dates of these purchases, in this case both plaintiffs are on a footing of equality, as each of them has established the right of property of his respective seller, and hence the case is the same as if the two sellers were themselves present and claimed their respective rights.—Each plaintiff, therefore, is at liberty to take the half of the thing at half of the price, or the relinquish his purchase entirely, for the reason before explained. If the witnesses of one of the parties specify a determinate time of payment, and not the witnesses of the other, still the Kazee must adjudge one half to each; because a knowledge of the length of credit does not imply priority in point of purchase;—may, it is even probable that the other's right of property may have been of prior date, as the case supposes two different sellers.—(It is otherwise where there is only one seller, as in that case both parties are agreed in the derivation of their right of property from one and the same seller).

Unless one only adduce evidence to a date, when it must be adjudged to him:—If, on the other hand, one of the plaintiffs prove a date of purchase, and not the other, a decree must be passed in favour of the claimant whose date of purchase is ascertained, unless the purchase of the other can be proved to have preceded his.

Where four claimants plead a right in a thing, as derived from four different persons, the article is adjudged among them in equall lots.—If one plaintiff claim a right to an article from his having purchased it from Zeyd;—a second, from a gift of it to him by Omar,—a third, from inheritance from his father,—and a fourth, from its having been bestowed upon him in charity by a particular person —and each of the four claimants adduce evidence in support of his claim in this case the Kazee must adjudge the article among them, in four equal lots: because each of them pleads his right, as derived from a different person, and the case is therefore the same as if these four different persons had themselves appeared in court, and each proved his absolute right of property.

The evidence of the possessor must be preferred to that of the plaintiff, where it proves a prior date of right—If a plaintiff adduce evidence to prove his right of property in a thing from a particular period, and the possessor of the thing adduce evidence to prove his right from a prior period, the evidenee of the possessor must be preferred.—This is according to Haneefa and Aboo Yoosaf.—It appears also (from one tradition) to be the opinion of Mohammed.—According howevers, to another tradition, Mohammed is of opinion that the evidence of the possessor ought not to be preferred (and this is the sentiment he adopted and acted upon); because, as each party produced evidence in support of his absolute right of property, without explaining the cause of that right, it follows that priority or posteriority of date is in this instance immaterial.—The reasoning of Haneefa and Aboo Yoosaf is that wherever a person proves his right of property in a thing at a particular period the right of property of another in that thing at a subsequent period cannot otherwise be established than by its being derived from the former; but in the case in question, the plaintiff has not pleaded the derivation of his right of property from the possessor: and therefore the evidence of the possessor is preferred.

The evidence on the part of the plaintiff is preferred, where the claim is laid absolutely.—If a plaintiff and possessor, respectively, bring evidence to prove each his right of property, in an absolute manner (that is, without explaining the instrument or cause of it), and the witnesses of one the parties declare the date of his right, and not those of the other, in this case (according to Haneefe and Mohammed) the evidence of the plaintiff must be preferred.—Aboo Yoosaf alleges that the evidence of the claimant of known date must be preferred (and this, according to one tradition, is also the opinion of Haneefa); because the right of property of the claimant of known date is established in the past, whereas that of the other, in consequence of his evidence not mentioning any date, is only established in the present; and the past has precedence of the present;—in the same manner as where one of two claimants from purchase proves the date of his purchase, and the other does not; in which case the evidence of the former is preferred—The reasoning of Haneefa and Mohammed is that the evidence adduced by the possessor of an article in dispute is admitted only as it tends to repulsion;—but, in the case in question, no property of repulsion exists, because it is this instance doubtful whether the plaintiff may have derived his right in the article from the possessor or not, since it is possible that if the plaintiff's witnesses were to mention a date that date might prove to be prior:—the evidence adduced by the plaintiff is therefore preferred

And the same, where the subject in dispute is immoveable property.—A SIMILAR disagreement subsists with respect to a contested house in the possession of two plaintiffs: for, according to Haneefa and Mohammed, the house must be left in their possession, as before, and no regard whatever paid to the evidence on either part: whereas, according to Aboo Yoosaf, a decree must be passed in favour of him who proves a date.—Supposing, however, the house to be in the possession of a third person; and all the other circumstances to be the same, in that case according to Haneefa, both the claimants are upon an equal footing; whereas, according to Aboo Yoosaf the evidence on the part of him who proves the date must be preferred.—Mohammed, on the other hand, alleges that the evidence on the part of him who does not show any date must be preferred because he claims a prior right of property, on the ground that when a person claims property in an absolute manner, without specifying any date; and establishes his claim, he is entitled to more than one who specifies a date; as holds in a case of claim of acquisition by labour.—The argument of Aboo Yoosaf is that the mention of a date is a certain corroboration of the claimant's right of property at that time; whereas the omission of a date admits of two constructions, as it leaves it doubtful whether the right of the other had existed prior or posterior to that period; and as certainty is always a cause of preference, he whose evidence goes to establish a date is therefore preferred;—in the same manner as where two persons claim the purchase of the same thing, and one of them specifies the date and not the other.—The argument of Haneefa is that the date mentioned by the dating claimant bears the construction either of priority or posteriority, in the same manner as the claim of the other, which is absolute.

also bears two constructions: the claims of both are, therefore, on a footing of equality. It is otherwise in the case of two purchasers, where one specifies the date, and not the other: because purchase being a supervenient circumstance, is therefore, when doubtful, referred to the nearest period;' and hence, in that case, the reason for preferring the known date.

Case of claims to animals, founded upon generation.—If a plaintiff and possessor should both bring evidence to prove a generation, as if each should bring evidence to prove that "such a camel (for instance) is the offspring of a particular camel, which had brought it forth whilst in his possession,"—in this case the claim of the possessor must be preferred; because, as the evidence is adduced upon a point which derives no additional proof from actual possession, it follows that the plaintiff and the possessor are both upon a perfect equality with respect to plea and evidence; and the evidence on the part of the possessor afterwards acquires a superiority from the circumstance of his possession: the Kazee must therefore adjudge the camel to him.—This is approved.—Yeesa Ibn Ayam, however, has asserted the contrary: for he maintains that as both evidences are in opposition to each other, they must both be rejected, and the camel left, as it was, in the hands of the possessor; but that it ought not to be decreed to him by the Kazee.

If, in a suit respecting a horse, the plaintiff assert that he had purchased it from Zeyd, and that it was the offspring of a horse of Zeyd, and the possessor assert that he had bought it from Omar, and that it was the offspring of a horse of Omar's, and each bring evidence in proof of the horse having been produced from a claim in the possession of the seller, it is the same as if each had adduced evidence in proof of the horse having been produced in his own possession. If, on the other hand, one of the parties bring evidence in proof of his right of property, and the other in proof of the contrary, in this case the claim of the party proving the generation of the horse is preferred, whether he be the possessor or not; because, as the evidence adduced by him goes to prove his right of property abinitio, it follows that the right cannot afterwards exist in another, unless by a derivation of it from him.—In the same manner also, if, where neither of the parties is possessed of the horse, one prove that it was produced in his possession, and the other prove his right of property, a decree must pass in favour of him who proves the generation of the horse.—It is to be observed that if the Kazee pass a decree in favour of the person who proves the production of the horse from one in his possession, and another person then prove, by evidence, the generation of it to have been from his property, the Kazee must, in that case, pass a decree in favour of that third person, unless the possessor again produce evidence in proof of the generation, in opposition to that person.

Or to any other property founded upon a cause of right equivalent to generation.—The same rule holds with respect to materials for making cloth, where they have undergone only one opearation (such as spinning, for instance).—Thus, if a plaintiff and a possessor, respectively, assert that "the yarn in dispute is his property, and he has spun it himself," and each bring evidence in support of his claim, in that case the Kazee must pass a decree in favour of the poessessor, in the same manner as in a case of claim founded upon generation: and the same of every cause relating to property which is simple and not complicated, such, for instance, as the extracting of milk from an animal, the making of cheese, or of felts, the sheering of wool, and the like.—If, on the other hand, the cause of right of property be of a complicated nature, such as the wearing of cloth, the planting of trees, or the sowing of wheat, and a dispute arise between a plaintiff and possessor of any of these articles, the Kazee must pass a decree in favour of the plaintiff, and not of the possessor,—and so also, if a plaintiff and possessor, respectively, adduce evidence in proof of his absolute right of property, without explaining the cause.—If the cause be doubtful (that is, if it be unknown whether complicated or simple), recourse must be had to skilful persons; and if it appear doubtful to them also, the Kazee must in that case decree in favour of that plaintiff who is not the possessor; because the original principle is to pass the decree in conformity with the evidence adduced by the plaintiff; and although an exception be established in cases of claim founded upon generation (because of a tradition of the Prophet, who, upon a certain occasion, decided, in such a case, in favour of the possessor), still; in a case where the cause is doubtful, and where of course it cannot be ascertained whether the article is comprehended within the exception, recourse must be had to the original principle of the law.

The possessor of an article, proving his having purchased it from the claimant, sets aside his plea.—If a plaintiff produce evidence in support of his absolute right of property in an article, and the possessor bring evidence to prove his having purchased the article from the plaintiff, the evidence of the possessor must be preferred; because, although the plaintiff plead that his right of property was of prior date, yet the possessor appears to have afterwards purchased the article from him (which is in no respect repugnant thereto), and hence the case is the same as if the possessor were first to acknowledge that the article had formerly belonged to the plaintiff, and then to assert that he had purchased it from him.

If each party prove a purchase from the other (without specifying a date) no decree can take place.—If a plaintiff bring evidence to prove his purchase of the article in dispute from the possessor, and the possessor, on the other hand, bring evidence in proof of his having purchased it from the plaintiff, and neither party specify the date of his purchase, in this case the evidence of both falls to the ground, and the thing in dispute is left in the hands of the possessor.—The compiler of the Hedaya observes that this is according to Haneefa and Aboo Yoosaf: but that Mohammed has said that the Kazee must admit the evidence of both, and that then the thing goes to the plaintiff; because a conformity to the evidence of both is practicable, since it is possible that the possessor may have purchased the thing from the plaintiff, and having then received possession of it may have afterwards sold it to him again.—This construction ought therefore to be adopted; more especially as seisin implies that the possessor must have made the first purchase; nor can the contrary, indeed, be supposed, because (according to Mohammed) a thing cannot be sold previous to the seller's possession of if, although it be land.—The reasoning of Haneefa and Aboo Yoosaf is that each of the parties in pleading a purchase from the other, virtually makes an acknowledgment of the right of property in the other; and as, where each party makes an acknowledgment in favour of the other, the evidence of both must be set aside, according to all our doctors, so also in the case in question.—In reply to the assertion of Mohammed, it is to be observed that a conformity to the evidence of both is impracticable, in as much as the cause, namely, the purchase, is an object only as far as it is necessary to prove the existence of the effect, namely, right of property.—Now in the case in question, it is impracticable to pass a decree in favour of the possessor's right of property, but by previously admitting the plaintiff's right; and hence if the Kazee were to pass a decree in favour of the possessor, it is a decree upon the cause, namely, the purchase, which would be vain and useless.

And so also, if each prove payment of the price.—If, in the case now under consideration, the witnesses of each party should give evidence of the payment of the price (one thousand dirms, for instance), in that case (according to Haneefa and Aboo Yoosaf) a Mokasa, or mutual liquidation, takes place with respect to both prices, provided the prices be on an equality either with regard to prompt payment, or to a payment at a limited period, beeause in this case the seisin of each party induces responsibility.—If no evidence be given of the payment of the price, in this case also, according to Mohammed, a mutual liquidation takes place, because the price is due from each party to the other respectively, provided the witnessess of each separately testify to the sale, and also to the seisin of the article sold.—And here, in the opinion of all our doctors, the evidence of both parties falls to the ground; since, even according to Mohammed, a conformity to the evidence of both is impracticable in this instance; because both the sales are valid, as being both made after seisin: moreover, no date is specified, nor does any argument of a date exist by which a preference might be given to the one claim rather than to the other; they are therefore of equal force, and no superiority is assigned to the one over the other: and the evidenee of both parties consequently is accounted of no force.—It is otherwise in the preceding case, because, as no mention is there made of the seision of either party, a conformity of the evidence of both is practicable, as has been already explained.

In disputes concerning land, a decree must be passed in favour of the last purchaser—If the thing in dispute be land, and the witnesses of both parties specify the dates of purchase, without making any mention of the seisin of either party, in that case, where the date of the plaintiff's purchase precedes that of the possessor, the Kazee (according to Haneefa and Aboo Yoosaf) must pass a decree in favour of the possessor; and the dispute is settled as if the plaintiff had first purchased the land, and then sold it to the possessor previous to his own seisin of it, which in their opinion is lawful. Mohammed, on the other hand, contends that the Kazee ought to pass a decree in favour of the plaintiff; because, as (according to him) the sale of land previous to the seisin of it is not lawful; the land ought necessarily to remain with the plaintiff.—If, on the other hand, the witnesses of both parties give evidence also to the seisin, in that case the Kazee must pass a decree in favour of the possessor, according to all our doctors; because both sales are in such an instance universally admitted to be valid. Thus, however, proceeds upon a supposition of the date of the plaintiff's purchase being prior to that of the possessor's: for if the date proved by the possessor be prior to that proved by the plaintiff, the Kazee must pass a decree in favour of the plaintiff, whether the witnesses may or may not have specified the seisin; and the matter is adjusted as if the possessor had first purchased the thing from the plaintiff, and having received seisin of it, had afterwards sold it to the plaintiff, without having as yet delivered it to him; or as if, having delivered it, it had reverted to him again from some other cause.

The production of any number of witnesses above the lawful number makes no difference with respect to the decree.—If one of two plaintiffs produce two, and the other plaintiff produce four witnesses still they are on an equal footing; because, as the testimony of each two of the four witnesses is a complete cause, or ground of decision, it follows that the evidence of four witnesses amounts merely to two causes; and a multiplicity of causes is no argument of superiority, since it is in the strength of a cause, and not in the number, that a superiority lies.

Case of a claim made by two persons to a house; where one claims the half and the other the whole.—If a house in possession of any person be claimed by two other persons, one of them alleging his right to the whole, and the other to the half, and each bring evidence in proof of his claim, in this case the Kazee must adjudge three-fourths to the claimant of the whole, and one-fourth to the claimant of the half, according to Haneefa, because (agreeable to his tenets) regard must be had to the nature of the dispute; and as, in the present instance, no dispute subsists with respect to one half, that half goes exclusively to the claimant of the whole; but as there is a dispute between the parties respecting the other half, and as they are both upon an equal footing with regard to the ground of their claim, that half therefore goes to them both in equal proportions.—The two disciples allege that the house must be divided between the claimants in three equal lots, two going to the plaintiff for the whole, and one to the plaintiff for the half; because, according them, regard must be had to arithmetical proportion; in other words, the plaintiff for the whole in consideration of his claim, which is to the two halves, is entitled to two lots, and the plaintiff for the half, in consideration of his claim, which is to one half, is entitled to one lot: the house, therefore, is divided between then in three lots.—If, on the other hand, the house in dispute be in the possession of the parties the whole of the house in that case goes to the claimant of the whole; for he receives the half possessed by the claimant of the half in consequence of a decree of the Kazee (which decree must necessarily be granted him, since in being a claimant for the whole, he is a claimant for that half, without having possession of it, and judgment must therefore be given according to his evidence); and he keep the other half, of which he was himself possessed, as it is a necessary inference that the claim of the other plaintiff related only to that half of which he was in possession, since if he were to prefer a claim to the other half, it must follow that the half of which he is in possesion is held by an unjust tenure:—and as no claim subsists with respect to the half in the hands of the claimant of the whole, it consequently remains with him.—In short, the whole house remains with him.

In claims founded upon generation regard must be paid to the date stated by the claimant.—If two persons lay claim to an animal, and each adduce evidence to prove its production, at the same time specifying the date, in this case the animal must be adjudged to the claimant whose witnesses specified a date apparently according with the age of the animal; because, as probability is an argument in his favour, he is therefore entitled to a preference.—If, however, the age of the animal be doubtful, and an agreement with the date on one side or the other not apparent, it must then be adjudged in an equal degree to both, and the specification of dates set aside: that is, the case must be considered in the same light as if no dates had been mentioned.—If, on the other hand, both the dates be repugnant to the apparent age of the animal, the evidence of each party is nugatory (and such also is reported from Hakim), because the falsity of the evidence on both parts is in such a case manifest:—the animal is therefore left with the person who may be in possession of it.

One party pleading a trust, and the other asserting an usurpation, each is upon an equal footing.—If two persons severally prefer a plea against other who is in possession of a slave; the one pleading that "the possessor has usurped the said slave from him," and the other, that "he has committed the said slave to him in trust;" in this case the Kazee must decree one half of the slave to each, as their claims are equally strong.

Section
Of disputes concerning Possession.

The possession of an animal is ascertained by any act which implies a use of the animal If two men dispute the possession of an animal, one of them being mounted upon it, and the other holding the bridle, in this case the claim of the rider is the strongest, since his act of riding upon it is an act in virtue of right of property—In the same manner, also, if one of them be riding on the saddle, and the other on the croup, the claim of the person seated upon the saddle is preferable. It is otherwise, however, if they be mounted upon an animal without a saddle; for this case the property of the animal is divided between them, as both are, with respect to the act of riding, upon an equal footing in such an instance.

If two men contend concerning a camel, the one having a burden, his own property, upon it, and the other having in his hand the Mohr or rope that guides it, the right of the person having the burden upon it is preferable, as the camel is employed in his service.

The right of one using a thing is preferable to that of one laying hold of it.—If two men dispute respecting an under garment, the one wearing it, and the other holding the sleeve of it, the claim of the wearer is preferable, as his act is evident.

If two persons should dispute concerning a carpet, the one being seated upon it, and the other having hold of it with his hand, the Kazee must not pass a decree in favour of either.

If two persons dispute concerning a piece of cloth the one enclosing great part of it in his hand, and the other having hold of the border of it, in this case the cloth is equally parted between them, because the greater quantity held by the one than the other does not give a superiority of claim, as it goes only to furnish one argument or poof

Right of possession over a foundling is established by his own acknowledgment.—If a boy* be in the possession of any person, and, being capable of explaining his own condition, declare that "he is free", his assertion must be credited, in as much as he is his own master.—If, on the other hand, he declare himself to be the slave of some other person than the possessor, he is adjudged to be the property, of the possessor, because, in declaring himself a slave, he acknowledges that he is not his own master.—If, also, the boy be not capable of explaining his own condition, he is adjudged to be the property of the possessor, because not being his own master he is considered in the same light as clothes or any similar article :—and if, after attaining maturity, he claim his freedom, his plea will not be admitted, because his slavery during his childhood became apparent ; and no matter that becomes apparent can afterwards be set aside excepting upon proof.†

The court of a Serai is adjudged between the disputents.—If there be ten apartments of a Serai in the possession of one man, and one apartment in the possession of another, and they enter into a contention respecting the court of the Serai, in this case the claim of both must be adjudged to be equal, since both have an equal right to the use of it, and to pass through it.

A decree cannot be issued, respecting a claim to land, without the adduction of evidence.—If two men claim a piece of ground, each, respectively, asserting it to be "in his possession," the Kazee in this case must not pass a decree in favour of the possession of either, until evidence be produced ; since possession of land is not of a nature to be actually seen by the Kazee, because of the impracticability of producing it in court ; and also, because it is necessary to prove by evidence whatever is concealed from the knowledge of the Kazee.—If, therefore, either of the parties produce evidence in support of his claim, the land must be adjudged to be in his possession ; because of the establishment of proof, and also because possession is a right which is the object of desire In the same manner as other rights.—If both parties produce evidence in support of their claims, the ground must in that case be adjudged to be jointly in possession of both —If, however, one of the claimants should have made bricks upon the ground, or should have built upon it, or dug a well or a ditch in it, in all these cases the possession must be adjudged to him on account of those acts.

CHAPTER V.

OF CLAIM OF PARENTAGE.

A claim made by the seller of a female slave to a child born of her within less than six months after the sale, is established.—If a person sell a female slave, and she afterwards bring forth a child, and the seller claim it.—in that case, provided the birth take place in less than six months from the sale, the child is adjudged to the seller, and the mother is his Am-Walid.—This is according to a favourable construction of the law. In the opinion of Ziffer and Shafei the claim is null ; and this is agreeable to analogy ; because the seller, in making the sale, has virtually acknowledged the child to be a slave, which is inconsistent with his plea of its being his child.—The reason for a more favourable construction in this particular is, that as the birth happened in less than six months from the sale, it is evident that the conception must have existed whilst the slave was in the possession of the seller ; and this argues the conception to have proceeded from the seller, since there is no reason to suppose that the woman was guilty of wheredom. As pregnancy moreover, is a circumstance which may remain unknown for a time, the seller is on this account vindicated from the charge of prevarication or inconsistency and his claim is consequently valid.—Now as his claim of parentage is valid, it is therefore referred to the period of conception ; and hence it appears that the man has sold his Am-Walid ; and as the sale of an Am-Walid is unlawful, it must therefore be annulled, and the price must be returned by the purchaser, as having been unjustly obtained

And if the purchaser make the same claim, still the claim of the seller is preferred.—If, on the other hand, the purchaser should, either at the same time with, or posterior to, the claim of the seller, claim the parentage of the child, in that case, also, the claim of the seller is preferred, because of its having existed prior to that of the purchaser, as being referred to the period of conception.

If the birth happen within from six months to two years after the sale, his claim is not admitted without the verification of the purchaser—Supposing, however, the child to be born two years after the sale, the seller's claim of parentage is not in that case valid ; because the conception, in this instance, could not possibly have taken place during his possession of the slave, and this is the only idea under which a decision could pass in his favour :—his claim, therefore, cannot be admitted unless it be confirmed by the

---

*Undoubtedly meaning a foundling, or strayed child.

†The translator has omitted a case of considerable length, which immediately follows, relative to the claim of sundry persons to a wall, founded upon different circumstances which argue right of property.—These circumstances the translator has not been able to procure a satisfactory explanation of ; and they are probably such as relate to antiquated customs in Arabia.

purchaser; in which case the parentage of the child is established in the seller, as on a supposition of marriage:—for this reason, however, the child is not free, nor is the sale annulled, since it is evident that the conception did not take place whilst the slave was in the seller's possession:—the child's freedom, therefore, is unestablished, as well as the eventual freedom of the mother. —Supposing, also, the child to be born at any period more than six months and less than two years from the date of the sale, the claim of parentage by the seller cannot be admitted unless it be verified the purchaser; since, in this instance also, it is not absolutely certain that the conception took place during the seller's right of property, therefore there is no proof, and hence the necessity of the verification of the purchaser.—If, therefore, the purchaser verify the claim of the seller, the parentage is established in him and the sale is annulled, and the child is free, and the mother becomes an Am-*Walid*, in the same manner as in the first instance; because the seller and the purchaser are both agreed in the circumstance of conception having taken place during the right of property of the seller.

The mother becomes his Am-Walid if the child be living at the time of the claim.—If the child, having been born in less than six months from the sale, should die, and the seller should afterwards claim his parentage, the mother does not in that case become his Am-Walid; because she is a dependant on the child, with regard to her eventual claim to freedom; and the child not being extant to admit of its issue from the seller being proved, she cannot of course become his Am-Walid.—If, on the other hand the mother were to die, where the child had been born in less than six months from the sale, and the seller claim his parentage, in this case the parentage of the child is established in the seller, and he is entitled to resume the child; because the child is the principal with respect to the establishment of the parentage and cannot therefore be affected by the extinction of a dependancy in the death of the mother. —In this case the seller, according to Haneefa must return the whole of the price, because it becomes apparent that he sold his Am-Walid, and Haneefa holds that the property involved in an Am-Walid is not of, an appreciable nature. in sales and usurpations, and that therefore the purchaser is not responsible for it in the present instance.—In the opinion of the two disciples, however, he ought only to terun a proportion of the price adequate to the value of the child, because, (according to them) the property involved in an Am-Walid is of an appreciable nature, and consequently induces responsibility in a purchaser.

If made by the seller, after the mother has been emancipated by the purchaser, it is valid: but if the child should have been emancipated by him it is null.—It is related, in the Jama Sagheer, that if a female slave, being pregnant, should be sold by her master, and having afterwards brought forth a child, the seller should claim the child after she had been emancipated by the purchaser; in this case the child is considered as the offspring of the seller, and he must return to the purchaser a part of the price proportionate to its value. This also accords with the opinion of the two disciples, Haneefa alleges that the seller must return the whole of the price, in the same manner as in case of the mother's death; and this is approved. —If, however, the purchaser should have emancipated the child only, in this case the claim of the seller is null.—The reason for the distinction between these two cases is as follows:—In the former case, the child being the principal with regard to the claim, and the mother only a dependancy (as has been already explained), it follows that the bar to the claim of parentage and claim of offspring (namely, emancipation) exists in the dependant, that is, in the mother;—and consequently cannot operate upon the child, who is a principal:—the claim to the child is therefore approved, and it is accordingly free; and the parentage is established in the seller. The freedom of the child, moreover, or the establishment of parentage, do not necessarily infer that the mother also is emancipated—(whence it is that the child of a Magroor is free, whilst the mother remains a slave:—and also; that if a person marry the female slave of another, and beget a child upon her, the parentage is established in him, whilst the mother continues the slave of her master).—In the second case, on the contrary. the bar exists in the child, who is the principal, and hence the claim cannot be made good either with respect to the principal or the dependancy.—The freedom of the child is a bar to validity of the claim, because, as emancipation is incapable of annulment, in the same manner as a claim of parentage or of offspring are incapable of it, they are therefore both of equal force Now, in the case in question, an actual manumission has been established on the part of the purchaser, whilst on the part of the seller, on the other hand, is established a right of claim in regard to the child, and a right of emancipation in regard to the mother; but a mere right to a thing cannot be opposed to the actual thing itself.—It is also to be abserved that the purchaser's creating the child a Modabbir is, in this respect, equivalent to the complete emancipation of him, as that also is incapable of annulment, and is, moreover, followed by certain of the effects of emancipation,—such, for instance, as preventing sale.

A claim made by the original seller, after a second sales is valid; and that sale is null.—If a person sell a slave, that has been born

* Namely, her becoming an Am-Walid; which would have given her an eventual claim to freedom.

of a female slave, who was his property at the time of the birth,* and the purchaser afterwards sell him to another person, and the first seller then claim him, in that case the slave in question is his child, and the sale in null; because sale is capable of annulment, whereas the right of this person to claim the parentage of the slave is incapable of it; the sale is accordingly annulled.—In the same manner, if the buyer, after, the purchase of the mother and son, should make a Mokatib of the former, or pledge him, or let him out to hire—or, if he should make a Mokatiba of the mother, or pledge her, or give her in marriage to some person, and the seller afterwards claim the child,—in any of these cases his claim must be admitted; and all the several contracts mentioned are annulled, as they are all capable of annulment.—It is otherwise where the purchaser emancipates or makes a Modabbir of the child,—as has been already explained:—and it is also otherwise where the purchaser first claim him as his child, and afterwards the seller.—because the parentage, after having been established in the purchaser, cannot again be established in the seller, as it is a right which is incapable of annulment, and hence the case is the same as if the purchaser had emancipated him.

A claim established with respect to one twin establishes it with respect to the other also.—If a female slave bring forth twins, and the proprietor claim the parentage of one of them, in this case the establishment of parentage in him, with, respect to one of them, necessarily involves the same with respect to the other; because they must both have been conceived from one seed; for this reason, that by twins is understood two children born of the same mother, and between the birth of whom a period of less than six months has intervened,—and it is therefore impossible that the conception of the other child should have been supervenient and separate, as pregnancy† cannot be short of six months—It is related, in the Jama Sagheer, that if a person be possessed of two slaves, twins, who had been born his property, and he should sell one of them and the purchaser emancipate him, and the seller afterwards avow, as his issue, the one who remains in his hands; in this case both the twins are his children, and the emancipation of the purchaser is null;‡ because, upon the parentage being established of the one in his possession, by which he becomes free; the parentage and consequent freedom of the other are necessarily involved, as they are twins Hence, as it appears that the purchaser bought a person who was originally free, it follows that his purchase and consequently his emancipation of him is null.—It is otherwise where there is only one slave, for in this case the buyer's purchase and consequent emancipation are not liable to be annulled upon the seller establishing his claim; whereas, in the case now under consideration, the emancipation of the purchaser is rendered null dependantly; in other words freedom is first established in the slave who remained in the claimant's hands, and is then, dependantly, established in him who was sold and afterwards emancipated. There is therefore a material difference between the cases,*

A claim of offspring cannot be established, after on acknowledgment in favour of another person.—If a person be possessed of a boy, and declare the boy to be the son of a certain absent slave, and afterwards declare him to be his son, in this case the parentage although the absent slave were to deny the boy to be his son,—This is according to Haneefa. The two disciples have said that in case the denial of the slave, the parentage of the possessor is established.—A similar disagreement subsists where the possessor declares the boy in his possession to be the son of a particular person, and born of his wife, and afterwards himself claims the parentage of him.—The reasoning of the two disciples is that the ackowledgment, by the master, of the boy being the son of his slave, is repelled by the denial of the slave, whence the case becomes the same as if no such acknowledgment had ever been made.—Now, although parentage cannot be annulled after the establishment of it, yet acknowledgment of parentage is set aside by the denial of the person who is the object of it, and the acknowledgment is ascribed to levity or compulsion (as if a person, by way of levity, or under the influence of compulsion, should make an acknowledgment that his slave was his son, in which case his acknowledgment is not valid):—the case in question, therefore, becomes the same as if a purchaser of a slave should acknowledge that the "seller had emancipated him," and the seller deny the same, and the purchaser then say that "he had himself emancipated him; for in this case last assertion of the purchaser is credited, and the willa-right with respect to the slave thus emancipated rests with him; and his ackcowledgment with regard to the seller is considered as never having existed; so also in the case in question.—It would be otherwise if the boy should verify the first assertion of the possessor (that "he is the son of a certain absent slave,")

*This case supposes the child and the mother to be sold together, as appears by the context a little further on.

†Meaning the pregnancy requisite to produce a perfect child.

‡One effect of which is to destroy his right of Willa, which he would otherwise have enjoyed.

*This case has been somewhat abridged in the translation, and in particular the matter part of it is entirely omitted as being a mere repetition.

and the possessor himself should then claim the issue; because the claim would in such a case be invalid, as having been preferred after the proof of parentage in another. It would also be otherwise if the slave should remain silent, without either confirming or denying the claim for, in this case also, the subsequent claim of the possessor would be invalid, because the right of the person acknowledged relates to the boy, and there is a possibiiity that he may varify the assertion of the possessor.—The boy, therefore, in this instance, stands in the same predicament with the son of a woman who has been required to make assevation, and whose parentage cannot be proved by any other than the imprecator (namely, the husband of the woman), who has the power of afterwards contradicting himself, and declaring that the said son is his issue.—Haneefa, on the other hand, argues that parentage is a matter which, after proof, cannot be set aside; nor can the acknowledgment of such a matter be undone by the rejection of the person who is the object of it; it therefore continues in force notwithstanding the rejection; and hence the claim of the master, sabsequent to such acknowledgment, is invalid, although the slave should contradict the acknowledgment; in the same manner as if a person should bear testimony to the parentage of an infant, and his testimony being set aside from suspicion, he should then claim the said infant as his son; in which case his claim would not be valid; and so also in the case in question. The ground on which this proceeds is that the right of the person in question (namely, he slave) relates to the boy. insomuch that, if the slave should verify the assertion of the master subsequent to a contradiction, the parentage of the boy is established in the slave: and, in the same manner, the right of the boy is connected with the acknowledgment of the master; and hence the acknowledgment cannot be set aside by the contradiction of the slave.*—With respect to the case of a purchaser acquiring the right of Willa, adduced by the two disciples as analogous to this, it may be replied that a disagreement subsists concerning this case also; as Haneefa does not admit the doctrine there advanced:—or, if it be admitted, still there subsits this difference between it and the case in question, that Willa is capable of annulment,—in other words, the right of Willa in one person is sometimes set aside in favour of another, when any supervenient circumstance occurs to strengthen the claims of that other. Thus, if Zeyd should contract his female slave in marriage with the slave of Khalid, and after their having issue should emancipate the mother, in this case the right of Willa, or patronage, over the child, belongs to Zeyd; but if afterwards Khalid should emancipate his slave, who is the father of the child. then the right of Willa over the child would be annulled in Zeyd, and would vest in Khalid, the emancipator of the father, since the right derived from the emancipation of the father is stronger than that derived from the emancipation of the mother:—whereas, in the case exemplified by the two disciples, the establishment of the right of Willa in the seller of the slave rests on the supposition of the seller, after having contradicted the purchase, again contradicting himself, and verifying the assertion of the purchaser; and when, in this state of suspended Willa, a circumstance intervenes which operates as a stronger cause for the establishment of the Willa in the purchaser, the suspended Willa in the seller becomes null.—The circumstance here alluded to is the assertion of the purchaser that "he emancipated the slave;" and this operates as a stronger cause since it gives immediate freedom to the slave in consequence of his being the property of the purchaser, whereas the emancipation of the seller does not give immediate freedom, as it rests upon the verification of the purchaser, and hence becomes null on the supervention of a stronger cause; because Willa is capable of annulment; contrary to parentage, as has been already explained.—From this doctrine of Haneefa, that the possessor's acknowledgment of the boy being the son of his slave cannot afterwards be set aside by the contradiction of the person who is the subject of that acknowledgment,—and that, consequently, and subsequent claim of the possessor to the parentage of the child will not be valid,—it follows that a decree may be founded upon it for establishing the validity of a father's selling his son begotten upon his slave; for, in order to remove any apprehensions from the mind of the purchaser of his afterwards claiming his son, and thereby rendering the sale null, he may make an acknowledgment of the issue in favour of another, by which means he will effectually preclude the possibility of himself afterwards preferring a valid claim to him

A claim of parentage made by a Christian is preferable to a claim of bondage advanced by a Mussulman.—If a boy be in the possession of two men, of whom one is a Mussulman and the other a Christian, and the Christian assert that "he is his son," and the Mussulman that "he is his slave," he must in this case be decreed to be the son of the Christian, and free; because, although the religion of Islam have a superiority, yet that superiority is allowed to operate only in cases which are balanced against each other; but there is no balance between a claim of offspring and of bondage: the claim of the Christian is therefore admitted; because this is attended with a great benefit to the boy, since it procures him immediate free-

*Because a declaration which tends to establish a right cannot be revoked: and, in the case in question, the right of the boy is to have his parentage established and ascertained.

dom, and (as may also be expected) future faith, inasmuch as the arguments for the unity of the Godhead are evident and plain; whereas, if a contrary decree be passed (that is, if the boy should be decreed to be the slave of the Mussulman, and not the son of the Christian), in that case the true faith in the boy would be established merely from dependance, whilst he must be precluded from freedom, as not having the power himself to acquire it.—If, however both the Mussulman and the Christian claim the issue, the claim of the Mussulman must in that case be preferred, on account of the superiority due to the true faith, and because of the superior advantage that would result to the boy.

A claim of parentage, by a married woman, is not admitted, unless at least one woman testify to the birth.—If a married woman should claim parentage, as if she should say, "this boy in my arms is my son," her claim is not valid unless the birth be attested by the testimony of one woman; because the claim so made relates to another, and is therefore not admitted unless supported by proof: in contradiction to the case of a father, as his claim of parentage relates purely to himself.—(It is to be observed that the testimony of the midwife alone is sufficient with respect to birth, since the object of the testimony is merely to ascertain that the child in question is the identical child which the said woman brought forth; whilst parentage, on the other hand, is established on the ground of the mother of the child being the wife of the husband:—it is, moreover, recorded, in the Nakl Saheeh, that the Prophet accepted the testimony of a midwife, in a case of birth.)

Or (if she be in her edit) one man and two women.—If however the woman in question be in her edit from a complete divorce, the testimony of the midwife alone does not suffice with respect to the birth:—on the contrary, that of two men, or of one man and two women, is requisite —(This is the doctrine according to the opinion of Haneefa, as has been already mentioned in treating of divorce.)

If the woman be neither married, nor in her edit from divorce, in this case lawyers have asserted that the parentage of the child is established by herself; her own assertion on this head being admitted; since, in this case, it does not operate upon, or affect, any other person.—But if, being married, she should say, "this is my son, begotten by this my husband," and the husband verify the same, there is in this case no occasion for one witness to prove the birth, since the acknowledgment of the husband renders it unnecessary.

But if her husband verify her claim, there is no occasion for such evidence.—If the boy be in the joint possession of the wife and her husband, and the husband should say "this boy is my son, begotten not on this woman but on another," and the woman should say "this is my son, begotten by another husband," in this case the boy is decreed to be their son, because of the probability of the thing founded upon their joint possession of the boy, and their connection with each other as husband and wife. Besides, the assertion of each has a tendency to destroy the right of the other, and therefore that of neither out to be adopted.—This case resembles that where each of two men, having jointly the possession of a piece of cloth, asserts that it is the joint property of himself and some other person, in which case the cloth is adjudged to be the property of the two possessor.—There is, however, this difference between these two cases,—that in the case of the cloth, the other persons, in favour of whom the parties have respectively made an acknowledgment, are admitted to a participation in the shares of their respective acknowledgers, because of the subject of contention (namely, the cloth) being capable of division;—whereas, in the case in question, the persons referred to are not admitted to a participation in the right of the acknowledger, since parentage (which is the subject of it) does not admit of participation.

Case of a person begetting a child upon a female slave, under an erroneous possession.—If a person purchase a female slave, and beget a child upon her, and claim it, after its birth, as his issue, and it afterwards appear that the slave had not been the property of the seller, in this case the purchaser must give, to the rightful master of the slave, the value which the child may bear at the time of contention,—and the child is free; first, because he is the offspring of a Magroor: for a Magroor is defined to be a person who begets a child upon a woman, on the belief of her being his property—(or whom he has in that belief married),—and who afterwards proves to be the property of another; and this definition of a Magroor is exactly applicable to the person in question; the issue of a Magroor is therefore free for an equivalent, according to all the companions:—in the second place, a regard must be had to the right of both parties.—The said child is therefore completely free, in behalf of his father, and a slave in behalf of the plaintiff, namely, the proprietor of his mother.—Now, since the child remains in the possession of the father without any transgression or unwarrantable act on the part of the father, the father is therefore not responsible for it unless he become a bar to the seisin of it by the proprietor (in the same manner as is decreed in the case of the child of an usurped female slave); and he is a bar only where, the plaintiff having demanded the child, he [the father] refuses to surrender him; whence it is that the value of the child is estimated from the day of contention, as it is then that the bar begins to operate. If, therefore, the child should die in the possession of the father, without any contention having happened, the father is in no degree responsible, since no bar had taken place; and hence, also, if the child should die possessed of property, the father inherits it, as the child was completely free in right of his father.—If, on the other hand, the father should kill the son, he must in this case make compensation for the value, since he himself operated as a bar the proprietor's right—In the same manner also, if any other than the father were to kill the child, and the father exact the fine of blood, he must pay the value to the proprietor; because, although the child be destroyed, yet the compensation remains whole and entire in the hands of the father (since the fine of blood is a compensation); and, as the existence of the compensation is equivalent to the existence of the thing itself, and the bar the compensation is equivalent to the bar to the thing itself, it follows that it is incumbent on him to give the value, in the same manner as it would have been incumbent on him in case of the existence of the child.—It is to be observed that the purchaser, after paying a compensation for the value of the child, is entitled to receive the said value from the seller, since the seller was responsible to him for the safety and preservation of it; he is therefore entitled to exact from the seller the value of the child, in the same manner as the price of the mother.—It is different, however, with respect to the Akir, or fine of trespass, as he is not entitled to exact that from the seller.—The purchaser, therefore, as having had carnal knowledge of a woman who was the property of another, although he be exempted from punishment for whoredom, because of the doubt which existed, is notwithstanding required to pay to the proprietor an Akir, or fine of trespass;—but he must not demand a reimbursement for the Akir from the seller, because he became liable to pay it for the commission of an act of which he himself reaped the sole benefit.

BOOK XXV.

OF IKRAR OR ACKNOWLEDGMENTS.

Definition of the term.—Ikrar, in the language of the law, means the notification or avowal of the right of another upon one's self.—The person making such acknowledgment is termed Mookir;—the person in whose favour the acknowledgment is made is termed Mookir-lee-hoo; and the thing which is the subject of the acknowledgment is termed Mookir-be-hee.

CHAPTER I.

Acknowledgment, proceeding from a competent person, is binding upon the acknowledger.—When a person possessing sanity of mind, and arrived at the age of maturity, makes in acknowledgment of a right, such acknowledgment is binding upon him, whether the subject of it be known or unknown; because acknowledgment (as has been already explained) is an avowal of the right of another upon one's self: and by acknowledgment the right of another becomes binding;—and this argues the establishment of such right; because, property being desired by all men, it is not likely that any person would falsely establish the right of another to a part of his own Besides, the Prophet ordered Maaz to be stoned in consequence of his acknowledgment of whoredom.

But not upon any other person.—It is proper, in this place, to observe that acknowledgment is a defective proof,—in other words it operates only upon the person of the acknowledger, and not upon that of another, since over that he has no power.

The points that establish competency are freedom—Freedom is established as a necessary qualification in an acknowledger, in order that his acknowledgment may be valid, absolutely—(that is to say, with respect to property and the like): for although a privileged slave be, virtually, the same as a freeman with respect to acknowledgement, yet the acknowledgment of an inhibited slave is not valid with respect to property, but merely with respect to punishment or retaliation.—The reason of this is that the ackowledgment of an inhibited slave induces the obligation of a debt upon himself; and his self being the property of his master, it is consequently the same as if he had made an acknowledgment in regard to another which is not lawful.—It is otherwise with respect to a privileged slave; for his acknowledgment is valid, as his master, in privileging him, does virtually assent to his contracting debts—It is otherwise, also, with respect to the acknowledgment of inhibited slaves, in cases of punishment and retaliation; for if an inhibited slave should say "I have committed whoredom with a certain woman,"—or "I have killed a certain person,"—his acknowledgment would in these cases be valid; since a slave, in matters relative to punishment and retaliation, is allowed to assume his original condition of freedom (whence it is that the acknowledgment of his master with regard to him in these cases is invalid).

Sanity of mind, and maturity.—Sanity of mind, and maturity of years, are also necessary conditions in acknowledgment, because the acknowledgment of an infant or an idiot is invalid, as neither has any power to assume an obligation upon himself. The acknowledgment of a privileged infant is, however, valid, as he virtually a major.

Acknowledgment is not invalidated by ignorance of the subject.—Ignorance, with respect to the subject, is not destructive of the validity of acknowledgment, since it sometimes happens that an unknown right is due; as where, for instance, a person destroys something belonging to another of which the value was not known to the owner,—or gives a person a wound, of which the specific fine is not known at the instant.—or, where a person has accounts to settle with another, and of which he knows not the exact balance in favour of the other. Acknowledgment, moreover, is an intimation of the right of another; and the acknowledgment of an unknown right is therefore valid.

But it is so, by ignorance of the person in whose favour the acknowledgment is made—(IT is otherwise where the person in whose favour the acknowledgment is made is unknown; for this is invalid: as a right or claim cannot rest in an unknown person.)—As the acknowledgment, therefore, of an unknown right is valid, the acknowledger must be required to define the unknown thing, since it is with him that the ignorance originates;—in the same manner as where a person emancipates one of two slaves,—in which case he is required to specify the one to whom the emancipation applies—If the acknowledger should refuse to make the specification, then the Kazee must compel him; since it is incumbent upon him to disengage himself from the responsibility founded upon a valid acknowledgment, which he has incurred, and this cannot be effectual but by a specification.

Acknowledgment generally made must be specified to relate to something of a valuable nature—IF a person say "I owe a thing (or a right) to a certain person," it is incumbent on him to specify something valuable; because he has acknowledged an obligation; and a thing which does not bear value induces no obligation: if, therefore, he specify something which bears no value, it is considered as a retractation of his acknowledgment; which in temporal concerns is not admitted.—In the same manner, also, if a person should say "I have usurped a thing from a certain person," it is incumbent on him to explain it to be something bearing value, and to the taking of which there existed some bar and prevention; since usurpation is not established unless there be a bar to the taking of it; and according to established custom there is no bar where the thing in question bears no value.

And if more be claimed than the acknowledger specifies, his assertion, upon oath, is credited.—IF a person make an acknowledgment with respect to an unknown thing, or an unknown right, and define it to be something bearing value, and the person in whose favour the acknowledgment is made should claim more than is defined by the acknowledger,—in this case the assertion of the acknowledger, corroborated by an oath, must be credited

An acknowledgment, expressed under the general term property, must be received according to the explanation of the acknowledger—IF a person say "property* is due by me to a certain person," he must explain the amount; and his explanation must be credited, whether it be great or small, since great and small are alike applicable to property.—If, however, he specify less than one dirm, it is not to be admitted, since, in common usage, any thing short of a dirm is not reckoned property.

But if made to a great property, it cannot means less than what constitutes a Neisab in the property to which it relates.—IF he should say "a great property is due by me,", then, provided he explain it to be less than two hundred dirms, it cannot be admitted according to the two disciples (and also according to one report from Haneefa); because, where he describes the property in question, as being considerable, his explanation to any amount short of two hundred dirms is not to be credited; for, if it were otherwise, his description of great would be idle and nugatory, since the smallest sum which can properly be termed great is that which constitutes a Nisab in Zakat †—namely, two hundred dirms; as it is the possession of this sum which brings a person within the description of wealthy.—There is another opinion ascribed to Haneefa that the explanation, if it be less than ten dirms (which is the Nisab fixed for theft) must not be admitted; because ten dirms are what may property be termed a great property, whence it is that, for the theft of that quantity, the hand of man (which is otherwise sacred) is cut off.—What is here advanced respects an acknowledgment of great property in dirms.—But if he should have said "I owe great property of deenars," then the amount due is fixed at twenty Miskals. In camels it is twenty-five; because the smallest Nisab of camels upon which a camel is due in Zakat, is twenty-five ‡—In all property not subject to Zakat, the explanation is required to amount to a Nisab with respect to the value; § that is to say, if the acknowledger explain to the value of a Nisab his acknowledgment is to be credited; but if to less, it must be rejected.—IF the acknowledger should say, "I owe large properties," the smallest specification that can in that case be admitted is three Nisabs, of that species of property to which the acknowledgment relates; because the word properties is

*Arab. Mal; meaning property in each, or in the precious metals, &c,, in opposition to Rakht and Matta, which are particularly applied to goods and effects.

†See Vol. I., p. I.

‡Upon which a Zakat is paid of a yearling camel's colt. (See Vol. I. p 5).

§.See Vol., pp. 9 and 10.

plural, and the smallest degree of plurality is three.

Cases of acknowledgment relating to many dirms.—IF a person should say "I owe many dirms," his explanation is not admitted to an amount short of ten dirms, according to Haneefa.—The two disciples maintain that it is not to be admitted to an amount short of two hundred; because a proprietor of a Nisab (namely, two hundred dirms) is held to be opulent—(not one who is possessed of a smaller number,) whence it is that the proprietor of a Nisab is required to aid and assist others, and not he who is possessed of a smaller number.—The reasoning of Haneefa is founded upon principles peculiar to the Arabic language.

Or to dirms generally.—IF the acknowledger should say "I owe dirms," he is supposed to mean three, as that is the least number of plurality. But if he should himself explain a larger number, it must be admitted, as the word dirms may be applied to any number,—The weight of the dirms must be estimated from what is customary.*

Section

Acknowledgement made in favour of an embryo (in virtue of bequest or inheritance is valid.—IF a person say "I am bound, for a thousand dirms, to the conception in the womb of a certain woman; and afterwards add that "the said sum is due in virtue of a bequest of a particular person"—or that "it is the right of the conception in virtue of inheritance from its parent"—the acknowledgment so made is valid, in as much as it relates (in these instances) to a cause which is fit and adequate to the establishment of a right to property in a conception.

Provided the birth take place within a probable period.—IF, therefore, the woman should afterwards bring forth a living child within such a period as evinces the conception to have existed in the womb at the time of the acknowledgment, the acknowledger is bound to the child for a thousand dirms.

And if the embryo prove still born, the thing acknowledged must be divided among the heirs; or, if twins be born, it must be divided between them.—IF, on the other hand, the woman should bring forth a dead child, the acknowledgment in that case relates to the testator or the inheritee, and the amount of it must accordingly be divided amongst their heirs; because the acknowledgment was in reality in favour of the testator, or the inheritee, and was to vest in the offspring only on condition of its being born alive, which did not afterwards take place.—If the woman should bring forth two living children, then the thing acknowledged must be divided equally between them.

But if such acknowledgment be ascribed to an impossible cause, it is null.—IF a person say "I am bound to the conception of a certain woman for a thousand dirms, being the price of an article I purchased from the said conception," or "being money borrowed from it."—no obligation rests upon the acknowledger, as he explained it to arise from a cause which could not have happened, since a conception is incapable of either lending or selling.

And so also if it be made without specifying any cause.—IF a person acknowledge his being bound to a conception, without specifying the cause, such acknowledgment (according to Aboo Yoosaf) is invalid.—Mohammed maintains that it is valid; for, as ackowledgment is proof, it is necessary to fulfil it a far as may be practicable; and it is practicable to fulfil it, in the present instance, by construing the cause to have been such as was competent to the establishment of a right of property in the conception.—The argument of Aboo Yoosaf is that an acknowledgment, when absolute, is construed to be in virtue of traffic (whence it is that the acknowledgment of a privileged slave, or of one out of the two partners by recipocity, is understood to be an acknowledgment founded upon traffic); the case, therefore, is the same as if the acknowledger had expressly specified the cause to be traffic;—and as that would have been invalid, so also is it invalid where the cause is understood to be such from implication.

Acknowledgment relating to a thing existing, but not yet produced, is valid.—IF a person acknowledge the conception of a female slave, or the offspring of a goat, to be due to another, such acknowledgment is binding; since it would have been valid if he had bequeathed either of these, and his intention is it therefore construed to be such.

Acknowledgment of a debt, under a condition of option, is valid, and the condition becomes null.—IF a person should make acknowledgment that "he owes another a thousand dirms upon an optional condition" (in other words, if he should say "the said amount is due by me (or, from me), but I have an option of three days"),—the condition of option is in this case null, since optional conditions are instituted with a view to annulment, whereas an acknowledgment is a notification or avowal, which is binding; the acknowledgment, therefore, is in this case binding, and is not rendered null by the nullity of the condition.

---

*A considerable portion of the text which immediately follows has been omitted by the translator, as the cases which it contains, relating entirely to verbal criticism, cannot easily be translated, and are such as belong more properly to the province of grammarians than of lawyers.

CHAPTER II.

OF EXCEPTION ; AND WHAT IS DEEMED EQUIVALENT TO EXCEPTION.*

The exception of a part of the thing acknowledged is valid, if immmediately joined with the acknowledgment ; but if the whole be excepted, the exception is not attended to.—If a person make an acknowledgment of a thing in favour of another, adding an exception of part of the thing so acknowledged, uch exception is valid ; and the acknowledger becomes bound for the remainder, whether the exception be great or small ; provided, however, that it be immediately joined to the acknowledgment.† If, on the contrary, he except the whole of the thing acknowledged, the acknowledgment is in that case binding, and the exception null ; because this is in fact a retractation, not an exception ; for exception supposes the remainder of a part after the deduction of the thing excepted from the whole ; but after the deduction of the whole there is no remainder : it is therefore a retractation, and consequently null.

The exception must be homogeneous with the acknowledgment : otherwise it is invalid.—If a person say "I am bound to a certain person for a hundred dirms, with the exception of one deenar" (or "of one Kafeez of wheat‡"), then according to the two disciples he is bound for a hundred dirms, with the exception of one deenar (or of one Kafeez of wheat).—If, on the contrary, he should say "I owe a hundred dirms, with the exception of one piece of cloth:" the exception so made is not valid.—Mohammed maintains that the exception is invalid in both cases.—Shafei, on the other hand, holds that in both cases it is valid.—The argument of Mohammed is that an exception means a deduction from the thing mentioned in the preceding part of the sentence, which cannot be established where the thing excepted is not of the same genus with the thing from which it is excepted. The argument of Shafei is that the thing excepted, and that from which the exception is made, are of one and the same genus, as being both valuables,—The argument of the two disciples is that in the former instance, the thing itself, and the exception from it, are of the same genus as they are both pice :—deenars are evidently so :—and things estimable by weight, or by measurement of capacity, are so likewise, according to their qualities ;—is other words they become so upon their qualities being explained.—In the second instance, on the contrary (where the exception is cloth), the thing excepted, and that from which the exception is made, are of different genus, as cloth is not price in any shape, neither in respect of itself, nor in respect of its description or quality ; and accordingly, cloth is not due in any contract of exchange, excepting that of Sillim (that is, where the price is advanced to the seller beforehand).—Now whatever is price has this fitness, that it may be set in comparison with dirms or deenars, and may consequently, in a proportionate degree, be excepted from them ;—whereas on the other hand, whatever cannot be stated as price has not a fitness of being compared with dirms and deenars, and consequently cannot be stated as an exception from them, since the proportion cannot be ascertained.

A reservation of the will of God renders the acknowledgment null.—If a person make an acknowledgment, with this proviso "if it please God," he is not then liable for any thing; because (according to Aboo Yoosaf), a reservation of the pleasure of God is either an annulment of the acknowledgment, or a suspension of it ; and the achnowledgment is null on either supposition :—or, because (as Mohammed argues) it is equivalent to an acknowledgment suspended upon a condition, which is null, as in acknowledgment does not admit of being suspended on a condition, since acknowledgment is an avowal, which cannot be made conditional ; for if it be true it cannot be rendered false by a default of the condition; or on the contrary, if it be false it cannot be rendered true by the fulfilment of the condition :—or, lastly, because the acknowledgment is suspended on a circumstance which it is impossible to ascertain.—It is otherwise where a person says "I acknowledge a hundred dirms to be due by me to a particular person on my death,"—or "upon the arrival of a particular month,"—or "upon the festival of breaking Lent,"—because in these cases the acknowledgment is not suspended upon a condition, as this is merely an explanation of the time and is therefore a postponing of the thing ackowledged, and not a suspension ; whence it is that if the person in whose favour the acknowledgment is made can prove the falsity of the postponement, the thing becomes due to him immediately.

In an acknowledgment regarding a house, an exception of the foundation is invalid.—If a person make an acknowledgment of a house in favour of another, and except the foundation, both the house and the foundation are the right of the person in whose favour the acknowledgment is made; because the foundation is included in the house from its dependancy, and not from its being comprehended in the word house ; and an exception is valid only where it relates to something comprehended in the thing expressed, according to the meaning of the word. It is to be observed

*"What is deemed equivalent to exception,"—that is, reservation of any kind, &c.

† That is, that it be expressed in the same sentence with the acknowledgment.

‡ Grain is united with money in accounts, both being considered as of the same genus, since both are equally price (that is, standards of value), and may be equally used to represent property. (See Partnership, note Vol. II, p. 222.)

that the stone in a ring, or the trees of an orchard, stand, in the same relation to the ring or the orchard as the foundation does to a house, because neither the word ring nor orchard applies to the stone or the trees, but are both included merely as dependants. It is otherwise where a person makes an acknowledgment of a house in favour of another, excepting from it an indefinite portion, or a specific apartment, as the exception in these cases relates to a thing which is comprehended in the word house.

An exception of the court-yard of a house is admitted.—IF a person say "the foundation of this House belongs to me, and the Sihn (meaning the court-yard) to a particular person:" then the person in whose favour the acknowledgment is made is entitled to the court-yard, and the foundation is the property of the acknowledger. It is therefore, in fact, the same as if the acknowledger had declared that "all the ground free of building is the property of such a person." It would be otherwise if, instead of Sihn, he were to mention the word Arz [earth], for in that case the foundation as well as the house would become the property of the person in whose favour the acknowledgment is made; because an acknowledgment of the ground is an acknowledgment of the foundation, as much as an acknowledgment of the house itself; for the ground is the original thing, and the foundation is included along with it as a dependant.—In an acknowledgment of the ground, therefore, the foundation is included as a dependant, in the same manner as it would be included in the house itself; and hence the exception is invalid.

A reservation of non-delivery of the article is done away by the delivery of it to the acknowledger.—IF a person acknowledge a debt of a thousand dirms to another, as the price of a slave which he had purchased from that other, but which he had not received from him, in that case, if the slave be specific (as if he had said, "as the price of this slave"), the person in whose favour the acknowledgment is made must be desired to deliver up the slave and receive a thousand dirms, on pain of forfeiting his claim.—The compiler of the Hedaya remarks that this case admits of several statements.—I. That which has been already made, and which proceeds on the supposition of the acknowledger's assertion of the purchase and the non-delivery being verified by the person in whose favour the acknowledgment is made; and in which the law stands as above expounded, because the mutual agreement of the parties is equivalent to actual inspection.—II. Where the person in whose favour the acknowledgment is made denies the sale of the particular slave alleged by the acknowledger, and declares that "the slave in question in his property and it is another slave he sold to him,"—in which case the acknowledger is liable for the amount; since he acknowledges a sum due, on the supposition of the existance of a slave which he had purchased; and consequently upon the other person's declaration of the existence of the slave sold, he becomes liable for the amount.

OBJECTION.—It would appear that the acknowledger is not responsible for the amount, since he acknowledges his debt of a thousand dirms for the purchase of a specific slave; whereas the person in whose favour the acknowledgment is made claim the said debt for the sale of another slave.—Now as acknowledgment is binding only from the particular cause which is assigned for it and the cause in this case is contradicted by the person in whose favour the acknowledgment is made it follows that the acknowledgment is not valid.

REPLY.—The contradiction, with respect to the cause, after their mutual agreement as to the existence of the obligation, is of no effect. Thus if a person acknowledge his responsibility to another for a thousand dirms, as "for goods purchased from him," and the person in whose favour the acknowledgment is made assert the obligation in question to have arisen from usurpation or loan, still the acknowledger is responsible for the amount: and also in the case in question.—III. Where the person in whose favour the acknowledgment is made declares the slave in question to be his own property, and denies his having sold him; in which case the acknowledger is exempted from any obligation, because he has acknowledged the property to be due only as in return for the slave, and consequently, without that, it is not due from him.

But in case of a disagreement with respect to the article, both parties must be sworn.—IF, however, in this case, the person in whose favour the acknowledgment is made should further declare that "he had sold another slave to him [the acknowledger]," both parties must be sworn: because they are both defendants, as they reciprocally deny the assertions of each other:—and upon each taking on oath, the obligation involved in the acknowledgment is annulled, and the slave remains with the person in whose favour the acknowledgment was made.

If the article be not specific, the reservation is not regarded.—WHAT is here advanced proceeds on a supposition of the slave being specific: for if a person acknowledge a debt of a thousand dirms, due to another, for a slave that he had purchased from him, without specifically describing the slave, the acknowledger is in that case responsible for a thousand dirms:—and his assertion, that "he had not received the slave," is not to be regarded, according to Haneefa, whether he connect such assertion with his acknowledgment, or make it separately: because such assertion is a retraction of his acknowledgment; for this reason, that in acknowledging a thousand dirms to be due from him, he assumes an obligation to that amount; and his denial of the receipt of the indefinite slave is repugnant to this obligation, as the price is not due for an indefinite slave, because of the uncertainty :—and this, whether the uncertainty be interwoven in the contract (as where a person purchases one of two slaves), or supervenient upon it (as where a person purchases a specific slave out of a great number, and afterwards both the buyer and the seller forget the slave that had been purchased) ; because the uncertainty is a bar to the delivery, since the purchaser may always deny whatever slave is produced by the seller to be the one purchased : the uncertainty, therefore, is a bar to the obligation of the price ; and such being the case, the acknowledger, in denying the receipt of the slave, virtually retracts his acknowledgment, which is not allowed —The two disciples allege that if the person in whose favour the acknowledgment is made should verify the acknowledger's assertion, by declaring the debt of one thousand dirms to be due for the price of a slave, the acknowledger's declaration of his not having received the slave is in that case to be credited ; nor is any thing whatever due from him, whether such declaration have been conjoined with the acknowledgment, or otherwise.—But if the person in whose favour the acknowledgment is made contradict the acknowledger, with respect to the debt being for the price of a slave, asserting it to be due for some other goods, then the acknowledger's declaration of his not having received the slave is not to the credited, unless it be conjoined with the acknowledgment. Their reasoning in support of this opinion that the acknowledger having acknowledged the obligation of the debt upon himself, and having explained the cause of it (namely, sale), it follows that if the person in whose favour the acknowledgment is made verify his declaration so far as relates to the cause of the obligation, the sale is fully proven and established ; the obligation, however, towards the discharge of the debt, can be established only by the receipt of the subject of the sale : and as this is denied by the acknowledger, his assertion is therefore credited —If, on the other hand, the person in whose favour the acknowledgment is made should contradict the assertion of the acknowledger in regard to the cause of obligation, then the acknowledger's explanation of the cause may be regarded as a modification (that is, he by it modifies the tenor of the first part of his speech) ; because the tenor of the first part of his speech goes to show that an obligation is at present actually operating upon him ; whereas the latter part, in denying the receipt, tends to prove that no obligation subsists, since the obligation to pay is not established till after the receipt : the last part of the speech, therefore, is an explanatory modification ; and a modification is not admitted unless it be conjoined with the acknowledgment.

A reservation of non-receipt of the thing acknowledged must be credited.—IF a person acknowledge the purchase of an article from another, at the same time declaring that "has not yet received it," his assertion must in that case be credited, according to all our doctors : because he has merely acknowledged a contract of sale ; and an acknowledgment of sale is not an acknowledgment of receipt, since a receipt does not necessarily follow a conclusion of sale.—It is otherwise where a person acknowledge the obligation of the price of an article purchased ; for in that case his assertion of non-receipt is not approved, as payment of the price is not obligatory until after the receipt of the goods.

A reservation of the cause of obligation being illegitimate does not annul the acknowledgment.—IF a Mussulman declare that "he owes such a person a thousand dirms, on account of wine or pork," he is bound for the thousand dirms :—and his explanation of the cause is not admitted, according to Haneefa, whether it be conjoined with the acknowledgment, or otherwise ; because it is a retraction of his acknowledgment as the price of wine or pork cannot be obligatory on a Mussulman ; and in the preceding part of his speech he expressly declares the existence of an obligation upon him to the amount stated. The two disciples allege that if the explanation be conjoined with the acknowledgment, nothing is due from the acknowledger, since the latter part of his speech evidently shows this to have been his meaning, it being in fact the same as if he had added "if it please GOD." To this however, it may be replied, that there is no analogy between the two cases, as a reservation of the pleasure of GOD is a suspension of the matter upon a condition of which it is impossible to obtain a knowledge. Besides the suspension on a condition is a modification, and consequently admissible, provided it be conjoined with the speech : in opposition to an acknowledgment of the price of wine or pork, which is not a suspension, but an annulment of the acknowledgment, as has been already explained.

An exception with respect to the quality of money acknowledged to be due, is set aside by the counter assertion of the person in whose favour the acknowledgment is made.—If a person declare that "a thousand dirms are due from him to such a person, as the price of certain effects," or "on account of a loan ;" and afterwards allege the said thousand dirms to be Zeyf, or Binhirja, or Satooka, or Arzeez, and the person in whose favour the acknowledgment is made allege them to be Jeed,* in that case, according to Haneefa, the acknowledger is responsible for Jeed dirms, whether his latter assertion be conjoined with his prior declaration, or otherwise.—The two disciples maintain that the latter assertion of the acknowledger is to be credited, in case only of its being con-

*Pure money, of the current standard. The other descriptions are explained a little further on.

joined with the former, and not otherwise, —The same difference of opinion obtains where a person declares that "he owes another a thousand dirms" adding, that "they are Zeyf," or that "another has lent him a thousand dirms, but that they are Zeyf," or, that "he owes another a thousand dirms on account of certain goods, but that they are Zeyf."—(Zeyf dirms are such as are not accepted at the public treasury, but which pass amongst merchants; the Binhirja is of a kind still worse, which does not pass amongst merchants; and the Satooka and Arzeez, are the worst of all, and in which the mixture of base metal preponderates). The argument of the two disciples is that the above explanation is a modification, and is consequently valid if conjoined, in the same manner as a condition, or an exception; for the word dirm is literally applicable to Zeyf and metaphorically to Satooka; the acknowledger's declaration, therefore, of their being Zeyf or Satooka is merely a modification, in the same manner as for a person should declare that "he owes a thousand dirms, but of such a kind that ten of them weigh five miskals. The reasoning of Haneefa is that his assertion of their being Zeyf or Satooka is equivalent to a retraction; for an absolute contract presupposes dirms free from defect; whereas Zeyf and Satooka are both defective. Now the plea of a defect is a retractation of part of the obligation involved in the acknowledgment; and the case is therefore the same as if the seller of a thing should say to the purchaser of it, "I have sold you a thing with a defect, of which you were apprised," and the purchaser deny his knowledge of the defect, in which case the denial of the purchaser is credited, as probability argues in his favour, since every absolute contract supposes a freedom from defect. Besides, Satooka dirms do not constitute price, and as a contract of sale is never concluded but for price, it follows that his explanation is, in effect, a retraction. (With respect to the case adduced by the two disciples of "an acknowledgment of a debt of a thousand dirms, accompanied with a declaration that the dirms due are of that kind of which ten are equivalent to five miskals,"—It is to be observed, in reply, that the reservation is admitted, for this reason, that the acknowledger, in this instance, speaks with a reservation merely of the degree or proportion of the dirms, and to that the word dirms applies.—It is otherwise in a description of the goodness of the dirms, for as to this the term dirms does not properly apply, it is not considered as a reservation, any more than the exception of the foundation of a house.)

But not when the exception relates to the species and not to the quality.—THE case is different where a person acknowledges that he is indebted to another a Koor of wheat, as the price of a slave, but that the wheat is of a coarse kind; because coarsness, with relation to wheat, is not a quality but a species, and an absolute contract does not necessarily require that the wheat be other than coarse.—IT is related as an opinion of Haneefa, in other books than the Zahir Rawayet, that in a case of borrowing, the acknowledger's assertion of the dirms being Zeyf ought to be credited, provided this assertion be conjoined with the acknowledgement; because the act of borrowing is not complete until after the seisin of the borrower; and it often happens that dirms are Zeyf in borrowing, in the same manner as in usurpation. The reasoning of the Zahir-Rawayet is that the common custom is to deal in good dirms, and therefore when the explanation is absolute, good dirms must be understood.

An exception with respect to the quality is admitted, if the case of the obligation be not mentioned by the acknowledger.—IF a person acknowledge that he owes another a thousand Zeyf dirms, but without reciting the case (such as sale or loan), some authorities say that this assertion with respect to the quality of the dirms is to be credited, according to all our doctors. Others, however, allege that, according to Haneefa, it is not to be admitted, because, as the acknowledgment is absolute, it may relate either to legal contracts, or to acts of violence, such as usurpation or destruction, which are illegal:—and the former supposition is adopted, as acknowledgment is rather to be attributed to a lawful than to an unlawful cause

And also where it is mentioned, if it be either usurpation or trust.—IF a person acknowledge his having usurped a thousand dirms from another, or his having received them in deposit; and afterwards assert that the said dirms were Zeyf or Binhirja; in that case his assertion must be credited, whether it be conjoined with or separate from the acknowledgment; because mankind are accustomed to usurp whatever they can find, and to place in deposit whatever they possess;* and therefore neither of these acts necessarily infers the dirms to have been Jeed (that is, good). The acknowledger's assertion, therefore, of the dirms being either Zeyf or Binhirja is equivalent to an explanation of the species, and is consequently admitted, even though it should not have been conjunctively made.—For the same reason, also, if an usurper produce a defective article, as the thing he had usurped,—or a trustee produce a defective article, as the thing he had received in deposit,—the declaration so made must in either case be admitted.—It is reported, from in Aboo Yoosaf, that in case of an acknowledgment of usurpation, the acknowledger's assertion of the dirms being Zeyf ought not to be credited where it is made separately

* Without any regard to the species or quality.

from the acknowledgment; because of the analogy of this case to that of a loan, on the principle of seisin including responsibility in both cases, that is, in a case either of usurpation or of loan; for he holds that, in a case of loan, the acknowledger's assertion of the money borrowed being Zeyf cannot be credited, if separately made; and so also in the case in question.

Acknowledgment with respect to the deposit or usurpation of Satooka dirms.—If a person acknowledge his usurpation of a thousand dirms or his receipt of that sum in deposit, and assert that they were Satooka, in that case his assertion must be credited, if conjoined with the acknowledgment; but not otherwise; because although Satooka be not in reality a species of dirms, still it is customary to apply that word to them figuratively:—the mention of this term, therefore, is a modification, and must consequently be conjoined.

An exception of a part from the whole is not to be credited, if made separately.—If a person declare that "he owes such an one a thousand dirms, on account of certain goods," or that "he has borrowed a thousand dirms," or that "he has received a thousand dirms in deposit," or that "he owes a thousand Zeyf dirms," or that he has usurped a thousand dirms,"—and he afterwards except a particular number of dirms from the obligation.—in none of these cases is his assertion to be admitted, if made separately from the acknowledgment,—whereas if it be conjoined with the acknowledgment it must be admitted, as the assertion is in this case an exception, and an exception is valid when conjunct. It is otherwise if he assert the dirms to be Zeyf, as a reservation of this nature is not valid, since Zeyf relates to quality: but expression applies solely to quantity, not to quality;* and exception is not admitted with respect to any matter but what may be precisely expressed.

Unless this arise from some unavoidable accident.—It is to be observed, however, that if the exception should have been disjoined by necessity (such as by a cough, or a shortness of breath), it is then considered as conjunct, because of the interruption being unavoidable,

In an acknowledgment of usurpation a damaged article must be accepted.—If a person acknowledge the usurpation of cloth, and then produce damaged cloth, it must nevertheless be admitted, as usurpation is not restricted to perfect things.

Where the property is lost, if the acknowledger allege a trust, and the other party assert an usurpation, the acknowledger is responsible.—If Zeyd say to Omar, "I took from you a thousand dirms by way of trust, and they are lost," and Omar reply, "no; you took them by way of usurpation;" in that case Zeyd is responsible for the loss—if Zeyd, on the contrary, say, "you gave me a thousand dirms by way of deposit, and they are lost," and Omar reply, "no; you took them by way of usurpation;" in that case Zeyd is not responsible for the loss. The difference between these two cases is, that Zeyd (in the former case) first acknowledges a thing which is a cause of responsibility, namely, taking, and afterwards asserts an exemption from responsibility, by declaring that he held it as a deposit. Now a deposit implies the consent of Omar; but Omar denies his assent; and therefore, as defendant, his assertion supported by an oath must be credited. In the second case, on the contrary, Zeyd does not make any acknowledgment subjecting him to responsibility; because, in using the word given, he refers the action to Omar and not to himself: and no one is subject to responsibility for the actions of another Omar, on the other hand, asserts, against Zeyd, a cause of responsibility, namely, usurpation; which Zeyd denies; and consequently, as defendant, his word supported by an oath must be credited.—It is to be observed that the word receive, in this case, is equivalent to take; and the word remove to that of give. Thus, if the acknowledger, instead of taken, should say that he had received a thousand dirms, he is in that case subject to responsibility. If, on the contrary, he say, "you have removed to me," instead of "you have given me," he is not in that case subject to responsibility.

Objection.—Neither giving nor removing can be carried into execution without receipt on the part of the other party. An acknowledgment of giving or of removing, therefore, is virtually an acknowledgment of receiving; and consequently it would appear that, in either case, the acknowledger is subject to responsibility.

Reply.—The giving and removing of one thing to another is sometimes performed by a mere relinquishment of the right in an article (that is, by a non-prevention of the other from taking it); and sometimes by placing the article before the other.—Giving and removing may therefore be carried into execution without a receipt or taking: and hence an acknowledgment of giving or removing does not involve an acknowledgment of receiving or taking. Besides, admitting that receipt is established from giving or removing, still it is established only by implication is adopted only in cases of necessity; but there exists no necessity, in the present instance, to establish responsibility for the loss.

But not if he assert a trust, and the other assert a loan.—If a person say to another, "I have taken a thousand dirms from you by way of deposit"—and the other reply, "no; you have taken them by way of loan,"

* Meaning, perhaps, that number admits of a precise and definite expression, whereas quality can be assertained only by examination and inspection.

—in this case the assertion of the acknowledger, notwithstanding his use of the word taking, must be admitted: for both parties are agreed in the taking of the dirms with the consent of the person in whose favour the acknowledgment is made; but he asserts a loan (which is a cause of responsibility), whereas the acknowledger asserts a deposit. —There is an evident difference between this case and that which has already been explained, in which the person in whose favour the acknowledgment is made asserts usurpation; because that person stands as defendant, since he denies his consent.

Case of acknowledgment of the receipt of money, with a reservation of its being the property of the acknowledger.—If a person say, "this sum of a thousand dirms, my property, was in trust with such a person, and as such I have taken it from him," and the other deny this, and declare the said sum to be his own property; he is in that case entitled to take it from the acknowledger; because the acknowledger confesses that he took the sum in question from him on the claim of its being his own property, which the other denies; and hence his assertion, as defendant, must be credited.

Case of acknowledgment of the receipt of specific property, with a reservation to the same effect.—If a person affirm that he had hired out an animal of carriage to another, who, after riding upon him, had returned it to him,—or, that he had hired out a garment to another, who, after wearing it, had returned it to him,—and the other contradict this, declaring the said animal or garment to be his own property, in that case, according to Haneefa, the assertion of the acknowledger must be admitted, upon a favourable construction.—The two disciples maintain that the assertion of the other party must be credited; and this is agreeable to analogy. —(The same difference of opinion also obtains where, instead of hiring out, the acknowledger says that he had lent his horse to the other to ride on, or his house to reside in,—or, had given his garment to another to mend, or hire,—and had afterwards resumed the article, and the other declare it to be his property.—(Analogy would suggest, as has been already mentioned in the example of deposit) that the acknowledger, in these cases, has confessed his having taken and possessed himself of things which, however, he asserts to be his own property; but which is denied by the person in whose favour the acknowledgment is made; whose assertion, as defendant, must therefore be credited.— The reasons for a more favourable construction, in this particular, are twofold.—First, the establishment of the receipt, in cases of hire and of loan, is not admitted from itself, but from necessity (that is, from the necessity of answering the object of the contract, namely, the usufruct of the article); and the effect is therefore restricted to the point of necessity. Hence the acknowledgment of hire or of loan does not involve the acknowledgment of receipt, as in the case of a deposit.—Secondly, as in the cases of hire, loan, and residence, the possession of the person in whose favour the acknowledgment is made is established solely by the avowal of the acknowledger, his explanation of the nature of that possession must be admitted. It is otherwise in the example of deposit, since a deposit may be made without a delivery; as where, for instance, a person's gown is blown, by the wind, into another person's house, in which case the gown remains a deposit with the owner of the house, although not formal delivery have been made. The author of this work observes, that the point upon which the difference between the cases of hire, loan, or residence, and that of deposit (as before explained) turns, is not that the word take is recited in the latter and not in the former cases; because this word is used by Mohammed, in the case in question, in the Mabsoot, treating of acknowledgments;—but that it rests upon the two reasons for a favourable construction of the law in this particular, as recited above.

If a person says "I have received from such a person his acquittance, of a thousand dirms which he owed me,"—or, "I lent such a person a thousand dirms, and have received back the same,"—and the other deny the previous existence of the debt, our doctors are, in that case, unanimously of opinion that the assertion of the person in whose favour the acknowledgment is made is to be credited: because a debt must be discharged by means of a similar; and this cannot otherwise be accomplished than by the creditor's receiving a portion of the debtor's property, equivalent to the debt, in such a manner as may induce responsibility. The acknowledger, therefore, in saying that he had received from the other an acquittance of the debt with that other owed him, confesses a circumstance which is a cause of responsibility; and he afterwards claims the right of property in the same, in virtue of its having been given to him in exchange for his debt, which is denied by the other; he therefore stands as defendant, and his assertion must consequently be credited. It is otherwise in assertions of hire, loan, or residence, because the thing seized, in those instances, is an dentic article, for which the acknowledger claims the hire, or so forth: there is therefore an evident difference between the cases.

Case of dispute with respect to immovable property.—If a person acknowledge that another has cultivated a particular piece of land, or built a particular house, or planted grapes in a particular orchard, the said land, house, or orchard being in the possession of the acknowledger, and the person in whose favour he acknowledges claim the property of these things, and the acknowledger, on the other hand, declare them to be his own property, and that the other, in the cultivation, building, or planting, had only acted by his desire, as his assistant or as his hireling—in that case the assertion of the acknowledger must be credited, according to all our doctors; because he does not make an acknowledgment of the possession on behalf of the other, but merely of the above-mentioned acts as performed by that other, and these do not argue a right of possession, since the person in whose favour the acknowledgment is made might have lawfully performed these acts upon things that were in the possession of the acknowledger. The case, therefore, is the same as if a person were to declare that a particular tailor had sewed his garment for half a dirm, but that he had not received the garment from the tailor; and the tailor claim the property of the garment: for there the acknowledgment so made is not supposed to allude to the possession on the part of the tailor, and therefore the assertion of the acknowledger is credited; and so also in the case in question. It is otherwise if the acknowledger say that "he has received possession from the tailor;" for concerning that case there is a disagreement amongst our doctors, similar to what has been described.

CHAPTER III

OF ACKNOWLEDGMENT MADE BY SICK PERSONS,*

Debts acknowledged on a deathbed (without assigning the cause of them) are preceded by debts of every other description.—If a person, in his last illness, acknowledge a debt, as being due to another and he also owe other debts contracted during health, or debts contracted during his sickness for known causes (such as the purchase or the destruction of property, and of which proof may be obtained by other means than though his acknowledgment, or be indebted to his wife married during his sickness, for her Mihr-Misl (or proper dower),—all these debts so contracted during health or sickness have a preference to that other which he so acknowledges during his sickness, and of which the cause is unknown, Shafei maintains that the debts of the healthy and the sick are alike valid, since acknowledgment, which is the cause of both, is in both instances equal, inasmuch as it is derived from the understanding. Debt, moreover, and the responsibility of the person to which the obligation relates, are capable of comprehending the rights of a variety of persons, An acknowledgment of debt, therefore, resembles the settlement of a contract of purchase or of marriage;—that is to say, if a sick person purchase goods, and remain indebted for the price,—or marry on a proper dower, and remain indebted for the same,—debts so contracted are upon an equal footing with debts contracted during health; and so also in the case in question.—The argument of our doctors is that acknowledgment is not valid when it tends to prejudice the right of another; and the acknowledgment of a sick person does induce this consequence, since the rights of the creditors of debts contracted during his health are connected with his property, inasmuch as they may seize it for the payment of what is owing to them;—whence it is that deeds of a gratuitous or benevolent nature are not allowed, in a sick man, beyond the extent of a third of his estate.—It is otherwise with respect to marriage on a proper dower,* as marriage is one of the most essential wants of a sick person, since in the same manner as man is impelled to his own preservation so also is he impelled to the propagation of his species.—It is otherwise. also, with respect to the purchase of property for an equivalent price; because the right of the creditors is connected with the substance of the property and not with the form of it; and in an instance of purchase the substance is extent. —During health, moreover, the right of the creditors is connected with his person, not with his property, since whilst he is in a condition to acquire property, it is supposed that the property will increase:—a state of sickness, on the contrary, is a state of inability, and therefore the right of the creditors is then connected with his property.†

OBJECTION.—If the connection of debts contracted during health, with the property of the sick person, be a bar to the obligation of other debts, because of the priority of the former, it follows that if a sick person, having made an acknowledgment in favour of a person, should afterwards make an acknowledgment in favour of another, it is not valid, because the first acknowledgment is preferable, as being connected with his property; whereas, according to law, they are both valid.

REPLY.—The whole period of sickness is considered as one and the same, because the whole of it is a time of restriction, and therefore one part or period of it is the same as another.—It is otherwise with respect to health, as health is not a period of restriction, and therefore deeds are then lawful,

*By sick persons, throughout the whole of this chapter, is meant such as are effected with a mortal disorder.—(The analogical principle on which the law upon this head proceeds is set forth in treating of the divorce of the sick.—See Vol I., p. 99.)

*That is to say, without any particular specification of a dower: for if a sick person marry upon a specified dower, the agreement holds to the extent only of one-third of his whole property.

†What is here said merits some attention, as it elucidates a very important point in the laws of property.

whereas, sickness being a time of restriction, many needs are then unlawful.

It is to be observed that debts contracted during sickness, of which the cause of the obligation is known, are preferable to debts of sickness which are supported merely upon acknowledgment; because the former are free from suspicion It is also to be observed that debts of sickness, of which the cause is known, are upon a foot of equality with debts of health, neither having a preference over the other;—a debt of a proper dower, because of the necessity for marriage; and debts contracted on account of purchase, or of a loan, because of the existance of an equivalent.—The right of the creditors, moreover, is connected merely with the substance; and as, in the establishment of these debts, there is no doubt or suspicion, they are therefore on a foot of equality with debts of health.

A dying person cannot concede any specific property by acknowledgment.—If a sick person make an acknowledgment in favour of any person, of something he holds in his hand, such acknowledgment is not valid, because of the injury it induces to the creditors, whose right is connected with that thing.

Nor make a partial discharge of his debts (excepting those contracted during his illness).—It is not lawful for a sick person to discharge the debts of part of his creditors, because such partial discharge is a destruction of the right of the others; and in this respect the creditors of health and of sickness are upon an equality:—excepting, however, where the sick person restores something he may have borrowed during his sickness, or pays the price of something he may have purchased during his sickness; and the obligation admits of being proved by witnesses:—in other words, if a person borrows, during his last illness, a thousand dirms, and keep the same by him, or purchase anything with them to that value, and afterwards repay the loan, or pay the price of the purchase, it is lawful, where it admits of being proved by evidence, because these payments are attended with no injury to the creditors, as the acknowledger has obtained an equivalent for what he pays.

A debt acknowledged upon a death-bed is discharged after all other debts.—If, after the discharge of the whole of the preferable debts, there still remain some property of the sick man's estate,* such residue must be applied to the discharge of the debts acknowledged during his sickness; because such acknowledgments were in themselves valid, and having been annulled merely from a regard to the rights of the creditors, they resume their original validity when the bar to their operation is removed.

If there be no other debts it is discharged previous to the distribution of the inheritance.—The acknowledgments of debt, by a sick person who does not owe any debts of health, are valid, as they occasion no injury to others.—In such case, also, the said debts are preferable to the claims of the heirs; because Omar has said, "whenever a sick person acknowledges debts, they must be considered as obligatory, and discharged from his effects."—Besides, the discharge of his debts is a matter of necessity; and the right of the heirs is connected with his estate on the sole condition of its being free from incumbrance; whence; it is that the discharge of the funeral expenses precedes the right of the heirs, as that is also a matter of necessity.

An acknowledgment in favour of an heir is not valid, unless admitted by the co-heirs.—If a sick person make an acknowledgment in favour of any of his heirs, it is not valid, unless it be verified by the other heirs.—Shafei, in one report of his opinion upon this point, says that it is valid; because acknowledgment is the manifestation of an established right; and the probability is that the acknowledger has spoken truth, since reason forbids falsehood, more particularly in time of sickness.—Besides, as religion and justice, when joined to reason, must restrain a man from falsehood, the acknowledgment of a sick person in favour of his heir is like an acknowledgment in favour of a stranger;—or, like an acknowledgment in favour of an additional heir—(as if a person should acknowledge that "a particular person is his son," —which acknowledgment is valid, notwithstanding it diminish the rights of the other heirs);—or, like an acknowledgment of the destruction of a deposit, the property of an heir (as where, for instance, a person lodges a deposit of one thousand dirms, during either health or sickness, with his father, in the presence of witnesses, and the father afterwards, whilst dying, acknowledges that he had destroyed the deposit of his son,—in which case the acknowledgment, is valid, and the person in whose favour it is made is entitled to a thousand dirms from the estate of the acknowledger, although it diminish the right of the heirs;—and so also in the case in question].—The arguments of our doctors upon this point are threefold.—First, the Prophet has said "there is no legacy to an heir, and no acknowledgment of a debt in favour of an heir."—Secondly, as the right of the heirs is connected with the property of a person in his last sickness (on which account he is not permitted, at that period, to do any deed of gratuity or affection), an acknowledgment in favour of some of the heirs is invalid, as being prejudicial to the right of the others.—Thirdly, as the sick person, in his last illness, is above the want of his property, and as affinity is the cause of connection the right

*This case supposes a disribution of the effects of the acknowledger, after his decease; and the term sick man is applied to the defunct, in this instance, merely to distinguish him, as having acknowledged debts whilst he was sick of a mortal illness.

of the whole of the heirs with the property, when the want of it no longer exists in the sick person, it follows that at such period an acknowledgment in favour of a part of them must be an injury to the whole. This connexion, however, does not operate with respect to strangers because of the necessity the sick man was under, during health, of entering into concerns* with them; for many of the concars of the sick (such as purchase, sale, and the like) are entered into with strangers during heath; and if their acknowledgment of these during th ir sickness were not valid, people would be cautious of dealing with them during their health, and their affairs would of consequence suffer.—Such an acknowledgment, therefore, is preferable to the claims of the heirs—It is to be observed that the connexion here mentioned does not operate to the destruction of a sick man's acknowledgment of percentage, by which an additional heir is occasioned; because the sick man also is necessitous in this particular, as percentage exists after death, and a man is held to continue in existence, after death, in the person of his offspring; whence parentage is one of the wants of the dead.

And so also of an acknowledgment in favour of a part of the heirs.—If a sick man make an acknowledgment in favour of part of his heirs, and the others verify the same, such acknowledgment is valid, because of the removal of the only obstacle, namely, the connexion of the right of the other heirs with his property, which they themselves relinquish.

The acknowledgment of a dying person in favour of a stranger is valid, to the amount of the whole estate.—If a sick person make an acknowledgment in favour of a stranger, it is valid, although it be tantamount to the whole of his property,—because Omar has said "the acknowledgment of debt by a sick person is valid; and the debt is due from the whole of his estate"—(as before quoted).—Analogy would suggest that the acknowledgment does not operate in a degree beyond the third of his property; as it is in that degree only that the LAW admits of the deeds of a sick man with regard to his property.—Our doctors, however, remark upon this that as the acts of a sick person are valid with respect to a third of his property, it follows that the acknowledgment of a sick person is valid in the same proportion; and it then becomes valid with respect to the remaining thirds also; because, upon the sick person acknowledging one third of his property to belong to another, it becomes from that moment the property of that other and as the remaining two third then from the whole of the property of the acknowledger, he may lawfully make an acknowledgment of one third of it, and so on, until nothing remain.

Objection.—It would hence appear that bequest to the extent of the whole property as also valid.

Reply.—In bequest, the third of the estate does not become the property of the legates until after the death of the testator; and accordingly, they cannot claim their legacies before that event. It is otherwise with respect to an acknowledgment of debt, as the person in whose favour the acknowledgment is made becomes immediate proprietor.—There is therefore an evident distinction between the cases.

But it is annulled by a subsequent acknowledgment of the stranger being his son.—If a sick person make an acknowledgment in favour of a stranger, and afterwards declare that "he is his son," the parentage is established accordingly, and the acknowledgment is null.—If, on the contrary, a sick person make an acknowledgment in favour of a strange woman, and afterwards marry her, the acknowledgment does not become null. The difference between these two cases is that, in the former upon the sick person declaring the other to be his son; his parentage is established in the acknowledger from the instent of conception in the mother's womb; whence it is evident that the person in whose favour the acknowledgment was made was the heir of the acknowledger at the period of his acknowledgment; and consequently, that he has made an acknowledgment in favour of his own son, which is invalid of course.—It is otherwise with respect to marriage; for, as the relationship produced by that takes piece only from the time of contracting it, it follows that the women was not the acknowledger's heir at the time of the acknowledgment; and consequently, that his acknowledgment in her favour remains valid.

Case of acknowledgment in favour of a repudiated wife.—If a sick person repudiate his wife by three divorces, and then make an acknowledgment of debt due to her, and die,* she is in that case entitled to whichever of the two claims (namely, her portion of inheritance, or the amount of the debt acknowledged) may be the smallest.—The reason of this is that both the woman and the man are in this case liable to suspicion; for as the edit, or term of probation was not expired, the woman, after his death, is an heir, and an acknowledgment in favour of an heir is not valid.—Hence there is possibility that the woman may have requested her divorce as the means of her acquiring a right to the acknowledgment; and that the husband may have divorced her with the view of giving her more than she was entitled to as an heir. As, therefore, both husband and wife are liable to suspicion, the smallest of the two claims is decreed to the woman, since concerning that there can be no suspicion.†

* Arab, Moalikat; meaning concerns of a suspended nature,—such as purchase with a suspension of payment of the price, and so forth.

* Before the expiration of her edit.

† See this treated of at large under the head of the divorce of the sick. (Vol. I. p. 99.)

Section

Miscellaneous Cases,

Acknowledgments of parentage with respect to infants.—If a person acknowledge the parentage of a child who is able to give an account of himself, saying, "this is my son," and the ages of the parties be such as to admit of the one being the child of the other, and the parentage of the child be not well known to any person, and the child himself verify the acknowledgment, his parentage is established in the acknowledger, although he [the acknowledger] be sick; because the parentage in question is one of those things which affect the acknowledger himself only, and no other person.—It is made a condition, in this case, that the ages of the parties be such as to admit of the relation of parentage; for if it were otherwise, it is evident that the acknowledger has spoken falsely.—It is also made a condition that the parentage of the boy be unknown; for if he be known to be the issue of some other than the ackowledger, it necessarily follows that the acknowledgment is null. It is also made a condition, that the boy verify the acknowledgment; because he is considered as his own master, as he is supposed able to give an account of himself.—It were otherwise if the boy could not explain his condition; for then the acknowledgment would have operated without his verification.—It is to be observed that the acknowledgment, in this instance, is not rendered null by sickness; because parentage is an original and not a supervenient want. By the establishment of the parentage, therefore, the boy becomes one of the acknowledger's heirs, in the same manner as any of his other heirs.

Acknowledgments with respect to parents, children, and patrons, are valid.—If a person acknowledge his parents or his son (as if he should declare that "a certain man is his father," or, that "a certain woman is his mother," or, that "a certain person is his son,"—and the ages of the parties admit of those relations),—or, if a person acknowledge a particular woman to be his wife, or a particular person to be his Mawla (that is, either his emancipator, or his freedman),—in all these cases the acknowledgment is valid, as affecting only himself, and not any other.—In the same manner, also, if a woman acknowledge her parents, or her husband, or her Mawla, it is valid, for the same reason.—A woman's acknowledgment of a son, however, is not valid, as such acknowledgment affects her husband, in whom the parentaga is established: her acknowledgment of a son, therefore, is not valid, unless the husband confirm her declaration (as the right appertains to him), or, that it be verified by the birth being proven by the evidence of one midwife, which suffices in this particular.—(Concerning the acknowledgments made by women of their children, there are various distinctions, as set forth at large in treating of claims.)

If confirmed by the parties.—It is to be observed that in all these cases the confirmation of the party concerning whom the acknowledgment is made is requisite, excepting in the acknowledgment with respect to a child, when so young as not to be able to give any account of himself.—It is also to be observed that the confirmation concerning parentage is valid, although made after the death of the acknowledger; because the relation of parentage exists after death.—In the same manner, also, the confirmation of a wife after the death of her husband, is valid; because the edit is one of the effects of marriage; and that exists after the death of the husband, whence it may be said that the marriage itself endures in one shape; and therefore the confirmation of the wife after the death of her husband, is valid.—So also (in the opinion of the two disciples) the confirmation of the husband is valid, after the death of the wife; because inheritance, which is one of the effects of marriage, exists after the death of the wife; whence the marriage itself endures, in one shape; for which reason his confirmation is valid.—According to Haneefa the confirmation of the husband is not valid, because the marriage expires upon the death of the wife; on which account it is not lawful for a husband to wash the body of his wife after her death.—In regard to the assertion of the two disciples, that "the marriage endures, in one shape, after the death of the wife, because of inheritance," it is not admitted; for the inheritance," does not take place until after death, and was therefore a nonentity at the time of the acknowledgment.—Now a confirmation, in order to be valid, must be directed to the period of the acknowledgment: and as, that period, the inheritance did not exist, it is therefore invalid.

The acknowledgment of a dying person with respect to an uncle or brother, entitles them to inherit (if he have no other heirs), but does not establish their parentage.—If a person acknowledge an uncle or a brother, such acknowledgment is not credited, so far as relates to the establishment of the parentage, because of its operating upon another than the acknowledger. If, therefore, the acknowledger have a known heir, whether near or remote, the whole of the inheritance goes to him, and not to the person in whose favour the acknowledgment is made, since the parentage not having been established on the part of the acknowledger, no obstacle can thence arise to the inheritance of a known heir.—If, however, the scknowledger have no other heir, the person in whose favour he makes acknowledgment is in that case clearly entitled to the inheritance, as every person has full power over his estate when he has no heirs; whence it is that a person may bequeath the whole of his property in legacy, provided he have no heirs. The person in whose favour the acknowledgment is made is therefore in this case entitled to the whole of the property. although the parentage;be not proven, (that is, although he be not admitted to be the brother or uncle of the acknowledger); as that would tend to affect another, namely. the father or grandfather of the acknowledger.*—It is to be observed that the acknowledgment, in this case is not in reality a legacy; because, if a man should acknowledge a particular person to be his brother, and afterwards bequeath the whole of his property to another, the legatee would in that case be entitled only to one third of the whole of the property; whereas, if the acknowledgment had been in reality a legacy, the person in whose favour the acknowledgment is made, and the legatee, would in that case share the whole of the property equally between them. The acknowledgment, however, is equivalent to a legacy, on this consideration, that the person in whose favour it is made is entitled to the property merely because of the declaration of the acknowledger, and not from any other cause whatever, as in bequest: for which reason, if a sick man should acknowledge a certain person to be his brother, and this person confirm the same; and the acknowledger afterwards deny his right of inheritance, and bequeath the whole of his property to some other, the legatee is entitled to the whole of his estate;—or, that, if he should not bequeath his property to another, the whole of his estate goes to the public treasury; because retraction is in this case valid, for this reason, that the parentage, which annuls the validity of the acknowledgment, is not established.

The acknowledgment of a brother, by the heir, entitles to inheritance, but does not establish parentage.—If a person die, and his son acknowledge another to be his brother, the parentage of the person in whose favour the ackgowledgment is made is not established, but he is entitled to a share in the inheritance with the acknowledger:—because the acknowledgment in question involves two consequences; namely, the establishment of the parentage, which, as affecting another, does not take place,—and the participation of the acknowledgee in the property, which, being a power he possesses, as affecting himself only, does therefore take place.—In the same manner as where a purchaser acknowledges that the slave he has bought had been emancipated by the seller, in which case the acknowledgment (so far as it relates to the seller) is not to be credited; and on this account the buyer is not entitled to retake the purchase-money from the seller:—the acknowledgment, however, is credited so far as it relates to himself, and thefore the slave is free.

Case of acknowledgment, made by a co-heir, of the partial payment of a debt owing to the person from whom the inheritance descends.—If a person, to whom a debt is owing by another of one hundred dirms, should die, leaving two sons, and one of these acknowledge that his father had received payment of fifty dirms of the said debt, in that case the acknowledger is not entitled to any thing; and the other is entitled to the remaining fifty dirms; because, as the acknowledger has here made an avowal which operates upon himself, his brother, and the deceased, it is therefore valid only so far as it relates to himself, and not with respect to any other; for his acknowledgment that the deceased had received fifty dirms of the debt, is equivalent to an acknowledgment that the deceased owed fifty dirms, since the receiving payment of a debt cannot be established but by the receipt of a thing involving responsibility —(that is to say, by the receipt of a thing which induces responsibility on the receiver. so as that this responsibility may stand as a debt against him, and that then a mutual liquidation may take place, by the opposition of the debt of one to the debt of the other).—Upon the other brother, therefore, contradicting the acknowledgment, the debt which it in consequence established upon the deceased, is opposed to the share of the acknowledger, in conformity with the tenets of our doctors; for with them it is an established tenet that if one of the heirs acknowledge a debt due by the deceased. and the other heirs contradict the same, the debt is in that case charged to the share of the acknowledger.—In short, both brothers agree in this, that the sum to be received by the brother who is not the acknowledger (namely, fifty dirms) appertains equally between them.—it is to be considered, however, that if the acknowledger were to take the half from his brother upon his receiving payment of these fifty, he would then take it from the debtor; and the debtor again, would take the same from the acknowledger; which revolution would be totally useless; and this is the true meaning of the Der, or revolution, as mentioned in the Hedaya.

BOOK XXVI.

OF SOOLH, OR COMPOSITION

Definition of the term.—SOOLH, in the language of the LAW, signifies a contract by means of which contention is prevented or set aside, The essentials (or pillars of it are declaration and acceptance; and the conditions of it, that the subject of the composition (that is, the thing with relation to which the contract is formed) be property; and also, that it be defined, provided there be a necessity for seision, but not otherwise.—

* Because, if he were admitted to be actually the uncle or the brother of the acknowledger, that would induce, in his favour, a claim of inheritance from them

Thus if a person claim some degree of right in a house belonging to another,—and that other claim some degree of right in a shop belonging, to this person, and they come to a compromise, by relinquishing their respective rights in favour of each other, such compromise or composition is valid, although they should not have explained the extent of their right; since ignorance with respect to a claim which is to be annulled is not a cause of contention.

CHAPTER I.

Composition may be made in three modes—with acknowledgment, under silence, and after denial.—Composition is of three kinds or description.—I. Composition with acknowledgment (as where the defendant acknowledges the right of the plaintiff, and then compounds it for some other thing): II. Composition under silence (as where the defendant neither acknowledges nor denies the claim): and, III. Composition after denial.—All these descriptions of composition are lawful; because God says, in the Koran, "composition is laudable;" and this ordinance being absolute, necessarily includes all these species of it;—and also, because the Prophet has said "every composition is lawful amongst Mussulman, excepting such as renders lawful what is unlawful, or renders unlawful what is lawful."—Shafei maintains that compositions after denial or under silence are unlawful, because of the above tradition; for in these two cases it necessarily follows that what is unlawful becomes lawful, and what is lawful becomes unlawful, since the thing given in composition was, previous to the conclusion of the contract. unlawful to the giver, and lawful to the receiver; but afterwards becomes the reverse, Besides, in both these cases, the defendant gives property for the removal of contention; and this is bribery.—The arguments of our doctors, in support of their opinion upon this point, are threefold. First, the texts of the Koran, as above quoted. Secondly, the first part of the above tradition concerning the Prophet, comprehends both the cases in question; whereas the latter part applies solely to a composition which renders lawful something in itself originally unlawful, such as wine;—or, which renders unlawful something that in itself was originally lawful; as where a man agrees with a wife, for a certain consideration, not to have carnal connexion with another of his wives. Thirdly, composition after denial, or under silence, is a composition in consequence of a valid claim, and is therefore effectual, since the claimant receives the thing given in composition in lieu of a right of his own which in his opinion was a just one; and this is lawful, and the defendant, on the other hand, pays it to remove from himself a contention;—and this also is lawful; because the object of property is self preservation; not to giving of a bribe, with a view to remove oppression from himself, is lawful in the giver. Besides this cannot be strictly termed a bribe, as a bribe is what is taken by the receiver for the reason assigned by the giver, whereas here it is otherwise, for the giver gives it in order to prevent contention, and the receiver takes it because in his opinion it is his just right.

Composition by a concession of property for property is equivalent to sale.—In a composition made after acknowledgment, all the effects of sale take place, provided it be a composition of property for property; because it then corresponds, in its nature, with sale, which is an exchange of property for property by mutual consent of the parties;—whence it is that; if it relate to land, it admit of the right of Shaffa; and also, that the consideration may be returned on account of a defect; and that the conditions of inspection and of option exist with respect to it

And is rendered invalid by an ignorance of the thing to be given in composition.—This species of composition therefore, is rendered invalid by an ignorance of the consideration for the composition, as such ignorance may be a cause of contention, whereas an ignorance of the subject of the composition cannot afford any cause of contention, as that merely ceases (in consequence of the composition), whence there is no occasion for taking possession of it.—It is, moreover, a condition, that the defendant be competent to make good the amount of the consideration in question.

Composition by a concession of usufruct is equivalent to hire.—If, however, composition be a stipulation of usufruct in lieu of property, then the laws and rules incident to hire take place with regard to it; because the characteristic of hire (namely, an endowment with usufruct in exchange for property) exists in it.

But the term of usufruct must be specified.—And as, in contracts, regard is had to the spirit of the agreement, it is also requisite that the period of right to the usufruct be fixed.—The composition is also rendered null by the decease of any of the parties during that term,* because a composition of this nature is a species of hire.†

Compositions after denial are equivalent to an exchange with respect to the plaintiff, but not with respect to the defendant.—Compositions subsequent to denial are, with respect to the defendant, equivalent to an atonement

*That is during the term of usufruct.

†A contract of hire is rendered null by the demise of either of the contracting parties during its term.

for an oath*—and subsequent to silence, they stand (with respect to him) merely as a removal of strife;—but they do not stand as a mutual exchange, with respect to him, in either case.—With respect to the plaintiff, on the contrary, they are in the nature of a mutual exchange; because the plaintiff accepts the composition in lieu of an article which in his belief was his right; and one contract may lawfully bear different interpretations with regard to the two parties, in the same manner as the dissolution of sale is an annullment of the contract with respect to the seller and purchaser, but with respect to others, a new sale. The reason of a composition after denial standing, with respect to the defendant, as an atonement for an oath is obvious;—and it stands after silence as a mere removal of strife, because silence admits of two suppositions, namely, acknowledgment or denial, and hence, with respect to the composition in question being a contract of exchange, there is a doubt: and, in consequence of this doubt it cannot be established as an exchange with respect to the defendant.

The concession of a house by a composition, does not induce a right of Shaffa.—If a person claim a house from another, and that other either deny the claim, or remain silent, but afterwards compound the matter with the claimant for a certain amount, in that case the right of Shaffa does not operate with respect to that house; because the defendant receives it as his original right, and not in virtue of exchange; since he gives the amount of the composition to the plaintiff merely to put an end to the contention.

OBJECTION.—Although the defendant, in his own belief, receive the house as his original right, and pay the composition to put an end to the contention, yet the plaintiff believes that he receives the composition in lieu of the house, and therefore (on the grounds of the belief of the plaintiff) the right of Shaffa ought to operate.

REPLY.—The belief of the plaintiff has no effect upon the defendant, since a man is judged by his own belief, and not by that of other.

But Shaffa is induced by the act of giving a house in composition—It is otherwise where a house is given in composition (as where, for instance, a person claims some property from another, and that other, after denying the right, or remaining silent, compounds the claim by giving up a house); for in this case the right of Shaffa takes place, as the plaintiff receives the house in exchange for his property; and the composition is therefore, with respect to him, a contract of exchange (for which reason the right of Shaffa operates upon his own acknowledgment, notwithstanding the defendant contradict him).—It is therefore the same as if he were to declare that "he has purchased the house from the defendant,"—and the defendant deny the same; in which case the right of Shaffa operates; and so also in the case in question.

Case in which part of the thing given in composition must be restored—If a person claim something from another, and that other, having acknowledged the claim, compound it with the plaintiff for something else; and it afterwards appear that the thing claimed was in part the property of another,—in that case the defendant is entitled to take back from the plaintiff a part of the thing given in composition, proportionate to that part of the article claimed, which afterwards proved the property of another, because the composition in this case is, like sale, a contract of exchange with respect to both parties: and such is the law in sale, when a part of a thing sold proves the property of another.

If the composition be after denial or silence and the thing compounded for prove the right of another, the consideration must be returned and the plaintiff must lay his claim against him who has the right.—If a person claim a thing from another, and that other either deny it or remain silent, and then compound with the plaintiff from some other article, and it afterwards appear that the thing claimed is the right of another and not of the plaintiff in that case the plaintiff must prefer his demand against the person who claims the right, and return to the defendant whatever he may have received from him in composition; because the defendant gave his property merely for the purpose of removing contention; but when, afterwards it appear that the thing claimed is the property of another, it becomes evident that he was not liable to a contention with the plaintiff. Hence he is entitled to take back the article given in composition, as a condition on which he give it (namely, a right to detain in his possession the subject of the claim) is rendered void.

And the same proportionably, where any part of it proves the property of another.—IF on the other hand, a part, only, of the thing claimed prove the right of another, the plaintiff must in that case return to the defendant a proportionate part of the thing given in composition and make a demand for the same upon the person possessing the right; because the intent of the defendant does not comprehend that proportion.

If the thing given in composition after acknowledgment, prove the right of another, it must be restored, and the plaintiff is entitled to an equivalent from the defendant.—IF the thing given in composition prove the right of another, the plaintiff is in that case entitled to receive from the defendant the whole amount of the composition, provided it be

*Supposing him (as defendant) to have sworn to the fallacy of the plaintiff's claim; in which case, if he afterwards enter into a composition with the plaintiff, it is evident that he swore falsely, and consequently, that atonement or expiation is due for his prejury.

after acknowledgment, as this species of composition is equivalent to sale (as was before explained).—If also, the right of another appear to part of the composition, the plaintiff is entitled to a proportionate part of it, for the same reason.

If this happen in composition after silence or denial, the plaintiff must claim from the defendant the article in dispute.—If in a case of composition after silence or denial, it appear that the whole or a part of the thing given in composition is the property of another, the plaintiff must prefer a claim against the defendant for the thing in dispute between them, either wholly, or in part, as the case may be.—It is otherwise in case of sale after denial; as where, for instance, a person lays claim to a house, and the person upon whom the claim is made denies his right, but afterwards compounds the matter by means of a slave, using, however, the word "sold" instead of "compounded," as if he should say, "I have sold this slave for the said house;" for in that case, if the house afterwards prove to be the property of another, the plaintiff, instead of claiming, is entitled atcually to take the house from the defendant; because the defendant, in selling the slave for the house, does virtually acknowledge the house to be the property of the plaintiff:—contrary to a case of composition, as compositions are frequently made merely to remove contention —It is to be observed that, in case the thing given in composition be either lost or destroyed in the hands of the defendant, previous to the delivery of it, the law is the same as where it proves the right of another;—that is, if the composition follow acknowledgment, the plaintiff is entitled to take the article claimed; or, if it follow denial or silence, he must prefer a claim for it against the defendant.

A composition for an undefined part of a thing is not affected by the right of another afterwards appearing to a part of that thing.—If a person claim a right in a house, without explaining the extent of it (such as a third, a forth, or the like), and the defendant under this state of uncertainty, give him something in composition for his claim, and the right of another afterwards appear to a part of the house, the plaintiff is not in that case obliged to return to the defendant any part of the thing received in composition, since it is possible that the right may relate to some other part of the house, and not to that part which the plaintiff had claimed. It is different when the whole of the house proves to be the property of another; for in that case the whole of the thing given in composition must be returned to the defendant; since it would otherwise necessarily follow that the defendant had received nothing in exchange for the thing he gave in composition; and this is unlawful; as has been already explained under the head of sale.

Composition in consideration of a part of the subject is invalid.—If a person claim a house, and the defendant compound the claim for a part of the house, composition is unlawful, because what the plaintiff receives is already his actual right, and the rest of his claim remains unsatisfied. There are two devices, however by which this composition may be rendered lawful.—The one is, by the plaintiff adding a dirm to the share of the house; in which case, the dirm is considered as an equivalent for the remaining part of the claim:—the second is, by the plaintiff exempting the defendant from the remaining part of the claim.

Section.

Disputes concerning property may be compounded.—Compositions are lawful in claims of property; for a composition (as was before explained) being in the nature of a sale, it follows that whatever may be lawfully sold may also be lawfully compounded.

And also claims of usufrut.—Compositions are likewise lawful in claims of usufruct; as for instance, where a person prefers a claim, against the heirs of a person deceased, to the usufruct of, or right to dwell in a particular house, in virtue of the bequest of the deceased; in which case, if the heirs, having either denied or acknowledged the claim, should compound it with the plaintiff for something else, such composition is valid. The reason of this is that usufruct is considered as a property, in a contract of hire, and so also in a case of composition—for it is a general rule, to consider the composition as partaking of the nature of that contract to which it bears the nearest resemblance, in order to render it valid.—Thus, if the composition be of property for property, it is considered as a sale, because of its near resemblance to that contract—If on the other hand, it relate to usufruct, it is considered as a species of hire, because of its resemblance to it.

Compositions are lawful in homicide.—Compositions are lawful in case either of wilful or erroneous bloodshed.—They are lawful in the former instance, because God has said, "If a portion of the property of the murderer, being a believer, be offfred, by way of composition, to the representative of the murderer, let him accept the same,"—which passage Ibn Abbas reports to have been revealed upon the subject of compositions for wilful bloodshed.—It is to observed that composition for wilful bloodshed resembles marriage, because in both cases property is given without receiving property in return; accordingly, whatever is capable of constituting a speceific dower, is also capable of being given in composition for wilful bloodshed.—There is this difference, however, between marriage and the composition in question, that whenever the recital of the thing to be given in composition is invalid (as where an animal is mentioned indefinitely, or cloths are recited without a specification of them), a Deyit or fine of blood must be paid; — because such is the rule in case of bloodshed; and an invalidity in the nomination does not prevent the remission of retaliation, in the same manner as it does not prevent the validity of marriage.

But if acceded to for an unlawful article, nothing is due—If, however, a composition of wine or pork be stipulated for wilful bloodshed, nothing whatever is due; because neither of these articles are valuable property; it is therefore understood t at the avenger of blood, in agreeing to receive a composition which is not property, has, in effect, remitted the retaliation; and as, in a remission of the retaliation, no property is due, so neither is it in the case in question.—In marriage, on the contrary, a Mihr-Misl (or proper dower) is due in either case, (that is, in case of the invalidity of the recital,—or, where the dower is stipulated to be paid in wine or pork); because the dower is one of the essential requisites of marriage, and is therefore due in LAW, although no recital should have been made of it. • It is to be observed that as the crime expressed in this case of composition is absolute, it relates both to the members of the body, and to the body itself that is to say, the life.—It is also proper to observe that, although compositions for wilful bloodshed be lawful, as above related, yet it is otherwise with respect to compositions of property for the right of Shaffa (by a person receiving property from a purchaser, in composition for his right of Shaffa, which is invalid, because the proprietor of the right of Shaffa has no absolute property from it, but merely a right to become proprietor if he please until, therefore, he become the proprietor, he has no right to compound for it. —Retaliation, on the other hand, means a right of property in the subject, with respect to the action: in other words, the heir or representative is proprietor of the subject so far as relates to the action, inasmuch as he has a right to take retaliation, and may consequently, if he choose, receive a composition for not taking of it: in opposition to the case of Shaffa.—Now, since a composition of property for the right of Shaffa is invalid, it follows that nothing is on that account due from the purchaser, and that he right of Shaffa is lost, in the same manner as in a case of non-opposition or silence.—Bail for the person is also like the right of Shaffa, and therefore nothing is due in case of a composition of property for it —With respect, however, to the annulment of the bail, in such a case, there are two traditions, both of which have been already recited in their proper places.—Compositions are also lawful in the latter case (namely, erroneous bloodshed), because they in this instance relate to property, and therefore resemble sales. Still, however, they are not lawful when they exceed the amount of the fine of blood; because the rate of that as having been fixed by the LAW, cannot be set aside: anything, therefore, beyond the fine of blood, must be rejected.—It is otherwise in retaliation, for there the composition may exceed the fine of blood, as retaliation is not property, and therefore cannot be converted into it but by a special contract.—What is here advanced proceeds upon the supposition that the composition consists of one of the three species of Deyits namely, dirms, deenars, or camels. —If, however, it consist of any other species of property, it is lawful, because it is in that case an exchange for the Deyit, or ordained fine. But yet it is requisite that the delivery be made upon the spot where the contract is concluded, because it must otherwise follow that one debt (namely, the Deyit) remains opposed to another debt (namely, the composition), which is declared, in the sacred writings, to be illegal. If the Kazee should pass a decree directing the murderer to pay the Depit is one of the three modes to the avenger of blood; and he [the murderer] enter into a composition with him [the avenger] for another species of property, in a degree exceeding the Deyit, such composition is lawful, provided it be from hand to hand; because, after the decree of the Kazee, the right of the avenger of blood to the amount decreed by the Kazee becomes fixed and determined; and his composition of it, in that case, is merely an exchange.—It is different where the parties themselves, in the beginning, enter into a composition for one of the three kinds, exceeding the amount of the Deyit; because the consent of the parties to one of the three kinds is equivalent to the decree of the Kazee in respect of fixing it—(that is, in the same manner as it it fixed by the decree of the Kazee, so also is it fixed by their consent); and as the Kazee is not empowered to pass a decree exceeding the amount of the Deyit, so neither are they permitted to fix it at a superior rate. Hence it is not lawful to exceed the rate of a thing already fixed by the sacred writings.

There is no composition for punishment.—COMPOSITION for claim of Hidd, or stated punishment, is not lawful.—Thus if a person should apprehend another in the act of whoredom, or of stealing the goods of another or of drinking wine, or whilst in a state of intoxication; and, intending to carry the culprit before the Kazee, should notwithstanding accept something for suffering him to escape such composition is invalid; because punishment is a right of GOD, and it is not lawful to accept a composition for the right of another.

Claim of parentage.—For the same reason, also, it is not lawful to composition with a woman for a claim of parentage. For instance, a divorced woman, having brought forth a child, says to the divorcer, "this is your child," and he denies the same, but compounds with the woman for withdrawing her claim; which composition is invalid, because the claim of parentage was not her right, but that of the child; and the acceptance of a consideration for the right of another is not valid.

Or, for sufferance of a standing on the highway.—In the same manner if a person erect a bathing-house, or a place for sitting in, on the high road, and another having required him to put it down, he compound with him to withdraw his claim, such composition is invalid, because, the high road being the right of the community, no individual is singly entitled to compound for it.—It is to be observed that the punishment mentioned on this occasion comprehends punishment for slander, because in such punishment the right of God is predominant.

A claim of marriage may be compounded,—whether the claim proceed from a man.—If a person claim marriage with a woman, and she deny the same but compound with the man for his claim, the composition in that case is valid, because there is a possibility of reconciling it to the LAW, by supposing that the man conceives the contract of composition to be in the nature of a Khoola; and, on the other hand, that the woman pays the money to remove strife.—Lawyers, however, have asserted that, in the sight of God, it is not lawful for the person, in this case, to take the composition, if his claim be unfounded.

Or a woman.—If a woman claim marriage with a man, it is lawful for him to compound the claim with her. The author of the Hedaya remarks, upon this, that although the law be thus stated in several copies of the compendium.* yet is other copies such composition is declared to be illegal.—The legality of it is established by supposing that the thing given in composition is an increase of her dower; and that he afterwards sells her a divorce for the amount of her original dower † so that the increase, or the amount of the composition, remains binding upon him. The reason of its illegality is, that the man having given something by way of composition to the woman, to induce her to retract her claim, it follows that this retraction must either be considered as equivalent to a separation between them, or as not equivalent to a separation: now, if it be equivalent to a separation, it is invalid, because no property is given for a separation, since it operates of itself upon the parties (as, for instance, where a woman admits the son of her husband to carnal connexion, in which case the LAW enjoins a separation between them):—if however, on the other hand, the retractation from the claim be not considered as equivalent to a separation, then the case remains as before; and the composition is consequently invalid, as not being opposed to any advantage in exchange,

A claim of bondage may be compounded.—If a person claim another as his slave, and that other compound with him for his claim, by giving him some specific property, such composition is valid, as being, with respect to the plaintiff, an emancipation in exchange for property: because in his belief the defendant gives the composition in exchange for his freedom; and therefore considered in the light of a Mokatib.—It is for this reason, also that the composition in question is valid, if made in consideration of an animal due, and to be delivered at a fined future period; because it would not be valid if it were considered as an exchange of property for property instead of an emancipation for property: for an animal cannot exist as a debt in exchange for property, as has been explained in treating of the Sillim sale of animals: but it may exist as a debt for something else than property, as in the case of marriage or a fine of blood—It is therefore requisite that the composition in question be considered as an emancipation, and not as an exchange.—With respect to the defendant, the composition, in this case, is merely a removal of contention, since he believes himself to be originally free.

But it leave no right of Willa in the claimant.—It is to be observed that in this case no right of Willa over the defendant rests with the plaintiff, because of the denial of the former.—If however, the plaintiff prove by witnesses that the defendant was his slave, such evidence is admitted, and the right of Willa then rests with him.

A privileged slave cannot compound for offences committed by himself; but he may for offence committed by his slave.—If a Mazoon: or privileged slave, wilfully kill a person he is not of himself entitled to compound for the number: but if his slave should commit murder, he may then lawfully compound for it. The distinction between these two cases is that the person of a privileged slave not being a subject of traffic, he is not entitled to dispose of it in any manner (such as, for instance, to sell himself), and in the same manner he is not entitled to redeem his person by means of the property of his master, being considered with respect to his person as a stranger. His slave, on the contrary, is a subject of traffic, whence he is at liberty to sell, or otherwise to dispose of him, and consequently may also redeem him. The reason of this is that the slave, on committing the crime, ceases to be his property; whence the composition resembles a purchase of him; and this it is lawful for a privileged slave to make.

Case of composition for a property usurped; and which perishes in the usurper's hands.—If a person usurp cloth from a Jew, of which the value was less than a hundred dirms, and having lost or destroyed the same, compound the matter with the Jew by agreeing to pay him a hundred dirms previous to any judicial decree upon the subject, in that case the composition is lawful, according to Haneefa. The two disciples

* The Mookhtassir; a compendium of the commentary of Kadooree.
† See Khoola.

maintain that the composition, in the case, is not lawful in the degree in which it exceeds the appraised value of the cloth: because nothing was due from the usurper but the value; and the value of any article is to be known only by appraisement; any thing beyond that must therefore be considered as usury.—It is otherwise, however, if the composition for the cloth be made in articles of furniture, or so forth, exceeding in value the article usurped; for such composition is valid, because the difference of the value not being obvious, from the articles being of a different genus, no usury can be inferred It is otherwise also, if the difference of value be such as may come within the estimation of some of the appraisers, because the observance of an excessive degree of caution is impracticable. The reasoning of Haneefa, in support of his opinion, is that the right of the proprietor of an usurped article continues in it after its destruction, until his right to an equivalent be established; as is evident from this circumstance, that if an usurped slave should die, and the master refuse to accept an equivalent, he must in that case defray the expences of his burial. Now from this it appears either that the right of the proprietor of an usurped article remains in it after its destruction,—or, that the has a right, if he choose, to a similar, both in appearance and in reality,* because reparation for a transgression must be made in a similar,—But his right is not transferred to the value until such time as the Kazee pass a decree to that effect: any agreement, therefore, exceeding the value, which the parties themselves may conclude previous to such decree, being merely a compensation for the article destroyed, or for one similar to it in appearance and reality, cannot be considered as usurious.—It is otherwise if such agreement be made after the decree of the Kazee; for, in that case, according to all our doctors, the composition is not valid, as far as it exceeds the value; because, in this instance, the right of the pronietor to the value has become fixed and determined by the decree of the Kazee, and any thing beyond it is therefore usurious.

Case of composition for a share in a partnership slave.—If a man who is rich emancipate a slave held equally in partnership between himself and another, and compound with that other for a sum exceeding the value of his half such composition is invalid, according to all our doctors:—according to the two disciples, because (as they hold) nothing is due from the emancipator beyond half the value, which is to be ascertained by appraisement; whence any degree beyond that is usurious:—and, according to Haneefa, because the value, in emancipation, is decreed by the LAW; now the rate fixed by the LAW is not short of the rate fixed by the Kazee; and as in a case where the Kazee passes a decree for the value, a composition for any thing beyond the value is dull; it is in the present instance null a fortiori.—It is otherwise in the example concerning the cloth, as before recited, because the value of that if not decreed, by the LAW.—It is to be observed that if, in the case in question, a composition exceeding the value of half the slave be made in specific goods or effects, it is valid, because the excess in the value is not obvious where the articles are of a different genus; and hence no usury can be inferred.

* Independent of and judicial decree.

CHAPTER II

Of Gratuitous or Voluntary Composition; and of the Appointment of Agents for Composition.

An agent for composition in a case of bloodshed or debt is not responsible for the consideration, unless he expressly agree to be so.—If a person appoint another his agent for composition, and the agent accordingly enter into a composition on his behalf, he [the agent] is not responsible for the thing to be given in composition, unless, in setting the contract, he stipulate it is as a condition that "he himself shall be ansewerable for it."—This is where the composition is on account of wilful bloodshed, or of some claim in the nature of debt, in either of which case the composition is a mere annulment ; and as the agent, in either case, is merely a messenger, he is therefore subject to no responsibility, any more than an agent for marriage;—unless he himself engage in the responsibility,—in which case he becomes answerable, because of his contract of security, but not from his contract of composition.

But he is responsible where the composition is of property for property.—Where, however, the composition is of property for property, it is equivalent to a sale, and the rights of it appertain to the agent.—In such a case therefores the claim for the property (that, is: for the article to be given in composition) lies against the agent, not against the constituent.

Fazoolee composition are of four descriptions.—Fazoolee compositions (that is, such as are concluded by a stranger, in behalf of the defendant, without his desire) are of four kinds.

I. Of a debt by property (for which the compounder is responsible).—I Where a person compounds for a claim of debt by property, and makes himself responsible for the property:—in which case the composition is complete, because the defendant acquires nothing from it, but is merely exempted from a debt, and in this respect a stranger and the party that is the defendant are considered as the same.—It is also proper to remark further, that in the same manner as the condition of responsibility for the thing to be given in composition is lawful to the defendant, so also is it lawful to the stranger : a stranger, therefore, is capable of standing as the principal in composition, and in the obligation of the property, when he makes himself responsible for the thing to be given in composition ; in the same manner as a Fazoolee who concludes a Khoola in behalf of a wife.—In other words, if a person propose a Khoola to his wife, and another, without the desire of the wife, conclude the contract of Khoola with the husband on her behalf, making himself responsible for the consideration of Khoola, it is valid, and he is responsible for the consideration ;—and so also in the case in question, the Fazoolee is responsible for the thing to be given in composition.—He moreover, stands, with respect to the defendant, as one who acts gratuitously, in the same manner as a person who voluntarily pays the debts of another, in as much as he exempts the defendant from responsibility ; he therefore is not entitled to any return from the defendant : but it is otherwise where the compounder acts by the desire of the defendant, for in that case he is not a voluntary agent. The compounder in question, moreover, is not entitled to any part of the debt ; but that is cancelled with respect to the defendant ; for the principle, with respect to the legality of the composition, in this case, is that the plaintiff annuls the operation of the debt upon the defendant, and not that he renders the compounder proprietor of it and this, whether the defendant acknowledge the debt, or deny it ;—in a case of denial, evidently, because the defendant does not in his own opinion owe any thing, and the opinion or belief of the plaintiff cannot operate upon him ;—and in a case of acknowledgment, also, because the property of, or right to the debt, cannot be conveyed to another but by the person who is immediately indebted : it is therefore impossible, in this instance, to render the composition valid on any other principle than that of the annulment of the debt.—It is otherwise where the plaintiff claims some specific article in the possession of the defendant, who acknowledges the same, and another person, unauthorized, gives him something as a composition for his claim — because in this case the unauthorized person, in compounding for his claim with the plaintiff, does virtually purchase the article claimed ; and his purchase of a thing from the proprietor is lawful, although it be not in his possession.

II. Of any thing for a specific property (which must be immediately delivered by the compounder.)—II. Where the compounder says, "I have compounded for these thousand dirms of my own," or "this slave of my own ;" in which case the composition is valid ; and it is incumbent on the compounder to deliver over the article stipulated to the plaintiff ; because in referring the composition to his own property, he renders obligatory upon himself the delivery of it ; on which account the composition so made is valid.

III. Of any thing for unspecified property (but which the compounder delivers),—III Where the compounder says, "I have compounded for a thousand dirms," and immediately delivers a thousand dirms to the plaintiff, in which case the composition is valid ; for on the delivery of the thousand dirms the plaintiff obtains his object, and the contract of composition is thereby completely fulfilled.

IV. Of any thing for unspecified property (and which the compounder does not deliver),—IV. Where the compounder says, "I have compounded for a thousand dirms," but does not deliver them ; in which case the composition remains suspended on the consent of the defendant. If he confirm it, he becomes responsible for the sum stipulated ;—or, if he withhold his assent, the composition is annulled,—The reason of this is that in composition of this nature, the defendant is a principal, because of their operating to free him from contention ; but the compounder is also a principal because of his charging himself with the consideration of composition, either expressly (as where he says, "I am responsible for the thousand dirms") or directly (as where he compounds for one thousand dirms, and delivers them).—Now, if he should not so have charged himself (as the present example supposes), the part of the defendant only ;* and the validity of it consequently rests upon his concurrence.

Case of a Fazoolee compounding for a specific article, without referring the same to his property.—The compiler of the Hedaya remarks that a fifth kind of composition may be added to the preceding ; as, for instance, where a Fazoolee says, "I have compounded for this thousand dirms," or "for this slave," without referring these to his own property ;—which sort of composition is valid, because, in specifying the thing to be delivered to the plaintiff, the compounder does, as it were, establish it as a condition that the said thing shall become the right of the plaintiff. If, however the slave should afterwards prove to be the property of another;—or, if it should become known that he was free, or a Mokatib or Modabbir,—or, if the plaintiff should return him, on account of a defect, to the compounder in none of these cases is the plaintiff entitled to take anything from the compounder, since he engaged for nothing further than the delivery of a specific article : if, therefore, that article remain safe for the plaintiff, the contract is valid ; if otherwise he is not entitled to take any thing from the compounder, but must prefer his claim against the defendant.—It is otherwise

*That is to say, he alone is concerned in it

where the compounder stipulates dirms, and makes himself responsible for the same, and they afterwards prove the right of another, or of bad quality, and the plaintiff returns them; for in that case the plaintiff is entitled to take an equal number of good dirms from the compounder, because of his having made himself a principal with respect to security; and, accordingly, if the compounder refuse to comply, he must be compelled to make the delivery.

CHAPTER III.

OF COMPOSITIONS OF DEBT

A debt owing in consequence of any contract concluded upon credit may be compounded by payment of a part.—IF the thing to be given in composition be of the same nature with the debt which is to be compounded for, and which is owing to the plaintiff under an Akid Moodainat, or contract concluded upon credit,* the composition is not in that case construed to be an exchange, but the plaintiff is considered as taking a part of his right, and annulling or relinquishing the remainder.—An Akid Moodainat, or contract concluded upon credit, is where a person purchases the goods of another, for a thousand good dirms (for instance), and then the parties separate, without the seller receiving the price, of a time of payment being agreed upon:—in which case, if the purchaser should compound the said thousand for five hundred good dirms (or five hundred bad dirms), and the seller agree to the same, such composition is valid; and it is thus construed, that he [the seller] agrees to accept a part of his right, and to relinquish the remainder;—not that he accepts the five hundred in exchange for the thousand.—The reason of this is, that it is necessary, as far as possible, to give validity to the acts of rational persons; and this may be done, in the former instance, by the claimant relinquishing a part of the dirms to which he is entitled,—or, in the latter instance, by conceding that and the goodness of them.—Such also is the rule where the debt has been incurred, on the part of the defendant, by a usurpation or destruction of property.

And the same of similar compositions of debt, owing in consequence of any act which subjects to responsiblity.—THE restriction to debts owing "in consequecce of a contract concluded upon credit" (as here set forth), is for this reason, that it is originally requisite that debt be incurred in consequence of a contract agreeable to LAW.

Debt may be compounded by a forbearance, for the same sum.—IF, in the case in question, the composition consist of a thousand dirms payable at a distant time, for a thousand dirms immediately payable, it is valid; because the construction then given to it is that the plaintiff agreed to postpone his claim,—not that he entered into an exchange;—as a future period, is not lawful.

But not if the postponed payment be stipulated in money of a different denomination.—IF, on the other hand, the thousand dirms be compounded for a proportionable number of deenars, payable after the expiration of a month (for instance, it is unlawful; because it is impossible to consider it merely as a delay of the claim; since the claim related to dirms, not to deenars; nor is it possible to construe it into a sale, because a sale of dirms, for deenars payable at a future period, is unlawful. The composition, therefore, in this case, is invalid.

A postponed debt cannot be compounded by the immediate payment of a part.—IF a person have a debt of one thousand dirms, payable at a future period, owing to him by another in consequence of a contract upon credit, and compounded the same for five hundred dirms payable immediately, such composition is invalid; because ready money is better than future payment; and ready money not being his right, the composition therefore takes place in a thing which is not his right, whence it is impossible to consider the composition as a dereliction of part of the claim:—it must therefore be necessarily considered as an exchange (in this way, that the debtor gives up his right, namely, the delay of payment, in return for the five hundred remitted):—those five hundred, therefore, are in exchange for the forbearance; and the acceptance of any thing in consideration of forbearance is not lawful.

A debt of bad money cannot be compounded by the payment of a smaller sum in good money.—IF a person have a debt owing to him by another, in consequence of a contract upon credit, of a thousand adulterated dirms; and compound it for five hundred pure dirms, it is not valid; because pure dirms are not the right of the seller, as those exceed his right with respect to their quality, and it accordingly cannot be considered as a concession: it must therefore be construed into an exchange of one thousand for five hundred, superior with respect to quality.—and that is usurious, as quality is not regarded in transactions of exchage.

But a debt of good money may be compounded by bad, whether the sum be smaller

---

*The commentators define Moodainat to signify "the act of selling to a person upon credit;" or "the act of granting credit."—The composers of the Persian version of the Hedaya have evidently mistaken the sense of the text in the beginning of this passage. The Arabic simply states it "in all compositions for a thing claimed under a contract upon credit, the transaction is not considered as an exchange, but as an acceptance of a part of the right, and a relinquishment of the remainder.

than, or equal to the demand.—IT is otherwise where a person compounds a debt of a thousand good dirms for five-hundred bad dirms, because that is a concession with respect both to number and quality. It is otherwise, also, where a person compounds a debt due to him of a thousand bad dirms for a thousand good ones; because this is an exchange of like for like; and in that no regard is paid to quality.—It is, however, a condition, in this case, that the plaintiff take possession of the thing given in composition upon the spot, as this a Sirf sale

A debt in money of two denominations may be compounds by a smaller sum of either denomination.—If a person have a debt of a thousand dirms and a hundred deenars owing to him by another, in consequence of a contract upon credit, and compound the same for a hundred dirms, ready money, or payable at the expiration of a month (for instance), such composition is lawful, as it is possible, in this instance, to give validity to the contract of composition, by supposing that the creditor remits the whole of the debt owing to him except one hundred dirms. payable immediately, or (as in the second case) within a month. It therefore is not to be regarded in the light of an exchange; for if it were so considered, the contract would not be valid, as it would be usurious. In compositions moreover, a concession is always understood; and as, in the case in question, concession is the prevalent idea, the matter must be regarded as a concession rather than as an exchange.

Case of proposal from a creditor to grant his debtor a complete discharge, on condition of his paying one-half of the debt within a limited time.—If a person, having a debt due to him of a thousand dirms, payable at a future period, should say to the debtor, "pay me five hundred dirms tomorrow, upon this [condition], that you are exempted from the remainder of the debt;" and the debtor act accordingly, he is then exempted from the remainder. If, however, in such case, the debtor should not pay the five hundred dirms on the morrow, he remains responsible, according to Haneefa and Mohammed, for the thousand dirms. Aboo Yoosaf maintains that five hundred dirms are immediately remitted, and that the claim to them cannot afterwards be revived: for (in his opinion) the exemption here is absolute;* because the plaintiff has established the payment of five hundred dirms as an exchange for the exemption of five hundred dirms; but the payment of these five hundred dirms cannot be considered as an exchange for the remainder, payment of which still continues incumbent upon the debtor and is not at all suspended upon the exemption. To make it an exchange, therefore is nugatory;—consequently there remains only the absolute exemption; and hence the whole of the original debt cannot revive from a failure of the payment on the morrow any more than if the creditor had said. "I have exempted you from five hundred dirms out of one thousand dirms upon this [condition], that you pay me, tomorrow, five hundred dirms;" in which case the exemption is absolute, and so also in the case in question.—The reasoning of Haneefa and Mohammed is that the exemption, in this case, is not absolute, but conditional. Upon failure of the condition, therefore, the exemption does not ake place, for two reasons. FIRST, because the creditor begins his speech with requiring the payment tomorrow, and this may be considered in itself as an object, since it is possible that the creditor is afraid of losing the whole of the money in the event of the debtor's becoming poor, which induces him to use expedition; and also, because he perhaps wishes to get the money, in order that he may acqui[re] profit from it in trade. The express[ion] moreover, bears the construction of be[ing] [conditional], and is therefore to be take[n] in that sense, in order to give validity to the contract.—SECONDLY, such conditions are common in compositions; and an exemption may be restricted to a condition, although it be not suspended upon it. Thus a transfer of debt (for instance) is restricted to the condition of safety; in so much that if the person who had agreed to accept the transfer* should die insolvent, the debt reverts upon the person transferring it; the transfer, therefore is restricted, in this instance [to the condition of safety] and so also in the case in question. With respect to the reasoning of Aboo Yoosaf, an answer will soon be given to it.

Which admits of three different statements. I. Where the proposal has no condition annexed, that in failure of payment. II Where it is annexed that. in failure of payment the proposal shall be void. III. Where the discharge is primarily stated.—THE compiler of the Hadaya remarks that this case admits of three separate statements.—I. That which has been already explained.—II. Where the creditor says, "I have compounded with you the thousand dirms for five hundred dirms; which you must pay me to morrow, and then you shall be exempted from the remainder; provided, however, that if you do not pay them to morrow, the thousand dirms shall remain due by you as before;"—in which case according to all our doctors, if the payment, be made on the next day, the exemption holds good; but if otherwise, it is void.—III. Where the creditor says. "I have exempted you from the payment of five hundred dirms out of a thousand, on this

*That is, not suspended upon the condition of payment on the morrow.

*That is, to take upon him the responsibility for the debt (in the manner of an acceptor or endorser of a bill of exchange).

[condition] that you give me five hundred dirms to-morrow ;"—in which case the debtor is exempted from the payment of the five hundred dirms ; and this, whether he pay the five hundred on the ensuing day or not, because the exemption is here primarily stated.*

An acknowledgment may be stipulated for a composition.—If a person say to another, "I will not acknowledge your right of property until you first fix a distant time for the delivery, and promise me an indulgence in the payment,"—or, "until you first remit to me the whole (or a part) of the property," —and the person so addressed act accordingly, his thus fixing a time, or remitting a part or the whole of the property is lawful, because he does this of his own accord, and not by compulsion.

But if the stipulation be publicly proposed. the composition is of no effect.—This is where the acknowledger addresses the other party, as above, secretly and in a covert manner.—Where, however he addresses him publicly, he becomes liable nor the whole of the subject of acknowledgment upon the instant.

Section.

Of Participated Debt.

One of two partners compounding his share of a debt due to them jointly, the other partner may either take his proportion of the composition, or look to the debt for his share.—If there be a debt owing to two men, jointly, from a third, and one of the two compound with the debtor his share of the debt for a piece of cloth, the fellow-creditor has it in his choice either to demand the other half of the debt, which is his due, from the debtor, or to take the half of the cloth from the compounder ; unless, however, he [the compounder] pay him a quarter of the whole debt ; for, in that case, he is not entitled to take the half of the cloth.—in short, in all cases of the nature here exemplified, it is a rule that whatever, in a partnership debt, one of the partners receives a part of it, the other partner is entitled to an equal share in the part so seized ; because although debt become a sort of increase from seisin (since debt is not considered as substantial property until it be taken possession of), still this increase has reference to the original right ; and as the original right was equally divided, so also is the increase ; in the same manner as offspring or fruit. The partner, therefore, has a right of participation in the part which is taken possession of.—Still, however, previous to the operation of such right, the part or thing taken is the sole property of the receiver, because substance is totally different from debt, and the receiver has taken the article in question in exchange for his right.—He is consequently the proprietor : and accordingly all acts of his with regard to the substance in question are valid, and he remains responsible, in a proportionate degree, to his partner.—It is to be observed that by a partnership debt is meant such a debt as becomes due to two or more persons from one case ; such as the price of goods sold by two proprietors under one contract ; or a debt inherited by two men ; or the value, of a joint property destroyed by any person. Now such being the established rule, it follows that, in the case in question, the partner is at liberty either to demand his half of the debt from the debtor (since his share still remains due to him, in as much as the other partner has only received the amount of his own right), or to take the half of the cloth from the other partner, because of his right of participation in it.—If, however, the other should give him a composition, by paying him the quarter of the debt, he then has no right to half of the cloth, as his right is only to quarter of the whole debt.

One of two partners receiving payment of his share in a debt due to them jointly, and paying the other his proportion of what is so recovered, has still a claim upon the remainder.—If one of two partners in a debt should receive, from the debtor, the half of his portion of the debt, the other partner is then at liberty either to participate in the half so received, or to look to the debtor for his full share, for the reasons recited in the preceding example.—If, therefore, he should participate with the compounding partner, both partners are in that case entitled jointly to take from the debtor what remains due, because having shared equally in what was received, they are of consequence entitled to share equally in the remainder.

If the other prefer receiving payment of his part, solely. from the debtor and the property be lost, or the debtor prove insolvent. he has then a claim to his proportion of what has been received by this partner ; but not where this partner has compounded for his share by a commutation.—If, on the contrary, he should prefer demanding his share in full from the debtor, to an equal participation in the part received by the other creditor, and that part of the debt which has been received should remain safe, and that which remains due be lost, or destroyed, either by the debtor's dying insolvent, or by his denial of the debt upon oath, he is in that case still entitled to a participation with the other creditor in what has been received ; because he declined it before only on the supposition of the safety of the remaining part of the debt ; and when the event proves otherwise, he of course becomes entitled to an equal participation. Supposing, however that one of the joint creditors, instead of receiving his share of

---

*Two other statements, together with a long discussion, are omitted by the translator, as the whole turns upon certain points of verbal ctiticim, not capable of an intelligible translation.

he debt, should commute it for a debt which he had previously contracted to the debtor,—then the other sharer, in case of the destruction of that portion of debt due to himself, is not entitled to any participation with him since he is in this instance, held to have paid a debt, not to have received payment of one —The law is also the same, where one of the creditors exempts the debtor from that share of the debt which is due to him, because an exemption is a destruction and annulment, and not a receipt.

In a release from a part of his share, by one partner, the right of the creditors continues in proportion to their remaining claims.—If one of two partners in a debt release the debtor from a part of his proportion of the debt (such as an half, for instance), the remaining part of the debt is, in that case, due to the two creditors in degrees proportionate to their respective rights.—As, for instance, if the debt due to them were originally twenty dirms, and one of them afterwards release the debtor from the half of his share, the remaining debt will then be fifteen dirms, of which five are due to the exempting partner, and ten to the other partner,

One of two partners may agree to a postponement of payment.—If one of two partners should protract the period of payment of his share it is valid, according to Aboo Yoosaf, because of its analogy to an absolute exemption or release—in other words, as a suspension of the payment is equivalent to a restricted release, it is therefore valid, in the same manner as an absolute release.—According to Haneefa and Mohammed this is not valid:—as in such a case it must follow that a division of debt takes place prior to seisin,—since protracting the period of payment with respect to one share, and not to the other, is, as it were, a partition of the share; and a partition of debt previous to seisin is not lawful; because partition bears the sense of endowment with a right of property, and the endowment with a right in a debt, made to any other than the debtor himself, is not lawful.—Moreover, partition implies distinction: and as distinction cannot exist with respect to any obligation upon the person, it is therefore invalid.

One of two partners receives his share by usurping anything from the debtor: or by losing or destroying anything belonging to him; or, by accepting a lease in composition; or, by burning a piece of cloth, his property.—If one of two partners usurp some specific article from the debtor, or purchase something from him by an in invalid contract, and lose or destroy the some, these acts are considered as equivalent to a receipt of his debt.—So also if one of two partners accept a lease from the debtor in lieu of his debt, he is in that case held to have received his debt. If, also one out of two partners should burn a piece of cloth belonging to the debtor of equal value with his share of the debt. this is a receipt according to Mohammed. but not according to Aboo Yoosaf. (Some, however, observe that this difference proceeds on the supposition of his having thrown fire on the cloth, without having previously laid hold of it; for if he should have first laid hold of the cloth, and then burned it, all our doctors are of opinion that he has received his share, because he is considered first to have usurped the cloth, and then to have destroyed it)

One of two partners annuls his share by marrying the debtor (being a female) and settling his share of the debt as her dower; or, by compounding with it for an offence.—If the debtor be a female, and one of two partners, in the debt should marry her, and stipulate his share of the debt as her dower, this, according to the Zahir Rawayet. is an annulment.—and so also if he compound with his share, for a wiful offence,—It is, however, to be observed, that if one of the partners in a debt should marry the woman who is their debtor, without stipulating his share of the debt as her dower, in that case the other share has a claim upon him, as under such circumstances he is held to have made commutation with his wife of his claim for hers. It is otherwise where he stipulates his share of the debt as her dower; for then he is held to have annulled, and not to have commuted his right, and on this account the other share can have no future claim upon him.—It is an invariable rule that, where a receipt has been made, by one partner, the othe partner, in case of the destruction of his right, by the debtor's dying insolvent, or otherwise, is entitled to participate with the receiving partner;—but he has not such right in the case of an annulment.

One of the partners compounding his share of the debt by a purchase, the other may either take his share from the debtor, or an equivalent for his proportion in the receipt from the purchaser.—If one of two partners in a debt purchase something from the debtor (such as cloth, for instance) in lieu of his share of the debt, then the other partner is at liberty, either to require his share of the debt from the debtor (in which case all the effects take place, as described in the preceding example, where the partner requires payment from the debtor),—or to take an equiavlent from the purchaser of a fourth part of the debt;—because he [the purchaser] has taken complete possession of his debt, since in paying and selling there is no degree of loss or disparity admitted in the things exchanged,—He, therefore, is responsible for a fourth part of the debt, and has no option of either giving a quarter of the debt, or a half of the cloth, —It is otherwise in a composition, because, as composition generally proceeds upon a principle of lenity and abatement, it would be an injury to the compounder to force him to give a fourth part of of debt, and therefore an option is afforded him either to give a fourth part of the debt, or the half of the article received in composition.—The non-receiving partner, moreover, is not entitled to any part of the cloth purchased, as the purchasing partner has become proprietor or the same in virtue of contract of sale.

OBJECTION.—The cloth in question ought to be divided between the two partners, as it has been acquired in exchange for a joint debt.

REPLY.—The cloth in question has not been acquired in exchange for a joint debt, but merely in exchange for the share of the purchaser, in this way, that it produces a commutation of the price of the cloth for that part of the debt which is due to him.

OBJECTION.—If the price of the cloth be a commutation of his share of the debt, it induces a partition of the debt prior to the seisin of it, which is lawful.

REPLY,—A wilful partition of debt, previous to the seisin, is unlawful, but an unintentional partition of it (by that being comprehended, for instance) is lawful: and, in the case in question, it is comprehended in the validity of the sale: in the same manner as (in the preceding case) the partition of the debt. previous to the seisin, is interwoven with the validity of the composition.

One of two partners in a sillim contract cannot compound for his share.—IF two persons conclude a Sillm contract (that is, advance money for goods, to be delivered at a future period), and one of them afterwards compound his share of the goods for his share of the stock advanced, it is not lawful, according to Haneefa and Mohammed—Aboo Yoosaf maintains that it is lawful, as he considers this to be analogous to any other debt: and also to a case where two persons purchase a slave, and one of them afterwards dissolves the contract with respect to his share, which is lawful; and so also in the persent case.—The arguments of Haneefa and Mahammed, upon this point, are twofold.—FIRST, if the composition in question be lawful with respect only to the share of one of the partners it must necessarily follow that a partition of the debt has been made prior to the seisin of it; which is unlawful; for as the debt, prior to the seisin, is not extant, it is impossible to discriminate part from part. If, on the other hand it be lawful with respect to the shares of both, then the consent of the other must be had—it is otherwise where two persons purchase a slave, and one of them dissolves the contract with respect to his share, because the slave in question is extant, and the partition of an extant thing is not impracticable, since part can be discriminated from part, whether before seisin or after it.—SECONDLY, if the composition in question be valid, it must follow that the right of the purchaser to the goods for which the advance has been made is annulled, and established in the capital (that is, in the price advanced), and that it afterwards reverts with respect to the goods for which the advance has been made. For supposing the composition to be valid, and that one of the partners receives, in consequence, his share of the capital, the other partner has then a right to take from him his proportion of it; and the compounder again has a claim upon the other partner for a proportionate part of the goods. Hence it follows that the right of the compounder reverts, with respect to the goods of which the advance has been made, after annulment;—but an annulment cannot take place without a dissolution: a dissolution, therefore is primarily established.—Now, upon his right reverting, and annulment of the dissolution is induced; and this unlawful, as a dissolution in contracts of Sillim cannot be annulled.—Lawyers have observed that this case proceeds on a supposition of the purchasers having mixed together their capital: for, if their shares of the capital should not have been mixed or complicated, then (according to the first of the above arguments) the same disagreement must still subsist; since a division of the debt previous to the seisin must then also necessarily follow: but, according the second argument. the composition is valid in the opinion of all our doctors; for, in such a case, the non-compounding partner would not participate with the cumpounder in that part of the capital which he receives back, as they were not copartners in the capital, and hence it does not follow that the right of the purchaser, to the goods for which the advance was made, reverts after annulment.—It is recited in the Auzih that this assertion concerning the unanimity of our doctors, as stated in the second argument, is not well founded: because a right to participate in the article received is founded on this circumstance, that the goods which the advance has been made constitute a joint debt, as it arises from one contract in which they are alike concerned; and hence the non-compounding share has a right to participate with the compounder in whatever he may have received in virtue of their partnership in the goods for which the advance was made, whether their shares of the capital have been complicated or not.

Section

Of Takharij.

Definition of the term.—TAKHARIJ, in the language of the LAW, siginifies a composition entered into by some heirs with other heirs, for their share of the inheritance, in consideration of some specific thing, which excludes them from inheritance.

Heirs may compound with a co-heir for his share of inheritance, consisting of land or effects, by any equivalent.—IF the estate of a persons, consisting of land, or of goods and effects, be liable to be shared among several heirs: and the heirs compound with one amongst themselves for his share of the inheritance, by giving him some specific article, such composition is lawful, whether the thing given be superior or inferior to his right: because it is possible to legalize this composition, by construing it in the nature of a sale. and also, because it is related that. in the time of Osman, Tamazir the wife of Abdul-Rihman, the son of Auf, who had been divorced by her husband in his last illness, compounded her share of the inheritance, which was a fourth of the eighth, for one half of the fourth of an eighth: as is evident from this circumstance, that Abdul-Rihman, who, besides children, had four wives, left an estate of five millions three hundred and twelve thousand DEENARS; and the share she received was eighty three thousand deenars, which is one half of the fourth of an eighth.

Or, by one precious metal, where the inheritance is in another precious metal.—IN the same manner also, if the estate consist of silver, and gold be given to one of the heirs as a composition.—or, if it consist of gold. and a composition be given in silver, it is valid, whether the thing given be inferior or superior, because this is a sale of one species for another, and in it the condition of equality between the consideration and the return is not required.—It is requisite however, that the subjects of the composition be mutually interchanged and taken possession of by the parties at the place where the contract of composition is concluded; for this is a Sirf sale, and in it mutual seisin at the meeting is a necessary condition.—But if the heir, in whose possession the remainder of the estate it, should deny the possession then the former seisin suffices, because it is a seisin of responsibility (since it is in the nature of usurpation), and may therefore stand for a seisin of composition.—If, on the contrary. he should acknowledge the possession, then it is necessary that a new seisin be made; because the seisin, in that case, being in the nature of a trust, and consequently unattended with responsibility is weak in comparison with a seisin of composition, which is attended with responsibility, and therefore cannot be substituted in the place of it.

An inheritance of bullion and effects may be compounded for by gold or silver; but this gold or silver must exceed the share of the same metal inherited; and the heir must be put in possession of such excess at the time of adjusting the composition.—IF the estate consist of gold, silver, goods, and effects, and the heirs compound the share of one amongst themselves for silver or for gold: it is in that case requisite that the gold or silver given in composition be somewhat greater than his share of the gold or silver by inheritance, in order that, after opposing an exact equality of the two similar species to each other. there may remain some excess to oppose as a composition for his share of the other articles, to the end that the imputation of usury may be avoided.—In this case, also, it is requisite that possession be taken, at the meeting. of the thing opposed to his share of the gold or the silver, because the composition to the extent is considered in the nature of a Sirf sale.—If, in the case in question, the composition be made for goods and effects, it is lawful, absolutely,—that is, whether seisin be made by the parties at the meeting, or otherwise,—and whether the thing given in composition be inferior or superior to the share of the inheritance.

An inheritance of money may be compounded for by money; each species being opposed to the other respectively.—IF the estate consist of dirms and deenars, and the composition also consist of dirms and deenars, it is lawful, whether the amount given in composition exceed or fall short of the share of inheritance compounded for, because each kind is opposed to its opposite, in the same manner as in sale—It is a requisite, however, that the seisin be made at the meeting, because the composition in question is in the nature of a Sirf sale.

The inheritance of a debt cannot be compounded.—IF there be a debt due to the deceased, and it be included in the composition.—by the compounding heir giving up his share of it, and agreeing that it shall go entirely to the other heirs, such composition is null;—because in this case the heir renders the other heirs proprietors of his share of a debt, which is unlawful. as the property of a debt cannot be conveyed to any but the person indebted.—The composition, therefore, is null;—because it is null in that part which relates to the debt; and when a contract is null in part, it becomes null in the whole,—since where a contract is invalid with respect to a part of its its subject, it is invalid in toto.

Except by the heir agreeing to release the debtor from his proportion.—IF, however, the composition be made on this condition. that the compounding heir shall release the debtor from his share of the debt, and that the others shall not exact it, the composition is valid, as it is either an annulment of the debt. or a conveyance of it to the debtor This is one expedient for legalizing the composition.

Or by the other heirs paying him that proportion gratuitously.—ANOTHER expedient is, by the heirs paying, in a gratuitous manner, to the compounding heir, the share of the debt which is due to him, and then making a composition with him for his share of the collected part of the estate.—In both these expedients, indeed, an injury results to the other heirs:—in the latter, evidently, as there they pay his demand, out of their right, without any return;—and in the former, because it is possible that they may never receive the debt, nor any part of it, from the property of the debtor.

Or lending it to him, to transfer to the debtor.—THE best expedient, therefore, is that the heirs lend the compounding heir the amount of his share of the debt, and then compound with him for his share of the collected estate; and that he then transfer the said loan to the debtor, in order that the other heirs may lawfully receive from the debtor the share of the debt which is due to him.

Case of composition of an inheritance where the particulars of the estate are not known.—If there be no debts due to the estate of the deceased, and it be not known of what species the articles of the estate consist, and one of the heirs compound his share for articles of weight, or measurement of capacity,—some have said that this composition is not lawful, because of the semblance it bears to usury.—Others, however, maintain that it is lawful, as the semblance to usury is dubious in this instance; for, in the first place, it is possible that the articles may consist of articles of weight and of measurement of capacity, and it is also possible that they may not;—and, in the next place, if they do consist of such articles, it is possible that the quantity of the composition may be unequal to his right, and it is also possible that it may be equal to it.—The semblance to usury is therefore dubious; and regard is had to an actual semblance only, not to a dubious semblance.

Case of the same, where the particulars are only known in part.—If the estate consist of something else than articles of weight or measurement of capacity, but of which the particular substances are unknown, and one of the heirs compound his share for articles of weight or measurement of capacity,—some have said that this is unlawful; because the composition, in this case, is in the nature of a sale, or an exchange of property for property; and this is not lawful when one of the articles opposed in exchange is uncertain. The most approved opinion, however, is, that it is lawful; since the uncertainty here cannot be productive of strife, inasmuch as the thing for which the composition is made, and which is the subject of the uncertainty, is in the hands of the rest of the heirs.

The inheritance of an insolvent estate can neither be compounded for nor distributed.—If the estate be completely overwhelmed with debt, neither composition nor division of it amongst the heirs is lawful; because the heirs are not, in this case, masters of the property, as inheritance takes place only with respect to such property as in unincumbered with some essential requisite of the deceased; and the payment of the debts of the deceased is one of his essential requisites. If, also, the estate be not completely overwhelmed with debt, it is not even then becoming to enter into any composition until the debts be discharged. Lawyers, however, have said that if, in such case, a composition or a division be made, prior to a discharge of the debts, it is valid.—Koorokhee, in treating of partition, observes that it is not valid according to a favourable construction of the law; but that it is valid upon the principle of analogy.

BOOK XXVII.

OF MOZARIBAT, OR COPARTNERSHIP IN THE PROFITS OF STOCK AND LABOUR.

Definition of the term.—MOZARIBAT is derived from Zirrib, and means, in its literal sense, to walk on the ground. In the language of the LAW, Mozaribat signifies a contract of copartnership, of which the one party (namely, the proprietor) is entitled to profit on account of the stock, he being denominated Rabbi Mal, proprietor of the stock (which is termed Ras Mal); and other party is entitled to a profit on account of his labour; and this last is denominated the Mozarib (or manager) inasmuch as he derives a benefit from his own labour and endeavours.

A participation in the profit is an essential of the contract.—A CONTRACT of Mozaribat, therefore, cannot be established without a participation in the profit; for if the whole of the profit be stipulated to the proprietor of the stock, then it is considered as a Bazat; or, if the whole be stipulated to the immediate manager, it be considered as a loan.

CHAPTER I.

Contracts of Mozaribat are lawful.—CONTRACTS of Mozaribat are authorized by the LAW from necessity; since many people have property who are unskilled in the art of employing it; and others, again, possess that skill without having the property;—hence there is a necessity for authorizing these contracts, in order that the interests of the rich and poor, and of the skilful and unskilful, may be reconciled:—moreover, people entered into such contracts in the presence of the Prophet, who did not prohibit, but confirmed the same: several of the companions, also, entered into these contracts.

The stock is a trust in the manager's hands.—WHATEVER may be given by the proprietor of the stock to the manager is considered as a trust, because the manager takes possession of the same at the desire of the proprietor, and neither with a view to purchase nor to pawn.—The manager is also an agent on the part of the proprietor in regard to the employment of the stock, as he acts in that respect by the orders of the proprietor. Whenever, therefore, any profit is acquired, the proprietor and the manager are joint shares in it, inasmuch as it proceeds jointly from the stock of the one, and the labour of the other.

If the contract be of an invalid nature, the manager, in lieu of profit, receives an adequate hire.—WHEN a contract of Mozaribat is invalid: it is, in effect, an invalid hire; because, as the manager acts for the proprietor, with regard to his stock, the profit which is stipulated to him is similar to hire for his labour. The contract of Mozaribat, therefore, where it is invalid, bears the construction of an invalid hire; and such being the case, the manager is entitled only to a hire adequate to his labour.*

A manager opposing the proprietor, stands as an usurper.—IF the manager should oppose the proprietor, he is then held to be an usurper, since he wilfully transgresses with respect to the property of another,

A Mozaribat holds only in such stock as admits of partnership.—CONTRACTS of Mozaribat are valid only with respect to stock in which contracts of copartnership are valid; namely, dirms and deenars (according to Haneefa) and also current Faloos (according to the two disciples), as has been already treated of at large, under the head of Partnership.—Hence if a proprietor of stock should give goods or effects to another; and desire him "to sell them, and then to act as a Mozarib with regard to the price,"† the contract of Mozaribat would in such case be lawful, because it is not referred to the goods or effects, but to the price of these, and this is a thing respecting which a contract of Mozaribat is valid.—In regard to his referring the contract to a price at a future period, it is lawful to do so in contracts of Mozaribat; because such contracts are either in the nature of a commission of agency, or of hire; and neither of these is preventive of the validity of a reference to a future period.—In the same manner, also, if the proprietor should say, "receive the debt due to me by a particular person, and act as manager with regard to it;" the contract of Mozaribat is then lawful, because, by being referred to the period of seisin, it relates to substanee and not to debt, and it is lawful to refer it to a future period, for the reason above mentioned.—It is otherwise, however, where the proprietor of the stock says, "act as a Mozarib with respect to the debt due by you;" for this is not lawful either according to Haneefa or the two disciples:—according to the former, because he holds an appointment of agency of this nature to be unlawful (as has been before explained in treating of agency and sale): and also according to the two disciples, because, although such an appointment of agency (as they hold) be lawful, yet as a thing purchased by a pesson so instructed is the property of the instructor, it follows that the contract of Mozaribat relates to goods and effects,* and is accordingly unlawful.

It requires that the profit be determinate.—IT is one of the conditions of a contract of Mozaribat, that the profit of the proprietor and the manager be indeterminate; that is to say; that neither of them be entitled to a specific number of dirms: for if the condition of a specific number of dirms be stipulated with respect to one or other of the parties, the partnership between them with respect to the profit ceases to exist, since it is possible that the whole profit might not exceed the number fixed, and it is essential that they be partners in the profit. If, therefore, ten dirms (for instance) be fixed as the portion of one of the parties, the manager is entitled to an hire adequate to his labour, because the contract of Mozaribat has become invalid, since it is possible that the whole profit acquired may not exceed the amount fixed, in which case there could be no copartnership with respect to it.—The manager is, in this case, entitled to an adequate hire, because his object in his labour was to receive a return, and he is prevented from receiving such return by the invalidity of the contract: it is therefore indispensable that he be paid an adequate hire.—In regard to the profit which in such case may be acquired, it goes to the proprietor, being considered as the offspring of his property.—This is the law in every case of an invalid contract of Mozaribat.—It is to be observed that an adequate hire, in the case of an invalid contract of Mozaribat, cannot, in the opinion of Aboo Yoosaf, exceed the quantity stipulated. According to Mohammed, on the contrary, what it may be adequate, without any regard to the quantity stipulated, must be given: as has been already explained in treating of partnership.—In a case where the contract proves invalid, an adequate hire is declared, in the Rawayet Aasil,† to be due, although no profit should have been acquired, because the hire of a hireling is due upon the delivery either of profit or of labour, and the delivery of one or both of these here takes place.—It is recorded from Aboo Yoosaf that nothing in such case is due, because of its analogous resemblance to a valid contract of Mozaribat—that is to say, as in a valid contract of Mozaribat nothing is due to the manager in the event of there being no profit, so if the contract be invalid, nothing is due to him a fortiori.—It is further to be observed that the stock of an invalid contract of Mozaribat is not to be replaced or accounted for in case of its loss or destruction:—that is to say, indemnifica-

* To understand this it may be proper to remark, that where a contract of hire is rendered invalid by the invalidity of any of its conditions, the person hired is entitled only to a hire proportionable to the subject, and not to the hire stipulated in the contract.

† That is, "to employ them in trade, in the manner of MOZARIBAT."

* Arab. Rakht woo Mattaa, as distinguished from Mal. See Vol. I., p. 10.

† The original traditons. A law-book so called.

tion is not incumbent upon the manager;—because, as there is no responsibility for a loss of stock in a valid contract, so neither is there any in an invalid contract: and also, because, as the manager in the case of an invalid contract is only a hireling, and the stock remains in his possession merely that he may employ it, no indemnification is due from him on account of its destruction.

And not subjected to any uncertainty—ANOTHER requisite, in contracts of Mozaribat, is that there be no condition creative of an uncertainty with respect to the profit; for such a condition invalidates the contract, from its destruction of the object of it. Any other invalid condition, however, excepting this, or such as are opposite to the nature of the contract, do not invalidate the contract, but of themselves fall to the ground, as in the case of a condition of loss to the manager (where it is stipulated that "whatever profit may accrue shall be shared between the proprietor and the manager, according to their agreement; but that if any loss result, it shall fall entirely on the manager"). The contract of Mozaribat, therefore, is not annulled by the stipulation of coditions of this nature, but the condition itself is null; because, as the condition is merely redundant, and is neither productive of a dissolution of the partnership, nor of uncertainty with respect to the profit, the contract of Mozaribat is not thereby rendered invalid; in the same manner as agency does not become invalid from the invalidity of its conditions.

That the stock be completely made over to the manager.—ANOTHER requisite in Mozaribat, is that the proprietor deliver over the stock to the manager, and retain no seisin of it, because it is in the manager's hands in the nature of a deposit, and must therefore be in his sole possession, and in no respect in possession of the proprietor. It is otherwise in a contract of partnership; because, in a contract of Mozaribat, the property is supplied by the one party, and the labour by the other; whence it is indispensable that the property remain entirely with the manager, in order that he may be competent to perform the necessary labour with regard to it; whereas, in partnership, the labour is supplied by both parties: whence, if it were stipulated that the property shall remain entirely with one of the parties, a contract of partnership would not be established.*

A condition of management by the proprietor invalidates the contract.—A CONDITION of management by the proprietor of the stock invalidates a contract of Mozaribat; because where such a condition exists, the stock can never be possessed solely by tho manager, wherefore he cannot be competent to act with respect to it, and thus the object of the contract (namely, participation in the profit) cannot be effected;—and this, whether the proprietor be of sound understanding or otherwise (such as an infant), because, as the possession of the stock is established in the proprietor in virtue of his right of property, so long as it continues in his possession no delivery of it to the manager can be certified.—In the same manner, also if one of two Mozaribat partners, or one of two Ainan partners, deliver stock to any person in the way of a Moz ribat, and stipulate that the other partner shall also engage in the management of it, such contract of Mozaribat is null,—because the other partner is also a proprietor of the stock in question, although he be not a party to the Mozaribat agreement.

And so also, a condition of management by the contracting party, although he be not the proprietor.—IF the contractor of a Mozaribat agreement be not the proprietor of the stock, and stipulate that he also shall unite with the Mozarib, or manager, in the management of the stock, such agreement or contract is invalid, where the contractor happens to be incumbent,—that is, where he is a person who (like a privileged slave) cannot lawfully undertake the management of stock, in the way of Mozaribat.—Where, therefore, a privileged slave give stock to another to manage in the way of Mozaribat, stipulating that he shall, conjunctly with the manager, act with regard to the stock, for a proportion of the profit, the contract is invalid, because although t e slave be not actual proprietor of the stock, yet as he has a possession of it, with the power of employment, he is held to be the same as the proprietor, and therefore his possession of it is destructive of the validity of the contract.

Unless he be campetent to undertake it.—But if the party be competent to receive stock, and act as a manager then the contract in question would not be invalid;—as where, for instance a father, or a guardian, give the property of his infant charge to any person, to manage in the way of Mozaribat, stipulating that he himself, in exchange for a certain share of the profit, shall joint in the management of the stock;—in which case the contract is valid; because, such a person being himself entitled to undertake the management of the infant's property, in the way of Mozaribat, is equally entitled to join in the management of it in the way of Mozaribat, with others.

The manager is at liberty to act with the stock according to his own discretion.—As contracts of Mozaribat are absolute, that is to say, are not restricted to time, place, or other circumstances, It is therefore lawful for the manager to purchase or sell, or to eat of, or travel with, the stock; or to lodge it, either as a Bazat or a deposit; because the contract is unrestricted; and the object of it is the acquisition of profit; and as this cannot be accomplished but by trade, the contract of course extends to every occurrence in commerce, and the appointment of an agent, or the giving property by way of

* See Partnership, Vol. II p. 233.

Bazat, or the deposit of property are all occurrence of commerce;—and in the same manner, travelling is evidently so, because a trustee, who has no power of action with respect to his trust, has yet a power of travelling with it, and therefore a manager, who has the power of action with regard to the stock, entitled to travel with it a fortiori:—besides, the word Mozaribat in itself implies this power, as it is derived from Zirrib, which signifies to walk on the ground, or, in other words, to travel.—It is recorded from Aboo Yoosaf that a manager is not at liberty to travel, and he has also related an opinion of Haneefa, that if the proprietor should give the stock to the manager in his own city, the manager is not in that case at liberty to travel, because to travel with property is an unnecessary endangerment of it; but that, if the proprietor give the stock to him in some other city than his own, he may then travel to his own city, because it is not likely that a man should continue always travelling; and as the proprietor knowingly gave him the stock in another city than his own, it may be presumed that he thereby consented to his travelling with the property to his own city.

But he cannot entrust it to another in the manner of Mozaribat without the proprietor's consenu.—It is not lawful for a manager to make over the stock to another, in the way of Mozaribat, unless with the consent of the proprietor, or unless he should have empowered him to act according to his own judgment and discretion; because a thing cannot include its like, since both being of equal force, one cannot yield to the other.—Hence it is necessary either that an express permission should have been given, or an absolute and discretionary power have been delegated.—This case, therefore, is similar to that of the appointment of an agent; for one agent has not the power of appointing another agent, unless the consitituent should have said "act according to your own judgment and discretion."—It is different with respect to the depositing of property, or giving it by way of Bazat, because these acts are lawful to a manager, as they are of a nature inferior to a contract of Mozaribat, and a thing may include its inferior.

Nor lend it to another, although his powers be discretional.—It is not lawful for a manager to grant a loan to any one out of the Mozaribat stock, although the proprietor may have said to him "act according to your own discretion;" because the proprietor of the stock, in giving this discretional power, means to give a latitude with respect to such things only as are relative to trade; and loan is not connected with trade, but is a gratuitous dead, in the same manner as charity, or a gift; wherefore, by giving a loan, the object (namely, profit) cannot be obtained, since to receive back more than what is lent is not lawful.—Giving property in the way of Mozaribat, on the other hand, is in the nature of trade, and therefore a manager in such a case may give the stock which is the subject of it, by way of Mozaribat, to another, provided the proprietor have empowered him to act according to his judgment and discretion.—The case is the same with respect to partnership and commixture of the stock with the manager's own property;—that is to say, if the manager should commix the stock with his own property and thus because a partner therein, it is lawful, provided the proprietor have empowered him to act according to his judgment and discretion, because mixture and copartnership are in the nature of trade, and the power so given is therefore held to extend to it.

The manager cannot deviate from any restrictions imposed upon him in the contract.—If a person give property to another by way of Mozaribat, and restrict his management of it to a particular city or to particular articles, it is not lawful for the manager to deviate therefrom; because this is in the nature of a commission of agency; and as restriction is attended with an advantage, it is therefore allowed to operate.—(An explanation will hearafter be given of the nature of restriction.)—Neither is it lawful for the manager under such circumstances to give the stock by way of Bazat to another person, to be carried by him from that particular city: for as it is not lawful for the manager himself to carry it from that city, he therefore is not entitled to delegate such a power to another.

Upon violating the restriction, the manager becomes responsible for the stock.—If the proprietor restrict the management of the stock to a particular city, and the manager nevertheless carry it to another city; and there purchase something with it, he becomes in that case responsible for the stock; and whatever he may have purchased with it becomes his property, as well as the profit which may arise therefrom; because he stands as a usurper, since he has assumed a power of action with respect to the property of another without that other's consent.—If, however, the manager, having carried the stock out of the particular city, should not purchase anything with it until he had returned to the city to which the proprietor had restricted his power of action, he becomes freed from responsibility (in the same manner as a trustee who has opposed the depositor becomes freed from responsibility on the cessation of such opposition),—and the stock resumes its former nature of Mozaribat, in virtue of its continuance in the possession of the manager, under the original contract.—In the same manner; also, if the manager, having brought something with part of the stock in the city in question, should depart from it with the remaining part of the stock, and again return without having purchased anything with it, in that case both the purchase which was at first made, and the part which was afterwards brought back, are considered in the nature of Mozaribat, for the reason above-mentioned.—It is to be observed that what has been here related with respect to the manager's becoming responsible upon carrying the stock to another city, and there making a purchase with it, is recited from the Jama Sagheer.—In the Mabsoot, treating of Mozaribat, it is related that the manager becomes responsible immediately on carrying the stock from the prescribed city.—The more approved doctrine, however, is that the manager becomes responsible immediately on carrying away the stock from the prescribed city; and that upon his making a purchase with it in another city the responsibility becomes fixed and permanent, since there then exists no probability of his bringing it back to the prescribed city.—The condition stated in the Jama Sagheer, therefore, of the manager making a purchase out of the city, relates to the confirmation of the responsibility, and not to the original birth of it, which takes place immediately on carrying the property out of the city.

A restriction to any particular part of a city is invalid—If, a person give stock to another by way of Mozaribat, on condition of his making a purchase with the said stock in the market-place of a particular city, the condition is invalid; because a city, notwithstanding the distinction of its parts, is yet like one place and such a restriction is therefore useless.

Unless stipulated under an express exception of any other place.—If, however, he expressly limit the purchase to the market-place, by saying, "purchahse with this stock in the market-place and nowhere else," a purchase made out of the market-place is in that case unlawful, because the proprietor in this instance has expressly declared that 'he shall not make a purchase out of the market-place,"—and the proprietor is authorized to lay this restriction.—The restriction here mentioned is to be understood in the proprietor saying to the manager. "I give this stock to you on condition that you act with it in such a manner" ("that you purchases cotton with it," for example);—or, on condition that "you employ it in such a place;"—and so also, from his saying, "Take this stock and employ it in Koofa;" or, "Take this stock on condition of half the profit arising from it in Koofa."—If, however, the proprietor were simply to say, "employ this stock in Koofa," the manager may then employ it in Koofa or out of Koofa.—The proofs, upon these profits, are connected with Arabic grammar.

The manager may be restricted, in his transactions, to particular persons.—If the proprietor say to the manager, "Take this stock, on condition that you purchase and sell with it with a particular person," such restriction is valid, being founded on the particular credit in business of the person to whom it relates.—It is otherwise where the says "Take this stock on condition that you purchase with it from the people of Koofa," or "sell it to them;—or, "Take this stock for a Sirf-sale, on condition that you purchase with it from Sirrafa [bankers], or sell it to them;"—for if the manager (in the former instance) sell the stock in the city of Koofa, to a person who is not an inhabitant of that city, or (in the latter instance) sell it to some one who is not a Sirraf, his act is lawful;—because the first of these restrictions is merely a restriction in point of place; for as the people of Koofa are all different in regard to their judgments and manner of transacting business, the restriction to them in general could be attended with no advantage, whereas the restriction to the place is advantageous in regard to the preservation of the stock: and the second of these restrictions is a restriction to a particular mode of sale; for as he did not confine the restriction to any one individual, but to a particular set of people who prosecute the business of Sirrafs,* it is evident that the restriction was meant merely to a Sirf sale—Such is the meaning, in common acceptation, of the restriction in these two particular cases; but not in others,

The contract may be restricted, in its operation, to a particular period.—If the proprietor limit the Mozaribat to a particular period, the contract becomes null at the expiration of that period; because, as this is a commission of agency' its continuance is therefore restricted to the period specified; and as the restriction of its duration may be advantageous, it therefore operates in the same manner as a restriction to a particular place, or to a particular mode of sale.

Nothing can be purchased, by the manager, which is not a subject or property, in virtue of seisin: with respect to the proprietor.—A manager is not at liberty to purchase, with the stock, a slave, who would become free by being transferred to the proprietor, whether from the circumstance of affinity, or from any other cause (as if the proprietor had already vowed to emancipate him), because the contract has been made with a view to the acquisition of profit, which can be obtained only by repeated acts such as previous purchase and subsequent sale; and to this last the freedom of the slave operates as a bar:—and for this reason the purchase of all such things as do not become property, in virtue of seisin (such as wine or carrion) is not comprehended in a Mozaribat contract. (It is otherwise with respect to the purchase of a thing under an invalid sale;

*Sirraf is derived from Sirrif, which signifies a pure sale or the act of exchanging one sort of specie for a another: hence Sirraf means not only a banker or money changer, but also any one whose dealing are of that nature, and consequently a negotiator of Sirf sales.

for this is comprehended in a Mozaribat contract, since the manager may lawfully sell that thing again after seisin: and consequently profit, which is the object of the contract, may in that case be obtained,)—If therefore, a manager purchase a slave who becomes free with respect to the proprietor of the stock, such purchase is not included in the Muzaribat stock, but is considered to have been made for the manager himself; for the bargain being valid with respect to the purchaser, is therefore effectual with respect to him, in the same manner as in the case of an agent for purchase who opposes his constituent.

The manager cannot purchase a slave free with respect to himself, where any profit has been previously acquired upon the stock.—It is not lawful for a manager to purchase a slave who is free with respect to the manager himself, where a profit has been gained upon the stock; because the slave of the manager (namely, in the profit) would in this case become emancipated from the whole stock, and consequently the share of the property would be valid,* according to Haneefa (The two disciples hold that it would become emancipated, because of the known difference of their opinion from that of Haneefa concerning the divisibility or indivisibility of manumission)—Now, where a slave becomes emancipated, either wholly, or in part, he is no longer a lawful subject of sale; and consequently the end of the contract (namely, the acquisition of profit) cannot by this means be obtained. Hence it is not lawful for a manager, where a profit has been gained upon the stock, to purchase a slave who, with respect to himself, becomes free.—If, however, he should make this purchase, under such a circumstance, he becomes responsible for the amount of the Mozaribat stock so expended, because he is then held to have made the purchase for himself, and he has paid the price out of the stock.—But if there have been no accession of profit to the stock, the manager may lawfully purchase a slave that is free with respect to himself, because there exists no bar, in this case, since the manager has no share in the purchase, † so as to render his portion in the slave free.—And if, after the purchase, a profit should arise, from the slave increasing value, the manager's portion of the slave, involving his share of the profit, is emancipated; and he is not, in this case, in any respect responsible to the proprietor of the stock,* because neither the increase of the value, not the share acquired by the manager, were effected by his means, but operated of themselves independent of his will or endeavour. Hence this case is the same as where a person becomes heir to a relation, or to some one else; as if a wife should purchase the son of her husband, and should afterwards die, leaving behind her husband and brother; in which case the child becomes free, and the father is not in any degree responsible; and so also in the case in question.—(It is to be observed that the slave in question must perform emancipatory labour to the proprietor of the stock, to the amount of his share in him, as the proprietor's property is involved in his person; he must therefore perform emancipatory labour; in the same manner as in a case of inheritance.

Case of the manager purchasing a famale slave, and begetting a child upon her.—If a person give one thousand dirms to be managed, in consideration of a moiety of the profit, in the way of Mozaribat, and the manager purchase, for the thousand dirms, a famale slave of the value of these thousand, and afterwards have carnal connexion with her, and she in consequence produce a child also valued at one thousand dirms, and the manager claim the child, and the child afterwards increase in value to fifteen hundred dirms, in this case the proprietor of the stock has it at his option either or claim emancipatory labour from the slave [the manager's child] to the amount of one thousand two hundred and fifty dirms: or to emancipate him: but the manager does not owe any indemnification to the proprietor for his share, though he be rich. The reason of this is that there is a presumption of the validity of the claim here made since it is possible that the female slave may be the wife of the manager, by her former proprietor having first contracted her in marriage to him, and afterwards sold her to him on behalf of the Mozaribat stock: and that the child which she produced may have been the issue of his cohabitation with her:—but his claim to the child was not effectual (that is to say, the child was not emancipated), because of the condition of its emancipation (namely, his right of property in the slave) did not in any respect appear, as no profit had as yet arisen from her: for the value of each (namely, of the mother and child) was exactly equal to the amount of the stock, and consequently no profit existed in either of them; in the same manner as where the Mozaribat stock consists of different substances, and the value of each substance is equal to the stock,—in this way, that a person purchases, with a stock of one thousand dirms, two slaves, and each of them after-

* Because the slave, by becoming free in part, is rendered unsaleable; and obtains a claim to freedom.

† For, as no profit has been, as yet, gained upon the stock, and as the profit is the only thing in which the manager has any share, it follows that no part of the manager's property is expended in the purchase.

* That is, he owes him no indemnification for the vitiation of his property in the slave from this circumstance.

wards because worth one thousand dirms,—in which case no profit is held to exist in either of them; and so also in the case in question: and as no profit appears, it follows that the manager obtains no share whatever in either the slave or the child, and consequently that his claim is invalid: but upon the child exceeding the stock in value, a profit then appears, and consequently the claim formerly made then becomes valid.—It were otherwise if the manner were first to emancipate the child, and afterwards the value of him to rise, for this emancipation would be altogether invalid (that is to say, would be ineffectual after the appearance of profit, as well as before), because the libration is an indication of manumission, and the indication being null at the time, from non-existence of a present right of property†, cannot afterwards become effectual in consequence of a supervenient right: whereas claim, on the other hand, is an express notification, and hence may lawfully be admitted as effectual, in consequence of a supervenient right—(in the same manner as where a person, having declared the slave of another to be free, afterwards purchases him; in which case the slave, after the purchase, becomes free, in virtue of the previous declaration);—and the claim being effectual after the existence of profit, and the parentage, also, being established, it follows that the child is free in virtue of the manager's right of property in a part of him: and no compensation for any part of his value is due from the manager to the proprietor of the stock, whether the manager be rich or poor because the feedom of the child is established in virtue of the parentage, and also in virtue of the manager's right of property (that is to say, virtue of both):—but as the right of property is established subsequent to the parentage, the freedom is therefore referred to the right of property which takes place independent of the will and endeavour of the manager, and in which therefore he is guilty of no transgression; and as the indemnification for emancipating a slave ‡ is an indemnification for damages, it is not due but in a case of transgression.—The proprietor of the stock is entitled, on this occasion, to demand emancipatory labour of the male slave, because the property which he had in him remains, as it were, detained in him;—and he is also at liberty or emancipate him, because a slave who owes emancipatory labour is (according to Haneefa) like a Mokatib: and the proprietor is therefor empowered to emancipate him.—If the proprietor require the labour, the slave must perform it to the amount af one thousand two hundred and fifty dirms; for the proprietor is entitled to one thousand on account of the stock; and the remaining five hundred, which is the profit, is equally shared between him and the manager; the labour, therefore, must be performed to the amount above stated; and upon the proprietor thus obtaining that amount, of him, he is then entitled to take an equivalent for half the value of the mother; because the propeietor being entitled to one thousand DIRMS out of the twelve hundred and fifty, on account of the stock (which claim must always be first satisfied), it follows that the female slave is altogether profit, and is therefore equally shared between the proprietor of the stock and the manager; and as the manager formerly preferred a claim that was valid (since there was a presumption that he might have cohabited with the famale slave in virtue of marriage), and the efficiency of which remained suspended only on account of the defect in his right of property, and became effectual on the establishment of that right, by which means the female slave becomes his Am Walid,—he [the manager] is therefore responsible for the share of the proprietor, whether he be rich or poor, because the responsibility in this instance is responsibility for assumption of property, and a responsibility of the nature does not remain suspended on transgression;—in the same manner as where a person, in virtue of marriage, cohabits with the female slave of another, and child is born of her, and this person afterwards obtains, by inheritance, a right of property in her, jointly with another person,—in which case the person in question is responsible to the other for his share; and so also in the case in question:—contrary to responsiblility for the child as before treated of.

* That is to say, "it were otherwise if the manager's claim (involving the emancipation of the child) were first admitted, &c."

†As the manager acquires no right of property is in the child until such time as a profit be obtained upon it.

‡As where a partner (for instance) emancipates his share in a slave, which induces his ultimate freedom in toto, and is therefore, in its consequence, destructive to the property of the other partners.

CHAPTER II

OF A MANAGER ENTERING INTO A CONTARCT OF MOZARIBAT WITH ANOTHER.

A manager entrusting the stock in his hand to a secondary manager, is responsible to the proprietor, upon any profit being acquired on it —If a mananger give stock to another person, in the way of Mozaribat, without authority from the proprietor of the stock, in that case the first or principal manager is not responsible [for the stock] either on account of having so given the stock to the other, or on account of that other's employment of the same, until such time as profit shall have been acquired thereon: but whenever profit takes place, then the principal manager becomes responsible to the proprietor of the stock.—This is recorded by Hasan as an opinion of Haneefa. The two disciples maintain that the primary manager becomes responsible, immediately upon the action of the secondary manager, whether profit may have been acquired or not : and this is agreeable to the Zahir Rawayet.—Ziffer holds that the primary manager is responsible for the giving of the stock to the other. whether that other may have acted with regard to it or not (and there is an opinion recorded from Aboo Yoosaf to the same effect) ; because it is lawful for a manager to give the stock by way of deposit, but not by way of Mozaribat ; and as, in the case in question, it was given by way of Mozaribat, the manager was therefore guilty of a trespass, and is consequently liable to responsibility.—The argument of the two disciples is that the stock is here in reality given as a deposit ; and is only rendered Mozaribat by the action of the secondary manager ;—therefore (say they) there are two circumstances in this case, and we pay attention to both circumstances and determine, accordingly, that responsibility takes place in case of the action of the secondary manager : but if he do not act, and the property be lost in his possession without any transgression, responsibility is not in that case incumbent."—The reasoning of Haneefa is that the mére act of giving, previous to the action, is a deposit, and after the action it is an entrusting, in the manner of a Bazat ; and as both these deeds are lawful to a manager, he is not consequently responsible for either of them :—but upon profit secruing, the first manager renders the secondary one a sharer with him in the stock, and is therefore responsible in the same manner as if he had mixed the stock with the property of another, in which case he would have become responsible in consequence of his having rendered that other a sharer in the stock ; and so also in the case in question. All this proceeds on a supposition of both of the Mozaribats being valid : but if one or both of them be invalid, then the primary manager is not responsible, though the secondary manager should have acted with regard to the property ; because, in such case, the secondary manager is considered as a hireling, entitled to an adequate hire, and not to any share in the profit. Mohammed, in the Mabsoot, observes that in case of the validity of the Mozaribat, the primary manager becomes responsible ; but he has not stated the consequences with regard to the secondary manager. Some have said that he is not responsible, according to Haneefa, and that he is so according to the two disciples ; proceeding on the different opinions which they have maintained with regard to the trustee of a trustee,—Haneefa holding the principal and not the secondary trustee to be responsible ; and the two disciples holding the proprietor to be at liberty to take the compensation from whichever he chooses ; and so also in the case in question.—others, again, have said that the proprietor, is at liberty, in the opinion of all our doctors, to take a compensation either from the principal or the secondary manager : and this is the common opinion. This is evidently the opinion of the two disciples because, according to them, a secondary trustee is responsible :—and it is also evidently agreeable to the opinion of Haneefa ; because the principal manager was guilty of a transgression, in giving the stock to the secondary manager without the proprietor's permission ; and the secondary manager was also guilty of a transgression, in taking possession of the property of another without his consent. Respecting the two cases of a manager and a trustee, the difference between them according to Haneefa, is that the secondary trustee takes possession of the deposit with a view to the benefit of the principal trustee, and is therefore not responsible : whereas the secondary manager seizes the stock with a view to his own profit; on which account it is proper to make him responsible. It is to be observed that upon the primary manager becoming responsible for the stock, the contract of Mozaribat between him and the secondary becomes valid ; and the profit is participated between them agreeably to their stipulation ; because the primary manager becomes proprietor of the Mozaribat stock, in consequence of his responsiblity, from the time that he exceeded his authority, by making it over to another without the owner's consent, whence it is the same as if he had so given his own property. If the proprietor, on the other hand, should require the indemnification of the secondary manager, then the secondary must revert for satisfaction to the primary manager. because of their contract of mozaribat, as he acts on behalf of the primary manager ;—in the same manner as where a proprietor takes a compensation from the turstee of an usurper, in which case the trustee has recourse to the usurper ; and so likewise in the case in question ; and also, because the principal manager deceived him in the body of the contract And in this case also the contract of Mozaribat between the primary and the secondary managers is valid, because responsibility ultimately falls upon the primary manager, and it is therefore the same as if the proprietor had taken a compensation from him first : but the profit, in this case, is fair and lawful to the secondary, and not to the primary manager : because the secondary is entitled to the profit on account of his management, in which there is no baseness ; but the principal is entitled to profit merely from his right of property. which being founded only on the payment of the compensation, is not altogether free from baseness, since a right of property merely constructive is in one shape established, but in another shape it is not established.

Case of manager entrusting the stock to a secondary manager, with the proprietor's concurrence.—If a person give property to another by way of Mozaribat, on condition of half the profit, and with permission to him to give the property to another in the way of Mozaribat, and the manager, accordingly, give the said property to another by way of Mozaribat, on condition of a third of the profit; and the secondary manager employ the said stock, and acquire profit upon it in that case, if the proprietor should have said to the first manager, "Whatever advantage GOD Almighty may grant upon it is between you and me in an equal degree," then a half of the whole profit is due to it the proprietor, one third to the secondary manager, and one sixth to the primary manager;—because the act of the primary manager, in giving the stock to the secondary manager by way of Mozaribat, was lawful, as he had the consent of the proprietor thereto; but as the proprietor stipulated to himself one half of the whole profit, he is therefore entitled to it, and the remaining half is all with which the manager has any concern; and as he agreed to give a third of the whole to the secondary manager, these will remain of course only one sixth of the whole to him. —One half of the profit is, in this instance fair and lawful to the two managers, although the primary manager has not employed himself [with regard to the stock], because the industry of the secondary manager is held to be that of the primary:—in the same manner as where a person hires another to make him a garment for one dirm; and the person hired hires another to do the work for half a dirm; in which case, although the principal hireling does no work, yet he is fairly and lawfully entitled to the profit of an half dirm, as the work of the secondray is considered as his work. But if, in the case in question, the proprietor should have said, "Whetehr advantage GOD Almighty gives to you, is between you and me in an equal degree;" then the secondary manager is entitled to one third, and the remainder is divided in an equal degree between the proprietor and the principal manager;—because, in this instance, the proprietor commits the disposal of the property to the first manager, stipulating for himself one half of the whole profit which may accrue from it; and as, by this statement, two thirds of the profit accrue, those two thirds are equally divided between the proprietor and the manager.—It is otherwise in the preceding case, because there the proprietor had stipulated for himself one half of the whole profit: hence there is an evident difference between the two cases.

If the proprietor of the stock say to the manager, "I gave this stock in order that whatever profit may result to you thereform be equally divided between us;" and, at the same time, give him permission to have it managed by Mozaribat, and if, accordingly the manager entrust it to another manager with an agreement of half the profit to him, in this case one half of the profit goes to the secondary manager, and the other half is divided equally between the proprietor and the primary manager; because the primary manager has agreed to let the secondary manager have one half of the whole profit, and the proprietor of the stock having already agreed to this, the secondary manager is entitled to one half accordingly; and as the proprietor established for himself one half of the profit that might accrue to the primary manager, and one half only on the whole accrues to him (as the half which goes to the secondary must necessarily be deducted), if follows that this half is divided between them.

IF a proprietor give stock to any person by way of Mozaribat, upon condition that, of whatever advantage may accrue thereon, one half shall come to him,—or that, one half of the increase, above the original amount, shall be divided equally between him and the manager,—and at the same time permit the manager to entrust the stock in the way of Mozaribat to another, and the manager accordingly give it to another in the way of Mozaribat, with an agreement of one half of the profit to him,—in that case the proprietor is entitled to one half of the profit, and the secondary manager to the other half, whilst nothing whatever is due to the primary manager; for the stockholder having conditioned for himself one half of the property in an absolute manner, one half therefore goes to him; and as the principal manager agreed to give one half (which is the share that would be due to himself) to the secondary manager, the same must therefore be given to him; hence he himself is entitled to nothing;—in the same manner as where a person hires another to make him a garment for one dirm, and the person so hired again hires another to do the work for one dirm also—in which case the secondary hireling would be entitled to the dirm, and nothing whatever would be due to the principal; and so also in the case in question,—But if the primary manager to give the secondary one two thirds of the profit instead to one half, then the proprietor is entitled to one half, and the secondary to the other; and the principal manager must make good of the secondary, from his own property, to the amount of one third of the profit, in order that a complete share of two thirds may be thus rendered to him: for here the primary manager stipulated to the secondary a thing which was the right of the proprietor; and hence, in respect to the proprietor, his agreement is of no effect, since, if such were the case, it must necessarily follow that the condition he had himself established was null; —yet there is no illegality in referring the obligation of it to his own person, since it relates to a fixed and certain object, interwoven in a contract which he was competent to make. Hence he becomes responsible for the safe delivery of two thirds to the secondary, and consequently the discharge of the same is incumbent upon him. Besides, he deceived the secondary in the body on the contract, which a cause of recourse,—that is to say, entitles the secondary to revert and have recourse to the principal :—in the same manner as where a person has been hired to make a garment for one dirm, and be again hires another to do the work for one dirm and an half.—in which case the secondary hireling is entitled to an half dirm from the property of the principal hireling :—and so likewise in the present case.

Section.

The contract may stipulatel a proportion of the profit to the slave of the proprietor.—If a manager st'pulate to give one third of the profit to the proprietor of the stock, one third to the slave of the proprietor (on condition of assistance in the labour), and the remaining third to himself, it is lawful whether the slave be indebted or not : because the s isin of slave is valid (sepecially where he is a Mazoon, or privileged slave ; and in the present case the slave is priviledge, inasmuch as the condition of his working with the manager endows him with a privilege ; and already to the rule of the seisin of a slave being valid, a master is not permitted to take from a trustee the deposit which may have been made by his slave, although the slave be not privileged ; and on the same principal, also, a master may sell any thing to his slave, provided he be privi-ledged) :—and the seisin of the slave being valid,* tt follows that the condition of his uniting in the management is not repugnant either to the delivery of the stock,* or to the distinction between the stock and the manager : the condition is therefore approved † (It is otherwise where it is made a condition that the proprietor of the stock shall himself work, because that is preventive of delivery,‡ and consequently invalid, as has been already explained.)—The contract of Mozaribat, therefore, being valid, one third of the profit goes to the manager, and two thirds to proprietor of the stock ; because the earnings of the slave are the property of the master, if he be not indebted ; and if he be indebted they are the property of the creditors.—The doctrine here laid down proceeds on a supposition that the master, and not the slave, has concluded the contract of Mozaribat.

But if a slave engage in such a contract on behalf of his master it is invalid.—For if a privileged slave enter into a contract of Mozaribat with a stranger, stipulating that his master shall act with the manager in the management of the stock, the contract is invalid, provided the slave be free from debt : because in that case the Mozaribat stock is the property of the master ;* and as it is stipulated that the master shall unite in the management, it is requisite that he make seisin of it for that purpose ; but the seisin of the proprietor is repugnant to a due delivery.† If, however, the slave be insolvent, the contract is valid, as in that case the master stands in the same relation as a stranger, according to Haneefa.

CHAPTER III

OF THE DISIMISSION OFF MANAGER ; AND OF THE DIVISION OF THE PROPERTY.

The contract is dissolved by the death of either party.—If either the proprietor of the stock or the manager should die, the contract becomes null ; because a contract of Mozaribat (as has been already explained) is in the nature of an appointment of agency ; and agency ceases by the death either of the constituent or of the agent ; and inheritance does not take place with regard to agency, as has been already demonstarted.

Or by the apostacy and expatriation of the manager.—If the proprietor of the stock become an apostate, and be united to a foreign country, ‡ the contract of Mozaribat becomes null ; because his being united to a foreign country is equivalent to his death (whence it is that his property is then divided amongst his heirs).—If, on the other hand he should not be united to a foreign country, the transactions of his manager remain suspended in their effect.—(that is to say, if he again becomes a Mussulman, they then take effect) ; but if he die in his apostacy, they then become null (according to Haneefa because his manager's transaction [with the stock] is the same as his own transaction, since the manager acts on his own account : and as (according to Haneefa) the acts of an apostate are suspended in their effect, so, in the same manner the acts of his manager are suspended.

If the manager apostatize, without going to a foreign country the contract still continues

*To the slave, for the purpose of management.

†If a slave were incapable of making seisin, it would follow that a delivery of the stock to the slave (for the purpose of managing it) would, in fact, be a return of it to the proprietor, his master, and consequently the contract would be rendered nugatory.

‡Since such delivery would be return of it to the proprietor, which would invalidate in contract.

*Whereas, if the priviledged slave were involved in debt, the stock entrusted by him to the manager would (in common with his other property) be the right of his creditors.

†Because, as the property of the slave is, in effect, the property of his master, it follows that a delivery to the master would be nugatory.

‡By a sentence of the Kazee.

in force.—IF the manager become apostate, yet the contract still continues to exist in its original state, because the actions of a person are suspended in their effect, only on account of a suspension of his right property : but the apostate in question has no right of property in the Mozaribat-stock, as that belongs solely to the proprietor of the stock : and as the proprietor's right of property is not suspended, the contract of course still continues in force.

All acts of the manager are valid, until he be duly apprized of his dismission.—IF the proprietor of the stock dismiss the manager, and he should not be acquainted with his dismission until after he had transacted by purchase and sale then those transactions are valid ; because he acts as an agent on behalf of the proprietor ; and the dismission of an agent, if it be voluntary and intended (that is to say, not virtual, such as by death), remains suspended upon a knowledge of it ; for dismission is a prohibition from action ; and prohibition in injunctions respecting any matter, do not operate until after knowledge of them, as in the case of the commands and prohibition of the LAW.

The manager, after being apprized of his dismission, may still convert what remains on his hands into money.—IF the proprietor of the stock dismiss the manager, and he be apprized thereof, he may nevertheless sell such of the Mozaribat-stock as consist of chattels and effects, because his dismission from the agency is not preventive of a sale of articles of that kind, since he has a right to profit, which cannot be obtained otherwise that by a division ; and this can be effected only by turning the subject of the stock into species.—From this necessity, therefore he is at libery to sell such stock : but after the sale, it is not lawful for him to make any purchase whatever with the price he procure for these effects ; because there is no necessity for his so doing, and the sale is admitted only from necessity, as has been already explained.

But if it have been already converted into money, he cannot transact, with it.—IF the proprietor of a stock, which had originally consisted of dirms or deenars, dismiss the manager at a time when it has been reduced to specie, and the manager be apprized thereof, in that case he is no longer entitled to act with regard to it, since there exists no further necessity for his so doing.

Unless this money be of a species different from the original stock.—in which case he may contract it into money of the same species:—THE author of the Hedaya remarks that the law here proceed on the supposition that the stock has been converted into the very same specie with the original stock : but that, if it should have been converted into specie of a different denomination (as if the stock had originally consisted of deenars, it be now converted into dirms, or vice versa), the manager is by the benevolence of the law, allowed the liberty of selling it for the same specie as the original stock ; because it is incumbent upon the manager to return a similar to the original stock, which is impracticable otherwise than by selling what he has on hand for the same specie as the original stock ; and also, because, as the profit cannot be ascertained until the property on hand be converted into something of the very same nature as the original stock, the case becomes exactly the same as if the property consisted of goo s and effects.—It is to be observed that all the rules here laid down with respect to the dismission of a manager are applicable to the case of the death of the proprietor of the stock.—Thus, if the proprietor should die, the manager is entitled to sell the Mozaribat stock, where it consists of goods and effects :—but he is not allowed afterwards to purchase any thing whatever with the priee so obtained. If, on the other hand, the stock has been turned into dirms or deenars, he is not entitled to act with respect to it, provided the money into which it is converted correspond with the specie of the original stock : but if it be different from the specie of the original stock he is at liberty to convert, by sale, into the same specie with the original.

If, at the dissolution of the contract, the stock consist of debt, the manner must be compelled to collect them where any profit has been acquired.—IF the proprietor and the manager dissolved the contract, and the stock should at that time consist of debts due from other, in this case, where any profit has been acquired, the magistrate must compel the manager to possess himself of these debts ; since he is held to be equivalent to a hireling, and his profit to be like hire. But if no profit have been acquired, it is not incumbent upon the manager to receive payment of these debts ; since he is merely a voluntary agent, and no compulsion can be used for the fulfilment of a voluntary engagement (as where a person makes a grant to another without delivering the thing granted, in which case the donor cannot be compelled to make delivery of the grant). The manager, however, is in this case to be instructed to appoint the proprietor agent in his behalf for the receipt of these debts ; for as the right of the contract appertain to the contractor, it is indispensably necessary that he thus appoint the proprietor his agent, to prevent the loss of his right. Mohammed, in the Jama Sagheer, observes that "the manager ought to be instructed to make a transfer of his claim upon the debtors to the proprietor ;" the meaning of which also is, that he should appoint the proprietor his agent for the receipt of the debt ; because if such transfer were sufficient, the proprietor must necessarily be injured in case of the debtors not acceeding to the same. It is to be observed that this is the rule in all cases of agency. Thus, when an agent for sale (for instance) is dismissed, he must be told to appoint his constituent agent for the receipt of the debt, in the manner above mentioned. A broker, however, must himself be compelled to receive any debts that may be, due because with brokers the custom is to act for hire.

All lost upon the stock is placed against the profit—Whatever may be lost or destroyed, of the Mozaribat stock, must be placed to the account of the profit, and not of the original stock, because the profit being a dependant, it is most eligible to refer the loss to it; in the same manner as a loss in property subject to Zakat is referred to what is exempt,* and not to the actual Nisab, as the exempt property is a dependant of the Nisab

If more than the profit be lost, the responsibility does not fall on the manager, as he is merely a trustee.

If the profit be divided previous to a restoration of the capital and any accident afterwards befell the stock, the manager must return the portion of profit he had received.—If the stockholder and the manager devide the profit between them, and continue the contract in existence as before, and the whole or part of the stock be afterwards lost, the manager must, in that case, return the profit to the proprietor, in order that he may appear to recover this capital; because a division of the profit pervious to a restoration of the capital is not valid, since the profit cannot be ascertained until the proprietor shall have recorded his capital for the capital is the principal, and the profit the dependant; and hence, when what remained in the hands of the manager is lost or destroyed, as he is in this case subject to no responsibility (it being only a trust with him), it follows that what he and the proprietor had before taken possession of is capital, and consequently that he is responsible for the portion he had taken, and that the portion taken by the proprietor as also accounted as part of the capital

The manager is not responsible for deficiency.—If, when the proprietor has received back the whole capital, any excess remain, such excess must be divided between him and the manager, as being profit: but if there be a deficiency, no compensation is due from the manager, as he is only a trustee.

The profit received by the manager is no way implicated, with respect to any new contract between the same parties—If the manager and the proprietor, having divided and taken the profit, and annulled the contract of Mozaribat, should again enter into a new contract of Mozaribat and the stock be afterwards lost, in this case the profit gained upon the first Mozaribat is not to be returned to the proprietor, because that Mozaribat was completed, and the second Mozaribat is a new contract;—and the destruction of the stock of the second Mozaribat cannot effect the first;—in the same manner as if the proprietor should have given some other property than that which was the subject of the former contract to the manager, in which case, if the said additional property should be lost, it does not affect the contract; and so also in the case in question.

CHAPTER IV.

OF SUCH ACTS AS MAY LAWFULLY BE PERFORMED BY A MANAGER.

A manager may sell the stock either for ready money, or upon trust.—It is lawful for a manager to sell the stock either for ready money, or upon trust; because these acts are in the nature of traffic, and, as such, are included in an absolute contract,—The period of trust, however, must not be extended beyond what is customary amongst merchants (such, for instance, as a period of ten years); because he is only permitted to act according to the common practice, and custom of merchants; whence it is that he may lawfully purchase a quadruped for conveyance; but he can only hire a boat: for such is the custom amongst merchants.

According to the Rawayet Mashoor, a manager is at liberty to give the privilege to trading to slave whome he may have purchased with the stock, since this is in the nature of traffic.

Or entrust a slave with the management of it: or (having sold it for ready money) may grant a suspension of payment.—If a manager should sell part of the stock for ready money, and afterwards admit of a suspension in the payment, it is lawful according to all our doctors:—according to Haneefa and Mohammed, because, as an agent is permitted to grant a suspension of payment, a manager, as having a share in the profit, is entitled to do so a fortiori (the manager, however, is not responsible because, as he has a power of dissolving the sale, and afterwards selling the thing upon trust, the deferring of payment is accordingly lawful: contrary to an agent, as he is responsible to his constituent for the price of what he sells, because he is not at liberty to dissolve a sale and sell the article over again upon trust):—and according to Aboo Yoosaf, because a manager may, if he please annul the sale, and sell the article over again: contrary to an agent, who has no power of dissolving a sale.

Or allow the purchaser to transfer the payment upon another person.—If a manager should sell something to Zeyd upon trust and Zeyd, with the consent of the manager, should transfer the payment of the price upon Omar, this is lawful, whether Omar be rich or poor, because transfer of debts is customery amongst merchants.—It is other.

*Arab. Afoo.—See Vol. I. p. 43.

wise where a guardian assents to such a transfer with respect to the property of his orphan ward, as he cannot lawfully accept, in his ward's behalf, of a transfer upon a person that is poor; because the interest of the orphan is what must be consulted (whence the power of a guardian is restricted to what may conduce to the interest of his ward); and as the acceptance of a transfer upon a person that is poor is destructive of the orphan's interest, it is therefore illegal.

The acts of manager are such as he is empowered to perform by the contract.—THE acts of a Mozarib, or manager, are of three kinds. I. Such as he is competent to perform in virtue of the absolute contract of Mozaribat; including all deeds partaking of the nature of Mozaribat, or of its dependences; such for example, as agency for purchase or sale, because of the necessity for those acts; and also pawn, as this is in the nature of a discharge or satisfaction; and like wise deposit, hire, entrusting in the manner of Bazat, and also travelling with the stock, as before mentioned.

Or in virtue of general and discretionary power versted in him by the proprietor,—II. SUCH deeds as he is not competent to perfrom in virtue of the absolute contract, but in virtue of a general power granted him by the proprietor, to act agreeably to his own judgment and discretion; including all such deeds as may have a probable connexion with a contract of Mozaribat; and which are accordingly held to be connected with it, when there exists any argument for their being so;—such as the giving of the stock to another in the way either of Mozaribat, or of partnership, or the mixing of it with the manager's own property, or with that of another;—to which acts a manager is not competent, merely in virtue of the absolute contract, except where something argues a connexion between the act and the contract; because it is presumed that the proprietor of the stock intends that the manager alone should be his partner, and not any other person; and these acts are not in the nature of traffic (as traffic does not depend upon such acts), and consequently are not comprehended in the absolute contract: yet, as they are all instruments of an increase of profit, and are therefore admissible in a contract of Mozaribat, they are accordingly included in the contract, where any argument exists of their so being; and the power granted to the manager by the proprietor "to act according to his own discretion," clearly argues thus much.

Or such as he is not empowered to perform in either way.—III. SUCH deeds as the manager is not competent to perform, either in virtue of the absolute contract, or from the discretionary power granted him by the proprietor, being neither in the nature of traffic, nor having any probable connexion with the contract, but such as he may perfrom in case of an express power from the proprietor of the stock. These are termed Istidanit*; such as where a manager purchases something in exchange for dirms and deenars, after having laid out the whole capital in the purchase of goods and effects in which case the transaction relates entirely to the manager, and he is entitled to all the profit as well as subject to the loss or debts that may result from it: or, where a manager lays, out, in purchasing goods, more than the amount of the capital, in which case what is tantamount to the stock is considered as belonging to the Mozaribat; and the profit, loss, or debts resulting from the excess relate solely to the manager: or, where the stock consists of dirms and deenars, and the manager purchases something in exchange for articles of weight, measurement of capacity, or of s le; for, in that case, as the manager makes the purchase with something else than the stock, it is considered as an Istidanit, and operates entirely with respect to the manager: that is to say, the profit, loss, and debts arising from it, relate entirely to him, and not to the proprietor of the stock; the reason of which is, that Istidanit is a transaction with respect to other property than the capital; and as the agency is confined to the capital, the manager is of course not competent to such transaction.—Moreover, the property, in this case, exceeds the amount of that which was the subject of the contract, to which the proprietor has not assented: and although, in such excess of property, there be advantage: yet it is not free from the risk of loss, and of its producing debts. If, however the stockholder give his assent to the Istidanit, then the thing which the manager may have purchased is participated between him and the stockholder, in the manner of a Shirkat Wajooh, or partnership upon personal credit,† which signifies, where two persons are partners without either stock or labour, and purchase something upon credit, to be paid for at a future period, and sell it again. Of the third species of acts in Mozaribat is also the taking of Sifatja, which is a species of Istidanit, and the giving of Sifatja, which resembles a loan.—Sifatja means the delivery of property to another by way of loan, and not by way of trust, in order that that other may deliver it to some friend of his, and the object of it is to avoid the dangers of the road.—In the same manner also emancipation, either in exchange for property, or without property in exchange, and contracts of Kitabat, are of the third species of acts in Mozaribat, as not being in the nature of traffic;—and the same of gifts, loans, and charities, which are mere gratuitous acts.

A manager is not allowed to contract male

---

* Anglice.—Desiring to borrow.—In its common acceptation, it signifies contracting debt, on behalf either of one's self or of another.

† See Vol. p. 226.

and female slaves (forming a part of the stock) in marriage to each other.—It is not permitted to a manager, according to Haneefa and Mohammed, to join in marriage male and female slaves which are of the stock of the contract.—It is recorded as an opinion of Aboo Yoosaf, the he may contract in marriage a female but not a male slave, because the bestowing of a female slave in marriage is in the nature of acquisition; since her dower is obtained from it, and her maintenance annulled.—The argument of Haneefa and Mohammed is, that the bestowing of a female slave in marriage is not in the nature of traffic, and a contract of Mozaribat includes only agency in such things as relate to traffic, whence this is the same as the making a slave Mokatib; or the emancipating him in exchange for property; for in both these cases there is an acquisition of property; but as neither of them relates to traffic, they are not included in a contract of Mozaribat; and so also in the case in question.

Any part of the stock delivered by the manager of the proprietor in the manner of a Bazat, still continues to appertain to the Mozaribat stock.—If the manager deliver any part of the Mozaribat stock to the proprietor as a Bazat, and he make purchase and sale with it, it continues to belong to the Mozaribat stock, in the same manner as before. Ziffer says that the Mozaribat is annulled; because the proprietor, in this instance, acts with what is his own, and he is incapable of being the manager's agent in work which he performs with his own property; the proprietor, therefore, on this occasion, may be said to have taken back so much of the Mozaribat stock; whence it is that a contract of Mozaribat is not valid where the labour of the proprietor is stipulated for at the time of making the contract. The argument of our doctors is, that after the Mozaribat stock has been duly delivered to the manager, and taken possession of by him; and the manager has thus acquired a right of transacting with it, the proprietor is fully capable of acting as an agent on behalf of the manager, in transacting with the stock; and as making it over in the way of Bazat amounts to a commission of agency, it follows that (in this view) the proprietor cannot be considered merely as receiving back his stock It is otherwise where the proprietor's uniting in the management is made a condition of the contract, originally, as this is repugnant to the delivery of the stock to him for the purpose of management, and also to his taking possession of it. It is also otherwise where the manager makes over the stock to the proprietor in the way of Mozaribat, which is not lawful; because a contract of Mozaribat is a contract of partnership in the profit derived from the stock of the proprietor, and the labour of the manager; and, in the case in question, none of the stock appertains to the manager; whence if this were allowed, it would follow that both the stock and the labour proceed from one party, and this defeats the use of the contract.

Objection —Making it over as Bazat also defeats the use of a contract of Bazat, as a contract of Bazat signifies the stock being found by one party, and the labour by another; and if, in the case in question, this were admitted, it would follow that both the stock and the labour proceed from one party.

Reply.—Bazat signifies, simply, agency; and as a manager is endowed with a power of transaction, it follows that his delivering the stock, as a Bazat, is a commission of agency, proceeding from him, in regard to a thing concerning which he is empowered.

It is to be observed that, the secondary Mozaribat not being valid, the proprietor's management with the property still remains subject to the orders of the manager; and hence the primary Mozaribat is not annulled.

No part of the stock delivered by the defrayed unless he travel.—If the manager transact his business in his own city, his maintenence does not fall upon the stock If, however, he travel with it, his provisions and clothing are to be furnished out of the stock;—and the same, also, of his conveyance (that is to say, it is also lawful for him to purchase or hire a quadruped to carry him from place to place at the expense of the stock), for this reason, that a subsistence is due to him on account of his confinement, in the same manner as the subsistence of a Kazee, who, as being in a state of confinement, in the exercise of his public duties, is entitled to a recompense from the public treasury,—or like a wife, who is entitled to subsistence from her husband, because of her being in his custody:—for the manager, so long as he remains in his own city, resides there merely as it is his home, and not on account of the Mozaribat in particular: but upon his travelling he becomes confined on behalf of the Mozaribat, and is therefore entitled to subsistence out of the Mozaribat stock.—It is otherwise with an hireling, who is not entitled to any subsistence although he travel because he is already entitled to a compensation, namely, his wages, which are certain, and for which, if he were subsisted out of the stock entrusted to his management, there would be no absolute necessity:—whereas a manager, on the contrary, is not entitled to anything but his share of the profit: but profit is uncertain (in other words, it is possible that a profit may be gained; and it is also possible that he profit may be gained); if, therefore, the manager were obliged to furnish his own maintenance, he might be a loser.—It is otherwise, also, in a case of invalid Mozaribat, because the manager, in such a case, is entitled to wages: and it is likewise different from a case of Bazat, since a person who undertakes the management of a bazat gives his labour gratuitously, and is therefore not entitled to a subsistence.—It is to be observed that if, on the manager's return into his own city, there remain any victuals or clothing in his hands, he must return them into the Mozaribat stock, since his right to those articles no longer remains, because of his return into his own city.

To a distance beyond a day's journey from the usual place of his abode.—If a manager go forth from his place of residence to a distance short of what constitutes a journey, his maintenance does not fall upon the stock; for where he goes only to such a distance as that, if he set off in the morning, he may be the evening return and pass the night at home with his family, he is as any other merchant of the place.—If however, he go to such a distance as not to be able to return home the same evening, his maintenance is due from the stock, since he is absent upon the business of the Mozaribat,—Nifka, or subsistence, signifies such things as are expended in the supply of our daily wants, such as meet, drink, and clothing; and among these things, also, is the hire of a washerman, and other servants, and the maintenance of a quadruped for riding; and oil for anointing, where that is commonly used, as in Mecca.—It behoves the manager not to expend any of those articles of subsistence in a degree beyond what is customary; insomuch that, if he exceed in his expenses what is customary among merchants, he is responsible for the excess. Medicine used by a manager, however, must be furnished at his own cost, according to the Zahir Rawayet. It is recorded from Haneefa, that medicine is included in the subsistence: because this is taken for the preservation of health; and as it is impossible that he should engage in commercial transactions unless he be in nealth, it consequently partakes of the nature of subsistence.—The reason for what is said in the Zahir Rawayet upon this point is, that the necessity of subsistence is known and certain. Medicine, on the contrary, is necessary only in case of supervenient sickness; and as sickness sometimes occurs, and sometimes does not occur it follows that medicine is not part of maintenance; and hence it is that, although a wife's maintenance must be furnished by her husband, yet she finds herself in medicine at her own expense.

And it is defrayed out of the profit, not out of the stock.—When a profit is gained, the proprietor first takes the whole capital stock, and then the remainder is divided between both the parties according to stipulation; the subsistence of the manager, therefore, is taken from the profit, and not from the capital, although the manager should have expended out of the capital for his subsistence.

All expenses incident to the sale of stock must be defrayed out of that.—If the manager sell goods and effects in the way of traffic, he must charge the expense attending these goods and effects (such as porterage and brokerage) to the account of the capital stock:—but he is not to charge the capital with what he expends upon himself for subsistence; for this reason, that it is the custom of merchants to charge the former to the account of their capital, but not the latter; and also, because the former enhances the value of the goods, but not the latter.

All expenses upon articles purchased which do not substantially add to the article, are voluntary on the part of the manager.—If a manager have in his hands one thousand dirms, and lay them all out in the purchase of cloth, and expend one hundred dirms of his own property in bleaching and porterage and the proprietor of the stock had desired him to act according to his own discretion,—in this case the manager is accounted to have acted voluntarily, because as he hereby subjects the proprietor of the stock to a debt, it follows that the proprietor's instruction to him to act according to his own discretion does not include a transaction of this nature, as was formerly explained.—If, on the other hand, the manager, in the case in question, expend one hundred dirms of his own in dying the cloth red, he is a partner in the excess occasioned by the dying, because the colour is a substantial property existing in the cloth: hence, when the cloth is sold, the manager receives his share in respect to the colour; and also his proportion of the cloth as undyed, according to the contract of Mozaribat: contrary to the case of bleaching and porterage, as that does not occasion any additional substantial property to exist in the cloth;—whence it is that if any usurper bleach cloth which he has seized, without the consent of the owner, and the value be enhanced by the bleaching, yet the proprietor is at liberty to take back the cloth without making him any compensation;—whereas, if the usurper dye the cloth red or yellow, the owner is not at liberty to take it back without making a compensation, but has it at his option either to take the cloth, allowing the usurper the difference occasioned in the value by dying,—or to take an indemnification for the value of the cloth as it stood at the time of dying, and suffer it to remain with the usurper. It is to be observed that, on the manager becoming a partner in the cloth in consequence of the dying, he is not responsible for any things, because the proprietor's direction to him, "to act according to his own discretion", comprehends a liberty to manager to mix his own property with the Mozaribat stock; as was before mentioned

Section.

Case of loss of the stock after a profit having been acquired and a debt incurred upon it.—If a manager, having one thousand dirms in his hands, under an agreement of half the profit, purchase linen (for instance) to the amount of one thousand dirms, and sell the same for two thousand dirms, and again purchase a slave for two thousand,—and should not pay the price of either article (that is, of the cloth, or of the slave) until such time as these two thousand dirms perish in his hands, in this case the proprietor of the stock must make satisfaction to the amount of fifteen hundred dirms, and the manager to the amount of five hundred; and one fourth of the slave appertains to the manager, and three fourths to the Mozaribat stock.—The compiler of the Hedaya remarks that what is here said is the necessary result of the case; for the whole of the price is incumbent upon the manager (since he is the contracting party in the purchase); but yet he is entitled to call upon the proprietor of the stock for fifteen hundred dirms; the proprietor, therefore, is responsible for fifteen hundred (at the end of the transaction, not at the beginning of it), for this reason, that when the Mozaribat stock* was converted into cash, a profit appeared upon it, of which five hundred dirms go to the manager: consequently upon his purchasing the slave for two thousand he purchases one fourth of the slave on his own account, and three fourths on account of the Mozaribat (according to the division of the two thousand); and upon the two thousand perishing, the price of the slave is due from him, as it is he who made the bargain for him; but he is entitled to call upon the proprietor for three fourths of the price, because he acts as his agent in the purchase thereof. The manager's share, which is one fourth, is detached from the Mozaribat stock for that is secured (that is to say, is incumbent upon the manager to give one fourth of the price to the sellers [of the slave and cloth] after the destruction of the stock); but the Mozaribat stock is a trust; and a property secured is inconsistent with a property in trust: it is therefore indispensable that the manager's share be so detached;—and three fourths of the slave continue in the Mozaribat stock, for in that there is nothing inconsistent with Mozaribat;—consequently the capital then becomes two thousand five hundred, because the proprietor of the stock has given to the manager, in the first instance, one thousand dirms, and fifteen hundred in the second instance.—The slave, however, cannot be sold, so as to make any profit of him, for less than two thousand because he has been bought for two thousand.—With respect to what is above said, that "the fourth of the slave is detached, and the other three fourths continue in the Mozaribat stock,"—the use of this appears where the manager sells the slave (suppose) for four thousand dirms,—for in this case the capital, which is two thousand five hundred dirms, must be deducted from that proportion which appertains to the Mozaribat, which is three thousand dirms.—and consequently a profit of five hundred remains to be shared between the parties.

Cases of sale by the employer to the manager.—If the manager be possessed of one thousand dirms, and the proprietor of the stock purchase a slave for five hundred dirms, and sell him to the manager in return for the capital stock (namely, one thousand dirms) he [the manager] is considered as selling him [the slave] by a Morabihat sale at the rate of five hundred dirms;* for such sale is lawful, because of the difference of views in it,—since the view of the proprietor of the stock is to obtain one thousand dirms, at the same time securing the continuance of the Mozaribat contract; and the view of the manager is to obtain possession of the slave.—The sale, therefore is lawful, that the ends of both parties may be answered, although it be a sale of property belonging to the party for property belonging to the party.—There is however, in this sale, a semblance of illegality; since the slave does not, in fact, pass out of the property of the proprietor of the stock; and a semblance is connected with a reality in any matter concerning which caution is requisite.—Now caution is requisite in a Morabihat sale, since the points on which it turns are confidence, and a caution against the semblance of deceit: and accordingly in the Morabihat sale, regard is had to the lowest price, which is five hundred dirms.

Or by the manager to the employer.—If a manager, possessed of stock to the amount of one thousand dirms purchase a slave for those thousand, and sell him to his employer for twelve hundred, he is considered as selling him, by a Morabihat sale, for eleven hundred, since the contract in question is considered, with respect to one half of the profit (which is the proprietor's share) as non-existent:—as was formerly explained in treating of Morabihat sales.

Cases of a slave purchased by the manager and who is afterwards quality of homicide.—If a manager be possessed of one thousand dirms, under a condition of half the profit, and with these thousand purchase a slave valued at two thousand, and the slave accidentally slay a person. three fourths of the atonement rest upon the proprietor of the stock and one fourth upon the manager;—because, at the atonement is an expense attendant upon the right of property, the proportions of it are, consequently, according to the proportions of right of property. Now the property is here held between the parties in four lots, three of which appertain to the proprietor of the stock, and one to the manager; because, upon the capital being resolved into one specific article, the profit (namely, one thousand dirms) becomes evident; and that is between the two in equal shares; and one thousand (the original capital) appertains to the proprietor of the stock, as the value of the slave is two thousand. Upon each party paying his proportion of the atonement. the slave becomes excluded from the Mozaribat stock:—

*Namely, the linen.

*See sales of profit.

the manager's share in him; because, in the present instance, his responsibility with respect to that share operates upon him, and hence that share is no longer as a deposit with him; and Mozaribat stock is a deposit, as was formerly explained:—and the proprietor's share; because, upon the magistrate decreeing the atonement to be divided between both, the slave also becomes divided between them; and a contract of Mozaribat is dissolved by a participation in the stock. —It is otherwise in the case exemplified in the beginning of this section (where two thousand dirms perish in the manager's hands), for three the three fourths which form the share of the proprietor of the stock do not become excluded from the Mozaribat contract.—The difference between that case and the case now under consideration, exists in three shapes. I. In the former case the responsibility of traffic only is incumbent; and responsibility of traffic is not repugnant to Mozaribat, since Mozaribat itself is a branch of traffic;—whereas, in the case in question, responsibility for offence is incumbent; and responsibility for offence is not a branch of traffic.—II In the former case the whole price is incumbent upon the manager, although he have a right to revert upon the proprietor of the stock;—in that instance, therefore. there is no necessity for division.—III. The slave, in the instance of offence, escapes, as it were, from the property of both parties, in consequence his offence, and their paying an atonement for him, is, as it where, a purchase of him de novo.—He. therefore, no longer appertains to the Mozaribat stock, but is held between the parties in four lots, performing service to the manager one day, and to the stock proprietor three days, alternately—contrary to the former case.

The manager bargaining for an article, and then losing the stock, must have recourse to his employer for another stock, to enable him to fulfil his engagement.—IF a manager be possessed of a thousand dirms, and therewith purchase a slave, but neglect paying the price to the seller, and the thousand dirms perish in his hands, the proprietor of the stock must, in this case, made over another thousand to the manager, and the Mozaribat stock is then two thousand dirms.—The reason of this is, that as the stock is merely a deposit with the manager, he therefore cannot be considered as having duly received the price in virtue of his seisin [of the one thousand dirms], since a receipt in virtue of seisin is not established unless it involve responsibility —Now, as a due receipt of the price, by the manager, is not established, it follows that he is entitled, even repeatedly, to take the price from the stock proprietor, that is to say, if he take the price from the proprietor, and it be again lost in his hand, he may again take the price from him; and so on, repeatedly, until the seller's demand be satisfied;—and the whole of what the proprietor thus makes over to the manager becomes stock.—It is otherwise in the case of an agent commissioned to purchase a specific slave for one thousand specific dirms,—where the constituent delivers the price to the agent before the purchase, and they are lost in his hands after the purchase; for in this case the agent cannot take the price from his constituent more than once, since it is possible to consider him as having already made a due receipt of the price from his constituent: for agency is not repugnant to responsibility, but is rather involved with it;—as where, for instance, an usurper is commissioned by the proprietor to sell the thing he has usurped.—It is to be observed that, in the case of agency, as here adduced, the agent reverts to his constituent only once.—If, however, the agent were first to make the purchase, and then to receive the price from his constituent, he cannot afterwards revert to him at all; because, as the agent becomes endowed with a right to call upon his constituent on the instant of the purchase, it follows that his seisin of the price, after that was due, is a complete receipt on his part:—he is therefore considered as having duly received the price, in virtue of his seisin of it after the purchase:—on the contrary, what the constituent makes over to the agent before the purchase is merely a deposit in his hands; and after the purchase it still remains a deposit with him, since, in this instance, no cause of responsibility appears even after the purchase.—The agent, therefore in this case, is not considered as having duly received the price; and consequently, upon that being lost in his hands, he may take it again from the purchaser:—but if, again, it be lost in his hands, he cannot again revert upon the purchaser, since here a due receipt has been established, as before explained.

CHAPTER V

OF DISPUTES BETWEEN THE PROPRIETOR OF THE STOCK AND THE MANAGER

In disputes respecting the acquisition of profit upon the existing stock, the assertion of the manager is to be credited.—IF the manager have two thousand dirms in his hands, and say to the stock-proprietor, "you entrusted me with one thousand. and one thousand has accrued as profit," and the proprietor reply, "I entrusted you with two thousand,"—the assertion of the manager is to be credited.—Haneefa was at first of opinion that the assertion of the proprietor should be regarded: and such is the doctrine of Ziffer; because the manager here appears as a plaintiff, claiming a partnership in the profit,—and the proprietor as a defendant, denying his claim; and the assertion of the defendant is to be credited.—Haneefa, however, afterwards retracted, this opinion, and admitted that the assertion of the manager must be credited; because the dispute here turns upon the amount received; and concerning that the assertion of the receiver must be credited, whether he be merely a trustee, or otherwise, since he best knows what he was received.

But in disputes concerning the proportions of profit, that of the proprietor.—If the parties dispute, not only concerning the amount of the stock, but also concerning the proportion of the profit,—the manager affirming it to be between them in equal shares, and the proprietor asserting it to be in three lots, two for himself and one for the manager, the assertion of the proprietor is to be credited; because the manager here claims profit in virtue of a condition, which condition operat s. to the prejudice of the proprietor; his assertion, therefore, is to be credited.—But if either of the two produce evidence, his declaration must be admitted as evidence is positive proof.

As also in disputes concerning the nature of the agreement under which the stock was entrusted to the manager,—If a person, having one thousand dirms in his hand, say, "such a person entrusted me with these in the way of Mozaribat. under a condition of half the profit,"—and the person alluded to say, "I gave him the one thousand dirms as Bazat," the declaration of the proprietor is to be credited; because the manager is plaintiff in this instance since he either claims from the proprietor a recompense for his service, or alleges a condition to his prejudice, or a partnership in the profit,—all of which the proprietor denies.

If a person. having in his hands one thousand dirms, the property of another, assert that "those thousand had been lost to him by that other," and the other assert that "he entrusted him with them in the manner of Bazat, deposit, or Mozaribat." the assertion of the proprietor is to be credited on the one hand, or evidence adduced by the person in question on the other;—because he asserts his having obtained possession of the sum in dispute, by a loan; which the proprietor denies

If the proprietor assert a restriction, the denial of the manager is credited.—If the proprietor of the stock advance an allegetion, against the manager, of restriction to one mode of traffic. affirming, for instance, that "he had directed him to trade in cloth and in no other article,"—the assertion of the manager. upon oath, must be credited,—for, as universality is the original thing in a contract of Mozaribat. and restriction cannot be impossed in it but by particular stipulation, if follows that the assertion of the party who rests upon the. original thing must be credited. It is otherwise in agency, for in that restriction is the original thing.

But if each allege a different restriction, the allegation of the proprietor is credited.—If the proprietor allege a restriction to one particular mode of traffic, and the manager allege a rectriction to another particular mode, the assertion of the proprietor must be credited; for here both parties agree in the contract being restricted, and the proprietor's admission, in this particular, is pleaded against him.—His assertion, therefore, is to be credited on the one hand; or evidence adduced by the manager, on the other;—for the manager stands in need of evidence to disprove his responsibility; but the proprietor does not stand in need of evidence.

In disputes concerning restriction to time, the evidence which proves the latest date is preferred.—If the proprietor allege a restriction in point of time, and produce evidence thereto, and the manager allege a restriction to another time, and produce evidence thereto,—the proprietor, on his part, asserting that "he entrusted him [the manager] with one thousand dirms, in the manner of Mozaribat, for the purpose of purchasing what in the month of Ramzan" (producing evidence in support of his allegation),—and the manager, that "he [the proprietor] gave him one thousand dirms for the purpose of purchasing wheat in the month of Shawal" (producing evidence in support of his allegation),—the evidence which tends to prove the latest date must be preferred; because the condition last stipulated annuls the condition first stipulated.

BOOK XXVIII,

OF WIDDA, OR DEPOSITS.

Definition of the terms used in deposit.—Widda, in the language of the law, signifies a person empowering another to keep his property.—The proprietor of the thing is styled Modee, or the depositor;—the person so empowered, the Moda or trustee:—and the propery so left with another, for the puropose of keeping it, is styled Widdeeyat, because Widda literally means to leave, and the thing in question is left with the Moda or trustee.

A trustee is not responsible for a deposit unless the transgress with respect to it.—A deposit remains in the hands of the person who receive charge of it, as a trust,—that is to say, he is not answerable for it. If, therefore, a deposit be lost or destroyed in the trustee's hands, without any transgression on his part, he is not in that case responsible for it; because the prophet has said, 'an honest trustee is not responsible;"—and also, because there is a necessity, amongst mankind. for deposits; and this necessity could not be answered in case of making trustees responsible, as no one would then accept the trust

He may keep it himself, or commit the care of it to and of his family.—A trustee may either keep the deposit himself, or commit for that purpose to some one of his family such as his wife his son, his mother, or his father; because it is evident that a trustee does not engage to keep the property of another with more care than he does his own; and he sometimes keeps his own himself, and sometimes commits it to one of his family. Besides, there exists an absolute necessity for committing the trust to his family, since it is neither possible for him to remain always in the house, nor, when he goes out, to carry the deposit with him — For all those reasons, therefore, the consent of the proprietor is understood to extend to the trustee's committing the deposit to the care of his family.

But if he give charge of it to a stronger he becomes responsible.—BUT if the trustee should commit the deposit to the charge of any other than a member of his family (as if he were either to hire some person out of his family, for the purpose of keeping it,—or to give it in deposit to some one out of his family), he is then responsible, in as much as there is a difference between the care of different people, and it was his own care, and not that of another, to which the proprietor assented. Besides, a thing does not involve its similar; and hence a trustee is not empowered to constitute another the trustee of the same thing; in the same manner as an agent is not permitted to constitute another agent. (By the term family, in this place, is to be understood all such as live with the trustee, or whose maintenance is incumbent upon him, or his upon them, as a wife or adult son.)

And so also, if he lodge it in a place of custody belonging to another.—IF a trustee lodge the deposit in a place of custody* belonging to another, he becomes responsible for it; becomes the lodging it in another's place of custody is, in effect, depositing it with that other,—It is otherwise, however, if he hire the said place; for in that instance his lodging it there is considered in the same light with his keeping it himself, and therefore does not induce responsibility.

He is not made responsible by putting it out of his own possession with a view to the immediate preservation of it.—IF the house of a trustee take fire; and he deliver the deposit to his neighbour,—or if, being in a boat on the point of sinking, he throw the deposit into another boat,—and it in either case be lost he is not responsible, since he acted only for the preservation of it, and consequently according to the consent of the proprietor. But the assertion of the trustee, in such cases, is not to be credited unless supported by witnesses, since, upon the establishment of a cause of responsibility, he pleads the existence of a necessity, which invalidates the responsibility, and the case is therefore the same as if he were to plead that the proprietor had empowered him to consign the deposit to another.

He becomes responsible on neglecting to deliver it on demand.—IF the proprietor of the deposit demand it from the trustee, and he neglect delivering it to him, being at the same time capable of such delivery, he becomes in that case responsible for it, since his neglecting or refusing to deliver it, under a capacity to do so, is a transgression.—The ground of this is, that the demand of the proprietor clearly indicates his dissent from the trustee's retaining possession any longer, and is therefore a dismission of him from the trust.—Hence the trustee is responsible, because of his retaining possession after such dissent.

If he mix it inseparably with his own property, he must make the proprietor a compensation—IF the trustee mix the deposit with his own property, in such a manner that a separation becomes difficult, he must in that case make an adequate compensation, and the proprietor (according to Haneefa) has not the option of sharing the mixed property, whether the mixture be of a homogeneous nature (such as milk with milk, what with wheat, or white dirms with white dirms), or of a heterogeneous nature (such as oil of sesame with oil of olives, or wheat with barley). The two disciples allege that where the mixture is of homogenous articles not of a liquid nature (such as white dirms with white dirms, or wheat with wheat), the proprietor of the deposit has the option either of becoming a sharer with the trustee, or of taking a compensation for the value; because although it be impossible in such a case, for the proprietor to receive his right with respect to appearance; still it is possible for him to receive it with respect to reality (that is in effect), by making a division, since, in all articles of weight, or measurement of capacity, a delivery by division is equivalent to a delivery of the actual article, according to all authorities.—Such, therefore, being the case, it appears that mixture in the instance in question, is a destruction in another respect; and consequently, that the proprietor of the articles placed in deposit has the option either of taking a compensation on the principle of the mixture being a destruction, or of becoming a sharer (if he please) on the principle of its not being a destruction.—The argument of Haneefa is that mixture is in every respect a destruction, because of its being an action which occasions an impossibility of returning the thing to the proprietor in its original substance,—In regard to what the two disciples advance, that "it is possible for the proprietor to receive his right with respect to reality, by means of a division," it is answered that the proprietor cannot attain his actual right by means of division, Besides. division has been instituted

* Arab, Makan Mohirrez; meaning a chest, or other place of security. (See Hirz,)

from necessity, merely as a mode of advantage in cases of partnership. Division, therefore. is merely an effect of partnership, and is incapable of being a cause of it, for otherwise the principal would become secondary, and the secondary principal.—The result of this disagreement is that if the proprietor should exept the trustee, where he makes the mixture, by saying to him "I exempt you from the compensation due by you on account of the mixture," in that case, according to Haneefa, his right becomes entirely cancelled, since (agreeably to his tenets) the proprietor's right is limited to the compensation, which he expressly forgog ;—where as, according to the two disciples, the proprietor's right of option to a compensation ceases in consequence of such exemption, and resolves itself into a share in the mixed property ; because although by the exemption, his right of option be destroyed, still his actual property is not destroyed.—It is to be observed that the mixture of one liquid with a different liquid (such as of oil of Sesame with oil of olives) destroys the right of the proprietor to a participation in the mixed property, and fixes and determines it to a compensation, according to all our doctors, as such a mixture is a destruction with respect both to appearance and reality ; since a division is in this instance impracticable, because of the difference of species.—Of the same class, according to the Rawayet Saheeh, are all cases of an admixture of different articles, not liquids, where the separation is difficult, as in the mixture of wheat with barley.—In cases where the separation requires a process, or is attended with some difficulty (such as if dirms should be melted and incorporated with others), the depositor's right to the substance ceases, and he is entitled to a compensation, according to Haneefa, as before stated. Aboo Yoosaf holds that in this case the smaller is subordinate to the greater (for, according to his tenets, superiority must be regarded), and that therefore, the person who possessed the largest share of the property becomes proprietor of the whole, and liable to compensate to the other for the value of his quantum.—Mohammed, on the other hand, maintains that the proprietor of the deposit becomes a participator with the other in either case, because according to his tenets, species cannot acquire a superiority over the same species, as has been already explained in treating of fosterage.

If the mixture be occasioned by accident, the proprietor becomes a proportionate sharer in the whole.—If a deposit be mixed with the property of the trustee, not by any act of the latter, but by accident (as if a bag containing tha deposit, and another containing property of the trustee, should both be torn, and the contents mingled together), in that case the trustee becomes a sharer in the property with the depositor, and is not responsible for a compensation, since he did not commit any act inducing responsibility—They therefore become partners in the whole according to all our doctors.

If the trustee expend a part, and supply the deficiency, by mixture, from his own property, he is responsible for the whole.—If a trustee expend part of the deposit, and then produce a similar to what he had expended, and mix it with the remaining part, in such a manner that a separation is difficult, he is, in that case, responsible for the whole of the deposit ; because the part expended is a debt due by him, which he cannot otherwise discharge than in the presence of the owner.—When, therefore, he mixes his own property with the remainder of the deposit, he in fact destroys that remainder ; as was before explained.

In cases of transgression respect to the deposit, the trustee is responsible so long as the transgression continues.—If a trustee transgress with respect to the deposit, by converting it to his own use (as if, being a quardruped, he should ride upon it,—or, being a gown, he should wear it,—or, being a slave, he should use his services),—or by committing it to the care of a stranger, and he afterwards refrain from the use of it, or receive it back from the stranger, his responsibility thereupon ceases. Shafei maintains that he does not become exempted from responsibility ; because the contract of deposit ceases and determines immediately on the existence of responsibility, since responsibility and deposit are irreconcileable :—the trustee, therefore, in such case, cannot be exempted until he made actual restitution to the proprietor. The argument of our doctors is, that the order of the depositor to preserve the property continued to operate, as it was absolute, and not restricted to any particular time ; it being understood, in this case, that the proprietor had generally desired him to preserve the property, without restricting such desire to any particular time.—As, therefore, the order is still in force, it follows that the trustee, after abstaining from the transgression, becomes again trustee, because the object of the contract was preservation.—The contract, moreover, was suspended in its effect merely from the necessity of establishing a branch of it : when, therefore, the branch is removed, the contract becomes revived in its effect ; in the same manner as where a person hires another to guard his property for a month, and the person so hired remits his guard for part of the month. in which case he is entitled to wages in proportion to the number of days he did watch.—In answer to Shafei s assertion, that "the trustee cannot be exempted from responsibility until he make actual restitution to the proprietor," it is to be observed that, as the original order still continues in force, and the trustee ceases from his transgression, a recovery of the deposit is obtained into the possession of the trustee, who is the substitute or confidant of the proprietor ; and as this recovery is equivalent to a restitution of it to the proprietor.

himself, he [the trustee] is consequently not responsible for it on the ground of destruction.

If the trustee deny the deposit, upon demand, he is responsible in case of the loss of it.—IF the proprietor of the deposit demand it of the trustee, and the trustee deny the deposit, and it be afterwards lost, the trustee is in that case responsible; because, as the depositor, in making the demand, dismisses the trustee from his charge, if follows that the trustee, in retaining the deposit after such demand, is an usurper, and is consequently responsible.—If, also, after the denial, the trustee should acknowledge the deposit, still he does not thereby become exempted from responsibility, because the contract had been previously done away, inasmuch as the demand of restitution by the depositor was a dissolution on his part, and the denial of the deposit was a dissolution on the part of the trustee; in the same manner as the denial of agency by the agent, or of sale either by the buyer or seller, is a dissolution on their part—Now when a dissolution takes place on both sides, the contract to which it relates is done away; and cannot afterwards be revived, unless by a new formation, which does not appear in the case in question.—In this case, therefore, a recovery into the possession of the proprietor's substitute cannot be understood.—It is otherwise where the trustee deviates from his instructions by transgressing upon the property, and afterwards ceases from such deviation, and conforms to his orders, for in this case a recovery appears into the possession of the proprietor's substitute, as was before explained.

But not if the denial be made to a stranger.—IF the trustee deny the deposit to some other than the proprietor, he is not responsible, according to Aboo Yoosaf (contrary to the opinion of Ziffer), because denial to any other than the proprietor may be for the sake of preservation. The trustee, moreover is not competent to his own dismission, unless in the presence of the depositor, or unless the depositor claim his property from him. The order for keeping the property, therefore, still continues in force:—contrary to where the denial is made to the depositor.

A trustee is at liberty to carry the deposit with him upon a journey.—A TRUSTEE is at liberty, according to Haneefa, to carry the deposit with him when he travels, although carriage and other expenses be thereby incurred.—The two disciples maintain that that is not permitted to him where carriage or other expense is incurred. Shafei, on the other hand, maintains that it is not allowable in either case, because he considers an order to keep the article in the common acceptation of keeping, namely, keeping in cities; in the same manner as where a person hires another for the preservation of his goods for a stated time, in which case the person hired is not at liberty to travel with the goods,—or, if he should do so, becomes responsible for them. The argument of Haneefa is, that the proprietor's commission for preservation is absolute and unconfined; and that a plain is a place of preservation, provided the road be secured; on which principle it is permitted to a father or guardian to travel with the property of their ward. The reasoning of the two disciples is that, in case of travelling, where carriage for the deposit is necessary, the expense of it must fall on the depositor; and as it is probable he may not assent to this, his commission for keeping the article must, in such a case, be considered as limited to a city.—The answer to this is that the circumstance of the expense of removal falling upon the proprietor is of no moment, as it may be a consequence of an attention to the preservation of his property, and the fulfilment of his commission.—The answer to Shafei is that although are articles chi fly abound in cities, still the keeping or preserving of them is not particularly confined to cities, but extends alike to cities and to plains; since the inhabitants of plains must necessarily keep their property in plains.—Besides, a removal of the deposit may sometimes be a desirable object to the proprietor: as where it is made from a city in danger to one in security; or to the particular city in which the proprietor dwells,—Now as the keeping of an article is not, in its common acceptation, limited to cities, it follows that a commission for keeping is not limited to any particular city. It is otherwise in a case of hire for keeping, as hire is a contract of exchange, which requires a delivery of the subject of the contract (namely, keeping or guarding) in the place where the contract is executad

Provided the contract be absolute, the road safe, and the journey necessary—It is to be observed that this case proceeds on a suppesition of the contract being absolute, the road which the trustee travels safe, an . the journey necessary: for, if the road be dangerous, or the journey not necessary, the trustee is responsible, according to all our doctors.—If, also, the journey be not necessary, and the trustee travel with all his family, he is not responsible: but if, the journey not being necessary, he should leave his family behind, he becomes responsible, as in that case it was his duty to have left the deposit with his family.

Unless this be expressly prohibited.—IF the proprietor expressly prohibit the trustee from carrying the deposit out of the city, and he nevertheless carry it out, he becomes in that case responsible for it, as the restriction so imposed is a valid one since keeping the article in a city is most eligible.

In case of a deposit by two persons, the trustee cannot deliver to either his share, but in presence of the other.—IF two men deposit something jointly with another, and one of them afterwards appear, and demand his share of the deposit, the trustee must not give it, unless in the presence of the other depositor, according to Haneefa. The two disciples maintain that the trustee must deliver the claimant his share;—and the same is also said in Kadooree's compendium. In the Jama Sagheer is said that if three men deposit one thousand dirms with a particular person, and two of them afterwards disappear, the third is not entitled to take his share, according to Haneefa; but according to the two disciples he is entitled to take it. (It is to be observed that this difference of opinion relate solely to articles of weight, or measurement of capacity.) The argument of the two disciples is tha, the depositor claims his own share only, and is therefore entitled to receive it, where it is attainable, in the same manner as a copartner in a debt. The argument of Haneefa is that the person present, in claiming his on share, necessarily claim half of the absentee's since he claim a separate and determinate portion, whereas his right is indefinite. Now where a right is mixed indefinitely with another, it is to be rendered separate and determinate only by means of division; but the trustee has no power to make a division; and accordingly, if he were to give the present claimant his share, it is not account a division by any of our doctors.—It is otherwise in a case of a participated debt, because, in that instance, the present creditor claims from the debtor a delivery of his right, which may be made without a division, since debt is discharged by means of similars.—With respect to what is advance by the two disciples that "the depositor is entitled to receive his share where it is attainable." it may be answered, that it does not from hence follow that the trustee is liable to any compulsion on that head:—in the same manner as where, for instance, a person deposits one thousand dirms with another, who is indebted in one thousand dirms to a third person; in which case, although it be lawful for the creditor to take his due wherever it be attainable, still it is not lawful for the trustee to pay him with the said deposit.

Two persons receiving a divisible article in trust, must each keep on half.—If a person deposit, with two men, an article capable of division, it is not lawful for either of these trustee to commit such article entirely to the other, but they must divide it, and retain each an half; whereas, if the article were incapable of division, either might lawfully keep it entirely with the consent of the other.—This is the doctrine of Haneefa; and such also is the law, according to him, in a case of two pawnees, to whom a thing incapable or a division is jointly pledged; for in that case either of them, with the consent of the other, may retain sole possession of it:—and so likewise, in the case of two agents empowered to buy anything, and entrusted jointly with the purchase money, for in that case, also, one of the parties may retain the whole of the money with the consent of the other.—The two disciple allege that it is lawful for one of the parties to take entire charge, with the consent of the other, in either case; for as the proprietor has manifested his confidence in the integrity of both, it, is therefore lawful for either to deliver the deposit to the other without being re[illegible]ible, in the same manner as where the deposit is incapable of division.—The argument of Haneefa is, that the proprietor has given his approbation to the charge being united in two, but not to its being vested entirely in one; because the act of keeping, where it relates to a divisible article applies only to a part of the article, not to the whole. —The delivery therefore, of the whole by either party to the other is without the proprietor's consent; and the party who makes such delivery is accordingly responsible.—But the receiver is not responsible, since (according to his tenets) the trustee of a trustee is not subject to responsibility. It is otherwise where the deposit is incapable of division; for where an article of that nature is deposited with two persons, it is impossible for them jointly to be concerned in the case of it every hour of the day and night, unless by turns; and the approbation of the proprietor, with respect to the whole, is therefore of necessity construed to extend to either of them in particular.

Restrictions are not regarded where they are repugnant to custom or convenience.—If the proprietor of a deposit say to the trustee "deliver not the deposit to your wife," and he nevertheless deliver it to his wife, he becomes in that case responsible.—It is recorded, in the Jama Sagheer, that if the proprietor prohibit the trustee from delivering the deposit to any one of his family and he nevertheless deliver it to one of his family from any unavoidable necessity, he is not made responsible by having so delivered it; —as if, for instance, the deposit be an animal, and the proprietor prohibit the trustee from giving charge of it to his slave;—or as if, being of the description of things usually committed to the care of women, he should prohibit him from delivering it to any of his wives. The compiler of the Hedaya remarks, that as the former of these reports is absolute, and that quoted from the Jama Sagheer restricted, the first ought also to be understood as restricted; for this reason, that it is impossible to manage the conservation with an observance of the condition, which is therefore nugatory But if she trustee should not act from necessity,—as if, having two wives, or two slaves, the proprietor should prohibit the delivery to one particular wife, or to one particular slave, and the trustee nevertheless commit the deposit to the particular wife or slave so prohibited,—he becomes responsible, since the condition in this case is useful, as same of the family may not be trustworthy: and, as the conservation of the deposit is not incompatible with the observance of the condition, it is therefore valid.

Or where they relate to the particular apartment in a house.—If the proprietor say to the trustee. "Keep the deposit in this apartment of the Sarai," and he keep it in another apartment of the same Sarai, in that case he is not responsible for it; because the condition was useless, inasmuch as there is no difference with respect to keeping in different apartments of the same Serai.—(If, on the contrary, he were to keep it in a different Serai, he is responsible; because, as a difference of Serais occasions a difference in the keeping, the condition is therefore of use, and the restriction is consequently valid.)—If, however, there be an evident different between two different apartments of the same Serai (as if, the Serai being extensive, the apartment prohibited should be full of holes and crevices), the condition so made is valid, and the trustee becomes responsible in case of preserving it in that apartment.

Where the deposit is transferred to a second trustee, and lost, the proprietor receives his composition from the original trustee.—IF a person deposit something with another, and that other again deposit it with a third person, and it be lost in this person's hands, in that case the proprietor of the deposit, according to Haneefa, must take a compensation from the first trustee, not from the second. The two disciples allege that the proprietor is at liberty to take the compensation either from the first or second trustee; and that, in case he should take it from the first, he [the first] is not empowered to take an indemnfication from the second; but that, in case of his taking it from the second, the is second then entitled to take an indemnification from the first.—The reasoning of the two disciples is that the second trustee has received the deposit from the hands of a person who has himself become reponsible,* and is therefore responsible;—in the same manner as the trustee of an usurper;—that is to say, if an usurper deposit with any person the goods he has usurped, and they be lost in the trustee's hands, the proprietor is at liberty to take a compensation either from the usurper or the trustee; and so also in the case in question.—The ground of this is, that the proprietor of the deposit not having given his approbation to the second deposit; the first trustee was guilty of a transgression; and the second trustee was also guilty of a transgression in having received it without the consent of the proprietor.—The proprietor, therefore, has the option of taking a compensation from either.—If, however, he take the compensation from the first trustee, he [the first trustee] is not in that case entitled to indemnify himself from the second; because, upon paying the compensation, he becomes proprietor, which constitutes the second a legal trustee; and a legal trustee is not responsible for the deposit.—If, on the contrary, the proprietor take the compensation from the second trustee, he [the second] is in that case entitled to an indemnification from the first; because, as not being a legal trustee; he must be considered merely as an agent for conservation on behalf of the original trustee; and as such he is entitled to an indemnification for whatever losses he may sustain, connected with the agency.—The reasoning of Haneefa is, that the second trustee received the article from the hands of a trustee, and not of a responsible person; because the first trustee does not become responsible until the thing be separated from the second trustee; since so long as it is in existence with him, the wisdom and judgment of the first trustee are considered to be, as it were, extant and at hand with regard to it.—The proprietor, moreover, is supposed assenting to any mode of keeping his property which may be agreeable to the trustee's judgment; and as that still continues to be exerted, it follows that no transgression whatever has as yet taken place.—But. upon the article being lost by the second trustee, the first trustee it held to abandon the charge he had undertaken, and is therefore responsible. The second trustee, on the other hand, continues in his original predicament; that is, his ceisin is a seisin of trust in the end, in the same manner as it was at the beginning; and as he is not found in any transgression, he therefore is not responsible for the deposit;—in the same manner as where the wind blows a gown near to any person, and it is afterwards destroyed.—in which case that person is not responsible.

Case of claim advanced by two persons to a sum of money in the possession of a third.—IF two persons should separately claim a thousand dirms in the possession of a third; each asserting that he had deposited them with him; and the possessor deny their claims, but refuse to take an oath to that effect, the thousand dirms must, in that case, be divided between the two-claimants, and the defendant remains answerable to them for one thousand more.—The reason of this is, that the claim of each several claimant is valid, as the claim of each has the probability of truth—Hence each is entitled to exact an oath from the defendant, who, on his part, is required to make a separate deposition with respect to each, as the right of each is distinct. The Kazee, in administering the oaths, may lawfully being with either, since it is impossible to administer both at the same time, and neither has ground of preference over the other.—If however, a contention should take place between the claimants on this point, the die must be thrown in order to satisfy them, and to remove any suspicion of partiality on the part of the Kazee.—If he then take an oath in denial of the claim of one, let another oath be administered to him in denial of the second's claim; and if he thus made denying the claims of both, nothing

*In consequence of the deviation from is trust.

from him, for want of proof.—If he should refuse to take the second oath, a decree must be passed in favour of the second claimant, since the proof is established.—If, on the contrary, he refuse to take the first oath, a decree must not be passed in favour of the first claimant, but an oath must be tendered to him with regarded to the claim of the second.—It were otherwise if, at the time of refusing, he were be make an acknowledgment in favour of the first; for in that case a decree would immediately pass; since acknowledgment is proof and a cause of property in itself; whereas a refusal to take an oath is neither proof: nor a cause of property, unless in conjunction with the decree of the Kazee. It is therefore lawful for the Kazee, in such a case, to suspend his decree until he shall have tendered the second oath, that he may be apprised of the full extent to which his decree is to go:—and if the defendant refuse to take the second oath also, the Kazee must then pass a decree equally in favour of both; because neither party has a superiority over the other in point of proof; and no regard whatever is paid to priority of refusal [to swear], since the two refusals do not constitute proof separately, but together and at one period, namely, at the period of the decree of the Kazee;—and as, if both had adduced evidence, no superiority would have been given to either evidence on the ground or priority, to also in the present instance.—The defendant must also give a compensation of another thousand dirms to the claimants, since in paying them the one thousand which was present he only pays each half his due.—supposing that the Kazee, in consequence of a refusal to take the first oath, should immediately pass a decree in favour of the first claimant, without waiting to tender an oath with respect to the claim of the other, in this case Imam Alee Yezadee, in this commentary upon the Jama Sagheer, says that an oath must be tendered with regard to the second;—and if the difendant refuse to take it, a decree must then be passed jointly, in favour of both claimants, in an equal degree; because the decree in favour of the first claimant was not destructive of the right of the second, since the precedence, in the administration of the oath, was determined either by the will of the Kazee, or the chance of the die; and neither of these have power to destroy the second's right.—Khasaf has substituted a slave in this case; that is, instead of one thousand dirms, he has supposed the dispute to relate to a slave, and he maintains that the sentence ought to be executed in favour of the first claimant, since the matter is uncertain, in as much as several of the learned have given it as their opinion, that a decree should be passed in favour of the first without waiting for the second, as a denial to take an oath is equivalent, by implication, to an acknowledgment.—He, moreover, remarks, that the oath with respect to the second claimant must not be administered to this effect, "this slave is not the slave of such as one," because a refusal on the part of the defendant to take such an oath is of no consequence, after the slave in question had been proved to be the property of another.—The tenor of the oath, therefore, must be "there is nothing due from me to this man; not this slave, nor the value of him (which is so much), nor less than the said value."—He also observes, that it is requisite this oath be administered, according to Mohammed; but not according to Aboo Yoosaf; because if a trustee should make an acknowledgment of the deposit in favour of a certain person, and the thing acknowledged should by a decree of the Kazee be given to another, then, according to Mohammed, the acknowledger is responsible but not according to Aboo Yoosaf.—Now the case in question is a branch of this case relative to the acknowledgment of a deposit, and consequently the law in the one case is the same as in the other.—The case of acknowledgment here alluded to, is where a person first acknowledges a particular slave to be the property of a particular person, and afterwards denies it, averring that another person had deposited the slave with him, and a decree is passed in favour of the first acknowledge, because of the second acknowledgment being a retraction of the first;—in which case, if he should have given the slave to the first without a decree of the Kazee he is responsible, in the opinion of all our doctors; or if he should have given the slave by the decree of the Kazee, in that case also, according to Mohammed, he is responsible, because he acknowledges his obligation to keep the slave on account of the second and yet he destroys the said slave (that is, so far as relates to the claim of the second), by means of his acknowledgment, and is consequently responsible.—According to Aboo Yoosaf he is not responsible in this instance, because he as holds, it is not the immediate act of acknowledgment that destroys the slave, so far as relates to the right of the other, but the giving of him to the other, which is the necessary consequence of the order of the Kazee. Mohammed, on the other hand, maintains that it was he who urged the Kazee to pass that decree; whence he is responsible. Now the reason for assimilating the case in question with this one is, that the acknowledgment in favour of the second claimant, after the first had acquired a right to the thing, is useful to the second claimant in as much as (the opinion of Mohammed, it induces a responsibility in his favour. Hence in this case, it is requisite, according to Mohammed, to administer an oath to the second claimant, notwithstanding the slave have been proved to be the right of the first, because the object from it is to obtain a refusal to take the oath, which is equivalent to an acknowledgment; and an acknowledgment, even in that case, is useful, as it induces responsibility. According to Aboo

Yoosaf, on the contrary, an oath is not to be administered; because, in this same manner as the defendant is not made responsible by an acknowledgment, so neither is he by a refusal to swear, and hence the tendering of in oath is useless.

BOOK XXIX.

OF AREEAT OR LOANS.

Definition of Areeat, and the nature of the use granted in a loan.—AREEAAT, according to our doctors, signifies an investiture with the use of a thing without a return.—The person who so grants the use is termed Moyeer, or the lender; the person receiving it, Moostayir, or the borrower; and the article of which the use is granted, Areeat, or the loan—Koorokhee and Shafei define Areeat to signify, simply, a license to use the property of another because it is settled by the world Ibahit, signifying license or permission. Besides, a specification of the period is not a necessary condition in a loan: but if a loan were an investiture, it would not be valid without such specification, since without a specification of the period the full extent of the use cannot be ascertained, and an investiture with anything uncertained is invalid. A loan, moreover, is rendered null by a recall, whereas if it were an investiture with the use, it could not be rendered null by a recall, in the same manner as a lease cannot be annulled by a recall. Further, the borrows is not entitled to hire the loan; whereas, if it were an investiture, he might let it out to hire, because whosoever is himself proprietor of a thing may constitute another proprietor of it. Our doctors, on the other hand, argue that the word Areeat indicates an investiture, since it is derived from Areeya, which signifies a grant; and that, accordingly, in forming the contract the expression investiture is used. The use of a thing, moreover, is capable of being property, in the same manner as the actual thing itself; and as investiture with the latter may take place either with or without a return, so also with respect to the former.—With respect to what Koorokhee urges concerning for term Ibahit, it may be replied that this term is not uncommonly used to express investiture, since it is used in setting contracts of lease, which are an investiture with respect to the use of the thing hired.—With respect to his conclusion, that "if a loan were an investiture it would not be valid without a specification of its period, because of uncertainty,"—it may be replied that uncertainty, in loans, is of no consequence, as if cannot be productive of strife, inasmuch as loans are not binding,* whence the uncertainty cannot be injous, uri It is to be observed that a recall operates in a loan, because a recall is a prohibition with respect to the enjoyment of the use, and after such prohibition the use, of consequence, ceases to be the property of the borrower. The borrower, moreover, is not competent to let out to hire the thing borrowed, since that is attended with an injury to the lender, as will be hereafter explained.—It is also to be observed that investiture is made in four different shapes. I. By sale, which is an investiture with substance, for a return.—II. By gift, which is an investiture with substance, without a return.—III. By lease or hire, which is an investiture with the use of a thing for a return.—IV. By loan, which is an investiture with the use of a thing without a return, as before explained; and which is lawful, as being a species of kindness; because GOD has said "DO KINDNESS TO EACH OTHER;" and also, because the prophet borrowed a suit of armour from Sifwan.

Forms under which it is granted.—A DEED of loan is rendered valid by the lender saying "I have lent you this," as there the purpose is expressly mentioned; or, by his saying, 'I have given you to eat of this earth,' because such an expression is used to denote a loan metaphorically; for as it is impossible to eat of the earth itself, the meaning is therefore construed "to eat of the produce of it,"*

The lender may resume it at pleasure.—THE lender is at liberty to resume the loan whenever he pleases; because the prophet has said "MOONHA is liable to be recalled, and a loan must be returned to the proprietor (Moonha is a species of loan, where a person lends another a goat, a cow, or a she-camel, for instance), that he may use their milk;—and also, because the produce, or use of the thing lent, becomes property, particle by particle, merely according as it is brought into being; hence, with respect to such part of the produce as is not yet brought into being, there is merely an investiture, but no seisin: retraction with respect to such part is therefore valid.

The borrower is not responsible for the lost of it, unless he transgress respecting it.—A LOAN is a trust. If, therefore, it be lost in the hands of the borrower, without any transgression on his part, he is not answerable for it, whether the loss happen at the period of his using it, or otherwise.—Shafei maintains that he is responsible for it in case the loss should take place at a time when he is not using it; because he has taken possession of the property another without a right in it; and also, because as the borrower is liable to the charges of removal, in case of the existence of the substance, so also he is answerable for the value, in case of its

---

*That is, may be retracted at pleasure.

*Some cases are here omitted, as they turn entirely upon different modes of expression, in the original idiom.

destruction, in the same manner as an usurper the article standing in the same predicament with merchandise detained with a view to purchase.—With respect to the permission of seisin, established on the borrower's behalf that was granted merely with a view to enable him to enjoy the use; and hence. where the use ceases it no longer operates; in other words, where the loan is destroyed during his enjoyment of the use; he is not responsible, because of the existence of the necessity; whereas, if it be lost at a time when he is not using it, he is responsible, because of the non-existence of the necessity at the time. The argument of our doctors is, that the term Areeate does not indicate responsibility; for (according to their exposition) it is an investiture with the use without a return or (according to Shafei and Koorokeee) a permission of the use; and the seisin of it is not a transgression on the part of the borrower, since it was made with the consent of the lender; and although that consent was merely with a view to enable the lender to use the article, still to borrower did not make the seisin with any other intention; he therefore, is not guilty of any transgression; and consequently is not responsible.—In reply to what Shafei urges it may be observed, that the expense attending a removal of the article is incumbent on the borrower, merely on account of the advantage he derives from it, in the same manner as the maintenance of a loan is incumbent upon the borrower, on account of the advantage he derives from it, and not on account of any defect in his tenure. It is otherwise in the case of an usurper, where the charges of removal are due merely because of the defect in his tenure.—With respect to seisin with a view to purchase, the responsibility in that instance does not arise from the seisin, but from the design with which it was made; for as seisin in virtue of a contract of sale induces responsibility, so also seisin with an intention of purchase induces responsibility, since seisin with a view to any contract is subject to the same laws with that contract, as has been explained in its proper place.

He cannot let it out to hire.—It is not lawful for a borrower to let out a loan. If, therefore, he should let it out, and it be afterwards lost, he is in that case reponsible for it; because a loan is inferior to a lease, and an inferior cannot comprehend his superior; and also, because if the hire be valid. it can only be so on the supposition of its being binding; and that cannot be supposed otherwise than with the consent of the lender; for if it were binding without his consent, it would be a great injury to him, as it would deprive him of the power of resuming the loan, until the expiration of the lease.—The lease of a loan is therefore invalid.

Or, if he let it, he becomes responsible.—It is to be observed that, in case of letting out the loan, the borrower becomes responsible for it immediately upon the delivery to the lessee; for as the act of lending does not comprehend hire, it follows that such delivery is an usurpation. The lender is in this case at liberty to take the compensation, if he please, from the lessee, because of his having taken the property of another without his consent. If, however, he take it from the borrower, he is not then entitled to any indemnification from the lessee, since, in consequence of his receiving a compensation from the borrower, it becomes evident that the borrower only let his own property.—If he take the compensation from the leasee, the lessee is in that case entitled to an indemnification from tha borrower, who is the lessor, provided he [the lessee] had not known that the lease was a loan, as in that case he suffers an imposition. It is otherwise where he takes the lease knowing it to be a loan, as there he suffers no imposition.

He may lend it to another person, unless this subject it to be differently affected.—It is lawful for a borrower to lend the thing borrowed, provided it be of such a nature I may not subject is to be differently affected by different uses.*—Shafei is of opinion that the borrower is not entitled to lend the loan to another, because (according to him) a loan is merely a permission of the use, and a person to whom the use of a thing is permitted is not entitled to communicate that permission to another, for this reason, that the use of a thing is not capable of being property, as it is a non entity, the use being considered is an entity in the case of a lease merely from necessity, which in a loan may be completely answered by permission.—Our doctors, on the other hand, argue that as loan is an investiture with the use of a thing, the borrower may therefore lend the loan, in the same manner as a person to whom the use of a thing devolved by request.—Besides, in the same manner as the use is made property in the case of a lease, so also is it from a principle of necessity, in the case of a loan.

Objection.—If a loan signify an investiture with the use, it would necessarily follow that the borrower is at liberty to lend the loan even where a difference of use may occasion a different affection in the thing; whereas the law is otherwise.

Reply.—It is not permitted to the borrower to lend the thing borrowed when of a nature to be differently affected by different use, because of the possibility of the use of the second borrower being more injurious to

---

*Thus if the loan be a cow or a goat, as the object from these is milk, it matters not whether for this purpose they remain with Zeyd or Omar.—But if the loan be a riding-horse, it may be consequence that Zeyd be should not lend it to Omar, for if Zeyd be thin and Omar fat, Omar's use of the horse would in that case affect it more than the use of it by Zeyd.

the thing than that of the first ; and the consent and approbation of the first lender is give to the use of the first borrower, but not to that of the second.—The compiler of the Hedaya remarks that what is here related proceeds on the supposition of the loan being absolute ; for that loans are of four kinds. I. Loan that are absolute with respect both to the period and the use ; in which case the borrower is entitled to take the use in any manner and at any time he pleases because of the loan being absolute. —II. Loans that are restricted both as to the use and the time, in which case the borrower is not allowed to depart from these restrictions, excepting where the deviation is in an instance that is similar to the one prescribed, or of a better kind ; as where a person borrows a quadruped in order to load it on a particular day with ten measures of a particular kind of wheat ; and he loads it on that day with ten measures of a different kind of wheat, or with less than ten measures of the same or a different kind of wheat.—III. Loans that are restricted in point of time but absolute with respect to the use ;—and IV. Loans that are restricted with respect to the use, but absolute with respect o time ;—in either of which it is not lawful for the borrower to depart from the restrictions.—If therefore, a person borrow a quadruped without any conditions whatever, he is in that case entitled either to load it on his own account, or to lend it to another for the purpose of landing, as in landing there is no difference ; and, in the same manner, he may either ride upon it himself, or lend it to another for that purpose ;—but as riding is supposed to be of different kinds, he is not entitled to more than one kind, which his own act must fix and determine ; and hence, if he should ride upon it himself, he is not afterwards at liberty to lend it to another to ride ; or, if he should lend it to another to ride upon, he is not afterwards entitled to ride upon it himself.

Loans of money, &c., as opposed to loans of specific property.—The loan of dirms and deenars, and of articles estimated by measurement of capacity, by weight, or by tale, is considered in the light of Karz.*—The principle on which this proceeds is. that Areeat is an investiture with the use [of the property lent] ; and as this cannot be obtained, with regard to these articles, without a destruction of the substance. it must, with respect to him, be necessarily considered as an investiture with the substance,—Now an investiture of this nature is to be considered in two lights,—a gift or a loan :*—the act is, however, regarded as a loan in this instance, either because loan is more probable than gift, or because the objects of a loan are two-fold,—namely, the use of the article, and the restitution of the substance : and in the loan of the articles in question, a restitution of an equivalent is admitted in place of the identical substance.—Lawyers, however, have observed t at this doctrine proceeds on the supposition of the loan being absolute : for if it be limited (as if a person should lend another a quantity of dirms merely to place in his shop and attract customers from the persuasion of his being rich). it is not in this case a Karz-loan, but an Areeat-loan, whence he is not entitled to derive any other use from it then what was specified : the case, therefore, becomes the same as if he had borrowed a vessel or a sword to decorate his shop,

Land may be borrowed for the purpose of building or plantations . but the lender is at liberty to resume it.—If a person borrow land, with a view to build upon it, or plant trees in it, it is lawful ; because the use to which the loan is to be applied is here ascertained ; and as such use is the subject of property in leases, so also in loans.—But in this case it is permitted to the lender to resume the land ; and as he is to receive it back in the state in which he lent it, he is therefore empowered to compel the borrower to remove his houses or trees.—It is to be considered, however whether or not any period was fixed for the loan.—If no period was fixed, then no compensation is due by the lender for the loss he may have occasioned to the borrower by the destruction of his buildings or trees, since no deceit was practised on the borrower, but rather he deceived himself, in trusting to a contract which was absolute and unaccompanied with any condition.—If, on the other hand, a period was fi ed for the loan, and it be resumed before the expiration of that period, the resumption so made is valid, since a lender (as was before explained) may resume a loan when he pleases : but it is nevertheless abominable in this instance, as it involves a breach of promise, and the lender is responsible to the borrower for the loss he sustains

*Areeat and Karz are, in common conversation, used indiscriminately to denote a loan ; but there is a distinction in law with regard to them. Areeat is used with respect to such things as, after being lent to another, are identically returned to him ; and Karz, with regard to such things are returned, not idenfically, but equal in point of number, weight, or measurement of capacity.—Thus where a person, having borrowed a book, and read it, afterwards borrowed a book, and read it, afterwards returns it, it is considered as Areeat ; but if a person should borrower one bundred dirms from another, and after using them should return another hundred dirms, it is considered as Karz.

*Arab. Karz.—As the English language makes no distinction between the termr Karz and Areeat (although essentially different in their effect), the translator is under the necessity of adopting the term loan in both instances ;—leaving it to the reader to conceive the original term from the context.

in the removal of his trees and buildings, in as much as he deceived the borrower in fixing a period which it was natural to suppose he would adhere to:—the borrower, therefore, is entitled to a compensation from the lender, in consideration of the damage he receives; and the same is mentioned by Kadoree in his compendium.—Hakim Shaheed maintains that the borrower is at liberty either to take from the lender the value of the trees and buildings (in which case they become the property of the lender), or to take a compensation for his loss (in which case he is at liberty to carry away the trees and the buildings). Lawyers have observed that if the removal of the trees and buildings be detrimental to the ground, the choice of the alternative rests with the proprietor of the ground, as he is the principal, and the borrower the secondary, and a preference is always given to the principal.

Land borrowed for the purpose of tillage cannot be resumed until the crop be reaped from it.—If a person borrow a piece of land for the cultivation of grain, the lender has not the power of resuming the loan until the gathering in of the grain, whether a period have been fixed or not; because the gathering of the crop comes within a certain and known period; and in suffering it to remain on the ground, an observance of the right of both the lender and borrower is maintained; in the same manner as, under similar circumstances, in the case of a lease. It is otherwise with respect to trees; because, as the period of their existence is uncertain, the suffering them to remain would be an injury to the lender.

The borrower must defray the charges attending the restoration of a loan.—The charges of returning the loan must be defrayed by the borrower; because, as the restitution of it is incumbent on him (since he took it with a view to his own benefit), he is consequently liable to the expenses attendant on such restitution.—It is to be observed that the expenses attending the return of the subject of a lease are incumbent on the lessor; because the rent being a return for the benefit arising from the tenure of the article let, all that is required from the lessee is merely to put it in the power of the lessor to recover it, by divesting himself of it, and not that he should return it to him.—The expense of returning the subject of an usurpation, on the contrary, must be defrayed by the usurper: for as the return of the article to the proprietor is incumbent on the usurper of it in order to remedy the injury he occasioned, as the expense attendant on such return must of consequence be borne by him.

In restoring an animal borrowed it suffices that it be returning to the owner's stable.—If a person, having borrowed a quadruped from another, should restore it to the stable of the proprietor, and it be afterwards lost, in that case he is not responsible for it, on a favourable construction.—Analogy would suggest that he is responsible, since he has neither restored it to the proprietor nor his agent, but merely to his ground.—The reason for a more favourable construction of the law in this instance is, that a restitution has here been made according to general custom, since it is customary to restore loans to the house of the proprietor; as where, for instance, vessels or utensils belonging to a house are borrowed, in which case it is usual to return them, not into the proprietor's hands, but merely to his house.—Besides, if he had returned the quadruped to the proprietor, he [the proprietor] would have sent it to the stable and therefore his doing so at once is considered as a valid return.

And, in restoring a slave, that he be returned to his master's house.—If a person borrow a slave, and aftewards return him to the house of his master without delivering him, personally, to the master himself, he is not in that case responsible for him for the reasons above mentioned,—Is, on the contrary, an usurper or a trustee return the subject of the usurpation or the trust to the house of the proprietor, without delivering it to the proprietor, they are in that case responsible for the eventual loss of it:—the usurper, because it was incumbent on him to undo his act, and his act cannot be undone but by a delivery to the proprietor himself; and the trustee, because the proprietor did not wish that he should deliver the deposit merely to his house or his family, for if that had been the case, he would not have deposited it with him.—It is otherwise with respect to loans, as these are commonly returned to the house: excepting, however, where they consist of jewels, for in that case they must be returned to the proprietor, and not to the house or family.

It suffices to return the loan by a slave or servant either of the borrower.—If the borrower send the quadruped he had borrowed to the proprietor of it; by his own slave or his hireling, and it be lost in the way, in that case he is not responsible for it.—(By hireling is here to be understood a servant who receives yearly wages.)—The reason of this is that a loan is in the nature of a trust; and the borrower may commit it, for the sake of preservation, into the hands of any of his family, in which relation a slave and a yearly servant stand.—It is otherwise with respect to a daily servant, as he is not held to be one of the family.

Or lender.—If a borrower should send back the horse or other animal he had borrowed to the proprietor, by the slave or the hireling of the proprietor, and it be lost or destroyed on the way, he is not responsible for it, since the proprietor is virtually supposed to have approved of this, in as much as he himself, if a delivery had been made to him, would have consigned the horse to one of these:—Some have said that the law here proceeds on the supposition of the slave or hireling, to whom the quadruped is consigned, being the one to whom the care and management of it is always given. Others, again, have said that it matters not whether it be consigned to such a slave, or to any other slave of the proprietor; and the latter is the most approved doctrine.

If it be returned by a stranger, the borrwer is responsible.—IF a borrower should send the quardruped to the proprietor by the hands of a stranger, he becomes in that case responsible for it, and must make good the value in the event of its loss.—It is to be observed that the case seems to imply the illegality of a borrower's depositing a loan with a stranger; since, if that were lawful, he would not, in the present instance, be responsible.—Such also is the opinion of some of our modern doctors.—Others of them have said that it is lawful for a borrower to deposit the loan, because the contract of deposit is inferior to that of loan; and they have reconciled the doctrine, in the present case, by observing that the borrower does necessarily become responsible on sending the loan by a stranger, since from the moment of his consigning it to a stranger the loan determines, and being no longer a borrower, he becomes of consequence responsible.—Our doctors, however, do not admit the legality of a borrower's deposit, unless he be the borrower of a borrower, which in fact is not a borrower.

Terms in which a contract of loan with respect to land must be expressed.—IF a person lend a piece of fallow ground to another, that he may cultivate it, the borrower must insert, in the contract of loan, the words, "You have given me to eat of this land."—This is according to Haneefa. The two disciples have said that the term Areeat or loan must be inserted; because the term Areeat is particularly used to express a loan; and it is preferable that a contract of loan be expressed in terms particularly appropriated to loans:—as in the loan of a house, for instance, where the borrower expresses the contract. "You have lent me this house." The argument of Haneefa is, that the words "You have given me to eat of this land," are more expressive of the fact, since the term Itam [giving to eat] is particularly restricted to the produce of land; whereas the words "You have lent me this ground,' may apply to any other object, such as building, or the like.—The use of the former, therefore, in the case in question. is by much the most advisable.—It is otherwise with respect to a house, because the loan of it is given for no other purpose than that of residence.

BOOK XXX.

OF HIBBA, OR GIFTS.

Definition of the terms used in gift.—HIBBA. in its literal sense, signifies the donation of a thing from which the donee may derive a benefit: in the language of the LAW it means a transfer of property, made immediately, and without any exchange.—The person making the transfer is termed the Wahib, or donor:—the person to whom it is made the Mohoob-le-hoo; or donee;—and the thing itself the Moohoob, or gift.

Chap. I.—Introductory.

Chap. II.—Of Retractation of a Gift.

CHAPTER I.

Gifts are lawful.—DEEDS OF GIFT are lawful; because the Prophet has said "Send ye presents to each other for the increase of your love," which implies the legality of gifts, as by presents is meant gifts. All our doctors, moreover. concur in the validity of them.

And rendered valid by tender, acceptance, and seisin.—GIFTS are rendered valid by tender, acceptance, and seisin—Tender and acceptance are necessary, because a gift is a contract, and tender and acceptance are requisite in the formation of all contracts; and seisin is necessary in order to establish a right of property in the gift, because a right of property, according to our doctors, is not established in the thing given merely by means of the contract, without seisin.—Malik alleges that right of property is established in a gift antecedent to seisin, because of its analogous resemblance to sale: and the same difference of opinion obtains with respect to alms-gift.—The arguments of our doctors upon this point are twofold, —FIRST, the Prophet has said, "A gift is act valid without seisin" (meaning that the right of property is not established in a gift until after seisin).—SECONDLY. gifts are voluntary deeds; and if the right of property were established in them previous to the seisin, it would follow that the delivery would be incumbent on the voluntary agent before he had voluntarily engaged for it, —It is otherwise with respect to wills; because the time of establishment of a right of property in a legacy is at the death of the testator: and he is then in a situation which precludes the possibility of rendering any thing binding upon himself,

OBJECTION —Although a dead person be not capable of being bound, still an obligation may he against his heir, who is his successor and representative,

REPLY.—The heir is not proprietor of the legacy, and cannot therefore be subjected to obligation on account of it.

A gift may be taken possession of on the spot where it is tendered, without the express order of the donor: but not afterwards.—IF the donee take possession of the gift, in the meeting of the deed of gift,* without the order of the giver, it is lawful, upon a favourable construction.—If, on the contrary, he should take possession of the gift after the breaking up of the meeting, it is not lawful, unless he have had the consent of the giver so to do.—Analogy would suggest that the seisin is not vaild in either case as it is an act with respect to what is

---

*Arab. Majlis Akidal Hibba;—meaning, the place where the deed is executed.

still the property of the giver; for as his right of property continues in force until seisin that is consequently invalid without his consent. The reason for a more favourable construction of the law, in the instance in question, is that seisin, in a case of gift, is similar to acceptance in sale, on this consideration, that in the one the effect of the deed (that is, the establishment of a right of property) rests upon the seisin, and in the other upon the acceptance.—As, moreover, the object of a gift is the establishment of a right of property, it follows that the tender of the giver is, virtually, an empowerment of the donee to take possession.—It is otherwise where the seisin is made after the breaking up of the meeting; because our doctors do not admit of the establishment of the power over the thing but when seisin is immediately conjoined with acceptance; and as the validity of acceptance is particularly restricted to the place of the meeting, so also is the thing which is conjoined with it. —It is also otherwise where the giver prohibits the donee from taking possession in the place of meeting, for in that case the seisin of the donee in the place of the meeting would be invalid, as arguments of implied intention cannot be put in competition with express declaration.

A gift made from divisible property must be divided off;—but not a gift made from indivisible property.—*A gift of part of a thing which is capable of division is not valid unless the said part be divided off and separated from the property of the donor: but a gift of part of an indivisible thing is valid. Shafei maintains that the gift is valid in either case; because a gift is a deed conveying property, and valid, as such, with regard either to things that are connected or separated: in the same manner as in sale,—The ground of this is that as an indefinite share has the capacity to constitute property, it is consequently a fit subject of gift: nor is a voluntary deed rendered null by the indefiniteness of the subject of it: as in a Karz-loan, for the subject of person gives another one thousand dirms, of which one half is to be in the nature of a loan, and the other of copartnership: or as in bequest; or in the gift of indivisible things—The arguments of our doctors upon this point are twofold.—First, seisin in cases of gift is expressly ordained, and consequently a complete seisin is a necessary condition: but a complete seisin is impracticable with respect to an indefinite part of divisible things, as it is impossible, in such, to make seisin of the thing given without its conjunction with something that is not given; and that is a defective seisin.—Secondly, if the gift of part of a divisible thing, without separation, were lawful, it must necessarily follow that a thing is incumbent upon the giver which he has not engaged for,—namely, a division which may possibly be injurious to him (whence it is that a gift is not complete and valid until it be taken possession of; since if it were valid before seisin, a thing would be incumbent upon the donor which he has not engaged for,—namely, delivery).—It is otherwise with respect to articles of an indivisible nature; because in those a complete seisin is altogether impracticable, and hence an incomplete seisin must necessarily suffice, since this is all that the article admits of:—and also, because in this instance the donor does not incur the inconvenience of a division

Objection.—Analogy would suggest that the gift of a part of an indivisible article is invalid: because, although the donor do not in such a case, incur the inconvenience of a division, still he incurs a participation in the property; and this also is a sort of inconvenience.

Reply.—The donor is subjected to a participation in a thing which is not the subject of his grant, namely, the use [of the whole indivisible article], for his gift related to the substance of the article, not to the use of it;—hence the necessity of a participation is not incurred by him with respect to the thing which is properly. the subject of his grant.

With respect to the analogy advanced by Shafei between the case in question and that of Karz-loan, or bequest, it is totally unfounded; because in bequests the seisin [of the legatee] is not a necessary condition; neither is it so in a valid sale;—and although seisin be requisite in Sillim and Sirf sales, still is not ordained with respect to them and hence is not required to be complete in those instances. Besides, as all those contracts [of sale] are contracts of responsibility, the obligation of a division is agreeable to them.—With respect to a Karz-loan, it is a voluntary contract in the beginning, but a contract of responsibility in the end (since it involves responsibility for a similar); and hence, in consideration of its resemblance to both, an incomplete seisin is made a condition in it, not a division: besides, seisin is not especially ordained in this instance.

If a person make a gift to his partner, of his share in the partnership-stock, capable of division, it is invalid, because of the invalidity of the gift of an undefined part of a divisible subject, as before explained.

If a person make a gift, to another, of an undefined portion of land (such as an half, or a fourth), such gift is null, for the reasons already set forth.—If, however, he afterwards divide it off, and make delivery of it, the gift becomes valid: because a gift is rendered complete by seisin; and in this case nothing else remains indefinitely involved with the gift at the time of seisin.

* A small portion of the text immediately preceding, which relates to words synonimous, either directly or by implication, to the word Hibba, or gift, has been necessarily omitted in the the translation.

A gift of an article implicated in another article is utterly invalid.—If a person make a gift of the flour of Sessame which is yet in grain, or of oil of Sessame which is not yet expressed from the seeds, such gift is invalid; and if he afterwards grind the wheat into flour; or extract the oil from the Sessame seeds; and so deliver them to the donee, still the gift is not thereby rendered valid,—The same rule also holds with respect to butter which is yet in milk.—The reason of this is that the thing given, in all these cases, is a nonentity (whence it is that if an usurper of wheat, or of seeds, should either grind the one into flour, or press the other into oil, he then becomes proprietor of them); and as a nonentity cannot be a subject of property; the deeds in question are therefore null, and cannot afterwards be rendered valid otherwise than by being executed de novo.—It is different in the preceding case. because an undefined portion of any thing is nevertheless capable of being transferred.

The gift of milk in the udder, of wool upon the back of a goat, of grain or trees upon the ground, or of fruit upon trees, is in the nature of the gift of an undefined part of a thing, because in these instances the cause of invalidity is the conjunction of the thing given with what is not given, which is a bar to the seisin, in the same manner as in the case of undivided things.

The gift of a deposit to the trustee is valid without a formal delivery and seisin.—If the thing given be in the hands of the donee, in virtue of a trust, the gift is in that case complete, although there be no formal seisin since the actual article is already in the donee's hands, whence his seisin is not requisite. It is otherwise where a depositor sells the deposit to his trustee, for in this case the original seisin does fiot suffice, because seisin in virtue of purchase is a seisin inducing responsibility, and therefore cannot be substituted by a seisin in virtue of a trust; but seisin in virtue of gift, on the contrary, as not being a seisin inducing responsibility, may be substituted by a seisin in virtue of a trust.

The gift, by a father to his infant son, of any thing rather actually o virtually in his possession, is valid in virtue of his [the father's] seisin.—If a father make a gift of something to his infant son, the infant, in virtue of the gift, becomes proprietor of the same, provided the thing given be, at the time, in the possession either of the father or of his trustee; because the possession of the father is capable of becoming possession in virtue of gift and the possession of the trustee is equivalent to that of the father. (It were otherwise if the thing given have been pawned or usurped by another, or sold by an invalid sale: because a pawn and an usurpation are in the possession of another. and the subject of an invalid sale is the properrty of another.)—The same rule holds when a mother gives something to her infant son whom she maintains, and of whom the father is dead, and no guardian provided; and so also, with respect to the gift of and other person maintaining a child under these circumstances.—It is to be observed that the law with respect to seisin in cases of alms-gift is similar to that in gifts.—Thus if a person should bestow in alms, upon a pauper, any thing of which the pauper has possession at the time, he [the pauper] in that case becomes proprietor of the same, without the necessity of a new seisin; and so also, if a father should bestow in alms, upon his infant son. something of which he himself or his trustee has the possession, the infant becomes proprietor thereof;—contrary to where the thing so bestowed has been pawned, lost by usurpation, or sold by an invalid sale.

And so also, a gift to an infant by a stranger.—If stranger make a gift of a thing to an infant, the gift is rendered complete by the seisin of the father of the infant: for as he if master of deeds with respect to the child liable to both goc and evil (such as sale) he is consequenty, in a superior degree, master of gift, which is purely advantageous.

Gift to an orphan is rendered valid by the seisin of his guardian.—If a person make a gift of a thing to an orphan, and it be seised in his behalf by his guardian.—being either the executor appointed by his father,—or his grandfather, or the executor appointed by his grandfather, it is valid; because all these relatives have an authority over the orphan, as they stand in the place of his father.

And, to a fatherless infant, by the seisin of his mother.—If a fatherless child be under charge of his mother, and she take possession of a gift made to him, it is valid; because she has an authority for the preservation of him and his property: and the seisin of a gift made to him is in the nature of a preservation of himself, since a child could not be subsisted without property.—The same rule also holds with respect to a stranger who has the charge of an orphan:—because as his seisin is of legal force (whence it is that another stranger has not a right to take the orphan from him). he is consequently competent to all such things as are purely for the advantage of the orphan.

Gift to a rational infant is rendered valid by the seisin of the infant himself.—If an infant should himself take possession of a thing given to him, it is valid, provided he be endowed with reason; because such an act is for his advantage; and he has a capability of performing it, as capability depands on reason and understanding, which he possesses.

It is lawful for a husband to take possession of any thing given to his wife, being an infant, provided she have been sent from her father's house to his; and this although the father be present; because he is held, by implication; to have resigned the management of her concern to the husband. It is otherwise where she has not been sent from her father's house because then the father is not held to have resigned the management of her concerns. It is also otherwise with respect to a mother, or any others having charge of her; because they are not entitled to possess themselves of a gift in her behalf, unless the father be dead, or absent, and his place of residence unknown; for their power is in virtue of necessity, and not from any supposed authority; and this necessity cannot exist whilst the father is persent.

A house may be conveyed in gift by two persons to one.—If two persons, jointly, make a gift of a house to one man, it is valid: because, as they deliver it over to him wholly, and he receives it wholly, no mixture of seisin.

But not by one person to two.—If one man make a gift of a house to two men, the deed is invalid, according to Haneefa. The two disciples hold it to be valid, because as the donor gives the whole of he house to each of the two donees, (in as much as there is only one conveyance) there is consequently no mixture of property; in the same manner as where one man pawns a house to two men, —The arguments of Haneefa upon this point are twofold.—First, the gift, in this case, is a gift of half the house to each of the donees (as is evident from this; that if one man give to two men something incapable of division, and one of them accept the same, the gift becomes valid with respect to his share);—and such being the case, it follows that, at the time of seisin by each of the donees, a mixture of property take place. Secondly, as a right of property is established in each of the donees, in the extent of one half, it follows that the conveyance or investiture must also be in the same proportions, since the right of property is an effect of the conveyance: on this consideration, therefore, that right of property is established in each with respect to one half, an indefinite mixture of their respective share in the gift is fully established.—It is otherwise in a case of pawn, because the effect of that is detention, not right of property, and the right of detention is wholly and completely established in each of the pawn holders, respectively, insomuch that if the pawner should discharge the debt of one of them, still the right of the other to a complete detention remains unimpaired.

Distinction between joint gift or alms to the rich and to the poor.—It is recorded, in the Jama Sagheer, that if a rich man bestow ten dirms, in alms, upon two poor men, or make a gift of that sum to them, it is valid, but that if the said charity or gift be made to two rich men, it is invalid. (The two disciples maintain that in this last instance both gift and alms are valid),—From this it appears that Haneefa has construed a gift into alms, when the object is a poor man; and alms into a gift, when the object is a rich man,—because of the similarity betwixt these deeds, as each is a conveyance of property without an exchange. Hence Haneefa has made a difference with respect to them, as appears by the case recited in the Jama Sagheer, since he has admitted of charity to two poor men, but not of a gift to two rich men; whilst in the Mabsoot he has made no difference between them, but on the contrary has declared them to be equal, as he there declares "neither a gift nor alms to two men is valid, because the mixture of property is a bar in both cases, as both are dependant on a perfect seisin."—The reason of the distinction in the Jama Sagheer is that the end of alms is to give to God, who is one: and the alms comes not to the poor men, but as their daily food from God Almighty; whereas the gift goes directly to the object of it, namely, the two men.—Some have said that the recital in the Jama Sagheer is the most approved doctrine; and that the meaning of the doctrine in the Mabsoot is that charity to two rich men is invalid; in the same manner as a gift to two men or any description.

Case of the gift of a house inseparate lots.—If a person make a gift to two men, of one third of his house to one of them, and of one third to the other, it is invalid according to the two disciples, and according to Mohammed it is valid. If, however, he make a gift of one half to one, and one half to the other, there are in that case two reports with respect to the opinion of Aboo Yoosaf.—According to the two principles maintained by Haneefa, the gift in that case is invalid; whereas, according to the principles of Mohammed, it is valid —The reason of the distinction, in the latter instance, as maintained by Aboo Yoosaf, is that because of the express apportioning of the gift, it becomes evident that the object of the giver was to establish a part of the property in each, by which means a mixture of the property must inevitably take place;—whence it is that it is not lawful for a person to pawn a thing into the hands of two, by apportioning an half of it separately to each.

CHAPTER II.

OF RETRACTATION OF GIFTS.

The donor may retract his gift to stranger.—It is lawful for a donor to retract the gift he may have made to a stranger: Shafei maintains that this is not lawful; because the Prophet has said. "Let not a donor retract his gift; but let a father, if he please, retract a gift he may have made to his son;" and also; because retractation is the very opposite to conveyance,—and as a deed of gift is a deed of conveyance, it consequently cannot admit its opposite. It is otherwise with respect to a gift made by a father to his son, because (according to his tenets) the conveyance of property from a father to the son can never be complete; for it is a rule with him that a father has a power over the property of his son.—The arguments of our doctors upon this point are twofold.—First, the Prophet has said. "A donor preserves a right to his gift, so long as he does not obtain a return for it."—SECONDLY, the object of a gift to a stranger is a return;—for it is a custom to send presents to a person of high rank that he may protect the donor; to a person of inferior rank that the donor may obtain his services; and to a person of equal rank that he may obtain an equivalent;—and such being the case, it follows that the donor has a power of annulment, so long as the object of the deed is not answered, since a gift is capable of annulment. With respect to the tradition of the Prophet quoted by Shafei, the meaning of it is that the donor is not himself empowered to retract his gift, as that must be done by a decree of the Kazee, with the consent of the donee,—excepting in the case of a father, who is himself competent to retract a gift to his son, when he wants it for the maintenance of the son; and this is metaphorically termed a retractation.—It is to be observed, however, that although a retractation of a gift be agreeable to the letter of the law, still it induce abomination; for the Prophet has said. "The retractation of a gift is like eating one's spittle."

But there are various circumstances which bar the retractation.—IT is further to be observed, that the bars to a retractation of a gift are many,—amongst which are the following:—I. The donee giving the donor a return of consideration; because this fulfils the donor's object.—II. The incorporation of an increase with the gift: because in that instance a retractation cannot take place without including the increase, as that is implicated; and it cannot take place so as to include the increase, since that was not included in the deed of gift,—III. The death of one of the parties; for if the donee should die, his property shifts to his heir, and becomes the same as if it had shifted during his lifetime; and if the donor should die, his heirs are strangers with respect to the contract, since they made no tender of the thing given.—IV. The alienation of the gift from the donee's property during his lifetime; because this is a consequence of the power vested in him by the gift, which power therefore, cannot then be retracted; and also because the right of property has regenerated in another person, in virtue of a fresh cause, namely, conveyance to a second donee; and as a regeneration of the right of property is equivalent to an essential change in the thing, the case is therefore the same as if the gift were to become, in effect, a different thing from what it was, and consequently not liable to retractation.

A gift of land cannot be retracted after the donee has built or planted on it.—IF a person make a gift to another of a piece of land destitute of buildings or plantations, and the donee plant trees in it, or build a house, a stable, or a shop of such a size as to be deemed an increase, in that case the donor is not entitled to retract the gift, because of the increase which it has received.—The restriction is stated with respect to the shop, because shops are sometimes so small as not to be deemed an increase, and sometimes the land is very extensive, the shop occupying only one particular part of it: in which case the bar operates only with respect to that part.

After the sale of a part of the land by the donee. the donor may resume the remainder.—IF the donee sell one half of granted land undivided. the donor may in that case resume the other half, as to the resumption of that no bar exists. If, on the other hand, the donee should not have sold any part of the land, the donor may resume one half of it, for as he is entitled to resume the whole, it follows that he is entitled to resume the half, a fortiori.

A gift to a kinsman cannot be resumed.—IF a person make a gift of anything to his relation within the prohibited degrees, it is not lawful for him to resume it, because the Prophet has said. "When a gift is made to a prohibited relation, it must not be resumed;"—and also because the object of the gift is an increase of the ties of affinity, which is thereby obtained.

Nor a gift to a husband or wife during marriage.—IF a husband make a gift of any thing to his wife, or a wife to her husband, it cannot be retracted, because the object of the gift is an improvement of affection (in the same manner as in the case of presents to relations); and as the object is obtained, the gift cannot be retracted.* This object, however, is to be regarded only during the existent period of the contract; insomuch that if a person give something to a strange woman, and afterwards marry her, he may retract the gift;—whereas, if a man give something to his wife, and afterwards divorce her three times, he is not entitled to retract the gift.

The receipt of a return prohibits retractation.—IF the donee say to the donor. "Take this thing in exchange for your gift," and he accept it, the right of retractation is annulled, because of the donor having obtained the object of his gift.

Although the return be given by a stranger,—IF a stranger, on behalf of a donee, give something gratuitously † to the donor in exchange for his gift, and the donor accept the same, the right of retractation then ceases; because a stranger may lawfully give a compensation for the relinquishment of a right, in the same manner as in cases of Khoola or composition.

If a part of the gift prove the property of another, a proportionable part of the return may be resumed.—IF the half of a gift prove

*Because of the existence of the first bar before mentioned: for the increase of affection excited in the wife by the gift is supposed, by the law, to be a return which she pays for it, and which consequently deprives the donor of the power of retractation.

†Arab. Tibbarran; that is, of his own accord, and without solicitation.

the property of some other than the donor, the donee is in that case entitled to take back from the donor half of return he may have made him for the gift, since the thing opposed to that half was not secured and rendered safe to him. If, on the contrary, half the return prove the property of some other than donee, the donor is not in that case entitled to take back from the donee a particular part of the gift ; but he may restore the remaining part of the return, and then resume the whole of the gift from the donee.—Ziffer maintains that the donor may take back half of the gift, as he considers this case to be analogous to that of part of the gift proving the property of another.—The reasoning of our doctors, in support of the their opinion, is that the remaining part of the return has a fitness to be considered as a return for the whole of the gift from the beginning : as, moreover, in consequence of half the return proving the right of another, it becomes apparent that there is no other return for the gift than the remaining part, it follows that the donor is not entitled to resume an equivalent from the gift.—He is, however, allowed an option in this instance, with respect to the whole gift, because he did not relinquish his right of retractation on any other condition than that of the security of the whole of the return ; and as that does not prove completely secure to him, he is therefore at liberty to restore the remaining half of the return, and to take back the whole of the gift.

When the return is opposed only to a part the remainder of the gift may be resumed.—If a person make a gift of a house to another, and the donee give a return to the donor for a half only of the house so given, the donor may in that case resume the half of the house for which he received no exchange, since a bar to his retractation existed only with respect to the other half

Retractation requires mutual consent, or decree.—A gift cannot lawfully be retracted but with the consent of both parties, or by a decree of the Kazee, because the retractation of a gift is a disputed point amongst the learned. There is, moreover, a degree of weakness in a retraction, because the admission of it contrary to analogy, since it is a power over the property of another, as the right of property in a gift is established in the donee. Besides, as there may arise contention with respect to the object in lieu of it (since the donor may claim something which the donee may refuse), the contention, therefore, cannot possibly be settled but by the consent of the parties, or by a decree of the Kazee,—insomuch that if the gift be a slave, and the donee should have emancipated him previous to the decree of the Kazee, the emancipation holds good. If the donor should prohibit the donee from keeping possession of the gift, and he nevertheless retain possession of it, and it be lost or destroyed in his hands, he is not responsible for it, because his right of property in it is held still to continue in force.—The same rule also holds where the gift is lost or destroyed in the possession of the donee, subsequent to the decree of the Kazee, but prior to the demand of it by the donor, because the original tenure by which he held it was not a tenure of responsibility, and that tenure still exists.—But if the donor demand the article, and prohibit the donee from keeping possession of it, subsequent to a decree of the Kazee, and the donee nevertheless continue to retain it, he is responsible for it, as he is then guilty of a transgression

The donor's re-possession of the gift is not requisite to the validity of retractation.—When a person retracts his gift, either in virtue of a decree of the Kazee, or of the mutual consent of the parties, it is an annulment of the original gift, and not a gift, de novo on the part of the donee, and therefore seisin by the donor is not in such case a requisite condition. Retractation, moreover, is lawful with respect to an undivided portion ; but if a retractation were a gift de novo seisin would be a requisite condition, and consequently retractation with respect to an undivided portion would not be lawful. The reason of this is that a deed of gift is valid under the reservation of a right of annulment. The donor, therefore, in annulling the deed, does no more than possess himself of his own established right : and hence a retractation is an annulment in all cases, that is, whether it take place in virtue of a decree of the Kazee, or by the consent of both parties.—it is otherwise with respect to a buyer's return of goods on account of a defect without a decree of the Kazee ; for that with respect to a third person, is considered as a contract de novo, since the purchaser has not a power of annulment but has merely a right to the quality of safety in the goods ; and in defect of that quality, he is, from a principle of necessity, allowed to annul the contract. —Its being an annulment, therefore, with respect to any third person, must depend upon the Kazee's decree.—Hence there is an essential difference between the retraction of a gift, and the return of goods on account of a defect.

The donee, incurring any responsibility in consequence of a gift, receives no compensation from the donor.—If the substance of a gift prove the property of another after it has been destroyed, and the donee make good the loss to the proprietor, in that case he is not entitled to receive anything in compensation from the donor ; because a gift is a gratuitous contract, and a donee has no right to the security or safety of the gift, nor is he entitled to act in behalf of the donor.—Hence he is not entitled to any thing from the donor, notwithstanding the fraud that has been practised upon him ; for although fraud be a cause of resumption in a contract of mutual exchange, it is not so in contract not of mutual exchange.

A mutual gift requires mutual seisin.—IF a person give something to another on condition of that other giving something to him in exchange for it, the mutual seisin of the respective returns is regarded; that is to say, the contract is nothing until the two seisins take place, and is made null by the subject of it, on either side, being mixed with other property.—The reason of this is, that a deed of this nature is in its original a gift; but when the two seisins take place, it becomes, in effect, a sale; and, as such, return may be made on account of a defect or from an option of inspection: and the right of Shaffa is also connected with it.—Ziffer and Shafei maintain that this is a sale both original and ultimately, in as much as the characteristic of sale, namely, a conveyance of property for a return, exists in it; and in all contracts regard must be paid to the spirit of them, insomuch that if a master should sell his own slave to the slave himself, he [the slave] is in that case free.—The arguments of our doctors are, that the contract comprehends two different shapes or descriptions.—I. It is a gift with respect to the letter.—II. IT is a sale with respect to the spirit. It is therefore requisite to pay attention to both in the utmost possible degree. Now, in the deed at present under consideration, an observance of both is practicable; because, in a gift, the right of property is suspended till seisin: and; in a sale, the right of property is undone in case of any invalidity. The effect of sale moreover is obligation: and a gift also becomes obligatory upon giving a return for it.—Out of attention, therefore, to both shapes, the contract is considered as being originally a gift, and ultimately a sale. It is otherwise with respect to the sale of the person of a slave to the slave himself; for it is impossible in any respect to consider this as a sale, since a slave cannot possibly be master of himself.

Section

The gift of a pregnant slave includes a gift of her fœtus.—IF a person make a gift to another of a female slave, and except the child in her womb, the gift is valid:—but the exception is null; because an exception is never valid unless it relate to such a thing as might have been the subject of the deed; and a child in the womb cannot be the subject of gift, because it is equivalent to a constituent part, like the members of the body, as has been already shown in treating of sale;—such, therefore, being the case, the exception is in effect the same as an invalid condition: hence the gift remains in force; and the exception is null.—The same rule also holds in cases of marriage, Khoola, and composition for wilful bloodshed:—that is to say, if a person assign a female slave (for instance) as the dower, in marriage, or as the consideration for Khoola, or the composition for wilful bloodshed, and except the child in her womb, the deed is valid, but the exception is null; because none of these contracts are invalidated by the insertion of an invalid condition.—It is otherwise in cases of sale, lease, or pawnage; for these are all rendered invalid by involving an invalid condition.

Unless that have been previously emancipated—IF a master emancipate the fœtus in the womb of his female slave, and afterwards make a gift of the slave to some person it is valid; because as the fœtus is not, in this instance, the property of the donor, it therefore is not dependant on the gift, in the manner that an exception is.

If the fœtus have been previously created a Modabbir, the gift is null.—IF a master create the fœtus in the womb of his female slave a Modabbir, and afterwards make a gift of the slave to some person, the gift is not valid: because the child of the said slave still remains his property, and therefore his act of making it Modabbir does not resemble an exception, but rather operates as a total bar to the legality of the gift: for as it is impossible to render the gift valid with respect to the child, because of his being a Modabbir it becomes the same as the gift of an undivided portion, or as the gift of a thing involved with the property of the donor.

The gift of a thing renders all provisional conditions respecting it nugatory—IF a person make a gift of his female slave to another, on condition that he restore her to him, or that he emancipate her, or create her an Am-Walid, or, if a percent make a gift of a house to another, on condition that the donee give back a part of it,—or, if a person make a gift of his house in charity to another on condition that the receiver of the charity give him something in exchange for part of the house,—such gift or charity is valid; but the condition annexed is invalid, because it is contrary to the spirit or intendment of the contract; and neither gifts not charities are affected by being accompanied with an invalid condition, because the Prophet approved of Amrees [gifts for life], but held the condition annexed to them by the granter* to be void—It is otherwise in sale; because the Prophet has prohibited sale with an invalid condition; and also because invalid conditions, as being in the nature of usury manifest their effects in contracts of exchange, but not in such as are not of the description of exchange.

The gift of a debt, by a conditional exemption from it, is null.—IF a person, having a debt due to him of one thousand dirms, should say to the debtor "when to-morrow arrives the said thousand dirms are your property,"—or, "you are exempted from the debt,"—or, if he should say "whenever your pay me one half of the said thousand the other half is your property," or "you are exempted from the debt of the other half,"—the gift so make is null. The reason of

*Namely, the condition of restoration upon the demise of the grantee.

this is that the gift of a debt to a debtor is an exemption: but an exemption has two meanings:—I. It is a conveyance of property, on the principle of debts being property, on which account lawyers have held that "an exemption may be undone by a rejection:"—II. It is an annulment, since debt is in the nature of a quality, on which account an exemption does not rest upon acceptance,—Now nothing can be suspended on a condition excepting an utter annulment, such as a divorce or an emancipation;—and an exemption (as has been already said) is not an utter annulment, and therefore cannot be suspended on a condition, but on the contrary is perfectly nugatory.

Case of life-grants.—An Amree: or life-grant, is lawful to the grantee during his life, and descends to his heirs, because of the tradition before quoted.—Besides, the meaning of Amree ir a gift of a house (for example) during the life of the donee, on condition of its being returned upon his death.—The conveyance of the house, therefore, is valid without any return; and the condition annexed is null, because the Prophet has sanctioned the gift in this instance, and annulled the condition, as before mentioned. An Amree, moreover, is nothing but a gift and a condition; and the condition is invalid; but a gift is not rendered null by involving an invalid condition, as has been already demonstrated.

If one person say to another, "my house is yours by way of Rikba," it is null, according to Haneefa and Mohammed. Aboo Yoosaf has said that it is valid, because his declaration "my house is yours," is a conveyance of the house; and the condition of Rikba is invalid; because the meaning of this phrase is "if I die before you then my house is yours,"—that is to say, he waits in expectation of the other's death, that that the house may revert to himself:—Rikba, therefore, resembles Amree.—The arguments of Haneefa and Mohammed upon this point are twofold,—First, the Prophet has legalized Amree and annulled Rikba.—Secondly, the meaning of "my house is yours by way of Rikba," is "if I die before you, my house is yours," which is a suspension of the conveyance of property upon the decease of the donor previous to that of the donee: and this is a matter of doubt and uncertainty, and consequently null.—It is to be observed that Rikba is derived from In tikab, which means expectation; for the donor is, as it were, an expectant of the death of the donee.

Section.

Of Sadka, or Alms-deed.

Alms-deed requires seisin of the subject.—Alms-deed, like gift, is not valid unless attended with seisin, as it is gratuitious, in the same manner as a gift. Neither is an alms lawful, where it consists of an undivided part of a thing capable of division, for the reasons already explained in the case of a gift under these circumstances.

And cannot be retracted.—Retractation of alms is not lawful; because the object, in alms, is merit in the sight of God, and that has been obtained. If, also a person bestow alms upon a rich man it is not lawful to retract therefrom, on a favourable construction of the law, because to acquire merit in the sight of God may sometimes be the object in bestowing alms upon the rich.—In the same manner also, if a person make a gift of any thing to a poor man, it is not lawful to retract it, because the object in such gift is merit, and that has been obtained.

Distinction between votive vows of Mal and Milk, in alms.—If a person vow to devote his property [Mal] in charity, let him give of that kind on which it is incumbent upon him to pay Zakat.—If, on the other hand, he vow to devote his possessions [Milk], he must give the whole of his property.—It is related that there is no difference between these two cases.—We have, however, in treating of the duties of the Kazee, shown the difference between Mal and Milk; and also the principles on which both these traditions proceed,—It is to be observed that, in this case, the person that made the vow must be told to reserve for himself and his family as much of his property as may suffice for their maintenance until he able to acquire more. The remainder, after such reservation, must be bestowed in charity; and after he has acquired more, he must then give in charity a portion equal to what he had reserved for the subsistence of himself and family.—An explanation of this has already been given in treating of inheritance, under the head of duties of the Kazee.

BOOK XXXI.

OF IJARA, OR HIRE.

Definition of the terms used in hire.—Ijara, in its primitive sense, signifies a sale of usufruct; namely, a sale of certain usufruct for a certain hire, such, as rent or wages In the language of the law it signifies a contract of usufruct for a return.—(Analogy is repugnant to the validity of hire, as the thing contracted for, namely, the usufruct, is a nonentity: and the referring an investiture to a thing which is forthcoming is in valid.—The contract in question is however valid: because mankind stand in need of such contract; and also, because the Prophet has said, "Pay the hireling his wages before the sweat has dried from his brow;" and also, "If a person hire another, let him inform him of the wages he is to receive."—The hirer or the lessee is termed Ajir, or Mawjir; and the lessor, or the person who receives the wages or rent; is denominated the Moostajir,

Chap, I,—Introductory.
Chap. II.—Of the Time when the Hire-may be claimed.
Chap. III.—Of Thinge the Hire of which is unlawful or otherwise;—and of disputed Hire.
Chap. IV.—Of invalid Hire.
Chap. V.—Of the responsibility of a Hireling.
Chap. VI.—Of Hire on one of two Conditions.
Chap, VII.—Of the Hire of Slaves.
Chap. VIII.—Of Disputes between the Hirer and the Hireling.*
Chap. IX.—Of the Dissolution of Hire,

CHAPTER I.

The usufruct and the hire must be particularly specified.—A CONTRACT of hire is not valid unless both the usufruct and the hire† be particularly known and specified, because of the saying of the Prophet, "If a person hire another, let him inform him of the wages he is to receive."

OBJECTION.—It would appear, from that saying, that a knowledge of the hire alone is requisite, not a knowledge of the usufruct.

REPLY.—The usufruct is the subject of the contract, and the hire the thing contracted for.—Now the subject is the principal in a contract, and the thing contracted for the dependant : as therefore a knowledge of the dependant (namely the hire) is requisite, it follows that a knowledge of the principal is requisite a fortori :—consequently a knowledge of the usufruct is established, from the tradition in question, by inference.—and also, because ignorance with respect to the subject of the contract, and the return, tends to excite contention, in the same manner as ignorance with respect to the price and the article in a contract of sale.

The hire (or recompense) may consist of anything capable of being price.—WHATEVER is lawful as a price, is also lawful as a recompense in hire ; because the recompense is a price paid for the usufruct, and is therefore analogous to the price of an article purchased—All articles, moreover, which are incapable of constituting price (like things not of the description of similars, such as a slave, or cloth), are nevertheless a fit recompense in hire, since those constitute a return consisting of PROPERTY.

The extent of the usufruct may be defined by fixing a term—THE extent of usufruct may be defined by fixing a term ; as in the hire of a house for the purpose of residence, or the hire of land for the purpose of cultivation.—A contract of hire, therefore, stipulated for a certain term, to whatever extent, is valid : because, upon the term being known, the extent of the usufruct for that term is also known. This proceeds on a supposition of the use not being various.—Where, however, the uses to which the article is to be applied are various, the usufruct cannot be ascertained by the mere declaration of a term : as in the case, for instance, of hiring ground, for a certain term, for the purpose of cultivation, which contract is invalid unless it express the particular species of cultivation, since some modes of tillage are injurious to the land, and others are not so.—It is to be observed that the expression of our author "for whatever term," denotes that hire is valid, whether it be for a long or a short term, as the term is ascertained, and men, moreover, frequently require a long term, If, however, the Mootwalee [procurator] of a charitable appropriation let out the appropriated article, the hire of it for any long term is made unlawful, lest the lessee might be enabled to advance a claim of right to it.—Hire for a long term, signifies for any term beyond three years This is approved.

Or (in hiring servants, &c.) by specifying the work to be performed.—USUFRUCT may also be ascertained by a specification of work, as where a person hires another to dye or sew clothe for him, or an animal for the purpose of carrying a certain burden, or of riding upon it a certain distance,—because, upon showing the cloth, and mentioning a particular colour, and the degree of the dyeing (such as dipping once or twice, of instance) in the first case,—or explaining the nature of the needlework (such as whether it is to be after the Persian or Turkish fashion) in the second case,—or explaining the weight and nature of the load in the third case,—or the length of the journey in the fourth case,—the usufruct is fully ascertained ; and the contract is consequently valid.—It moreover frequently happens that a contract of hire is a contract for work, as in the case of hiring a fuller or a tailor, where it is requisite that the work be particularly specified, It is also sometimes a contract for usufruct, as in the case of hiring a domestic servant ; and in this case a specification of the term is requisite.

Or by specification and pointed reference.—USUFRUCT may also be ascertained by specification and pointed reference ; as where a person hires another to carry such a particular load to such a particular place ; because, upon seeing the load and the place to which it is to be carried, the service to be performed is precisely ascertiained : and the contract is consequently valid.

---

* The former of these terms is remarkably ambiguous in our language. It sometimes serves to express the person who lets to hire, as we speak of a man who hires horses. For the sake of accuracy, however, the translator has uniformity, in this treatise, employed the word "hirer," to express the person who engages the service of another, or the use of any article, as we commonly mean when we speak of a person who hires a servant, &c.

† Arab. Ujara ; meaning the wages, rent, recompense, &c., according to the subject to which it applies.

CHAPTER II.

OF THE TIME WHEN THE HIRE MAY BE CLAIMED.

Hire can only be claimed in virtue of an agreement, or in consequence of the end of the contract being obtained.—Hire is not due immediately on concluding the contract, but becomes claimable on one of three grounds : for it is claimable in advance, in virtue of a previous agreement —or in advance, independent of such agreement,—or, in consequence of the hirer obtaining the thing contracted for.* Shafei maintain that it becomes a property immediately upon the conclusion of the contract ; because a non-existent usufruct is accounted existent from the necessity of giving validity to the contract ; and consequently the effect (which is right of property) is established with respect to the thing opposed to the usufruct, namely. the consideration or recompense,—The argument of our doctors is that a contract of hire is renewed every instant according to the occurrence of the usufruct, as has been already explained.—Now the contract in question is a contract of exchange, which requires that the consideration and the return be equal. Hence, because of the unavoidable delay attending the usufruct, there must also be a delay with respect to the return for it, namely, the hire ; but upon the usufruct being obtained, a right of property takes place with respect to the hire, in order that equality may be established ;—and so also, where it is stipulated that the hire shall be in advance, or where it is paid in advance ; because equality was required on account of the right of the hirer, who, in this instance, foregoes his right.

The tenant becomes bound for the rent by a delivery of the house, &c , to him.—Upon a tenant taking possession of a house he becomes bound for the rent, although he should not reside therein ; because as it is impossible to make delivery of the usufruct, the delivery of the subject from which the usufruct is derived it a substitute for it ; since in delivering the article an ability to enjoy the usufruct is established.

So long as it is not usurped from him—If, therefore, any person were to usurp the house from the tenant he [the tenant] is no longer responsible for the rent ; because a delivery of the article was admitted to be a substitute for a delivery of the usufruct only, as this enabled the tenant to enjoy the usufruct ; but when the one no longer remains, the other ceases of course ; and as the contract is thereby broken. the rent consequently ceases,—If, also, a person usurp the house at any time before the expiration of the term of the lease, the agent drops in proportion, since the contract is broken in that proportion.

If it be not otherwise specified in the contract, rent may be demanded from day to day.—If a person hire a house, the lessor is at liberty to demand the rent from the tenant from day to day, because the object was daily use, and that has been obtained ; the lessor may therefore insist upon his rent from day to day, unless the time for claiming the rent be specified in the contract, as if that were to express that "the rent shall be paid at such a time"—or, "at the expiration of such a month."—since this amounts to a stipulation of ready payment.—The same rule also obtains with respect to a lease of land, for the same reason.

Or the hire of an animal (upon a journey) from stage to stage.—In the same manner also, if a person hire a camel to Mecca (for instance) the owner is at liberty to insist upon the hire stage by stage. because the object was to travel by stages.—What is here advanced is an opinion which was subsequently adopted by Haneefa. He was at first of opinion that the rent is not due, in the former instance, until the expiration of the term ; nor the hire, in the latter, until the end of the journey (and such is the doctrine of Ziffer) ; because, as the object of the contract is the whole of the usufruct within the time or journey specified, it follows that the hire cannot be separately applied to separate portions of it :—in the same manner as where the object of the contract is labour, by a person hiring a tailor (for instance), to sew his garment.—The reason for the last opinion of Haneefa is that analogy requires that the hire be demanded from instant to instant ; in order that equally may be established. If, however, the demand were admitted every instant, it would follow that the hirer or lessee would be perpetually employed in paying the hire, without leisure to attend to any thing else, which would be highly inconvenient and injurious to him.—For this reason: therefore, the proportion is determined at the rate of one day, in the hire of a house or land,—and at one stage, in the hire of a quadruped.

A workman is not entitled to any thing until his work be finished.—A workman is not at liberty to demand his hire until his work be finished, unless an advance of payment were stipulated ; because some of the work still remains unobtained, whence he is not entitled to his hire.—The some rule also holds if the workman perform his business in the house of his employer ; for in this instance he is not entitled to his hire before his work is finished, since same of his work still remains unobtained. as has been mentioned above—This is what occurs in the Hedaya upon this subject ; and the same is also to be found in the Tijreed.—The compiler of the Maheet and Kadooree likewise mention the same—It is, however, contrary to the Mabsoot, for there it is mentioned that "hire is due in proportion to labour ;" and Timoor Tashee, and others, have thus eexpoundd the law in this particular.—Concerning this case, therefore, there are

*Namely, the usufruct, work, or so forth.

two opinions, as is mentioned in the Jama Ramooz.—If an advance of hire be stipulated in the agreement, the workman is in such case at liberty to require his pay before his work be finished, as a stipulation of this nature, in a contract of hire, is binding.

Case of a baker hired to bake bread.—If a person hire a baker to bake bread in his [the hirer's] house, at the rate of one Kafeez of flour for a dirm, the baker so hired is not entitled to his wages until he draw the bread out of the oven, since until this be done his work is not completed. If, therefore, the bread be burnt, or fall out of his hands, and thus be spoiled, he is not entitled to his hire, because of the destruction of the bread before delivery of it to the hirer—If, on the other hand, he draw the bread out of the oven and it be afterwards burnt or otherwise destroyed, without his act, he is entitled to his hire, because he has made a due delivery of it to the hirer, in virtue of having deposited it in his house; neither is he, in this instance, liable to make any compensation, as he has not been guilty of any transgression.—The compiler of the Hedaya remarks that this is according to Haneefa, proceeding on the idea that the bread is a trust in the baker's hands;—but that the two disciples maintain that the hirer has it in his option to exact a compensation for the value of the flour only; and that in this case he is not to pay the baker any part of his hire, since (as they hold) the bread is insured with the baker, whence he is not exempted from responsibility until he duly deliver it to the hirer:—or, if he please, he may exact a compensation for the bread, paying the hire for the baking.

And of a cook.—If a person hire a cook to prepare an entertainment, he [the cook] must also dish the meat, as this is customary.

And of a brickmaker.—If a person hire another to make him a certain quantity of bricks, he [the brickmaker] is entitled to his hire when he sets up the bricks,* according to Haneefa.—The two disciples hold that he is not entitled to his hire until he collect the bricks together and build them up, because it is this which completes his work, since bricks are not secured from injury until they be so collected and built up—the collecting them together, therefore, is analogous to drawing bread out of the oven.—Besides, this is what is always customary with persons hired for such work; and custom is regarded in every matter concerning which we have no express ordinance.—The argument of Haneefa is that the work is completely finished by setting up the bricks, the collecting them together and stacking them being an extra business, in the same manner as removal from one place to another; and accordingly people take bricks, to build with, from the place where they have been set up, without waiting for the stacking of them.—It is otherwise before they are set up, since the clay is not then hardened: and it is also otherwise with bread, as the use of that cannot be obtained until it be drawn out of the oven.

The article wrought upon may be detained by the workman until he be paid his hire.—Every artificer whose work produce a visible effect upon an article (such as a dyer or fuller) is at liberty to detain such article until he receive his hire; because in this instance the subject of the contract is descriptively existent in the article, whence he is allowed to detain it with a view to receiving the return for such subject, in the same manner as if it were an article of sale;—in other words, as the seller is allowed to detain the article sole until he receive the price, so also in the case in question.

And he is not responsible, in case of accidents, during such detention.—If, therefore, a dyer or fuller detain cloth for the purpose of being paid his hire and the cloth perish in his hands he is not responsible, according to Haneefa, inasmuch as he has not transgressed in so detaining it, the cloth remaining as a deposit with him after detention, in the same manner as before.—He is not, however, in this case entitled to any hire, because of the subject of the contract perishing before delivery;—The two disciples hold that the cloth is a subject of responsibility before detention, and so also after detention: but that the owner of the cloth has it at his option either to take a compensation for the value of the cloth as it stood before the fulling or dyeing,—in which case the workman is not entitled to any pay—or to take a compensation for the value of it as it stood after the work,—in which case the workman is entitled to his hire.—This shall be more fully explained hereafter.

If the work be of a nature not to produce any visible effect in the article, it cannot be detained.—A workman, the effect of whose labour is not visibly extant in an article (such as a boatman, or a porter), is not at liberty to detain the article with a view to receiving the hire; because, in this instance, the subject of the contract is merely labour, which is in no manner existent in the article conveyed or carried:—and the washing or bleaching of cloth is analogous to the porterage of it in this particular. From this analogy in regard to washing or bleaching it may be inferred that the term fuller [Kissar] in the preceding example, applies solely to one who uses starch, or such other material; but, that where such a person, in cleaning cloth, makes use of things of no estimable value, such as water and sunshine, he has no right of detention, since in such case nothing remains that can be termed an effect from his labour, the whiteness being

* The case here considered has a reference to the various stages of brick-making, and relates merely to sun-dried bricks, the burning being a different trade.—The bricks are first molded; then, when half dried, set up on end; and when completely dried, built into stacks for use.

an original quality inherent in the cloth. Kazee Khan says, that if a fuller wash cloth, and an effect be produced from his work by means of starch (for instance), he has a right of detention; but that if he merely whiten the cloth, there is in that case a difference of opinion. The approved doctrine, however; is that he has a right of detention in either case; because the whiteness was a quality concealed in the cloth, and brought forth by his labour. This is different from the case of a fugitive slave; for the restorer is entitled to detain a fugitive slave with a view to his reward, notwithstanding there be no visible effect produced in the slave; the reason of which is, that the slave was in danger of being altogether lost, and was preserved only by the restorer bringing him back; whence he may be said to sell the slave to his owner, and consequently, that he has a right of detention. What is here advanced is according to our three doctors. Ziffer maintains that a workman possesses no right of detention in either case; that is, whether the effect be existent in the article, or otherwise;—because, where his work is attended with an effect existent in the article he has already made a delivery of the same to the hirer, as having blended it with his property; and a right of detention necessarily ceases upon delivery. Our doctors, on the other hand, argue that the workman, in blending the effect of his work with the hirer's property, has acted merely from necessity, since unless he were so to do it would be impossible to perform the work. This implication, therefore, does not infer that the workman intends or designs a delivery; and hence his right to detention does not cease; in the same manner as where, in a sale, the purchaser takes possession of the merchandise without the seller's consent: in which case the seller's right of detention with a view to receiving the price, does not ceases; and so also in the case in question.

A workman, if the contract be restricted to his work, cannot employ any other person.—If the hirer stipulate with the workman that he shall himself perform the work, he [the workman] is not at liberty to employ any other person; because the subject of the contract is the work of this person and not of any other, and therefore the right of the hirer is connected with his work in particular, in the same manner as the right of the person who hires a place or an article is connected with the use of that particular place or article. If, on the other hand, the work be absolute, without any stipulation that the workman shall himself perform it (as if a person were to say to a tailor "Make up this garment") the workman is at liberty to hire any other person to perform the work, as the right of the hirer, in this instance, is merely to tailor's work, which may be performed either by this or by any other tailor: in the same manner as the payment of a debt, which may be made either by the debtor himself, or by any other person.

Section

Cases in which (from an unavoidable accident) the contract cannot be completely fulfilled.—If a person hire another to go to Basra, and bring his family thence, and this person accordingly go to Basra, and there find some of the family dead, and bring away the remainder, he is entitled to his whole hire for the journey to Basra, and to a hire for returning back in proportion to the number he brings with him; because, as he has performed a part of his contract, and not the whole, it follows that he is entitled to an equivalent for what he performs, and that his right is annulled in proportion to what he does not perform. The compiler of the Hedaya remarks that this proceeds upon a supposition of the number of the family being greviously ascertained, so as to oppose the hire agreed upon to the whole; for otherwise the whole hire is due. This rule, moreover, obtains only where the expenses of the remainder are materially lessened by the death of some; for if the expense of the whole be not thereby diminished (as where those who died were not grown up, but yet able to travel on foot), the person in question is still entitled to his whole hire.

If a person hire another to carry a letter to Basra and bring back an answer, and he accordingly go to Basra, and there find the person dead, to whom the letter is addressed, and come back and return the letter, he is not entitled to any wages whatever. This is according to the two disciples. Mohammed maintains, that he is to receive the usual hire for going to Basra, since in so doing he has performed a part of the contract, namely, the journey; the reason of which is that the hire or recompense is in lieu of the journey, as it is that which is attended with labour, not the carriage of the letter. The argument of the two disciples is, that the carriage of the letter is the thing contracted for; either because that is the design (the letter being intended as a compliment to the person to whom it is addressed), or because the carriage of the letter is a means of accomplishing the design of it, namely, a communication of its contents. The title to wages, therefore, depends upon the carriage of the letter; but, upon the messenger returning the letter; the contract is broken, an his claim to wages consequently ceases;—in the same manner as in the next following example concerning wheat. If, however, in the case in question, the messenger leave the letter at Basra, and return, he is entitled to a hire for the journey thither, according to all our doctors, since what was contracted for has been in part performed in this instance

If a person hire another to carry wheat to a certain person at Basra, and he accordingly carry the wheat to Basra, and then find the person dead to whom it was consigned, and he bring back and return the wheat to the hirer, he is not entitled to any thing whatever, according to all our doctors, as he has failed in the performance of what he had contracted for. It is otherwise (according to Mohammed) in the case of the letter, because in that case (agreeably to his tenets) the journey was the thing contracted for, as has been already explained.

CHAPTER III.

OF THINGS THE HIRE OF WHICH IS UNLAWFUL OR OTHERWISE; AND OF DISPUTED HIRE.

A house or shop may be hired without specifying the particular business to be carried on in it.—IT is lawful to hire a house or shop for the purpose of residence, although no mention be made of the business to be followed in it; because, as the ostensible purpose to which it is to be applied is residence, this must be taken for granted: and residence does not admit of various descriptions. The contract in question is therefore valid: and the lessee is at liberty to carry on in the place any business he pleases, as the case is absolute.

Unless it be of a nature injurious to the building.—A BLACKSMITH, however, or a fuller or miller must not reside in the house, as this would be evidently injurious, since the exercise of those trades would shake the building. Although, therefore, the contract in question be absolute, still it is virtually restricted to what may not be injurious to the building.

In a lease of land, the renter is entitled to the use of road and water.—IT is lawful to hire land for the purpose of cultivation, as this is the use to which land is commonly applied. In this case also, the hirer is entitled to the use of the road leading to the hand, and likewise to the water (that is, to his turn of watering) although no mention of these be made in the contract; because land is hired with a view to the use of it, which cannot be obtained without a right to road and water:—both are therefore included, although no mention of them be made at the time of concluding the contract:—in opposition to a case of sale; for in that instance a right to road and water is not included unless particularly specified, the end of sale being appropriation, not present use; whence it is that it is lawful to sell an ass's colt, or saltpetre grounds, but not to hire them.

But the lease is not valid, unless the use to which it is to be applied be specified.—A LEASE of land is not valid unless mention be made of the article to be raised in it, because land is hired, not only with a view to cultivation, but also for other purposes, such as building, and so forth; moreover, the articles sown in the land may be of different qualities since some vegetables come quickly to maturity, whilst others are slower of growth. It is therefore requisite that the article be specified, to avoid disputes between the lessor and lessee; or, that the lessor declare "I let the land on this condition, that the lessee shall raise whatever he pleases in it," in which case, as the lessor expressly leaves the lessee at full liberty, the uncertainty which might occasion a dispute is removed.

At the expiration of the lease, the land must be restored in its original state.—IF person hire unoccupied land, for the purpose of building or planting, it is lawful, since these are purpose to which land is applied. Afterwards, however, upon the term of the lease expiring, it is incumbent on the lessee to remove his buildings of trees, and to restore the land to the lessor in such a state as may leave him no claim upon it, becauses houses or trees have no specific limit of existence, and if they were left upon the land it might be injurious to the proprietor. It is otherwise where land is hired for the purpose of tillage, and the term of the lease expires at a time when the grain is yet unripe; for in such case the grain must be suffered to remain upon the land, at a proportionable rent, until it be fit for reaping, because, as the time that may require is limited and ascertainable, it is possible to attend to the right of both parties. In the case, on the contrary, of trees or buildings, it is impossible to pay attention to the right of both parties; and it is therefore incumbent on the lessee to remove his trees or houses from the land;—unless the proprietor of the soil agree to pay him an equivalent, in which case the right of property in them devolves to him (still, however, this cannot be, without the consent of the owner of the houses or trees; except where the land is liable to sustain an injury from the removal, in which case the proprietor of the land is at liberty to give an equivalent, and appropriate the trees or houses without the lessee's consent);—or unless the proprietor of the land assent to the trees or houses remaining there, in which case they continue to appertain to the lessee, and the land to the landlord; for as the right of removing them belongs to the landlord he is at liberty to forego that right. It is written in the Jama Sagheer that if the term of the lease be expired' and the land be occupied by pulse or other garden stuffs, those must be removed; because as those have no fixed term of existence, they are therefore analogous to trees.

An absolute contract leave the hirer at liberty to give the use to any person.—THE hire of an animal is lawful, either for carriage or for riding, as to those uses animals are applied. If, therefore, the riding be absolutely expressed, the hirer is at liberty to permit any person he pleases to ride upon the animal, because of the riding being contracted for in an absolute manner. Upon the hirer, however, either mounting the animal himself, or admitted another to ride on it, he is not at libery to ses any person on it besides, because the actual object of the contract is then ascertained and determined. Men, moreover, differ in their mode of riding, whence it in fact becomes the sams as if the particulars of the riding had been expressly stipulated in the contract. In the same manner also, if a person hire a dress for the purpose of wearing it unrestrictedly, and in an absolute manner, he is at liberty either to wear it himself, or to give it to any other person to wear: but upon putting it on himself, or permitting another so to do, he is not at liberty to clothe any one in it besides.

But in a restricted contract, any deviation with respect to the use renders the hires responsible for the article hired.—If a person let a quadruped to hire, on condition that a particular person shall ride upon it, or let a dress to hire, on condition that a particular person shall wear it,—and the hirer set upon the quadruped some other than the person specified, or give the dress to some other person to wear, and the quadruped or dress be destroyed, he [the hirer] is responsible; because, as men differ in their manner of riding, and of wearing clothes, the specification of a particular person is valid, and consequently it is not lawful for the hirer to swerve therefrom. The same rule also obtains with respect to every thing liable to be differently affected by a different occupant: in other words, if the person who lets to hire restrict the use, it is restricted accordingly; and if the hirer swerve therefrom, he is responsible in case of the destruction of the article, for the reason above stated.

Unless that be of a nature not liable to injury from such deviation.—Land, however, and every other article not liable to be differently affected by a different occupant (such as a tent or pavilion), is not restricted in point of use by the mention of a particular person; and consequently, the hirer is at liberty to put any one to reside in it that he pleases, since the exclusive restriction is of use only because of its preventing a difference of effect. But the residence of persons whose business is of injurious tendency to a building (such as blacksmiths, and so forth), is always excepted from the contract, as was before explained.

Or, unless the deviation be not of a nature to injure the article.—If a person hire an animal to carry a burden, and the person who lets it to hire specify the nature and quantity of the article with which the hirer is to load the animal,—as if he were to say, for instance, "You shall load it with five Kafeezs of wheat"—the hirer is in this case at liberty to load the animal with an equal quantity of any article not more troublesome or prejudicial in the carriage than wheat, such as barley, or ape-seed, as all articles of that description are included in the permission contained in the contract, because of their not occasioning and difference, or because they may be even preferable to what was specified in it, as being less prejudicial. The hirer, however, is not at liberty to load the animal with any article of a more prejudicial nature, in the carriage, than wheat (such as salt, for instance), since to this the lessor had not assented.

If a person hire an animal th carry a certain quantity of cotton, he is not at liberty to load the animal with a similar quantity of iron, since it is highly probable that the carriage of the iron may be more prejudicial to the animal than the carriage of the cotton, for this reason, that the iron presses chiefly on one spot of the creature's back, whereas the cotton presses on it equally in all parts.

An excess in the use induces a proportionable responsibility in case of accident.—If a person hire an animal to carry a certain quantity of wheat, and load it with a greater quantity, and the animal perish, he is responsible in the proportion of the excess load Thus a person, for instance, hires an animal to carry ten Kafeezs of wheat, and loads him with fifteen Kafeezs, and the animal perishes:—in which case he is responsible for one third of the value of the animal. The reason of this is that the animal in question has perished in consequence both of what has been permitted to the hirer, and also, of what has not heen permitted; as, therefore, the destruction has been occasioned by the whole burden, it is divided between both parts respectively; and accordingly, nothing is accounted upon the proportion allowed, but an indemenification is due upon the proportion unallowed. If, however, the hirer had overloaded the animal to a degree beyond what it was able to bear, he is, in this case, responsible for the whole of the value, since he was utterly unauthorized to act thus, as it is altogether unusual to do so.

A rider, taking up an additional rider, incurs responsibility for half the value of the animal.—If a person hire an animal for his own riding, and he take up another person behind him upon the animal, and the animal perish, he is responsible for one half of the value.—No regard is paid to the load in this instance, because a person who does not understand riding will hurt an animal's back, although he be of light weight, as, on the contrary, a complete rider sits right on horseback, although his person be heavy.—Besides, a man is not an article of weight, whence his weight cannot be ascertained; and accordingly regard must be paid to the number of the riders, in the same manner as, in offences against the person, regard is paid to the number of the offenders;—in other words; if one person accidentally give another ten wounds, and a second person give him one wound, and the wounded person die, the fine of blood is due from both in equal shares —What is here advanced proceeds on a supposition of the animal in question being capable of carrying double: for if it be incapable of carrying double, the hirer is responsible for the whole value, in the same manner as in the case of wheat.—It is also to be observed that, in the same manner as this rule applies to adults, so does it likewise to infants capable of riding alone upon an animal: but if the hirer place behind him an infant incapable of riding alone, it is the same as goods or effects, and he is, in such case, responsible only in proportion to the additional load.

An hired animal perishing from ill usage subjects the hirer to responsibility.—IF a person hire an animal for riding, and pull the halter, or beat the animal, so as to occasion its death, he is responsible for the whole value, according to Haneefa. The two disciples maintain that he is not responsible where he only pulls the halter or beats the animal in such a degree as is customary, since every thing customary is included in the contract, and therefore the case is the same as if he were to perform those acts by express permission of the owner, whence he is not responsible.—The argument of Haneefa is that the owner's permission is restricted to the condition of safety, since an animal may be driven without either pulling the halter or beating it, both of these being an excessive and unnecessary exertion: the use, therefore, is restricted to the condition of safety, in the same manner as the travelling upon the public highway.

In the hire or loan of animals, responsibility is induced by any deviation from the prescribed journey.—IF a person hire an animal to carry him to a particular place (Medina, for instance), and he go out of his way, and proceed to another place, and then return with the animal to Medina, and it die, he is responsible for it. The same rule also holds with respect to an animal lent.—Some have said that this example proceeds upon a supposition of the animal being hired merely to go to Medina (not to go and return), in which case the hirer is not, in fact, required to restore it to the owner: but that where it is hired for the purpose both of going and coming, the hirer is in the same predicament with a trustee who first swerves from the terms of his trust, and afterwards accords to them, in which case he is not responsible for the deposit in his hands.—Others, again, say that the rule is absolute; and consequently that responsibility attaches in either case: for there is an essential difference between a hirer or borrower, and a trustee; because the trustee is directed to keep the deposit, independently, and consequently the order of conservation still remains in force after the trustee ceases from his deviation and reconforms to the terms of trust, whence he reverts to his situation of representative of the owner: whereas, in a case of hire or loan, the hirer or borrower are directed to keep the article dependently of the use, and not independently; and consequently, upon the use ceasing, they no longer continue representatives of the owner; whence they are not discharged from responsibility by their return to Medina.—This is approved.

The change of a saddle for another of the same sort does not induce responsibility.—IF a person hire an ass with its saddle, and fasten upon it another saddle, of the same sort as is commonly used upon such an ass, he is not responsible if the ass perish; because where the saddle is proportionate to the animal, the owner's assent extends to it, as the restriction is advantageous only in case of the other saddle being heavier than the one specified in the contract, when, if the ass were to perish, the hirer would be responsible in proportion to the difference.

Unless the weight be different, when responsibility attaches in proportion to the excess.—IF, on the contrary, the hirer were to fasten upon the ass a saddle of a sort not commonly used upon such an ass, he is responsible for the whole value; for as this is not included in the lessor's assent, it follows that the hirer, in so doing, acts contrary to engagement.

If the nature of the saddle be different, responsibility attaches in toto—IF a person hire an ass with its saddle, and fasten upon the ass a pack-saddle, of a sort not commonly put upon such an ass, he is in this case responsible for the whole value of the animal for the reason alleged in the example of the saddle; nay, the obligation rests upon him in this case, a fortiori, since a pack-saddle or panniers are not of the same nature as a riding-saddle, and are, moreover, heavier. If, also, he fasten upon the ass a pack-saddle of a sort commonly used upon such an ass, he is responsible for the whole value, according to Haneefa.—The two disciples allege that, in this instance, he is responsible only in proportion as the load of the pack-saddle exceeds that of the riding-saddle; because, where the pack-saddle is of a sort commonly put upon such an ass, it follows that the riding-saddle and the pack-saddle are equal, and consequently that the owner of the ass assents,—except the latter exceed the former in weight, in which case the hirer is responsible in proportion to the excess of weight, as to that the owner is not assenting.—The excess, therefore, in this instance, is analogous to a case where the person who lets out an animal to hire specifies the quantity of wheat he is to carry, and the hirer loads it with a larger quantity.—The argument of Haneefa is that a pack-saddle is not in the nature of a common saddle:—it is not so in appearance, since it is more spread upon the animal on one side than on the other;* nor is it so in reality, since a pack-saddle is for carrying burdens, whereas a common saddle is for riding.—The hires, therefore, in fastening a pack-saddle upon the ass, acts contrary to his engagement with the owner, in the same manner as a

* This alludes to the particular fashion of the Palan, or Persian pack-saddle, with which the translator is unacquainted.

person who hires an animal to carry wheat, and loads it with iron.

A porter is not made responsible by any immaterial deviation from the prescribed road.—IF a person hire a porter to carry a load of wheat to a certain place, by a particular road, and he take another frequented road, and the wheat be lost, he is not responsible; and if he carry the wheat safe to the place, he is entitled to his hire.—This proceeds upon the supposition that the roads are not widely different, for in this case the restriction to either in particular is useless.—Where, however, the roads are widely different, that taken by the porter being dangerous or round about, or of difficult passage, the porter is responsible in case of the wheat being lost, since the restriction is of use in this instance, and therefore, valid.—It is to be observed that Mohammed does not make this distinction, but alleges that the porter is not responsible if he carry his load by any other than the road specified, provided it be one commonly used; because, where it is a beatan path, there is no apparent difference between the two.—If, on the contrary, he carry the load by an unrequented road, and it be lost, he is responsible for the value, as the restriction is valid, and the porter acted contrary to his instructions.—If, however, in this case, he carry the wheat safe to the place, he is entitled to his hire; because upon so doing his deviatation from his orders is rectified, and the end is obtained.

Any injurious deviation from the prescribed culture of hired land induces a proportionable responsibility—IF a person hire land for the cultivation of wheat, and sow therein trefoils or clover, he is responsible in proportion to the damage the land sustains, because the cultivation of any species of grass* is more injurious to the land than the cultivation of wheat, as those require more water, and their roots spread more in the ground.—In this instance, therefore, the lessee has acted contrary to his agreement with the lessor, inasmuch as he had done a thing more injurious to the land than what the lessor had specified. But if the lessor require this compensation, he is not entitled to any rent, as the lessee in that case stands as an usurper, because of his acting contrary to engagement, as before explained.

A tailor is responsible for deviating from his orders.—IF a person deliver a piece of cloth to a tailor, directing him to make it into a Peerahin, or shirt, for a particular hire and he make it into a Kabba, or short vest, the person has it in his option either to take a compensation from the tailor for his cloth, or to receive the Kabba, paying him an adequate hire, which, however, is not to exceed what had been at first agreed upon.—This is according to the Zahir Rawayet.—Some have said that the Peerahin is merely a Kabba, or vest, of one fold.—Others, again, say that the Peerahin is not particularly restricted to vest of one fold, as both are used indiscriminately at all seasons.—It is reported from Haneefa, that the proprietor of the cloth is to take a compensation from the tailor, and that he has no option of any thing else; because as the Kabba is a species of apparel totally different from the Peerahin, the tailor stands in the predicament of an usurper.—The reasons of the doctrine, as reported from the Zahir Rawayet, is that the Kabba is in one shape a Peerahin, as it is occasionally used instead of the Peerahin, and in another view it is not so.—Hence there is both a similitude and a dissimilitude; and accordingly the proprietor of the cloth has it at his option to take a compensation for the value (in which case the cloth becomes the property of the tailor), or, to take the Kabba, paying an adequate hire:—an adequate hire only is due, because the tailor has not completely fulfilled his agreement; and it must not exceed what was at first agreed upon, as obtains all cases of invalid hire.

IF a person deliver a price of cloth to a tailor, directing him to make it into a Kabba, and he make it into a Shilwar, or drawers, some allege that the proprietor must accept a compensation; and that he has no other option because of the different uses to which those two sorts of apparel are applied.—It is certain, however, that the proprietor has it at his option, in this instance, either to take a compensation for the value of his cloth, or to take the Shilwar, paying an adequate hire; because the use, namely, clothing and covering nakedness, is the same in both; and the case is therefore analogous to where a person orders a brazier to 'make him a dish of this brass, and the brazier makes him a brazen plate, in which instance the proprietor of the brass has an option, and so also in the case in question.

CHAPTER IV.

OF INVALID HIRE,

In invalid condition invalidates hire.—HIRE is rendered invalid by involving an invalid condition, in the same manner as sale, for hire stands in the place of sale, whence it is that a contract of hire may be dissolved in the same manner as a contract of sale.

But a proportionate hire is in much case due, to the extent of the hire specified.—IN a case of hire rendered invalid by involving an invalid condition, a proportionate hire is due where that does not exceed the hire, specified in the contract,—in othre words, of the specified hire and the proportionate hire, the smallest is due.—Ziffer maintains that

*The term, in the original, is Katba, which applies to all the more succulent species of field herbage.

a proportionate hire is due, to whatever amount it may extend; for he conceives an analogy between the case in question and a case of invalid sale, in which the value of the article is due, to whatever amount.—The argument of our doctors is that usufruct cannot be appreciated but by a contract entered into to answer the necessity of mankind, whence, in valid hire, the degree is measured by the necessity.—As, however, invalid hire is a dependant of a contract of valid hire, it has a relation to a valid contract, and consequently regard is paid in it to what may be the customary recompense in valid hire, which is a proportionate hire.—Now the parties, in a case of invalid hire, having agreed upon a specific amount, it follows that both, in making such specification agreed to remit whatever may be beyond the specified hire, where that is exceeded by the proprotionate hire; in this case, therefore, the specified hire; is due:—but if, on the other hand, the proportionate hire fall short of the specified hire, the excess of the specified hire is not due, as the specification itself was invalid.—It is otherwise in an invalid sale, for as an article of sale is appreciable to its extent, there is no necessity for a regard to the contract in order to manifest its value. Now this value is the original thing: if, therefore, the specification of a price be valid (as in a case of valid sale), the effect passes from the original thing to the said price; but if, on the contrary, the specification of a price be invalid (as in a case of invalid sale), the effect does not pass from the original thing to the price.

A contract indefinitely expressed closes at the expiration of the first term.—If a person hire a house, on a condition thus expressed, that "he shall pay one dirm every month," such contract is valid for one month, but invalid for every subsequent month, unless the whole of the months for which it is to be hired be specified, in which case it continue valid.—The arguments on which this is founded are drawn from the construction of the words in the Arabic idiom.—It is to be observed that as the contract in question is valid for one month only, it belongs to both the lesser and lessee, respectively, to dissolve the contract at the end of the month, as the valid contract is then complete and finished.—If, therefore, in this instance, the lessee, after the expiration of the said month, continue in the house for a single instant of the second, the contract remains in force for the second month, nor is the lessor at liberty to put out the lessee until the end of this month (and the same rule holds with respect to every month in the beginning of which the lessee continues to occupy the house); because the contract appears to be renewed, with the consent of both parties, in virtue of the lessee still continuing to occupy the house in the succeeding month.—This, however, proceeds merely upon analogy; and has been adopted by some of our modern doctors.—According to the Zahir Rawayet, an option of dissolution remains in the next month, to either party, to the end of the first day of the month; for in having regard to the very first instant only of that month, a restriction is induced so narrow as not to admit the exercise of an option.

Rules with respect to annual leases.—IF a person hire a house for a year, at the rate of twelve dirms, it is lawful, although no mention is made of the rent of each month respectively; because, as the whole term of the lease is known without division, it is therefore the same as hiring for a single month, which is lawful, although no mention be made of the rent of each day respectively.—It is to be observed that if the day of the year's commencement be specified (as if the lessee were to say, "I take this house, for a year, from the first of the month Rajab"), the lease commences from that date.—If, on the contrary, no date of commencement be specified, the lease commences from the date of the deed itself; because all dates are equal with respect to hire, and therefore a lease in this particular resembles a vow; in other words, if a person make a vow that "he will not speak (for instance) to a particular person for one month," the observance of his vow commences upon the instand of expressing it, all dates being equal with respect to vows; and so also in the case in question.—It is also to be observed, that if in this instance, the contract of hire be concluded on the first day of the month, all the succeeding months of the year are counted from the appearance of the new moon as this is the original standard of calculation.—If, on the contrary, the contract be concluded after the lapse of some days from the commencement of a month, the lease is in that case for three hundred and sixty days, according to Haneefa; and there is one report from Aboo Yoosaf to the same effect.—According to Mohammed, and another report of Aboo Yoosaf, the first month is to be counted by days, to be completed from the next succeeding month; and the other months must be counted from the appearance of each new moon: because a calculation by the number of days is admitted purely from necessity which exists in the first month only.—The argument of Haneefa is that upon the first month being completed by the deduction of a certain number of days from the second, that also must, from necessity, be counted by days; and so of the rest to the end of the year;—in the same manner as obtains with respect to the Edit;—that is to say, if a divorce take place in the middle of a month, it must be counted by days, and so also in the present instance.

Wages are due to keepers of baths and cuppers.—KEEPERS of baths and cuppers are lawfully entitled to wages:—the former because it is an invariable custom, among all Mussullmans, to pay them wages, and the Prophet has said. Whatever seems good unto the body of the MUSSULMANS is also good before God;"—and the latter, because the Prophet paid a recompense to a person who performed the operation of cupping upon him: and also, because this is a certain recompense for a certain service, and is therefore lawful.

But there is no hire for the covering of mares, &c.—There are no wages for the covering of animals,—that is, for bringing a male to copulate with a female: because the Prophet has said, "Assib-tees is among the things prohibited;" and by Assib-tees is understood the recompense for the copulation of a stallion, or so forth.

Nor for the performance of any religious duty.—It is not lawful to accept a recompense for summoning the people to prayers, or for the performance of a pilgrimage, or of the duties of an Imam, or for teaching the Koran, or the law; for it is a general rule, with our doctors, that no recompense can be received for the performance of any duty purely of a religious nature.—According to Shafei, it is allowed to receive pay for the performance of any religious duty which is not required of the hireling in virtue of a divine ordinance, as this is only accepting recompense for a certain service; and as the acts above described are not ordained upon the hireling, it is consequently lawful to receive a recompense for them.—The arguments of our doctors upon this point are twofold—First the Prophet has said, "Read the Koran, but do not receive any recompense for so doing:", and he also directed Othman-bin-Abeeyas, that if he were appointed a Mawzin [a cryer to prayer] he should not take any wages. Secondly, where an act of piety is performed, it springs solely from the performer (whence regard is had to his competency), and consequently he is not entitled to any recompense from another, as in the cases of fasting or prayer.—A teacher of the Koran, moreover, is incapable of instructing another in it, but by means of qualities existing in his scholar, namely; capacity and docility, and therefore undertakes a thing the performance of which does not depend upon himself which is consequently invalid.—Some of our modern doctors, however, hold it lawful to receive wages for teaching the Koran in the present age, because an indifference has taken place with respect to religion, whence if people were to withhold from paying a recompense for instruction in the sacred writings, they would in time be disregarded;—and decree pass accordingly.

Nor for singing or lamentation.—It is not lawful to receive wages for singing or lamentation * or for any other species of public exhibition, as this is taking a recompense for an act which is of a criminal nature, and acts of that nature do not entitle to a recompense in virtue of contract.

Hire of Indefinite articles.—The hire of any thing indefinite is invalid, according to Haneefa, unless from a partner.—The two disciples maintain that such hire is valid;—and decrees pass accordingly.—(This rule chiefly applies to such cases as where, for instance, a person lets a share or portion of his house to another, or lets his own share in a partnership-house to any other than his partner).—The argument of the two disciples is that an indefinite part is capable of being used (whence a proportionate hire is due), and the delivery of it is practicable, either by the lessor vacating his share to the lessee, or by agreeing to hold it with him alternately.—The case is therefore the same as if he were to let it to a partner, or between two, which would be valid: consequently this resembles a case of sale.—The argument of Haneefa is that as the lessor, in this instance, lets to hire an article which he is incapable of delivering, the deed is consequently invalid.—The ground of this is that the delivery of an indefinite part of any thing is inconceivable; because delivery cannot be completely executed on one part without seisin on the other; and seisin, as being a perceptible act, cannot take place but upon a specific subject.—With respect to execution, it is regarded as a delivery, because it amounts to investiture, an act through which occupancy, or, in other words, a power of seisin, is obtained. With respect to alternate occupancy, on the other hand, that cannot be established but in virtue of a right of property in the use, which is an effect of the contract of hire. Now as the effect of any thing must be subsequent to that thing, it follows that the alternate occupancy is subsequent to the execution of the contract of hire: but ability to make delivery is one condition of the contract; and as the condition to a thing must precede that thing, it follows that the ability to make a delivery must precede the contract of hire. A thing, however, which is subsequent cannot be considered as antecedent; and hence the alternate occupancy, which is subsequent, is incapable of being accounted a delivery.—Where, on the contrary, the lease is to a partner, the whole use arising from the article become, the property of the lessee, and consequently no part of what he holds can be termed indefinite: neither is the difference in the nature of the usufruct (from part of it being in virtue of right of property, and part of it in virtue of a lease) injurious to the lessee in this instance.—Besides, the hire of an indefinite subject is unlawful from a partner also (according to an opinion of Haneefa, as reported by Hasan).—It is otherwise in a case of supervenient indefiniteness, as that does not occasion contention. (A supervenient indefiniteness is where a person lets an article to two persons, and one of the lessees dies,—or where two persons let an article to one person, and one of the lessors dies,—in which case the lease continues in force with

---

* Arab, Nooha, Crying over the dead (by female mourners, who make it a profession).

respect to the other's share, indefinitely, and does not become invalid, according to the Zahir Rawayet, for this reason, that ability to make delivery is not a condition merely because of the contract, but because of the obligation of delivery,—which obligation exists in the beginning, not afterwards whence the ability of delivery is not a condition in the continuance) It is also otherwise where an article is let to two persons, because in this instance a delivery of the whole is established, after which an indefinite division supervenes, because of the right of property of each party being separate.

Hire of a nurse.—It is lawful to hire a nurse to suckle a child, at a certain rate of wages: because God has said in the Koran, "IF THEY SUCKLE YOUR CHILDREN, PAY THEM THEIR HIRE;" and also, because, in the time of the Prophet, such was the practice, and likewise both before and since his time,—Some have said that the contract of hire, in the case in question, is a contract for serving the infant, the particulars of such service (namely, attendance and milk) following as dependants, in the same manner as the colour in a contract for dying cloth (Others maintain that the contract is a contract for the milk, the attendance following as a dependant: and accordingly, if a goat be hired to give milk to an infant, no recompense is due.—The former opinion, however, is more conformable to LAW; because contracts of hire are not concluded for destruction or expenditure of an actually existent article; as where, for instance, a person hires a cow for the purpose of using her milk, which is invalid, as shall be shortly shown to its proper place.)—Such, therefore, being the case, the contract in question is valid, provided the rate of hire be specified, considering it as hiring a person for the sake of her attendance.

It is lawful to hire a nurse to suckle an infant in return for meat and clothing, on a favourable construction, according to Haneefa.—The two disciples maintain that this is not lawful, because as the recompense is indeterminate and unknown, the case is therefore the same as if a woman were hired to bake bread, or so forth, in return for her meat and clothing.—The argument of Haneefa is that the indeterminateness in question is not likely to engender strife, since it is customary to feed nurses in a liberal manner, with a view to render them kind and tender to the children under their care.—This case; therefore, resembls the selling of a measure of wheat out of a heap, which is lawful, although the seller be at liberty to give the wheat from whatever part of the heap he pleases, as an ignorance in that particular does not engender strife.—It is otherwise in the case of hiring a woman to bake bread, or the like, because an ignorance in that instance is calculated to occasion contention.—What is here advanced proceeds upon a supposition that no explanation has been given concerning the quantity or quality of the food and clothing agreed for to the purse,—It is written in the Jama Sagheer that if a nurse be hired to suckle a child for her victuals and clothing,—in this way, that an explanation be given of the kind and fashion of her apparel, and the time of giving it, and a specific number of dirms appointed for her board,—and victuals be afterwatds given in lieu of the money, it is lawful according to all, because in this case there is no ignorance.—Or, if the victuals be specified, and the quantity and quality explained, this also is lawful, for the same reason; and in this instance it is not requisite that any time be fixed for giving the victuals because articles of weight, and measurement of capacity, when described, become a debt, and a debt is sometimes prompt and sometimes deferred, like price, which consists of money,—It is, however, a condition, with Haneefa, that an explanation be given of the place where the victuals are to be delivered in case of any expense (of porterage, and so forth) attending it.—The two disciples, on the contrary, maintain that this is not a condition, as has been fully stated under the head of Sale.—It is otherwise with respect to apparel: for in that instance an explanation is requisite, not only of the place, but also of the time of delivery, as well as of the quantity; becouse clothing is not construed to be a debt except in a case of Sillim sale: and as, in that instance, a prompt payment is requisite, so also where the nurse is hired for a recompense in clothes, it is requisite that a prompt delivery be specified, as well as the quantity and the quality.

The hirer, in the case above stated, is not at liberty to prevent the husband of the nurse from having carnal connexion with her; because as such connexion is the husband's right, it is not in the hirer's power to annul it.—for this reason, that the husband, in case of his not being informed of the contract at the time of concluding it, is antitled to dissolve it for the purpose of preserving his own right.—The hirer, however, may prevent the husband from having such carnal intercourse in his house, since that place is his exclusive right,—If, also, in consequence of such connexion, the nurse prove pregnant, the infant's guardians are at liberty to dissolve the contract, provided there be any apprehension of injury to the child's health from the use of her milk, as is most probable in such instances;—and for the same reason also, they are at liberty to dissolve the contract where the nurse falls sick.—It is also incumbent upon the nurse to prepare the child's victuals by mastication, and to avoid every species of food which might prove injurious to her milk, in pursuance or her duty.—In short, in all matters of this nature, regard is had to custom, where there is no divine ordinance. The performance, therefore, of every usual service to a child (such as washing its linen, preparing its victuals, and so forth) is incumbent upon the nurse. The victuals, however, must be provided by the father. With respect to what has been observed by Mohammed, that, "it is incumbent upon the nurse to provide oils and perfumes,"—this is according to the custom of Koofa.

IF the nurse above mentioned feed the child with goat's milk, during the term of hire, she is not entitled to any wages, as not having performed what was her duty, namely, fosterage, or, in other words the feeding the child with milk from her own breasts; for feeding it with milk from a goat is not fosterage, but merely feeding it with milk. Wages, therefore, are not due to her in this instance, as she has not performed what she had contracted for.

A contract of hire, stipulating that the recompense shall be paid from the article manufactured or wrought upon is invalid—IF a person deliver thread to a weaver, to make it into cloth, in consideration of an half thereof to himself, he is to receive a recompense proportionate to his work; and the same rule also holds if a person hire an ass to carry wheat, paying, in consideration a measure of such wheat. The contract, therefore, is invalid in both these instances, because the recompense is made to consist of a thing obtained by the labour of the person or animal hired, and hence the case is analogous to that of an allowance made for grinding,* which has been prohibited by the Prophet. (The case of allowance for grinding is where a person hires an ox to grind grain in consideration of a proportion from the flour or meal:—and this case is the grand criterion by which a judgment is formed of the invalidity in various instances of hire, more especially in our country.) The reason of the prohibition, in this instance, is that the hirer is incapable of delivering the recompense (namely, a part of the woven cloth, or a part of the carried grain); for as the obtaining of it depends upon the act of the person or animal hired, the hirer cannot be accounted capable of making delivery merely in virtue of the capacity of that person or animal. The contract is therefore invalid and an adequate hire is due. It is otherwise where a person hires an ass to carry one half of a parcel of wheat, in consideration of the other half; for in this instance no hire is due on account of the animal hired, as the hirer has constituted the owner of the ass proprietor of half of the grain upon the instant, in the manner of a prompt or advanced payment, and consequently the wheat is in partnership between them, for reasons which will be explained in a future example. It is to be observed that where a person hires an ass, to carry wheat, in consideration of a measure of such wheat, or an ox, to grind grain; the hire allowed must not exceed the value of what has been specified, because, as the hire is invalid, the least only of the two (the hire named, or an adequate hire) is due, since the person who lets the animal has agreed to remit any thing beyond. It is otherwise where two men enter into a partnership in collecting wood, and one of them says to the other. "I will take the whole wood; and pay you a recompense for your share in the collecting of it," for in this case an adequate recompense is due, to whatever amount (according to Mohammed), inasmuch as no sum has been specified in this instance, whence no remission of any excess can be inferred.

Partners do not owe hire to each other with respect to their stock.—IF a person hire another to carry wheat which is in partnership between them, no recompense is due; for in all grain so carried the porter works on his own account, whence a complete delivery is not made of the thing contracted for.

Any uncertainty in the terms invalidates the contract.—IF a person hire another to back ten particular saas of wheat into bread, "this day," for a dirm, it is invalid, according to Haneefa. The two disciples in the Mabsoot, article Hire, maintain that the contract in question is valid: because in this instance the performance of the task [of baking the bread] is the thing really contracted for, the mention of a time being considered merely as for the purpose of expendition, in order that the contract may be valid; and consequently the objection of uncertainty is removed The argument of Haneefa is that the thing contracted for is uncertain; because the specification of a time argues that the thing contracted for is general usufruct, or, in other words, the hireling's surrender of himself [to service]; and, on the other hand, the specification of a particular act argues that such act is the thing contracted for. Now general usufruct and a particular act cannot be united; for where a particular act is the thing contracted for, no hire is due for the labourer's surrender of himself. As, moreover, neither of these has a preference over the other, and the advantage is to the hirer, in the latter instance, and to the hireling in the former, it follows that a contract of this nature would lay a foundation for strife. It is reported, from Haneefa, that where the hirer, instead of "this day" says "within this day," the hire is valid, as in such case the thing contracted for is the particular act or task specified: contrary to where he says "this day." The arguments upon this point are connected with Arabic grammar, and have already been stated in treating of Divorce.*

*Expressed by an Arabic phrase (Kafeez Tehan), which will not bear a literal translation. It is more fully explained in Vol. IV, in treating of Compacts of Cultivation.

*The arguments in this example turn upon the distinction between the performance of a thing by general service, and the

A lease of lands is not invalidated by stipulating a right to perform any act which does and leave lasting effects—If a person hire land, stipulating that he shall be at liberty to plough and cultivate it or to water and cultivate it, such contract is valid: because he is entitled to cultivate the land in virtue of the contract; and as this is impracticable unless he plough and water it, he is consequently entitled to perform these acts upon it likewise; and every other act of this nature in the same manner a requisite of the contract; nor does the mention of it cause invalidity. If, on the contrary, he stipulate that he shall be at liberty to plough the land twice, or to dig trenches in it, or to dung it, the contract is invalid; because, in this instance, an effect remains after the expiration of the term of hire, which is not a requisite of the contract. This condition, moreover, is advantageous to one of the contracting parties; and every stipulation of that nature invalidates a contract. Besides, in this instance, the lessor becomes, in fact, a tenant of the lessee with respect to such advantage as may remain to the land after the expiration of the lease; and consequently the contract involves one bargain within another, which is not lawful. Some explain ploughing twice to signify ploughing the land a second time, after having reaped a crop from it, and then returning it in that state to the owner; and concerning the invalidity in this instance no doubt can be entertained. Others, again explain it to mean ploughing the land twice, and then sowing the grain in it. What is here advanced (with respect to the invalidity occasioned by stipulating a right of ploughing twice) applies solely to cases where the land is of a nature to be productive from once ploughing, and the term of hire only one year;—for if the term of hire be three years (for instance), the advantage derived from ploughing twice swears out and no longer remains. By the term trenches, as here used, small temporary trenches are not to be understood, but watercourses, such as are calculated to last, and yield an advantage the year ensuing.

A contract stipulating the recompense to consist of a similar usufruct is nugatory.—If a person hire land to cultivate, in return for the right [on the part of the lessor] of cultivating other land, it is nugatory; in other words, it is utterly invalid. Shafei maintains that it is valid. Analogous to this is the hire of a dwelling-house, in return for residence in another house; the hire of apparel in return for the use of other apparel;—or the hire of a quadruped for riding, in return for a right of riding upon another quadruped. The argument of Shafei, is that the advantage is the same as actual substance; and it is on this idea that hire is valid in return for a debt of wages;* for if those were not the same as actual substance, it would follow that the transaction is the exchange of one debt for another debt, which is null. The arguments of our doctors upon this point are twofold.—First, contracts upon credit are rendered invalid by an unity of species alone; and as an unity of weight or measure is not essential (according to our doctors, as has been already explained in treating of sale), the contract in question, therefore, resembles the sale, upon credit, of cloth of a particular description in return for cloth of the same description.—Secondly the validity of hire is admitted (in opposition to what analogy would suggest) from convenience and necessity; but no convenience or necessity whatever exists where the advantage is exactly the same on both sides, contrary to where the advantage derived on each part is different.

Objection.—Where hire of one kind is in return for hire of another kind, although it be not rendered invalid by a non-existence of necessity or convenience, still it would follow that it is invalid, as being the sale of a debt for a debt.

Reply—In this instance the subject from which the advantage accrues is made a substitute for the advantage, from necessity:—the recompense, therefore, is as a price; and accordingly, the transaction is a sale of substance for something else than substance; which is lawful.

Case of two partners.—If a quantity of wheat be between two men in partnership, and one of them hire the other, or his ass, to carry his share to a certain place, and he, or his ass, carry the whole of the wheat thither, he is not entitled either to the recompense specified, or to a proportionate recompense. Shafei maintains that he is entitled to the specified recompense; because, according to his tenets, advantage is the same as actual substance; and as the sale of an undefined substance is lawful, it follows that it is also lawful to receive a recompense in return for an underfined advantage. The case in question, therefore, is similar to where a person hires a building; held in partnership between himself and another, for the purpose of keeping grain,—or, a slave held in partnership between him and another, for the pur-

---

performance of the same thing in a particular instance; that is, between hiring a person for any business by the day, or so forth, and engaging him for the performance of the same business by the particular task. If the contract for a particular task be so expressed as to leave it uncertain whether the recompense specified be for the day's service, or for the particular work required, it is in that case invalid according to Haneefa), and consequently no regard is had to the sum mentioned as the recompense, but the workman receives a proportionate hire for his day's work.

*That is, wages owing from the person hired to the hirer (as where the hirer had previously performed service to the person whom he now hires, and for which this person still owes him wages.

pose of making up apparel. The arguments of our doctors upon this point are twofold — First. the person in question here hires another for the performance of a matter the existence of which cannot be conceived; because the carriage or porterage of any thing is a sensible or perceptible act, which is impossible with respect to a thing undefind : —and as the performance of the thing contracted for is impossib'e. it follows that no recompense is due —Secondly, the person hired is a partner of the hirer with respect to every particle he carries. whence he carries on his own account also, and consequently does not perform what he had contracted for It is otherwise where the thing contracted for is a partnership house, for keeping grain. for in this instance the thing contracted for is the use of the house and a delivery of that may be effected. without the person depositing his grain therein, by the other evacuattng it to him.

A lease of land is invalid unless it specify the purpose to which the land is to be applied —If a person hire land, without mentioning that it is for the purpose of cultivation, or, without mentioning what species of cultivation he means to employ it in, the contract is invalid : because land is hired for tillage, and also for other purposes ; and, in the same manner, it is cultivated for various uses, some more and some less injurious to the soil. The thing contracted for is therefore uncertain : and accordingly, the contract is not lawful. Notwithstanding this, however, if the person who hires the land should cultivate it, and the term of the lease expire, he is entitled to the specified rent, on a favourable construction. According to analogy he is not so entitled (and such is the opinion of Ziffer), because the contract, as being once invalid, cannot afterwards become valid.—The reason for a more favourable construction, in this particular, is that, before the complete fulfilment of the contract, the uncertainty has been done away ; and it therefore becomes valid, in the same manner as where the uncertainty is done away before the contract has been yet concluded ;—the case being analogous to where a seller and purchaser do away an undefined time of promise for payment or delivery, in sale, before the usual term of credit expires, or do away a right of option extended beyond the term of three days, before the expiration of those three days,—If, in this case, the lessor and lessee dispute before cultivation, the lessee being desirous of cultivating the land, and the lessor forbidding him, the contract becomes dissolved, in order that strife may be prevented,

Responsibility does not attach, from the customary use of an article, under an indefinite contract.—If a person hire an ass to Bagdad (for instance) for one dirm, without specifying what it is to carry, and load upon it such a burden as men usually put upon that animal, and it die before it has proceeded more than half way, he is not responsible ; because the article hired is as a trust in the hands of the hirer; although the contract be invalid. If, on the other hand. the ass arrive at Bagdad, the owner is entitled to the hire stipulated, upon a favourable construction; because in this instance the uncertainty has been done away, in the same manner as in the preceding example.—If, also, a dispute arise between the hirer and the owner of the ass, before it be loaded, the contract is dissolved, in order that strife may be prevented.

CHAPTER V.

OP THE RESPONSIBILITY OF A HIRELING.

Difference between common and particular hireling.—Hirelings are of two description common and particular.—A common* hireling is one with whom a contract of hire is concluded for work of such a nature as may be perceived by examining the subject : —and in this instance there is no occasion for any mention of a term; nor is he entitled to his hire or recompense until the work he has engaged for (such as dying or fulling) be executed, because the work is the only thing contracted for, where he engages to perform it in person, or the effect of such work, where he has not particularly engaged to peform it in person.—It is therefore lawful for him to work for the public at large. since no partcuar person has any exclusive claim to his service ; and accordingly, he is termed Ajeer Mooshtarik, that is, a general or common hireling.—(The rules with respect to particular hirelings shall be discussed in their proper place.)

The article committed to a common hireling is deposit.—An article delivered to common hireling is a deposit in his hands. If, therefore, it perish whilst in his possession heis not in any degree responsible for it, according to Haneefa, and such also is the opinion of Ziffer.—The two disciples maintain that he is responsible, except where the article is lost or destroyed by any irremediable and irresistible accident, such as a fire burning down his house, or robbers, in such force as not to be repelled : because it is recorded of Alee and Omar that they understood a common hireling to be responsible : and also, because the care of the article is incumbent on him; as without such care he cannot perform his work upon it. When, therefore, the article is lost from any cause which might have been avoided, such as usurpation or theft, this proves him to have been negligent, and he is consequently responsible in the same manner as a trustee who lets to hire the deposit in his hands,—It is otherwise

* Arab. Mooshtarik, literally held in common,—meaning one whose services are open to all (such as a tradesman), in opposition to a particular servant,

where the article is lost from some unavoidable cause, such as fire, sudden death, and so forth, since in this case he cannot be accused of negligence.—The argument of Haneefa is that the article is merely a deposit in the workman's hands, the possession of which does not involve responsibility, inasmuch as he took possession with consent of the proprietor; and accordingly, if it were lost from any unavoidable cause, he is not responsible,—whereas, if his possession of it involved responsibility, he would owe a compensation for it at all events, in the same manner as in a case of usurped property.—The care; moreover, of the article is incumbent upon the proprietor dependatly and not essentially, and accordingly no hire is due for such case. This case is different from that of an hired trustee; for the care of the deposit is essentially incumbent upon a trustee who acts for hire, because of the wages he receives.

But he is responsible if it be destroyed in the course of his work.—A COMMON hireling is resposible in case of the loss or destruction of any article in the course of his work: as where a dyer or fuller tears the cloth entrused to him, or a porter stumbles, or the tying of his load breaks, or the girth of a camel breaks, and thus the goods with which he is loaded fall to the ground, or a boat sinks from the mismanagement of the boatman,—Ziffer maintains that the hireling is not responsible in those cases, because the hirer had ordered him to work in an absolute manner, and hence his order extends as well to dangerous as to safe operations,—in other words, to operations which subject his property to damage, and also to operations under which it continues uninjured.—The hireling in question, therefore, is in the same predicament with a particular hireling, or any assistant of a workman.* The argument of our doctors is that the orders of the hirer do not extend to any operations but what are mentioned in the contract; and those are to be supposed of a safe nature, since in virtue of them is obtained the thing contracted for, namely, the effect of them,—whence it is that if this effect be obtained through the work of any other than the hireling, still the recompense is due. The orders of the hirer, therefore, do not comprehend any operations that may be injurious, since through such the thing contracted for, namely, the effect, cannot be produced. It is otherwise with respect to the assistant of a workman; because, as he works gratuitously, his work cannot be restricted to the condition of safety, for if it were so restricted, he would decline working gratuitously. It is also otherwise with respect to a particular hireling, as shall be hereafter explained.—(It is to be observed that the breaking of a camel's girth, or so forth, is supposed to originate with the hireling, inasmuch as the accident may be attributed to his want of care.)—A common hireling, therefore, is responsible for any thing which may be destroyed in the course of his work; excepting, however, where a MAN is destroyed, either by the sinking of a boat, or by falling from a camel or other animal (athough those accidents should have been occasioned by the driving of the camel or the navigating of the boat); for in this instance the hireling is not responsible, as responsibility for a MAN cannot be incurred in virtue of a contract, or in virtue of any thing but a Janayat, or offence against the person, whence it would be due, in this instance, not from the hireling, but from his Akila, who, however, cannot be made responsible by a contract.

IF a person hire a porter to bring an earthen jar from the banks of the Euphrates (for instance), and he fall down upon the way and break the jar, the hirer has it at his option either to take the value which the jar bore at the place where it was taken up (in which case the porter is not entitled to any recompense), or to take a compensation for the value it bore at the place where it was broken, paying the porter a proportionate hire.—Responsibility is incurred in this instance, because (as was before said) the falling of the jar was either owing to the porter stumbling, or his rope breaking, which is attributed to him:—and an option is allowed to the hirer; because, where the jar is broken upon the road, the cricumstance admits of two construction: for the hireling is in one shape guilty of a transgression from the beginning, inasmuch as the carriage of the jar from the place where it was taken up to the place directed is one act; and in another shape he is not guilty from the beginning, since the carriage was undertaken with the consent of the owner, and consequenty no transgression took place until the breaking of the jar;—the owner, therefore, has it at his option to proceed upon either ground;—if he proceed upon the second ground, the hireling is to receive a recompense in proportion to the work he has rendered to the hirer: but if upon the first ground, he is not to receive any thing, since in this view he has not rendered the hirer any service whatever.

A surgon, or farrier, acting agreeably to customary practice, is not responsible in case of accidents.—IF a surgeon perform the operation of phlebotomy in any customary part, he is not responsible in case of the person dying in consequence of such operation,—This is according to the Mabsoot.—It is written, in the Jama Sagheer, that if a farrier bleed an animal for a danik, and the animal die in consequence, or if a cupper perform the operation of cupping upon a slave by direction of his master, and the slave die in consequence, no responsilility is incurred.—It is to be observed that the doctrine of the Mabsoot, in this particular, proceeds upon the idea of a restriction to

* Meaning a person who assists the workman gratuitously (as will be perceived by the context a little further on).

the performance of the operation in some customary part; but it is unrestricted with respect to the assent of the party or otherwise; whereas the doctrine in the Jama Sagheer proceeds upon the idea of a restriction with respect to the assent [of the owner of the slave or animal], but is unrestricted with respect to the part on which the operation is performed. Each of these reports, therefore, affords an argument with respect to the other; and consequently the cases in both are restricted to this, that the operation be performed in the usual part, and with consent of the party,—The ground on which the LAW proceeds in this particular is, that it is impossible for the operators to guard against consequences, as those must depend upon the strength or weakness of the constitution in bearing any disorder or pain; and as this is unknown, it is therefore impossible to restrict the work to the condition of safety.—It is otherwise with respect to tearing cloth, as before treated of, because the strength or weakness of cloth may be known by skill and attention, whence it is possible in that instance to restrict the work to safety. Thus much with respect to common or general hirelings.

A particular hireling.—A PARTICULAR hireling signifies one who is entitled to his hire in virtue of a surrender of himself during the term of hire, although he do no work; as, for instance, a person who is hired as a servant for a month, or to take care of flocks for a month, a certain rate, under a condition that he shall not serve or tend the flocks of any other person during that term —An hireling of this description is denominated an Ajeer Wahid, or singular hireling, because the advantage of his service belongs exclusively to a single person during the term of his engagement, and the wages he receives are opposed to such advantage: —and as the hireling, in this instance, is entitled to his hire in virtue of his surrender of himself, for the term of hire, he is entitled to his wages although he do no work, or although his work be afterwards undone; as where, for instance, a person is hired to make up a dress, and he sew it accordingly, and the sewing be afterwards ripped out, in which case he is nevertheless entitled to his hire.

Is not responsible for any thing he loses or destroys.—IF an article be lost whilst in the hands of a particular hireling, without his act; by a thief stealing it (for instance), or, an usurper carrying it away,—or, if it be lost by his act, he is not responsible for it.—He is not responsible in the former instance, because the article is a deposit in his hands, since he took possession of it with the owner's consent.—(This, according to Haneefa, is evident:—and it is also evident according to the two disciples, because they hold that the obligation of responsibility upon a common hireling proceeds upon a favourable construction of the LAW, in order that men's property may be in security; but as a particular hireling does not engage to work for every person, it is still more likely that property is safe with such an hireling: and therefore, in this case, the law proceeds upon analogy,)—He is also not responsible in the second instance, because, as the advantage of this hireling's service is the property of the hirer, it follows that, where he directs him to act with his property, such direction is valid: consequently the hireling is his deputy; his acts, therefore, are the same as the acts of his principal, the hirer, and of course he is not responsible.

CHAPTER VI.

OF HIRE ON ONE OF TWO CONDITIONS.

The hire is valid, of a tradesman, under an alternative with respect to work.—IF the owner of cloth say to the tailor whom he has engaged, "If you make up this cloth in the Persian fashion, you shall have one dirm, and if in the Turkish fashion, you shall have two,"—it is valid, and the tailor is entitled to a recompense according to whichever of the two fashions he makes up the cloth in. In the same manner, also, if he say to a dyer, "If you dye this cloth purple, you shall have one dirm, and is yellow, you shall have two," the dyer is entitled to a recompense, according as he dyes the cloth purple or yellow.

Or of an article under an alternative of another article.—THE same rule also holds if the proprietor of the article hired leave two things at the option of him who hires it;—as if he were to say to him " I let to you this house, for one month, for five dirms, or this other house, for one moth, for two dirms. "

Or with respect to the use.—And so likewise if he leave at his option two different distances; as if he were to say "I hire to you this camel, to Koofa, for five dirms; or this, to the half-way station, for so much:"—and the same, also, if the proprietor give an option of three things: but if he give an option of four things, it is invalid.—In all these cases regard is had to sale; in other words, they are judged of by sale; for if in person agree to sell cloth, under this condition, that the purchaser shall take either of two particular pieces, as he pleases, it is valid (and so likewise, if he allow the purchaser an option of one out of three pieces): but it is not valid if he allow him an option of one out of four pieces.—The reason of this is that as cloth is of three descriptions, a good sort, a bad sort, and a medium sort, an option of three is of use, and necessity is thereby answered; but as, in a case of four pieces, necessity is answered by a choice from a smaller number, so an option out of four is useless.—In the same manner, also, in hire, necessity is answered by an option from three things, as those comprehend a good, a bad, and a middling sort: and there is no occasion for four, as necessity is answered by fewer,—There is, however, this difference between sale and hire, that sale is not valid unless an option of determination be stipulated; for if a person sell one of two slaves, it is valid only in virtue of stipulating an option of determination.—A contract of hire, on the contrary, is valid, for one of two advantages, without stipulating an option of determination, because the recompense is not due in virtue of the contract, but in virtue of the usufruct or work; and consequently, when the party commences the enjoyment of one of the advantages, the thing contracted for becomes known: but as, in a case of sale; the price of the article is due in virtue of the contract, uncertainty consequently exists in that instance to such a degree as leaves room for strife, unless the purchaser possess an option of determination.

Case of a tradesman hired under an alternative with respect to time.—If a person say to a tailor whom he hires, "If you make up this garment this day you shall have one dirm; and if to-morrow, you shall have half a dirm." in this case, provided the tailor finish the garment within the day, he gets a dirm, or if he finish it the next day, he receives a proportionate hire (according to Haneefa) where that does not exceed half a dirm: in other words, he gets the least of the two, between a half dirm and his proportionate hire.—It is written, in the Jama Sagheer, that he is entitled to his proportionate hire, not being less than half a dirm, not more than one drim.—The two disciples allege that both conditions are valid, and consequently, that if he perform his work on the morrow he gets an half dirm.—Ziffer maintains that both the conditions in question are invalid; because sewing, or tailor's work, is one thing to which the hirer, in this instance, opposes two returns (namely, one dirm, and half a dirm), in the manner of a consideration: the recompense, therefore, is uncertain.—The reason of this is that the mention of this day is merely for the purpose of hastening; and the mention of to-morrow for the purpose of giving ease; and there is no suspension; for if the hirer were to express the contract "make up this garment by to-morrow, for half a dirm," the contract is established, insomuch that if he make up the garment within the persent day, he is entitled to half a dirm. Hence it appears that the mention of to-morrow is merely for the sake of ease, and is not a suspension; and consequently two specifications are united in one day.—The arguments of the two disciples upon this point are twofold, First, the mention of this day is for the purpose of determining a time, and the mention of to-morrow is by way of a condition: consequently two specifications are not united in one day. Secondly, quickness and delay are the designs: and the case therefore resembles that of two species of work, such as Persian and Turkish. The argument of Haneefa is that the mention of to-morrow is certainly by way of a condition,—The mentioning this day, moreover, cannot be construed to imply fixing a time; for otherwise the contract of hire would be invalid, because of its uniting time and work Such, therefore, being the case, it follows that two specifications are united in the mention of to-morrow, not in the mention of this day; consequently the contract with respect to this day is valid, whence the hire mentioned is due [in case of the work being finished within the day]; but it is invalid with respect to to-morrow, whence [in case of the work being finished on the morrow] a proportionate hire is due,—not exceeding, however, half a dirm, as that is what was specified for to-morrow.—With respect to the quotation from the Jama Sagheer upon this subject, that "he is entitled to his proportionate hire, not being less than half a dirm, nor more than one dirm," the ground on which it proceeds is, that the first specification does not become extinct on the second day, because then both specifications unite: regard, therefore, is had to it, with respect to preventing any excess beyond it; and to the second specification, with respect to preventing any deficiency:—If, in the case in question, the tailor finish the garment on the third day, he gets whatever is least of the two, his proportionate hire, to half a dirm. This is approved; because, as the hirer was unwilling to have the work delayed for one day, it follows that he was still more unwilling to have it delayed longer than one day.

Case of hire of a shop, under an alternative with respect to the business to be carried on in it—If the lessor of a shop say to a person about to hire it "If you place a perfumer in this shop the rent is one dirm, or if a blacksmith, it is two," the contract is valid, and the lessor is entitled to one or other of the rents specified according to which of the two trades may be exercised in the shop. This is the doctrine of Haneefa. The two disciples maintain that a contract thus expressed is invalid.—In the same manner, also, if a person hire a house, under this condition, that "if he reside in it himself, the rent shall be one dirm, or if he place a blacksmith in it the rent shall be two dirms," it is valid, according to Haneefa, whereae the two disciples deem it invalid.

And of an animal, under a condition with respect to the journey it is to perform.—If a person hire an animal of Heera for one dirm; under a condition that if he proceed on to Kadseea he shall pay two dirms, it is valid: and in this instance, also, the above difference of opinion may be inferred: that is to say, this example is stated in the book [of Kadooree] generally, without mentioning any difference of opinion; but it bears the construction of a difference of opinion, and also of an agreement of opinion.

Or the load it is to carry.—If a person hire an animal to Heera, under this condition, that "if he load it with a Koor of barley he shall pay one dirm, or if with a

Koor of wheat he shall pay two dirms," it is valid according to Haneefa. The two disciples maintain it to be invalid,—The ground on which the two disciples proceed is, that in all the instances here recited the thing contracted for is uncertain; and in the same manner, the hire, as being one of two things, is also uncertain: and uncertainty occasion nvalidity.—It is otherwise in the examp'e of making up apparel after the Pers an or the Turkish fashion, because the hire is due on account of the work, and in his instance the uncertainty is removed as oon as the work is begun; whereas in the examples in question the hire is due on account of the relinquishment and delivery of the house or animal, whence the uncertainty still continues, because after delivery, in case of no use being made of the article, it is not known which of the two hires specified is due (for it is a principle, with the two disciples, that hire is due on account of relinquishment and delivery.)—The argument of Haneefa is that the lessor, in the case in question, gives the lessee an option of either of two valid contracts. of different descriptions; for the hirer himself residing in the house is different from his placing a blacksmith to reside in it: and such being the case, the contract is valid, in the same manner as in the example of making up apparel after the Persian or the Turkish fashion.—With respect to what is advanced by the two disciples, that "the hire is due on account of relinquishment and delivery whence the uncertainty still continues" it may be replied that the design of the contract of hire is advantage or usufruct; because, as such contracts are legalized to answer the necessity of mankind, it is evident that they are never entered into but with a view to such advantage; and the uncertainty is removed upon the advantage commencing, —As, moreover, the relinquishment and delivery, without any enjoyment of the use (which alone constitute endowment), are not principles, but rather mere accidents, there is no necessity to guard against uncertainty at the period of delivery.—Besides, if it be required, in a contract of hire, that the hire be due on the instant of delivery, it follows that the smallest of the two hires specified is due, as that is undoubted:—the hire, therefore, is not uncertain.

CHAPTER VII.

OF THE HIRE OF SLAVES.*

An hired servant cannot be taken upon a journey, unless it be so stipulated in the contract.—IF a person hire a slave, as a servant, he is not at liberty to carry such slave along with upon a journey, unless this be a condition of the contract; because, as travelling is attended with additional trouble, a contract in general terms is not held to extend to it: whence it is that travelling is a sufficient plea for breaking off a contract of hire. It is therefore requisite t at, in the the contract in question, travelling be particularly stipulated, in the same manner as the residence of a blacksmith or fuller in a dwelling-house.—Besides. the difference between stationary service and travelling service is evident; and consequently. upon stationary service being ascertained or specified, the other description (namely, travelling service) cannot be included;—in the same manner as riding upon an animal; as. for instance, where a person in general terms hires an animal to ride, and the rider is afterwards ascertained, the hirer is not at liberty to set any other person upon the animal; and so likewise in the present case.

Wages paid to an inhibited slave, hired without the consent of his owner. cannot be resumed.—IF a person hire an inhibited [absolute] slave for the term of one month, and pay him his wages after the performance of service. he is not at liberty to resume such wages. The ground of this is that the hire in question is valid, on a favourable construction, where a slave is not otherwise occupied. Analogy would suggest that it is invalid, as the proprietor of the slave has not given his consent, and the slave is a Mahjoor, or inhibited:—in the same manner as if the slave were to die before the completion of the service; in which case the hirer would be responsible for his value; but he would not be responsible for any wages on account of the service performed, since in employing the slave he becomes an usurper,—whence he is, in case of the slave's death, required to pay a compensation for his value; and as, upon so doing, he becomes proprietor of the slave from the first instant of employing him, he thus appears to have derived an advantage from his own slave: wherefore, in such case, no wages are due.—The reason for a more favourable construction, in this instance, is that the transaction in question may be considered in two shapes: for first, it may be regarded as advantageous on the idea of the slave being unoccupied by any other business, and remaining in safety; and secondly, it may be regarded as injurious, on the idea of the slave dying before he finishes his service.—Now, on the idea of the transaction being advantage, the slave is licensed therein, in a manner analogous to the acceptance of a gift. The contract of hire therefore is valid; and such being the case, it follows that the hirer is not at liberty to take back the wages.

The usurper of a slave is not responsible for what the slave earns during the term of usurpation.—IF a person usurp a slave, and the slave afterwards let himself to hire, and

* It is a common practice, in Arabia, Persia, &c., for slaves to hire themselves in the capacity of menial servants, being accountable to their master for the wages they receive.

the usurper receive his wages, and expend the same, he is not responsible for them, according to Haneefa.—The two disciples allege that he is responsible for the wages, because he has acted with the property of the master without his consent (for the contract of hire is valid, on the grounds stated in the preceding example). The argument of Haneefa is that responsibility does not attach except in the case of destruction of protected property* (for the fixing of a price upon property is for the purpose of protecting it). Now the wages in question are not in a state of protection or custody in regard to the master, although they be so with respect to another, because the protection or custody of property is established only by actual possession, such as may admit of the care of it, like the possession of the proprietor, or his deputy; and the seisin of the slave is not the seisin of his master, since the slave himself is in the possession of an usurper, and being thus incapacitated from protecting his own person, is therefore incapable of protecting his wages from the usurper,—If, however, the master find the wages in the usurper's possession, he is entitled to take them from him as he in this case discovers his own property.—In the case in question, also, it is lawful for the slave to take possession of his wages from the usurper, according to the opinion of our three doctors, since, if not otherwise employed, and remaining safe, he is licensed with respect to the transaction, because of its being advantageous, as was before mentioned.—It is different where a master lets his slave to hire; for in this case the slave is not at liberty to take possession of his wages unless his master constitute him his agent for that purpose, because receiving the wages is one of the rights of the contract.

Case of a slave hired for different terms.—If a person hire a slave for two months, with this distinction, that he shall serve one month for four dirms, and one month for five dirms, it is lawful; and the hire is for four dirms in the first month; because the month first mentioned must be construed to mean the month immediately succeeding the execution of the contract, in order to its validity; for otherwise the contract would be invalid, since in this case a month would appear included in it which is not specified, and this would be invalid.—Besides, the act of hiring infers that the hirer has immediate occasion for the service of the slave, whence the month in question must necessarily be construed to mean the month immediately succeeding the execution of the contract, in order that the hirer's necessity may be answered: and such being the case, the second month must in the same manner be necessarily construed to mean the month immediately succeeding the first month.

Case of hired slave absconding before the expiration of the term.—If a person hire a slave for one month, at the rate of one dirm, and take possession of the slave in the beginning of the month, and at the end of the month, the slave having absconded or fallen sick, the hirer and the owner or master dispute,—the hirer asserting that the slave had absconded or fallen sick in the beginning of the month, and the master, that he had not fallen sick or absconded until within a short time,—the assertion of the hirer must be credited.—If, on the other hand, the hirer produce the slave, he being then present and in good health, the assertion of the master must be credited; because, as the parties differ upon a point which is of a problematical nature, a preference must be given to the side of the question which is best supported by apparent circumstances. The principle upon which the LAW in this instance proceeds is to be found in the case of the running or stopping of a mill-stream; for if the hirer of a mill dispute with the proprietor concerning the running of the stream during the term of hire,* in this case the assertion of that party is credited on whose behalf apparent circumstances bear testimony.†—If, on the contrary, they dispute concerning the deficiency in the running of the stream,—as if the lessee were to say that it had not run for ten days, and the lessor that it had not run for five days, in this case the assertion of the tenant must be credited, or evidence on the part of the lessor.

CHAPTER VIII.

OF DISPUTES BETWEEN THE HIRER AND THE HIRELING.

In cases of dispute with a tradesman concerning the orders he has received, the assertion of the employer must be credited.—If a dispute arise between the tailor and the owner of cloth,—the owner asserting that "he had directed the tailor to make the cloth into a vest," and the tailor that "the owner had directed him to make it into drawers,"—or if a similar dispute happen with a dyer, the owner of the cloth affirming that he had directed him [the dyer] "to colour the cloth yellow," and the dyer that he [the owner] "had directed him to dye it red,"—in either case the declaration of the owner of the cloth must be credited, since it is from him that the orders proceed.—The ground of this is, that as, if the owner of the cloth were to

* Arab, Mal Mohirrez.—The meaning of this has been fully explained elsewhere. (See Hirz, and Mohirrez.)

* He asserting that the stream had not run at all, and consequently that the mill stood still during the whole term

† That is to say, if, at the time of the assertion, the stream be running, the proprietor must be credited; but if otherwise, the tenant

deny the original order,* by disavowing the contract of hire, his word would be credited —so, in the same manner, his word must be credited where he denies the description or qualification of the order.—He must, however, be sworn, because he in this instance denies a thing which, if he were to acknowledge it, would be binding upon him. Upon the owner of the cloth swearing, the tailor becomes responsible; that is, the owner of the cloth has it at his option either to take the value of the cloth,—or to take the drawers, paying the tailor an adequate hire. —In the same manner, also, in the case of dyeing, upon the owner of the cloth swearing, he has it at his option either to take a recompense for the value of the cloth uncoloured, or to take the dyed cloth, paying the dyer an adequate hire not beyond the value,— because the dyer, in acting contrary to his instructions, stands in the same predicament with an usurper.

And so also, if the dispute be with regard to wages.—If a dispute arise between the owner of cloth and the dyer, tailor, or other workman,—the owner asserting that "he [the workman] had agreed to execute the work without hire," and the workman that "he wrought for hire," the assertion of the owner must be credited, inasmuch as he both denies any price having been put upon the workman's labour (which can only be effected by a contract), and also any responsibility, or, in other words, any hire being due, which the owner claims; and the assertion of the defendant [upon oath] must be credited. Aboo Yoosaf maintains that if the workman be one commonly employed by the owner of the cloth, and with whom it has been usual for the owner to fix a hire for his work, he is entitled to a hire proportionate to what he performs; but that, if he was not commonly employed by the owner he gets nothing whatever; and the reason is, that it is only former practice which can furnish a ground of requisition of wages, and establish the rate at which they are to be fixed in the present instance. Mohammed says that if it have been a general and known practice of the workman to work for hire, his word must be credited, because whenever he opens a workshop for the purpose of carrying on his business, this stands in place of an express declaration that he works for hire, as apparent circumstances signify thus much. It is to be observed that the opinion of Haneefa, as, here stated, proceeds upon analogy, the owner of the cloth standing as the denier, or defendant. The opinion of the two disciples, on the other hand, proceeds upon a favourable construction.—In reply to what they advance in this particular it may be observed that apparent circumstances may suffice to repel, but are not sufficient to establish to claim; in other words, if a person advance a claim, such claim may be set aside by apparent circumstances, but apparent circumstances are incapable of constituting proof, or of establishing anything in his behalf; and, in the present instance, it is required that a claim be established. Sheikh-al-Islam remarks that decrees pass according to the opinion of Mohammed,—as is also mentioned in the Kafees.

*That is, were to deny his ever having given any order (with respect to dyeing or making up the cloth).

CHAPTER IX.

OF THE DISSOLUTION* OF CONTRACTS OF HIRE.

A contract for the hire of a house is dissolved by a defect in it.—If a person hire a house, and then discover a defect in it, such as renders it uninhabitable, he is at liberty to dissolve the contract: because the contract was executed with a view to advantage; and as that continually, from time to time, is the object of the hire, it follows that the defect discovered in the house had existence previous to his obtaining possession of the thing actually contracted for, although it had occurred subsequent to taking possession of the house, in the same manner as where a defect has taken place in merchandise before the purchaser obtains possession of it. If, however, the hirer derive the advantage [that is make use of the house], he assents to the defect; and in such case the whole consideration (namely, the rent) is incumbent upon him, in the same manner as in sale. If, also, the lessor perform what is requisite to remedy the defect, the hirer is in that case without an optien, as the reason for such option is then done away.

Or by its falling to decay; and the hire of land, by its wells being dried up,—or of a mill, by the mill-stream stopping.—If a house fall to decay, or the wells for watering land dry up, or a mill-stream cease to run, the contract of hire is dissolved, because in such case the thing contracted for (namely, exclusive advantage) is defeated before possession; and the case is therefore the same as where merchandise perishes before possession, or where a hired slave dies.—Some of our modern doctors hold that the contract of hire is not dissolved in this instance, because the advantage has been defeated in a manner which admits a recovery of it. The case is therefore the same as where a slave dies after purchase, but before delivery; and as, in that case, the contract [of sale] is not dissolved, so likewise, in the present instance, the contract [of hire] is not dissolved.—It is recorded, from Mohammed, that if, in the, case is question, the lessor remove the defect by repairing the house, the hirer must abide by the contract, and also the lessor.—From this it is to be inferred that the contract is not dissolved.—It is, however, dissolved.

*Arab. Fiskh; literally, a breaking off.

But if the mill-house be used, a proportionate rent is due.—IF a mill-stream cease from running, and the mill-house be applicable to any other use than that of grinding grain, the hirer must pay a rent proportionable to the use derived from such house, as that is a part of what was contracted for.

A contract of hire is dissolved by the death of one of the contracting parties, being a principal.—IF one of the contracting parties die, and the hirer had entered into the contract of hire on his own account, it [the contract of hire] is dissolved; because if the contract were still to remain in force, it would follow that the usufruct, or rent, then becomes the right of a person who was not party to the contract, namely, the heir (since it would shift from the deceased to his heir), which is unlawful. Besides, with respect to the lessor, it is the use of his property which forms the subject of the contract; and as in consequence of his decease, this property changes to his heir, it follows that the contract of hire becomes null, because of the subject being lost; for a change in the right of property is the same as a change in the thing itself.—With respect to the hirer, or renter on the contrary, if the contract were to remain in force after his decease, it can only do so upon the principle that his heir is his substitute. But the use of a house cannot be a heritage without the house itself, because inheritance is a succession, which is impossible except with respect to a thing which endures at both times, so as to be at first the right of the person through whom inheritance descends, and at last to be succeeded to by his heir. —As, therefore, inheritance cannot hold with respect to the use, the contract of hire is necessarily annulled. It is otherwise where a person enters into a contract of hire on behalf of any other than himself, such as an agent, an executor, or the procurator of a Wakf: for in that case the contract is not annulled, since if the contracting party die, the contract is then transferred to him in whose behalf it was executed, and he consequently becomes, by construction of LAW, the contractor.

It admits a reserve of option—A RESERVE of option is valid in hire. Shafei maintains that it is invalid; because if a right of option be reserved to the hirer, it is impossible for him to reject, that is, to return the thing contracted for complete, since in such case some part of that thing is lost: or if, on the other hand, a right of option be reserved to the lessor, it is impossible for him to make a complete delivery; and either circumstance is repugnant to the validity of option. The argument of our doctors is that a contract of hire is a contract of commerce, in which it is not required that possession be taken at the meeting of the contract;* and a condition of option may therefore be lawfully inserted in it, in the same manner as in a contract of sale.—The cause, moreover, of the validity of option, in a contract of sale (namely, convenience), is also to be found in a contract of hire.—In answer to the arguments advanced by Shafei, it may be observed that the circumstance of a part of the subject of the contract being lost is not repugnans to a rejection: in opposition to sale, as in that instance the circumstance of any part of the subject of the contract being lost is repugnant to a rejection under conditional option; or option from defect.—The reason of this is that, in sale, a complete return of the article is practicable, under conditional option, or option from defect, whereas in hire this is impracticable; a complete return of the subject of the contract is therefore required in the one case, but not in the other.—As, moreover, a complete delivery is impracticable in hire, the hirer may be compelled to take possession, in case of the lessor making delivery of it at a time when part of the term has elapsed:—in other words, where a person takes a house (for instance) for a year, and the lessor does not deliver it until after the lapse of a month, the lessee is not at liberty to decline taking possession of it for the rest of the year.

It is dissolved by the occurrence of any sufficient pretext for dissolution.—A CONTRACT of hire is dissolved by a pretext,* according to our doctors—Shafei maintains that it is not dissolved but by a defect or failure, because as (agreeably to his tenets) the advantage stands in place of actual substance (whence it is that a contract holds with respect to it), the case therefore bears a resemblance to sale.—The argument of our doctors is that advantage is the thing contracted for; and as that is not a subject of seisin, a pretext in hire resembles a failure or defect in merchandise existing before it be taken possession of,—in which case the contract of sale is annulled, as the seller cannot carry it into execution without bearing or occasioning an injury, not incurred by it: and the same reason holds in hire also, as this is the meaning of an Oozir, or pretext, according to our doctors.

Circumstance which from a pretext for dissolving contracts of hire.—IF a person, being afflicted with the toothache, hire a surgeon to draw one of his teeth, and the pain afterwards cease,—or hire a cook to prepare a marriage-feast, and afterwards repudiate the bride by her own desire,† the

*Meaning, at the time and place where the contract is executed.

*Meaning (in this place) any circumstance which would render it impossible to carry the contract into execution without inducing, to one or other of the parties, an injury not provided for mentioned in the contract.—It is more fully explained a little farther on.

†See Khoola.—his species of divorce most commonly happens in consequence of an aversion conceived by a wife to her husband at their first meeting.

contract of hire is dissolved, because if it were to continue in force, the hirer would suffer a superinduced injury not incurred by the contract:—and the same rule also holds, if a person hire a shop for traffic, and his property be all afterwards disposed of.

IF a person let to hire a house or shop, and afterwards become poor and involved in debt to degree which he is unable to discharge but by the price of the house or shop, the Kazee must in this case dissolve the contract of hire, and sell the place for payment of the debt: because in the endurance of the contract the lessor sustains a superinduced injury not incurred by the contract,—which superinduced injury, in this instance, is that the Kazee will otherwise seize and imprison him on account of the debts, as he cannot be certain whether the debtor speaks truly in declaridg that "this is his only property." From the expression "the Kazee must in this case dissolve the contract," it may be inferred that a decree of the Kazee is requisite to the dissolution; and the same is mentioned in the Zeeadath, treating of a pretext of debt. Mohammed, on the other hand, in the Jama Sagheer, says "Whatever I have described to be a pretext, is competent to the annulling of hire;"—whence it may be inferred that there is no occasion for a decree of the Kazee: because, as a pretext, in hire, is the same as a defect in merchandise before seisin (as was before mentioned), it follows that the contracting party may of himself dissolve the contract.—The ground of the opinion in the Zeeadat is that as, concerning the dissolution of hire on account of a pretext, there is a difference of opinion, it is therefore requisite that the Kazee issue a decree and render it obligatory. Some of the Haneefite doctors endeavour to reconcile both opinions, by explaining that if the pretext be not of an evident nature (such as debt), there is no occasion for a decree of the Kazee: but if it be not evident, a decree of the Kazee is requisite to render it so.

IF a person hire an animal to carry him upon a journey, and something afterwards occur to prevent his proceeding, this is a pretext; for if the contract were put in force, he might be subjected to injury,—as a person may go upon a pilgrimage, and the proper season for it may in the meanwhile pass away,—or he may go in search of a person who is indebted to him, and that person in the mean time may appear,—or he may proceed upon a trading excursion, and may in the mean time become poor.—If, on the contrary, the obstacle to the journey occur to the Makar, or person who lets the animal to hire,* it is not admitted as a pretext because it is in his power, if he do not choose to go himself, to send the animal under the care of one of his servants or apprentices.—If, also, the Makar fall sick, so as to be incapable of proceeding upon the journey, this is not a pretext, according to the Mabsoot,—Koorokhee is of opinion that it is a pretext, since sending his animal under the care of another person is not altogether void of injury:—the contract, therefore, is set aside in a case of unavoidable necessity, as in sickness, but not in a case of mere option, as in health.

IF a person let his slave to hire, and afterwards sell him, this is not a pretext, because he sustains no injury in case of the contract being put into force, the only consequence incurred being, that his right of advantage (from the slave's hire) is lost, which is out of the question in the present instance.

IF a tailor hire a servant to saw for him, and he afterwards become bankrupt, and quit his business of tailor, this is a pretext; for if the contract were to continue in force he would sustain injury, because of his means (namely, his capital) being lost.—It is proper to remark, that by the tailor mentioned in this example is to be understood one who carries on business on his own account: for with respect to a tailor who works for hire, his only capital is needle, thread, and scissors, whence he cannot be considered as becoming bankrupt. If a tailor, who has hired an assistant as above, be desirous to quit his business of tailor and to pursue the business of money-changer, this is not a pretext, as it is in his power to place the hireling in a particular part of his shop for the purpose of exercising the business of a tailor, whilst he himself pursues the business of a money-changer in another part.—It is otherwise where a person hires a shop to carry on the business of a tailor, and is afterwards desirous to exercise some other trade, for this is not a pretext; the reason of which (as mentioned in the Mabsoot) is that one person cannot exercise two different professions.—In the instance, however, of a tailor hiring a servant to sew, the persons are two, and consequently may exercise two different trades.

IF a person hire a servant to attend him in a city, and afterwards travel, this is a pretext, as not being altogether void of injury; for the trouble of attendance is greater in travelling; whence if the servant were to go upon the journey, he would sustain an injury; or if, on the other hand, the hirer were prevented from undertaking the journey; he on his part would be injured; and as neither is to incur an injury by the contract, it follows that the circumstance in question forms a pretext.—The same rule also holds if the servant be hired in an absolute manner, by the hirer saying to him (or to his master, supposing the hireling to be a slave) "I hire you" (or "I hire your slave") "to wait upon me," without restricting the service either to a stationary or a travelling description, because it has been already mentioned that the hire is in such case restricted to stationary service.

IF a person let land, and be afterwards

*Maker is a person whose business it is to let horses, camels, &c., to hire.

desirous to make a journey, this is not a pretext, because it does not induce any injury, since the lessee or hirer has it still in his power to derive his advantage from the land, after the lessor's departure.—If, on the contrary, the lessee be desirous to make a journey, this is a pretext, since a continueance of the lease must either prevent the journey, or induce an obligation of rent without residence, which would be injurious.

Section

Miscellaneous Cases.

A hirer or borrower of land is not responsible for accidents in burning off the stubble. &c.—IF a person either hire or borrow land, and in burning the Hissayed, or stubble and roots of the soil, happen to burn anything upon the neighbouring lands, he is not responsible; because as, in exciting the cause to the destruction, he was not guilty of any transgression or trespass, he therefore stands in the same predicament with a person who digs a well in his own house.*——Some say that this holds only where he sets fire to the stubble during a calm; the wind rising afterwards;—for if he set fire to it whilst the wind is blowing, he is responsible, as he must in such case be sensible that the fire will extend beyond his land.

A tradesman may unite with another, for a moiety of the hire acquired upon the work.—IF a fuller, tailor, or dyer who keeps a public shop, and is possessed of credit, but unskilled in his trade, place any person in his shop who is skilled in the business, with a view that he shall himself procure cloth to be wrought upon, and the person in question work with it, under a condition that a moiety of the recompense or hire shall go to him, this is lawful and valid, as being a Shirkat Wadjooh, or partnership upon credit; because, as the shop keeper procures the cloth to be wrought with upon his own credit, and the person in question works upon it, the ends of both parties are thus completely answered:—neither is the uncertainty with respect to the amount of the time injurious, since that must be in proportion to what is acquired.

Hire of a camel to carry a litter with two persons.—IF a man hire a camel to carry a litter with two persons to Mecca, it is valid, on a favourable construction,—and he is at liberty to put upon the camel a litter of the usual dimensions.—Analogy would suggest that a contract of this nature is invalid (and such is the doctrine of Shafei), because the quality of a litter, with respect to its length, breadth, and weight, is uncertain, and may possible occasion disputes. The reason for a more favourable construction of the LAW, in this instance, is that the intent of the rider is merely the conveyance of his person upon the animal, the litter being a subordinate consideration. Besides, as any uncertainty is removed by supposing the litter to be such as is commonly used, there can be no occasion for contention.—The same rule holds, although the owner of the camel should not have seen the carpet and other appurtenances.—It is, however, preferable that he view the litter, &c., as thus uncertainty is removed, and his assent indubitably established.

A sumpter camel may be loaded with other articles in proportion as the provisions he carries are consumed.—IF a person hire a camel to carry provisions upon a journey, he is entitled to load the camel with other articles during the journey, in proportion as the provisions are consumed, because, as being entitled to the carriage of a specific load for the whole journey he is therefore entitled to exact such carriage complete.—The same rule also holds with respect to any thing else besides provision, provided it be an article of weight, or measurement of capacity.

OBJECTION.—It is not customary for travellers to impose any additional load upon an animal in lieu of the provision they consume upon the way;—and as absolute contracts must be construed agreeably to custom, it would follow that it is not lawful to load the animal with other articles in lieu of the consumed provisions.

REPLY.—Custom admits of either construction, since in some instances it is usual to supply the defect in the article consumed, as in the case of water, for instance;—and where custom is various, it is agreeably, in absolute contracts, to act agreeably to the requisites of them.

*A person digging a well on the public highway, or in any other place of general access, is responsible for the fine in case of any person being killed by falling into it; but a perron digging a well in his own house or land is not responsible.

BOOK XXXII

OF MOKATIBS.

Definition of the terms—KITABAT, in its literal sense, signifies a slave purchasing his own person from his master, in return for a sum to be paid out of his earnings,—according to the exposition in the Jama Ramooz.—(From what occurs in the course of the present work it appears that the literal meaning of Kitabat is junction, or union.)—In the language of the LAW it signifies the emancipation of a slave,—with respect to the rights of possession and action (in other words, the conveyance and appropriation of property) at the time of the contract, and with respect to his person at the time of his paying the consideration of Kitabat.

Chap. III.—Of Acts lawful to a Mokatib, or otherwise.

Chap IV.—Of a Person transacting a Kitabat on behalf of a Slave.

Chap. V.—Of the Kitabat of Partnership Slaves.

Chap VI.—Of the Death or Insolvency of the Mokatib; and of the Death of his Master.

[*Since the abolition of slavery this subject has become comparatively useless, and the learning upon it is therefore omitted.*]

BOOK XXXIII.

OF WILLA.*

Definition of the term.—WILLA literally means assistance and friendship. In the language of the LAW it signifies (according to the exposition in the Inayat) that mutual assistance which is a cause of inheritanee.

Willa is of two descriptions, Ittakit and Mawalat.—WILLA is of two species or descriptions. I. Willa Ittakit† (which is also termed Willa Niamit‡), the occasion of which is manumission from right of property (act cording to the Rawayet-Saheeh), whence it is that if a person become proprietor of his kinsman by inheritance, such kinsman is free, and his Willa goes to that person.—II. Willa Mawalat, § the occasion of which is a contract of Mawalat [mutual amity—or patronage and clientage], as shall be explained in its proper placc.—The occasion of the first species, therefore, being manumission, and of the second, a contract of mutual amity, they are termed the WILLA of manumission, or the WILLA of mutual amity, by a reference of the effect to the cause. Both species, moreover, bear the characteristic of assistance:—and as the Arabs were accustomed to assist each other in various ways, and the Prophet interpreted such mutual assistance into Willa of both species, he used to say of them, indiscriminately. "They have WILLA people among them," and also. "They have HALEEFS [sworn confederates] among them;" by which last is understood the relation of Mala Mawalat; as the Arabs were accustomed to confirms their contracts of Mawalat, or mutual amity, by oaths.

The Willa of a slave appertains to his amancipator, rendering him liable to fines incurred by the slave, and endowing him with a right of inheritance.—IF a master emancipate his slave, the Willa of such slave appertains to him;—because the Prophet has said. The WILLA of a slave belongs to the person who emancipates him;" and also, because* [two consequences arise from manumission: I. Liability to the Deyit. or fine of blood,—the cause of which liability is assistance, exhibited and obtained by means of manumission; and, II Inheritance,—because the emancipator has given life to the emancipated by means of removing his bondage, and consequently inherits of him. The relationship of Willa, moreover, resembles relationship of blood, with respect to inheritance, and the obligation of atonement by fine, the Prophet having said. "The relationship of WILLA is like the relationship of consanguinity."

OBJECTION.—From this it would follow that the emancipated also inherits of his emancipator, where he is destitute of kindred (and such is the opinion of Hasan Bin Zeeyad); whereas it is otherwise.

REPLY.—An emancipated slave is a stranger with regard to his emancipator, and consequently does not inherit of him. The emancipator's right, moreover, to inherit of the emancipated, is founded on a paticular text of the KORAN, in opposition to analogy, which, therefore, must not be abandoned or departed from with respect to any other instance of inheritance.

Another reason, also, why the Willa of an emanipated slave appertains to his emancipator is, that there must be an acquisition for a surrender,—or, in other words, an advantage in lieu of a loss; and as, in consequence of emancipation, the property involved in the slave is destroyed, the Willa thereof consequently belong to his emanci-

---

*There is no single word in our language fully expressive of this term. The shortest definition of it is "the relation between the master (or patron) and his freed-man;" but even this does not express the whole meaning.

†The Willa of manumission.

‡The Willa of beneficence, or of favour.

§The Willa of mutual amity, or of confederacy.

*The passage between the crochets is in some places rather obscure; and affords an instance of the great liberty occasionally taken by the Molovees employed in the composition of the Persian Hedaya, for which indeed they have endeavoured to apologize, by alleging the excsssive closeness and obscurity of the original text. (See introductory address.] The whole passage, in the Arabic, stands verbatim thus,—"because he assists him thereby, and consequently attaches him; and he likewise, in his bondage, whence he inherits, of him; and his Willa, with respect to him, resembles relationship; and also, because [there must be] an acquisition for a surrender." What mentioned of "the liability to the fine of blood being induced by manumission" is because an emancipator is the Akila of his freed-man. (See Moakli).

pator]. It is to be observed that a woman is entitled to the Willa of her emancipated slave in the same manner as a man ;—because of the tradition before quoted ;—and also because it is recorded the upon a freed-man of Hamaza dying, and leaving a daughter (Hamza also being dead and having left a daughter), the Prophet divided his effects equally between this daughter and the daughter of Hamaza.—It is also proper to observe that manumission for a compensation, and manumission, without a compensation, are alike with respect to this rule, as the tradition above mentioned is absolute.

A stipulation of waving the claim to inheritance is invalid.—If a person emancipate his slave, engaging, at the same time that "he will not claim the right from him," such engagement in null, and the Willa appertains to the emancipator notwithstanding ; because the condition here mentioned is contrary to the text [of the Koran], and is consequently invalid.

The Willa of a slave emancipated by Kitabat appertains to his master.—Upon a Mokatib paying his ransom he is free, and the Willa belongs to his master, although he become free after his [the master's] decease ;* because he becomes free in consequence of a contract of Kitabat to which his master was a party ; and as a Mokatib, like a Modabbir, is not a subject of inheritance, he is consequently emancipated while the master's right of property continues —The same rule also holds with respect to a slave whose master has bequeathed him manumission,—or a slave whom a person directs, in his will, to be purchased and set free upon his decease —for the act of the executor, after the testator's death, is equivalent to the act of the testator.

Objection.—The slave in question cannot be considered as emancipated from the testator, except where he is his actual property ; and he discontinues from being his property because of his death.

Reply.—The whole estate of the testator is regarded as his property as long as there is occasion,—that is, until his will be executed.

And the same of the Willa of Modabbirs, Am-Walids.—If a master of slaves die his Modabbirs and Am-Walids are free (as has been explained in treating of manumission), and the Willa of them belongs to him,† as he emancipated them by making them Modabbirs and Am-Walids.

And slaves emancipated by affinity.—If a person become proprietor of a relation within the prohibited degrees, such relation is free, (as has been explained under the head of manumission), and the Willa of him belongs to his person, as he is emancipated from his property.

In the emancipation of a pregnant female slave, the Willa of the fœtus belongs to her emancipator.—If a slave marry the female slave of any person, and she become pregnant, and her master then emancipate her, she is accordingly free, together with the fœtus in her womb ;—and the Willa of the foetus belongs to her master, and never can shift from him : because he has emancipated it, not as a dependant of the mother, but independently; and of itself, as being a portion of the mother, and it is capable of being so emancipated.—The Willa of the child, therefore, cannot shift from him, because the Prophet has said. "The Willa belongs to the person who emancipates."—The same rule holds if the female slave be delivered of a child at any time short of six months from the date of her manumission, because in this case the existence of the fœtus at the time of manumission is certified. The same rule also holds if she be delivered of two children, one within the six months, and the other after they have expired ; because those are twins, as having been begotten from one seed. It is otherwise where a female slave, being pregnant, enters into a contract of Mawalat with any person, and her husband also enters into a similar contract with any other person ; for in this case the Willa of the child belongs to the master of the father, because an embryo cannot of itself be a party to a Mawalat contract, as that is concluded by proposal and acceptance, of which an embryo is incapable.

But if she be not delivered within six months from the date of her manumission, it may gifts from him to the father's emancipator.—If the female slave mentioned above be delivered of a child after six months from the date of manumission, the Willa belongs to the mother's because the child is in this case free as a dependant of the mother, and is therefore a dependant of her with respect to the Willa. As, however, in this case, it is no certain that the child existed at the time of manumission so as that it should be emancipated independently and of itself, if the father be afterwards emancipated the Willa shifts from the master of the mother to the master of the father, because of the child having become free, not of itself, but depently. It is otherwise where produces a child within six months, for in that case the Willa would not shift from the one master to the other. The ground of this is, that Willa stands in the same predicament with parentage ; for the Prophet has said. Willa is a relationship as much as the relationship of parentage; and cannot be sold, or given away, or inherited." In the same manner, moreover, as parentage is established on the part of the father, so also is Willa. Besides, the Willa was referred to the mother's master, of necessity, merely because of the father's incapacity : but upon the father becoming capable, the Willa reverts to his master ;—in the same manner as the child of

*In which case the Willa appertains to his heirs.

†Descending, as a heritage, to his heirs.

an asseverating woman* is of necessity referred to her family; but if her husband afterwards retract his assertions, the parentage of it is then established in him—It is otherwis where a female slave is emancipated during her edit from the death of her husband, who was a Mokatib, and who has left effects sufficient to discharge his ransom,—and she brings forth a child at any time within two years from the time of his decease; because in this case the Willa of the child appertains to the master of the mother; for as it is here impossibie to refer the conception to a period subsequent to the father's decease, it must therefore be referred to some time during his life;—and as the foetus existed† at the time of her manumission, the Willa of it therefore belongs to the mother's master, since he has emancipated the child by itself and independently. It is also otherwise where a famale slave is emancipated whilst in her Edit from divorce, and brings forth a child within less than two years from the date of her manumission; for in this case also, notwithstanding her husband be emancipated, the Willa of the child belongs to the mother's master, whether the divorce she was under be reversible or irreversible. It belongs to him in the case of irreversible divorce; because after such divorce the begetting of the child cannot be attributed to the father, as his having connexion with the female slave in question after an irreversible divorce would be unlawful, and we must always, as far as possible, put a fair construction on the acts of a Mussulman. The begetting of it is therefore refrred to him antecedent to divorce: and as the foetus exists at the time of emancipation the Willa of it consequently belongs to the mother's master, as he has emancipated it of itself and independently. In the same manner also, it belongs to him in the case of reversible divorce; because the child being born of the slave in question within less than two years, it is possible that the foetus may have existed during divorce, in which case there is no occasion for a reversal of the divorce in order to the establishment of the parentage;—or, on the other hand, it is possible that the foetus may not have existed during divorce, in which case a reversal of the divorce is essential to the establishment of the parentage:—now such reversal is doubtful:—no regard, threfore, is paid to that, but the conception is referred to the time of the marriage; and as the foetus exists at the time of manumission, the child is therefore emancipated independently and of itself. It is written in the Jama Sagheer, that if a slave marry a freed-woman, and they have children, and those children commit any offences, the fine falls upon the Mawlas of the mother: because they have become free as dependants of their mother. Their father, moreove, is not possessed either of Akilas or of Mawals by manumission. Consequently, they are of necessity attached to the Mawlas of the mother, in the same manner as in the case of in asseverating woman, before alluded to: but if, afterwards, the father be emancipated, the Willa of them shifts to the Mawlas of the father, as was before explained. The Mawlas of the mother, however, are not in this case entitled to recover, from the Mawlas of the father, the fine they have paid on account of the children's offence, because at the time they paid it the Willa of the children appertained to them; and the Willa is not established to the master of the father until he [the master] emancipate him [the father]: because the occasion of Willa, namely manumission, cannot be referred to an antecedent time, but is restricted to the time of emancipation.—It is otherwise with respect to the child of an asseverating woman, where the mother's tribe pay the fine on account of any offence committed by such child, and the husband afterwards retracts his imputation against her:—for in this case the parentage is established by referring it to the conception of that child; and as the mother's Mawlas have not paid the fine willingly, but per force, they are accordingly entitled to recover it.

Case of a Persian marrying a freed-woman.—If a Persian* marry a freed-woman, and they have children, the Willa of those children rests with the Mawlas of the mother, whether she was emancipated by an Arab or a Persian. The compiler of the Hedaya remarks that this is the opinion of Mohammed; but that Aboo Yoosaf maintains that the child is in this case subject to the same rule with the father, inasmuch as its parentage is established in the father, in the same manner as if the person who married the slave in question were an Arab.—It is otherwise, however, where the person who marries her is a slave; for as a slave is, constructively, a mere dead matter, the case is therefore the same as if those children had no father whatever. The argument of Haneefa and Mohammed is that the Willa of manumission is strong, and worthy of regard with respect to its effects, whence equality is attended to in it, insomuch that a Persian emancipator is not equal to an Arab emancipator. The parentage of a Persian, moreover, is weak, as they pay no regard to genealogy (whence no attention is paid by them to equality in point of family); and that which is weak cannot oppose that which is strong. It is otherwise where the

* Meaning a woman repudiated in consequence of Laan.

† Meaning "the child existed as (or, in the state of) a foetus."

* Arab, Ajmee. This term applies not only to the natives of Persia, but of all other countries except Arabia. The case here considered turns upon the superiority which the Arabs claim, in point of privileges, over all others.

father is an Arab, because the parentage of an Arab is strong, and is regarded with respect to equality and the payment of fines;—for as the assistance they afford to each other is an account of a affinity or genealogy, there is therefore no necessity, in the case of an Arab, to have regard to the Willa—It is related, in the Jama Sagheer, that if a Nabathean infidel merry a freed-woman who is a Christian, and become a Mussulman, and enter into a contract of Mawalat with any person, and they afterwards have children, the Willa of those children (according to Haneefa and Mohammed) appertains to the Mawlas of the mother. Aboo Yoosaf, on the contrary, maintains that their Willa appertains to the Mawlas of the father (namely, his Mawla Mawalat); because, although the contract of Mawalat be but weak, still it is on the part of the father:—and hence the children in question resemble the child of a Persian man and an Arab woman;—in other words, as, if a Persian marry an Arab woman, and she bring forth a child, it is referred to the father's tribe, so also in the present case—(The ground on which this proceeds is that the parentage of a child is weaker on the part of the mother than on the part of the father.) The argument of Haneefa is that the Willa of Mawalat is weak (whence it is capable of dissolution), whereas the Willa of manumission is strong (whence it is incapable of dissolution); and the weak cannot oppose the strong.

If the father and mother are both freed-persons, the Willa of their children belongs to the father's tribe—IF the father be a freed-man, and the mother a freed-woman, the parentage of their children is referred to the father's tribe; because in this instance the parents are both upon an equality: and the father's side has the preference, as protection is on his side more effectual.

Heirship is established by the Willa of manumission—BY the Willa of manumission Asoobat* is established;—in other words; where a person emancipates his slave he is Assaba † to such slave, and is entitled to inherit of him in perference to his maternal uncles or aunts, or other uterine kindred; because the Prophet said to a person who had purchased a slave and afterwards emancipated him, "He whom you have thus emancipated is your brother; and if he manifest his gratitude, it is the better for him, but the worse for you;—or, if he do not manifest his gratitude, it is the worse for him, but the better for you; and if he die without leaving heirs, you are his ASSABA."—The daughter of Hamaza, moreover, emancipated her slave: and the slave died, leaving a daughter; and the Propht constituted the daughter of Hamaza her heir in the manner of an Assaba, that is, notwithstanding there was a daughter.—Where, therefore. Asoobat is established on the part of the emancipator, he precedes the relations (and such is the opinion of Alee). If, however, the emancipated have any Assaba by blood, they precede, as the emancipator comes after the paternal kindred.—The ground of this is that, in the saying of the Prophet above quoted, "if he die without leaving heirs," by the term heirs is to be understood those the description of Assaba. as may be inferred from the tradition concening the daughter of Hamaza, The emancipator, therefore, follows after the Assabas, but not after the maternal kindred.* If, on the contrary, the emancipated have no Assabas by blood, the whole inheritance belongs to the emancipator This is where there is no participating heir. But where there is a sharer the emancipator is entitled to what remains after paying the sharer his [or her] portion; because the emancipator is the Assaba, agreeably to the tradition before quoted, The grounb of this is, that the Assaba is one who protects and assists his family;—and as a master aids and assists his freed-man (according to what has been already stated), he is therefore his Assaba, Now an Assaba takes what remains after paying the portions:—hence the person in question takes what thus remains—If, therefore, the emancipator were first to die, and then his freed-man, the estate of the latter would go to the sons of the emancipator, not to his daughters.

An emancipatress is entitled to the Willa of her freed-men, &c., but not of their children—A WOMAN is entitled only to the Willa of the person whom she has herself emancipated, or of the person whom she (again) has emancipated, or of the person whom she has created a Mokatib, or whom her Mokatib has created a Mokatib, or of the person whose Willa has been transferred† to her by her freed-man; because

* Asoobat, in its literal sense, signifies binding together the branches of a tree, a bundle of arrows, or so forth,—IN its secondary sense it is used to express the descent of inheritance in the male line.

† Assaba, in its primary sense, signifies a nerve, sinew, or tendon, of an ox or other animal, with which bundles of arrows, &c., are tied together. Hence Assaba is used to express the first heir or head of a family, since the various branches of the family are represented and (as it were) bound up in his person—Assobat might be rendered heirship, and Assaba the heir; but as the translator is apprehensive this might confound those terms with Wirasit and Waris [inheritance and heir in the most extensive sense]. he has therefore thought it advisable, in this palace, to preserve the original terms, for the sake of distinction.

* That is, he precedes the maternal kindred.

† Arab. Jurra, literally "drawn over."—A case of transferring or drawing over the Willa, is where (for example) the male slave of a woman marries a female slave,

such is the recorded opinion of the Prophet upon this subject; and also because, as power, and the right of possessing property, are established in the person emancipated by the act of the emancipatress; this person is accordingly referred (in regard to Willa) to her; and in the same manner is referred to her the person who is referred to her freed-man. It is otherwise with respect to parentage* (that is, the Willa of manumission may be established on the part of a woman, but parentage cannot be so established); because Willa is established in consequence of the occurrence of a power to possess property, occasioned by and arising from the emancipation which may proceed from a woman in the same manner as from a man;—whereas parentage is established by regular cohabitation [Firash], and it is the husband that possesses the right of cohabitation, not the wife; for she is the appropriated, not the appropriator:—hence perentage cannot be established in a woman

The estate of a freed-man descends to the lineal heir of the emancipator, and not to his heirs general.—IT is to be observed that the estate of a freed-man goes to the Assaba [lineal heir] of the emancipator,—to the nearest, and after him to the next of kin.—and not solely to his children; because inheritance does not hold with respect to Willa, for if such were the case, the property of the free-man would at all events descend to the sons and daughters of the emancipator (the sons receiving two shares each, and the daughters one),—whereas it is not so—Hence it is evident that inherirance does not hold in Willa.—Succession, however, holds with respect to it:—but succession cannot be established with regard to any except a person from whom proceeds protection and aid; and protection and aid are afforded by men only, not by women.—Now it being proved that the estate of a freed-man goes to the emancipator's Assaba,—to the nearest, and after him to the next of kin,—it follows that if a freed-man die, leaving the father and the son of his emancipator, the right of Willa descends to the son, not to the father (according to Haneefa and Mohammed), because the son is the nearest Assaba [lineal heir];—and, in the same manner, it would go to the master's grandfather, not to his brother (according to Haneefa), since (as he holds) the grandfather is the nearest of the two.—In the same manner also, the Willa of her freed-man descends to the son of his emancipatress, not to her brother, for her son is the nearest in lineal succession.—If, however, the freed-man were to commit an offence, the fine for it would fall upon her brother; because the offence of the freed-man is the offence of the emancipatress, and her brother is of her paternal kindred, whereas her son is not so.—If, also, a freed-man die, leaving a son of his master, and the children of another son, his estate goes to the son, not to the grand-children, because the Willa descends to the nearest. This is recorded from several of the companions; and among the rest from Amroo, Alee, and Ibn Masaood.

Section

Of the Willa Mawalat, or Willa of Mutual Amity.

Nature and effect of a contract of Mutual lat.—THE case of Willa Mawalat is where (for instance) a stranger* says to the person whose proselyte be is,† or to any other person. "I enter into a contract of Mawalat with you, so that if I die my property shall go to you, or if (on the other hand) I commit an offence, the fine is upon you or your Akila," and the person thus addressed assents accordingly,—in consequence of which he becomes the Mawla of the stranger, and upon his decease without heirs inherits his property.—The stranger is termed the Mawla Asfal, ‡ and the person who thus accedes to the contract the Mawla Aaila. §—Shafei maintains that a contract of Mawalat does not occasion inheritance in any respect, and is of no force whatever, as it tends to annul the right of the public treasury ¶—whence the invalidity of it with respect to any other heir: for if it were valid with respect to such, his right of heritage would be annulled;—and on this ground also it is, that (according to Shafei) a man's bequest of his whole property is invalid although the testator be destitute of heirs; for still (according to him) such bequest holds good to the amount

---

and the master of the female slave afterwards emancipates her, and she brings forth a child in six months from the date of her manumission; when the Willa of such child belongs to the mother's master; but if, afterwards, the woman emancipate her slave, the Willa of the child then shifts to her, as being the emancipatress of the father.

*This means that an emancipatress is entitled to the Willa of her freed-men, &c., but not to the Willa of their children.

*Arab Ajimee. This term (as has been already remarked) signifies, generally, any person not an Arab. It is also used in the same sense among the Arabs as Barbarian with the Greeks, or Gentile among the Jews. The case here stated applies to any infidel alien coming into a Mussulman territory under protection, and there embracing the faith, in which case it was customary for some Mussulman to adopt him as his proselyte.

†Literally, "in whose hands he has embraced the faith."

‡Literally, "the inferior Mawla," or the client

§Literally, "the inferior Mawla," or the client.

¶Where a stranger dies without heirs the whole of his property goes to the public treasury.

only of a third of his property, since if it were effectual to the amount of the whole, the right of the public treasury would be annulled.*—The arguments of our doctors upon this point are twofold.—FIRST, GOD has said, in the KORAN, "ALLOW, TO THOSE WHO ENTER INTO CONTRACTS, THEIR SHARE OF INHERITANCE," which text related to contracts of Mawalat:—and it is also recorded that the Prophet, upon being questioned concerning a certain person who had become the proselyte of another, and entered into a contract of Mawalat with that other, replied. "This person is endowed with a right with regard to that man, superior to all others, both during life and in death."—from which it may be inferred, that during his proselyte's life he is subject to fines on his account, and upon his decease is his heir.—SECONDLY; the property of the proselyte is this person's right, whence he is at liberty to make use of it in any manner he pleases: for the property would fail to the public treasury only from this necessity, that there are no claimants to it, not because the public treasury has any right in it.—If, however, the proselyte leave any natural heir, such heir precedes the Mawla Mawalat, notwithstanding he be of the uterine kindred (such as a maternal uncle for instance); because the two person in question are the only parties to the contract, whence it is not binding upon any other; and an uterine relation is entitled to inheritance.—It is to be observed' that in the contract in question the parties must particularly mention and stipulate fine and inheritance, as has been explained in the exemplificaiion of the case. If, therefore, the stipulation of inheritance be made on both parts, whoever dies first inherits of the other; but if on one part only, heritage holds agreeably to stipulation. In the same manner also, if responsibility for fines be stipulated on both parts, each is responsible for the fines incurred by the other; but if on one part only, responsibility holds accordingly: for a thing is rendered obligatory only by undertaking for it; and it cannot be undertaken for but by stipulation. It is also to be observed, that it is essential in contracts of Mawalat, that the Mawala, Asful, or, client, be a stranger [Ajmee], and not an Arab; because among the Arabs aid and patronage run in families or tribes—(that is, one Arab aids or patronizes another where they are both of the same tribe or family),—whence they have no occasion for engaging in contracts of Mawalat.

Either party may dissolve the contract in presence of the other.—THE Mawla Asfal, or client, is at full liberty to desert from his Mawla Aaila, or patron, and to enter into a contract of Mawalat with some other person, so long as the first shall not have paid any fine of his incurring; because a contract of Mawalat is, like bequest, a reversible deed.—In the same manner, also, the Mawla Aaila, or patron, is at liberty to relinquish his right of Willa, and to break off the contract of Mawalat, because such a contract is not binding.—It is requisite, in case of either party dissolving the contract, that it be dissolved in the presence of the other, in the same manner as in the case of dismissing an agent, where the dismission is express, and not implied, or virtually induced.

Or the inferior party may breach it off in the superior's absence, by engaging in a Mawalat with some other person.—IT is otherwise, however, where the client enters into a contract of Mawalat with a person in the absence of the former patron; for in this case the first contract of Mawalat is dissolved without the presence of the party, this being a dissolution by effect, and necessarily resulting;—in other words, the dissolution of the first contract is a necessary consequence of the formation of the second.—In this case, therefore, the presence of the other party is not requisite; in the same manner as the presence of an agent is not requisite where he is virtually dismissed from his employment, by the constituent (for instance) himself selling the article concerning which he had constituted him his agent for sale.

But he cannot do so after the other has paid a fine incurred by him.—WHERE the patron pays the fine incurred for an offence committed by his client, the latter is incapaciated from quitting him and engaging in a contract of Mawalat with any other person;—because the right of another then becomes implicated; and also, because the fine was decreed by the Kazee—Besides, the fine paid by the patron on his account stands as a valuable consideration, in the same manner as the return for a gift; whence he has it not in his power to turn from his patron, in the same manner as a donor, after receiving a return, cannot recede from his gift.—In the same manner also, the child of the client cannot turn from the patron who has paid a fine on account of its father; and so likewise, if the patron pay a fine on account of the child of his client, neither the client not his child can afterwards turn from the patron, because with regard to the Willa Mawalat they are as one person.

A freed man cannot engage in a contract of Mawalat.—AN emancipated slave, as having a Mawla in his emancipator, is not at liberty to enter into a contract of Mawalat with any person; because the Willa of Manumission is binding, whereas the Willa of Mawalat is not so; and during the existence of a thing which is forcible and binding, a thing which is not so cannot take place.

*He holding that, in case of a person dying without heirs, two thirds of his property must go to the public treasury at all events.

BOOK XXXIV.

OF IKRAH, OR COMPULSION.

The nature of compulsion defined—IKRAH, or compulsion, applies to case where the compeller has it in his power to execute what he threatens,—whether he [the compeller] be the Sultan, or any other person, as a thief (for instance).—The reason of this is, that compulsion implies an act which men exercise upon others, and in consequence of which the will of the other is set at nought, at the same time that his power of action still remains.—Now this characteristic does not exist unless the other (namely, the person compelled) be put in fear, and apprehend that if he do not perform what the compeller desires, the threatened evil will fall upon him;—and this fear and apprehension cannot take place unless the compeller be possessed of power to carry his menace into execution; but provided this power does exist, it is of no importance whether it exist in the Sultan or in any other person. With respect to what is recorded from Haneefa, that "compulsion cannot proceed from any except the Sultan," the learned remark that this difference originates merely in the difference of times, and not in any difference of argument; for in his time none possessed power except the Sultan, but afterwards changes took place with respect to the customs of mankind.—It is to be observed that, in the same manner as it is essential, to the establishment of compulsion, that the compellor be able to carry his menace into execution, so likewise it is requisite that the person compelled be in fear that the thing threatened will actually take place; and this fear is not supposed except it appear most probable to the person compelled that the compeller will execute what he has threatened, so as to force and constrain him to the performance of the act which the compiler requires of him.

A person forced into a contract may afterwards dissolve it—IF a persen exercise compulsion upon another, by cutting, beating or imprisonment, with a view to make him sell his property, or purchase merchandise, or acknowledge a debt of one thousand dirms to a particular person, or let his house to hire, and this other accordingly sell his property, purchase merchandise or so forth, he has it afterwards at his option either to adhere to the contract into which he has been so compelled or to dissolve it, and take back or restore the article purchased or sold; because one essential to the validity of any of these contracts is that it have the consent of both parties, which is not the case here, as the compulsion by blows or other means rather occasions a dissent; and the contract is therefore invalid.

Unless the means of compulsion be trifling.—(THIS rule, however, does not hold where the compulsion consists only of a single blow, or of imprisonment for a single day, since fear is not usually excited by this degree of beating or confinement. Compulsion, therefore, is not established by a single blow, or a single day's imprisonment:—unless the compelled be a person of rank, to whom such a degree of beating or confinement would appear detrimental or disgraceful; for with respect to such a person compulsion is established by this degree of violence, as by it his volition is destroyed.)

The purchaser becomes proprietor of goods sold upon compulsion.—IN the same manner, also, an acknowledgment extorted by any of the above modes of compulsion is invalid; because acknowledgment is a species of proof, inasmuch as truth is more probable, in acknowledgment, than falsehood; but in a case of compulsion falsehood is most probable as a man will acknowledge falsely where, by so doing he may avoid injury.

An acknowledgment extorted by compulsion is invalid. WHERE a person sells goods by compulsion, as above stated; and makes delivery of them under the influence of such compulsion, the purchaser becomes proprietor of them, according to our doctors.—Ziffer maintains that he does not become proprietor, because a sale by compulsion depends, for its validity, upon the assent of the seller, and a sale so circumstanced cannot endow with a right of property until such assent be signified. The argument of our doctors is that, in the case in question, the pillar of sale (signified by proposal and acceptance) has proceeded from fit persons with respect to a fit subject; the sale being merely invalid, from a want of one of the essentials of sale, namely, the mutual consent of the parties; and the purchaser, in an invalid sale, becomes proprietor of the article upon obtaining possession of it: whence it is that if a person take possession of a slave purchased under an invalid contract, and then emancipate him, or perform such other act with respect to him as cannot afterwards be annulled, it is valid, and he must pay the seller the value, as is the rule in all cases of invalid sale.—After the compulsion has ceased, however, if the seller signify his assent, the sale then becomes lawful and valid, because by such assent the causes of invalidity (namely, compulsion and unwillingness) are removed.

But the seller may resume the article, provided he does not signify his assent to the sale.—WHERE a person thus sells his property by compulsion, he has still a right, as long as he does not signify his assent to the sale, to take back the article, although the purchaser should have sold it into the hands of another person.—It is otherwise in all other cases of invalid sale; for in those, after the purchaser has sold the article; the seller has no right to take it back; because the invalidity of sale in those cases is on account of the right of the LAW; and when the purchaser sells the article to any third person, the right of that person becomes involved in this second contract; and his right precedes the right of the LAW, as the individual is necessitous, whereas the LAW is not so.—In a case of compulsion, on the contrary, the invalidity of the sale is on account of the right of the seller; and as he is an individual, it follows that, in this case, notwithstanding the right of the second purchaser be involved in the second contract, still both rights are upon a par, as being both rights of the individual; and consequently, the right of the first cannot be annulled by the right of the second.

Case of a Waffa sale.—IT is to be observed that some consider a Waffa sale* to be invalid, in the same manner as a compelled sale, and apply to it the rules of sale by compulsion; whence (according to them) if the purchaser in a Waffa sale sell the article purchased. the sale so made by him may be broken through, as the invalidity of the sale, in this case' is on account of the non-consent of the seller, in the same manner as in a case of compulsion.—Waffa sale is where the seller says to the purchaser, "I sell you this article in lieu of the debt I owe you, in this way, that upon may paying the debt the article is mine"—Some determine this to be, in fact, a contract of pawn; for between it and pawn there is no manner of difference. as; although the parties denominate it a sale, still the intention is, in effect, a pawn. Now in all acts regard is paid to the spirit and intenion; and the spirit and intention of pawn exist in this instance,—whence it is that the seller is at liberty to resume the article from the purchaser upon paying his debt to him.—Some, again, consider a Waffa sale to be utterly null, as the purchaser, in the case in question, resembles a person in jest since he (like a jester) repeats the words of sale, at the same time that the effect and purpose of sale are not within his design. Such sale is therefore utterly null and void, in the same manner as a sale made in jest. The Haneefite doctors of Samarcand, on the other hand, hold a Waffa sale to be both valid and useful, as it is a species of sale commonly practised from necessity and convenience, and is attended with advantage in regard to some effects of sale, such as the use of the article, although the purchaser cannot lawfully dispose of it.

A compelled sale is rendered valid if the seller willingly receive the price.—IF, in a case of compulsion, the seller take possession of the price readily and willingly, the sale is valid, as his thust taking possession of the price is an argument of its validity; in the same manner as where, in a suspended sale, the seller readily and willingly receives the price of the article, such receipt argues the validity of the sale.—So, likewise, if a person advancing part of the price conclude a Sillim contract by compulsion, and the party who received the advance should afterwards readily and willingly deliver the article for which the advance had been paid, his so doing is an argument of the validity of the transaction. It is otherwise where one person compels another to make a gift, saying to him, "make a gift of this article to such a person,"—but without adding to the word gift "and delivery," and the person thus compelled make gift and delivery of the article to the person named; for such gift is utterly null, becaese the design of the compeller is that the donee shall be endowed with a right in the article upon the instant of donation; and this design cannot be obtained, in a case of gift, but by delivery of the article to the person specified. In a case of sale by compulsion, on the other hand, the end of the compeller is obtained on the instant of compelling the party to accede to the contract of sale Gift upon compulsion, therefore, comprehends a delivery of the article to the donee; whereas sale upon compulsion does not comprehend a delivery of the article sold to the purchaser,—whence it is that if the seller, after acceding to the contract from compulsion, make delivery of the arttcle without compulsion, the sale is rendered valid by such delivery,—whereas the gift in question is not rendered valid by a delivery of the article to the donee.

But it is not valid if he be compelled to receive it.—IF, in a case of compulsion, the seller take possession of the price by compulsion, such receipt does not render the sale valid; and it is accordingiy incumbent on him to return the price to the purchaser, if it remain in his hands, because of the contract being invalid. If, howevery, the price have been lost, or have perished in his hands, nothing can be taken from him in lieu of it, because it was merely a trust with him, inasmuch as he took possession of it by consent of the proprietor, namely, the purchase.

A sale in which the seller is compelled, but not the purchaser, leaves the latter responsible for the article, in case it be lost in his hands.—IF one person compel an other to sell an article to a third person, but do not compel this person to purchase the article, and it afterwards perish in the purchaser's hands he [the purchaser] is responsible to the seller for the value, as the article is insured in his hands, such being the law of invalid sale, It is to be observed, however, that in this case the seller is at liberty to take the compensation from the compeler; because as it was (in a manner)* he who gave the article to the purchaser, it may be said that it is he who has lost or destroyed the seller's property. In short, the seller, in the case in question, is at ful liberty to take the compensation from either of the two; in the same manner as the proprietor of an usurped article is at liberty to take his compensation from either party, where the article has first been usurped from him, and then usurped by some other from the first ururper

* Literally, "a security sale;" so termed because, by it, the seller insures to the purchaser the debt he owes him,

If, however the seller take his compensation from the compeller, he [the compeller] is entitled to recover the value from the purchaser, since, in consequence of paying the compensation for the article, he stands as substitute to the seller.—It is to be observed that, in a case of usurpation, if the usurper sell the article to Amroo, and he (again) sell it to Khalid, and he (again) sell it to Bikroo, and so on, from hand to hand, and the proprietor take his compensation from Khalid (for instance), in the case every purchase subsequent to that of Khalid is legal and valid; because as Khalid, in consequence of paying the compensation, becomes proprietor of the usurped article, he then appears to have sold his own property; where as every purchase made before, and even the purchase of Khalid himself, is invalid: because the article usurped becomes the property of Khalid, by retrospect, from the time only that he took possession of it. It is otherwise where similar circumstances follow a compulsive sale; for if, in such case, the party compelled (namely, the first seller) signify his assent to any one of the subsequent contracts, every other contract antecedent to that one is valid, and so likewise every subsequent contract; because the invalidity of these contracts was on account of the right of the proprietor, as he had sold his property upon compulsion; and he therefore possesses a right to resume the property, until he signify his assent: but upon his assenting to any of these contracts, he relinquishes this right; and all the contracts become valid of course.

Section

A person may lawfully eat or drink a prohibited article, upon a compulsion which threatens life or limb.—If one person use compulsion towards another, by imprisonment or blows; with a view to make him eat carrion or drink wine, still it is not lawful for the person thus compelled to eat or drink of those articles,—unless he be threatened with something dangerous to life or limb, in which case he may lawfully do so and the same rule obtains if compulsion be used to make a person eat blood or pork;—because the eating of such prohibited articles is not permitted except in cases of extremity, such as famine, since in any other case the argument of illegality still endures. Now extremity, or unavoidable necessity, do not exist, to require the eating or drinking of the article, except the not eating it be attended with danger to life or limb; but as the eating or drinking is in such case permitted, it follows that it is so permitted where this danger is to be apprehended from imprisonment or blows. Neither is the person, who is thus put in fear, under any obligation to suffer the thing menaced; but rather, if he do suffer it, and refrain from eating or drinking the prohibited article until he die, or lose any of his limbs, he is an offender; because as, under such circumstances, the eating or drinking is permitted to him, it follows that, if he refuse, he is an accessory with another to his own destruction, and is consequently an offender, in the same manner as if he were to refrain from eating carrion when perishing for hunger. Aboo Yoosaf maintains that he would not be an offender from persisting, unto death or dismemberment, in his refusal; because the eating or drinking, in the case in question is merely licensed (since the articles still continue prohibited).—whereas the refraining from them is an observance of the LAW; and consequently, in persisting to refuse, he acts in obedience to the LAW.—To this, however, it may be replied, that in the case in question the illegality no longer remains; because, as a situation of compulsion or indispensable necessity is particularly excepted in the KORAN, it follows that under the circumstances here described the argument of illegality does not exist: hence the eating is positively lawful, and not merely lincensed. It is to be remarked, however, that in the case in question the compelled person is an offender only where he knows the eating to be lawful and nevertheless refrains: because as its legality is a matter of a concealed nature, it follows that he stands excused, from ignorance —in the same manner as men are excused for omissions or neglects, from ignorance, in the beginning of their conversion to the faith, or during their residence in a hostile country.

A person must not declare himself an infidel, or revile the Prophet, upon compulsion, unless he be in danger of otherwise losing life or limb.—If one person compel another to turn infidel, or to revile the Prophet, by imprisonment of blows, still compulsion [in its legal and exculpatory sense] is not established; but if he menace him with something which puts him in fear, and gives room to apprehend danger to life or limb, in this case compulsion is established.—The reason of this is; that as by mere blows or imprisonment compulsion is not established with regard to eating prohibited meats (as was before explained), it follows that it is not established with regard to infidelity a fortiori, since the illegality of infidelity is much greater. When, therefore; a person is put in fear for his life or limbs, so as that compulsion is established, it is lawful for him to make an exhibition of infidelity (that is, to repeat infidel expressions),—and if he merely exhibit this with his lips, but keep his heart steady in the faith, he is not an offender; because when Amar had fallen into the hands of the infidels and they had compelled him to revile the Prophet, he said to him. "If you find your heart still firm in the faith, your uttering infidel expression is immaterial;—nay, if they again should compel you, you may again repeat such infidel expressions;"—and a passage in the KORAN was also revealed to the same effect. Another reason is that by uttering infidel expressions faith is not destroyed, since the actual faith (by which it is understood rectitude of heart) still continues unaffected, and if he were to refuse uttering such infidel expressions he would incur actual destruction, as the infidels would in that case dismember or put him to death.—Yet if he persist in refusing unto death, he has a claim to merit, and is entitled to his reward; because Jeeb persevered in refusing, and suffered death in consequence; and the Prophet gave him the name of Seyd al Shaheed [the martyr], and declared, in afterwards speaking of him, "he is my friend in heaven;" and also because, in thus acting, his honour is effectually preserved. A refusal, moreover, for the sake of religion, to utter any infidel expressions, is an observance of the LAW: in opposition to the case before stated, as there the eating of carrion, or so forth, is positively lawful, because of the exception cited on that subject.

A person destroying the property of another upon compulsion is not responsible; but the compeller is so.—If one person compel another to destroy the property of a Mussulman, by menacing him with something dangerous to life of limb, it is lawful for the person so compelled to destroy that property: because the property of another is made lawful to us in all cases of necessity (such as in a situation of famine for instance), and in the case in question this necessity is established.—The owner of the property must in this instance take the compensation from the compeller: because the compelled is merely the instrument of the compeller in any point where he is capable of being so; and the destruction of property is of that nature.

A person murdering another upon compulsion is an offender; but the compeller is liable to retaliation—If one person compel another, by mencing him with death, to murder a third person, still it is not lawful for the person so menaced to commit the murder, but he must rather refuse, even unto death.—If therefore, he notwithstanding commit the murder, he is an offender, since the slaving of a Mussulman is not permitted under any necesssity whatever.—In this case, however, the retaliation is upon the compeller, if the murder be wilful.—The compiler of the Hedaya remarks that this is according to Haneefa and Mohammed; and that Ziffer, on the contrary, maintains that the retaliation, is upon the compelled person;—whereas Aboo Yoosaf holds that there is no retaliation upon either party.—and Shafei (on the contrary) contends that it is incurred by both.—The argument of Ziffer is, that the act of murder has proceeded from the compelled person, both de facto and duo animo, and the LAW, also, has attached to him the effect of it, namely, criminality: consequently he incurs retaliation—(It is otherwise in the case of destroying the property of another upon compulsion; since as the LAW has not attached the effect thereof, namely, the criminality, to him, it is consequently referred to another, namely the compeller) Such also is the argument of Shafei for awarding retaliation upon the compelled person: and his argument for awarding it upon the compeller is, that from him proceeded the moving cause of the murder, as the compulsion was the cause of it; and the moving cause in murder stands (according to him) subject to the same rule with the actual perpetration;—as in the case of witnesses whose evidence induces retaliation; in other words, if two witnesses give evidence of a wilful murder, and in conformity with their testimony retaliation be executed upon the accused, and the person to whose murder they had borne testimony afterwards prove to be still living, those witnesses are then put to death in retaliation. The argument of Aboo Yoosaf is that concerning the propriety of awarding retaliation upon the compelled person there is a doubt; and, in the same manner, there is also a doubt concerning the propriety of awarding it upon the compeller; for in one way the view is to fix the murder upon the compelled, because of his being an offender, and it is also fixed upon the compeller, because of his being the mover:—thus a doubt opposes itself with respect to each; and hence neither of them is liable to retaliation. The argument of Haneefa and Mohammad is that the compelled person is in this instance, forced to the commission of the murder by a natural instinct, which leads a man to prefer his own life to that of another; and he must therefore, as for as is possible, be regarded as the instrument of the compeller. He is accordingly considered as his instrument in the commission of the murder, in the manner of a weapon. He cannot, however, be his instrument with regard to the criminality of the murder, in such a way as that no part of the criminality would attach to himself, but the whole be imputable to the compeller; and hence the murder, with regard to its criminality, is restricted to the person compelled.—This is therefore in some measure analogous to a case of compulsive manumissinn,—or of a person compelling a Magian to slaughter a goat: that is to say, if one person compel another to emancipate his slave, and he emancipate him accordingly, in this case the emancipation is referred and imputed to the compeller, whence he is answerable for the value of the slave,—but the emancipation is imputed to the compelled with regard to the execution of it, for if it were in this respect also imputed to the compeller, the slave would not become free;—and, in the same manner, if a person compel a Magian, or other idolator, to slaughter the goat of another. his act is referred and imputed to the compeller, with regard to the destruction of the property, but not with regard to a lawful Zabbah, whence the goat is pro-

*Arab. Zabbah. (It is fully explained under its proper head.)

hibited and carrion:—and so likewise, in the case in question, the act of the compelled person is imputed to the compeller with respect to the destruction, not with regard to the criminality.

Case of compelled divorce or emancipation.—If one person compel another to divorce his wife, or to emancipate his slave, and this person accordingly divorce his wife or emancipate his slave, such divorce or emancipation takes effect: according to our doctors; in opposition to the opinion of Shafei as has been already stated under the head of Divorce.—In the case of compulsive manumission, the person compelled is entitled to take the value of the slave from the compeller, because as in this case the compelled admits of being considered as the instrument of the compeller with regard to the destruction of property; to him such destruction is accordingly referred and imputed. Hence he is at liberty to seek a compensation from the compeller, whether rich or poor; and the slave is not liable to emancipatory labour, as that could only be due from him either with a view to his emancipation, or on account of the right of some other person being involved in him, neither of which motives exist in the present instance.—It is also to be observed that the compeller, in this case, is not entitled to take from the slave his value as paid to his proprietor; because as he [the compeller] is sued on the score of a destruction of the slave, it may therefore be said that he has (as it were) murdered or made away with the slave; and he [the slave] consequently cannot be responsible.—In the case of compelled divorce, also, the person compelled is entitled to take from the compeller half the dower, provided the divorce be before consummation:—or, if no dower was mentioned in the marriage contract, he may take from him that for which he is himself in such case responsible, namely, a Matat, or present, as that is what he incurs by the divorce *—It is otherwise where the compelled divorce is pronounced after consummation; for in that case the dower has been already made due by the consummation, and is not made so by the divorce.

Case of a compelled appointment of agency for divorce or emanciption.—If a person, upon compulsion, create another his agent for divorce or emancipation, and the agent divoce the wife, or emancipate the slave, of the person thus compelled to authorize him, such divorce or manumission is valid, on a favourable construction; because a compelled contract or commission, provided it be such as is rendered invalid by involving an invalid condition; is invalidated by the compulsion; but a commission of agency is not rendered invalid by involving an invalid condition.—In the case of divorce, the compelled constituent is entitled to take half the dower from the compeller,—and, in the case of manumission, to take from the compeller the value of the slave; because in both cases the end and design of the compeller was to destroy the constituent's right of property, in performing the act for which he appointeth him agent.

No deed, in itself irreversible, can be extracted after being executed by compulsion.—It is to observed, as a rule, that in all deeds or contracts which, after engagement, do not admit of reversal or dissolution, compulsion has no effect whatever, but they are equally obligatory and under compulsion as otherwise Hence compulsion has no operation upon a vow, since this (unless it be of a suspended nature) incapable of dissolution; and accordingly, the person compelled into such a vow is not entiled to take any thing whatever from the compeller, in consideration of the loss he incurs by such vow.—In the same manner, also, compulsion is attended with no effect in oaths, or in Zihar, as those do not admit of retraction: and reversal of divorce and Aila are also subject to the same rule, as well as a recantation of an Aila oath at the time of making the assertation. In Khoola, also, as being a suspension of divorce on the part of the husband (for he suspends it on the payment of the consideration), compulsion is attended with no effect, since it is incapable of reversal or dissolution; and accordingly, if the husband be compelled into it, not the wife, she is answerable for the consideration, since she assents to it, as having undertaken for it without compulsion.

Whoredom by compulsion incurs punishment.—If a person upon compulsion, commit whoredom, he is liable to punishment, according to Haneefa,—except where the compeller is a Sultan.—The two disciples, on the contrary, maintain that he is not liable to punishment in either case.

Case of apostacy upon compulsion.—If person, upon compulsion, become an apostate by pronouncing a renunciation of the faith, yet his wife is not separated from him, because apostacy has a connexion with belief, whence if his mental faith continue firm, he does not become an infidel by the mere verbal renunciation.—In the case in question, moreover, his infidelity is dubious, and consequently his wife is not separated from him, because of the doubt.—If, therefore, the husband and wife differ, she insisting that she has been separated, and he that his renunciation was only pronounced outwardly, but that this faith still remains firm, his declaration must be credited; because a declaration of apostacy is never used with a view to effect a matrimonial separation, but merely signifies a change of belief: and the compulsion, on the other hand, affords an argument that the belief has not been altered:—consequently his declaration must be credited.—It is otherwise with respect to a man turning Mussulman upon compulsion; as a man who embraces the faith upon compulsion is nevertheless admttied to be a Mussulman, because of the

* See Vol. I., p. 464.

possibility that his faith accords with his words.—In short, in both cases (namely, compulsion to apostacy, and compulsion to Islam) a preference is given to Islam, as it is the superior, and cannot be overcome.—What is here advanced relates merely to the award of the Kazee;* for with God, if the person do not believe in his heart, he is not a Mussulman.

Case of Islam upon compulsion.—If a person become a Mussulman upon compulsion, so as to decreed a Mussulman, and afterwards apostatize, still he is not worthy of death, since his Islam is doubtful, and doubt prevents the execution of death upon him.

Case of a husband acknowledging his having apostatized upon compulsion.—If a person, after having made, upon compulsion, a declaration of infidelity, should say to his wife, who claims a separation, "I said a thing in which I was not serious" in other words, ("I spoke falsely"), in this case his wife is separated from him in the conception of the Kazee,† and he [the Kazee] must issue a decree accordingly, although there be no separation before God —The reason of this is, that from his acknowledgment it is established that he was not compelled into his declaration, but made it without compulsion, as the compeller used compulsion towards him not with a view to extort the declaration from him, but with a view to make him change his faith; and as he, of his own choice, made the declaration of infidelity, and his wife claims a separation, his allegtion that "he intended nothing" cannot be credited with the Kazee, who must therefore issue a decree of separation, although there be no separation in the sight of God.—If, on the other hand, he allege that "he intended merely to fulfil the design of the compeller, namely, to make a declaration of infidelity, at the same time that he spoke under a mental reservation," in this case his wife is separated from him both with the Kazee, and also in the sight of God; because in this case he appears to have made a serious declaration of infidelity, notwithstanding he may have screened himself under the mental reservation.—In the same manner: if a person compel another to worship a cross, or to revile the holy person of the Prophet, and he do so accordingly, and afterwards plead that "his design in worshipping was the worship of God,"—or "by Mohammed he ment some other than the Prophet," his wife, claiming separation, is separated from him with the Kazee, but not in the sight of God;—whereas if he were thus to worship a cross, or to revile the Prophet, under a mere mental reservation his wife would be separated from him both with the Kazee, and also in the sight of God, for the reasons above stated.

* That is, "relates to the mere point of law."

† That is, "in the eye of the law."

BOOK XXXV

OF HIJR, OR INHIBITION.

Definition of the term.—Hijr, in its primitive sense, means interdiction or prevention. In the language of the law it signifies an interdiction of action, with respect to a particular person, who is either an infant, an idiot, or a slave.—the causes of inhibition being three,—infancy, insanity, and servitude.

CHAPTER I.

Inhibition operates upon infants, slaves, and lunatics.—The acts of an infant are not lawful unless authorized by his guardian, nor the act of a slave unless authorized by his master;—and the acts of a lunatic, who has no lucid intervals, are not at all lawful. The acts of an infant are unlawful, because of the defect in his understanding; but the license or authority of his guardian is a mark of his capacity: whence it is that in virtue thereof an infant is accounted the same as an adult. The illegality of the acts of a female or male slave is founded on a regard to the right of the owner:—for if their acts (such as purchase and sale) were valid and efficient, they would be liable to debt, and their creditors might appropriate their acquisition, or even sell their persons for the discharge of their demands, whence the master's advantage would be defeated. If, however, the master signify his assent to their acts, he thereby agrees to the destruction of his right. With respect to the acts of a lunatic, they are not lawful under any circumstance, as he is utterly incompetent to act at all, although his guardian should agree to his so doing. It is otherwise with respect to a slave or an infant: for a slave is possessed of personal competency, and there is hope of an infant in due time attaining that competency,—whence there is an evident difference between those and lunatics.

Whence purchase or the sale by them requires the assent of their immediate superior.—If a slave, an infant or a lunatic, should sell or purchase any article, knowing at the time the nature of purchase and sale, and intending one or other of those, the guardian, or other immediate superior, has it at his option either to give his assent if he see it advisable, or to annul the bargain; because, as the control and suspension with regard to the acts of a slave are on account of the right of his master, it follows that he has an option with respect to them; and as the same con-

*Arab. tæserrif, meaning transactions of any kind, such as purchase, sale, or so forth.

trol and suspension as to the acts of an infant or a lunatic are with a view to the security of their interest, their guardians are therefore to examine and attend to what may be good for them in their acts. It is requisiie, morever, . that the persons here described know the nature of sale, in order that the pillar of the contract may exist, and the sale be concluded so far as to remain suspended upon the guardian's consent ;— and a luntic sometimes knows the nature of sale, and designs it, although he be incapable of distinguishing between the profit and loss attending it.—(A lunatic of this description is termed a Matooa ;—and his agency is likewise valid,— as has been already mentioned in treating of agency.)

Objection.—Suspense obtains only in sale; the original rule in purchase being that it takes effect upon the agent :* but in the present instance, purchase by an infant or a lunatic depends upon the ascent of the guardian, in the same manner as sale by them.

Reply.—The non-suspense of purchase is only where its taking effect upon the agent is possible, as in the case of purchase by a Fazoolee, or unauthorized person ; but in the case in question it is impossible that the purchase should take effect upon the agent, because of his incompetency where he is an infant or a lunatic, and because of the injury to the master where he is slave.—Purchase by them, therefore, is also suspended.

But it operates upon them with respect to words only, not with respect to acts.—It is to be observed that the three disqualifications in question, namely, infancy, insanity, and servitude, occasion inhibition with respect to words, but not with respect to acts;† because acts, upon proceeding from the actor, are existent and perceptible, whereas mere words, such as purchase, sale, and so forth, are accounted existent only where they are of lawful force and authority, which depends upon the design of them, a thing which, in the case of infants and lunatics, is not regarded, because of their want of understanding; or in the case of slaves, because of the injury to their master.—In short, the disqualifications here considered occasion inhibition with respect to speech, but not with respect to actions ;—unless, however, those be of such nature as to induce an effect liable to prevention from the existence of a doubt, such as punishment or retaliation, in which case infancy or lunacy occasion inhibition; whence it is that infants or lunatics are not liable to punishment or retaliation. since no regard is paid to their design.

All contracts or acknowledgments by an infant or lunatic are invalid; and so likewise divorce or manumission pronounced by them.—No contract entered into, nor acknowledgment made by an infant or lunatic is valid, for the reason before assigned ;— and, in the same manner, divorce or manumission pronounced by them does not take place, the Prophet having said, "every divorce takes place except that pronounced by an infant."—It is to be observed, moreover, that manumission is peculiarly prejudicial :—and an infant does not understand the nature of divorce, as not being capable of desire; and his guardian cannot possibly know whether the infant and his wife may not agree together after he attains maturity. —Hence the divorce or manumission pronounced by an infant are not suspended, in their effect, upon the consent of the guardian.

Or by their guardians on their behalf.—If, also, the guardian himself pronounce a divorce upon the infant's wife, or grant manumission to his slave, it does not take place:— in opposition to other acts, such as purchase, sale, and so forth.

They are responsible for destruction of property.—If an infant or a lunatic destroy any thing, they are liable to make a recompense, in order that the right of the owner may be preserved. The ground of this is that destruction occasions responsibility, independent of the intention or design:—as where, for instance, a man's property is destroyed, from being fallen upon by a person walking in his sleep, or from the falling of an inclined wall, after due warning; in which cases ihe sleeper or the owner of the wall are responsible, although they did not design the destruction.

Acknowledgment by a slave affects himself, not his master; and takes effect upon him on his becoming free.—An acknowledgment made by a slave is efficint with respect to the slave himself, because of his competency; but it is inefficient with respect to his master, from tenderness to his right; for if he were liable to be affected by it, the debt or obligation contracted by the slave's acknowledgment would attach to his [the slave's] person or to his acquisitions, which would be destructive of his [the master's] property.—If, therefore, a slave make an acknowledgment concerding property such property is obligatory upon him after he shall become free; because a slave is in himself competent to make a valid acknowledgment, the validity of which is however obstructed by the right of his master; but that right is extinguished upon his becoming free, and consequently the obstruction then ceases to exist.

Or on the instant, if it induce punishment or retaliation.—If a slave make an acknowledgment inducing punishment or retaliation, those are exceuted upon him on the instant, since he is accounted free with respect to his blood, whence it is that his

* Arab. Mobashir : meaning the actor or performer of any thing; whence, in treating of crimes, it is translated the perpetrator. (The translator thinks it is proper to explain this distinction. because of the equivocal nature of the term agent.)

† Arab. Ifyal. Meaning overt acts, such as a destruction of property, and so forth.

master's acknowledgment affecting his blood is not admitted.

Divorce pronounced by him is valid.—Divorce pronounced by a slave is valid and efficient; because of the saying [of the Prophet] before quoted; and also because the Prophet has said, "a slave and a Mokatib are not masters of any thing except divorce."—Besides, as a slave knows what is advisable for him with regard to divorcing his wife, he is therefore competent to that act. His master's right of property in him, moreover, or the advantage he derives from his services, are not liable to be thereby lost or defeated.—Divorce by a slave is therefore lawful and effectual.

CHAPTER II

ON INHIBITION FROM WEAKNESS OF MIND.*

Inhibition with respect to a prodigal.—Haneefa has declared it as his opinion that there is no inhibition upon a freeman who is sane and adult notwithstanding he be a prodigal; † and also, that the acts of such a person, with regard to his property, are valid, although he be one of an extravagant and careless disposition, who throws away his property on objects in which neither his interest nor his inclination are concerned. A prodigal [Safeeya] signifies one who in consequence of a levity of understanding acts merely from the impulse of the moment, in opposition to the dictates of the law and of common sense.—Aboo Yoosaf, Mohammed, and Shafei maintain that a prodigal is under inhibition, and is interdicted from acting with his own property, as he expends his substance idly, and in a manner repugnant to the dictates of reason. Hence he is placed under inhibition for his own advantage, because of the analogy between him and an infant:—nay, he is to be inhibited rather than an infant since in an infant carelessness and extravagance are only to be apprehended, whereas in him they are certain,—whence it is that he is not entrusted with the care of his own property. Besides, if he were not under inhibition, there would be no advantage in withholding his property, since in such case he might still destroy what is kept from him by his words or declarations. The argument of Haneefa is that as a prodigal is still supposed to be a person naturally endowed with sense and understanding, as much as one who acts discreetly, he therefore is not subject to inhibition any more than a prudent person. The ground of this is, that if the prodigal were subject to inhibition (that is, if his power of acting were doubted), he would be excluded from humanity and connected with brutes, an exclusion still more injurious to him than any extravagance of which he could be guilty; and to remedy the smaller evil by the greater would be absurd. If, however, in laying an inhibition upon a free man who is sane and adult any general evil be remedied (such as in disqualifying an unskilful physician, or a profligate magistrate, or a mendicant imposter), the inhibition is lawful (according to what is reported from Haneefa), since in this instance the smaller evil is used to remedy the greater, which is just and reasonable. With respect to the argument for inhibition upon a prodigal, from the circumstance of his not being entrusted with his own property, it is not admitted, since inhibition is a still greater hardship upon him than withholding his property; for the legality of the smaller hardship does not prove the greater hardship to be legal. In the same manner, also, the analogy adduced between a prodigal and an infant is not admitted, since an infant is incapable of pursuing his own advantage, whereas a prodigal is capable of so doing. Besides, although in subjecting the prodigal to inhibition his interest and advantage be consulted, still, however, the law exhibits in one particular a tenderness towards him, by enabling him to pursue his own advantage, which he acts contrary to only from the vice or folly of his disposition. In withholding his property from him, moreover, there is one particular advantage; for the dissipation of property by extravagance chiefly consists in making idle and unnecessary donations; and as his making these must depend upon the property being in his hands, there is therefore an evident advantage in detaining it from him.

May be imposed by one magistrate and removed by another.—If a magistrate lay an inhibition upon a prodigal, and the matter be referred to another magistrate, and he annul the inhibition, and leave the prodigal at full liberty, it is lawful; for the inhibition imposed by the former magistrate is merely an opinion [Fitwa], not a decree, since to a judical decree a plaintiff and a defendant are requisite, and those do not exist in the present instance. Besides, if the act of the magistrate, in thus imposing an inhibition,

---

* Arab. Fisad; meaning (in this place) any species of mental depravity (not occasioned by a defect of understanding), or the practice of any folly, such as extravagance, or so forth.

† Arab. Safeeya. According to the lexicons it signifies light-minded. Prodigal may appear, in many places, to be rather too harsh a term. The word might more literally be rendered indiscreet, it being frequently opposed, in the sequel, to Rasheed, a discreet person. As, however, the translator does not recollect any sustantive in our language perfectly correspondent with this idea, he has thought it advisable to adopt that term which most nearly answers to the definition of the Mussulman doctors, although it be not precisely what he could wish.

be considered as a decree, there is a difference concerning its being actually such, as Haneefa is not of this opinion. It is, however, incumbent upon the second magistrate, in this instance, to maintain the virtue of the sentence [of inhibition]. in order that it may continue in force :—and accordingly, if the prodigal perform any act after inhibition, and the act in question be referred to the magistrate who imposed the inhibition (or to any other), and this magistrate issue a decree annulling such act, and again the matter be referred to another magistrate, he is bound to uphold and adhere to the sentence of the first magistrate, and not to annul it ; for as the first or other magistrate, upon the matter being referred to them, had confirmed and subscribed to the sentence of inhibition, it cannot afterwards be reversed.

The property of a prodigal youth must be withheld from him until he attain twenty-five years of age.—Haneefa has delivered it as his opinion, that if an infant be a prodigal at the time of his attaining maturity, his property must not be delivered to him until he be twenty-five years of age (still, however, if he should perform any act with respect to his property prior to that period, it takes effect, since, according to Haneefa, prodigals are not liable to inhibition) :—but upon completing his twenty-fifth year, his property must be delivered to him, although his discretion should not be ascertained. The two disciples maintain that his property must not be delivered to him until such time as his discretion be fully known ; and that in the interim all acts performed by him are invalid ; for as mental imbecility is the occasion of the obstacle to his power of action, it follows that the obstacle continues as long as the occasion of it remains ;—as in the case of an infant, who remains subject to inhibition during the continuance of his infancy. The argument of Haneefa is that, withholding to property from the person in question is intended to operate merely as instruction, or as a species of discipline ; and it is most probable that a person, after attaining the age mentioned, will not be disposed to receive instruction, since it frequently happens, that a man arrived at those years is a grandfather, his son having a son born to him : hence in withholding his property there is no advantage whatever, since the view in withholding it is to make him submit to instruction, which upon his attaining the age mentioned can no longer be answered; —and it is therefore indispensable that his property be delivered to him. Besides, the reason for withholding his property from the person in question after he has attained maturity, is in consideration of the vestiges or remaining impressions of infancy ;—and as these continue only in the beginning of maturity, and are terminated by time, it follows that upon a time passing sufficient for this purpose, his property must be delivered to him ;—whence Haneefa maintains that if an infant be discrent at the time of his majority, and afterwards become prodigal, still his property must be delivered to him, since the prodigality, in this instance, cannot be regarded as a vestige of infancy. It is to be observed that as according to the tenets of the two disciples, an inhibition upon the prodigal in question is valid, it follows that a sale concluded by him is of no effect, in order that the advantage proposed in the inhibition may be obtained. If, however, the sale be deemed advisable, the magistrate must give his assent to it ; because here the sale possesses all the essentials of sale, being suspended in its effect merely for the advantage of the prodigal, and from a regard to his interest , and as the magistrate is appointed his office for the purpose of watching over and consulting the interest of the individual, it is therefore requisite that he examine whether the sale be advisable, in the same manner as it is his duty to investigate into a sale made by an infant who intends and is acquainted with the nature of sale.

But a sale concluded by him after maturity, and before inhibition, is valid.—If the prodigal, considered in the preceding example, conclude a sale before any inhibition has been laid upon him by the magistrate such sale is valid, according to Aboo Yoosaf, since (agreably to his tenets) to render the acts of the prodigal invalid, it is requisite that the magistrate lay an inhibition upon him, in order that inhibition may be fully established. According to Mohammed, on the contrary, the sale in question is unlawful, since (agreeably to his tenets) the prodigal is in fact under inhibition after majority, as the cause of inhibition, namely prodigality, stands in the place of infancy. The same difference of opinion obtains concerning an infant who if discreet at the time of attaining majority and afterwards becomes prodigal.

And he may grant manumission.—If the prodigal in question emancipate his slave, it is valid and effectual, and the slave becomes free, according to the two disciples ; whereas according to Shafei it is not effectual. In short, it is a rule with the two disciples that every act liable to be affected by jesting is also liable to be affected by inhibition, as (on the contrary) any act not affected by jesting is not affected by inhibition ; for a prodigal is, in effect, a jaster, inasmuch as the words of a jester, spoken to an unwise or absurd effect, proceed from mere passion or waywardness, not from a want of understanding, and the same also of a prodigal ; and as manumission is one of those things not affected by jesting, but valid even when spoken in jest, so in the same manner manumission pronounced but a prodigal is valid. With Shafei, on the contrary, it is a rule that inhibition in consequence of prodigality is in effect the same as inhibition in consequence of servitude (whence it is that after inhibition in consequence of prodigality no act whatever of the prodigal is valid except divorce, which is effectual in the same manner as divorce pronounced by a slave); and as manumission by a slave is invalid, so in the same manner is manumission by a prodigal. It is to be observed that as, according to the two discipies, a manumission pronounced by the prodigal is valid, the slave therefore owes to his master (the prodigal) emancipatory labour the amount of his whole value; because inhibition is laid upon the master with a view to his interest and advantage; and as the preservation of his interest by a rejection of the manumission itself is impossible it must therefore be rejected so far as to subject the slave to emancipatory labour for his full value; in the same manner as holds in the case of inhibition with respect to a dying person for if a dying person emancipate his slave, he [the slave] must perform emancipatory labour on behalf of the creditors, where the person was involved in debt: or on behalf of the heirs, for two thirds of his value, where he died free from debt. It is elsewhere recorded, from Mohammed, that emancipatory labour is not incumbent upon the slave thus emancipated by his master, being a prodigal; for, if it were due from him, it could only be so on behalf of the emancipator; and the LAW does not authorize the obligation of emancipatory labour on behalf of the emancipator, but of others.

Or Tadbeer.—If the prodigal in question constitute his slave a Modabbir, it is lawful; because Tadbeer gives a title to manumission: and as actual manumission, proceeding from a prodigal, is valid, that which merely entitles to it is certainly valid.—Emancipatory labour, however, is not incumbent upon the Moodabbir during the prodigal's life, since he still continue his property. But if the prodigal die, without discretion having been ascertained in him, the Modabbir is in that case to perform emancipatory labour [to the prodigal's heirs or creditors, as the case may be], for the value he bore as a Modabbir: because he becomes free upon his master's decease, at which time he is a Modabbir, and the case is therefore the same as if the master had first constituted him a Modabbir, and then emancipated him.

Or claim a child born if his female slave.—If the prodigal's female slave bring forth a child and he claim it, the parentage is established in him, and the child is free, and the mother becomes his Am-Walid; for as the prodigal has occasion to make the claim in question, with a view to posterity, he is therefore accounted a discreet person with respect to the claim offspring advanced by him.

Or create his female slave Am-Walid, independent of such claim.—If the prodigal's female slave be not in possession of any child, and the prodigal avow her to be his Am-Walid, she accordingly becomes his Am-Walid, to this effect that he has it not in his power to sell her. If, however, the prodigal die, she must perform emancipatory labour [to his heirs or creditor] for her whole value; because his avowal of her being Am-Walid is the same as his acknowledgment of her being free, since the child, which would be an evidence of her freedom, does not exist in this case; and as, if he had declared her to be free, she would owe emancipatory labour, so likewise in the present instance. It is otherwise, in the example before stated (where the child is supposed to be existing), since in that case an evidence exists of the slave being free. Analogous to this example is the instance of a dying person laying claim to a child born of his female slave; for in that case also the same rules prevail.

He may also marry.—If the prodigal here treated of marry any woman, such marriage is legal and valid; because jesting has no effect in materimony; and also, because marriage is one of his original indispensable wants. If; also, he specify any dower, it is valid to the amount of the woman's proper dower, as that is one of the pertinents of marriage; but any thing beyond the proper dower is null, since for that there is no occasion, it being binding only in consequence of specification, which in this instance is no way advantageous to the prodigal:—the excess, therefore, is invalid, in the same manner as where person affected with a mortal disease marries, and specifies a dower greater than the proper dower. If, also, he divorce his wife before consummation an half dower is due to the woman from his property, as his specification of a dower is valid to the amount of the proper dower. In the same manner also, if he marry four wives, or a new wife every day, it is valid, for the reasons above specified.

Out of his property is paid Zakat; and also maintenance to his parents, children, &c.—Zakat is levied upon the property of the prodigal in question, as Zakat is incumbent upon him. In the same manner also, substance is provided to his parents and children, his wife or wives, and all relations who have a claim upon him for maintenance; because the preservation of his wife and children is among his essential wants, and maintenance is due to his relations by right of affinity; and no person's right is annulled by his prodigality. It is to be observed that it is the Kazee's duty to give the amount or proportion of Zakat into the prodigal's hands, in order to his expending it upon the proper objects of Zakat; for as Zakat is a matter of piety, intention is therefore requisite in the payment of it. The Kazee must, however, depute one of his Ameens to see that the Zakat be applied to its proper objects:—and in the case of maintenance to relations, he must pay the necessary sum into the Ameen's hands, that he may distribute the same among those entitled to maintenance; for as this duty is not a matter of piety, the intention of the donor is not requisite in the fulfilment of it.

It is otherwise where the prodigal swears, or makes a votive engagement, or pronounces a Zihar upon his wife; for in these cases he does not forfeit any property, but has only to perform an expiation for his oath, vow, or Zihar, by fasting, this expiation being incurred by his own act; and therefore if his performance of expiation by a payment of property were required, he would be allowed himself to expend his property to the degree necessary;—but it is not so where any thing is due from him not incurred by his own act, such as Zakat, and so forth.

He cannot be prevented from performing pilgrimage.—If the prodigal be desirous of performing the ordained pilgrimage, he must not be prevented, since this is a matter rendered incumbent upon him by a commandment of God, independent of an act on his part. The Kazee must not, however, entrust to him the sum requisite for his travelling expenses, but must lodge it in the hands of some trusty person among the pilgrims, to provide him a maintenance out of it upon the journey; for otherwise he would throw it away, or expend it on something not relating to pilgrimage.—In the same manner also, if the prodigal be desirous of performing the Amrit,* he must not be prevented; for as concerning the obligation of that there is a difference of opinion, caution dictates that no obstruction be offered to the observance of it.—In the same manner also, if he be desirous of perfoming a Kiran,† he must not be prevented since by Kiran is understood the perfomance of Amrit and pilgrimage‡ in one journey; and as he is not prevented from performing those separately, it follows that he is not to be prevented from performing the whole in one journey.

His bequests (to pious purposes) hold good.—If the prodigal fall sick, and make a variety of bequests to pious and charitable purposes, they hold good to the amount of a third of his whole property; for rendering them valid is advantageous to him, since when the bequests take effect he has no longer any occasion for the property; and those bequests are used as a mean either of manifesting the testator's gratitude to God, or of acquiring merit in his sight.

There is no inhibition upon a Fasik.—Our doctors are of opinion that no inhibition is to be imposed on a reprobate [Fasik] with respect to his property, provided he be endowed with discretion;—and original or supervenient depravity of manners are alike as far as regards this rule. Shafei maintains that inhibition is to be imposed upon a person of this description as a punishment, in the same manner as on a prodigal; whence it is that (according to him) an unjust person is incapable of exercising jurisdiction or bearing evidence.—The arguments of our doctors upon this point are twofold. First the word of God, in the Koran, says, "Whenever ye perceive them to be discreet, deliver to them their property;"—and the reprobate, in the case in question, is supposed to be discreet with regard to the expenditure of his property. Secondly, a reprobate (according to our doctors) is competent to exercise authority, as being a Mussulman, and is consequently empowered to act with regard to his own property.

People are liable to inhibition from carelessness in their affairs.—The two disciples allege that the Kazee is at liberty to lay an inhibition upon persons on account of carelessness or neglect in their concerns, although they be not prodigal. Their argument is that an inhibition imposed upon a person of this description is advantageous to him. Shafei concurs with the two disciples in this opinion.

Section.

*Of the Time of attaining Puberty.**

The puberty of a boy is established by circumstances, or upon his attaining eighteen years of age;—and that of a girl, by circumstances, or upon her attaining seventeen years of age.—The puberty of a boy is established by his becoming subject to nocturnal emission, his impregnating a woman, or emitting in the act of coition; and if none of these be known to exist, his puberty is not established, until he have completed his eighteenth year.—The puberty of a girl is established by menstruation, nocturnal emission, or pregnancy; and if none of these have taken place, her puberty is established on the completion of her seventeenth year. What is here advanced is according to Haneefa. The two disciples maintain that upon either a boy or girl completing the fifteenth year they are to be declared adult; there is also one report of Haneefa to the same effect; and Shafei concurs in this opinion.—It is also reported, from Haneefa, that to establish the puberty of a boy nineteen years are required.—Some, however; observe that by this is to be understood

*This is also pronounced Omara. It applies to certain ceremonies used by the pilgrims at Mecca, namely, compassing the Kaba, or temple, seven times, and running between Siffa Mirwa, which must be performed before the visitation to the temple: but concerning the necessity of those observances there is a difference of opinion among the Mussulmen doctors.

†Kiran signifies performing the ceremonies of pilgrimage in company with others.

‡As the Amrit is not regarded as an essential part of pilgrimage, that and the visitation to the temple (properly termed the pilgrimage) are considered under different heads.

*Puberty and majority are, in the Mussulman law, one and the same.

merely the completion of eighteen years and the commencement of the nineteenth; and consequently, that this report perfectly accords with the other. Some, again, affirm that this is not the sense in which the last report is to be received; for there have been other opinions reported from Haneefa on this point, different from that first recited as above; because some authorities expressly say that (according to him) the puberty of a boy is not counted by years until he shall have completed his nineteenth year. It is to be observed that the earliest period of puberty, with respect to a boy, is twelve years, and with respect to a girl, nine years.

Their declaration of their own puberty, at a probable season, must be credited.—WHEN a boy or girl approaches the age of puberty, and they declare themselves adult, their declaration must be credited, and they become subject to all the rules affecting adults; because the attainment of puberty is a matter which can only be ascertained by their testimony; and consequently, when they notify it, their notification must be credited, in the same manner as the declaration of a woman with respect to her courses.

CHAPTER III.

OF INHIBITION ON ACCOUNT OF DEBT.

A debtor is not liable to inhibition.—HANEEFA is of opinion that no person can be laid under inhibition on account of debt. If, therefore, a debt be proved against any person, and the creditors require the Kazee to imprison him and lay him under inhibition, still the Kazee must not do the latter; because as laying him under inhibition is a destruction or suspension his competency, it is not therefore allowable for the remedy or removal of a particular injury.

Nor can his property be made the subject of any transaction.—IF, also, the debtor be possessed of property, still the Kazee is not at liberty to perform any act with it,* as this would be a species of inhibition, and his thus acting with the property would, moreover, be an act of conversion without the assent of the proprietor, and consequently null, according to both the KORAN and the Sonna.

But he may be imprisoned.—IT is, however, requisite that the magistrate imprison the debtor, and hold him in durance, until such time as he sell his property for the discharge of his debts, and the rendering of justice. The two disciples say, that if the creditors require the Kazee to impose an inhibition upon their insolvent debtor, it is requisite that he impose an inhibition upon him accordingly, and prevent him from selling, or transacting, or making acknowledgments, in order that his creditors may not sustain an injury; because restriction is imposed upon a prodigal only out of a regard for his interest; and in imposing the same upon a debtor a regard is manifested to the interest of his creditors; for if an inhibition upon him were not authorized, it is not improbable that he might act collusively, or, in other words, might declare that "the property in his possession belong to a particular person," notwithstanding it actually belongs to himself and not to the other, his declaration being made merely with a view that the property might not go to his creditors,—whence the right of the creditors would be defeated.—(It is to be remarked, that what the two disciples say of an inhibition being laid upon the debtor with respect to sale, applies only to the sale of anything for a price short of its real value; as the right of the creditors is not injured by his selling an article for an adequate price. Besides, the prohibition of the sale exists only on account of the creditors right; and as their right is not annulled by such a sale, he need not be prohibited from concluding it)—It is also lawful (according to the two disciples) for the Kazee to sell the debtor's property, where he himself declines so doing, and to divide the price of it among the creditors in proportion to their respective claims; because it is incumbent upon the debtor to sell his property for the payment of his debt; and consequently, upon his declining so to do, the Kazee is his substitute for that purpose, in the same manner as a Kazee is the substitute of the husband for pronouncing a separation between him and his wife, where he is an eunuch, or impotent. The argument adduced by our doctors on behalf of Haneefa, and in reply to the two disciples, is that collusion is a matter of uncertanity. And with respect to sale, it is not to be particularly appointed for the payment of debts, since it is in the debtor's power to discharge what he owes by various other means, such as borrowing or begging; whence it is not lawful for the Kazee to appoint a sale. It is otherwise in the case of a husband who is an eunuch or impotent, as in that instance separation is the appointed remedy. The debtor, moreover, is not impisoned with a view to sale (as alleged by the two disciples), but with a view to the payment of his debts, and to constrain him to adopt some method for the discharge of them.—Besides, if it were lawful for the Kazee to set up the debtor's property to sale, he could not lawfully have recourse to imprisonment, since that would be injurious both to the debtor and the creditors, as being vexatious to the former, and creating a delay in the discharge of the latter's right, whence the imprisonment would not be sanctioned by the LAW;—whereas it is in fact strictly lawful.

If he be possessed of money, of the same denomination as his debt, the Kazee may make payment with it; or, if the species be

* That is, to purchase, or sell with it, &c.

different, he may sell it for this purpose.—IF the debts owing by the debtor in question consist of dirms, and the property possessed by the debtor also consist of dirms, the Kazee may in this case discharge the demands upon him without his consent. This is a point in which all our doctors coincide: for as the creditor is here at liberty to take his right without the debtor's consent, it follows that the Kazee is at liberty to assist him in the recovery of it. If, on the contrary, the debt consist of dirms; and the property in the debtor's hands be deenars, or vice versa, the Kazee is in this case empowered to sell such property for payment of the debt. This is according to Haneefa, and proceeds upon a favourable construction.—Analogy would suggest that the Kazee is not at liberty to sell the property in this instance, in the same manner as he is not at liberty to sell the debtor's household goods, or other effects. The reason, however, for a more favourable construction of the LAW, in this particular, is that dirms and deenars are both alike with regard to their constituting price and representing property, as, on the other hand, they differ from each other with regard to appearance: hence, because of their similarity in the one shape, the Kazee is empowered to act with respect to them; and because of their dissimilarity in the other shape, the creditor is not at liberty to take them without the debtor's consent. It is otherwise with respect to goods and effects, since those are objects of desire and use, both in appearance and reality, whereas dirms and deenars are mereby a means of obtaining such objects.

Rule in selling off a debtor's property:—IN discharging debts, that part of the debtor's property which consists of money* is first disposed of, then his effects and household furniture; and last of all his houses and lands; for in this mode of adjustment a regard is paid to the ease and convenience of both parties. The debtor's clothes, also, must be sold, excepting only one suit, which is sufficient to answer necessity. Some, however, say that two suits must be left with the debtor, one suit being in use whilst the other is washing.

Acknowledgments by a debtor are not binding on him until his debts be paid.—IF a debtor make an acknowledgment whilst under inhibition, †such acknowledgment is not binding upon him until he shall have satisfied his creditors; for as their right was first connected with his property, he is therefore not at liberty to annul it by an acknowledgment in behalf of any other person. It would be otherwise supposing the debtor to destroy a person's property; for in that case he would be responsible; and the owner of the property so destoryed would come in upon an equal footing with the other creditors, as the destruction of property is a sensible and perceptible circumstance, and therefore cannot possibly be set aside. If, also, the debtor acquire or obtain property after inhibition, his acknowledgment, as above, takes effect with respect to such property; because the right of the former creditors is not connected with this property, it not existing at the time of inhibition.

A debtor (being poor) gets a subsistence out of his property: and also his wives, children, and uterine kindred.—A SUBSISTENCE must be paid to the debtor out of his property (provided he be in poverty), and also to his wives, infant children, and uterine kindred; because his indispensable wants precede the right of his creditors; and also because; as the maintenance of his wife, &c,, is their right, it cannot be annulled by inhibition, whence it is that if he were to marry, his wife comes in upon an equal footing with his other creditors, to the amount of her proper dower.

A debtor, on pleading poverty, is imprisoned.—IF the debtor be not possessed of any known property, and the creditors require the Kazee to imprison him, he at the same time declaring that "he has nothing," the Kazee must in this case imprison him on account of such debts as he may have incurred by contracts such as a dower, or an obligation undertaken by his becoming bail for property.—(Those cases have been already discussed at large in treating of the duties of the Kazee, and therefore a repetition in this place is unnecessary.)

General rules with respect to him whilst in prison.—IF the debtor who pleads poverty, as above, fall sick in prison, he is nevertheless continued in durance, provided he have an attendant to wait upon him and administer medicine to him:—but if he have no such attendant he must in that case be liberated from confinement, lest he perish. If he be an artisan, he must be prevented from following his trade and must not be suffered to do any work, in order that, from distress, he may be compelled to pay his debts.*—This is approved. If he be possessed of a female slave, under such circumstances as that he may cohabit with her,† he must not be prevented from so doing; since carnal connexion is required to satisfy a man's appetite in the same manner as eating or drinking; and he therefore must not be pre-

---

* Arab. Nakd, which literally signifies cash, but in this place comprehends all sorts of property which come under the denomination of Mal, as opposed to Rakht and Matta [goods and effects].

† Proceeding on the idea of the two disciples, that "he may be put under inhibition."

* This, at first sight, does not appear consistent with the tenderness exhibited towarde a debtor in other instances. It is to be recollected, however, that the debtor in question is imprisoned on suspicion of his being possessed of property, which he denies.

† That is, under such circumstances as make her lawful to him.

vented from indulging himself in this, any more than from eating or drinking.

After liberating, the creditors are at liberty to pursue him.—UPON his being liberated from prison,* the creditors must not be obstructed in enforcing their claims against him, but are at liberty to pursue him.† They must not, however, prevent him from transacting business or travelling. The reason of this is that the Prophet has said, "the proprietor of a right has a hand and a tongue," meaning, by the hand, the power of pursuing, and by the tongue, the power of demanding the right. The creditors are also at liberty, in this case, to take the excess‡ of the debtor's earnings, and divide it among themselves in proportion to their respective claims; for as their right is equal with regard to power, attention must be paid equally to that of each. The two disciples maintain that upon the Kazee declaring the debtor's poverty [insolvency] the creditors must be obstructed (that is, must be prevented from pursuing the debtor), unless they adduce evidence to prove his being possessed of property; for as (according to them) the Kazee's decree of poverty on behalf of the debtors is valid, his inability to discharge his debts is there by fully established, and this being the case, he is entitled to an indulgence until he may acquire property, and thereby become solvent. According to Haneefa, on the contrary, the Kazee's decree of poverty on behalf of the debtor is not valid; because property comes in the morning and goes in the evening. Besides, as witnesses possess a knowledge of property only with regard to appearance, evidence therefore, although it be proof sufficient to release the debtor from prison, is yet not proof sufficient to annul the right of the creditors, that is, their title to pursue the debtor. With respect to the exception stated in relating the opinion of the two disciples, that "the creditors must not be obstructed unless they adduce evidence to prove the debtor's being possessed of property," it is an argument that evidence of wealth has a preference over evidence of poverty: because the former tends to prove new matter, since the possession or acquisition of wealth is supervenient, whereas indigence is original. With respect, on the other hand, to what has been said, in speaking of the right of pursuing, &c., that creditors "must not prevent the debtor from transaction business; or travelling," it is an argument that the creditor is at liberty to pursue the debtor by accompanying him wherever he goes, but not by fixing him in any particular place; for this would be imprisonment. If, also, the debtor go into his house upon any business, the creditor is not at liberty to enter with him, but must stand at the door until he come forth; because men stand in need of some private and secluded place.

And have an option, if he prefer continuing in prison.—IF a debtor be desirous of continuing in prison, and his creditor be rather desirous of holding him in pursuit, regard is paid to the option of the creditor, as that is the most effectual towards obtaining the desired end, since he, it is to be supposed, will adopt such measures as may distress the debtor, and thus compel him to do justice. If, however, the Kazee perceive that the debtor is subjected to any particular injury (from the creditor in the exercise of the right of pursuing, as, for instance, not permitting him to enter his own house), in this case he [the Kazee] must imprison him [the debtor] in order to repel such injury.

A male creditor cannot pursue his female debtor.—IF the debtor be a woman, and the creditor a man, the creditor must not be suffered to pursue her, since if this were admitted, it would induce the retirement of a man with a strange woman. The creditor, however, is at liberty to depute a confidential female to attend the debtor in the exercise of his right.

Case of a purchased article being in the debtor's hands upon his failure.—IF a debtor become poor* having at the same time in his hands effects purchased from a particular person, this person, in recovering the price of such effects, is upon an equal footing with the other creditors. Shafei maintains that in this case it is the duty of the Kazee to lay an inhibition upon the purchaser, provided the seller require him so to do; and then that the seller has it at his option to dissolve the sale; for the purchaser has become incapable of paying the price; and this occasions a right of dissolution, in the same manner as the inability of the seller to deliver the article sold. The ground of this is that sale is a contract of exchange, which requires perfect equality:—in the same manner as a contract of Sillim; in other words, if the person who receives the advance, in a contract of Sillim, be incapable of delivering the article advanced for (from its not being procurable, for instance), the advancer has it at his option either to wait until the other may procure the article, or to dissolve the contract and take back what he had advanced; and so likewise in the present instance. The argument of our doctors is that poverty occasions an inability

*In consequence of the Kazee passing a decree of insolvency in his behalf.

† Arab. Molavimat, meaning a continual personal attendance upon or watch over him. This is a customary mode of proceeding, with respect to debtors, among all Mussulmans, and is termed, in Persia and Hindostan, Nazr-band; which may be rendered holding in sight.

‡ Meaning any balance which may remain after the maintenance of the debtor and his family

* This, in effect, signifies the same as failing or becoming bankrupt.

to make a specific delivery.* In the case in question, however, the purchaser is not under any obligation to make a specific delivery, but merely to make a delivery of the price [of the article purchased], which is a debt upon him. Hence the seller is not endowed with a right of dissolution in consequence of the purchaser's inability to make such specific delivery.

OBJECTION.—If debt in general be obligatory upon the purchaser, and not a particular substance, it would follow that the purchaser is not discharged of the demand by his giving money, and the seller taking possession of it, since substance is different from debt.

REPLY.—By the seller taking possession of the particular money, a substitution is established between this substance and the debt owing by the purchaser; and as this is the original object in paying debts, regard must therefore be had to it, unless that be impossible, which however is not the case in the example here considered.—It is otherwise in a contract of Sillim; for there no regard can be paid to substitution, as it cannot there be admitted;—whence it is that, in contracts of Sillim, the sustance, or particular sum taken possession of, is accounted to be, in effect, the thing for which the advance is made, and which remains a debt upon the person who receives such sum.

BOOK XXVI.

OF MAZOONS, OR LICENSED SLAVES.

[This has been omitted for the same reason as Book V.]

BOOK XXXVII.

OF GHAZB, OR USURPATION.

Definition of the term.—GHAZB, in its literal sense, means the forcibly taking a thing from another. In the language of the LAW it signifies the taking of the property of another, which is valuable and sacred, without the consent of the proprietor, in such a manner as to destroy the proprietor's possession of it.

Acts by which usurpation is established.—WHENCE it is that usurpation is established by exacting service from the slave of another, or by putting a burden upon the quadruped of another; but not by sitting upon the carpet of another; because by the use of the slave of another, and by loading the quadruped of another, the possession of the proprietor is destroyed; whereas by sitting upon the carpet of another the possession of the proprietor is not destroyed.

A wilful usurper is an offender.—IT is to be observed that if any person knowingly and wilfully usurp the property of another, he is held in law to be an offender, and becomes responsible for a compensation. If on the contrary, he should not have made the usurpation knowingly and wilfully (as where a person destroys property on the supposition of its belonging to himself, and it afterwards proves the right of another), he is in that case also liable for a compensation, because a compensation is the right of man; but he is not an offender, as his erroneous offence is cancelled.

The usurper of an article of the class of similars is responsible for a similar, if it be destroyed in his possession.—IF a person usurp any thing of the class of a similars, such as articles estimable by weight, or by measurement of capacity, and of which the particulars are nearly equal, and it be afterwards destroyed in his possession, he is in that case responsible to the proprietor for a similar; because GOD has so ordained in the KORAN; and also, because the giving of a similar in return is the justest method, since a regard is thereby shown both to the genus and the substance, and consequently the injury to the proprietor is thereby removed in the most eligible manner. If, however, the usurper be not able to give a similar, because of no similar being to be found, he in that case becomes responsible for the value which the article bears at the time of the suit or contention. This is according to Haneefa. Aboo Yoosaf maintains that he becomes responsible fot the value the thing bore upon the day of usurpation. Mohammed, on the other hand, has said that he becomes responsible for the value it bore upon the day when the similar was not to be found or procured. The reasoning of Aboo Yoosaf is, that whenever a similar became unattainable, the thing then became the same as if it was not of the class of similars. Hence it is necessary to have regard to the value on the day of usurpation; because usurpation, being the cause which induces responsibility, it follows that the value on the day of the establishment of the cause ought to be regarded. The reasoning of Mohammed is, that the usurper is responsible for a similar; and that, as this responsibility is afterwards referred to the value, for no other reason than that a similar is not to be found, it follows that regard is to be had to the value the article bore on that day.* The

*Arab.. Ain, meaning (in this place) the particular sum of money owing to the seller. It is proper here to observe that the Arabian lawyers make an essential distinction between debt and substance, the former being considered as merely ideal, until it be realized.

* Arab Yawm-al-Inkatta—Literally, the day of terminatian; meaning, the day on which the power of returning a compensation by a similar terminated.

reasoning of Haneefa is, that the responsibility is not referred to the value immediately upon the extinction of a similar, since the proprietor may, if he please, delay until a similar shall be found : but that the responsibility is referred to the value merely on account of the decree of the Kazee ; and that therefore the value on the day of contention (which is the day of the decree of the Kazee) ought to be regarded. It is otherwise with respect to a thing which is not of the class of similars ; because in such case the value is demanded from the usurper in virtue of the original cause, namely, the usurpation ; and therefore the value it bore on the day of usurpation is to be regarded.

If the article be of the class of non-similars, he is responsible for the value.—If a person usurp any article of the class of non-similars (such as where the particulars are different, like household goods), he is in that case responsible for the value the article bore on the day of usurpation ; for as it is here impossible to preserve the right of the proprietor with respect to quality, it is therefore necessary to preserve that right with respect to substance only, in order that the injury to him may be done away in the utmost possible degree. (It is to be observed, that if a person usurp wheat in which there is a mixture of barley, he becomes than responsible for the value, as that is of the class of non-similars.)

The actual article usurped must be restored to the proprietor, if it be extant.—It is incumbent upon an usurper to restore the idential article usurped to the proprietor of it provided it be extant in his possession ; because the Prophet has said, "It is incumbent upon a person who takes a thing from another to restore it to him ;" and also, "It is not lawful for a person to take the goods of his brother in any manner" (that is, neither in a familiar easy way, nor by violence and contention) ; "and therefore, if a person do take any thing, he must restore it to its owner :"—and also, because the proprietor's seisin or possession of his property be this shown right, which the usurper has destroyed, it is therefore incumbent on the usurper to restore the right the actual thing that is to say, to give back that is originally taken. This, moreover, is what is originally incumbent, agreeable to the opnion of most of the learned ; and the giving of the value to the proprietor is merely a cause of release from strife, inasmuch as it is defective ; whereas the perfection lies in the restoration of the actual thing. Some of the learned, whoever, have said that the original obligation is that of giving the value ; and that the restitution of the actual article is merely a cause of release. A result of this disagreement appears in the different deductions arising from it ; as where, for instance the proprietor exempts the usuper from the value, at a time when the actual thing is extant in his possession ; in which case, according to the latter opinion (above mentioned, of some of the learned), the exemption is valid ; whence if the article be destroyed in the possession of the usurper subsequent to the exemption, he does not (according to their tenets) become responsible for a compensation : whereas, in the opinion of most of the learned, he becomes responsible.

In the place where it was usurped.—It is to be observed that, according to the opinion of most of the learned, it is incumbent upon the usurper to restore the thing to the proprietor in the place where he had usurped it, because the value of things varies in different places.

And failing of this, the usurper must be imprisoned until he make satisfaction.—If the usurper plead that he has lost the article, the magistrate must cause him to be imprisoned for a length of time sufficient to ascertain whether or not he has the thing in his possession, and must then enjoin him to give the value of it. The reason of this is, because the original obligation is the restoration of the actual thing, and the circumstance of the loss of it being merely an accident, is not credited, as it is contradicted by appearances : in the same manner as where a person who owes the price of goods pleads poverty, in which case he must be confined until the truth of his plea be ascertained.—Whenever, therefore, it becomes known that the article usurped has really been lost in the possession of the usurper, the obligation to restore the actual thing is annulled, and a compensation (that is, the value of the thing) becomes obligatory.

Usurpation (so as to occasion responsibility) cannot take place but in moveable property.—It is further to be observed, that usurpation (so as to occasion responsibility)—takes place only with respect to moveables, such as a garment, or the like : for the destruction of the proprietor's possession cannot otherwise be effected than by removal. If, therefore, a person should usurp land, and the land be destroyed in his possession (that is, be rendered useless by an inundation, or the like), the usurper is not responsible for it. This is the opinion of Haneefa and Aboo Yoosaf. Mohammed alleges that the usurper is responsible for the land ; and this is the first opinion of Aboo Yoosaf, which has likewise been adopted by Shafei. The arguments in favour of the latter opinion are, that the possession of the usurper is established with respect to the land usurped, which occasions a destruction of the proprietor's possession, since it is impossible that one thing can be in the possession of two people at one and the same time.—Usurpation, therefore, which means the annihilation of the proprietor's possession, and the establishment of the usurpers, exists in the case of land : hence land is in this respect the same as moveable property and therefore the usurper of it is responsible for it ; in the same manner as a denying trustee ; that is, if a person deposit land in the hands of another, and that other afterwards deny the deposit, in that case he becomes responsible for the land, and so also in the case in question. The arguments of Haneefa and Aboo Yoosaf are, that usurpation is the establishment of the usurper's possession by a destruction of that of the proprietor, in such a manner that the cause of the establishment of the possession, and of the destruction of it, is the action of the usurper with respect to the thing usurped, such as the removal of it from one place to another. Now this is impracticable with respect to land or houses, because the proprietor's possession of these cannot otherwise be destroyed than by driving him from them. But the driving away of the proprietor from his house (for instance) is not an action of the usurper with respect to the thing but with respect to the person of the proprietor, and therefore amounts to the same as if he were to remove the proprietor from his cattle. In the usurpation of moveables, on the contrary, the removal is the action of the usurper operating with respect to the article; and this is usurpation. With respect to the case of a trustee who denies the deposit (adduced by Mohammed as being analogous to the case in question), it is not admitted to be such; but allowing that it were, it is answered that the necessity for a compensation in that instance arises from the want of care which is manifested by the denial of the trustee.

The usurper of a house is responsible for the furniture.—An usurper is responsible, according to all our doctors, for whatever he breaks of a house, either by his residence in it, or by his pulling it down, because that is wilful destruction, and compensation for fixed property is incurred by wilful destruction,—as where, for instance, a person removes the manure or water from land that being an act with respect to the substance of the land.

But if he sell the house, and the proprietor have no witnesses, he is not responsible.—If a person usurp a house, sell it, and delver it to the purchaser, and afterwards acknowledge the usurpation, and the purchaser deny it; and there be no witnesses on the part of the proprietor to prove it, in this case there is a disagreement between Haneefa and Aboo Yoosaf on one side, and Mohammed on the other; for, according to the two disciples the seller of the house is not responsible on account of the sale and delivery of it to the purchaser (contrary to the opinion of Mohammed); because sale and delivery to the purchaser is merely an usurpation on the part of the seller; and usurpation of moveable property (according to the two disciples) does not induce compensation.

A usurper of land is responsible for any damage occasioned by the cultivation of it.—If usurped land be damaged by the cultivation of it, the usurper must compensate for the damage, since he has destroyed part of the land.—He must, moreover, deduct from the produce of the land the amount of his stock, that is to say, the quantity of the seed sown, and also the amount he may have paid for the damage; and if any surplus should then remain, he must bestow it in charity.—The compiler of the Hedaya remarks that this is according to Heneefa and Mohammed; but that Aboo Yoosaf has said that it is not necessary to bestow the surplus in charity. Their arguments shall be recited at large hereafter.

The usurper of a moveable is responsible for the value in case of its destruction.—When an article of usurped moveable property is destroyed in the possession of the usurper, whether by his act, or by the act of another, in either case he is responsible for the value of it:—according to those who hold that the giving of the value is originally incumbent, and the restitution of the actual thing a release, because the releasement being here impracticable, the giving of the value which was originally due is therefore established;—and also according to those who hold that the restitution of the actual thing is originally due and that the giving of the value is merely subordinate thereto; because the fulfilment of what is originally due being impracticable, in consequence of the destruction of the actual thing, the value of it is therefore due.

If he himself render it defective he is responsible for such defect.—If an usuper should, with his own hands, render defective the thing he had usurped, he is in that case responsible for such deficiency; for as, in consequence of the usurpation, he is responsible for the thing usurped, in all its parts, it follows that whenever the restitution of any part of it becomes impracticable, the value of that part is due from him.

But not for any depreciation it may have sustained in his hands.—It is otherwise with respect to a diminution of the value by depreciation; since for that the usurper is not resposible, provided he restore the thing in the place of usurpation; because a diminution of the price arises from the diminution of desire on the part of the purchaser, and not from the ruin or destruction of any of the parts of the thing.—It is also otherwise with respect to things sold which become defective in the possession of the seller prior to his delivery of them; for he is not in that case under a necessity of compensation to the purchaser; because responsibility for the article of sale is a responsibility involved in the contract; and the subject of the contract is the actual wares, and not the qualities of them. With respect to usurpation, on the contrary, that is an act, and qualities are liable to be compensated for by an act, but not by a contract, as has been already demonstrated. The author of the Hedaya has said that this case alludes to usurped articles which are not of an increasing nature; but that with respect to things of an increasing nature, a compensation for the damage must not be taken along with the actual restitution, as that would necessarily induce usury.

The usurper of a slave, hiring him out to service, is responsible for any damage he may sustain, must and bestow the wages in charity.—If a person usurp a slave and hire him out to work, and receive his wages, and the slave be thereby affected in his value, in that case (upon the principle laid down in the preceding example) the usuper must compensate for the damage, and must bestow the whole of the wages in charity. The compiler of the Hedaya remarks that this is according to Haneefa and Mohammed; but that according to Aboo Yoosaf there is no necessity for his bestowing the wages in charity: and that the same disagreement subsists with respect to the case of a borrower hiring out the subject borrowed. The reasoning of Aboo Yoosaf is, that the profit in question has been acquired by the usurper upon his responsibility with respect to the subject, and upon his own property: the former of which, namely responsibility, is evident: and so likewise his right of property; because whatever is a subject of responsibility becomes the property of the usurper, in consequence of his making compensation, by the way of transition. The reasoning of Haneefa and Mohammed is that the profit in question has been acquired by a cause in which baseness exists, namely, by an exertion over the propety of another; and that such profit ought to be bestowed in charity; because the cause (that is, the exertion over the property of another) is the trunk, and the profit so acquired is a branch from it; and the qualities of the trunk, or original, communicate with the branches spring from it; whence a baseness exists in the profit also, as well as in the original. With regard to what Aboo Yoosaf alleges, that "whatever is a subject of responsibility becomes the property of the usurper. In consequence of his making compensation, by the way of transition," it is answered that a right of property established merely by the way of transition is a defective right of property and therefore baseness is not removed by it.

But if the slave be destroyed, the wages may by given in part of the compensation.—If, however, the slave be destroyed in the possession of the usurper, so as to make him liable for his complete value, he may in that case give the wages in payment of the compensation, because the baseness which exists with regard to such wages is only on account of the right of the proprietor (whence, if they were paid to the proprietor, it would be lawful for him to receive and convert them to his own use): they may therefore be paid to him; and, in consequence of such payment, the baseness which would otherwise attach to them is removed. It is different where the usurper sells the slave, who is afterwards destroyed in the possession of the purchaser, and is then proven to be the right of another, for which the purchaser pays a compensation, because in such case it is not lawful for the usurper to give the wages to the purchaser in payment of the price, since the baseness which exists in the wages is not on account of the right of the purchaser. Still, however, if the usurper in this case, be not possessed of any other property than the wages, he may then lawfuly give that to the purchaser in return for the price which he had taken from him, because under these circumstances the usurper stands in need of it, and he is therefore permitted to apply it to the answering of his necessities If, however, he should afterwards acquire other property, he must bestow from it in charity an amount equal to the wages, provided he was rich at the time he made use of the price he received from the purchaser; but if, on the contrary, he was at that time poor, he is not required to bestow any thing in charity

All monied profits acquired by means of usurped money must be bestowed in charity.—If a person usurp one thousand dirms, and with those thousand purchase a female slave, whom he afterwards sells for two thousand, and then with these two thousand purchase another female slave, whom he again sells for three thousand, in that case the usurper must bestow in charity the whole of the profit namely, two thousand dirms. This is according to Haneefa and Mohammed; and the principle of it is, that whenever, either an usurper or a trustee perform any act with respect to the thing usurped, or the deposit, and thereby acquire profit, such profit (according to Haneefa and Mohammed) is not lawful and sanctified to them; in opposition to the opinion of Aboo Yoosaf. The opinion of Haneefa and Mohammed, in this particular, with regard to a deposit, is evident, since the property of it is not referred to a period antecedent to the act of the trustee; for, as the property cannot be proven from responsibility at that time it follows that the act of the trustee was not exerted upon his own property. It is to be observed, however, that what is here mentioned of the opinion of Haneefa and Mohammed being evident with regard to a deposit, alludes to such deposits only as consist of goods, and not of money; for if the deposit consist of money, and the trustee, at the time of purchasing the female slave say "I purchase her with this money" (pointing to the identical money in deposit), and he accordingly discharge the price with that very money, in that case the profit must be bestowed in charity; whereas if, on the contrary, at the time of making the bargain, he point to the money in deposit, and pay the price with other money,—or point to other money, and pay the price with the deposited money,—or; if he should not point to any money; but express himself in an absolute manner, saying "I purchase this slave for one thousand dirms" (not "for these thousand dirms") and he pay the price with the thousand dirms in deposit,—

in all these cases the profit acquired is free and lawful to the trustee. Such also is the opinion of Koorokhee: and the reason of it is, that by pointing to specific dirms at the time of purchasing, the dirms are not thereby rendered fixed and specific, but that, on the contrary, it is lawful for the purchaser to give other dirms than those referred to; and that, therefore, in such case, the profit acquired is not base; excepting when, in purchasing the said slave with the thousand dirms in deposit, he points to these very dirms, and pays the price with the same.— The Haneefite doctors; on the contrary, allege that the profit is not lawful to the trustee, neither before the giving of compensation, nor after it: and this is approved; because this law has been recited in an absolute manner, both in the Jama Sagheer and the Jama Kabeer, in treating of Mozaribat.

But not profits of any different description.—If a person purchase with one thousand usurped dirms a female slave worth two thousand, and make a gift of her to any person; or purchase wheat with the said thousand, and eat the same; he is not, under such circumstances, required to bestow any thing in charity This is a case in which all are agreed; and the principal of it is that although the female slave be worth two thousand dirms, yet she is not of the species of dirms, so as to occasion usury: for usury does not take place excepting when the profit is of the same description as the principal.

Section.

Of usurped Articles altered by Acts of the Usurper

An alteration wrought upon the article usurped vests the property of it in the usurper; who remains responsible to the original owner for the value of it; and cannot lawfully derive any advantage from it, until such compensation be paid.—Whenever an article usurped is altered in consequence of an act of the usurper, in such a manner that it loses both its name and its original purpose, it is then separated from the right of the proprietor, and becomes the property of the usurper and the usurper becomes responsible for it: but he is not entitled to derive any advantage from it until he pay the compensation. An example of this occurs where a person usurps a goat, kills it, and afterwards roasts or boils it; or usurps wheat, and afterwards grinds it into flour;—or usurps iron, and makes a sword from it;—or usurps clay, and makes a vessel from it. What is here advanced is according to our doctors. Shafei maintains that, after the alteration in the article, the right of the proprietor to it is not extinguished, but he is entitled to take from the usurper the flour of his wheat. There is also a report from Aboo Yoosaf to the same effect. He, however, maintains that in case the proprietor choose to take the flour of the wheat, he is not entitled to a compensation for the damage, as that would induce usury; whereas Shafei holds that he is entitled to a compensation from the usurper for the damage. It is also related, as an opinion of Aboo Yoosaf, that the right of property with respect to an usurped article which has been altered ceases in the proprietor, but that it may be sold to answer the debt due to him (namely, the compensation), and that, in case of the death of the usurper, he has a preferable claim to the other creditors with respect to the article in question. The reasoning of Shafei is, that the substance of the thing being extant, notwithstanding it have undergone an alteration, it follows that the right of property still remains in the proprietor, since the quality is merely a dependant on the substance;—as where, for instance, the wind blows wheat into the mill of another person, and it is ground into flour; in which case it continues the property of the original proprietor of the wheat; and so also in the case in question. With respect to the act of the usurper by which the thing is altered, it is not to be regarded, since it is an underact, and consequently incapable of becoming the cause of property, as has been explained in its proper place. The case is therefore the same as if the act had never existed,—in the same manner as holds where an usurper kills an usurped goat, and tears the skin of it in pieces The argument of our doctors is, that in the case in question the usurper has performed an operation which bears a value, and has therefore destroyed the right of the proprietor in one respect, inasmuch as the appearance is no longer the same, whence it is that the name is changed and many of the original purposes of the article defeated; as grains of wheat, for instance, which are fit for being sown or roasted, but after being converted into flour are no longer fit for these purposes. In short, by the alteration of an article usurped the right of the proprietor is destroyed in one shape, and that of the usurper with respect to the qualities is established in every shape; and hence the right of the usurper has a superiority with respect to the original of that thing which has been in one shape destroyed. (With respect to the act of the usurper, it is not made the occasion of property because of its illegality, but because of its being the performance of a valuable operation. It is otherwise with regard to a goat slain by the usurper, and the skin of it torn to pieces; for, after the killing of a goat, and the destruction of its skin, the name of goat is still retained, since it is common to say "a slaughtered goat." With respect to what has been recited, that "the usurper is not entitled to derive any profit from the article until he pay the compensation." it is according to a favourable construction of the law. Analogy would lead us to conclude that it is lawful to derive a profit from the article before the payment of a compensation. This is the opinion of Hassan and Ziffer, and there is also a report to that effect from Haneefa, of which the relater is the lawyer Aboo Lays. The reason derived from analogy is because, after, the alteration, the usurper becomes the proprietor of the thing, and may therefore perform any act with repect to it, or derive profit from it, in the same manner as he might lawfully give it away or sell it. The reason, however, for a more favourable construction is, that in the days of the Prophet a goat having been killed and roasted without the consent of the proprietor, the Prophet ordered that the prisoners should be fed with it, meaning, that it should be bestowed in charity upon them. Now this order of the Prophet evinces that upon an alteration in the state of an article usurped, it is separated from the property of the proprietor, and that it is unlawful for the usurper to derive a profit from it until he have satisfied the proprietor. Moreover, if it were lawful to the usurper under these circumstances to take a profit, a door would be opened for usurpation; and, therefore, to prevent such mischievous consequences, the acquisition of a profit before satisfaction being made is not permitted. With respect to the assertions of Hassen and Ziffer adduced in support of their opinion, that "the gift or the sale of the thing is lawful;" it is answered, that notwithstanding the illegality of deriving profit from the article usurped, still the sale or gift of it is lawful, because the article in question is the property of the usurper, and the gift or sale of property held under an invalid right is lawful. Where, however, the usurper makes a compensation for the thing usurped, he is entitled to derive an advantage from it, because the right of the proprietor has been transferred to him in consequence of his making compensation; and it becomes the same as an exchange between the usurper and the proprietor with their mutual consent. In the same manner, also, he is entitled to derive profit from the thing in question when the proprietor exempts him from responsibility for it; because in consequence of such exemption the right of the proprietor ceases: and so likewise where the proprietor takes the compensation from the usurper, or where he demands it and the usurper assents thereto, as in that case the consent of the proprietor is obtained; and so also where the Kazee passes a decree directing the usurper to pay a compensation to the proprietor,—or where the usurper pays the compensation upon the decree of the Kazee, because in that case likewise the consent of the proprietor is obtained, since the Kazee passes the decree at his suit. It is to be observed that in the same manner as a disagreement subsists between our doctors and Shafei concerning these cases, so likewise with respect to the case of a person usurping wheat and sowing it, or usurping the stones of dates and planting them. In the opinion of Aboo Yoosaf, however, it is lawful even in these cases for an usurper to enjoy profit before the payment of compensation, because in both these cases the usurper has destroyed the substance of the thing usurped in every respect. It is otherwise in the cases before recited: for in those instances the usurper is not entitled to derive pofit, since there the substance of the article continues in one respect extant. In the case, therefore, of sowing usurped wheat, is not necessary (according to Aboo Yoosaf) to bestow in charity such part of the produce of it as exceeds the quantity sown and the expense of the labour; contrary to the opinion of Haneefa and Mohammed, as has been already explained.

Any alteration wrought upon gold or silver does not transfer the property of it.—If a person usurp gold or silver, and convert it into dirms or deenars, or make a vessel from it, such silver or gold does not separate from the property of the proprietor, according to Haneefa.—whence he is entitled to take it from the usurper without giving him any compensation. The two disciples maintain that the usurper, in such case, acquires a property in the metal, and owes a compensation of a similar quantity; of gold or silver to the original proprietor; because he has performed a valuable operation upon the metal, which in one shape destroys the right of the proprietor, since in so doing he has broken it down so as to destroy its original purposes, inasmuch as bullion is unfit to become the stock in a contract of Mozaribat, or of partnership, whereas coined money has this fitness. The reasoning of Haneefa is, that in the case in question the substance of the thing usurped is extant in every respect, insomuch that it still preserves its name; and the purposes to which gold and silver relate, such as price and weight, are also extant, insomuch that usury by weight takes place in them when coined, in the same manner as before coinage.—With regard, moreover, to the fitness of them (when coined) for constituting stock, it is an effect of the workmanship, and not a quality inherent in the substance of the thing Besides, the workmanship in question does not always increase the value, but is sometimes attended with value, and sometimes not; as where, for instance, genus is opposed to genus —in which case workmanship is of no value.

The construction of a a building upon an usurped beam transfers the property of the beam to the usurper.—If a person usurp a beam, and build a house upon it, the beam is, in that case separated from the property of the proprietor, and the usurper must make a compensation to him for the value of it. Shafei maintains that the proprietor is entitled to take it. The arguments of the two parties on this point have been already recited; but in this case there is another reason in addition to those of our doctors, namely, that if (according to the opinion of Shafei) the proprietor were to take the beam, an injury would result to the usurper, as his house would thereby be demolished without his receiving any compensation.—Where, on the contrary (according to the opinion of our doctors), the beam is separated from the property of the proprietor, and becomes the property of the usurper, although an injury be thereby occasioned to the proprietor, yet that is done away by the usurper making compensation. The case is, therefore, analogous to one where an usurper sows the belly of his male or female slave with an usurped thread,* or inserts an usurped plank into his own boat; for in these cases the proprietor is not permitted to take away the thread or the plank, but is entitled to a compensation for their value.

In the case of slaying an usurped animal, the proprietor has an option of taking the carcase (receiving a compensation for the damage), or making it over to the usurper for the value.—If a person usurp and slay the goat of another, the proprietor has it in that case at his option either to take compensation for the value from the usurper, making over the goat to him, or to keep the goat, receiving from the usurper a compensation for the damage done by slaughtering it. Such also is the law with respect to a camel; or where a person cuts off one of the legs of a goat or camel belonging to another. This is according to the Zahir Rawayet; and the reason of it is, that a destruction of the animal is occasioned in one respect in a termination of many of its uses, such as milk, and progeny, and the transportation of burdens, whilst some of its uses still continue, such as that of the flesh, for instance; whence the case is similar to that of a large rent in cloth. If, however, a person slay or cut off the leg of a quadruped of which the flesh is not edible, the proprietor is entitled to take from him a compensation for the whole of the value; for in such case the slaying or maiming is in every respect a destruction. It is otherwise where an usurper cuts off the hand or foot of a male or female slave; for in that case the proprietor must receive back the slave, together with the fine, since the capability of yielding profit still exists in man after the loss of a foot or a hand.

A small damage committed upon usurped cloth does not transfer the property of it; but a considerable damage gives the proprietor an ovation of taking it back (with a compensation for the damage), or making it over to the usurper for the value.—If a person tear a piece of cloth the property of another so as to occasion a small rent in it, he is in that case responsible for the damage, and the cloth remains with the proprietor, since the substance of it is extant in every respect, nothing more having happened to it than a defect; — whereas if the rent were large, so as to destroy many of its uses, the proprietor would in that case have it in his option either to take the whole of the value from the usurper and give him the cloth (since he has destoryed it in every respect, even as much as if he had burnt it), or to keep the cloth and take a compensation for the damage; because a large rent is in one respect merely a defect, inasmuch as the substance of the cloth is still extant, as well as some of its uses likewise. It is to be observed that what is recited by Kadooree upon this subject implies that a large rent is such as occasions a destruction of many of the advantages. In fact a large rent is such as occasions a destruction of some parts of the cloth, and also of some of its uses; some of the parts and some of the uses still remaining (as where, for instance, before the accident of the rent, the cloth was capable of being made into an upper or under garment; and afterwards loses that capability); whereas a small rent is such as does not induce a destruction of any of the uses, but merely occasions a damage; for Mohammed, in the Mabsoot, has said, "the cutting of a garment is a great damage, notwithstanding it occasion only a destruction of some of the uses."

Case of planting or building upon usurped land.—If a person usurp land, and plant trees in it, or erect a building upon it, he must in that case be directed to remove the trees and clear the land, and to restore it to the proprietor; because the Prophet has said "there is no right over the seed of the oppresser" (alluding to the planting of trees; and also, because the property of the proprietor still exists as it did before, since the land has not been destroyed, nor has the usurper become proprietor, inasmuch as he cannot become the proprietor but by some one of the causes which establish property, of which none here exist. In this case, moreover, usurpation is not established;* and therefore the person who has so employed the land of another is ordered to clear and restore it to the owner, in the same manner as in the case of his putting his food into the vessel of another. If, however, the removal of the trees or the building be injurious to the land, the proprietor of the land has, in that case, the option of paying to the proprietor of the trees or the building a compensation equal to the value they would bear when removed from the ground, and thus

*This is the literal meaning in both the Arabic and Persian version; but what custom or particular operation it alludes to the translator has not been able to discover.

* There appears, at first sight, a sort of incongruity in opening the case "If a person usurp, &c.," and then saying "usurpation is not established."—The expression, however, only means that "usurpation, in the sense of the LAW, as requiring atonement, is not established," the reason of which is, 'that usurpation cannot take place with respect to fixed property, as has been already explained.—See p. 534.

possessing himself of them; because in this there is an advantage to both, and the injury to both is obviated. By the expression "paying a compensation equal to the value they would bear when removed," is to be understood paying the value which the trees or house bear upon the proprietor being directed to remove them; because his right exists only with respect to the trees or building "as required to be removed," since he is not at liberty to leave them upon the ground. It is therefore requisite to appreciate the land without the trees or the building, and afterwards to appreciate it with the trees or building (as removeable at the landholder's desire); and whatever may be the excess of the second appreciation over the first is the amount of the compensation which the proprietor of the land is required to pay to the proprietor of the trees or building-- (It is to be observed that the value of trees or of a building which are liable or required to be removed is less than that of trees or a building which are permitted to stand, since the expense of removal must be deduced from the value of trees or buildings which are removeable.)

Case of dying usurped cloth, or grinding usurped wheat into flour.—IF a person usurp the cloth of another and then dye it red, or the flour of another and then mix it with oil in that case the proprietor has the option of taking from the usurper a compensation equal to the value of the white cloth, or an equal quantity of flour, giving the red cloth or the mixed flour to the usurper,—or, of taking the red cloth or the mixed flour, giving to the usurper a compensation equal to the additional value these articles may have acquired from the red dye, or the mixture of oil. Shafei maintains that in the case of dyed cloth the proprietor of it has a right to take it, and then to tell the usurper to separate and take, to the utmost of his power, his dye from it; for he holds this case to be analogous to that of a plot of ground (in other words, if a person usurp a piece of ground belonging to another, and afterwards erect a building upon it, the proprietor is entitled to take the ground, desiring the usurper to dig up and carry away his building); because the separation of a dye from stained cloth is equally practicable with the removal of a building from the ground on which it stands. It is otherwise in the case of oil mixed in flour, because the separation of the oil is then impracticable. The argument of our doctors in that, in what they have advanced on this point, an attention is shown to the interests of both parties, an option, however, being allowed to the proprietor of the cloth, as he is the original. It is otherwise in the case of a plot to ground; for in that instance the usurper is entitled to the fragments of the house after its being pulled down (that is, to the bricks, wood, &c.); whereas a dye, when separated from cloth, is lost, and cannot be collected by the usurper of the cloth. It is also otherwise in the case of a garment blown by the wind into the vat of a dyer, and becoming stained in consequence; for in that case the dyer is not responsible for the garment: on the contrary; the proprietor of the garment must take it so stained, and pay to the dyer the value of his dye, as in this case nor degree of blame is imputable to him. It is to be observed that Aboo Assama has said that when a person usurps the cloth of another, and dyes it, the proprietor of the cloth may, if he please, sell it, and deduct from the price a proportion equal to the value of the white cloth, and give to the dyer a proportion equal to the value of his dye: for as the proprietor of the cloth has it in his power to refuse taking the dye and paying a compensation for its value, it follows that when he does refuse to take it, the cloth must be sold; that he may receive his proportion, and that the interests of both may be attended to. This reasoning of Aboo Assama equally holds in the case where a garment is stained in consequence of being blown by the wind into the vessel of a dyer; and in the same manner, the reasoning adduced in the case of cloth equally holds in the case of flour. As flour, however, is of the class of similars, it must be compensated for by a similar; whereas cloth, as being an article of price, must be compensated for by a payment of its value. Mohammed, in the Mabsoot, has said that flour must also be compensated for by value, because flour is altered by being baked, and is no longer of the class of similars. (Some have explained the meaning of the value of flour to be a similar quantity; and that Mohammed has used the term value instead of similar, because a similar is an equivalent, in the same manner as value.) It is to be observed that a yellow dye is the same as a red dye: but that with regard to a black dye there is a difference of opinion; Haneefa holding it to be a defect, whereas the two disciples maintain that it is not a defect, but, on the contrary, the cause of additional value. Some have said that this difference of opinion arises from the different periods of time; and others have said that if the cloth be of such a nature that a black dye occasions a diminution of its value, the dying of it must in that case be considered as a damage or defect; but that if it be of such a kind as to receive an increase of value from a black dye, the black dye is the same as a red dye. If, however, the usurped cloth be of such a nature that a red dye occasions a diminution of its value (as if, for instance, the value of it having been thirty dirms, it should, after receiving the red dye, be worth only twenty dirms), in that case it is related as an opinion of Mohammed, that regard must be had to the additional value which the red dye may have occasioned in some other piece of cloth; and if it amount to five dirms, that then the proprietor of the cloth has a right to take it, and to receive, besides, five dirms from the usurper: for the proprietor of the cloth is entitled to a compensation of ten dirms from the usurper for the amount of the damage occasioned to his cloth: and the usurper is entitled to five dirms from the proprietor as the value of his dye, having operated that increase upon another piece of cloth. Hence the proprietor is entitled to take five dirms from the usurper, and the remaining five is cancelled by the value of the dye thus estimated at five dirms.

Section.

An usurper, damaging the article usurped, becomes proprietor of it upon the owner demanding the value.—If a peson usurp any article of goods or furniture,* and damage it, and the proprietor demand a compensation for the value from the usurper, he [the usurper] in that case becomes the proprietor of such article, according to our doctors. Shafei maintains that the usurper does not become proprietor, because the act of usurpation, as being oppressive and illegal, is therefore incapable of occasioning a right of property; in the same manner as where a person usurps a Modabbir, and injures him, and the proprietor takes from him the value of the Modabbir as a compensation for the injury, —in which case he [the usurper] does not thence become proprietor of the Modabbir. The reasoning of our doctors is, that in the case in question the proprietor of the article obtains a return for it; and as the article usurped is fit to be shifted from the property of one person to that of another, the usurper becomes the proprietor of it, in order to remove the injury he would otherwise sustain. It is different with respect to a Modabbir, as he is not fit to be removed from the property of one person to that of another. (The contract of Tadbeer, however, is sometimes annulled by order of the Kazee; in which case the sale of the Modabbir is lawful, as it then is the sale of mere property, since he becomes such by the annulment of the contract.)

The amount of which is ascertained by the declaratian of the usurper upon oath,—or by evidence adduced by the proprietor.—It is to be observed that, in ascertaining the value of the article usurped, the assertion of the usurper, confirmed by an oath, is to be credited, since the proprietor is the claimant of a large value, and the usurper is the denier of the same, and the assertion of the denier upon oath must be admitted;—unless, however, the proprietor bring evidence in support of his claim; for then the assertion of the proprietor must be credited, as being supported by evidence, which is convincing proof.

And after accepting this, the proprietor cannot remand the article, if the compensation be given in conformity with his claim.—If, therefore, the substance of the article usurped appear or be found at a period when the value of it is greater than the compensation given by the usurper, and such compensation have been given in consequence of the claim of the proprietor, or of evidence adduced by him, or of the non-denial of the usurper,—the proprietor, in that case, has not the option of taking the substance of the thing usurped: on the contrary, it remains the property of the usurper, since his property in it has been rendered complete in consequence of a cause conjoined with the consent of the proprietor, inasmuch as he claimed that extent of value:—whereas if, on the contrary, the proprietor have taken a compensation in consequence of the assertion of the usurper, corroborated by an oath, he has in that case the option either to adhere to the compensation he has taken, or to take the substance of the article usurped, and restore to the usurper the compensation he may have taken; for under such circumstances the consent of the proprietor was not complete with respect to the quantity, since he claimed a larger quantity, but was obliged to take the quantity in question from his want of proof to establish the other. If on the other hand, the substance of the article usurped be found at a period when its value is equal to, or less than, the compensation taken,—and the proprietor should have taken the compensation in conformity with the assertion or oath of the usurper, the law (according to the Zahir Rawayet) is the same as already recited; that is, the proprietor has the option of either adhering to the compensation he had taken, or of taking back from the usurper the substance of the article, and restoring to him the amount of the compensation. This is approved; because the consent of the proprietor to take the compensation in question was not complete, inasmuch as he claimed a larger sum; which he did not get, and hence he has the option, because of the non-existence of his consent.

The sale of an usurped slave by the usurper is valid upon the owner receiving the value as a compensation;—but the emancipation of him would be invalid.—If a person usurp a salve, and sell him, and the proprietor take the value of him from the usurper as a compensation, the sale is in that case valid. If, on the contrary, the usurper emancipate the slave, and the proprietor afterwards take a compensation, the emancipation is not valid; because the right of property established in the usurper by his paying the compensation is defective, as being established by a retrospective reference, from a principle of necessity (whence it is that the right of property in an usurper takes place with respect to earnings of labour, but not with respect to progeny;—in other words, if a person usurp a female slave, and take to himself the earnings of her labour, and afterwards pay a compensation to the proprietor, the earnings are in that case his property; but if she should bear children whilst in his posses-

* Arab. Rakht wa Matta: household goods, &c., as opposed to Mal.—The distinction is fully explained elsewhere.

sion, and he afterwards pay a compensation to the proprietor, the children are not his property.—In short, the right of property established in an usurper in virtue of his payment of compensation is defective; and a defective right of property is sufficient to legalize sale, but not emancipation; in the same manner as the right of property established in a Mukatib with respect to the earning of his labour is defective: yet if he should sell a slave whom he may have earned by his labour it is valid: whereas if he were to emancipate him, the emancipation would be invalid.

The produce of an usurped property is a trust in the usurper's hands.—The fruit of an usurped orchard, and the children of an usurped female slave, together with their produce (such as their increase of stature and beauty), are a trust in the hands of the usurper. If, therefore, they be destroyed, he is not responsible for them;—unless, however, he should have committed a trespass with regard to them, or refused to answer the demand of the proprietor to deliver them up to him; for in these cases he is responsible. Shafei maintains that the increase of an article usurped, whether it be conjoined (such as increase of stature or of beauty) or separated (such as progeny), is a subject of responsibility; because usurpation is established with respect to it; for usurpation means the establishment of possession over the property of another without the consent of that other: and as this definition applies equally to any increase which may accrue upon such property, it is therefore a subject of responsibility, although the usurper have not dispossessed the proprietor of it; in the same manner as the fawn is a subject of responsibility, in a case where a person takes a deer out of an inclosure * and it afterwards brings forth whilst in his possession, notwithstanding that it [the fawn] had not before been in the possession of any one, so as to establish a dispossession. The reasoning of our doctors is, that usurpation means "the establishment of possession over the property of another, so as to destroy the possession of the proprietor" (as has been already explained). Now the possession of the proprietor had not been established, with respect to the increase, so as to admit the destruction of it. Besides, if the possession of the proprietor with regard to the increase be admitted by way of dependancy on his property, still his possession continues, and the usurper has not destroyed it; for it is apparent that the usurper has not hindered him from taking his increase;—yet if he refuse to give it to him upon his demand, he is then responsible to him for it; in the same manner as where he commits a trespass with regard to it, by destroying it, or killing and eating it, or selling it and delivering it to the buyer.—With respect, moreover, to the fawn before mentioned, it is not a subject of responsibility when destroyed prior to the ability of the trespasser to place it in the inclosure, because he is not, before that, guilty of any obstruction or hindrance;—in short, he is liable to responsibility only where he destroys the fawn after his ability to place it in the inclosure; and this because he is then guilty of an obstruction after the establishment of the claimant's right.*

The usurper of a female slave is not liable for any damage she may receive by bearing a child, provided the value of the child be adequate to such damage.—If a female slave be injured by bearing a child whilst in the possession of the usurper, and the value of the child be equal to the damage sustained, the usurper is not liable for a compensation. Shafei and Ziffer maintain that the value of the child be equal to the damage sustained, injury; because the child is the property of the proprietor of the slave; and consequently cannot be applied to remedy the damage sustained by her;—in the same manner as in the case of the fawn above recited;—that is to say, if a person drive a deer out of an inclosure, and she then bring forth a young one, and be injured by such delivery, and the value of the young be adequate to the damage, in that case the person is not only obliged to restore the deer and its young one to the inclosure, but must also make good the damage sustained. It is also the same where the child dies prior to the usurper's restoration of the mother; or where the mother dies in consequence of the delivery of the child, and the value of the child is adequate to remedy the loss; or where a person shears the wool of a sheep belonging to another, or lops off the branches of a tree belonging to another, or castrates the slave of another, or teaches him the knowledge of some art in consequence of which he is rendered in any respect defective;†—for in all these cases the person so acting is responsible for the injury, notwithstanding the value of the article be increased in consequence. The arguments of our doctors are that, in the instance in question, the cause of the increase and of the injury is the same, namely, childbirth;—and

*In the text the case is supposed that of a pilgrim driving a deer out of the sacred territory round Mecca.—The translator has hazarded a small deviation from the original in this instance, merely with a view to familiarize the allusion in the mind of an European reader.

* A small portion of the text is here omitted, as it relates merely to the prohibition against trespassing upon game in the sacred territory (round Mecca), a subject the discussion of which is of little importance to the point in question, and which is treated of at large elsewhere.—(See Seyid.)

†That is, defective in regard to the purpose for which his master had intended him; as by a loss of health, or any accident sustained in the course of his learning the art.

such being the case, the injury is not taken into the account, because, in opposition to it, an increase has been obtained. Hence an injury of this nature does not occasion responsibility; it being, in fact; analogous to where a person usurps a fat female slave, who afterwards becomes lean, and then grows fat again; or who losses two of her fore teeth, and then acquires two new ones;—or where a person cuts off the hand of an usurped slave whilst in the possession of the usurper, and the usurper receive the fine from him, and gives it with the slave to the proprietor;—for in all these cases no compensation for the injury is incumbent upon the usurper.—With respect to the case of the fawn, as adduced by Ziffer and Shafei, it is not admitted as applicable.—With respect, moreover, to the death of the mother, in consequence of her delivery (as also adduced by them) there are two opinions on record,—The first is, that if the value of the child be adequate to remedy the injury, it is then taken as such; and the second (which is according to the Zahir Rawayet) is, that the value of the child cannot be taken as a compensation for the injury, for this reason, that the delivery is not to be considered as the cause of the mother's death since delivery is not necessarily connected with death, being more frequently attended with safety. Where, on the other hand, the child dies prior to the restoration of the mother the injury is not remedied; because there was a necessity for the restoration of the original (namely, the mother) in the condition in which she was at the period of usurpation: and as she afterwards sustained an injury by the birth of a child, and the fruit of the injury (namely, the child) cannot, because of its death; be given along with the mother, it follows that the mother is not restored in the condition in which she was at the period of usurpation. With respect to the castration of a slave, it is not an increase, being an object only with some loose people;—and as to the other instances adduced by Ziffer and Shafei, the case in them of the increase and the damage is not one and the same thing: for the cause of damage in a tree is the cutting off its branch, whilst the cause of increase is the growth; the case of damage in a sheep is the shearing of its wool, whilst the cause of increase is the growth of the animal; and the cause of damage in the slave is the teaching or instructing him, whilst the cause of increase is the intellect of the slave.

The usurper of a female slave, impregnating her, is responsible for her value, in case she die of childbirth after restoration.—If a person usurp a female slave, and cohabit with her, and she become pregnant, and he restore her in that state to the proprietor, and she then die of childbirth, the usurper must in that case pay a compensation equal to the value which she bore on the day of her impregnation; whereas, if she were free, no compensation would be required, according to Haneefa. The two disciples maintain that neither is any compensation due in the case of her being a slave. The argument of the two disciples are, that in the case in question, upon the usurper restoring the slave to the proprietor, and the restoration, being made valid and complete, the proprietor is held to have received her into his property; and as, afterwards, the disorder of which she dies, namely, childbirth, is thus considered to have happened to her whilst in the possession of the proprietor, the usurper is, therefore, not liable for her; in the same manner as where an usurped female slave, having been seized with some disorder, such as a fever, the usurper restores her in that condition to the proprietor, and she afterwards dies in his possession; or where an usurped female slave commits whoredom with some person whilst in the usurper's possession, and he restores her to the proprietor, and she afterwards suffers punishment for whoredom and dies of the same; in neither of which cases is the usurper responsible, any more than the seller, in the case of his selling a pregnant female slave, who afterwards dies of childbirth in the possession of the purchaser. The arguments of Haneefa are, that as the usurper, in the case in question, usurped the female slave at a time when the cause of destruction did not exist in her and restored her at a period when such cause did exist in her, he therefore has not restored her in the state in which he took her:—consequently, the restoration was not valid and complete, being, in fact, the same as if an usurped female slave, having committed a crime in the usurper's possession, should afterwards, on account such crime, be put to death whilst in the possession of the proprietor,—or be given up to the avenger of the offence, in consequence of her having committed the crime inadvertently, instead of wilfully,—in either of which cases the proprietor is entitled to take the whole of the value from the usurper, and so also in the case in question. It is otherwise where the woman usurped is free; because no responsibility takes place from the usurpation of a free woman, and consequently the usurper is not responsible after the restoration, although such restoration were invalid. With respect to what has been alleged of the purchase of a pregnant female slave, it is answered, that the delivery not having been incumbent upon the seller on account of his having before taken her, so as to require a delivery in the state in which he had taken her (which is a condition of validity in the case of usurpation). it follows that the analogy here does not hold good. With respect, also, to the case of an usurped female slave committing whoredom, and dying in consequence of the punishment on that account inflicted upon her, the answer is, that whoredom merely occasions scourging, which is a case of pain, but not of death, and therefore, in this case, a cause of destruction did not take place whilst the slave was in the possession of the usurper.

There is no hire for the use of an usurped article: but the usurper is responsible for any damage it may sustain—An usurper is not responsible for the use of the article usurped:* but if it be injured he is responsible for the damage. Shafei maintains that an usurper is liable for the use of a thing usurped, and consequently, that he owes an adequate rent of hire for it. It is to be observed that there is no difference between the doctrine of Shafei and that of our doctors, in the case where a person usurps a house and leaves it unoccupied, or occupies it himself; for in such case, according to both doctrines, the usurper is not liable for the use of it.—Malik maintains that if the usurper himself occupy the house he is responsible for an adequate rent; but not in case of his leaving it unoccupied. The argument of Shafei is that the use of property is estimable (whence it is a subject of responsibilty from contracts and agreements), and consequently is a subject of responsibility from usurpation. The arguments of our doctors on this point are twofold.—First, the use of an article usurped is obtained by the usurper in consequence of its occurring during his occupancy (for it had not existed in the hands of the proprietor, as use is a passing accident which does not endure); and such being the case, he is entitled to it, and consequently is not responsible for it, as no man is responsible for that to which he is entitled.—Secondly, there is no similarity between use and property, such as dirms and deenars; for use is an accident, whereas property is a substance. Use therefore, cannot be a subject of responsibility in substantial property; because a similarity is requisite between the compensation and the thing for which the compensation is given.—With respect to the assertion of Shafei, that "the use of property is estimable," it is not admitted use being considered as estimable only in the case of contracts of hire, from necessity; but in the case of usurpation there exists no contract whatever.—Where, however, the article usurped is damaged, whilst in the possession of the usurper, in consequence of his use of it, a compensation for the damage is incumbent upon him, because of his having destroyed part of the substance of the thing usurped.

Section

Of the usurpation of things which are of no value.

A Mussulman is responsible for destroying the wine or pork of a Zimmee.—If a Mussulman destroy wine or pork belonging to a Zimmee, he must compensate for the value of the same; whereas, if he destroy wine or pork belonging to a Mussulman, no compensation is due.—Shafei maintains that in the former case also no compensation is due. A similar disagreement subsists with respect to the case of a Zimmee destroying wine or pork belonging to a Zimmee; or of one Zimmee selling either of these articles to another; for such sale is lawful, according to our doctors,—in opposition to the opinion of Shafei. The argument of Shafei is that wine and pork are not articles of value with respect to Mussulmans,—nor with respect to Zimmees, as those are dependant of the Mussulmans with regard to the precepts of the law. A compensation of property, therefore, for the destruction of these articles is not due. The arguments of our doctors are that wine and pork are valuable property with respect to Zimmees: for with them wine is the same as vinegar with the Mussulmans, and pork the same as mutton; and we, who are Mussulmans, being commanded to leave them in the practice of their religion, have consequently no right to impose a rule upon them.—As, therefore, wine and pork are with them property of value, it follows that whoever destroys these articles belonging to them does, in fact, destroy their property of value: in opposition to the case of carrion or blood, because these are not considered as property according to any religion, or with any sect.¶

And must compensate for it by a payment of the value.—Hence it appears that if a Mussulman destroy the wine or pork of a Zimmee, he must compensate for the value of the pork,—and also of the wine, notwithstanding that be of the class of similars; becausa it is not lawful for Mussulmans to transfer the property of wine, as that would be to honour and respect it. It is otherwise where a Zimmee sells wine to a Zimmee, or destroys the wine of a Zimmee; for in these case it is incumbent upon the seller to deliver over the wine to the purchase, and also upon the destroyer to give as a compensation a similar quantity of wine to the proprietor, since the transfer of the property of wine is not prohibited to Zimmees:—contrary to usury, as that is excepted from the contracts of Zimmees;—or to the case of the slave of a Zimmee, who having been a Mussulman becomes an apostate; for if any Mussulman kill this slave, he is not in that case responsible to the Zimmee, notwithstanding the Zimmee consider the slave as valuable property, since we Mussulmans are commanded to show our abhorrence of apostates. It is also otherwise with respect to the wilful omission of the Tasmeea, or invocation, in the slaying of an animal, where the proprietor considers such omission as lawful, being, for instance, of the sect of Shafei;—in other words, if a person of the sect of Haneefa destroy the flesh of an animal so slain by a person of the sect of Shafei, the Haneefite is not in that case responsible to the Shafeyite, notwithstanding the latter did, according to his tenets, believe the slain animal to have been valuable property; because the authority to convince the Shafeyite of the illegality of his practice is vested in the Haneefite, in-

*Meaning he does not owe any hire for the use.

asmuch as it is permitted to him to establish the illegality of it by reason and argument.

A change wrought upon an usurped article by any unexpensive process does not alter the property; but if the process be expensive, the property devolves to the usurper, who, must make a compensation.—If a person usurp wine belonging to a Mussulman, and convert it into vinegar by placing it alternately in the sun and in the shade,—or the skin of a carrion, and tan or dress it by the application of some valuable article,—the proprietor of the wine is entitled to take the vinegar, without giving any thing to the usurper, and the proprietor of the skin is entitled to take it, upon paying to the usurper the increase it may have received from the dressing: for in the former case, the conversion of the wine into vinegar is merely a purification of it, in the same manner as the bleaching of unclean cloth; and hence the property of the vinegar continues vested in the proprietor, since a property is not created in the liquor by the operation of making it into vinegar; whereas, in the second case, a valuable article belonging to the usurper is united to the skin, in the same manner as a dye in cloth, and this case is therefore the same as the dyeing of a garment.—Accordingly the proprietor of the wine is entitled to take the vinegar from the usurper without making him any compensation; and, on the other hand, the proprietor of the skin is entitled to take it from the usurper, upon making a compensation to him for the increase which it may have received from the dressing. The mode of ascertaining the amount of this increase, is by first estimating the value of the skin supposing it undressed; and then the value which it bears dressed; when the difference must be paid to the usurper. In this case, also, the usurper is entitled to detain the article adopted until he obtain his right, in the same manner as a seller is entitled to detain the goods sold as a security for the price.—If in the cases here considered, the usurper should destroy the vinegar, or the dressed skin, he is responsible for the vinegar,—but not for the skin, according to Haneefa The two disciples maintain that he is responsible for the skin also,—being entitled, however to the increase of value from the dressing. The reason of responsibility for the vinegar is, that as it still continues in the property of the first proprietor, being, at the same time, an article of value, it follows that the usurper is liable for the destruction of it: and as vinegar is of the class of similars he must compensate for it by a similar quantity—With respect to the skin, the reasons of responsibility for it (as maintained by the two disciples) are twofold—FIRST, it still continues the property of the proprietor, in asmuch as he is entitled to take it back from the usurper; and as it is an article of value, it follows that, in consequence of the destruction of it by the usurper, he [the proprietor] is entitled to take from him [the usurper] a compensation adequate to the value of the dressed skin; paying him afterwards the increase of value it has received from the dressing; in the same manner as where a person usurps the cloth of another, and dye it, and then destroys it,—in which case he is responsible for it to the proprietor, receiving from him, at the same time, the difference occasioned in the value of the cloth by the dyeing—SECONDLY, the restoration of the skin dressed was incumbent on the usurper; whence, upon his destroying it, he is bound to give a consideration for it, namely, the value;—in the same manner as where a borrower destroys the article borrowed; in which case he is responsible for the value—It is to be observed, however, that if the destruction of the skin take place whilst in the possession of the usurper, without his being the occasion of it, in that case, according to all our doctors, he is not responsible for it, whether he have dressed it by the application of something valuable, or otherwise (With respect to what is advanced by the two disciples, "that the proprietor must take the value of the dressed skin from the usurper, paying him afterwards the increase of value it has received from the dressing"—it proceeds on the supposition that the value of the skin and of the operation of dressing is of different kinds,—as if the skin should be valued in deenars and the workmanship in dirms; for if both be estimated in the same species, the proprietor must at once deduct from the value of the skin the value of the workmanship, and take the difference from the usurper; as it would be needless first to receive the whole from him, and the then to pay back a part of it)—The reasoning of Haneefa is, that the skin in question has been rendered valuable by the workmanship of the usurper, namely, the dressing, which is of a valuable nature, as he mixed with it valuable property (whence his right to detain it until he receive the increase of value from the dressing),—The workmanship, therefore, is his right; and the skin is, with respect to its being valuable, a dependant of the workmanship, that being the original;—and as the usurper is not responsible for the original, namely the workmanship, so neither is he responsible for the dependant namely, the skin; in the same manner as he is not responsible where the skin is destroyed in his possession without his act. It is otherwise where the skin is extant; for in such case it is incumbent upon the usurper to restore it to the proprietor, because the restoration of it is a consequent of the proprietor's right of property, and the skin is not a dependent of the operation of dressing it, with respect to right of property, since the property of the proprietor is established in it prior to the dressing, although, whilst in that condition, it was not an article of value:—in opposition to the case of cloth, or the skin of an animal killed according to the prescribed forms; for the proprietor of these is entitled to a compensation from the usurper, as both are articles of value prior to the dressing or dyeing, and consequently not dependent upon the workmanship with respect to their being valuable. It is to be observed that, in the case in question (that is, where the usurper has dressed the skin with something of value, and it remains extant in his possession), if the proprietor be inclined to leave it in the possession of the usurper, and take from him a compensation for the value, some have said that it is not permitted to him so to do, because of the skin being of no value.—(It is otherwise in the case of dyeing cloth, the dye being an article of value).—Some, again, have said that this is not permitted to him according to Haneefa;—but that according to the two disciples it is permitted to him; because when the proprietor refuses to take back the dressed skin, and, leaving it in the possession of the usurper, demands from him a compensation, the usurper has it not then in his power to restore it; and the case is, therefore, the same as if it had been destroyed, concerning which the two disciples and Haneefa have disagreed.—Some have said that, according to the doctrine of the two disciples, the proprietor is to take from the usurper the value of the dressed skin, and return to him whatever increase it may have received from the dressing, in the same manner as in the case of a destruction: whilst others have said that the proprietor is entitled only to the value of an undressed skin of an animal killed according to the prescribed form.—All that has been advanced on this topic proceeds on the supposition of the usurper having dressed the skin with something of value; for if he should have dressed it with something of no value, such as by means of moisture, or the heat of the sun, the proprietor is then entitled to take it from him without making him any return since a dressing of that nature is equivalent to the washing of cloths. If, also, in this case, the usurper destroy the skin, he is responsible for the value of it in its dressed state. Some, on the contrary, have said that he is responsible for the value of it in its undressed state, because the dressing, as being an acquisition of his own, ought not to subject him to responsibility. The first opinion is adopted by most of the modern lawyers; and the reason of it is, that the quality of dressing, as being a dependent of the skin, cannot be separated from it; and consequently, when responsibility takes place with respect to the original [the skin] it must also operate with respect to the dependent, namely, the quality, [of dressing].

Case of converting usurped wine into vinegar, by means of mixing in it some valuable ingredient.—If an usurper of wine convert it into vinegar by throwing salt into it, lawyers have said that, according to Haneefa the vinegar becomes the property of the usurper without any thing being due from him; whereas, according to the two disciples, the proprietor is entitled to take the vinegar, making a compensation to the usurper for the increase of the article by means of the salt (that is to say, he must give him a quantity of vinegar equal to the weight of the salt). If, on the contrary, the proprietor wish to leave the vinegar with the usurper, and take a compensation from him for its value, the same two opinions that have been given with regard to the case above recited of the dressing of a skin, prevail with regard to this case. If, also, the usurper destroy the wine, he is no ways responsible, according to Haneefa—in opposition to the opinion of the two disciples, as has been already recited in the case of dressing a skin.—If the usurper convert the wine into vinegar by means of pouring vinegar into it, in that case it is related as an opinion of Mohammed that, provided the wine be turned into vinegar within the hour in which the usurper poured the vinegar into it, it is his property, without his being subject to any compensation: because the pouring of the vinegar, in such case, is equivalent to a destruction of the wine; and wine is not an article of value. If, on the other hand, the wine because of the quantity of vinegar poured into it being small, should not become vinegar until after the lapse of a considerabe period, it must in that case be divided between the usurper and the proprietor, according to its measure; that is the usurper is entitled to a part of it in proportion to the quantity poured in, and the proprietor to a part of it in proportion to the quantity of wine; because in this case the usurper has mixed his vinegar with what eventually became the vinegar of the proprietor; and this (in the opinion of Mohammed) is not a destruction. In the opinion of Haneefa, however, the vinegar, in both cases, becomes the property of the usurper; because the immediate act of his pouring vinegar into the wine is (according to him) a destruction of it; and this destruction does not, on any supposition, occasion responsibility, because if considered as a destruction of wine, it is destruction of a thing that bears no value, or if considered as the destruction of vinegar, it is a destruction of his own property, inasmuch as the vinegar becomes the property of the usurper. According to Mohammed the usurper is not responsible where he destroys the liquor after its having become vinegar on the hour in which he put the other vinegar into it; for as, in this case, he acquires a right in the whole, he of course merely destroys his own property; whereas if he destroy it where it has become vinegar after a length of time, he is responsible, since in this case he destroys the property of another. With respect to what has been recited in Kadooree, some of our modern lawyers have said that it is absolute; that is, that in all conversions of usurped wine into vinegar, the proprietor is entitled to take it without making any compensation to the usurper; because the thing thrown into the wine by the usurper is of no value, inasmuch as, by the mixture of it with wine, it becomes virtually wine, which is a thing of no value. There are variety of opinions concerning this case, which the author of this work has recited in the Kafayat al Moontihee.

A person is responsible for destroying the musical instruments, &c., or the prepared drink of a Mussulman.—If a person break the lute, the tabor, the pipe, or the cymbal of a Mussulman, or spill his Sikker,* or Monissaf,† he is responsible, the sale of such articles being lawful; according to Haneefa. The two disciples maintain that he is not responsible, they holding such article to be unsaleable. Some say that this difference of opinion obtains only concerning such musical instruments as are merely used for amusement; but that if a person break a drum, such as are allowed to be used in celebrating a marriage, he is responsible, according to all our doctors. Some, also, say that in decreeing responsibility, opinions are given according to the doctrine of the two disciples. By Sikker is understood the juice of unripe dates, which is sufferred to ferment and acquire a spirit without boiling; and by Monissaf, the juice of unripe grapes, boiled until only one half remain. Concerning liquor boiled in the smallest degree, which is termed Bazik,‡ there are two opinions reported from Haneefa, one, that it is a lawful subject both of sale and responsibility,—and another, that it is not so. The arguments of the two disciples on this point are,—First, that these articles are all made for the purpose of doing that which is offensive to the law, and therefore are not valuable property,—Secondly, what the person in question has done was in reformation of an abuse; and as we are directed to reform abuses wherever they occur, he therefore is not responsible, in the same manner as he would not be responsible, if he were to destroy those articles by order of the magistrate. The argument of Haneefa is that the articles in question are property, as being capable of yielding a lawful advantage, although they be also capable of being used unlawfully, and therefore resemble a female singer, —whence there is no reason why they should not be considered as valuable property. As, therefore, those articles are (according to Haneefa) of a valuable nature, a reparation is due from the destroyer of them; and if a person were to sell them, the sale is lawful; for the obligation of reparation, and the legality of sale, depend upon an article being property, and capable of valuation, circumstances which exist with respect to the articles in question. The reformation of abuses, moreover, is committed to the hands of magistrates: as they are enabled, by the nature of their office, to carry it into effect: but it is not entrusted to others, excepting merely to the exent of verbal instruction and advice.

And must compensate for them by paying their intrinsic value.—Proceeding upon the doctrine of Haneefa, the destroyer, in the case here considered, is responsible for the value the articles bear in themselves, independent of the particular amusement to which they contribute. Thus if a female singer (for instance) be destroyed, she must be valued merely as a slave girl; and the same of fighting rams, tumbling pigeons, game cocks, or eunuch slaves; in the other words, if any of these be destroyed, they must be valued and accounted for at the rate they would have borne if unfit for the light and evil purposes to which such articles are commonly applied; and so likewise of pipes, tabors, and other musical instruments. It is to be observed that, in the case of spilling Sikker or Monissaf, the destroyer is responsible for the value of the article, and not for a similar, because it does not become a Mussulman to be proprietor of such articles. If, on the contrary, a person destroy a crucifix belonging to a Christian, he is responsible for the value it bears as a crucifix; because Chirstians are left to the practice of their own religious worship.

The usurper of a Modabbira is responsible for her value if she die in his possession, but not the usurper of Mokatiba.—If a person usurp the Modabbira of another, and she die in his possession, he is responsible for her value; whereas, if a person usurp the Am-Walid of another, and she die in his possession, he is not responsible. This is according to Haneefa. The two disciples maintain that the usurper is responsible for the value in either instance.—The reason of this difference of opinion is, that a Modabbira is universally admitted to be valuable property; and an Am-Walid is not valuable, according to Haneefa; whereas the two disciples hold an Am-Walid to be valuable. The arguments on both sides have been already detailed at length in treating of Manumission

BOOK XXXVIII.

OF SHAFFA.

Definition of Shaffa.—Shaffa, in the language of the law, signifies the becoming proprietor of lands sold for the price at which the purchaser has bought them, although he be not consenting thereunto. This is termed Shaffa, because the root from which Shaffa is derived signifies conjunction, and the lands sold are here conjoined to the land of the Shafee, or person claiming the right of pre-empion.

*A sort of intoxicating liquor.

†Half boiled wine. (These terms are fully explained in Book XLVI., treating of Prohibited Liquors.

‡ A species of date wine.

Chap. I.—Of the Person to whom the Right of Shaffa appertains.
Chap. II.—Of Claims to Shaffa; and of Litigation concerning it.
Chap. III—Of the Articles concerning which Shaffa operates.
Chap. IV.—Of circumstances which invalidate the Right of Shaffa.

CHAPTER I

OF THE PERSONS TO WHOM THE RIGHT OF SHAFFA APPERTAINS.

The right of Shaffa appertains to a partner in the property, a participator in the immunities of the property, and a neighbour.—THE right of Shaffa appertains,—I. to a partner in the property of the land sold,—II. to a partner in the immunities and appendages of the land (such as the right to water, and to road): and III. to a neighbour.—The right of Shaffa in a partner, is founded on a precept of the Prophet, who has said, "The right of SHAFFA holds in a partner who has not divided off and taken separately his share"—The establishment of it in a neighbour is also founded on a saying of the Prophet. "The neighbour of a house has a superior right to that house; and the neighbour of lands has superior right to those lands; and if he be absent, the seller must wait his return; provided however, that they both participate in the same road;"—and also. "A neighbour has a right, superior to that of a stranger, in the lands adjacent to his own."—Shafee is of opinion that a neighbour is not a Shafee; because the Prophet has said, SHAFFA relates to a thing held in joint property, and which has not been divided of:" when therefore, the property has undergone a division, and the boundary of each partner is particulary discriminated- and a separate road assigned to each, the right of Shaffa can no longer exist. Besides, the existence of the right of Shaffa is repugnant to analogy, as it involves the taking possession of another's property contrary to his inclination: whence it must be confined solely to those to whom it is particularly granted by the LAW. Now, it is granted particularly to a partner; but a neighbour cannot be considered as such; for the intention of the LAW; in granting to it a partner, is merely to prevent the inconveniences arising from a division; since if the partner were not to get that share which is the subject of the claim of Shaffa; a new purchaser might insist upon a division, and thereby occasion to him a great deal of unnecessary vexation;—but as this argument does not hold good in behalf of a neighbour, he therefore is not entitled to the privilege of shaffa.—We,* on the contrary, allege that the precept of the Prophet, already quoted, is a sufficient ground for establishing the right of Shaffa in a neighbour.—Besides the reason for establishing this right in a partner is the circumstance of his, property being continually and inseparably adjoined to that of a stranger† (namely, the purchaser), which is injurious to him, because of the difference of a stranger's disposition and so forth; and certainly a greater regard is due to the partner than to the stranger who may have made the purchase, since the vexation that would ensue to the partner from forcing him to abandon a place which, from long residence, may have acquired his affections would doubtless be greater than that to which the stranger is subjected; for, although he may thus be dispossessed, contrary to his inclination, of a property over which he has acquired a right by purchase, yet still the grievance is but inconsiderable, since he is not dispossessed without receiving a due consideration:—and as all these reasons equally hold in behalf of a neighbour, he is therefore entitled to the privilege of Shaffa as well as a partner.—The reasons, moreover, on which Shafei grounds the right of a partner, and the distinction he makes betwixt a partner and a neighbour, can by no means be admitted: since the inconveniences attending a division of property are allowed by the LAW; and are not of such a nature that the preventing of them should justify the injury which must be committed in depriving another of his property contrary to his inclinations.—The order in which we have classed the persons entitled to the privilege of Shaffa is founded on a precept of the Prophet, who has said, "A partner in the thing itself has a superior right to one who is only a partner in its appendages; and a partner in the appendages of the property precedes a neighbour." Besides, the conjunction occassioned by a partnership in the property itself is of all others the strongest; and next to it is that occasioned by a partnership in the appendages (since here the party participates in the immunities of the property, which is not the case with a neighbour): and a superiority of right in every instance, depends on the strength, in the case, or fundamental principle—The vexations, moreover, and inconvenience arising from a division may be admitted as an additional argument, although it be not of such weight as to form a ground for injury to another.

No person can claim it during the existence of one who has a superior right—A PARTNER merely in the road or the rivulet, or a neighbour, cannot be entitled to the privilege of Shaffa during the existence of one who is a

* In other words, "is entitled to the right of SHAFFA;"—Shaffa being the term used to express the person endowed with that right.

* Meaning, the Haneefites (in opposition to the followers of Shafei)

† Arab. Dakheel; meaning, literally, "an arrival;" i.e a new comer.

partner in the property of the land; for his is the superior right, as has been already shown.

Unless he first relinquish it, when the title devolves to the next in succession.—If a partner in the property of the land relinquish his right of Shaffa, it devolves next to him who is a partner in the road: and if he also relinqish his right, it falls to the Jar Molasick, or person whose house is situated at the back of that which is the object of Shaffa, having the entry to it by another road. Aboo Yoosaf is of opinion that during the existence of partner in the ground, whether he resign or insist upon his right, no other person is entitled to the privilege of Shaffa; for by his existence all others are excluded; and whilst the excluder remains the excluded have on right: as holds in inheritance.—The ground on which the Zahir Rawayat (first quoted as above) proceeds is, that the cause of the privilege of Shaffa exists with respect to each of the above-mentioned persons. The partner, however, has the superior right. Upon his relinquishing it, therefore, the one who is next to him in order of precedence will assume it;—in the same manner as holds with respect to debts contracted during health, when they came in competition with debts contracted in sickness; that is, the former are first discharged; but if the creditor whose debt was contracted in health relinquish his claim, the estate of the deceased is then appropriated to discharge the claim of him whose debt was contracted under sickness

A person who is a joint proprietor of only a part of the article has a title superior to a neighbour.—A person who is a joint proprietor of only a part of the property sold (such as a partner in a particular room or wall of a house), as he has a right superior to one who is neighbour to that particular part, so likewise has he a right superior to one who is a neighbour to the rest of the house. This is an approved maxim of Aboo Yoosaf; for the conjunction holds stronger in the case of a person who is a joint proprietor of only a part of the house, than in that of one who is merely a neighbour. It is necessary that the road or rivulet, the joint participation in which gives a claim to the privilege of Shaffa, be private. By a private road is understood a road shut up at one end: and by a private rivulet we understand a steam of water in which boats cannot pass and repass; for otherwise it is a public river. (This is according to Haneefa and Mohammad. It is reported from Aboo Yoosaf, that a private rivulet is a stream which affords water to two or three pieces of ground; but if it exceed that, it is a public one).

The relative situation of the property determines the right, when claimed on the plea of neighbourhood—If a house be sold, situated in a short lane, shut up at one end, communicating through another lane, shut up also at one end, but of greater extent, in this case the inhabitants of the short lane only are entitled to the privilege of Shaffa: whereas, if a house situated in the long lane be sold, the inhabitants of both lanes are so entitled. The reason of this is, that the right of egress and regress in the short lane is participated only by its own inhabitants, whereas the right in the long lane appertains equally to the inhabitants of both:—as has been already explained under the head of "Duties of the Kazee." The same rule also holds good in the case of a small rivulet issuing out of another.

The laying of beams on the wall of a house gives a right of Shaffa from neighbourhood, but not from partnership, since this act does not constitute a partnership in the property of the house. In the same manner, also, a person who is a partner in a beam laid on the top of the wall is only held in the light of a neighbour.

The right of all the Shafees (claiming upon equal ground) is equal, without any regard to the extent of their properties. When there is a plurality of persons entitled to the privilege of Shaffa, the right of all is equal, and no regard is paid to the extent of their several properties. Shafei maintains that the right of Shaffa in this case is possessed by the parties in proportion to their several properties; because Shaffa is one of the immunities of their property, and must therefore be held, like the profits of trade, the produce of lands, the offspring of slaves, or the fruit of trees, inproportion to their respective shares in the joint property. The argument of our doctors is, that the parties being all equal with respect to the principle on which their right of Shaffa is grounded (namely, a conjunction with the lands sold), they are all consequently equal in the right itself,—whence if only one partner were present, however inconsiderable his share might be, he would be entitled to the whole of the Shaffa.—In reply, moreover, to the arguments used by Shafei, it is to observed that the disseising another of his property contrary to his inclination, is not one of the immunities of property, and is very different from the profits of trade, the fruits of trees, or the like, which are produced absolutely from the property itself.

If one of the parties relinquish his right, it devoles to the others, and is participated equally amongst them; for although the grounds of their right were complete, yet they were obstructed from enjoying the entire privilege by the intervention of his right: but that right being resigned the obstruction consquently no longer remains.

If some be absent, the Shaffa in adjudged equally amongst those who are present;—but the absentees appearing receive their shares.—If some of the partners happen to be absent, the whole of the Shaffa is to be decreed equally amongst those who are present; for it is a matter of uncertainty whether those who are absent would be inclined to demand their right; and the rights of those who are present must not be prejudiced on a mere uncertainty.—If, however, the Kazee should have decreed the whole of the Shaffa to one who is present, and as absentee afterwards appear and claim his right, the Kazee must decree him the half: and so likewise if a third appear, he must decree him one third of the shares respectively held by the other two in order that thus an equality may be established amongst them.

IF the person present should relinquish his Shaffa after the whole has been decreed to him by the Kazee, and the absentee afterwards appear, he is in this case entitled to claim only one half ' because the decree which the Kazee has passed, awarding the whole to the other, absolotely extinguished one held of the absentee's right.—It were otherwise if the person present relinquish his right previous to any decree being passed by the Kazee, and afterwards the absentee appear: for in this case he [the absentee] is entitled to the whole of the Shaffa.

The right does not operate until after the sale of the property.—THE privilege of Shaffa is established after the sale; for it cannot take place until it be manifest that the proprietor is no longer inclined to keep his house; and this is manifested by the sale of it. It is therefore sufficient, in order to prove the sale and establish the privilege of Shaffa, that the seller acknowledge the sale, although the person said to be the buyer deny it.

Nor until it be regularly demanded.—THE right of Shaffa is not established until the demand be regularly made in the presence of witnesses;—and it is requisite that it be made as soon as possible after the sale is known; for the right of Shaffa is but a feeble right, as it is the disseising another of his property merely in order to prevent apprehended inconvenience.—It is therefore requisite that the Shafee without delay discover his int ntions, by making the demand; which must be done in the presence of witnesses, otherwise it cannot be afterwards proved before the Kazee.

Neither does the property go to the Shafee but by the surrender of the purchaser, or a decree of the magistrate.—WHEN the demand has boen regularly made in the presence of witnesses, still the Shafee does not become proprietor of the house until the purchaser surrender it to him, or untii the magistrate pass a decree: because the purchaser's property was complete, and cannot be transferred to the Shafee but by his own consent, or by a decree of a magistrate; in the same manner as in the case of a retraction of a grant, where the property of the grantee being completely established by the grant it cannot be transferred to the granter, but by the surrender of the grantee, or, by a decree of a magistrate. The use of this law appears in a case where the Shafee, after having preferred his claim before witnesses previous to the decree of the magistrate or the surrender of the purchaser, dies, or sells the house from whence he derived his right;—or where the house adjoining to that to which the right of Shaffa relates is sold for in the first of these instances the house is not a part of his hereditaments, because it was not his property; and the right of Shaffa fails in the second instance, as the fundamental principle of that right is extinguished previous to his becoming the proprietor: and in the third case, he has no right of Shaffa with respect to the house which is sold, since the house from which he would have derized that right is not his property.

CHAPTER II.

OF CLAIMS TO SHAFFA, AND OF LITIGATION CONCERNING IT.

The claims are of three kinds. I. The immediate claim (which must be made on the instant, or the Shafee forfeits his title).—CLAIMS to Shaffa are of three kinds.—The first of these is termed Talb Mawasibat, or immediate claim, where the Shafee prefers his claim the moment he is apprised of the sale being concluded; and this it is necessary that he should do, insomuch that if he make any delay his right is thereby invalidated; for the right of Shaffa is but of a feeble nature; as has been already observed; and the Prophet, moreover, has said "The right of SHAFFA is established in him who prefers his claim without delay.

IF the Shafee receive a letter which, either in the beginning or the middle apprises him of the circumstance of his Shaffa, and he read it on to the end, his right of Shaffa thereby invalidated. Many of our modern doctors accord in this opinion; and it is in one place recorded as the doctrine of Mohammad.—In another place, however, it is reported from him, that if the man claim his Shaffa in the presence of the company amongst whom he may be sitting when he receives the intelligence, he is the Shafee, his right not being invalidated unless he delay asserting it till after the company have broke up. Both these opinions are mentioned in the Nawadir;—and Koorokhee passed decrees agreeably to the last quoted report; because the power of accepting or rejecting the Shaffa being established, a short time should necessarily be allowed for reflection; in the same manner as time is allowed to a woman to whom her husband has given the power of choosing to be divorced or not.

IF the Shafee, on hearing of the sale, exclaim "Praise be to GOD!" or "There is no power or strength but what is derived from GOD!" or "GOD is pure!" his right of Shaffa is not invalidated, insomuch that if, immediately on pronoucing these words he without delay claim his Shaffa, he will accordingly get it; because the first of these is considered as a thaknsgiving on his being freed of the neighbourhood of the seller; the second (which is an expression of admiration) is supposed to proceed from the astonishment with which he is struck at the intention manifested by the seller of doing a thing which would be vexatious to him; and the last is considered as an exclamation prefatory to further discourse. None of these expressions, therefore, can imply a refusal or rejection of the Shaffa.—In the same manner also, if on receiving the news of the sale, he ask "Who is the purchaser, and how much is the price?" it does not invalidate his right: since these questions cannot be considered as a refusal, but on the contrary it may be concluded from them that if the price be reasonable, and the purchaser a person whom he would not like as a neighbour, he will afterwards claim his right of Shaffa.

It is not material in what words the claim is preferred; it being sufficient that they imply a claim. Thus if a person say "I have claimed my Shaffa," or "I shall claim my Shaffa," or "I do claim my Shaffa," all these are good; for it is the meaning, and not the style or mode of expression, which is here considered.

When news of the sale is brought to the Shafee it is not necessary, according to Haneefa, that he assert his intention of claiming the Shaffa before witnesses unless the news be communicated to him by two men, or one man and two women, or one upright man The two disciples maintain that he ought to declare his intentions before witnesses as soon as the news is communicated to him by one person, being either a freeman or a slave, a woman or a child,—provided, however, that the person be, in his belief; a true speaker—It is otherwise where a woman is informed that her husband has given her the power of divocing herself; for in that case it does not signify who is the informer, or what is his character.

If the person who gives the intelligence to the Shafee be himself the buyer it is not (according to Haneefa) in such case necessary that he be an upright man: because he is the opponent; and uprightness is not requisite in him.

II. The claim by affirmation and taking to witness (which must be made as man as conveniently may be af'er the other).—The second mode of claim to Shaffa is termed the Talb Takreer wa Ish-had, or claim by affirmation and taking to witness;—and this also is requisite; because evidence is wanted in order to establish proof before the magistrate; and it is probable that the claimant cannot have witnesses to the Talb Mawasibat, as that is expressed immediately on intimation being received of the sale. It is therefore necessary afterwards to make the Talb Ish-had wa Takreer, which is done by the Shafee taking some person to witness,—either agains the seller, if the ground sold be still in his possession,—or against the purchaser,—or upon the spot regarding which the dispute has arisen; and upon the Shafee thus taking some person to witness, his right of Shaffa is fully established and confirmed The reason of this is, that both the buyer and seller are opponents to the Shafee in regard to his claim of Shaffa; the one being the possessor, and the other the proprietor of the ground;—and the taking evidence on the ground itself is also valid; because it is that to which the right relates. If the seller have delivered over the ground to the buyer, the taking evidence against him is not sufficient, he being no longer an opponent; for having neither the possession nor the property, he is as a stranger. The manner of claim by affirmation and taking to witness is, the claimant saying "Such a person has bought such a house, of which I am the Shafee. I have already claimed my privilege of Shaffa, and now again claim it: be therefore witness thereof" (It is reported from Aboo Yoosaf that it is requisite the name of the thing sold, and its particular boundaries, be specified: because a claim its not valid unless the thing demanded be precisely known,)

And III. claim by litigation—The third mode of claim to Shaffa is termed Talb Khasoomat, or claim by litigation,—which is performed by the Shafee petitioning the Kazee to command the purchaser to surrender up the ground to him: the method of doing which will hereafter be particularly explained.

A delay in the litiga ion does n t invalidate the claim—If the Shafee delay making claim by litigation still his right does not drop, according to Haneefa Such also is the generally received opinion; and decrees pass accordingly. There is likewise one opinion recorded from Aboo Yoosaf to the same effect. Mohammed maintains that if the Shafee postpone the litigation for one month after the taking of evidence, his right drops. This is also the opinion of Ziffer; and it is related as an opinion of Aboo Yoosaf, that the right of the Shafee becomes null if he delay the litigation after the Kazee has held one court: for, if he willingly and without alleging any excuse, omit to commence the the litigation at the first court held by the Kazee, it is a presumtive proof of his having declined it. The reasoning on which Mohammad founds his opinion in this particular is, that if the right of the Shafee was never to be invalidated by his delaying the litigation it would be very vexatious to the buyer: for he would be prevented from enjoying his property, in the apprehensioon of being deprived of it by the claim of the Shafee—"I have therefore (says Mohammed) limited the delay that may be admitted to one month, as being the longest allowed term of proc astination."—In support of the opinion of Haneefa, it is urged that the right of the Shafee being firmly established by the taking of evidenoe, it cannot be extinguished but by his own rejection, openly declared:—in the same manner as holds in all other matters of right —With respect to what is mentioned by Mohammed, that "the delay would be vexatious to the buyer," it is of no weight; for in case of the absence of the Shafee, his right is not invalidated by the litigation being delayed; and the vexation sustained by the buyer from the delay is equally the same, whether the Shafee be present or absent.

Particularly, if it be occasioned by the absence of the magistrate.—If it appear that the Kazee was not in the city, and that on that account the litigation was delayed, the right is not invalidated, according to the concurrent opinion of the three above-mentioned sages; for the litigation can only be made in the presence of the Kazee; and the delay is therefore excused

Rules to be observed by the magistrate on an appeal.—When the Shafee goes to the Kazee and claims his right, alleging that "such a person has purchased a house, in which he has the right of Shaffa," the Kazee must first question the purchaser (the defendant in the cause) concerning the property on which the Shafee grounds his right, of Shaffa: and if he acknowledge it, this is a sufficient ground for the Kazee passing a decree:—but if he deny it, the Kazee must then order the Shafee to bring witnesses to prove his property; for the possession which is apparent, may be owing to other causes than property; and a thing which is thus doubtful cannot be admitted as a proof to the detriment of another Kadooree alleges that the Kazee, before he applies to the defendant, ought to ask the plaintiff regarding the situation of the house and its boundaries; because if a man sue for the property of a house, it is requisite that he describe its situation and boundaries; and therefore he must do the same in claiming his right of Shaffa. When he has done this, the Kazee must next interrogate him regarding the grounds of his right of Shaffa; for the grounds of Shaffa are various, and possibly he may set forth grounds according to his own imagination, which do not, in reality, constitute any ground If he reply that "he is the Shafee, because of his house being situated next to that which is the present object of dispute," his claim (as Khasaf observes) is complete. It is also mentioned in the Fatavee, that he must describe the boundaries of the house from whence he derives his right to the Shaffa in question.

And the mode prescribed for his examining the parties.—If the Shafee, being unable to bring witness, require that the purchaser be put to his oath, it must be tendered merely according to the best of his [the purchaser's] knowledge (that is he must be required to say, "By God, I know not that the plaintiff is the proprietor of the house on which he founds his claim of Shaffa"); because his deposition relates to a thing which is in the hands of another, and therefore he can only swear as to his own knowledge, and not positively as to the fact in question, namely, whether the house be, for certain, the property of the plaintiff or not.—If the purchaser refuse to swear, or the Shafee bring evidence, his property is proved in that house from which he derives his claim of Shaffa, and the neighbourhood of that house to the one in dispute is also proved. The Kazee must next ask the purchaser whether he has bought the house or not? and if he deny it, the Kazee must order the Shafee to bring witnesses to prove the puachase: for the Shaffa cannot be established until the sale be proved; which must be done by witnesses —If the Shafee cannot bring witnesses, the Kazee must administer an oath to the purchaser to this effect, that "he has not purchased the house," or that "the plaintiff is not entitled to the privilege of Shaffa to the manner in which he has claimed it;" for here he swears regarding an act committed by himself, and relative to a thing which is in his own possession: and therefore it is necessary that the oath be positive as to the certainty of the fact

The cause may be litigated and determined independent of the price of the property in dispute.—The Shafee may litigate his claim of Shaffa although he do not produce in court the price of the ground in dispute: but when the Kazeee has decreed to him the privilege of Shaffa, it is necessary that he bring the price. This is the doctrine of the Zahir Rawayet, as quoted in the Mabsoot It is reported, from Mohammad, that the Kazee ought not to pass the decree until the Shafee produce the price (and the same is also cited by Hasan from Haneefa); because possibly the Shafee may be indigent, and the Kazee must therefore delay the decree, in order that the purchaser may not lose his property.—The reason assigned in support of the first opinion quoted from the Zahir Rawayet, is that the price does not become due from the Shafee to the purchaser until the Kazee have passed his decree: and as the purchaser is not obliged to surrender up the ground previous to the decree so in the same manner the Shafee (as has been mentioned above) is under no necessity of previously producing the price:—nor can there be any apprehension of the purchaser losing his property, since he has the right of detention, as will more particularly be shown in the ensuing examples.

But the defendant may retain the one until the other be produced—When, previous to the Shafee producing the price, the Kazee has commanded the purchaser to deliver up the ground [to the Shafee], still he may retain it in his own hand until the price be brought to him.

The privilege is not forfeited by a delay in the payment.—If the Shafee delay to pay the price to the purchaser, after the Kazee has ordered him, still his privilage of Shaffa is not invalidated; for it has become firmly established by the litigation and the decree of the Kazee.

The seller may be sued whilst the house is in his possession.—If the Shafee bring the seller into court whilst the house is still in his possession, he [the Shafee] may commence his litigation against him, and the seller may retain the house in his own possession until he receive the price from the Shafee. The Kazee, however, is not in this case to hear the evidence until the purchaser also appear, as for his presence there is a twofold reason; for FIRST, the purchaser is proprietor of the ground, and the seller the possessor; and as the decree of the Kazee must be against both, both therefore must be present. (It is otherwise where the purchaser has obtained possession; for then there can be no occasion for the presence of the seller, as he has become like a stranger, having neither the property nor the possession.) SECONDLY, the sale or bargain which had been concluded in favour of the purchaser is to be dissolved by decree; and it is therefore requisite that he be present, in order that the Kazee may decree the dissolution against him.

An agent for the purchaser may be sued (before delivery to his constituent).—If an agent on behalf of another purchase ground, the Shafee must sue the agent. If, however, the agent have delivered over the ground to his constituent, the Shafee must not institute his suit against the agent (as he is neither the propietor nor the possesor), but against his constituent; for the agent then stands as the seller, and his constituent as the purchaser; and when (as has been already explained) the seller delivers up the ground to the purchaser, the Shafee's suit is against the latter.

And so also an agent for the seller, or an executor.—If the agent of a person who is absent sell ground on account of his constituent, the Shafee may claim his right and obtain the ground from the agent, provided it be in his possession. The same rule also holds in the case of an executor authorized to sell lands.

The Shafee, after gaining his suit, has an option of inspection, and also an option from defect.—If the Kazee decree, in favour of the Shafee, at a time when he has not yet seen the property in dispute, he [the Shafee] has an option of inspection; and if any defect be afterwards discovered in it, he has an option from defect* and may, if he please, reject it, notwithstanding the purchaser should have excepted such defect from the bargain, or, in other words, should have exempted the seller from responsibility for such defect; because, as the transfer of property by right of Shaffa is the same as a transfer of property by sale, the Shafee has therefore, under both the above circumstances, the power of rejection, in the same manner as any other purchaser; and this power in the Shafee is not destroyed by the purchaser having seen the property, or having so exempted the seller; for he [the purchaser] was not deputed by the Shafee, and his act, of course, does not affect the Shafee's power of rejection.

Section.

Of Disputes relative to the Price.

In disputes concerning the price, the assertion of the purchaser, upon oath† must be credited.—If the purchaser and Shafee differ regarding the price, the former alleging one hundred, for instance, and the latter only eighty, and neither of them be able to bring any evidence, the assertion of the purchaser must be credited in preference to that of the Shafee; because here the Shafee alleges a right in the purchaser's property for a sum short of one hundred, which the purchaser denies; and, according to the LAW, the declaration of a defendant, upon oath, must be credited:—neither is the oath of both parties* required in this case for the Shafee is plaintiff against the purchaser, but the purchaser is not plaintiff against the Shafee, he being at liberty either to claim or resign the thing in question; and it is a rule that both parties cannot be called on to swear, unless where both are in some manner plaintiff, or in some particular cases, where it is expressly ordained by the LAW, neither of which reasons exist in the present instance.

And so likewise evidence produced by him.—If both the purchaser and the Shafee produce evidence, that produced by the Shafee must be credited, according to Haneefa and Mohammed.—Aboo Yoosaf on the contrary maintins that the evidence produced by the purchaser must be credited; because it proves a larger sum than the other, and it is a general rule that regard is had to the evidence which proves the most,—as where, for instance, a difference arises regarding the amount of the price betwixt a purchaser and a sellers or an agent and his constituent, or a person who buys a thing from an infidel enemy, and the original proprietor of the thing;—in all which cases, if both parties bring evidence, the evidence of him who proves the largest sum is admitted.—The difference here alluded to, betwixt one who buys a thing from an infidel enemy, and the former proprietor of the thing, will be better elucidated by the following case.—A Mussulman merchant goes upon a voyage, arrives in the country of the infidels, receives their protection, and, whilst he remains there purchases a slave, who had formerly belonged to Zeyd, from an infidel, who had carried him away as his plunder; and, on the merchant's return, Zeyd claims his slave, offering the price which the merchant had given to the infidel; but a difference arising betwixt them regarding the amount

*Option of inspection and option from defect are fully explained under the head of SALE (See Vol. II. p. 255 and 258.)

Arab. Tahalif.—For a full explanation of this term see p. 417 of this Vol.

of the price, both adduce evidence to prove the sum they asserted;—in which case the evidence of the merchant, which goes to prove the largest sum, is admitted, in preference to that of Zeyd.—In support of the opinion maintained by Haneefa and Mohammed on this point, two arguments may be urged—FIRST, the evidence of the Shafee subjects the purchaser to an obligation; whereas the evidence of the purchaser does not subject the Shafee to any obligation, since he has it in his option to take the thing in dispute or not; and the intention of establishing evidence is to impose an obligation.—SECONDLY, if it be possible, a regard should be paid to the evidence of both parties; and here it is possible, for there is no absolute contradiction in this allegations of the two parties, since the purchaser may perhaps have twice purchased the thing; and both purchases being thus apparently proved, it remains in the option of the Shafee to prefer whichever he pleases; that is to say, if the purchaser have bought the thing twice, viz. once for one thousand, and another time for two thousand, the Shafee has it in his option to take the thing for whichever of these prices he thinks proper.—With respect to the analogy urged by Aboo Yoosaf betwixt the case in question and that of a purchaser and a seller differing concerning the amount of the price, it cannot be admitted; for if two different sales take place betwixt the parties, one immediately after the other, regarding the same thing, the one sale invalidates the other: and it being thus impossible to admit the allegations and evidence of both parties that evidence which proves the largest sum must be superior; and the superiority is therefore allowed to the evidence of the seller over that of the purchaser, because it proves the largest sum. In the case of the Shafee, on the contrary, as the maxim of one sale invalidating the other does not affect him both the sales hold good with respect to him;—whence if the purchaser choose to purchase the same thing twice, the Shafee has it in his option to take it for either of the prices, as has been mentioned above. Beside, as an agent is supposed to stand in the place of a seller, and his constituent in that of a purchaser, the same laws will of course hold with respect to them as are established in the case of a buyer and a seller; and this is confirmed by a precept quoted from Mohammed, in which it is expressly said, that "the evidence brought by the constituent is preferable."—With respect, also, to the analogy urged [by Aboo Yoosaf] betwixt the case in question and that of a dispute between the purchaser of a slave from an infidel and the former master of such slave, it is entirely unfounded since it cannot be admitted that the effect of the branch is the same as that of the root, as we find it expressly declared in the Seyir Kabeer; that the evidence adduced by the former master of the slave is superior. But even admitting the above-mentioned proposition still the argument is of no weight; for in the case of the merchant two bargains could not be made successively without the one of them being invalidated; whereas in the case of the Shafee (as we have already observed) both bargains may be effective.

And also his assertion, if the seller allege a larger amount.—IF the seller and purchaser differ regarding the price, and the seller (supposing him not yet to have received it) allege the smallest sum, the Shafee may take the house for the price alleged by the seller the assertion made by him of a smaller sum being considered as an abatement in favour of the purchaser, of which the Shafee is entitled to avail himself. We shall have occasion in the ensuing section to explain the ground on which this law is founded; and shall therefore in this place assign only one reason, namely, that the right given to the Shafee over the seller arises from his own declaration, in saying, "I have sold it for such a price;" and therefore, so long as he has not received the price, his allegation must be credited regarding it,—whence the Shafee is entitled to take the property at a rate agreeable to his assertion.—If, on the contrary, the seller allege the largest sum, both parties must be required to swear, and the contract of sale is then dissolved. If, in this case, either of them refuse to swear, that price is established which has been set forth by the other, and the Shafee is consequently entitled to take the house for that amount. If, on the other hand, both parties swear, the Kazee, at the requisition of one or both of them; must dissolve the sale; and the Shafee (whose right is not be prejudiced by such dissolution) may then take the house for the amount alleged by the seller.

IF the seller should have received the price, the Shafee may take the house for the amount set forth as the price by the purchaser; and here the allegation of the seller is of no weight or credit, for having received the price, the sale, as far as relates to him, is finally concluded, and he becomes only as a stranger; the dispute then lying betwixt the purchaser and the Shafee, regarding which we have already been very explicit in a former part of this section.

Case in which the seller's assertion may be credited concerning the price.—IF the Shafee be not apprized of the seller's having received the price and the seller should say, "I have sold the property for one thousand dirms, which I have received," in this case the Shafee is entitled to take the property for one thousand dirms; for, as the beginning of the seller's speech, in which he acknowledges the sale, creates the Shafee's right of Shaffa, the subsequent sentence, in which he asserts his having received the price, as tending to extinguish that right which he has himself created, must not be admitted. But if the seller should say, "I have sold the ground and received the price," and then should add, "which was one thousand dirms," his evidence with respect to the amount of the price cannot be admitted, because by the prior acknowledgment of his having received the price, he becomes like a stranger. and has no further concern or interest in the matter.

Section

Of the Articles in lieu of which the Shafee may take the Shaffa Property.

The Shafee is entitled to the benefit of any abatement made to the purchaser, but not to that of a total remission.—If the seller abate a part of the price to the purchaser, the Shafee is entitled to the benefit of such abatement; whereas if the seller; after the sale, remit the whole of the price to the purchaser, the Shafee is not allowed to avail himself of such indulgence. The reason of this distinction is, that an abatement of a part is an act connected with, and referring to, the original bargain or sale; and the Shafee is entitled to be benefit of it, because that sum which remains after deducting the abatement is the price; whereas an entire remission has no connexion with the original bargain. In the same manner also, if the seller abate a part of the price, after the Shafee has become seised of his Shaffa property, he [the Shafee] is entitled to the benefit of such abatement, and accordingly receives back the amount abated by the seller to the purchaser.

He is not liable for any augmentation agreed upon after the sale.—If, on the contrary, the purchaser after the bargain is concluded, agree to an augmentation of the price in favour of the seller, the Shafee is not liable for such augmentation, because his privilege of Shaffa is established for the prior originally settled: and if any subsequent augmentation were admitted to operate with respect to him, it would be a loss to him; whereas, on the contrary, any subsequent abatement is a benefit. Analogous to this case of augmentation is that formerly stated, in which it was remarked, that if a man make a purchase for a certain price, and afterwards renew the purchase of the same thing, and settle a large price, the Shafee is not prejudiced by such augmentation, but is entitled to his Shaffa for the price first agreed upon.

If the price consist of effects, the Shafee may take it on paying the value of those effects: but if it consist of similars he is to pay an equal quantity of the same.—If a man sell a house for a certain quantity of goods or effects, the Shafee is entitled to take it for the value of such effects; for effects are amongst the things denominated Zooat-al-Keem, or things which, being estimable, are compensable by an equivalent in money.—If, on the other hand, a man sell a house for a compensation in wheat, silver, or any other articles estimable by measure or weight, the Shafee may take it for an equal quantity of the same article; because these are of the class of Zooat-al-Imsal, or things compensable by an equal quantity of the same species. The reason of this is that the revealer of the LAW* has established in the Shafee a right to take possession of the property of the purchaser, on giving him a compensation similar to the price which he has paid;—it is therefore necessary that a similarly betwixt the compensation and price be observed as nearly as possible, in the same manner as in cases of destruction of property.—(It is to be observed that articles which differ very little in their unities, such as walnuts or eggs, are included under the denomination of Zooat-al-Imsal, or things compensable by an equal quantity of the same species. If, therefore, a man purchase ground for walnuts or eggs, the Shafee may give him a compensation in walnuts or eggs and is not required to pay an equivalent in money.)

And so likewise, if the price consist of land.—If a man sell a piece of ground for another piece of ground, in this case, as each piece of ground is the price for which the other is sold. the Shafee of each piece is entitled to take it for the value of the other, land being of the class of Zooat-al-Keem, or things compensable by an equivalent in money.

In case of a term of credit, the Shafee may either wait the expiration of the term, or take the property immediately, upon paying the price.—If a house be sold for a price payable at a distant period, the Shafee may either wait until that period be expired, and then take the house for the same price,—or he may take it immediately, on paying the price in ready money; but he is not entitled to take it immediately and demand a respite to the period settled by the purchaser. Ziffer maintains that the Shafee is entitled to take the house immediately, and demand a respite of the payment (and such also is the opinion of Shafeei): for the respite is a modification of the price, in the same manner as if it were stipulated to be paid in coin of an inferior species; and as the Shafee is entitled to take the house for the price itself, he is of course entitled to take it for the price under its modification. The argument adduced by us, in support of the former opinion, is that a delay or respite cannot be established but by a positive stipulation betwixt the parties: and in the present case there is not any stipulation, either betwixt the Shafee and the seller, or the Shafee and the purchaser.—nor can the seller's consenting to a respite in favour of the purchaser be construed into a consent to respite in favour of Shafee; for men, as they differ in their circumstances, are more or less capable of discharging their debts.—With respect, moreover, to the arguments used in behalf of Ziffer's opinion, it is true that the respite is a modification of the price; yet the law is not to be bent thereby; for the respite is in fact, a right of the purchaser;

*Meaning, the Prophet, who is often termed Shari, or the lawgiver.

but if it were admitted a modification of the price, it would be a right of the seller, like the price itself :—this case being analogous to where a man purchases a thing for a price payable at a distant time, and afterwards sells it again by a tawleeat ;—in which instance, if no such stipulation be expressed, the second purchaser is not entitled to a term of credit,—and so here likewise.—If in the case here considered, the land be still in the possession of the seller, and the Shafee take it and pay him the price in ready money, his [the seller's] claim against the purchaser ceases ; for the bargain with respect to him is dissolved, and the Shafee is substituted in his place, as has been already explained.—If, on the contrary, the land be in the possession of the purchaser, and the Shafee take it from him, still the seller must allow to the purchaser the term of credit originally settled : because the bargain betwixt them is not dissolved by the Shafee's taking the land, and the case is therefore the same as where a person makes a purchase upon credit, and then sells the article for ready money, in which case the first seller is not entitled to demand ready money from him. It is, however ; lawful for the Shafee to defer taking the land until the term of credit be expired ; but he must make his demand without delay ; for if he neglect to make an immediate demand, his right of Shaffa, according to Haneefa and Mohammed, becomes null :—contrary to be opinion of Aboo Yoosaf.—The reason for the opinion of Haneefa and Mohammed upon this head is, that as the Shaffa has existence from the time of the sale, it is therefore requiste that the claim be made upon the instant of the sale being known. The reason for Aboo Yoosaf's opinion is that "the only use of the claim is to enable the Shafee to take the land, which end cannot be at present effected, whence he remains silent ; and as this silence does not argue any recession from his right, that is consequently not in validated. To this, however, it may be replied, that the taking of the land is a matter posterior to the claim ; and the Shafee has it, moreover, in his power to take it on the instant, by paying down the price.

Case of property subject to Shaffa, purchased by a Zimmee for a price consisting of unlawful articles.—IF a Zimmee purchase land for wine or pork, and the Shafee be also a Rimmee, he [the Shafee may take the land for an equal quantity of similar wine, or for the value of the pork, because a bargain of this kind is held valid amongst Zimmees; and as the right of Shaffa is enjoyed in common by both Mussulmans and Zimmees, and wine, amongst the latter, is held as vinegar amongst the former, and hogs as sheep, it follows that, vinegar being included under the denomination of Zooat-al-Imsal, and sheep under that of Zooat-al-Keem, the Shafee is at liberty to take the land for an equal quantity of wine, or for the value of the pork. If, on the contrary, the Shafee be a Musalman, he is to take the land for the value of the wine as well as of the pork ; for the giving or receiving of wine amongst Mussulmans is prohibited by their relig on, and it is therefore, with respect to them; reckoned also amongst the things which are of the denomination of Zooat-al-Keem —If, on the other hand, there be two Shafee, the one a Mussulman and the other a Zimmee, the former must take half of the land for half the value of the wine, and the latter the other half, for half the quantity of the wine.—If, also, the Zimmee Shafee become a Mussulman, as his right is strengthened, not invalidated, by his conversion, he is therefore to take his half of the land for half of the value of the wine ; because, by his embracing the faith, he is incapacitated from paying the actual wine, which then (as it were) becomes non-existent with respect to him ;—in the same manner as where a person makes a purchase of a house for a measure of green dates, and a Shafee afterwards appears, at a time when the season for green dates is past; in which case he must take the house for the value of the dates,—and so likewise in the present instance, as wine is, in effect, non-existent with respect to Mussulmans, they being prohibited by the LAW, from using it in any shape.

Section,

The Shafee may either take the buildings or plantations of the purchaser (paying the value), or may cause them to be removed.—IF the purchaser of ground subject to a claim of Shaffa erect buildings or plant trees upon it, and the Kazee afterwards order the ground to be delivered to the Shaffee, it in this case rests with him [the Shafee] either to take the ground, together with the building or trees, paying the value of both, or to oblige the purchaser to remove them. This is the doctrine of the Zahir Rawayet. It is recorded from Aboo Yoosaf that the Shafee cannot oblige the purchaser to remove his buildings ; but he must either take the ground, paying the value of the trees or buildings, or relinquish the whole. This is also the opinion of Shafei. He, however ; admits that the Shafee may cause the buildings or the trees to be removed, on indemnifying the purchaser in the loss he may thereby sustain. In short, according to him, the Shafee has three things in his option : for he may either take the land, together with the trees and buildings, paying the value of those,—or he may cause them to be removed, indemnifying the purchase,—or, lastly, he may relinquish the whole. In support of the opinion of Aboo Yoosaf two arguments are urged. FIRST, the purchaser was justifiable in erecting the buildings; since the ground was his own property, and it would therefore be unjust to oblige him to remove them ;—in the same manner as where ground is for a short time transferred by a great, or by a defective sale, and afterwards taken back,—in which case the granter or the seller has it not in his power to oblige the grantee or the purchaser to remove any buildings he may have raised upon the ground whilst it was in his possession,—or (in cases of Shaffa) where the purchaser has raised a crop of grain from the ground,—in which case the Shafee cannot oblige him to remove it until it be fit for reaping.—Secondly, in the present case one of two grievances must follow; for either the Shafee must suffer a grievance in being obliged to pay an enhanced price for his Shaffa on account of the additional value of the buildings, or also the purchaser must suffer a grievance is being compelled to remove them. Now the latter of these grievances is the heaviest, for it is a loss without any recompense; whereas the increase of price paid by the Shafee is not without a consideration;—and where the Shafee either takes the ground, paying for the trees and buildings, or relinquishes the whole, the greater of the two grievances is obviated, and the smaller one only is induced. The reasons urged in behalf of the opinion quoted from the Zahir Rawayat are, that as the purchaser has planted trees or erected buildings on ground over which the rights of another extended, without first obtaining the sanction of that other, they must be removed, in the same manner as where a person who holds ground in pledge builds upon it without the permission of the pledger.—Besides, the right of the Shafee is stronger than that of the purchaser, as being of prior date; whence it is that any act of the purchaser, even such as the selling or granting of the ground, may be dissolved. It is otherwise with respect to a grantee, or a purchaser under an invalid contract (according to Haneefa); because they act under a permission from the possessor of the right; and also, because the right of resumption, in cases of gift or invalid purchase, is but of a weak nature,—whence it discontinues upon the erection of buildings. The right of Shaffa, on the contrary, still continues in force; and therefore the rendering absolutely obligatory the value of the trees or buildings, upon the Shafee, in case of his claiming his right, would be absurd; in the same manner as holds in cases of claim of right;*—in other words, if a person purchases land, and plant or build upon it, and it afterwards prove the right of another, the purchaser recovers the price of the land and the value of the trees and buildings from the seller, and not from the claimant of right; and in the present instance the Shafee stands as the claimant of right. Analogy would suggest that grain also should be removed from the land; but, by a more favourable construction of the LAW in this particular, it is not to be removed; because the term of its continuance is limited and ascertainable; and as the delay may be recompensed to the Shafee by a rent or hire, it cannot therefore be very grievous to him.

The Shafee is not entitled to any remuneration for buildings erected or trees planted on land which proves the property of another:—but he may remove them.—If a Shafee having obtained possession of his Shaffa land, erect buildings, or plant trees upon it, and it afterwards appear that the land was wrongfully sold, being the property of another, the Shafee recovers the price,—from the seller, where he had taken the land from him,—or from the purchaser, where he had taken it from him; because it is evident that it was wrongfully taken. He is not, however, entitled to recover from either party the value of his buildings or trees, but is at liberty to carry the wherever he pleases.—It is recorded from Aboo Yoosaf that the Shafee may also recover the value of the buildings or trees from the person from whom he received the ground; because that person, under such circumstances, is considered as the seller, and the Shafee as the purchaser; and it is an established rule that the purchaser may recover from the seller the value of such buildings as he has erected on the ground, if it appear that the ground sold to him was not the property of the seller, but of another person. There is, however, a difference, in this case, betwixt a Shafee and an ordinary purchaser; for the latter is deceived by the seller, and is empowered by him to take the ground,—whereas the Shafee is not deceived by the purchaser, nor can he be said to be empowered by him to take the ground, since the purchaser himself is compelled, the Shafee taking possession of the ground without his consent.

If the property have sustained any accidental or natural injury after sale, still the Shafee cannot take it for less than the full price.—If a man purchase a house or garden subject to a claim of Shaffa, and the building (owing to some unforeseen calamity) be destroyed, of the trees decay, it rests in the option of the Shafee either to resign the house or garden, or to take it and pay the full price: because as buildings or trees are mere appendages of the ground (whence it is that they are included in the sale of land without any particular mention being made of them), no particular part of the price is set against them,—unless where they have been wilfully destroyed by the purchaser, in which case it is lawful for him [the purchaser] to sell the appendages so destroyed, and make a profit by them, exclusive of the full price of the ground. It is otherwise when one half of the ground is inundated: for in such case the half of the thing itself being destroyed, the Shafee may take the remainder paying only half the original price.

If the injury be committed by the purchaser, the Shafee may take the ground alone at its estimated value.—If the purchaser wilfully break down the erections, the Shafee may either resign his claim, or may take the area of ground for a proportionable part of the original price; but he is not entitled to

* Arab, Istihkak, meaning, a claim set up to the subject of a sale. (See Vol II. p. 294.)

the ruins, because they become a separate property, and are no longer appendages of the ground; and the right of Shaffa extends only to the ground, and to things so attached to it as to be appendages.

Case of a Shafee taking ground with fruit trees.—If a man purchase a piece of ground, having date trees upon it bearing fruit at the time, the Shafee is entitled to take the fruit, --provided particular mention have been made of it in the sale, for otherwise it is not comprehended. What is here advanced proceeds upon a favourable construction. Analogy would suggest that the Shafee is not entitled to take the fruit; because, as the fruit is a dependant both of the tree and of the ground (whence it is not included in a sale of ground unless it be particularly mentioned), it therefore resembles the furniture of a house. The reason for a more favourable construction, in this particular is that the fruit, in consequence of its connexion with the tree, is a dependant of the land, in the same manner as an erection, or any thing inserted in the wall of a house, such as a door, for instance; and therefore the Shafee is entitled to take it. The same rule also holds where the ground is purchased at a time when there is no fruit upon the trees and the fruit is afterwards produced whilst it [the ground] is yet in the purchaser's possession;--in other words, the Shafee is here also entitled to take the fruit, because that is a dependant of the original article: in the same manner as in the case of a female slave who is sold.—if she be delivered of a child previous to her being given over to the purchaser, still the child, as well as its mother, is the property of the purchaser.

In either of the two preceding cases if the purchaser have gathered the fruit, and the Shafee afterwards come and claim his privilege he is not entitled to the fruit so gathered; for it is no longer an appendage of the ground. It is said, in the Mabsoot, that if the purchaser have gathered any of the fruit, a proportionable abatement should be made in the price to the Shafee. The compiler of the Hedaya remarks, that this is in the former only of the two above-mentioned cases; for the fruit being produced at the time, and being actually and expressly included in the sale, it is natural to suppose that a part of the price was given in consideration of it; whereas, in the latter case, the fruit was not produced, and could only be included in the sale as a consequent, whence no part of the price could have been set against it.

CHAPTER III.

OF THE ARTICLES CONCERNING WHICH SHAFFA OPERATES

The right of Shaffa holds with respect to all immoveable property.—The privilege of Shaffa takes place, with respect to immoveable property, notwithstanding it be incapable of division, such as a bath, a mill, or a private road. Shafei maintains that nothing it subject to Shaffa but what is capable of being divided: because (according to his tenets) the end of Shaffa is to obviate the inconveniences attending a division of property, which does not hold in a property incapable of division. Our doctrine, however, is grounded on a precept of the Prophet, who has said "Shapea takes place with regard to all lands or houses." Besides, according to our tenets, the grand principle of Shaffa is the conjunction of property, and its object (as we have already explained) to prevent the vexation arising from a disagreeable neighbour; and this reason is of equal force whether the thing be divisible or otherwise.

The privilege of Shaffa does not extend to household effects or shipping;* because of a saying of the Prophet, "Shaffa affects only houses and gardens;" and also, because the intention of Shaffa being to prevent the vexation arising from a bad neighbour, it is needless to extend it to property of a moveable nature.

Unless it be sold separate from the ground on which it stands—It is observed. in the abridgment of Kadooree, that Shaffa does not affect even a house or trees when sold separately from the ground on which they stand. This opinion (which is also mentioned in the Mabsoot) is approved; for as buildings and trees are not of a permanent nature, they are therefore of the class of moveables. There is, however, an exception to this in this case of the upper storey of a house; for it is subject to Shaffa —whence the proprietor of the under storey is the Shafee, as is also the proprietor of the upper the Shafee of the under one, notwithstanding their entries be by different roads.

A Mussulman and a Zimmee are on an equality with respect to it.—A Mussulman and a Zimmee; being equally affected by the principle on which Shaffa is established, and equally concerned in its operations, are therefore on an equal footing in all cases regarding the privilege of Shaffa, and for the same reason, a man or a woman, an infant or an adult, a just man or a reprobate, a freeman or a slave (being either a Mokatib or a Mazoon), are all equall with respect to Shaffa.

It holds with respect to property transferred in any shape for a consideration.—When a man acquires a property in land for a consideration (in the manner, for instance, of a grant for a consideration), the privilege of Shaffa takes place with respect to it, because it is in the power of the Shaffa to fulfil the stipulation.

It does not hold in a property assigned in dower, or as a compensation for Khoola, or

---

*The term, in the original, signifies boats including every species of water-carriage *as a hire. or in composition for murder, or as the price of manumission.*—The privilege of Shaffa cannot take place relative to a house assigned by a man as a dower to his wife, or by a woman to her husband as the condition on which he is to grant her a divorce, or which is settled on a person as his hire or reward, or made over in composition for wilful murder, or assigned over as the ransom of a slave; for with us it is a rule that Shaffa shall not take place unless there exist an exchange of property for property, which is not the case in any of these instances, as the matters to which the house is opposed are not property. Shafei holds Shaffa to take place in all these cases; because, although the matter to which the house is opposed be not property, it is nevertheless capable of estimation (according to his tenets), and therefore the house may be taken upon paying the value of the matter to which it is opposed, in the same manner as in the sale of a property for a consideration in goods or effects. It is to be observed, however, that this opinion of Shafei obtains only with respect to a case where a part of a house is assigned as a dower, or made over as a consideration for Khoola, a composition for murder, and so forth: for, according to his tenets, there is no Shaffa except in cases of joint property.

It holds with respect to a house sold in order to pay the dower.—If a man marry a woman without settling on her any dower, and afterwards settle on her a house as a dower, the privilege of Shaffa does not take place, the house being here considered in the same light as if it had been settled on the woman at the time of the marriage.—It is otherwise where a man sells his house in order to discharge his wife's dower either proper stipulated: because here exists an exchange of property for property.

If a man, on his marriage, settle a house upon his wife as her dower, and stipulate that she shall pay him back, from the price of the house, one thousand dirms, according to Haneefa the privilege Shaffa does not take place relative to that house: whereas the two disciples hold that it affects a port of the house equivalent to one thousand dirms.*

It does not hold with respect to a house the possession of which is compromised by a sum of money.—The privilege of Shaffa does not operate relative to a house concerning which there has been a dispute betwixt two men, compromised by the defendant (who was the possessor) paying the plaintiff a sum of money, after denying his claim: for in this case, the compromise being made after the denial, the house, in the imagination of the defendent, still belongs to him under his original right of property, and consequently no sale or exchange of property for property can here be established in regard to him;—and so likewise if he refuse to answer to the suit, and then compromise it with a sum of money.—since it may be supposed that he has parted with his money rather than be under the necessity of taking an oath, even with truth on his side, or of involving himself in litigious disputes and broils. If, on the contrary, he confess the justness of the plaintiff's claim, and then compromise with a sum of money, the privilege of Shaffa takes place; because as he has here acknowledged the plantiff's right to the house, and retained it afterwards in virtue of a compromise, an exchange of property for property is clearly established in this instance.

It holds with respect to a house made over in composition.—If a defendant compromise a suit by resigning or making over a house to the plaintiff, after having either denied his claim or acknowledged it, or refused to answer it, the right of Shaffa is established with respect to the house: because, as the plaintiff here accepts the house in consideration of what he conceives to be his right, he is therefore [in adjudging the right of Shaffa against him] dealt with according to his own conceptions

But not with respect to property transferred by grant.—The privilege of Shaffa is not admitted in the case of grants,—unless when the grant is made for a consideration, in which case it is, in effect, ultimately a sale. Still, however, the privilege of Shaffa cannot be admitted, unless both parties have obtained possession of the property transferred to them by the terms of the grant (nor if the thing granted on either side be an indefinite part of any thing); for a grant on condition of a return is still a grant in its beginning, as has been already explained in treating of gifts. It is further to be observed that the privilege of Shaffa cannot be admitted, unless the return be expressed as a condition on making the grant; for if it be not so expressed, and the parties give to each other reciprocal presents, these presents on both sides are held as pure grants, although each of them having met with a requital of his generosity, neither is allowed the power of retreating.

It cannot take place with respect to a property sold under a condition of option.—If a man sell his house under a condition of option,* the privilege of Shaffa cannot take place with respect to that house, the power reserved by the seller being an impediment to the extinction of his right of property but when he relinquishes that power, the impediment ceases, and the privilege of Shaffa takes place, provided the Shafee prefer his claim immediately. This is approved.

* The reasonings on both sides are here recited at large; but are omitted in the translation, as containing merely a string of metaphysical subtilties or little or no use.

* That is, "reserving to himself the power of hereafter dissolving the sale." (See Vol. II. p. 220 to 256.)

But it holds with respect to a property so purchased.—If, on the contrary, a man purchase a house under a condition of option, the privilege of Shaffa takes place with respect to it; for such a power reserved by the purchaser is held, in the opinion of all the learned, to be no impediment to the extinction of the seller's right of property: and the right of Shaffa is founded and rests upon the extinction of the seller's right of property, as has been already explained.

And on the Shafee taking possession, the purchaser's right of option ceases.—If the Shafee take the house during the purchaser's right of option (namely, three days), such right ceases; and the sale is completely concluded; for the purchaser, as no longer having the house in his possession is no longer capable of rejecting it; and the Shaffa cannot pretend to claim the power of dissolving the bargain, since that power was founded in a condition established in favour of the purchaser only.

In a case of sale upon option, the possessor of the option is Shafee of the adjacent property.—If, whilst one of the parties, either purchaser or seller, has the power of dissolving the bargain, the house adjoining to the one in question be sold, he who possessed such power is the Shaffee of the adjoining house.—If it be the seller, he is the Shafee, because whilst he retained the power of dissolving the bargain, his right of property remained unextinguished;—or, if it be the purchaser, his claiming the Shaffa of the second house is a proof of his inclination to keep the first, and not to avail himself of his power of dissolving the bargain:—his right of property is therefore held to commence from the time of adjusting the bargain; and in consequence of his right of property in the first house, he has the right of Shaffa with respect to the second. If, in this case, the Shafee of the first house should afterwards come and claim his right, he is entitled to the Shaffa of the first home;—but he is not entitled to that of the second, because the first house was not his property at the time when the second was sold.

If a man purchase a house without seeing it, and afterwards, in virtue of his privilege of Shaffa, take the adjacent house, which happens to be sold, still his power of rejecting the first house on seeing it does not cease; for as it would not be annulled even by an express renunciation; it consequently is not annulled by an act which affords only a presumption of renunciation.

The right does not hold with respect to a property transferred under an invalid sale—The privilege of Shaffa cannot take place regarding a house transferred by an invalid sale, either before or after the purchaser obtaining possession of it; for, before the purchaser obtains possession, the house belongs as usual to the seller, and his right of property is not extinguished; and after he has obtained possession there is still a probability that the bargain may be dissolved, since the LAW admits the dissolution of a sale, in a case of invalidity, in order to obviate such invalidity, an effect which could not be produced if the privilege of Shaffa were allowed. If, however, the purchaser put an end to the possibility of the dissolution by any particular act, such as by erecting buildings on the ground, or the like, the privilege of Shaffa may take place, since the impediment then no longer exists.

The seller of a property, under an invalid sale is still Shafee of the adjacent property.—If the house adjacent to one which has been transferred by an invalid sale be sold whilst the one so transferred is still in the possession of the seller, he [the seller] is the Shafee of the adjacent house, because of the continuance of his right in the other.

Until he deliver the property sold to the purchaser, who then has the right.—If the seller have delivered over the first house, previous to the Kazee decreeing to him the Shaffa of the adjacent one, the purchaser, because of the property he has acquired in obtaining possession of the first house, is the Shafee of the second. It is otherwise where the seller delivers over the first house after the Kazee has decreed to him the Shaffa of the second; for in this case his right of Shaffa is not invalidated: because, after the decree of the Kazee has passed, it is no longer necessary that he preserve his right of property in that house from which he derived his right of Shaffa,

Which, however, falls upon the seller resuming his property.—If the seller take back the first house, previous to the Kazee decreeing the Shaffa to the purchaser; his [the purchaser's] right of Shaffa becomes null; because his right of property in that house from which he derived it has ceased previous to its being granted him by a decree of the Kazee. If, on the contrary, the seller do not take back the first house until after the Kazee has decreed the Shaffa of the second to the purchaser, his [the purchaser's] right of Shaffa is not invalidation; because, at the time it was decreed, the house from which it was derived was his property; and (as we have already observed) after the decree of the Kazee has passed it is no longer necessary that he preserve his right of property in that house from which he derived his right of Shaffa.

A right of Shaffa is not created by partners making a partition of their joint property.—If two or more partners divide the ground in which they have hitherto held a joint property, the privilege of Shaffa cannot be claimed by any neighbour; because, although the division of joint property bear the characteristic of an exchange, yet it also bears the characteristic of a separation, namely, a separation of the rights of one person from those of others, a thing which may be done by compulsion, since any one of the partners may cause it to be effected by an application, to the Kazee, notwithstanding it be contrary to the inclination of the others. It is not therefore a pure exchange, which admits of no compulsion, but must be accomplished by the concurrence of both parties: and the privilege of Shaffa is admitted by the LAW to operate only in cases of a pure exchange.

The right once relinquished cannot afterwards be resumed.—IF a man purchase a house: and the Shafee relinquish his privilege, and the purchaser afterwards reject it in virtue of an option of inspection, or a condition of option, or by a decree of the magistrate in virtue of an option from defect, the Shafee is not entitled to claim his privilege, whether the man had ever taken possession of the house or not; and so likewise, if the man, before taking possession, reject the house on discovering a blemish, without a decree of the Kazee; for as, under all those circumstances, the rejection is a dissolution of the bargain, the house reverts to its original proprietor; and the privilege of Shaffa is not established but on the notification of a new sale. If, on the contrary, the purchaser reject the house on discovering a blemish in it, after having taken possession without a decree of the Kazee,—or, if the seller and purchaser agree to dissolve the contract.—the privilege of Shaffa is established to the Shafee; because in those instances the rejection or dissolution is a breaking off with respect to the seller and purchaser, inasmuch as they are their own masters, and moreover will and intend a breaking off:—yet with respect to others it is not a breaking off, but is rather, in effect, a new sale, since the characteristic of sale, namely, an exchange of property for property with the mutual consent of the parties, exists in it; and as the Shafee is another, it is therefore a sale with respect to him, whence his right of Shaffa must be admitted.

—

CHAPTER IV.

OF CIRCUMSTANCES WHICH INVALIDATE THE RIGHT OF SHAFFA.

A right of Shaffa is invalidated by the Shafee omitting to procure evidence in due time.—IF the Shafee omit to procure evidence of his having claimed his Shaffa on being informed of the sale, notwithstanding his ability so to do, his right of Shaffa is void, because of his neglecting to claim it.—In the same manner also, if he prefer the Talb Mawasibat, or immediate claim, and omit the Talb Ish-had wa Takree, notwithstanding his ability to make it, his right of Shaffa is void, as has been already explained.

Or by his offering to compound it.—IF the Shafee agree to compound his privilege of Shaffa for a compensation, he thereby invalidates his right, and is not entitled to the compensation; for he has no established right or property in the place in dispute, but merely a power of insisting on becoming the proprietor exclusion of the purcahser: and as, therefore, a renunciation of Shaffa (understood in renouncing all right to disturb the proprietor in the enjoyment of the property) is not a subject of exchange, it follows that no consideration can be demanded for it As, moreover; the relinquishment of the right could not lawfully be suspended even upon a valid condition, that is, a condition proper to it (such as a stipulation of giving up something in return which is not property), it follows that it cannot be lawfully suspended upon an invalid condition, or condition not proper to it (such as a condition of giving up property in return for a mere right, which is not property). a fortiori. The condition of a return is therefore null, and the relinquishment of the right remains valid without a return:—and the case of a person selling his right of Shaffa is subject to the same rule—It is otherwise in a case of composition for retaliation; because retaliation is a right established against the person of the murderer in behalf of the representative of the murdered, who is the avenger of his blood.—It is also otherwise with respect to a consideration received for manumission or divorce; because that is a consideration for a right of property established in the subject of the manumission or divorce.—Analogous to the case of relinquishment of Shaffa for a compensation by composition is that where a man says to his wife, being under an option of divorce; "Choose me, for one thousand dirms." or where an impotent person tells his wife that "if she will relinquish her right of dissolving the marriage he will give her one thousand dirms;" for if, in either of these cases, the wife accept the proposal, she forfeits the power she possessed, and the husband cannot be compelled to pay the compensation.—Bail for the person, also (commonly termed Hazir Zaminee), bears a resemblance to Shaffa in this particular; for if a person who is bail for the appearance of a debtor apply to the creditor and prevail upon him to compromise with him, by relinquishing his claim on him as security, for a certain compensation, the surety is in this case released from his engagement, and at the same time is not liable for the compensation. This is one tradition. According to another tradition, the surety can neither be made liable for the compensation, nor yet released from his engagement of bail. Some also, contend that this last is the case with respect to Shaffa, whilst others maintain that the rule applies to bail only.

Or by the death of the Shafee before the Kazee's decree.—IF the Shafee die, his right of Shaffa becomes extinct. Shafei maintains that the right of Shaffa is hereditary.—The compiler of the Hedaya remarks that this difference of opinion obtains only where the Shafee dies after the sale, but previous to the Kazee decreeing him the Shaffa; for if he die after the Kazee has decreed his Shaffa, without having paid the price, or obtained possession of the property sold, his right devolves to his heirs, who become liable for the price. The argument of our doctors upon the point in which they differ from Shafei is, that the death of the Shafee extinguished his right in the property from which he derived his privilege of Shaffa; and the property did not devolve to his heirs until after the sale. Besides, it is an express condition of Shaffa, that a man be firmly possessed of the property from which he derives his right of Shaffa at the time when the subject of it is sold, a condition which does not hold on the part of the heirs. It is, moreover, a condition that the property of the Shafee remain firm until the decree of the Kazee be passed; and as this does not hold on the part of the deceased Shafee, the Shaffe is therefore not established with respect to any one of his descendants, because of the failure of its conditions.

It is not invalidated by the death of the purchaser, and therefore cannot be disposed of on his behalf.—If the purchaser die, yet the right of Shaffa is not extinguished, for the Shafee who is entitled to it still exists, and no alteration has taken place in the reasons or grounds of his right. The house, therefore, is not to be sold for the payment of the purchaser's debts, or disposed of according to his testament; and if the Kazee or executor sell it in order to discharge the debts of the estate, or if the purchaser have bequeathed it, the Shafee may render any of these transactions void, and may take the house; for the right of the Shafee is antecedent,—whence he has the power of annulling the purchaser's acts with respect to the property, even during his lifetime.

It is invalidated by the Shafee selling the property whence he derived his right.—If the Shafee previous to the decree of the Kazee sell the house from which he derives his right of Shaffa, the reasons or grounds of his right being thereby extinguished, the right itself is invalidated, notwithstanding he be ignorant of the sale of the house to which it related;—in the same manner as where a man relinquishes his Shaffa without being informed of the sale, or acquits a person of a debt without knowing the amount; in the first of which cases the right of Shaffa is invalidated, and in the second the debtor is acquitted. It is otherwise where the Shafee sells his house upon a condition of option: for as, whilst a power of option remains in the seller, his property is not totally extinguished, it follows that the ground of Shaffa (namely, a conjunction of property) still continues.

Or by his acting as agent for the seller.—If the Shafee act as agent of the seller, and sell the house on his behalf, his right of Shaffa is thereby invalidated:—whereas if he act as agent for the purchaser, and purchase the house on his behalf, his right of Shaffa is not invalidated. In short, it is a rule, that if a person, an agent for another sell the land, &c. of that other, the right of Shaffa in both is thereby invalidated: whereas; if an agent (such as a manager, for instance) purchase land, or so forth, the right of both continues unaffected; for the former, if he were afterwards to contest his right, must in so doing labour to annul the sale which was completed by him,—whereas the latter, in so doing does not annul the purchase made by him. the taking of a property in virtue of Shaffa being itself a sort of purchase. In the same manner also, if the Shafee become Zamin be'l Dirk, or bail for what may happen.* by engaging to be responsible to the purchaser for the amount of the price in case the house should afterwards prove the right of another person, his right of Shaffa is thereby invalidated. So also, if a man sell a house, stipulating the option of a third person, meaning the Shafee, and he [the Shafee] confirm the sale, he thereby forfeits his right of Shaffa; whereas, if a man purchase a house, stipulating the option of a third person, who is the Shafee, and he [the Shafee] confirm the purchase, his right of Shaffa is not invalidated.

He may resume his right where he had relinquished it upon misinformation concerning the price.—If intelligence be brought to the Shafee, of the house which is the subject of his right being sold for one thousand dirms, and he relinquish his right of Shaffa, and afterwards learn that the house was sold for a less price, his resignation is not binding, and he may still assert his right of Shaffa: for it was the dearness of the price which induced him to resign; but upon the diminution of the price becoming known, the reason of his reisgnation no longer exists, and it is consequently void. In the same manner also, if news be brought that the house is sold for one thousand dirms, and the Shafee afterwards learn that it was sold for a quantity of wheat or barley, equivalent to one thousand dirms, or even more, his resignation is void, and he may still take his Shaffa; because it is to be supposed that his reason for resigning it was his inability to furnish the amount of the price in that species (namely, dirms) for which he first heard the house was sold; but upon his understanding that it was sold for wheat or barley, it is probable that he may be able to furnish the quantity, since it frequenty happens that men who are unable to pay one thousand dirms are capable of furnishing an equivalent, or even more than an equivalent, in barley or wheat. This rule also holds regarding every other article sold by weight or measure, or which differs so little in its species that it may be sold by number (such as eggs or walnuts), in the same manner as with respect to barley or wheat. It is otherwise with respect to goods or effects; for if the Shafee, hearing that the house is sold for one thousand dirms, resign his right, and afterwards learn that it was sold for goods

* For an explanation of this phrase see Vol, II. p. 255.

equal in value to one thousand dirms, or more, his resignation is nevertheless binding, and he not entitled to his Shaffa, because he would in this case be liable for the price of the goods, which consists of dirms and deenars.—So, likewise, his resignation is binding if he afterwards learn that the house was sold for a certain number of deenars equivalent to one thousand dirms, or more.

Or the purchaser.—If the Shafee be first informed that a particulars person is the purchaser, and thereupon resign his Shaffa, and he afterwards learn that the purchaser was another person, he is still entitled to his Shaffa, because a man might not wish to have one person for his neighbour, although he may very readily choose to have another. In the same manner also, if he afterwards learn that two persons are the purchasers (viz. the one whose name he first heard of, and another), he is entitled to take his Shaffa from the one in whose favour he had not resigned it.

Or where he has been misinformed concerning the article sold.—If news be brought to the Shafee that one half of the house is sold and he resign his right, and it after wards appear that the whole was sold, he must still in such case claim his Shaffa, since it is to be supposed that he at first resigned his right in order to avoid the convenience of a partner, whereas if the whole be sold there is no occasion for his being a subject to any such inconvenience. If, on the contrary the case be reversed, that is to say, if he first learn that that the whole, and afterwards that only the half is sold, he is not (according to the Zahir Rawayet) entitled to claim his Shaffa, because his resignation of the whole comprehended his resignation of a part.

Section.

Device by which the right of Shaffa may be evaded.—Where a man sells the whole of his house, excepting only the breadth of one yard extending along the house of the Shafee, he [the Shafee] is not in this case entitled to claim his privilege, because of his neighbourhood being thus cut off This is a device by which the Shafee may be disappointed of his right : and it is still the same, if the seller grant the intervening part of his house as a free gift to the purchaser, and put him in possession of it.

Case of a house purchased in shares, by the same person, at different times.—If a man purchase, first, a share of a house, such as a a third or a fourth, and afterwards the remainder,—the neighbour has the privilege of Shaffa over that share which was first bought, but not over that which was last bought; for although, as being a neighbour, he is entitled to that privilege over both, still the purchaser has a superior right to the Shaffa of the remainder of the house, as being a partner therein, the right of a partner superseding that of a neighbour, as has been already explained. If, therefore, a man wish to disappoint a neighbour of his right of Shaffa, he may do it by first purchasing a part of the house, for the price he means to give for the whole, excepting only a single dirms, which he may afterwards give as the price of the remainder.

Where the price of the property sold is compromised for a specific article, the Shafee, if he insist on his right, must pay the price.—If a man purchase a house for a certain price, and afterwards, in lieu of that price, give a Jamma, or gown; to the seller, the Shafee must take the house for the price first settled, and not for the value of the gown ; for, the exchanging of the price for the gown was a distinct and separate bargain ; and the price which the Shafee is to pay is on account of the house, not on account of the gown. The compiler of the Hedaya remarks that this also is a device, by which the right of Shaffa, either in a partner or a neighbour, may be eluded ; as the house may be sold for a price equal to twice its value, and then, in lieu of that price, a gown may be given to the seller equal to the real value of the house. Such an evasion, however, may be productive of loss to the seller in case the house should afterwards prove to have been the right of another; for then the purchaser of the house is entitled to receive back, from the purchaser of the gown (that is. the seller of the house) ; the whole price of the house, which was much more than adequate to its value, the bargain regarding the gown remaining undissolved. There is, indeed, one mode by which the seller may avoid the risk of such a loss ; and that is, by purchasing, in lieu of the number of dirms for which the house was sold, a quantity of deenars ;—for, as this is a Sirf sale, it follows that upon the right of another appearing to the house, the agreement becomes null, as mutual seizin, which is a condition of Sirf sale, does not here exist ; because as it here appears that the seller was not entitled to the price of the house in lieu of what he purchased or accepted deenars. he is obliged to restore the deenars, but nothing more.

A device, as above described, for eluding the privilege of Shaffa, is not abominated by Aboo Yoosaf. According to Muhammad, however, it is abominable ; because (as he argues) the privilege of Shaffa is instituted solely with a view to prevent the inconvenience which might otherwise ensue to the Shafee ; but if devices are admitted to elude and set at nought his privilege, the inconveniences which may ensure will not be prevented, and the end of the institution will be defeated. The argument of Aboo Yoosaf is, that as the above devices prevent the right of Shaffa from ever being established, the inconveniences that may accrue to the Shafee ought not to be considered.

Section

MISCELLANEOUS CASES.

The Shafee may take a share from one of

several purchacers: but if there be several sellers, and only one purchaser, he must take or relinquish the whole.—If five persons purchase a house from one man, the Shafee may take the proportion of any one of them. If, on the contrary, one man purchase a house from five persons, the Shafee may either take or relinquish the whole, but is not entitled to take any particular share or proportion. The difference between these two cases is that if, in the latter instance, the Shafee were allowed to claim a part, it would occasion a discrimination in the bargain to the purchaser, and be productive of very great inconvenience to him; whereas in the former instance; the Shafee being merely the substitute of one of the five purchasers, no discrimination in the bargain is occasioned. There is no difference in the law in either of these cases, whether in making the purchase, a certain proportion of the price had been set against each proportion of the house, or whether one price had been in general terms agreed upon for the whole; for the law is grounded only upon the discrimination in the bargain. Neither is there any difference whether the Shafee take his right before the purchaser has obtained possession; or delay it until after.—This is approved. It must, however, be observed, that if one of the purchasers have not obtained possession, although he have paid his proportion of the price, the Shafee is not entitled to take his share of the house until the rest of the purchasers have also paid their respective proportions of the price; for otherwise, a part of the house being in the possession of the Shafee, and a part still remaining it that of the seller, it is to be apprehended that the seller might suffer vexation from having a bad neighbour. In short, the Shafee here stands in the room of one of the purchasers; and one of the purchasers, on paying his proportion of the price, may not take possession of his share until the rest [of the purchasers] have also paid their proportion. it is otherwise after possession; for in that case the Shafee may assert his privilege, as the possession of the seller is then destroyed.

In case of the sale and partition of half a house, the Shafee may take the purchaser's lot.—If a man purchase one half of a house, and afterwards the seller and purchaser make the partition betwixt themselves. the Shafee may either take or relinquish that half which fell to the lot of the purchaser, on whichever side it happens to be situated, but he cannot object to the partition, and insist upon a new one: for a Shafee is not entitled to disturb the possession of the seller, and as partition is an act investitute, he is therefore not entitled to disturb the partition also. This is related as the opinion of Aboo Yoosaf. It is recorded from Haneefa, that the Shafee is not authorized to take the half in question, unless it happen to be on that side next to the house from which he derives his right, for if the purchaser's lot fall in the other part of the house, he [the Shafee] is not the neighbour.

If one partner sell his share, the Shafee may annul any subsequent position, and take it for the price.—If one of two partners in a house sell his share, and afterwards the purchaser and the remaining partner make the partition together, the Shafee may object to such partition, and insists upon a new one because, as no sale took place betwixt the purchaser and the remaining partner this partition is not, strictly speaking, an act of investiture, but merely an exercise of right of property, and consequently, the Shafee is entitled to annul it, in the same manner as he may annul any other act of property, done by the purchase, such as sale or gift.

A licensed slave (involved in debt) and his master may be Shafee to each other's property.—If a man being possessed of a Mazoon [licensed] slave, involved in debt, sell his house, that slave may be the Shafee of it. And in the same manner also, if such a slave sell a house, his master may be the Shafee of it, for the act of taking a property by privilege of Shaffa stands as a purchase, and purchase and the sale is admitted betwixt them, as being attended with advantage since it is here considered to be on behalf of the creditors. It is otherwise where the slave is not involved in debt, for then if he sell a house, it is on account of his master, and the man on whose account the house is sold cannot be the Shafee.

Act of a father or guardian with respect to the Shaffa of an infant ward.—If a father or guardian resign the right of Shaffa belonging to their infant ward, such resignation is lawful, according to Aboo Yoosaf and Haneefa. Mohammad and Ziffer say that it is not lawful, and that the right of the infant Shafee being still extant, he is entitled to claim it as soon as he attains maturity. The learned in the law observe that there is the same difference of opinion in the case of a father or guardian omitting to make the claim of Shaffa on being apprised of the sale of the house;—or of an agent resigning the claim before the tribunal of the Kazee. The arguments used by Mohammad and Ziffer are twofold.—First, it is alleged that the right of Shaffa being firmly established in the infant, the father or guardian have not the power of annulling it, any more than of annulling his right to a fine of blood or retaliation.—Secondly, their authority over the affairs of the infant is vested in them in order that they may prevent him from suffering and injury; and if they were to annul his right of Shaffa they would occasion an injury instead of preventing one. The arguments, on the other hand, in support of the doctrine of Aboo Yoosaf and Haneefa are likewise twofold.—First, the taking by privilege of Shaffa is virtually traffic, since it stands as purchase; and the father or guardian may therefore reject it, in the same manner as a thing offered for sale.—Secondly, the taking by privilege of Shaffa is an act of a doubtful tendency, as it may either be productive of loss or of gain: the relinquishing of it may therefore be sometimes the most for the minor's benefit, inasmuch as the price of the house will still remain his property; and as the power of a father or guardian is granted them with a view to the benefit of the infant, they ought consequently to have the power of rejection.

The silence of the father or guarding or their omitting to claim the Shaffa, being considered as a rejection, annuls the right. It is to be observed that the difference of opinion above mentioned obtains only in cases where the house in the neighbourhood of the infant is sold for a price nearly adequate to its value: but that where the house is sold for more than its value, beyond what appraisers would rate it at, and which it would be most advisable to avoid, some say that the resignation of the father and guardian is admitted to be lawful by all authorities, as being purely advantageous; whilst others, on the contrary, maintain that, according to all, it is not lawful; for as the father and guardian are not empowered, in such a case, to take the Shaffa, so also they are not empowered to reject it, but are as strangers; and the right of the infant still continues to exist.

If a house in the neighbourhood of an infant be sold for a price much inferior to its value, it is recorded as an opinion of *Haneefa* that in such case the resignation of a father or guardian is invalid.

END OF THE THIRD VOLUME.

VOL. IV.

BOOK XXXIX

OF KISSMAT, OR PARTITION.*

CHAPTER I.

Partition involves a separation, in articles of weight or measurement of capacity.—The partition of things held in joint property is lawful and valid, because the Prophet was accustomed to make a partition of plunder and hereditaments: and it is moreover a practice which no one pretends to controvert. It is to be observed, however, that partition may be received in two senses; for, considered in one view, it is separation, as it separates or distinguishes the right of one man from that of another; and considered in another view it is an exchange; because, the share or portion which falls to one of the parties in consequence of the partition is partly his own original right; but part of it was the right of the other during their joint property; and this he receives in lieu of that part of his own right, which remains involved in the other's share. It is more particularly a separation with respect to articles of weight or measurement of capacity such as wheat or silver, because of the similitude of their parts; or of these articles do not differ in their properties, the end to be answered by one parcel of wheat or silver being just the same as by another (since there is nothing in the one that was not in the other), it follows that each person receives his entire right, and nothing is left in the share of the one which of right belongs to the other:—whence it is that one partner may lawfully take his share during the absence of the other; and also, that if two men make a joint purchase of any article of weight or measurement of capacity, and afterwards divide it each may separately sell the share which falls to him for a determinate profit on half the original price.

And an exchange, in articles of dissimilar parts or unities.—It is, on the other hand, more particularly an exchange with respect to articles dissimilar in their parts or unities, such as animals or household goods;—whence it is that one of two partners in such articles cannot lawfully take his share in the absence

* Partition, in the Mussulman law, applies to joint property in whatsoever manner obtained or acquired. It more immediately relates, indeed, to the distribution of inheritance: but as the Mussulman doctors make no distinction, in terms, between a partner and a parcener (co-inheritance being defined to be one mode of partnership, Vol. II. p. 210), the translator uses the terms partner and partnership throughout.

of the other; and also, that if two men buy any thing of this species, and afterwards make a division, they cannot separately sell their respective shares at determinate profit on half the original cost. Here, however, if those articles be all of one particular species, such as a herd of goats, the Kazee, at the requisition of only one of the partners, must enforce a partition; for the properties of all the goats being nearly the same, such a partition is, in effect only a separation;—and the intention of such a equisition being, that the partner who makes it may enjoy the use of his own share solely, without any other person being able to interfere in his property, it is incumbent on the Kazee to comply with his requisition. Where, on the contrary, the joint property consists of articles of different species, the Kazee must not enforce a partition, as it cannot be made equitably where each particular thing differs from the rest in properties.—If, however, both the partners consent to a partition of things of various species, it is lawful.

The magistrate must appoint a public partitioner; and must appoint him a salary,—IT is incumbent on the Kazee to appoint a person to make partitions, and to settle on him an allowance from the public treasury so as that partitions may be made for the people without his receiving any hire; because, as the making of partitions is a part of the duty of the Kazee himself (it being necessary in order to terminate dispute), the allowances of the person appointed for this purpose must be defrayed from the public treasury, in the same manner as those of the Kazee: and also because, as the appointment of a person to make the partition is a benefit which extends to all Mussulmans, the charge of his maintenace must be defrayed from the public treasury, which is the property of all.

Or establish a particular rate of hire for his work.—IF it be not in the power of the Kazee to settle the allowance from the public treasury, he must at all events appoint a person who will make the partition for a certain rate of hire, to be paid by the parties who are concerned and particularly benefited by the division. In this case, the rate must be moderate and fixed, so that the partitioner may not be able to make exorbitant demands.—It is, however, more eligible that his allowances be paid from the public treasury, as this is easier for the people in general, and precludes, in a greater degree, the imputations of corruption and injustice.

The partitioner must be just, and skilful.—THE partitioner must be a man noted for justice and integrity; and he must also possess a knowledge of that particular business.

But must not always be the same person.—THE magistrate must not compel the people always to accept of one particular person for their partitioner; because the transaction which passes betwixt the partners and the partitioner is a species of contract; and it is not lawful to compel any person to enter into a contract;—and also, because, if such a practice were admitted, the person possessing the exclusive appointment would demand an immoderate rate of hire.

The partners may agree to a partition, procuring (if one be an infant) an order from the magistrate.—IT is lawful for several partners to agree amongst themselves, and to make a division of their joint property. But if there be an infant among them, it is requisite that they procure an order from the magistrate; for they possess no power over the infant.

One public partitioner cannot be concerned with another.—THE Kazee must not suffer the persons employed in making partition to be concerned together in the hire or profit arising from their business, such a conjunction tending to raise the hire to an exorbitant rate; for each of them, when applied to, will make some excuse for declining the employment, and they will refer the party who has occasion for their services from one to another, until at length he be constrained to consent to immoderate terms;—whereas, if every man is concerned only for himself, each will readily consent to be employed for a moderate hire, rather than lose it altogether.

The partitioner is paid in proportion to the number of claimants.—THE rate of wages to a partitioner is regulated by the number of persons for whom the division is made, according to Haneefa. The two disciples maintain that it is determined in proportion to their respective shares the wages of the partitioner being on account of their property, and therefore determined according to its extent, like the wages of a public weigher, or a measurer, or of a person who digs a well to be held, in joint property,—or like the maintenance of a slave belonging to several partners. The argument of Haneefa is, that the wages of the partition are given to him for discriminating and separating the shares, in doing which it signifies not whether the shares be large or small, since the shares of the inferior partner is distinguished and severed by his work, as well as that of him who holds a large proportion. It moreover sometimes happens that the labour in calculating a small share is more than in ascertaining a large share; and sometime the reverse: hence it is difficult to determine how far the one or the other is attended with the most trouble; and therefore the hire must be referred to the mere act of dividing off or discriminating. It is otherwise in digging a well; for, in that instance, the wages are on account of digging and carrying away the earth, in which there is difference in the labour performed for each partner's proportion. With respect to weighing or measuring, if those be performed in order to effect a partition of any thing (such as wheat held in partnership) it is affirmed by some that the same difference of opinion subsists betwixt Haneefa and the two disciples :—but if they be performed merely to ascertain the quantity of the whole or for any other purpose than partition, the wages are then on account of the weighing or measuring, which is greater in the larger than in the smaller share. There is also another opinion maintained upon the authority of Haneefa, —that the hire of the partitioner falls entirely upon the one who solicits the partition, and not on the one who has not solicited it, because of its being advantageous to the one, but not to the other.

In the distribution of hereditaments, the magistrate must previously ascertain the circumstances.—When several co-partners appear before the Kazee, and represent that a tenement or piece of ground which is in their possession has devolved to them as the heirs of a certain person, the Kazee must not make a partition of the house or ground until they have proved by witnesses the death of the person, and the number of his heirs. This is according to Haneefa. The two disciples say that if they all concur, the Kazee may make the partition, taking care, however, to insert in the Kissmat Namma, or deed of partition, that it was made in consequence of their declarations.

But not if the property consist of moveables.—If, on the contrary, the joint property be moveables and not lands or tenements, and the parties represent that it is their inheritance the Kazee may, on their representation, order the partition.

Nor in the case of property acquired by purchase.—Or, if the joint property be lands or tenements, and they represent that they acquired it by purchase, the Kazee may order a partition. The argument of the two disciples, is, that possession is an apparent proof of property, and the concurrent declaration of all the parties with respect to their several claims is a proof of their veracity. Besides, there is no person who either disputes or denies their allegations ; and where there is no denier the law require no evidence. Hence the Kazee must order the partition in the instance above mentioned, as well as in cases which relate to moveable property acquired by inheritance, or landed property acquired by purchase. It is requisite, however: that he specify, in the deed of partition, that it has been made in consequence of their declarations, in order that his decree may extend only to those who have attended, and not to others who may (perhaps) afterwards appear. The argument of Haneefa is, that the order which the Kazee gives for the partition is in fact a decree against the defunct, by which his right is terminated ; for until a partition take place, the hereditaments are still considered as his estate, insomuch that if any increase be produced upon it, such increase is subject to the will of the deceased declared in his testament, or is appropriated to the payment of his debts, neither of which could be the case after partition has been made. The partition, therefore, being in fact a decree of the Kazee affecting the defunct, the concurrence of a part of the claimants to the suits of the others is not admitted as an argument of sufficient weight ; and hence they must support their claims against the defunct by evidence ; in which case a part of the heirs are considered as litigants on behalf of the defunct.

Objection.—A part of the heirs cannot be considered as litigants on behalf of the defunct, since each individual acknowledges the claims of the others and a man who acknowledges another's claim cannot be regarded as his opponent.

Reply.—A part of the heirs may be considered as litigants on behalf of the defunct, although they do acknowledge the claims of the others, their acknowledgment being of no weight ;—in the same manner as where a man sues for a debt against an estate, and an heir or executor acknowledges his claim, in which case such acknowledgment, as being to the detriment of the others, is not sufficient, but the claimant must produce evidence before the Kazee in his suit, even against that heir or executor, before he can establish his claim against the estate in general to the prejudice of the whole of the heirs. The acknowledgment of the heir or executor being therefore of no weight, he may, with propriety, be considered as an opponent or litigant.

What is here mentioned is the law with respect to immoveable property.* It is otherwise with respect to moveable property ; † because that requires care in keeping, and there is an advantage arising from the immediate partition of it ; whereas immoveable property, being by its nature safe, requires no care ;—besides, the person in whose possession moveable property remains is responsible for it ; whereas (according to Haneefa) he is not so with regard to immoveable property. It is also otherwise with respect to landed property acquired by purchase ; because an article sold is no longer accounted the property of the seller, although it still remain undivided ; and the partition of it, therefore, cannot be regarded as a decree of the Kazee, passed against an absent person, by which his right is terminated.

Nor in case of a partition being demanded without the parties specifying the manner in which the joint property was acquired.—If the joint owners of a property request a partition of it, without specifying whether it was acquired by inheritance, or by purchase, or by any other means the Kazee may order the partition, this being, in fact, not a decree against another person, since no other is acknowledged by them. The author of this

---

* Arab. Akbar ; meaning houses, tenements, &c., such as is termed, in our law, real property.

† Arab. Mankool ; comprehending every species of personal property.

work says, that this adjudication is to be found in the Kitab al Kissmat.*—It is mentioned in the Jama Sagheer that when two men apply for a partition of lands which they prove by witnesses to be in their possession, the Kazee must not order the partition until they also prove, by evidence, that the lands are their property ; for otherwise it is possible that they may belong to another person. Some say that this is agreeable to the opinion of Haneefa alone ;—but others aver that it is agreeable to the opinion of all the learned; and this is approved, since it is unnecessary to order the partition of landed property in order to preserve it. Besides, the right of property being the ground on which partition is made, it cannot take place until that right be established by evidence.

A partition may be granted on the requisition and testimony of any two heirs ; but an agent or guardian must be appointed to the charge of the shares of the absent or infant heirs.—WHERE two heirs appear and produce evidence to prove the death of their ancestor, and the number of his heirs, and the house or other inheritance is in their possession, but one of the heirs is absent,—in this case the Kazee may order a partition, if the heirs who attend require it, appointing an agent to take possession of the portion of the absentee ; or if, under the same circumstances, one of the heirs be an infant, the Kazee may order a partition, appointing a guardian to take possession of his portion ;—because in so doing the interest of the infant or absentee is promoted.—(But here likewise the production of evidence is indispensable, according to Haneefa, in opposition to the opinion of the two disciples, as before stated.) It would be otherwise if they had become proprietors of the house by purchase ; for in that case no partition could be made in the absence of any of the partners. This distinction between the case of property acquired by inheritance and property acquired by purchase is made on the following grounds.—An heir is master of his ancestor's estate as his substitute, insomuch that he has the power of returning (on discovering a defect) any thing which his ancestor may have bought, or, in like manner, he may be compelled (on the discovery of defect) to take back any thing which his ancestor may have sold ; and he is likewise subject to become deceived † in consequence of the purchases of his ancestors (that is to say, if the ancestor purchase a female slave and die, and the heir afterwards have a son by her, and the slave then prove the property of another person, the son born of her is free, but the heir must pay the value of him to the paoprietor of the slave, and he may again recover it from the person who sold the slave, in the same manner as if he were the ancestor who made the purchase). One of the heirs, therefore, stands as litigant on behalf of the ancestor, and the other is litigant on his own behalf ; and the partition, under such circumstances, is in fact a decree passed in the presence of both the parties. The purchaser, on the contrary, becomes the proprietor of the thing bought by a recent title of property, and not in the manner of a substitute, insomuch that he cannot, on discovering a defect, return the article to the person from whom the late seller had before bought it. Hence neither of the two present purchasers can stand as litigant on behalf of an absentee. Thus there is an evident difference between the two cases.

And it cannot be granted where the property, or any part of it, is held by an absent heir, or his trustee, or an infant.—IF the land,* or a part of it, be in the possession of the absent heir, or of his trustee, or in that of an infant heir, the partition must not be ordered, whether the heirs who are present produce the evidence or not. This is approved ; for the partition, in such a case, would in fact be a decree of the Kazee against an absentee, or an infant, divesting them of something they possess without any litigant appearing on their behalf :—nor can the trustee of the absentee stand as litigant on his behalf in any thing which may be attended with loss to him ;—and it is illegal in the Kazee to pass a decree without all the litigants being present.

IF only one heir appear, a partition must not be ordered, although he produce the necessary evidence, for it is requisite that both the litigants be present ; and one man cannot stand as litigant on both sides. It is otherwise where two appear, as has been already shown.

The partition may be ordered although one of the requiring parties be an infant, or, one an infant heir, and the other a legatee.—IF two heirs appear, one an adult, and the other an infant, the Kazee must appoint a guardian to the infant, and order the partition as soon as evidence is produced ; and in the same manner, if an adult heir appear, and also a legatee of one third of the estate, and they demand a partition, and produce evidence (one to prove that he is heir, and the other that he is legatee), the Kazee must order the partition ; for in each of these cases the litigating parties are both supposed to appear,—the adult heir being litigant on the part of the deceased, and the legatee on his own behalf,—and, in the same manner, the guardian being litigant on behalf of the infant,—whence it may be said that the infant (as it were) has appeared in his own proper person as an adult, because of the guardian being his substitute.

* A collection of laws compiled by Mohammed, the disciple of Haneefa.

† Arab. Magroor. The meaning of this term has been fully explained elsewhere.

* Arab, Akkar ; meaning any immoveable property (and in this sense is the term land to be understood throughout).

CHAPTER II.

OF THINGS WHICH ARE FIT OBJECTS OF PARTITION.

An estate may be distributed on the requisition of any one partner, whose share separately is capable of being converted to use.—Where the respective share of each of the partners is capable of being separately converted to use, if any one of them demand a partition it must be granted ; because partition is an indisputable right, when required in any article capable of partition; as has been before explained. If, on the contrary, the share of one partner only be fit for use, and not that of the other, because of its being extremely small, and the owner of the greater share demand a partition, the Kazee must grant it ; but he must not grant it at the requisition of the other partner; for as the former can reap a benefit from his share, his demand is worthy of regard; but as the latter can have no other motives for his requisition than malice, and a desire of giving trouble, it is not to be attended to. Khasaf holds the reverse of this doctrine, "because (says he) the great partner, in making his demand, occasions an injury to another, whereas the small partner, in making his demand, submits to his own injury."—Hakim Shaheed, on the other hand, mentions in his abridgment, that "the Kazee must order the partition at the request of either of the partners; for the great partner is desirous of enjoying the use of his share, and the small partner voluntarily submits to his own injury." The first of these opinions, however, is the most authentic.

If the shares be separately useless, the assent of all the parties is requisite.—If the shares of each of the partners be so very small that they would separately be of no use, the Kazee must not order a partition unless both partners acquiesce ; for whenever partition is compulsively made, it is with a view to promote utility; but, in the present instance, all utility would be destroyed by it, and therefore it cannot take place without the consent of both the partners, as they must necessarily be the best judges in a matter which concerns themselves, and the Kazee can only be guided by appearances.

A partition must be ordered where the property consists of articles of one species (not being land or money)—When the joint property is Arooz* (that is, neither dirms, deenars, lands, nor houses). the Kazee must order the partition, provided it [the property in question] be all of one species, such as articles of weight or measurement of capacity, or similars of tale, or gold, silver, iron, or copper, or cattle of one species, whether camels, oxen, or goats ; for as, in this case, there can be no difference in the design, the partition may be effected with equity, and utility may thereby be accomplished.

But not where it consists of various species.—The Kazee must not order a partition when the joint property is of various species, such as a camel and a goat, or a house and an ass; because, as articles of different species cannot be indiscriminately blended, the partition, in this instance. would not be a separation and distinction, but rather an exchange, which must always be effected by a mutual concurrence of the parties, not by the decree of a magistrate.

Or of household vessels—The Kazee must not order a partition of household vessels, as those are subject to the rule of diversity of species, because of difference of workmanship.

A partition may be made of cloth of an equal quality.—He may make a partition of Herat cloths, as those are all of one quality; but he must not make it of a single piece of cloth which is not uniformly alike throughout; for the division of one piece or cloth occasions an injury, as it cannot be effected without cutting it; neither must he make a partition of two pieces of cloth where they are of unequal value. It is otherwise where there are three pieces, the value of one of which is equal to that of the other two: or where the value of one of them is one dirm, that of another one dirm and a quarter, and that of the third one dirm and three quarters; for, in the first case, he must give one piece to the one partner, and the other two to the other partner; and, in the second case, he must give to one of the partners the second piece, valued at one dirm and a quarter; to the other the third piece, valued at one dirm and three quarters, and must leave the first still to be held in partnership, one fourth appropriated to one partner, and three fourths to the other, as it is lawful to divide a part of a joint property, and to leave a part undivided.

But not of jewels or slaves.—Haneefa is of opinion that slaves and jewels must not be divided by the Kazee, because of the great difference which is to be found amongst them. The two disciples hold, that he may make a division of slaves, for this reason, that they are of one species, like camels, or goats, or captives taken in war. The argument of Haneefa is, that among the individuals of the human species there is a wide difference, because of their various characteristics; and hence slaves are. in effect, of different kinds. It is otherwise among animals, for with them there is little difference to be found betwixt the individuals of the same genus; and although the male and female of the human race be held as different species, yet the male and female amongst animals are reckoned as the same species. It is also different with respect to slaves taken in war, as it is in their value that the captors hlod a right, whence it is lawful for

*Some lexicographers define Arooz to signify household furniture. (Sooraj-al-Loghat.)

the Sultan to sell them and make a division of the price; whereas, in a case of partnership, the right of the partners is connected with the substance of the article, as well as with the property it involves. Hence there is a difference betwixt plunder and partnership property.—Some are of opinion that jewels cannot be divided when they are of different species, such as pearls and rubies. Others say, that where the jewels are of large grains they cannot be divided, because of the great difference that may be betwixt them; but that when the grains are small, the difference being inconsiderable, the jewels may be divided. Others, again, maintain that no jewels, whether of small or large grains, can be divided, because the difference betwixt them, and the difficulty of ascertaining their value, is greater than in the case of slaves, insomuch that if a man marry a woman, and in general terms stipulate to give pearls or rubies as her dower, such stipulation is invalid;—whereas if he stipulate, in general terms, to give slaves, it is valid. The Kazee, therefore, is not to exert his authority in making a partition of jewels.

Partition cannot be made of a bath, mill, or well, without the consent of all the parties.—THE Kazee must not order the partition of a joint mill, bath, or well, unless with the concurrence of all the partner (and such also is the rule with respect to a wall which stands betwixt two houses); for if, in these cases, a partition were to take place, it would be injurious to all parties, as the individual share of each would then be useless.

Partition of houses and tenements.— T is proper to remark, that a single roofed place, surrounded with walls, with a door or entry, is termed a Bait, or room. A Manzil, or tenement, on the contrary, is a place composed of different rooms, a roofed court,* and a kitchen, such as a man may reside in with his family. A Dar, or house, on the other hand, is a place consisting of various rooms or tenements, with an open court. A tenement is therefore superior to a room and inferior to a house. These are the definitions of Shims-al-Ayma in his book on Shaffa. In this work, whenever the general word Khanna [house] is used, we mean such an one as we have now described, under the denomination of Dar, excepting only where we mention an under house in contradistinction to an upper house, and then we only mean a Bait or a Manzil.

IF there were several houses held in partnership or coparcenary in one city, each house must be separately divided, according to Haneefa. The two disciples say, that if it be expedient for the partners the whole of the houses must be united in one general partition, and not divided separately. All the houses, therefore, must be considered merely as one house consisting of various apartments, and all the shares of each partner must consequently concentre in one of the houses, so that it may be his entirely. The same difference of opinion also subsists regarding the case of lands held in partnership or coparcenary, and dispersed in different situations. The argument of the two disciples is, that all the houses are, on the one hand, of one species with respect to name, appearance, and original design; as, on the other hand, they* are of different species with regard to their particular qualities, and their commodiousness for habitation, which depends on size: and so forth; whence it must be left to the Kazee to determine their different degrees of superiority.—The argument of Haneefa is, that regard should be paid only to what they are in reality, with respect to their qualities; and that in them they may greatly differ on account of the difference of the cities, lanes, or neighbourhood, in which they are situated, and their proximity to or distance from water or a mosque; and that therefore it is impossible to observe an equality in the partition without dividing each house separately;—whence it is that a man cannot appoint an agent to purchase a house in general terms;—and so likewise, that if a man marry, assigning as a dower "a house" (in general terms), his mention of the house is invalid,—in the same manner as holds where a man assigns "cloths" (generally) as a dower, or appoints an agent to purchase "cloths."—It is otherwise with respect to a single house, held in partnership or coparcenary, composed of different rooms; for as, in such case, to divide each room amongst the copartners would be productive of inconveniency to all; the whole house is therefore divided at once.

WHEN two houses, held in partnership, are situated in different towns, we learn from Hillal that it is the concurrent opinion of Haneefa and Aboo Yoosaf that both houses shall be divided separately. Mohammed, on the contrary, maintains that they must be divided at once, as well as the houses situated in the same town.

ROOMS, whether situated all in the same quarter, or in different quarters, must be divided at once, for the difference amongst them is inconsiderable. Manazil Molazika (that is to say, adjoining tenements, or such as are in the same house, one part of them being contiguous to another), are considered as rooms: whereas, Manazil Motbayena (which is the term used for apartments not adjoining, in contradistinction to the other), are considered as houses,—a Manzil or tenement being the middle term betwixt a house and a room, and resembling both.

IF there be a partnership in immoveable property of two species such as in a house and a piece of ground, or in a house and a shop, the Kazee must divide eac separately, they being of different species.

*Arab. Sahn; meaning the interior square of a dwelling, common to all the family and which, in large edifices) is open, but in small ones is covered in.

CHAPTER III.

OF THE MODE OF ACCOMPLISHING PARTITION.

The partitioner must draw a plan; and must make the distribution equitably by measurement or appraisement.—It is incumbent upon the partitioner to draw on paper a plan of the thing which he divides, so that it may remain on his memory.—He must likewise observe an equality in the partition, that is to say, he must divide the article into due proportions; and it is also recorded that he ought to separate each share and measure it, so that its extent may be known. He must, moreover, appraise the article, as it is requisite, for his further guidance, that the value be ascertained.

Partition of houses how accomplished.—Supposing the article to be a house, in separating the shares he must also separate the road and the drain belonging to it, if possible, so that one share may no longer have any connexion with the other, in order that every cause of dispute may be terminated, and that the intention of partition may be completely accomplished. In doing this he must term one share the first share, that which lies next to it the second, and that which lies next to it the third share, and so on; and he must then write down their names, and draw them like lots; and he that draws the first name gets the first share, he that draws the second gets the second share, and so on to the end. The article must, moreover, be divided into fractions equal to the smallest proportion; that is to say, if the smallest proportion held by any of the partners or coparteners be a third, the whole must be divided into three parts; or if the smallest proportion be a sixth, the whole must be divided into six parts; so that the division may be made accurately. Thus, if an estate is to be divided betwixt two heirs, the one being the son and the other the daughter, it must be divided into three shares, one termed the first, the next to it the second, and the next the third; and the partitioner is to write the names upon billets, and cause them to be drawn like lots; and if the son's name come up first, he gets the first share, and the one next to it, and the third goes to the daughter;—or, if the daughter's name come up first, she gets the first share, and the other two fall to the son.

The drawing of lots is proposed in order to give satisfaction to the parties, and to prevent the partitioner from being influenced by partiality or favour. It is not, however, absolutely necessary; and if the partitioner choose to appoint a particular share to each, it is valid; for the making the partition is an act of magistracy, and the authority of the partitioner must therefore be enforced.

In the partition of landed property, a composition in money cannot be admitted.—The partitioner, in making a division of landed property, must not annex a consideration in dirms or deenars without the concurrence of the parties; that is to say, if he make one share less than the other, and, as a compensation, annex to it a sum in dirms, it is not valid, unless they consent;—for the partnership is not in dirms, and partition is one of the rights of the partnership. Besides, if dirms be admitted into the transaction, it destroys the equality of the partition; because one of the partners gets the property; and is liable for the dirms which have become the right of the other; and there is a possibility that he may never pay them, by which means the other would lose his right.

Partition of a house, with a piece of ground:—If the partnership property consist of two things, namely a house, and a piece of ground each, according to Aboo Yoosaf, must be divided separately, agreeably to its value; for it is only by ascertaining the value of each that an equality can be observed in the partition. It is recorded from Haneefa that the ground may be divided agreeably to its measurement, and afterwards he on whose share the house is situated, or whose share is the most eligible, must pay a sum in dirms to the other, so that an equality may be effected.;—and that therefore dirms may be introduced as auxiliaries in the division when necessity requires it. Mohammad in this case maintains that the person on whose share the house is situated must give to the other partner a space of ground equal in value to it. If, however, his share (from its containing the house) be still the most valuable and it be impossible for him to effect an equality for want of enough of ground to compensate for the value of his house, he may then give dirms equivalent to the excess; for as the necessity exists only in that degree, the original rule of partition by measurement must not in any greater degree be abandoned. This is conformable to the opinion delivered in the Assil [the Mabsoot].

Partition of land where there is a road or drain.—If the partitioner so divide the property, that the road or drain of one runs through the share of the other, and no condition had been expressed regarding this matter the case then admits of two predicaments.—I It is possible for him to turn the road or drain another way, so that it pass not through the share of the other;—in which case the partition is valid;—for it is not proper that he let the road or drain of one man pass through the share of the other; on the contrary, it is incumbent on him to turn it another way, even though each individual may have mutually stipulated that they were to enjoy their respective shares "with all the rights and immunities belonging to them;" because the intention of portion is to separate and discriminate the proportions of each partner; and as it is possible, in the present instance, without injury to either, to effect such a separation and discrimination completely, so as that no connexion or dependance may remain betwixt the shares, this is therefore indispensable.—It is otherwise with respect to lands sold with an express condition that "they are sold with their immunities," for here, notwithstanding the connexion or dependence which may subsist betwixt them and the lands of another, the intention of selling, which is to transfer the right of property, is nevertheless fully accomplished. --II. It is (or may be) impossible to turn the road or drain another way, so that it pass not through the share of the other:—and this may happen under two different circumstances:—FIRST, where the parties have not stipulated to one another the enjoyment of their shares "with all the rights and immunities belonging to them;"—in which case the partition must be annulled, an account of the connexion and mixture of property, which renders it inefficient, the ends of partition (namely, separation and discrimination) not being thoroughly accomplished;—the partition must therefore, in this instance, be made anew, in such a manner, that the road and water-drain of each may be separate. (It is otherwise with respect to lands sold; for the object of a sale is the transfer of right of property, which the purchaser may fully possess without being able to enjoy immediately the use of it, whereas the intention of partition is that the use of the property may be enjoyed in the fullest degree, which it cannot be unless a separate road be made.)—SECONDLY, where all the parties have stipulated that they shall enjoy their respective shares with all the rights and immunities belonging to them; in which case, the partition is valid, and the road and water-drain are included in it, since the end of partition is that each may enjoy the use of his property, and it is impossible perfectly to enjoy the use of the grounds without a road and water-drain. The road and water-drain are therefore, in this instance, included in the partition, provided the parties mutually stipulate to each other the enjoyment of their shares with all their respective rights: as however, the object of partition is to discriminate, which requires a complete separation of all connexion in their respective shares, the road and water-drain are not included, unless such a stipulation be particularly made. It is otherwise with respect to lands farmed; for the intention of farming being to enjoy the use of the lands, which cannot be done without having road and water-drain, it follows that if these articles should not have been expressed, they are nevertheless included in the farm.

In case of a dispute concerning the road, it must be divided.—IF the parties differ regarding the road, some of them desiring that it should remain, as formerly, in common, but that all the rest of the property be divided, and others of them opposing this, in such case, provided it be practicable, the magistrate must divide the road, and assign a part of it to each particular share;—or, if this be impracticable, he must leave the road out of the partition, which must nevertheless be made, in order that the parties may enjoy the full use of all their property excepting the road.

IF the parties differ regarding the extent of the road (that is, regarding the height and breadth which ought to belong to each), the Kazee must regulate their proportions by the breadth and height of the doors of their respective houses as that is sufficient to answer their necessary occasions. The advantage of this arrangement is, that if any of them be desirous of making a projection or terrace from his house over the street he may do it above the height of his door, but not below it; and the road will still remain in common, according to their several proportions, in the same manner as before the partition; for the partition (as we have observed above) did not take place regarding the road

The parties may make a private agreement with regard to it.—IF two partners in dividing a road, agree that the one shall have two thirds and the other only one third, such a partition is valid, although the house be held betwixt them in equal proportions; for in partiton it is lawful to give more or less than his proportion to one partner, provided both of them agree to this

Complicated partition of different houses and tenements.—IF two partners hold a house, the upper floor of which is held by a stranger, or which has no upper floor and likewise another house, the under floor of which is held by a stranger, and also a complete house (that is, one of two stories), in this case the Kazee must appraise each house separately, and make his division accordingly. Mohammed alleges that this is the only lawful mode. Aboo Yoosif and Haneefa are of opinion, that he ought to make the partition according to measurement. The argument of Mohammed is, that the lower floor has many advantages and conveniences which the upper floor cannot possess, such as walls, necessary houses, stables, and so forth; and that therefore the equality of partition cannot be effected but by an appraisement. The argument of the two disciples, on the other hand, is, that the partition, if possible, ought to be made by a measurement, since the partnership subsists in a thing capable of measurement, and not in the value of that thing. They afterwards however, differed regarding the mode of measurement; Haneefa contending that one span of the lower floor should be held equivalent to two spans of the upper floor; and Aboo Yoosaf maintaining that a span of the one is equivalent to a span of the other. Some have thought that the contradictory opinions of these three ages ought to be ascribed to their different places of abode, and the periods in which they lived; for during the time of Haneefa the inhabitants of Koofa (the place of his residence) preferred the under floor to the upper; whereas afterwards, in the time of Aboo Yoosaf, the people of Bagdad (where he lived) held the upper and the under floor in equal estimation; and Mohammed observed that, on the contrary, the taste of mankind differed, some preferring the upper and some the under floor, and others holding them in equal estimation. There are again some who, instead of ascribing the opinions of the three sages to the prevailing customs and notions of the ages and places in which they lived, are rather for deriving the origin from different principles of law. Thus, in support of Haneefa's doctrine, it is argued, that the advantages of an under floor are double those of an upper one; for the advantages of the under floor remain after the upper one is ruined and destroyed, whereas those of the upper floor do not remain after the destruction of the under one. In the under floor, moreover, there are not only the advantages of habitation, but also those of foundation; for the proprietor of the under floor may build if he pleases, but the proprietor of the upper floor can only enjoy the advantages of habitation, as it is not lawful for him to erect any buildings without the consent of the proprietor of the ground floor; and upon these considerations a span of the under floor should be reckoned equivalent to two spans of the upper. In favour of Aboo Yoosaf's opinion, on the other hand, it is alleged, that habitation is the great end of both, and that both are equally fit to answer that end; whence it is lawful for the proprietor of either of them to erect any buildings that are not productive of injury to the other. Lastly, it is urged, on the part of Mohammad, that the advantages of an upper and an under floor are according to the seasons of summer or winter, the violence of the wind, the temperature of the air, and the different climates or countries in which they are situated; whence it is impossible to establish any just rule of partition, but by appraisement. In modern times the law is administered agreeable to the adjudication of Mohammed, which does not require any comment or elucidation.—The mode of partition prescribed by the doctrine of Haneefa, in the case in question, is as follows.—The partitioner must first set against the upper floor house (which we shall suppose measures one hundred spans) a part of the complete house equal to thirty-three one-third spans; because an upper floor is rated at half the value of an under floor; consequently thirty-three and one-third spans of the under floor of the complete house are equal to sixty-six and two-thirds of the upper-floored house; and as those sixty-six and two-thirds, together with the thirty-three and one-third spans of the under floor, form the complete house; the whole amount exactly to the one hundred spans of the upper floor house. The partitioner must then set sixty-six and two-thirds spans of the complete house against the under floor house (supposing it to measure one hundred spans), for the upper floor of the complete house is rated at one half the value of the under floor house, and sixty-six and two-thirds spans of both the floors of the complete house are equal to the one hundred spans of the under floor house. The mode, on the other hand, of making the partition, according to Aboo Yoosaf's doctrine, is as follows. Let one hundred spans of the upper floor house be set against fifty spans of the complete house: or, let one hundred spans of the under floor house be set against fifty spans of the complete house; for, according to him, the upper and the under floor are held in equal estimation; wherefore fifty spans of the complete house, comprehending fifty spans of the under floor, and fifty spans of upper floor, must be equal to one hundred spans.

In disputes after partition, the evidence of two partitioners must be admitted.—If the partners differ after partition, one pleading that "he has not received the whole of his share, a part of it still remaining in the possession of the other"—and the other denying this, and the two partitioners (or any other two person) testify that: "they have made a partition," their evidence, according to the two disciples, must be admitted. Mohammed says that it cannot be admitted, because the evidence they give relates to their own act, and is consequently inadmissible in the same manner as the evidence of a man relative to some act of his own, on the occurrence of which a person may have formerly suspended the emancipation of his slave. The argument of the two disciples is, that the witnesses, in fact, testify to the act of others (namely, the act of seising and possessing), and not to their own act; because their act was merely discriminating and separating, to which evidence is not required; hence their testimoney must be admitted. Tahavee observes that where the partitioners receive pay for making the partition, it is universally allowed that their evidence cannot be admitted; and indeed several doctors of our sect are of the same opinion; alleging that as in that case, their evidence tends to prove that they have fully and accurately performed the work for which they received pay, it is in the nature of a representation on their own behalf. Our author, however, does not subscribe to this reasoning; for he remarks, that the two partitioners could not have a view to their own interest in their evidence, as the partners have agreed that they fully and accurately performed the work of partition for which they receive their pay, the only question in dispute being the seisin and possession; wherefore no imputation of falsehood ought to fall on them.

But not that of one partitioner.—If only one partitioner give evidence, it must not be admitted; for the evidence of one man alone against another is not sufficient.

CHAPTER IV

OF PLEAS OF ERROR IN PARTITION; AND OF CLAIMS OF RIGHT IN REGARD TO IT.

A plea of error cannot be admitted, where the party acknowledges having received his share, unless it be supported by evidence.—Where one of the partners complains of an error in the partition, and that a part which ought to have fallen to him by the partition is in the possession of another, in this case; if he has before acknowledged that he had received his share, his complaint must not be admitted unless supported by evidence; for it is, in fact, sueing to cancel the partition after it has been accomplished; and it is to be presumed that there is no error, and that his complaint is false. If the complainant cannot support it by evidence, the other must be required to deny the complaint upon oath; and if they refuse to swear, their refusal is construed as proof in favour of the complaint, and the Kazee must cause their property to be divided anew, agreeably to their several proportions, as this is dealing with them according to their own suspicions. The author of this works thinks that in the above case the complainant's suit should, on account of his contradicting himself, be wholly rejected.

A complaint of after-assumption is a complaint of usurpation.—If the complainant allege that he receive his whole right, but that the otherwards took a part of it, the denial of the other, on oath, must be credited, as this is in fact a complaint of usurpation.

In case of a complaint of non-delivery: both parties are sworn, and the partition is dissolved and made anew.—If he allege that "a certain village fell to him in consequence of the partition, but that the other had not delivered it up to him," in this case provided he have not previously acknowledged the obtaining possession of his share, and the other contradict him, both must be required to swear;—because the dispute is with respect to the quantity which the complainant received in consequence of the partition; and hence the difference in the present instance is analogous to a dispute concerning the quantity of an article of sale,—in which case a mutual oath is tendered to the parties (as has been fully explained under the head of Sales); and so here likewise.

A plea of error cannot be heard, if the partition was made by the parties.—If one of the parties complain that an error took place in the division, his complaint must not be attended to, it being held in the same light as a complaint of a fraudulent bargain, which in case of sales concluded by the principals themselves cannot be heard. In partition, there, as in sales, since both parties have mutually concurred, such a complaint cannot be heard. If, however, the partition was made by the order of the Kazee, and extreme fraud be alleged, the complaint must be heard, as the stability of the Kazee's authority depends on justice.

Case of a claim laid to a particular room in a house, after partition.—If a house be divided betwixt two partners, each receiving a part and afterwards one of them claim a room in the possession of the other, alleging, that "it is one of the things which ought to have fallen to him in consequence of the partition," and the other deny this,—in the case, as the plaintiff complains of usurpation, it is requisite that he bring proper evidence; and if both bring evidence, that adduced on the part of the plaintiff, who is not in possession, must be admitted in preference to that of the other; for it is a maxim of the law that the evidence on the side of the party who is out of possession is preferable to that on the side of him who is in possession.

If the complaint above mentioned be previous to an avowal of the plaintiff's having ever acquired possession, both parties must be required to swear, and the partition must be annulled, and performed anew. In the same manner, also, if two partners differ regarding their boundaries, the one alleging that "a certain boundary belongs to him, but has fallen into the possession of the other," and the other alleging the same thing regarding another boundary, and both produce evidence, the Kazee must decree, in favour of each, that boundary which is in the possession of the other. If only one produce evidence, the Kazee must pass a decree only in his favour; but if neither of them produce evidence, they must both be required to swear, in the same manner as in cases of sale.

Section

*Of the Laws which prevail in a Claim of Right**

In a case of claim set up to an indefinite part, after partition, it must be dissolved and made anew.—If a house (for instance) held in partnership be divided, and afterwards an undefined part of the whole (such as a half or a third), prove the right of another, the partition, according to all our doctors, is null, and must be made anew.

If a definite part be claimed, after partition, it must be compensated for from the shares of the other partners, or, the partition must be dissolved and executed anew.—If a particular and defined part of what has fallen to one of the partners, in consequence of partition should prove the right of another person, the partition is valid, according to all our doctors, and become not void with respect to what remains after the right of the other person has been separated:—but the party from whose share that right is taken has in his option either to dissolve the portion (thereby restoring the property to the state in which it stood previous to the partition) and then to demand a new one,—or, if he choose, he may let the partition hold good, and exact from his partner's share a compensation for that part of which he has

* Arab, Ishthikak; meaning a claim set up to the subject of a deed or contract, by some person not concerned in such deed or contract.

been deprived by its proving the right of another.

And so likewise, if an undefined part be claimed.—If, after partition, an undefined part of the share of one of the partners (such as a half), prove the right of another person, the partition is valid with respect to the remainder, and does not become void according to Haneefa and Mohammed; but the partner upon whose share the claim operates has it in his option to annul the partition (restoring the concern to the state on which it previously stood), and then to demand a new partition;—or, if he choose, he may let the partition hold good, and exact from his partner a compensation for the half of his share which he has lost, and which is equivalent to one fourth of the share in that partner's possession. According to Aboo Yoosaf, the partition is in this case null, since by an undefined proportion of one of their shares proving the right of another person, a third partner is created, without whose concurrence the partition is void; in the same manner as where an undefined part of the whole article proves the right of another person. The reason of this is, that where an undefined proportion of one of their shares becomes the right of another; one of the objects of partition (namely, separation) is destroyed, sinch the share of one of the partners by that means becomes in itself a matter of partnership; and he must have recourse to the share of the other for an undefined part, equal to that proportion of his right of which he has been deprived. It is otherwise in the preceding case, where a particular and defined part of one of their shares proves the right of another; for in that case the object of partition (namely, separation) still exists with respect to the remainder. The argument of Haneefa and Mohammed is, that the object of partition, namely separation, is not defeated by an undefined proportion of one of the partner's shares becoming the right of another person. Hence a partition of this nature, originally made, would be valid;—as where, for instance, the first half of a house is jointly held by two partners, Zeyd and Amroo, and by a third person, named Khalid, one half thereof by Khalid, and the other half betwixt Zeyd and Amroo; the second half being held jointly between Zeyd and Amroo, Khalid holding no share thereing—in which case Zeyd and Amroo might lawfully make a partition betwixt themselves, Zeyd getting the whole of their joint share in the first half of the house and one fourth of the second half; and Amroo getting three fourths of the second half; and it is in the same manner ultimately valid; the case becoming similar to that in which a defined proportion of one of the shares proves the right of another. It is otherwise where an undefined proportion of the whole house, including both shares, proves the right of another; because in this latter case, supposing the partition to be valid, an injury is sustained by the third person, whose right was manifested after the partition, since he must then accept his proportion, not in a compact manner, but dispersed, from the shares of each of the others; whereas, in the former case (in which an undefined proportion of one of the shares proves the right of another), he suffers no injury. Thus there is an evident difference between two cases. In short, the nature of the case in question is this that one of two partners takes one third of a house, and the other takes the remaining two thirds; the value of the first third being equal to that of the other two thirds; and afterwards one half of the first third proves the right of another person;—in which case (according to Haneefa and Mohammed), the first partner has it in his option to annul the partition; for if it continue valid, his share is defective, because of its being dispersed, part in the first third of the house, and part in the two last thirds;—or, if he please, he may take one fourth of the share which fell to the second partner; for if the whole of his [the first partner's] share had proved the right of a third person, he would have been entitled to take one half of the second partner's share; wherefore (arguing of a part from the whole) since one half of his share proved the right of the third person, he is entitled to take one half of a half of the second partner's share, which is equal to one fourth.

If the partner to whose for the first half falls should sell a moiety of it, and afterwards the other moiety prove the right of another, he is still entitled to one fourth of the second half in the possession of his co-partner, for the reasons before assigned; and his option of annulling the partition drops, because of his having sold a part of his share. This is according to Haneefa and Mohammad Aboo Yoosaf maintains that the second half, in the possession of the co-partner, must be divided equaly betwixt them; and that the first partner forfeits to his co-partner one half of the price for which he sold a part of his share; for (agreeably to his tenets) the original partition is invalid; and as an article of which a person obtains possession by an invalid deed becomes his property, he may lawfully dispose of it by sale; but he is responsible for the value of it; and hence in the case in question, the first partner is responsible for the value of an half of what he has sold, as that is a moiety of the other's half

A debt proved against an estate, annuls the partition of it among tha heirs.—If the estate of a daceased person be divided amongst the heirs, and afterwards a debt be proved against the estate equal to the whole; the partition must be annulled, because the debt prevents the estate from being the property of the heirs;—and the same rule holds where the debt is not equal, because the right of the creditor attaches equally to the whole fortune of the deceased. The partition must therefore be annulled, unless there be left after it a sum sufficient to discharge the debt, in which case it is not annulled, since the annulment of it is not necessary for the discharge of the debt.

Unless the creditor remit it, or the heirs discharge it.—IF the creditor, after the partition; remit the debt, or if the heirs discharge the debt from their own fortunes, the partition remains valid, whether the debt be equal to the estate or exceed it, the obstacle to its validity being thus removed.

An heir may prefer a claim upon an estate after partition.—IF one of the heirs prefer a claim of debt against the deceased, after the admissible; of the hereditaments. his claim is admissible; for in this case there is no contradiction, since the debt relates to the spirit of value, and not to the substance of the particular hereditaments, and it was in the substance of the hereditaments that the partition took place.

A claim cannot be set up, by an heir, to any particular article, after distribution—IF a part of the heirs, after partition, prefer a claim for a particular thing, included in the estate, on whatever ground the claim be built, it cannot be admitted, on account of the contradiction, which is here evident, as their acquiescence in the partition implies an acknowledgment in them that particular thing, which has been divided, was a part of the co-parcenary.

CHAPTER V.

OF THE LAWS OF MAHAYAT.

Mahayat is a partition of usufruct.—MAHAYAT, in the language of the LAW, signifies, the partition of usufruct; and it is allowed; because it is frequently impossible for all the partners to enjoy together, and at one time, the use of thing held in partnership. Mahayat, therefore, resembles the partition of property (whence it is that the Kazee may enforce it in the same manner)—with this difference, however, that in the partition of property each partner enjoys the use of his respective share at the same time, whereas in the partition of usufruct each most frequently enjoys the use of the thing held in partnership only when it comes to his turn, by rotation. Partition of property is therefore more effectual than partition of usufruct in accomplishing the enjoyment of the use; for which reason, if one partner apply for a partition of property, and another for a partition of usufruct, the Kazee must grant the request of the former; and if a partition of usufruct should have taken place with respect to a thing capable of a partition of property such as a house or a piece of ground), and afterwards one of the partners apply for a partition of property, the Kazee must grant a partition of property and annul the partition of usufruct.

And is not annulled by the decease of the parties.—A PARTITION of usufruct is not annulled by the death of one of two partners, nor even by the death of both, for if it were annulled, it must (most probably) be renewed (since the heirs of the deceased may lawfully demand a partition of usufruct), and therefore it would be to no purpose to annul it.

Partners may make it by allotting to each the use of a particular part of the joint concern.—IF two partnes, by a mutual contract, make a partition of usufruct respecting a house, to this effect, that one of them shall inhabit one part of it and the other another,—or, that one shall inhabit the upper floor and the other the under, such contract is valid; for as a partition of property executed in this mannar is lawful, so likewise is a partition of usufruct. It is proper to remark, that a partition of usufruct, when thus executed, is in reality a separation, that is, a division of the whole of the shares of usufruct of one partner from those of another partner, and a concentration of both into one place: but the cantract does not comprehend an exchange, whence it is that a limitation of time is not required in it;—for if it comprehended an exchange, a limitation of time would have been requisite because of its being (in that case) a lease.

In which case either is at liberty to let his share.—IT is lawful for each partner to let out on rent that part of which the usufruct has fallen to him, and he may appropriate to himself the rent accruing therefrom, whether it be a condition in the agreement of partition of usufruct or not; for every use which accrues from that part becomes (in consequence of the partition of usufruct) his property and the rent which he receives is nothing more than a compensation given him in lieu of the use accruing from it.

Or by stipulating an alternate right to the use.—IF two partners make an agreement of partition of usufruct regarding a slave, in this manner, that the one day he shall serve the one, and the next the other, it is lawful (and so likewise if they make a similar agreement regarding a small room); for partition of usufruct is sometimes effected by means of time, and sometimes by means of place; and in the present instance it is effected by means of the former.

A difference between the parties must be settled by the interference of the Kazee.—IF two partners disagree concerning the terms of their contract of partition, the one alleging that it related to time, and the other that it related to place; the Kazee ought to enjoin them to agree regarding one or other of these methods. The reason of this is that the partition of usufruct with respect to place is the more equitable, since by that means each partner enjoys the use at the same time that the other partner enjoys it also; but partition of usufruct with respect to time (on the other hand) is the more complete in regard to the use, since each individual then enjoys it entire. As, therefore, the reasons in favour of these two methods are different, it is requisite that the partners agree on one of them;—and if they choose partition with respect to time, the Kazee, to prevent the imputation of partiality, must draw lots, in order to determine which of them shall have the first turn.

Case of partition of the use of two slaves.—If two partners (whom we shall suppose Zeyd and Amroo) make a partition of usufruct regarding two slaves, to this effect, that the one shall serve Zeyd, and the other Amroo, it is valid, according to the two disciples; for as (by their doctrine) partition of property with respect to slaves, is lawful, whether performed by the authority of the Kazee, or by the mutual agreement of the parties, it follows that partition of usufruct, with respect to slaves, is also in the same manner lawful. Some (by inference from the doctrine of Haneefa) maintain that the Kazee must not enforce the partition of usufruct with respect to slaves (and such is reported as his opinion by Khasaf); because compulsion being (as we have formerly shown) disallowed by Haneefa with respect to partition of property in the case of slaves, it evidently follows that the Kazee cannot enforce a partition of usufruct in a similar case. The truth is, that if the Kazee enforce a partition of usufruct in this way, it is lawful, according to Haneefa,—whereas, if he were in this way to enforce a partition of the substance it would be unlawful; because in the service of slaves there is no great difference, but in their persons they differ considerably

If a partition of usufruct be made regarding the above two slaves in this manner, that the maintenance of the one whom Zeyd takes for his service shall be defrayed by Zeyd, and the maintenance of the one whom Amroo takes shall be defrayed by Amroo, it is valid, on a favourable construction. Analogy would suggest that it is not valid, because the maintenance of each of the slaves is incumbent on both the masters:—but when it is stipulated that the maintenance of one of them shall fall solely on one of the masters, and that of the other on the other master, it may be called an exchange; and as the consideration (supposing it an exchange) is uncertain, it is therefore invalid. The reason for a more favourable construction in this particular, is that in feeding slaves strictness is not particularly regarded. It were otherwise, however, if each partner stipulated to clothe his slave, as strictness is regarded with respect to clothing them.

Or, of two houses.—If two partners make a partition of usufruct regarding two houses; in this manner, that the one shall inhabit the one house, and the other inhabit the other, it is valid: and the Kazee may enforce it, according to the two disciples and such is also the opinion of Haneefa, as mentioned in the Zahir Rawayet. The reason of this, with the two disciples, is that as (agreeably to their tenets) a partition of property, made in this manner, is valid, so likewise is a partition of usufruct. Some say that according to Haneefa such a partition of usufruct, when made by the mutual agreement of the parties, is valid; but that it cannot be enforced by the Kazee; for although a partition of property of this nature, by the consent of the parties, be valid, still (agreeably to his tenets) the Kazee cannot enforce it; and the same of a partition of usufruct. There is another opinion transmitted to us from Haneefa, that a partition of usufruct in the manner above mentioned is utterly invalid, whether enforced by the Kazee (for the reasons which have been stated above), or made by mutual agreement; because it would be a sale of residence in one house for residence in another, which is not legal, as has been already shown in treating of Hire. It is otherwise with respect to partition of the substance of two houses; for the sale of a part of the one house for a part of the other is lawful. The reasons for the opinion quoted from the Zahir Rawayet are, that as the difference between the usufruct of the one and of the other is inconsiderable, a partition of the nature described is in the manner of a separation, and is therefore lawful when made by the mutual agreement of the parties, and may be enforced by the Kazee. The difference, on the contrary, between the substance of the houses may be very considerable; hence a partition of the substance of them, in the manner described is (in effect) an exchange, and may accordingly be made by the consent of the parties, but cannot be enforced by the Kazee.

Or, of two quadrupeds.—If a partition of usufruct be made regarding two quadrupeds, to this effect, that the one partner shall have the riding, of the one, and the other the riding of the other, it is not valid according to Haneefa. According to the two disciples it is valid; since a partition of property made in this manner is (by their doctrine) valid; and partition of usufruct is only a branch of partition of property. The argument of Haneefa is, that there is a difference in the use and riding of one or another quadruped, because of the difference in riders, some being expert and knowing in the art of riding, and others the reverse. The same difference of opinion also obtains concerning a partition of usufruct, by rotation, with respect to one quadruped;—in opposition to a slave; for a slave serves according to his own reason, and will not suffer a greater burden than he is capable of bearing, whereas a quardruped must submit.

Partition of the advantage from a house may be effected by each party letting in to hire alternately.—If a partition be made regarding the produce of a house, to this effect, that the one partner shall let it out to rent for one or two months, and enjoy the produce or rent, and that afterwards the other partner shall let it out in the same manner, and enjoy the rent, such a partition is valid, according to the Zahir Rawayet; but a similar agreement regarding a slave or a quadruped is not valid. The reason of this distinction is, that in the case of the slave or quadruped the equality of the several shares, which is a necessary condition, is lost,—whereas in the case of the house it is preserved; for slaves and quadrupeds are changed and prejudiced by the lapse of time and severe labour, and it is probable that their hire will be less the second than it was the first turn, where as house may be supposed to continue in the same state during both turns, and the rent may be equal.

Any occasional excess in the rent being divided equally between them—IF it should happen that the rent of a house is greater during the turn of one partner, than in that of the other, they are both to participate in the excess, or difference betwixt the one rent and the other, so that an exact equality may be effected between them. It is otherwise where they make a partition respecting the use of the house, and it afterwards yields a greater produce to the one in his turn than to the other, for as, in this case an equality has still been preserved in that which was the subject of partition (namely, the use), the excess of acquisition, received in return for the use, is immaterial, since it frequently happens that there are two things exactly equal, and yet the return received for the one is greater than that received for the other.

In a case of partition of the advantage from two houses, neither party is accountable for any excess of rent to the other—A PARTITION concerning the rent of two houses is likewise lawful, according to the Zahir Rawayet for the same reasons as have been assigned in the case of one house. If, however, one house yield a greater rent than the other, still the partners do not both share in the excess. The reason of this distinction is that, in the case of two houses, when a partition of their rents is made, separation is the prevailing principle; because as each partner enjoys the rent of his particular house, at the same time, it follows that each obtains the whole of his respective rights, without leaving any part of them with the other,—whereas in a partition of the usufruct of one house, the partners receive the rent by rotation (that is, the one receives the rent the one month, and the other receives it the other), and it may therefore be said that they successively grant to each other a loan of their shares of the rent,—the partner who holds the second month lending to him who holds the first month his share, or half of the rent for the first month, which he is again to receive out of the rent of the second month;—and it may be also said that during their respective months each acts as agent for the other in receiving his share; and when the other has received his share from the rent of the second month, if there be an excess, it is divided betwixt them; but if, on the contrary, he be not able to recover the whole amount of his loan from the rent of the second month (it being less than the first), the excess which is on the side of him who held the first month must be divided betwixt the partners, so that a perfect equality may be thus accomplished.

Case of partition of the advantage from two slaves.—ACCORDING to the two disciples, a partition with respect to the hire of two slaves, made in the manner of the preceding case, is lawful, as well as a partition with respect to the service and use of two slaves, Haneefa maintains that it is not valid; because the difference to be found in two slaves is greater than that which is to be found in one slave at two separate periods. As, moreover, a partition with respect to the gain required from a single slave, by rotation, is invalid, it follows that such a partition with respect to the gain acquired from two slaves is invalid a fortiori. Besides, a partition regarding the service and use of slaves is admitted from necessity, slaves being of themselves indivisible; but there is no necessity in the case of the hire of slaves, as that is a thing which is capable of division. In the case moreover, of service, it may not be requisite to consider matters strictly;—whereas, in the case of hire (which is a money transaction) matters must be considered strictly. Hence there is no analogy between the cases.

A partition of advantage from two quadrupeds—A PARTITION of usufruct concerning the hire of two quadrupeds is invalid, according to Haneefa, in opposition to the two disciples. The arguments used on both sides are the same as those which have been set forth in the case of a partition of usufruct concerning the use of service of a quadruped.

A partition of usufruct cannot be made with regard to productive articles.—IF two partners make a partition of usufruct regarding an orchard of dates, or a garden containing trees, in this manner, that each shall take a part and cultivate it, and enjoy the fruits produced from it,—or, if they make a partition of usufruct regarding a herd of goats, in this manner, that each shall take a certain number, and feed them, and enjoy the milk produced by them, neither of these partitions of usufruct is valid; because partition of usufruct regarding use, as well as partition of usufruct regarding service, is admitted only from necessity, as being unsubstantial, and therefore incapable of division; but, in the present instances, the fruit and the milk, when once produced, are capable of division, being things which substantially exist, and therefore there is in these instances no necessity. The device here is for one of the partners to sell his share to the other, who may first enjoy the fruit and milk, and afterwards, when the other's turn is expired, his partner may again purchase the whole, and enjoy the fruit and milk in his turn. Or, one may enjoy the produce of the other's share in the manner of a loan, and ascertain the quantity thereof, for the loan of indefinite things is lawful.

BOOK XL.

OF MOZAREA, OR COMPACTS OF CULTIVATION.

Definition of the term.—MOZAREA, in the lanugage of the LAW, signifies a compact betwixt two persons, one being a proprietor of land, and the other the cultivator, by which it is agreed that whatever is produced from the land shall belong to both in such proportions as may be therein determined.

Difference of opinions concerning compacts of cultivation.—A COMPACT of cultivation is not valid according to Haneefa. The two disciples maintain it to be valid; because it is related of the Prophet that he entered into such a compact with the people of Kheebir, by which it was agreed that they should manage the gardens and lands of Kheebir, and enjoy one half of the fruits and grain produced from them, and that they should give the other half to him. Besides, a compact of cultivation is, in fact, a compact of partnership in regard to stock and labour, in this way, that one of the parties being the proprietor of the ground, and the other the tiller of it, the product is between them.—It is therefore valid from its analogy to a contract of Mozaribat; for contracts of Mozaribat are valid on a principle of conveniency; since, as it often happens that there are men possessed of property who have not a capacity for trade or business, and again, that there are others endowed with such a capacity who have no property, it is therefore convenient that a contract of Mozaribat be established betwixt them, by which means the desires of both are accomplished; and as the same reason subsists in the case of compacts of cultivation, they are therefore valid as well as compacts of Mozaribat. It is otherwise where one man gives to another goats, fowls, or silkworms, to take care of, on condition that he who thus takes care of them shall have one half of the produce and the proprietor the other half; for this is disapproved; because as the care and mangement of the keeper has no effect in creating the produce, patnership is therefore not sufficiently established in that instance. The arguments of Haneefa on this point are threefold. FIRST, the Prophet has expressly prohibited Mokhabera, which in the dialect of Medina has the same signification as Mozarea, namely, compacts of cultivation.—SECONDLY, to make a compact of cultivation is to hire a labourer for a part of that thing which is produced by his labour; it is therefore, in effect, a Kafeez Teham, and as that is unlawful, so likewise is this.—(Tehan signifies a miller or grinder of wheat, and Kafeez a cup used for measuring; Kafeez Tehan, therefore, means to hire a person to grind wheat into flour, in consideration of a measure of the flour for his hire)—THIRDLY, the rate of hire, in such cases, is uncertain, when any produce is reaped; or it is annihilated when no produce is reaped; and in either case the hire if invalid. With respect, moreover, to the transaction which passed betwixt the Prophet and the people of Kheebir, it was not a compact of cultivation, but was rather in the nature of a tributary revenue, allowed to be paid in kind, as an indulgence or compromise. As compacts of cultivation are thus deemed invalid by Haneefa, it follows that (agreeably to his doctrine), where the labourer waters, tills, and sows the land, and it nevertheless proves unproductive, he is entitled to the customary rate of hire adequate to his labour, since (according to Haneefa) the compact of cultivation is, in effect, as an invalid hire. This is where the seed sown is furnished by the proprietor of the ground; for if the seed be furnished by the cultivator, he is liable for the rent of the land at the customary rate:—and if, in either case, any produce be reaped, it belongs to him who supplied the seed, since it is an increase from his property;—and the other, if he be the cultivator, is entitled to a rate of hire adequate to his labour,—or, if he be the proprietor of the ground, to an adequate rent for his ground. In the present times however, the adjudication of the courts is given according to the doctrine of the two disciples, both because compacts of cultivation are convenient to mankind, and also because they have become everywhere customary.

They require that the ground be capable of cultivation.—The following conditions are essential to the validity of a compact of cultivation. I. That the ground be capable of cultivation, for otherwise the object of the compact cannot be accomplished.

That the parties be duly qualified.—II. THAT the proprietor of the ground and the manager be both qualified to make such a compact; that is to say, that they be both in their right reason, of age and conversant in such compacts; for unless the parties be so qualified no compact whatever is valid.

That the term of their continuance be expressed.—III. THAT the period or term be expressed; for such a compact is in the nature of an agreement, either for the use of the ground (as when the cultivator supplies the seed), or, for the use of the labour (as when the seed is supplied by the proprietor of the ground), and the determinate use of either can be ascertained only by the period.

That the party be specified who is to supply the seed.—IV. THAT it be expressly stipulated by whom the seed is to be supplied, in order that the grounds of the compact may be known;—in other words, in order that it may be known whether it is founded on the use of the labour, or on the use of the land, and that no source of dispute may remain.

That the share of the other party be expressed.—V. THAT the particular share which is to fall to him who does not supply the seeds be expressed; for in consequence of the agreement he is entitled to a share; and it is requisite that the proportion be determined, because a thing which is unknown cannot be established by the compact, not withstanding a share be in general terms stipulated.

That the land be delivered up to the cultivator—VI. THAT the proprietor of the land deliver up the land to the cultivator, in order to the cultivation of it, and that he himself abstain from any mangement or enjoyment of it; insomuch that if it be stipulated in the compact of cultivation that he also shall manage, the compact is null, because of the invalidity of such stipulation.

That both parties participate in the produce.—VII. THAT both parties participate in the produce of the ground after it is reaped; for a compact of cultivation is ultimately a compact of partnership; wherefore every stipulation repugnat to partnership invalidates the compact. (For example, if a precise quantity of the produce be stipulated for one of the parties, it is invalid; since, as it is uncertain whether so much will be produced, the partnership is therefore defeated).

And that the particular seeds be mentioned.—VII. THAT the particular species of seed, such as wheat, barley, &c., be expressed, in order that the species in which the hire of the labourer is to be paid may be known.

Of compacts of cultivation four descriptions are valid.—COMPACTS of cultivation (according to the two disciples) are of four different kinds:—I. Where the ground and the seed are supplied by the one, and the cattle and the labour by the other:—and this is lawful for the cattle are considered as implements of labour, and the case is therefore similar to that of a man hiring a tailor to sew his robe with his (the tailor's) own needle. II. Where the ground alone is supplied by one of the parties, and the labour, seed, and cattle by the other:—and this also is lawful for in this case the labourer has hired the ground for a known proportion of its produce, and it is therefore lawful, in the same manner as if he had hired or rented it for a certain number of dirms. III. Where the ground, the seed and the cattle, are supplied by the one, and the labour alone by the other:—and this likewise is lawful; for in this case the proprietor of the ground hires a labourer to work with implements belonging to him (the hirer); and it is consequently analogous to the case of a man hiring a tailor to sew his robe with his (the hirer's) needle, —or, to that of a man hiring a labourer to dig with his (the hirer's) hoe. IV. Where the ground and cattle are supplied by one of the parties, and the seed and labour by the other.—This is not valid, according to the Zahir Rawayat:—but it is reported from Aboo Yoosaf that this also is valid; for as, if it were agreed that both the cattle and the seeds should be supplied by the proprietor of the land, it would be valid, it is in the same manner valid where he supplies the cattle only; being, in fact, the same as where the cattle are furnished by the cultivator. The reason on which the opinion in the Zahir Rawayet is grounded are, that the use of cattle is different, in its nature from the use of ground; for the use of ground arises from a strength in the soil which occasions vegetation, whereas the use of cattle consists in their fitness for labour; these two things therefore, not being of the same species, the use of the cattle cannot be a dependent on the use of the ground. It is otherwise where the cattle are supplied by the cultivator; for the use of cattle and the use of a cultivator or labourer are of the same species, the product being equally derived from the work of both.

And two are invalid.—IT is here proper to remark, that besides the four species of compacts of cultivation above enumerated, there are two more, which are, however, invalid I. Where it is stipulated that the seed shall be supplied by one of the parties, and the ground, the labour, and the cattle, by the other; which is invalid, because the sixth condition before mentioned is not found in it. II. Where it is stipulated that the seed and cattle shall be furnished by one of the parties, and the ground and labour by the other, which is likewise invalid, for the same reason. In both these cases the produce of the lands (according to the one opinion*), belongs to him who supplied the seed, upon the same principle that it belongs to him in any other cases of compacts of cultivation which are invalid. But according to the other opinion,† the produce belongs to the proprietor of the land he therefore stands (as it were) as merely a borrower of the seed of which he has obtained possession by its being sown in his ground.

The period of their duration must be known and the produce must be participated between the parties, in definite proportions.—COMPACTS of cultivation are not valid unless the period of their duration be known;—nor unless the produce of the land be indefinitely participated between the parties (such as in a third, a fourth, &c.) in order that partnership may be established betwixt them. If, therefore, it be stipulated that either of them in particular shall receive a certain number of measures of grain from the produce of the ground the compact is null as in this case partnership is defeated (in other words, is not established) since it is possible that no more may be produced from the ground than what is thus stipulated to one of the parties —and the case is therefore similar to that of two men concluding a contract of Mozaribat, in which it is stipulated that one of them shall receive a certain number of dirms.

IN the same manner also, compacts of cultivation are invalid where it is stipulated that he who supplies the seed shall receive an equal quantity of grain from the produce of the ground, and that the rest shall be divided betwixt the parties;—for, in case the

*The opinion of Haneefa, as before stated.
†The opinion of the two disciples.

produce exceed the quantity of seed, a stipulation of this nature defeats the partnership with respect to that particular quantity; or with respect to the whole, in case the produce should not exceed the quantity of the seed. A stipulation of this nature, moreover, is similar to where the paties agree, regarding tribute-land, that the rest of the produce shall be divided after deducting tribute. It is otherwise where two men agree that one tenth of the produce shall go to one of the parties, and that the remainder shall be divided betwixt both; for a stipulation of this nature does not defeat partnership, because the remaining nine-tenths still continue participated between the parties; whence this is similar to a stipulation, regarding tithe-lands, that "after deducting the tithe, the remainder shall be divided betwixt the parties."

In the same manner also, a compact of cultivation is invalid if it stipulate that whatever is produced on a particular spot (such as on the banks of a rivulet), shall belong to one of the parties, and that the remainder of the produce of the whole ground shall be divided betwixt both; for such a stipulation defeats partnership, since it is possible that nothing may be produced except upon that particular spot:—and it is in like manner invalid where it is stipulated that the produce of one spot of ground shall go to one of the parties, and the produce of another spot to the other.

In the same manner also, a compact of cultivation is invalid where it is stipulated that the one shall get the straw, and the other the grain; for it is possible that nothing may be produced but straw: and it is equally invalid if it be stipulated that the straw shall become their joint property, and that the grain shall belong to one of them only; for here a partnership is not established with respect to the grain, which is the particular object of cultivation.

If the grain alone be mentioned, the straw goes to him who supplies the seed.—If it be stipulated, in the compact of cultivation, that the grain shall be divided equally betwixt the parties, and no mention be made of the straw, still the compact is valid, because a partnership is stipulated in that thing which is the chief object of cultivation; and in this case the straw will belong to him who supplied the seeds, as of that the straw is the produce. (The Shiekhs of Balkh* are of opinion that the straw should also be divided equally betwixt the parties; because such is the usual practice when no mention is made of the straw; and also because as the straw is subordinate to the grain it should, as well as the grain, be held in partnership.)

And it may be stipuluted to go to him.—If it be stipulated that the grain shall be divided equally, and that the straw shall go to him who supplied the seed, it is valid; because this is consistent with the spirit of compacts of cultivation.

But it cannot be stipulated to go to the other—If, on the contrary, it be stipulated that the straw shall go to him who did not supply the seed, it is invalid, as such a stipulation defeats the partnership in case nothing but straw should be produced. The difference betwixt these two cases is, that the person who did not supply the seed has no other claim to the straw than what he acquires from the stipulation, whereas he who supplied the seed has a right to the straw in consequence of its being the produce of his seed; and whether the straw be stipulated to him or not his right to it holds equally good.

The produce is participated according to agreement: and if nothing be produced, the cultivator has no claim—When a compact of cultivation is valid, the produce of the ground is the joint property of the parties, in such proportions as they may have stipulated, such as an half, a third, or the like.—If, on the contrary, nothing be produced, the cultivator is not entitled to any thing; for he has a right only to a share of what may be produced. It is otherwise where the compact of cultivation is invalid; for in that case an adequate hire falls due upon the person [of one of the parties], not upon the produce; and the person is not absolved by a failure of produce.

Where the compact proves invalid, the produce goes to him who furnishes the seed; and the other party.—When a compact of cultivation proves invalid, the crop belongs to him who furnished the seed, it being the produce of his property. Besides, the other has no right therein except what he acquires in virtue of express conditions in the compact; and where that proves invalid, it follows of course that the entire crop belongs to the person who supplied the seed.

If he be the cultivator; gets wages (not exceeding his right under the compact).—If the seed be supplied by the proprietor of the ground, the cultivator is entitled to a suitable hire for his labour, provided it do not exceed what he would have received in consequence of the conditions of the compact; because, in subscribing to these conditions, he consented to relinquish his right to the excess. This is the law, as laid down by the two elders. Mohammed maintains that he is entitled to a suitable hire, to whatever amount; for as the master of the land has obtained his services in consequence of an invalid compact, he is of course liable for the value thereof, service not being of the calss of similars;—as has been fully explained in treating of Hire.

Or, if the proprietor of the ground, an adequate rent—If the seed be supplied by the cultivator, the proprietor of the ground is to receive a suitable rent for his ground, whether there be any produce or not. Tha:

*Balkh is a city in Turan.

reason of this is, that as the cultivator has acquired the use of the ground in consequence of an invalid compact, he ought therefore to restore the use itself; but that being impossible, and there being no similar in which he might make a return, it is therefore incumbent that he make a return in the value to an amount not exceeding what the other would have received in virtue of the stipulations of the compact. This is the doctrine of the two elders. Mohammed is of opinion that he must pay an equivalent, whatever it may be.

And also an adequate hire for the cattle, if supplied by him.—IF the cattle be provided by the proprietor of the ground, so as that the compact (according to the Zahir Rawayet), becomes invalid, the cultivator is in that case liable for a suitable hire on account both of the cattle and the ground:—and this is certainly just; since the cattle are equally included in the contract of hire (the compact of cultivation being, in fact, a contract of hire in this instance); and the use of the cattle and the use of the ground are uses of different kinds

If it be the proprietor who thus gets the produce, he may keep the whole; but if the cultivator, he must bestow the surplus in charity.—WHERE the proprietor of the ground, in consequence of having supplied the seed, is entitled to the produce, he may lawfully on the compact proving invalid, enjoy the whole, since it was yielded from ground which was his own property. If, on the contrary, the cultivator, in consequence of having supplied the seed, be entitled to the produce he is to reserve for his own use a quantity equal to the seed he supplied, and also a quantity equivalent to the rent he is to pay to the proprietor of the ground,—and the rest of the produce he must apply to charitable purposes; because the produce springs from the seed, but grows out of the ground, whence his right to the use of the ground is invalid; and as invalidity in regard to the use occasions a baseness in regard to the product, it follows that what remains with him as a return is lawful to him, and that every thing else must be bestowed in alms.

The party who agrees to supply the seed is at liberty to retract previous to the sowing.—WHERE two men enter into a compact of cultivation, and he who was to supply the seed afterwards retracts, previous to the sowing, the Kazee must not compel him to abide by the compact, because he cannot abide by it without sustaining an immediate loss from the sowing of his seed, and the case is therefore similar to where a man hires another to break down his house, in which instance, if the hirer were to retract, the Kazee could not compel him to abide by his agreement. If, on the contrary, the party retract who was not to supply the seed, the Kazee may compel him to fulfil the compact; for in so doing he does not sustain any loss; and compacts of cultivation, like compacts of hire, are binding, unless when some plea can be alleged sufficient to dissolve compacts of hire, in which case a compact of cultivation is also dissolved.

And if the proprietor of the ground thus retract, the cultivator is not enttitled to anything.—IF the proprietor of the ground, being to furnish the seed, should retract, after the cultivator has tilled the ground, the cultivator is not entitled to receive anything for the work he has performed. Some, however, are of opinion, that although in point of law, there be no compensation due to the cultivator, still, in point of conscience, it is incumbent on the proprietor of the ground to satisfy the cultivator for the work he has performed, as he has been deceived in this instance.

The compact is annuled on the decease of either party.—WHEN one of the parties dies, the compact of cultivation, like compacts of hire, becomes dissolved. (The reason of this is fully set forth in treating of Hire.)

If the proprietor of the ground die, when the crop has appeared; the compact is dissolved at the end of that year.—IF a man give up a piece of ground to another for a term of three years, and afterwards, when the first year's crop has begun to grow, but is still unfit for reaping, the man die, the ground. in this case, remains in the hands of the cultivator until the crop be fit for reaping, and the produce is then divided according to the conditions of the compact;—and the compact is dissolved with respect to the remaining two years of the term; because analogy would suggest that it discontinues even for the first year, as the duration of a compact depends on the duration of the parties; but it is continued throughout the first year, in order to the preservation of the rights of both parties (that is, the cultivator and the heirs of the proprietor), since, if it were to discontinue, the cultivator would sustain an injury. It is otherwise in regard to the second and third years, because in the discontinuance of the compact for those years no injury is sustained by the cultivator; and accordingly the compact is dissolved for these years, agreeable to analogy.

But if he die before that, it is dissolved immediately.—IF the proprietor of the ground die after the cultivator has ploughed the land, and dug rivulets for watering it, but previous to the crop appearing, the compact is dissolved, since in such case the dissolution of it is not injurious to the cultivator's property. (It is otherwise where the proprietor of the ground dies after the crop has begun to grow, and appears like grass; for in that case the compact is not dissolved, as the cultivator would then be injured in his property by the dissolution of it). In this case the cultivator is not entitled to any thing for his labour; because the use of a person's service cannot be appreciated but by a compact; and when the compact becomes null, the estimation of the service no longer remains.

The proprietor of the ground may dissolve the compacts with a view to sell the ground for the discharge of his debts.—It is lawful for the proprietor of the ground to dissolve the compact, in case he have occasion to sell the ground to discharge considerable debts which he may have incurred, for this is a pretext, which he may avail himself of, in the same manner as in Hire: *—and in this case the cultivator has no right to claim from him any expense which may have attended the tilling of the land, or the digging of drains; because service is not appreciable but in consequence of a compact; and as the price set on the service, in the present instance, was upon the supposition of a produce, it follows that upon the produce being prevented the cultivator is not entitled to any thing.

But if the crop be growing, the sale must be delayed until it be ready for cutting.—If, however, the crop have begun to grow, although it be still unfit for reaping, the land must not be sold for the payment of the proprietor's debts until the grain be ready to cut down; because if the lands were to be sold, under such a circumstance, the sale would be injurious to the right of the cultivator; whereas, by waiting until the crop is ready, it only occasions a small delay in the payment of the proprietor's debts, which is the lighter evil of the two. The Kazee must also, in this case, enlarge the proprietor, if he have been imprisoned on account of his debts, for it being unlawful immediately to sell the lands, the proprietor, in delaying to pay his debts, is guilty of no injustice, and imprisonment is intended as a retribution for injustice.

Rules in case of the compact expiring before the crop is ready to cut.—If the term of the compact of cultivation should expire before the crop be ready for cutting, the cultivator must pay to the proprietor of the land a hire or rent for his [the cultivator's] proportion of the ground until the crop be ripe; and in the mean time any work which it may require must be performed by both parties according to their respective proportions. The reason of this is, that in thus prolonging the compact, and ordaining the payment of a rent, a regard is paid to the benefit and interest of both parties, wherefore it is necessary that it should be prolonged;—and it is also necessary that both should bear their proportions of the work or expenses; because the compact which they entered into is expired, and the crop remains their joint property, and in cases of joint property the work is incumbent on both parties, in the same manner as the subsistence of a partnership slave. (It is otherwise where the proprietor of the land dies whilst the crop is yet green; for in that case it is incumbent on the cultivator to perform the whole of the work that may be required; because in such an event the compact is continued during the remainder of its term: and it [the compact] obliges the cultivator to sustain the whole burden of the work;—whereas, in case of the term of the compact expiring, it is no longer binding, and therefore the cultivator alone is not obliged to perform the work.) If, therefore, either party incur any expense after the expiration of the term, without consulting the other, or without an order from the Kazee, he must bear it himself as he had no right of himself to subject the other to any charge.

If, in the example above recited; the proprietor of the land should be desirous of taking the crop (which is still green) after the expiration of the term of the compact, yet he must not be allowed to do so, because it would be an injury to the cultivator. If, on the contrary, under the same circumstance, the cultivator be desirous of taking the green crop, the proprietor of the land has three things in his option; for he may either pull up the crop and divide it; or he may keep it altogether and make an allowance to the cultivator, equivalent to his share of it; or he may take care of the crop until it be fit for reaping, in which case he may deduct from the share of the cultivator the amount of the expense, incurred on that account;—because if the cultivator should choose to desist from labouring, on the expiration of the term of the compact, he cannot be compelled, since it is prolonged with a view to his benefit, which he himself has forsaken; and no injury is occasioned to the proprietor of the ground, as he has three modes in his option, by either of which injury is prevented.

If the cultivator die, his heirs may continue the cultivation, but are not entitled to wages.—If the cultivator should die after the crop has begun to grow, and his heirs should offer to continue the cultivation until it be fit for reaping, and the proprietor of the land should not consent, in this case they are nevertheless authorized to continue the cultivation, as the proprietor will sustain no injury thereby; but they are not entitled to any hire or wages, as the compact is continued with a view to their benefit. If on the contrary, the heirs should desire to pull up the crop, and not to continue to cultivate, they cannot be compelled to continue to cultivate, for the reason above assigned; but the proprietor of the ground has in his option the three modes already recited.

The incidental charges are sustained by the parties in proportion to their respective shares.—The expense of cutting down the crop, of carrying it to the stack, of thrashing it, and of cleaning the grain from the straw, falls upon both the parties in proportion to their several shares. If, therefore, they were to stipulate in the compact that the expenses shall fall on only one of them, the compact would be invalid. In short, all the above mentioned charges must be sus-

* See Vol, III. p. 510.

tained by both parties in proportion to their several shares, and not by any one of them in particular; because, when the crop is ready, the object of the compact being accomplished, the compact itself is at an end; and as the crop remains the joint property of the parties, and no compact or stipulation is left in force betwixt them, it follows that any expenses which may be afterwards required on account of their joint property ought to fall upon both. Besides, if they stipulate that those expenses shall fall on one of them only, such a stipulation is inconsistent with the true spirit of the compact, as it tends to the advantage of one party over the other; and all stipulations having such a tendency invalidate the compact itself, in the same manner as a stipulation by which the cultivator is bound to carry the grain, or to grind it into flour. Aboo Yoosaf is, however, of opinion that where the parties agree that the operations above-mentioned shall fall upon the cultivator, it is lawful, because of custom. The sages of Balkh concur in this opinion; and the Shims-al-Ayma observes, that this doctrine is authentic, and that the practice prevails in his country.

General rules in compacts of cultivation.—IN fine, every operation of agriculture, previous to the maturity of the crop (such as watering and watching it), falls upon the cultivator; and every subsequent operation requisite until the partition (such as reaping, & c.) falls equally upon both; and lastly, every operation that is necessary after the partition (such as carrying watching, &c,) falls upon each of them severally, for their respective shares.

And of gardening.—THE foregoing rule holds good, also, in cases of Mosakat, or compacts of gardening; that is to say, all operations previous to the maturity of the fruit, such as watering, grafting, and watching the trees, fall upon the gardener; and all subsequent operations, such as gathering the fruit, and watching it, previous to a partition, fall upon both. If, therefore, it be settled betwixt the parties that the trouble of gathering the fruits shall fall upon the gardener, it is disapproved, according to all our doctors, as being uncustomary;—and all operations, after partition, must be performed by each with respect to his own share.

IF, in compacts of cultivation, the parties be desirous of cutting down the crop whilst it is young,—or, in compacts of gardening, of pulling the dates whilst they are sour or moist, the labour of these operations falls upon both, for the intention and desire of performing them terminates the compact, in the same manner as if the crop or dates had arrived at maturity.

BOOK XLI.

OF MUSAKAT, OF COMPACTS, OF GARDENING.*

Nature of a compact of gardening.—MOSAKAT, in the language of the law, signifies, a contract entered into by two men, by which it is agreed that the one shall deliver over to the other his fruit-trees, on condition that the other shall take care of them, and that whatever is produced shall belong to them both, in the proportions of one half, one third, or the like; as may be stipulated. Haneefa alleges, that a compact of gardening, stipulating an indefinite proportion of the produce, such as an half, or a third, is invalid. The two disciples, on the contrary, maintain that it is valid, provided a term or period be expressed; and this is approved. It is to be observed, that compacts of gardening are frequently termed Mamilat as well as Mosakat; and the same laws hold with respect to them as those which have been laid down with respect to compacts of cultivation.

Doctrine of Shafei upon this subject.—(SHAFEI is of opinion that compacts of gardening are valid; and that compacts of cultivation are only so, where they happen in subordination to the former; as, for example, where the fruit trees grow in fertile and clean ground, which is watered for the nourishment of the trees, and the proprietor of them directs the cultivator to sow a crop on the ground on condition that he shall get a share, such as one half of the produce. The reason he assigns is, that the original thing, in this point, is, a contract of Mozaribat; and to that a compact of gardening bears a nearer resemblance than a compact of cultivation; for as, in compacts of gardening, the partnership subsists in the produce, and not in the principal thing (namely, the trees), so in contracts of Mozaribat the partnership subsists in the produce or profit, and not in the principal or stock;—whereas, in compacts of cultivation, if it be agreed that a partnership shall exist in the produce, and not in the principal (namely, the seed)—in other words, if the parties agree that the one who furnished the seed shall receive an equal quantity of seeds from the crop, and that the remainder shall belong to them both, the compact is invalid.—As, therefore, compacts of gardening bear a nearer resemblance to Mozaribat than compacts of cultivation, it follows that they are the primary object, and that compacts of cultivation are lawful only as a dependant; like a right of drawing water, which cannot be sold separately, but is included, subordinately, in the sale of the land; or like a moveable article

* Applying, more particularly, to the plantation and culture of date and other fruit trees.

(such as the furniture of a house), which cannot be separately appropriated in Wakf, but is included in the appropriation of the house or ground on which it stands.*)

Analogy requires the specfication of a term; but it is not essential —The specification of a term is requisite in compacts of gardening, by analogy, in the same manner as in compacts of cultivation, the one being, in reality, a contract of hire, the same as the other. According to a more favourable construction, however compacts of gardening are lawful without any specfication of a term. Thus, if two men enter into a compact, by which it is agreed that the one shall deliver his date trees to the other, who shall water and nourish them until they produce fruit, and it become ripe, and no particular period (such as a year; or the like) be specified, the compact is nevertheless valid, and continues in force with respect to the first fruit that may be produced; for the season for producing and ripenning fruit is known, and seldom differs much. In the same manner also, if two men enter into a compact, and agree that the one shall deliver to the other the roots of shrubs, which are in the ground,† and that to other shall water and nourish them until they yield ripe seed, to be shared between them without mentioning any term, the compact is neverthless valid, and takes place with respect to the first seed that shall be produced and arrive at maturity because as seed is of the same nature as fruit, the period of its maturity being equally known, it is therefore, needless to settle any limited time. It is otherwise with regard to compacts of cultivation, which are invalid unless a period be settled; because the time of commencing the cultivation differs greatly, some crops being sown during the autumn, some during the winter, and others during the spring; and as there is thus a difference in the time of beginning the cultivation, the period of its ending can not be known, for the ending depends on the beginning.

Except where the trees are newly planted. —It is also otherwise in case of gardening, where one man delivers to another his young trees newly planted, for in that case the compact is not valid unless a period be fixed, it being very uncertain when the trees may arrive at that stage in which they are capable of bearing fruit, as that is a circumstance which depends on the strength and fertility of the soil.

Or, *where the compact is declared to be for as long trees, &c., shall last,*—It is also otherwise, where a man delivers to another his date garden, his herb roots, desiring him to water and nourish them always until they die, or until their roots be pulled, and their vegetation be thereby terminated,—or where he sets no bounds whatever to the duration of the compact with respect to the herbs; for in this case the compact is invalid, its period, being uncertain, because herbs grow as long as their roots are suffered to remain in the ground.

The specification of too short a term invalidates the compact.—If the parties, in a compact of gardening, settle a period during which it is certain that the trees cannot bear fruit, it is invalid; because the object of such compact, which is a partnership in the produce, is thus defeated

But not where it is possible that the end of it may be answered within that period.—If the parties settle a period during which the trees may bear fruit, although they be frequently later in bearing, it is valid, because the object of the compact is not to a certainty defeated in this instance. If, therefore, the trees bear fruit within the prescribed term, it belongs to them both in the proportions which they may have previously settled; or, if they should not yield fruit until after it is expired, the gardener is entitled to a suitable hire for his labour because the compact has in this case been rendered abortive by the error of the parties, in fixing a period too short for the trees to yield fruit, and which invalidates the compact in the same manner as if it had been known to be too short at the beginning. It is otherwise, however, if the trees afterwards yield no fruit; for in that case it is supposed owing to a blight, and not to the shortness of the period, that the compact proves abortive; the compact therefore holds good, and neither of the parties is entitled to receive any thing from the other.

The compact is valid, with respect to fruit trees, vines, herbs, and roots.—Compacts of gardening are lawful with respect to date-trees, vines &c., and also with respect to herbs and roots. According to the first opinion of Shafei, they are lawful with respect to date-trees and vines only; because the validity of such compacts is founded on the sentence of the Prophet regarding Kheebir, which is confined solely to these two. The argument of our doctors is, that the validity of such compacts is founded on their utility, and consequently is established regarding other things as well as dates and vines;—and in answer to Shafei, it is observed, that the sentence of the Koran regarding Kheebir does not admit of so confined a construction; for the inhabitants of that country cultivated all kinds of trees and herbs.

The compact cannot be dissolved by either party, but under some plea or pretext.—The proprietor of the orchard cannot dissolve the compact unless he have some plea for so

* It would appear that this opinion of Shafei is introduced merely for the purpose of elucidation, as it is not opposed to any different opinions, and his doctrines are seldom adduced in practice by the followers of Alee.

† Meaning such vegetables as renovate from the root every season.

doing, such as when the claims of his creditors oblige him to sell it. In the same manner also, the gardener cannot cease to work, and thereby dissolve the compact unless he adduce some plea, such as sickness. It is otherwise in compacts of cultivation; for (as has been already observed) in those instances the party who supplies the seed is at liberty to dissolve the compact at any time previous to the sowing.

A compact may be entered into whilst the fruit is green: but not after it is ripe.—IF two men enter into a compact of gardening, to the effect, that the one shall deliver over to the other his date orchard, at a time when the fruit has already appeared, but is, still very small, and may, by watering and proper care, become full and large, it is valid;—whereas, if the fruit were arrived at perfection, and were incapable of being further improved by care, it would be invalid. In the same manner also, if two men enter into a compact of cultivation, by which it is agreed, that the one shall deliver over to the other his crop, being yet green, and unfit for reaping, the compact is valid; whereas if the crop be fit for reaping it is invalid. The reason of this is, that the labourer is entitled to a share of the produce on account of his labour; but if the compact were to hold good when his labour can have no effect, he would be entitled to a share without labour, and this is not admitted in this Law.

If the compact be invalid, the gardener gets wages.—WHEN compacts of gardening are invalid, the gardener is entitled to suitable wages, as an invalid compact of gardening is equivalent to an invalid contract of hire, and therefore resembles an invalid compact of cultivation.

The compact is annulled by the decease of either party.—Rules in case of the proprietor dying.—IF, in a compact of gardening, one of the parties should die, the compact becomes null, because it is in reality a contract of hire.—If the owner of the orchard die whilst the fruit is yet green, the gardener may continue to work as usual until it be ripe, notwithstanding the dissent of the heirs. —(This proceeds upon a favourable construction for by continuing the compact, the gardener is prevented from suffering an injury, and none is occasioned to the heirs)—But if the gardener should rather choose to submit to the injury, the heirs have in that case three things at their option;—in other words, they may either divide the green fruit, agreeably to the proportion stipulated, —or, they may keep the whole of the green fruit, and pay to the gardener the value of his proportion,—or, lastly, they may take care of the fruit until it be ripe, and expend such sums as may be necessary for that purpose, and afterwards recover a proportionable part of the expense from the share of the gardener—for the gardener is not at liberty to occasion an injury to the heirs.

Rules in case of the gardener dying.—IF the gardener die, his heirs may continue to work, although the proprietor should not consent thereto, because it tends to their mutual benefit. If, on the contrary, the heirs of the gardener decline working, and rather choose to gather the fruit whilst it is still green, the proprietor of the orchard has the three things in his option, as mentioned above.

Rule in case of both parties dying.—IF both the parties die, the heirs of the gardener may continue to work; for as, if the gardener had lived, and the proprietor of the orchard had died, he [the gardener] might have continued to work, it follows that his heirs, as being his substitutes, have the same thing in their option. If, however, they should decline it, the heirs of the proprietor are in that case at liberty to pursue either of the three ways above mentioned

Rule in case of the compact expiring whilst the fruit is yet green.—IF the term of the compact should expire whilst the fruit is still green and unripe; the gardener may continue in his employment until it become ripe; and in this case he is not liable for any rent on account of the trees, the letting of trees being unlawful. It is otherwise with respect to compacts of cultivation; for if their term expire whilst the crop is yet green, the cultivator may continue to work until it be fit for reaping.—but he is liable for the rent of the ground, the letting of ground being lawful.

IF the term of a compact of gardening expire at a time when the fruit is still green; the gardener alone is obliged to perform the rest of the work; whereas, on the contrary, if the term of a compact of cultivations expire at a time when the crop is still green, both parties are obliged to work until the crop be brought to maturity.—The reason of this distinction is that, in compacts of cultivation, the cultivator being liable for the rent of the ground after the expiration of the term of the compact, it would be unjust that he alone should afterwards perform the labour; whereas, in cases of compacts of gardening, the gardener, as not being liable for any rent is obliged to perform the work alone, after the expiration of the term, in the same manner as before

The compact may be dissolved by any plea or pretext.—COMPACTS of gardening may be dissolved by particular pleas,—such as where the gardener is a thief, and there is reason to be apprehensive of his stealing the branches or leaves of the date trees, or the fruit, before it is ripe,—or, where he [the gardener] is disabled from working by sickness.

A question has arisen whether, if the gardener be desirous of relinquishing his work, it is lawful for him so to do?—concerning which two opinions are recorded, ONE, that it is lawful; and ANOTHER, that it is not so, —This apparent difference may, however, be reconciled, by supposing that the former opinion alludes to cases wherein it is stipulated that the gardener shall work with his own hands, which condition he is, by reason of sickness, unable to fulfil.

A lease of open land, for planting, in consideration of a part of the produce, is invalid.—If a man deliver to another a piece of open ground, for a certain number of years, that he may plant trees thereon, and stipulate that the trees and the ground shall be in partnership between them, each holding a half,—it is invalid, for two reasons; First, because they have stipulated a partnership in the ground, being a thing which already exists without the previous aid of the gardener's labour: and Secondly, because such a compact is liable to the same objection as Kafeez Tehan; for in this instance the master of the orchard in effect hires the gardener, and settles, as his wages, a part of the thing produced by his labour, namely, one half of the trees.—In this case, therefore, the whole of the fruit and trees go to the master of the ground; and the gardener is entitled to the price of his trees, and also to an adequate consideration as the hire of his labour; for as it is impossible to restore to him the trees, because of their adhesion to the ground, he necessarily gets their value, and also an adequate hire;—nor is his hire included in what he receives for the trees; that is to say, they are both due, distinctly; the use of labour being in this case of itself capable of estimation.

BOOK XLII.

OF ZABBAH OR THE SLAYING OF ANIMALS FOR FOOD.*

All animals killed for food, except fish and locusts must be slain by Zabbah.—All animals, the flesh of which is eatable, except fish and locusts, are unlawful, unless they be slain by Zabbah:—but when slain by Zabbah they are lawful, as by means of Zabbah the unclean blood is separated from the clean flesh,—whence it is that all animals not eatable (such as rats, dogs, or cats), are rendered clean† by Zabbah, excepting only hogs and men.

Zabbah is of two kinds, by choice, and of necessity.—Zabbah is of two kinds;—I. Ikhtiaree, or of choice (that is, voluntary, or at pleasure), which is effected by cutting the throat above the breast;—and II. Iztiraree, or of necessity (that is, at random, from necessity), which may be affected by a wound on any part of the animal's body.—The latter kind, however, is merely a substitute for the former, and accordingly is not of any account unless the former be impracticable, as the former is more effectual in extracting the blood; but the latter suffices where the other is impracticable; as mankind are required to act only according to their ability.

It must be performed by a Mussulman, or a Kitabee.—It is one of the laws of Zabbah that the person who performs it be either a Mussulman or Kitabee.—The Zabbah of a Mussulman is therefore lawful; and so also the Zabbah of a Kitabee, although he should not be a subject of a Mussulman state,—provided, however, that it be done in the name of God, for in the Koran we find these words, "The victuals of Kitabees are lawful to you."

Provided he be a person acquainted with the form of invocation, whether man or woman, infant or idiot.—The Zabbah is lawful provided the slayer be acquainted with the form of the Tasmeea, or invocation in the name of God, the nature of Zabbah, and the method of cutting the veins of the animal; and it signifies not whether the person be a man or a woman, an infant or an idiot, a circumcised person or an uncircumcised.

It cannot be performed by a Magian.—An animal slain by a Magian is unlawful; because the Prophet has said. "Ye may deal with them as well as with Kitabees; but ye must not marry their women, nor eat of animals slain by them;"—and also, because a Magian is a polytheist, and does not acknowledge the unity of God.

An apostate.—The Zabbah performed by an apostate is unlawful; because he is not permitted to continue in the faith to which he has turned, but must rather suffer death. —It is otherwise with respect to a Kitabee; for if he change his religion, he is permitted (according to our doctors) to continue in that which he has adopted; and the law will still consider him, with respect to Zabbah, in the same light as the people of that faith which he has embraced.

Or an idolater.—The Zabbah of an idolater is unlawful; because he does not believe in the Prophets.

Games slain in any place by a Mohrim is unlawful, or slain by any other person in holy ground.—Any species of game slain by a Mohrim* is unlawful, although it be not slain within the holy territory:†—and in the

* The Arabic lexicographers define Zabbah to signify, in its literal sense, the act of cutting the throat; in the language of the law it denotes the act of slaying an animal agreeably to the prescribed forms, without which it is not considered as eatable.

† That is to say, their flesh may be used in medical compositions; but still it cannot be eaten as ordinary food.

* The appellation given to a pilgrim during his residence at Mecca—It is also applied to any person who; having resolved to undertake a pilgrimage, lays himself under particular restrictions.

† Arab. Arzal haram: the territory in the neighbourhood of Mecca, where no animal of the game species is ever put to death.

same manner, any game slain in the holy territory is unlawful, although the slayer be not a Mohrim. It is otherwise where a Mohrim or any other person, slays an animal that is not game either in the holy territory or in any other place; for this is sanctioned by the LAW, because the holy territory affords no protection to goats, and the slaying of goats by a Mohrim is not prohibited.

Rules with respect to the Tasmeea or invocation.—IF the slayer wilfully omit the Tasmeea, or invocation "in the name of GOD," the animal‡ is carrion, and must not be eaten. If, however, he omit the invocation through forgetfulness, it is lawful, in either case.—Malik, on the contrary, maintains that it is unlawful in both; and that Mussulmans and Kitabees are considered as the same, with respect to the omission of the invocation. The same difference is to be found in the opinions of our doctors concerning a man omitting the invocation on letting loose a hound or flying a hawk at game, or when he shoots his arrow. The opinion of Shafei, in this particular, is opposite to that of all our sages; for, previous to his time, it was the universally allowed opinion, that an animal slain under a wilful omission of the invocation was unlawful; the only point on which they differed being respecting the omission of it from forgetfulness. The sect of Abdoola Ibn Omar were of opinion that an animal slain under an omission of the invocation from forgetfulness is also unlawful; whilst, on the contrary, the sects of Alee and Ibn Abbas deemed it lawful, but not under an omission made wilfully.—Hence Aboo Yoosaf and the other Haneefite doctors have declared an animal slain under a wilful omission of the invocation to be utterly unlawful: and that the Kazee cannot authorize the sale of meat so killed, it being contrary to the current opinions of all our doctors. The arguments of Shafei on this point are twofold. FIRST, the Prophet has said, "Let MUSSULMANS slay in the name of GOD, whether they mention it with their tongues or not,"—SECONDLY, If the invocation were essential to the legality of the animal, it could never be remitted on a plea of forgetfulness, any more that the purification essential to prayer.—Besides, admitting the invocation to be essential, still the Mussulman faith is a substitute for it, in the same manner as in a case of omission through forgetfulness. The arguments of our doctors, on the other hand, are twofold. FIRST, GOD has said, in the KORAN, "EAT NOT ANY THING OVER WHICH THE NAME OF GOD HAS NOT BEEN MENTIONED."—SECONDLY, it is the universal opinion, as has been already remarked.—SECONDLY, the Prophet has said, regarding Addee the son of Hatim, "When thou hast let loose thy hound after game, and repeated the name of GOD, thou mayest eat of that game; but if another dog assist thine in killing the game thou shalt not eat of it, because thou repeatedst the name of GOD over thine own dog and not over the other:" it is therefore evident that the omission of the name of GOD renders the game unlawful. The argument of Malik is founded upon a literal construction of the passage of the KORAN, which we have quoted above, it not being particularly expressed therein that the wilful omission is unlawful, and the omission from forgetfulness lawful. But the answer which we give to this argument is that the passage plainly alludes to an animal with respect to which the invocation has been wilfully omitted, the latter being here different from the spirit of the text, for if the spirit were according to the latter; the companions of the Prophet (who hold the first rank in point of authority) would doubtless have drawn arguments from it, and the difference of opinion that is to be found amongst them would not have existed. The answer to Shafei is, that the analogy which he establishes betwixt wilful omission and omission from forgetfulness; is not just: because he that forgets acts under necessity, and the Mussulman faith is admitted as a substitute in his behalf; whereas he who wilfully omits acts under no necessity.—With respect, moreover, to the saying of the Prophet quoted by Shafei, it evidently alludes to a case of omission through forgetfulness.

In the first species of Zabbah, it must be pronounced whilst the animal's throat is cutting; and in the second species, upon shooting the arrow, or letting loose the dog or hawk at the game.—IT is a condition of Ikhtiaree Zabbah, that the invocation be pronounced over the animal at the time of slaying it.—whereas, in the case of Zabbah Iztiraree (or of a man slaying an animal in hunting), the condition is that the invocation be pronounced at the time of letting loose the hound or hawk, or shooting the arrow, which is termed an invocation over the instrument. The reason of this distinction is, that in the first case the power of the man extends to the slaying; whereas in the second it is confined to the act of letting loose the hound or hawk, or of shooting the arrow, and does not extend to their reaching the animal; wherefore the invocation must be pronouced at the instant of such act, which is in the power of the man.—Hence if a man throw a goat on its side; with an intention of slaying it, and then pronounce the invocation, and afterwards let that goat loose, and then, without repeating the invocation, slay another, this is not admissible, and the meat is unlawful; whereas if a man shoot an arrow at an animal, and pronounce the invocation, and the arrow, instead of the one which he aimed at, hit another animal, it is lawful;—and the same law holds in the case of letting loose a hound or hawk.—If the man, having thrown the animal on its side and pronounced

‡ Arab. Zabeeha, meaning (literally) the creature slain

the invocation, should cast away the knife from his hand and take up another, and with it slay the animal, it is lawful;—whereas if he pronounce the invocation over one arrow, and then take another and shoot the game with it, it is unlawful, the instrument over which the invocation was pronounced having been changed.

It is abominable to add any other thing to the name of God at the time of performing the Zabbah, such as if a man were to say "O God, accept this from me!"—This may occur in three different shapes; as first; where he says anything besides the name of God, without pausing between them, or making use of the conjunction "and," as in the example cited above,—or, where he says, Bism Illah, Mohammed Rassool Illah, "in the name of God, Mohammad is His Prophet," which would be abominable, but the meat would not be unlawful;—secondly, where he says anything besides the name of God, without making a pause, but using the conjunction; as if he were to say, "Bism Illah wa Ism Falan," "in the name of God and the name of another;" or "Bism Illah wa Falan," "in the name of God and another;"—in either of which case the animal slain is unlawful; and, thirdly, where he says anything besides the name of God, separately, and by itself, either before or after the invocation, and the throwing down of the animal, which is of no consequence, and does not render the meat unlawful for it is related of the Prophet, that he said prayers immediately after performing Zabbah.

Nothing must be said except the invocation—It is a condition of Zabbah that nothing but the invocation be said: that is, that no prayer or other matter be mentioned. If, therefore, a man, during the Zabbah, instead of "Bism Illah" ("in the name of God"), were to say, "Illahoom agfar lee," ("O God, forgive me!") the animal slain is not lawful, as this is a prayer or entreaty. If, however, instead of "Bism Illah," he say "Alhumdolillah" ("praise be to God"), or "Subhanillah" ("God is purest"), and mean this as an invocation it is sufficient. But if he sneeze during the Zabbah, and exclaims "Alhumdolillah!" ("praise be to God!") it is not sufficient (according to the Rawayet-Saheeh), because the exclamation will then be considered as thanks, and not as the invocation. The method which has frequently prevailed of saying "Bism Illah or Illa Akbaro" ("in the name of God, and God is the highest"), during the Zabbah, is copied from Ibn Abbas.

Proper method of slaying animals.—The place for slaying is betwixt the throat and the libba [the head of the breast-bone] because the blood freely issues from a wound given in that place: the Zabbah, therefore, when performed anywhere within that space, is lawful.

The vessels which it is requisite to cut in Zabbah are four; namely, the Halkoom, or windpipe; the Mirree, or gullet; and the Wadijan, or two jugular veins.—This is founded on a saying of the Prophet. According to Shafei it is sufficient if two of these vessels (namely, the windpipe and gullet) be cut. According to Malik, on the contrary, three of the four do not suffice, but it is requisite that they be all cut. According to Haneefa the animal is lawful where three of the four vessels are cut, whichever they may be. Aboo Yoosaf was also at first of this opinion; but he afterwards declared it indispensably requisite that the windpipe and gullet should be cut, and one of the two blood-vessels: because as the effusion of the blood is the design of cutting the blood-vessels, one of them may serve as a substitute for the other:—but as the gullet and windpipe, on the contrary, answer two different purposes (the one being the channel of food, and the other the channel of respiration), it is requisite therefore that they be both cut, the one being unfit to stand in the place of the other. The argument of Haneefa is that the majority represents the whole in many rules of the LAW; and when three of the four vessels are cut, the majority is cut, and the object (which is the speedy effusion of the blood and deprivation of life) is effected, since upon three of the above-mentioned vessels being cut, the animal cannot remain alive. If, therefore, to avoid giving additional pain, only three vessels be cut, it is sufficient.—It is otherwise where only two are cut; for as, in that case, a cutting of the majority, representing a cutting of the whole, does not exist, it follows that the animal so slain is not lawful—Mohammed is of opinion that the greater part of each of the four vessels should be cut, because every one of them may be considered as a principal of itself, being separated from the rest. In the Jama Sagheer, also, he alleges that if one half of the windpipe, and one half of each of the blood-vessels, be cut, the animal is not lawful; but that if the greater part of the windpipe, and the greater part of each of the blood-vessels be cut, previous to the death of the animal, it is lawful;—and he has not made mention of any difference of opinion.

It may be performed with nails, horns, or teeth (detached from their native place).—If a man slay an animal with nails, horns, or teeth it may be eaten without apprehension, provided the nails, horns, or teeth be detached from the place in which they grew. The act, however, is abominable,* because it introduces the use of human members, and further, because it is productive of too much pain to the animal, and we are directed to perform the Zabbah in such a manner as may be most easy to it. Shafei is of opinion that an animal slain in the above manner is

* The force of this term is explained in a note a little farther on.

unlawful, and carrion; because the Prophet has said, "the ZABBAH is lawful when performed with any thing that can draw blood, or cut the vessels, excepting the teeth and the nails, which are the instruments of the ABYSSINIANS;"* and also, because it is a thing not allowed by the LAW any more than if the teeth or nails had been fixed in the place in which they grew. Our arguments, on the contrary, are that the Prophet has said, "Spill the blood with whatever thing it may please thee;" and it is likewise related that he said, "Cut the vessels with what thing soever thou pleasest." With respect to the saying quoted by Shafei, it alludes to nails and teeth fixed in their native place; for it was a frequent custom amongst the Abyssinians to slay cattle in that manner. —Nails, moreover, when removed from their place, are instruments for cutting; and the object of Zabbah, namely, the effusion of the blood, may be accomplished with them, whence they are the same as a sharp iron or stone. But when they are in their place they slay by means of the force or weight applied to them, and the animal so slain is, in effect, strangled.

Or with any sharp instrument.—IT is lawful to slay with the kind of a reed, with a sharp stone, and with every thing that is sharp and capable of cutting the vessels and drawing the blood excepting teeth and nails fixed in their native place.

Precautions to be observed by the slayer.—IT is laydable in the slayer to sharpen his knife; for the Prophet has said, "GOD has enjoined us to be merciful to all; wherefore, when ye slay, let it be done in the most merciful manner; and when ye perform the ZABBAH, let one of ye sharpen your knife and do it in the easiest manner for the animal.

IT is abominable first to throw the animal down on its side, and then to sharpen the knife; for it is related that the Prophet once observing a man who had done so, said to him, "How many deaths do you intend that this animal should die?—Why did you not sharpen your knife before you threw it down?"

IT is abominable to let the knife reach the spinal marrow, or to cut off the head of the animal. The meat, however, in either of these cases is lawful. The reasons of the abomination in cutting into the spinal marrow are, FIRST, because the Prophet has forbid this; and, SECONDLY, because it unnecessarily augments the pain of the animal, which is prohibited in our LAW.—In short, everything which unnecessarily augments the pain of the animal Zabbah is abominable.

IT is abominable to seize an animal destined for slaughter by the feet, and drag it to the place appointed for slaying it.

IT is abominable to break the neck of the animal whilst it is in the struggles of death; but when the struggles are over it is not abominable to break the neck and strip off the skin, for then it is insensible to pain.

The animal is lawful although it be wounded previous to cutting its throat—IF a man slay an animal by first cutting it in the back of the neck, doing it, however, in such a manner as to cut the vessels whilst the animal is still alive, the meat is lawful, because the animal dies by Zabbah: but the act itself is abominable, as it unnecessarily augments the pain of the animal, being in effect the same as if he had first wounded the animal, and afterwards cut its vessels. If, on the contrary, the animal die previous to the cutting of the vessels, the meat is not lawful, because in this case the animal dies before the Zabbah has taken place.

All tame animals must be slain by cutting the throat; and wild animals by chasing or shooting them.—IN the case of all animals attached to man, and which do not fly from him, the Zabbah is performed by cutting the vessels:—but in the case of those which have become wild, and fly from him, the Zabbah is performed by chasing and wounding them; because where the Zabbah Ikhtiaree, or Zabbah of choice, is impracticable, there is occasion for the Zabbah Iztiraree, or Zabbah of necessity; and there is such an impracticability regarding the latter class of animals, but not regarding the former. The Zabbah Iztiraree is also lawful regarding an animal which has fallen into a well, provided the other sort of Zabbah be impracticable.—Malik maintains that the meat is unlawful in both the foregoing cases,—that is, in the case of a wild animal, and of one which falls into a well,—because such instances are rare. We, again, say that as the impracticability of the Zabbah Ikhtiaree (which is allowed to be a valid argument), exists in both these cases, it follows that the substitute, namely, Zabbah Iztiraree, may be adopted: nor is what he observes (that "such instances are rare") admitted: on the contrary, they very frequently happen. In Kadooree, moreover it is expressly said that it is lawful to use the Iztiraree Zabbah towards all animals that fly from man;—and it is reported, from Mohammed, that if a goat become wild in the plains, the Iztiraree Zabbah is lawful with respect to it; but if it become wild in the city, the Iztiraree Zabbah is not lawful, because in the city it may be caught, and consequently the Ikhtiaree Zabbah is not impracticable. With respect to cows and camels; however, the city and plains are alike; because these animals attack, with their horns or their teeth, any person that attempts to catch them; whence it is impossible to catch them, even though it be in the midst of the city that they have become wild; and the Ikhtiaree Zabbah is therefore impracticable. When, also, these animals attack a man, they are considered as wild, provided it be not in his

* The Abyssinians are held in great contempt by the Mussulmans.

power to catch them; wherefore if one of them should attack a man, and he with an intention of Zabbah kill it, the flesh of it may be eaten lawfully.

Camels must be slain by Nahr, rather than by Zabbah.—THE most eligible method of slaying a camel is by Nahr, that is, spearing it in the hollow of the throat, near the breast-bone, because this is agreeable to the Sonna, and also because in that part of the throat the vessels of a camel are combined. It is also lawful to slay it by Zabbah, although this be considered as abominable, since it differs from the Sonna. In regard to goats and oxen, it is most eligible to slay them by Zabbah, as being agreeable to the Soona, and also because the vessels of a goat are assembled together in the upper part of the throat:—but they may also be speared like a camel, although this method be not approved, as being contrary to the Sonna.

The fœtus of a slain animal is not lawful. IF a person, having slain a camel or cow, should find a dead fœtus in the womb, such fœtus is unlawful, whether it be covered with hair or not. This is the opinion of Haneefa; and it has been adopted by Ziffer and Hasan bin Zeeyad. The two disciples maintain that if the fœtus be complete in its form, it is lawful, (and Shafei concurs with them in this opinion); because the Prophet has ordained the Zabbah of a fœtus to be the Zabbah of the mother; that is to say, the Zabbah of the mother answers for that of the fœtus likewise. Besides, the fœtus is, in reality, a constituent part of the mother, as it is joined to her until separated by a pair of scissors or knife subsists on the same food, and lives by the same breath;—and it is likewise considered as such in law, insomuch that it is included in the sale of the mother, and is rendered free by the emancipation of the mother. The fœtus, therefore, being a constituent part of the mother, it follows that the Zabbah of the mother serves also for it, when a separate Zabbah is impracticable, in the same manner as a wound in the case of game serves as a substitute for Zabhah. Haneefa, on the other hand, argues that a foœtus if complete with respect to life; that is to say, that it has a separate existence, inasmuch as it may surive after the death of the mother, whence it is that a separate Zabbah is necessary, in case of its being alive. Moreover, if a person destroy a fœetus he is subject to a pecuniary penalty; and the owner of it may emancipate it alone, without including the mother. It is also lawful to bequeath it in legacy, or to leave a legacy to it. Besides, the object of Zabbah is to separate the blood from the flesh; an object which cannot be accomplished, in the case of a fœtus, by the Zabbah of the mother alone. It is otherwise with respect to wounding game, as in that case the blood is separated from the flesh, and though it be in an imperfect manner, yet as any other mode is impracticable, it is therefore considered as Zabbah. A foetus, moreover, is included in the sale of the mother, because the sale would otherwise be invalid, and from this necessity it is included. And it is likewise rendered free by the manumission of the mother, in order that a bond-infant may not be born from a freed-woman.

Section

Of the Things which may lawfully be eaten, and of those which may not.

All beasts and birds of prey are unlawful.—ALL quadrupeds that seize their prey with their teeth, and all birds which seize it with their talons, are unlawful, the Prophet having prohibited mankind from eating them.—The reason of this prohibition is because MAN is held particularly dear, and it is to guard him, lest by eating of these animals their bad qualities might be communicated to him, and effect his disposition.

HYENAS and foxes, being both included under the class of animals of prey, are both unlawful.—(Shafei maintains that they are both lawful.)—Elephants and weasels are also accounted animals of prey:* and pelicans and kites are abominable, because they devour dead bodies.

Rocks are neuter: but carrion crows and ravens are unlawful.—Magpies, the crocodile, otter, all insects, and the ass and mule are unlawful:—CROWS which feed on grain [rooks] are neuter:†but the crow of the wilderness [the carrion crow] and the raven, are not lawful.—According to Haneefa the magpie is neuter, like poultry; although it be said (upon the authority of Aboo Yoosaf) that it is abominated, because it frequently eats dead bodies.—The crocodile and the otter, wasps, and in general all insects, are abominated. The ass and the mule are unlawful, because they are prohibited by the Prophet.—The flesh of horses is held in abomination by Haneefa and Malik. According to the two disciples and Shafei it is neuter: for it is mentioned in the Hadees Joabir that the Prophet permitted it; and some are of opinion that the milk of mares is also neuter.

Hares are neuter.—According to Haneefa, the flesh of hares is neuter, because the Prophet eat it, and commanded his companions to eat of it.

---

* Arab. Zoo-Nab; meaning, literally, creatures which have canine teeth. The elephant (although certainly not a beast of prey) is perhaps classed with those, because of his tusks.

† It is here proper to remark that, in the Mussulman law, there are four gradations from legality to illegality I. Hilal, or positively lawful. II, Mobah, or neuter (that is, indifferent, and which may either be pursued or avoided). III. Makrooh or abominable (that is, reprobated, but which is nevertheless lawful). IV. Hiram, or positively unlawful (that is, prohibited).

THE flesh and skin of all unlawful animals become pure after they have been killed according to the laws of Zabbah, excepting only men and hogs.—According to Shafei they do not become pure.

No aquatic animal is lawful except fish.—No animal that lives in water is lawful except fish. Malik and and number of other learned men are of opinion that all water animals are lawful, others again say that sea-dogs, sea-hogs, and mair-men, are unlawful.

Fish which perish of themselves are not lawful.—FISHES which, dying of themselves, float upon the surface of the water, are abominated. According to Shafei and Malik they are neuter. The rule observed amongst our sect is this.—Fishes which are killed by any accident are lawful, like those which are caught; whilst, on the contrary, such as die of themselves without any accident are unlawful, like those which are found floating on the surface of the water. There are, however, different opinions regarding such as die of extreme heat or cold. Fishes and locusts are lawful without being killed by Zabbah.

BOOK XLIII.

OF UZHEEA, OR SACRIFICE

Sacrifice must be performed at the Yd. Kirban.—IT is the duty of every free Mussulman, arrived at the age of maturity to offer a sacrifice on the Yd Kirban, or festival of the sacrifice,* provided he be then possessed of a Nisab,† and be not a traveller. This is the opinion of Haneefa, Mohammed, Ziffer and Hasan; and likewise that of Aboo Yoosaf, according to one tradition, and also in the opinion of Shafei, sacrifice is not an indispensable duty, but only laudable. Tahavee reports that in the opinion of Haneefa it is indispensable; whilst the two disciples hold it to be in a strong degree laudable.

It is incumbent on a man, for himself, and for his infant children.—THE offering of a sacrifice is incumbent on a man on account of himself, and on account of his infant child. This is the opinion of Haneefa in one tradition. In another (which is recorded in the Zahir Zawayet) he has said that it is not incumbent on a man to offer a sacrifice for his child.—In fact, according to Haneefa and Aboo Yoosaf, a father or guardian are to offer a sacrifice at the expense of the child, where he is possessed of property), eating what parts of it are eatable, and selling the remaining parts that are valuable in their substance) such as the skin, &c Mohammed, Ziffer, and Shafei, have said that a father is to sacrifice on account of his child at his own expense, and not at that of the child.

The victim for one person is a goat; and for any number from one to seven, a cow or camel.—THE sacrifice established for one person is a goat; and that for seven, a cow or a camel.—IF a cow be sacrificed for any number of people fewer than seven, it is lawful; but it is otherwise if sacrificed on account of eight. If, also, in an association of seven people, the contribution of any one of them should be less than a seventh share, the sacrifice is not valid on the part of any.

An animal held in joint property may be jointly offered in sacrifice.—IF a camel that is jointly and in an equal degree the property of two men, should be sacrifised by them on their own account, it is lawful, according to the most authentic traditions:—and in this case they must divide the flesh by—weight, as flesh is an article of weight. If, on the contrary, they distribute it from conjectural estimation, it is not lawful; unless they add to each share of the flesh part of the head, neck, and joints.

Others may be admitted to a share in an animal purchased for sacrifice—IF a person purchase a cow, with an intent to sacrifice it on his own account, and he afterwards admit six others to an association with him in the sacrifice, it is lawful.—It, is however most adviseable that he associate with the others at the time of purchase, in order that the sacrifice may be valid in the opinion of all our doctors; as otherwise there is a difference of opinion.—It is related, from Haneefa, that it is abominable to admit others to share in a sacrifice after purchasing the animal; for, as the purchase was made with a view to devotion, the sale of it is therefore an abomination.

It is not incumbent on the poor or travellers—SACRIFICE is not incumbent on either a poor man or a traveller; for Aboo Bickir and Omar Farook did not offer the sacrifice of the Yd during their travels: and it is, moreover, related that Alee said, "neither the prayers of Friday, nor the sacrifice of the Yd are incumbent on travellers."

The time of performing it.—THE time of the offering is on the morning of the day of the festival; but it is not lawful for the inhabitants of a city to begin the sacrifice until their priest shall have finished the occasional prayers. Villagers, however, may begin after break of day. The place, in fact, must regulate the time. Thus, where the place of celebration is in the country, and the performers of it reside in the city, it is lawful to begin in the morning: but if otherwise, it must be deferred until the prayers be ended.

* This festival happens on the tenth of Zee-hidja, and was instituted in commemoration of Abraham having offered up his son Ishmael as a sacrifice to GOD, in consequence of a vision he had.—(See Sales's Koran, Vol, II. p. 312.)

† For the amount of Nisab, see Vol. I. p. 1 to 6

If the victim be slain after the prayers of the mosque, and prior to those offered at the place of sacrifice, it is lawful; as is likewise the reverse of this.

Sacrifice is lawful during three days,—that is, on the day of the festival, and on the two ensuing days. Shafei is of opinion, that it is lawful on the three ensuing days. The sacrifice of the day of the festival is, however, far superior to any of the others. It is also lawful to sacrifice on the nights of those days, although it be considered as abominable.—Moreover, the offering of sacrifices on these days is more laudable than the custom of omitting them, and afterwards bestowing an adequate sum upon the poor.

If the sacrifice be delayed beyond the proper time, the victim be bestowed in charity.—If a person neglect the performance of the sacrifice during the stated days, and have previously determined upon the offering of any particular goat, for instance; or, being poor, have purchased a goat for that purpose;—in either of these cases it is incumbent on him to bestow it alive in charity. But, if he be rich, it is in that case incumbent on him to bestow, in charity, a sum adequate to the price, whether he has purchased a goat with an intent to sacrifice it, or not.

The sacrifice of a blemished animal is not admitted.—It is not lawful to sacrifice animals that are blemished,—such as those that are blind, or lame, or so lean as to have no marrow in their bones, or having a great part of their ears or tail cut off. Such, however, as have a great part of their ears or tail remaining may lawfully be sacrificed.—Concerning the determination of a great part of any member, there are indeed various opinions reported from Haneefa.—In some animals he has determined it to be the third; in others more than the third; and in others, again, only the fourth.—In the opinion of the two disciples, if more than the half should remain, the sacrifice is valid; and this opinion has been adopted by the learned Aboo Lays.

But a trifling blemish does not render it exceptionable.—If an animal have lost the third of its tail, or the third of its ear, or eyesight, it may be lawfully sacrificed:—but if, in either of these cases, it should have lost more than a third, the offering of it is not lawful. The rule which our doctors have laid down to discover in what degree the eyesight is impaired, is as follows. The animal must first be deprived of its food for a day or two, that it may be rendered hungry; and having then covered the eye that is impaired, food must be gradually brought towards it, from a distance, until it indicate, by some emotion, that it has discovered it.—Having marked the particular spot at which it observed the food, and uncovered the weak eye, the perfect eye must then be bound, and the same process carried on, until it indicate that it has observed it with the defective eye. If then the particular distance from those parts to where the animal stood be measured, it may be known, from the proportion they bear to each other, in what degree the sight is impaired.

An animal wanting a horn, or mad, or castrated, may be sacrificed.—If a person sacrifice an animal without a horn, it is lawful;—and so likewise where the horn is broken, or where the animal is mad or castrated.—Many, however, have said, that it is not lawful to sacrifice a mad animal, unless it eat food, in the same manner as it is not lawful to sacrifice a Gurgeen [the offspring of a wolf and goat] unless it be fat. With regard to animals that want teeth, it is reported from Aboo Yoosaf that they may be lawfully sacrificed, provided they be able to chew.—or (according to another report) provided the greatest of their teeth be remaining. Animals, however, that are born without an ear cannot lawfully be sacrificed. What is here said respects such blemishes as may have existed in the animal previous to the purchase of it: for if it be perfect at the time of purchase, and afterwards contract such a blemish as to render the sacrifice of it unlawful, and the proprietor be rich, it is in that case incumbent on him to sacrifice another; whereas, if he be poor, he may lawfully sacrifice the same. The reason of this is, that as an offering is incumbent on a rich man originally, and not on account of his purchase, the animal, therefore, which he buys is not particularly set aside for the offering; whereas, on the contrary, an offering not being incumbent on a poor man, except when he purchases an animal with that intent, the animal so purchased is therefore particularly destined for the purpose:—and accordingly, our doctors hold that if an animal, purchased with a view to be offered, should die, it is incumbent on the proprietor, if he be rich, to substitute another, but not if he be poor;—or, if the animal be either lost or stolen, and the purchaser, having bought another, should then recover the first, in such case it is incumbent on the proprietor, if he be rich, to sacrifice one of them, whether it be the first bought or the second; but if he be poor, he is under an obligation to sacrifice both.

Any accident befalling the victim at the time of slaying it does not invalidate the sacrifice—If it should happen that the goat, having been turned over in order that the sacrifice might be performed, in the struggle breaks one of its legs, in that case, provided the sacrifice be immediately made it is lawful and sufficient. So also, it is lawful, if the animal, in that situation, having received any hurt, should run away, and having been immediately and without delay taken, should then be sacrificed. Mohammed has likewise judged the sacrifice lawful, if, in this case, the animal should not be retaken until after some delay;—in opposition to the opinion of Aboo Yoosaf.

Goats, camels, and cows alone are lawful

in sacrifice.—It is not lawful to offer a sacrifice of any animal except a camel, a cow, or a goat ; for it is not recorded that the Prophet or any of his companions ever sacrificed others. Buffaloes, however, are lawful, as being of the species of a cow. Every animal of a mixed breed, moreover, is considered as of the same species with the mother.

Age at which an animal is fit for sacrifice. The sacrifice is lawful of any animal of the three species above mentioned, although it be only a Soonee :* but not of younger ; excepting, however, a sheep, which may be sacrificed when a Judday, or so young as to have no teeth ; and in this case our doctors have made it a condition that the sheep be of large stature, insomuch as to have the appearance of a Soonee at a little distance. The period of Juddy in sheep (according to our doctors) is at the expiration of six months, and the commencement of the seventh. The time of Soonee in goats or sheep is at the age of one year ; in cows, at the age of two ; and in camels at the age of five years.

If one of seven joint sacrificers die, the consent of his heirs is requisite to the sacrifice.—If seven persons purchase a cow for sacrifice, and one of them afterwards die, and his heirs desire the other six to sacrifice a cow on account of themselves, and on account of the dead, it is lawful ;—whereas if they sacrifice it without the consent of the heirs it is not lawful.

If a Christian, or any person whose object is the flesh, and not the sacrifice, be a sharer with six ethers, the sacrlfice is not lawful on the part of any.

Rules with respect to the disposal of the flesh, &c , of the victim.—It is lawful for a person, who offers a sacrifice, either to eat the flesh, or to bestow it on whomsoever he please, whether rich or poor ; and he may also lay it up in store.

It is most advisable that the third part of the flesh of a sacrifice be bestowed in charity.

It is lawful either to bestow the skin of a sacrifice in charity, or to make any utensil of it, such as a bucket, sieve, or the like. It is likewise lawful to barter it for any unconsumable article that yields profit in its substance ;—but it it not allowable to barter it for any thing consumable, as vinegar, and such like. Flesh, in these respects, is considered in the same light as the skin, according to the most authentic traditions.

If the flesh of a sacrifice be sold along with the skin of it for money, or for any thing that is not profitable but in consumption, it is incumbent on the seller to devote the price to the poor ; and the sale is valid.

It is not lawful to give a part of the sacrifice in payment to the butcher.

*The sheep and the goat are held to be of the same species.

It is abominable to take the wool of the victim and sell it before the sacrifice be performed ; but not after the sacrifice. In the same manner, it is abominable to milk the victim and sell the milk.

It must be slain by the sacrificer, or in his presence.—It is most advisable that the persons who offers the sacrifice should himself perform it, provided he be well acquainted with the method ; but if he should not be expert at it, it is then advisable that he take the assistance of another, and be present at the operation.

A Kitabee may be employed to slay it, but not a Magian.—It is abominable to commit the slaying of the victim to a Kitabee. If, however, a person order a Kitabee to slay his victim, it is lawful. It is otherwise where a person orders a Magian, or worshipper of fire, to slay his victim, for this is inadmissible.

Two persons slaying each other's victim by mistake must make a mutual compensation.—If two persons commit a mistake, each slaying the offering of the other, it is lawful ; and no compensation is on that account due from either. If, also, having erred in this manner, they should eat the flesh, and then discover the mistake, in this case it is requesite that they sanctify the act of each other, and sacrifice is then fulfilled. If, on the contarary, they refuse to do so, and dispute the matter, each is in that case entitled to take a compensation for the value of the flesh of his offering from the other and must then bestow such compensation in alms, as it is a return for the flesh of his offering : and the same rule also obtains where a person destroys the flesh of the offering of another.

Case of sacrifice of an usurped animal.—If a person usurp a goat and sacrifice it, he is in that case bound to compensate for its value, and his offering is thereby rendered valid ; because upon paying the compensation he is held to have been proprietor of the goat from the time of his having usurped it. It is otherwise where a person sacrifices a goat committed to him as a deposit ; for this is not valid ; because he is obliged to compensate for it (not on account of the animal, but) on account of the sacrifice, and hence his property in it is not established until after he has sacrificed it.

BOOK XLIV

OF KIRAHEEAT OR ABOMINATIONS

Difference of opinions concerning the extent of the term Makrooh.—The author of the Hedaya remarks that our doctors have disagreed concerning the extent in which the term Makrooh* is to be received — Mohammed was of opinion that every thing Makrooh is unlawful; but as he could not draw any convincing argument from the sacred writings in favour of this opinion, he renounced the general application of unlawfulness, with respect to such articles, and classed them under the particular description of Makrooh, or abominable. It is recorded, on the other hand, from Haneefa and Aboo Yoosaf, that Makrooh applies to any thing which, in its qualities, nearly approaches to unlawful, without being actually so.—This article is comprehended under a variety of heads or sections.

Section I.
Of Eating and Drinking

It is abominable to eat the flesh or to drink the milk of an ass, or to take the urine of a camel, unless medicinally.—Haneefa has said that the flesh and milk of an ass, and the urine or a camel are abominable.—According to Aboo Yoosaf the urine of a camel may be taken as a medicine; but with respect to milk, it is a secretion from the blood, and is therefore subject to the same rule with the flesh of the animal from which it is produced.

Or to use vessels of gold or silver.—It is not allowable, either to men or women, to use a vessel of gold or silver in eating, drinking, or in keeping perfumes; because the Prophet has said, with respect to any person who drinks out of a vessel of silver or gold, that "the fire of hell shall enter into his belly:" and it is also related, that a person having brought water for Aboo Hareefa in a silver vessel, he refused to drink, declaring that the Prophet had prohibited him from drinking out of such a vessel. The prohibition, therefore, being established with respect to drinking, it follows that the rule extends to the using of oils, and similar articles, that being in effect the same with drinking, since in both cases the use of a vessel of gold or silver is induced,—whence it is that the use of a golden or silver spoon is abominable, as also the use of a silver or golden bodkin for drawing antimony along the eyelids, or of boxes for holding antimony, or any other thing, made of those metals.

It is allowable to use vessels of lead, glass, crystal, or agate.—The use of vessels of lead, glass, crystal, and agate, is permitted. Shafei maintains that those are abominable, because they resemble gold or silver in point of splendour.

Or to drink out of vessels, or ride upon a saddle, or sit upon a chair or sofa, ornamented with gold or silver.—It is allowable, according to Haneefa, to drink out of a wooden vessel ornamented with silver, provided the particular part to which the lip is applied be void of it. In the same manner, also, it is permitted to ride upon a saddle interwoven with silver, provided the space allotted for the seat be plain; and this rule likewise holds with reepect to a couch or sofa. —According to Aboo Yoosaf, on the contrary, all those are abominable.—From Mohammed there are two traditions on this point; one corresponding with the opinion of Haneefa, and the other with that of Aboo Yoosaf. After the same manner they have disagreed concerning the use of a vessel or chair adorned both with gold and silver; concerning swords mosques, frames of glasses, and books, when they are ornamented either with gold or silver; and also concerning stirrups, bridles, or cruppers of that description.—These differences of opinion, however, exist only where the gold and silver is so applied, in any of these cases, that it is to be separated only by means of some difficult process; but the gilding of things, either with gold or silver, in such a manner as to require art to separate it, is unanimously allowed.—The argument of the two disciples is that the use of one part of a vessel includes the use of the whole; wherefore they hold it equally abominable as if the part applied to use were likewise of gold or silver. Haneefa, on the other hand, argues that ornaments of gold or silver, when not applied to use, are merely appendages, and therefore not to be regarded; whence the use of the article is allowable, in the same manner as wearing a garment which is trimmed with silk, or a ring which has a piece of gold set in it.

The information of an infidel may be credited with regard to the lawfulness of any particular food.—If a person send his servant, or a hireling, being a Magian, to purchase meat, and he purchase meat accordingly, and acquaint his master that he had bought it from a Jew, a Christian, or a Mussulman, it is lawful for him [the master] to eat the food so purchased: because the word of an infidel is creditable in all matters of a temporal nature, as he is presumed to be possessed of reason, and falsehood is prohibited in his religion: besides, there is a necessity for believing his assertion in temporal concerns, from their frequent occurrence. If, on the contrary, the servant inform his master, that "he purchased the meat from an infidel who is not a scripturist, and it was slain by one who was neither a scripturist nor a Mussulman," it is in that case unlawful for the master to eat the flesh so purchased; for as the word of an infidel is credited with respect to the legality of meat, it is credited with respect to the illegality, in a superior degree.

A present may be accepted by the hands of a slave or an infant.—If a slave, either male or female, or an infant, should carry something to a person, saying, "such an one has sent this to you as a present," in that case

* Makrooh is the participle passive of Kuriha, to abominate; this word is frequently taken in a milder sence; and may relate to any thing improper or unbecoming.

the person may justly credit the information, as it is a frequent custom to send presents by such messengers. In the same manner, if either of these should intimate to a slave that his master had given him a licence to trade, he is allowed, accordingly, to accept of it: because it is perhaps impossible for them to bring witnesses to attest the intention of the master, whence, if there word were not credited, it would occasion an obstruction to business, and an unnecessary restraint amongst mankind.—It is related, in the Jama Sagheer, that where a slave girl comes to a person and says, "my master has sent me as a present to you," it is lawful for that person to accept of her.

The word of a reprobate may be taken in all temporal concerns, but not in spiritual matters.—IN all temporal concerns the word of a reprobate* may be taken; but in matters of a spiritual nature the word of an upright man only is to be credited. The reason of this distinction is, that affairs of a temporal nature are of frequent occurrence amongst every sect of men; whence if, in the transaction of them, anything more than maturity of age and sanity of intellect (such as integrity, &c.) were required, it would occasion a restriction in business; to obviate which; the word of one person, in such case, is creditable, whether that person be virtuous or dissolute, a Mussulman or an infidel, a man or a woman. Concerns of a spiritual nature, on the contrary, are not of such frequent occurrence; hence it is requisite that in relation to them a greater caution be used. The word, therefore, of none but an upright Mussulman is admissible in spiritual matters; because an unjust man lies under a suspicion of falsehood; and an infidel, as not following the LAW himself, has no right of enforcing it upon others. The case is different with respect to temporal matters; for an infidel is permitted to reside in a Mussulman terrirory purely on account of his temporal business, for which he would be incapacitated if his word in temporal matters were to be rejected. From this necessity, therefore, credit is given to it.

And the same of a person of unknown character.—A person, also, whose character is unknown is considered in the same light as an unjust man or reprobate; and his word relative to matters of faith is inadmissible. It is, however, related in the Zahir Rawayet, that suspicion and probable conjecture are the grounds on which it is lawful to determine in this point;—in other words, practice must accord with the conjecture which appears most probable or best supported. There is also another tradition from Haneefa, that the word of a person of unknown character may be believed in matters of a spiritual nature

The word of an upright person, whether freeman or slave, may be taken in spiritual matters.—THE word of a freeman or slave, whether male or female, is admitted in spiritual concerns, provided they be upright; for, in consequence of integrity, veracity preponderates; and this is a cause of belief.—IT is to be observed, that what was before related; of licensing a slave to trade, sending presents and messages, and the like, are of the class of temporal matters; as is also the investing of another with the power of agency.—Information, on the contrary, concerning the impurity of water (for instance) is a matter of a spiritual nature. In this instance, therefore, if the former be an upright Mussulman, the person who receives the information is at liberty; in performing his purification, to substitute sand for the water, in the manner of teyummim,† and must not perform it with the water.—If, on the contrary, the informer be a profligate, or of unknown character, it is incumbent on the person who receives the information to consider the matter deliberately; when, provided he conclude the informer to be a person of veracity, he must perform teyummim instead of ablution—(In this case, however, he should use the precaution of first pouring out a little of the water, and may then perform teyummim; whereas, if the informer be of an upright character, as there is in that case no suspicion of falsehood; the pouring out the water by way of precaution, is entirely unnecessary.)—If, on the contrary, the result of his reflection be that the information was false, he must perform ablution, but not teyummim with the water. This is what the law enjoins; but in this case also it is a requisite precaution that, after ablution; he perform teyummim, as the judgment he has formed in this case is entirely from conjecture. It is also to be observed that legality and illegality are considered as of a spiritual nature where they affect not the property of any person. Where, on the contrary, the testimony of one upright person tends to injure the property of another, it is not in such case of any weight;—as where, for instance, an upright person testifies that a certain person has married his own foster-sister; in which case his testimony is not creditable, as tending to hurt the property of the husband, inasmuch as he would be deprived of the effects of the woman, to which the marriage had entitled him;—or where a person informs another, who had purchased a slave girl, that she is his own foster-sister, or that she is a free woman.

It is laudable to accept an invitation to a marriage-feast, notwithstanding any irre-

* Arab, Fasik, in opposition to Adil, a just or upright person.—The distinction between these terms has been fully explained elsewhere.

* Arab, Adil; in opposition to Fasik.

† For a further explanation of this, see Vol. I. p. 105.

gularities which may be practised there.—If a person be invited to a marriage-feast, and, upon going there, observe the company to be engaged in wanton amusement, or in singing, still it is laudable in him to sit down and partake of the entertainment; for the acceptance of such invitation is strictly orthodox, as the Prophet has said, "whosoever refuses an invitation is certainly not obedient to me."—He is not, therefore, to leave the entertainment on account of any irregularities committed by others; in the same manner as, at the ceremony of a funerel prayer, a person is not to absent himself, although people hired for the purpose of lamentation may there be present.—If, however, he have power to prohibit these irregularities, it is incumbent on him to exert it: but if he possess not such power, he must then remain with patience.—This is where the person invited is not a Mooktidda,* or holy man; for, if such a person should be present and have it not in his power to restrain these irregularities, it is then incumbent on him to withdraw, as his presence in such a place shows a relaxation of religion. If also, irregularities be committed during the time of eating, it is improper that any person should remain there, whether he be a Mooktidda or not; GOD having prohibited us, in the KORAN, from sitting in company with the wicked. All this proceeds on the supposition of the invited person being actually present at the marriage-feast, before he is aware of those irregulaties.

Unless those irregularities be known beforehand.—FOR if he be previously aware of such irregularities being practised, it is incumbent on him to stay away, whether he be a Mooktidda or otherwise.

Section II.

Of Dress

Women may dress in silk; but men must not.—A DRESS of silk is not lawful for men; but women are permitted to wear it; for it is related by several of the companions of the Prophet, of whom was Alee in particular, that one day the Prophet appeared with a piece of silk in one hand, and of gold in the other, and said, "Both these are prohibited to the MEN of my tribe, but are lawful to the WOMEN."

Farther than what is merely ornamental.—A SMALL quantity of silk, such as three or four fingers breadth, used as a fringe or border to a garment, or applied to any such purpose, is allowable; because it is related that the Prophet prohibited the wearing of silk, excepting a shred of the breadth of three or four fingers in a garment; and it is moreover related, that the Prophet wore a robe with an edging of silk to it.

A pillow of silk is allowable.—ACCORDING to Haneefa, it is allowable to make a pillow of silk, and to sleep upon it. The two disciples, on the contrary, hold this to be abominable: and the same difference of opinion obtains concerning making curtains of silk, and hanging them upon doors. The arguments of the two disciples on this point are twofold. FIRST, the use of silk in general is prescribed by the Prophet. SECONDLY, the making of pillows and curtains of silk is a custom of the proud; and the imitation of such is forbidden. —The argument of Haneefa, on the other hand, is that the Prophet sat upon a pillow of silk; and that there was one laid upon the sofa of Abdoola Ibn Abbas.

And a dress of silk to warriors.—IT is allowed to warriors, in the opinion of the two disciples, to wear a dress of silk or satin in the time of war; because there is a tradition, recorded by Shaaby, that the Prophet permitted the wear of silk during the time of battle. Moreover, it is in a manner necessary, as being best adapted to counteract the hard pressure of armour, and tending to excite horror in the eyes of the enemy. Haneefa, on the contrary, holds this to be abominable, because the traditions which point out its illegality are absolute, without distinguishing between any particular period or juncture, such as war, or the like; and the necessity may be answered in a dress of Makhloot,—that is having the wool of silk, and the warp of anything else. Besides, silk, and every other thing that is proscribed, becomes allowable in no case but that of necessity;—and with respect to the tradition recorded by Shaaby, it alludes to dress of Makhloot.

Or of mixed cloth—A GARMENT of cloth, the woof of which consists of silk, and the warp of anything else, such as wool or cotton, is allowable to wear during war, because of its being necessary: but it is abominated at any other junction because then there is no necessity for it. The same rule also obtains with respect to cloth of which the warp is silk and the woof wool or cotton; and for the same reason.

Section III.

Of Ornaments.

Men are not to wear ornaments of gold or silver, except on signet-rings, girdles, and swords—MEN are prohibited from the use of ornaments of gold, such as rings, and the like, because of a saying of the Prophet to that effect. Ornaments of silver are likewise unlawful; because silver is, in effect, the same as gold. An exception, however, is made with respect to signet-rings, girdles, or swords; the use of silver in ornamenting those being approved.—In the Jama Sagheer, it is related that silver rings only should be used; whence it may be inferred that rings

---

* Literally, an exemplary person, as being eminent for sanctity of character.—whence the term is applied to priests, or other persons who exercise a holy office.—The Persians term such a person a Peishwa, or one who leads the way.

of stone, iron, or brass, are forbidden. It is also related, that, the Prophet on seeing a ring of brass upon the finger of a man, said, "I perceive the smell of an image," and again, that having seen, upon the finger of another person, a ring of iron, he spoke to him thus, "I see upon your finger the ornament of the people of hell,"—What is here said respects the circular hoop, and not the setting or beazel of the ring. Hence it is lawful that the setting be of stone. It is proper, however, that men, in wearing rings, turn the setting or beazel towards the palm of the hand, and women otherwise, because, with respect to them, rings are considered as ornaments.—Sovereigns and judges, moreover, wear rings, only as having occasion to seal with them; but with respect to other people, it is most advisable that they never wear rings, as a like reason does not operate with them.

The setting of a ring may be of gold.—IF a piece of gold be inserted in the setting of a ring, it is allowable; for, in that case, the gold is only a dependant on the ring, in the same manner as a shred of silk upon a garment.

Gold is not to be used in any cases of necessity, where silver will answer equally well.—IT is forbidden, in the opinion of Haneefa, to bind the teeth* with a thread of gold. Mohammed, on the other hand, maintains that this practice is unobjectionable. Of Aboo Yoosaf there are two opinions recorded; one corresponding with the opinion of Haneefa, and the other with that of Mohammed. The two disciples, in support of their opinion, quote the case of Arifja the son of Assad, who, having lost his nose by a wound he received at the battle of Goolab, made a false one of silver, which occasioning a very offensive smell, the Prophet commanded him to make another of gold. The argument of Haneefa is, that gold is in its nature unlawful whence the use of it is allowable only in a case of necessity; and as the necessity may in general be equally well answered by substituting silver, gold therefore remains subject to its original state [of prohibition]: this necessity, however, could not be answered, in the case of Arifja, but by a substitution of gold, because of the silver occasioning a nauseous smell.

Infants must not be sumptously apparelled.—IT is abominable in any person to clothe has infant child in a dress of silk, with ornaments of gold; for, since that dress is proved to be prohibited to men, they are consequently forbidden to dress others in it; in the same manner as it is unlawful to give wine to drink, because of the illegality of drinking it.

Vain superfluities are not allowable.—THE custom of keeping handkerchiefs, as is frequently practised, is abominable. Many, however, hold that it is allowable, if done from motives of necessity. This is approved: for the practice is abominable only when done ostentatiously, in the same manner as the mode of sitting with the knees on a line with the chin, and the hands folded round the legs.*

IT is allowable to bind the finger with a string, or a ring, with a view to aid the memory concerning some business relative to another person.

Section IV.

Of the Commerce of the Sexes; and of looking at or touching any Person.

Men must not look at strange women, except in the face, hand, or foot—IT is not permitted for a man to look at strange women, except in the face, and palm of the hands, which is allowable, because women being frequently concerned in business with man, such as giving taking, &c., it would therefore subject them to great inconvenience if these parts were veiled, whence there is a necessity for leaving them bare.—It is reported, from Haneefa, that it is allowable to look at the feet of a woman; because of there being sometimes occasion for it. From Aboo Yoosaf there is a tradition that the seeing of the shoulder is likewise allowed; because that, from the influence of custom, it is left exposed. If, however, a man be not secure from the impulse of lust, it is not allowable to look even at the face of a woman, except in cases of absolute necessity.

A man (if young) must not touch a strange woman.—IT is not lawful for a man to touch the hand of a strange woman, notwithstanding he have a control over his lust; because the Prophet has said, "whosoever toucheth a strange woman, shall be scorched in the hand with hot cinders on the day of judgment".—This, however, proceeds on a supposition of the woman being young; for if she be old, insomuch as to be insensible to lust, in that case it is lawful to touch her at the time of salutation. The case is similar where the man, being old, is insensible to passion himself, and not such as to excite it in the woman he touches.

A female infant may be touched or looked at.—IT is lawful to touch or look at a young girl insensible of the carnal appetite; as in that case there is no apprehension of seduction.

Rules to be observed by a magistrate with respect to woman, when acting in his judicial capacity or by a witness.—A KAZEE may look in the face of a strange woman, when he passes a decree upon her, notwithstanding

* This possibly means where a supposititious tooth is placed in the head to supply the loss of one.

* Meaning, that when a person sits in the manner so described, from ostentation, it is abominable, but that it is allowable when done with a view to obtain rest.

there be an apprehension of lust; because he is under a necessity of so doing, for the purpose of expediting his decrees, in order that the rights of mankind may sustain no injury.—Witnesses also, are under the same necessity, in order to their giving evidence; and hence it is lawful for them likewise to look in the face of a strange woman, where they are desirous of giving evidence concerning her.—With respect, however, to looking merely in order to bear testimony, it is certain that this is not allowable where there is any apprehension of lust, since others might be found free from such influence; which argument does not apply at the time of actually giving evidence.

A woman be looked at with a view to marriage.—A MAN may without blame look on a woman whom he has an inclination to marry, notwithstanding he knows that it will inflame his passion.

Rules to be observed by a physician in prescribing for women.—A PHYSICIAN, in administering to a strange woman, is permitted to look at the part affected. It is, however, most advisable that he instruct another woman how to apply the remedy, as the circumstance of an individual of one sex looking at another of the same is of less consequence. If he should not be able to procure a fit woman to instruct, it is in that case incumbent on him to cover all the members of the woman, leaving exposed only the particular part affected, when he may look towards it; refraining from it however as much as is possible, since anything the sufferance of which is prompted by necessity, ought to be exercised with as much restriction as the circumstances of the case will admit.—In the same manner also, it is lawful for a man, in administering a glyster to a man, to look at the proper part.

A man may view or touch any part of another man, except his nakedness.—ONE man may, without blame, look at any part of another, except from beneath the navel up to the knee; because the Prophet has said, "the nakedness of a man is from the navel to the knee;" and as, in another tradition, it is said, "from beneath the navel," it may thence be inferred that the navel is not included, but that the knee is so.—Still, however, in this a gradation is observed; for the exposure of the knee is of less consequence than that of the thigh, as on the other hand the exposure of the thigh is not so bad as that of the positive nakedness, or genitals; wherefore a person is to be reproved mildly when he leaves his knee bare; to be treated more harshly when he covers not his thigh; and, in the case of exposing his genitals, must be compelled by punishment to cover them.

EVERY part of a man, which it is proper for another to look at, may likewise, without blame, be touched by him; for the sight and the touch of those parts of a man which are not nakedness are considered in the same light.

A woman also, may look at any part of a man except his nakedness (provided she be free from lust.)—WOMEN may lawfully look at a man, except in the space from the navel to the knee; provided, however, they be secure from lust; for men and women are considered as alike, in looking at parts not private, the same in looking at a dress or a quadruped. (In the Mabsoot, under the head of Hermaphrodites, it is related that a woman looking at a strange man resembles a man looking at his female relation in which case it is unlawful that he look at her back or belly,* lest he thereby excite lust.)—If, however, a woman be inflamed with lust, or harbour a strong suspicion that looking at a man would create it, or be in any degree doubtful about it, in either of these cases it is most becoming that she shut her eyes, and avoid looking at a strange man; and if a man also be thus circumstanced, it is incumbent on him to close his eyes, nor must he look at a strange woman; because lust having great power over women, is considered as always operating upon them; and when men are also subject to a passion of that nature, it exists then on the part of both; and this is a weighty reason for rendering their looking at each other illegal. It is otherwise where the woman is influenced and not the man, for then there is not an equally cogent reason to render it unlawful, one party only being in that case inflamed with lust.

Or at any such part of another woman.—A WOMAN is permitted to look at any part of another except from under the navel to the knee. This is according to one tradition of Haneefa; but according to another tradition, the looking of one woman at another of her sex, is the same as that of a man at his female relation; that is, they are not permitted to look at the back or belly. The first tradition is, however, the most authentic

A man may view his wife or his slave in any part.—IT is lawful for a man to look at his slave girl in any part, provided he be not related to him within the prohibited degrees; and also at his wife in any part, even in the pudenda, if he please; because the Prophet has said, "shut your eyes from all excepting your wives and female slaves." Nevertheless, it is most becoming that a husband and wife should neither of them look at the genital parts of the other, as the Prophet has said, "when ye copulate with women of your own tribe, you must conceal as much as possible; and be not then naked, as that savours too much of the custom of asses."

A man may look at the person of his kinswoman.—IT is lawful for a man to look at his female relation either in the face, head, breast, shoulder, or legs: for as it is usual

* The reason of this is explained hereafter.

with relations to visit one another without any previous intimation, and unattended with any retinue, and as women, in their house, generally wear a dress adapted to service, if, therefore, the sight of these parts were culpable, it would impose too great restraint upon them. It is different with respect to other parts ; and hence proceeds the illegality of looking at the back or belly. (It is proper to observe that by the term relation [Mohrim], as here used, it to be understood any person between whom and the beholder marriage is utterly and perpetually illegal, in consequence of affinity by either blood or marriage)

Male and female relations may touch each other (if there be no apprehension of passion.)—EVERY part in a relation which it is lawful to look at may likewise be touched ; unless, however, there be a dread of its inflaming the passion of either, in which case neither the sight nor the touch is approved.

Or sit in private of travel together.—THERE is no impropriety in a man sitting in private with his female relation, or travelling with her ; because the Prophet has said, "No woman shall travel more than three days and three nights, unless accompanied by her husband, or her relation ; and if, in this case the woman should have occasion to mount upon, or descend from a horse the man may then, in assisting her, without blame, touch her back or belly, if covered, and provided he be sure of his passion, but otherwise he must beware of touching her."

A man may look at the female slave of another, in the same manner as at his kinswoman.—EVERY part which it is lawful for a man to look at in his female relation, may likewise be viewed by him in the female slave of another, whether she be an absolute slave, a Modabbira a Mokatiba, or an Am-Walid ; for as a slave is necessitated to wear clothes adapted to servile employments, that she may discharge the business of her master, and attend upon his guests, her condition without the house is therefore the same, in relation to stranger, as that of a free woman without the house, in regard to her kinsman.—With respect to privacy, or travelling with the female slave of another, many have said that it is allowed, in the same manner as in the case of a female relation.—Some however, declare it improper, as not being justified by necessity. Mohammed; in the Mabsoot, has said that the assisting of a female to ascend or descend from a horse is approved, provided it be in a case of necessity.

And may also touch her with a view to purchase—IT is permitted to a man to touch a female slave when he has an inclination to buy her, notwithstanding he may be apprehensive of lust. It is so related in the abridgment of Kadooree ; and Muhammad, in the Jama Sagheer, has given a similar absolute opinion in this case, without making any exceptions as to the circumstance of lust. The two disciples, on the other hand, maintain that although on account of necessity, it be proper for a person to look at a slave girl when he is about to purchase her, notwithstanding it may be the means of inflaming his passion, still it is improper to touch her when under the impulse of passion, or where there is a probability of its being excited. In case of an exemption from passion, however, they hold it allowable either to touch or look at her.

An adult female slave must be put in a decent habit.—WHEN a female slave arrives at maturity, it is improper to leave her in drawers only : on the contrary, it is requisite that she have two clothes, in order that her back and belly may be covered, as these, with regard to her, may be considered as privy parts It is moreover reported, from Mohammed, that when a female slave reaches the age of puberty, she must not be exposed in drawers only as that may occasion lust.

An eunuch or hermaphrodite is the same as a man with respect to those rules.—A KHASEE, or simple eunuch, is considered in the same light with a man, whence anything prohibited to a man is so likewise to him, for he possesses virility, and is not disabled from copulation : and the same, also, of a Majboob or complete eunuch ; for he is likewise capable of friction, and has the power of passing semen ; and so likewise of an hermaphrodite, as he is merely a defective man.

A male slave must not view his mistress but in the face or hands—IT is not lawful for a male slave to view his mistress, except in the face, or palm of the hands, in the same manner as a strangers. Malik maintains that a slave is in the predicament of a kinsman within the prohibited degrees (and such also is the opinion of Shafei) ; because his mistress is subject to his entering her apartment frequently without intimation. The arguments of our doctors are, that the slave is a man neither related to her as a kinsman nor husband ; that he is liable to be influenced by a passion towards her, as marriage may eventually be lawful between them (that is, in case of his emancipation) ; and that there is no necessity for his approaching her without leave, as the business of a slave properly lies without the house.

A man may gratify his passion with his female slave in whatever way he pleases.—IT is lawful for a man to perform the act of Azil* with his female slave without her consent, whereas he cannot lawfully do so by his wife unless with her permission.—The reason of this is that the Prophet has forbidden the act of Azil with a free woman without her consent, but has permitted it to a master in the case of his female slave. Besides, carnal connexion is the right of a free woman for the gratifying of her passion, and the propagation of children (whence it is that a wife is at liberty to reject a husband who is an eunuch or impotent) ; whereas a slave

* For a definition of Azil, see Vol. I. p 60

possesses no such right.—A man, therefore, is not at liberty to injure the right of his wife, whereas a master is absolute with respect to his slave. If, also, a man should marry the female slave of another, he must not perform the act of Azil with her without the consent of her master.

Section V.

Of Istibra, of waiting for the Purification of Women.

A man must not have connexion with his purchased female slave until one term of her coureses have elapsed.—A MAN, when he purchases a female slave, is not permitted either to enjoy her, or to touch, or kiss her, or look at her pudenda, in lust, until after her Istibra, or purification from her next ensuing courses; for when the captives taken in the battle of Autass were brought thence, the Prophet ordained that no man should have carnal connexion with pregnant women until after their delivery, or with others untit after one menstruation; which evinces that the abstinence so enjoined is incumbent on a proprietor; and further, that the occurrence of right of property and of possession is the occasion of its being incumbent. The end proposed in this regulation is, that it may be ascertained whether conception has not already taken place in the womb, in order that the issue may not be doubtful.

But this rule operates only on the purchaser, not on the seller.—ABSTINENCE until after purification is incumbent on the buyer, but not on the seller; for the true reason of its necessity is the desire of copulation; and as the buyer is presumed to possess this desire, and not the seller, the observance of it is therefore enjoined him, and not the other. If, moreover, desire be an internal operation of the mind, the obligation of the law in this particular, rests upon the argument of such desire. Now the mere power of committing the carnal act is an argument of the desire for such act; and as this power is established only by property and possession it follows that property and possession are the occasions of this obligation of abstinence.—This law, therefore, extends to a right of property, in all its different modes of being acquired, such ar by purchase, donation, legacy, inheritance, covenants, &c., whence it is that this abstinence is enjoined upon a person, who buys a female slave, either from an infant, or a woman, or from a slave licensed to trade, * or from a person who is by law prohibited from having any carnal connexion with her. In the same manner also, this abstinence is incumbent where a person buys a female slave who is a virgin; for the law proceeds according to the proof of the cause which prompted it, and not according to the proof of the propriety or expediency, as these relate to what is internal and unknown.

In the purchase of a menstruous female slave, the purchaser must wait for another complete term.—IF a person purchase a female slave during her menstruation, no regard is paid to this menstruation with respect to determining the abstinence.† In the same manner, also no regard is paid to a menstruation which occurs between the time of taking possession and the time of the right of property being established, by purchase, or the like;—and so likewise, regard is not paid to the delivery of a female slave between the establishment of a right of property in her, and the act of taking possession (contrary, however, to the opinion of Aboo Yoosaf). The reason of this is, that the occurrence of right of property and possession is the cause of purification being required; and the obligation of observing the purification is an effect of property and possession; and the effect cannot take place before the occurrence of the cause. The same rule holds with regard to such menstruous purgations as may happen previous to the procuring of sanction, in the case of an unauthorized sale of a female slave, notwithstanding the purchaser may be seised of her;—and so likewise, where the courses happen after the seisin in the case of an illegal contract of sale, and before the slave is purchased by a valid contract; for in none of all these do the present courses determine the abstinence.

A person purchasing his partner's share in a female slave must wai tuntil her next purification. ABSTINENCE is requisite in the case of a partnership female slave, where one of two partners purchases the other's share: for here the cause is complete, and upon the completion of the cause the effect takes place.

Other rules to be observed respecting female slaves.—IF a person purchase a Magian female slave, or receive her in donation, and

* A phraseology runs throughout this section which renders the translation of it into English particularly difficult, as the precise meaning of the term Istibra cannot be expressed by any single word in our language.—The best Arabic lexicons define Istibra to signify "the purification of the womb."—The term, however, must here be received in a more involved sense; for Istibra does not, in fact, mean simply purification, but a desire of, or (as rendered in the text) a waiting for purification; for which reason the translator renders it purification, or abstinence, as best suits the context.

* The slave licensed to trade is, in this case, supposed to have been prohibited from cohabiting with the slave, as the goods he sells or purchases are presumed to be the property of another, namely, his master.

† Arab, Fee babal Istibra; (literally) "In point of purification," meaning that purification requisite to determine the abstinence imposed on the purchaser of a female slav

she, after his taking possession of her, have her courses, and then become a Muslima,—or, if a person purchase a female slave, and make her a Mokatiba, and she, after his taking possession of her, having voided her courses, prove unable to discharge her ransom,—such courses are sufficient to establish the requisite purification, in either of these cases, as having happened after the occurrence of the cause for waiting, namely, right of property and possession.

IN cases where a female slave, having eloped, returns to her master,—or, having been taken away, or hired out, is restored,—or, having been pawned, is redeemed,—abstinence is not requisite, for the cause of it (namely, the acquisition of property and possession) does not exist in either instance.

Where the carnal act is unlawful, all incentives to it are prohibited.—IN every case where abstinence is enjoined, and carnal connexion prohibited, all sorts of allurements and dalliance, such as kissing and hugging, are likewise prohibited, as these lead to the commission of unlawful acts. Add to this, the possibility of their being committed on the property of another, as may happen if the slave prove with child and the seller lay claim to her. (It is reported from Mohammed that dalliance with a captive slave girl is lawful.)

Pregnant women are purified by delivery, and immature females by the lapse of one month.—THE purification of a pregnant female slave is established by her delivery, and that of a girl in whom the menses have not yet appeared, by the lapse of a month, that space being, with respect to such an one, a substitute for the courses, in the same manner as holds in the case of a woman under Edit.* If, however, the menstrual blood should discharge itself before the expiration of the month, the purification by lapse of time is annulled, because of the ability with respect to the original circumstance, prior to accomplishing the object of the substitute.

Rule respecting adult females not subject to the courses.—IF the courses be delayed in a female slave who is of age to be subject to them, it is in that case requisite to refrain from any carnal connexion with her, until it appear that she is not pregnant, when it becomes lawful to cohabit with her. (This opinion is quoted from Haneefa, in the Zahir Rawayet, without specifying any particular term.)

Devices used to elude the abstinence required.—IT is allowable, according to Aboo Yoosaf, to elude the abstinence by the practice of a device; in opposition to the opinion of Mohammed. The arguments of each on this point have been already detailed under the head of Shaffa.—The opinion of Aboo Yoosaf has been adopted by Kazees in their decisions, where it has appeared that the seller had not cohabited with the slave from the period of her courses antecedent to the sale;—and, according to the opinion of Mohammed, when the contrary has been proved. The device which may be practised in a case where the purchaser is not married to a free woman,* is that he may first marry the slave, and then purchase her.—If, on the contrary, he be already married to a free woman, the device in that case is that the seller, previous to the sale, or the purchaser, before taking possession, give the slave in marriage to another person (who must, however, be one in whom they can confide, that he will not cohabit with her, and that he will divorce her), and then, that the party purchase the slave, in the former instance, or take possession of her, in the latter,—and the husband divorce her:—because as the purchaser was at any rate prohibited from cohabiting with the slave at the time when the cause of the abstinence first operated (that is, when he first acquired property and possession), no abstinence is therefore required after she did become lawful to him, as regard is paid to the time and circumstances under which the cause takes place;—in the same manner as where a person purchases and takes possession of a slave who is in her Edit,—in which case, upon the expiration of the term of Edit, abstinence is no longer required, since in this case the slave was nor lawful to the purchaser at the time of the cause taking place.

A person pronouncing Zihar must entirely abstain from his wife until he have made expiation.—It is not lawful for a person who has given abusive language to his wife,‡ either to look at her pudenda in lust, or to cohabit with her, or to kiss or touch her until such time as he have performed expiation; because, as it is unlawful for him to copulate with her until after expiation, it is, consequently, unlawful that he enter into dalliances with her, since the cause of an illegal act is likewise illegal;—in the same manner as holds in cases of Yttikar§ and

*See Edit, Vol. I., p. 128.—There seems here to be a small mistake in the text, as the Edit of a female slave not subject to the courses is determined by the lapse of a month and an half.

* This condition is here made, because it is not lawful for a Mussulman to marry a slave if he should be previously married to a free woman. (See Vol. I, p. 31.)

† It is here understood that marriage exempts from abstinence.

‡ Literally, " it is not lawful for a Mozahir,"—meaning a person who has, pronounced a sentence fo Zihar upon his wife. (This whole passage will be better understood by a reference to a Zihar. Vol. I., p. 117.)

§ Yttikaf is a religious austerity practised by the most pious of the Mussulmans in the last ten days of the month of Ramzan; they remain during that, period in a mosque, without ever departing from it but

Ihram;* or where a person, by mistake, cohabits with the wife of another,—in which case she must observe an Edit; during which, as it is unlawful for the husband to have connexion with his wife, so it is likewise unlawful for him to use any of its incentives with her. It is otherwise during the courses or fasting, for, although copulation be at such time prohibited, yet dalliance is lawful, because the courses are frequent and of long continuance, engrossing a great part of life, as they happen once every month, and cotinue ten days every time;—and, in the same manner, the days of fasting are protracted to one month by the divine ordinances, and (among pious persons) voluntarily occupy a considerable part of life;—whence if dalliances were forbidden during those terms, it would tend to restrain men too much in their enjoyments.

A person indulging in wantonness with two female slaves who are sisters, must put one of them away before he can have connexion with the other.—If a person, incited by passion, should kiss two female slaves who are sisters, he is not in that case permitted to have carnal connexion with either of them, or to kiss, touch, or look at the pudenda of either in lust, until he render one of them unlawful to him, either by making her the property of another, in whatever manner he may choose, or by giving her to another in marriage, or by emancipating her; because it is not lawful either to copulate or to enter into dalliance (such as kissing and hugging) with two sisters. But whenever one of them is rendered unlawful, the enjoyment of the other is permitted to him.—(The transfer of a part of the slave in this instance, is the same as a transfer of the whole, with respect to the illegality of enjoyment; † and so likewise the emancipating her, or rendering her a Mokatiba in part.) If, on the contrary, he let one of them to hire, or pawn her, or create her a Modabbira, the other is not thereby made lawful to him, as he does not by any of these acts relinquish his property in her. If, also, he should give one of them in marriage to any person by an invalid contract, he does not thereby acquire a right to enjoy the other; unless, however, the husband of that one consummate the marriage, in which case an Edit is incumbent upon her, and this is the same as a valid marriage, with regard to rendering the enjoyment of her illegal. If, also, he once carnally enjoy one of them, he may afterwards continue to do so;—but he cannot then lawfully have connexion with the other; for if so, it would be a connexion with two sisters, which is unlawful: but this consequence is not induced by connexion with one of them.

Any two women who are related to each other in a degree that prevents their being lawfully married to the same person, are considered as sisters, and are consequently subject to the rules exhibited in the preceding case.

Men must not kiss or embrace each other.—It is abominable for one man to kiss another either in the face or hand, or on any other part; as it is likewise for two men to embrace each other. Tahavee reports that this is the opinion of Haneefa and Mohammed; but that Aboo Yoosaf holds it not improper for a man either to kiss or embrace another; because it is related that when Jaffer came from Abyssinia the Prophet embraced him and kissed him between the eyes. The argument advanced by Haneefa and Mohammed is a tradition that the Prophet prohibited both kissing and embracing; and with respect to the circumstance adduced by Aboo Yoosaf, it must be construed as having happened prior to the prohibition. The learned, however, have said that this disagreement between our doctors concerning the act of embracing, respects only a case where men are not properly dressed, as where, for instance, they are in drawers only; but that those acts are allowable, in the opinion of all our doctors, when the parties are clothed with an under and upper garment.—This is the most approved doctrine.

But they may join hands.—The joining hands by way of salutation is allowable; for the Prophet has said. "Whosoever joins his hand to that of his brother Mussulman, and shakes it, shall be forgiven of his sins"

Section VI.

Of the Rules to be observed in Sale

Dung may be sold; but not human excrement.—Three is no impropriety in the sale of dung; but it is abominable to sell human excrement. Shafei maintains that the sale of dung is likewise abominable, because of its being actually filthy; in the same manner as excrement, or the undressed skin of a dead animal.—The argument of the Haneefites upon this point is, that dung is capable of yielding profit, as it is commonly strewed upon land, in order to render it more fertile: and as it thus yields a profit, it is therefore is a valuable property, the sale of which is lawful.

Unless mixed with mud.—It is otherwise with respect to excrement, as that is incapable of profit, unless it be mixed with mud,

when the calls of nature absolutely force them, abstracting themselves at the same time from all enjoyments.

* Ihram is the the period during which pilgrims remain at Mecca.—They are then subject to a number of strict regulations, and are particularly enjoined to refrain from all worldly pleasures.

† That is to say, he will as completely render one of the sisters illegal (or forbidden) to him (and consequently legalize his connexion with the other) by selling or otherwise transferring his property in a part of her, as by transferring her in toto.

when the sale of it becomes lawful,* according to what is reported from Mohammed; which is approved.

A person may purchase and have connexion with a female slave on the faith of the seller's assertion respecting her.—If a person see another selling a female slave, he at the same time knowing her to be the property of some other person, and he be informed by the seller that "he has been empowered by that other to dispose of her," it is in that case lawful for him to purchase her, and have carnal connexion with her; and the word of one man, although he be not upright,† may be received in temporal matters, provided there by no oppenent to shake the credit of his testimony.—The same rule also holds if the seller allege that he had received her in donation from the other, or that he had bought her from him; with this difference, however, that he is here required to be of an upright and trustworthy character;—and so likewise if he be not trustworthy, provided the purchaser believe that he speaks truth; but if he disbelieve him, it is not lawful for him to purchase the slave. The law is the same, if the purchaser, not having previously known the female slave, be informed by the seller, that "she is the property of another who has empowered him to sell her,"—or that "he has purchased her from such a person."—If, on the other hand, knowing her to have been in the possession of another he do not receive any information from the seller, he cannot in that case lawfully purchase her until he know by what means the seller has acquired a property in her; for her having been in the possession of another is on argument of her being the property of another. If, on the contrary, he should not know her to have been before the property of another, he may then lawfully purchase her, notwithstanding the seller bear a bad character; because possession, even with an unjust man, argues property; and suspicion, or probable conjecture lose all force in any case where a legal argument can be urged. Where it is evident, however; that a person of such appearance as the seller is not likely to be the proprietor of her, it is most prudent on that account to avoid buying her. Nevertheless, if the purchase be made— there are hopes of its being lawful, because of its being supported by a legal argument.

But if the seller be a slave, precaution must be used.—If the person who offers the female slave to sale be a slave, male or female, in that case the other must neither accept nor purchase her until he enquire into the circumstances; because as property cannot be a proprietor, it is evident that some other is the proprietor of her. If, however, the seller inform him that "his master had licensed him to sell her," his word may in that case be taken, provided he be upright and trustworthy; but if he be otherwise, the purchaser must be guided by probable opinion; and if he have not the means of forming any opinion of him, whether good or bad, he must not in that case purchase her, or admit his allegation concerning her.

A woman may marry (after observing her Edit) on receiving authentic information of her widowhood or divorce.—If a person of an upright and trusty character inform a woman that her husband who was absent had died, or that he had divorced her thrice,—or, if a person of a reprobate character deliver her a letter from her husband, wherein he acquaints her of his having divorced her, and she, not knowing for certain that the letter was written by her husband; should however be led to think so,—in either of these cases she may lawfully observe her Edit, and then marry;—because in this instance a circumstance destructive of the former marriage has occurred without any person appearing to contradict it. In the same manner, also, if a woman inform a man that her husband had divorced her, and that the stated period of her forbearance had elapsed, the man may lawfully marry her. If also, a woman inform her former husband who had divorced her thrice, that "after the lapse of her Edit she had married another, with whom she had cohabited, and that having divorced her she had again completed her Edit from that divorce," the first husband may in that case lawfully marry her again. The law is also the same where a woman informs a person that, having been a slave she had received her freedom.

Information tending to annul a marriage, must not be credited unless supported by testimony.—If a person inform a woman that her marriage had been originally unlawful, inasmuch as her husband was at that time an apostate, or her foster-brother, his word is not in that case to be credited, unless confirmed by the evidence of two men, or of one man and two women. So likewise, if a person inform another that his wife had been an apostate at the time of marriage, or that she is his foster-sister, he is not in that case permitted either to marry the sister of that woman, or to marry other four women, until the information so given be fortified by the attestation of two upright men. For here the husband is informed of an illegal circumstance co-existent with the marriage; whereas his execution of the contract of marriage is an argument in favour of its validity, and a denial of its illegality; and hence the information of the other is apparently, contradicted. The case is otherwise, however, if a person, having married a child, should be informed that she had afterwards sucked the milk of his mother or sister; for the information so given is to be believed.

* Because in this case the mud or manure is the article sold, the ordure being merely a dependant.

† Arab. Adil, in opposition to Fasik.

since here the bar to the marriage is subsequent to, and not co-existent with, the contract; and the execution of the contract, being antecedent to the circumstance of its illegality, does not therefore afford any proof of its non-existence; whence the information is not controverted.

A man is not at liberty to marry a female slave on her informing him that she is free.—IF a girl, so young as to be unable to give any account of herself, being in the possession of a man who asserts her to be his property, should be afterwards when she arrives at the age of maturity, met in another city by a man who formerly knew her, and tell him that "she is a free woman," he is not, on the strength of her word, permitted to marry her, as there is an argument against the truth of it, namely, her having been in the possession of another.

A Mussulman is not allowed to pay his debts by the sale of wine; but a Christian may pay his debts in this manner.—IF a Mussulman, involved in debt, should sell wine, it is abominable in his creditor to receive payment in the money so obtained; whereas, if the debtor were a Christian, it would be allowable so to do. The reason of this distinction is, that in the former instance the sale was invalid, as wine is not valuable to Mussulmans, and the price of it being therefore the property of the purchaser, cannot be lawfully received in payment. In the latter instance, on the contrary, the sale was lawful, wine being a valuable commodity amongst Christians; and as, consequently the price of it is the property of the seller, the discharge of a debt from such price is lawful.

It is abominable to monopolize the necessaries of life; or to forestall the market.—IT is abominable to monopolize* the necessaries of life, and food for cattle, in a city where such monopoly is likely to prove detrimental. So likewise is it abominable to forestall † as where people leave a city to meet a caravan with a view to purchase goods and lay them up. This however, is immaterial, when it tends not to the injury of any one. The argument, in this case, is a tradition of the Prophet, who said, "Bleassed is the JALIB, and accursed is the monopolizer." (By Jalib is to be understood a merchant who brings camels, goats, and so forth, for sale.) Another argument is, that grain is connected with the rights of every one, whence the withholding it from sale is an invasion of the general rights of mankind, and an occasion of scarcity in their necessary food. Such an act is therefore abominable where the effects of it are extended to the people; as is the case when the monoply is made in a small city. It is otherwise, however, where it carries not along with it any sensible detriment to the people, as where it is done in a large city. Thelaw is similar in the case of forestalling. The learned, however, remark that this is where the purchasers neither conceal from the merchants the price current of the market, nor deceive them in it; for if they either conceal or deceive them in the established prices, the anticipation of the market is in such case abominable, whether it be hurtful in its consequences or otherwise. The restriction of the term Ihtikar, or monopoly, to the necessaries of life and the food of animals is according to Haneefa. Aboo Yoosaf has said that the hoarding of anything, the detention of which from circulation produces bad consequences, although it be such articles as gold, silver, or cloth, comes equally within the definition of a monopoly. It is reported from Mohammed, on the contrary that the withholding of cloth from the market does not constitute a monopoly. It therefore appears that, according to Aboo Yoosaf, regard is paid to the actual detriment in determining the monopoly, as that is the cause of its being abominated; whereas, according to Haneefa, regard is paid to the particular detriment. Decrees pass according to the latter opinion. It is to be observed that, if the period of detention be short, it is not a monopoly, as not being then attended with any detriment. If, on the contrary the period be long, it becomes an abominable monopoly, as it then induces detriment. Some have said that by a long period is to be understood at least forty days, because of a saying of the Prophet, "Verily, whosoever hoards victuals for the space of forty days is at variance with GOD, and GOD is at variance with him." Others have said that a month is a long space, and that any time less is a short space, and that the degree of guilt rises in proportion to the necessities of the people, and the effect of the monopoly in producing a famine. Others, again, have said, that although there be a fixed period for rendering it punishable in this world, still it is criminal, however short the period may be. In short, it is not good to trade* in grain, or commodities of that nature.

But a person may monopolize the product of his own grounds, or what he brings from a distant place.—IF a person should hoard a quantity of grain, being the product of his own cultivation, or which he had brought from another city,—in either of these cases it is not deemed an abominable monopoly:—

* Arab, Ihtikar. It is explained in the text to signify, in its literal sense, the laying up of anything; and in the language of the LAW, the purchasing of grain, or other necessaries of life, and keeping them up with a view to enhance the price.

† Arab. Talakkee.

* By trading is not here to be understood simple purchase and sale, but the usual practice of merchants in keeping up their commodities, and watching the turns of the market, in order to sell to the greatest advantage.

it is not so in the first case, because such product being an unmixed right of his own, without any relation to that of other people, he is therefore permitted to hoard it up; and in the same manner as it is lawful for him not to cultivate the seed, so is it lawful for him not to sell the product:—nor is it so in the second case, according to the opinion of Haneefa, the reason in support of which is, that the rights of the people extend only to what is collected in the city, or what is brought thither from its dependancies. Aboo Yoosaf, on the contrary, deems this practice abominable, because the tradition recorded on this head is absolute. Mohammed, also, has said that every place from which grain is frequently brought to a particular city may be deemed a dependancy of it; and that a monopoly of whatever may be brought from such place is forbidden, as the rights of the people are connected with it. It is otherwise, however, where goods are brought from a distant place, such as it is not customary to bring them from; since in that case the rights of the community are not concerned.

Sovereigns must not fix prices.—IT is not the duty of sovereigns to establish fixed prices to be paid by the community; because the Prophet has forbidden this, saying, "Establish not prices, as these are regulated by GOD." Besides, the price is the right of the merchant, and the measure of it is therefore left to him; and sovereigns are not entitled to invade any such right.

Except in cases of necessity. —EXCEPT where the welfare of the community is concerned, as shall presently be made appear.

A monopolizer, upon information, must be required to sell his superfluous provisions.—IF a person guilty of a monopoly be brought before the Kazee, he must direct him to sell whatever he may have laid up more than is amply sufficient for the subsistence of himself and family, and must prohibit him from the like practice in future;—and if, after this, he should again monopolize, the Kazee may then chastise him at his own discretion.

A combination to raise the price of provisions must be remedied by the magistrate fixing a rate.—IF victuallers, taking advantage of the necessity of the people, raise the market to an exorbitant rate, and the Kazee be otherwise unable to maintain the rights of the people; he may in that case regulate the prices, with the assistance of men of ability and discernment.—Notwithstanding if this, however, they should continue to sell their grain at a rate exceeding the fixed standard, the Kazee must confirm the sale, nor has he the power of annulling it. This, according to Haneefa, is evident; for he holds it unlawful to inhibit a freeman in this respect—and so likewise, according to the two disciples, unless the inhibition affect only some particular people, since (agreeably to their tenets) inhibition is not allowed where it is indefinite.

Is it lawful for a Kazee to sell the grain of a monopolizer without his consent?—Some say that upon this point there is a diversity of opinion, in the same manner as in the case of selling the effects of a debtor;—whilst others maintain that it is lawful in the opinion of all our doctors, because Haneefa holds it just to inhibit a freeman, with a view to removing a common evil, as is the case in the present instance.

Arms must not be sold to seditious persons—IT is abominable to sell arms in the time of sedition to a person whom the seller knows to be a rebel, as this is a cause of evil. If, however, the seller should not know the purchaser to be engaged in the rebellion, he may then without blame sell arms to him.

The crude juice of fruit may be sold for the purpose of making wine.—THERE is no impropriety in selling the juice of dates or grapes to a person whom the seller may know intends making wine of it for the evil does not exist in the juice, but in the liquor, after it has been essentially changed. The case is different with respect to selling arms at a time of tumult, since in that instance the evil is established, and exists in the original thing, arms being the instruments of sedition and rebellion.

A house may be let to hire anywhere out of a city for the purpose of a pagoda or a church.—IF a person let a house to hire in a village, or in the neighbourhood of a city, in order that the lessee may convert it into a pagoda, or a Christian church, or that he may sell wine in it, it is immaterial, according to Haneefa. The two disciples hold such lease to be improper, as tending to promote sin. The arguments adduced by Haneefa are, that the compact is formed with a view to obtain profit from the house, which becomes due immediately upon the delivery; that the guilt exists only in the act of the lessee; and that, as he is a free agent, no crime of his can therefore be reflected upon the lessor. The reason of restricting the place, in this instance, to a village, or the neighbourhood of a city, is because it is illegal to let out a house in a city for any of the above-mentioned purposes as there the light of the Mussulman religion is supposed to blaze, which is not always the case in other places. The learned, however, have said, that this refers only to the neighbourhood of Koofa, because many infidels reside there: but that in any other place where the Mussulman religion prevails it is unlawful. This latter opinion is the most authentic.

A Mussulman may carry wine for an infidel, and receive wages for so doing.—IF an infidel hire a Mussulman to carry wine for him, and afterwards pay him for his labour, the money so obtained is lawful to the Mussulman. The two disciples have said that it is abominable, as being the instrument of sin, and likewise because the Prophet (according to the Rawayet Saheeh has denounced curses upon ten several people who are concerned in wine, amongst whom are they who carry it. The argument of Haneefa is, that the sin lies only in the drinking of it, which is the act of a free agent; that the carrying it is no ways allied to the drinking of it; and that the object of the porter is not that another should drink it, but only that he himself should obtain the reward of his labour;—and with respect to the tradition above alluded to, it refers only to a case where the wine is carried with intent to promote sin.

Rules respecting the ground and houses of Mecca.—There is no impropriety in the sale of the walls of the houses at Mecca, but it is abominable to sell the ground on which they stand. This is the opinion of Haneefa. The two disciples have said that the ground of Mecca may likewise be sold; and it is also related that Haneefa accorded in this opinion; because in the same manner as the houses are property, so likewise is the ground. The real opinion of Haneefa, however, is that it is improper; because the Prophet has said, "Mecca is sacred, and the houses there can neither be sold nor inherited." Mecca, moreover, is sacred, as the being a dependancy of the Kaba, and the place where reverence is particularly shown to it; whence it is not lawful either to hunt at Mecca, or to cut the thorns or grass which grow there (except when they have faded and become parched); or to shake the leaves off the trees growing there.

It is abominable to let the ground at Mecca, because the Prophet has said, "Whosoever hires out the ground of Mecca is guilty of usury; whoever has use for the ground at Mecca, let him reside in it; and whoever possesses more than is sufficient for his own purposes, let him bestow it upon others."

Implied usury is abominable.—If a person take from a merchant something he may have occasion for, and leave with him a certain number of dirms (for example) he is guilty of an abomination; because, in thus taking what he wants, he derives an advantage from a loan (namely, the money he leaves with the merchant;) and the Prophet has prohibited us from taking interest on loans. He must therefore first deposit the dirms with the merchant, and then take from him whatever he may want; as the money is in this case a trust, and not a loan, insomuch that the merchant is not subject to pay a compensation in case of the loss of it.

Section VII.

Miscellaneous cases

The Koran ought to be written without marks or points.—It is abominable to distinguish the sentences of the Koran by marks, or to insert in it the points or short vowels. Nevertheless the learned amongst the moderns have said that these distinctions are proper when made for the use of a foreigner.

Infidels may enter the sacred mosque.—There is no impropriety in a Polytheist* entering the sacred mosque.† Shafei held this to be abominable; and Malik has said, that it is improper for such to enter into any mosque.—The argument of Shafei in support of his opinion is, that God has said in the Koran. "Associators are impure, and therefore must not be permitted to enter the sacred mosque." Another argument is, that an infidel is never free from impurity, as he does not perform ablution in such a manner as to work a purification; and an impure man is not allowed to enter into a mosque. The same arguments have been urged by Malik; but he extends them to any mosque. The argument of our doctors in this point is drawn from a tradition that the Prophet lodged several of the tribe of Sakeef, who were infidels, in his own mosque. Besides, as the impurity of an infidel lies in his unbelief, he does not thereby defile a mosque. With respect, moreover, to the text above quoted, it merely alludes to infidels entering a mosque in a haughty and forcible manner, and to a custom which was practised in the days of ignorance of walking about the mosque naked.

It is abominable to keep eunuchs—It is abominable for a Mussulman to keep eunuchs in his service, as the employment of them is a motive with men for reducing others to a like state, a practice which is proscribed in the sacred writings.‡

It is allowed to castrate cattle.—It is not abominable to castrate cattle, or to make a horse copulate with an ass, as these tend to the benefit of mankind. Besides, it is related, in the Nakl Saheeh, that the Prophet rode upon a mule, which if such promiscuous procreation of animals had been prohibited, he would never have done, as thereby a door would have been opened to sin.

A Jew or Christian, may be visited during sickness.—There is no impropriety in visiting a Jew or Christian during their sickness, as this affords them a kind of consolation; and the law does not prohibit us from thus consoling them. Nay, we are told in the Nakl Saheeh, that the Prophet visited Jew who lay sick in his neighbourhood.

Vain invocations in prayer not allowed.—It is abominable that a person, in offering up prayers to God, should say, "I beseech thee, by the glory of thy heavens!" or "by the splendour of thy throne!" for a style of

* Arab. Moshirrak i. e. an associator, including all who deny the unity of the Godhead, and therefore applying to (trinitarian) Christians as well as to Idolators.

† This is a mosque in Mecca, so called because the Prophet most frequently offered up prayers in it.

‡ That is, in the Koran, which is termed, by way of pre-eminence, the Sharra, or law.

this nature would lead to suspect that the Almighty derived glory from the heavens; whereas the heavens are created, but GOD, with all His attributes, is eternal and immutable. It is, however, recorded by Aboo Yoosaf, that there is no impropriety in this (an opinion which has been likewise adopted by Aboo Lais), because it is related of the Prophet that he offered up a similar prayer to GOD. Our doctors, on the other hand, have urged that this tradition is uncertain; and that to abstain from whatsoever is suspected of being wrong is most prudent and advisable.

IT is abominable to say, in a prayer, "I beseech thee, O GOD, by the RIGHT of" (any particular person), or "by the RIGHT of" (any of the Prophets); because none of his creatures is possessed of any right with respect to the Creator.

Gaming is disallowed.—IT is an abomination to play at chess, dice, or any other game; for if anything be staked it is gambling, which is expressly prohibited in the KORAN; or if, on the other hand, nothing be hazarded, it is useless and vain. Besides the Prophet has declared all the entertainments of a Mussulman to be vain excepting three; the breaking in of his horse; the drawing of his bow; and the playing and amusing himself with his wives. Several of the learned, however, deem the game of chess to be allowed, as having a tendency to quicken the understanding; which opinoin has also been ascribed to Shafei.—Our doctors have founded their judgment in this particular on a saying of the Prophet, "Whosoever plays at chess or dice does as, it were, plunge his hand into the blood of a hog." Moreover, plays of this nature are apt to withhold men from the adoration and worship of GOD at the set periods; and the Prophet has said, "Whatsoever tends to relax men in their duty to GOD is considered in the same light with the practice of gaming." It is also proper to remark, that if a man play at chess for a stake, it destroys the integrity of his character, and renders him a Fasik, or reprobate: but if he do not play at it for a stake, the integrity of his character is not affected. Aboo Yoosaf and Mohammed hold it abominable to salute any person that is engaged in play: since, in thus refraining, our abhorrence of gaming may be expressed. Haneefa, on the contrary, holds to proper, as being the means of diverting the parties from their game.

Presents (except of cloth or money). and entertainments may be accepted from a mercantile slave.—THERE is no impropriety in a person receiving a present from a slave who is a merchant; or in accepting from him an invitation to an entertainment; or in borrowing his carriage; but it is abominable to receive from him a persent either of cloth or money.—What is here advanced proceeds upon a favourable construction of the law. Analogy would suggest that there is no difference whatever between his invitations and his presents consisting of cloth or money;—in other words, they are all equally abominable in the acceptance, as being all gratuitous acts, to which a slave is not competent.—The reason, however, for a more favourable construction of the law, in this particular, is that the Prophet accepted a present from Soliman when he was a slave, and from Bareera when she was a Mokatiba. A number of the companions, also, accepted an invitation jrom the freedman of Aboo Russaid whilst he was yet a slave. There is, moreover, a sort of necessity which operates upon a mercantile slave, and obliges him to give into these several customs. Thus, for instance, if a person, having gone to his shop with a view to purchase wares, and having requested of him something to drink, should be refused by him, in that case he would consequently incur the imputation of covetousness, few people would frequent his shop, and his trade would thereby be ruined; Besides, when a slave is permitted to trade, he implicitly possesses all the power of a merchant in its full extent But he is under no necessity of clothing people, or of distributing money to them; and hence it is not allowed to him to perform such acts, in conformity with what analogy suggests upon this subject.

General rules with respect to infant orphans or foundings.—IF a person bestow anything in gift or alms upon an orphan* under the protection of a particular person, it is lawful for that person to take possession of such gift or alms on his behalf.—It is here proper to remark, that acts in regard to infant orphans are of three descriptions.—I. Acts of guardianship, such as contracting an infant in marriage, or selling or buying goods for him; power which belongs solely to the Walee, or natural guardian, whom the LAW has constituted the infant's substitute in those points.—II. Acts arising from the wants of an infant; such as buying or selling for him on occasions of need; or hiring a nurse for him, or the like; which power belongs to the maintainer of the infant, whether he be the brother, uncle, or (in the case of founding) the Mooltakit, or taker-up, or the mother, provided she be maintainer of the infant; and as these are empowered with respect to such acts, the Walee, or natural guardian, is also empowered with respect to them in a still superior degree;—nor is it requisite, with respect to the guardian, that the infant be in his immediate protection.—III. Acts which are purely advantageous to the infant, such as accepting presents or gifts, and keeping them for him; a power which may be exercised either by a Moltakit, a brother, or an uncle, and also by the infant himself, provided he be possessed of discretion, the intention being only to open a door to the infant's re-

* Arab. Lakeet. Properly, a foundling. (See Vol., II., p. 206)

ceiving benefactions of an advantageous nature.—The infant, therefore, is empowered in regard to those acts (provided he be discreet), or any person under whose protections he may happen to be.

It is notl awful for the Mooltakit [taker-up] of a founding to hire him out in service; nor is it lawful for an uncle to do so by his infant nephew, although he be under his immediate care. It is otherwise with a mother; for she may lawfully let her infant child to hire, provided she have immediate charge of him; because a mother is empowered to use the services of her infant child by employing him, without tendering him any return,—whereas a Mooltakit or an uncle has not this power.—If the child should of himself enter into an engagement of service, it is not valid, as there is a possibility of its tending to his prejudice.—Still, however, if after having hired himself out he should fulfil his engagement, it is then valid; because in thus confirming it his advantage only is consulted; and he is consequently entitled to the hire agreed for.

A master must not fix an iron collar on the neck of his slave.—It is abominabe for a person to fix an iron collar on the neck of his slave in such a manner as to deprive him of the power of moving his head, according to the custom of tyrants; because a punishment of this nature is like the torments of the damned, and is consequently unlawful, in the same manner as scorching with fire.

But he may imprison him.—A Mussulman may imprison his slave; for as a custom prevails amongst the Mussulmans of confining people who are mad or seditious, so in a similar manner it is lawful for a person to confine a slave, that he may prevent his absconding, and thus secure his property.

Glysters are allowed in cause of necessity.—It is not abominable to apply a glyster in a cause of need; because medical practices are approved, in the united opinion of all our doctors, as well as by the traditions of the Prophet. An application of this kind is, moreover, equally proper, whether it be administered to a man or woman. It is not allowable, however, to have recourse to any forbidden thing, such as wine, or the like; for it is unlawful to seek health by unlawful means.

The allowances of a Kazee are to be defrayad from the public treasury.—It is not improper to defray the allowances of a Kazee from the public tresaury, because the Prophet nominated Atab Bin Osaid Kazee of Mecca, appointing him his allowance from the public treasury there; and he also nominated Alee to be Kazee of Yemn, appointing him his allowance from the treasury there.—Besides, as a Kazee is, by the nature of his office, confined to the business of guarding the rights of Mussulmans, his maintenance is therefore drawn from their property (and the public treasury is the property of the Mussulman community); for a confinement to any particular office or duty entitles to maintenance; as holds in the case of an executor, or a Mozaribat factor who travels, with the stock.—It is to be observed, however, that the propriety of the Kazee receiving his allowance from the public treasury is only where he takes it in a satisfactory manner, without any condition; for if he should refuse to undertake the office, unless the sovereign allow him a certain salary, it is unlawful; because he in such case demands a reward for the discharge of an act of piety; for such the office of a Kazee is; nay, the exercise of jurisdiction is the noblest species of devotion.—It is also proper to remark, that if a Kazee be poor, it is most eligible, or rather incumbent on him to receive his maintenance from the public treasury; for otherwise he would be unable to support the dignity of his office from a necessary attention towards the concerns of his subsistence. If, on the contrary, he be rich, some deem it most eligible that he should not receive his allowance from the public treasury; whilst others maintain that it is incumbent on him so to do. The latter is the better opinion; because otherwise the office might be rendered low and contemptible: and also because, if an indigent person should succeed a rich Kazee, it would then be difficult for him to procure a salary, as that had been, perhaps, for a long time relinquished.

Case of a Kazee dismissed after having received his allowance.—If a Kazee, having possessed himself of one year's allowance, should be dismissed from his office before the expiration of that year, there is in this case a disagreement amongst our doctors, in the same manner as they have differed in opinion where a wife dies in a similar predicament.* The better opinion, however, is that he should restore the excess.

Female slaves may travel without being attended by a kinsman.—There is no impropriety in a female slave or an Am-Walid travelling without being attended by a kinsman; because a stranger (as has been already explained) is considered the same as a kinsman with respect to looking at or touching a female slave; and an Am-Walid is also a slave, as being property, although she cannot be sold.

BOOK XLV.

OF THE CULTIVATION OF WASTE LANDS.†

Definition of Mawat.—Mawat (which is here rendered waste land) signifies any piece

---

*See Vol. I., p. 143.

† Arab. Ahya-al-Mawat, meaning, literally, the revival of the dead.

of ground incapable of yielding advantage, either from a want of water, an inundation, or any other cause, such as prevents tillage; and it is termed Mawat, or dead, because, like the dead, it is of no use.

And description of the land so termed.—Any piece of ground which, from a long time, has lain waste without belonging to any person, or which has been formerly the property of a Mussulman, who is not then known and is likewise so far removed from a village that, if a person call out from thence his voice cannot there be heard, is termed Mawat. The compiler of the Hedaya remarks that this is the explanation of it as delivered by Kadooree. It is reported from Mohammed that it is requisite the ground be neither the property of a Mussulman nor a Zimmee; and likewise, that it be of no use; in which case it becomes absolutely Mawat; but that ground which is the property either of a Mussulman or a Zimmee is not Mawat.—If the proprietor be unknown, the ground in the mean time belongs to the Mussulman community;—but if he afterwards appear, it must be restored to him, and the cultivator is responsible for whatever damage he may have occasioned.—With respect to the ground being distant from a village, as mentioned by Kadooree, Aboo Yoosaf is of opinion that this is a condition, for this reason, that where the ground is contiguous to a village it cannot be said to be entirely useless to the inhabitants of it. Mohammed holds it sufficient that the villagers do not in reality make use of the ground, whether it be contiguous or not. The same opinion has been delivered by the Imam styled Khahir Zada; but Shims al Ayma, the Siruckshian, has adopted the opinion of Aboo Yoosaf.

The cultivation of waste lands invests the cultivator with a property in them.—Whosoever cultivates waste lands, with the permission of the chief, obtains a property in them; whereas, if a person cultivate them without such permission, he does not in that case become proprietor, according to Haneefa. The two disciples maintain that, in this case also, the cultivator becomes Proprietor; because of a saying of the Prophet, "Whosoever cultivates waste lands does thereby acquire the property of them." and also because they are a sort of common goods and become the property of the cultivator in virtue of his being the first possessor; in the same manner as in the case of seizing game, or gathering firewood. One argument of Haneefa on this point is a saying of the Prophet, "Nothing is lawful to any person but what is permitted by the Imam:"—and with respect to the saying quoted by the two disciples, it is to be construed merely into a judicial permission (for the Prophet was himself an Imam),—in the same manner as where he said, "Whoever kills an infidel is entitled to his armour."—Besides, all waste lands are plunder, seeing that the Mussulmans acquired the possession of them by conquest; and hence no person can assume a property in them without the consent of the Imam— as holds in all cases of plunder.

Tithe only is due from land so cultivated, unless it be moistened with tribute water.—If a person cultivate waste land, a tithe only is due from it, for it is unlawful to chage a Mussulman with tribute in the beginning: but if the land be moistened with tribute water, tribute may lawfully be imposed, as it then becomes due on account of the water.—If, also, a person cultivate waste lands, and afterwards relinquish them, and another then cultivate them, some have said that the second cultivator is best entitled to the property; for the first was owner of the profits merely, and not of the land itself; and therefore, upon his relinquishing it, the second obtains a superior claim. It is certain, however, that the first cultivator may resume the lands from the second, because he is proprietor of them in virtue of having brought them to a state of cultivation (as appears from the saying of the Prophet quoted in the preceding case), and does not forfeit his property by the relinquishment.

In the cultivation of the circumjacent grounds, a road must be left to it.—If a person cultivate a piece of waste land, and four others afterwards so cultivate the circumjacent ground as to obstruct the passage into his property, it is reported, from Mohammed, that his road is lead through the ground of him who cultivated last; for, after three of the sides bordering upon his property had been cultivated, the other of consequence remains for his ingress and egress; and therefore the person who cultivates it wilfully aims at the destruction of his right.

A Zimmee acquires a property in the land he cultivates, as well as a Mussulman.—If a Zimmee cultivate waste lands, he becomes proprietor of them, in the same manner as a Mussulman; because cultivation endows with a right of property. (Haneefa, however, holds that the consent of the Imam is requisite.)—A Zimmee and a Mussulman, therefore, are alike in this respect, in the same manner as in all other points of property.

If the land be not cultivated for three years after it is marked off, it may be transferred by the Imam.—If a person circumscribe a piece of ground, and set marks upon it with stones or such like, and keep it in that state for the space of three years without cultivating it, the Imam may in the case lawfully resume it, and assign it to another; because the ground was given to the first with a view to his cultivating it, so that a benefit might ensue to the Mussulmans from the collection of the tithe and tribute; and as he neglected this, it is therefore incumbent on the Imam to deliver it over to another, that the end for which it was given to the first may be answered.—Moreover, the encompassing of the ground with stones, &c., does not, like cultivation, create a right of property, since by cultivating the land is understood rendering it productive, whereas the encompassing it with stones serves merely to designate the boundaries: the land, therefore, still remains unappropriated as before.—With respect to the specification of three years, as here mentioned, it is founded on a saying of Omar, "The marker has no right after three years have elapsed."—It also proceeds on this principle, that three periods of time are requisite for a person who marks lands; one, that he may go to his place of abode after having set the marks; another, that he may there settle his affairs; and a third that he may return to his land; and each of these several periods is determined at a year, as it is probable any less division of time, such as an hour, a day, or a month, might not suffice to answer the purpose. If, therefore, after the elapse of three years the marker return not to his lands, it is presumed that he has relinquished them.—Lawyers remark that what is here advanced proceeds upon a principle of equity; but that, in strictness of law, if a person cultivate the lands which another has marked before the elapse of the period above mentioned he becomes the proprietor of them, as in this case he is the cultivator, and not the other.

Manner of marking off waste land.—It is here proper to observe that waste lands may be marked by other modes beside setting stones, such as by surrounding them with the branches of trees; by burning the underwood and thorns which may be growing upon the lands; or by collecting them together and scattering them, mixed with a little earth, about the borders, without carrying them so uniformly round as to form a continued boundary or, lastly, by digging a trench one or two yards in width.

Cultivation is established by digging and watering the ground.—It is related, as an opinion of Mohammed, that if a person dig up and water a piece of waste land, he is then the cultivator of it; whereas, if he dig it up or water it singly, he is only held to have set a mark upon it.—In the same manner, if he dig a trench or ditch without watering the land, it is considered only as marking; whereas, if he moisten it with water, after digging a trench, it is cultivation.

Enclosing it, or sowing it with seed.—If, moreover, a person raise an enclosure round the land so high as to be a dam to the water; he is held to have cultivated it; and so likewise if he sow seed in it.

It must not be practised on the borders of land already cultivated.— It is not permitted to cultivate a piece of waste land immediately bordering upon lands that are in a flourishing state; as it is requisite that a space be left for the use of the cattle of the other proprietor, and also for piling up his stacks, whence such land does not come under the description of waste any more than a river or a highway;— and accordingly, our doctors have said, that it is not lawful for the Imam to bestow on a person any article of indispensable use to the Mussulmans, such as a salt-pit, or a well from which the people draw water to drink.

A space is appropriated to wells dug in waste lands.—Whoever digs a well in waste land is entitled to a space or piece of land* round it. If, therefore, the well be dug for the use of camels, a space of forty yards is annexed to it.—This is related in the traditions. Several of our doctors have construed the forty yards to mean the aggregate space. The better opinion, however, is that forty yards are annexed to each side of the well; for as many lands are of a soft and humid soil, it might happen that if another person should dig a well at a less distance from the first than forty yards, the water of the one might ooze through the earth and communicate with the other. If the well be dug with a view to drawing water from it by means of camels or other animals,† in that case the space of sixty yards is annexed, according to the two disciples. Haneefa holds that in this case likewise only forty yards are allowed.—The arguments of the disciples upon this point are twofold.—First, a saying of the Prophet, "The precincts of a fountain are five hundred yards, of a well from which camels may drink forty, and of a well from which water is drawn sixty yards."—Secondly, there is a necessity that a considerable space be annexed to a well of this nature, since the camels may be required to be led to a distance from it, as the rope by which the water is drawn up is often of long extent; but where wells are so made that the water may be taken out by the hand, it is not necessary that any great space be allotted on this account; and therefore a difference should certainly be made between the two sorts of wells. Haneefa argues from the tradition before cited, in which forty yards are mentioned, without distinguishing between the two species of wells. The objection, moreover, started by the two disciples may be obviated by making the camels revolve round the well with the rope, instead of driving them directly from it.

If the well have a fountain in it, the space annexed to it is five hundred yards; because of the tradition before quoted; and also, because a large space is here absolutely requisite; for as the fountain is brought out to water the ground, one space is required through which the water may be conducted from the fountain; another for a reservoir wherein the water may be collected, and a third for conveying the water from the reservoir to moisten the lands for cultivation. A considerable space is therefore required; which is determined at five hundred yards,

* Arab Hareem; meaning, literally prohibited to others.

† See note in Vol. II., p. 220.

by the tradition; and this, according to the most authentic opinions, means five hundred yards. on each side of the fountain; the yard measuring six spans.—(Some have said that the annexation of five hundred yards to a fountain is only in the country of Arabia, where the soil is hard; but that in our country, where it is soft, a larger extent is required as otherwise the water of one fountain might transude through the earth and communicate with that of another.)

Within the limits of which no other person is entitled to dig.—IF a person attempt to dig a well within the limits of the proprietor of another well, in that case the other may prohibit him; because the limits of his well are his property (as has been explained), and therefore none has a right to encroach upon them. If, also, a person should actually dig a well within the limits of another the first proprietor has in that case the option either of filling it up himself gratuitously, or of forcing the other so to do.—Some have said that in this case, the first proprietor is to take a compensation for the damage from the other, and then to fill up the well himself:—in the same manner as where a person destroys a wall the property of another, in which case he must make reparation to the proprietor, who must rebuild it himself. This is approved. It is related in Khasaf's treatise upon the duties of a Kazee, that the damage, in this instance, must be computed by a comparison of the value the first well bore before the other was dug, with what it bears afterwards; the difference showing the loss sustained.

Or, if any do so, he is responsible for such accidents as it may occasion.—THERE is no responsibility for any thing which may happen to be destroyed by falling in to the first of the two wells, as the proprietor, in digging it, was not guilty of any trespass.—This is evident, in the opinion of Haneefa, if he dug it with the consent of the Imam; and also in the opinion of the two disciples, whether it was done with the consent of the Imam or not;—according to Haneefa, because the digging of a well, in this instance, was the same as the setting of marks, which may be done without the consent of the Imam, although the property cannot be acquired without his permission.—If, on the contrary, anything be destroved by falling into the second well, it must be atoned for as the proprietor of this well has been guilty of a trespass in having dug upon the property of another. If, on the other hand, a person dig a well bordering on the precincts of another, without however encroaching upon it, and the water of that other should then decrease, he is not liable to make any compensation, as he is not here guilty of any transgression.—In this last case, morover, the second digger is entitled only to the ground on three sides of his well, as the ground on the side of the first well is the property of the first digger.

A space is also appropriated to a water-course.—WHOEVER digs a channel * for conducting water to any place, has a space annexed to it, according to his want. It is related by Mohammed that an aqueduct is the same as a well, so far as regards the annexing of land to it.—Some say that this is the doctrine of the two disciples; but that, according to Haneefa, no space is allowed, except when the water appears above ground; for as an aqueduct is in fact merely a rivulet, it is therefore subject to the same rules. Several doctors have, however, maintained that when an aqueduct appears above ground, it is then considered in the same light as a spring or fountain: and that consequenty the same quantity of land is annexed to it, namely, five hundred yards.

Or to a tree planted in waste land.—IF a person plant a tree in a waste spot of land, he is entitled to a small spaces an appendage to it: wherefore no other person is allowed to plant tree on the ground within his precincts, as this space is useful to him for collecting his fruits, and heaping them upon it. The space allotted to a tree is the measure of five yards, agreeably to what occurs in the traditions upon that subject.

The deserted beds of rivers must be cultivated.—LANDS through which the Euphrates; the Tigris, or any similar river formerly ran; must not be cultivated, if it be possible that the river may again run over them; as the people whose lands lie adjacent to the river in its former course have an interest in desiring that the river may not be prevented from returning to it. If, however, the lands be not likely to be again overflowed, they are then held to be waste, provided they do not adjoin to any cultivated spot:—because such lands are not the property of any one; for the superiority of water repels all other superiority; but as soon as the land appears above the water it beomes subject to the Imam.

A space is not allowed to an aqueduct running through another's land without proof of prior right.—WHOEVER has the property of an aqueduct, which runs through land belonging, to another, is not (according to Haneefa) entitled to any adjacent space, unless he produce evidence to prove his right.—The two disciples, on the contrary; maintain that he is, in virtue of his property in the aqueduct, entitled to the banks on which people pass, and which the earth thrown up by the excavation of it occupies. Some have said that the difference of opinion in this case is founded on that which obtains where a person digs a canal in waste lands by permission of the Imam; for in this case, according to Haneefa, he is not entitled to any space; whereas the two disciples maintain that he is so entitled, since he can derive no advantage from the canal unless he possess a space annexed to it, as he must

* Arab, Kanat, Pers, Kareez. It is generally understood to mean a subterraneous aqueduct or drain.

often be bliged to walk along the banks of it to clear away any incumbrances that may stop the course of the water, it being impracticable for a person, in the common course of things, to walk in the middle of it.—As, moreover, he is often necessitated to dam it with earth and clay, and it is impossible for him to bring these from any distance without incurring an extraordinary expense; he is therefore entitled to a space of ground, in the same manner as a person who digs a well.—The argument of Haneefa is, that the claim to any space is repugnant to analogy, the right to it being established, in the case of a well, solely on the ground of the precept before quoted. Besides, the necessity of a space, in the case of a well, is more urgent than in the case of a canal or aqueduct; for, in the latter, the use of the water may be enjoyed without any space,—whereas, in the former, this is impossible, as the water must be pulled up by a rope, to effect which a space is requisite, as has been before explained. Hence there is an obvious difference between a well and a canal; and consequently they can bear no analogy to each other. The reason for founding the case in question on this is, that if the proprietor of the aqueduct be entitled to a space of land, he is held to be seised of the said space as a dependency of the aqueduct; and the evidence of the possessor is valid in case of a contest; whereas if, on the contrary, he be not entitled to any space, he is not held to be seised of it, and circumstances therefore testify for the proprietor of the land; as shall shortly be explained—If, however, the case in question be considered separately, and not as founded on the above, then the two disciples argue that the space is in the hands of the proprietor of the aqueducet, as he preserves the water by means of it,—whence it is that the 'proprietor of the land is not entitled to break it down.—Haneefa, on the other hand, argues that the dependent land resembles the other land, of the proprietor, with respect both to appearance and substance:—with respect to appearance, because it is on a level with, and joins to it; and with respect to substance also, because it is of the same soil, and is equally capable of nourishing trees and vegetables; and circumstances testify for him who is in possession of what bears the greatest resemblance to the dependent ground, namely, the land adjacent to it;—in the same manner as where two people contend for a door-plank in the possession of some other person, and which exactly quadrates with another that is possessed by one of the litigants; for in that case the Kazee must abjudge such plank to be the property of him who possesses the correspondent one, —In reply to what the two disciples further urge— it may be observed that the contest here does not hinge upon what was placed for the conservation of the water (the banks), but upon what is independent of it, and fit for producing treat, &c. Besides supposing that the proprietor of the aqueduct preserves the water only on account of the dependent space of land, it may be answered that the proprietor of the ground preserves it only on account of the dependent space of land likewise.—With respect, moreover, to what they urge, that "the proprietor of the land is not entitled to break down the banks of the aqueduct," it is to be observed that this is not because they are the property of the proprietor of the aqueduct, but merely because he has an interest in them;— in the same manner as where a person is possessed of a wall, and another, having the property of a wall near it, lays beams across both with the assent, of the other; for in such case the other has not afterwards the power of pulling down his own wall, since he must thereby injure the right of this person.

Differences of opinion concerning aqueducts.—It is related, in the Jama Sagheer, that if a person possess an aqueduct having banks on each side, and adjacent to them a piece of land belonging to some other person, and the banks be not in the hands of any one, that is to say, be destitute of marks, such as trees, stones, or the like, to determine the property, those banks belong to the proprietor of the land, according to Haneefa; —whereas the two disciples hold that they, appertain to the proprietor of the river.—If, on the contrary, the marker of any person be left upon them, they are then unanimously, of opinion that the marker has the better claim,—Stil, however, they differ in opinion where there is a tree upon the banks, and it is not known who planted it;—for Haneefa is of opinion that to plant a tree is the right of the proprietor of the grounds, whilst the two disciples hold this to be the right of the proprietor of the aqueduct.—With respect, also, to throwing up earth, many have said that, there is a disagreement; whilst others have said that this belongs to the proprietor of the aqueduct, provided he do not exceed the prescribed bounds. With regard to walking upon the banks, some have said that it is not permitted, in the opinion of Haneefa; whilst others have said that it is not prohibited, because of there being a necessity for it. The learned Aboo Jafir has said that he would decree according to the opinion of Haneefa in the case of planting a tree,—and according to that of the two disciples, in the case of throwing up earth. It is reported, from Aboo Yoosaf, that the width of the dependent space of an aqueduct is half the breadth of the aqueduct; but according to Mohammed it is the whole breadth : and this opinion is the most favourable to mankind.—It is here proper to onserve, that the subject resolves itself into several sections, treating of the cases of Shirba, or a right; to water, whether derived from the the possession of land, or from other causes.

Section I.
Of Waters.

All people have a right to drink from a well, canal, or reservoir, and also cattle.—

If a person have the property of a canal, a well, or a reservoir, he cannot prohibit either man or beast from drinking of it.—Here it is necessary to premise that water is of four kinds. I. The water of the ocean, which every person has a right to drink, or to carry away for the purpose of moistening his lands.—If, therefore, a person incline to dig a canal, and convey the water in it from the ocean to his land, no person has power to prevent him from so doing; for the enjoyment of the water of the ocean is common to every one, in the same manner as the light of the sun or moon, or the use of the air.—II. The water of large rivers, such as the Oxus, the Euphrates, or the Tigris, in which every person has an absolute right to drink, and also a conditional right to use it towards moistening his lands;—that is to say, a person, if he cultivate waste land, may dig a channel for the purpose of conveying water to it from the river, provided his doing so be not detrimental to the people: but if there be a probability of its being hurtful in its consequences (as if, by opening the banks, the water should overflow the country and villages around), in that case he is not permitted to dig a channel for the watering of his land, as the prevention of a public evil is a consideration of greater moment.—Analogous to this, also, is the erection of a mill on the banks of a river; for the demolition of the banks by the mill is the same as by watering land.—III. Water in which several have a share;—and in which, likewise, the right of drinking is allowed to every one; for it is recorded in the traditions that three things are common to all, namely, water, grass, and fire. Besides, wells, and the like, are not dug for the purpose of preserving water; and hence the water of them is not the property of anyone; for it is common, and as such cannot be made a particular property until it be separately kept and preserved;—as holds with respect to a deer that only sleeps upon a person's ground There is, moreover, a necessity for establishing this common right with regard to water, since it is impossible for every person to carry it along with him; and as a person may be in want of it for himself and his horse, mankind would therefore be too much cramped if an unlimited use of it were not granted them. If, however, a person incline to bring water to moisten the land he had cultivated from a river or canal which belongs to others, the proprietors may prevent him, as otherwise their right of watering* would be entirely destroyed.—IV, Water which is preserved, or in other words kept in vessels. Water of this description is property, because of its detention; and the right of others no longer extends to it;—in the same manner as holds with respect to game, after being taken by any person. Nevertheless, it is doubtful whether this water may not also be participated, because of the tradition before quoted. Hence, if a person, in a time of scarcity, steal a quantity of water equivalent to the amount which constitutes theft, he is not liable to amputation.

Unless there be other water at a little distance.—If a person be possessed of a well, fountain, or rivulet, he may prevent any one from drinking the water of them, or encroaching on his property, provided there be other water at a little distance, and which is not the particular property of any one. If, however, this be not the case, the proprietor must then either bring him water to drink, or permit him to take it himself, on condition that he destroy not the banks. What is here advanced is reported from Tahavee,—Some have said that this is approved, in case the possessor of the well have dug it himself in land which is his own property: but that, if he should have dug it in waste lands, he is not, in that case, on any account permitted to prohibit others from entering on his premises to drink water; for the waste lands are a common right; and as the well was dug towards the promoting of a common right, namely, tithe and tribute, it follows that the digging of it is not destructive of the liberty of drinking, If, therefore, the proprietor refuse the other permission to drink, and that others be apprehensive either of the death of himself or his horse from an excess of thirst, he may then lawfully oppose the proprietor with weapons, as he has already aimed at his destruction in withholding his right, namely, the water: for the water of a well is common, and is not property.—It is otherwise with respect to water kept in vessels; for a person in want of it where it is so kept, is only permitted to contend with the possessor of it without weapons. The same law obtains in the case of a person oppressed with hunger. Many have said that in the case of a wall it is not lawful to use weapons; but that it is allowable to contend with a stick; for the possessor is guilty of an offence in refusing the water; and the application of a stick is a substitute for correction.

Water may also be carried away for the purpose of ablution.—It is lawful for men to carry away water from a rivulet to perform their ablutions, or to wash their garments,—This is approved; because, to desire men to purify themselves, or to wash their garments with such water, without carrying it away as mentioned by some), would be attended with much inconvenience.

Or for watering trees or parterres.—If, also, a person be inclined to water the trees or small parterre before his house, he may lawfully carry away water for that purpose from the rivulet of another; for the law allows great liberty in the case of water, and considers the refusal of it as truly opprobrious.—A person is not, however,

*Arab, Shirba, a particular right to water, explained in the course of this book

allowed to carry away water either from the rivulet, well; or aqueduct of another, for the use of his orchard or fields, unless he be expressly permitted so to do; and the proprietor may prohibit him from it; because when water is possessed in joint property, none but the proprietors have any right to the use of it, as otherwise their right would be defeated.—Still, however, the proprietor of the river may, if he coose, either give or land, the water of it to another, because it is his property; and because the gift of such is customary; in the same manner as holds with respect to water preserved in vessels.

Section II.

*Of digging or clearing Rivers.**

River are of three descriptions.—RIVERS are of three kinds.—I. Such as are not the property of any; and of which the waters have not been divided, like the Tigris, Euphrates, &c.—II. Such as, being appropriated and divided, are at the same (time public rivers, in which boats sail.—III. Rivers that are held in property, and divided; and are also private, in which no boats sail.

Great public rivers must be cleared and repaired at the expense of the public treasury.—IN the first kind of rivers, if the river fill up so as to require digging, the care thereof devolves upon the chief, †who is to defray the charges of it from the public treasury; for as the work is performed for the advantage of the Mussulman community, the expense attending it must be defrayed from the property of the community;—those expenses must, however, be disbursed from the funds of tribute and capitation-tax, and not from those of tithe and alms: for the latter are appropriated solely to the use of the poor, whereas the former are intended as a provision to answer contingencies.

Or by a general contribution of labour.—IF there be not any money in the public treasury, the chief is in that case at liberty; with a view to promote the public utility, to compel the people to repair the damage in question, as it is presumed they would not of themselves apply to the work,—whence it was that Omar Farook said to the people, "Were I to leave you to your own direction, without ever using compulsion, verily, matters would come to such a pass that you would even sell your children."—None, however, must be compelled but such as are able to work; and such as are not able to work, and are rich, must pay a certain sum, according to their particular station and ability.

And appropriated rivers, at the expense of the proprietors.—WITH respect to the second kind of river, it must be cleared, when requisite, at the expense of the proprietors, without any supply from the public treasury; for the right of the river particularly belongs to them, as does also the use of it.—If, therefore, any one of them should refuse to assist in digging, the chief may compel him, to the end that the others may not suffer any injury by his refusal.

OBJECTION.—It would appear that, in being thus forced to work, the refuser suffers an injury.

REPLY.—Such injury is particular, and is not without its use, for in recompense thereof the party obtains his share of the water; it is not, therefore, to be put in competition with the common injury that would otherwise be suffered by the rest.

If, also, some of the proprietors of the river be desirous of strengthening the banks, from an apprehension that they might give way, and it be probable that bad consequences may ensue from their decay (such as inundating the neighbouring country, and breaking up the roads), the chief may in that case use compulsion with any of them who refuse to assist in the undertaking. He must not, however, use force where the decay of the banks cannot produce any bad consequence; for the fall of the banks is an event merely probable. It is otherwise with respect to clearing a river in a case of necessity; for that is a matter of certainty,—whence it is that compulsion may be used to effect it.—With respect to the third kind of rivers they are particularly appropriated and therefore the digging of them is entirely the duty of the proprietors.—Some have alleged that the magistrate may employ force with any who refuse to dig; in the same manner as in the case of the second kind of rivulets. Others, again, have maintained that the magistrate has not a power of this kind; since both of the injuries, namely, that of the partner on whom compulsion is used, and also that which the other partners sustain in consequence of his refusal, are private; and the injury to the other partners may be remedied by their taking from the one who refuses to work a part of the expense incurred in digging the rivulet, proportionately to his share (provided, however, that the work be executed at the instance of the magistrate).—It is otherwise with respect to the second kind of rivers, as there one of the injuries is public.

ORJECTION.—Here likewise is a conjunction of two injuries and as one of these (namely, that sustained by those who have a right to drink the water) is public, it would follow that, to prevent this public injury, compulsion may be used in the case of private rivers likewise.

*Arab. Nihr.—It is a term of very general application, signifying not only rivers properly so called, but also canals, or any other species of aqueduct constructed by art.

† Arab. Walee; meaning, generally, the governor of a province or district.

REPLY.—No compulsion is used in digging towards obtaining water to drink;—thus if the whole should refuse to dig, the magistrate cannot employ force.*

Rules with respect to drains, watercourses, &c.—IN digging a watercourse, the expense incurred in the upper part is equally defrayed by the whole of the partners; but when the work is carried beyond the land of any one of them, he is then, according to Haneefa, exempt from all further charge. The two disciples maintain that the expenses of digging from the head to the end of the watercourse is jointly defrayed by the several partners, according to the extent of their shares; because the partner possessing the higher share has likewise a right in the lower ones, they being needful to him, in receiving the discharge, from his part, of the superfluous water. Haneefa, in support of his opinion, argues that the end of digging the watercourse being to obtain water for the purpose of cultivation, the object of the higher sharer is consequently obtained when his part is finished; and he is not, therefore, under any obligation after that to assist in prosecuting the work solely for the benefit of others.—With respect, moreover, to what the two disciples urge, it may be replied that, although the higher partner do indeed stand in need of the lower shares, for the passing away of the superfluous water from his share, yet he is not, on that account, obliged to dig these lower shares;—in the same manner as where a person has a right of passing the water from his house upon the terrace of another; in which case he is not under any obligation to unite in building or repairing such terrace.—Besides, the higher partner may at any time prevent the water from overflowing his land, by occasionally damming up the source or spring, thereby preventing the flow of any superfluity of water into his share.

WHEN, in digging a watercourse common to several partners, the work is carried beyond the share of one of them, who is thus exempted from any further charge, some have alleged that he may then immediately open the spring-head, or inlet, in order to obtain water for cultivation, as the watercourse, with respect of him, is wholly dug. Others have said that he cannot do so until the shares of the other partners be likewise completed; in order to prevent any preference among them.

SUCH persons as have only a right to drink the water, are not subject to pay any part of the charges of digging, as those are numberless, and are, moreover, subordinate to the actual sharers.

*When water is wanted, towards moistening lands for cultivation, the magistrate may then employ force in causing a rivulet to be dug; but not where the water is wanted only to drink.

Section III.

Of Claims of Shirb, and of Disputes and particular Privileges with respect to it.*

A right to water may exist independent of the ground.—A CLAIM of Shirb, or right to water, is valid independent of any property in the ground, upon a favourable construction of the law; for a person may become endowed with it, exclusive of the ground, either by inheritance or bequest; and it sometimes happens that when a person sells his lands he reserves to himself the right of Shirb. Besides, Shirb being a desirable object, and also capable of yielding advantage, the claim to it is therefore valid.

No person can alter or obstruct the course of water running through his ground.— IF a person be possessed of a rivulet running through lands which are the property of another, and the proprietor of these lands, being desirous that it should not run through them, attempt to prevent it, on the plea of its being his property, he must not be permitted to do so but the rivulet must be suffered to flow in its usual channel,—for, as the rivulet is in the possession of the person who has the property of it, because of his water running in the bed of it, his word, in case of a litigation, is therefore to be credited in preference to that of the other;—whereas, if the rivulet were not in his possession (as if it should contain now water), in that case the word of the proprietor of the lands would be credited;—unless the other could prove by witnesses that the rivulet is his property, or that he formerly conveyed water through it towards his own grounds for the purpose of watering them,—when the Kazee must decree it to him, as he thus substantiates his claim.—(Analogous to this is a contention concerning the property of a river-head, or a water drain, a spout, or a road through the court of another.)

In case of disputes, a distribution of the right to water must be made.—IF a rivulet be jointly held by several persons, and they dispute concerning their particular proportions of right to water, a distribution must be made according to the extent of land which they serverally possess;—for as the object of right to water is to moisten their lands, it is consequently fit that each receive in proportion to his territory:—It is otherwise in the case of a road; for the object in that being to pass and repass, the smallness or largeness of the house is of no weight in the division:—that is to say, if the partners in a road dispute concerning their shares, it is decreed that they shall hold it equally, and that no distinction shall be made from the difference of their houses.

* This term, which is purely technical, the translator, for the convenience of the English reader, has rendered, in general, a right to water.

A rivulet must not be dammed up for the convenience of one partner, without the consent of the others.—If it happen that the person who possesses the highest part of rivulet be nor able, without stopping the current, to enjoy his right to water in a satisfactory manner (for this reason; that his lands, being high precipitate, the water from them with great velocity); still he must not be permitted to dam the rivulet, as he would thereby destroy the right of the others: he must, therefore, take his share without stopping the current. If, however, the others assent to his stopping the current that he may the better water his land, or enter into an agreement that each shall stop it in his turn, it is lawful, as being their right. But if it be possible to effect the stoppage with a board, they must not use clay, or any kind of plaster, without the consent of the whole, as an injury would be thereby occasioned to the other shares.

One partner in a rivulet cannot dig a trench or erect a mill upon it without the general consent.—It is not permitted to any of the sharers to dig another rivulet leading from the common one, or to erect a water mill upon it;—because, in the former instance, the bank of a common rivulet must necessarily be broken; and in the latter, an erection is made of a building upon a partnership concern;—unless, however, the mill be stationed on the builder's land, and be not injurious, either to the ground, by breaking down the banks, or to the water, by diverting it into another channel;—in which case it is lawful, as being the exercise of a power derived from property, and from which there results not any injury to others.

Nor construct a water-engine or a bridge.—(The erecting of a machine for raising water by camels, or oxen, is considered in the same light as the erecting of a mill.)—It is likewise unlawful for any of the sharers either to erect a small bridge which may be occasionally withdrawn, or a large one of stone or bricks which is durable and fixed.—In short, a private rivulet is considered in the same light as a private road, in which several participate, but in which none have any particular privileges.—It is otherwise where a person possesses a small private rivulet brought out from a large private, one jointly held by several; for in that case, if the proprietor of the little rivulet choose he may erect upon it a large solid bridge; or, if there was previously a bridge over it, he may, if he please, pull it down (provided a greater quantity of water than formerly do not, by that means, flow into his rivulet) for under these circumstances the demolition of the bridge is lawful, being in virtue a power derived from his own property, which occasions no detriment to others. He must not, however, extend the inlet of the smaller rivulet; as he would thereby destroy the banks of the large one, and likewise draw a greater quantity of water into his own than is his due,—Neither must he be suffered to enlarge the sluice through which he receives his share of water, where the distribution is made in that manner,—that is, where boards with holes are fixed on the bank of the river contiguous to the lands of each partner, that he may receive, as his share, whatever quantity of water issues through his board.—But any of them who chooses may either heighten or lower his particular board, as the equality of the division depends upon the largeness or smallness of the holes, and upon the height or lowness of them, for an alteration in that respect occasions no difference in the distribution.

One partner cannot alter the mode of partition without the others' consent.—If where the distribution is made by sluices, in the manner above described, one of the partners choose that the partition be made by the measure of time, he is not at liberty so to adjust it, unless with the concurrence of the others; for whatever is the establised mode must be continued; as the right of every one is by that means more clearly distinguished.

Or increase the number of openings through which he receives his share.—If each partner in an appropriated rivulet have a specific number of holes or sluices allotted to him, it is not permitted to any of them to increase that number, notwithstanding it may occasion no injury to the others; for here exists a partnership in particular property, and in which the right of each is particularly specified.—It is otherwise in the case of large rivers, such as the Tigris or the Euphrates; for as there any person is at liberty to dig a small rivulet, and fill it from them, he is consequently at liberty to increase the hole or sluices through which the waters pass from them.

Or convey his share into lands not entitled to receive it.—It is not lawful for any of the partners in a river to convey his share of water into such of his lands as are not entitled to receive water from that river; for this circumstance might, in process of time, furnish an argument of his having a right to water these lands from that river.

Or through such lands into those that are entitled.—Neither is it lawful for a partner to convey his share of water through such of his lands as are not entitled to it, into others that are: for, in this case, it is probable he would receive a greater quantity of water than his due, as part would be absorbed by the lands through which they first passed. (This is analogous to the case of a joint road, where one of the partners wishes to open a road to the inhabitants of a house, in the same range, whose road lies through another way, by permitting them to pass through his house in their way to their own).

Neither can he shut up any of the water-vents.—If two persons possess a rivulet jointly, and receive their shares by water issuing through sluices, and the one whose share lies nearest to the source be inclined to stop several of the sluices allotted to him, to prevent the issue of a superfluity of water into his lands, he must not be allowed so to do, as he might thereby subject the lands of the other sharer to be overflowed

Or adopt a partition by rotation.—Neither is he at liberty to change the mode of participations; by taking the use of the whole in rotation, instead of each receiving a moiety of the whole quantity; for as the division has already been settled by the mode of vents or sluices, he cannot afterwards require any other mode,—unless the other assent, in which case he may do so;—is still, however, remaining at the option of this partner (or of his heir, after his decease) to annul this, and revert to the former mode;—because the establishment of division, by giving the whole to each in rotation, in a case where each had formerly held a separate share, is, in fact, lending a right to water (as an exchange of Shirb for Shirb is null): and a right to water is inheritable, or the use of it may lawfully be left in legacy; but it can neither be sold nor bestowed in gift, nor left in legacy to sell, give away, or bestow in alms, these several deeds being unlawful on account of the uncertainty to which they are liable, either from ignorance or deceit, with regard to the quantity of water,—or because Shirb is not, in itself, a substantial property, but rather a privilege or immunity, insomuch that if a person water his lands from the Shirb of another, he is not liabe to make compensation for it;—and these several deeds being void, a legacy for any of these purposes is also void.

A right to water cannot be consigned as a dower.—A RIGHT to water is incapable of being assigned as a specific dower in a contract of marriage; wherefore if such be mentioned in a marriage contract, Mihr-Misl, or proper dower, is due.

Or given as a consideration for Khoola.—In the same manner, also, it cannot be given as a consideration for Khoola;—whence, if a wife bargain for her divorce, in consideration of her making over such right, the husband may restore it to her, and; in lieu of it, take from her the dower he had assigned her on their marriage. The ground on which the law in these cases proceeds is, that right to water is a matter the extent of which cannot be ascertained with any precision.

Or in composition for a claim.—A RIGHT to water is incapable of being given in composition for a claim; for as it cannot, by means of any deed whatever, be rendered property, a composition in conideration of it is consequently null.

Or sold (without ground) to discharge the debts of a defunct—(mode to be pursued in this last instance)—A RIGHT to water, without ground, cannot be sold after the death of any perosn to discharge his debts,—in the same manner as it cannot be sold during his lifetime. What, then, shall the Imam do, in this case, towards settling the debt of the deceased?—This question has given rise to a diversity of opinions; but the most advisable method of proceeding, in such an instance, is to join the right to the lands of another person not possessing such right, and then, with his consent, to dispose of both:—when, computing how much the value of the lands has been increased by the addition of the right, he may apply the difference towards paying off the debts of the deceased. If he be not able to procure land in this manner, he may buy a piece of land payable from the effects of the deceased, and having joined it to the right, sell them together; when with the price so obtained he must first discharge the purchase-money discharging the debts of the deceased.

Any accident from the use of the water does not induce responsibility.—IF a person, having moistened his lands, or filled them with water, should by that means overflow the lands of his neighbour, he is not, in such case, liable to make a compensation, as he was not guilty of any transgression

---

BOOK XLVI.

OF PROHIBITED LIQUORS.

There are four prohibited liquors. I. Khamr (the crude juice of the grape).—THERE are four prohibited liquors,—the first of which is termed Khamr,* meaning (according to the exposition of Haneefa) the crude juice of the grape, which, being fermented, becomes spirituous,—first gathering foam and settling, and then possessing an inebriating quality. According to the two disciples; the juice becomes Khamr upon its fermenting, and being spirituous without the condition of its gathering foam;—for whenever the juice of grapes becomes spirituous, the appellation of Khamr, and the characteristic of it, namely, illegality, are both established.—The argument adduced by Haneefa is, that fermentation is the commencement of the process by which liquor becomes spirituous, and which is completed when it foams and settles, as by that means the dregs are separated from the finer particles;—and the ordinances of the LAW regarding Khamr (which are decisive), such as punishment for drinking it, the holding him an infidel who shall deem it lawful, and the prohibition against selling it,—have all a reference to the completion. Some of the learned allege that it is declared unlawful to drink after having become spirituous, purely

---

* The translator has, in the course of the work rendered every inebriating drink under the general term wine, which comprehends all descriptions of prohibited liquors.—In this book, however, he retains the original terms for the sake of distinction,

from motives of caution.—Others, again, maintain that the term Khamr is applicable to whatever is of an inebriating quality; because it is mentioned in the traditions, that "whatever inebriate is KHAMR;"—and (in another tradition) "KHAMR is produced from two trees, namely, the VINE and the DATE." The term Khamr, moreover, is derived from Mokhamira, signifying, stupefaction, or deprivation of sense, which is a consequence of drinking any inebriating liquor. In reply to this, however, Haneefa argues that the term Khamr, according to the concurrent opinion of all lexicographers, is used only in the sense above mentioned, whence it is that to liquors of other descriptions other terms are applied, such as Nabeez, Tabeekh, and Mosillis.* Another argument is that the illegality of Khamr is indubitable,—whence, if every inebriating liquor were Khamr, all such would of course be likewise indubitably illegal,—whereas this is not the case, for there is a doubt regarding them. In reply, moreover, to the arguments of some of the learned as above adduced, it is to be remarked that the first-recited tradition is not perfectly authentic, Yehya Ibn Mayeen having disputed it;—and with respect to the second quoted tradition, the intention of it was merely to explain the LAW, or, in other words, to show that all liquors extracted from either of the two trees mentioned, being of an inebriating quality, are unlawful as well as Khamr.

Which is unlawful in any quantity.—KHAMR is in itself unlawful, whether it be used in small or great quantities, the illegality not depending on drinking it to such a degree as to produce intoxication Some of looser principles reject the absolute illegality of Khamr, alleging that its effects only are the cause of its illegality; because the evil of it is, that it creates an inattention towards the worship of GOD; and as this evil is occasioned only by intoxication, it follows that where this does not take place it is not unlawful.—This, however, is gross infidelity, and in direct contradiction to the KORAN, GOD having there termed such liquor filth, a thing which is unlawful in its own nature. Bsiedes, the Prophet has decreed Khamr to be unlawful, according to various traditions; and all the doctors are unanimously of this opinion. It is to be observed, however, that although Khamr be unlawful, even is so small a quantity as may not be sufficient to intoxicate, yet the same law does not hold with respect to other things of an inebriating quality; for a little of them if not sufficient to intoxicate, is not forbidden. Shafei, indeed, is of opinion that these are likewise unlawful, in any quantiy.

Is filth in an extreme.—KHAMR is filth in an extreme degree, in the same manner as urine; for the illegality of it is indisputably proved, as has been already shown.

WHOSOEVER maintains Khamr to be lawful is an infidel,* for he thereby rejects incontestable proof.

And cannot constitute property with a Mussulman.—KHAMR is not a valuable commodity with respect to Mussulmans. If therefore, it be destroyed or usurped by any person, there is no responsibility. The sale of it is moreover unlawful; for GOD, in terming it filth, manifested a detestation of it; whereas, if it had been a commodity of value, some respect would have been shown to it.—Besides, it is recorded in the traditions, that "he who prohibited the drinking of it; did likewise prohibit both the sale of it and the use or enjoyment of the price of it."

Nor be employed in the discharge of his debts.—IF a Mussulman be indebted to another, and wish to discharge the debt with the price of Khamr, in that case both the payment and receipt is unlawful because such price is produced from an illicit sale, and is considered either as an usurpation or a trust in the Mussulman's hands, according to the different opinion of the doctors on this subjects; in the same manner as in the case of the sale of carrion. If, on the contrary, the debtor be a Zimmee, it is lawful for his Mussulman creditor to receive such payment; as the sale of Khamr is legal amongst Zimmees.

Or used by ihm.—IT is unlawful to derive any use from Khamr, either as a medicine, or in any other manner; because the use of filth is forbidden; and also, because abstinence from it is enjoyed and this injunction could not be observed in case of its use being allowed.

And the drinking of which, in any quantity induces punishment.—WHOEVER drinks Khamr incurs punishment, although he be not intoxicated: for it is said, in the traditions, "Let him who drinks KHAMR be whipped;—and if he drink it again, let him be again in he same manner punished." The whole of the companions are agreed upon this point; and the number of stripes prescribed is eighty, as has already been shown in treating of punishments.

Unless it be boiled.—IF a person boil Khamr until two-thirds of it evaporate, it is not thereby rendered lawful. If, however, a person drink of it after such process, he is not liable to punishment, unless he be intoxicated.

But it may be converted into vinegar.—IT is lawful to make vinegar of Khamr. Shafei, however, holds a different opinion.

II. Bazik (the boiled juice of the grape), termed (when boiled away to one half) Monissaf.—THUS much with respect to Khamr, the first in order of prohibited liquors.—The second species of prohibited liquor, is the juice of grapes boiled until a

* These are different kinds of liquor, extracted from dates, which are more particularly described a little farther on.

* And consequently becomes exposed to the penalties of apostasy.

quantity less than two-thirds evaporate. This is denominated Bazik. It is also termed Monissaf; but that is only where exactly one half of it evaporates in boiling. This kind of liquor is unlawful, according to all our doctors;—according to the two disciples, when it only ferments and become spirituous;—and according to Haneefa, when if foams and settles. Oozrai has said that Monissaf is lawful (and several of the tribe of Mutazali* have seconded this opinion); because it is a good liquor, or, in other words, is pleasing to the, palate and also, because it is not Khamr. The argument of our doctors, that as Monissaf is pure, and equally delicious with Khamr, a number of the idle and dissolute are consequently tempted to drink it; and it is therefore prohibited, with a view to prevent that dissipation which it is found to occasion.

III. Sikker (an infusion of dates).—The third species of unlawful liquor is termed Sikkir; and is made by steeping fresh dates in water unitl they take effect in sweetening it; when it is both unlawful and abominable to drink of it. Shareek-Ibn-Abdoola alleges that it is lawful, as God, speaking of his bounty in the Koran, says, "Ye enjoy Sikker from the grape and the date;" whence we may infer that it is allowable—,as bounty cannot apply to any thing unlawful. The argument of our doctors is the concurrent opinion of all the companions upon this point; and with respect to the text above cited, it has a reference to a particular period, having been revealed in the infancy of the religion of Islam, when all sorts of spirituous liquors were lawful.

IV. Nookoo Zabeeb (an infusion of raisins).—The fourth species of prohibited liquors is Nookoo-Zabeeb,† that is, water in which raisins are steeped until it become sweet, and is affected in its substance. This kind is, however, lawful when merely it possesses a sweet quality;—and is prohibited only when it ferments and becomes spirituous. Oozrai is of a different opinion regarding this liquor likewise.

The three last are not so illegal as Khamr.—They may be held legal, without incurring a change of infidelity.—It is to be observed that the illegality of these liquors, namely, Bazik, Monissaf, and the Nookoo of dates and raisin, is inferior to that of Khamr. If, therefore, any person hold these lawful, still he is not deemed an infidel. It is otherwise in the case of Khamr; for, with respect to the liquors here mentioned, the illegality a mere matter of opinion; whereas, with regard to Khamr, the illegality is undisputed.

And may be drank (so as not to intoxicate) without punishment.—Punishment, moreover, is not inflicted for drinking these liquors, except in a quantiy sufficient to produce intoxication; whereas the drinking of one drop only of Khamr induces punishment. The filth of these liquors, likswise, according to one tradition, is of a slight degree, and according to another, of an extreme degree; but the filth of Khamr is of an extreme degree, according to every tradition.

They may also be sold: and are a subject of responsibility.—The sale of the liquors in question is lawful, according to Haneefa, and a compension is due from the destroyer of them. The two disciples, on the contrary, hold that the sale of them is unlawful, and that no reparation is due from the destroyer of them; in the same manner as in the case of Khamr.

But they must not be used.—It is unlawful to derive any kind of use from the abovementioned liquors, as they are prohibited. It is related that Aboo Yoosaf holds the sale of any of the aforesaid liquors, excepting Khamr, to be lawful,—if more than one half, and less than two-thirds, should have evaporated in the boiling.

Mohammed, in the Jama Sagheer, remarks that every sort of liquor excepting those above mentioned is lawful. This opinion, the learned say, is recorded only in the Jama Sagheer, and is not to be found in any other book. It, however, affords an agrument that any kind of strong liquor extracted from wheat, barley, honey, or millet, is lawful in the opinion of Haneefa, if not drank so as to occasion intoxication; and he, in fact, maintains that punishment is not inflicted even in the case of intoxication. If, therefore, a person intoxicated with these liquors should divorce his wife, it is void, in the same manner as divorce pronounced by a person in his sleep or by one whose faculties are impaired from the use of opium, or from having drank the milk of a mare in a medical composition. It is elsewhere related, as an opinion of Mohammed, that every sort of strong drink, excepting those above specified, is prohibited:—that if a person drink them to intoxication he is to be punished;—and that a divorce pronounced by him when so intoxicated is valid;—in the same manner as holds in the case of liquors; and decrees pass according to this opinion. He has also said, in the Jama Sagheer, that Aboo Yoosaf had first declared every sort of wine to be unlawful which fermented and became spirituous, and afterward remained ten days without spoiling: but that he afterwards adopted the opinion of Haneefa. In other words, he first, according to the adjudication of Mohammed deemed all inebriating liquors unlawful; but afterwards adopted the opinion of Haneefa. Aboo Yoosaf was singular in making it a condition that the liquor should remain ten days without being spoiled, He, however, afterwards receded from this opinion, and gave into that of Haneefa and Mohammed on this point. In the Abridg

*A particular heretical sect of the Mussulmans. (See Sale's Prelminary Discourse, Sect. 8.)

† Nookoo signifies water in wheih anything is steeped and Zabeeb means raisins.

ment (of Kadooree) it is said, that the steeping of raisins or dried dates, when boiled a little, even so as to become spirituous, may lawfully be drank in such a quantity as not to inebriate, povided it be done without wantonness or joy,—his is according only to the two Elders; for Mohammed and Shafei deem it unlawful.

Khoolteen (a mixture of the infusion of dates and raisins) may be drank.—There is no impropriety in drinking Khoolteen; that is, water in which dates have been steeped, mixed with that of raisins, and boiled together until they ferment and become spirituous. This is grounded on a circumstance relative to Ibn Zeeyad, which is thus related by himself:—"Abdoola, the son of Omar, having given me some Sherbet to drink, I became intoxicated to such a degree that knew not my own house. I went to him next morning, and having informed him of the circumstance, he acquainted me that he had given me nothing but a drink composed of dates and raisins."—Now this was certainly Khoolteen, which had undergone the operation of boiling; because it is elsewhere related by Omar that it is unlawful in its crude state.

Liquors produced by means of honey or grain are lawful.—Liquor produced by means of honey, wheat, barley, or millet, is lawful, according to Haneefa and Aboo Yoosaf, although it be not boiled,—provided, however, that it be not drank in a wanton or joyful manner. The argument they adduce is the saying of the Prophet "Khamr is the product of these two trees" (meaning the vine and the date);—that is to say, he confined the prohibition to these two trees, as his intention was to explain the law.—It is to be observed that several of the learned have made the boiling of these liquors a requisite towards their legality. Others, on the contrary, hold it to be no way necessary (and such is the opinion recorded in the Mabsoot): because these liquors are not of such a nature that a little induces a wish for more, whether they be boiled or crude. It has likewise been disputed whether a person who gets drunk with any of these liquors is to be punished. Some have said that he is not.

But any person drinking them to intoxication incurs punishment.—The learned in the law, however, have determined otherwise; for it is related by Mohammed that punishment is to be inflicted on whoever is intoxicated with any of the aforesaid strong liquors; for this reason, that in the present age they are as much sought for by the dissolute as other liquors were formerly; nay even more so.—The same law holds with regard to strong drinks extracted from milk. Many have said that any drink made from the milk of a mare is unlawful, in the opinion of Haneefa, because it is derived from the flesh, which (according to him) is unlawful. Lawyers, however, remark it as the better opinion that the milk is not unlawful according to Haneefa; for although he have pronounced the flesh to be abominable, yet the reason is either because, if it were otherwise, the means of conquest would thereby be destroyed; or because the horse is a noble animal: neither of which reasons hold with regard to the milk.

Mosillis (grapejuice boiled down to a third) is lawful.—If the juice of grapes be boiled until two-thirds of it evaporate (being then termed Mosillis), it becomes lawful, according to the two Elders, notwithstanding it be spirituous. Mohammed, Shafei, and Malik, say otherwise. (This difference of opinion, however, exists only on the supposition that it is used with a view to strengthen the constitution; for if it be drank from pleasure or joy they are unanimous in judging it unlawful.) Mohammed, Shafei, and Malik, in support of their opinion, have cited a saying of the Prophet, "Every inebriating drink is Khamr; and whatever in excess produces intoxication is prohibited, even in moderation;" and in another place. "Any drink of which one cupful occasions intoxication, is unlawful in a single drop."—Another argument is, that every inebriating liquor tends to stupefy the senses, and is consequently prohibited either in a small or large quantity, in the same manner as Khamr. The two Elders, in support of their opinion, have quoted the saying of the Prophet; "Khamr is unlawful in its very nature:" and in another place, "Little or much of it is alike unlawful; and inebriation from every other strong drink (that is to say, every kind besides Khamr) is forbidden." Now since the Prophet has specified intoxication as a condition with respect to other drinks than Khamr, we may conclude that on that circumstance only their illegality depends. Besides, stupefaction of the senses takes place only when liquors are used in such excess as to inebriate which is allowed to be dregal. A little, therefore, of any strong rink other than Khamr is never illegal, except when, on account of its fineness or purity, a little of it invites to more,—in which case the law regards every quantity of it in the same light. This, however, is not the case with Mosillis, a little of which, because of its thickness, does not induce a wish for more; and which, in its substances, is food,—wherefore when used in a moderate quantity it retains its original legality.*

General rule with respect to it.—If a little water be poured into Mosillis to render it fine, and it be afterwards boiled for a short time it is still Mosillis, that addition of

* By original legality Haneefa alludes to an opinion he maintained in opposition to Malik, that every thing is originally lawful in its nature, being rendered otherwise only by the prohibition of the sacred writings:—whereas Malik holds every thing to have been originally unlawful, until sanctified by the Koran.

water tending only to weaken it.—It is otherwise where water is mixed with crude juice, and this mixture is then boiled until two-thirds of it evaporate; for here, either the water purely evaporates altogether, or it evaporates jointly with the juice; and in either case it is plain that two-thirds of the pure juice of the grapes or dates does not evaporate, which is requisite to render it a legal drink.

Rule in the boiling of unpressed grapes.—IF grapes be first boiled, and afterwards pressed until their juice be extracted, in that case a very little more boiling is sufficient to render the drinking of the liquor lawful, according to one tradition of Haneefa. According to another tradition it does not become lawful until two-thirds of it evaporate in boiling; and this is the better opinion; because the juice remaining within the film. and not being in any manner affected by the boiling, it is consequently similar to juice which is not boiled.

Or grapes mixed with dates.—IF fresh or dried grapes; being mixed with dates, be then boiled, two-thirds of the mixture must evaporate before it becomes lawful; for although, with respect to dates, a small boiling be often sufficient, yet with respect to the juice of grapes two-thirds are always required to have evaporated in boiling The same rule also holds where the juice of grapes is mixed with the water in which dates have been steeped. If, however, dried grapes, being mixed with the water of dates, should be boiled for a little, and afterwards some dates or dried grapes be thrown into it, in that case, provided the quantity thrown in be small, and not so much as is generally used to make Nabeez, it is lawful. It is otherwise, indeed, if the quantity be not small;—in the same manner as where a pot of the water of dates or raisins is mixed with the bolied juice Still, however, the person who drinks it is not subject, to punishment, because its illegality is adjudged merely on principles of caution; and endeavours must always be used to avoid the infliction of punishment.

Liquor, having once acquired a spirit, is not rendered lawfu by boiling.—IF Khamr, or any other spirtuous liquor, be boiled until two-thirds of it evaporate, still it is not lawful; for the illegality of it, which was previously established, is not removed by boiling.

Rule with respect to the use of vessels.—THERE is no impropriety in squeezing juice into pots or vessels of a green colour, or of which the interior part has been varnished with oil. The reason of this is, that formerly, in the infancy of the Mussulman religion, it was customary to keep Khamr in such vessels; and, on this account, when Khamer was rendered illegal, the Prophet prohibited the use of them likewise, that the greater caution might be observed. He afterwards, however, permitted the use of them, seeing that the vessels of themselves did not render any thing unlawful. If, therefore, Khamr have been kept in these vessels, it is necessary they be washed before they are applied to use. If a vessel be old, it becomes clean by three washings: but if it be new it can never be cleansed, in the opinion of Mohammed; for then the wine penetrates, and makes a deep impression in it; contrary to the case of an old one. Aboo Yoosaf holds that it may be cleansed by washing it thrice, and drying it after each washing.—Several have said that, in the opinion of Aboo Yoosaf, the mode of cleansing it is by filling it with water, and letting it remain for a short time; and then emptying it and filling it again; and so repeating this process until the water poured out be perfectly pure; when the vessel is clean.

Vinegar may be made from Khamr.—When Khamr is converted into vinegar, it is then lawful, whether it have been made so by throwing any thing into it (such as salt or vinegar), or, have become so of itself.

VINEGAR made of Khamr is not abominable. Shafei maintains that it is abominable; and that all vinegar obtained from Khamr by means of some mixture is unlawful.—With respect, however, to such as turn so from Khamr of itself, he has given two different opinions.

And the vessel in which it is so made becomes pure.—When Khamr is changed into vinegar, the vessel in which it is contained becomes clean according to the quantity of the Khamr. With regard to that part of the vessel that was empty, several have said that it also becomes clean, as being dependent on the other: but others have said that, as it is battered over with dried Khamr, it does not become clean until it be washed with vinegar, when it is immediately purified. In the same manner also, if Khamr be poured out of a vessel, and the vessel be then washed with vinegar, it becomes (as lawyers have said) instantaneously clean.

Rules with respect to the dregs of Khamr.—IT is abominable to drink the dregs of Khamr, or to use it in combing the hair as some women do; for the dregs are not entirely void of the particles of Khamr, and it is unlawful to apply any unlawful thing to use;—whence the illegality of using it in healing a wound, or applying it to a sore on the back of a quadruped.—It is also unlawful to administer it to an infidel or an infant; and whosoever does so is chargeable with the crime of it. In the same manner, it is unlawful to give it to a quadruped to drink.—Concerning this point, however, several have said that although it be unlawful to carry Khamr to a quadruped, yet if the animal, being brought to it, should drink of it, there is no impropriety;—in the same manner as in the case of a dog and carrion; that is to say, carrion must not be thrown to a dog; but if a dog be carried to where carrion is, he may, without any impropriety, be suffered to eat it.

IT is allowable to mix the dregs of Khamr with vinegar. In this case, however, it is required, that the vinegar be carried to the place where the dregs are, and be there mixed, for otherwise it is unlawful.

A PERSON who drinks the dregs of Khamr without being intoxicated is not liable to punishment. Shafei is of a different opinion; for in this case several of the particles of Khamr must necessarily be drank likewise. Our doctors, on the contrary, argue that as the dregs, of Khamr are disagreeable to the palate, a little of it does not, by consequence, beget an inclination for more; and thus, being like other strong drinks, the drinking of a little, unless it be attendedwith intoxication, is not punishable.

An injection of Khamr is unlawful but not punishable. An injection of Khamr into the anus or penis is unlawful as being a benefit derived from an unlawful article. It is not, however, punishable, as punishment. is inflicted only in the case of drinking it.

And so likewise a mixture of it in viands —IF a person throw Khamr into soup, it is not then lawful for him to eat the soup—because of its being rendered impure. Nevertheless, if he eat it, he is not liable to punishment, for in this case the Khamr is as it were boiled.

IF a person knead flour with Khamr, in that case it is unlawful to eat the bread or paste so made, as many of the particles of the Khamr still remain in it.

Section.

Of boiling the Juice of Grapes.

There are three general principles to be observed upon this subject.—IN boiling the juice of grapes there are three principles.— The first principle is, that whatever quantity may run over the pot from the agitation in boiling, or from the foaming of the juice, is not taken into account, but if considered as not having belonged to it; and the residue is to boiled until two-thirds of it evaporate, in order that the remaining third may be rendered lawful. To illustrate this:— suppose a person inclined to boil ten cups of juice; in that case, if one cup be lost from its boiling over the pot, he must boil the remainder until six cups have evaporated and three remain in the pot, when it becomes lawful.

THE second principle is, that if water be first poured into the juice, and the whole be then boiled, and the water, on account of its subtletv, be soon wasted, it is requisite that whatever remains after the evaporation (of the water) be boiled until two-thirds of it be wasted. If, on the contrary, the water and juice evaporate together, it is in that case requisite that the mixture be boiled until two-thirds of the whole evaporate, that the remaining third may be rendered lawful; for here the third of the mixture of water and juice which remains becomes the same as if, a third of the pure juice having remained. water had then been poured into it To exemplify this;—suppose a person should mix ten cups of juice with twenty cups of water;—in that case, if the water purely evaporate, the mixture must be boiled until a ninth of it remain, which is equi alent to one-third of the pure juice:—wher as, if the juice and water ev porate conjunctly, the whole must then be boiled until two-thirds of it evaporate.

IF juice be boiled with fire,* at one or several different times before it be inebriating or prohibited, it is lawful. If, also, the juice, being taken from the fire, should continue to boil until two-thirds of it evaporate, it is lawful, as in this case the evaporation is the effect of the fire.

THE third principle is, in boiling juice, after part of it has evaporated, and part has likewise been poured out,—to know how much more must evaporate, that the remaining part may be rendered lawful;— and, in order to this, the following rule must be observed.—The quantity which remains after part has been poured out must be multiplied by the third of the whole; and this sum being divided by the quantity which remains after part of it only has evaporated, the quotient is the quantitythat is lawful. Thus, if a person boil ten cups of juice, and after one cup had evaporated three cups more should be poured out; then three cups and one-third (the third of the whole) being multiplied into six, the number which remains after the loss of evaporation and pouring out amounts to twenty, and this sum being divided by nine, there remains two cups and two-ninths; the quantity which is lawful, when the rest has evaporated.

BOOK XLVII.

OF HUNTING.

Section I.

Of catching Game with Animals of the Hunting Tribe, such as Dogs. Hawks, &c.

It is lawful to hunt with all animals of the hunter tribe that are duly trained. It is lawful to hunt with a trained dog, a panther,† a hawk a falcon, and in short with every animal of the hunter tribe that is trained. It is related in the Jama Sagheer that game caught with a trained animal of the hunter tribe, whether bird or beast, is lawful; but that, caught with any other animal it is not lawful, unless when taken alive, and slain by Zabbah. This doctrine is established by a text of the KORAN, in which mention is made of trained dogs. The term Kalb [dog] comprehends, in its general

* The common method of making strong drink, among the Asiatics, is by fermenting the juice in the sun.

† YUZ.—It is an animal of the leopard on lynx species, hooded and trained to catching game, nearly on the same principle as the hawk.

acceptation every carnivorous animal even to a tiger.* It is, however, related as an opinion of Aboo Yoosaf, that tigers and bears are excepted, as neither of them hunt for others,—the tiger because of his ferocity, and the bear because of his voraciousness. Some of the kite tribe have likewise been excepted because of their voraciousness; and the hog has been excepted because it is essential filth, and because it is unlawful to derive any adventage from it. It is to be observed that it is a condition of the lawfulness of game that the animal which takes it be of the hunter tribe, and trained; and also that the master let slip† the animal in the name GOD; for it is so related in a tradition of Audee, the son of Hatim Tai.

Rules for ascertaining whether a dog, &c. be duly trained.—THE sign of a dog being trained is, his catching game three times without eating it; whereas the sign of a hawk being trained is, merely, her returning to her master, and attending to his call These signs are adopted from Abdoolla Ibn Abass. The body of a hawk, moreover, is not capable of enduring blows; but as, on the contrary, the body of a dog has this capability, a dog is therefore to be beaten until he desist from eating the game. Besides, one sign of being trained is; to desist from that which custom and habit have made agreeable; and as it is the custom of a hawk to be wild and to fly from man, it follows that its paying attention to its master's call, and showing no wildness, is a sign of its being trained. With respect to a dog, on the contrary, he is attached to man; but his custom is to tear and eat; and consequently, when he preserves game and does not eat it, it is a sign of his being trained, —It is to be observed that the condition hererecited, of a dog desisting, and not eating three times, is the doctrine of the two disciples (and there is also one tradition from Haneefa to the same effect);—and the reason of it is that, in less than three times there is a probability of the dogs forbearance having proceeded from satiety or some such cause; but that when he desists from eating for three different times, it is a proof that such forbearance has become a custom; for this particular number of three is the established standard for experiments, and for the discovery of an evasion. —in the same manner as it is used in determining the period of an option. It is also recorded to have been adopted in the story of Moses and Khizzir;‡ for Khizzir, upon the third instance, said, "Now there is a separation between you and me." Another reason is that plurality is a sign of knowledge; and as three is the smallest number of plurality, it has therefore been adopted as the standard. In the opinion of Haneefa, however, as recorded in the Mabsoot, a training does not take place, so long as the hunter does not conceive the animal to be trained; —and he holds it improper to fix on the number three; because the fixing on a particular number cannot be done by the forethought of man, but must be regulated by the precepts of the sacred writings; and as no precept has been issued on this head, it is proper to consign it to the judgment of him who is best acquainted with the matter, namely, the hunter. According to a former tradition. Haneefa holds the game of the third time to be lawful;—whilst the two disciples maintained that it is not lawful, as the animal does not become trained until after the third time; and consequently the game of the third time is the game of an untrained animal, and, as such, is unlawful: this beings like the act of a slave in the presence of his master; in other words, if a slave perform any acts in the presence of his master, such as purchase or sale, and the master, seeing and knowing the same, remain silent, the slave in that case becomes licensed,—not only with respect to the act in question, but also with respect to every act which he may afterwards perform:—and so likewise in the case in question. The reasoning of Haneefa is, that when the animal takes the game the third time, and instead of eating preserves it, this argues it to have been trained at the time of taking the game, and consequently the game of the third time is the game of a trained animal. —It is otherwise in the case above cited, because license is a notification, and cannot take place without the knowledge of the slave; and the slave cannot acquire this knowledge until after he has performed the act, and his master remained silent.

The invocation must be repeated (or, at least, must not be wilfully omitted) at the time of letting slip the hound, &c.— If a person let slip his trained dog, or his trained hawk, and at the time of letting them slip repeat the name of GOD, or omit it from foregetfulness, and the dog or hawk catch the game, and wound it so that it dies, the game may in that case lawfully be eaten. —If, however, he should wilfully, and not from forgetfulness, omit the name of GOD, it is not then lawful to eat the game so taken. It is mentioned in the Zahir Rawayet that the wounding of the game is a condition of its lawfulness, as it furnishes the means of a Zabbah Iztiraree. (The meaning of Zabbah Iztiraree has already been explained in treating of Zabbah.)

* Arab, Assid; including lions, and every other creature of the feline tribe, except the panther before mentioned.

† The expression in the original, signifies to send off.—It here means the act of casting off the hound or hawk, and hunting them at the game.

‡ This story (of which an explanation was given to the translator) is probably the original of Parnell's Hermit.

The Arabs, having a dual number, do not of course admit two to constitute plurality.

A hunting quardruped eating any part of the game renders it lawful.—IF a dog or panther eat any part of the game, it is unlawful to eat of such; but if a hawk eat part of it, it may lawfully be eaten.—The distinction between these two cases has already been explained.

IF a dog (for instance) catch game several times without eating it, and afterwards catching game eat part of it, such game cannot lawfully be eaten, as the circumstance of the dog eating it is a proof that he has not been properly trained. In the same manner also, the game which he may afterwards take is not lawful until he shall have been trained anew, concerning which the same difference of opinion obtains as that already set forth concerning a training in the beginning. With respect to the game previously taken by him, illegality does not attach to such parts of it as have been eaten, since there the subject no longer remains; but with respect to such parts as have not been preserved (that is, have been left upon the plain), they are unlawful according to all our doctors. As to what may have been preserved (that is, what the hunter may have carried to his own house), it is unlawful, according to Haneefa. The two disciples maintain it to be lawful; for they contend that the circumstance of the dog eating at that time is no argument of his not having been previously trained, as an art may be acquired and afterwards forgotten. The argument of Haneefa, on the contrary, is that the dog's eating of the game at that period is a proof of his never having been properly trained from the first.

Game caught by a hawk, after it has returned to its wild state, is not lawful.—IF a hawk fly from its master, and remain for a while in a state of wildness and flight, and afterwards catch game, such game is not lawful, as the hawk in that state is not trained; for the sign of being trained is to return to its master; and as it did not so return, the sign no longer remains; whence it is considered in the same light as a dog which eats his game.

A dog does not render his game unlawful by taking its blood.—IF a dog eat the blood of his game, and not the flesh, the name is lawful, and capable of being eaten, as the dog has preserved it for his master, which argues him to have been well trained, since he eat merely what was unfit for his master, and preserved what was fit for him.

Or by eating a piece of the flesh cut off and thrown to him by the hunter.—IF a hunter, having taken the game from his trained dog, cut off a piece of it, and throw it to the dog, and the dog eat the same, still the remaining part of it is lawful, as it is not then game; the case being, in fact, the same as if a person were to throw to a dog any other kind of food. The law is the same where a dog leaps upon his master; and takes from him part of the dead game in this hands and eats it; this being similar to where a dog attacks his master's goat, and kills it, which is no proof of the dog's not being trained.

Case of a dog biting off a piece in the pursuit of his game.—IF a dog lay hold of game with his teeth, and having bitten off the part eat it and afterwards catch the game and kill it, without eating any other part of it, the game is unlawful; because upon the dog eating part of his game it becomes evident that he is not trained. If, on the contrary, he drop the part bitten off, and having pursued the game kill it and deliver it up to his master without eating any part of it; and having afterwards passed by the part bitten off eat the same, the game is lawful; for as, if the dog, under these circumstances, had eaten part of the body of the game in the hands of his master it would have been of no consequence, it follows that it is, a fortiori, of no consequence where he eats what was separated from it, and unlawful to the master to eat. It is otherwise in the former case; because there the dog eat in the very act of hunting; and also, because the tearing off a piece of flesh with teeth admits of two explanations; for first, this may be done with a view to devouring,—and secondly, it may be done with a view merely to weaken the animal, in order the more easily to catch it;—and the eating of the piece before catching the animal argues the first of these,—whereas the eating of it after catching and delivering the game to the hunter argues the second, whence no inference can be drawn that the dog is not trained.

Game taken alive must be slain by Zabbah.—IF a hunter take game alive which his dog had wounded, it is incumbent upon him to slay it according to the prescribed form of Zabbah], and if he delay so doing until it die, it is then carrion and incapable of being eaten. The law it the same with respect to game taken by a hawk, or the like; and also with respect to game shot by an arrow. The reason of it is, that in this case the hunter is capable of the original observance, namely, Zabbah Ikhtiaree, before the occurrence of the necessity for the substitute, namely, Zabbah Iztiraree; and therefore the validity of the substitute is annulled. This law, however, supposes a capability in the hunter to perform the Zabbah; for where he takes the game alive, and is incapable of performing the Zabbah, and there exists in the animal more life than in one whose throat has been just cut, such game (according to the Zahir Rawayet) is not lawful. It is related, as an opinion of Haneefa and Aboo Yoosaf, that it is lawful (and this opinion has been adopted by Shafei); because the hunter is not in this case capable of the original observance, and is therefore in the same situation as a person necessitated to use sand instead of water, notwithstanding he be in sight of water. The reason alleged in the Zahir Rawayat is, that the hunter's finding the animal alive is equivalent to his capability of performing the Zabbah, since it enables him to reach the throat of the animal with his hand. Hence he has, in a manner, the power of performing the Zabbah, which he neglects. It is otherwise where only as much life exists in the animal as in one whose throat has been cut; because it is then, in effect, dead,—whence it is that if, in that state, it should fall into water, it is not unlawful, any more than is it had fallen into water when actually dead, the dead not being a fit subject for Zabbah. Some of the learned have entered more perticularly into this case, alleging that if the inability to perform the Zabbah arise from the want of an instrument, it is not then permitted to eat it; and that if the inability arise from the want of time, in that case likewise it is not permitted to eat it, according to our doctors,—in opposition to the opinion of Shafei. The argument of our doctors is, that when the animal is taken alive it is no longer game, because the term game is applicable only to what is wild and free; and that therefore the Zabbah Iztiraree is then of no effect. What is here recited proceeds on the supposition of the animal being taken alive, and of there being a possibility of its continuing to live; for if there be no possibility of its continuing to live (as where its belly has been torn, and part of his entrails have come out), it may lawfully be eaten without the performance of Zabbah, because the life that remains in it is equivalent only to the struggling of an animal whose throat had been cut, and is consequently of no effect;—in the same manner as where a goat falls into water, after having had its throat cut.

Provided it live long enough to admit of performing this ceremony.—If the hunter find the game alive, and do not take it from his dog till it be dead, and there have been sufficient time, after he found it alive, to perform the Zabbah, it is not in that case lawful to eat it: because this is equivalent to an omission of the Zabbah, notwithstanding an ability to perform it. If, on the contrary, he had found it alive at a period when, if he had taken it, there was not sufficient time to perform the Zabbah, it is lawful.

The game taken is lawful although it be not the same that wae intended by the hunter,—If a hunter let slip his dog at game, and the dog take some other game, the game so taken is lawful. Malik has said that it is not lawful, since the dog took this game without having been let slip at it, as it was at another specific animal that the hunter let him slip. Our doctors, on the other hand, argue that the object of the hunter is merely the acquisition of game; and all game is the same to him. Besides, the specification of the particular animal is of no advantage, as it is impracticable to teach a dog to take that particular animal.

Rule in casting off a panther at game.—If a person let slip a panther at game,* and the panther lie for a while in ambush, and then catch and kill the game, it is lawful to eat it; because the lying in ambush being with a view to catch the game, and not to take rest, does not of consequence terminate the act of letting it slip. The same rule also holds with respect to a dog, when trained in the manner of a panther

All the game caught by the dog, &c., under one invocation, is lawful. Rule for determining this with respect to dogs.—If a dog be let slip at game, and take and kill it and afterwards take and kill other game, both are lawful; because the act of letting him slip continues to operate, and is not terminated until after the taking of the second game; this case being similar to that of a person shooting at an animal with an arrow, which not only his and kills it, but also hits and kills another. If, on the cntrary, the dog, after killing the first game, lie down upon the ground and rest for a long time, and then, some other game passing by, he rise up and kill it, it is not lawful to eat that other game; because when the dog lay down and took rest, he thereby determined the act of letting him slipssince his sitting down was with a view to take rest, and not to deceive the game: in opposition to what was before recited.

And hawks.—If a hawk, being let slip (cast off) at game, first perch upon some,—thing, and afterwards, going in quest of the game, take it and kill it, it is lawful to eat it. This, however, proceeds on the supposition of the hawk neither tarrying long, nor with a view to rest, but merely a short time, and with a view to surprize her prey.

Game is not lawful when caught (by a hawk, &c.) independent of the act of the hunter.—If a trained hawk catch game and kill it, and it be not known whether any person let her slip at such game, it is then unlawful to eat it; because in this case a doubt exists with respect to the letting slip; and game is not lawful unless the animal which takes it be let slip at it.

It is requisite to its legality (when caught dead) that blood have been drawn from it.—If game be strangled by a dog, and not wounded, it is not lawful to eat it; because the wounding of it is a condition of its legality, according to the Zahir Rawayet (as has been before mentioned); and this condition implies that where merely particular members of the game are broken by the dog it is not lawful to eat it.

Game is rendered unlawful by the conjunction of any cause of illegality in the catching of it.—If a trained dog be assisted

* The lynx or panther used in hunting is generally kept hooded, and is conveyed from place to place upon a sort of litter. When the hunters have approached within sight of their game, they unhood the panther and cast off his chains, and he instantly springs at his prey, if within his reach, or if otherwise, practises a variety of stratagems to get near to it.

in killing the game by a dog that is not trained, or by a dog belonging to a Magian, or by one upon which the invocation had been wilfully omitted, in that case the game is unlawful; because two causes are here united, namely. a cause of legality, and a cause of illegality, and caution dictates a preference to the cause of illegality.

Game hunted down by any person not qualified to perform Zabbah is unlawful.—Any person not permitted to perform Zabbah (such as an apostate, a Mohrim, or a person who wilfully omits the invocation) is the same as a Magian with respect to letting loose an animal of the hunter tribe.

If a dog, without being let slip, should of himself pursue game, and a Mussulman repeat the invocation, and then make a noise and incite the dog to run faster, and the dog catch the game, it is in that case lawful to eat it.

Game killed at a second catching of it (either by the same or a second dog) is lawful.—If a Mussulman, having repeated the invocation, let slip his dog at game, and the dog having pursued and caught the game and thereby rendered it weak, let it go, and afterwards catch it a second time and kill it, it is in that case lawful to eat it,—and so likewise where a Mussalman lets slip two dogs, and one of them renders the game weak, and the other kills it;—and also, where two men let slip their dogs (that is, each of them one dog), and one of the dogs renders the game weak, and the other kills it. In this last case, however, the game is the property of him whose dog rendered it weak; because he deprived it of the quality of game, as he disabled it from running.

Section II.

*Of shooting Game with an Arrow.**

Game slain by a hunter shooting &c. at random, on hearing a noise, is lawful, provided the noise proceed from game.—If a person hear a noise, and, imagining it to be that of game, shoot an arrow, or let slip his dog or hawk and in either case game be killed, and it be afterwards discovered that the noise did actually proceed from game, it is then lawful to eat the game so killed by the arrow, dog, or hawk, whether it were the game of which the noise was heard, or not; because the object of the hunter was merely to game of whatever kind. This is according to the Zahir Rawayet,—It is related as an opinion of Aboo Yoosaf, that a hog is in this case an exception;—in other words, if it be afterwards known that the noise proceeded from a hog, the game killed by the arrow, hawk, or dog, is not lawful; because a hog is in an excessive degree impure;—whence it is that no part of it is rendered allowable by hunting:— contrary to other quadrupeds, for of those the skin by their being hunted, is rendered lawful Ziffer has likewise excepted al those animals of which the flesh is not fit for eating, inasmuch as the hunting of these is not with a view to render them lawful.

Game shot by an arrow aimed at an other animal is lawful.—If an arrow beshot at a bird and hit other game, and the bird shot at fly away, without its being known whether it was wild or tame, the game is in that case lawful, because the probability is that the bird was a wild one. If, on the contrary, an arrow be shot a camel, and hit game, and the camel having escaped, it be not known whether it was a wild one or otherwise, the game in that case is not lawful, because the natural condition of a camel is that of tameness and attachment to man.—If, on the other hand, an arrow be shot at fish or locusts, and hit game, such game is lawful in the opinion of Aboo Yoosaf, according to one tradition, inasmuch as it is game: but according to another tradition it is unlawful; because hunting is equivalent to the performance of Zabbah, which is not requisite with respect to fishes and locusts.

If a person, hearing a noise, and imagining it to be that of a man, should in consequence shoot an arrow, and kill game, and it be afterwards discovered that the noise proceeded from the game, in that case the game so killed is lawful; because, when it actually proves to be game, the imagination of the person who shoots is of no consequence.

Invocation must be made on the instant of shooting; but if the animal be taken alive, it must still be slain by Zabbah.—If a hunter, upon shooting his arrow, repeat the invocation, and the arrow wound and kill the game it is lawful to eat it; because the shooting of an arrow along with the invocation, and the wounding of the animal, is equivalent to the performance of Zabbah. Nevertheless, if the animal be taken alive, it is incumbent to slay it by Zabbah, as has been already set forth in the first section.

Game wounded, and afterwards found dead by the person who shot, is lawful.—If an arrow hit game, and the game fly away with the arrow until it disappear, and the hunter go in search of it, and find it dead, it is in that case lawful to eat it. If, on the contrary, he should not follow or go in search of it, and afterwards happen to find it dead, it is not in that case lawful; because it is related that the Prophet held it abominable to eat that game which disappeared from the sight of the bowman; and also, because there is a possibility that it may have died from some other cause.

Unless he then discover another wound upon it.—If the hunter above mentioned find another wound in the game besides that of his arrow, it is not lawful to eat it, not

* The title of this section, in the Arabic version, is simply Rama, signifying the use of any missile weapon whatever.

withstanding he may have continued in the search of it until he found it; because in this case two causes are conjoined,—one of illegality, namely, the other wound,—and one of legality, namely, the wound of his arrow; and it is the established custom to give the preference to the cause of illegality. Moreover, caution is easily observed in this case, as it is an uncommon one. All that has been above recited relates to the shooting of an arrow; but it is equally applicable throughout to the letting slip of a dog, or so forth.

Game which, being shot, falls into water, or upon any building, &c., before it reaches the ground, is unlawful.—If a person shoot at game with an arrow, and hit it, and it fall into water, or upon the roof of a house, or some other eminence, and afterwards upon the ground, it is not lawful to eat it; because the animal is a in this case a Mootradeea, the eating of which is prohibited inthe KORAN; and also, because there is a suspicion that the death may have been occasioned by the water, or by the fall from the eminence and not by the wound.*

Rule with respect to water-fowl.—If a water-fowl be wounded, and the member wounded be not a part under water, it is lawful,—whereas, if it be a part under water, it is not lawful, in the same manner as a land bird, which being wounded falls into water.

Game slain by a bruise, without a wound, is not lawful.—GAME hit (stunned) by an arrow without a sharp point is unlawful, as it is so recorded in the traditions. It is to be observed, moreover, that the wounding of game is a condition of its legality; because a Zabbah Iztiraree cannot otherwise be established,—as has been already mentioned.†

GAME killed by a bullet from a cross-bow is not lawful, as this missile does not wound, and is therefore like a blunt arrow. A stone, also, is subject to the same rule, as it does not wound:—and game is also unlawful when killed by a great heavy stone, notwithstanding it be sharp; because there is a probability that the game may have died from the weight of the stone; and not from the sharpness of it. If, however, the stone be sharp, and not weighty, the game killed by it is lawful, as it is then certain that it must have died in consequence of a wound from it.

GAME killed by a small pebble stone, and of which no part has been cut by the stone, is not lawful, because in this case t[illegible] is bruised and not wounded. If, also game be beaten by a stick or piece of wood until it die, it is not lawful, as the death is then occasioned by the weight of the stick or piece of wood, and not by any wound: yet if, in his case, the stick or piece of wood, because of their sharpness, occasion a wound, there is no impropriety in eating the game, as the stick and piece of wood are then equivalent to a sword and spear. The general rule, in short, in these cases, is that when it is known with certainty that the death of the game was occasioned by a wound, it is lawful food; but unlawful where the death is known with certainty to have been occasioned by a bruise, and not a wound; and that, in case of the existance of a doubt (that is, where it is not certainly known whether the death was occasioned by a bruise or by a wound), it is then also unlawful, from a principle of caution.

If a person throw a sword or a knife at game, and the game be struck by the handle of the sword, or the back of the knife, it is not lawful; whereas if struck by the edge, and wounded, it is lawful.

Case of cutting off the head of an animal.—If a person cut off the head of a goat, it is lawful to eat it, as the jugular veins have been cut through; but it is nevertheless abominable. If, however, a person perform this action by beginning with the spine, so as to occasion the death of the animal before the jugular veins be cut, it is not lawful: but it is lawful if the animal do not die until after the jugular veins are cut.

A Magian, an apostate, or an idolator are not qualified to kill game.—GAME killed by a Magian, an apostate, or a worshipper of images, is not lawful, because they are not allowed to perform Zubbah (as has been already explained in treating of that subject), and Zabbah is a condition of the legality of game. It is otherwise with respect to a Christian or a Jew, because, as their performance of a Zabbah Ikhtiaree is lawful, it follows that their performance of a Zabbah Iztiraree must also be lawful.

Case of game wounded by one person, and then slain by another.—If a person shoot an arrow at game, and hit it, without rendering it so weak as to prevent it from running, and in that state another person shoot at it, and kill it, the game is the property of the second hunter, because he was the person who took it, and the Prophet has said, "Game belongs to him who takes it." If, on the contrary, the first hunter render it too weak to run, and another person then kill it, it is in that case the property of the first hunter. Nevertheless, he must abstain from eating it, as there is a probability that it may have died in consequence of the second wound; and as it had not the power of running after the first wound, it ought to have been slain by a Zabbah Ikhtiaree, no regard being, in such an instance, paid to the Zabbah Iztiraree, in opposition to the

* Amidst such a mass of frivolous absurdity, the translator thinks it unnecessary to offer any apology for the omission, in this place, of a long discussion still more futile than any thing which has gone before.

† From this, and various preceding passages, it appears that it is requisite to draw blood in order to the rendering game lawful.

former case.—This prohibition, however, against eating the game, proceeds on the supposition of its being in such a condition as to induce us to believe the continuance of its existence possible; since under these circumstances its death is referred to the second shot: but if the first wound be such as to render the continuance of its existence impossible (as if it have as little life in it as an animal with its throat cut, having, for instance, had its head cut off), in that case it is lawful to eat it, as its death is not then referred to the second shot it being at that period in a state equivalent to annihilation.. If, however, the first wound be such as to render the survival of the game impossible, and there nevertheless be more life in it than in an animal with its throat cut (as if, for instance, it be capable of living one day), in that case, according to Aboo Yoosaf, it is not rendered unlawful by the second shot, because such a degree of life (in his opinion) is of no effect; but according to Mohammed it is unlawful, as such a degree of life (in his opinion) is of effect.

IN the foregoing case, the second hunter is responsible to the first for the value which the game bears after receiving the first wound; because he (the second hunter) has destroyed game the property of the first hunter (who became the proprietor of it in consequence of his wounding it, and thereby incapacitating it from running); and the game is, by such wound rendered defective and in all cases of responsibility for destruction of property a regard is paid to the time of the destruction. The compiler of the Hedaya remarks that in this case there is a distinction;—in order words, responsibility takes place where it is known that the game in question died in consequence of the second wound (that is, where the wound of the first hunter was such that the animal lived after it,—and the wound of the second hunter such as to destroy the existence); and the second hunter is accordingly responsible for the value of the game, in its wounded and defective, not in its unwounded and perfect state; in the same manner as where a person kills the sick slave of another. If, however, it be known that the game died inconsequence of the first wound, or if it be uncertain of which wound it died, Mohammed has said, in the Zeeadat, that it is incumbent upon the second hunter, first to pay a compensation for the damage he may have occasioned to the game by the wound; and, secondly, to pay a compensation for half the value which the game bore after receiving both wounds; and, thirdly, to pay a compensation of half the value of the flesh. The reason for the first compensation is that the second hunter, having occasioned a damage to an animal which was the property of another, is bound, in the first instance, to make good the amount of that damage. The reason for the second compensation is that, as the animal died of both wounds, the second wound must have been the immediate cause of its destruction; and as it was at that time the property of another person, it is incumbent upon him to make a compensation for half the value which it bore after receiving both wounds, as the first wound did not proceed from him, (With respect to the damage occasioned by the second wound, having paid it before, he is not required to pay it again.) The reason for the third compensation is that as the game, after receiving the first wound, was in such a state as to have rendered it lawful by a Zabbah Ikhtiaree, if it had not received the second wound, it follows that the second hunter inconsequence of the second wound, did render unlawful half of the flesh with respect to the first hunter. He is only required, however, to pay a compensation for one half of the flesh, as he paid the other half before in as much as he paid half the value which included the flesh.

Case of game first wounded, and then killed by the same person.—IF, instead of two persons shooting the game, one person shoot the same game twice, the law is then the same with respect to the illegality of the game as when it receives two wounds from two different persons;—this being similar to where a person, having shot game upon any eminence, and rendered it weak and feeble, afterwards shoots it a second time, and brings it to the ground,—in which case the game so killed is unlawful, inasumch as the second wound is the cause of illegality; and so also in the case in question.

All animals may be hunted.—THE hunting of every species of animal is lawful whether they be fit for eating or otherwise, because the legality of hunting has been absolutely declared in the KORAN without restricting it to animals fit to eat. Another reason is, that the hunting of animals not fit for eating may proceed either from a desire to obtain their skin, their wool, or their feathers, or from a wish to exterminate them on an account of their being mischievous or hurtful; and all these motives are laudable.

BOOK XLVIII.

OF RAHN, OR PAWNS.

CHAPTER I.

Definition of Rahn.—RAHN literally signifies to detain a thing on any account with ever. In the language of the LAW it means the detention of a thing on account of a claim which may be answered by means of that thing; as in the case of debt.—This pactice is lawful, and ordained; for the word of GOD, in the KORAN, says, GIVE, AND RECEIVE PLEDGES;"—and it is also related, that the Prophet, in a bargain made with a Jew for grain, gave his coat of mail in pledge for the payment.—Besides, all the doctor have concurred in deeming pawn legal; and it is, moreover, an obligatory engagement, and consequently lawful, in the same manner as bail.

Pawn is established by declaration and acceptance; and confirmed by the receipt of the pledge.—CONTRACTS of pawn are established by declaration and acceptance, and are rendered perfect and complete by taking possession of the pledge.—Several of the learned have said that the contract is complete immediately upon the declaration; for as it is a deed purely voluntary, it therefore obtains its completion from the voluntary agent alone; as in cases of gift and alms. The seisin of the pledge is, nevertheless, absolutely requisite to the obligation of the deed, as shall be shown in its proper place. Malik has said that a contract of pawn becomes valid and binding immediately upon the concurrence of the parties; because they relate to the property of both, and are consequently similar to sale.—One of the arguments advanced by our doctors is, the text of the KORAN, above quoted; and another argument is, that as the act of pledging is purely voluntary (whence it is that there is no compulsion on the pawner towards the act), it must therefore be effectually concluded, in the same manner as in the case of legacies:—and a contract of pawn can only be effectually concluded by the seisin, in the same manner as as a legacy is effectually concluded by the testator dying without having receded from his bequest. It is to be observed, that if the depositor reliquish the pledge to the pawnee, his so doing is equivalent to an acceptance; in other words, his not obstructing the pawnee from taking possession of the pledge is equivalent to his actually investing him with the possession, and is a sufficient proof of his having so done. This is recorded in the Zahir Rawayet; and the reason of it is, that as the seisin of the pledge is sanctioned in virtue of the agreement, it therefore resembles the seisin of a thing sold. It is recorded from Aboo Yoosaf, that the seisin of a movable pledge can only be accomplished by the laying hold of and removing it, not by the pawner's merely relinquishing it, as above mentioned; for the seisin of a pledge is an occasion of responsibility from the first, in the same manner as usurpation. The former is, however, the better opinion.

Upon the pawnee taking possession of the pledge, the contract becomes binding.—UPON a person receiving a pledge which is distinguished and defined (that is, unmixed and disjoined from the property of the depositor) the acceptance being then ascertained, the contract is completed, and consequently binding. (Until, however, the seisin actually take place, the pawner is at full liberty either to adhere to, or recede from the agreement, as the validity of it rests entirely upon the seisin, without which the end and intention of a pledge cannot be answered).

And he [the pawnee] is responsible for the pledge.—UPON the pledge, therefore, being delivered to the pawnee, and his taking possession of the same, he becomes answerable in case of its being destroyed in his hands. Shafei maintains that a pledge being a trust in the hands of the pawnee, if it be destroyed in his possession still he does not on that account forfeit his due; because it is recorded in the traditions, that "no pledge shall be distrained for debt, and the pawner shall be liable for all risks," meaning (according to Shafei), that if the pledge be destroyed, still the debt is not annulled on account of any responsibility arising therefrom;—and further, because a pledge being merely a testimony, the loss of it does not annual the debt, seeing that a debt still exists after the loss even of a written bond; and reason of which is, that the use of taking such a testimony is to add greater security to the pawnee's debt and therefore if, from the decay or destruction of the pawn or testimoney, the debt of the pawnee were cancelled, it would be opposite to the spirit of the agreement, since it would admit a possibility of the pawnee's right becoming extinguished, a thing repugnant to conservation and security. The arguments of our doctors upon this point are two fold.—FIRST, a tradition of the Prophet, who once decreed the claim of a pawnee to be annulled, on account of the death of a horse which he had in a pledge (although, indeed, several of the learned, in their comments on this tradition, have remarked, that it was made at a time when the value of the horse could not be ascertained).—SECONDLY, all the companions of the Prophet, and their followers, have declared a plege to be a subject of responsibility; that is to say, that if it decay in the hands of the pawnee, he sustains the loss.—With respect, moreover, to the assertion of Shafei, that "a pledge is a trust," it is inadmissible, as being in direct contradiction to the concurrent opinion of the companions above-mentioned. With respect, also, to the tradition adduced by him as an argument, the real meaning of it is, "that a pledge cannot be completely seised, so as to, render it the absolute property of the pawnee in the room of his other claim," an explication which Koorokhee has transmitted to us, as delivered by former sages.—As, moreover the pawnee is entitled to take possession of the pledge as a security for his claim, and to detain it (for Rahn, in its literal sense, signifies detention), it necessarily follows that a pledge is not a trust,

Which he is entitled to detain until he

receive payment of his debt.—In short, in the opinion of our doctors, a contract of pawn requires that the pledge be continually detained in the hands of the pawnee in lieu of his debt, in this way, that it remain in his possession as a security for the fulfilment of his claim:—whereas, in the opinion of Shafei, the claim of the pawnee is connected with the substance of the pledge, as a satisfaction for his claim,—in this way, that he may sell it, and thereby obtain a discharge,—it being until such sale a trust reposed in him, and the property of the depositor;—and agreeably to these different tenets several cases occur concerning which there is a disagreement between our doctors and Shafei.

Without admitting the pawner to any use of it.—For instance,—if the pawner be desirous of resuming his pledge for a short time, that he may enjoy the use of it (as in the case of taking milk from a cow, or so forth), he is not so allowed, according to our doctors, unless by the consent of the pawnee as the object of the agreement of pawn (namely, a constant possession) would by that means be entirely defeated,—whereas, according to Shafei a pawner may even forcibly take back his pledge for a temporary enjoyment of the use, nor can he be prevented from this; because (in his opinon) a pledge may be sold conformably to the nature of the agareement; and the resumption of it towards an enjoyment of the usufruct cannot be considered as a subversion thereof.—(More cases of this kind shall be exhibited in the sequel.)

The debt to which the pawn is opposed must be actually due.—A contract of pawn is not valid unless opposed to a debt due at that time; for the end of such contract is to establish possession in order to the obtaining of payment: and the obtaining of payment presupposes an obligation of debt.

The responsibility or the pledge extends to the amunt of the debt owing to the pawnee.—A pledge is insured in the possession of th pawnee* to whatever is the smallest amount,—the debt of the pawnee, or the value the pledge bore at the time of its being deposited. Thus if a pledge equivalent to the amout of the debt perish in the pawnee's hands, his claim is rendered void, and he thereby, as it were, obtains a complete payment. If, on the contrary, the vlaue of the pledge exceed the amount of the debt, the excess is in that case considered, as a trust, and the whole of the pawnee's claim is annulled, on account of the decay of that part of the pledge which is equivalent to the amount thereof; and the remainder (the excess), as being held in trust, is not liable to be compensated for, and consequently the pawner sustains the loss of it. If, on the other hand, the value of the pledge be less than the debt, the pawnee forfeits that part of his claim only which is equal to the value of the pledge, and the balance, or excess, must be paid to him by the pawner. Ziffer maintains that a pledge is liable to be compensated for according to its value;—whence if a pledge of the value of one thousand five hundred dirms at the time of delivery be destroyed, and the debt of the pawnee be one thousand dirms, the pawner has a claim upon the pawnee for the difference, namely, five hundred dirms.—His arguments upon this point are twofold.—First, a saying of Alee, "The pewner and pawnee shall mutually restore to each other the excess, whether the pledge exceed in value the debt, or the debt the pledge."—Secondly, the amount in which the pledge exceeds the debt being (as well as the sum equivalent to the debt) given in pledge, the excess is of consequence a subject of responsibility as much as that part which is equivalent to the debt. Hence, when the debt is annulled, a restitution must be made of the surplus. The opinion of our doctors upon this subject is adopted from Omar Farook, and Abdoola-Ibn Masaood. They moreover, argue, that as the pledge was taken possession of purely for the purpose of obtaining payment it is therefore a subject of responsibility only in that degree of value from which the payment of the debt might have been made, as in the case of a real payment, the surplus being pawned merely from necessity (as it was impossible to have pawned the exact value of the debt), and therefore not demanding restitution.—With respect, also, to the saying of Alee (as quoted by Ziffer), the meaning of it is, that the parties shall mutually return the excess, in case of sale (that is to say, if the pawner sell the pledge), not in case of destruction, for he has elsewhere declared the surplus to be held by the pawnee in trust.

The pawnee may demand payment of his debt, and imprison the pawner in case of contumacy.—It is lawful for the receiver of a pledge to made a demand of his debt, and even to imprison the pawner in case of refusal; because the claim still exists after the receipt of the pledge, which is not considered as a fulfilment, but merely as a preservative of it. The pawnee, therefore, is not prohibited from making the demand; and if the circumstance of the evasions and delays of the pawner be made known to the Kazee, he must imprison him, as has been formerly explained.*

It is required of the pawnee, before payment to produce the pledge.—Whenever a pawnee demands payment of his debt, it is requisite that the Kazee order him first to produce the pledge; because as he possesses that for the purpose of obtaining payment, it is not lawful for him to take his due at the same time that he retains possession of the pledge, which he holds as a security; since

* In other words. "The pawnee is responsible for it,"

* In treating of the duties of the Kazee, (See Vol. II., p. 338.)

if in such case, the pledge were to perish in his hands, a double payment would be induced, which is inadmissible. And when the pawnee shall have produced the pledge, the Kazee must order the depositor first to discharge the debt, in order to ascertain the pawnee's right, in the same manner as the right of the pawner is ascertained, to the end that both may be placed upon an equal footing: as in the case of bargains, where the seller having produced the goods, the buyer then lays down the purchase-money.

But if the demand payment in a distant place, he is not required to produce it unless this can be done without expense.—If the pawnee demand payment in a city different from that wherein the contract of pawn was concluded, and the pledg be of such a nature as neither to require charge of carriage or expense, the same rules which have been laid down in other cases hold good in this; as the place for the surrender of a pledge of this kind being entirely immaterial and indifferent, the doctors have therefore assigned no particular rules or conditions regarding it. If, on the contrary, the pledge be of such a nature as to require carriage and charges of removal, the pawnee is not desired to prodcue it; for such a requisition would necessarily oblige him to have it carried from place to place. It is, moreover, incumbent on him to relinquish the pledge to the pawner, and to allow him to resume it; but he is not required to remove it from one place to another, as that would be a loss to him which he had not stipulated.

The pledge may be sold, at the desire of the pawner; and the pawnee cannot afterwards be required to produce it.—If the pawner empower the trustee * to sell his pledge, and he sell it accordingly, either for ready money or on credit, it is lawful, the power of the pawner to sell it being indisputable. If, therefore, the pawnee afterwards demand payment, he is not desired to produce the pledge, as that in such case, is not in his power.—The same rule also holds where the pawnee, at the instance of the pawner, having sold the pledge, does not possess himself of the purchase-money; for then the Kazee may compel the pawner to discharge his debt, without requiring the pawnee to produce the pledge, which because of its having been sold at the desire of the pawner, has become converted into a debt;—wherefore the pawner himself did, as it were, pawn the purchase-money (that is, the debt).—If, on the contrary, the pawnee possess himself of the purchase-money, he must in that case be required to produce it upon demanding his debt; for as the money is a commutation for the pledge, it is therefore a substitute for it. It is to be observed, however, that in the above case the pawnee has a right to the possession of the purchase-money; for as he himself made the sale, the rights of the cantract consequently appertain to him.

He must produce it on receiving a partial pament, as well as in case of a complete discharge.—In the same manner as the pawnee is required to produce the pledge when he is about to receive payment of his debt in full, he is also required to produce it when he receives part payment, provided the term stipulated be expired; because his thus producing it can be of no prejudice to him) whilst at the same time it serves to dissipate any apprehension of the loss of the pledge which may have arisen in the mind of the pawner. The pledge, however, is not to be restored until a complete discharge be made. If, also, the pledge should have been sold by the pawnee, and the purchase-money taken possession of by him he is required to produce such purchase-money upon demanding payment of his debt, or of part of it, in the same manner as he is required to produce the pledge itself, in case of its being extant, as the purchase-money is a substitute for the pledge.

If a person should, by misadventure, kill a pawned slave, and the magistrate decree the value of such slave to be made good by the Akilas of the slayer within the term of three years, the pawner must not be compelled to discharge the pawnee's debt until he (the pawnee) shall have produced the full value of the slave; for in this case, the value is a substitute for the slave who was in pawn; and it is consequently incumbent on the pawnee to produce the whole of his value, in the same manner as he is required to produce the whole pledge where it is extant. Here, moreover, the pledge has not become converted into value by any act of the pawner:—whereas, in the case formerly stated (namely, where the pawnee sold the pledge at the desire of the pawner without possessing himself of the purchase-money) the pledge was converted into debt by the act of the pawner, since he invested the pawnee with a power of disposal. There is consequently an essential difference between these two cases;—whence it is that, in the present instance, it is incumbent on the pawnee to produce the value received for the slave, whereas, in the former case, he is not required to produce the pledge, nor yet its price, as of that he had never received possession.

Cases in which he is not required to produce it.—If the pawner deliver the pledge into the hands of a trustee, ordering him, at the same time, to resign it in charge to some one else than the pawnee, and he accordingly do so, in that case the pawnee is not required to produce the pledge upon demanding pay-

* Arab. Adil; meaning (literally) an upright person,—one in whose hands the parties mutually agree that the pledge shall remain until it be redeemed. The translator substitutes the term trustee throughout this book, because (although not the literal meaning of Adil) it best expresses the sense of the author.

ment of his debt, for this is rendered impossible, from its not having been intrusted to his care, but to that of another.— If, also, the trustee, having committed the pledge into the hands of one of his relations, should then abscond, and the person to whom it was given acknowledge, upon its being demanded from him, that "he had indeed received it in trust, but was ignorant of the real proprietor," the pawner may be compelled to discharge his debt, without the pawnee being required to produce the pledge, as he had never received it (and the same rule also holds, where the trustee absconds, carrying the pledge along with him, without its being known whither he is gone).— If, on the other hand, the trustee deny the goods entrusted to him to be a pledge, asserting that "they are his own property," the pawnee cannot take anything from the pawner until the contrary be proved; because the denial of the trustee is tantamount to a destruction of the pledge and when a pledge is destroyed, the pawnee is considered as having received payment of his debt. after which he is no longer at liberty to claim it.

The pawner cannot reclaim the pledge on the plea of selling it for discharge of his debt.— If the pawner demand a restitution of the pledge with a view to sell it, and thereby pay off his debt, still it is not incumbent on the pawnee so to do, as the contract of pawn requires that the pledge be continually detained in the hands of the pawnee until such time as his debt be paid.— If, also, the pawner discharge the debt in part, still it remains with the pawnee to keep possession until he shall have received payment of the balance; but whenever a complete payment is made the pawnee must be directed to restore the pledge to the pawner, as the obstacle to his so doing no longer exist, the claimant having obtained his due.

The pawnee must restore what he has received in payment, if the pledge perish in his hands.— If, after the discharge of the debt, the pledge should be destroyed with the pawnee, he must return the money he received in payment; for as, upon the pledge perishing in the hands of the pawnee, he appears to have received payment in virtue of his previous possession of it, he therefore appears to have taken payment twice, and consequently must return what he has received. In the same manner, if the pawner and pawnee should, by mutual consent, dissolve the contract of pawn, the pawnee may, nevertheless, keep possession of the pledge until such time as he receive payment of the debt, or exempt the pawner therefrom.

The contract is not dissolved until the pledge be restored.— A contract of pawn is not rendered void until the pawnee restore the pledge to the pawner, according to the prescribed mode of annulment.

The debt is discharged by the loss of the pledge.— If the pledge perish in the hands of the pawnee, after the parties have in concert dissolved the contract, his debt is in that case considered as discharged, provided the value of the pledge be adequate to it, the agreement being still held in force.

The pawnee is not entitled to use the pledge.—It is not lawful for the pawnee to enjoy, in any shape, the usufruct of the pledge.—If, therefore, a slave be pawned, the pawnee must not employ him in service; if a house, he must not dwell in it; and if clothes, he must not wear them;—for the right of the pawnee is in the possession, not in the use.—Neither is a pawnee authorized to sell the pledge, unless at the desire of the pawner.

Or to lend or let it to hire.— A pawnee is not permitted to let out, or give the pledge in loan; for as he is himself prohibited from enjoying any use of it, he consequently is not authorized to confer the power of enjoyment upon another. If, therefore he do so, it establishes a transgression: but a transgression does not occasion a dissolution of the contract.

He may consign it in charge to any of his family.— A pawnee may either watch over the pledge himself, or he may devolve the care of its preservation upon his wife, child, or servant, provided they be of his family. If, on the contrary, he commit the care of it, or resign it in trust, to one who is not of his family, he becomes the security, and the person to whom he gave it the secondary security. Concerning this, however, there is a difference of opinion between Haneefa and his two disciples; for he does not consider the other person to be a secondary security; whereas they have declared it to be in the option of the pawner to make whomsoever he may please the secondary security.

If he transgress with respect to it, he is responsible for the whole value.—If a pawnee commit any transgression* with respect to the plege, he must make reparation to the whole amount of the value; in the same manner as in a case of usurpation; for the amount in which the value of the pledge exceeds the debt is a trust: and a transgression with respect to a trust, renders the person who commits it liable to make complete reparation.

The use of the pledge is determined by the pawner's mode of keeping or wearing it.— If a person pledge a ring, and the receiver put it on his little finger, and it be afterwards lost or destroyed, he is responsible, as he has transgressed in making use of the pledge instead of using means for its preservation:—and, in this case, the right or left hand is indifferent, there being no uniform custom of wearing a ring invariably upon either.— If, on the contrary, the pawnee wear the ring upon any other than his little finger, this is not considered as an enjoyment of use, but as a means of preser-

* Such as converting it to his own use, &c. (as prohibited above).

vation, as it is contrary to the customary mode of wearing a ring.—So likewise, if the pawnee wear a sheet (which he has received in pledge) after the customary mode, he is responsible for it; whereas, if he spread it over his shoulders, he is not responsible.

If a person pawn two or three words, and the pawnee sling them over his shoulder, then, provided there be only two, he becomes responsible for their value in case of their loss, but not if there be three; the reason of which is, that amongst warriors it is a frequent custom to sling two words on their shoulders in battle, but never to sling three.

If a person pawn two rings, and the pawnee put them both on his little finger, and it appear that he was accustomed to adorn himself in this manner, he is liable to make compensation in case they be by any means destroyed; but if the contrary be proved, he is exempt from any responsibility.

The expenses of conservation (of the pledge) rest upon the pawnee; and those of subsistence upon the pawner.—The rent of the house wherein the pledge is kept, as well as the wages of the keeper, rest upon the pawnee:—but if the pledge be a living animal, and require a keeper and maintenance, the expense of these must be defrayed by the pawner.—It is to be observed that the wants of a pledge are of two kinds; I. such as are requisite towards the support of the pledge and the continuance of its existence:—II. Such as may be necessary towards its preservation or safety, whether wholly or partly. Now, the absolute property of the pledge appertains to the pawner, the expenses of the first class must therefore be defrayed by him; and as he has, moreover, a property in the usufruct of the pledge, its support and the continuance of its existence for this reason also rest upon him, being an expense attendant upon his property;—in the same manner as holds in the case of a trust. (Of this class are the maintenance of a pledge in meat and drink, including wages to shepherds, and so forth, and the clothing of a slave, the wages of a nurse for the child of a pledge, the watering of a garden, the grafting of fig-trees, the collecting of fruits. &c.) The expenses of the second class, on the contrary, are incumbent on the pawnee; because it is his part to detain the pledge; and as the preservation of it therefore rests upon him, he is consequently to defray the expense of such preservation. (Of the second class is the hire of the keeper of the pledge; and so likewise the rent of the house wherein the pledge is deposited, whether the debt exceed or fall short of the value of the pledge.)—All that is here advanced is according to the Zahir Rawayet. It is recorded, from Aboo Yoosaf, that the rent of the house is defrayed by the pawner, in the same manner as maintenance, it being his duty to use every possible means towards securing the existence of the pledge: but that a Jual, or reward for restoring fugitive slave, is of the second class: for as the pawnee is necessitated to use every possible expedient to recover the possession of the slave, the reward, as being connected with preservation, must be defrayed by him. This, however, holds only with respect to such pledges as do not exceed the amount of the debt; for where the value of the pledge exceeds the amount of the debt, the pawnee must not be taxed with the payment of the whole, but with such share of it only as is proportionate to the value of the pledge; whilst the remaining part, in proportion to the surplus, falls on the pawner; for the excess not being held by the pawnee in pledge, but in trust, the restitution of the salve, in regard to the excess, is, as it were, made to the absolute owner, to whom, therefore, the surplus must be charged.

But those incurred by sickness, or by offences must be defrayed by both.—THE expense of healing the wounds, of curing the disorders, and of pecuniary expiations for the crimes of pledges, are defrayed by the pawnee and pawner proportionably to the amount of the debt, and the excess of the value of the pledge over the debt.

Taxes are defrayed by the pawner.—THE taxes on pledges are levied from the pawner as they are necessary towards the subsistence of his property.

Tithes (upon pawned land) have preference to the right of the pawnee.—THE tithe from the revenue of tithe-lands held in pawn precedes the right of the pawnee; because it is connected with both the substance and the property of the pledge, whereas the right of the pawnee is connected with the property of it only, not with the substance.—Still, however, the contract of pawn is not invalidated in regard to the sum remaining after the payment of the tithe, as the obligation of tithe in no respect impugns the pawner's right of property. It is otherwise where an undefined part of a pledge proves the right of another; for in that case the contract becomes null with respect to the remainder, because this shows that the pledge was not wholly the pawner's property.

If either party voluntarily defray what is incumbent on the other he has no claim upon him on that account.—IF either party defray any of the expenses incumbent on the other, it is deemed a voluntary and gratuitous act. If, on the contrary one of them should, by order of the Kazee, fulfil a duty incumbent on the other, he has in that case a claim on the other for so doing, in the same manner as if he had done it at his instigation; for the Kazee's jurisdiction is general: It is recorded, from Haneefa, that no claim can be made on the other, notwithstanding the expense be defrayed by order of the Kazee unless he were then absent. Aboo Yoosaf, on the contrary, has said that a claim is valid in both cases; that is, whether the other were present or absent.

CHAPTER II.

OF THINGS CAPABLE OR BEING PAWNED; AND OF THINGS FOR WHICH PLEDGES MAY BE TAKEN.

An indefinite part of an article cannot be pawned.—It is unlawful to pawn an indefinite part of anything. Shafei maintains that it is lawful.—On behalf of our doctors two reasons are urged. First, this disagreement arises from the difference of opinions regarding the object of pledges; for according to us, pledges are taken to be detained with a view to obtain payment of a debt, which cannot be effected in case the pledge be an undefined part of property; because a seisin of things of that nature cannot be made a real seisin being only practicable with respect to things which are defined and distinguished;—whereas, according to Shafei, the object of pledges is that the pawnee may sell them to effect a discharge of his debt; and with this object pledges of the nature above mentioned are not in any shape inconsistent.—Secondly, it is an essential part of the contact of pawn, that the pledge be constantly detained in the hands of the pawnee until the redemption of it by the pawner; a condition which cannot be fulfilled with respect to pledges, of the above nature; for in such cases it would be necessary that the pawner and the pawnee have possession of the article alternately, whence it would be the same as if the pawner were to say to the pawnee, "I pawn it to you every other day."—As, therefore, a constant detention is in such case impossible, it follows that the pledge of an undefined part of anything, whether capable of division or incapable, is illegal.

Even to a partner in the article.—It is not lawful to pledge any undefined part of joint property, even to a copartner; for, besides that the detention of such pledges cannot be made, the receiver would in such case retain possession of it, one day in virtue of property, and another in virtue of the contract of pawn, and thus he would hold it one day in pledge, and another not.

If the pledge be rendered indefinite by any supervenient act or circumstance, the contract of pawn is annulled.—A supervenient indefiniteness in repugnant to the continuance of a contract of pawn, according to the Mabsoot;—in other words, if a person pledge a piece of ground, for instance, and afterwards desire a trustee* to sell the half thereof, and the trustee accordingly do so, the contract of pawn no longer exists.—It is recorded from Aboo Yoosaf, on the contrary, that a supervenient indefiniteness does not dissolve a contract of pawn,—in the same manner as it has no effect in the case of donations;—in other words, if a person bestow anything in gift upon another, and afterwards retract the half, the gift still remains valid with respect to the other half.—The reason for what is quoted from the Mabsoot, as above, is that, in the case there stated, the subject of the contract does not exist as before; and a subsequent circumstance, as far as it has a tendency to annihilate the subject of the contract, operates equally as if it had existed from the beginning:—in the same manner as where a person (whether knowingly or unknowingly) marries within the prohibited degree.—It is otherwise with gifts: for the effect of gift is investiture with right of property; and an undefined part of a thing is capable of being property. The reason, moreover, why seisin, in the case of a gift, is requisite before the right of property can be acquired, is to prevent the possibility of compulsion: for if the grantee should become proprietor of the gift immediately upon its being offered, and without taking possession, the giver (who ought to act of his own accord) would then be constrained to do that to which he has not yet assented; namely, to deliver up the gift.

An article naturally conjoined to another cannot be pawned separately.—It is not lawful to pledge fruit without the trees which bear it, crops without the land on which they are produced, or trees without the ground on which they stand; for as the pledge, in all these cases, has a natural connection with an article which is unpledged, it is therefore, in effect, indefinite, until such time as it separated from that article. In the same manner also, it is unlawful either to pawn a piece of ground without the trees which are produced upon it, a fi ld without its produce, or a tree without its fruit; because, in these cases, a mortgage is induced of an article naturally conjoined with another which is not pledge. In short, it is a rule that when a pledges is joined to something not in pawn, the contract is not valid, since in such case possession cannot be taken of it. Haneefa has judged it lawful to pawn a piece of ground without its trees; for as the trees have no connection with the ground, except in that part only from which they vegetate, they may therefore be excepted, together with the particular spot on which they stand It is otherwise when a person pawns the court-yard of a house without the building itself; for then the part of the ground on which the building stands remains unpledged, whereas it is requisite that the whole of the ground be pledged.

Trees: however, may be pawned with the immediate spots on which they grow, without including the est of the land.—It is lawful to pawn trees, together with the particular sports of ground on which they grow: for here subsists a vicinity only with the pawner's property, which is not repugnant to a contract of pawn.—If, in this case, there be fruit upon the trees, it is included in the contract; for as the fruit is an appendage of the tree, because of the connection between

*Arab, Adil. (See note, p. 632.)

them, it is therefore included in the contract in order that the same may be valid.—It is otherwise in the case of sale, for as trees may be sold without their fruit, unless that be expressly stipulated, it is not included in the sale. It is also otherwise with respect to valuables deposited in a house; for these not being appendages to the house are not included in the pledge, unless they be expressly stipulated. Grain, however, and herbs are considered as included, in case of their ground being pawned; but not in case of the sale of it. Buildings, also, and trees, are included in the contract of pawn, when the ground or villages to which they belong are pledged.—A person may also lawfully pawn a house, together with whatever it contains.

A claim of right established in a separable part of a pledge does not annul the contract with respect to the remainder.—If another person prove his right to part of a pledge, and the remaining part be of such a nature that it might with propriety be distinctly pawned (as where another proves his right to the court-yard only of a pledged house, without the building), the contract still subsists with respect to the remaining part; in other words, if the residue be destroyed in the hands of the pawnee, his debt is divided between such residue and the value of what had proved the right of another: and the proportion which the residue bears to the whole is struck off from the debt, and that which the other part bears to the whole remains due from the pawner.* If, on the contrary, the residue be of such a nature that it cannot be separately pawned (as where another proves a right to a pledged house without its court-yard), the contract of pawn becomes absolutely void; for it cannot operate upon any thing except what remains after deducting what has proved the right of another; and such residue is incapable of being pawned.

Occupancy, so as to obstruct a delivery of the pledge to the pawnee, prevents his becoming responsible for it.—It is to be observed that the continuance of the pawner, or of his goods, in the house which he has pledged are obstructive of a regular delivery of the house:—in other words, if a person pledge or mortgage his house, and remain himself, or keep his goods therein, a delivery to the pawnee is not established until he evacuate it, or withdraw his goods therefrom, whence, if it be destroyed in the interim, the pawnee is not answerable.—In the same manner, the continuance of any thing within a pledged vessel is repugnant to the delivery of it; and so likewise the continuance of a burden on a pawned quadruped,—whence the contact is not complete until the burden be taken off, as the animal otherwise continues occupied. It is different where the burden is pawned and not the animal; for in this case the contract is valid, and the burden is pledged immediately upon the pawner delivering over the animal, it being occupied by the burden, not the burden by it; in the same manner as where things contained in a house or vessel are pledged without that house or vessel.—It is otherwise, however, where a person pawns a saddle or bridle upon a camel, and delivers the camel to the pawnee; for in that case the contract is not valid until the saddle or bridle be taken off the camel and delivered separately to the pawnee; these being dependents of the camel, in the same manner as fruit is a dependent of the tree:—whence it is that (as lawyers have remarked) whenever a camel is pawned with a saddle or bridle on it, these are likewise included in the contract, although not particularly specified.

Pledges cannot be taken for trusts.—It is not lawful to take pledges for trusts, such as deposits, loans, or Mozaribat, or partnership stock;—in other words, if a person commit his goods in trust to another, taking a pledge for the same, it is invalid, as the receipt of the pledge would subject the receiver to responsibility; for if the pledge were destroyed in his hands; his claim would be extinguished in a degree proportionate to the value. In short, it is requisite that something lie against the pawner of a nature to subject him to responsibility, in order that, opposed to it, the possession of the pledge, in the event of its destruction, may subject the pawnee to responsibility and operate as a discharge of his claim; but there is no responsibility with respect to trusts.

Not for any thing not insured with the holder of it.—It is not valid to take a pledge for articles which do not subject the holder to responsibility,—such, for instance, as an article sold, and which still remains in the hands of the seller; for if the purchaser be desirous of taking a pledge from the seller to answer the delivery, it is invalid, an article sold, not being insured in the hands of the seller. (Still, however, if the article sold perish in the seller's hands, his claim on the buyer for the price ceases; or, if he should have previously received the price from the buyer, he must restore it).—With respect, on the contrary, to articles which subject the holder to responsibility that is, those for which, when destroyed, the holder is responsible,—for a similar, if of the class of similars;—or for the value, if of a different description.—such as usurped property, the consideration for Khoola, the dower to a wife and the composition for wilful murder), it is lawful to take pledges for them, as responsibility attaches to all such matters, since if the article be extant the delivery of it is incumbent, or the value if it be destroyed. Opposing a pledge to such articles, therefore, is taking a pawn in security for that which

* The mode of calculation, in this case, will be exhibited in a note in the last section of this book.

is itself a subject of responsibility, and is consequently valid.

Nor as a security against contingencies.—IT is nof lawful to take a pledge as a security against contingencies;—in other words, if a person sell an article and receive the price, and the purchase, from an apprehension that the property might afterwards prove the right of another, and that he might thereby be rendered liable to a loss, should on that account demand a pledge from the merchant securing him against such a circumstance, it is invalid; for it is an established maxim that a pledge is to be taken as a security for the discharge of a claim then extant; and in the above case the claim does not exist, but is only what may possibly happen. If, therefore, a pledge be in such a case taken, it is considered as taken in trust, and not in pawn, and is in no respect subject to the laws of pledges. In a similar manner, if a person deposit any thing in pledge with another, in security for any thing which may in future be due from him, it is invalid.—It is, indeed, otherwise in the case of a promised debt;—as where a person gives a pledge to another on the strength of his promising to lend him one thousand dirms, and the other takes the pledge and promises to lend the money, and the pledge perishes in his hands; for in this case he is responsible in proportion to the sum promised, in the same manner as if it had been actually paid, the promise of debt being considered as an actual existence of it, for this reason, that it was made at the earnest desire of the borrower.

Case of pawns in bargains of Sillim or Sirf.—IF a person, having bespoke goods of a merchant, pawn something in security for the payment of the purchase-money, or haveing sold silver to a banker, receive a pledge in security for the price, or if a merchant give a pledge to a person who has bespoke goods from him, as a security for his delivery of them,—the contract is valid. Ziffer has said that the contract, in these instances, is not valid, inasmuch as the object of the pawn in such cases is that it may be a security for the discharge of the several claims, namely, the purchase-money, of the goods bespoken, the value of the silver sold to the banker, or the goods bespoken,—which is not allowable, because an exchange is here induced of things not delivered for things of a different species; and an exchange of such things, previous to seisin being obtained of them is unlawful. The argument of our doctors is, that as a parity of species betwixt the things which were to be delivered, and the pledge, holds good with respect to their worth, by means of their worth the engagement may be fulfilled;—and the possession of a pledge induces a responsibility in regard to its worth, although with respect to its substance it be considered merely as a trust.—If, also, the pledge opposed to the price of the article bespoke, or the value of the silver sold, be destroyed at the time of making the contract (that is, before the company in whose presence it was made breaks up), the bargain is accomplished, and the pawnee or seller is reckoned to have received his right; because by the destruction of the pawn he is virtually considered to have received the price of his silver, or the amount of money which was to have been advanced.—If, on the contrary, the buyer and seller should have separated previous to the destruction of the pledge, the bargain becomes invalid; because the receipt of the price of the silver or the advance of money for the goods at the time of making the bargain (which is a condition), is not here established either in reality or in the construction of law.—If, moreover, a pledge taken, in security for the delivery of the goods bespoken be destroyed, the bargain is completed, and the pawnee (who advanced the money) is held to have received the goods which he bespoke.

In the dissolution of a contract of Sillim, the pledge remains as a security for the advanced capital.—IF the parties to a contract of Sillim dissolve the bargain in a case where a pledge has been given for the delivery of the goods, it still remains as a security for the refunding of the money which had been advanced, as that then stands in lieu of the goods;—in the same manner as where goods are usurped, and the Kazee having ordered their restoration, a pledge is given for that purpose, and afterwards the goods are destroyed,—in which case the pledge remains a security for the value of the goods.

And if it be lost in the advancer's hands his claim of restitution is annulled.—IF, in the above instance, the pledge be lost after the parties had agreed to annul the bargain of Sillim, the bespoken article is in that case considered as delivered, and the purchaser (the advancer) has no further claim.—It is, however, incumbent on him to give to the seller as much grain as he should have received from him, in order to his recovering the money he had advanced,—in the same manner as where a person, having sold a slave and delivered him to the purchaser, takes a pledge in surety for the price,—and they afterwards mutually consent to annul he bargain,—in which case the seller is entitled to retain possession of the pledge as a security for the restoration of the slave; and if the pledge be destroyed in his hands, he is considered to have received the purchase-money; and it is incumbent on him to pay the sum of the purchase-money to the buyer, and thereby recover his slave.

A freedman, a Madabbir, a Makatib, or an Am-Walid, cannot be pawned.—IT is not lawful to pawn either a freedman and Modabbir a Makatib, or an Am-Walid; because the end of a contract of pawn is to establish the pawnee's possession of the pledge, with a view to obtaining payment of his claim; a view which cannot be accomplished in any of the above-mentioned instances, as a freedman is not property, and the sale of the others is contray to law.

Pledges cannot be taken to secure the appearance of a surety; or of a criminal liable to retaliation.—If a person agree to be bail for the appearance of another it is not allowable to demand a pledge from him on this account.—In the same manner also, it is not lawful to take a pledge as a security for a criminal condemned to suffer retaliation either in life or limb, as in such case the right could not be obtained by means of the pledge. It is otherwise in the case of offences by misadventure; for there the fine may be discharged by means of the pledge.

Or in security for a right of Shaffa.—It is not lawful to take a pledge opposed to a right of Shaffa:—in other words, if a person appeal to the Kazee (for instance), and claim his privilege of Shaffa, and obtain from him a decree to that effect, and demand of the purchaser a pledge for the house over which his privilege of Shaffa extends, the pawn is not valid, ; for here the article is not insured in the hands of the purchaser: (that is to say, if the house suffer any damage in the possession of the purchaser, he is not responsible for it); and a pledge cannot be taken but for matters that induce responsibility.

Or for a criminal slave, or the debts of a slave.—It is not permitted to take a pledge opposed either to a slave guilty of a crime, or to the debt of a slave; because the master is not in either instance responsible, since, in case the death of the slave, he is not obliged to discharge his debts.

Or for the wages of a public singer or mourner.—It is not lawful to give a pledge for the wages either of a mourner* or of a singer. If, therefore, a pawn be given in such case, and be afterwards destroyed in the hands of the pawnee, he is not responsible for it, as the thing in security for which it was pledged is not a subject of responsibility.

A Mussulman cannot give or take wine in pawn: but if he so receive wine from a Zimmee, and it be destroyed, he is responsible.—It is unlawful for a Mussulman either to give or take wine in pawn, whether from a Mussulman or a Zimmee. Notwithstanding this, however—if the Zimmee be the pawner and the Mussulman the pawnee, and the wine be lost or spoiled, the Mussulman is accountable for it, in the same manner as in the case of his having usurped it; whereas, if the Mussulman were the pawner and the Zimmee the pawnee: and the wine be lost in the hands of the latter, he would not owe any compensation to the Mussulman, any more than a person who had usurped wine from a Mussulman. It is otherwise where the pawner and pawnee are both Zimmees; for wine is property with them. Carrion, on the contrary, is not property with them any more than with Mussulmans; and accordingly a pawn of carrion is not valid among them by more than with us.

A pawnee is still responsible for the pledge, although it appear that the debt to which it was opposed is not due.—If a person purchase vinegar, a slave, or a slaughtered goat, and having given a pledge for the purchase-money, afterwards discover the vinegar to be wine, the slave to be a freeman, or the goat to be carrion,* still the seller is responsible for the pawn in case of its being lost or destroyed; for it was deposited in opposition to a debt to all appearance due. The same rule also holds in a case where a person, having killed a [supposed] slave and given a pledge for the payment of his value, afterwards discovers that he was a freeman. So, likewise, where the parties in a suit compromise the business for a part of the plaintiff's demand and the defendant deposits a pledge to answer the same, and they afterwards agree that nothing was owing from the defendant, the pledge is insured in the hands of the holder of it.

A father or guardian may pledge the slave of his infant ward for a debt owing by himself.—It is lawful for a father to pledge, in security of his own debt, the slave of his infant child; for a father has the privilege of depositing the goods of his infant child in trust; and to pledge them is still more conducive to the interest of the proprietor than to place them in trust, since if a pledge be lost it must be accounted for, whereas a trustee is not responsible for the deposit in his hands. A guardian also is the same as a father in this particular, because such an authority vested in him is beneficial to the child. Aboo Yoosaf and Ziffer maintain that this is not lawful either to the father or guardian (and such is what analogy would suggest); for a pledge is, in effect, equivalent to a payment; and as a father is not privileged to pay off his debts with the goods of his child, it follows that he has no power of giving them in pledge. To this, however, it may be replied, that there is an obvious difference between the act of pledging and that of payment; for discharging the debts by means of the child's property is a destruction of his right without any equivalent; whereas, placing his property in pledge is providing it a guardian, for the interim, without in any degree affecting his right.

But they are accountable in case of loss.—As, therefore, the contract of pawn is valid in this instance, it follows that in case of the

* Meaning, a person employed, on occasions of grief, in making lamentations. It is a custom amongst the Mussulmans to employ such persons; although prohibited by the Law,—whence it is that they cannot legally sue for their hire.

* As having died a natural death.—The term carrion is applied to the flesh of all animals not slain according to the prescribed form.

pledge being destroyed in the pawnee's hands, he is considered to have received payment of his debt, and that the father or guardian are responsible to the infant, as having discharged their debt by means of his peoperty.

And they may also authorize the pawnee to sell the slave.—IN like manner it is lawful for a father or guardian to order the pawnee to sell the pledge; for both of these have the privilege of selling the goods of their infant ward. The learned have said, that this is founded on the law in a case of sale; for where a father or guardian gives the goods of his ward to his own creditors, in payment of his debt, it is lawful; and a commutation being thus made of the debt for the price, the father or guardian, in the opinion of Haneefa and Mohammed, become answerable to the ward for the value.—According to Aboo Yoosaf, on the contrary, a commutation does not take place:—and the same difference of opinion obtains where an agent for sale disposes of the goods of his constituent to a person to whom he is indebted. The contract of pawn, however, is in these instances similar to that of sale with respect to its effects; for in both the object is to discharge the debts of the father or guardian with the goods of the infant, and to become answerable for them.

A father may retain the goods of his infant child in pledge for a debt owing from the infant to himself, or to another infant child, or to his own merchantile slave.—IF a father pawn the goods of his infant child into his own hands for a debt due from the child, or into the hands of another of his children being an infant, or of his slave, being a merchant and not in debt, it is lawful; because a father, on account of the tender affection which he is naturally supposed to have for his child, is considered in a double capacity, and his bare inclination as equivalent to the assent of both parties; in the same manner as where a father sells the property of his infant child to himself.

But a guardian has not this privilege.—IT is not lawful for a guardian to pledge into his own hands goods belonging to his ward on account of a debt due to him, or into the hands of his child being an infant, or into the hands of his slave being a merchant and free from debt nor is it permitted to him to give anything of his own in pawn into the hands of an orphan for a debt owing to the orphan from himself); for a guardian, being merely an agent, cannot of course have a double capacity in contracts. A guardian, moreover, is more deficient in tenderness than a father, and therefore cannot, like a father, stand in a double capacity in making contracts. Besides, a guardian pawning the property of his ward into the hands of his infant child, or his slave, being a merchant and free debt, is in effect the same as pawning it to himself.—It is otherwise where a guardian pawns the property of his ward to his adult son, to his father, or to his indebted slave, since over these he has no authority.

Yet he also may retain the goods in pawn for necessaries furnished by him.—IF a guardian purchase victuals or apparel for the use of his ward, and, having debited him for the price, take in pawn part of his goods as a security for the debt, it is valid; for, as he is permitted to borrow for the use of the orphan, and as taking a pawn is like the discharge of a claim, it is of consequence legal. Besides, as it is lawful for a guardian to trade on account of his ward, it follows that it is also lawful for him to give and receive pawns, they being similar to receipts and payments.

A child cannot recover property which had been pawned by his deceased father, but by redeeming it.—IF a father pawn the goods of his infant son, and the infant attain maturity, still he is not at liberty to annul the contract of pawn and take back the pledge until he shall have discharged the debt; for the contract is binding upon him; as the act of a father on behalf of his infant child is binding upon the child after he shall have attained maturity, a father being his infant child's substitute.

If he redeem it during the father's life-time, he has a claim on him for what he pays.—IF a father pawn the goods of his son on account of his own debt, and the son, by a discharge of the debt, redeem the same, he has a claim on the father for the sum; for it was necessary that the son should discharge the debt, having occasion to release his goods out of the hands of the pawnee;—in the same manner as holds with respect to the lender of a pledge; in other words, if a person lend any thing to another with a view to that other's pawning it, it is lawful to him to redeem the article from the pawnee by a discharge of the borrower's debt, and then to prefer a claim of debt against the borrower; and so here likewise.

And the father is responsible in case of the pledge being lost.—IF, also, on this case, the pawn be lost or destroyed before the son's release of it by discharging his father's debt, it is lawful for him to prefer a claim upon the father, as he has in effect discharged his debt by means of his (the son's) property.

IT is lawful for a father to pawn the goods of his son for a debt jointly due by both. If, therefore, the pledge be destroyed, the father must compensate to the son by the payment of a sum equivalent to his [the father's] share of the debt; because he has paid off so much by means of the sons' property.—The same rule also holds with a grandfather, or a guardian, in case of the non-existence of the father.

Case of a guardian pawing the goods of his ophan ward, and then borrowing and losing the pledge.—IF a guardian purchase victuals for an orphan, so as that the price is a debt upon the orphan, and pawn an article belonging to the orphan as a security for the debt, and the pawnee take possession of the same, and the guardian then borrow it from the pawnee for the use of the orphan, and it be destroyed in his (the guardian's) hands, it is no longer included in the contract of pawn, nor is any person responsible for it; for the act of the guardian in this instance is the same as that of the orphan when he has attained maturity, her having borrowed the article for his use,—in which case such is the rule. The debt of the orphan, in this case, still remains due; and the creditor is to receive payment from the guardian, who is reimbursed by the orphan; because the guardian, in borrowing the pledge, was not guilty of any transgression, as it was borrowed for the orphan's use, If, on the contrary, it have been borrowed on his own account, he is responsible for it to the orphan; because in borrowing it for his own use he is guilty of a transgression, as having usurped a privilege which does not belong to him. It, also, he were to usurp it from the pawnee and apply it to his own use, he is responsible for the value, as having been guilty of a transgression,—with respect to the pawnee, by the usurpation,—and with respect to the orphan, in having applied the article to his own use. He is, moreover, in this instance bound to discharge the debt of the pawnee, if the term stipulated should have expired. If, therefore, the value of the pawn be equivalent to the debt, he must discharge it in full, without any reimbursement from the property of the orphan; for the same that was before due from the orphan to him becomes now so from him to be orphan, and hence a commutation takes place. If, on the other hand, the value of the pledge be short of the debt, he must discharge from his own property a sum equivalent to the pledge, and the residue from that of the orphan; for he is only liable for the amount of the value of the pledge. If, on the contrary, the value of the pledge exceed the debt, he must pay the amount of the debt to the pawnee in discharge of his claim, and the remainder is the right of the orphan. If the stipulated term of payment should not have expired, the value of the pledge must be deposited in pawn with the pawnee; for the guardian having destroyed one of the established rights of the pawnee, the value of it therefore must be given in pledge into his hands;—and upon the term if payment arriving, the same rules are to be observed as are above fully set forth.—It is to be observed, however, that the guardian, in case of having extorred the pawn and applied it to the use of the orphan, becomes (if under these circumstances it should be destroyed) liable only to make reparation for violating the rights of the pawnee, as in applying it to the use of the orphan he does not violate his right; neither is his taking it from the pawnee any transgression with respect to the orphan, as a guardian is authorized to take the goods of his ward;—whence it is that Mohammed, in the Zeeadat (under the head of Acknowledgements), has said, "Where a father or guardian acknowledges having usurped the goods of his infant ward, nothing is chargable to them in case of loss or decay; because this is not an usurpation, they having an unlimited power to take the goods of their ward." In the above case, therefore, the guardian is answerable to the pawnee; and at the expiration of the stipulated term he must discharge his debt and charge it to the account of the orphan; for he has in no respect perjudiced him, but has on the contrary applied the pawn in his use. If, however, the term of payment be not arrived, the thing given in reparation must, until then, remain as a pledge in the hands of the pawnee, when he is to obtain payment of his debt, and the guardian to recover the amount from the orphan's property.

Money and all weighable and measureable articles may be pawned.—Rules to be observed in those instance.—IT is lawful to pawn dirms, deenars, or any article of weight or measurement of capacity; for as a debt may be discharged by means of such articles, they are consequently fit to be pawned. If, therefore, any such articles be pawned in security for an article of the same kind or species, and be lost in the pawnee's hands, the debt becomes cleared in a degree, proportionate to the value of the pledge, if that be either equal to, or less than the amount of the debt. If, on the contrary, the value of the pledge exceed the amount of the debt, the whole of the debt is in that case held to be discharged, notwithstanding the one be base and the other pure; for where the pawn, and debt are of the same kind, the quality is not to be considered. This is the opinion of Haneefa; for (according to him) the pawnee in the above case is to receive payment of his debt by weight, and not by value.—The two disciples, on the contrary, hold that the pawnee, on the loss of the pledge, becomes responsible for its value in something of a different species, which value he holds (as it were) in pawn in lieu of the original pledge.* The argument of Haneefa is, that any regard to quality drops in the case of usurious, property† when opposed to its own species.—A discharge in a pure article of this nature, moreover, in return for a base article, is lawful,—as where, for instance, a debtor, through inattention,

* Here follows a case in point, quoted from the Jama Sagheer, with the author's remarks, and the difference of opinion among the Mussulman doctors concerning it, which is omitted by the translator, as it interrupts the discussion of the point in question, and the arguments adduced have been before fully detailed under the head of Usury.

† Arab. Imwal Rabwee, meaning any sort of grain,—and also gold or silver;—in short, everything with respect to which usury can be conceived possible.

repays a debt of base money in pure money.

Case of a silver vessel pawned,—and afterwards lost.—If a silver vessel equiponderant to ten dirms be pawned for a debt of ten dirms, and afterwards lost in the hands of the pawnee, the whole amount of the debt stands discharged. The compiler of the Hedaya remarks that this rule universally obtains with our doctors where the value of the vessel is either equal to, or greater than the weight of it; but that where the value, by being short of the weight, is short of the debt, there is a difference of opinion; for, according to Haneefa, the whole debt, in that case, stands discharged (he holding the pawnee to have received payment by the weight of the vessel);—whereas the two disciples teach that the pawnee remains responsible for the value, which continues, with him (as it were) in pawn, his claim still existing as before.

Or broken.—If, on the contrary, the vessel be not lost, but broken, then, on the first supposition (that is, supposing the weight and value to be the same), according to Haneefa and Aboo Yoosaf the pawner is not compellable to redeem it; for if he were to redeem it by paying the greatest part of his debt, and deducting some small part of it in consideration of the loss arising from the breakage, it would in that case appear that he considered the quality separately, and on this account paid only part of his debt, which is illegal; or if, on the other hand, he were to redeem it by paying the whole of his debt, and thus taking the broken vessel, it would be a loss to him.—The pawner, therefore (according to the two Elders), is at his own option, either to redeem the broken vessel by paying the whole of his debt, or to relinquish it and compound with the pawnee for its value, which may either be of the same or of a different species from the vessel; and this value remaining (as it were) in pawn, the pawnee becomes proprietor of the vessel, because of his having thus made compensation for it. In the opinion of Mohammed, on the contrary, the pawner may either redeem the broken vessel by a payment of the whole of the debt, or he may give it to the pawnee as discharge of it, in the same manner as in the case of the loss of the pawn. Hence Mohammed conceives an analogy between a pawn damaged and a pawn lost, for this reason, that when a redemption cannot be made without a compensation, it is then the same as if the pawn were lost; and as, when the pawn is actually lost, the debt becomes (in the opinion of all our doctors) annulled, it is so likewise in the present instance, which is a case of loss in effect.—Haneefa and Aboo Yoosaf have said, that when a pawn is lost the pawnee is held to be paid in respect of the worth,—in this manner, that he becomes immediately answerable for the value of the pawn to compensate for its loss, and that a commutation for the debt takes place.—But when a debt is annulled for a pawn then extant, though somewhat damaged, on absolute appropriation of it takes place; that is to say, it must be so detained as to render the substance of it the property of the pawnee. This is, however, a mistaken determination, and is rejected in law: wherefore it is most proper that a substitute be made of the value.*

A pledge may be stipulated, in sale, for the price of the article sold.—If a person sell a slave on condition that the purchaser shall deliver to him in pawn some specified thing, it is lawful on a flavourable construction, whereas analogy would suggest that it is unlawful. So also, it is lawful for a person to sell a slave, on condition that the purchaser give, as his security, a third person who is present at the conclusion of the bargain, and who consents to be security. The objection suggested by analogy, in this instance, is that the agreement entered into forms a double compact, or one compact within another, which is prohibited in the LAW.—Besides, it contains a condition which is not conformable to the object of the agreement, and from which there results an advantage to the seller, who is a party in both the compacts; and such a condition renders a contract of sale void. The reason, however, for a more favourable construction of the law, in this particular, is that such a condition in the agreement is no way repugnant to the contract, since bail or pawn tend to ensure and strengthen the agreement, and are in strict conformity with the obligation of the price. If, therefore, the proposed surety be present at the conclusion of the agreement, or the pledge be specified, attention is paid to the condition of bail or pawn; for, as being proper to the agreement, they are consequently legal.

But the agreement is not valid unless the pledge be particularly specified—If, on the other hand, the surety be not present, nor the pledge specified, the agreement is invalid; for the intention of giving bail or pawn does not in that case exist, inasmuch as the pledge or surety is unknown; and as there remains only a nugatory condition, the agreement is therefore invalid. Still, however, if the proposed surety appear before the parties have separated, and acquiesce in the bail, the agreement then becomesvaild,

Nor can the purchaser be compelled to deliver it.—If the purchaser, after the pawn had been agreed upon, should refuse to deliver the pledge specified, the Kazee must not compel him thereunto, as it is the delivery alone that determines the agreement.—Ziffer has said, that when the condition of pawn is included in the sale, a fulfilment of it is

* A long discussion which follows upon this subject is omitted by the translator, as containing merely a train of subtle and frivolous distinctions relative to usury, of no practical utility.

absolutely necessary; and that therefore the Kazee may enforce it; for the condition having been stipulated as an article of the sale, becomes one of the rights thereof, and is equally binding, although it be not in itself of any force;—in the same manner as a power of agency included in a contract of pawn, which is binding because of the contract being so; in other words, if the pawner of a thing were to stipulate that the pawnee shall undertake the sale of it, such agency would be binding;—whence it would not afterwards be in the power of the pawner to retract it. In reply to this, however, it is to be observed, that the agreement of pawn is voluntary on the part of the pawner; and there is no compulsion to the execution of a voluntary deed. The seller, however, may, at his discretion, either relinquish the agreement of pawn, or he may invalidate the sale; for as he had earnestly desired the detention of the pawn, and as it was on the strength of that condition only that he had agreed to the sale, he is not, consequently, in default of it, obliged to adhere to his agreement, unless the buyer should in the mean time either have paid the price, or pawned, in place of the thing specified, the worth of it in dirms or deenars, in which case the sale becomes complete and binding, since, in the first instance, the seller obtains his object, and in the second he obtains the fulfilment of a conditon with which he was satisfied, the pawn of the value being the same as that of the substance, for the end of the agreement is to obtain payment and that can only be obtained by means of the product of the pledge, namely, the value.

An article tendered by a purchaser in security for the price of the merchandize is considered as a pledge, although the term pawn be not expressly mentioned by him.—IF a person purchase anything for a particular sum, and request of the seller "to keep his robe until such time as he pays him the purchase-money," the robe is considered as a pledge; for the buyer, in saying that the seller should detain the robe until he render him the purchase money, spoke in a manner which implied an intention of pawn, although he did not expressly mention the word pawn: and in every agreement regard is to be had to the spirit, not to the letter. Ziffer maintains that, in this case, the robe is not pawned, in which opinion Aboo Yoosaf likewise concurs; and the reason they allege is, that the expression used by the buyer does not only imply an intention to pawn, but may likewise signify a deposit, which construction, as being the most favourable, ought to be adopted.—It is otherwise where a person expresses himself, "keep, this robe in security of your debt (or goods)," for then, in mentioning security, it becomes obvious that his object was to pawn it.—In answer to this, however, it is to be observed, that in either case his intention was to pawn he robe; for although the expression, "keep his robe," may admit of the interpretation either of pawn or deposit, yet when the speaker subjoins, "until such time as I pay you the purchase-money," it is no longer doubtful that he means to pawn, and not to deposit it.

Section.

Where two (or more) articles are opposed in pledge to one debt, hey cannot tbe redeemed separately.—IF a person pawn two slaves for a debt of one thousand dirms, and afterwards pay the proportion of one of these slaves, still he is not permitted to take back that slave until such time as he render to the pawnee the residue of the debt. (By the proportion of the slaves is to be understood the particular sum for which each is pawned, when they are both opposed to the amount of the debt.) The argument in support of this determination is, that as a pawn is detained in behalf of the whole debt, it is therefore detained in behalf of every part of it, in order the more strongly to bind the pawner to the payment of his debt; in the same manner as hold with respect to an article sold, where, if the seller, having paid part of the purchase-money, be desirous of taking in lieu thereof a proportionate part of the article, it is not allowed: on the contrary, he must wait until the payment of the whole price be made, when he may take the whole of the goods purchased.

Notwithstanding each article be opposed to a particular part of the debt.—THE same rule also holds, according to the Mabsoot, when the depositor previously specifies the particular value of each of the component parts of his pledge; as, for instance, when a person, having pledged two slaves against a debt of one thousand dirms, declares the value of each to be five hundred dirms. It is related in the Zeeadat, on the contrary, that in this case the pawner is permitted to take back the slave upon paying to the pawnee the sum which he had before specified to be his value. The argument of the Mabsoot is that, in the case in question, there is only one agreement; and that no separation takes place in it on account of the distinct specification;—in the same manner as in sale; in other words, if a person sell two slaves for one thousand dirms, and particularly mention the price of each to be five hundred dirms, still there are not two distinct bargains; and so likewise in the present instance. The argument of the Zeeadat is that in the above case there subsists two agreements; and that it is unnecessary to consider them as one; for, if they be considered as two, it amounts merely to this, that it would follow that the one is a condition of the other, a conclusion which does not invalidate the agreement, but rather the condition itself is invalid (whence it is that if the pawnee acquiesce in the agreement respecting only one of the two slaves, it is lawful). It is otherwise in the case of sale; for if there be two contracts of sale, it leads to this, that the one is a condition of the other; a conclusion which would invalidate the sale altogether.

An article pawned to two persons (in security of a debt jointly owing to both) is pledged in toto to each.—IF a person pawn any specific article into the hands of two people, in security of a debt which he jointly owes to both it is lawful;—and in this case the articles is held to be completely pledged into the hands of each of the creditors; because the spirit of the agreement is, that the article is held entire and in one pledge:—nor does it hence follow that the pledge is undefined, because of the separateness of rights; for each has a claim to the whole,—the object of the agreement being a detention in security of debt; and as that is a thing incapable of severalty, the pawn is therefore detained wholly in security of the debt of each. It is otherwise where a person bestows anything in gift to two people; for this is not lawful, according to Haneefa, as the object of a gift is an endowment with right of property, and two men cannot lawfully have each the complete property of one thing, since this would induce the consequence of a moiety being appropriated to each indefinitely, which in gifts is not admissible.

And if they agree to hold it alternately, each is in his turn trustee on behalf of the other.—IF, in this case, the parties agree to a Mahayat, or alternate possession of the pledge, each is, during his term of possession, a trustee on behalf of the other;—and if it be destroyed, each is responsible according to his respective share,—for upon this happening each is held to have received a discharge of his claim, a discharge being capable of partition. If, also, the pawner pay off the debt of either, the article in that case remains wholly in pledge with the other, since it was before completely so in the hands of each without any separation. Analogous to this is the detention of things which have been sold to two or more jointly; for one of the buyers, after paying his proportion of the price, is not entitled to take from the merchant his share of the goods purchased; on the contrary, the merchant may detain the whole until such time as he shall have received the remaining part of the price from the other purchaser.

IF two people, by one agreement, pawn a certain thing into the hands of one person in security of a debt which they jointly owe to him, it is lawful, and the thing so pledged is detained in security of the whole of the debt. The pawnee is, moreover, at liberty to detain the pledge until he receive a complete discharge; for the two having pawn the article together, the pawnee is therefore held to have received a complete and undivided seisin of it.

If two persons, respectively, claim an article from a third, in virtue of an alleged pawn, and both produce evidence, the claim of both is null.—IF two persons prefer a claim to a slave in the possession of a third, each separately asserting "that the possessor had formerly completely pawned the slave into his hands, and had afterwards borrowed or usurped him," and each produce an evidence in support of his declaration, the claims and evidences are null and inadmissible; for each of the claimants having a maintained and supported by evidence that the possessor had pawned the slave completely into his hands alone, it is not, therefore, in the power of the Kazee to decree him to either, as it is impossible that the same slave should be pawned wholly into the hands of one person, and at the same time wholly into the hands of another:—neither could he decree wholly the substance of the pawn to any one of them; since he has no reason to prefer one to the other; nor could he decree each of them an half, as a pawn is indivisible. As, therefore, it is impossible, to decide according to the evidences of either they are both set aside.

OBJECTION.—It would appear that the Kazee ought to decree the slave to be the pledge of both, since they have both, as it were, received him at the same time, the period when he was pledged not being ascertained.

REPLY.—The Kazee has no power to pass a decree of that nature, as he would thereby depart from the evidence adduced by the parties, each having expressly declared, that the slave was wholly pawned into his hands towards obtaining a satisfaction for the whole of his particular claim. If, on the other hand, he were to decree an half to each, he would act in opposition to the evidence, which a Kazee is not at liberty to do.

If a pawner die, leaving an article in pledge with two pawnees, it is sold for the discharge of their claims.—IF a pawner die, leaving a pledged slave (for instance) in the hands of two pawnees, and each of them produce evidence to prove that the slave had been pledged wholly to him, a moiety of the slave is in that case awarded in pldege to each, and may respectively be sold by them in satisfaction of their claims, upon a favourable construction; and such is the opinion of Haneefa and Mohammed.—Analogy would suggest that the pawn is in this instance null (and such is the opinion of Aboo Yoosaf); for as the intendment of a contract of pawn is that the pledge shall be detained towards obtaining payment of a claim, it follows that the decree of the Kazee, awarding a moiety of the slave to each, proves the pawn to have been indefinitely held in severalty, which is unlawful now, in the same manner as in the lifetime of the pawner.—The reason, however, for a more favourable construction of the law in this particular is, that the object is not the mere contract itself, but its utility. Now the utility of the agreement in the lifetime of the pawner consists in a detentions of the pledge, which cannot be accomplished in the case of an indefinite severalty of claim; but the utility of it after his death is, that the pawnee may sell it in order to discharge his debt, which a severalty of claims does not prevent,—the case being the same as where two men contend that they are married to the same woman,—or where two sisters contend that they are married to the same man, and evidences are produced to prove it by both ;—for in this case the evidence adduced is disregarded during the lifetime of the man ; but after his death a decree is passed assigning them their respective shares of inheritance, as that is capable of division.

CHAPTER III

OF PLEDGES PLACED IN THE HANDS OF A TRUSTEE*

The parties may, by agreement, entrust the pledge to the custody of any upright person.—IF the pawner and pawnee agree to place the pledge in the hands of any upright person (to act as trustee for both), it is lawful. Malik is of opinion that this is not lawful; because the seisin of the trustee is the same as that of the pawner (whence it is that the trustee has recourse to him for indemnification where the pawn is lost in his possession, and another, having proved a right to it, takes a compensation from him for its loss) ; and such being the case, no account is made of the seisin of the pawnee ; wherefore the contract of pawn is incomplete, because of the failure of one of its conditions, namely, the seisin of the pawnee. The argument of our doctors is that the seisin of the trustee is apparently the same as that of the pawner, with respect to preservation (the substance of the pawn being a trust), and with respect to worth it is the same as that of the pawnee, as it subjects him to responsibility in case of its loss, a pawn being insured with regard to its worth ; wherefore the trustee stands in the place of two parties, the pawner and the pawnee, to strengthen the object of both, namely, the contract of pawn. (With respect to the trustee's right of having recourse to the pawner, in case of the loss, and so forth, as mentioned above, it is admitted solely in consideration of his being the pawner's deputy for the conservation of the substance of the pledge, in the manner of any ordinary trustee.)

After which neither of them is at liberty to take it out of the trustee's hands.—THE pawnee is not at liberty to take the pledge from the trustee, inasmuch as the right of the pawner is still connected with it, in this way, that the pledge is a deposit in the trustee's hands. Neither is the pawner at liberty to take it, because of the pawnee's right being connected with it for the purpose of obtaining payment of his debt. Neither party, therefore, is at liberty to invalidate the right of the other.

But the pawnee is responsible in case of loss.—IF the pledge be destroyed in the possession of the trustee, the pawnee is responsible ; for the seisin of the trustee is the same as that of the pawnee in regard to the worth of the pledge ; and responsibility attaches only on account of worth.

Unless the trustee have transgressed, in which case he is responsible.—IF, on the contrary, the trustee deliver the pawn either to the pawner or pawnee, he is responsible ; for this reason, that he is the pawner's trustee with respect to the substance of the pledge, and the pawnee's trustee with respect to its worth ; and each of these parties stands as a stranger towards the other ; and a trustee is rendered responsible by delivering the object of his trust into the hands of a stranger. The trustee, therefore, being in this case responsible, cannot retain the value by way of the pawn in his own possession ; for as he has become indebted for the value, it follows that, if he were to retain it by way of the pawn, he becomes at once the claimant and claimee, and the payer and receiver ; in which is implied an obvious inconsistency.

Rules to be observed in this instance.—THE pawner and pawnee must therefore, in this case, concur to take the value from the trustee, and deliver again to him, or to any other person, in place of the original pawn. If, however, they should not concur in so doing, either of them may in that case refer the matter to the Kazee, who may take the value from the trustee, and again deliver it to him, or to any other, in the place of the original pawn. If the Kazee do so, and the pawner afterwards discharge his debt, then, supposing that the responsibility for the value had attached to the trustee in consequence of his having restored the pledge to the pawner, the value in question remains secure to the trustee, as the pawner here appears to have recovered his pledge, and the pawnee his debt. If, on the contrary, the responsibility had attached to the trustee in consequence of his having surrendered the pledge to the pawnee, the pawner, upon discharging the debt, is entitled to take from him the value in question ; for as, in case of the existence of the pawn, he would immediately on payment of the debt resume it, he is by consequence at liberty to take the substitute. It is to be observed, in this case, that if the trustee have given the pledge to the pawnee in loan or trust, and it have been destroyed without any transgression on his part, he (the trustee) is not entitled to take the value from him (the pawnee) ; — whereas, if the pawnee have occasioned the loss, he is so entitled ; for as the property of the thing has before vested in him in virtue of his having compensated for its loss, it was of course his own property that he lent ; and the borrower is therefore liable for its loss when occasioned by himself, but not otherwise. If, also, the trustee give the pledge to the pawnee, "in order that he may preserve it himself as a security for, his debt," and it be afterwards destroyed,

---

* Arab, Adil, an upright person. (See note in p. 632.)

he is entitled to take the value from the pawnee, whether, he (the pawnee), were the occasion of its loss or not; for it was not given to him in the nature of trust or loan, but on terms which implied a liability to make compensation.

The pawner may commission the pawnee, or any other person, to sell the pledge, and discharge the debt; but he cannot reverse the commission, if it be included in the contract.—If the pawner constitute the pawnee, or an other person of character, an agent for the sale of the pledge, towards effecting a discharge of his debt at the expiration of the stipulated term, such agency is valid; because here the pawner has merely created an agent for the sale of his own property. If, also, such agency be expressed as an article in the contract of pawn, the pawner has not afterwards the power of reversing it; because where the agency is thus stipulated, it is one of the rights of the contract, and is therefore binding, in consequence of the contract being so;—and also, because, as the right of the pawnee is connected with it, the annulment of it would be a destruction of his right;—the case here being similar to that of an agent for a defendant, who has been so created at the instance of the plaintiff; for such agent cannot be dismissed from his employ but in the presence of the plaintiff.

Rules with respect to an agent appointed to sell a pledge.—If the pawner constitute any person his agent to sell the pledge, without restricting him to ready money or credit, so as to leave him entirely at his own option in those points, and afterwards prohibit him from selling it on credit, such prohibition is of no effect; for the agency (as was before mentioned) being at first absolute, is not afterwards subject to the restriction of the pawner. In the same manner, the agent cannot be dismissed by the pawnee, as on him he is no way dependent, having been created agent by the pawner. If, also, the pawner die, the agency nevertheless continues in force; for as the contract of pawn becomes not void upon the death of the pawner, so neither does the agency, that being expressly included therein. Besides, if the contract were by this event rendered void, it would be so only with respect to the rights of the heirs of the pawner, to which the rights of the pawnee are superior. The agent, moreover, is empowered to sell the pawn without the consent of the heirs, in the same manner as he would have done in the lifetime of the pawner without his consent.—So likewise, if the pawnee should die the agency does not determine; for a contract of pawn is not rendered void, either by the death of both the parties, or of one; but continues, as before, with all its rights and privileges; such as possession, discharge, and the agency in question. The power of agency, however, ceases on the death of the agent; and his heir or executor cannot stand in his place; because agency is not an inheritance, the constituent being supposed to have confided in his agent alone, and not in any other person. It is recorded from Aboo Yoosaf, that the agent's executor may sell the pledge; for as the agency is binding, the executor has a power of selling it;—in the same manner as where a Mozarib, after having exchanged the capitel stock for any species of merchandize, dies,—in which case his executor is permitted to dispose of the merchandize, the compact being still binding. To this, however, it may be replied, that agency is the right of a principal over his factor; and the heirs of an agent can inherit only his own rights. It is otherwise with respect to Mozaribat, as the rights of that appertain to the Mozarib, or manager.

The pawnee cannot sell it without the pawner's consent.—A pawnee has not a power of selling the pledge without the consent of the pawner, as the property of it belongs absolutely to him. Neither can the pawner sell it without the consent of the pawnee; for, as the thing pledged is, with respect to its worth, the right of the pawnee, it follows that the pawner, if he were to sell it without the concurrence of the pawnee, would not have it in his power to surrender it to the purchaser.

The agent at the expiration of the term of credit, may be compelled to sell the pledge.—If, at the expiration of the stipulated term of credit, the agent refuse to sell the pledge deposited for that purpose with him, and the pawner have absconded, the Kazee must compel him to execute the sale, by imprisonment, or other compulsatory means, the agency being binding for two reasons;—First, because, when expressly included in the contract of pawn, it becomes one of the rights thereof; and, Secondly, because the right of the pawnee is connected with it: and the dismission of the agent annihilates that right. The same rules, in short hold in this instance, as in the case of an agent for the adjustment of a cause of dispute created by the defendant at the instance of the plaintiff; for if the defendant abscond, and the agent refuse to settle the cause, he is compellable thereunto by the Kazee, for the second reason above-mentioned, that the right of the plaintiff would else be destroyed. (It is otherwise with respect to a mere agent for sale; for if he refuse to execute the sale, he cannot be compelled thereto; as his constituent may still sell the article, whence his right is not destroyed.) What is here advanced proceeds on the supposition of the agency being included in the contract of pawn; for if it have not been stipulated until after the execution of the contract, there is in that case a difference of opinion; some asserting that the agent cannot be compelled to execute the sale, whilst others maintain that he may be compelled. Of these the compiler of the Hedaya remarks that the last is the better opinion. Aboo Yoosaf has said that the agency is equally binding in both cases (that is, when included in the contract, and also when made posterior thereto). And the Jama Sagheer and Mabsoot tend greatly to corroborate this opinion for in treating of this species of agency they have supposed it absolute, and not discriminated between that included in the contract of pawn and that agreed upon posterior thereto.

If the pledge be sold by commission from the trustee, the purchase-money is substituted in place of it.—When the agent of a trustee in whose hands a pledge has been deposited sells it, it is no longer in pawn, and the purchase-money stands in its place (that is to say, is, as it were, in pawn), although the agent may not yet have received it, as being the substitute for a thing which was before in his possession. Hence, if the purchase-money should be lost, by the purchaser (for instance) dying insolvent without having discharged it, the loss falls upon the pawnee; because the contract of pawn still continues in force with respect to the purchase-money, since that stands in the place of the thing sold, namely, the pledge. In the same manner, where a pawned slave is slain, and the murderer accounts for his value, the contract still continues in force, as the owner of the slave is entitled to the value in virtue of his property, notwitstanding such value be paid in atonement for blood. The same rule also holds where a slave, having killed another pawned slave, is commuted for the one so killed,—the murderer being in that case substituted for the murdered.

If the trustee, having sold the pledge and paid off the pawnee, be exposed to any subsequent loss, he may reimburse himself from either party.—If a trustee, having been appointed agent for the sale of the pledge, should sell it, and deliver the price to the pawnee by way of payment, and another afterwards prove a property in the pledge, and he accordingly pay that other a compensation for its value, it then remains in his option, either to take the value from the pawner, or the amount of the purchase-money from the pawnee: but he is not permitted to take more from the pawnee than the purchase-money.—The compiler of the Hedaya remarks that this case may occur under two different circumstances or predicaments:—I, where the pledge is destroyed after the sale; and II. where it remains whole and complete.—In the former of other, the owner of the pledge is at liberty there to take a compensation for the value from the pawner, who is an usurper of his right, or form the trustee, who has invaded it, in having sold his property and delivered it to another. Should he, therefore, take it from the pawner, the sale of the trustee becomes valid, as does also the pawnee's seisin of the price in satisfaction for his debt; because, as the pawner, by making compensation, becomes proprietor of the pledge and effaces the usurpation, it then appears that he had authorized the trustee to sell that which was his own.—If, on the contrary, he take the compensation from the trustee, he (the trustee) may, if he choose, have recourse to the pawner; that is to say he may take from him the value of the pledge; for, as being his agent, and the manager of his affairs, he is consequently entitled to an indemnification for whatever loss he may have unavoidably sustained in the execution of his commission. And in this case, also, the sale of the pledge is valid, as well as the pawnee's seisin of the purchase-money in satisfaction for his debt,—whence, in this case, he (the pawnee) cannot urge any future claim against the pawner on the score of his debt.—Or, if the trustee choose, he may have recourse to the pawnee; that is to say, he may resume from him the purchase-money which he had unjustly received from him; unjustly, because it proved in the end to be the trustee's property, by his having afterwards made good the loss to the proprietor. For when he gave it to the pawnee, he supposed it to have been the property of the pawner: but he may not, perhaps, when it proves his own property, be inclined to confirm the transfer, and he is therefore allowed to resume it. As, however, the resumption of the purchase-money from th pawnee deprives him of a discharge of hi^e claim, which the seisin of it was intended to effect, he therefore remains at liberty to demand payment from the pawner in this instance. In the latter of the above circumstances, on the contrary (where the pledge remains whole and complete after the sale), it is incumbent on the owner of the pledge to resume it from the purchaser, as he possesses the substance of his property; and the purchaser is entitled to a restitution of the purchase-money from the trustee, because of his being the seller; after which the trustee may, at his option, receive an indemnification either from the pawner or pawnee,—from the former, because he occasioned him to enter into the agreement, from which he is consequently bound to release him,—and from the latter, because, when the thing sold was proved to belong to another, the money obtained in lieu thereof is no longer formed purchase-money, and the pawnee having received it only as such his seisin is no longer of effect. If, therefore, he take the value from the pawner, the pawnee's seisin of the price is rendered valid:—whereas, if he resume the purchase-money from the pawnee, his seisin being thereby destroyed, his former righ (namely, the claim against the pawnee) exists as before.

But if he was commissioned by the pawner after the contract, he must recur to him alone for indemnification.—All that is here advanced proceeds on the supposition of the agency having been included as an article in the contract of pawn; for if the pawner appoint the trustee his agent for the sale of the pledge after the contract, he (the agent) is in this case to indemnify himself for any loss he may sustain, in consequence of selling the pledge from the pawner, not from the pawnee, notwithstanding he may have made over to the pawnee the price he had received for the pledge, since with this agency the pawnee has no concern, insomuch that the pawner may rescind the agency without consulting him.

A stranger proving his right in a pledged slave, who had died with the pawnee, may seek his compensatiin from either party.—If a pledged slave die in the possession of the pawnee, and it be afterwards discovered that he was the property of another, and not the pawner, it remains with the proprietor to demand a compensation from either the pawner or pawnee; for both are violators of his right,—the one in having delivered the pledge to another, and the other in having received it. If, therefore, he take a compensation from the pawner, the pawnee, because of the slave having died in his possession, is held to have received payment of his debt; for as the pawner has obtained a property in the slave by indemnifying his owner, the payment of his debt is therefore effected by the slave dying in the pawnee's hands. If, on the contrary, he take a compensation from the pawnee, he (the pawnee) is not only entitled to an indemnificatory satisfaction from the pawner, but his claim upon him still exists as before:—he is entitled to an indemnification from the pawner, because of his having deceived him; and his claim of debt exists as formerly, because the discharge effected by the pledge having died in his possession ceases to be of force upon his making good the value, whence his right reverts.

Objection (by the Kazee Aboo Khazim). —It would appear that in this case the pawnee's claim does not exist as before, but that the death of the slave in his hands establishes a satisfaction for it; because, upon the pawner compensating for the slave's value (by the pawnee recovering such value, from him as above), he becomes, in virtue of such compensation, proprietor of the slave, whence it appears that he, in fact, pledged that which was his own, and that the case is the same as if the properietor had taken the compensation, from the pawner, which ould exempt him from all further obligation to the pawnee.

Reply.—As the pawnee first pays the compensation, he first becomes proprietor of the slave from the time of possession; and when, afterwards, he retakes that sum from the pawner, his property in the slave is annulled, and the pawner becomes proprietor of him. The pawner's property in the slave therefore, takes place, in this instance, posterior to the contract of pawn (the pawnee having, as it were, sold the slave to the pawner, and received the price for him);—and this debt to the pawnee remains against him as before,—whence the pawnee is entitled to take it from him. It is otherwise in the former alternative (where the owner takes the compensation from the pawner); for in this case the pawner becomes proprietor from the time of the slave being in his possession (which was prior to the contract of pawn), whence it may eb said that he merely pawned what was his own;—and upon the slave dying in the pawnee's hands, he stands acquitted of his debt, which the pawnee, therefore, cannot afterwards claim from him.

CHAPTER IV.

OF THE POWER OVER PAWNS; AND OF OFFENCES COMMITTED BY OR UPON THEM.

A pledge cannot be sold without the pawnee's consent.—If the pawner sell the pledge without the consent of the pawnee, the sale remains suspended upon his will because of his right being involved in the pledge notwithstanding such sale be an act of the pawner with respect to what is his own property; in the same manner as where a person bequeaths the whole of his state, in which case legacy is suspended in its effect, with respect to the excess, above one-third, upon the consent of his heirs—because of their right being connected therewith. If, therefore, the pawnee assent to the sale, it is vaild; for it was before suspended only on account of his right, which he here consents to forego: and it is also valid if the pawner discharge his debt; for the sale is an act of the proprietor upon his property, being suspended in its effect only because of an obstacle,* which obstacle is here removed.†—In the former case, upon the pawnee having given his consent, and the sale having been thereby rendered valid, the right of the pawnee is transferred from the pledge to the thing given in exchange, namely, the price,—which, in the case here considered, then becomes a substitute for the original pledge. This is approved; because the right of the pawnee is connected with the worth of the pledge; and the return is in effect the same as the consideration:—this being analogous to where an indebted slave is sold by the consent of his creditors in which case their right is transferred from the slave to the value received for him, as they are supposed, in assenting to the sale, to have agreed to the transfer of their right from the slave to the value, but not to the total a bolition of it. If the pawner refuse his assent, and annul the contract of sale, it is null of course (according to one tradition), where, if the pawner redeem the pledge, still the purchaser is not at liberty to take

---

* Namely, the pawnee's right connected with the pledge.

† By the discharge of the debt, which of course disengages the pledge from any claim the pawnee might otherwise have upon it.

it; for as the right of the pawnee is equivalent to his actual property, he therefore stands the same as the proprietor of the pledge (whence his power acceeding to, or annulling the contract of sale). According, however, to a more authentic tradition, the pawnee has not the power of annulling the sale; for his right can sustain no detriment, as the sale cannot, at all events, be carried into execution until he assent to it. The execution of the sale, therefore, being in this manner suspended, the purchaser has the option of waiting until the pawner may redeem the pawn, and resign it to him conformable to the contract, or of carrying the matter before the Kazee; for the seller has it not in his power to deliver the goods, and the power of dissolving the contract rests with the Kazee alone; this being similar to where a slave, having been sold by his master, elopes before the purchaser has received possession of him, in which case the purchaser may either wait until the slave return, or he may prefer a complaint to the Kazee, in order (as the seller is incapable of delivering the goods) to obtain an annulment of the contract.

Who, if the pawner sell it more than once, may ratify either sale.—IF the pawner sell * the pledge without the consent of the pawnee, and again, before the pawnee has signified his assent, sell it to another person, in that case whichever of these two contracts the pawnee may confirm is valid; for as the first sale is dependent on the consent of the pawnee, it cannot prevent the second from being so likewise. If, therefore, the pawnee choose, he may ratify the second sole. If, on the contrary, the pawner, after having first sold the pawn as above, should let, give, or pawn it to another person, and the pawnee give his consent to such lease, gift, or pawn, the sale which preceded either of these deeds is valid. The difference between these two cases is, that in the first (where one sale is made after another) the pawnee may derive an advantage from confirming either of them (as his right lies in the price and whichever, therefore, he approves is valid. In the case of a lease or gift, on the contrary, no advantage can accrue to the pawnee, as his right lies in the return, for the article, not in the usufruct. If, therefore, the pawnee approve of either of these, he by consequence impliedly assents to the abolition of his own right; and the previous sale (which was suspended on his consent only because of his right) becomes valid of course.

A pawned slave may be emancipated by the pawner.—IT is permitted to a pawner to emancipate the slave whom he has deposited in pawn; for as he is sane and adult, he may of course render free his own property which the pawn indisputably is. As, moreover the contract of pawn does not induce any destruction of the pawner's property in the pledge, his act with respect to it is not rendered void by the pawnee withholding his assent to it, notwithstanding the pawnee's right (of detention in regard to the worth) be thereby defeated:—in the same manner as where the purchaser of a slave emancipates him without having taken possession; in which case the slave is free, notwithstanding the seller's right (of detention of the article in satisfaction for the price) be thereby rendered null.

OBJECTION.—If a person bequeath a slave to another upon his deathbed, and leave no other effects except that slave, and the heirs of the testator afterwards emancipate the slave, such manumission is not valid, because of the right of the legatee; and hence it would follow that a pawned slave cannot be emancipated, because of the right of the pawnee.

REPLY.—The manumission of the slave by the heirs of the testator is not (in the opinion of Haneefa) void, but is merely suspended until such time as he (the slave) shall have performed emancipatory labour.

The sale, moreover, or gift of a pawn is null, for this reason, that the pawner is unable to surrender it to the purchaser or donee,—an objection which does not obtain in the case of manumission, since in that instance a delivery is not required. The manumission is therefore valid, and takes immediate effect,—whence the contract of pawn is null, as the subject of it no longer remains.

Who, if he be rich, must substitute the value in pawn for the slave.—CONSEQUENTLY, if the pawner be rich and the debt to the pawnee be then due, he (the pawnee) may require payment of it immediately;—or, if it be not due until after the expiration of a term, he may take from the pawner the value of the slave, and return it as a substitute until his debt become payble, when he may take it in satisfaction of his right, restoring any surplus which may remain from it to the pawner.

But if he be poor, the slave must perform emancipatory labour to the amount of his value for the discharge of the pawnee's claim.—THIS is supposing the pawner to be rich for, if he be poor, the slave in (question must perform emancipatory labour to an amount adequate to his value; and with this (which, if it be of a different species from the debt, must first be converted into the same) the debt of the pawnee is to be discharged; for a discharge from the pawner being here impossible, it is consequently made from him who enjoys the advantage of the manumission, namely, the slave. The slave however, when his emancipator afterwards becomes rich, is entitled to take from him the sum he earned; because he has, in fact paid his debt, not voluntarily or gratuitously,

*The sale here mentioned does not signify an absolute, but a conditional sale, depending, for its ratification, upon the pawnee's concurrence, as before mentioned.

but in conformity with the ordinance of the LAW in this particular.*

Although he should have denied his being in pawn previous to such manumission.—IF a person make a declaration of having pawned his slave, by saying to him, "I have deposited you in pledge with such a person." and the slave deny it, and the master afterwards emancipate him, at a time when he is poor, it is incumbent upon the slave to perform emancipatory labour, according to our doctors. Ziffer is of a contrary opinion; for he holds this case to be analogous to where a master first liberates his slave, and then declares his having pawned him; in which case, if the master be poor, and the slave deny it (as above), emancipatory labour is not incumbent on the slave; and so. here, likewise. Our doctors, on the other hand, argue that, in the case in question, the master declare the pawn at a time when he is undoubtedly competent to it, as he still possesses a property in the slave, not having yet emancipated him; and consequently his declaration is valid.—It is otherwise where the declaration of pawn is made subsequently to the emancipation, as the master's power of pawning is then terminated;—whence there is no analogy between the cases.

A pawner may create his pawned slave a Modabbir or Am-Walid.—IF a pawner create the slave whom he has pawned a Modabbir, it is valid, according to all authorities:—according to our doctors, because, as the complete emancipation would be lawful, it follows that this qualifiede macipation is lawful, a fortiori; and according to Shafei, because the granting Tadbeer to a slave does not (as he holds) prevent the sale of him. In a similar manner, it is in the power of a pawner to constitute his pawned female slave an Am-Walid; for as a father has this privilege with respect to the female slave of his child, because of the right which he has in his property, notwithstanding such right be inferior to that of the child himself, it follows that thexertion of the same privilege by a pawner, in virtue of his right in the pledge, is valid a fortiori the right of the pawner being superior to that of any other person, as he is the proprietor.

And if he be rich, he must substitute the value in pawn; but if he be poor, the slave must perform emancipatory labour to the full amount of the debt.—When, therefore, a pawned slave is constituted either Modabbir or Am-Walid, such slave is excluded from the contract of pawn, as the intention is defeated, since a debt cannot be discharged by means of a Modabbir or Am-Walid;*—whenceif the pawner be rich, he is responsible for the value, after the manner before shown in the case of pawned slaves emancipated; but if, on the contrary, he be in indigent circumstances, the pawnee may require from the Modabbir or Am-Walid emancipatory labour to the amount of the debt, as the fruit of their labour is the property of their master. It is otherwise in the case of a pledged slave emancipated by an indigent pawner; for the fruits of his labour being his own property, he is obliged to labour to the amount of his value only, or that of the debt of the pawner, in case of its being less than his value.

The pawner, on becoming rich, is responsible for the emancipatory labour in the former instance, but not in the latter.—IT is not permitted either to a Modabbir or Am-Walid to resume from their master when he becomes rich what they paid on his account when poor, because they in fact paid this from his property; † but when a poor pawner emancipates the slave whom he had pledged, he [the slave] is entitled to take whatever he may have paid on account of his emancipator; because he has paid it from his own property, ‡—and this from necessity, in conformity with the precepts of the LAW (as before observed), whence such payment cannot be considered as gratuitous.§ Some have said, that if the debt be not due at the time, the Modabbir or Am-Walid are compellable to earn their value; which, as being a substitute for the pawn, must be detained as such in lieu of the original: but that if, on the contrary, the debt be then due, it is in that case necessary to discharge it from the stock of the pawner; and as the earnings of the Modabbir or Am-Walid are considered as the property of the master, they must therefore labour towards obtaining a sum adequate to the whole of the debt.

An emancipated Modabbir does not owe the pawnee labour beyond his value.—IF a pawner emancipate the slave whom he had created a Modabbir, as above, it is not then incumbent on the freedom to earn, a greater sum than his value, although he should be thereunto commanded by the Kazee; for after emancipation, the fruits of his labour are his own property. Still, however, he cannot recover from his master what he had paid on his account prior to his freedom; as that was, in fact, the property of the master.

Destruction of the pledge by the pawner.—IF a pawner destroy the thing he had pledged.

* The remainder of this discussion is omitted by the translator, as being merely a repetition of what has been already set forth at large under the head of Manumission.

* Because Modabbirs and Am-Walids cannot be sold..

† To earnings of their labour being his right.

‡ The labour and earnings of a freedman being considered as his own property..

§ A person is not entitled to recover, who pays the debts of another in a gratuitous manner.

the same rules hold as are established in the case of emancipating the pledge.

By a stranger.—If a stranger (that is, a person unconcerned in the contract) destroy the pledge, the pawnee (not the pawner) is litigant against him, and may take from him a compensation for the value, which he must retain in pawn in place of the original pledge; for the pawnee, as being the most entitled to the substance of the pledge, is also most entitled to its substitute, namely, the value. It is here to be observed, that the stranger must compensate for the pledge according to the value which it bore at the time of its being destroyed. If, therefore, it be valued at five hundred dirms at the period of its destruction, and at one thousand dirms on the date of the contract, the stranger must account for five hundred dirms to the pawnee, who must retain the same in pawn;—and five hundred dirms are remitted from the debt; for the deficiency to the amount is a destruction which has occurred in the hands of the pawnee, occasioned (as it were) by the visitation of heaven; and as the property has thus perished in his hands, a proportionable amount is therefore deducted from his claim.

Or by the pawnee.—If the pawnee destroy the pledge before the expiration of the stipulated term of payment, he is responsible for the value, because of his having destroyed the property of another;—and this value he is to retain in pawn until the term of payment arrive; for as it is a substitute for the substance of the pledge, it is consequently subject to the same rule. As soon, therefore, as the debt becomes due, the pawnee may take it from the va'ue and if When a balance remain, it must be restored to the pawner, as being a return for his property, with which the pawnee has no concern.

A depreciation in the value of the pledge occaesons a proportionable deduction from the pawnee's claim.—If a person pawn any article estimated at one thousand dirms, in security of a debt of the same amount payable at some future period, and the article, in consequence of a fall in the price, bear afterwards a value of five hundred dirms, and be then destroyedin the pawnee's hands, he [the pawnee] is responsible for five hundred dirms, and five hundred are also remitted from his debt; for the deficiency of five hundred dirms arising from the fall in the price being (as it were) a decay of part of the pawn whilst in the hands of the pawnee, an adequate sum is therefore retrenched from his claim; and the remaining five hundred dirms are likewise due from him in consequence of the decay, and remain with him in pawn, as before stated.

The pawnee lending the pledge to the pawner, is freed from responsibility during the loan.—In a person, having received slave in pawn, lend him to the pawner, in order that he may enjoy the use of his service, or for any other purpose, and the pawner take possession, the slave is no longer a subject of responsibility with the pawnee (in other words, if he be killed or lost in the hands of the pawner, the pawnee is not thence held to have received payment of his debt); because he has passed out of the possession of the pawnee; and the seisin of the pawner in virtue of a loan does not stand as the seisin of the pawnee, as the tenure of loan is repugnant to that of a pawn, since the latter induces responsibility, whereas the former does not.

But he may resume it at pleasure, and then his responsibility reverts.- The pawnee, however, is at liberty at any time to resume the pledge from the pawner; because he holds it by the tenure of a loan which is not binding; and also, because the contract of pawn still subsists;—whence it is that if the pawner were to die without having returned the pledge, the pawnee would in that case have a claim upon it in preference to the other creditors (that is to say, he would be entitled first to take a satisfaction for his claim from the pledge; which done, if any part should remain it would be distributed among the other creditors).

Objection.—If a pawnee be not held liable for a pledged slave after he is lent, how is the contract of pawn supposed then to exist, Rerly— Responsibility is not, . in every instance, one of the requisites of a contract of pawn;—whence it is that the effect of the contract reaches to the child of a pawned female slave, although such child be not a subject of responsibility from loss or destruction.

As, therefore, the contract still subsists, the pawnee resume the pledge from the pawner, he again become liable for it, in the same manner as formerly, having again taken possession of it in virtue of the contract of pawn.

The pledge being lent to a straanger by either party. is no longer a subject ofresponsibility.—If either of the parties to a contract of pawn lend the pledge with the concurrence of the other to a stranger, it is not in this case a subjectof responsibility to the pawnee, any more than in the former instance of but the contract of pawn still continues in force, and either party is entitled to resume the pledge from the borrower, and to place it in pawn as before, from the interest each has in it.

The pledge, on being disposed of by either party, with the consent of the other, is excluded from the contract.—If either party, with the consent of the other, let, sell, or bestow the pawn in gift to stranger, it is excluded from the contract, and cannot again be subject to it, unless the parties conclude a fresh agreement. It is to be observed that if, in any of these cases, the pawner die before a restitution of the pledge be made to the pawnee, he (the pawnee) is upon the same footing with the other creditors; ; because as, in consequence of these acts, a binding right of others is connected with the pledge, the effect of the contrsate no longer remains:—whereas no binding right is connected with a pledge in consequence of the loan of it:—for which reason there is an essential difference between the cases here considered and that of loan.

If the pawnee borrow the pledge from the pawner for any particular purpose, and it be destroyed previous to his having applied it to that purpose, he is responsible for it,—that is to say, a sum proportionate to its value is retrenched from his claim; for until he apply it to that use for which he has borrowed it, the seisin which he had made in virtue of the contract of pawn still subsists. The law is similar where the pawn is destroyed after the pawnee has accomplished the service for which he had borrowed it; for then his seisin of loan exists no longer. If, on the contrary, it be destroyed during the period in which he enjoys the use of it, he is not responsible, as at that time he holds it in loan, not in pawn. (The same rule also holds where the pawner consents to the pawnee's making use of the pledge.)*

A person borrowing an article, with intent to pawn it is restricted in the pawn according as he specifies the particulars of the debt, &c., or otherwise.—If a person borrow a robe from another, with an intent generally declared "to pawn it," he may accordingly pawn it in security for any debt whether great or small;—whereas, if the lender particularly specify the sum; in security for which the borrower may pawn the robe, he is not, in that case, permitted to pawn it for a sum either large or smaller than what is so specified;—not for a larger sum, because the intention of the lender is, that the robe shall be pawned for a debt which may be easily discharged, an intention which is obviously defeated in the case of pawning it for a large sum:—nor for a smaller sum, because the view of the lender here is, in case of its loss, the obtaining from the pawner that sum which he would receive from the pawnee in consideration of the extra value of the pledge. The same rule also holds where the lender specifies either the particular species of debt, the person who is to receive the pawn, or the city in which the contract is to be concluded;—such restrictions being severally attended with particular advantage; for the payment of some debts is more easily effected than of others,—and it is also more convenient to make payment in some cities than in others, and so likewise it is of advantage to particularize the persons, as some men are just and careful, whilst others are not so.

And if he transgress, is responsible for the value in case of loss.—If, therefore, in any of these cases, the borrower act contrary to the directions of the lender, he becomes responsible for the value of the article in case of loss;—and when this happens, the lender has it in his option either to take a compensation from the borrower (in which case the contract of pawn subsists entirely between the borrower and the pawnee, since the former, by paying a compensation for the pledge, becomes sole proprietor of it), or from the pawnee, who will take an indemnification from the pawner, and likewise receive payment of his debt, as has been before explained in the cases of claims laid to pledges. If, on the contrary, the borrower conform to the directions of the lender, by pawning the robe for the exact sum to which he was restricted and the value of the robe be equal to, or greater than the amount of the debt, the pawnee is held, in case of its loss, to have received payment of his debt, and the proprietor of the robe receives from the pawner the amount of the debt, being the sum which the borrower had cleared by means of his property (and it is on this account that the borrower must pay the amount of the debt,—not because he was seised of the robe, as that was in virtue of a free loan from the proprietor).—In the same manner if, when the pawner had conformed to the direction of the lender, the robe be in any degree depreciated, the pawnee forfeits a proportionate part of his claim, and a like sum is due from the borrower to the lender, because of so much having been retrenched from his debt. If the value of the robe be short of the amount of the debt, and it be lost in pawn, a sum equivalent to its value is retrenched from the claim, and the remainder of the debt is due from the pawner, as no discharge of debt is effected beyond the amount of the value of the robe; and the pawner is, moreover, indebted to the lender for the value of the robe, having by means of it made payment of as much of his debt.—If, also, the value of the robe be adequate to the amount of the debt and the proprietor be desirous of redeeming his property, on the part of the pawner, by paying the amount, the pawnee is not in that case allowed to object to the restoring of it; because the robe being the property of the lender, he does not, consequently, by redeeming it, officiously intermeddle in an affair which does not concern him (whence he is entitled to take from the pawner (the borrower) the sum which he pays towards the redemption of the pawn); and the Kazee must therefore compel the pawnee to surrender the robe. It is otherwise where an unconcerned person pays the debt of the pawner; for as, by endeavouring to redeem a thing which is not his own property, he interferes in a business which does not relate to him, the pawnee is not therefore compellable to surrender the pledge to him.

But not if it be lost before pawn, or after

* That is,—where the pawnee, being already possessed of the pledge, obtains the owner's consent to make use of it.—For the elucidation of what is here advanced it is proper to remark, that a pledge may either be delivered to the pawnee, given in trust to an Adil, or retained in the hands of the owner [the pawner] under a responsibility to account for it if necessary.

redemption.—If the borrowed article be lost in the hands of the borrower, either prior to his having pawned it, or posterior to his having redeemed it, he is not responsible; for here he has not accomplished any discharge by means of the value, which (as we have shown in the above case) is the sole cause of responsibility.

On disputes concerning the loss of the pledge, the deposition of the borrower is credited with respect to the person in whose hands it was lost, and that of the lender with respect to the restrictions of the loan.—If a dispute arise between the lender and borrower after the loss of the pledge, the lender asserting that it had been lost whilst in the hands of the pawnee, and the borrower on the other hand maintaining that it was lost in his own possession, either before he had pawned it or after he had redeemed it, the declaration of the borrower, upon oath, must be credited, because he is, in this case, the defendant, as he denies having paid the debt by means of the other's property.—If, on the contrary, they disagree concerning the amount of the debt to which the lender had restricted the pawning of the robe, the declaration of the lender is credited; for as his deposition would be credited if he wese to deny the loan itself, it follows that where he merely denies a quality of the loan it is credited a fortiori.

A person receiving a borrowed article in pledge on the faith of a promise, must pay the sum promised to the pawner, who again pays the same to the lender.—If the borrower of the robe pawn it on the faith of a promise, —that is, on a person promising to lend him a certain sum of money, and that promise accept the pledge, and make the promise accordingly, and the pledge (which is supposed to be equal to the amount of the debt) be lost before the pawnee had fulfilled his engagement, he [the pawnee] is in that case responsible for the sum so promised, as a promise is held to be the same as a real debt; —and the lender is entitled to receive from the pawner the sum which he takes from the pawnee.

The lender of a slave to pawn may emancipate him, lodging the value with the pawnee, in substitute for the pledge.—If a person lend his slave to another, that he may pawn him, and the borrower pawn him accordingly, and the lender afterwards emancipate him, he is accordingly free; for the owner's property in him is not destroyed by the circumstance of his being pawned. And in this case the pawnee may either receive payment of his debt from the pawner (who is still indebted to him), or he may take from the lender the value of the slave by way of compensation, as the right which he had in the worth of the slave was destroyed by the lender emancipating him;—and having thus received the value, he may retain it in pawn until such time as he obtain payment of his debt, upon which he must restore the said value to the owner.

The borrower transgressing upon the article (before pawn or after redemption) and then ceasing from such transgression is not responsible in case of loss.—If a person borrow a slave or a camel with intent to pawn it, and having first employed the slave in service, or rode upon the camel, he then pawn it in security of a debt adequate to its value, and having afterwards discharged the debt, the pledge be completely destroyed in the hands of the pawnee before restoration, in that case the pawner is not responsible; for when he concluded the pawn he became exempt from responsibility, notwithstanding he had previously enjoyed the usufruct; since although he at first transgressed, yet he afterwards retracted, and acted in conformity with the intention of the lender. In the same manner, if the pawner, after having redeemed the pledge, employ it in service, without occasioning any detriment to it, and it be afterwards destroyed by some unforeseen contingency, he is not responsible; because the term of the loan having expired upon the redemption of the pawn, he is no longer a borrower, but becomes from that period a trustee; and although, in taking the service of the pawn, he was guilty of a transgression, yet as he afterwards retracted, and conformed to the intention of the lender he becomes thenceforth free from all responsibility. It is otherwise in the case of a person who has borrowed any thing not with an intent to pawn it; for his seisin, being derived merely from the loan, is not therefore the same as that of the proprietor, to whom he is consequently bound to restore the thing which he borrowed. In the case, on the contrary, of a loan with intent to pawn, when the thing is pawned the object of the lender is obtained; for his views is to have recourse to the borrower; that is to say, that when the pawn is destroyed in the possession of the pawnee, and a discharge of debt thereby proved, he may take from the borrower a sum adequate to what he is held to have discharged by the loss of the pawn: wherefore if it be destroyed in the hands of the borrower, without a transgression on his part, he is not responsible.

A pawner destroying the pledge, is responsible to the pawnee for the value.—If the pawner kill the slave whom he had pledged he is responsible for the value; because by the murder of the slave he destroys the right of the pawnee, which is sacred and inviolable; and a right of this nature, attaching to the property of any person, renders him [the proprietor] the same as a stranger with respect to responsibility; like the connexion of the right of the heirs with the property of a dying person, which prevents the effect of his gratuitous acts in any thing beyond the third of his estate; or like the connexion of the right of a legatee with the legacy bequeathed to him, which, if the testator's heirs should destroy the article (bequeathed to him in legacy), renders them responsible for the value as a substitute.

And so in proportion for any injury he

may do to it.—IF the pawnee commit any offence upon the pledge,* a sum is remitted from his debt equivalent to the atonement for such offence; because the substance of the pledge belongs to the proprietor (the pawner): and as the pawnee has transgressed upon it in this instance, he is consequently responsible to the proprietor for having so done.

Any finable offence committed by a pledged slave upon either the person or property of his pawner is of no account.—IF a pledged slave be guilty of an offence against the pawner, either in person or property, such offence is of no account,—that is to say, is not attended with any effect;—and in this our doctors have been unanimous for as the offence is here committed by the property on the proprietor, the cognizance of it would tend to no advantage. (By the offences here alluded to it is to be understood merely such as induce fine, not such as occasion retaliation.)

Nor such offence committed by him upon the person of the pawnee.—IF a pledged lave be guilty of an offence against the person of the pawnee, this likewise (in the opinion of Haneefa) is of no account—The two disciples have judged otherwise.—The argument adduced by them is that as, in this case, the offence does not affect the proprietor, an advantage may be derived from a cognizance of it, since the slave may be made over [to the pawnee] in reparation of the injury.—The offence is therefore of account in this instance; and such (according to them) being the case, it follows that if the pawner and pawnee concur in dissolving the contract of pawn, and the pawner either deliver the slave, or pay a sum to the pawnee in atonement for the offence, the obligation of debt is void: †—but if the pawnee should signify that "he does not desire any compensation for the offence," the slave remains in pawn as before. The argument of Haneefa is, that no advantage can possibly result from taking cognizance of the offence in question; for if cognizance of it be taken on account of the pawnee, it is then incumbent on him to extricate the slave from the guilt in which he is involved; ‡ wherefore he must first pay the expiatory sum, and then again receive it which there is evidently no advantage.

Nor upon his property, provided his value do not exceed the debt for which by stands pledged.—IF a pledged slave commit an offence upon the property of the pawnee, such offence is of no account, according to all our doctors, provided the value of the slave be adequate to the amount of the debt: for here no advantage can result from taking cognizance of the offence; as the remedy applicable in this case is an appropriation of the slave to the pawnee, in compensation for the injury he had sustained,—a remedy which cannot here be effected, as the slave is not made over in atonement for the offence, but is sold, and a compensation for the injury he has done to the property of the pawnee discharged from the purchase money;—and as the sum appropriated to the discharge of the compensation is deducted from the debt, there is finally no advantage in taking account of the offence in this instance. If, on the contrary, the value of the slave exceed the amount of the debt, there are two opinions recorded from Haneefa upon the case.—One is, that [the offence may be redressed in the proportion in which the value [of the slave] exceeds the debt, a pledge being a trust with respect to any excess, and the injury in this case being similar to that committed by a slave in deposit on the property of the trustee. The other is, that the offence cannot be redressed at all; for as the effect of the contract of pawn (namely, the detention of the slave on account of debt) applies to the excess as well as to any other part of the pledge, it may therefore be said that he is a subject of responsibility in toto.

But his offence against the son of the pawnee is cognizable.—IF an offence be committed by a pledged slave on the son of the pawner or pawnee, it is cognizable; for, as the right of property of a father is, in reality, distinct and separate from that of his son, the crime is therefore the same as if committed upon a stranger.

If the pledge be destroyed after depreciation, the pawnee must remain satisfied with the compensation he recovers from the destroyer.—IF a person pawn a slave estimated at one thousand dirms, in security for a debt of the same amount, payable at some future period, and the value of the slave be afterwards lowered to one hundred dirms from a fall in the price,* and a person then kill the slave, and pay a compensation of one hundred dirms (being the value he at that time bears), and the time of payment arrive, the pawnee must in this case keep possession of the hundred dirms aforesaid in lien of his debt and has no further claim whatever upon the pawner.—This is founded upon an established rule, that no regard is paid to any depreciation of a pledge from a fall in the price, regard being had solely to the value it bore at the time of the contract of pawn;—whence it is that (as is here mentioned) diminution of the value of a pledge from a fall in the price does not occasion a remission of the debt, according to our doctors:—contrary to the opinion of Ziffer, who contends that, upon the pledge sustaining any loss with respect to its worth, it may be

* Such as by maiming, or otherwise.

† Because the slave here appears to have been "lost in the hands of the pawnee," a circumstance which liquidates his debt.

‡ Because he is possessed of the slave in a way which induces responsibility.

* That is, from a fall (for instance) in the current or market price of slaves.

said to sustain a loss with respect to the substance also. The argumet of our doctors is that a fall in the price arises merely from a decrease of desire in men towards the article,—a circumstance to which no regard is paid in the case of sale (whence the purchaser has on option in consequence of any casual fall in the market, but owes the whole price agreed for), nor in the case of usurpation (whence an usurper, upon restoring the article he has usurped, is not responsible for any depreciation it may have sustained in the interim of usurpation from a fall in the price). As, therefore, no art of the debt is remitted in consequence of a fall in the price, the slave continues in pledge opposed to the whole of the debt;—and upon any person killing him, he pays the value which he [the slave] then bears, namely, one hundred dirms (for, in exacting compensation, regard must be paid to the value at the time of the destruction taking place);—and the pawnee takes the hundred dirms, as being a compensation for the worth of the pledge with respect to the owner of it. But, after this, the pawnee has no further claim on the pawner; because the seisin of the pawnee stands as a seisin of payment from the time of his obtaining possession of the pledge-which payment is confirmed in the event of the loss of the pledge whilst in his possession. The value of the slave, moreover, at the beginning was (one thousand dirms, and upon his being destroyed in the hands of the pawnee, he [the pawnee] is accounted to have received payment of his whole debt in virtue of his original seisin. But since, in consequence of his having received one hundred dirms, it is impossible that the can also be thus accounted to obtain payment of one thousand dirms (the original value of the slave) without inducing usury, the matter is therefore settled thus,—that he received these hundred dirms as part payment of his debts of one thousand dirms, and that there still remain nine hundred dirms annexed to the substance of the pledge;and that, upon the pledge being destroyed in his possession, he is in consequence of such destruction accounted to receive payment of nine hundred dirms. It is otherwise where the slave dies a natural death in the hands of the pawnee; for as, in that case, there can- be no imputation of usury, he is therefore held to have received payment of the whole of the debt in that instance.

But if (after such depreciaiton) he sell it by desire of the pawnee for payment of his claim, he is still entitled to any deficiency.—If a person pawn a slave estimated at one thousand dirms in security of a debt of the same amount, and the value of the slave be afterwards lowered to one hundred dirms by a fall in the price, and the pawnee be authorized by the pawner to sell the slave, and accordingly sell him for one hundred dirms, and take possession of the price towards the discharge of his debt,—he is still entitled to receive from the pawnee the remaining nine hundred dirms: for as the pawnee sold the pledge at the instance of the pawner, it is effect the same as if the pawner had taken it back and sold it himself— in which case the agreement would be dissolved and the debt would continue in force, except in regard to tha sum which the pawnee had received — and so here likewise.

The pawner must redeem a slave of less value received by the pawnee in compensation for having slain the slave in pledge) by payment of his whole debt – If a person pawn a slave valued at one thousand dirm against a debt of the same amount, and afterwards a slave valued at one hundred dirms kill the slave in pawn, and having been given in compensation for his blood, be detained in pawn in lieu of him, the pawner is in that case compellable to redeem him by the payment of the whole of the debt, namely, one thousand dirms. This is the opinion of Haneefa and Aboo Yoosaf. Mohammed maintains that the pawner is in this case at liberty either to redeem the pledge by discharging the whole of the debt or to transfer the property of it to the pawnee as a commutation. Ziffer, on the other hand, contends that the slave who perpetrated the murder is to remain in pawn in security of one hundred dirms; and that the remaining sum of nine hundre d dirms is accounted to be discharged; because (as he argues) the seisin of the pawnee in virtue of the contract is a seisin of payment, which is fulfilled in this cas by the destruction of the pledge; but as the pledge has left behind it a return or consideration, equivalent to the tenth part of the debt, such part is therefore still due and the slave is detamed in pawn in security thereof. The argument of our doctors is, that in his case no part of the debt is remitted; because the second slave is a substitute for the first, in regard merely to flesh and blood (that is, in regard to appearance); and as, in case of the existence of the first slave, if the value were be diminished by a fall in the price, still no part of the debt (as we have before shown, would be on that account annulled, so neither is any part a annulled when another slave is substituted for the one originally pledged. Mohammad has indeed said that the pa ner may nevertheless refuse to redeem the pledge; for when a change and diminution of value took place in the pawn whilst in the possession of the pawnee (which is a cause of responsibility), the pawner became empowered to object to the redemption of it;—in the same manner as where a slave kills a purchased slave antecedent to the delivery of him,—in which case the purchaser has it at his option either to accept the slave who committed the murder in lieu of the one he purchased, or to annual the contract [of sale]. To this, however, the two Elders reply, that upon the second salve being, with regard to appearance, substituted for the first, it may be said that in change takes place in the identity of the slave; and as the substance of a pawn is a trust in the hands of the pawnee, it follows that the pawner cannot render it the property of the pawnee unless he should consent there unto.—Moreover, the transfer of a pledge in commutation of the debt to which it stood opposed was a common practice in times of ignorance, but has since been proscribed by the LAW. It is otherwise with respect to the case of sale adduced as a parallel by Mohammed; for there the buyer has the option of annulling the contract of sale; and the annulment of sale is permitted by this LAW.

The fines incurred by a pledged slave must be defrayed by the pawnee.—IF a pledged slave slay a person by misadventure, the fine of blood is in that case chargeable to the pawnee, who must defray it accordingly —nor is he at liberty to commute the slave for it, as he has not the power of transferring the property of him to any person. If, therefore, the pawnee dischange the whole fine, the slave is thereby rendered pure; and the stains of guilt being thus effaced, his [the pawnee's] claim of debt subsists as before: but he is not entitled to make any demand on the pawner on account of the sum which he paid in expiation of the crime of the slave; for as it was committed whilst in his possession a circumstance which occasions responsibility),* the atonement for it therefore rests upon him.

But if he refuse, they are defrayed by the pawner, who charges the pawnee accordingly, in liquidation of his debt.—IF, however, the pawnee object to the payment of the penalty, the pawner must in that case be ordered either to pay the fine, or to make over the slave in lieu of it; for the pawner is the proprietor of the slave; and the fine was chargable to the pawnee merely for this reason, that his right is connected with the slave [in virtue of pawn], and not because of his being in any respect the proprietor. Upon his refusal, therefore, the claim of atonemet for the offence lies against the pawner, as being proprietor of the salve; and the atonement, in the present instance, is either paying the fine of blood, or making over the slave in lieu of it. If the pawner adopt the latter alternative, his debt to the pawnee is held to be completely discharged; for the transfer having been incurred by an offence committed by the slave whilst in the pawnee's possession, he therefore, as it were, perishes in his hands. If, also, he adopt the former alternative (that of paying the fine), his debt is extinguished; for as the slave was (as it were) lost by the offence, the recovery of him was incumbent on the pawnee, by the payment of the atonement. Upon the pawner, therefore, discharging such atonement, he, as it were, retrieves the slave, and is consequently entitled to payment from the pawnee; for which reason the debt is held to be annulled. It is otherwise where a person pawns a slave girl who bears a child whilst in the possession of the pawnee; for if that child should either kill a man, or trespass upon any person's property, it s incumbent on the pawner in the first instance to make over the child in expiation for the murder, or in compensation for the damage he may have occasioned; as the child is not a subject of responsibility with the pawnee. If, therefore, the child be given in lieu of the blood or property, it is excluded from the contract of pawn, but is not deducted from the pawnee's debt,—in the same manner as where it dies a natural death:—or, if, on the other hand, he pay the atonement, the child in that case remains in pawn with its mother as before.

Rule with respect to the debts increased by a pledged slave destroying the property of a stranger.—IF a pledged slave destroy the property of any person to an equal or greater amount than his value, and the pawnee discharge the debt thus incurred by the slave, his claim upon the pawner holds good as before, in the same manner as where he pays a pecuniary atonement for any offence committed by the slave. In case, however, of his objecting to such payment, the pawner is then required either to sell the slave towards discharging of the debt, or to pay it himself. If he adept the latter alternative, the claim of the pawnee is cancelled, in the same manner as explained in the example of atonements. If, on the contrary, he prefer the former alternative and (declining to pay the debt himself) sell the slave towards the discharge of it, in that case the person who sustained the injury must first take what is due to him from the price (his claim having preference to that of the pawnee), and then, if anything remain, in inquiry must be made whether the claim of the proprietor of the goods was greater equal to, or less than that of the pawneee?—If it be either equal to, or greater than the claim of the pawnee, the residue of the price is appropriated to the pawner, and the debt of the pawnee is held to be annulled; for upon the slave being sold towards the discharge of a debt attaching to him in consequence of an offencé committed whilst in the possess'on of the pawner, the case becomes in effect the same as if he had been destroyed in the pawnee's possession. If, on the contrary, the claim of the proprietor be less than that of the pawnee—the claim of the pawnee is in that case annulled only in proportion to the sum disbursed to the proprietor and the remainder is detained in pawn in lieu of the slave:—wherefore, if the pawnee's debt be at that time due, he may then take this sum as a satisfaction for it but if the term of payment should not have arrived, he must retain it in his hands until his debt become payable. If, on the other hand, it should so happen that the price of the slave does not

* The immediate possessor of a slave is in a certain degree responsible for his conduct.

altogether suffice towards the discharge of the proprietor's debt, he [the proprietor] may in that case take the whole of the price, but without making a demand on any person for the remainder, until such time as the slave may have become free; for his right relates to the slave; and as the slave has been sold towards making satisfaction for it, his claim therefore to whatever part of the right may not have been thus discharged, is suspended until the slave obtain his freedom, when it may be again urged;—and if the slave, after obtaining his freedom, should thus discharge the remainder, he is not then entitled to claim a reimbursement from any person, as the money be disbusred was due from him on account of his own act.

If the value of the slave be twice the amount of the debt, the fines incurred by him are defrayed equally by both parties.—If a person pawn a slave valued at two thousand dirms in security of a debt of one, thousand, and the slave commit an offence in that case the pawner and pawnee must both be ordered to pay the atonement;* for a moiety only of the slave is insured with the pawnee, the other moiety being with him as a trust; and accordingly the atonement for the insured moiety is chargable to him, and that of the other moiety to the pawnee. If, therefore, the pawner incline to give the slave as a composition for the offence, and the pawnee assent thereto, his [the pawnee's] debt is extingusihed. If, on the contrary, the parties disagree (one of them inclining to give the slave in composition, and the other wishing to discharge the atonement), the declaration is in that case accepted of the party who perfers paying the atonement, whether it be the pawner or pawnee; for if the pawnee pay the atonement, still the right of the pawner is not annulled; whereas the pawner, in commuting the slave for the penalty, would destroy the right of the pawnee. If the pawnee pay the atonement, a part of the payment, in proportion to the part [of the slave] he held in trust, is considered as gratuitous (for this reason, that if he had not chosen to pay it, the matter would have rested upon the pawner), and such being the case, he has no claim upon the pawner for an indemnification.—If, on the contrary, the pawnee refuse to pay the atonement, and the pawner discharge the whole, a moiety of it is in that case placed to the account of the pawnee (that is to say, is deducted from his claim); for as, in all cases where pledged slaves commit a crime, the debt of the pawnee is held to be extinguished upon the pawner either making over the slave, or paying the atonement, it follows that the pawner, in paying the atonement, does not act gratuitously. As, therefore, a moiety of the atonement is due from the pawnee, if such moiety be equal to, or greater than his claim, the whole of his debt is extinguished; or, if it be less, a proportionate part; whilst the slave is detained in pawn in security of the part remaining due.

The executor of a deceased pawner may sell the pledge, and discharge the debt, with the pawnee's consent.—IF a pawner die, his executor is empowered to sell the pledge, and discharge the debt, provided he obtain the consent of the pawnee; for as the executor represents the pawner, he has consequently the same power and privilege as had appertained to him during his lifetime. But if a pawner die without leaving an executor, it then belongs to the Kazee to appoint a person to act in that capacity; as it is his duty to conserve the rights of those who are themselves incapable of maintaining them; which purpose is fulfilled in the appointment of an executor, who may discharge the debts of the deceased, and receive payment of his claims upon others.

An executor cannot pawn effects of the defunct to any particular creditor.—IF an executor pawn part of the effects of the defunct to one of his creditors, it is illegal, and the other creditors may compel him to revoke the pawn;—for an executor, not having the power of paying some of the creditors, and of excepting others, cannot therefore give pledges to some and not to others; as a pledge is held to be the same, in effect, with an actual payment. If, therefore, the executor should, in the meantime, discharge the claims of the other creditors, the pawn which he before made is valid, since in satisfying them he removes the bar to its legality.

Unless there be only one.—But if the defunct should leave only one debt against him, in that case the executor is justified in pawning part of the effects in security of it; for, since he has a power of giving part of the effects, in payment of the debts of the deceased, he may consequently deposit part of them in pledge; and if, afterwards, he sell the pledge as a means of discharging the debt, it is lawful, because the sale of the effects of the defunct with a purpose to pay off his debts being lawful when they are not pawned, it is consequently so likewise when they are pawned.

He may receive pledges in security for debts owing to the defunct.—IF an executor take a pawn in security of a debt due to the defunct, it is lawful; because the seisin of a pawn is the same as a receipt of payment; and it is the duty of an executor to receive payment of the debts of the deceased. (A more particluar explanation of the powers of an executor, with respect to pawns, shall be given in treating of Executorships.)

Section.

Grape-juice still remains in pawn after having become wine and then vinegar.—IF a

* This does not mean that each is to pay the atonement [for that would be to pay it twice], but that the obligation of atoning of the offence rests upon the one as well as upon the other.

person pawn, in security of a debt of ten dirms, a quantity of the juice of grapes the same value, which afterwards becomes wine,* and then vinegar, and the value of the vinegar be also ten dirms, it in that case remains in pawn for the debt of ten dirms; because whatever is fit to be sold is likewise fit to be pawned, since worth is requisite to the fitness in the one instance as well as in the other; and wine, although not at first qualified for sale, does yet possess that fitness ultimately;—whence it is that if a person purchase the juice of grapes, and it become wine prior to his taking possession, still the compact of the sale is not dissolved, but the purchaser has, in such case, the option of either adhering to, or receding from the bargain; as the goods which he purchased, having been changed, are thereby as it were damaged.

A pledge destroyed in part is still retained in pawn with respect to the remaineder.—IF a goat, estimated at ten dirms, having been pawned for a debt of the same amount, should afterwards die, and its skin be preserved so as to bear a value of one dirm, it is detained in pawn in security of a like part of the debt; for as a contract of pawn is completed and perfected by the destruction of the pledge (since the object of it namely, a payment of debt, is then obtained), it follows that where a part of the pawn remains, the contract continues in force in proportion to that part. It is otherwise where a goat, having been sold, dies before the purchaser takes possession, and the skin is preserved; for in that case the contract is completely void (that is to say, it does not subsist even in regard to the skin);—because sale is rendered void, and entirely done away, be a destruction of the goods before the delivery of them to the purchaser; and such being the case, it cannot (in this instance) revert with respect to the skin.

Any increase accruing from the pledge is deatined in pawn along with it.—EVERY species of increase according from a pledge after the execution of the contract (such as milk, fruits, wool, or progeny), belong to the pawner, as being the offering of his property:—but they are, nevertheless, detained with the original in pawn; for branches are dependent on the stock; and the contract of pawn, being of a binding nature, extends over all its branches. If, however, this off spring be destroyed in the pawnee's hands, he is not responsible for it; because no part of the sum opposed to the original is opposed to the offspring, as that was not originally included in the contract, since the proposal and acceptance which form the contract did not relate to, or comprehend it. If, on the contrary, the original be destroyed, and the offspring remain whole, it is incumbent on the pawner to redeem the same, by paying its proportionate value; that is to say, the debt must be divided proportionately to the value which the original bore at the time of concluding the bargain, and that which the offspring bears at the time of redeeming it; and the proportion given to the original is, upon the loss of it, held to be annulled; but that of the offspring remains due, and must be paid by the pawnee towards the redemption of it.* (A variety of cases are determined by this rules, several of which are set forth in the Kafayat-al-Moontihee; and the whole are enumerated in the Jama Sagheer and Zeeadat.)

The pawnee, using the product from the pledge by permission of the pawner, is not liable for any thing on that account.—IF a person, having pawned a goat, desire the pawnee to milk it, giving him, at the same time, permission to enjoy whatever quantity he might milk, and the pawnee act ccordingly, he is not liable to compensate for the milk he may have thus consumed, nor is his claim, on that account, in any measure diminished, since he used the milk at the instance of the pawner. If, therefore, the goat die unredeemed in the hands of the pawnee, the debt owing to him must be divided into two parts, proportionate to the value of the goat and of the milk; and that part opposed to the goat is cancelled; whilst the other part, opposed to the milk, remains due from the pawner; because, although the milk be the property of the pawner, yet as the pawnee consumed it by his desire, the case is the same as if the pawner had himself taken and destroyed it. The pawnee, therefore, is not answerable for the milk: but (if the goat die) his claim still exists with respect to that proportion which corresponds with it. The same rule also obtains with regard to the offspring of a goat, which a pawnee eats at the desire of the pawner; and, in

* By fermentation. (For an explanation of this, see Prohibited Liquors.)

*As this is somewhat obscure, it may be proper to render it more clear, by a statement of the case according to the rules of proportion. Suppose, therefore, the debt to be one hundred dirms, the original pledge valued at one hundred, and its offspring at fifty,—in that case the original and offspring, amounting to one hundred and fifty dirms, are pawned in security of one hundred dirms. —Now, in order to know the proportions of pawn which the original and the offspring respectively bear to the whole debt, the latter must first be multiplied by the original; and the multiple divided by the whole value of both (original and offspring), and the product gives the proportion of the original; after which the same process must be observed with respect to the offspring;—when the calculation will stand thus.

150 : 100 : : 100—66⅔ the proportion of the original pledge.

150 : 100 : : 50—33⅓ the proportion of the offspring.

fine, with respect to every increase accruing from pledges posterior to the contract.

The pledge may be augmented, but not the debt.—THE augmentation of a pledge is lawful, in the opinion of all our doctors;—as where, for instance, a person, having pawned a slave for a debt of one thousand dirms, afterwards gives the slave a garment to be detained likewise in pawn in security of the same debt;— in which case the addition so made to the original pledge is lawful, and the garment is included in the agreement; the case being, in short, the same as if the slave and garment had been originally pawned together. On the other hand, the increase of a debt in security or which a pawn has been taken is not lawful (according to Haneefa and Mohammed); that is to say, the pledge opposed to a particular debt does not also stand opposed to any increase upon it. Aboo Yoosaf holds that both debts are liquidated.—The addition to a pledge, as here stated, is termed Zeeadit Koosdee, or intentional increase;* and the debt is to be between the value the original pledge bore at the time of pawning it, and that which the addition bears on the day of its delivery.—Hence if the value of the latter was then five hundred dirms, and that of the original pledge at the time of concluding the agreement one thousand, and the amount of the debt likewise one thousand, the debt is in that case divided into three shares, two of which are opposed to the original pledge, and the remaining one to the increase; and according to this proportion they are respectively charged for, if lost or destroyed in the hands of the pawnee.

Case of increase to a pledged female slave.—IF a person, in security of a debt of one thousand dirms, pawn a female slave of the same value, who afterwards brings forth a child likewise estimated at one thousand dirms, and the pawner then increase the pledge by the addition of a slave also valued at one thousand dirms (saying to the pawnee, "I have added this slave to the child of the pledge"), the slave is in that case pawned with the child only. If, therefore, the child afterwards die, the slave is no longer in pawn, insomuch that the pawner may resume him from the pawnee without making him any return. If, also,the slave should die, or be lost, nothing is chargable on that account to the pawnee,—If, on the other hand, the mother should die, the debt must in that case be divided between the value she bore at the time of concluding the contract, and that which the child bears on the day of redemption;—and since the slave was attached solely to the child, the share of the child must therefore be proportionably divided between it and the slave, agreeably to their respective values, in order that if either of them should die he may be charged for accordingly. If, on the contrary, the pawner attach the slave to the mother (saying to the pawnee. "I have placed him with her in addition to the pledge"), the debt must in that case be proportionably opposed to the mother and the slave, according to the value which they severally bore at the time of seisin; and from the sum opposed to the mother a proportionate part must be allotted to the child; for the pawner, in having placed the slave with the mother, joined him (as it were) to the original matter of the agreement—; whence the child is included in the proportion of the mother only.

Case of a pawner committing one slave in pawn for another.—IF a person pawn a slave valued at one thousand dirms in security of a debt of the same amount and afterwards give the pawnee another slave, likewise of the same value, to be detained in place of the former, in that case the first slave is considered as being in pawn until such time as the pawnee restore him to the pawner in the way of annulment, the second slave being merely a deposit in his hands until he be regularly rendered a substitute for the other; for the first slave was included in the responsibility of the pawnee only because of his being possessed in security of debt; and as both the seisin and the debt still exist, the slave therefore continues a subject of responsibility until the seisin be formally voided; and such being the case, the pawnee is not liable for the scond slave, as the parties intend one of them only to be included in the pawnee's responsibility :—but upon the pawnee restoring the first slave to the pawner, he becomes responsible for the second.

The pawnee is not responsible for the pledge after having acquitted the pawner of his debt.—IF the pawnee acquit the pawner of the debt, or bestow it on him in gift, and the pledge, be afterwards destroyed in his (the pawnee's) possession, he is not responsible for it, according to our doctors, proceeding upon a favourable construction of the LAW:—contrary to the opinion of Ziffer. The reasons for a favourable construction of the LAW in this particular are twofold.—FIRST, a pledge is insured on two conditions;—one, that it be actually possessed by the pawnee; and another, that it be opposed to a debt either due or promised. Now, compensation for a pledge in the case of a debt then due, is made in this manner,—that if the pawn be lost in the hands of the pawnee, his debt is extinguished, provided the value of the pledge be adequate to the amount of the debt; whereas compensation in the case of a promised debt is made by constraining the pawnee, in case of the decay of the peldge in his hands, to make good to the pawner the sum he had promised;—and in a case where the pawnee acquits the pawner of the debt, or bestows it on him in gift, the second condition is wanting, as no debt exists in that instance either due or promised. SECONDLY, one object of a pawner in delivering the pledge to the pawnee is that, in

* To distinguish it from accidental increase by breeding, vegetation, &c.

case of its loss, he may be absolved from any further obligation; but where the pawnee acquits the pawner of the debt, and the pawn is afterwards lost in his hands, the desire of the pawner being accomplished, the pawnee is not therefore liable for it (unless however, the pawnee, having remitted the debt, refuse to restore the pawn, and prevent the pawner from resuming it; for, in that case, if the pledge be lost, he is responsible for the value, since by such obstruction he becomes an usurper, as he no longer possesses a power of obstruction).— In the same manner, if a woman take a pledge from her husband in security of her stipulated dower, and afterwards exempt him from the payment of it, or apostatize from the faith befor consummation, and the pledge be then destroyed in her hands, she is not responsible for it, as the dower (like the debt) was remitted.

If the pledge be destroyed with him after he has received payment of his debt, he must return what he has received, and the debt stands liquidated.— If a pawnee receive paymet of his debt, either from the pawner or from an unconcerned person, in a gratuitous manner, and the pledge be afterwards destroyed in his possession, his debt is in consequence extinguished, and it is incumbent on him to restore what he had received to the person from whom he received it, whether the pawner or any other; for the seisin of he pawnee is equivalent to a receipt of payment in case of the loss of the pledge; and in the present instance, upon the pledge being destroyed, the pawnee is accounted to to have received payment from the time he was first seised of it; and as he is not entitled, after that, to a second discharge, and the payment he had received as above then becomes such in effect, it must therefore be refunded.— In short, the discharge of the pawnee's claim, whilst he remains seised of the pawn, does not take place, but continues suspended until he deliver it to the pawner; and such being the case, the pawner is not therefore, during that time, held to be acquitted of the debt;— and upon the pledge being afterwards destroyed in the hands of the pawnee, his possession of it under such a circumstance is, in effect, a receipt of payment, and the othe payment received whilst he was in possession of the pledge is annulled and done away, for otherwise a repetition of discharge would be induced;— for which reason he must refund the money he received in payment,— and also for this reason that if he were not to refund it the intent of the pawner would be defeated.

And so likewise, if he compound the debt, — If a pawnee purchase some specific article from the pawner in lieu of his debt, or compound the debt with him for some specific article; and the pawn be afterwards lost in his possession, he is still responsible, and may therefore be compelled to restore the article which he had either received in purchase or composition; for the seisin of that article, in either case, is equivalent to an acceptance of payment; and consequently, if he do not refund it, a double receipt of payment is induced, as mentioned in the preceding example.

Or if the pawner (with his concurrence) transfer the debt upon another person.— If a pawner transfer the debt which he owes the pawnee upon another person (such as Zeyd, for instance), who agrees to pay the same, and the pawnee, having assented to such transfer, acquit the pawner of the debt and the pledge be afterwards destroyed in the pawnee's hands, the transfer is thereby rendered ineffectual, and the claim of the pawnee is annihilated; for although, in consequence of the transfer, the transferred [the pawner] be acquitted of any further concern in the mater, yet this acquittance is the same as an actual payment, inasmuch as the sum, the payment of which he had transferred upon the other person, is ultimately disbursed by him, he having so transferred it in consequence of his having a claim upon the transferee for a like sum, whence the payment it made from him in effect;— or, if that person was not indebted to him, still the pawner must afterwards repay whatever sum he may have disbursed in consequence of the transfer, as in that case he acted in the capacity of an agent on his behalf.

If the pledge be lost after the parties agreeing that no debt had existed, it stands as a discharge of the supposed debt.— If a person pawn any thing into the hands of another, and both parties afterwards concur in saying that no debt had ever subsisted between them, and the pledge be then destroyed in the hands of the pawnee, it is answered by the debt; in other words, the debt in security of which the thing had been pawned is extinguished;— for there is still a probability of the debt being established by the parties at some future period concurring and agreeing that it did exist; whence it is possible that the debt may be claimed,— a circumstance which cannot happen in a case of acquittal of debt.

BOOK XLIX.

OF JANAYAT, OR OFFENCES AGAINST THE PERSON.

Definition of Janayat.— Janayat, in the language of the law, is a turn expressive of any prohibited act committed either upon the person or property:—in the practice of lawyers it signifies that prohibited act committed upon the person,* which is called

* Arab, Zat, signifying the body connected with the soul; in opposition to Badn, which means simply the material body. The translator renders it person or life, as best suits the context.

murder, or upon a part of the body, which is termed wounding or maiming.

(This subject, coming under the Penal Code, is omitted here.)

BOOK L.

OF DEENYAT OR FINES.

Definition of Deenyat,—DEENYAT is the plural for Deyit, which signifies the fine exacted for any offence upon the person..

CHAPTER I.

(This subject has been omitted in consequence of its forming part of the Penal Code.)

CHAPTER II.

OF NUISANCES PLACED IN THE HIGHWAY.

Buildings or timbers placed in or projecting over the highway may be removed by any person whatever.—IF any person construct a bath, or set out a water-spout, or erect a wall, or set out timbers from his wall to build upon, or set up a shop or both.—in the public road, every other person is at liberty, however mean and humble his condition, to pull down the same, and remove it; because all people are entitled to a free passage along such a road for themselves and their cattle; and the case is therefore the same as where a stranger erects a building upon a partnership property; in which instance any one of the partners is at liberty to remove such building; and so here likewise the removal is lawful to all, as all are alike partners in the rights of the road. It is lawful, however, for the person in question in all the above cases to make use of the bath, fountain, or so forth, where they are no way injurious to the community; for as he has the right (in common with others) of passing and repassing, it follows that, provided there be no injury sustained, the obstructing him in the enjoyment would be vexatious. But if they be injurious to the community, the use of them is abominable.

They cannot be erected or set up in a closed lane without she conset of the inhabitants.—IT is not lawful for an inhabitant of a lane shut up at one end to construct in it a bath, set out a spout, on so forth, without the consent of the other inhabitants, whether it be injurious to them or otherwise; for as the lane is, in fact, their property (whence it is that the right of Shaffa with respect to the houses in it appertains equally to them all), their acquiescence is therefore indispensable. In a public road, moreover, the conversion to particular use is lawful to all men indiserminately, excepting only in instances where it may prove detrimental; for as it is impossible to obtain the acquiescence of every individual of the community, each is therefore accounted a proprietor, lest his right of use should be altogether defeated:—but it is not so in a closed lane; for as it practicable to obatin the acquiescence of all the inhabitants of the lane, the privileges of partnership therefore hold good both actually and virtually, with respect to each individual of them.

A person erecting a building, &c., in the highway incurs a fine for any person.—IF a person erect a building in the public highway, as before mentioned,and it happen to fall upon and destroy any one, a fine is due from the Ak ilas of the person in question; because he as the occasion of the destruction, and was guilty of a transgression in having erected a building such a situation and a person who occasions a destruction is responsible where he has in any respect transgressed, as in the case of digging a well in the highroad. The same rule also obtains where the building fails upon and thus destroys a man or an animal.

(Or number of persons) it may occasion the destruction of.—IF a man stumble over the ruins of such building, and fall upon another man, and they both die, the person who erected it is responsible for both, and nothing is due from him who fell upon the other; for as the builder was the primary cause of the accident, the case is therefore the same as if he had struck the person who fell, and so caused him to fall upon the other, and they had both died inconsequence.

Case of death occasioned by the fall of a spout.—IF a water-spout, set out from a house over the public road, fall upon any person, and kill him, an examination must be made to discover which part of the spout it was that hit the person; and if it appear that he was struck by the end next the house from which it had projected, no atonement is due from the person who set it up, because with respect to that part he is not a transgressor, since he had placed that in his own property; but if it appear that the deceased was struck by the projecting end, the person who set it up is responsible, because with respect to that part he is a transgressor, as having caused the spout to project over the road without any necessity, since he might to as good purpose have fixed it up so as not to project over the road at all.—(It is to be observed that in this instance expiation is not incumbent on the fixed up of the spout;—nor is he excluded from inheritance; for he is not actual perpetrator, but stands merely guilty of homicide by an intermediate cause.)—If, on the other hand, it appear that the deceased was struck by both ends of the spout, the fixer-up is responsible for an half of the fine, and the other half drops; in the same manner as where a person is wounded by another, and also by a lion or tiger, and dies,—in which case an half only of the fine is due from the wounder. If it cannot be discovered which part of the spout struck the deceased, in this case also an half of the fine is due; for the accident may have happened in either of two ways, in one of which the complete fine is due, and in the other nothing whatever; and therefore, in contemplation of both circumstances, an half is imposed.

A person having fixed up a nuisance upon his house, is responsible for any damage it may occasion even after he has sold the house.—IF a person construct a balcony, projecting from his house, and then sell the house, and the balcony afterwards fall upon any person and destroy him,—or, if a person set up a piece of timber in the middle of the highway, and afterwards sell it, and delivery it to the purchaser, and he [the purchaser] declare him acquitted of all accidents which may happen from it, and leave it there until it fall and kill some person,—the seller is responsible in both instances, and nothing whatever falls upon the purchaser; because the act of the seller (in constructing the balcony, or setting up the timber) is not done away by the extinction of his property; and as such act occasions responsibility, he is responsible accordingly and not the purchaser, who has not done any act to occasion responsibility.

A person laying fire in the highway is responsible for any thing which may be burnt in consequence.—IF a person, lay fire in the highway, and any thing be burnt in consequence, he as having transgressed, is responsible for the damage. If, however, after the fire being thus laid in the highway, the wind should blow it to another place, and any thing be burnt in consequence, he is not responsible, as by the wind carrying off the fire his act is done away. Some, indeed, say that if the fire was laid in the highway at a time when the wind was high, he is responsible; because he laid the fire there, notwithstanding his knowledge of the probable consequence; and therefore the act of the wind, in carrying it off, is in effect the same as if he had himself carried it to the place which was burnt.

Workmen constructing a nuisance are responsible for any accident it may occasion before their work be finished.—IF a person hire workmen for the purpose of constructing a balcony, or a penthouse, and such balcony or penthouse fall upon and kill a man before the workmen had finished it, the responsibility falls entirely upon the workmen; for the deceased was destroyed in consequence of their act; and so long as they continue engaged in the work, the balcony or penthouse is not held to be delivered to their employer. Their act is therefore construed into homicide, insomuch that they must perform an expiation for it. Besides, as their employer did not hire them to kill any person, but to construct an erection, the accident has therefore no relation to the contract of hire, but attaches to the workmen alone, whence the damage also attaches solely to them, as being a consequence of their act. If, on the contrary, the balcony or penthouse in question fall after the work is finished, the owner of the house is responsible, on a favourable construction; for in this case the contract of hire has been completely fulfilled, insomuch that the workmen have become entitled to their wages. Their act has therefore devolved upon their employer, who consequently stands in the same predicament as if he had himself performed the work; and he is responsible accordingly.

A person is responsible for any accident occasioned by his throwing water in the highway.—IF a person spill water on the highway, either purposely, or by performing his ablutions there, and a man or animal perish in consequence, a fine for the man is due from the person's Akilas, or a compensation for the animal from the person himself; because he has been guilty of a transgression, injurious in its consequences to the passengers upon the road. It is otherwise here water is spilled in a closed lane by one of the inhabitants, and a man or animal perishes in consequence; or, where an inhabitant of such a lane sets down any thing in the middle of it, and a man or animal falls over the same, and so perishes; for in none of these cases does responsibility attach to him, as any inhabitant of a closed lane is entitled, in virtue of his residence, to perform these acts in such lane, in the same manner as in a partnership house. Lawyers remark that what is here advanced applies only to a case where water is spilled upon the road in large quantities, such as commonly renders the footing insecure;—but that if the water be only in a small quantity, and not in a degree to endanger the passenger, there is no responsibility.

Unless the person who sustained the damage had wilfully passed over such water.—IF a person knowingly and wilfully pass over a road in which water has been spilled, as above, and perish in consequence of falling in it, nothing whatever is incurred by the person who spilt the water, since here the deceased has perished from his own wilfulness or obstinacy. Some, however, remark that this rule obtains only where the water is spilled over a part of the road, for in that case a part remains unaffected by it;—whereas, if it extend over the whole road, the passengers have no option; and (as they further observe) the same distinction holds with respect to timbers, or other nuisances, act up in the highway.

The person who directs water to be sprinkled in the road is responsible for accidents.—IF a shopkeeper desire a person to sprinkle water in the front of his shop, and another person fall there, and die in consequence, the responsibility rests upon him who gave the order (the shopkeeper), on a favourable construction (and so likewise, if a shopkeeper hire a workman to erect a stall or other edifice in the front of his shop, and after it is finished a person fall over it and die);—because the order given by the shopkeeper is of a lawful nature, his right to the precincts in front of his shop being superior to that of any other person; and therefore the act of the person whom he directed must be referred to himself.—It is otherwise where a person orders another to throw water, or erect an edifice on the middle of the highway; for in this case the responsibility rests upon him who obeyed the order, as an order to this effect is unlawful, the man who gave the order posssessing no superior right in the highway.

Case of a person digging a well or laying a stone, in the highway.—IF a person dig a well, or lay a stone, in the middle of the highway, and a man perish in consequence, a fine is due from the Akilas of the person who placed such nuisance there. If, on he contrary, an animal were thus to perish, the compensation for the same would be due from the property of the person in question; because, as he has been guilty of a transgression, he is therefore responsible for any accidents it may occasion; and as the Akilas are not implicated except in offences against the person, it follows that, in cases of property merely, the responsibility rests solely upon the offender himself.

The throwing dirt, or digging a hole, in the highway is the same as placing a stone there.—THE throwing of dirt or earth in the highway, or the carrying away of earth thence, so as to occasion an hollow, is the same as placing there a stone or log of wood, for the reasons already explained. It is otherwise where a person merely sweeps the road,; for in this case he is no way liable to responsibility, as his act of sweeping does not occasion any nuisance. but rather the contrary. If, however, this person leave an heap of the sweepings in the road, so as to occasion accidents, he is responsible, since in acting thus he is guilty of a transgression.

The remover of a nuisance to another spot incurs responsibility for any accident it may afterwards occasion.—I a person lay a stone in the highway, and a second 'person remove the stone to another part of the road, and a man be thereby destroyed, the responsibility rests upon the remover of the stone; because the act of the original depositor is abrogated in its effect, by the place which he had occupied with the stone being cleared, and another place being occupied with it by the act of the remover,—who is therefore responsible for the consequence.

There is no responsibility for accidents occasioned by a sewer constructed in the highway by public authority.—IT is related in the Jama Sagheer, that if a person construct a common sewer in the public highways, by the order or compulsion of the Sultan, he is not responsible for consequences; because, in constructing the sewer, he has not committed any transgression, for in so doing he acted by order of the Sultan, who possesses a paramount authority with respect to all public rights. It is otherwise where a person does so without such an order; for in that case he is responsible, as having transgressed, in presuming to encroach upon the 'public rights without a sufficient authority:—besides, acts with respect to the highway are permitted under a condition of safety,—that is, under the condition that they be not injurious. It is to be observed that this distinction holds in all cases of acts with respect to the highway, as the same reasoning equally applies to every other instance.

A person digging a well in his own land is not responsible for any death it may occasion.—IF a person dig a well in his own land, and another be killed by falling into it, the digger of the well, is not responsible, as he has not transgressed; and the same rule also hold where a person digs a well within the precincts of his house, a man being entitled so to do, for the purposes of domestic convenience. Some say that this rule with respect to a well dug in the precincts of a house holds only in cases where the householder has either a property in such precincts, or possesses a right, by immunity, of digging therein;—but that where the precinct is public, or held in partnership (as in the case of a court or closed lane), the digger is responsible, since in digging the well under such circumstances he is guilty of a transgression.—This is approved.

A person falling into a well and there dying of hunger, does not occasion responsibility.—IF a person dig a well or pit in the highway, and another happen to fall in, and there persih of hunger, the digger is not responsible, according to Haneefa, because the deceased has here died of hunger, and not in consequence of the excavation, as he death cannot be attributed to the latter unless he be killed by the fall, which is not the case in this instance.

Workmen employed to dig a well in another's land are not responsible for accidents unless they be aware of the tresspass—

If a person hire workmen to dig a well the precincts of his neighbour's habitation and they dig it accordingly, and a man be killed by falling into it, the responsibility rests upon the employer, not upon the workmen, provided they dug the well under the idea of the place being within the precincts of their employer; because, as a contract to hire, ignorantly engaged in, is lawful and valid in appearance, their act is therefore referred to the hirer, they themselves having proceeded under a deception:—the case being, in fact, the same as where a person desires another to slay "such a goat," and he does so accordingly, and it afterwards appears that the goat was the property of another,—in which case the compensation is paid by the person who gave the order. It is otherwise where the workmen dig the well, knowing, at the same time, that the place is not within the precincts of the employer; for in this case they are responsible; because the contract is not here valid in appearance, as they have not been deceived.

The builder of a private bridge, &c., is not responsible for any life which may be lost in passing over it.—If a person construct a bridge, or lay a plank, in the highway [over a stream] without authority, and another, wilfully passing over such bridge or plank, fall off and perish, still the person in question is not responsible; because although he be the creator of the cause, and therefore a transgressor, yet as the deceased was a wilful agent* and transgressed in his own act† his destruction is therefore referred to himself; and also, because where the act of one who has an option intervenes, it precludes the reference of the destruction to the first agent; as where (for instance) a person digs a well in the highway, and another gives a man a push, and thereby causes him to fall into the well, so that he dies,—in which case the responsibility rests upon the person who gave the push, since his act, being the act of a wilful agent, precludes a reference of the destruction to the digger of the well.

A porter is responsible for accidents occasioned by his load.—If a person be carrying a load upon the highway, and the load fall upon any person so as to kill him, or fall in the road so as to cause a preson to stumble and thereby occasion his death, the responsibility rests upon the carrier;—whereas, if a person be wearing a cloak upon the highway, and it fall upon any person, or upon the road so as to occasion death, the carrier of the cloak is not responsible. The difference between these two cases is, that as the business of the carrier is to take care of his parcel or load, the circumstance of restricting his liberty of carrying it to the condition of safety does not operate as a hardship upon him;—whereas, the business of the wearer is not merely the taking care of his garment, but the wearing of it; and therefore, as the restricting his liberty of use to the condition of safety would operate as a hardship, his use of it is not restricted to any particular conditions, but is allowed to him generally.

A stranger hanging up a lamp, or strewing gravel, &c., in a mosque, is responsible for any accidents which may arise therefrom.—If a person hang up a lamp, or spread a carpet, or strew gravel in a mosque appropriated to any particular tribe or people, and any person perish in consequence, nothings is incurred, provided the person who hung up the lamp, or so forth, be one of that people;—whereas, if a stranger do any of these acts, he is responsible. In the same manner, if one of the people of a mosque sit in that mosque, and any person perish in consequence, he is not responsible, provided he be, at the time engaged in prayer: but if he be engaged in reading the Koran, or teaching, or be waiting for the time of prayer, or sleeping (eithr during prayer or at any other time), or conversing, he is responsible. The reason for the law in the former instance is, that as all the regulations of a mosque, such as the appointment of a priest or a supervisor, the opening and shutting of the doors, and so forth, appertain solely to the people to whom the mosque belongs, and not to any others, their acts are therefore of a natural nature, and are not restricted to the condition of safety; whereas the acts of all others with respect to it are either transgressive, or permitted under the condition of safety; and a pious intention does not prevent responsibility where the person errs in the manner of his piety. The reason for the law in the second instance is, that a mosque is constructed particularly for the purpose of prayer, to which reading the Koran, teaching, or so forth, are only (as it were) appendages; and as it is indispensable that a distinction be made between the original and the branch, or dependent, the act of prayer (which is the original) is therefore permitted generally, without any restriction to the condition of safety, whereas all other acts or employments are so restricted.

But he is not responsible for accidents occasioned by his own person.—If a stranger to the people of the mosque be at prayers in it, and a person fall over him, and die in consequence, the stranger is no way responsible; because (as has been already observed) a mosque is constructed for the purpose of prayer; and although the right of public prayer appertain solely to the people of that mosque, yet any person is entitled to pray there alone.

Section.

Of buildings which are in danger of falling

The owner of a ruinous wall is responsible for any accident occasioned by it after having

* Arab. Mohashir;—literally a perpetrator.

† (Probably) as having passed over the bridge, &c., without leave from the builder of it.

received due warning, and requisition to pull it down.—IF a wall belonging to any person lean towards the public highway and a person require the owner to pull it down, and call people to witness his requisition, and the owner neglect taking it down until at length it fall and destroy either man or property, the owner is responsible for the damage so occasioned, on a favourable construction. Analogy would suggest that he is not responsible (and such is the doctrine of Shafei); for he has neither perpetrated the destruction himself, nor done any thing transgressively to occasion it, as he built the wall in his own right, and its tottering, or the wind shaking it, were not his acts, whence the case is the same in effect as if the wall had fallen previous to the requisition and calling of witnesses, as aforesaid. The reasons, however, for a more favourable construction of the LAW in this particular are twofold.—FIRST, upon a wall leaning over towards the highway, the public communication becomes interrupted, and the way* occupied by the property of the owner of that wall. When, therefore, any person makes application to him, and requires him to clear the way, it is incumbent on him so to do; and he is consequently guilty of a transgression in neglecting it, and therefore remains responsible for any damage it may occasion;—in the same manner as where a man finds his garment upon another, and demands it of him; in which case, if that other refuse to deliver it, he is guilty of a transgression, and is consequently responsible for the garment if it should be lost whilst in his possession.—SECONDLY, if the owner of the wall were not made responsible for any damage its falling might occasion, he would neglect to remove the nuisance, and consequently passengers would sustain an injury, as they would be deterred from going by the place, for fear of the wall falling on them. The removal, moreover, of any thing injurious to the community is a duty incumbent upon the person to whom it belongs; and as the owner of the wall is the person immediately concerned in the present instance, it is therefore incumbent on him to take it down, notwithstanding his so doing may be prejudicial to himself, since private interest must yield to public benefit. It is requisite, however, that such a time be allowed as may admit of the owner taking down his wall, this being indispensable to the establishment of offence from neglect or delay. If (after the requisition for pulling it down), any person be destroyed by the wall falling, a fine is due from the Akilas of the owner, not from the owner himself; for as the offence, in this instance, is still short of homicide by misadventure, an alleviaton is admitted fortiorii lest the owner should suffer too severely:—but if, on the contrary, property (such as an animal, or household goods) be destroyed, the compensation for it must be paid by the owner of the wall, as the Akilas are not implicated in the responsibility for property. It is to be observed that the application (that is, the requisition for pulling down the wall) is a condition of responsibility, but not the taking to witness; for the latter is called in aid merely with a view to establish the former, in case of the owner of the wall denying it, and is therefore used only out of caution. The application is made by the claim at saying to the owner of the wall, "Your wall has become dangerous;—you must therefore take it down lest it prove destructive;" and the taking to witness is effected by his saying to the bystanders, "be ye witness that I have required this person to take down his wall."—It is proper, however, to remark that the taking to witness before a wall has become ruinous or crooked is not valid, as transgression cannot established previous thereto.

A person building a crooked wall is responsible for the damage occaioned by its falling.—IF a person build a wall in the highway, leaning over from the first, lawyers remark that he is responsible for any thing which may be destroyed by its falling, independent of the requisition before mentioned, as having been guilty of a transgression in the building of it, in the same manner as a person who constructs a balcony or gallery projecting over the highway.

The requisition is established upon the evidence of one man and two women.—THE evidence of one man and two women suffices to establish the application above described for it is not here requisite, as in cases of murder, that both the witnesses be males, the death occasioned by the falling of a wall not amounting to murder.

A Zimmee, may make it, as well as a Mussulman.—A MUSSULMAN and a Zimmee are upon an equal footing with respect to the requisition for pulling down the wall, as all mankind are partners in the right of passing along. The application is therefore valid, by whomsoever it be made,—whether a man, a woman, a free man, a Mokatib, a slave (provided his master give him permission to litigate the point), or an infant (with permission to litigate from his guardian).—It is also valid whether made by the Sultan or any other; for as the application affects a matter of right in which all are equally concerned, all are therefore equally entitled to make it.

Or the inhabitants of a neighbouring house.—IF a wall lean over towards a neighbouring house, the owner of the house is entitled to require it to be pulled down,—or the tenants whether they be hirers or borrowers,—for to such persons in particular the right appertains in this instance.

And if those last grant a term of delay, it is valid.—IF the owner or tenants of the

* Arab. Hawa; literally, the air, or atmosphere; a phrase generally used where the nuisance or obstruction is not immediately upon the ground.

house grant the owner of the wall a term of delay, or exempt him from responsibility for any damage which may be occasioned by it, it is lawful, and the owner of the wall is not responsible in case of any thing being destroyed by its fall, because the right of the owner or tenant alone is concerned. It is otherwise where a wall leans over a road, and the magistrate, or the person who made the requisition for pulling it down, grants a term of delay, or an exemption; for this is not valid; and the owner of the wall consequently still remains responsible in case of its falling and destroying any thing: because here the right of every one is concerned: and the magistrate, or the person who made the requisition, is not at liberty to annul a right of the public.

A person selling a ruinous house, after requisition, is not responsible for any accidents it may occasion.—IF, after application, a person sell a house, the wall of which leans over, and the purchaser take possession of it, and any thing be then destroyed by its falling, there is no responsibility whatever upon either party.—The seller is not responsible, as offence cannot be established in him unless it apeared that he neglected to take down the wall, having at the same time ability so to do; and here his ability has terminated with the sale:—neither is the purchaser responsible, because no application has been made to him. But if application be made to the purchaser after the sale, he then becomes responsible, as in that case he possesses the ability of complying with the requisition.

The requisition (to be valid) must be made to a person capable of complying with it.—THE application and requisition for pulling down a ruinous wall are valid when made to any one who possesses the power of pulling it down;—but not when made to one who is not possessed of his power, such as a pawnee, a trustee, a borrower, or a renter. The application and requisition in question are therefore valid when made to the pawner of a house, as he has it in his power to pull down the wall by redeeming his house. They are also valid with respect to a wall belonging to an infant when made to the infant's parents or guardians; and if, after the requisition, they neglect to pull down the wall, and any thing be destroyed by the fall of it, the compensation falls upon the infant's property, because their act is in effect the act of the infant. They are likewise valid with respect to a Mokatib, as he may be authorized to pull down a wall; and also, with respect to a trading slave, whether indebted or otherwise, for the same reason; —and if, in this last instance, the slave neglect to pull down the wall, and any property be destroyed by the wall falling, the compensation for it rests upon the slave's person;*—or, if a man be destroyed, the fine is due from the master's Akilas.

The requisition, made to one of several coparceners, affects that coparcener in particular.—IF a ruinous wall be held in coparcenery by several heirs, and a person apply to one of the heirs, requiring him to pull down the wall, the application affects that heir in particular; and accordingly, if any thing be afterwards destroyed by the falling of the wall, the heir who was applied to is responsible in proportion to his share of inheritance; for it was in his power to have remedied the nuisance by referring the matter to the Kazee, and representing the circumstance to him, requiring his order to his coparceners (if present) to pull down the wall,—or (if absent) his authority to do so himself.

After a wall falls, it is the duty of the owner to remove the ruins, and failing of this, he is responsible for subsequent accidents.—IF a ruinous wall fall upon a man, after application, and destroy him, and another person fall over the corpse, and so perish, the proprietor of the wall incurs nothing for this second person, because the removal of the corpse was incumbent upon the heirs, not upon him. If, on the contrary, another person, after the wall falling, be destroyed by stumbling over a fragment of the ruins, the owner of the wall is responsible, as it is his business to clear the road of all such fragments, since those are his property, and an application with respect to the wall itself is (as it were) an application with respect to the fragments, the intention of it being to clear the highway.

The owner of a ruinous wall is not responsible for accidents occasioned by the fall of any article from it, unless such article belong to him.—IF a person make application concerning a wall which leans over towards the highway, and it afterwards fall, throwing down a vase or urn, which had stood upon it, and a man be thereby destroyed, the owner of the wall is responsible, provided the vase or urn was his property, as the freeding the road from it rested upon him. If, on the contrary, the vase or urn be the property of some other, the owner of the wall is not responsible, since the freeing the road from the vase or urn rests upon him to whom it belongs.

CHAPTER III.

OF OFFENCES COMMITTED BY OR UPON ANIMALS.

The rider of an animal is responsible for any damage occasioned by it, which it was in his power to prevent.—THE rider of an animal is answerable for any thing which the animal may destroy by treading it down, or by striking it with his head, his fore feet, or his body; but he is not respon-

*That is, he must either be made over or redeemed, as in other cases of offence

sible for any thing which the animal may destroy by striking it with his hind fact or his tail.—In short, it is a rule that the right of passing on the highway is allowed to the whole community, under the condition only of safety; for it is the exercise of a privilege in the passenger, with respect to himself in one shape, and with respect to others in another shape, the right of passage being participated among the whole community, —whence it is adjudged to all, under the condition of safety, with a view to the interest of both parties.—It is moreover to be observed, that a restriction to the condition of safety can obtain only in matters where an attention to safety is practicable; for if it were imposed where such attention is impracticable, the exertion of the privilege [of travelling on animals] would be altogether precluded. Now it is possible for a man to guard against the animal he rides treading men or property under foot, and such like, since a person who rides is under no necessity of treading down every thing that lies in his way: but he cannot guard against the animal striking things with his hind feet or tail, since an animal unavoidably uses these parts, in travelling, without any immediate control from its rider. Accordingly he is restricted to the condition safety in the former instance, but not in the latter.

Any if the stop the animal in the road, he is responsible for all accidents.—If, however, he stop the animal in the highway, he is responsible for any destruction which may be occasioned by a kick of its hind feet, or a stroke of its tail, since it is possible for him to avoid stopping, although it be not in his power to guard the animal from kicking, or so forth; and therefore, as he transgresses in so stopping, he is responsible for any damage which may ensue in consequence.

He is also responsible for any injury sustained from a large stone, thrown up by the animal's hoof.—IF an animal's hoof strike upon and throw up gravel or small stones, and a person's eye be put out, or his clothes damaged thereby, the rider is not responsible; whereas, if the animal so throw up a large stone, he is responsible. The reason of this is that in the former case it was impossible to guard against the accident, since an animal cannot move without being liable to it; whereas, in the second instance, it is possible to guard against the accident, since animals may easily be so guided as to avoid large stones. It is to be observed that, in all these cases, a second rider (that is, one who rides behind the first) is in the same predicament as the first, with respect to responsibility.

But not for any accident occasioned by its dung or urine.—IF an animal, whilst travelling, discharge its dung or urine on the highway, and any person perish in consequence, the rider is not responsible, since it was impossible to guard against this; and the same rule also holds where the animal stands still whilst discharging its dung or urine, or when the rider stops it for this purpose, since there are several animals which cannot perform these whilst in motion.

Unless he had stopped it on the road unnecessarily whilst discharging those.—IF, however, the rider have stopped the animal for any other purpose, and it discharge its dung or urine, and any person perish in consequence, he (the rider) is responsible, as in so doing he was guilty of a transgression, since he stopped the animal without any absolute necessity, knowing, at the same time, that this must be injurious to the passengers.

Responsibility attaching to the driver or leader of an animal.—THE driver of an animal is responsible for any damage the animal may occasion with either its fore or hind feet, whereas the leader of an animal is responsible for the damage occasioned by its fore feet only, not by its hind feet. The compiler of the Hedaya remarks that this is what is said by Kadooree in his compendium; —and several of our modern doctors coincide in the same opinion; because, as a person who drives an animal before him has a view of his hind feet, it is therefore in his power to avoid accidents from them; whereas, a person who leads an animal after him, not seeing or having any command over its hind feet, cannot possibly guard against such accidents. Most of our modern doctors, however, are of opinion that as the driver of an animal has no more command over its hind feet than a person who leads it, he therefore is not responsible, any more than the other, for the damage which may be occasioned by them;—and this is approved.

IT is written in the Jama Sagheer, that the driver or leader of an animal is responsible in all the instances in which responsibility lies against the rider; for as they (as well as one who rides) occasion the damage by taking the animal to the place where it is committed, their so doing is therefore restricted to the condition of safety, as far as may be practicable, in the same manner as holds with respect to the rider.

Expiation is required from the rider of an animal,—not from the leader or driver.—THE rider of an animal is required to perform expiation only where he has happened to tread down a person,—not in any other instance;—but no expiatory act whatever is required from the leader or driver of an animal. The reason of this is that, in the case of treadings down a person, the rider is, in effect, the perpetrator of the homicide, as it is by his weight that the person is destroyed,—the weight of the animal being merely a dependent upon the weight of its rider, since to him the motion of its must be referred, it being the instrument of such motion. It is otherwise with the leader or driver of an animal: for those are only the producers of the intermediate cause, and not the actual perpetrators of the homicide, as their acts did not immediately affect the subject (and the same reasoning holds with respect to the act of the rider in all cases except that of treading down);—and expiation is enjoined, in cases of homicide, only where the offender is the actual perpetrator of the homicide, not where it is effected by an intermediate cause. In the same manner, the rider of an animal is excluded from his succession to the deceased by bequest or inheritance, in case of treading down, but not the leader or driver, exclusion from bequest or inheritance being restricted to the actual perpetrator.

If there be a rider, as well as leader or driver, responsibility, attaches to the former, not to the latter.—IF one man ride upon an animal whilst anothr drivers or leads it along; and it tread down a man, some say that no part of the responsibility falls upon the driver or leader; because the rider (as has been already explained) is accounted the actual perpetrator of the homicide, and the driver or leader the producer of the intermediate cause; and the accident must be referred to the actual perpetrator, rather than to the producer of the cause.—This is approved.

Case of two riders driving against and killing each other.—IF two men be riding on two different animals, and rush with violence against each other, so that they both die, the fine for each is due from the Akilas of the other. Shafei and Ziffer maintain that in this case the Akilas of each party owe a half fine only, on account of the other.* each having died as much in consequence of his own act as of that of the other, whence one half of the homicide, on each part, is of no account.—The argument of our doctors is, that the death of each party must be referred solely to the act of the other, and not in any degree to his own act, for his act (namely, passing along the highway) is purely of a neutral nature, and an act of such a nature does not admit of the death being referred to it so as to occasion responsibility. It may indeed be objected, that upon this ground the whole of the blood is of no account, and of course that nothing whatever is due from the Akilas on either side;—for as the act of both (namely, passing along the highway (is of a neutral nature, it cannot be made the occasion of responsibility. In reply, however, to this it is to be observed, that although the act of each party, respectively, be of a neutral nature, still it is restricted to the condition of safety; and a neutral act, restricted to the condition of safety, notwithstanding that it be not an occasion of responsibility with respect to the party himself, is nevertheless so with respect to the other party. It is to be observed however, that a complete fine for each rider is due only where they have happened to rush against each other (as above) by misadventure; for where they have done so wilfully, a half fine only is due on account of each. All that is here advanced proceeds on the supposition of the parties being freemen; for if they be both slaves, the blood of each is of no account: *—it is not of any account in a case of misadventure; because the offence of a slave effects only his own person, in this way, that his master makes his person over to the avenger of offence, or days him an atone ment in lieu thereof; but in the present instanc the persons of both slaves are destroyed, in such a manner that the masters have no concern with it; nor have they left any thing in lieu thereof; and hence the blood of each must needs be of no account: —and so likewise in a wilful case; because each of them has perished at the time of his offence, without leaving any thing in lieu of his person, and in such a manner that the masters have no concern in it,—whence the blood of each must needs be of no accoun in this instance also. If one of the parties be a slave, and the other a freeman, then, in a case of misadventure, the freeman's Akilas are responsible for the value of the slave, which must be paid to the freeman's heirs, whose right is extinguished with respect to any thing beyond such value (as if, for instance, the value of the slave were one thousand dirms; in which case the freeman's heirs would be entitled to take, from his Akilas, one thousand dirms, the remaining nine thousand of the freeman's fine being remitted);—because, in conformity with the tenets of Haneefa and Mohammed, the value of the slave is due from the freeman's Akilas as the compensation for his [the slave's] person, for which the Akilas are responsible;—and of this the freeman's heirs are entitled to possess themselves, because it is (in effect) an equivalent for the slave;—but their right to any thing beyond the value of the slave drops, as the slave has left nothing behind him to answer such excess. If, on the contrary, the parties being a slave and a freeman, rush against each other wilfully, the freeman's Akilas are accountable only for half the value of the slave (a wilful case only inducing half of the responsibility), which must be paid to the freeman's heirs; for as, in this instance, a moiety of the fine for the freeman was due from the slave, and he left nothing except the half of his value (as above), they are therefore entitled to possess themselves of the same, and the remainder of the half fine, beyond half the value of the slave, is remitted.

The driver of an animal is responsible for any accident occasioned by its saddle, &c.,

* The fines here (as in all other cases) go to the heirs of each party respectively.

* Literally, "goes for nothing."— The translator adopts the phrase here used in preference, as beings omewhat more elegant, and expressing the sense of the author with equal correctness.

falling off.—IF a person be driving an animal along, and the animal's saddle or load, or any thing else which may be upon it, fall off, and kill a man, the driver is responsible, as having been guilty of a transgression, in neglecting to secure the load, or so forth, properly upon the animal, for if it had been sufficiently secured, it could not have fallen off.

Responsibility in the case of a string of camels.—THE person who leads a string of camels is responsible for any thing which they may tread down. If, therefore, the camels tread down a man, the fine for him is due from the leader's Akilas, or, if they tread down property, he is to make compensation for the same; because it was his business to look to the camels, in the same manner as a driver; and as, where he neglects so to do, he is guilty of transgression, and transgression occassions responsibility, he is responsible accordingly:—but the responsibility for the person rests with this Akilas, and that for the property with himself, as has been already explained. If there be a driver to the string, as well as a leader, the responsibility rests equally with both; because, as the leader of one camel is the leader of the whole, so the driver of one is the driver of the whole, the halter of each being fastened to the one immediately before him. This rule, however, obtains only where the driver is at the end of the whole string; for if he be in the middle, and there lay hold of the halter of one of the camels, he alone is responsible with respect to such damage as may be occasioned by the camels which come after him; because the leader at the head of the whole cannot be said to lead those, on account of the string being thus interrupted;—but both are equally responsible for any damage occasioned by the camels before him, since he drives those at the same time that he leads the others.

IF a person fasten a camel to a string of camels, with the leader's knowledge, and the camel so fastened tread down a man, the fine for him is due from the leader Akilas because it was in his power to have looked after and watched his camels, so as to prevent an additional one being joined to the string; and in neglecting so to do he was guilty of a transgression; which occasions responsibility. Now the homicide, in this instance, is homicide by an intermediate cause; and the fine for it therefore falls upon the Akilas, in the same manner as in a case of homicide by misadventure. But the leader's Akilas are entitled afterwards to reimburse themselves by taking the amount of the fine from the Akilas of the person who fastened the additional camel to the string; because it was by his act that they became subjected to the payment of it; and the only reason why the responsibility did not fall upon them at the first is, that the act of fastening the additional camel was a sort of creation of a cause, whereas the leading of the string is, in the eye of the law, equivolent to the actual commission of the homicide, the destruction having been occasioned by the leading of the string, not by fastening the additional camel;—and as the actual perpetration of the homicide is a thing of a more forcible nature than the mere creation of the cause of it, the responsibility consequently first falls upon the Akilas of the leader. Laywers remark that what is here advanced (of the leader's Akilas having recourse to the Akilas of the fastener) applies only to a case where the additional camel was fastened to the string at a time when it was moving forwards; for as in this case, the fastener does, as it were, direct his camel to be led, he therefore impliedly assumes the responsibility for such damages as it may occasion:—but where the additional camel was fastened to the string at a time when it stood still, and the leader afterwards leads it on, and a man is trodden down by this additional camel, the responsibility rests with the leader's Akilas, who are not entitled, in this case, to reimburse themselves from the Akilas of the fastener, because here the leader appears to have led on the camel of another without that other's concurrence, as he has not signified his consent either expressly or by implication.

A person is responsible for the damage occasioned by hunting his dog at anything.—IF a person let slip* his dog, and drive him (that is, run after him), and the dog, without stopping, destroy any thing, the responsibility for it rests with the person who let him slip, the act of the dog being attributed to him because of his driving him;—whereas, if a person cast off his hawk, and drive her (as above) and she, without stopping, destroy any thing, she person who cast her off is not responsible.—(The reason of this distinction between a dog and a hawk is, that a quadruped is capable of being set on or driven, whereas a bird is not so,—whence a regard is paid to the driving of the one, but not of the other).

But not unless he drive or encourage the dog.—IF, on the contrary, a person let slip his dog without driving him (that is, with out running after him), and he destroy any thing without stopping, the person who let him slip is not responsible; because, as the dog, in this instance, acts from his own option, his act cannot be attributed to the person who let him slip.—It is related as an opinion of Aboo Yoosaf that, in all those cases, the person who fast off the hawk or let slip the dog is to be held responsible, out of a regard to the preservation of property. Mohammed also observes, in the Mabsoot that where a person lets slip or casts oft any animal upon the highway, and the animal, without stopping, kills a man, the responsibility for the same rests upon the person who cast it off, or let it slip, whether he have driven it, or otherwise, the motion of the

* Literally, give head to. (See Hunting, p. 624.)

animal being referred to the person who let him slip, so long as it continues to move on in a straight line:—but that upon the animal turning off to the right or left, the effect of letting it slip terminates,—in other words, the person is no longer responsible in case of any damage:—and the same rule also holds where the animal stops, and then moves on of itself; for if, afterwards, anything be destroyed, there is no responsibility.

Nor where he has let him slip at game.—IF a person let slip his dog at game, and the dog destroy any thing else, without stopping, yet the person who let him slip is not responsible, provided he did not drive (that is, run after) him; for as hunting is a thing unlimitedly lawful, and is not restricted to the condition of safety (it not being an exertion which can effect any other than the hunter himself), transgression (which is the occasion of responsibility) cannot be established in this instance. If, on the contrary, a person let slip his dog on the highway, and the dog destroy any thing without stopping, compensation must be made by the person who let him slip; because, although the occupancy of the highway be a matter of a neutral nature, still it is restricted to the condition of safety, as being an exertion affecting the community; and the letting slip the dog, being an endangering of the safety of the highway, is therefore a transgression, and consequently induces responsibility.

A man, casting off his animal on the highway, is responsible for any depradation it may commit.—IF a person cast off or set loose an animal on the highway, and the animal move straight on, and then, turning to the right or left, tread down corn, or so forth, the person who cast it loose is responsible; but not if there be more roads than one. If, on the contrary, an animal break loose, and the , moving on of its own accord, kill a man, or tread down property, either by night or day, the owner is not responsible; because the Prophet has so ordained: and also, because the fact of the animal cannot, in this case, be attributed to the owner since he neither cast it off nor drove it.

For the eye of a goat an adequate compensation is due; and for the eye of a labouring animal a fourth of the value.—IF a person put out one of the eyes of a goat, he must compensate (not for any determinate part of the whole value, but merely) for the defect thereby occasioned; because, as the only use of a goat is its milk or its flesh, not its labour nothing more can be required than merely the diminution occasioned in its value. For the eye, on the contrary, of an ox, a camel, a dromedary, an ass, or a horse, of whatever description, a compensation mus tbe made of one fourth of the value; because the Prophet has said, "For the eye of every animal except a goat yet must pay a fourth of the value of the animal;"—and also because, as the work of the animal cannot be performed but by means of four eyes (two of the animal, and two of his diriver), the animal may therefore be said to have four eyes,—whence a fourth of his value is due for the loss of one eye.

Cases of damage occasioned by an animal, having a rider on its back.—IF a person be riding upon his beast on the highway, and another person strike or goad the beast, without the consent of the rider, so as to cause it to kill a man by kicking, or treading him down, or running over him, the responsibility rests upon the person who so struck or goaded it, not upon the rider; because the former was the instigator of the animal's act, which must therefore be referred to him; and also, because this person is the producer of the cause of the accident (for an animal naturally kicks upon being struck or goaded), and, as such, is guilty of a transgression, having goaded the beast without the rider's consent; and as the rider has not in any respect transgressed, he [the goader] is therefore soley responsible.—(If, however, the rider, at the time of the other person striking or goading the beast, had stopped it in the highway, the responsibility rests upon him and the goader in equal shares, as in this case he also has transgressed, in having stopped the animal upon the road.)—If, on the contrary, the beast strike out at the person who goaded or struck him, as above, and he die of the kick, his blood is of no account, as he may be said to have slain himself. If, on the other hand, the beast throw his rider, and kill him, the fine for him is due from the Akilas of the goader or striker, he having transgressed in producing the cause of the accident.

IF a person be riding or stopping upon his beast on his own land, and another goad or strike the beast without the rider's consent, and the beast fly out and tread down a man, the responsibility rests upon the person who so goaded or struck it, and not upon the rider, for the reasons before explained.—If, on the other hand, a person be riding upon his beast on the highway, or stopping upon it on his own land, and another goad or strike it by his desire, and it fly out and tread down a man, neither the rider nor the other are in any degree responsible:—the latter is not so; because his act of striking or goading the animal is in such a case tantamount to that of the rider himself;—nor is the former (the rider) so, as he has here authorized an act to which he is perfectly competent, the goading of an animal being equivalent to driving it. But if the rider be moving along the road upon his beast, and another then strike or goad it by his desire, and it tread down a man, both parties are responsible in an equal degree, provided the man was trodden down without the beast making any stop, because, in this case, its motion is referred to both alike.*

* A frivolous discussion, on this point, of considerable length is omitted by the translator.

Or being led in hand.—If a man be leading an animal, and another strike it, and it break away from the leader, and commit any damage without stopping, the person who struck it is responsible (and so likewise where the animal was driven by any person, instead of being led); because as the breaking away of the animal was owing to the act of the striker, any accident that may ensue is referred to him.

A person wantonly striking an animal, so as to occasion mischief, is responsible.—If the striker, in the examples here recited, be a slave, he is responsible in his person for any damage which may ensue;—or, if he be an infant, the responsibility (for property destroyed, or for any personal injury short of a Mawziha wound) lies against his estate because slaves and infants are liable to be prosecuted for their acts.

And so likewise, a person who sets anything in the highway, which renders the animal mischievous.—If a beast be struck by any thing which a person may have set in the highway— and fly out, and kill a man, the responsibility rests with the person who placed the thing there; for as he transgressed in so doing, the striking is therefore referred to him, the cause being in effect the same if he had himself struck the animal.

CHAPTER IV.

OF OFFENCES COMMITTED BY OR UPON SLAVES.

[*This subject has been omitted in consequence of the abolition of slavery.*]

BOOK LI.

OF MAWAKIL, OR THE LEVYING OF FINES

Definition of terms.— MAWAKIL is the plural of Makola, signifying a Deyit, or fine of blood; and Akilas are those who pay the fine, which is termed Akkil and Mawakil, because it restrains men from shedding blood,—Akkil (among a variety of other senses) meaning restraint.

(*This is also omitted, as it is comprised in the Penal Code, &c.*)

BOOK LII.

OF WASAYA, OR WILLS.

Definition of the terms used in wills.—WASAYA is the plural of Waseeat.—Waseeat means an endowment with the property of any thing after death,—as if one person should say to another, "give this article of mine, after my death, to a particular person."—The thing so given is termed the Moosee be hee, or legacy;—the person who wills that it be given is denominated the Mawsee, or testator; the person in whose favour the will is made is called the Moosee le hoo, or legatee;—and the person appointed to carry the will into execution is called the Wasee, or executor.

CHAPTER I.

OF WILLS THAT ARE LEGAL, AND WILLS THAT ARE LAUDABLE; AND OF THE RETRACTATION OF WILLS.

Wills are lawful and valid.—Wills are lawful, on a favourable construction. Anology would suggest that they are unlawful; because a bequest signifies an endowment with a thing in a way which occasions such endowment to be referred to a time when the property has become void in the proprietor [the testator];—and as an endowment with reference to a future period (as if a person were to say to another, "I constitute you proprietor of this article on the morrow"), is unlawful, supposings, even, that the donor's property in the article still continues to exist at that time, it follows that the suspension of the deed to a period when the property is null and void (as at the decease of the party), is unlawful, a fortiori. The reasons, however, for a more favourable construction, in this particular, are twofold.—FIRST, there is an indispensable necessity that man should have the power of making bequests; for MAN from the delusion of his hopes, is improvident, and deficient in practice; but when sickness invades him he becomes alarmed, and afraid of death. At that period, therefore, he stands in need of compensating for his deficiencies by means of his property;—and this in such a manner, that if he should die of that illness, his objects (namely, compensation for his deficiencies, and merit in a future state) may be obtained, —or, on the other hand, if he should recover, that he may apply the said property to his wants;—and as these objects are attainable by giving a legal validity to wills, they are therefore ordained to be lawful*—SECONDLY,

* In this place are stated an objection and reply, which the translator has omitted in

wills are declared to be lawful in the Koran and the traditions; and all our doctors, moreover, have concurred in this opinion.

To the extent of a third of the testator's property.—If a person make a will in favour of a stranger, to the amount of a third of his property, it is valid, although the heirs of the testator should not be consenting thereto; for it is so recorded in the traditions.

But not to any further extent.—A bequest to any amount exceeding the third of the testator's property is not valid. In proof of this the following tradition is quoted, as delivered by Abee Vekass,. "In the year of the conquest of Mecca, being taken so extremely ill that my life was despaired of, the Prophet of God came to pay me a visit of consolation. I told him, that, by the blessing of God having a great estate, but no heirs except one daughter, I wished to know 'if I might dispose of it ALL by WILL." He replied, 'No!' and when I severally interrogated him 'if I might leave TWO THIRDS, or ONE HALF; he also replied in the negative;—but when I asked 'if I might leave a THIRD', he answered, 'Yes, you may leave a THIRD of your property by will; but a third part, to be disposed of by will, is a great portion; and it is better you should leave your heirs rich, than in a state of poverty, which might oblige them to beg of others.' "—Besides, the right of the testator's heirs is connected with his property; for when he is in his last illness he has no further use for it; and as this is the cause of the title to it becoming null and void in him, and vesting in the heirs, their right therefore, at that period, becomes connected with it accordingly. This right, however, is not recognized by the law, with respect to a stranger, to the extent of one third of the estate, in order that the testator may be enabled, by bequeathing a third of his property out of his family, to atone for his past deficiencies, as before mentioned. With respect to the heirs themselves on the contrary, this connexion of right is, recognized to the extent of the whole of the testator's property (whence it is that if a person should dispose of a third of his property to a part of the heirs, it would not be valid); for if no regard were paid to the connexion of their right with the whole of the property, with respect to themselves, so as to legalize the bequeathing a third of it to a part of them, in that case the object of a will (namely, a compensation for deficiencies) might not be attended to, as it is possible that the testator, instead of including the whole of the heirs, might leave the third only to a select part of them; and this would be an injury to the others, and would consequently induce a breach of the ties of kindred, which is unlawful.

Unless by the consent of the heirs.—It is to be observed, however, that although a will, bequeathing more than a third of the testator's property, be not lawful, yet if the heirs, being arrived at the age of maturity, should give their consent to it, after the death of the testator, it then becomes valid; for the objection to its validity is founded merely on a regard to their right, and therefore does not operate any longer, after they themselves agree to forego such right. Their consent, indeed, during the lifetime of the testator, is not regarded; for as this is an assent previous to the establishment of their right, they are therefore at liberty to annul it upon the death of the testator. It is otherwise where the consent is given after that event; for as this is an assent subsequent to the establishment of their right they are not afterwards at liberty to annul it.

A bequest to an heir is not valid unless confirmed by the other heirs.—Where a person makes a will in favour of part of his heirs, the same rule holds as in the case of bequeathing more than a third to a stranger;—in other words, the deed is not valid, unless the other heirs give their consent to the disposition after the death of the testator; and their consent previous to his death will have no effect. It is to be observed that, in every instance where a will is rendered valid by the consent of the heirs, the legatee derives his property from the testator, not from the heirs. This is the opinion of our doctors. Shafei maintains that he derives his property from the heirs. The opinion of our doctors is approved; for the will of the testator is the occasion of the property, the consent of the heirs being only the removal of a bar; and as the law has regard to the cause, not to the removal of a bar, the property is therefore derived from the testator, not from the heirs (whence it is that seisin is not requisite;* for if the property were derived from the heirs, seisin would be requisite; because the transfer of property from a living proprietor, without receiving any thing in return, is in effect a gift, to the establishment of which the seisin of the donee is a necessary condition); in the same manner as where a pawner sells the pawn in which case the ratification of the deed of sale rests entirely on the pawnee, and if he give his consent, the sale is valid, and the purchaser derives his property in the article sold from the pawner, not from the pawnee.

A bequest to a person from whom the testa-

---

the text, in order to avoid an interruption of the subject.– Viz.

"Objection.– If the right of property in the proprietor become extinct at his decease, how can his act of endowment be then valid?

"Reply.– His right of property is accounted to endure at that time from necessity,—in the same manner as holds with respect to executing the funeral rites, or discharging the debts of the dead."

* Meaning, "the testator's taking possession of the bequest is not requisite for the establishment of his right in it."

tor had received a mortal wound is not valid.—IF a person make a bequest in favour of another from whom he has received a mortal wound, it is not valid; whether the murderer be one of his heirs, or a stranger, or whether he may have wounded him wilfully or by misadventure, provided he be the actual perpetrator of the deed; because it is recorded in the traditions, that "there is no legacy for a murderer;" and also, because, as the person who gave the wound has hastened the death of the testator, he is, by way of punishment, excluded from the benefit of the will, in the same manner as a person under similar circumstances is excluded from inheritance.

And if a legatee slay his testator, the bequest in his favour is void.—So likewise, where a man, having made a bequest in favour of a particular person, is afterwards killed by that person, such bequest is invalid.—If, however, in these cases, the heirs should give their consent, the bequest then becomes valid, according to Haneefa and Mohammed.—Aboo Yoosaf is of a contrary opinion; because the offence of the murderer, which is the cause of the invalidity of the will, still exists.—The arguments of Haneefa and Mohammed upon this point are twofold.—FIRST, the defect in the validity of the will; with respect to the murderer, is on account of the right of the heirs; because the advantage of such defect results to them, as in the case of exclusion from inheritance.—SECONDLY, the defect in the validity of the bequest, as made in favour of the murderer, is owing to the heirs withholding their consent, in the same manner as in the case of a will in favour of part of the heirs; and consequently, as the consent of the remaining heirs, in that instance, establishes the validity of the will, it follow that the consent of the heirs at large must have the same effect in the case in question.

A bequest to a part of the heirs is not valid.—IF a man make a bequest in favour of a part of his heirs, it is not valid; because of a traditional saying of the Prophet, "GOD has allotted to every heir his particular right;" and also, because a will in favour of a part of the heirs is an injury to the rest; and therefore, if it were deemed legal, would induce a breach of the ties of kindred.—Besides, it is said, in the traditions, "a bequest to particular heirs is unjust."—It is to be observed that in judging whether the legatee be an heir, or otherwise, regard is paid to the time of the testator's death, not to the period of making the will; because the efficacy of the will is established after the death of the testator.—(The gift of a dying person* is in this respect of the same nature with a legacy, both being the same in effect and is therefore executed to the amount of a third of the property.)—If, on the contrary, a dying person make an acknowledgment in favour of a part of his heirs, regrd is paid to the time of such acknowledgment; because the acknowledgment of a dying person is an immediate and complete act of his own, and has not any reference to a future period;—and such being the case, it follows that it is not valid in favour of any who were actually heirs at the time of making it,—and that it is valid with respect to such as were not heirs at that time; although they should become so afterwards;—as where, for instance, a person makes an acknowledgment in favour of his child, who is a slave, and the child recovers his freedom before the death of the father; in which case the acknowledgment so made is valid, notwithstanding the child, by the recovery of his freedom, became one of his father's heirs; for as, at the time of the acknowledgment, he was not an heir,* any acknowledgment made in his favour was virtually made in favour of his master, who was a stranger;—and the validity of the acknowledgment being once established, it does not afterwards admit of being annulled from the circumstance of the child's becoming an heair.—It is to be observed, however, that although a bequest in favour of a part of the heirs be not valid, yet it is rendered so by their consent, as was already mentioned.—If, moreover, a part should give their consent, and part withhold it, the bequest then becomes valid in proportion to the amount of the shares of those who consent, and invalid in proportion to the amount of the shares of the othrs.

Bequests are valid between Mussulmans and Zimmees.—THE bequest of a Mussulman in favour of a Zimmee or of a Zimmee in favour of a Mussulman, is valid, the former, because GOD has said, in the KORAN, "YE ARE NOT PROHIBITED, O BELIEVERS, FROM ACTS OF BENEVOLENCE TOWARDS THOSE WHO SUBJECT THEMSELVES TO YOU, AND REFRAIN FROM BATTLES AND CONTENTIONS;"—and the latter, because Zimmees, in virtue of their compact with the Mussulmans, are considered in the same light with them in all temporal concerns; and as, on this principle, an intercourse of good offices towards each other is held lawful during life, they are therefore in the same manner permitted to extend beyond the grave.—It is related in the Jama Sagheer that a will in favour of an hostile infidel is not valid, as GOD has prohibited, in the KORAN, the exercise of benevolence towards them.

The acceptance or rejection of them is not determined until after the death of the testator.—THE acceptance or rejection of a bequest is not established until after the death of the testator; for as the bequest does not take

* Arab, Mareez. Literally, sick,—but always (in the language of the LAW) meaning, 'sick of a mortal illness."

* A slave cannot possess any right of inheritance.

effect before that event, those cannot be previously regarded.—Hence the acceptance or rejection during the life of the testator has no effect, in the same manner as an acceptance declared before the existence of a contract.—If, therefore, a legatee accept a bequest after the death of the testator, it is valid, notwithstanding he may have rejected it during his lifetime.

It is laudable to avoid making them where the heirs are poor.—It is preferable and most advisable not be leave legacies, if the heirs be poor, and their particular portions not such as to enrich them; because this manifests benevolence to the heirs, who have a superior claim to it from the relation in which they stand, God having declared, in the Koran, "The exertions of generosity towards relations is more laudable than towards strangers."—Besides, in this an observance of twoo claims is maintained, namely, that of poverty and consanguinity. If, on the contrary, the heirs be rich or the particular portions assigned to them be such as to enrich them, it is most advisable to leave something short of a third of the estate in legacies, as a legacy to a stranger is an act of charity, whereas the bestowal of the whole upon the heirs is a gift; and the former is more laudable than the latter, being calculated to gain the favour and good will of God. Some have said that in such case the proprietor is under no restraint, but is perfectly at liberty to make a will in favour of strangers, or to suffer the whole to pass to the heirs, as each has its particular merit, the first being an act of generosity, and the second an obedienc to the dictates of natural affection.

The legatee becomes proprietor of the legacy by his acceptance of it.—The property of a legatee in a legacy is established by his acceptance of it. Ziffer is of opinion that a legacy is like an inheritance; because the legatee acquired the property by transition from, and succession to the testator, in the same maner as an heir acquires it by succession to and descent from the last possessor; and therefore his acceptance is not necessary towards the establishment of the property, in the same manner as holds in the case of inheritance.—Our doctors, on the contrary, argue that a legacy establishes the property in the legatee de novo, and does not vest by succession and descent as in the case of inheritance (whence it is that a legatee cannot reject the legacy on account of any defect; in other words, if a person, having purchased a slave, for example, should bequeath him to another, and the legatee, after the death of the testator, discover the slave to have some fault or defect, it would no, on this account, be in his power to return him to the seller, as an heir, in a similar case, would be entitled to do;—and likewise, that nothing can be returned to a legatee on account of a defect; in other words, if a person should bequeath his whole estate by will, and afterwards sell something belonging to it, and the buyer discover a defect in the same, still he would not have the power of returning it to the legatee, whereas he might to an heir);—and such being the case, it rests, therefore, entirely on his acceptance, as no person can be made proprietor of any thing against his will. Inheritance, on the contrary, is a succession (whence it is that the rules above mentioned have effect in it); and an heir is therefore, as it were, forcibly put in possession of his inheritance, by the especial ordinance of the law, to validity of it not being suspended on his acceptance or consent.

Which may be either expressed or implied.—It is to be observed that acceptance in cases of bequest, is of two kinds.—I. Express, which needs not to be explained.—II. Implied, which is where the legatee dies without having either declared his acceptance or refusal; for this also is in acceptance in effect; because the bequest as rendered complete on the part of the testator by his death (in other words, it cannot be rescinded after that event); and as it was susmpeded in its effect purely in deference to his right of rejection, it of course falls into his property upon his demise;—in the same manner as hold in a case of sale with a reserve of option to the purchaser; in which instance, if the purchaser die without formally signifying his assent to the sale, it is then regarded as complete, and the article sold is considered as part of his estate.

Bequest by an insolvent person is void.—If a person deeply involved in debt bequeath any legacies, such bequest is unlawful and of no effect; because debts have a preference to bequests, as the discharge of debts is an absolute duty, whereas bequests are gratuitous and voluntary; and that which is most indispensable must be first considered. If, however, the creditors of the deceased relinquish their claims, the bequest is then valid, the obstacle to it being removed, and the legatee being supposed to stand in need of his legacy.

And so likewise by an infant.—Bequest by an infant is not valid. Shafei maintains that it is valid, provided it be made to a discreet and advisable purpose; because Omar confirmed the will of a Yaffai (that is, a boy who has nearly reached the age of maturity); and also, because in the execution of it a degree of advantage results to the infant, inasmuch as he acquires the merit of the deed,—whereas in the annulment of it he is deprived of all advantage. The arguments of our doctors in support of their opinion upont his point, are two fold.—First, a will is a voluntary act, concerning which an infant has not a capacity of forming a proper judgment. Secondly, the declaration of an infnt is not of a binding nature; but if the validity of a bequest by such were admitted, that effect would follow of course.—With regard to the tradition of

Omar, the term Yaffai, there used, must be understood to mean a person just arrived at the age of maturity, or, "the will of the Yaffai" relates merely to the celebration of his obsequies, which is lawful in the opinion of our doctors. Besides, the annulment of the will is advantageous to the infant, since in allowing his property to pass to the heirs the rights of natural affection are maintained, as befor mentioned. With respect to the assertion of Shafei, that "in the execution of the will an advantage results to the infant," it may be replied that the point to be attended to, in case of advantage or loss, is the immediate tendency of any act or deed, and not what may eventually result from it ; in other words, if the deed itself, in its immediate tendency, produce advantage, the execution of it on account of the infant is preferable; but in the case here considered the deed (that is, the bequest), in its immediate tendency, leads to a loss of property, although eventually the infant have an advantage, the bequest having been made with a view to obtain merit in the eye of GOD; and since the bequest of the infant, in its immediate tendency, occasions a loss, it is not valid;-- in the same manner as holds in case of a divorce; in other words, if an infant divorce his wife, or his guardian do so on his behalf, it is not binding, notwithstanding a divorce may on many occasions be attended with advantage,- as where an infant, having a wife who is poor, wishes to divorce her, and marry her sister, who is rich and handsome - In short, bequest by an infant is invalid, accordng to our doctors;—and in the same manner, if an infant shoud make a will, and die after he had attained to maturity, the will is not valid, as having been made at a time when he was unqualified for such an act; and so likewise, if an infant should say, "It is my will, whenever I reach the age of maturity, that a third of my estate be considered as a legacy in favour of a particular person," the will is not valid; because an infant, being unqualified, is not competent to make a will that shall be deemed valid immediately; or that can be rendered so by being suspended to a future period; in the same manner as he is incapable of divorce or emancipation. It is otherwise with respect to a slave or a Mokatib; for they possess a complete competency, obstructed merely by the right of their master; and therefore all their acts (such as divorce, bequest, or so forth) are perfectly valid if referred to a period when that bar no longer exists; as where a slave (for instance) says "I declare my wife to be divorced whenever I am free."

Or a Mokatib.—BEQUEST by a Mokatib is not valid, notwithstanding he leave effects sufficient to discharge his covenanted ransom; because the property of a Mokatib is not a fit subject of gratuitous acts. Some assert that this is according to Haneefa; but that the two disciples hold a ontrary opinion.

A bequest of (or in favour of) a foetus in the womb is valid.—A WILL in favour of a foetus in the womb, and a will bequeathing a foetus, are both valid, provided the birth happen in less than six months from the date of the will. The ground on which te first case proceeds is, that a legacy is, in a manner, a succession to property; and as a foetus is capable to succeed in the case of inheritance, it is so likewise in the case of a legacy, that being analogous to inheritance. If, however, the legatee should reject the legacy, it is rejected accordingly, as a bequest bears also the sense of a endowment, which may be declined. It is different with inheritanee, as that is purely a succession, and is not annulled by the rejection of the heir.—Gift, moreover, differs from be quest, it not being (like bequest) admitted in favour of a foetus; for gift is purely an endowment; and no person can endow a foetus with any thing. The ground, on the other hands, on which the second case proceeds is, that the existence of the foetus is understood at the period of making the will ; and as the legacy of things not yet in being (such as the fruit a tree may hereafter yield) is valid, it follows that a legacy of a thing actually existing is valid a fortiori.

A female slave may be bequeathed with the exception of her progeny.—IF a person bequeath a female slave, and except the offspring of her womb, both the bequest and the exception are valid. The bequest is valid, because the words "female slave" do not include the offspring. As, however, in the bequest of a female slave, her offspring is included dependently, were the bequest is absolute, it follows that where a slave is bequeathed with an exception of her offspring, such bequest is valid. The exception also is valid; because as it is permitted to bequeath a foetus in the womb, it is also allowable to except it from a legacy; for it is a rule that whatever is in itself capable of being the subject of a deed may also be excepted from that deed; and vice versa. Besides, the acceptance of the legatee is suspended until the death of the testator; and the annulment of the declaration, previous to the acceptance is valid, as in a case of sale for instance.

A bequest is rescinded by the express declaration of the testator; or by any act on his part implying his retractation.—UPON the testator either expressly rescinding his bequest (as if he were to say, "I retract what I had bequeathed"), or performing any act which argues his having rescinded it, retractation is established. It is established, in the former instance, evidently; and so likewise in the latter; for as acts are demonstrative of the inclination as much as express words, they are consequently equivalent thereto.—It is to be observed, that if the testator perform, upon the article he had bequeathed, any act which, when performed on the property of another, is the cause of terminati g the right of the proprietor (such as the slaughter of a goat, or the flaying, roasting, or boiling of it, the fabrication of a vessel from a piece of copper, the grinding wheat into flour, or the fabrication of a sword from iron),—such act is a retractation of the bequest. If, also, he perform upon it any act creating an addition to the legacy, and this addition be so connected, that the legacy cannot be separately delivered (as where a person, bequeaths the flour of wheat, and afrerwards mixes it with oil,—or a piece of ground, and afterwards erects a building on it,—or undressed cotton, and afterwards dresses it,—or a piece of cloth, and afterwards lines or covers a gown with it),—such act is a retractation of the bequest. It is otherwise with respect to plastering the wall of a bequeathed house, or undermining the foundaction of it; for these fcts do not indicate a retractation of the bequest, as they affect the legacy in its dependencies only.

Or which extinguishes his property in the legacy.—EVERY act or deed which occasions an extinction of the property of the testator is a retractation from his bequest (as where for instance, a testator sells the article he had bequeathed, and afterwards purchases it, —or gives it to some person, and afterwards retracts the gift),—and consequently, the legacy does not go to the legatee after his [the testator's] decease:—because a will can hold good only with respect to the testator's property; and therefore, upon his property being extinguished, the bequest becomes null of course. (It is to be observed that the washing of a bequeathed garment is not a retractation from the bequest; on the contrary, it is rather a confirmation of it, as it is a custom to wash garments before they are given to any person).

The testator's denying his bequest is not a retractation of it.—IF a testator deny his bequest, and the legatee produce witnesses to prove it, there is in that case a difference of opinion among our doctors;—for according to Mohammed this is not a retractation;—whereas Aboo Yoosaf maintains that it is so, because retractation signifies the testator negativing his bequest at the present time; and as the denial is a negative applying both to the present and to the past, it therefore amounts to a retractations a fortiori. The argument of Mohammed is, that the denial of a bequest signifies the putting a negative upon it with respect to the past, of which its being negatived with respect to the present is a consequence; and upon the bequest being proved, by witnesses, to exist at present, the enial is of no effect, Another argument is, that as a retractation implies the former existence of a will, and the present annihilation of it, and denial (on the other hand) disavows both the former and the present existence of it, there is therefore an evident difference between a retractation and a denial; whence the latter ought not to be considered in the light of the former;—and accordingly, den al not being a retractation, if a husband deny his marriage, and the wife bring witnesses to prove it, still a separation does not take place between them.

Nor his declaring it unlawful or usurious.—IF a testator declare the will he has made in favour of a particular person to be unlawful or usurious, this is not a retractation, because the specification of it under the description of illegality or usury is a plain proof that the subject of the description (namely, the will) does actually exist. The case would be different if he should declare the will to be null; for that is evidently a retractalon; because, as a thing which is null is non-existent, the description of null evinces that the thing so described no longer exists. It is otherwise with the description of unlawful; for that indicates a continuance of the existence, as illegality cannot apply to a nonenity.

Or desiring the execution of it to be deferred.—IF a testator should desire that the execution of his will be suspended for some time after his death, this is not a retractation. If, on the contrary, he say "I depart from my will" he is then held to have retracted it.

A bequest to one person is annulled by a subsequent bequest of the same article to another.—IF a person say, "I will that a particular slave, which I formerly bequeathed to Zeyd, be given as a legacy to Amroo," in that case a retractation from the first will is established, as the tenor of his speech evidently shows that it was not his intention they should both partake of the legacy. It is otherwise where a person first leaves a particular article to one man, and then leaves the same thing to another;—as if he should say, "I will that this thing be given to Zeyd," and afterwards make a bequest of the same thing in favour of Amroo;—for in that case retractation of the first will does not take place; the subject being capable of division, and the separate sentences bearing that construction.

Unless that other be not than alive.—IF a person say, 'the slave which I formerly left to Zeyd I now bequeath to Amroo," and at that time Amroo be not alive, the first will, in favour of Zeyd, holds good for that was annulled only on account of the legacy having been completely devised to Amroo; and upon this no longer remaining in force, because of Amroo's death, the first will reverts. —If, on the contrary, Amroo be alive at the time of the bequest in his favour, and afterwards die before the testator, the legacy (the slave) in that case passes to the heirs, both bequests being void,—the first, because of the retractation,—and the last, because of the death of the legatee previous to that of the testator.

CHAPTER II.

CONCERNING THE BEQUEST OF A THIRD OF THE ESTATE.

Case of a person bequeathing two thirds of his property to two persons respectively.—If a person bequeath a third of his property to one man, and a third to another, and the heirs refuse their consent to the execution of both bequests, one third is in that case divided equally between the two legatees; for where the will exceeds a third of the estate, and the heirs refuse their consent to the execution of the whole, it is then restricted to one third, as has been already explained; and as, in the present instance, the right of the both claimants is equally good and the third is capable of division, it is therefore divided equally between them.

Or a third to one and a sixth to the other.—If a man bequeath a third of his property to one person and a sixth to another, and the heirs refuse to confirm the whole, in that case one third of the property is to be divided between the legatees in three equal lots, two to the legatee of the third, and one to the legatee of the sixth; because the bequest does not hold good for any thing beyond one third; and as both the legatees lay their claims on equally good ground, and it is impossible to discharge their demands (namely, a third and a sixth) with one third only, that is therefore shared between them in proportion to their respective claims, in the same manner as is practised with creditors, in discharging the debts of a person who dies insolvent. Here, moreover, the right of one legatee is to a sixth, and that of the other to a third; and as a third is twice the amount of a sixth, the third is therefore divided between the claimants in three shares, two shares going to the one, and one share to the other.

Cases of Mohabat wills.—(* A WILL by way of Mohabat, on a deathbed, is the same in effect as a bequest of property, and is therefore executed to any amount not exceeding a third of the testaor's estate. (Mohabat literally signifies a gift. In the language of the LAW it means a fight interwoven in some compact or deed, as if a person should sell part of his property to another at an inferior value.)

If a person, having two slaves, one estimated at thirty dirms, and the other at sixty, should on his deathbed will that the slave worth thirty dirms be sold to Zeyd for ten and that the other worth sixty, be sold to Omar for twenty,—in that case Zeyd obtains a Mohabat of twenty dirms, and Omar a Mohabat of forty dirms; and this is what is denominated a will by Mohabat. But if the testator should not be possessed of any other property than these two slaves, and the heirs refuse to ratify the will, in that case the Mohabat is executed only in the proportion of a third. Now the whole of the property is ninety dirms, that being the aggregate value of the two slaves; one third of that therefore (being thirty dirm), is divided into three shares, two of which are given in Mohabat to Omar, and one to Zeyd; that is, the slave worth sixty dirms is sold to Omar for forty, and the other, worth thirty, to Zeyd, for twenty.

If a person, having two slaves one valued at thirty dirms, and the other at sixty, should on his deathbed emancipate both, such manumission is in effect a bequest. If, therefore, the person in question leave no other property than these two slaves, and the heirs refuse their consent to the emancipation, it takes effect in the proportion of one third; that is to say, each of the slaves is rendered free in one third of his value, and must earn the freedom of the remaining two thirds by emancipatory labour.

And bequests of specific sums of money.—If a person bequeath a particular number of dirms without specifying the relative proportion they bear to his estate,—such as a half, a third, a fourth, or the like,—it is valid, but is executed only to the extent of a third of his whole property, unless the hairs be willing to confirm the whole. Thus if a person, having only ninety dirms, should bequeath thirty to Zeyd, and sixty to Omar, and the heirs refuse their assent to it, in that, case the sum of two legacies is reduced to thirty dirms, of which Zeyd receives ten and Omar twenty.)

Case of a person bequeathing the whole of his estate to one, and then a third of it to another.—If a person first bequeath the whole of his estate to one man, and then a third of it to another,* and the heirs refuse their assent, in that case one third of his estate is divided into four shares, of which three are given to the legatee of the whole and one to the legatee of the third. This is according to the two disciples. Haneefa alleges that the third of the estate must be divided equally between the two legatees; for in his opinion, when a legacy is extended beyond a third, the excess is of no weight in the determination. The argument of the two disciples is, that the testator has two objects in view; for first, he designs that

* The whole passage within the crochets seems to be an interpolation of Molovees employed in the composition of the Persian version of the HEDAYA, as the translator has consulted various Arabic copies, without finding it in any of them. It may possibly have been inserted in some copies of the work in the manner of marginal illustrations, which induced the Molovees to give it a place in the text.

* This supposes the testator, first, to say, "I bequeath the whole of my property to Zeyd" (for instance), and again at some future time, "I bequeath a third of my property to Amroo."

each of the legatees shall receive the whole of his legacy; and secondly, that a superiority of the one over the other shall be maintained. Now the attainment of the first of these objects is impossible, because of the right of the heirs, and is, indeed, in itself impracticable; but as there is no bar to the full accomplishment of the second object, the superiority of the one over the other is preserved, in the same manner as in the cases of bequest by Mohabat, or emancipation, or, of legacies of a specific number of dirms. The argument of Haneefa is, that a will is null and void in whatever degree it may exceed a third of the estate, where the heirs refuse their assent; and cannot on any sort of pretext be executed in that amount, as being repugnant to the ordinance of the LAW in this particular. Since, therefore, the will is rendered null in the excess above a third, one object of the testator (namely, to establish a superiority) is also rendered null, as being comprehended in it: in the same manner as a Mohabat is rendered null when interwoven in a contract or sale which is afterwards invalidated; as where, for instance, a person sells, by Mohabat, a slave valued at thirty dirms for twenty, and the sale afterwards becomes void in consequence of the loss of the subject of it previous to the delivery,—in which case the Mohabat also becomes void. It is otherwise in the cases of bequest by Mohabat or emancipation, or of legacies of a specific number of dirms; for there the validity does not rest on the consent of the heirs; it being eventually possible that the bequests may become valid notwithstanding the heirs should refuse to ratify them, by the testator (for instance), after making the bequest, increasing his property to a degree that might render the amount of the bequest no more than equal to, or less than, one third of the whole. Since, therefor, in these cases, the bequest is not in itself null, but rather stands within the possibility of being valid, a regard must consequently be paid, in such instances, to the superiority of one of the parties. It is otherwise in the case here considered; for it is in this instance impossible that the will should be valid, as has been already shown. It is also otherwise where a person bequeaths a particular slave, valued at one thousand dirms, to Zeyd, and another, valued at two thousand dirms, to Bicker, and has himself no other property than these slaves; for although, in this case, there be a possibility that the testator may so increase his property as to render the amount of the two slaves equal to, or less than, a third of the whole, yet Bicker would receive a proportion according to the third, not according to the amount of the legacy (viz. two thousand dirms); because here the right of the legatees is connected with the substance of the slaves, on this ground, that if the slave should be destroyed, the will would be rendered void, notwithstanding the testator might have acquired other property. Hence the apprehension before stated is of no weight in this instance, as the right of the legatee is here connected with the very article with which the right of the heirs has a connexion. In the case, on the contrary, of a legacy of a specific number of dirms, if the property of the testator be destroyed, and he afterwards acquire more, the legacy would be valid, and executed by means of the newly acquired property; whence it is plain that the right of the legatee, in the case of a legacy of a specific number of dirms, is not connected with the substance, and consequently is no annulled on account of its destruction.

The bequest of "a son's portion of inheritance" is void, but not the bequest of an equivalent to it.—If a person bequeath to another "his son's portion of inheritance,"* such bequest is null; whereas, if he bequeath "an EQUIVALENT to his son's portion," such bequest is valid; for the first is a bequest of what is the property of another, whereas the second is merely a bequest of something similar; and the semblance of a thing is different from the thing itself, notwithstanding its rate be determined thereby Ziffer is of opinion that a bequest of the former nature is likewise valid; because at the time of making it the portion belonged evidently to the testator. I reply to this, however, it is to be observed, that the legacy does not take place until after the death of the testator, when the property does not belong to him, and hence his bequest of his son's portion is a bequest of property not his own.

A bequest of "a portion" of the estate is executed to the extent of the smallest portion inheritable from it.—If a person bequeath "a portion of his estate," the legatee is in that case entitled to the smallest portion allotted to any of the heirs,—provided, however, that such portion be not less than a sixth, for then a complete sixth must be given to him; and if it should exceed a sixth, in that case also a sixth is given to him: for he is in no wise to get more than a sixth. A case in which one of the inheritable portions is less than a sixth is where, for instance, a person bequeaths to another "a portion of his estate," and leaves heirs, at his death, a son and a wife;—in which case, although the share of the wife be only an eighth, yet the legatee receives a sixth, and the remainder is then divided between the wife and son (the heirs) according to the ordinances of the LAW. A case on the contrary, in which all the inheritable portions exceed a sixth, is where, for instance, a

* In this, and several subsequent examples, the effect depends entirely upon the terms in which the bequest is conceived, and which must therefore be particularly attended to, —Thus, in the present instance, the testator is suppoed to say, "I bequeath to SUCH AN ONE my son's portion of inheritance:" and so of the rest.

person makes a bequest in the terms here stated, and dies, leaving heirs a full brother and wife; in which case, although the smallest portion be a fourth, yet the legatee is only entitled to a sixth; and that being paid to him, the remainder is then divided between the brother and wife, agreeably to the ordinances of the LAW. This is according to Haneefa. Aboo Yoosaf and Mohammed are of opinion that the legatee is entitled to the lowest share, whatever be its amount, provided it do not exceed a third; but if it exceed a third, an exact third must be given him, and not more, unless the heirs be consenting thereto. The argument on which they ground this opinion is, that the word Sehm [portion], both in its literal and received sense, means a portion allotted to an heir; and as the smallest share is a matter of certainty, it is therefore adopted as the standard; except where the smallest portion of inheritance exceeds a third, in which case the bequest is executed in the proportion of a third, as a legacy exceeding a third is not valid, unless confirmed by the heirs. The argument of Haneefa is; that Sehm, according to the interpretation of the LAW, means a sixth; a legacy of a Sehm having been left in the time of the prophet, who ordained that a sixth of the property of the testator should be given to the legatee. In its literal sense, moreover, it bears the same meaning, because Ayass, a man skilled in the Arabic language, who was Kazee of Bagdad, declared that Sehm literally signified a sixth. Since, therefore, Sehm, both in the practice of the LAW, and the literal signification, means a sixth, the legatees in cases of this kind is always entitled to it, and to no more.—(Several lawyers, however, remark, that although this was the received sense of Sehm in those days, yet in our time it means indefinitely, a portion, or part.)

A bequest of "part of the estate" undefined, may be construed to apply to any part.—IF a person bequeath "a part of his property" to another without specifying to what amount, the heirs are at liberty to give whatever they please to the legatee; for here the amount of the bequest is unknown; but as the uncertainty with respect to that is no bar to its validity, it is therefore valid; and such being the case, and the heirs being the representatives of the testator, it is consequently at their discretion to fix the amount, in the same manner as the testator himself might do if he were living.

Case of a person bequeathing first a sixth, and then a third, to the same person.—IF a person bequeath "a sixth of his property" to another, and afterwards, before the same or another company, bequeath "a third of his property" to that same person, in this case the legatee is entitled to a third of the testator's estate, whether the heirs be consenting or not, the sixth being included in the latter bequest of a third.

Or, first a third, and then a sixth, to the same person.—IF a person bequeath "a third of his property" to another, and afterwards, either before the same or another company, bequeath "a sixth of his property" to the same person, in that case the legatee is entitled only to the sixth. (The proofs, in this instance, are drawn from the Arabic).

A person bequeathing a third of any particular property, if two-thirds of it to be lost and the remainder come within a third of the testator's estate, the legatee is entitled to the whole of such remainder.—IF a person bequeath to another "a third of his DIRMS." amounting in all to three thousand, or "a third of his goats," amounting in all to three, and afterwards two-thirds of the dirms or goats be lost or destroyed, so that only one-third remains, and the remaining third do not amount to a third of the whole of the testator's property (he having been in possession of other things besides the dirms or goats), the legatee is entitled to the complete remaining third; that is, to a thousand dirms in the first case, and to one goat in the second. Ziffer maintains that the legatee is entitled only to one third of what remains, —that is, in the first instance to one third of one thousand dirms, and in the second to the third of the value of the goat; because the heirs and the legatee having had proportionate claims to the whole in an indefinite manner, are to participate in the loss according to the proportion of their claims;—in the same manner as holds where the effects are of different kinds, such as a gown, a slave, and a house; for if "one of these three" be bequeathed to a particular person in an indefinite manner, and two of them be afterwards destroyed, the remaining one is divided between the heirs and the legatee; and so likewise in the present instance. Our doctors, on the other hand, argue that it is possible completely to maintain the right of one of two partners (such as the legatee, in the present instance) in one of three articles, where they are all of the same class (whence it is that the holder of a partnership property may be compelled, if it be of a homogeneous nature, to make a division of it among the partners; the division, with respect to any unique and specific article, being the right of each partner respectively):—and as the bequest precedes the right of the heirs,* the right of the legatee is therefore completely maintained with respect to the thousand dirms in question,—the case being in fact the same as where a person bequeaths another three dirms, two of which are afterwards lost,—when the remaining dirm goes completely to the legatee, according to all our doctors. It is otherwise where the effect bequeathed are of different kinds; for there, after the loss or destruction of two of the articles, neither the complete right of the whole, nor the complete particular right of

* The debts and bequests due from an estate are discharged previous to the distribution of the portions of inheritance.

any one of the parties, can be maintained by means of the remaining article; and therefore the division is not set aside in favour of the legatee on account of the priority of his claim; on the contrary, the remaining article is divided among the parties, according to the nature of their respective claims.

A bequest of "the third of" an article, part of which is afterwards destroyed, holds with respect to a third of the remainder.—If a person bequeath to another "a third of his clothing," of which two thirds are afterwards destroyed, and the remaining third exceed in value a third of the whole property of the testator, the legatee is in that case entitled to only one third of the vestments that remain. Lawyers, however, have observed that this is only where the vestments are of different kinds; for otherwise they are considered in the same light as dirms;—and so likewise of all articles of weight, or measurement of capacity, as it is possible, in those also, to maintain complete the right of particular partners to particular portions, whence it is that a division of such among partners may be compelled.

If a person bequeath to another "the third of his three slaves," and two of them afterwards die, the legatee is entitled only to a third of the value of the remaining slave; and the same rule also holds with respect to different houses. Some say that this is according to Haneefa only; and others, that it is the opinion of all our doctors. The compiler of the Hedaya remarks that it is approved, proceeding upon the general rule before stated, that, 'in all articles which admit of the rights of the partners being united in them, it is practicable to unite the right of the legatee."

A legacy of money must be paid in full with the property in hand, although all the rest of the estate should be expended in debts.—If a person whos estate consists, partly of ready money, and partly of debts due to him from others, bequeath to another one thousand dirms, and that sum exceed not a third of the existent property, it is paid to the legatee without any deduction. If, on the contrary, it exceed a third of the ready property, he is only to receive a third of the amount in hand; and afterwards a third must be paid him, of whatever sums may occasionally be recovered by the heirs, until in this manner the amount of the legacy be completely dischraged. The reason of this is that the legatee is (as it were) a partner with the heirs; and therefore, if his claim in particular were discharge with the ready property (by its being applied to the payment of the whole of his legacy), an injury would be occasioned to the right of the heirs, as ready money is allowed to be preferable to money that is due.

A legacy left to two persons, one of them being at the time dead, goes entire to the living legatee.—If a person leave a third of his property, "to Zeyd and Omar," and Omar be at that time dead, the whole of the third is given to Zeyd, whether the testator, at the time of making the will, have been acquainted with the death of Omar or not; for as a defunct is not capable of becoming a legatee, he therefore cannot prevent a living person from being so;—in the same manner as where, for instance, a person bequeaths something "to Zeyd and to a wall." According to one tradition from Aboo Yoosaf it is said, that if the testator were not acquainted with the death of Omar, Zeyd is then entitled only to one half of the third; for on such a supposition the will in favour of Omar was valid in the opinion of the testator; which sufficiently indicates his will and intention to have been that Zeyd should receive only one half of the third. But it, on the other hand, he was acquainted with the circumstance of Omar's death it is evident that he intended that Zeyd should receive the whole, as a will in favour of a dead man is vain and useless.

A legacy being bequeathed to two persons indefinitely, if one of them die, a moiety of it only goes to the other.—If a person will that one third of his property "be divided, as a legacy, between Zeyd and Omar," and Omar be at that time dead, Zeyd is entitled to only one half of the third; for the words used by the testator clearly denote his intention that each should have an half; but Omar being at that time dead, the will with respect to him is void.

A bequest made by a poor man is of force if he afterwards become rich.—If a person who is poor bequeath to another "the third of his property," and afterwards become rich, the legatee is in that case entitled to a third of his estate, to whatever amount; for the bequest does not take effect until after the death of the testator, and therefore the condition of its validity is, his being possessed of property at the time of his decease. The law is also the same in case the testator, being rich at the time of making the will should afterwards become poor, and again acquire wealth.

A bequest of any article, not existing in the possession or disposal of the testator as his decease, is null.—If a person bequeath "a third of his goats" to another, and it happen either that he has no goats, or that such as he had were destroyed before his death, the bequest is null; for the condition or its validity is, the testator being possessed of the property at the time of his decease, which is not here the case. If, on the contrary, having no goats at the time of making the will, he should afterwards acquire goats, so as to leave some at his death, one thirds of them goes as a legacy to Zeyd (according to the Rawayet Saheeh); for here the condition of validity (namely, that the testato die possessed of the property) exists.

Unless it was referred to his property, in which case it must be discharged by a payment of the value.—If a person bequeath "a goat of his property" to Zeyd, and afterwards die without leaving any goats, the price of a goat must in that case be paid to Zeyd; for the testator's expression "a GOAT of his property" denotes his intention to bequeath the worth of the animal. If, on the contrary, he neither bequeath "a goat of his property," nor "one of his goats," but simply "a goat" (to Zeyd), without any relation to his property or herd of goats, in that case there is a difference of opinion, some saying that the bequest is not valid, as the absolute expression of the testator denotes his intention to have been a legacy of the aninmal itself, of which he had none,—whilst others maintain it to be valid, for this reason, that the testator having specified a goat, of which he had none, must be supposed to have intended the worth of it. If, on the other hand, the words of the testator were, "I bequeath one of my goats," in that case the bequest is evidently invalid; because the relation to his herd of goats determines the legacy to have been restricted to the animal itself. (A variety of cases of this nature occur, and are determined on the principle now stated.)

Distribution of a bequest made indefinitely to three different descriptions of persons.—IF a person bequeath "a third of his property to his AM-WALIDS, to the distressed, and to beggars," and the Am-Walids amount to three in all,—in that case, according to the two Elders, a third of his property is, after his death, divided into five shares, of which three are given equally among the Am-Walids, one to the distressed, and one to beggars. Mohammed, on the contrary, says that it is to be divided into seven shares, of which three are distributed in equal portions among the Am-Walids, two given to the distressed, and two to beggars.

Or, to an individual, and a particular class of people.—IF a person bequeath "a third of his property to a certain person and to the distressed," in that case, according to the two Elders, the thrid is divided into two equal parts, one of which is given to the person named, and the other to the distressed; whereas Mahommed maintains, that it must be divided into three shares, one to be given to the said person, and two to the distreesed.

Or to a particular class of people alone.—IF a person bequeath "a third of his property to the ditressed," the two Elders are of opinion that the executor may in that case give the whole of the third to one distressed person; whereas Mohammed holds that it cannot be given to fewer than two.

Case of a third person being admitted, by the testator, to a participation with two other legaters.—IF a person bequeath one hundred dirms to Zeyd, and one hundred to Amroo, and afterwards declare Bicker to be a participator with them, by saying, "I have made three Bicker a sharer with Zeyd and Omar," Bicker is in that case entitled to a third of each of their portions, in order that he may be put on an equality, as the words of the testator evidently imply that intention, for the term used by him [Shirkot] literally means equality which it is here possible to preserve, and there is no impracticability in the execution of the bequest. It is otherwise, where the portions of the legtees are unequal, as if the legacy of Zeyd were four hundred dirms and that of Omar two hundred, and Bicker were declared by the testator to be a sharer with them; for in that case the establishment of an equality is impracticable, and therefore Bicker is entitled to receive a moiety of each of their shares, that they may be brought as nearly on an equality as possible.

An acknowledgment of debt, upon a death-bed, is efficient to the extent of a third of the estate.—IF a person, on his death-bed, say be his heirs, "I am indebted to Zeyd, and you must credit what he says," in that case the claim of Zeyed, to any amount not exceeding a third of the estate, must be admitted, although the heirs should falsify it. This proceeds on a favourable construction. Analogy would suggest that the declaration of Zeyd is not to be credited; for although an acknowledgment concerning a thing undefined be approved, still its effect depends upon the ascertainment of it; and as that cannot be had, because of the death of the acknowledger, it would follow that the declaration of Zeyd is of no weight. The reason, however, for a more favourable construction, in this particular, is, that the object of the acknowledger is evidently to give Zeyd a preference over his heirs; and it being possible to execute his design in the way of a bequest, and men being (moreover) desirous of discharging themselves of obligations where they may know of the debt itself, but are uncertain as to the amount (as having forgotten it), the acknowledgment is therefore considered equivalent to a bequest of which the amount is left to the deterination of the legatee,—whence the matter is regarded in the same light as if the acknowledger had said to his heirs, "if Zeyd come and claim any thing from you on my behalf, pay him the same, to whatever amount,"—which declaration would be recognized and complied with, to the amount of one third of the estate; and the acknowledgment being thus equivalent to a bequest, the declaralon of Zeyd must be credited to the amount of one third of the acknowledger's estate, and no more. If, therefore, besides the acknowledgment in question, the dying person had made various bequests in favour of others, one third of his estate must be set apart for the legatees, and two thirds for the heirs, when both parties must be required "to verify the declaration of Zeyd to such extent as they may think proper." Now, if both parties acknowledge

* The arguments are here omitted, as (in this and some following instances) they turn on certain peculiarities in the grammar of the Arabic language.

that there is something owing to Zeyd, it is evident that there rests a debt upon the estate affecting the shares of each respectively; and accordingly, a deduction is made from the legatees, to the amount of one third of what they acknowledge to be owing to Zeyd, and from the heirs, to the amount of two thirds of what they have so acknowledged, in order tat the acknowledgment of each party may be carried into execution in proportion to his right in the whole estate. If Zeyd should claim still more than what falls to him in virtue of this acknowledgment of the parties, each party [the heirs and legatees] must be respectively required to make oath, to the best of their knowledge, or, in other words to this effect, that "they do not know of any more being due to Zeyd;"—for they cannot be required to swear positively, as their oath regards a matter between the claimant and the acknowledger merely, and in which they are not principals,

A joint bequest to an heir and a stranger is executed in favour of the latter only, to the extent of one half.—IF a person bequeath any article jointly to one of his heirs and a stranger, in this case the bequest in favour of the heir is not admitted, and a moiety only of the legacy is given to the stranger; because, as an heir possesses the capacity of being a legatee,* he therefore obstructs the stranger in the title which he would otherwise have to the complete legacy. It is not so where a legacy is left between one person living and another dead, for here the whole goes to the living legatee, since as a dead person is incapable of succeeding to a bequest, there is no obstruction in this instance.

And so likewise a joint bequest to the murderer of the testator and a stranger.—IF a person make a will jointly in favour of his murderer and a stranger, in that case the murderer is not entitled to any thing and the stranger receives only a moiety of the legacy, for the reason assigned in the foregoing case, to wit, that the murderer (like an heir) possesses the capacity of being a legatee, and therefore obstructs the stranger's title to the whole, as there stated, It is otherwise where a person, on his deathbed, makes a declaration of any specific thing or sum due by him to one of his heirs and a stranger jointly; for there the declaration is invalid as well with respect to the stranger as the heir. The reason of this distinction is, that a will or bequest is an indication of endowment; and as, by it, a joint concern is established between the two legatees, the bequest is therefore valid with respect to him, of the two, who is not under a legal incapacity, namely, the stranger;—whereas a declaration or acknowledgment is an annunciation of the right of the parties in whose favour it is made, referred to a past time, under the description of joint concern, a thing which cannot be established; for the establishment of it with respect to the stranger only, independent of the description of joint concern, is contrary to the tenor of the dying person's declaration; and the establishment of it (on the other hand) in the manner of joint concern, occasions the establishment of a declaralon in favour of an heir, upon a deathbed, which is unlawful.

Any accident occasinoing uncertainty with respect to the legatees annuls the will.—IF a person bequeath three garments of different prices, leaving the best to Zeyd, the next in value to Omar, and the worst to Bicker, and one of these garments be afterwards lost without its being known which of them it was, and the heirs of the testator declare, to each legatee in particular, that "his share is lost," the bequest is null in toto, as it is in this case uncertain who are the legatees, and such uncertainty occasions an annulment of the will, since the Kazee cannot pass a decree concerning a thing unknown. If, on the contrary, the heirs make over the two remaining garments to the legatees, the bequest is not null, but still continues in force, and those two garments are divided among them, by two thirds of the best being given to Zeyd, two thirds of the worst to Bicker, and the remaining third of each to Omar.

Bequest of an apartment in a partnership house.—If Zeyd bequeath to Omar a specific apartment of a house held in partnership between him and Bicker, it is requisite that a partition be made of the house; and then, if the apartment so bequeathed should fall within the share of Zeyd, it must be given to Omar as his legacy, according to the two Elders; whereas, according to Mohammed, he is entitled only to one half of it. If, on the other hand, the apartment so bequeathed should not fall within the share of Zeyd, then, according to the two Elders, a number of cubits equal to the size of the bequeathed apartment must be given to Omar from the share of Zeyd, whereas, according to Mohammed, he is entitled only to half that number. The argument of Mohammed is that in this case the testator has bequeathed partly his own property, and partly the property of another, inasmuch as the house was shared equally between him and Bicker in all its parts. The bequest, therefore, takes effect with respect to the former, but remains suspended with respect to the latter; and if, upon the partition (which is a species of exchange), the apartment fall within the share of Zeyd, still that part of the bequest which had remained suspended does not take effect, any more than where a person bequeaths to another some article which does

* The incapacity of an heir to succeed to a legacy does not arise from any natural or original defect in him, but is occasioned solely by the ordinance of the LAW in this particular, which suspends it upon the consent of his co-heirs.

not belong to him, and afterwards purchases that article. Where, moreover, upon a partition of the house, the apartment in question falls to the share of the testator, his bequest takes effect with respect to the actual legacy, namely, an half of the apartment; whereas if, on the contrary, it falls to the lot of Bicker, Amroo (the legatee) is to receive from the share of Zeyd, a number of yards equivalent to half the apartment; because, upon the actual legacy failing the bequest must be executed by means of the consideration received in exchange for it; in the same manner as where a person bequeaths a slave who is afterwards killed; in which case the legacy must be executed from the compensation received for his blood (contrary to where the slave is sold; for in this case the bequest has no connexion with the price received, but is completely annulled by the sale; whereas a bequest is not annulled by a partition, as that is also a species of separation of property).—The argument of the two Elders is, that the testator has certainly meant to bequeath an article in which his property may be firmly and solidly established by means of partition; for his apparent object is to bequeath an article which in every respect may be productive of use; and that can be accomplished only by partition, as the use of a thing of which the property is shared in common with another is defective.—Where, therefore, the apartment bequeathed, upon a partition being made, falls to the share of Zeyd, and his property in it is firmly established in toto, his bequest of it takes complete effect. With respect to what is urged by Mohammed, that "partition is a sort of exchange," it may be replied that the quality of exchange, in partition, is merely secondary, the original design of partition being, that each may enjoy the complete use of his own share (whence it is that the parties may be compelled to a partition of it); according to which original design the apartment may be said to have been in the possession of Zeyd from the beginning. Where, on the other hand, it falls to the share of Bicker, in that case the bequset of Zeyd takes effect from the share allotted to him, to the quantity of cubits of the whole apartment; because that quantity is the consideration for the apartment, as has been already stated:—or, because the bequest must be thus construed, that, the testator, by the apartment, merely meant a sum of measurement equivalent thereto, in order that his design may be answered as for as the nature of the case admits; *—or else, because the testator may have meant that the apartment should go to Omar, provided it fell to his share upon a partition, or otherwise a sum of measurement equivalent to it;—this case being analogous to that of a man suspending the freedom of a child born of his female slave, and the divorce of his wife, upon the circumstance of his female slave bearing the child (by saying, "upon my female slave being delivered of her first-born child, such child is free and my wife divorced"); which is construed to mean any child, to produce the divorce, and a living child to produce the emancipation.—‡ It is to be observed that where the apartment does not fall to the share of Zeyd, if the extent of the whole house be one hundred cubits, and that of the apartment ten, Mahommed in that case is of opinion that the share of Zeyd is to be divided into ten parts, of which nine must be given to the heirs, and one to Omar;—whereas the two Elders, hold that the share of Zeyd is to be divided into five parts, of which one must be given to Omar, and four to the testator's heirs. (With respect to what is mentioned in the Hedaya, that [according to the two Elders] "the share of the testator is divided into eleven parts, of which two are given to Omar and nine to the heirs," it is a mistake, for this mode of division obtains only in cases of declaration or acknowledgment.) It is here proper to remark that if a acknowledgment be made under the same circumstances as are here stated, as if Zeyd should declare an apartment of the extent of ten cubits, in a house of one hundred cubits, which he possessed in common with another to be the property of Omar, some say that in this case also a difference of opinion obtains between the two Elders and Mohammed; whilst others maintain that there is no difference of doctrine in this point, Mohammed also holding (in common with the two Elders) that in case the said apartment fall to the share of Zeyd, it goes complete to the acknowledgee [the person in whose favour the acknowledgment is made], or otherwise, that the share of the acknowledger is divided into eleven parts, of which two are given to the acknowledgee and nine to the acknowledger. The reason of this last adjustment is that the acknowledger here makes his

* An objection and reply are here stated, which the translator prefers inserting in a note, in order to avoid an interruption of the context.

"OBJECTION.—If such be the testator's meaning, why is the particular apartment given to Omar when it falls to the share of Zeyd?"

"REPLY.—The apartment in question is made the legacy, where it falls to the share of Zeyd, for this reason, that in thus settling the matter a regard is paid to the two chief distinguishing circumstances of the case, namely, the quantity or sum [of the thing bequeathed], and the investiture [of the legatee] with the actual apartment:- and as, where the apartment falls to the lot of Bicker, it is impossible to pay attention to both circumstances, it accordingly in that case suffices to pay attention to the first."

acknowledgment to this purpose; "the house which, exclusive of that apartment, measures ninety cubits, is the joint property of me and my partner,—of which forty-five appertain to me;" and the acknowledgee claims ten cubits from the fifty which fall to the share of the acknowledger. The fifty cubits therefore, which constitute a moiety of the house, are divided between the acknowledger and acknowledgee in this way, that the acknowledgee takes in the proportion of ten cubits, and the acknwledger in the proportion of forty-five, and accordingly that moiety of the house is disposed of in eleven shares. It is otherwise with respect to a bequest, as before stated; for there this mode of division cannot obtain, as the testator, in making bequest, cannot be supposed to have said "the house, except such an apartment, is in common between me and my partner," since if he were to speak thus his bequest would be null, as the bequest of another's property is not approved. Mohammed further remarks that the difference between a bequest and an acknowledgment is this, that an acknowledgment affecting the property of another is approved (insomuch that if a person were to declare that "such a thing, held by Zeyd, is the property of Amroo," and this person should at any time thereafter become proprietor of that thing, he is directed to deliver it up to Amroo), whereas a bequest of the property of another is utterly null and void, insomuch that if a person bequeath any thing belonging to another, and afterwards become proprietor of that thing, and die, still the bequest is of no effect.*

The validity of a bequest of money belonging to another rests upon the proprietor's consent.—IF a person bequeath a thousand dirms that belong to another, the execution of the bequest rests entirely on the consent of the proprietor, and it is optional in him to confirm it, or not, as he pleases. If he, therefore, after the death of the testator, give his consent, the bequest is valid, and the money paid to the legatee accordingly. This consent, however, is purely voluntary and gratuitous; whence if, after having signified it, the person refuse to pay the money, it is lawful.

An heir, after partition of the estate, acknowledging a bequest in favour of another must pay the acknowledged legatee his proportion of such bequest.—IF two sons make a partition of their father's estate, and one of them then declare that "his father had bequeathed a third of his property to Zeyd," he [the declarer] must in that case make over a third of his portion to Zeyd. This proceeds upon a favourable construction. Mohammed, on the contrary, maintains that the declarer is to make over an half of his portion to Zeyd (and such is what analogy would suggest) because when this son made the declaration that Zeyd was entitled to a third, he then in fact declared Zeyd to be entitled to as much as himself, whence it is requisite that he make over a moiety of his portion to him, in order that both may be placed on an equality. The reason, however, for a more favourable construction in this particuar is, that the son has here made a declaration, in favour of Zeyd, of one third, affecting the whole estate indefinitely; and as the whole estate has gone in two portions, each falling to each son respectively, it follows that the son has made his declaration in favour of Zeyd with respect only to a third of his own portion.

Bequest of a female slave who (previous to the partition of the estate) produces a child.—IF a person bequeath a particular female slave to Zeyd, and after his death the said slave bring forth a child, the legatee is in that case entitled to both the mother and child, provided, however, that their added value do not exceed a third of the estate, for then Zeyd is to receive the female slave, as far as a third of the estate, and if her value

---

* There being here a considerable deviation from the original text, and also some confusion in the subject (owing to the quantity of extraneous matter introduced by the Persian commentators, the translator thinks it his duty to give the whole passage literally; from‡ p. 682 to* p. 683, as stated in the Arabic copy.—" here the apartment falls to the other partner, not the testator, the house measuring one hundred cubits, and the apartment ten cubits, the testator's share is divided into ten lots, nine for the heirs, and one for the legatee.—This is according to Mohammed; for the suposes the legatee to multiply a moiety of the apartment by five (the number of cubits it measures), and the heirs the half of the remainder of the house by forty-five; and thus the whole will compose five lots [of ten cubits], which makes ten [lots of five cubits].—But according to the two [Elders] it is divided into eleven lots; because they suppose the legatee to multiply by ten, and the heirs by forty-five; and thus the whole composes eleven lots two for the legatee, and nine for the heirs;—If declaration [acknowledgment] be put in the place of bequest, it is said there is a difference of opinion:—but it is also said that there is no difference on the part of Mohammed,—the only difference, according to him, being that an acknowledgment affecting the property of another is valid,—insomuch that he who makes an acknowledgment concerning property possessed by another in favour of a different person, and afterwards obtains possession of the same, must be directed to give it up to the acknoledge;—whereas a bequest affectng the property of another is null; insomuch that if the testator should by any means afterwards became possessed of that property, and then die, still his bequest does not pass" [is of no effect].

be short of the third, the residue must be made up to him from the value of the child. This is according to Heneefa. The two disciples, on the contrary, maintain that in this case the legatee is to receive to the amount of a third of the property from both the mother and child, in proportion to their respective values. Thus if the value of the mother be three hundred dirms, that of the child the same, and the other effects amount to six hundred dirms, the whole forms an estate of one thousand two hundred dirms, of which a third is four hundred. Now Haneefa holds that in this case the female slave must be made over to the legatee in payment of three hundred dirms, and he also receives one hundred deducted from the value of the child ;– whereas the two disciples maintain that he is entitled to a deduction of two thirds from the value of each. The argument of the two disciples is, that the child is virtually included in the bequest, from its being (as it were) a dependent on the original subject of it, and that, therefore the bequest must be executed proportionally from both, without preference or distinction.– The argument of Haneefa is, that the mother is the original subject of the bequest, and the child only a dependent ; and the dependent cannot obstruct the original. If, moreover, the bequest were executed equally from both, it induces this consequence, that a part of the legacy is split off from the original subject, which is unlawful. All that is here advanced proceeds on a supposition of the birth of the child happening prior to the partition, and the acceptance of the legatee; for if it should take place afterwards, the child incontestibly belongs to him, as being the offspring of his property ; for his right in the slave was fully and completely established by the partition.

Section.

Of the Period of Making Wills.

Gratuitous acts, of immediate operation, if executed upon a death bed, take effect to the extent of one third of the peroperty only.– IT is to be observed, as a general rule, that where a person performs, with his property, any gratuitous deed, of immediate operation (that is, not restricted to his death), if he be in health at the time, such deed is valid to the extent of all his property,–or, if he be sick,* it takes effect to the extent of one third of his property ; and where a person performs such deed, with his property, restricted to the circumstance of his decease, it takes effect to the extent of a third of his property, whether, at the time, he be sick or in health. If, on the contrary, a person makes an acknowleagment of debt, such acknowldegment is of effect to the whole extent of his property, notwithstanding it be made during sickness, as this is not a gratuitous deed. Still, however, a declaration of this nature, made in health, precedes a declaration of the same nature made in sickness. It is also to be remarked, that a sickness of which a person afterwards recovers is considered, in LAW, as health.*

An acknowledgment on a death bed is valid in favour of a person who afterwards becomes an heir ; but not a bequest or gift.— IF a sick person make an acknowledgment of debt in favour of a strange woman, or make a bequest in her favour, or bestow a gift upon her, and afterwards marry her and then die, the acknowledgment is valid; but the bequest or gift is void ; for the nullity of an acknowledgment in favour of an heir depends on the person having been an heir at the time of making it, whereas the nullity of a bequest in favour of an heir depends on the legatee being so at the time of the testator's death, as has been already explained ; and as the woman was not an heir at the time of the acknowledgment, but had become so [by marriage] at the time of the testator's death, the acknowledgment is therefore valid, but the bequest is void ; and so likewise the gift, it being subject to the same rule as the bequest.

Neither is an acknowledgment so made valid, if the principle of inheritance had existed in the person previous to the deed.– IF a sick person make an acknowledgment of debt due by him to his son, or make a bequest in his favour or bestow a gift upon him, at a time when the son was a Christian, and he [the son] afterwards, previous to his father's death, become a Mussulman, all those deeds of acknowledgment, gift, or bequest, are void : the bequest and the gift, because of the son being an heir at the death of his father, as above explained ; and the acknowledgment, because, although the son, on account of the bar (namely difference of religion), was not an heir at the time of making it, still the cause of inheritance (namely consanguinity) did then exist, which throws an imputation on the father, as it engenders a suspicion that he may have made a false declaration, in order, to secure the descent of part of his fortune to his son. It is different in the case of marriage, as above stated ; far there the cause of inheritance (namely, marriage), occurred posterior to the acknowledgment, and had no existence prvious thereto ; for supposing the marriage to have existed at the period of making the acknowledgment, and that the wife, being then a Christian, should after-

* Arab. Mareez.– This term (as has been already observed) literally means sick. In the language of the LAW, however, it is always used to signify a dying person,– that is, "sick of a mortal illness ;" and in that sense it is invariably to be understood throughout this book.

* This passage has no place in the Arabic copy It has been introduced in the Persian version as a premiss necessary to the completely understandng of what follows

wards. before the husband's death, become a Mussulman, in that case it (the acknowledgment) would not be valid.

Such acknowledgment, gift or bequest, in favour of a son, being a slave, who afterwards becomes free previous to the father's decease, is nevertheless void.—IF a sick person make an acknowledgment of debt due by him to his son, who is an absolute slave or Mokatib,—or bestows gift upon him, or make a bequest in his favour, and the son should afterwards, before the death of his father, obtain his liberty, in that case none of these deeds are valid, because of the reasons explained in the preceding example. It is related, in the Mabsoot, under the head of Acknowledgments, that "the acknowledgment of a sick person in favour of his son who is a slave is valid, provided the slave be not in debt; for in that case the acknowledgment is, in effect, in favour of the master, who is a stranger; and an acknowledgment in favour of a stranger is valid;—whereas, if the slave were involved in debt, his father's acknowledgment in his favour would not be valid, as in such case it could not be construed to be in favour of the master, since an indebted slave is the proprietor of his own acquisitions."—The bequest is, however, invalid, because to establish it regard must be paid to the time of the testator's death, and the son is at that time an heir, as being then free. With respect, indeed, to the gift, it is said to be valid,* provided the slave be not indebted; because a gift is an immediate transfer and investiture; and as the son is at that period a slave, the gift is in effect in favour of the master, but if he be involved in debt the gift is invalid, as in that case he is master of his own acquisitions, and a gift is considered as such. According to the more commonly received authorities, however, the gift is void on either supposition; for as a gift during a mortal illness is equivalent to a bequest, it is therefore invalid, in the same manner as a bequest would be which was made in favour of the same person.

Rule for ascertaining a deathbed illness.—PARALYTIC, gouty, or consumptive persons, where their disorder has continued for a length of time, and they are in no immediate danger of death, do not fall under the description of sick [Mareez], whence deeds of gift, executed by such, take effect to the extent of their whole property; because, when a long time has elapsed, the patient has become familiarized to his disease, which is not then accounted as sickness. (The length of time requisite, by its lapse, to do away the idea of sickness in those cases is determined at one year; and if after that time the invalid should become bedridden, he is then accounted as one recently sick.) If, therefore, any of the sick persons thus described make a gift in the beginning of their illness, or after they are bedridden, such gift takes effect from the third of their property, because at such a time there is apprehension of death (whence medicine is then administered to them), and therefore the disorder is then considered as a deathbed illness.

* Probably meaning "in the Mabsoot."

CHAPTER III.

OF EMANCIPATION UPON A DEATHBED; AND OF WILLS RELATIVE TO EMANCIPATION.

Emancipation, gift, and acts of Mohabat, on a deathbed, take effect to the extent of a third of the property.—IF a person, on his deathbed, emancipate a slave, or give a portion of his property to another, or make a Mohabat,* in purchase or sale, by buying an article at an over-value, or selling it at an under-value,—or concerning the dower, hire, or so forth,—or become security for another all these deeds are considered in the light of a bequest, and take effect to the extent of a third of his estate

Case of a Mohabat, and an emancipation by the same person—IF a sick [dying] person make a Mohabat [of any kind], † and then emancipate his slave, and [after his death] the third of his prperty suffice not for both, in that case Haneefa is of opinion that the Mohabat has the preference;—in other words, if, after executing the Mohabat, any part of the third remain, the slave is, without recompense, free in that proportion, and must perform emancipatory labour for the remainder of his value,—or for his full value, if nothing remain.—If, on the contrary, the person first emancipate the slave, and then make the Mohabat, the slave, and the person in whose favour the Mohabat is made, are upon a perfect equality, and each takes from the third of the estate in proportion to his right:—as, for instance,

*Mohabat literally signifies connivance.—Thus, a purchaser or seller who gives more, or takes less, for an article than its real value, connives at the loss.—This term, therefore, is not confined to sale, but extends to every act in which the person connives at his own loss, such as (in the case of dower) paying the wife more than she is entitled to, or (in a case of hire) paying the hireling more than he had agreed for.—The translator preserves the original term, as it is purely technical.—The Arabic text expresses this passage with great brevity:'Whoso frees his slave in sickness, or sells, or connives, or gives, it is lawful, and recognized to the extent of a third of his property.''

† That is, "execute any contract, or perform any act, by which he sustains a wilful loss."

the slave is emancipated from the third of the estate in the proportion of his value, and performs emancipatory labour for the remainder,—and the person in whose favour the Mohabat is made takes in the proportion of his Mohabat, and makes good the remainder.—The two disciples maintain that the emancipation has the preference in both cases, for it is the stronger, inasmuch as it does not admit of retractation. Haneefa on the contrary, maintains that Mohabat is the stronger, as being interwoven in a compact of exchange: contrary to emancipation, for in that there is no exchange. If, therefore, the Mohabat be first made, it sets aside the emancipation, because of the comparative weakness thereof;—whereas, if the emancipation be first made, it obstructs the Mohabat, because of its priority, but still does not set it aside, as emancipation is incapable of setting aside a Mohabat;—whence, in this instance, both are placed upon a footing. According, therefore, to this difference of opinion, if a person be possessed of two slaves, one valued at two hundred dirms, and the other at one hundred, and first sell the former by a Mohabat sale, for one hundred dirms, and afterwards emancipate the latter and die, leaving no other property, in that case, according to Haneefa, the Mohabat is executed in full, and the other slave is required to perform emancipatory labour to the full amount of his value;—whereas if, on the contrary, the emancipation precede the Mohabat, then a third of the value of both slaves, amounting to one hundred dirms, is divided equally between both parties (that is, between the emancipated slave and the person in whose favour the Mohabat was made); and accordingly, a moiety of the slave is emancipated without any consideration, and he is to perform emancipatory labour for fifty dirms more, being the remaining half of his value;—and fifty dirms are deducted, in the manner of a Mohabat, from the slave sold by Mohabat, and his price is then one hundred and fifty dirms, for which the purchaser is accountable:—but the two disciples maintain that the slave is completely free in both instances. In the same manner, if a person, upon his deathbed, first sell a slave by Mohabat, then emancipate a second, and afterwards sell a third by Mohabat, and have no other property besides these three slaves, in that case, according to Haneefa, the half of the third of the property must be allowed to the person in whose favour the Mohabat was first made, and the remaining half of the third is equally divided between the emancipated slave and the one in whose favour the last Mohabat was made;—whereas, had he first emancipated one, then sold the second by Mohabat, and afterwards emancipated the third, in that case one third of the estate would be divided into two equal shares, of which one would be given to the person, in whose favour the Mohabat sale was made, and the other equally divided between the two emancipated slaves:—but the two disciples maintain that in both cases the emancipation is to be perferred.

Mohabat or emancipation precede, in their execution, the actual bequests.—It is to be observed, as a standing rule,* that where a person bequeaths several legacies, and the third of his property suffices for the payment of the whole, they are all carried into execution without a preference being given to either. But if, besides these legacies, he should in his last illness emancipate a slave, or direct the emancipation to take place after his death, or sell something by Mohabat,—in that case both kinds of emancipation, as well as the Mohabat, are preferred to the legacies, and must therefore be first executed from the third of the estate, and the remainder (if there be any) is then divided equally among the legatees.

The appropriation of a sum, by bequest, to the emancipation of a slave is annulled by the subsequent loss or failure of any part of it; but not the appropriation of a sum to the performance of a pilgrimage.—If a person, on his deathbed, set aside one hundred dirms, and will that "after his death the said sum be applied to the emancipation of a slave," and one dirm of the number happen to be lost, in that case Haneefa maintains that the will is annulled, and that the remaining ninety-nine dirms cannot be applied to the purpose of emancipating a slave If, on the contrary, the person will that "the said sum be appropriated to defray the expense of a pilgrimage to Mecca," in that case the loss or destruction of one dirm does not invalidate the will, but the remaining ninety-nine dirms are applied to the purpose prescribed by the testator, by deputing a person from such a distance as may enable him to reach Mecca by means of the said sum (If also, in this last case, part of the sum have been lost or destroyed, and there remain a part after the return of the pilgrim, it must be restored to the heirs.) The two disciples maintain that the will is valid in the former instance likewise, and the ninety-nine dirms applied to the emancipation of a slave, in the same manner as (in the other instance to the performance of the pilgrimage,. The argument of Haneefa, is that, in the former instance, the will direct the emancipation of a slave valued at one hundred dirms; and therefore, if it were executed with ninety-nine dirms, it would take effect in favour of a person different from the intended legatee, which is not lawful. It is otherwise with a bequest concerning pilgrimage, as pilgrimage is purely a religious duty, and religious duties appertain exclusively to GOD; and as GOD therefore is the legatee in this instance, a diminution of the sum does not induce an execution of the will in favour of any other than the legatee, since a pilgrimage for

* Arab. Asl; literally, a root; meaning (in this place) a principle or ground of decision in all parallel cases,

ninety-nine dirms is performed on behalf of God, as much as a pilgrimage for one hundred dirms. Some have observed that this difference of opinion between Haneefa and the two disciples is founded on the different sentiments they entertain with respect to the emancipation of a slave; the two disciples holding it to be a religious act, in the same manner as the performance of a pilgrimage; and Haneefa considering it as an act in favour of the slave alone. (The compiler of the Hedaya remarks that this last opinion is approved.)

A slave exceeding a third of the property, emancipated on a deathbed, is exempted from emancipatory labour by the heirs assenting to his freedom.—If a person during his last illness emancipate a slave valued at one hundred dirms, and die, leaving two sons and one hundred dirms, and the emancipated slave and his heirs give their consent to the emancipation, the slave is not required to perform any emancipatory service whatever, but is free without so doing; for although the manumission was equivalent to a bequest in the proportion beyond a third of the emancipator's property, yet it is valid on the heirs assenting to it.

A bequest of emancipation, in favour of a slave, is annulled by his being made over in compensation for an offence committed by him.—If a person will that "his heirs emancipate his slave at his decease." and the slave, after the death of the testator, commit an offence, and the heir surrender him, as a compensation, to the avenger of offence, the will is void; because the surrender of him in compensation for the offence is approved; for as the right of the testator must yield to that of the avenger of offence, the right of the legatee must consequently yield to it likewise, since a legatee obtains his right in the legacy from the testator;—and as, upon the slave being surrendered in compensation for the offence, he passes out of the property of the testator, the will is void of course. If, on the contrary, the heirs prefer paying a redemptionary atonement; the will remains valid, and does not become void (but in this case the redemptionary atonement falls entirely upon their property, as they have themelves undertaken the payment of it); and as the slave, by the payment of the redemption, is purified from the offence, the case is therefore the same as if he had not offended it all, and the will takes effect of course.

Where the heir and the lagatee agree concerning a slave having been emancipated by the testator, the allegation of the heir is credited with respect to the date of the deed.—If a person bequeath to another a third of his property," and leave, among his other effects, a slave, and the legatee and heirs agree that the testator had emancipated the slave, but differ with respect to the time of such emancipation (the legatee asserting that it was during his health, and the heirs, on the other hand, maintaining that it was during his sickness), in that case the word of the heirs must be credited, and the legatee is entitled only to what remains after the value of the slave is deducted from the third of the testator's whole property;* because the legatee here pleades his title to a third of what remains after the emancipation of the slave, since manumission granted during health does not stand as a bequest (whence it is that it takes effect from the whole of the property), and the heirs resist his plea, asserting that the testator had emancipated the slave during sickness; and as manumission during sickness is a species of bequest, and takes place of a bequest of a third of the property, the heirs are therefore negators; and as the assertion of a negator [the defendant], upon oath, must be credited, the legatee is therefore entitled to nothing whatever;—unless there should remain some excess in the third of the property over and above the value of the slave, in which case the legatee is entitled to such excess; or, unless the legatee confirm his assertion by evidences, in which case he is entitled to a third of what remains of the whole estate after the emancipation of the slave.

Case of an alleged emancipation and debt, credited by the heirs.—If a person die,, leaving no other property except one slave and the slave say so the heirs "your father whilst he was in health, emancipated me," and another person say to them "your father was indebted to me one hundred dirms," and the heirs credit both these assertions, (as, for instance, by replying to them together, "you both speak truly"), the slave is, in that case, required to perform emancipatory labour to the full extent of his value, according to Haneefa. The two disciples, on the contrary, maintain that the slave is emancipated without performing any service whatever, because the proof of the debt and of the emancipation during health are established, jointly, as the heirs have acknowledged both at the same time, and the emancipation of a slave during health does not induce the necessity of labour notwithstanding the emancipator should be involved in debt. The argument of Haneefa is, that the acknowledgment of the debt on the part of the heirs is stronger than that of the emancipation; because the former is valid at whatever period it may have been contracted, and is dischargable from the whole estate; whereas the latter, if performed during sickness, is limited to a third of the estate; and such being the case, it would follow that the emancipation is utterly annulled. As, however, emacipaton, after having been made, does not admit of being absolutely annulled, it is therefore virtually annulled, in this instance, by the

* Literally, "is entitled to nothing whatever." The translator renders the passage in a modified sense, because of the reservation afterwards stated.

imposition of emancipatory labour,—The same difference of opinion subsists in the case where a person, dying, leaves one thousand dirms, and one person asserts that the decease owed him one thousand dirms, and another, that he had deposited one thousand dirms in trust with the deceased, and the heirs confirm both assertions at one and the same time; for in such case the two disciples are of opinion that both claims are upon an equal footing, and the one thousand dirms are therefore to be divided equally between the parties; whereas Haneefa maintains that the claim of the depositor is the strongest, as his right relates to the identical dirms whilst the creditor has only a general claim on the person.

Section.

*Of Bequests for Pious Purposes.**

In the execution of bequestse to sundry pious purposes, the ordained duties precede the voluntary.—IF a person make several bequests for the performance of sundry religious duties, such as pilgrimage, payers, and so forth, it is requisite to execute first such as are absolutely incumbent and ordained;† and this, whether the testator have mentioned them first or not; for the discharge of the ordained duties is of more importance than that of acts which are merely voluntary; and the law therefore supposes that the object of the testator was to begin with the performance of them.

Unless all the purposes mentioned be of equal importance, in which case the arrangement of the testator must be followed.—BUT if the several duties, the objects of the will, be all of the same importance, and of similar force, and the third of the estate suffice not for the discharge of the whole, they must in that case be executed agreeably to the order in which they have been specified by the testator, as it may be inferred that those to which he gave the precedence were, in his opinion, the most urgent. Tahavee maintains that alms are to be executed before pilgrimage. There is also one report from Aboo Yoosaf to the same effect. Another opinion reported from him is, that pilgrimage precedes alms; and such is the opinion of Mohammed. The argument in favour of the first report is, that both are in an equally strong degree enjoined by GOD: but yet alms, as being connected with the rights of mankind, must be preferred, the right of the individual preceding the right of GOD.—The argument in support of the second report is, that the performance of pilgrimage, besides the expenditure of money, requires also an exertion of the body; and as this is not the case with alms, pilgrimage has therefore precedence. Either of those, however, is preferable to expiation, because they have been in a greater number of instances, and in a stronger degree enjoined by GOD.—Again: expiations for murder, for Zihar, and for a broken vow, are preferable to Sadka-fittir [charity given on the day of breaking fast]. because these expiations have been enjoined in the KORAN, whereas the latter has not. Sadka-fittir, on the other hand, is preferable to sacrifice, because it is an incumbent duty in the opinion of all our doctors, whereas a difference of opinion subsists with respect to the absolute obligation of sacrifice.

As well as where the purposes of the bequests are purely of a voluntary nature.—IN the execution of all pious wills, where the objects of them are not incumbent duties (such as the erection of a mosque of a receptacle for travellers, or of a bridge), it is requisite to follow the arrangement of the testator, since it may be inferred that he considered those first mentioned as the most urgent. Lawyers, moreover, have remarked that if a person make several bequests, some for the performance of religious duties immediately enjoined by GOD, and others for benovolent purposes amongst mankind, in that case a third of his property must be set aside for the execution of them; and whatever may be the share appropriated for the performance of the duties belonging to GOD, it must be applied agreeably to the order of arrangement, as already explained —It is to be observed, also, that every different duty is to be considered in the nature of a distinct legacy; for, the object of each being the attainment of the goodwill of the ALMIGHTY, every several duty has an object in itself, and each is therefore to be considered in the nature of a legacy left to a different person.

Rules in bequests towards the performance of a pilgrimage.—IF a person will that "the pilgrimage incumbent on him be performed on his behalf after his death," in that case the heirs must depute a person for this purpose from the city of the testator, and furnish him with such conveyances and equipments as are suitable to his [the testator's] rank; because, being performed on his account, it must be executed in the same manner as it actually performed by himself. But if the property of the testator be inadequate to the expense of sending a person from his own city, in that case a person must be sent from some other nearer place, the distance of which from Mecca may be proportioned to the amount of the property.

IF a person set out from his own city, with an intention of performing the pilgrimage to Mecca, and die on the road, after having willed that the pilgrimage be prformed [by others] on his behalf, a person must be deputed for this purpose from the city of the

* Literally, "of bequests to the rights of GOD."

† Arab. Farz: a term applied to any thing enjoined as an indispensable duty, and more particularly to the five primary duties; purification, prayer, alms, fasting, and pilgrimage.

testator, according to Haneefa (and such also is the opinion of Ziffer). The two disciples, on the contrary, maintain that a person is to be sent from the place at which the testator had arrived in the prosecution of his intention;—and the same difference of opinion obtains where a person, having undertaken the pilgrimage on account of another, dies in the like manner on the road. The reasoning of the two disciples is, that the performance of a part of the jounrey, with the intention of having prosecuted the remainder, is in itself an act of piety, which is entitled to merit with GOD, and which annuls, in a proportionate degree, the obligation of the duty. Hence the pilgrimage is to be recommenced from the place in which he died, and which in effect has become (as it were) his city. It is otherwise where a person, with a view of trading, sets out on a journey to Mecca, and does on the way, after having willed that the pilgrimage be performed on his behalf; for in this case the part of the journey already performed not being an act of piety, there is as evident necessity for sending person from the city of the testator.—The reasoning of Haneefa is, that the will must be construed as meaning a commencement from the city of the testator, in order that the pilgrimage may be completely performed in the manner in which it was originally incumbent on the testator.

CHAPTER IV.

OF WILLS IN FAVOUR OF KINSMEN AND OTHER CONNEXIONS.

A bequest to "a neighbour" is in favour of the owner of the next adjoining house.—IF a person make a bequest in favour of "his neighbour,"* this according to Haneefa, is a bequest to the person whose house is immediately adjoining to that of the testator. The two disciples, on the contrary, maintain that it comprehends all the inhabitants of the vicinity, who belong to the same mosque-without any regard to the immediate adjunction of the houses; since, according to the common acceptation of the word, they all fall equally under the description of neighbours. The arguments adduced by Haneefa in support of his opinion upon this point are two fold. FIRST, the person whose house adjoins to that of the testator is in reality the neighbour. —SECONDLY, the modes and descriptions of neighbourhood are many; and as it would be impracticable to carry the will into execution with respect to the whole, it is therefore necessary to restrict it to him whose title, from the circumstance of adjunction, is the most perfect and indisputable.

And comprehends all competent descriptions of persons.—IT is to be observed that the learned in the law are of opinion that every person may be included under this description of neighbour, whether the proprietor of a house or not, or, whether a man or a woman, a Mussulaman or a Zimmee, the term neighbour being equally applicable to all these. Haneefa also holds that an absolute slave, possessed of a house in the neighbourhood, is entitled to the benefit of the will.—The two disciples hold a different opinion; because, in such case, the benefit of the will would ultimately revert to the master of the slave, who is not supposed to be a neighbour. The argument of Haneefa, is that the term neighbour applies indiscriminately to all.

Rules in bequests to "the As'har" of the testator.—IF a person make a bequest in favour of "his As'har," * all the relations of his wife within the prohibited degrees (such as her father, brother, and so forth) are therein inculded; and likewise all the relations of his father's wife [his step mother] and of his son's wife [his daughter-in-law] within the prohibited degrees, as these all stand in the relation of As'har to the testator. This explanation of As'har has been followed by Mohammed and Aboo Obeydah. It is to be observed that all the kindred of the wife within the prohibited degrees are included in the bequest, notwithstanding she were, at the time of the death of the testator, in her edit from a reversible divorce. But if the divorce was irreversible, her relations are not to be included, as the existence of that degree of relation entitled As'har depends on the actual existence of the marriage at the time of the testator's death; and by an irreversible divorce marriage is utterly annulled.

And to his Khatn.—IF a man make a bequest in favour of "his Khatn," it is a bequest to the husbands of his female relations within the prohibited degrees; and in it are likewise included all the relations of these husbands within the prohibited degrees, these also falling under the description of Khatn.—(Some commentators remark, that this explanation is agreable to the ancient custom; but that in the present times Khatn comprehends only the husbands, as above.)—It is also to be observed that in this respect freemen and slaves, and the near and the distant relations are all upon a footing, because the terms Khatn comprehends the whole of these.

* Specifying the legatee by description only, without mentioning his name; as thus, "I bequeath one thousand DIRMS to MY NEIGHBOUR,"—In this and the succeeding examples, the effect turns entirely on the terms in which the testator signifies his bequest.

* As'har is the plurl of Sheral (pronounced, in Arabia, Dehr), which is a general term for all relations by marriage

And to his Akraba.—If a person make a will in favour of his "relations" [Akraba*], it is executed in favour of the nearest of kin within the prohibited degrees, and failing of them, in favour of the next in proximity, and so on with respect to the rest within the prohibited degrees, in regular succession. The will, in this case, includes two or more; but the father, mother, or children of the testator are not comprehended in it. This is the opinion of Haneefa. According to the two disciples, the will includes only such as are descended from the most distant progenitor of the testator, professing the Mussulman faith.—(Concerning the meaning of "the most distant progenitor professing the faith." there is a difference of opinion; some maintaining that this applies to the remotest ancestor who actually embraced the faith and others alleging that it extends to the remotest ancestor who may have known of the existence of the faith, although he himself may not have acceded to it; as is exemplified in the case of Aboo Talib, who although he understood the Mussulman faith, never embraced it.) The argument of the two disciples is, that the term relations being in general applied all of the same blood, the will therefore extends to all such as fall under this description, to whatever d. gree removed. The arguments of Haneefa are that legacies are a species of inheritance; and as, in inheritnce, the arangement here described is observed with respect to the heirs, it is also observed in the payment of legacies.—As, moreover, the plural term [Akraba] mentioned in inheritance means two, so likewise in bequest.†—Besides, the object of the testator, in his bequest, is, to compensate for his deficiencies, during life, with respect to the ties of kindred, ‡ which affects only his relations within the prohibited degrees. The parents or children, moreover, are not styled relations [Akraba], insomuch that if a person were to call his father "his RELATION" [Kareeb], he would be considered as denying his parentage. The reason of this is that, in common usage, by the term relation [Kareeb] is understood one related to a person by means of another: but the relation of parent and child is personal, and not by means of another.—In short, according to Haneefa, the will in question is restricted, in its operation, to the prohibited relations of the testator; whereas, according to the two disciples, it extends to [all the descendants of] the most ditant prgenitor professing the faith:—whilst Shafei maintains that it is confined solely to the testator's father [and his off spring].

If a person, having two parternal and two maternal uncles, make a will in favour of "his relations" [Akraba], it is in favour of the paternal unless only, accordingly to Haneefa, he holding that regard is to be paid to the order of relationship;—whereas, according to the two disciples, all the four uncles are included, they holding that no regard is to be paid to the order of relationship If, on the other hand, the testator have only one paternal and two maternal uncles, the half of the legacy, in that case, goes to the paternal uncle, and the other half to the two maternal uncles, out of attention to the plural number, which, in bequests, comprehends two (as before observed); for as, if there were two paternal uncles, the whole legacy would go to them, it follows that where there is one only, he gets no more than an half, and the other half goes to the two maternal uncles, It would be otherwise if the person had expressed his bequest for "his kinsman;" *for in this case the whole legacy would go to the paternal uncle, and nothing whatever to the two maternal uncles; because, as the term kinsman expresses a singular, not a plural number, the paternal uncle therefore takes the whole, he being next of kin.—If (in the case of a bequest to "relations") the testator have a paternal uncle only [and no maternal uncles], he is entitled to no more than a moiety of the third of the estate; for as, if there had been two paternal uncles, they would have had the whole between them, one consequently gets only an half.—If, on the contrary, he have a paternal uncle and aunt, and a maternal uncle and aunt, the legacy goes in equal shares between the paternal uncle and aunt, both being related to the testator within an equal degree of affinity —and their connexion being of a stronger nature than that of the maternal uncle or aunt.—A parternal aunt, moreover, although she be not entitled to inherit, is nevertheless capable of succeeding to a legacy,—in the same manner as holds with respect to a relation who is a slave or an infidel.—It is to be observed that, in all these cases, if the testator have no prohibited relation, the bequest is null, because it is restricted, in its operation, to these within the prohibited degrees, as before noticed.

Or to the Ahl of a particular person.—If a person make a bequest "to the Ahl† of such as one." it is a bequest to the wife of the person mentioned, according to Haneefa

* Akraba is the plural of Kareeb, and signifies (collectively) kindred.

† Here is something like a contradiction; for it was before said that "the will includes two or more." This, however, is not to be taken as excluding any number above two, but merely as comprehending the dual as well as any higher number.

‡ Arab. Silla Rihm.—It is a technical term, comprehending, in its application, the kindred within the prohibited degrees only

* Arab. Zee-Kirrabit.

† The word Ahl, in its most common acceptation, denotes a people or family, as Ahl Iran, "the people of Persia."—Ahlnee, "my family."—(This and several succeeding examples turn entirely upon the meaning of the terms used by the testator.)

The two disciples, on the contrary, maintain that the bequest comprehends every individual of the family, entitled to maintenance from that person, such being (with them) the common import of the word. The argument of Haneefa is that Ahl, in its literal sense, signifies a wife, a proof of which is drawn from this sentence of the KORAN. "MOSES WALKED WITH HIS Ahl" [wife], (whence also the common mode of expression "such a person made taahul [married] in a particular city ");—and as the word Ahl, in its literal sense, means a wife, it follows that whenever it is used absolutely it must be resolved into its literal sense, which is the true one.

(Or of the house of particular person.)—IF a person make a bequest " to the Ahl of the house of such an one." the father and grandfather of the person named are included in such bequest, as well as all the descendants from the remotest progenitor, on the paternal side, professing the Mussulman faith;—and if a person make a bequest "to the Arl of such an one." it is a bequest " to the Al of his house," the term Al applying to the tribe from which he is descended.

IF a person make a bequest. "to the Ahl of such a person's Nish [race] or Jins" [generation],—by the former is understood all those descended from his ancestors in general,—but by the latter these only descended from the paternal stock, not from the maternal, because men are said to be of the generation of their fathers, not of their mothers.—It is otherwise where the term Kirrabit (affinity) is used; for that appertains both to father and mother.

Or to the orphans, blind, lame, or widows, of a particular race.—IF a person make a bequest "to the orphans,—the blind,—the lame,—or the widows,—of the race* of such an one,"– and the individuals of the race name can be enumerated, the bequest includes them all indiscriminately, whether rich or poor, males or females; for the execution of the bequest is practicable in the instance, because of the ascertainment of the legatees.-- (It is to be observed that, concerning the exposition of the expression "if they can be enumerated,' here is a difference of opinion; for, according to Aboo Yoosaf, this phrase comprehends" as many as can be counted without the aid of written calculations" whereas Mohammed holds that it extends no farther than to one hundred, any greater number being considered as beyond enumeraton. Some, on the other hand, allege that the determination of this point rests entirely with the Kazee, and decrees pass accordingly).—But if the individuals of the race named be incapable of enumeration, the poor only are in that case included in the bequest, not the rich; for it [the bequest] is of a pious nature, and the object of it (namely, by removing the wants of best attainable by removing the wants of the poor, Besides, as the very descriptions used indicate a degree of want and distress in the legatee, it is therefore proper to admit this to have been the testator's meaning. It is otherwise where a person makes a bequest "to the youths (or the virgins) of a particular race," who are innumerable; for in such case the bequest is void; because, as the description used does not indicate want the words of the testator cannot be construed to apply to the poor: neither can the bequest possiby hold valid in favour of all the individuals of the class named, since, as they are not to be enumerated, it is impracticable to define them, and a bequest to unknown legatees is null,—for bequest is an act of endowment, and it is impossible to endow persons unknown. It is to be observed that, in the case of bequests "to the poor or distressed," the legacy must be paid to at least two paupers, two being the smallest number of plurality in bequest, as was before stated.

Or to the race of a particular person.—IF a person make a bequest "to the race of such on one," in that case, according to the two disciples, and also according to the first opinion of Haneefa, the women of the said race are included, the plural term Binnee extending to females as well as males. Haneefa, however, afterwards retracted this opinion, and maintained the males of the race only to be included, not the females; because the term Binnee applies to men literally, but to women only metaphorically; and a word must be taken in its literal not its figurative acceptation. It is otherwise where ' the race of such a person " is the proper name of any particular tribe; for in that case the bequest includes the women also, as the term Binnee, in such instance, comprehends the females of the tribe along with the males,—in the same manner as the general expression Benni.—Adim [the sons of Adam)] —whence the bequest includes the freedment, the sworn confederates [Haleefs], the slaves, and the Mawalat confederates of the tribe named.

Or to the awlad of a particular race.—IF a person make a bequest "to the children [awlad] of the race of such an one,"—the males and females have an equal right in such bequest, as the term awlad comprehends the whole

A bequest to the heirs of a particular person is executed agreeably to the laws of inheritance.—If a person make a bequest " to the heirs of such on one," the legacy is in that case divided among the heirs of the person named, in the manner of an inheritance, a male getting as much as two females; because there is reason to imagine that the object of the testator, in using the word heirs, was that the same distinction might be observed in the partition of he legacies as obtains in the case of inheritance.

* Arab. Binnee: It is an irregular plural from Ibn, "a son," and expresses a generation or tribe.

Case of a bequest to "the Mawlas" of the testator.—If a person make a bequest "to his Mawlas,"* and he have some Mawalas who had emancipated him, and others whom he had emancipated, the bequest is void; because the term Mawla partakes of two different meanings, an emancipator, and a freedman, and it cannot be discovered which of these the testator intended. Neither can the intention be construed to comprehend both; because a word bearing a double meaning cannot be used in more than one of its senses at a time; and as it is unknown which sense the testator meant it in, the legatee is therefore uncertain; and any uncertainty concerning the legatee annuls the bequest. (In several of the books of Shafei it is recorded that the bequest is construed in favour of all the Mawlas, both the emancipators and the emancipated, as the term used applies to both.) It is to be observed that where the term Mawla is mentioned, in bequest, it comprehends every one whom the testator may have actually emancipated, whether in health or in sickness; but not his Modabbirs or Am-Walids, as their emancipation does not take place until after his death, and his bequest is in favour of such only as are free previous to that event. Aboo Yoosaf maintains that a Modabbir or Am-Walid is also included, because, although these be not free previous to the testator's decease, still as a cause of freedom has taken place, and is established in them, they may be said to have been emancipated—In this bequest is also included any slave of the tetstator to whom he may have said, "you are free if I beat you not before my death" (provided he did not afterwards beat him); becasue the slave is in this case free before the testator's decease, and from the time that his strength and power of beating failed him. If the testator have Mawlas whom he had emancipated, and also the children of those Mawlas, and likewise Mawlas by Mawalat,† his freedmen Mawlas and their children are included in the bequest, but not his Mawlas by Mawalat. It is recorded from Aboo Yoosaf, that those last are likewise included, and that all those there description equally participate in the bequest, as the term Mawala comprehends the whole. Mohammed argues that Mawla is a term which partakes of two different meanings; but a word of double meaning cannot be used in more than one sense at a time; and as emancipation is an absolute and unretractable act, and a contract of Mawalat may be rescinded at pleasure, a Mawla by manumission has precedence of a Mawala by Mawlat, and those are consequently included in preference. But the Mawlas of the testator's Mawlas* are not included in the bequest, which relates only to the Mawlas of the testator, not to those of another. It is otherwise with the children of the testator's Mawlas; for they stand related to the testator because of their freedom proceeding from him. It is also otherwise where the testator has no Mawlas by manumission, nor children of those Mawlas: for in that case the Mawlas by Mawalat are included in the bequest, as the term Mawla applies to those by manumission, literally, and to those by Mawalat, metaphorically; and where the literal sense cannot be followed, the figurative sense may be adopted.

If, in the above case, the testator have only one freedman and several freedmen of his freedman, the half of the legacy goes to the freedman, and the remaining half reverts to the testator's heirs: and there is nothing whatever for the freedmen of his freedman; for the term Mawla applies literally to the freedmen of the testator, and figurativey to the freedmen of those freedmen; and it is impossible that the word should be meant in two senses, as it cannot bear, at once, a literal and a figurative meaning. Neither are the freedmen of the testator's parents or children included, they not being his freedmen either actually or virtually.

* Mawla is a term applying either to the patron or the client (see Willa); and expresses the relation between the emancipated and his emancipator.

† See Vol. III, pp. 513 and 517.

* That is, "the freedmen of his freedmen," or "the emancipators of his emancipators."

CHAPTER V.

OF USUFRUCTUARY WILLS.

An article bequeathed in usufruct.—If a person bequeath the service of his slave, or the use of his house, either for a definite or an indefinite period, such bequest is valid; because as an endowment with usufruct, either gratuitous or for an equivalent, is valid during life, it is consequently so after death; and also, because men have occasion to make bequests of this nature as well as bequests of actual property. So likewise, if a person bequeath the wages of his slave, or the rent of his house, for a definite or indefinite term, it is valid, for the same reason.

Must be consigned to the legatee.—In both cases, moreover, it is necessary to consign over the house or the slave to the legatee provided they do not exceed the third of the property, in order that he may enjoy the wages or service of the slave, or the rent or use of the house during the term prescribed, and afterwards restore it to the heirs

But if it constitute the sole estate, being a slave, he is possessed by the heirs and legatee alternately, or being a house, it is held among them, in their due proportions.—If the whole property of the testator consist of the slave or the house in that case the slave is to be possessed one day, by the legatee, and two by the heirs, alternately; but the house, on the contrary, is to be portioned into three equal parts, of which one is given to the legatee, and two to the heirs,—the legatee being entitled to one third,—the estate, and the heirs to two thirds. The reason of the distinction here made between a house and a slave is, that a slave is incapable of being divided, and therefore an alternate use of him is established from necessity; whereas a house, on the contrary, is capable of division; and as division is the most fair and equitable mode (since retaliation necessarily induces a preference of one over the other in point of time), it ought to be adopted where it is practicable. Still, however, if the parties agree to enjoy the house by turns, it is lawful, as the right rests entirely with them:—but division is the most equitable mode.

Nor are the heirs (in the latter instance) allowed to sell their share.—IT is not in this case lawful for the heirs to sell the two thirds of the house which are allotted to them. This is according to the Zahir Rawayet. It is recorded from Aboo Yoosaf that such sale is lawful, because these shares are purely their own property. The ground on which the Zahir Rawayet proceeds is, that a right of residence may eventually be established to the legatee in the whole house, by so much other property of the testator being afterwards discovered as may cause the house to come within a third of his property. Besides, the legatee has a controlling power over the heirs with respect to their portions, so far as to restrain them from executing any deed which may injure or affect his share.

The bequest becomes void on the death of the legatee.—IF the legatee should die before the expiration of the limited term of usufruct, the article bequeathed in usufruct immediately reverts to the heirs of the testator; for the bequest was made with a view that the legatee might derive a benefit from the testatore's property; but if the article were to devolve to the legatee's heirs, it induces the consequence of their being entitled to the use of the testator's property without his consent, which is contrary to law. If the legatee die during the testator's life time, the bequest is void; because the acceptance of it is suspended upon the death of the testator, as has been already explained.

A bequest of the produce of an article does not entitle the legatee to the personal use of the article.—IF a person bequeath the produce* of his house or of his salave to Zeyd, in that case some are of opinion that it is lawful for Zeyd to reside in the said house himself, or to use the slave for his own service, because, an equivalent for the use is in fact the same as the use itself, so far as relates to the accomplishment of the testator's object. The more approved opinion, however, is, that it is not lawful; for a bequest of produce is a bequest of money, as it is that which constitutes produce; whereas residence or service is an enjoyment of the use; and the effect of these is different with respect to the heirs; for if any just debt should afterwards appear against the testator, it might be repaid by means of a restitution of the rent by the legatee, which could not be done in case of his having had the actual use.

Nor does a bequest of the use entitle him to let it to hire.—IT is not lawful for the usufructuary legatee of a slave or a house to let them out to hire. Shafei maintains that he is at full liberty so to do, because, in consequence of the bequest, he becomes (as it were) proprietor of the article; and, as such, he is entitled to transfer it either for a return or otherwise, usufruct (according to him) being equivalent to actual property. It is otherwise with a loan, that being (according to his tenets) simply a licence [to the use of a thing], not an investitutre.* The arguments of our doctors upon this point are twofold.—FIRST, a bequest is an endowment with property, without a return, referred to the testator's decease; and hence the legatee is not empowered to make a transfer of the legacy even without a return, because of the analogy it bears to a loan; for a loan, according to our doctors, is an investiture with the use of a thing granted in the lifetime of the lender; and the borrower is not permitted to hire out the article lent (hire being an investiture for a return), so here likewise.—A proof of this is that an investiture for a return is strong and binding, whereas investiture without a return is weak and not binding; and a person who is not empowered with respect to the weakest of the two cannot be empowered with respect to the strongest. Bequest, moreover, as being a gratuitous deed, is weeak and not binding.—Now in gratuitous deeds to voluntary agent is at liberty to retract, not the other party:—but as, in the case of a bequest, the voluntary agent is the testator, and it is impossible for him to retract after his decease, retractation is therefore not supposed possible in this instance;—yet still as the bequest is not originally of a forcible and irrevocable nature, the legatee of usufruct is of course not at liberty to let the article to hire, since hire, as being a contract of exchange, is forcible and irrevocable. SECONDLY, usufruct (according to our doctors) is not property; but the investiture of it for property induces a creation of the character of worth in it, necessarily, in order to establish an equality between the articles opposed to each other in exchange. Now

* By the term "produce"; [Arab. Hasil] as here used, is to be understood the earnings or hire of a slave, or the rent of a house, &c.

* See Vol. III. p. 478.

the power of such creation rests only with one who is a proprietor of usufruct as a dependent of his right of property, or in consequence of a contract of exchange, and who is consequently empowered to make over the property to another in the same manner in which he himself may have held it. But when a person who acquires the property of usufruct without any return on his part, and in an original manner (that is, not in virtue of its subjection to something else), afterwards makes it over to another for a return, it follows that he makes another proprietor of a thing in a degree superior to what he himself in effect was, which is unlawful.

A bequest of the use of a slave does not entitle the legatee to carry him out of the place, unless his family reside elsewhere.—IF a person bequeath the service of his slave to another, the legatee it not entitled to carry the slave from the city of the testator; —unless his own family reside in another city, in which case he may carry him thither, provided he exceed not a third of the testator's property, The reason of this decision is, because the bequest must take effect and be executed in conformity with the intent of the testator; and in a case where the family of the legatee reside in the same city with testator, his intent is that the legatee shall take the service of the slave there, without exposing him (the slave) to the trouble of a journey elsewhere;—whereas, on the other hand, where the family of the legatee reside in a different city, the intent the testator is that the legatee shall carry the slave thither in order that the family may enjoy the use of his service, without putting them to the trouble of removing to his [the testator's] city to enjoy this advantage.

A bequest of a year's product, if the article exceed a third of the estate, does not entitle the legatee to a consignment of it.—IF a person leave one year's product of his slave or house to another, and he have no other property except such house or slave, the legatee in that case receives one third of a year's product; because product, as being property, is capable of division. If, therefore, the legatee require the heirs to make a division of the house, in order that he may himself collect the product from his own share (being a third), it would not be admitted. Aboo Yoosaf, indeed, according to one report, holds a contrary opinion; for he argues that the legatee is a partner with the heirs; and a partner has a right to demand a division of the common property. In answer to this, however, it may be observed that this right amongst copartners arises from their having a property in the article itself; whereas the legatee, in the present instance, has a property only in the product of the article, and consequently is not entitled demand a division.

In a bequest of the use of an article to one, and the substance of it to another, the legatee of usufruct is exclusively entitled to the use during his term.—IF a man bequeath the person of his slave to Zeyd, and the service of him to Omar, and the slave exceed not a third of the testator's estate, his person belongs to Zeyd, and his service to Omar; for as the testator has bequeathed a specific thing to each legatee respectively, each is therefore entitled to his own right. As, moreover (the bequest to the usufructuary legatee being at any rate valid), if the slave's person had not been bequeathed, that would have belonged to the heirs, at the same time that his services would have belonged to the legatee; so in the same manner his services belong to the legatee of usufruct where the testator has bequeathed his person to another; for bequest resembles inheritance, inasmuch as the right of property to the article is established after death in both instances.

A bequest of an article to one, and its contents to another, if connectedly expressed entitles the second legatee to nothing.—IF a person bequeath his female a slave to one and the child in her womb to another, or a ring to one and the stone of it to another, or a leathern bag, containing dates, to one, and the dates to another, and the legacy do not exceed a third of the estate,—in this case the first legatee gets his legacy, but the legatee of the contained article is not entitled to any thing. This is where the second bequest is immediately conducted in the same sentence with the first. But if they be mentioned separately (as if the testator should first say, "I bequeath my female slave to Zeyd," and then remain silent, and afterwards say, "I bequeath the child with which she is pregnant to Amroo"), the effect, according to Aboo Yoosaf, is the same as above mentioned; whereas Mohammed maintains that in this case the female slave goes to the first legatee, and her child is shared equally between the two (and the same holds with respect to the two other cases of the ring and the bag). The argument of Aboo Yoosaf is that as the testator first bequeathed the female slave, and afterwards the child in her womb, it may be inferred that his object in the first bequest was the female slave only, the second bequest being merely an explanation of his meaning in the first, —which explanation is approved, whether it be connected in the same sentence or not; for as the bequest is not binding till after the death of the testator, his explanation connectedly or unconnectedly is one and the same; in the same manner as holds where a person first bequeaths the person of his slave to one and afterwards the service of him to another,—in which case the legatee of the person is not a partner of the legatee of usufruct with respect to the service

* In other words, "he is at liberty, at any period after making the bequest, to alter or amend it."

the slave. The argument of Mohammed is that the word ring comprehends both the stone and the hoop, and so likewise, the word female slave comprehends both the slave herself and also the child in her womb,—and the word bag includes both the bag and its contents. With respect, therefore, to the ring-stone, the child, and the contents of the bag, there are two different bequests to two different persons, where both the legatees are equal partners in each. Nor is the second bequest, in this instance, a retractation of the first, it being, in effect the same as where a person first bequeaths a ring (for instance) to one, and again bequeaths the same ring to another,—in which case the second bequest is not a retractation of the first, but the two legatees are equal partners in the ring; and so here likewise. It is different where a man first bequeaths the person of his slave to one, and then the property of him to another, as the word slave does not comprehend the service of that slave. It is also different where a second bequest follows in immediate connexion with the first; for in that case the whole forms (as it were) one sentence indicating the design of the testator to be that the hoop of the right (for instance) shall go to one, and the stone to the other.

A bequest of the fruit of a garden implies the present fruit only, unless it be expressed in perpetuity.—If a person bequeath to any one "the fruit of his garden;" in that case the legatee gets the fruit actually in being at the time of the testator's death, not what may be produced afterwards. If, however, the testator say. "I bequeath the fruit of my garden perpetually to such an one," the legatee is in that case entitled to the fruit then existing, as well as to whatever may afterwards grow there during his life. But if, on the other hand, the testator bequeath the produce of his garden (not the fruit), the legatee is then entitled to the present produce and to whatever may be collected from it until his death, although the word perpetual should ot have been expressed; for as the word fruit, in its common acceptation, means a thing actually in being, it cannot therefore be applied to what is not in being, unless by an express provision for that purpose:—whereas produce, in the common acceptation of the term, comprehends not only what at present exists, but also what may hereafter exist in succession; and therefore its including what may appear after the testator's decease does not depend upon the mention of any particular provision or term.

A bequest of the produce of an animal implies the existent produce only, in every instance.—If a person bequeath the wool of a sheep, or its milk, or young, and then die, the legatee is in that case entitled to whatever may be extant (for these things) at the period of the testator's death, and not to what may afterwards appear notwithstanding the word "perpetual" have been expressed; as the term wool, or so forth (as mentioned above), do not comprehend what is not actually in being. It is otherwise with respect to fruit (although that term also, in it's common acceptation, comprehends only what is actually existent, and a bequest of non-existent fruit the never theless valid), because ordained contracts* (such as of gardening and hire) with respect to non-existent fruit being good in LAW, it follows that the word fruit, mentioned with a condition of perpetuity, comprehends also what is non-existent, and that a bequest of such is valid. It is otherwise with the wool, the milk, or the young of a sheep; for as, with respect to the non-existent of those articles, there are no ordained contracts, a bequest of such is not valid:—contrary to what is existent; for these are subjects of a valid contract (such as Khoola and the like), and therefore a bequest of them is likewise valid.

CHAPTER VI.

OF WILLS MADE BY ZIMMEES.

A church or synagogue, founded during health, descends to the founder's heirs.—If a Jew or a Christian, being in sound health build a church of a synagogue, and then die, such building is an inheritance, according to all our doctors; because Haneefa holds an erection of this nature to be equivalent to a Wakf, or pious appropriation, which (agreeable to his tenets) is not absolute,† but descends to the heirs of the founder; and the two disciples, on the other hand, hold all such erections to be sinful in their nature: whence they are of no validity [as a public foundation], and therefore descend to the heirs [in the same manner as any other of the founder property].

In the bequest of a house to the purpose of an infidel plach of worship, it is appropriated accordingly.—If a Jew or Christian will that, "after his death his house shall be converted into a church or synagogue for a particular set of people," the bequest is valid, according to all our doctors and takes effect to the extent of a third of the testator's property; because a bequest has two different characters, the appointment of a successor, and an actual endowment; and the testator is competent to either of these.

Whether any particular legatees be mentioned, or otherwise.—If a Jew or Christian will that "his house be converted into a church or synagogue for a sect of people," without specifying the particular sect, the bequest is valid, according to Haneefa.

---

* Ordained contracts are such as are authorized and sanctioned by the KORAN and concerning the validity of which, therefore, no doubt can be entertained.

† See Vol. II, p. 231.

According to the two disciples, on the contrary, it is not valid; for a deed of that nature is in reality sinful, although it may appear pious to the testator; and a will for a sinful purpose is null, because the execution of it would be a confirmation of sin. The argument of Heaneefa is, that the founding of churches or synagogues is held, by these persons, to be an act of piety; and as we are enjoined to leave them to the exercise of whatever may be agreeable to their faith, the bequest is therefore lawful, in conformity with their belief.

OBJECTION.—What is the difference between the building a church or synagogue in the time of health, and the bequeathing it by will, that Haneefa should hold it inheritable in the former instance, and not in the latter?

REPLY.—The difference is this: that it is not the mere erecting (of the church, &c.) which extinguishes the builder's property, but the exclusive dedication of the building to the service of GOD, as in the case of mosque erected by Mussulmans: and as an infidel place of worship is not dedicated to GOD, indisputably, it therefore still remains the property of the founder, and is consequently inheritable [in common with his other effects];—whereas a bequest on the contrary, is used for the very purpose of destroying a right of property.

THE bequests of Zimmees are of four kinds.*—I. Those made for purposes held pious in their belief, but not in the belief of Mussulmans, such as the building of a church or a synagogue (as already mentioned), or the slaughter of hogs to feed the poor of their sect; in which cases Haneefa holds the bequest to be valid, in conformity with the faith of the testator, whereas the two disciples deem it invalid, as being sinful.—II. Those made for purposes held pious with Mussulmans, but not with Zimmees, such as the erection of a mosque, a pilgrimage to Mecca, or burning a lamp in a mosque, in all of which instances the bequests is invalid in conformity with the belief the testator, according to all our doctors; unless, however, it be made in favour of some particular persons, in which case it is valid, as under such circumstance it is an investiture, the mention of "building a mosque," or so forth, being considered merely in the light of a counsel—(in other words, as if the testator had bequeathed his property to particular persons, counselling them therewith to erect a mosque). III Those made for a purpose held pious both by Mussulmans and Zimmees, such as burning a lamp in the holy temple (of Jerusalem), or waging war against infidel Tartars,†—which are valid, whether made in favour of specific persons or not.—IV. Those made for purposes not held pious either by Zimmees or Mussulmans, such as the support of singers and dissolute women.—which are invalid, as being of a sinful tendency;—unless, however, they be made in favour of particular persons, and then they are valid.

The will of a sensualist or innovator is the same as of an orthodox Mussulman, unless he proceed to avowed apostecy—A SENSUALIST,* or an innovator,† provided he proceed not to open and avowed infidelity, is, in point of bequest, in the same state with a perfect believer, because the law regards only his apparent state, which is that of a Mussulman; but if he proceed to open infidelity, he is then considered as an apostate; and with regard to his will there is a difference of opinion (in the same manner as our doctors have differed withregard to every other deed of such persons), —Haneefa holding, that in this case his bequest remains in suspense, and becomes valid upon his repentance, or null upon his death or expatriation,)—and the two disciples (on the contrary) maintaining that it is in every respect valid.

The will of a female apostate is valid.—The will of an apostate woman is valid. This is approved; because women in such cases are left to themselves, and not put death, as in the case of men.‡

A Moostamin may bequeath the whole of his property.—IF a Moostamin bequeath the whole of his property to a Mussulman or a Zimmee, it is valid; for a bequest of the whole of an estate is deemed illegal only as it affects the right of the testator's heirs (whence it is that if they assent such bequest is valid); but the heirs of the Moostamin are possessed of no cognizable rights, they being, as it were, dead, so far as relates to the Mussulman government, because of their being in a hostile country. Besides, the property of a Moostamin is in security only in virtue of the protection he receives from the state, which protection he enjoys in his own right; not in right of his heirs.

But if he bequeath a part only, the residue is ransmitted to his heirs.—IF a Moostamin bequeath part of his property, the bequest is executed accordingly, and the remainder is transmitted to his heirs, notwithstanding they be residents in an hostile country; such being the law with respect to Moostamins.

An emancipation, or Tadbeer, granted by him on his deathbed, takes effect in toto.—IF a Moostamin, immediately before his death.

* The distinctions here stated apply solely to bequests for particular purposes.

† Koofr at Toork: the name by which the hands of robbers who used to infest the northern provinces of Persia were formerly distinguished.

* Arab, Sahib-al-hawa. Hawa signifies the sensual passions, a complete conquest over which is essential to the chrracter of a good Mussulman.

† Arab. Sahib-al-biddat. A free-thinker or secrtary,—Abroacher of new and heterodox inions in matters of faith.

‡ See Vol. II. p. 229.

emancipate his slave, or make him a Modabbir in the Mussulman territory, it it valid, and the slave is accordingly free, notwithstanding his value exceed a third of his master's estate; for a bequest beyond a third of the property it is deemed illegal only as it affects the right of the testator's heirs; but a Moostamin's heirs possess no cognizable right, as was already mentioned.

Any bequest in favour of a Mussulman is valid.—If a Mussulman or Zimmee make a will in favour of a Moostamin, it is valid; for a Moostamin, so long as he resides in a Mussulman country, is considered in the light of a Zimmee; and as the exercise of generosity and benevolence in favour of such is therefore allowed to Mussulmans during life, it is also permitted them to extend such acts to a period after their death,—(It is related of Haneefa and Aboo Yoosaf, that they held wills in favour of Moostamins to be illegal, because of their intention to return to their own country; and also, because the Mussulmans not only allow this, but even do not suffer them to reside in their dominions more than a year, unless they submit to the payment of the capitation-tax.—The former is, however, the better opinion.)

The bequests of a Zimmee are subject to the same restrictions with those of a Mussulman.—If a Zimmee bequeath more than a third of his estate to a stranger, or to an heir, it is not valid, as being contrary to the laws of the Mussulmans to which they have laws to conform with respect to all temporal concerns.

He may make a bequest in favour of an unbeliever of a different sect.—If a Zimmee make a will in favour of an infidel of a different persuasion, it is valid, because of the analogy of legacies to succession by inheritance, all the different descriptions of those persons who disbelieve the true faith being considered as of one class.

Not being a hostile infidel.—If a Zimmee, residing in the Mussulman territory, make a will in favour of a hostile infidel, it is not valid for as inheritance does not obtain between those, because of the difference of country, it follows that a bequest from the one to the other is of no effect, bequest being similar to inheritance.

CHAPTER VII.

OF EXECUTORS AND THEIR POWERS.

An executor, having accepted his appointment in presence of the testator, is not afterwards at liberty to reject it.—If a person appoint another his executor, it remains with that other either to accept of or decline the appointment, in the presence of the testator; because no one has the power of compelling another to interfere in his concerns. But if the executor accept his appointment in the presence of the testator, and afterwards, either in his absence, or after his death, decline it, such refusal is not admitted; because the testator had placed a reliance on his consent; and therfore, if the rejection were allowed of either in his absence or after his decease, he would, necessarily be deceived.

His silence leaves him an option of rejection.—If a person appoint another his executor, and that other remain silent, without giving any indication of his acceptance or refusal, he is in that case at liberty, after the death of the testator, to accept on refuse the appointment, as may be most agreeable to him.

But any act indicative of his acceptance binds him to the execution of the office.—But if a person, under such circumstances, should, immediately after the death of the testator, dispose of any part of the effects by sale, then, as an act of this kind is a clear indication of his acceptance, the executorship becomes obligatory on him. The sale moreover, is valid in this instance, notwithstanding the executor may not have considered himself as such at that time; for his executorship (like inheritance, bequest being a sort of succession as well as inheritance), does not depend on his knowledge; and, as being an executor, a sale transacted by him is valid.

Having rejected the appointment, after the testator's decease, he may still accept of it, unless the magistrate appoint an executor in the interim.—If a person appoint another his executor, and the person so appointed, remain silent until the testator's decease and then reject the office, and afterwards declare his acceptance of it, such acceptance is valid, unless the Kazee, during the interim, should have set him aside, and appointed another, in consequence of his first declaration; because the refusal does not immediately annul the appointment, that being injurious to the decease; and although the continuance of it be prejudicial and troublesome to the executor, still he has the merit of it, which is an equivalent for the disadvantage,—whereas the injury to the deceased has nothing to counterbalance it, The executorship therefore endures in this case. If, however, the Kazee set him aside, his decree to that effect is valid, as he possesses the power of removing an inconvenience, to which executors are frequently subjected, and which may render the continuance of the office injurious to them. The Kazee, therefore, to remedy this, may discharge the executor from his office, and appoint another in his room, to act with the estate, thereby preventing an injury both to te excutor and the deceased. If, moreover, the executor, after being thus dismissed by the Kazee, declare his willingness to undertake the executorship, such declaration is not admitted or attended to, as he here assents after his appointment having been altogether annulled by the order of the Kazee.

Where a slave, a reprobate, or an infidel, are appointed, the magistrate must nominate a proper substitute.—A PERSON may appoint a slave, reprobate * or an infidel, to be his executor; but it is incumbent on the Kazee to annul such appointment, and nominate another person, because of the disadvantages which would attend the comfirmation of it in either of those instances; for a slave could not act but by the power of his master; a reprobate may be suspected of fraud; and it is not fit such a trust should be committed to an infidel, as the enmity which every infidel may be supposed to entertain towards a Mussulman on the score of religion will occasion a disregard to his interest. The dissolution of such appointments is therefore incumbent on the Kazee, notwithstanding their original validity.

The appointment of the testator's slave is invalid, if any of the heirs have a attained to maturity; but not otherwise.—IF a person appoint his own slave his executor, any of the heirs being arrived at the age of maturity, it is not valid; because such heirs may prevent the slave from the execution of his office by selling their property in him to another, and thereby rendering him incapable of acting but by the consent of the purchaser. If, on the contrary, the heirs be all infants, the appointment is in that case valid, according to Haneefa. The two disciples maintain that it is not valid (and such is what analogy would suggest); because slavery is incompatible with the exercise of power; and also because, in this particular instance, it would follow that the property was master over the proprietor, which is contrary to LAW. The argument of Haneefa is, that the slave is sane and adult, and therefore capable of the discharge of such trust. Neither has any person the power of prohibiting him from it, because the heirs, although they be his masters, yet cannot exert this power, on account of their youth. As, moreover, the deceased appointed him to this trust, it may hence be inferred that his tenderness, and regard for the heirs was superior, in his opinion, so that of any other. This appointment, therefore, is valid; in the same manner as that of a Mokatib;—in other words, if a person appoint his Mokatib his executor it is valid; and so here likewise.

In case of the executor's incapacity, the magistrate must give him an assistant.—IF an executor be unequal to the execution of his office, it is incumbent on the Kazee to associate another with him, in order that the duties of the office may be properly executed.

But he must not do so on the executor pleading incapacity, without due examination.—IF an executor represent to the Kazee his inability to execute the duties of his charge, it is requisite, in such case, that the Kazee, before he attends to his representation, make particular inquiry into the truth of it, as complainants of this kind often assert falsehoods, with a view to alleviate their own burden. But if it shall appear to the Kazee, on due examination that the executor is utterly incapable of the office, he must release him, and appoint another in his place, this being advantageous both to the executor and to the estate.

And if he appear perfectly equal to the office, he cannot be removed.—IF an executor be perfectly equal to the discharge of his office, and trust worthy therein, the Kazee is not at liberty to dismiss him; for any person whom the Kazee may appoint in his place must be less eligible, as the deceased had particularly selected him, and signified his confidence in him. He therefore must be continued in preference to all others; even to the testator's father, notwithstanding his supposed tenderness; and consequently to others a fortiori.

He cannot be removed on the complaint of the heirs, unless his culpability be ascertained.—IF all or part of the heirs prefer a complaint against the executor, still the Kazee must not dismiss him immediately, nor until his guilt be ascertained, as he acts under an authority derived from, the deceased. If, however, he prove culpable, it is incumbent on the Kazee to dismiss him and appoint another in his place; for the deceased nominated him to the office from supposing him worthy of confidence; but upon being found culpable he no longer continues so, insomuch that if the testator were living he would himself discharge him; and as he is incapacitated, by death, from so doing, the Kazee must take this upon him as his substitute.

One of two joint executors cannot act without the concurrence of the other.—IF a man appoint two executors, neither of them is entitled, according to Haneefa, and Mohammed, to act without the other, except in particular cases, of which an explanation shall be hereafter given.—Aboo Yoosaf is of opinion that in all cases either of them may act without the other, because, an executor is endowed with his power of action in virtue of the will of the testator; and as power of action is a thing sanctioned by the LAW, and incapable of division,* he enjoys his power complete and perfect in the same manner as a complete authority to contract their infant sister in marriage appertains to each of her brothers respectively.—(The ground of this is, that executorship is a succession, which succession cannot be established in the executor, unless the authority of the testator devolve to him in the same degree in which it had apertained to the

* Arab. Fasik. (The term has been repeatedly defined.)

* That is, cannot be enjoyed or exercised partially.

testator, that is, completely and perfectly.)—The testator's choice, moreover, of the two to be his executors is an argument of the particular attachment of each to his interest, which attachment is equivalent to the consanguinity of two brothers in the point of contracting their infant sister in marriage,—The arguments of Haneefa in support of his opinion are twofold.—FIRST, the power of an executor, being derived from the testator, is of consequence to be exercised in the manner prescribed by him ; and in the case in question the testator has entrusted this power to both the executors, on the condition of their being united in the trust, for he does not expressly assent to their acting otherwise than jointly, and the above condition is moreover attended with advantage, as the deliberations of two persons are better than of one. It is otherwise with two brothers, in the circumstance of contracting their infant sister in marriage (as adduced by Aboo Yoosaf), since the cause of such authority being vested in them is relationship, a cause which exists equally in each. The contracting in marriage, moreover, is a right of the infant, resting upon her guardian (insomuch that if the infant require her guardian to contract her to any person, being her equal, for whom she has a liking, he must comply), whereas, in the case here considered, the acting [with the estate] is the right of the executor himself not of another resting upon him. In the case of contracting the infant in marriage, therefore, if one of the two brothers so contract her, he merely discharges a duty incumbent on the other brother, and his act is therefore valid ; whereas, in the case of executorship, if one of the two act alone, he exercise a right appertaining to the other, and his so doing is therefore invalid ;—in the same manner as where two persons owe a sum of money to one, in which case it would be perfectly lawful for either of them to discharge the whole debt, whereas, supposing one man to owe a sum of money to two others, it would not be lawful for him to pay the whole to either of them.

Except in such matters as require immediate execution,—THE case excepted by Haneefa and Mohammed, in which they hold the acts of either executor, singly, to be valid, are such as require immediate execution. This it is lawful for either executor, singly, to disbusre the funeral charges, as a delay in this might occasion the body to become offensive ; whence it is that a similar power is vested in the neighbours. In the same manner, either of the executors, singly, may purchase victuals or clothes for the infant children of the testator, this being a matter of urgency, and which admits of no delay.

Or which are of an incumbent nature.—So likewise, it is lawful for either of the executor to restore a deposit, and usurped article, or a thing purchased by the testator under an invalid contract. In preserving the estate of the testator, also, and in discharging his debts, the act of either executor is lawful independent of the other. For none of these are considered as an exercise of power, but merely the performance of a duty,—insomuch that the depositor has himself a right to seize and carry away his deposit, if he find it among the effects of the deceased, and the creditor has a similar right with regard to his debt ;—and it is, moreover, the duty of every one into whose hands property may fall, to attend to the preservation of it, whence this comes under the description of aid and assistance, not of an exercise of power ;—neither do any of these acts require thought or consideration. Either of the executors has also a right singly to discharge a legacy, or emancipate a slave, if directed by the testator, because such deeds require no thought or consideration.

Or in which the interest or advantage of the estate are concerned.—IN the same manner, either of them may institute a suit in claim of the rights of the testator because a conjunction of both in so doing would be impracticable, since, if they were to do it at one and the same time in the assembly of the Kazee, they must occasion noise and confusion (whence it is that only one of two agents for litigation is allowed to plead at a time). The acceptance for a gift for an infant is likewise an act which neither may perform singly ; for in case of delay there is a possibility of the gift being rendered null by the death of the donor previous to the seizure. These acts,, moreover, being permitted to a mother and nurse, is a proof that they are not exertions of power. It is likewise permitted to any of the executors, singly, to sell goods where there is an apprehension of their spoiling, as in th case of fruit, and the like : and also to collect together and preserve the scattered property of the testator, as delay might occasion the destruction of it ; and such permission is, moreover, given to every person into whose hands property may fall, whence it may be inferred that this is not an exertionof power (It is recorded, in the Jama Sagheer, that none of the executors, where there are more than one, has singly the power of selling goods, or receiving payment of debts, because these are exercises of power which they must perform jointly, in conformity with the will and intention of the testator.)

Case of a testator appointing different executors at different times.—IF a person appoint two executors in a separate manner (as if he should first say to the one "I have appointed you my executor," and again, at a different period, to the other "I have appointed you my executor"), some allege that in this case each of them has individually a power of exercising the functions of his appointment, without consulting the other, in the same manner as two agents, where they are appointed by different commissions ;—the reason of which is that he testator, in appointing the two separately, indicates his assent each acting from his own judgment, without the other's asistance or advice. Others, again, say that concerning this case also a disagreement subsists between Haneefa and Mohammad on one side, and Aboo Yoosaf on the other; because a will is not established until the death of the testator; and at that time both are executors together, notwithstanding they had been appointed separately. It is otherwise with two agents appointed under different commissions; for the appointment of each of those still continues distinct and separate, as settled by the constituent.

In case of the death of a joint executor, the magistrate must appoint a substitute.—If one of two executors die, it is incumbent on the Kazee to appoint another in his room. This is the opinion of Haneefa and Mohammed; because, according to their doctrine, the remaining executor has not, of himself, power to act on every occasion, and he interest of the deceased therefore requires the appointment of another to operate with him; and it is also the opinion of Aboo Yoosaf, because, although the remaining executor be (according to him) empowered to act of himself; still it behoves the Kazee to appoint another his companion; for the design of the testator evidently as, to leave two successors the management of his concerns; and as this may be fulfilled by the appointment of a substitute for him who dies, one must be appointed accordingly.

Unless the deceased have himself nominated his successor.—If the deceased executor have appointed the living executor to act for him, it is in that case lawful for the latter (according to the Zahir Rawayet) to act alone, nor is it incumbent on the Kazee to appoint another in the room of the deceased; because here the judgment of the deceased executor virtually subsists in the living one, as it were, by succession.—(There is a tradition of Haneefa having contradicted this doctrine, because of its repugnance to the object of the testator, namely, the agency of two persons: in opposition to the case where a dying executor appoints some other person to succeed him; for such appointment is valid, because of its being attended with the advantage of the judgment of two distinct persons, as was intended by the tastator.)

The executor of an executor is his substitute in office.—If an executor, previous to his death, appoint another person his executor, in that case the person so appointed is entitled to act as executor, both to him, and also to the person to whose affairs his immediate testaor had acted as executor. This is according to our doctors. Shafei maintains that the person so appointed is not entitled to act as executor to the first deceased, because of the analogy his appointment bears to that of an agent; in other words, if a person, during his life time, appoint an agent to act for him, that agent is not permitted to delegate his powers to another without having previously obtained the consent of his constituent.—(The ground of analogy between these two cases is, that in the same manner as the constituent is supposed to place a reliance on the agent, and on him only, so also the testator may be supposed to act with regard to the executor.) The arguments of our doctors upon this point are twofold.—First, an executor derives his power from the testator: and it is therefore lawful for him to appoint an executor to succeed him;—in the same manner as in the case of a grandfather; in other words, a father has the power of bestowing his child in marriage, which devolves upon his father after his death; and the grandfather has in such case the power of appointing an agent for the execution of the child's marriage; and so likewise, it is lawful for an executor to appoint another executor, as the power appertaining to the testator devolves upon his executor, in the same manner as a father's right to dispose of his child in marriage devolves upon the grand father. As, moreover, the grandfather is the father's substitute with regard to the power which devolves to him, so in the same manner the executor is the substitute of the testator; because the nomination of an executor is, in effect, an appointment, by the testator, of a substitute with respect to the matters in which he is himslf empowered; and as the executor, at the time of his death, possessed a power with respect to both estates (his own, and also that of his testator), it follows that the second executor (that is, the one appointed by him) is his substitute with respect to both estates also.—Secondly, as the testator had recourse to the assistance of the executor, notwithstanding he knew there was a possibility of his dying in the interim, and thereby leaving his object unaccomplished, it may be inferred that his intention was that his, executor should in such case appoint another. It is otherwise with an agent; for he is not at liberty to appoint any other person his agent without the consent of his constituent; because, as the latter is still living, and consequently has it in his power to accomplish his object himself, it is therefore not to be supposed that he will consent to his agent appointing another agent under him.

An executor is entitled to possess himself of the portions of infant and absent adult heirs, on their behalf.—If an executor, the legatees being present, divide off the estate of the testator from the legacies, on behalf of his heirs who are infants, or adult absentee, and take possession of their portions, it is lawful; for an heir is successor to the deceased; and as an executor is also a successor to him, he is of course a competent litigant on behalf of infant or absent heirs, and may, of consequence, make a division, and possess himself of their portions on their behalf,—insomuch that if those portions were to perish in his hands, still they are not at liberty to participate with the legatees in what remained to them after such division.

But not of the legacies of infant or absent legatees.—IF, on the contrary, an executor, the heirs being adult and present, divide of the legacies from the estate, and take possession of them on behalf of infant or absent legatees, it is unlawful; for a legatees not a successor to the deceased in every respect, he being constituted a proprietor by a new and supervenient cause; and as, therefore, the executor does not stand as litigant on his behalf, his taking his [the legatee's] portion is not valid,—insomuch that if the legacy were to perish in his [the executor's] hands, the legatee would be entitled to take a third of whatever had remained to the heirs. Neither as any compensation due from the executor in this instance; because an executor is a trustee: and as the power of conserving the effects of the testator is lodged in him, the case is therefore the same as if the loss had happened previous to the division of the effects.

A legacy appropriated to pilgrimage, if lost, must be repaired, to the extent of a third of the estate.—If a person bequeath a sum for the performance of a pilgrimage to Mecca, and then die, and the executor divide off the said sum from the heirs, and take possession of it, and it be afterwards lost or destroyed, either in his charge, of in that of the person whom he had appointed for the performance of the pilgrimage, in that case, according to Haneefa, a third of the remaining property of the deceased must be appropriated for the pilgrimage. Aboo Yoosaf, on the other hand, holds that if the sum thus lost have been originally equivalent to a third of the property, nothing is afterwards to be taken from the heirs; but that if it was less, the deficiency must be applied to the purpose of the pilgrimage. Mohammed, on the contrary, is of opinion that in neither case is the executor to take any thing from the heirs: because the setting aside of a particular sum, for the performance of the pilgrimage, was the undoubted right of the testator; and as, if he had himself set aside the sum for that purpose, and it had afterwards been lost or destroyed, nothing further would have been required, and the legacy would have been void, it is in the same manner void where the sum was set aside by the executor, as he acts for, and stands in the place of, the deceased. The argument of Aboo Yoosaf, in support of his opinion, is that a third of the whole property is a fund for the execution of wills, to which extent only they are to be executed, and no farther. The arguments of Haneefa, in support of his opinion on this point, are twofold. FIRST, the performance of the pilgrimage was the object of the testator, not the setting aside a sum for that purpose, and therefore the appropriation or delivery of the money, without the accomplishment of the object, is of no consideration, it being, in effect, the same as if the sum had been lost previous to the division,—in which case a third of the remainder would be appropriated to the pilgrimage. SECONDLY, the division, with respect to the legacy, is not perfect and complete until the portion bequeathed for the purpose of pilgrimage be expended there upon as there is no person to take possession of it.* Where, therefore, this sum is not expended in the performance of pilgrimage, the partition is incomplete, and the case is (consequently) the same as if the sum had been lost or destroyed before the partition.

A legacy, after being divided off by the magistrate, descends to the legattee's heirs in case of his decease.—IF a person bequeath a third of one thousand dirms to another who is at that time absent, and the heirs consign the said sum to the Kazee, in order to divide and set apart the share of the absent legatee, the division thus made by the Kazee is valid because of the original validity of the will, insomuch that if the absentee should afterwards die, previous to his having declared his acceptance, the legacy nevertheless devolves to his heirs. The office of Kazee, moreover, is instituted with a view to the benefit of mankind, that he may attend to the conservation of their rights, especially with respect to such as are dead or absent;—and as among these attentions to the rights of mankind is the setting aside and taking posession of the portions of absentees, such acts by him on behalf of an absentee are valid of course:—insomuch that if such portion were destroyed in his possession and the legatee should afterwards appear, still he would have no claim upon the heirs.

An executor may sell a slave of the estate, for the discharge of the debts upon, it, in absence of the creditors.—IT is lawful for an executor, in order to discharge the debts of the deceased, to sell a slave for a suitable price, in the absence of the creditors; for as the testator might have done so during his lifetime the executor, as his representative, is entitled to do the same. The ground on which this proceeds is, that the right of the creditors to the effects of the deceased lies, not in the things themselves but in their worth; and the worth of the slave is not annihlated by the sale, as the price (which is in reality the worth) still remains.

Unless the slave be involved in debt.—IT is otherwise with respect to an indebted slave; for the sale of such in the absence of the creditors is not valid, as their right lies in the person of the slave, they having a claim to the earnings of his labour, which would be annihilated by the sale of him.

An executor, having sold and received the price of an article which afterwards proves to be the property of another, is accountable to the purchaser for the price he had so received.—IF a person appoint another his executor, directing him, after his decease, to

---

* In other words, there is no individual legatee.

sell a slave, and bestow the price in charity, and the executor accordingly sell the slave and take possession of the price, and it be afterwards lost or destroyed with him, and the slave prove to be the property of another person, he (the executor) is accountable to the purchaser for the price, agreeably to the laws of sale; and he is entitled to take an equivalent from the effect of the deceased, being, as it were, an agent on his behalf. This indemnification, according to Haneefa, he is to take from the whole of the estate at large, and such is the Zahir Rawayet. It is recorded from Mohammed, on the contrary, that he is to indemnify himself from the third of the effects as the instructions of the deceased were in the nature of a will; and the third of the property is the fund for the execution of a will. The ground of the doctrine of the Z-hir Rawayet is, that as the executor, in the sale of the slave, was deceived by the testator, the restitution made by him to the purchaser is therefore a debt due to him from the testator; and the debts are discharged from the whole of the estate, not from the third. It would be otherwise if the Kazee, or his Ameen, should sell the slave, and he afterwards prove the property of another; for in this case the obligations of the sale do not rest upon those officers, but the purchaser comes at once upon the estate for an equivalent to the price lost or destroyed as above; since otherwise the door of magistracy would be shut, and the rights of mankind consequently injured, as no man will undertake the office of Kazee unless he be exempted from responsibility. It is to be observed that what is now advanced, that "the executor is to take an equivalent from the effects of the deceased;" proceeds on the supposition of these being sufficient to answer this purpose; for if they be inadequate to it, the executor is entitled to an indemnification only in the greatest possible degree; and if the deceased should have no effects whatever, the executor (like any other creditor) has no claim for indemnification.

But if this have been lost, he may reimburse himself from the person to whom the article had fallen by inheritance.—If an executor sell a slave which had fallen to the share of a child of the deceased, and take possession of the price, and it be afterwards lost in his hands, and the slave prove the property of another person, the purchaser has in that case a claim for restitution from the executor, who is entitled to indemnify himself from the share of the child in whose behalf he acted;—and the child is entitled to an equivalent from the shares of the other heirs; for upon the slave proving the property of another person, the distribution of inheritance, as at first executed, is annulled, the case being, in fact, the same as if no such slave had ever existed, or been accounted upon as part of the estate.

An executor may accept a transfer for a debt due his infant ward.—If a person indebted to an orphan like a transfer on some other person, and the executor (the guardian of the orphan) accept the same, such acceptance is approved, provided it be for the interest of the orphan, because of the person on whom the transfer is made being richer (for instance) than the transferrer, and also a man of probity; for the power of acting is vested in the executor, merely that he may employ it for the interest of the orphan:—but if the transferrer be richer than the other, the acceptance is not approved, as being, in its tendency, prejudicial to the orphan.

Or sell or purchase moveables on his account.—It is lawful for an executor to sell or purchase moveables, on account of the orphan under his charge, either for an equivalent, or at such a rate as to occasion an inconsiderable loss,—but not at such a rate as to make the loss great and apparent; because, the appointment of an executor being for the benefit of the orphan, he must avoid losses in as great a degree as possible;—but with respect to an inconsiderable loss, as in the commerce of the world it is often unavoidable, it is therefore allowed to him to incur it, since otherwise a door would be shut to the business of purchase and sale.

An executor, in giving a bill of sale, must not insert his power as an executor in it, but must give a separate paper to that effect, out of caution; for if the latter also were inserted, it might happen that the witness to the sale might set his name to the bottom of the instrument without examination, which would implicate a false testimony, since with the executorship he has no concern. Some, moreover, have asserted that the attestation of the witness ought to run in this manner—"Sold by Zeyd the son of Omar," and not "by Zeyd te executor of such a person:"—but others maintain that this is immaterial, and that the latter mode may with propriety be adopted, as executorship in a matter of notoriety.

He may also sell moveable s on account of an absent adult heir.—An executor has the power of selling every species of property belonging to an adult absent heir, excepting such as immoveable:—for as a father is authorized to sell the moveable property of his adult absent son, but not such as is in moveable, his guardian (the executor) has the same power. The ground of this is that the sale of moveable property is a species of conservation, as articles of that description are liable to decay, and the price is much more easily preserved than the article itself. With respect, on the contrary, immoveable property, it is in a state of conservation in its own nature; whence it is ulawful to sell it,—unless, however, it be evident that it will otherwise perish or be lost, in which case the sale of it is allowed.

He cannot trade with his ward's portion.—It is not lawful for an executor to trade with the property of the orphan; for the conservation of it, merely, is committed to him, not the, power of trading with it,—according to what is mentioned in the Awzah upon this subject.

He may sell moveable property on account of the infant or absent adult brother of the the testator.—According to Mohammed and Aboo Yoosaf, the executor of a brother, with respect to an infant brother, or one of mature age, who is absent, stands in the same predicament as the executor of a father with respect to his adult absent son (in other words, he is empowered to sell the moveable property of the orphan or absentee); and so likewise of an executor appointed by the mother or uncle; for as the mother and uncle are permitted to interfere in the management of the property so far relates to its preservation, so also is the executor who represents them.

The power of a father's executor precedes that of the grand-father.—The power of the father's executor, in the management of the property of his orphans, is superior to, and precedes that of the grandfather. Shaikh is of opinion that in this respect the grandfather has the superior power; because the law has ordained him to be the representtive of the father, where the latter hasceased to exist,—whence it is that (failing the father) the grandfather inherits to his grandson. The argument of our doctors is, that as, in consequence of the will, the authority of the father devolves upon his executor, the executor's authority is therefore that of the father, in effect,—and consequently the father's executor precedes to grandfather, in the same manner as the father himself would. The ground of this is, that as the father, notwithstanding the existence of the grandfather, appointed another, to act for his children, it may be hence inferred that he considered such appointment more beneficial to them than if they had been left to the management of the grandfather.

If there be no executor, the grandfather is the father's representative.—If a father die without appointing an executor, the grandfather represents the father;* because a grandfather is most nearly related to the children of his son, and most interested in their welfare;—whence it is that the grandfather is empowered to contract the infant wards in marriage, in preference to the father's executor,—notwithstanding the latter take precedence of him in point of managing and acting with the property, for, the reasons already assigned.

CHAPTER VIII.

OF EVIDENCE WITH RESPECT TO WILLS.

The evidence of two executors to the appointment of a third is not valid unless he claim or admit it.—If two executors give evidence that the deceased had associated a third person with them, and that person deny his having done so, the evidence of the executors is of no effect; because their assertion having a tendency to their own advantage, in the case it will afford them from part of their labour, lays them open to suspicion. If, on the contrary, the third person claim or admit of the executorship, their evidence is valid, on a favourable construction. Analogy would suggest that here also the evidence is null, in the same manner as in the former instance, and for the same reasons. The ground of a more favourable construction, in this particular, is that as the Kazee has the power of either appointing an executor at the first, or associating a third person (by that person's consent) with the two executors, without any testimony on their part, it follows that their testimony merely prevents the Kazee from the trouble of nomination, by rendering it unnecessarry for him to seek out and name a proper person to assist in the executorship;—the person still, however, holding his office in virtue of the Kazee's nomination.

The evidence of orphans to the appointment of an executor is not admitted if he deny it.—If two orphans give evidence that their deceased father had appointed a particular person his executor, and the person mentioned deny the same, their evidence is not credible, being liable to a suspicion in the advantages they would draw from the labours of a person exerted towards the preservation of their property.

The testimony of executors with respect to property, on behalf of an infant.—If two executors give evidence, on behalf of an infant heir (their ward) concerning property of the deceased, or of any other person, it is of no effect; because their testimony merely tends to prove their right to the management of such property.

Or of an absent adult, is not admitted.—If two executors give evidence, on behalf of an adult heir, concerning property of the deceased, it is of no effects; but it is valid concerning property appertaining to any other person. This is the doctrine of Haneefa. The two disciples are of opinion that in both cases the evidence is valid, because it is not liable in either of them to any suspicion, as the power of an executor over the property ceases after the heir attains the maturity. The argument of Haneefa is, that as executors have the power of conservation and also of selling the moveable property of an adult heir in this absence, it follows that their evidence, in favour of an adult heir, concerning any part of the deceased's estate, is not altogether free from suspicion. It is otherwise with respect to their evidence, in behalf of an adult heir, concerning and other property, for over that the executors cannot possess any authority, as the deceased constituted them his substitutes with respect to his own estate only, not with respect to the property of others.

* Literally, "is in the stead of," or "stands in the place of."

The mutual evidecne of parties, on behalf of each other, to debts due to each from an estate is valid; but not their evidence to legacies.—IF two persons bear evidenc to a debt of one thousand dirms, due from a person deceased to Omar and Zeyd, and Omar and Zeyd give a similar evidence in favour of these two, the evidence on both parts is valid. If, on the contrary, each of the parties in the same manner give evidence that legacies had been left by the deceased to the other, their attestations are of no effect. This is the doctrine of Haneefa and Mohammed. Aboo Yoosaf maintains that in neither case are these evidences valid; and such also (according to the relation of Khasaf) is the opinion of Haneefa. There is also a tradition of Aboo Yoosaf having concurred in the opinion of Mohammed. The reasons urged in support the validity of the evidence, in the case of debt, is that debt relates solely to the person; and as the person admits a great variety of rights, the evidence of both parties is therefore admitted. —Neither does it follow, in this case, that either party is to partake of what may be obtained in payment by the other, so as to cause the evidence of this party to be a mere establishment of their own right of participation,—insomuch that if a stranger were to pay, to one of the perties. of his own accord, the debt alleged to be due to that party, still the other party is not at liberty to claim any share in such payment. The reasons, on the other hand, against the validity of the evidence,in this instance, are that as the death [of the debtor] occasions the relation to shift from the person to the property, since in consequence of the decease the person no longer remains (insomuch that if any one party were to obtain payment of his right from the estate of the deceased the other party participates with them therein, provided the estate suffice for the discharge of the debts of both), it follows that the evidence of each, respectively, in behalf of the other, tends to establish a right of participation in whatever payment that other may obtain in consequence; and accordingly, the testimony is here liable to suspicion. It is otherwise where the debtor is living; for in that case the testimoney of each party [of creditors] on behalf of the other is admitted; since as the debt, at that time, rests upon his person, not upon his property (the former still continuing existent), a participation, therefore, is not established in this instance.

Unless each legacy, respectively, consist of a slave.—IF two persons give evidence that a particular person had bequeathed his female slave in a legacy to two others, and the two others give evidence that the same person had bequeathed a male slave to these two, both evidences are valid; for as their testimony does not in any respect tend to establish a participation, it is terefore liable to no suspicion, and must be admitted accordingly.

A mutual evidence of this nature is void where it involves a right of participation in the witnesses.—IF two persons give evidence that a particular person had bequeathed the third of his property to Zeyd and Amroo,—and Zeyd and Amroo, on the other hand, give evidence that the same person had bequeathed a third of his property to these two, the evidence of both parties is void and of no effect (and so likewise if the two were to give evidence that the person had bequeathed his male slave to Zeyd and Amroo,—and Zeyd and Amroo, on the other hand, give evidence that the said person had bequeathed his female slave to those two);—because as the evidence on each part tends, in those instances, to establish a right of participation,it is therefore not altogether free from suspicion.

BOOK LIII

OF HERMAPHRODITES.

Section I.

Of who are Hermaphrodites.

Hermaphrodites are either male or female. —A KHOONSA, or hermaphrodite, is a person possessed of the parts of generation of both a man and a woman. If, therefore, such person discharge urine from the male member he* is accounted a male, or if from the female member, a female;—because it is so recorded in the traditions, and likewise reported from Alee; and also, because the circumstance of the urine being discharged from either member in particular, denotes that member to be the original, and the other merely a defect. If, on the contrary, the person discharge the urine from both members, regard is paid to that from which it first proceeds, as this denotes that member to be the original. If, on the other hand, the person discharge his urine from both members equally (that is, at one and the same time) he is a Khoonsamoosh'kil, or equivocal hermaphrodite, according to Haneefa.

Or ambiguous.—NOR is any regard paid to the superior or inferior quantity of the urine in this instance, because a superiority of discharge from either member does not denote that member to be the primary, since this circumstance arises merely from the urinary passage in the one being wider than in the other. The two disciples maintain that regard must in this case be paid to the comparative quantity of urine; and conse-

* The gender of an absolute hermaphrodite is dubious. The translator follows the Arabic text in expersing it throughout in the masculine, that being the most generally applicable.

quently, that the sex is determined according to the member from which the greatest quantity proceeds; because this denotes that member to be the superior and original and also, because the greater quantity is, in effect of law, the whole. From whichever member, therefore, the principal quantity of urine is discharged, that member is accounted the superior. If, however, the urine proceed from both passages alike (that is, at the same time, and in equal quantity), the person is accounted an equivocal hermaphrodite, according to all our doctors, as in this case neither member possesses any superiority over the other.—What is here advanced applies solely to hermaphrodites not yet arrived at the age of maturity;—for upon an hermaphrodite attaining to maturity, if his beard grow, or he have connexion with a woman, or nocturnal emissions, or his breasts appear as those of a man, he is accounted a male, those being indisputable tokens of manhood;—but if the breasts swell like those of a woman, or the menstrual discharge appear, or pregnancy, or carnal connexion with a man, the hermaphrodite is accounted a female, such being the tokens of womanhood. If, on the contrary, no distinguishing tokens of either sex appear, or the tokens of both (such as a beard, with the breast of a woman), the person is an equivocal hermaphrodite.

Section II.

Of the Laws respecting equivocal Hermaphrodites.

An equivocal hermaphrodite.—It is a rule with respect to equivocal hermaphrodites, that they are required to observe all the more comprehensive points of the spiritual law, but not those concerning the propriety of which [in regard to them] any doubt exists.

Must take his station, in public prayers, between the men and the women.—An equivocal hermaphrodite, in standing behind the Imam for the purpose of prayer, must take his station immediately after the man and before the woman, as it is possible that he may be a man, and it is also possible that he may be a woman. If, therefore, he chance to stand among the women, he must recite the prayers repeatedly, for as it is possible he may be a man they would otherwise be nuagatory. If, on the contrary, he stand among the men, his prayers are valid; but the men who are next to him are to recite their prayers repeatedly, out of caution, as it is possible that he may be a female.

Observing (in other respects) the customs of women.—It is laudable in an equivocal hermaphrodite to cover his head, during prayer, with the skirt of his garment, and also to sit in the posture of women; for if he be a man, this is merely a deviation from custom, which does not imply any positive illegality; but if he be a female, his neglecting so to do would induce an abomination, it being indispensably incumbent on women to be covered upon that occasion. It is also laudable in him, if he be without a garment, to recite the prayers repeatedly; but still the prayers are lawful although he should neglect so to do. It is, moreover, abominable in him to wear silk or jewels.

He must not appear naked before man or woman, or travel along with either, except a relation; and he must be circumcised by a slave purchased for that purpose.—It is abominable in an equivocal hermaphrodite to appear naked before either man or women, or to be in retirement with either man or woman except his prohibited relation. In the same manner, it is abominable in him to journey in company with a man other than his prohibited relation,—or with a woman notwithstanding she be a prohibited relation, as it is not lawful for two women to travel together, although they be relations. It is also abominable that he be circumcised by either a man or a woman; and therefore, to perform this ceremony, a female salve must be purchased at his expense;—or, if he be destitute of property, the price of such slave must be advanced to him, by way of loan, from the public treasury, with which he may purchase her for the purpose of circumcising him; and having so done, she is to be sold, and her price paid into the treasury, as he has then no farther occasion for her.

Rules to be observed by him during a pilgrimage.—If an equivocal hermaphrodite undertake a pilgrimage during his adolescence (that is, when nearly arrived at maturity), Aboo Yoosaf declares he is uncertain which modes of dress is most proper for him to adopt; for if he be a male, his wearing a seamed garment is abominable; and he be a female, it is abominable to wear any thing else. Mohammed, however, says that he ought to wear a seamed garment, in the same manner as woman; because it is still more abominable for a woman to neglect this during pilgrimage than for a man to wear it.

Divorce or emancipation, suspended upon the circumstance of sex, are not determined, in relation to an hermaphrodite.—If a man suspend the emancipation of his slave, or the divorce of his wife, upon the circumstance of her producing "a male child," and she be delivered of an hermaphrodite child the divorce or emancipation do not take place until the sex or condition of the child be fully ascertained, since the person canot incur the penalty, in this instance, because of the doubt.

Until his sex be ascertained.—If a man declare, "all my male slaves are free," or, "all my female slaves are free,"—and he be possessed of an hermaphrodite slave, this slave is not emancipated until his real condition be ascertained, since here the master cannot be forsworn, because of the doubt If, on the contrary, he thus mention his male and female slaves together, the hermaphradite is in that case emancipated, since one or other description applies to him indisputably, as he must be either a male or female.

His declaration of his sex is not admitted. IF an hermaphrodite declare himself to be a male, or a female, and he be of the equivocal description, his declaration is not credited as his plea is repugnant to the suggestion of proof. But if he be not of an equivocal description, his declaration may be credited, he being better acquainted with his own state than any other person.

Rules to be observed in his interment.—IF an equivocal hermaphrodite die before his condition be ascertained, the ceremony of ablution must not be performed upon his body by either man or woman, neither of those being allowed to perform it to the other. Ablution, therefore, being impracticable in this instance, the ceremony of teyummim [rubbing with dust or sand] must be substituted for it;—and it is mentioned in the Jama Ramooz, that if the teyummim be performed by any other than a prohibited relation, the hand must be covered with a cloth.

IF a hermaphrodite die at an age bordering on maturity (at twelve years of age, according to the Jama Ramooz), the corpse is not to have the ceremony of ablution performed upon it, whether it be male or female Upon depositing it, moreover, in the tomb or grave it is laudable to cover the same with a cloth, this being indispensable with respect to woman, although not with respect to men.

WHEN there is occasion to repeat the funeral prayers over a man, a woman, and a hermaphrodite, at the same time, the bier of the man must be placed next the Imam, that of the hermaphrodite next, and beyond all the bier of the woman.

WHERE there is any reason for interring a hermaphrodite in the same tomb [or grave] with a man, the former must be deposited after the latter, as it is possible that he may be a female; and a partition of earth must also be constructed between them. If, on the other hand, a hermaphrodite be interred in the same tomb [or grave] with a woman, he must be deposited first, as it is possible that he may be a man.

IT is laudable to shroud the body of a hermaphrodite in the same manner as that of a woman, by wrapping it in five cloths; for, if it be a female, such is that ordained practice with respect to women; and if it be a male, that is merely an excess of two cloths, which is a matter of no moment.

Rules of inheritance with respect to hermaphrodites.—IF a man die, leaving two children, one a hermaphrodite, and the other a son, in that case, according to Haneefa, the whole inheritance is divided between them in three shares, two going to the son, and one to the hermaphrodite; because he hold a hermaphrodite to be subject to the law of a woman, unless his condition be ascertained to be otherwise. Shobbaia, on the contrary, maintains that in this case the hermaphrodite is to receive half the share of a male heir, and half the share of a female,—by first calculating the amount of his shares, supposing him to be a male, and then the same supposing him to be a female, and adding the two together, and paying him a moiety of the added sums. Mohammed and Aboo Yoosaf subscribe to this opinion. They however, differ in their exposition of it—; for Mohammed holds that the whole inheritance is to be divided into twelve parts, seven of which go to the son, and five to the hermaphrodite;—whereas Aboo Yoosaf alleges that it is to be divided into seven parts, four of which go to the son, and three to the hermaphrodite. The argument of Aboo Yoosaf is that the son, if he stood alone, would be entitled to the whole inheritance; and the hermaphrodite, if he stood alone, would be entitled to three fourths of the inheritance,—he being entitled (when standing alone) to a half, if accounted a male, or to the whole, if accounted a female; for the whole property consists of four quarters, the half of which is two quarters,—and these, being added together, make six quarters, the half of which is three. Where, therefore, those two unite in one inheritance, the estate is divided between them according to their respective proportions of right; and as the right of the son is to four fourths, and that of the hermaphrodite to three fourths, the former gets in the proportion of four, and the latter in the proportion of three:—and accordingly, the whole inheritance is divided into seven parts, four of which go to the son, and three to the hermaphrodite. The argument of Mohammed is that, supposing the hermaphrodite to be a male, the inheritance would be divided between him and the son in equal shares; or supposing him (on the other hand) to be a female, it would be divided between them in three lots. We must therefore have recourse to the smallest number which admits of division by two and by three; and as this number is six, it follows that on the former supposition the inheritance is to be divided equally between the two, three shares of the six going respectively to each,—or that, on the latter supposition, it is to be divided between them in three lots, two shares of the six going to the hermaphrodite, and four shares to the son. The hermaphrodite, therefore, is entitled to two shares, unquestionably; and there being still a doubt with respect to the one redundant share, that is divided into two. Hence the hermaphrodite gets two shares and an half; and a fraction thus falling to his share, the root of the proposition (six) must be multiplied by two, in order that there may be no fractions; * and the whole calculation, being twelve, will come out right, in this way, that five go to the

* That is, in order to reduce the whole to integral parts.

hermaphrodite and seven to the son. The argument of Haneefa is, that it is necessary, in the first place, to establish the hermaphrodite's right in the inheritance; and as the smaller portion of inheritance (namely, that of a woman) is unquestionable, and any thing beyond it is doubtful, that alone is to be established, and due, which is certain and indisputable, not any more, as a right to property is not admitted under any circumstance of doubt,—the point in question being, in fact, the same as where a doubt exists with respect to a right in property, founded on any other cause beside inheritance, in which case the unquestionable proportion only would be decreed, and so here likewise;—excepting, however, in the case of a smaller share* going to the hermaphrodite, supposing him to be a male; for then he would be entitled to the share of a son, since, in such instance, that would be his indisputable right;as where, for instance, a woman dies, leaving heirs her husband, mother, and a full sister † who is an hermaphrodite,—or, where a man dies, leaving heirs his wife, two maternal brothers, and a full sister who is an hermaphrodite;—in the former of which cases (according to Haneefa) one half of the property would descend to the husband, a third to the mother, and the remainder to the hermaphrodite,—and in the latter, a quarter would descend to the wife, a third to the two brothers and the remainder to the hermaphrodite; for in both these cases the remainder is smaller than either of the two full shares, that is, the share of the hermaphrodite supposing him to be a man, and the same supposing the hermaphrodite to be a woman.

CHAPTER THE LAST

MISCELLANEOUS CASES

The intelligible signs of a dumb person suffice to verify his bequests, and render them valid; but not those of a person merely deprived of speech.—WHERE people read a deed of bequest to a dumb person, and desire to know whether they shall testify such deed on his behalf? and the dumb person makes a sign by an inclination of the head, equivalent the expression of assent "Yes!" or, where a dumb person himself writes such deed, and they thus desire to know whether they shall testify it on his behalf? and he makes a sign; by an inclination of his head in the affirmative,—the bequest, provided the sign be made in such a manner as is commonly used to denote affirmation, is valid:—but this mode of affirmation by a sign does not suffice with respect to a person whose inability to speak is superpenient, occasioned (for instance) by some recent disorder,—Shafei maintains that the sign in question is cognizable and valid equally with respect to both; for the inability alone is the cause of its being at all admitted as sufficient, a cause which exists alike in both.—Our doctors, however, conceive a natural difference between a person originally dumb, and one who merely labours under a recent incapacity of speech, for various reasons.—FIRST, signs are not cognizable, unless they be habitual and their meaning ascertained, which is the case with the signs of a dumb person, but not with those of one who has merely lost his speech. (Still, however, our doctors hold that if this person be so long deprived of speech as to render signs habitual to him, and their meaning ascertained, he then stands in the same predicament with a dumb person in this particular.)—SECONDLY, the person in question is chargeable with a neglect in not having made his will before he had lost his speech, whereas no such neglect can be charged to the dumb person.—THIRDLY, it is most probable that a recent incapacity of speech will be removed and yield to remedies which is not the case with dumbness, and therefore there is no analogy between them.

A dumb person may execute marriage, divorce, purchase or sale, and sue for or incur punishment, by means of either signs or writings; but he cannot thereby sue for or incur retaliation.—WHERE a dumb person is capable of either writing intelligibly, or making intelligible signs, marriage, divorce, purchase, of sale, declared by him, are valid, and retaliation is also execute on his behalf, or upon him; but he is not liable to punishment,* nor is punishment inflicted on his behalf.—His written deeds are valid, and cognizable, for this reason, that the writing of an absentee is equivalent to the oral declaration of a person actually present (insomuch that the Prophet, in promulgating his laws, sometimes used one mode, and sometimes another); and necessity is the ground of validity with respect to the writing of an absentee, which ground exists still more strongly in the case of a dumb person.—It is to be observed that writings are of three different sorts or descriptions: I regular testimonials† (meaning, such as are

---

* Namely, a smaller share than the half of the whole.

† This might be rendered, with more strict property, "a fraternal connexion," an hermaphrodite being, in fact, neither a brother nor sister. The translator, however, thinks it most advisable to adhere literally to the original.

* Meaning, punishment for offences against GOD, namely, for whoredom and slander; as is explained a little farther on.

‡ Arab. Moost'been Marsom. It is a technical term, applied to all regular deeds, contracts, &c.

executed upon paper, and have a regular title, superscription, and so forth, as is customary), which are equivalent to real declaration, whether the person be present or absent: II. irregular testimonials* (meaning, such as are not written upon paper, but upon a wall, or the leaf of a tree, or, upon paper without any title or superscription), which are not admitted as proof farther than merely as they signify the writer's object or design: and II. writings which are not testimonials in any sense † (meaning such as are delineated in the air, or upon water), which, as they are merely, equivalent to words not heard, are no way cognizable, nor attended with any effect.—With respect to signs made by a dumb person, they are recognize in the cases of marriage, divorce, and so forth (as mentioned above), from necessity, since those are matters in which the right of the individual alone is concerned, and which are not restricted to any particular form of words, but are even, in some instance (such as of Beeayo-Taata, or sale by a mutual surrender). effected without any words whatever; and retaliation also is a right of the individual, —But there is no necessity for punishment. as that is a right of GOD, whence the prevention of it by the existence of any doubt), and therefore, if a dumb person verify the report of a slanderer, still he is not liable to punishment.—neither is punishment inflicted upon him if he himself slander another by signs, because the slander is not express, which is the condition of its being punishable.—The difference between punishment and retaliation is, that the former is not established by doubtful evidence, whereas the latter is so;—for if witnesses charge a particular person with "illegal carnal connexion," or a person make confession of "illegal carnal connexion," till punishment is not to be inflicted; whereas if witnesses testify to "a murder" in general terms, or a person make a confession of "a murder,' retaliation is inflicted, although the term "wilful" should not have been expressly mentioned.—The ground of this is that retaliation possesses the character of reciprocity, as having been ordained for the preparation of injuries; and it is therefore admitted to be established notwithstanding a doubt, in the same manner as all other matters of reciprocity which concern the rights of the individual —With respect, on the contrary, in such punishments as are inflicted purely in right of GOD, they have been ordained for the purpose of determent; and as that does not bear the character of reciprocity, punishment, as not being a matter of necessity, is not established under any circumstance of doubt. — Mohammed, in treating of ACKNOWLEDGMENTS,* says "the writing of an absentee is not cognizable as proof, with respect to retaliation upon himself, such acknowledgment send a written acknowledgment, inducing retaliation upon himself, such acknowledgment is not cognizable). Our author remarks, upon this passage, that it may be taken in two ways. FIRST, by the absentee may be meant any absentee, whether dumb or otherwise; and on this construction the point admits of two determinations; the one what is here mentioned; and the other, what has been before recited. SECONDLY, by the absentee may be meant a person who is not dumb;— and if he [Mohammed] had said "the writing of an absentee, not being dumb, is not cognizable as proof with respect to retaliation, since, having the power of speech, it is possible that he may himself appear, and make an express confession by word of mouth;— an expectation which cannot be entertained with respect to a dumb person, since it is impossible that such person should speak, so as to make an express oral confession." Some of our doctors entertain an apprehension that the signs of a dumb person, who is at the same time able to write, are cognizable; because signs are admitted as proof purely from necessity, which does not exist in this instance.— This apprehension, however, is repugnant to what has been before mentioned, as from that we are to infer that the signs of a dumb person are cognizable, notwithstanding he be capable of writing; for as it is their said that " if a dumb person make signs, or write, it is valid," it follows that signs and writings are of equal weight, and that either of them suffices :— the reason of which is that signs and writings are, both of them, admitted as proofs purely from necessity; and as, on the one hand, writing possesses an explicitness of whole signs are destitute (the design or meaning of the person being ascertained indubitably from what he writes), whereas signs are of an ambiguous nature, so, on the other hand, signs possess an explicitness of which writings are destitute, as they approach still nearer to speed ;—and signs and writings are therefore upon an equal footing.

The writing of a person who has been deprived of the use of speech by any accident, for two or three days, is not cognizable, any more than that of an absentee who is not dumb, since there is still room to hope that he may be able to speak, as his organs of speech remain.

Case of slaughtered carcases being promiscuously mixed with carrion.—IF the carcases of slaughtered † goats be promiscuously

* Arab. Moost'been Ghayr Marsoom. This is the same term, only with the addition of the primitive Ghayr.

† Arab, Ghayr Moost'been.

‡ See Vol. II. p. 141.

* Probably in the Mabsoot.

† Arab. Mazboot, meaning those reugularly slain according to the. prescribed form of Zabbah. (See Vol. IV. p. 587.)

mixed with those of carrion* goates, and the one be not known from the other, and the number slaughtered exceed the number of carrion the persons about to use them must make a deliberate selection, and eat such only as they suppose most likely to have been lawfully slain.—But if the number of carrion exceed the number slaughtered, or if they be equal in number, none of them must be used.—What is here advanced applies solely to a situation which admits a latitude of choice; for in a situation of necessity the selection may be made under either circumstance, and those used which the people suppose most likely to have been lawfully slain; because as, in time of want, indubitable carrion is allowed to be lawful, it follows that what comes within the possibility of having been duly slain is lawful a fortiori: but still a deliberate selection must be made, since it is most likely that by this means those will be used which have been duly slain; and the selection is therefore not to be dispensed with except in cases of extreme urgency. Shafei maintains that, in a situation which admits a latitude of choice it is not lawful to eat any of the goats, notwithstanding the number of those duly slain exceed the number of the carrion; for as the selection is an argument of necessity, it is not to be practised except in a case of necessity, which does not apply to a situation admitting a latitude of choice. The argument of our doctors is, that the circumstance of the slain goats exceeding the carrion in number is equivalent to necessity, whence the eating of some of them is lawful after a due selection;—in the same manner as it is lawful to take and use articles sold in a Mussulman market, because of the greater number of commodities there exhibited being lawful, notwithstanding a market be not altogether free from certain prohibited articles, such as stolen or usurped goods, and the like; the ground of which is, that as it is not always possible to make a distinction with respect to small matters, a regard to them is remittled, since otherwise the business of life could not be carried on; and accordingly, a small degree of dirt, or of nakedness, in prayer, is not of any moment. In a case, therefore, where the number of slaughtered goats exceeds that of the carrion, the eating of some of them is allowed, from a species of necessity. I is otherwise where the number of the carrion exceeds or equals that of the slain; for in this case, supposing the situation to be such as admits a latitude of option, no necessity whatever exists.

* Arab. Moordar, meaning those which have died a natural death, or have not been slain according to the prescribed form.

THE END

INDEX.

B.

C.

E.

F.

G.

H

J.

K.

N

O

P.

Q.

R.

S

U

V.

W

Y

Z